Introducing
Autodesk® Maya® 2016

DARIUSH DERAKHSHANI

Acquisitions Editor: STEPHANIE McCOMB
Development Editor: STEPHANIE BARTON
Technical Editor: KEITH REICHER
Production Editor: CHRISTINE O'CONNOR
Copy Editor: KIM WIMPSETT
Editorial Manager: MARY BETH WAKEFIELD
Production Manager: KATHLEEN WISOR
Associate Publisher: JIM MINATEL
Book Designer: CARYL GORSKA
Compositors: KATE KAMINSKI AND MAUREEN FORYS, HAPPENSTANCE TYPE-O-RAMA
Proofreaders: JOSH CHASE AND SARAH KAIKINI, WORD ONE NEW YORK
Indexer: TED LAUX
Project Coordinator, Cover: BRENT SAVAGE
Cover Designer: WILEY
Cover Image: DARIUSH DERAKHSHANI

To Mom

Acknowledgments

As this book goes into its 12th edition, I am thrilled that the *Introducing Maya* book is a favorite resource for students and teachers of the Autodesk® Maya® software. Education is the foundation for a happy life, and with that in mind, I'd like to thank the outstanding teachers from whom I have had the privilege to learn. You can remember what you've been taught—or, just as important, you can remember those who have taught you. ■ I also want to thank my students, who have taught me as much as they have learned themselves. Juan Gutierrez, Victor J. Garza, Robert Jauregui, and Peter Gend deserve special thanks for helping me complete the models and images for this book. Thanks to my colleagues and friends at work for showing me everything I've learned and making it interesting to be in the effects business. Special thanks to HP for its support and keeping me on the cutting edge of workstations and displays. ■ Thanks to my editors at Sybex and the folks at Autodesk for their support and help and for making this process fun. Thanks to the book team for bringing it all together: Stephanie McComb, Stephanie Barton, Christine O'Connor, and Kim Wimpsett. My appreciation also goes tenfold to technical editor Keith Reicher. ■ Thank you to my mom and brothers for your strength, wisdom, and love throughout. And a special thank-you to my lovely wife, Randi, and our son, Max Henry, for putting up with the long nights at the keyboard; the grumpy, sleep-deprived mornings; and the blinking and buzzing of all my machines in our house. Family!

About the Author

Dariush Derakhshani is a VFX and CG supervisor and educator in Los Angeles, California. Dariush has been working in CG for more than 18 years and teaching classes in CG and effects production for close to 16. He is the best-selling author of a handful of books, including the popular *Introducing Maya* books. He is also co-creator of *Learning Autodesk® Maya®: A Video Introduction*, available from Wiley. You can find out information on this video series and more at www.koosh3d.com.

Dariush started using the Autodesk® AutoCAD® software in his architecture days and then migrated to using 3D programs when his firm's principal architects needed to show their clients design work on the computer. Starting with Alias PowerAnimator version 6, which he encountered when he enrolled in the University of Southern California Film School's animation program, and working for a short while in Autodesk® 3ds Max® before moving on to Maya® jobs, Dariush has been using Autodesk animation software for the past 18 years.

He received an MFA in film, video, and computer animation in 1997 from USC. Dariush earned a BA in architecture and theater from Lehigh University in Pennsylvania and worked at a New Jersey architecture firm before moving to Los Angeles for film school. He has worked on feature films, music videos, and countless commercials as a 3D animator and VFX supervisor, garnering honors from the London International Advertising Awards, the ADDY Awards, the Telly Awards, and a nomination from the Visual Effects Society Awards. He is bald and has flat feet.

CONTENTS AT A GLANCE

Contents

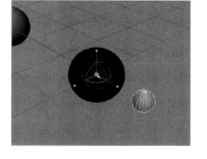

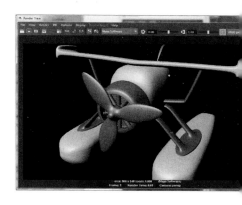

Introduction

Welcome to Introducing Autodesk® Maya® 2016 and the world of computer-generated imagery (CGI). Whether you're new to 3D graphics or venturing into Autodesk's powerhouse animation software from another 3D application, you'll find this book a perfect primer, freshly updated from the previous edition (Maya 2015) for the new interface introduced in Maya 2016. This book introduces you to the Autodesk® Maya® software and shows how you can work with Maya to create your art, whether it's animated or static in design.

Fourteen years ago, the first edition of this book was written out of the author's desire for solid, comprehensive, and yet open-ended teaching material about Maya for his classes. This book exposes you to all the facets of Maya by introducing and explaining its tools and functions to help you understand how Maya operates. In addition, you'll find hands-on examples and tutorials that give you firsthand experience with the toolsets. Working through these will help you develop skills as well as knowledge. These tutorials expose you to various ways of accomplishing tasks with this intricate and comprehensive artistic tool.

Finally, this book explains workflow. You'll learn not only how specific tasks are accomplished but why—that is, how they fit into the larger process of producing 3D animation. By doing that, these chapters should give you the confidence to venture deeper into the Maya feature set on your own or by using any of the other Maya learning tools and books as a guide.

It can be frustrating to learn a powerful tool such as Maya, so it's important to remember to pace yourself. The number-one complaint of readers of books like this is a sense that either the pace is too fast or the steps are too complicated or overwhelming. That's a tough nut to crack, to be sure, and no two readers are the same. But this book offers you the chance to run things at your own pace. The exercises and steps may seem challenging at times, but keep in mind that the more you try—even the more you fail at some attempts—the more you'll learn about how to operate Maya. Experience is the key to learning workflows in any software program, and with experience comes failure and aggravation. Nevertheless, try and try again, and you'll see that further attempts will be easier and more fruitful.

Above all, this book aims to inspire you to use Maya as a creative tool to achieve and explore your own artistic vision.

What You'll Learn from This Book

Introducing Autodesk® Maya® 2016 is updated from the previous version of the book to show the new interface and slightly different procedures introduced in Maya 2016, all within the same exercises used in the Maya 2015 version of the book.

The book aims to show you how Maya works and introduce you to every part of the toolset to give you a glimpse of the possibilities available with Maya.

You'll learn the basic concepts underlying animation and 3D and how to work with the Maya interface. You'll then learn the basic methods of modeling—creating objects and characters that appear to exist in three-dimensional space and that can be animated. You'll also explore shading and texturing—the techniques of applying surfaces to the objects you create—and you'll learn how to create lights and shadows in a scene. Animation is an enormously rich topic, but the practice and theory provided here will give you a solid footing. Next, you'll learn how to control the process of rendering, turning your images into files that can be viewed. Perhaps the most dazzling capability of Maya is its dynamics engine, software that allows you to make objects behave as if controlled by the real-world laws of physics.

After you've finished this book and its exercises, you'll have experience in almost everything Maya offers, giving you a solid foundation on which to base the rest of your Maya and CGI experience.

The goal of this book is to get you familiar enough with all the parts of Maya that you can work on your own and start a long, healthy education in a powerful and flexible tool.

You will, however, learn the most from yourself.

Who Should Read This Book

Anyone who is curious about learning Maya or who is migrating from another 3D software package can learn something from this book. Even if you're highly experienced in another 3D package such as the open source Blender or Autodesk® 3ds Max® or Softimage®, you'll find this book helpful in showing you how Maya operates so you can migrate your existing skill set quickly and efficiently. By being exposed to everything Maya has to offer, you'll better understand how you can use its toolset to create or improve on your art and work.

If you already have cursory or even intermediate experience with Maya, culled from time spent learning at home, you can fill many holes with the information in this book as well as expand your experience. Self-education is a powerful tool, and the more you expose yourself to different sources, opinions, and methods, the better educated you'll be.

In addition, this book is invaluable for teachers in the CG field. This book was written to cater to those who want to pick up the fundamentals of Maya as well as those who want to teach classes based on a solid body of course material. You won't find a better basis for a class when you combine this book with your own curriculum.

How to Use This Book

To begin reading this book, open it to some page, and read.

Introducing Autodesk® Maya® 2016 approaches the subject in a linear fashion that tracks how most animation productions are undertaken. But the book has numerous cross-references to make sure the chapters make sense no matter in which order you want to tackle them. You can open this book to any chapter and work through the tutorials and examples laid out for the Maya task being covered. Feel free to browse the chapters and jump into anything that strikes your fancy. However, if you're completely new to CG, you may want to take the chapters in order.

Although you can learn a lot just by reading the explanations and studying the illustrations, it's best to read this book while you're using Maya 2016 so that you can try the exercises for yourself as you read them. If you don't already have Maya, you can download an educational license if you are a qualifying student or faculty member at www.students.autodesk.com/ or a 30-day trial version of the software at www.autodesk.com/maya. This book refers to a companion web page (www.sybex.com/go/introducingmaya2016), containing all the example and support files you'll need for the exercises in the text as well as some videos to help you through some of the tutorials, which is a valuable educational aid. These videos will be updated over time, so make sure to check back in now and then for more material. You can use the example files to check the progress of your work, or you can use them as a starting point if you want to skip ahead within an exercise. The latter can save the more experienced reader tons of time. You'll also find it valuable to examine these files in depth to see how scenes are set up and how some of the concepts introduced in the book are implemented. Because Maya is a complex, professional software application, the exercises are both realistically ambitious and simple enough for new users to complete. Take them one step at a time and find your own pace, accepting aggravations and failures as part of the process. Take your time; you're not working on deadline—yet.

How This Book Is Organized

Chapter 1, "Introduction to Computer Graphics and 3D," introduces you to common computer graphics concepts to give you a basic overview of how CG happens and how Maya relates to the overall process. In addition, it describes basic animation concepts to better build a foundation for further study.

Chapter 2, "Jumping into Basic Animation Headfirst," creates a simple animation to introduce you to the Maya interface and workflow and give you a taste of how things work right away. By animating the planets in our solar system, you'll learn basic concepts of creating and animating in Maya and how to use its powerful object structure.

Chapter 3, "The Autodesk® Maya® 2016 Interface," presents the entire Maya interface and shows you how it's used in production. Beginning with a roadmap of the screen, this chapter also explains how Maya defines and organizes objects in a scene while you are set to the task of building a decorative box model.

Chapter 4, "Beginning Polygonal Modeling," is an introduction to modeling concepts and workflows. It shows you how to start modeling using polygonal geometry to create various objects, from a cartoon hand to a catapult, using some of the new tools incorporated into Autodesk Maya 2016.

Chapter 5, "Modeling with NURBS Surfaces and Deformers," takes your lesson in modeling a step further. It shows you how to model with deformers and surfacing techniques, using NURBS to create a glass candle jar to later light and render in a scene. You'll also learn how to create NURBS surfaces directly into polygon meshes easily.

Chapter 6, "Practical Experience!," rounds out your modeling lessons with a comprehensive exercise showing you how to model a child's toy airplane using polygons. The chapter also exposes you to the powerful File Referencing workflow available in Maya.

Chapter 7, "Autodesk® Maya® Shading and Texturing," shows you how to assign textures and shaders to your models. Using a toy wagon model, you'll learn how to texture it to look like a real toy wagon as well as lay out its UVs for proper texture placement. Then, you'll create detailed photo-realistic textures based on photos for the decorative box and toy plane models. You'll also learn how to use toon shading to achieve a cartoon look for your renders.

Chapter 8, "Introduction to Animation," covers the basics of how to animate a bouncing ball using keyframes and then moves on to creating and coordinating more complex animation—throwing an axe and firing a catapult. You'll also learn how to import objects into an existing animation and transfer animation from one object to another, a common exercise in professional productions. In addition, you'll learn how to use the Graph Editor to edit and finesse your animation as well as animate objects along paths.

Chapter 9, "More Animation!" expands on Chapter 8 to show you how to use the Maya skeleton and kinematics system to create a simple walk cycle. This chapter also covers how to animate objects by using relationships between them. A thrilling exercise shows you how to rig a hand for easier animation and then a locomotive model for automated animation, some of the most productive uses of Maya.

Chapter 10, "Autodesk® Maya® Lighting," begins by showing you how to light a 3D scene as you learn how to light the toy plane and box that you modeled and textured earlier in the book. It also shows you how to use the tools to create and edit Maya lights for illumination, shadows, and special lighting effects. The mental ray for Maya Physical Sun and Sky feature is explored in this chapter as an introduction to some sophisticated techniques for mental ray lighting.

Chapter 11, "Autodesk® Maya® Rendering," explains how to create image files from your Maya scene and how to achieve the best look for your animation using proper cameras and rendering settings. You'll work with displacement maps to create details in a model. You'll also learn about the Maya renderer, the Vector renderer, and Final Gather using HDRI and image-based lighting through mental ray for Maya, as well as raytracing, motion blur, and depth of field. You'll have a chance to render the table lamp and decorative box to round out your skills.

Chapter 12, "Autodesk® Maya® Dynamics and Effects," introduces you to the powerful Maya dynamics animation system as well as nParticle technology. You'll animate pool balls colliding with one another using rigid body dynamics, and you'll fire the catapult. Using nParticle animation, you'll also create steam to add to your locomotive scene. You will then be exposed to nCloth to create a tablecloth and a flag. This chapter also shows you how to use Paint Effects to create animated flowers and grass within minutes.

Hardware and Software Considerations

Because computer hardware is a quickly moving target and Maya now runs on three distinct operating systems (Windows 7/8, Linux, and Mac OS X), specifying which hardware components will work with Maya is something of a challenge. Fortunately, Autodesk has a "qualified hardware" page on its website that describes the latest hardware to be qualified to work with Maya for each operating system, as well as whether you're running the 32-bit or 64-bit version. Go to the following site for the most up-to-date information on system requirements:

www.autodesk.com/maya

Although you can find specific hardware recommendations on these web pages, some general statements can be made about what constitutes a good platform on which to run Maya. First, be sure to get a fast processor; Maya eats through CPU cycles like crazy, so a fast processor is important. Second, you need lots of RAM (memory) to run Maya—at least 4 GB, but 8 GB or more is better to have, especially if you're working with large scene files and are on a 64-bit system. Third, if you expect to interact well with your Maya scenes, a powerful video card is a must; although Maya will mosey along with a poor graphics card, screen redraws will be slow with complex scenes, which can quickly become frustrating. You may want to consider a workstation graphics card for the best compatibility (rather than a consumer-grade gaming video card). Several companies make entry-level through top-performing workstation cards to fit any budget. A large hard disk is also important— most computers these days come with huge drives anyway.

Fortunately, computer hardware is so fast that even laptop computers can now run Maya well. Additionally, even hardware that is not officially supported by Autodesk can often run Maya—just remember that you won't be able to get technical support if your system doesn't meet the company's qualifications.

Writing This Book with the zBook 14

As you consider the hardware requirements for running Autodesk Maya 2016, it's interesting to note that a good portion of this book as well as the previous edition was written and accomplished on an ultrabook-sized laptop workstation from HP, the zBook 14 (Figure FM.1). This little laptop has been a powerful ally in working on the scenes used throughout this book, as well as the actual writing of the book.

With a strong Intel i7 2.1GHz CPU, 16 GB of memory and an HD resolution 14″ LED display, I was able to write this book and work on the scene files for the exercises anywhere I went, even crushed in a coach-class airplane seat. The ultrabook's AMD FirePro c41i000 adeptly powered the graphics and even ran a second 24″ display without a hiccup.

This is the first thin and light ultrabook form factor I've seen that is capable of workstation graphics, and I'm grateful to HP for allowing me the pleasure of using the zBook 14 while writing this book. It allowed me to have the stability and power I need without having to be chained to my desk, and without toting around a much heavier 15″ or 17″ mobile workstation.

Figure F.1

The HP zBook 14 was a great little machine to run Maya while traveling around!

Free Autodesk Software for Students and Educators

The Autodesk Education Community is an online resource with more than five million members that enables educators and students to download—for free (see website for terms and conditions)—the same software used by professionals worldwide. You can also access additional tools and materials to help you design, visualize, and simulate ideas. Connect with other learners to stay current with the latest industry trends and get the most out of your designs. Get started today at www.autodesk.com/joinedu.

The Next Step

By the time you finish *Introducing Autodesk® Maya® 2016*, you'll have some solid skills for using Maya. When you're ready to move on to another level, be sure to check out other Maya books from Sybex at www.sybex.com and additional resources at www.koosh3d.com.

You can contact the author through www.koosh3d.com and Facebook at www.facebook.com/IntroMaya. You may also go to the book's web page for the project files and video tutorials from the book at www.sybex.com/go/introducingmaya2016.

CHAPTER 1

Introduction to Computer Graphics and 3D

This book will introduce you to the workings of 3D animation, also called *computer graphics* (CG), with one of the most popular programs on the market, the Autodesk® Maya® software. It will introduce you to many of the features and capabilities of Maya with the intent of energizing you to study further.

The best way to succeed at anything is to practice. Go through the exercises in this book (more than once if you care to), and also think of exercises and projects that can take you further in your learning process.

This is not to say you can't be a casual visitor to working in CG—far from it. Playing around and seeing what you can create in this medium is just flat-out fun. Understanding your own learning pace is important.

Throughout this book, you'll learn how to work with Maya tools and techniques at a pace you set for yourself. When you're learning how to work with Maya, the most important concept is discovering how you work as an artist.

Learning Outcomes: In this chapter, you will be able to

- ▪ Develop an appreciation for the CG process

- ▪ Discern between different types of digital image files

- ▪ Recognize key terms and principles in film and animation

A Preview of the CG Process

Try not to view this experience as learning a software package but as learning a way of working to an end. It's hard to relax when you're trying to cram so much information into your brain. You should try not to make this experience about how a software program works but about how you work with the software. Maya is only your tool; you're the boss.

CG and CGI are the abbreviations for *computer graphics* and *computer graphics imagery*, respectively, and are often used interchangeably.

The process of creating in CG requires that you either model or arrange prebuilt objects in a scene, give them color and light, and render them through a virtual camera to make an image. It's a lot like directing a live-action production but without any actor tantrums.

> A large community on the Web provides free and for-pay models and textures that you can use in your scenes. Sites such as www.turbosquid.com, www.cgtextures.com, www.doschdesign.com, and www.archive3d.net can cut out a lot of the time you might spend creating all the models or textures for a scene.

After you build your scene in 3D using models, lights, and a camera, the computer *renders* the scene, converting it to a 2D image. Through setup and rendering, CGI is born—and, with a little luck, a CG artist is also born.

The CG animation industry inherited a workflow from the film industry that consists of three broad stages: preproduction, production, and postproduction. In film, *preproduction* is the process in which the script and storyboards are written, costumes and sets are designed and built, actors are cast and rehearse, the crew is hired, and the equipment is rented and set up. In the *production* phase, scenes are taped or filmed in the most efficient order. *Postproduction* (often simply called *post*) describes everything that happens afterward: the scenes are edited into a story; a musical score, sound effects, and additional dialogue are added; and visual effects may also be added.

Preproduction for a CG animation means gathering reference materials, motion tests, layout drawings, model sketches, and such to make the actual CG production as straightforward as possible. Production begins when you start creating models of characters, sets, and props from the storyboards, model sheets, and concept art. Then these *assets* are animated, and finally, shots are then lit and ready for rendering. Postproduction for a CG project is where all of a CG film's elements are brought together and assembled into the final form through editing, adding sound, and so on.

The CG Production Workflow

Modeling almost always begins the CG process, which then can lead into texturing and then to animation (or animation and then texturing). Lighting should follow, with rendering pulling up the rear as it must. (Of course, the process isn't completely linear; you'll often go back and forth adjusting models, lights, and textures along the way.)

Modeling, the topic of Chapters 4 through 6, is usually the first step in creating CG. Downloading or purchasing models from the Internet can often cut down the amount of time you spend on your project, if you don't prefer modeling or texturing.

Knowing how an object is used in a scene gives you its criteria for modeling. Creating a highly detailed model for a faraway shot will waste your time and expand rendering times needlessly.

> Because your computer stores everything in the scene as vector math as opposed to pixels (called *raster*), the term *geometry* refers to all the surfaces and models in a scene.

When the models are complete, it's a good idea to begin *texturing* and *shading*, the process of applying colors and material textures to an object to make it renderable. In Figure 1.1, an elephant model is shown, with textures applied to its lower body.

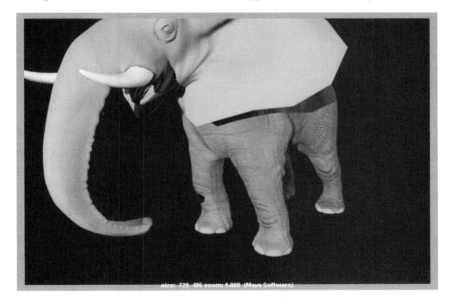

Figure 1.1

Texturing adds detail to an otherwise flat model.

Because the textures may look different after animating and lighting the scene, it's wise to leave the final adjustments for later. You'll learn more about texturing and shading in Chapter 7, "Autodesk Maya Shading and Texturing."

Next comes the process of animating. *Animation* shows *change over time*. All animation, from paper flipbooks to film to Maya, is based on the principle of *persistence of vision*: that when we see a series of rapidly changing images (called *frames*), we perceive the changing of the image to be in continuous motion.

You know when something doesn't look right, and so will the people watching your animation. So, to animate something properly, you may need to do quite a lot of setup beyond just modeling and texturing. In character animation, for example, you'll need to create and attach an *armature*, or skeleton, to manipulate the character and to make it move like a puppet. I cover animation techniques in Maya in Chapter 8, "Introduction to Animation," and Chapter 9, "More Animation!"

Next there is lighting. *CG is fundamentally all about light.* Without light, we wouldn't see anything; simulating light is the one of the most influential steps in CG. During the lighting step, you set up virtual lights in your scene to illuminate your objects and action, as you'll learn in Chapter 10, "Autodesk Maya Lighting." Before long, you'll start modeling and texturing differently—that is, working with the final lighting of the scene in mind.

When you're done lighting, you move to rendering; your computer takes your scene and makes all the computations it needs to render your scene into images. Rendering time depends on how much geometry is used in the scene as well as on the number of lights, the size of your textures, and the quality and size of your output: the more efficient your scene, the shorter the rendering times. The more experience you gain, the more efficient your eye will become.

Digital Images

When you're finished with your animation, you'll probably want as many people as possible to see it (and like it!). Here is a primer on the types of digital images and how they are discerned.

As mentioned, each image file holds the color information in *channels*. All color images have red, green, and blue color channels. Some images have a fourth channel called the *alpha* channel (a.k.a. *matte* channel), which defines what portions of the image are transparent or opaque (solid). You can read more about alpha channels in Chapter 7.

First, an image file stores the color of each pixel as three values representing red, green, and blue. The image type depends on how much storage is allotted to each pixel (the *color depth*).

Grayscale   The image is black and white with varying degrees of gray (typically 256 shades). These are good for use as texture maps such as bump and displacement maps.

8-Bit Image File (a.k.a. 24-Bit Color Display)   Each color channel is given 8 bits for a range of 256 shades of each red, green, and blue channel, for a total of 16 million colors in the image.

16-Bit Image   Used in television and film work with such file types as EXR and TIFF, a 16-bit image file holds 16 bits of information for each color channel, resulting in an impressive number of color levels and ranges.

32-Bit Image   32-bit image files, such as the HDR and OpenEXR formats, give you an incredible amount of range in each color channel. EXR files in particular are a standard at many film studios and are finding use with television productions more and more because of their impressive image range and quality.

File Formats

Several image file formats are available today. The main difference between file formats is how the image is stored. Some formats compress the file to reduce its size. However, as the degree of compression increases, the color quality of the image decreases.

The popular formats to render into from Maya are Tagged Image File Format (TIFF) and Targa. These file formats maintain a good color image, include an alpha channel, and are either uncompressed or barely compressed (lossless compression) for high quality. Note that some image file types such as TIFF may have 8, 16, or even 32 bits of color depth, while some other file types such as JPEG can have only 8-bit color depth.

To see an animation rendered in a file sequence of TIFFs or JPEGs, for example, you must play them back using a frame player, such as FCheck (which is included with Maya) or compile them into a movie file using a program such as Adobe After Effects.

Animations can also be output directly to movie files such as AVI or QuickTime. These usually large files are self-contained and hold all the images necessary for the animation that they play back as frames. Movie files can also be compressed, but they suffer from quality loss the more they're compressed.

Maya can render directly to a movie format, saving you from having to render a large sequence of files, though it's always best to render a sequence of files that can be compiled into a movie file later using a program such as Adobe After Effects, Adobe Premiere Pro, or QuickTime Pro.

Resolution, Aspect Ratio, and Frame Rate

Resolution denotes the size of an image by the number of horizontal and vertical pixels, usually expressed as #×# (for example, 640×480). The higher the resolution, the finer the image detail will be, and the larger the files. Full HD, for example, is defined as 1920×1080. *Aspect ratio* is the ratio of the screen's width to its height. Finally, the number of frames played back per second determines the *frame rate* of the animation. This is denoted as *frames per second* (fps). Most digital movie files are output at 24fps to mimic the frame rate of movies.

You should have your frame rate set properly before animating to match the frame rate you intend on using for playing the animation back. Playing back a 24fps animation at 30fps will show a slower-moving animation. Conversely, playing a 30fps animation at 24fps will create a faster-moving animation that will either skip some frames or end later than it should.

3D Coordinate Space, World Axis, and Local Axis

Space is defined in three axes—X, Y, and Z—representing width, height, and depth. The three axes form a numeric grid in which a particular point is defined by *coordinates* set forth as (#,#,#), corresponding to (X,Y,Z), respectively. At the zero point of these axes is the *origin*. This is at (0,0,0) and is the intersection of all three axes. The 3D space defined by these three axes is called the *World axis*, in which the *XYZ* axes are *fixed references*. The axis in *World Space* is always fixed and is represented in Maya by the XYZ Axis icon in the lower-left corner of the Perspective window.

Because objects can be oriented in all sorts of directions within the World axis, it's necessary for each object to have its own width, height, and depth axis independent of the World axis. This is called the *Local axis*. The *Local axis* is the *XYZ*-coordinate space that is attached to every object in Maya. When that object rotates or moves, its Local axis rotates and moves with it. This is necessary to make animating an object easier as it orients and moves around in the World axis. Figure 1.2 shows an example of a Local axis in action, where you can see a large yellow planet and its moon rotating around the central Sun.

Figure 1.2

The Sun at the origin, with Earth and other planets orbiting the World axis while rotating on their own axes

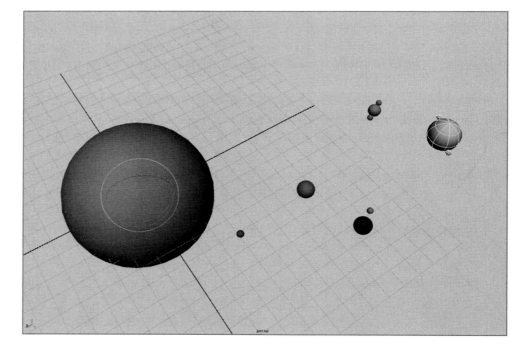

Basic Animation Concepts

The following sections define the key terms you'll come across numerous times on your journey into animation and CG.

Frames, Keyframes, and In-Betweens

Each drawing of an animation—or, in the case of CG, a single rendered image—is called a *frame*. The term *frame* also refers to a unit of time in animation whose exact chronological length depends on how fast the animation will eventually play back (frame rate).

Keyframes are frames in which the animator creates a pose or other such state of being for an object or character. Animation is created when an object travels or changes from one keyframe to another. In CG, a keyframe can be set on almost any aspect of an object—its color, position, size, and so on. Maya then interpolates the *in-between* frames between the keyframes set by the animator. Figure 1.3 illustrates a keyframe sequence in Maya.

Weight

Weight is an implied, if not critical, concept in design and animation. How you show an object in motion greatly affects its weight and therefore its believability. Weight in animation is a perception of mass. An object's movement, how it reacts in motion, and how it reacts to other objects together convey the feeling of weight. Otherwise, the animation will look bogus—or, as they say, "cartoonish."

Weight can be created with a variety of techniques developed by traditional animators over the years. Each technique distorts the shape of the object or character in some way to make it look as if it's moving. The following are a few animation principles to keep in mind:

Squash and Stretch   This technique makes a character, for example, respond to gravity, movement, and inertia by squashing it down and stretching it up when it moves. For example, a cartoon character will squeeze down when it's about to jump up, stretch out a bit while it's flying in the air, and squash back down when it lands.

Ease-In and Ease-Out   Objects never really stop suddenly; everything comes to rest in its own time, slowing before coming to a complete stop in most cases. This is referred to as *ease-out*. Objects don't immediately start moving either; they accelerate a bit before reaching full speed; this is referred to as *ease-in*. The bouncing-ball tutorial in Chapter 8 illustrates ease-in and ease-out.

Follow-Through and Anticipation   Sometimes you have to exaggerate the weight of an object in animation, especially in cartoons. You can exaggerate a character's weight, for instance, by using well-designed follow-through and anticipation.

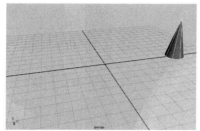

Keyframe at Frame 1

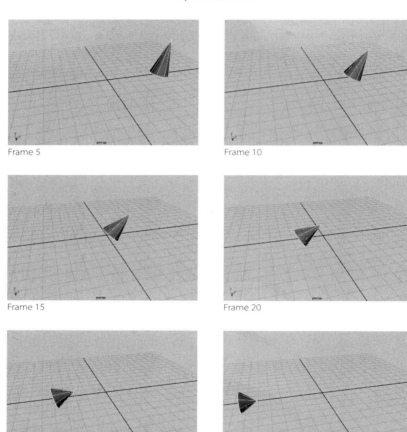

Frame 5

Frame 10

Frame 15

Frame 20

Frame 25

Keyframe at Frame 30

You should create a bit of movement in your character or object *before* it moves. *Anticipation* is a technique in which a character or object winds up before it moves, like a spring that coils inward before it bounces.

Likewise, objects ending an action typically have a *follow-through*. Think about the movement of gymnasts. When they land, they need to bend a bit at the knees and waist to stabilize their landing. In the same way, a cape on a jumping character will continue to move even after the character lands.

The axe tutorial in Chapter 8 will give you a chance to implement these two concepts.

FOR FURTHER REFERENCE

Some of the exercises in this book also have videos created for your use; you can find them at www.sybex.com/go/introducingmaya2016. For more video tutorials and reference on Maya, you can visit www.koosh3d.com.

Summary

In this chapter, you learned the basic process of working in CG, called a *workflow*. In addition, you were introduced to some fundamentals of digital images and animation principles.

Now that you have a foundation in CG and 3D terminology and core concepts, you're ready to tackle the software. Maya is a capable, intricate program. The more you understand how *you* work artistically, the better use you'll make of this exceptional tool. Have fun!

CHAPTER 2

Jumping into Basic Animation Headfirst

In this chapter, you'll start using the Autodesk® Maya® software and get your groove on. This will be a quick primer on the Maya interface so you experience tasks right away. The next chapter will show you more details and provide additional explanations and a reference of how the entire Maya interface functions as you work on another project.

In this chapter, you will follow an exercise for creating a solar system and learn the mechanics of animating orbits. With this exercise, you'll create simple objects, set keyframes, and stack your animation to get planets and moons to orbit each other and the Sun. These tasks will expose you to object creation, simple modeling, object components, pivot-point placement, grouping and hierarchies, basic keyframing, and timing.

Learning Outcomes: In this chapter, you will be able to

- Gain a working understanding of the user interface and how to navigate in 3D space

- Learn project structure in Maya and how to create projects in Maya

- Create, name, and manipulate simple objects with the Move, Rotate, and Scale tools

- Make and apply simple shaders to scene geometry through the Hypershade

- Add keyframes to objects to create animation

- Adjust pivot points

- Create and edit hierarchies by using groups

- Output your animation through playblasting

You Put the *U* in User Interface

Fire up your computer, and let's get going. This section will introduce you to getting around the Maya user interface (UI).

The overall goal of this chapter is to expose you to Maya UI basics as well as important scene creation and editing tools. You'll find more details on the interface in Chapter 3, "The Autodesk Maya 2016 Interface."

KEYBOARD AND SYMBOL CONVENTIONS USED IN THIS BOOK

The following terms are used throughout this book:

Click and LMB+Click These actions refer to a mouse click with the primary (left) mouse button.

RMB+Click This refers to a mouse click with the right mouse button.

MMB+Click This refers to a mouse click with the middle mouse button.

Shift+Click This indicates you should hold down the Shift key as you click with the primary (left) mouse button.

Shift+Select This indicates you should hold down the Shift key as you select the next object for multiple selections.

The □ Symbol This, next to a menu command, indicates you should click the box (□) next to the menu command to open the options for that command.

A Quick Screen Roadmap

Let's get to the basics of how Maya is laid out (see Figure 2.1). Running across the top of the screen, right under the application title bar, are the UI elements: the main menu bar, the Status line, and the Shelf. On Mac OS X, note that the main menu bar runs across the top of the screen, above the application title bar.

Figure 2.1 shows the major parts of the UI. In the middle of the interface is the *work-space*, which is host to your *panels* (or Scene windows) and their menu options (known as *views* or *viewports* in some other 3D packages). This is where most of your focus will be.

Click inside the large Perspective view panel (named *persp*) with the mouse to activate the panel, highlighting its border slightly. Press the spacebar to display a four-panel layout, which gives you top, front, and side views, as well as the perspective view. Press the spacebar in any of the panels to display a large view of that panel.

Figure 2.1

The initial Maya screen

Main Menu Bar Status Line Shelf

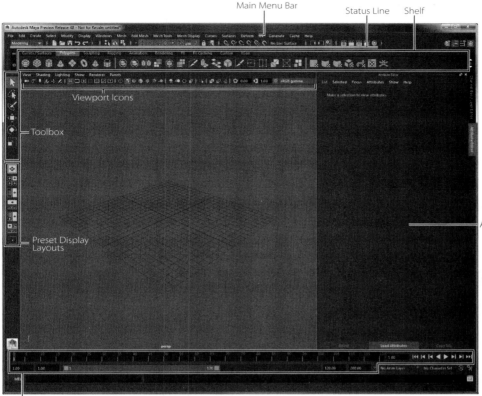

Viewport Icons

Toolbox

Preset Display Layouts

Attribute Editor / Channel Box

Time Slider, Range Slider, Playback Controls

To the right of the panels is the Attribute Editor/Channel Box/Modeling Toolkit. This is where most of the information (attributes) about a selected object is displayed and edited. Also, this is where you access the Modeling Toolkit suite of polygon tools. Simply click any of the tabs to access these functions. Furthermore, pressing Ctrl+A toggles between the Attribute Editor and the Channel Box.

In short, the Attribute Editor gives you access to all of an object's attributes, whereas the Channel Box is a quicker display of the most commonly animated attributes of the selected object.

Letter Keys and Syntax in Maya

Maya is case sensitive (meaning it distinguishes between lowercase and uppercase letters). The conventions of this book are to always print an uppercase letter to denote which key you must press. So, when I ask you to press the E key, for example, you should simply press the E key on your keyboard (thereby entering a lowercase *e*). When an uppercase letter is called for, the book tells you to press Shift+E, thereby entering the uppercase letter *E* into Maya. Also, make sure your Caps Lock key is turned off.

Mouse Controls

Maya requires the use of a three-button mouse, even on a Mac. The clickable scroll wheel found on most mice can be used as the third button by pressing down to click with the wheel.

SHORTCUTS TO NAVIGATING

Here's a rundown of how to navigate Maya. Keep in mind that the Option key is used on a Mac in place of the Alt key on a PC.

Alt+MMB+Click   Tracking moves left, right, up, or down in two dimensions; hold down the Alt key, press and hold the MMB, and drag the mouse.

Alt+RMB+Click   This dollies into or out of a view, essentially zooming the view in and out. Hold down the Alt key, press and hold the RMB, and drag the mouse.

Scroll Wheel   The scroll wheel acts as a middle mouse button when pressed and can also dolly into or out of a view just like the Alt+RMB+click combination when scrolling the wheel.

Alt+Click   This rotates or orbits the camera around in a Perspective window. To orbit, hold down the Alt key and the LMB. You can't tumble your view in an orthographic panel.

Alt+Ctrl+Click and Drag   Dollies your view into the screen area specified in your mouse drag. Hold down the Alt and Ctrl keys while using the LMB to outline a window in the panel to execute this *bounding box dolly*. This action is commonly referred to as a *window zoom* in other applications.

The ViewCube   The ViewCube is a navigational aid that is not visible by default when you launch Maya 2016. The ViewCube, when enabled, lets you easily change your current panel view. To enable the ViewCube in a viewport, select Renderer from the panel's menu bar (not the main menu bar) and select either Legacy Default Viewport or Legacy High Quality Viewport, and the ViewCube will appear in the upper-right corner of the panel.

By clicking an area of the ViewCube (shown here), you can switch to other views inside that panel. Clicking one of the conical axis markers gives you an orthogonal view from that direction. Clicking the center square gives you the perspective view. You can toggle the ViewCube on or off in the UI by choosing Display → Heads Up Display → ViewCube.

Mac Keys   The Option key on a Mac serves the same function as the Alt key on a PC. Although a few Ctrl key combinations in Windows are accessed via the Command key on a Mac, Mac users can use the Mac's Ctrl key for their key combinations just like PC users do.

In Maya, you press and hold the Alt key on a PC (or the Option key on a Mac) along with the appropriate mouse button to move in the view panel.

- The left mouse button (LMB) acts as the primary selection button and allows you to orbit around objects when used with the Alt key.
- The right mouse button (RMB) activates numerous shortcut menus and lets you zoom when used with the Alt key.
- The middle mouse button (MMB) used with the Alt key lets you move within the Maya interface panels, and the mouse's wheel can be used to zoom in and out as well.

Making Selections

Selecting objects in a view panel is as easy as clicking them. As you select an object, its attributes appear in the Attribute Editor or Channel Box on the right. To select multiple objects, simply hold the Shift key as you click objects to add to your current selection. If you press Ctrl+LMB (press the Ctrl key and click) on an active object, you'll deselect it. To clear all of your current selections, click anywhere in the empty areas of the view panel.

> Remember, when you press Shift+click to select, Maya adds to the current selection. When you press Ctrl+click, Maya deselects the object you clicked.

Manipulating Objects

When you select an object and enable one of the transformation tools (tools that allow you to move, rotate, or scale an object), you'll see a manipulator appear at or around the selected object. Figure 2.2 shows the three distinct and most common manipulators for all objects in Maya (Move, Rotate, and Scale) as well as the Universal Manipulator. You use these manipulators to adjust attributes of the objects visually and in real time.

To activate a transform tool, select an object and then click one of the transform tool icons in the Tool Box, shown in Figure 2.3.

> Press 4 for Wireframe mode; press 5 for Shaded mode.

Try This Let's put some of this into action.

1. Press 4 for wireframe mode. Choose Create → Polygon Primitives → Sphere. Drag in a view panel anywhere on its grid to create a wireframe sphere and then size it to your liking. If this does not happen and instead a sphere appears in your window, a default setting has previously been changed, which is okay. In this case, turn on Interactive Creation

Figure 2.2
The Maya manipulators

Figure 2.3
The transform tools in the Tool Box

Transform Tools

if it was previously turned off. Click Create → Polygon Primitives and make sure the check box next to Interactive Creation at the bottom is checked.

In one of the view panels, press the 5 key on your keyboard, and the display of the sphere will become solid gray. This is called *Shaded mode*. Press the 4 key to return to Wireframe mode. You should also see an in-view message at the top of your view stating "shaded display is now on. Press 4 to display objects in wireframe mode."

You can turn off in-view messages by toggling off the In-View Messages check box under Display → Heads Up Display.

2. With the sphere selected, select the Move tool (⊡) from the Tool Box. The first manipulator shown earlier in Figure 2.2 should appear in the middle of the sphere. The three arrows represent the three axes of possible movement for the object. Red is for the X-axis, green is for the Y-axis, and blue is for the Z-axis. Cyan is for free movement in both axes of the active panel view. Clicking any one of the three arrows lets you move the object only on that particular axis. The square in the middle of the manipulator lets you move the object freely around the plane of the view panel, regardless of the axis. The three squares represent planar movement in two of the three axes at a time, for example moving on the XY plane or the YZ plane.

3. Next, select the Rotate tool (◉) from the Tool Box, and you'll see the second manipulator from Figure 2.2. The three colored circles represent the three axes of rotation for the object—red for *X*, green for *Y*, and blue for *Z*. Select a circle to rotate the object on that axis. The yellow circle surrounding the three axis circles lets you freely rotate the object on all three axes.

4. Try selecting the Scale tool (▣) to see the third manipulator from Figure 2.2. By selecting one of the axis handles and dragging the mouse, you can scale the object in a nonuniform manner in that axis. The middle cyan box scales the object uniformly on all three axes.

5. Try selecting the Universal Manipulator, which is not shown in the Tool Box but is found by choosing Modify → Transformation Tools → Universal Manipulator. Its icon (▣) appears under the Tool Box after you select it from the menu. This tool acts in place of all three manipulators you just tried. Grabbing the familiar arrows translates the sphere. Selecting any of the curved arrows in the middle of the edges of the manipulator box lets you rotate the sphere in that axis. Finally, selecting and dragging the cyan boxes in the corners of the manipulator box lets you scale the sphere. If you hold down the Ctrl key as you drag, you can scale the sphere in just one axis.

Go ahead and click around the interface some more. Create more primitive objects and tool around a bit. Move around the view panels and see how it feels. Give the tires a good kick.

Enough chatting—let's jump into the solar system exercise.

Project: The Solar System

This project will familiarize you with the fundamentals of navigating Maya, object creation, hierarchy, and pivots, all of which are important concepts for scene manipulation and animation within Maya. In this exercise, you'll gain experience with UI elements while setting up a Maya project in which you create and manipulate objects. You will animate a simple simulation of your working solar system, making and adjusting hierarchies for animation and setting keyframes.

Starting with the Sun in the center, the planets in order are Mercury, Venus, Earth, Mars, Jupiter, Saturn, Uranus, Neptune, and Pluto. (Yes, yes, I know Pluto isn't classified as a planet anymore.) All these planets orbit the Sun in ellipses, but you'll give them circular orbits for this exercise. Most planets have a number of moons that orbit them, and a few, including Saturn, have large rings that circle them. For this exercise, you will create only two moons for any planet that has more than two moons, like Jupiter.

The more you run this exercise, the clearer the scene manipulation and hierarchy structure will become to you. Art is a marriage of inspiration, hard work, and practice.

Creating a Project

Projects are the way Maya manages a scene's assets. A file and folder structure keeps your files organized according to projects. You will want to create a new project for this new exercise.

The top level of this organization is the *project folder*. Within the project folder are numerous file folders that hold your files. When you set your workspace to a project folder (or when you create a new project), Maya will know where to look for elements and folders for that project. The two most important types are the Scenes and Images folders. The Scenes folder stores your scene files, which contain all the information for your scene. The Images folder stores images you've rendered from your scene.

NAMING OBJECTS AND KEEPING THE SCENE ORGANIZED

In Maya and most other CG packages, keeping things organized is important to workflow. When you pick up a disorganized scene, it is time-consuming to figure out exactly how everything works together. Get into the habit of naming your objects and keeping a clean scene or you'll be bombarded by dirty looks from other artists when they have to handle your cluttered scenes.

The scene files discussed in this chapter are included in the book's download, available at www.sybex.com/go/introducingmaya2016. They are in a project layout explained in the following text. Copy the scene files on the web page for this project into your own project folders after you create the project.

Figure 2.4

The completed Project Window

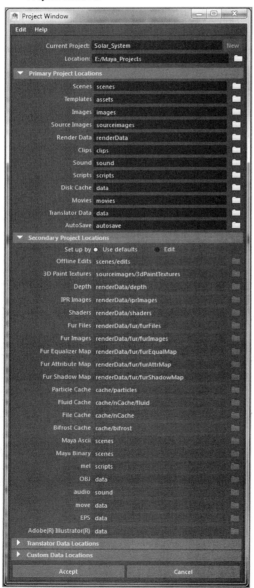

To create a new project for this assignment, follow these steps:

1. Choose File → Project Window to open the Project Window and then click the New button.

2. In the Current Project field in the Project Window, enter **Solar_System** as the name for your project. In the Location box, type the location where you want to store your projects.

   The default location for Windows XP, Vista, and Windows 7 is the current user's My Documents folder: My Documents\maya\projects; for Macs, the default location is Home (/Users/<yourname>) in the Documents/maya/projects/default folder; and for Windows 8 users it is found under the Documents location under the Start menu. If you prefer, you can put projects in a folder on a secondary or external hard drive to keep them separate from your operating system; this allows for easier backup and is generally a safer environment.

3. If you're using a Windows system, create a folder on your hard drive called **Projects** using Windows Explorer. If you're using a Mac, select a drive in the Finder and create a folder on the drive called **Projects**. In the Project Window, click the folder icon next to the Location field and select D:\ Projects (Windows) or <Hard Drive Name>/Projects (Mac) for the location. Maya will fill in all the other fields for you with defaults. Click Accept to create the necessary folders in your specified location. Figure 2.4 shows the completed Project Window in Mac OS X; except for the drive name, the values are the same on Windows.

After you create projects, you can switch between them by choosing File → Set Project and selecting the new project. Maya will then use that project's folders until you switch to or create another project. You may also select a recent project by choosing File → Recent Projects.

DON'T FORGET TO ALWAYS SET YOUR PROJECT FIRST!

You should make sure to set your project before continuing with your work. The exercises in this book are based on projects, and you'll need to set your project whenever you start a new exercise. Otherwise, the scene may not load properly, or your files may not save to the proper locations for that project. Don't say I didn't warn you!

The Production Process: Creating and Animating the Objects

In this project, you'll first create the Sun, the planets, and their moons; then, you'll animate their respective orbits and rotations.

USE CUBES INSTEAD OF SPHERES

Make the planets with cubes instead to make it easier to see them spin.

Creating the Sun and the Planets

The first thing you'll do is create the Sun and the planets. Follow these steps:

1. Choose File → New Scene (or press Ctrl+N). Maya asks if you want to save your current scene. Save the file if you need to or click Don't Save to discard the scene.

2. By default, the screen should begin in an expanded perspective view. Press the spacebar to enable the four-panel view. When you're in the four-panel view, press the spacebar with the cursor inside the top view panel to select and maximize it.

3. To create the Sun, you need to create a primitive sphere. A *primitive* is a basic 3D shape. First let's turn off a default feature called Interactive Creation. Uncheck Create → Polygon Primitives → Interactive Creation to toggle it off, as shown in Figure 2.5.

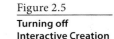
Figure 2.5

Turning off Interactive Creation

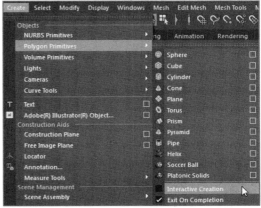

Interactive Creation lets you create a primitive by clicking and dragging to specify its size and position. You'll find this option when you choose Create → NURBS Primitives or Create → Polygon Primitives. When this option, at the bottom of each of those menus, is unselected or off, the created primitive appears at the origin in 3D space at a uniform scale of 1.0.

4. With Interactive Creation now turned off, choose Create → Polygon Primitives → Sphere. Doing so places a polygon sphere exactly at the origin—that is, at a position of 0,0,0 for X,Y,Z. This is good, because the origin of the workspace will be the center of the solar system, too. The sphere will be selected, and some of its attributes will show on the right of the UI in the Attribute Editor.

5. Press Ctrl+A to toggle off the Attribute Editor and toggle on the Channel Box in its place.

5. Select the word *pSphere1* in the Channel Box (shown in Figure 2.6) and enter **Sun** to rename it. If you don't see the Channel Box in your Maya window, press Ctrl+A to toggle the view from the Attribute Editor to the Channel Box.

Figure 2.6

Renaming the sphere in the Channel Box

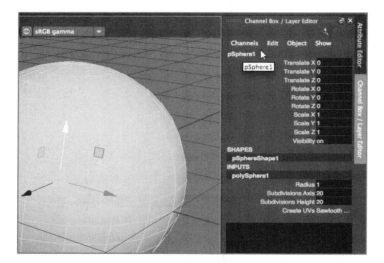

Naming your objects right after creation is a good habit to develop and is particularly important if anyone needs to alter your scene file; proper naming will keep them from getting frustrated when they work on your scene.

Always keep in mind that Maya is case sensitive. An object named *sun* is different from an object named *Sun*.

6. Choose the Scale tool in the Tool Box to activate the Scale manipulator, and uniformly scale the Sun sphere up to about four times its creation scale of 1. (Make it a scale of about 4 in all three axes.) For more precision, you can select the sphere and enter a value of **4** in all three entry fields (the white window next to the attribute)

for the Scale X, Scale Y, and Scale Z channels in the Channel Box shown in Figure 2.7.

7. After you enter the final value, press Enter, and the sphere will grow to be four times its original size. Entering exact values in the Channel Box is a way to scale the sphere precisely; using the manipulator isn't as precise.

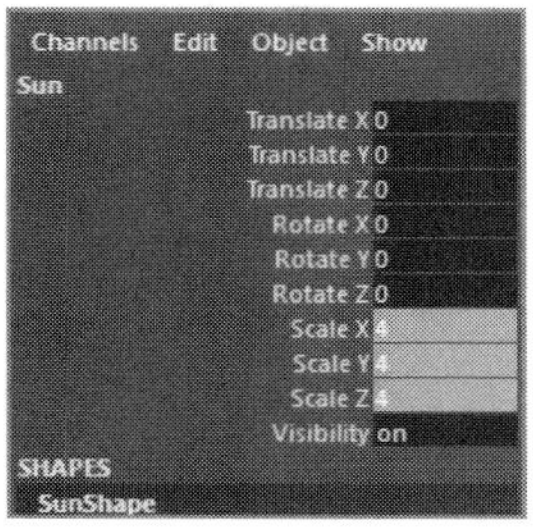

Figure 2.7

The Sun sphere's Scale values in the Channel Box

Creating the Planets

Next, you'll create the primitive spheres for the planets. Leave Interactive Creation off, and follow these steps:

1. Create a polygon sphere for Mercury just as you did before, by choosing Create → Polygon Primitives → Sphere. A new sphere appears at the origin. Click its name in the Channel Box and change it to **Mercury**.

2. Choose the Move tool from the Tool Box to activate the Move manipulator and move Mercury a few grid units away from the Sun sphere in the positive X direction. (Click the red arrow and drag it to the right.) Leave about 2 grid units between the Mercury sphere and the Sun sphere.

3. Because Mercury is the second-smallest planet and is tiny compared to the Sun, scale it down to 1/20th the size of the Sun sphere, or type **0.2** in all three axes of Scale in the Channel Box.

4. Repeat steps 1 through 3 to create the rest of the planets and line them up, placing each one farther out along the X-axis with about two grid units of space between them. If you run out of grid, simply select Display → Grid ❐, set the Length and Width value in the Grid Options window to 36 or more, and click Apply and Close.

5. Scale each planet sphere proportionally as shown in the chart on the right. Make sure to name each planet in the Channel Box (as in step 1 for Mercury) for each new planet sphere you create, using the chart on the right as reference.

Planet Sphere Sizes

Venus	0.5
Earth	0.5
Mars	0.4
Jupiter	1.0
Saturn	0.9
Uranus	0.7
Neptune	0.7
Pluto	0.15

These proportions aren't exactly real, but they will do nicely here. Figure 2.8 shows how your solar system should look now.

Figure 2.8

All the spheres are lined up in place.

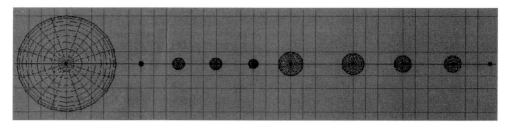

No, Pluto isn't actually a planet anymore, but for nostalgia's sake, we'll include it here in our solar system. Poor Pluto!

Using Snaps

Now is the perfect time to start using *snaps*. Table 2.1 shows some common snap icons. These icons run across the top of the UI just below the main menu bar, as shown here.

Table 2.1

Snap icons

SNAP ICON	NAME	DESCRIPTION
	Snap To Grids	Snaps objects to intersections of the view's grid
	Snap To Curves	Snaps objects along a curve
	Snap To Points	Snaps objects to object points such as CVs or vertices
	Snap To Projected Center	Snaps an object to the center of another object
	Snap To View Planes	Snaps objects to view planes

You use snaps to snap objects into place with precision, by placing them by their pivot points directly onto grid points, onto other object pivots, onto curve points, and so on. Here you'll reposition all the planets slightly to center them on the nearest grid line intersection:

1. Select the first planet, Mercury. Choose the Move tool from the Tool Box and toggle on grid snaps by clicking the Snap To Grids icon ( ).

2. The center of the Move manipulator changes from a square to a circle, signaling that some form of snapping is active. Grab the manipulator in the middle by this circle and move it slightly to the left or right to snap it onto the closest grid intersection on the X-axis.

3. Select the remaining planets and snap them all to the closest grid intersection on the X-axis, making sure to keep about two grid spaces between them. Because the Sun sphere was created at the origin and you haven't moved it, you don't need to snap it onto an intersection.

Making Saturn's Ring

Now, let's create the ring for Saturn. To do so, follow these steps:

1. Press the spacebar in the top view to maximize it. Choose Create → Polygon Primitives → Torus to place a donut shape at the origin (since Interactive Creation is still off). Use the Move tool to snap the ring to the same grid intersection as Saturn. This ensures that both the planet and its ring are on the same pivot point and share the same center.

2. Select the torus shape you've created and name it **Ring** in the Channel Box.

3. While the torus shape is still selected in the top view, press the spacebar to display the four-panel layout. Place the mouse cursor in the persp view and press the spacebar to maximize the Perspective window.

4. Press the F key to focus the perspective display on the ring and on Saturn. Pressing F centers and zooms in the panel on just the selected objects.

5. Press 5 to get into Shaded mode.

6. From the Tool Box, select the Scale tool and scale the torus down to 0 or close to 0 in the Y-axis (the torus's height, in this case) to flatten it.

   You need to edit the attributes of the ring to increase the inside radius of the donut shape and create a gap between the planet and the ring.

7. Press Ctrl+A (Ctrl or Cmd+A will work on a Mac) to toggle the Attribute Editor if it's not on and then click the polyTorus1 tab to select its creation node (see Figure 2.9).

8. Increase the Radius attribute to about 1.5 and decrease the Section Radius attribute to about 0.4 to get the desired effect.

   Now all your planets are complete, and you can move on to the moons.

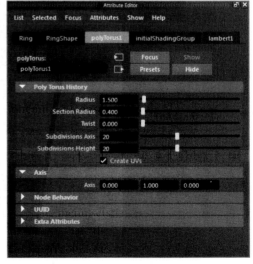

Figure 2.9

Changing the creation attributes of the polygon torus in the Attribute Editor

Saving Your Work

Save your work, unless you like to live on the edge. Power failures and other unforeseen circumstances (such as your pet jumping onto your keyboard) may not happen often, but they do happen. Because you created this as a new project, the Save File window will direct you to the Scenes folder of that project. Save your scene as **planets** in the .ma (Maya ASCII) format.

The file Planets_v1.ma in the Scenes folder of the Solar_System project, available on the book's web page, shows what the scene should look like at this point.

SAVING MULTIPLE VERSIONS OF YOUR WORK

Maya software's Incremental Save feature makes a backup of your scene file every time you save your scene with File → Save. To enable it, choose File → Save Scene ❏ and click the Incremental Save box. Every time you save, Maya will create a new backup (for example, planets_001.ma) in a folder in your Scenes folder.

The scene files for the projects in this book use a slightly different naming system than the names generated by Incremental Save, so there is no risk of files overwriting each other.

The AutoSave feature automatically saves your file at a set interval of time. To enable AutoSave, choose Windows → Settings/Preferences → Preferences. In the Categories column on the left, choose Settings → Files/Projects. You can enable AutoSave as well as set its time interval and save location under the AutoSave heading.

Creating the Moons

For the planets with moons, create a new polygon sphere for each moon. For simplicity's sake, create only two moons for any planet. The first moon will be Earth's. Use the top view to follow these steps:

1. Create a polygon sphere and scale it to about half the size of Earth using the Scale tool. Visually estimate the size of the moon.

2. Move the sphere to within half a unit of Earth, using the Move tool by the X-axis. There's no need to snap it to a grid point, so toggle off the Snap To Grids icon (⊕). Name the moon **earthMoon**.

3. Repeat steps 1 and 2 for the remaining moons, placing them each within half a grid unit from their respective planets. When placing two moons, place them on opposite sides of the planet. Make sure to name your moons.

4. After you've finished with all the moons, their placements, and their sizes, you should have a scene similar to Figure 2.10 in perspective view. If you don't, it's clear Maya doesn't like you.

Figure 2.10

The planets and moons in position in perspective view

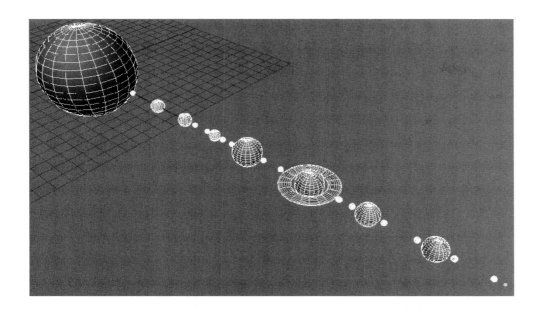

Applying a Simple Shader

To help distinguish one gray planet from another, let's attach simple shaders to each of the planets to give them color. Shaders, in short, are materials that give an object its particular look, whether it is color or a tactile texture. Follow these steps:

1. Choose Windows → Rendering Editors → Hypershade to open the Hypershade window. With this window, you create the look of your objects by assigning colors, surface properties, and so on. You'll notice three default (or initial) shader icons already loaded, as well as a new material you'll create in the next step (see Figure 2.11).

HYPERSHADE WINDOW LAYOUT

The Hypershade is customizable, so your initial Hypershade window layout may not exactly match the ones shown in this book. For example, in Figure 2.11 (which should match the initial view you see when you launch Maya for the first time), you can see there is a section called Bins immediately above the Create panel as well as a section called Material Viewer showing a thumbnail image of a sphere shape in the upper right corner of the Hypershade. Both the Bin and the Material Viewer have been turned off for the majority of this book, but they can be accessed through the Hypershade's Window menu. This window will be explained further in Chapter 3.

Figure 2.11

**The Hypershade
window**

2. In the Create panel on the lower left of the Hypershade window, click the Lambert icon (Figure 2.11) to create a new Lambert shader node. A new node called lambert2 appears in the top-left panel (called the Browser). This is where the Hypershade lists all the materials in the scene. In the top-right panel, called the Material Viewer, the Hypershade shows a rendered preview of the selected material. A selected material's more important attributes are listed in the Property Editor directly below the Material Viewer. Click the Lambert icon in the Create panel eight more times to create a total of nine new Lambert shading groups (lambert2 through lambert10).

3. In the Hypershade's Browser, click the first of the new Lambert nodes (select lambert2, do not select lambert1) to display its attributes in the Property Editor. (The material's complete list of attributes are shown in the Attribute Editor in the main Maya UI window.) At the top of the Property Editor, rename lambert2 to **Mercury_Color** to identify this material as the one you'll use for Mercury.

4. Name each of the remaining planets' materials in the Hypershade's Property Editor (Venus_Color, Earth_Color, Mars_Color, Jupiter_Color, Saturn_Color, Uranus_Color, Neptune_Color, and Pluto_Color) and save your work.

After you've created and named all the materials (a.k.a., shaders), you can assign appropriate colors to each of the shaders according to the planets that they represent.

1. Click Mercury_Color's lambert icon in the Hypershade to display its properties (see Figure 2.12).

2. To change the color of the shader, click the gray box next to the Color attribute. This opens the Color Chooser window, where you can choose a new color by using the color wheel or by adjusting values with the HSV sliders. Go with an orange color, such as in Figure 2.13 (take note of the HSV values, and see that Color Management is checked, otherwise your HSV values will differ from those shown in the figure).

3. Change the shaders as follows:

Mercury	Orange-brown
Venus	Beige-yellow
Earth	Blue
Mars	Red-orange
Jupiter	Yellow-green
Saturn	Pale yellow
Uranus	Cyan
Neptune	Aqua blue
Pluto	Bright gray

   Figure 2.14 shows the shading groups.

4. Next, let's apply the materials to the planets. Select a planet in the Perspective window, and RMB+click its corresponding

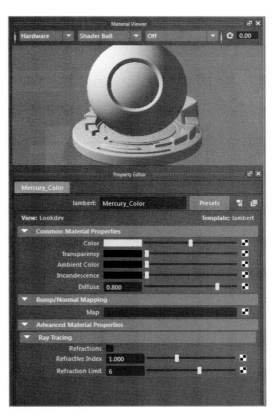

Figure 2.12

Mercury's material in the Hypershade Property Editor

Figure 2.13

The Color Chooser window

material in the Hypershade window to open a *marking menu*. Marking menus are a fast UI workflow to allow you to select commands and options as you work in your panels without having to access the main menu bar.

Figure 2.14

The Hypershade window with all the colored planet materials

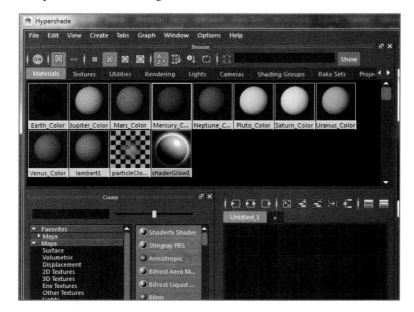

5. Still holding the right mouse button, drag up to highlight Assign Material To Selection and release the button to select it. You can also use the middle mouse button to drag the material from the Hypershade window to its planet. Leave the moons set to the default gray color. When you're finished, you should have a scene similar to Figure 2.15.

A marking menu is a context-sensitive menu that appears when you RMB+click an object or a shader. For example, clicking a polygon cube in a scene brings up a marking menu where you can select the cube's vertices, faces, edges, and so on, and where you can quickly access some often-used options and tools. The kind of marking menu that appears depends on the node you are RMB+clicking.

Now that you're finished, you're ready to animate. Save this file; if you enabled Incremental Save as recommended earlier, your file won't be replaced with subsequent saves.

Figure 2.15

The shaded planets in perspective view

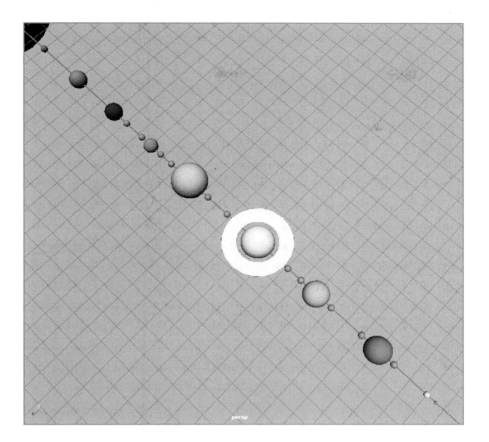

Creating the Animation

To begin this phase of the project, load the file `Planets_v2.ma` in the Scenes folder of the Solar_System project on the web page to your hard drive, or continue with your own scene file.

The animation you'll do for the planet's self-rotation is straightforward. You'll rotate the planets around their own axes for their self-rotation, and then you'll animate the moons around the planets for their lunar orbits. Finally, you'll make the planets and their moons orbit the Sun.

This exercise focuses on hierarchy and pivot points. A *pivot point* is an object's center of balance of sorts. Every object or node created in Maya has a pivot point, especially primitives like you're creating here. That pivot point is usually at the center of the primitive and moves along with the object if it's moved.

Now, you need to set up the animation settings for your scene file:

1. Press F4 to open the Animation menu set, or select it from the drop-down menu shown earlier in the chapter. *Menu sets* are groupings of menu headings in the main menu bar. They're organized according to the type of task at hand. You'll see the several menu headings change.

2. At the bottom of the UI, you'll notice a slider bar (the Range slider) directly below the strip of numbers counting off the frames (the Time slider) in the scene. Using the Range slider, you'll set the length of your animation to go from 1 to 240. Enter **1** in the Scene Start Frame and Range Start Frame boxes (Figure 2.16). Enter a value of **240** in the Scene End Frame and Range End Frame boxes, also as shown in Figure 2.16.

Figure 2.16

The Time and Range sliders

3. To the right of the Range slider, click the Animation Preferences icon ( ), click Settings (Figure 2.17), and make sure Time is set to Film (24fps).

Figure 2.17

Set Time to 24fps on the Settings tab of the Preferences window.

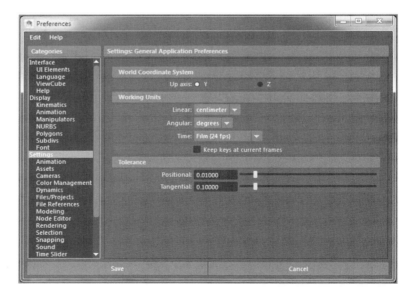

Choose Windows → Settings/Preferences → Preferences to open the Preferences window. Under Settings → Undo, make sure Undo is on and set Queue to Infinite, allowing you to press Ctrl+Z as many times as needed. To close the Preferences window, click Save.

Mercury's Rotation

Now you're ready to animate Mercury's rotation. Follow these steps:

1. Select Mercury, and press E to activate the Rotate tool. The E key is the hotkey to invoke the Rotate tool in Maya. Press F to focus on Mercury in the perspective view, or zoom in on it manually.

2. Make sure you're on frame 1 of your animation range by clicking and dragging the Scrub bar (refer to the earlier Figure 2.17) to place it at the desired frame. You can also manually type the frame value of **1** in the Current Frame box.

3. For Mercury, you'll set your initial keyframe for the Y-axis rotation. RMB+click the attribute name for Rotate Y in the Channel Box to select it and bring up a context menu, as shown in Figure 2.18. Select Key Selected from the context menu. This places a keyframe for a rotation of 0 in the Y-axis at frame 1 for the Mercury sphere, and the Value box in the Rotate Y attribute turns to pink to indicate that a keyframe exists for that attribute.

Conversely, instead of RMB+clicking Rotate Y in the Channel Box, you could also set a keyframe through the main menu bar (in the Animation menu set) by selecting Key → Set Key. However, this method will set a keyframe for *all* attributes of the Mercury sphere, which is not efficient. You should ideally try to set keyframes only on attributes you need.

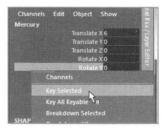

Figure 2.18

Setting the initial keyframe for Mercury's Y-axis rotation

4. Using the Scrub bar in the Time slider, go to frame 240. Grab the Rotation manipulator handle by the Y-axis (the green circle) and turn it clockwise a few times to rotate the sphere clockwise. You'll notice that you can rotate the object only so far in one direction before it seems to reset to its original rotation. Rotate it as far as it will go and release the mouse button. Then, click the manipulator again and drag to rotate the sphere as many times as necessary until you're satisfied with its spin.

5. RMB+click the Rotate Y attribute in the Channel Box and choose Key Selected again. This sets a keyframe for your new Y-axis rotation at frame 240 for the Mercury sphere.

6. To play back your animation, you can scrub your Time slider. Click in the Time slider on the Scrub bar, hold down the left mouse button, and move your cursor from side to side to scrub in real time. You'll see Mercury rotating in your active view panel, if you set your two keyframes as described.

You have the self-rotation for Mercury worked out. Mercury has no moon, so let's get Mercury orbiting the Sun.

Grouping Mercury for a New Pivot Point

You've learned that every object in Maya is created with a pivot point around which it rotates and scales and which acts as the placement for its X-, Y-, and Z-coordinates. To orbit Mercury around the Sun sphere, the sphere must revolve around a pivot point that is placed in the middle of the Sun sphere. If the pivot point for Mercury is already at the center of itself, how can you revolve it around the Sun sphere?

One idea is to move its current pivot point from the center of itself to the center of the Sun sphere. That would, however, negate Mercury's own rotation, and it would no longer spin around its own center, so you can't do that. You need to create a new pivot point for this object. This way, you have the original pivot point at Mercury's center so it can self-rotate, and you have a second pivot point at the Sun sphere so that Mercury can revolve around that point around the Sun sphere. You'll accomplish this by creating a new *parent node* above Mercury in the hierarchy. What does that mean?

To explain, I'll take time in the following section to introduce the concept of Maya object structure: nodes and hierarchies. Save your progress so far and open a new blank scene. After this explanation, you'll resume the solar system exercise.

Hierarchy and Maya Object Structure

On top of everything you see in Maya (its interface) is a layer you don't see: the code. The layer of code keeps the objects in Maya organized through a network of nodes. How you relate these nodes to each other defines how you've built your scene. So, having a solid understanding of how Maya defines objects and how they interact is essential to an efficient and successful animation process.

Understanding Nodes

At its core, Maya relies on packets of information called *nodes*, and each node carries with it a group of attributes that in combination define an object. These attributes can be spatial coordinates, geometric descriptors, color values, and so on. You can define, animate, and interconnect any or all of these attributes individually or in concert, which gives you amazing control over a scene.

Nodes that define the shape of a surface or a primitive are called *creation nodes* or *shape nodes*. These nodes carry the information that defines how that object is created. For example, a sphere's creation node has an attribute for its radius. Changing that attribute changes the radius of the sphere at its base level, making it a bigger or smaller sphere. This is different from scaling the sphere as you've done with the planets so far. Shape nodes are low on the hierarchy chain and are always child nodes of *transform nodes*. The sphere applies attributes from its creation node first and then moves down the chain to apply attributes from other nodes (such as position, rotation, or scale).

The most visible and used nodes are the transform nodes, also known as directed acyclic graph (DAG) nodes. These nodes contain all the transformation attributes for an object or a group of objects below it. *Transformations* are the values for translation (position), rotation, and scale. These nodes also hold hierarchy information about any other children or parent nodes to which they're attached. When you move or scale an object, you adjust attributes in this node.

Parents and Children

A *parent node* is simply a node that passes its transformations down the hierarchy chain to its children. A *child node* inherits the transforms of all the parents above it. So, by using hierarchies for the solar system exercise, you'll create a nested hierarchy of parents and children to animate the orbital rotation of the nine planets and some of their moons.

With the proper hierarchy, the animation of the planet (the parent) orbiting the Sun automatically translates to the moon (the child). In effect, the planet takes the moon with it as it goes around the Sun.

Child nodes have their own transformations that can be coupled with any inherited transforms from their parent, and these transformations affect them and any of their children down the line.

You're about to experience this first hand as you continue the solar system exercise. The more you hear about these concepts in different contexts, the easier they will be to master.

Figure 2.19 shows the Outliner and Hypergraph views with a simple hierarchy of objects for your reference. The Outliner and Hypergraph show you the objects in your scene in an outline and flowchart format, respectively. Both of these windows allow you to access the different levels of nodes (the hierarchy) in a scene and are discussed further in Chapter 3.

Figure 2.19

A simple hierarchy in both the Outliner and Hypergraph windows

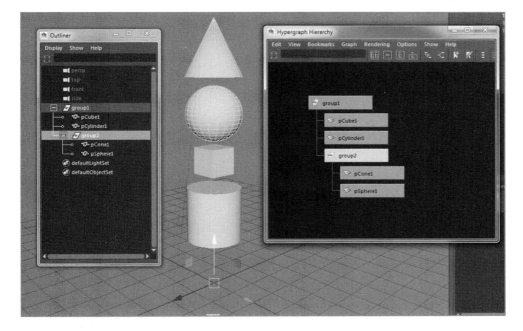

A top parent node called group1 holds its children pCube1, pCylinder1, and the nested group node group2. The node group2 is the parent node of pCone1 and pSphere1.

The Solar System, Resumed

If you still feel a little unsure about nodes and hierarchies, take the time to reread the previous section. You'll practice these concepts as you resume the solar system exercise. By the time you've finished this exercise, you'll have a strong sense of how hierarchies work in Maya, although you should feel free to repeat the entire exercise if you think that will help you master hierarchies. Understanding nodes and hierarchies is absolutely critical to animating in Maya.

If you're new to CG animation, take your time with the following section.

Animating Mercury's Orbit Around the Sun

Load your scene from where you last saved it. When you left off, you had created the self-rotation animation for Mercury and were about to create a second pivot point for the planet to orbit around the Sun sphere by creating a new parent node for the Mercury sphere.

To create a new pivot point by making a new parent node, follow these steps:

1. With Mercury selected, press E for the Rotate tool and then choose Edit → Group from the main menu bar (you can also press Ctrl+G). The Channel Box displays attributes for a new node called group1. Notice that nothing about the Mercury sphere changed, except that the Rotation manipulator handle jumped from where it was centered on Mercury all the way back to the origin, where the zero points of the X-, Y-, and Z-axes collide. Figure 2.20 shows the new Mercury group (called group1) and its new pivot location.

Figure 2.20

Grouping Mercury to itself creates a new pivot point at the origin.

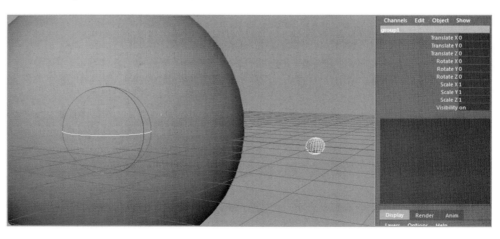

You just created a new Maya object by grouping Mercury to itself. In doing so, you also created a second pivot point for Mercury, which was placed by Maya at the origin by default. Because an object's manipulator always appears at the object's pivot point when it's selected, Mercury's Rotate manipulator jumped to the origin when the new parent node was created. That is fortunate for you because that happens to be the center of the Sun sphere—exactly where you need it to be for Mercury to orbit the Sun sphere properly.

2. Without unselecting anything, click the group1 name in the Channel Box, and change the name of this new group to **Mercury_Orbit**. It's important to make the distinction between node names so you never get confused. Now you know that the Mercury node is the planet sphere itself, whereas Mercury_Orbit is the name of the new parent node with which you'll orbit Mercury around the Sun sphere.

3. Click anywhere in an empty space in your view window to unselect Mercury_Orbit. Try selecting it again by clicking the Mercury sphere. Notice that when you click Mercury, you select only the planet and not the new parent node Mercury_Orbit, the group that has its pivot point at the center of the Sun sphere. This happens because you're in Object mode. To select the group Mercury_Orbit, switch into Hierarchy mode by toggling its icon ( ) on the Status line at the top of the UI, as shown in Figure 2.21. For more on selection modes, see Chapter 3. Now when you click Mercury, it selects the new Mercury_Orbit parent node you made.

4. Go back to frame 1 of your animation. Set a keyframe for Mercury_Orbit's Rotate Y attribute by RMB+clicking its name in the Channel Box and then choosing Key Selected.

5. Go to frame 240, grab Mercury_Orbit's Rotate manipulator handle by the green Y-axis, and spin it around the Sun twice in either direction. (It doesn't matter if you go clockwise or counterclockwise.) You can also enter **720** in the Rotate Y attribute field in the Channel Box (or **-720** to go in the other direction).

6. Set a keyframe at frame 240 for Mercury_Orbit's Rotate Y attribute, as you did in step 4. Scrub your animation to play it back.

7. Make sure to switch back to Object mode by clicking its icon ( ) in the Status line (Figure 2.21).

Does that make good sense? You'll have the chance to do this a few more times as you animate the other planets and their moons. However, if you still find yourself a little fuzzy on this concept (which is perfectly normal), repeat the steps to animate Mercury in a new scene file if need be. One down, eight to go.

Figure 2.21

Toggling on the Hierarchy mode

Creating Venus

For your next planet, Venus, follow the same procedure as for Mercury's self-rotation (steps 1–6 in the "Mercury's Rotation" section) and animate it so that it rotates around itself, just like Mercury. Then, create a new pivot point by grouping Venus to itself to create a new parent node (as you did for Mercury_Orbit in steps 1–2 in the previous section) and call the new parent node **Venus_Orbit**. Lastly, animate Venus_Orbit to revolve around the Sun sphere just as you did with Mercury_Orbit in steps 3–7.

Earth and the Moon

Now you need to animate the third planet, Earth, in much the same way, except that this time there will be the added complication of a moon. (Earth? Hey, I can see my house from here!)

To animate Earth and the moon, follow these steps:

1. Select Earth and give it its self-rotation animation as you did for Mercury.

2. Select the moon and give it its own self-rotation animation by spinning it around itself and keyframing it as you've just done with Earth.

3. To spin the moon around Earth, you'll do as you did earlier in this chapter to orbit a planet around the Sun: first, group the moon to itself by choosing Edit → Group; then, name the new parent node **Moon_Orbit**.

This time, however, you need the pivot point to be at the center of Earth and not at the center of the Sun object, where it is currently. Follow these steps:

1. Turn on the grid snap () and press and hold down the D key to be able to move the pivot point. The moon's manipulator changes from a rotation handle to the Pivot Point manipulator. This manipulator acts just like the Move manipulator, but instead of moving the object, it moves the object's pivot point as long as you keep the D key pressed. Just don't rotate the pivot using this Pivot Point manipulator; use just the move handles.

2. Grab the yellow circle in the middle of the manipulator and move the pivot point to snap it to the grid point located at the center of Earth (see Figure 2.22).

3. Now release the D key to return to the Rotation manipulator for Moon_Orbit. At frame 1, set a keyframe for the moon's Y-axis rotation. Then, at frame 240, rotate the moon around the Y-axis and set a keyframe. Return to frame 1.

Grouping the Moon with Earth

To animate Earth's orbit of the Sun, you need to make sure the moon will also follow Earth around the Sun sphere. Instead of just selecting Earth and grouping it to itself as you've done for the other two planets, you need to include the Moon_Orbit node in that group. Follow these steps:

1. Select Earth. Shift+click the Moon_Orbit group while in Hierarchy mode (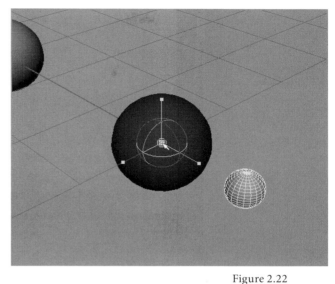) to make sure you get the topmost node of the moon and then choose Edit → Group. Name this new parent node **Earth_Orbit**. Remember, when you select just Earth or the moon in Object mode ( ), the Earth_Orbit node isn't selected. If you select Earth and then Shift+click the moon, you select both objects, but you still don't select the parent node Earth_Orbit, which is the group that contains both these objects and has its pivot point at the center of the Sun. Make sure you select the right group. Keep an eye on where the manipulator is when you make your selection. If you have the Earth_Orbit node selected, its manipulator should be in the middle of the Sun sphere. I'll deliberately illustrate this mistake and its consequences when you animate Pluto a little later.

Figure 2.22

Moving the moon's pivot point to the center of Earth

> Make sure you use Hierarchy mode ( ) when you click the moon object to select Moon_Orbit and not just the moon sphere. Otherwise, you'll lose the animation of the moon orbiting Earth.

2. Set a keyframe for Earth_Orbit's Rotate Y attribute at frame 1, again by RMB+clicking Rotate Y in the Channel Box and selecting Key Selected.

3. Go to frame 240, spin Earth and the moon around the Sun sphere a few times in whichever direction and for however many revolutions you want, and set a keyframe at frame 240.

Now the first three planets are going around themselves and around the Sun, with a moon for Earth. If you haven't been saving your work, save it now. Just don't save over the unanimated version from earlier.

Creating the Other Planets' Moons

Repeat this animation procedure for the remaining planets and moons, but leave out Pluto for now. (Poor Pluto: first it loses out on being a planet, and now it has to wait for last.)

If you find that one of your moons is left behind by its planet or that it no longer revolves around the planet, you most likely made an error when grouping the moon and planet. Undo (Ctrl+Z) until you're at the point right before you grouped them and try again. If that still doesn't work, start over from the earlier version of the file you saved just before you began animating it. You'll learn how to fix it in the section "Using the Outliner" later in this chapter.

Auto Keyframe

You can also use the Auto Keyframe feature when animating the planets and moons. Auto Keyframe automatically sets a keyframe for any attribute that changes from a previously set keyframe. For example, an initial keyframe for an attribute such as Y-Axis Rotation needs to be set at some point in the animation. The next time the Y-Axis Rotation is changed at a different frame, Maya will set a keyframe at that frame automatically.

To turn on Auto Keyframe, click the Auto Keyframe icon (⊙), which is to the right of the Range slider in the lower right of the main UI. When the icon is blue, Auto Keyframe is active.

To use Auto Keyframe to animate the moon orbiting Mars, follow these steps:

1. Turn on Auto Keyframe.

2. Start at frame 1. Select the moon of Mars and set a keyframe for its Y-axis orbit by highlighting Rotate Y in the Channel Box and selecting Key Selected.

3. Go to frame 240. Revolve the moon around Mars several times in a direction of your choosing. Maya automatically sets a frame for Y rotation at frame 240. Save your file.

Using the Outliner

The Outliner is an outline listing of all the objects and nodes in your scene. For an in-depth look at the Outliner, see Chapter 3. For now, let's look at how to use the Outliner to illustrate the hierarchies for the planets and moons. When all is good and proper, the Outliner should look like Figure 2.23. Choose Windows → Outliner to open the Outliner window and take a peek at what you have. If you haven't yet properly named everything, including the moons, take this opportunity to do so by double-clicking a name in the Outliner and entering a new name.

Let's look at the planet Mars and its layout in the Outliner to better understand the hierarchy for all the planets. All the other planets should be laid out exactly like Mars (except the planets that have just one or no moon).

At the bottom of the hierarchy are Mars's two moons, mars_moon and mars_moon2. Each of those moons is spinning on its own pivot point. You grouped each moon to itself, created the mars_moon_orbit and mars_moon2_orbit nodes, and placed their pivot points at the center of Mars to animate their orbits around Mars.

Mars is spinning on its own pivot point, but it needed another pivot point to be able to orbit the Sun. Because you had to make the moons go with it around the Sun, you selected Mars, mars_moon_orbit, and mars_moon2_orbit (the top nodes of the moons that circle the planet Mars) and grouped them all together, placing that pivot point at the center of the Sun. You called this node Mars_Orbit. This is the *parent node* because it's the topmost node for this group. Wherever this parent node goes, the child nodes that are under it will follow.

Hierarchies such as this are a cornerstone of Maya animation. It's imperative that you're comfortable with how they work and how to work with them. If you find yourself scratching your head even a little, try the exercise again. A proper foundation is critical. Remember, this learning 3D thing isn't easy, but patience and repetition help a lot.

Correcting Hierarchy Problems Using the Outliner

One of the most common problems you'll run into with this project is a planet revolving around the Sun without its moon. To illustrate how to fix it using the Outliner, as opposed to undoing and redoing it as suggested earlier, the following steps will force you to make this error with Pluto. Usually, people learn more from mistakes than from doing things correctly.

Go to Pluto, start the same animation procedure as outlined earlier, and then follow these steps to force an error:

1. Create Pluto's own self-rotation by spinning it around itself and keyframing as before.

2. Do the same for Pluto's moon's self-rotation.

3. Group the moon to itself and grid-snap the pivot point at the center of Pluto to create the moon's orbit of Pluto.

    When Pluto's moon (pluto_moon) is orbiting Pluto, you're ready to group the moon's orbit and Pluto together to create an orbit of the Sun sphere for both.

4. Here is where you make your mistake. In Object mode, select the sphere for Pluto's moon and select the sphere for Pluto. Your error is that you're in Object mode instead of switching to Hierarchy mode.

5. Choose Edit → Group to group them together and call that new node **Pluto_Orbit** (following the naming convention you used for the others).

6. Animate Pluto_Orbit revolving around the Sun.

7. Play back the animation.

Figure 2.23

The Outliner view of the planet hierarchies

Notice that the moon is no longer orbiting the planet. This is because you didn't include pluto_moon_orbit in your group Pluto_Orbit. The animation of the moon going around Pluto is stored in that node, and because it's no longer attached to Pluto_Orbit, there's no moon orbit of Pluto.

Figure 2.24 shows the hierarchy of Pluto and how it's different from that of the other planets: the moon's orbit node has been left out of the group. (Earth has been expanded as a contrasting example.)

Using the Outliner, you can easily fix this problem. Place the pluto_moon_orbit node under the Pluto_Orbit node. Go to frame 1 of the animation, grab the pluto_moon_orbit node in the Outliner, and use the middle mouse button to drag it to the Pluto_Orbit node so that it has a white dashed line around it to show a connection, as in Figure 2.25 (left). The proper grouping is shown in Figure 2.25 (right).

You've just grouped pluto_moon_orbit under Pluto_Orbit, a practice known as *parenting*. Now you need to parent pluto_moon under pluto_moon_orbit as well. Use the MMB to drag pluto_moon onto pluto_moon_orbit. When you play back the animation, you'll see that the moon is revolving around the planet and that Pluto and the moon are orbiting the Sun sphere. Now that you've corrected Pluto's layout in the Outliner, it's similar to the layouts for the other properly working planets.

The file Planets_v3.mb in the Scenes folder of the Solar_System project on the book's web page will give you an idea of how this project should look. The first five planet systems are grouped and animated as a reference, leaving the final four for you to finish.

Figure 2.24

Pluto's incorrect hierarchy

Figure 2.25

Actively regrouping objects in the Outliner (left). Pluto's moon is grouped properly (right).

You can add objects to a group by MMB+dragging their listing onto the desired parent node in the Outliner. You can also remove objects from a group by MMB+dragging them out of the parent node to a different place in the Outliner.

GROUPING TERMINOLOGY

Grouping terminology can be confusing. Grouping Node A under Node B makes Node A a child of Node B. Node B is now the parent of Node A. Furthermore, any transformation or movement applied to the parent Node B will be inherited by the child Node A.

When you group Node A and Node B, both nodes become *siblings* under a newly created parent node, Node C. This new node is created just to be the parent of Nodes A and B and is otherwise known as a *null node*. To group objects, select them and choose Edit → Group. Parenting nodes together places the first selected node under the second selected node. For example, if you select Node A, Shift+select Node B, and then choose Edit → Parent, Node A will group under Node B and become its child. This is the same procedure as MMB+dragging Node B to Node A in the Outliner, as you did with Pluto's moon and Pluto itself.

Outputting Your Work: Playblasting

What's the use of animating all this work and not being able to show it? There are several ways of outputting your work in Maya, most of which involve rendering to images. One faster way of outputting your animation in a simple shaded view is called *playblasting*. Playblasting creates a sequence of images that play back on your computer at the proper frame rate. Only if your PC is slow or if you're playblasting a large sequence of frames will your playback degrade. In this case, playblasting 240 frames shouldn't be a problem.

A *playblast*, as it's called in Maya, outputs the view panel's view into an image sequence or AVI movie. You can also save the image sequence or AVI to disk if you like. Playblasting is done mainly to test the look and animation of a scene, especially when its playback is slow within Maya.

When you have your solar system animated, output a playblast by following these steps:

1. With your animation completed, click in the perspective panel to make it active in the four-panel layout (don't maximize the Perspective window). Press 5 to enter Shaded mode.

2. RMB+click anywhere in the Time slider, and select Playblast ❐ from the context menu, as shown in Figure 2.26. The option box is shown for the Playblast options in Figure 2.27.

Figure 2.26

Selecting Playblast

CHAPTER 3

The Autodesk® Maya® 2016 Interface

This chapter takes you on a guided tour of all the elements visible on the screen for the Autodesk® Maya® 2016 program as you build a simple model of a decorative box. The chapter draws from the experience you had in Chapter 2, "Jumping into Basic Animation Headfirst," with the solar system exercise. You'll visit the menus, icons, and shelves to become familiar with the interface basics as you build a model.

This chapter also serves as a good reference when you're wondering about the purpose of a particular icon.

Learning Outcomes: In this chapter, you will be able to

- Recognize and use Maya UI elements

- Understand how Maya view panels and windows work

- Use manipulators to transform objects in 3D space

- Create and use reference planes for modeling from pictures

- Use polygon modeling techniques

  - Extrude

  - Bevel

  - Edge loops

  - Multi-Cut tool

  - Component editing—edges, faces, vertices

- Use the Layer Editor to organize your scene

- Render test frames to preview your work

- Gain confidence in using the Attribute Editor

- Better manage your scenes and object hierarchies with the Outliner

Navigating in Maya

The key to being a good digital artist or animator isn't knowing *where* to find all the tools and buttons but knowing *how* to find the features you need. The purpose of this chapter is to help you get to know Maya and how it operates, building on your experience so far.

Explore the interface. Using your mouse, check out the menus and the tools. Just be careful not to change any settings; the rest of this book and its projects assume your Maya settings are all at their defaults. If you do change some settings inadvertently, reverting to the defaults is easy. Choose Windows → Settings/Preferences → Preferences. In the Preferences window, choose Edit → Restore Default Settings. Now all the settings and interface elements are restored to their default states.

Exploring the Maya Layout

Let's take another look at the initial Maya screen in Figure 3.1—this time with the Full Perspective window and not the four-panel layout you saw in the previous chapter.

Figure 3.1

The initial Maya screen

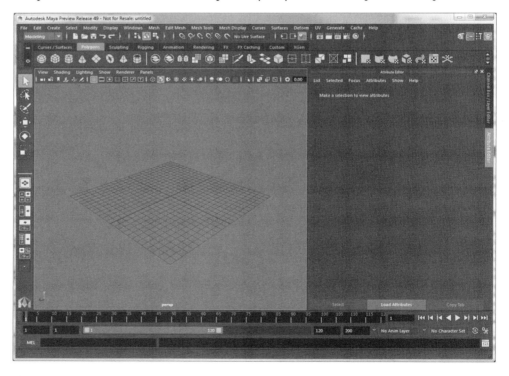

The *main menu bar*, *Status line*, and *Shelf* all run across the top of the screen. The Tool Box runs vertically on the left side of the screen. It contains icons for your transform tools (such as Move, Rotate, and Scale) as well as quick-view selections to allow you to customize your panel layouts quickly. The Attribute Editor, Channel Box/Layer Editor, and Modeling Toolkit (the Attribute Editor is currently displayed in Figure 3.1) run down the right side of the screen. Finally, listed from the top down, the Time slider, the Range slider, the Character Set menu, the Auto Keyframe button, and the Animation Preferences button, some of which you've already used, run across the bottom of the screen.

REMINDER: MAYA MOUSE CONTROLS

In Maya, holding the Alt key on a PC or the Option key on a Mac along with the appropriate button allows you to move in the view panel. The left mouse button (LMB) acts as the primary selection button and lets you orbit around objects when used with the Alt key. The right mouse button (RMB) activates numerous context menus and lets you zoom with the Alt key. The middle mouse button (MMB) with the Alt key lets you move within the Maya interface, and the mouse's wheel can also be used to zoom in and out.

The Main Menu Bar

In Maya, menu choices are context sensitive; they depend on what you're doing. The main menu bar is shown in Figure 3.2. By switching menu sets, you change your menu choices and hence your available tool set. The menu sets in Maya are Modeling, Rigging, Animation, FX, and Rendering.

Figure 3.2

The main menu bar is where the magic happens.

Menu Sets

The Menu Set drop-down is the first thing on the Status line, as shown in Figure 3.3.

No matter which menu set you're working in, the first seven menu items are constant: File, Edit, Create, Select, Modify, Display, and Windows, as is the last menu entry, Help.

Some plug-ins can also add menu items to the main menu bar. If the plug-in is turned off, that menu item is removed. So, don't panic if you don't see the same main menu bar pictured throughout this book.

Figure 3.3

The Menu Set drop-down menu

ADVANCED TIP: FLOATING MENUS

In Maya, you can *tear off* menus to create separate floating boxes that you can place anywhere in the workspace, as shown here. This makes accessing menu commands eas especially when you need to use the same command repeatedly. To tear off a menu, cl dashed line at the top of the menu and drag the menu where you want it.

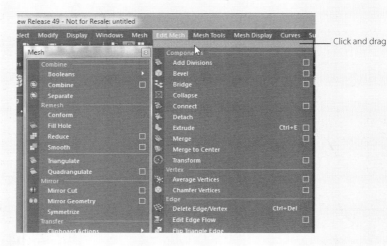

Figure 3.4

Submenus and the all-important option box

Submenus and the Option Box

You'll notice two different demarcations to the right of some menu items (Figu arrows and boxes (called *option boxes*). Clicking an arrow opens a submenu tha more specific commands. Clicking an option box (▢ opens a dialog box in which you can set the options fo particular tool.

Marking Menus

Marking menus are a fast UI workflow to allow you to commands and options without accessing the main me bar, as you did in the Hypershade in Chapter 2's solar sy exercise. For example, RMB+clicking any object in you scene gives you the marking menu shown in Figure 3.5 this particular marking menu, you can select vertices or

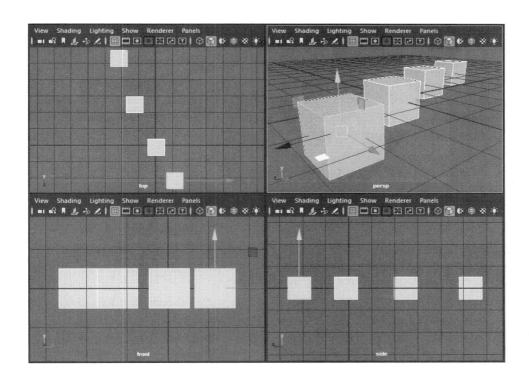

Figure 3.8

The four-panel layout

SHORTCUTS TO VIEWING

Here's a summary of the most important keyboard shortcuts. Keep in mind that the Option key is used on a Macintosh in place of the Alt key on a PC. See Chapter 2 for more details.

Alt+MMB+Click   Tracks around a window.

Alt+RMB+Click   Dollies into or out of a view.

Scroll Wheel   Dollies into or out of a view.

Alt+LMB+Click   Rotates or orbits the camera around in a Perspective window.

Alt+Ctrl+Click and Drag   Dollies your view into the screen area specified in your mouse drag.

ViewCube   Allows you to change views in a panel easily. This works only in legacy viewports and not the new Viewport 2.0 display that is default with Maya 2016. In other words, the ViewCube will not display by default, so the ViewCube will go largely unused, though you may notice it in some figures and images throughout the book.

Macintosh Keys   The Option key on a Mac is used as the Alt key on a PC.

WIREFRAME AND SHADED MODES

When you're working in the windows, you can view your 3D objects either as wireframe models (as in Figure 3.9) or as solid, hardware-rendered models called *Shaded mode* (see Figure 3.10). When you press 4 or 5, notice that a text helper opens to tell you your current viewing mode. These messages are called *in-view messages* and can be helpful as you learn the Maya workflow. You can toggle them on or off by choosing, in the main menu bar, Display → Heads Up Display → In-View Messages.

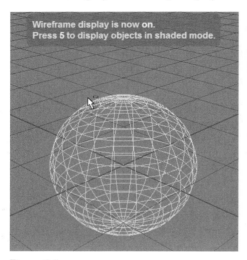

Figure 3.9

Wireframe display of the selected sphere

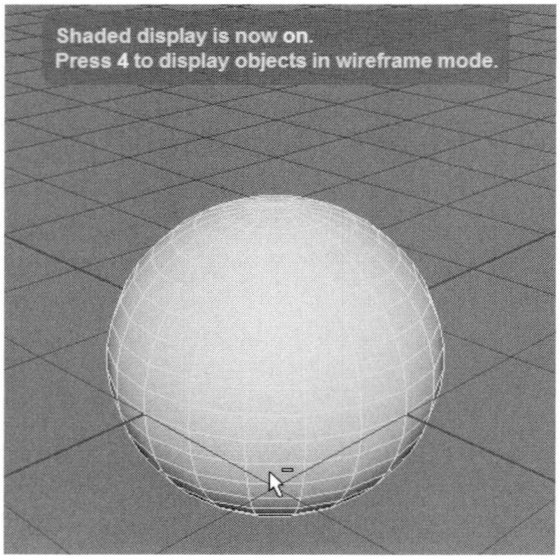

Figure 3.10

Shaded display of the selected sphere

You can cycle through the modes of display by pressing 4, 5, 6, and 7. Wireframe mode is 4, Shaded mode is 5 and shows you a solid view of the objects, Texture Shaded mode is 6 and shows any textures that are applied to the objects, and Lighted mode is 7 and shows a hardware preview of the objects as they're lit in the scene. Table 3.1 gives a quick reference for toggling display levels.

Table 3.1

Levels of display detail

KEY	FUNCTION
4	Toggles into Wireframe mode
5	Toggles into Shaded mode
6	Toggles into Textured mode
7	Toggles into Lighted mode

Pressing 5 for Shaded mode lets you see your objects as solid forms and volumes. Pressing 6 for Texture mode is good for the rudimentary alignment of textures. Pressing 7 for Lighted mode (Figure 3.11) is useful for spotting proper lighting direction and object highlights when you first begin lighting a scene.

Other display commands you'll find useful while working in the Modeling windows are found under the panel's (a.k.a. viewport's) View menu. Look At Selection centers on the selected object or objects. Frame All (hotkey = A) moves the view in or out to display all the objects in the scene, and Frame Selection (hotkey = F) centers on and moves the view in or out to fully frame the selected object or objects in the panel.

The Manipulators

Manipulators are onscreen handles that you use to manipulate the selected object with tools such as Move or Rotate, as you saw in the solar system exercise. Figure 3.12 shows three distinct and common manipulators for all objects in Maya: Move (press W), Rotate (press E), and Scale (press R). In addition, the fourth manipulator shown in Figure 3.12 is the Universal Manipulator, which allows you to move, rotate, or scale an object all within one manipulator (select Modify → Transformation Tools → Universal Manipulator or press Ctrl+T).

You can access the manipulators using either the icons from the Tool Box on the left of the UI or the hotkeys shown in Table 3.2.

KEY	FUNCTION		Table 3.2
W	Activates the Move tool		**Manipulator hotkeys**
E	Activates the Rotate tool		
R	Activates the Scale tool		
Q	Select tool; also deselects any Translation tools		

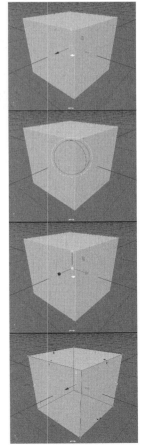

CAPS AND HOTKEYS

Keyboard shortcuts in Maya are *case sensitive* because in many cases, pressing a single letter key has a different effect than pressing Shift + that letter (which makes the letter uppercase). This book shows all single letters as capitals in the text (the same way they appear on your keyboard). The Shift key is included in the text only when it's part of an uppercase shortcut. So, if you find yourself wondering why pressing a hotkey isn't working, make sure you aren't pressing Shift or that the Caps Lock isn't enabled.

Try This   In a new scene, choose Create → NURBS Primitives → Sphere, drag in a view panel on its grid to create a sphere, and then size it however you like. If you have Interactive Creation already turned off for NURBS primitives, a sphere appears at the origin. Press the 5 key in one of the view panels for Shaded mode. In the previous chapter, you tried the manipulators on a sphere to get a feel for how they work. In Chapter 2 you may have noticed the feedback feature on the Universal Manipulator. Select Modify → Transformation Tools → Universal Manipulator,

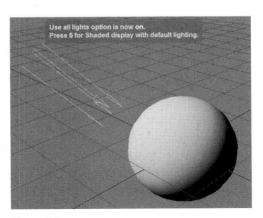

Figure 3.11
Lighted mode (press 7) showing a single directional light shining on the sphere

Figure 3.12
Using manipulators

and you'll notice the Universal Manipulator icon appear just below the Tool Box (). Manipulate the sphere in the view panel and take a look.

The Universal Manipulator interactively shows you the movement, rotation, or scale as you manipulate the sphere. Notice the coordinates that come up and change as you move the sphere. When you rotate using this manipulator, you see the degree of change. Notice the scale values in dark gray on the three outside edges of the manipulator box; they change when you scale the sphere.

You can scale any manipulator handle. Press the plus key (+) to increase a manipulator's size, and press the minus key (–) to decrease it.

Soft Selection

Soft selection is a way to select part of an object (like a vertex) and manipulate it so that neighboring vertices are affected as well, but in decreasing amounts. Soft selection is best described by seeing it in action.

1. In a new scene, create a polygonal sphere at the origin.

2. RMB+click the sphere to bring up a *marking menu*. Select vertices as shown in Figure 3.13.

3. Your display now shows the sphere as cyan and pink points indicating where the vertices are. (I cover vertices in detail in the next chapter.) Manipulating vertices allows you to alter the shape of the polygonal mesh. As you move your mouse over vertices, they turn into red blocks. Click a single vertex to select it.

4. Press W for the Move tool and move the vertex away from the sphere, as shown in Figure 3.14. Doing so creates a spike on the sphere.

5. This time, let's go into the options for the Move tool. Select Modify → Transformation Tools → Move Tool □ to open the Tool Settings window, shown in Figure 3.15. If you need to expand the window, click and drag the vertical bar on the right of the Tool Settings window to see the full width of the panel.

6. Scroll down to the Soft Selection heading and toggle on Soft Select, as shown in Figure 3.16.

7. In the persp view panel, RMB+click the sphere again and select Vertex. Select another vertex on the sphere. When you do, a gradient of color from yellow to red to black appears on your model. This gradient shows you the influence of your soft selection. Figure 3.17 shows you the falloff region on the sphere.

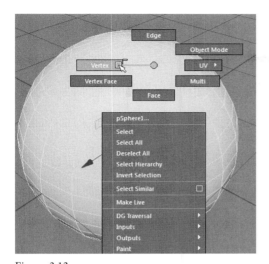

Figure 3.13
Selecting vertices

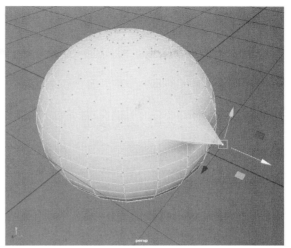

Figure 3.14
Pull a vertex to make a spike.

Figure 3.15
The option box for the Move tool opens Tool Settings.

Figure 3.16
Click Soft Select.

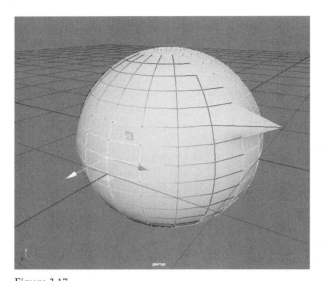

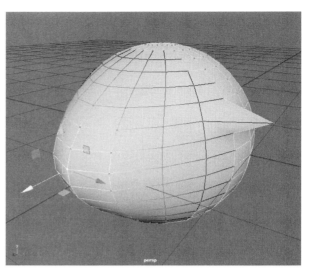

Figure 3.17

Soft Select shows you the falloff gradient.

Figure 3.18

Use soft selection to pull out a bulb rather than a spike.

8. The area of influence is too large for this sphere, so set Falloff Radius from 5.0 to 1.0 and move that vertex away from the sphere. This time, instead of a spike forming on the sphere, a much larger, but smooth, bulb forms out of the sphere, as shown in Figure 3.18, much like what would happen if you used the Soft Modification tool.

9. You can further adjust the size of the falloff area by adjusting the Falloff Radius attribute in the Tool Settings. Be sure to turn off Soft Select and close the Tool Settings window.

Using soft selection on a transform tool such as Move allows you to make organic changes to your mesh easily.

Figure 3.19

Hovering over the icon will give you some information for that tool. Double-clicking the icon will open the options for that tool.

Symmetry

Using the Symmetry transformation option makes symmetrical edits to a mesh. Follow these steps to experience Symmetry with the Move tool:

1. Create a polygonal sphere at the origin in a new scene.

2. Invoke the Move tool options by double-clicking the Move tool icon in the Tool Box on the left of the UI, shown in Figure 3.19. The options will open just as if you selected the option box through the menu.

3. At the bottom of the Tool Settings window (a.k.a. option box) in the Symmetry Settings section, as shown previously at the bottom of Figure 3.16, click the Symmetry pulldown menu's

down arrow (next to the box that says Off) and select an axis for symmetry. Select Object Z for now.

4. Enter component selection mode by RMB+clicking the sphere and choosing Faces from the marking menu that appears.

5. Move your cursor over a face, and it turns blue; a face on the opposite side of the sphere turns blue as well. Select a face on one side of the sphere, and a face on the opposite side of the sphere is also selected (Figure 3.20, top). Now when you try to move that selected face, the opposite face moves as well in the opposite direction, as shown in Figure 3.20 (bottom).

6. Make sure to turn off Symmetry when you're done.

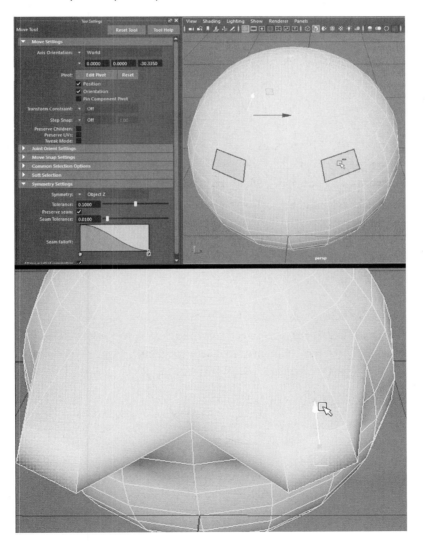

Figure 3.20

The user selected the face on the left and moved it. With Symmetry turned on, the opposite face along the Z-axis is also selected and moved.

Building a Decorative Box

Let's get back to making things and explore the interface as we go along. In this exercise, you'll build a decorative box, shown in Figure 3.21. You will learn to use reference images for modeling, model polygons with Bevel and Extrude tools, and then add edges with Edge Loop and Multi-Cut. Through the process, the Layer Editor helps you stay organized, and you can hide objects from view. This box will be a fairly simple model to make, but you'll use it extensively in Chapters 7, 10, and 11 when working with texture, light, and rendering.

Figure 3.21

A photo of the decorative box

Notice that the box has intricately carved grooves and surface features. You'll build the box to fit the reference and then rely on texture maps created in Chapter 7, "Autodesk® Maya® Shading and Texturing," to create the details on the surface of the box. You'll begin by creating *reference planes* in the next section.

Creating Reference Planes

You can use image references from photos or drawings to model your objects in Maya quite easily. These references are basically photos or drawings of your intended model, usually from three different image views of the model (front, side, and top).

The image reference views of the decorative box have already been created and proportioned properly. (You will see a more thorough review of this process for an exercise in Chapter 6, "Practical Experience.") You can find the images for the box in the Sourceimages folder of the Decorative_Box project. Table 3.3 lists their names, along with their statistics.

FILENAME	VIEW	IMAGE SIZE	ASPECT RATIO
boxFrontRef.jpg	Front	1749 x 2023	0.865:1
boxSideRef.jpg	Side	1862 x 2046	0.910:1
boxTopRef.jpg	Top	1782 x 1791	1.005:1

Table 3.3

Reference views and image sizes

The idea here is to map these photos to planes created in Maya. First, press Ctrl+A to toggle off the Attribute Editor if it currently appears to the right of the UI. Toggling off the Attribute Editor displays the Channel Box. Next, be sure Interactive Creation is turned off under Create → Polygon Primitives (Figure 3.22) and then create the reference planes in steps 1 through 3 with the ratios shown in Table 3.4.

Figure 3.22

Make sure Interactive Creation is toggled off.

1. In the front view panel, create a polygonal plane by choosing Create → Polygon Primitives → Plane ❑. This plane is for the front image, so in the option box, set Axis to Z, Width to **0.865**, and Height to **1.0**. Make sure the check box for Preserve Aspect Ratio is deselected, as shown in Figure 3.23. Setting Axis to Z will place the plane properly in the front view. Click Apply to create the plane and keep the option box open.

REFERENCE PLANE	WIDTH	HEIGHT
Front	0.865	1
Side	0.910	1
Top	1.005	1

Table 3.4

Reference planes and sizes

2. Switch to the side view panel. Create a second plane, this time with a width of **0.910** and height of **1**. Set Axis to X and make sure Preserve Aspect Ratio is unchecked. Click Apply to create the plane.

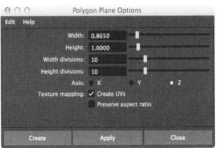

Figure 3.23

Option box for creating a plane for the front view

3. Switch to the top view panel. Create a third plane with a width of **1.005** and height of **1** and set Axis to Y. Make sure the Preserve Aspect Ratio box is still unchecked and click Create to create the plane and close the option box. Your planes should look like those shown in Figure 3.24.

4. Select the front image plane. In the Channel Box, double-click pPlane1 and rename it to **frontPlane**. Select the side plane and rename it from pPlane2 to **sidePlane**. Rename the top plane from pPlane3 to **topPlane**.

5. You still need to place and scale these planes to align them. Take a look at Figure 3.25 to size your reference planes and place them as shown. There are two ways to position these planes. You can manually scale and move them to visually match what you see in Figure 3.25, or you can enter the exact values for scale and translation as shown in Table 3.5 using the Channel Box or Attribute Editor (I discuss these windows next before continuing with the box exercise).

Table 3.5

Reference planes: scale and position

REFERENCE PLANE	XYZ SCALE	XYZ POSITION
Front	4.711, 4.711, 4.711	0.134, 0.017, –2.167
Side	4.856, 4.856, 4.856	–1.979, 0, 0
Top	4.28, 4.28, 4.28	0, 0, 0.133

6. Save your work using the main menu bar by choosing File → Save Scene As. Name your work, remembering to use version numbers to keep track of your progress.

You can compare your progress to boxModel01.mb in the Scenes folder of the Decorative_Box project on the book's web page, www.sybex.com/go/introducingmaya2016.

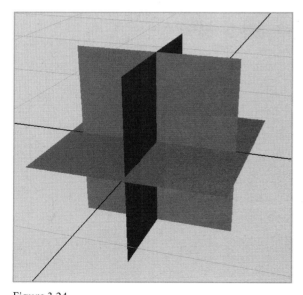

Figure 3.24

The three view planes are ready and waiting at the origin.

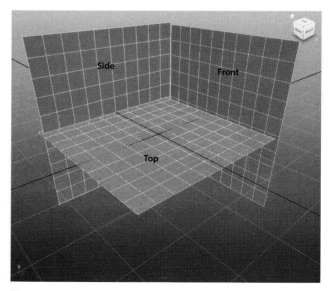

Figure 3.25

Arrange the reference planes for the box model.

The Channel Box/Attribute Editor Explained

To the right of the panels is the Attribute Editor/Channel Box. This is where you'll find (and edit) most of the information, or attributes, about a selected object. Pressing Ctrl+A toggles between the Attribute Editor and the Channel Box.

The Channel Box lists an *object's channels*—that is, the attributes of an object that are most commonly animated. When an object is selected in one of the main views, its name appears at the top of the Channel Box, and its channels are listed. You can edit all the channel values and rename the object itself here.

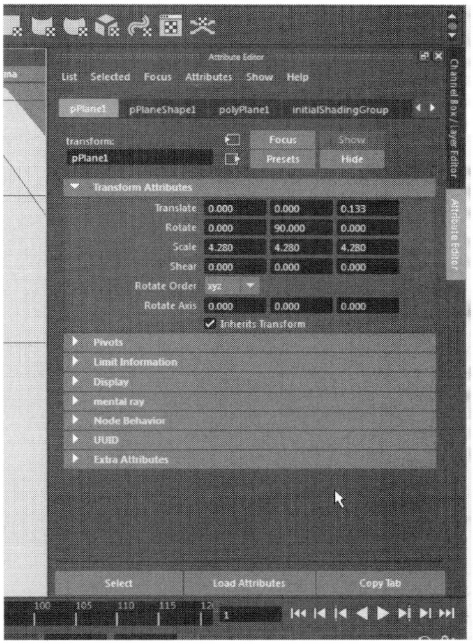

Toggle on the Attribute Editor by pressing Ctrl+A. This window gives you access to all of a selected object's attributes, whereas the Channel Box displays only the most commonly animated attributes.

Tabs running across the top of the Attribute Editor give you access to the other nodes related to that object, as shown in Figure 3.26.

You can click and drag the top of the Attribute Editor to undock it from the main UI. Once you have it in its own window, pressing Ctrl+A will open the Attribute Editor in its own window from then on. However, you can dock the Attribute Editor to the main UI by dragging it back over to the Channel Box area. After that, pressing Ctrl+A will toggle between the Channel Box and Attribute Editor again.

Figure 3.26

The Attribute Editor docked to the main UI

Mapping the Box's Reference Planes with Hypershade

Now you'll import the three reference JPEG images from the Sourceimages folder into Maya through the Hypershade window. Click Windows → Rendering Editors → Hypershade to open this highly powerful texturing window. In the top-left panel (called the Browser), click the Textures tab. This tab will be empty at first, but once you add the reference JPEGs, their icons will show here.

In a file browser (Windows Explorer in Windows or the Finder in Mac OS X) window, navigate to the Sourceimages folder of the Decorative_Box project from the companion web page. One by one, select `boxFrontRef.jpg`, `boxLeftRef.jpg`, and `boxTopRef.jpg` and drag them individually into the bottom panel (called the Work Area) of the Hypershade window, as shown in Figure 3.27.

Figure 3.27

Drag the JPEGs one by one into the Hypershade window's Work Area.

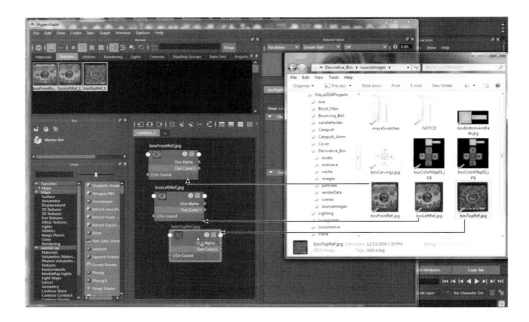

Once you have imported the JPEG images, the Hypershade displays them in the Work Area. You use the Alt+ LMB, RMB, or MMB key combinations to pan and zoom in the Hypershade window, like in other Maya views.

The Hypershade Browser panel has tabs along the top. Since you already clicked the Textures tab, you will see the three JPEGs there as well. Return to the Materials tab to display your scene's materials, a.k.a. shaders. There will be three defaults that are always in every Maya scene (lambert1, particleCloud1, and shaderGlow1), which you should leave alone.

The bottom-right panel is the Work Area and is just that: a work area for you to create and edit materials for your scene. The top section (the Browser) displays all the texture and shader nodes available in your scene, again, separated by tabs.

Any time you need to apply a new material to an object in your scene, you need to create a new shader. So for this example, you need to create three new shaders to assign to the reference plane objects. You can load the scene file to boxModel01.mb in the Scenes folder of the Decorative_Box project from the companion web page or continue with your own scene.

1. Create three Lambert shaders in the Hypershade by clicking three individual times on the Lambert button in the Create panel on the left side of the Hypershade window, as shown in Figure 3.28. Notice that the new Lambert shaders appear up in the Browser but not in the Work Area (which is disappointing!).

2. Simply MMB+click and drag the new Lambert thumbnail icons from the Browser to place them in the Work Area so you can see them all alongside the JPEG nodes of the textures you imported earlier. You can also click and drag the nodes in the Work Area around to arrange them all as shown in Figure 3.29.

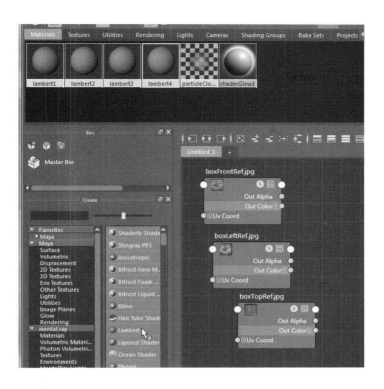

Figure 3.28

Create three new Lambert materials.

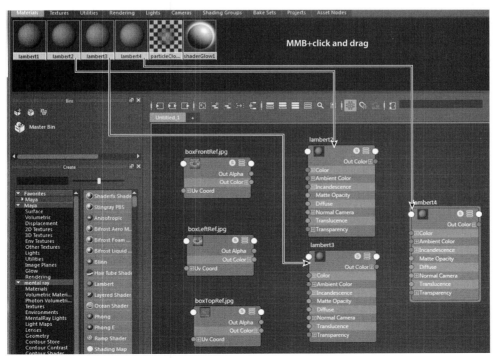

Figure 3.29

MMB+click and drag the three new Lambert shaders to the Work Area and arrange the nodes to see everything.

3. Select the lambert2 node, and you'll see some of its attributes in the panel to the right of the Hypershade, called the Property Editor. You will also see a sample render of that shader above the Property Editor in the Material Viewer window, as shown in Figure 3.30.

4. The nodes you see in the Work Area have colored dots on the left side, called Input Sockets. On the right, the dots are called Output Sockets. These sockets allow you to easily connect textures to shaders. Click the green Output Socket next to Out Color for the boxFrontRef.jpg node, and a rubber band pulls out. Drag the rubber band to the red Input Socket of the lambert2 node, as shown in Figure 3.31. This will make that JPEG image be the color of the lambert2 shader. Rename that Lambert material to **topImage**.

5. Repeat step 4 two times to connect and rename the materials for the front and side views. Make sure you label the materials properly; it's tough to tell the side and front images apart.

6. To assign the materials, simply MMB+drag each shader's thumbnail icon (or node) from the Hypershade to its respective reference plane in the persp view panel. Press 6 for Texture mode in the Perspective window, as shown in Figure 3.32. Close the Hypershade.

7. Choose File → Save Scene As to save a new version of your work.

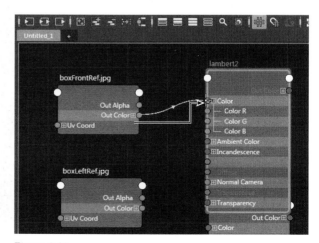

Figure 3.30

The Property Editor in the Hypershade with the Material Viewer above it displays information about the selected node.

Figure 3.31

Connect the Out Color socket of the reference image to the Color input of the lambert2 shader.

You can compare your progress to `boxModel02.mb` in the Scenes folder of the Decorative_Box project at the companion web page.

The Hypershade Explained

Just as the Outliner window lists the objects in your scene, the Hypershade window lists the textures and shaders. Shaders are assigned to objects to give them their visual appearance—their look and feel.

The Hypershade (Window → Rendering Editors → Hypershade) displays shaders and textures in a graphical flowchart layout (see Figure 3.33). The Hypershade window has a few main areas: the *Create* panel the *Bins* panel, the *Browser* panel, the Material viewer, the Property Editor, and the *Work Area*. The Window menu at the Hypershade's menu bar allows you to turn on and off any of these panels. You can also tear them off, or dock them into the Hypershade by clicking the top of any panel and dragging it around in the Hypershade.

Figure 3.32

The images are applied.

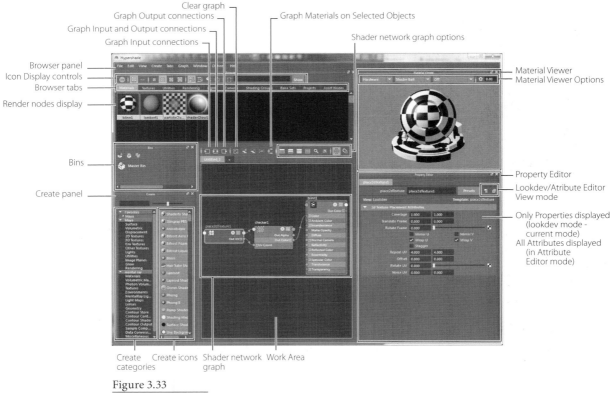

Figure 3.33

The Hypershade's default layout

The Create Panel and Bins Panel Figure 3.33 shows the Create Panel and Bins panel on the left side of the window. The Create panel gives you access to creating a variety of render nodes (shaders and textures, for example) by clicking them. Once you click an icon in the Create panel, it will show up in the Browser panel above. The Bins tab adds a level of organization by letting you store sets of shaders in different bins to sort them. The bar at the top switches between Create Maya Nodes and Create Mental Ray Nodes.

The Browser panel After you create a render node, it appears in the Browser area as a thumbnail icon. Clicking an icon opens its settings in the Property Editor on the right of the Hypershade window. You use the MMB to drag any icon from the Browser to the Work Area, where you can work on making or editing shading networks.

The Work Area The Work Area is a free-form workspace where you can connect render nodes to form-shading networks that you can assign to your objects for rendering. You can add nodes to the workspace by MMB+clicking and dragging them from the Browser panel of the Hypershade window.

The Material Viewer The Material Viewer panel gives you an icon representing how your currently selected material looks. This panel by default sits above the Property Editor. It is usually turned off throughout the figures in this book past this chapter to save space. It is turned on and off through the Window menu in the Hypershade.

Figure 3.34

The Hypershade layout used in this book

Bin Panel turned off

Material Viewer turned off

Property Editor view mode toggle

Attribute Editor mode

The Property Editor   The Property Editor panel gives you access to the settings of any selected node in the Hypershade. This panel has two view options: Lookdev display (shown in Figure 3.33) and Attribute Editor display (as shown in Figure 3.34, where the Material Viewer is also turned off). Lookdev display shows you only the more important settings, a.k.a. properties. The Attribute Editor view shows all the attributes and is almost identical to the main Attribute Editor window in the main Maya UI. You will primarily use the layout shown in Figure 3.34 throughout this book, where the Bins and Material Viewer panels have been turned off to maximize space. You can turn off panels by clicking the Close icon () in the upper right of any panel.

Figure 3.35

Turning parts of the Hypershade back on (top) and docking it to the Hypershade (bottom)

You can turn any of the panels on and off by accessing the Window menu in the Hypershade, as shown in Figure 3.35, to turn them back on as floating windows. Drag the floating panel to inside the Hypershade to dock it as you prefer.

Organizing Workflow with the Layer Editor

Now that you have the reference planes set up and mapped, you'll create *display layers* to help organize the scene before you actually start modeling. You can load the scene file boxModel02.mb in the Scenes folder of the Decorative_Box project from the companion web page or continue with your own scene.

Figure 3.36

The Display tab in the Layer Editor

1. Select the three reference planes and toggle off the Attribute Editor to show the Channel Box. Under the Channel Box is the Layer Editor. Click the Display tab, as shown in Figure 3.36.

2. With the planes selected still, click the Create A New Layer And Assign Selected Objects icon at the top of the Layer Editor, as shown in Figure 3.37. Doing so creates a new layer for these three reference planes.

Figure 3.37

Click to create a new display layer and add the selected objects automatically.

Figure 3.38

Name the new display layer.

Figure 3.39

Toggle the visibility of the reference layer.

Figure 3.40

Set the display to X-Ray mode so you can see how the poly cube and the decorative box line up.

3. In the Layer Editor, double-click the name layer1 to open the Edit Layer window. Rename the layer to **referenceLayer**, as shown in Figure 3.38.

4. Toggle the display of this layer by toggling the V icon, shown in Figure 3.39.

5. Save another version. You can compare your progress to boxModel03.mb in the Scenes folder of the Decorative_Box project.

Display layers allow you to easily turn on and off the display of the reference planes as you model the decorative box. Become familiar with this feature early because it will be a valuable asset when you animate complicated scenes.

To add items to an already created layer, select the objects; then RMB+click the desired layer and choose Add Selected Objects. You can also use the layers to select groups of objects by choosing Layers → Select Objects In Selected Layers or by RMB+clicking the layer and choosing Select Objects. To change the name and color of a layer, double-click the layer to open the Edit Layer window, as shown earlier in Figure 3.38.

Modeling the Decorative Box

Make sure you are in Texture mode (press 6) so you can see the reference plane and the images on them in the persp view panel. Also be sure to toggle on visibility of the references' display layer. In Chapter 4, I'll cover in more detail the modeling tools you'll use.

You can load the scene file boxModel03.mb in the Scenes folder of the Decorative_Box project from the companion web page or continue with your own scene. To model the box to fit the references, follow these steps:

1. With Interactive Creation turned off, select Create → Polygonal Primitives → Cube. Position and size the cube to roughly match the size of the reference planes for the decorative box.

2. To make it easier to see the reference planes and their images in relation to the box you just created, in the menu bar of the persp view panel, select Shading → X-Ray, as shown in Figure 3.40. Now you can see the box and the reference images at the same time.

3. Scale and position the cube to match the size of the main part of the box, as shown in Figure 3.41. Don't bother sizing the box to include the little feet on the bottom of the box. Use X-Ray mode in the Side, Front, and Top modeling panels in Maya to line up the cube as best as you can. This will be the base model for the decorative box.

4. Switch off X-Ray mode in your views (in the persp view panel's menu bar, select Shading → X-Ray). Let's work on the rounded bevel on top of the

box, where the lid is. Select the poly cube, open the Attribute Editor (Ctrl+A), and click the pCubeShape1 tab to access the shape node attributes.

5. Under Object Display → Drawing Overrides, check Enable Overrides to enable it. Deselect Shading to display the poly cube as a wireframe while the reference planes remain displayed as textured planes. This way, you can more easily match the cube to the decorative box (see Figure 3.42).

6. RMB+click the box and select Edge from the marking menu, as shown in Figure 3.43.

7. Select the top four edges of the cube and switch to the front view, as shown in Figure 3.44. Using the front view, you'll shape the top of the cube.

8. Make sure you are in the Modeling menu set; then select Edit Mesh → Bevel. Don't worry about the settings; you'll adjust them after the fact. You should now have something like Figure 3.45 if your bevel options were at the defaults. Because you created a bevel operation on the cube, Maya has created a new node connected to the cube. You will access this bevel node to adjust the bevel settings on the cube.

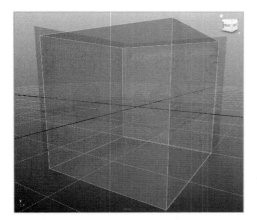

Figure 3.41
Size the cube to fit the box references.

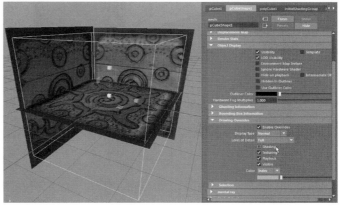

Figure 3.42
Display the cube as a wireframe.

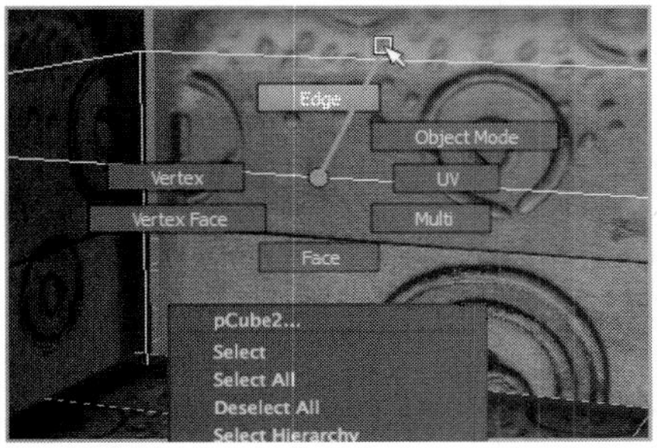

Select the top four edges

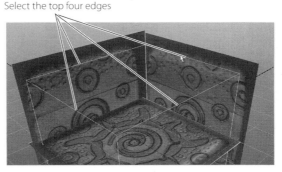

Figure 3.43
Select Edge from the marking menu.

Figure 3.44
Select the top four edges.

Figure 3.45

Default bevel

9. RMB+click the cube, select Object Mode from the marking menu, and then select the cube. Toggle on the Attribute Editor and select the new polyBevel1 tab. Using the front view panel, set Fraction so that it lines up with the rounded top of the box, at about **0.26**. Set Segments to **12**. Make sure Auto Fit, Offset As Fraction, and World Space are all checked (see Figure 3.46).

10. In the side view panel, move the bottom-corner vertices on the cube to line up the bottom corners of the box to the reference image.

11. In the front view panel, move the bottom-corner vertices to match the bottom of the box in the image (see Figure 3.47). Don't worry about the curvature in the middle of the box or the feet just yet. Save your work.

12. Let's take a quick look at how this box will look rendered now. Click anywhere in the persp view panel to make it the active panel. In the Status line (the group of icons at the top of the screen), click the Render The Current Frame icon, as shown in Figure 3.48.

13. Save your work. You can compare your progress to boxModel04.mb in the Scenes folder of the Decorative_Box project from the companion web page.

When you rendered your work in step 12, the Render View opened to show you a gray shaded box with the reference planes barely showing, as you can see in Figure 3.49.

Figure 3.46

Set the bevel to fit the rounded top of the box in the front view panel.

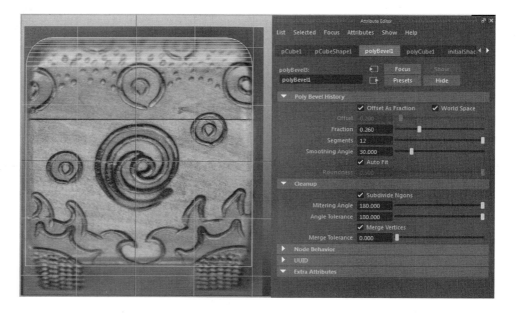

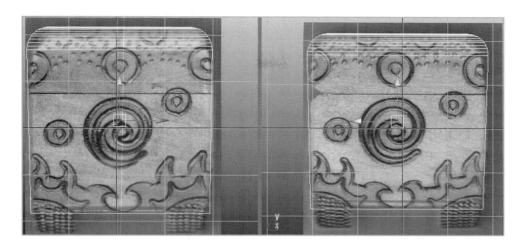

Figure 3.47

Taper the bottom of the cube.

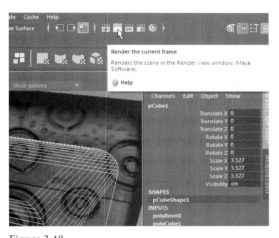

Figure 3.48

Render a frame of the box from the Status line.

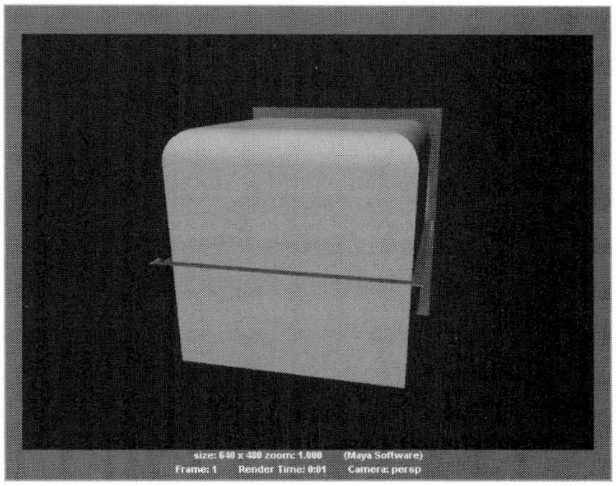

Figure 3.49

The model thus far is rendered.

Status Line Explained

The Status line (see Figure 3.50) contains a number of important and often used icons.

Figure 3.50

The Status line

The Status line begins with a drop-down menu that gives you access to the menu sets in Maya. You'll notice that intermittently throughout the Status line are white vertical line breaks with either a box or an arrow in the middle. Clicking a break opens or closes sections of the Status line.

Some of the most often used icons are identified here.

Scene File Icons

The tools in the first section of the Status line deal with file operations; they are Start A New Scene (▯), Open An Existing Scene (▯), or Save Your Current Scene (▯).

Selection Modes

Selection modes allow you to select different levels of an object's hierarchy (see Table 3.6). For example, using a selection mode, you can select an entire group of objects, only one of the objects in that group, or even components (vertices, faces, and so on) on the surface of that object, depending on the selection mode you're in.

Table 3.6

Selection modes

ICON	NAME	DESCRIPTION
	Hierarchy and Combinations mode	Lets you select groups of objects
	Object mode	Lets you select objects such as geometry, cameras, lights, and so on
	Component mode	Lets you select an object's components, such as vertices, faces, UVs, and so on

To switch between the two most often used modes—Object and Component—press the F8 key. You can also select among the Component and Object modes from the marking menu when you RMB+click an object.

You'll work with these selection mask filters throughout the book, but you will likely access them through marking menus as you have already done to select vertices and edges of a polygonal object. For a quick preview, hover your cursor over each of the icons to see a tooltip that gives the icon's name and describes its function.

Snapping Functions, or Snaps

The icons with the magnets are called *snaps*. They allow you to snap your cursor or object to specific points in the scene, as you saw in the solar system exercise. You can snap to other objects, to CVs or vertices (▯), and to grid intersections (▯) and other locations by toggling these icons. Table 3.7 shows the various snaps.

Figure 3.51

Attribute Editor/
Channel Box/Tool
Settings icons

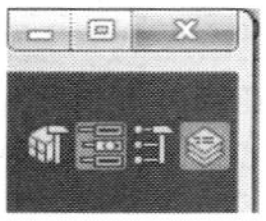

The Channel Box/Layer Editor Icons

These last four buttons on the Status line (Figure 3.51) toggle between the Attribute Editor, Channel Box, and Modeling Toolkit view on the right side of the UI. Clicking the first icon (▯) shows or toggles the Modeling Toolkit. The second icon (▯) toggles the Attribute Editor, much the same as pressing Ctrl+A. The third icon (▯) displays or hides the Tool Settings window along the left side of the UI, as you've seen with soft selections. The fourth icon here (▯) toggles the display of the Channel Box, again much the same as pressing Ctrl+A.

ICON	NAME	DESCRIPTION	
	Snap To Points	This icon lets you snap objects to object points such as CVs or vertices.	**Table 3.7**
	Snap To Grids	This icon lets you snap objects to intersections of the view's grid.	**Snap icons**
	Snap To Curves	This icon lets you snap objects along a curve.	
	Snap to Projected Center	This icon lets you snap to the center of a selected object.	
	Snap To View Planes	This icon lets you snap objects to view planes.	
	Make The Selected Object Live	This icon has nothing to do with snapping but is grouped with the Snap To icons. It lets you create objects such as curves directly on a surface.	

Editing the Decorative Box Model Using the Shelf

Back to work on the box model. You will use the Shelf in the UI to access some of the commands for the next series of steps as you continue working on the box. The Shelf runs directly under the Status line and contains an assortment of tools and commands in separate tabs, as shown in Figure 3.52.

Figure 3.52

The Shelf

You can load the scene file boxModel04.mb in the Scenes folder of the Decorative_Box project from the companion web page or continue with your own scene.

In the following steps, you have to add surface detail to the model so you can more adequately adjust its shape:

1. Orient the persp view panel so you can see the bottom of the box and then select the box model. In the Shelf, click the Polygons tab. Double-click the Multi-Cut tool (as shown in Figure 3.53). The Modeling Toolkit will open on the right showing you the Multi-Cut tool's settings (Figure 3.54).

2. Your cursor will change to a knife icon (it may also give you a cross shape). Click the back edge, as shown in Figure 3.55, and drag along that edge to select a point near the bottom-left edge of the box that corresponds with where the box's feet begin. The readout should show 75 percent or so.

Figure 3.53

The Multi-Cut Tool icon in the Shelf

Figure 3.54

The Multi-Cut Tool settings

Figure 3.55

Select the first point for the multicut.

Figure 3.56

Create a new edge line along the bottom of the box.

3. Click and drag a second point on the opposite edge on the bottom of the box (at about 75 percent again) to create a new edge line, as shown in Figure 3.56. Click the RMB to commit the new edge line. This creates surface detail along the bottom of the box for you to model the feet for the box. This methodology is explained in detail in Chapter 4.

4. Using the same procedures in steps 1 through 3, create three more edge lines for a total of four separate cuts in the bottom face of the cube that line up with the legs of the box, as shown in Figure 3.57. The preceding three steps have created a surface detail called *faces* that allow you to create the feet for the box.

Figure 3.57

Cut the bottom face four times to create divisions for the box's feet.

5. Click the Select Tool icon in the Tool Box to the left of the UI (shown in Figure 3.58) to exit the Multi-Cut tool. Your cursor returns to the regular Maya cursor.

6. RMB+click the box and select Face from the marking menu (Figure 3.59). As you hover your mouse over the parts of the box, the new faces in the four corners of the box you just created will highlight in red. Shift+click the four corner faces to select all four faces, as shown in Figure 3.60.

Figure 3.58

The Select tool in the Tool Box

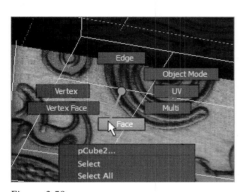

Figure 3.59

Select Face from the marking menu.

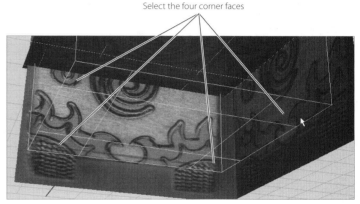

Select the four corner faces

Figure 3.60

Select the four corner faces.

7. With the four faces selected, go into the Shelf and select the Extrude icon shown in Figure 3.61. This tool is also accessible through the menu Edit Mesh → Extrude.

8. Your manipulator will change, as shown in Figure 3.62. Grab the Z-axis move handle and drag it down to "pull" the feet out of the bottom of the box as shown.

Figure 3.61

The Extrude icon in the Shelf

9. By moving vertices, taper the feet to match the reference images in the front and side view panels; see Figure 3.63.

10. Save your work. You can compare your progress to boxModel05.mb in the Scenes folder of the Decorative_Box project.

Figure 3.62
Extrude the feet.

Figure 3.63

**Move the vertices
on the feet to line
them up to the
reference images.**

Figure 3.64

The Tool Box

The Shelf and Tool Box Explained

Here is a brief explanation of the tools and icons in the Shelf and Tool Box.

The Shelf

The *Shelf,* shown earlier in Figure 3.52, is an area where you keep icons for tools. It's divided into tabs that define functions for the tool icons in the Shelf. Don't worry too much about the Shelf right now; it may be better to use the commands from the menus first before turning to icons and shelves.

The Tool Box

The Tool Box, shown in Figure 3.64, displays the most commonly used tools. Table 3.8 lists the icons and their functions.

In addition to the common commands, the Tool Box displays several choices for screen layouts that let you change the interface with a single click. Experiment with the layouts by clicking any of the six presets in the Tool Box.

Table 3.8

Tool Box icons

ICON	NAME	DESCRIPTION
	Select	Lets you select objects
	Lasso Select	Allows for a free-form selection using a lasso marquee
	Paint Selection Tool	Enables the Paint Selection tool
	Translate (Move)	Moves the selection
	Rotate	Rotates the selection
	Scale	Scales the selection
	Last Tool Used	Shows the last tool that was used (shown as Insert Edge Loop here, sometimes shown blank)

Continuing the Decorative Box Model

Back to work! You'll be spending more time getting the box in shape. You can load the scene file boxModel05.mb in the Scenes folder of the Decorative_Box project or continue with your own scene. In the following steps, you will add more faces and edges to the model surface (a.k.a. mesh) so you can add detail to the shape:

1. The middle of the box has a bit of a curve; you will need to create a new edge line that runs across the middle of the box so you can bow out the sides in the middle. In the Layer Editor, toggle off visibility for the reference images by clicking the **V** icon for reference planes. Now you can see just the model of the box.

2. Select the box, and in the Polygons tab of the Shelf, double-click the Multi-Cut Tool icon (▨). Click and drag your Multi-Cut cursor (▨) along the box's first edge to place a point in the middle of that edge (at about 50 percent), as shown in Figure 3.65.

4. Place a new split point in the middle of the next edge of the box (working from left to right), creating an edge line along one side of the box. Continue to place two more split points in the middle of each remaining edge to create a horizontal cut line in the middle of the box, as shown in Figure 3.66. Your last point will display the word *close* next to your cursor. Press Enter, and you now have a horizontal split along the middle of the box.

5. Click the Select Tool icon in the Tool Box to the left of the UI (▨) to exit the Multi-Cut tool. Your cursor returns to the regular Maya cursor. Turn on the referencePlanes layer to show the image references.

6. RMB+click the box and choose Vertex from the marking menu. Move the new vertices in the middle of the box to bow out the box slightly. Move the rest of the vertices to match the model to the box images in the side and front view panels (see Figure 3.67).

7. Save your work. You can compare your progress to boxModel06.mb in the Scenes folder of the Decorative_Box project.

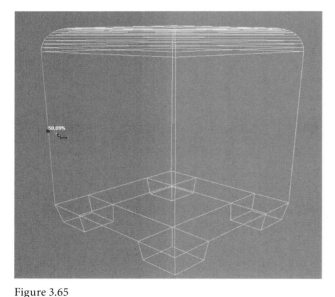

Figure 3.65

Insert the first point of a Multi-Cut at about 50 percent along this first edge.

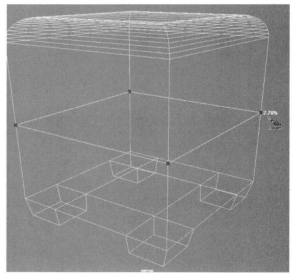

Figure 3.66

Create a horizontal edge line all the way around the box.

Figure 3.67

Adjust the cube to fit the reference images.

Time Slider and Help Line Explained

In this section, you will examine the bottom part of the UI where the Help line and Time slider live.

Time Slider/Range Slider

Running horizontally across the bottom of the screen are the Time slider and the Range slider, as shown in Figure 3.68. The Time slider displays the range of frames available in your animation and gives you a gray bar, known as the *Current Time indicator*. You can click it and then drag it back and forth in a scrubbing motion to move through time in your sequence. (When instructed in this book to *scrub* to a certain point in your animation, use this indicator to do so.)

Figure 3.68

The Time and Range sliders

The text box to the right of the Time slider gives you your current frame, but you can also use the text box to enter the frame you want to access. Immediately next to the current time readout is a set of DVD/DVR-type playback controls that you can use to play back your animation.

Below the Time slider is the Range slider, which you use to adjust the range of animation playback for your Time slider. The text boxes on either side of this slider give you readouts for the start and end frames of the scene and of the range selected.

You can adjust any of these settings by typing in these text boxes or by lengthening or shortening the slider with the handles on either end of the bar. When you change the range, you change only the viewable frame range of the scene; you don't adjust any of the animation. Adjusting the Range Slider lets you zoom into sections of the timeline, which makes adjusting keyframes and timing much easier, especially in long animations.

Command Line/Help Line

Maya Embedded Language (MEL) is the user-accessible programming language of Maya. Use the Command line (see Figure 3.69) to enter single MEL commands directly from the keyboard in the white text box portion of the bar.

Figure 3.69

The Command line and the Help line

Toggle between MEL and Python scripting

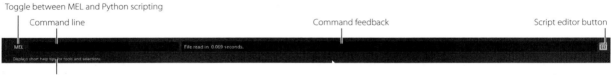
Command line

Command feedback

Script editor button

MEL

File read in 0.069 seconds.

Displays short help tips for tools and selections

Help line

Below the Command line is the Help line. This bar provides a quick reference for almost everything on the screen. It also prompts you for the next step in a particular function or the next required input for a task's completion. The Help line is useful when you're not really sure about the next step in a command, such as which object to select next. You'll be surprised by how much you'll learn about tool functions by reading the prompts displayed here.

Finishing the Decorative Box Model

Now that you have the overall shape of the box finished, you need to add a few finishing details to the box. You will round out the edges of the box so they are not sharp, as well as add a line around the top of the box for the lid's seam and hinges. You can load the scene file boxModel06.mb in the Scenes folder of the Decorative_Box project or continue with your own scene.

To make a model more dynamic, you can round or *bevel* the edges to heighten the realism of the model when it is lit and rendered.

1. Let's turn off the image reference planes again, but this time, let's do it a different way. Open the Outliner window by choosing Windows → Outliner. You are already

somewhat familiar with the Outliner from the solar system exercise in the previous chapter. Select frontPlane, sidePlane, and topPlane in the Outliner and hide them by selecting Display → Hide → Hide Selection or by pressing Ctrl+H. This way, you can individually hide any object in your scene. Notice that when an object is hidden, its Outliner entry is grayed out (Figure 3.70).

Figure 3.70

Hiding objects using the Outliner

2. Select the box and open the Attribute Editor. Under the Object Display → Drawing Overrides headings, uncheck the Enable Overrides box, as shown in Figure 3.71, to display the box in Shaded mode again. This will help you see how the bevel works.

3. You will bevel the edges of the box throughout to soften the crisp corners of the cube that the real box doesn't have. RMB+click the box and choose Edge from the marking menu. Shift+select all the outer edges of the cube, as shown in Figure 3.72.

4. With those edges selected, select Edit Mesh → Bevel ❑. Set everything to the defaults, but change Segments from 1 to **3**. Click Bevel, and your box should resemble the one shown in Figure 3.73.

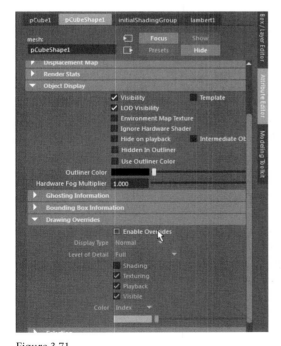

Figure 3.71

Uncheck the box for Enable Drawing Overrides in the Attribute Editor to display the box in Shaded mode again.

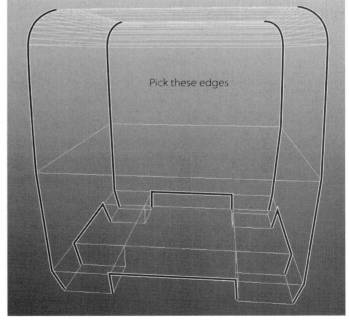

Figure 3.72

Select all of these edges for beveling.

Figure 3.73

**The beveled edges
of the box**

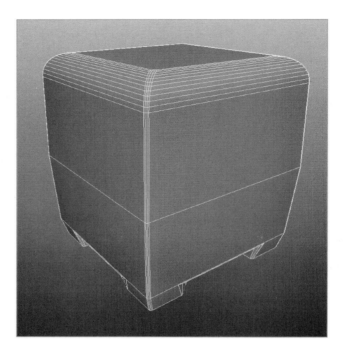

5. Select the cube and delete its history by selecting Edit → Delete By Type → History. This process essentially cleans up the model and the procedures it has undergone. You'll learn about History in the following chapters.

6. You have one final detail to tend to on the lid. You need to add the hinge area you can see in the side view panel's reference image. Select the reference planes in the Outliner (pPlane1, pPlane2, and pPlane3) and press Shift+H to unhide them (you can also choose Display → Show → Show Selection). Make sure you're in Texture Shaded mode in your views (press 6) to see the box images.

7. Select the box. Turn its display back to wireframe by going into the Attribute Editor and, in the pCubeShape1 tab, turning on Enable Overrides under the Object Display → Drawing Overrides heading.

8. Select Mesh Tools → Insert Edge Loop. This tool is like the Multi-Cut tool in that it inserts new edges into a model. Your cursor will change to the solid triangle. Click the upper edge of the box and drag a dashed line to line up with the lid's seam in the box reference images, as shown in Figure 3.74. Once it's placed and you release the mouse button, the edge line will be completed, and the dashed line will turn solid.

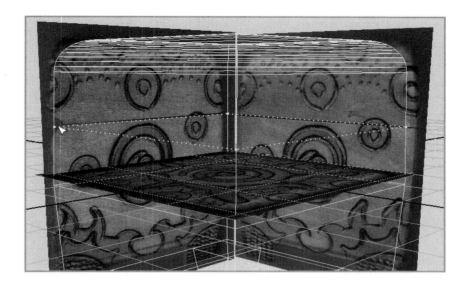

Figure 3.74

**Insert an edge loop
to line up with the
seam in the real box.**

9. In the side view panel, insert four more horizontal edge loops for a total of five edge loops, as shown in Figure 3.75. This gives you edges with which to create the wedge cutout where the box is hinged, and that gives you a little indentation where the lid meets the box. You won't create a separate lid because you won't animate the box to open or close, and you don't need to see the inside.

Figure 3.75

**Insert these five
edge loops for the
lid of the box.**

Insert these five edges

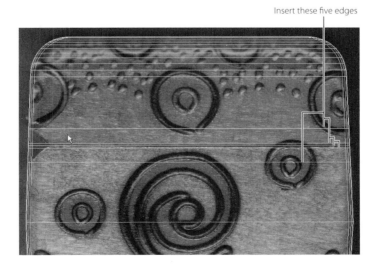

10. In the side view panel, select the appropriate vertices (see Figure 3.76) and move them to create the wedge-shaped indentation as shown.

11. Choose Select → Select Edge Loop Tool. Select the middle edge loop you created earlier for the indent where the lid meets the box, as shown in Figure 3.77. Press R to scale the edge loop slightly inward, as shown.

12. Hide the reference planes again through the Layer Editor and turn Shading back on for the cube in the Attribute Editor. Figure 3.78 (left) shows the completed box. But there's still a little snag. Notice the dark area where the lid meets the box, where you just created the slightly indented seam line. This is because of Normals. It makes the lid look as if it's angled inward.

13. Select the box and choose Mesh Display → Set Normal Angle. In the Set Normal Angle window that pops open, set Angle to the default of **30** and click Apply And Close. Doing so fixes the darkening, as shown in Figure 3.78 (right). For more on Normals, see the "Normals" sidebar. Select the box and delete its history by choosing Edit → Delete By Type → History.

14. Save your work, grab someone you love, and give them a hug.

Figure 3.76

Move the vertices to create the hinge area in the back of the box.

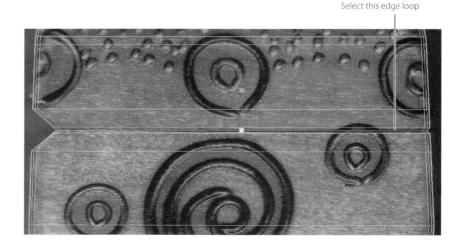

Figure 3.77

Select this edge loop and scale it to create an indent line where the lid meets the box.

Select this edge loop

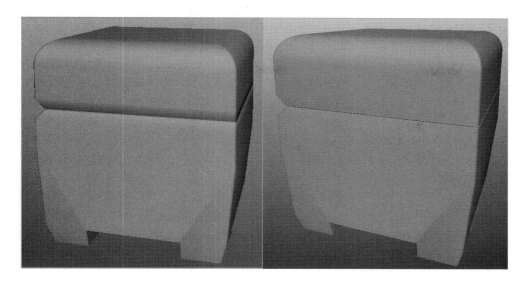

You're finished with the modeling portion of this decorative box, and you've gotten to know the interface much better. In later chapters, you'll texture, light, and render the box with photorealism in mind. You can load boxModel07.mb from the Scenes folder in the Decorative_Box project to compare your work.

NORMALS

Normals are imaginary lines that are perpendicular to a mesh's poly face and that define sides for that face. They also help determine how a renderer, such as mental ray®, shades the surface. In some cases when you're modeling, you may notice an action that causes part of your model to display a darkened area as you saw in the decorative box in Figure 3.78. By manually setting a Normal angle for the box as you did in step 13 of the exercise, you override the display anomaly. You'll learn more about Normals in Chapter 7.

The Attribute Editor and Outliner Explained

You have worked with the Attribute Editor and Outliner several times already. Here's a brief overview of these all-important windows in the workflow in Maya.

The Attribute Editor Window

To use the Attribute Editor, select Windows → Attribute Editor (Ctrl+A). The Attribute Editor window is arguably the most important window in Maya. As you've already seen, objects are defined by a series of attributes, and you edit and even set keyframes for these attributes using the Attribute Editor. Some attributes listed in the Attribute Editor are also shown in the Channel Box. These attributes, despite being shown in two places, are the same.

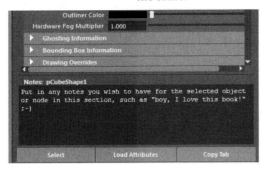

The Attribute Editor has tabs that correspond to the object's node structure. You learned a little about the Maya object structure in the previous chapter.

You'll see an area for writing notes at the bottom of the Attribute Editor. This is handy because you can put reminders here of important events, such as how you set up an object or even a birthday or an anniversary. If you drag the horizontal bar, you can adjust the size of the notes space, as shown in Figure 3.79.

The Outliner

The Outliner is perfect for organizing, grouping objects, renaming nodes, and so forth, as you've already seen.

To use the Outliner, select Windows → Outliner (see Figure 3.80). It displays all the objects in your scene as an outline. You can select any object in a scene by clicking its name.

The objects are listed by order of creation within the scene, but you can easily reorganize them by MMB+clicking and dragging an object to a new location in the window. This is a fantastic way to keep your scene organized. Additionally, you can easily rename an object by double-clicking its Outliner entry and typing a new name.

A separator bar in the Outliner lets you split the display into two separate outline views. By clicking and dragging this bar up or down, you can see either end of a long list, with both ends having independent scrolling control.

Introducing the Modeling Toolkit

As you've seen in the interface, alongside the right of the UI where the Attribute Editor and Channel Box reside is a third tab called Modeling Toolkit, shown in Figure 3.81. This suite of tools makes polygon modeling more efficient since the most often used tools are centralized into one place. In addition, the Modeling Toolkit, when activated, allows for faster and easier component selection and editing.

Figure 3.80

The Outliner

In the Modeling Toolkit, the top half centers around making selections, while the bottom half lists important polygon workflow tools such as Bevel and Extrude. All of the Modeling Toolkit tools work slightly differently than the standard Maya tools of the same name; however, the results of the executed tool are identical. This tool set is explored in depth and put to good use in Chapter 4.

Summary

In this chapter, you learned more about the user interface and the primary windows used in Maya as you worked on modeling the decorative box. The user interface combines mouse and keyboard input as well as plenty of menu and tool icons that you can select and use to accomplish your tasks.

You'll be quizzed in 10 minutes. Do you have it all memorized? Don't worry if you haven't absorbed all the information in this chapter. Now that you've had some exposure to the Maya user interface, you'll be familiar with the various windows when you really get to work. You can always come back to this chapter to refresh your memory. Remember, you should learn the Maya program using its default settings. When in doubt, remember to access the Maya Help system (F1 keyboard shortcut or the Help menu in the main menu bar).

Figure 3.81

Modeling Toolkit tab

CHAPTER 4

Beginning Polygonal Modeling

Simple objects call for *simple models*, and complicated objects call for a complex arrangement of simple models. Like a sculptor, you must analyze the object and deconstruct its design to learn how to create it.

The Autodesk® Maya® software primarily uses two types of modeling: polygons and NURBS. Both require a process that begins with deciding how best to achieve your design, although it's common to mix modeling methods in a scene.

To help you decide where to begin, this chapter starts with an overview of modeling, briefly describing the two popular methods and how they differ. You'll also learn about primitives. The second part of the chapter takes a detailed look at modeling with polygons. (The next two chapters cover the process of modeling with polygons and NURBS surfaces and how to bring them together in one model.)

Learning Outcomes: In this chapter, you will be able to

- Decide how to plan your model

- Edit polygon geometry in traditional Maya as well as Modeling Toolkit workflows

- Navigate the Modeling Toolkit interface

- Work with the Modeling Toolkit selection workflow

- Extrude, bevel, and wedge polygons

- Use edge loops to create detail

- Create curves and use the Revolve function to convert them to polygon meshes

- Adjust grouping and hierarchies in a complex model

Planning Your Model

When you dissect the components of an object into primitive shapes, you can then translate and re-create the object in 3D terms.

First, you should take reference pictures from many angles, get dimensions, and even write down a description of the object. The more perspectives from which you see your subject, the better you'll understand and be able to interpret your model.

You must also decide the purpose for your model and determine the level of detail at which it will be seen in your CG scene. Consider the two scenes in Figure 4.1. If you need to create a park bench for a far shot (left), it will be a waste of time and effort to model all the details such as the grooves in the armrest. However, if your bench is shown in a close-up (the images on the right), you'll need those details.

Figure 4.1

The level of detail you need to include in a model depends on how it will be seen in the animation.

If you aren't certain how much detail you'll need, it's better to create a higher level of detail rather than skimping. You can more easily pare down detail than create it later.

Keep in mind that you can also add detail to the look of your model in the texturing phase of production, as you'll see with the decorative box later in the book. (Chapter 7, "Autodesk® Maya® Shading and Texturing," covers texturing.)

Choosing a Method

Polygon modeling involves tearing and extruding from larger pieces to form a desired shape. This method is typically preferred by most digital artists in the field.

NURBS modeling is great for organic shapes because smooth lines, or *curves*, are the basis of all NURBS surfaces. However, NURBS tends to be more difficult in comparison since it's more difficult to create a complete model without several surfaces that must be perfectly stitched together, a process not covered by this book. Basic NURBS modeling techniques are covered in the next chapter.

An Overview of Polygons

Polygons consist of *faces*. A single polygon *face* is a flat surface made when three or more points called *vertices* are connected. The position of each *vertex* defines the shape and size of the face, usually a triangle. The line that connects one vertex to another is called an *edge*. Some polygonal faces have four vertices instead of three, creating a square face called a *quad*.

Polygonal faces are attached along their polygonal edges to make up a more complex surface that constitutes your model (as shown with the polygonal sphere in Figure 4.2). A camping tent is a perfect example. The intersections of the poles are the faces' vertices. The poles are the edges of the faces, and the cloth draped over the tent's frame is the resultant surface.

Figure 4.2

A polygonal sphere and its components

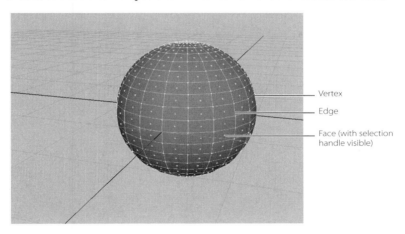

Vertex

Edge

Face (with selection handle visible)

Polygon models are the simplest for a computer to render. They're used for gaming applications, which need to render the models as the game is running. Gaming artists create models with a small number of polygons, called *low-count poly models*, which a PC or game console can render in real time. Higher-resolution polygon models are frequently used in television and film work.

Using Primitives

Primitives are the simplest objects you can generate in Maya (or in any 3D application). They are simple geometric shapes—polygons or NURBS. Typically, primitives are used to sculpt models because you can define the level of detail of the primitive's surface; they offer great sculpting versatility through vertex manipulation.

To get a better sense of how to begin a modeling assignment, you may find it helpful to analyze your modeling subjects into forms and shapes that fit in with Maya primitives. Figure 4.3 shows all of the primitives in Maya, including NURBS, polygons, and volume primitives. Quite different from geometry primitives, volume primitives are used for lighting and atmosphere effects, such as fog or haze, and don't play a part in modeling.

Figure 4.3

The Maya primitives

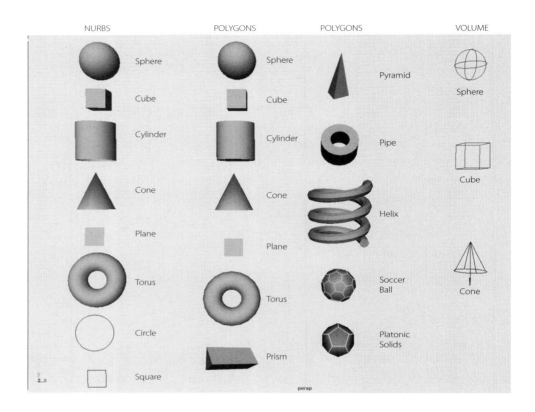

Polygon Basics

Polygon modeling is popular because its resulting models are usually one piece of geometry with many facets. You can, therefore, deform polygon models without fear of patches coming apart, as can happen with NURBS. Polygons, however, have a finite detail limitation and can look jagged up close or when scaled up. One solution to this problem in the Maya software is the Smooth tool, which smoothes your mesh into a more organic shape by increasing its polygon count and rounding off areas. You'll be using the Smooth tool later in this chapter.

A popular method of polygonal modeling called *box modeling* involves creating a base object (a.k.a. a primitive) such as a simple cube and then pulling and pushing faces to draw angles to create more faces. With NURBS you typically need to start by creating curves like outlines or shapes.

A second method for creating poly surfaces uses the same curves that NURBS surfaces use or even converts a completed NURBS surface model to polygons. A third method is to create poly surfaces directly with the Polygon tool, which allows you to outline the shape of each face, which is less often used.

Creating Polygonal Primitives

With a poly mesh, detail is defined by *subdivisions*, which are the number of rows and columns of poly faces that run up, down, and across. The more subdivisions you have, the greater definition and detail you can create with the mesh.

Choosing Create → Polygon Primitives gives you access to the poly primitives. Opening the option box for any of them gives you access to their creation options. To see an example, choose Create → Polygon Primitives → Sphere ☐ to open the option box.

To get started, first make sure History is turned on (▣) in the status bar along the top of the UI or there will be no creation node; then, click Create to make the poly sphere. Open the Attribute Editor and switch to its creation node, called polySphere1. In the creation node polySphere1 you'll find the Subdivisions Axis and Subdivisions Height sliders (in the option box, these are called Axis and Height Divisions), which you can use to change the surface detail retroactively.

The Polygon Tool

You use the Polygon tool to create a single polygon face by laying down its vertices (switch to the Modeling menu set and then choose Mesh Tools → Create Polygon). When you select this tool, you can draw a polygon face in any shape by clicking to place each point or vertex. Aside from creating a polygon primitive by choosing Create → Polygon Primitives, this is the simplest way to create a polygon shape. Figure 4.4 shows some simple and complex single faces you can create with the Polygon tool.

After you've laid down all your vertices, press Enter to create the poly face and exit the tool. For complex shapes, you may want to create more than just the single face so that you can manipulate the shape. For example, you may want to fold it.

Try This The poly shown in Figure 4.5 was created with the Polygon tool and has only one face. Therefore, adjusting or deforming the surface is impossible. To fold this object, you need more faces and the edges between them. Make your own intricate poly shape with the Polygon tool by clicking vertices down in the different views to get vertices in all three axes.

Figure 4.4

Polygon faces created with the Polygon tool

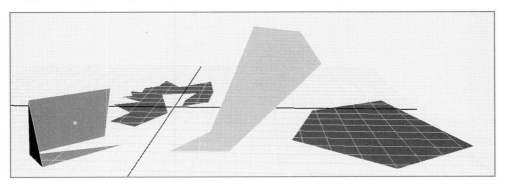

With the surface selected, choose Mesh → Triangulate (under the Remesh section of the menu). The custom shape now has more faces and edges and is easier to edit but was still simple to create. If you need a uniquely shaped poly, start with this tool and then triangulate your surface into several faces, as shown in Figure 4.6.

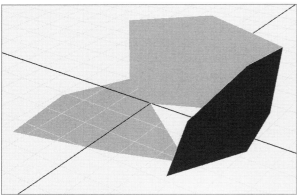

Figure 4.5
A single-faced polygon with a complex shape

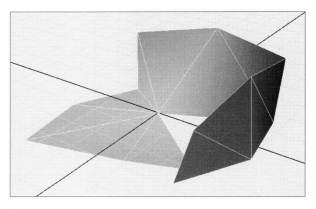

Figure 4.6
Complex shapes are better with more faces.

Faces that have too many edges (a.k.a. Ngons) may cause you trouble later in the workflow, particularly in further manipulation of the mesh containing any Ngons and also when rendering. It's recommended to always work with polygons with three (tri) or four (quad) sides, with quads being preferred.

Poly Editing Tools

Here's a brief preview of what to expect in the world of poly editing. You should experiment with each tool on a primitive sphere as it's introduced, so saddle up to your Maya window and try each tool as you read along.

Later in this chapter, you'll deploy these new skills. You'll create a cute toy airplane to exercise your modeling skills in Chapter 6, "Practical Experience!" For most of the work in this chapter, you'll use the Polygons menu.

Open the Edit Mesh menu, tear it off, and place it somewhere on your screen so you can get a good look at the tools and functions, which are separated into sections according to function type. For example, tools that work on vertices are found in the Edit Mesh menu's Vertex section. It's important to note these sections because some tools have the same name and may be repeated more than once in the menu but function differently when applied to vertices, faces, or edges. For tools repeated like this, I will call out the section name in the text to help.

Modeling Toolkit

Modeling Toolkit integrates component-level selection and editing tools (such as selecting vertices, edges, and faces, and extruding them, for example) for a more streamlined modeling workflow. Modeling Toolkit can make tedious modeling chores much easier, especially for advanced modeling techniques. I will be covering some of the Modeling Toolkit workflow and how it's integrated into Maya 2016 alongside Maya traditional workflows to give you a comparison and allow you to decide which workflow suits you. You'll take a look at Modeling Toolkit and its interface later in the chapter.

The Poly Extrusion Tools

The most commonly used poly editing tools have to do with extrusion. You can use Extrude to pull out a face, edge, or vertex of a polygon surface to create additions to that surface. In the Modeling menu set, you access the Extrude tool in the menu Edit Mesh → Extrude. Maya automatically distinguishes between edge, face, or vertex extrusion based on which of those components you've already selected. Follow these steps:

1. Select a face or multiple faces of a polygon and choose Edit Mesh → Extrude. The regular manipulator changes to a special manipulator, as shown in the left image in Figure 4.7.

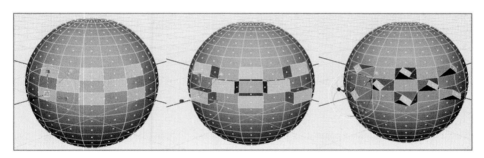

Figure 4.7

Extruding several faces at once on a sphere. The left image shows the selected faces, the middle image shows those faces extruded, and the right image shows those faces extruded with a rotation and smaller scale.

2. Grab the Z-axis move handle (the blue arrow) and drag it away from the sphere, as shown in the center of Figure 4.7.

3. Use the scale handles (the boxes) to scale the faces of the extrusion. The cyan circle rotates the face. The image at the right in Figure 4.7 shows the faces extruded, rotated, and scaled.

4. Choose the Extrude command again without deselecting the faces, and you extrude even more, keeping the original extrusion shape and building on top of that.

5. Select the edges of the poly surface instead of the faces and choose Edit Mesh → Extrude to extrude flat surfaces from the edges selected. The special manipulator works the same way as Extrude does for poly faces.

The faces you select will pull out from the sphere, and new faces are created on the sides of the extrusion(s). The Extrude tool is an exceptionally powerful tool in that it allows you to easily create additions to any poly surface in any direction. Later in this chapter, you'll use it to make a simple cartoon hand.

You can also use the direction and shape of a curve to extrude faces. Create a curve in the shape you want your extrusion to take, select the curve, Shift+select the faces, and choose Extrude ❑. Taper decreases or increases the size of the face as it extrudes. Twist rotates the face as it extrudes, and Divisions increases the smoothness of the resulting extrusion. Choose Selected for the Curve setting. When you have your settings for those attributes, click the Extrude button (see Figure 4.8).

Figure 4.8

Extruding a face along a path curve

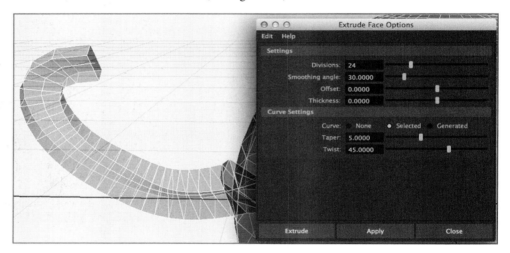

Although it seems to be strange behavior, the Twist and Taper values are taken into account in the extrusion. You can edit these values when you uncheck Selected, or you can reselect this option after you enter values for Twist and Taper. If your faces aren't extruding to the shape of the curve, increase the number of divisions.

Modeling Toolkit and Extrusions

Modeling Toolkit makes selecting and editing polygonal components more streamlined, accelerating some workflows by incorporating tools into one place for ease of access as well as by reducing how often you have to exit one tool or mode and enter another one. Since a lot of what Modeling Toolkit does centers around component selections, let's start there first.

Modeling Toolkit Interface

By default, the Modeling Toolkit plug-in should be enabled, which places the Modeling Toolkit menu on the main menu bar. If you don't see Modeling Toolkit, simply choose Windows → Setting/Preferences → Plug-In Manager. About halfway down the list, you should see ModelingToolkit.dll (or ModelingToolkit.bundle on a Mac). Check Loaded and Auto Load, as shown in Figure 4.9.

Modeling Toolkit also places an icon on your status bar, next to the XYZ input fields, shown next to the cursor and already turned on in Figure 4.10. When the Modeling Toolkit icon is turned on, Modeling Toolkit is automatically invoked whenever you enter component selection mode. Click the icon to turn Modeling Toolkit on if it isn't already.

In addition, Modeling Toolkit places a tab in the Channel Box, called Modeling Toolkit, to make display-ing its tool set easier, as shown in Figure 4.11. You will notice toward the top of the Modeling Toolkit panel four icons for selecting, moving, rotating, and scaling. These operate in the same way as transformation tools; however, they enable the Modeling Toolkit functionality. You'll see this in action throughout the book and intro-duced next.

Figure 4.9

Loading the Modeling Toolkit plug-in, if needed

Modeling Toolkit Extrusion

Now that you have a little background on how Modeling Toolkit integrates with Maya 2016, let's use it in comparison to the Maya Extrude tool you just used on a sphere.

Show/Hide Modeling Toolkit

Figure 4.10

The Modeling Toolkit icon button

1. Make sure the Modeling Toolkit icon ( ) in the status bar is active to see the Modeling Toolkit tab alongside the Attribute Editor and Channel Box/Layer Editor tabs.

2. Create a polygon sphere and press 5 for Shaded mode.

3. Right-click the sphere in your scene and select Face from the marking menu for face selection mode. This is the easiest way to select components in Maya, which also works the same while using Modeling Toolkit.

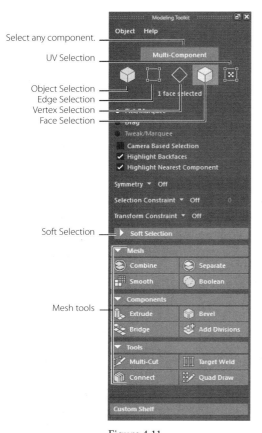

Select any component.

UV Selection

Object Selection
Edge Selection
Vertex Selection
Face Selection

Soft Selection

Mesh tools

Figure 4.11

The Modeling Toolkit panel

4. Hold down Shift to select two faces side-by-side on the sphere.

5. In the Modeling Toolkit panel, click Extrude under the Components heading, as shown in Figure 4.12. A floating options panel appears next to the selected faces.

6. In the floating panel, your cursor will change to a double-headed horizontal arrow as you hover over each of the attributes (such as Offset or Divisions). Hover over Thickness and click and drag left or right to set the amount of extrusion (Figure 4.13).

7. You can also enter numbers directly. In the floating panel, click in the Divisions text box and set the number to **3**. This will give you multiple sections along your extrusion. You can also click and drag in the floating panel to set the Divisions number interactively as you did with Thickness.

8. Click and drag on Offset in the floating panel to make the extruded faces bigger or smaller. You may also enter a value for Offset in the floating panel, since clicking and dragging is pretty sensitive. Figure 4.14 shows an extrusion of 0.29 with a Divisions of 3 and an Offset of 0.04.

9. Finally, click the Keep Faces Together text box to toggle the option on and off in the floating panel to see how the extrusion changes. Figure 4.15 shows the same extrusion as Figure 4.14, but with Keep Faces Together turned off. Whatever options you set will be used the next time you extrude in Modeling Toolkit. Simply turn off the Extrude button to exit the tool and commit the changes.

Figure 4.12

Click Extrude in the Modeling Toolkit panel.

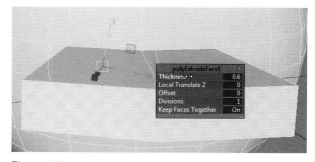

Figure 4.13

Click and drag the Thickness value to set the extrusion amount.

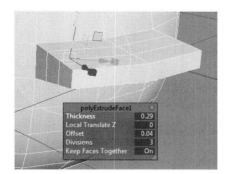

Figure 4.14

Modeling Toolkit extrusion in action

Figure 4.15

Keep Faces Together is turned off.

All of these extrusion options and settings are available in the Maya Extrude tool but are a little more streamlined in the Modeling Toolkit workflow. Experiment to see how you like to work. You will be using a combination of traditional Maya and Modeling Toolkit workflows throughout the chapter and other parts of the book.

The Wedge Tool

Similar to extruding faces, Wedge pulls out a poly face, but it does so in an arc instead of a straight line. For this tool, you need to select a face and an edge of the selected face for a pivot axis of the corner. Here's how to do this.

RMB+click a mesh and select Multi from the marking menu, which lets you select any type of component. Select a face, then Shift+select one of the face's edges, and finally choose Edit Mesh → Wedge (under the Face section of the menu).

A floating panel appears, and you can select the degree of turn in the Wedge Angle setting (90 degrees is the default) as well as the number of faces used to create the wedge (by changing the Divisions value), as shown in Figure 4.16.

The Wedge tool is useful for items such as elbows, knees, archways, and so on.

Figure 4.16

Executing a Wedge operation on a face of a sphere

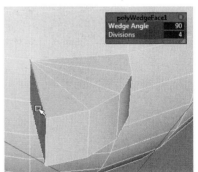

The Poke Tool

Poke is great for creating detailed sections of a mesh (poly surface) and bumps or indentations. To use the Poke tool to add detail to a face, select a face and then choose Edit Mesh → Poke.

A vertex is added to the middle of the face, and the Move manipulator appears on the screen for that new vertex, as shown in Figure 4.17. This lets you move the point to where you need it on the face. You can add bumps and depressions to your surface as well as

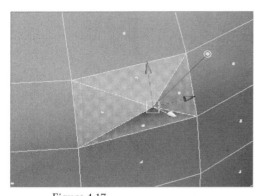

Figure 4.17

Poke helps create areas of detail in your model.

create regions of extra detail. By selectively adding detail, you can subdivide specific areas of a polygon for extra detailed work, leaving lower poly counts in less-detailed areas for an efficient model.

The Bevel Tool

Use the Bevel tool to round sharp corners and edges and to help catch light and generally make a model's edges look more polished. With the Bevel tool you must select an edge or multiple edges and then use them to create multiple new faces to round that edge or corner.

Select an edge or edges and choose Edit Mesh → Bevel (under the Components section of the menu). The Fraction value in the floating panel sets the distance from the edge to the center of where the new face will be. This basically determines the size of the beveled corner. The Segments number defines how many segments are created for the bevel: the more segments, the smoother the beveled edge (see Figure 4.18). Leaving Segments at 1 creates a sharp corner.

The setting of the Roundness slider specifies the roundness of the corner. Setting the number too high will make the beveled edge stick out, as shown in Figure 4.19, although that can be a valid design choice. You can allow Maya to set the roundness automatically based on the size of the geometry being beveled. Set the AutoFit value to Off to enable the Roundness slider so you can set your own roundness to the bevel. Remember to set the Segments value higher for a smoother bevel.

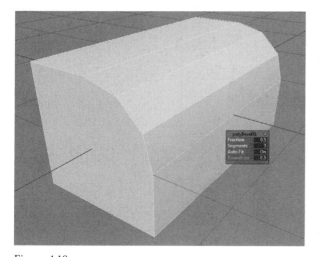

Figure 4.18

Increase Segments to create a rounder corner.

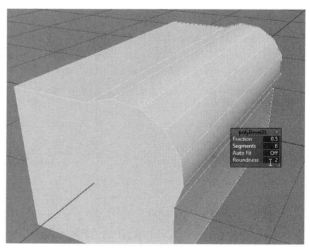

Figure 4.19

A poly bevel's roundness set pretty high

You can invoke the bevel tool through Modeling Toolkit as well. Simply turn on Modeling Toolkit () and click the Bevel icon instead of choosing Edit Mesh → Bevel as you did before, and you'll access the same Bevel tool, as shown in Figure 4.20.

Figure 4.20

Bevel icon in Modeling Toolkit

Additionally, Bevel responds to the type of selection you make. So far, you have beveled edges. This time, create a new cube and select the top face. In Modeling Toolkit, click Bevel and set Fraction to **0.2** and Segments to **3** in the floating panel. The tool will bevel all four edges around the selected top face (Figure 4.21).

Use the Bevel tool to round polygonal edges and add polish to your models.

> Having even a *slightly* rounded edge on a model—a box, for example—greatly enhances the look of that box when it's lighted and rendered because the edges catch much more light, helping define the shape of the box. A perfectly sharp corner with no bevel doesn't catch any light, making the model look less realistic.

Figure 4.21

Here you have beveled the top face of a cube, instead of just a single edge.

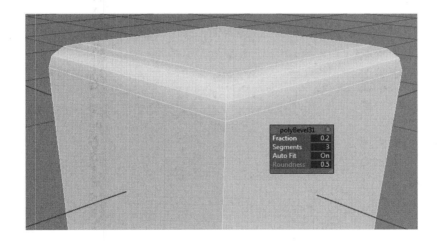

Putting the Tools to Use: Making a Cartoon Hand

Starting with a simple polygonal cube, you'll create a basic cartoon hand using a mix of Maya and Modeling Toolkit workflows.

> The book's web page (www.sybex.com/go/introducingmaya2016) as well as the author's website (www.koosh3d.com) will be hosting videos of some of the exercises in this book; these videos may be updated and added to over time, so make sure to check in on these links every now and then.

Download the entire Poly_Hand project from the web page (www.sybex.com/go/ introducingmaya2016) where you can also find a video for this tutorial. Set your project to this folder and follow these steps:

1. With Interactive Creation turned off, create a polygonal cube. Open the Attribute Editor and, in the polyCube1 tab, set Subdivisions Width to **3**, Subdivisions Height to **1**, and Subdivisions Depth to **1**. If you don't have that tab in the Attribute Editor, click Undo to remove the cube, turn on History, and re-create the cube.

2. Scale the cube to X = 4, Y = 1.3, and Z = 4.5 so that it looks like Figure 4.22.

Figure 4.22

The poly cube in position to make the hand

3. If Modeling Toolkit is off, turn it on with its icon (▨) in the status bar. RMB+click the cube and choose Face from the marking menu.

4. Select the front face in the corner closest to you. You'll extrude the face to make the first part of the index finger. Before you extrude, though, rotate the face a bit in the Y-axis, away from the rest of the hand, to angle the extrusion toward where the thumb would be, as shown in Figure 4.23 (left).

5. In the Modeling Toolkit panel, click the Extrude button. In the floating panel, set Divisions to **2**, Thickness to **3.7**, and Offset to **-0.1.** You can press W to exit the Extrude tool (and consequently enter the Move tool). Figure 4.23 (right) shows the full index finger with the slight rotation away from the hand from the previous step.

Save your work and compare it to the scene file poly_hand_v1.mb in the Poly_Hand project on the web page.

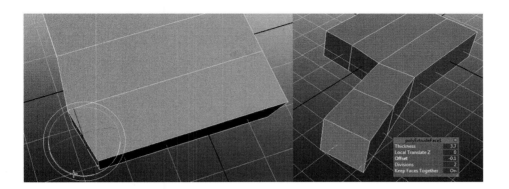

Figure 4.23
Rotate the face (left) and then extrude the index finger.

6. Repeat steps 4 and 5 for the remaining two fingers using the extrusion Thickness values shown in Table 4.1. Remember to rotate the initial face of each finger slightly away from the previous finger before extruding so that the extrusions will have small gaps between them, as shown in Figure 4.24. Otherwise, the fingers will extrude right up against each other, like a glove with the fingers glued together.

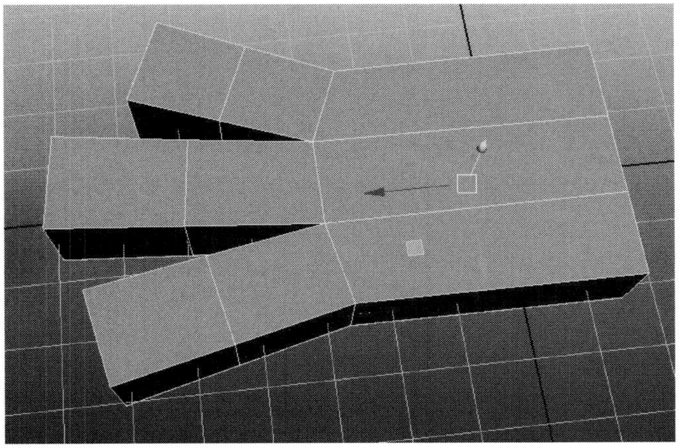

Figure 4.24
Three fingers

Use Table 4.1 as a guide for the Thickness values for the two fingers.

When you're finished with the three fingers, select the hand. In the Perspective panel, press 2 to give you a smooth preview of the hand. With a polygonal object, pressing the 1, 2, and 3 keys previews the smoothness your model will have when it's smoothed (a polygonal modeling operation about to be discussed). Pressing 2 also shows the original shape of the hand as a wireframe cage (see Figure 4.25, left) as reference.

FINGER	EXTRUDE LOCAL Z VALUE
Middle	4.2
Pinkie	3.0

Table 4.1
Extrusion length guide

Figure 4.25

A smoothed pre-
view of the hand,
with the original
shape shown as a
cage (left) and a full
smooth preview
without the cage
(right)

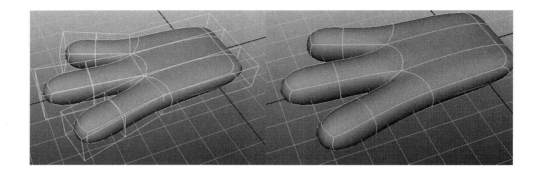

With the hand still selected, press 3. The original wireframe cage disappears, as shown in Figure 4.25 (right). This doesn't alter your model in any way; if you render, your hand will still be blocky, just as you modeled it. Press 1 to exit the smooth pre-view and return to the original model view. The scene file poly_hand_v2.mb shows the hand with the three fingers created.

7. Let's work on the thumb. You need to insert some new divisions on the body of the hand to extrude a thumb. With the hand selected, choose Mesh Tools → Insert Edge Loop and click the side edge of the hand, as shown in Figure 4.26. A dotted line appears. Drag along the edge you clicked to place the insertion and release the mouse button to place the new loop of edges.

8. Insert a second loop of edges at the middle of the hand, as shown in Figure 4.27. Press W to exit the Insert Edge Loop tool.

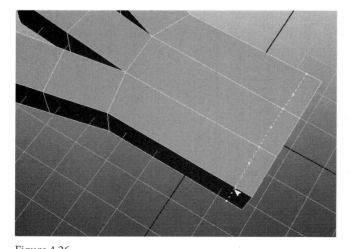

Figure 4.26

Insert an edge loop at the base of the hand.

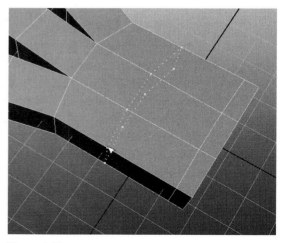

Figure 4.27

Insert a second loop of edges up toward the middle of the hand.

9. Rotate and then scale down the face shown in Figure 4.28 in the Z-axis to get ready to extrude the thumb.

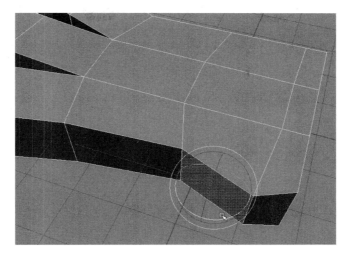

Figure 4.28

Scale and rotate the thumb's face to get it ready to extrude.

10. In the Modeling Toolkit, click Extrude and, in the floating panel, set Thickness to **3**, Offset to **-0.1**, and Divisions to **2**, as with the other three fingers (see Figure 4.29).

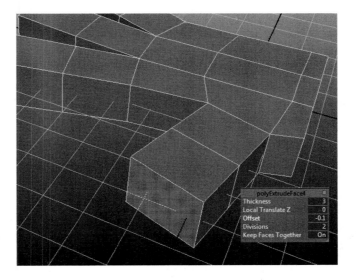

Figure 4.29

Extrude the thumb.

11. Select the three faces at the base of the hand (where it would meet an imaginary wrist) and scale them down in the X-axis and up in the Y-axis to create a flare, as shown in Figure 4.30.

Figure 4.30

Create a flare at the base of the hand.

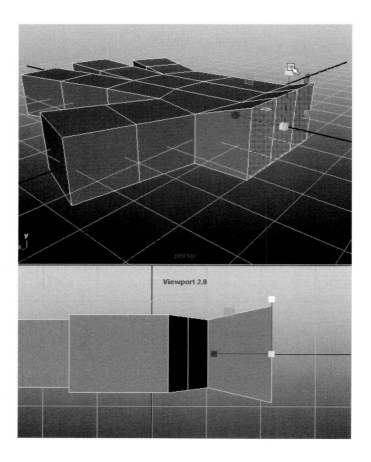

12. If you press 3 to preview the hand smoothed, it will lose a good amount of its detail and become too soft. Let's keep some of the angles of the hand by beveling the edges all around the hand. Select the outer edges all around the hand, as shown in Figure 4.31, in X-Ray view (which you invoke in a view panel by selecting in its menu bar Shading → X-Ray). Make sure to get all the edges around the outside of the hand, fingers, and thumb.

13. In Modeling Toolkit, click Bevel and in the floating panel set Fraction to **0.5** and Segments to **1**. Figure 4.32 shows the beveled hand (left) and again with Smooth Preview (right) enabled (by pressing 3).

14. While in Smooth Preview, select the ring of faces around the base of the thumb and scale them down a bit to accentuate the flare of the thumb, as shown in Figure 4.33. Make any additional adjustments to your liking by manipulating faces and vertices.

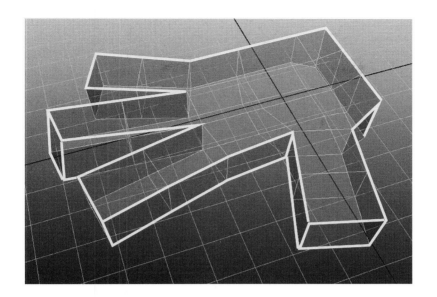

Figure 4.31

Select all the edges outlining the entire hand.

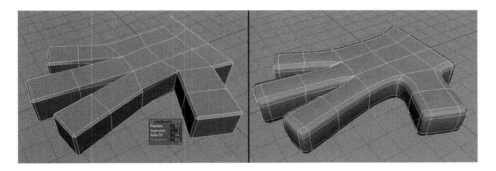

Figure 4.32

Beveling all around the hand (left) and shown with Smooth Preview (right)

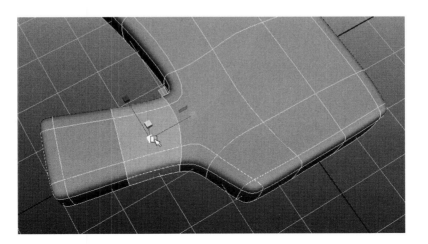

Figure 4.33

Scale down these faces to flare the thumb a bit more.

15. Exit Smooth Preview (press 1). To add more detail to the hand, you'll raise the knuckles. You need to create new vertices for the knuckles where each finger meets the hand. In the Modeling Toolkit panel, click the Multi-Cut icon (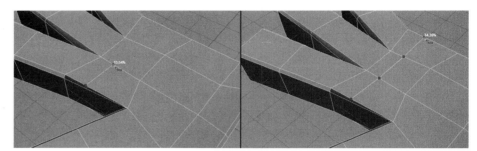). Click and drag along the edge of the hand, right below where the index finger attaches to the hand, until the yellow readout reads about 65%. Release the mouse button to lay down the first point of the Multi-Cut operation.

16. Now click the opposite edge across at about 34%, as shown in Figure 4.34 (left). You'll notice an orange line stretch across denoting where a new edge will be placed.

Figure 4.34

Use the Multi-Cut tool to lay down edges for the knuckles.

17. Click across the remaining knuckle faces to lay down a cut line across the top of the hand, as shown in Figure 4.34 (right).

18. RMB+click to commit, and the tool will add three new edges (and hence three new faces) along the back of the hand for the knuckles. Select each of those new faces and choose Edit Mesh → Poke (under the Face section) to subdivide them into five triangles, with a vertex in the center. A special manipulator appears when you invoke the Poke command. Use the Z translate handle to pull up those middle vertices to make knuckles (see Figure 4.35).

Figure 4.35

Use the Poke tool to raise the knuckles.

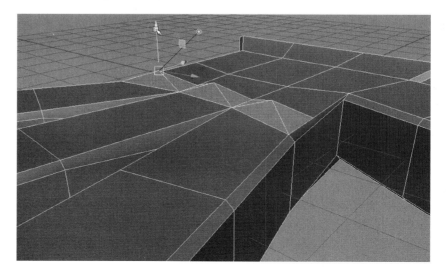

19. Now that you have a cartoon hand, you can smooth out the mesh to make it less boxy. In Object mode, select the hand and press 3 to see a preview of what the hand will look like after it's smoothed. Press 1 to exit the smooth preview. Choose Mesh → Smooth ❑ (under the Remesh section of the menu); in the option box, under Exponential Controls, select Maya Catmull-Clark for the Subdivision Type, set Division Levels to **2**, and leave the other options at their defaults (see Figure 4.36). The smoothed hand shows all of its history nodes in Figure 4.37.

20. Click Smooth. Your cartoon hand should take on a smoother, rounder look. This time, however, you've altered the geometry and actually made the mesh smoother and given it a higher density of polygons. Notice all the nodes listed under Inputs in the Channel Box in Figure 4.36 (right). This is because History has been on for the entire duration of this exercise. At any time, you can select one of those nodes and edit something—the extrusion of the pinkie, for example.

To verify that you've been working correctly, you can load the finished hand file (with its history intact), which is called `poly_hand_v3.mb`, available from the book's web page, www.sybex.com/go/introducingmaya2016. If you don't need any of the history anymore, then with the hand selected, choose Edit → Delete By Type → History to get rid of all those extra nodes.

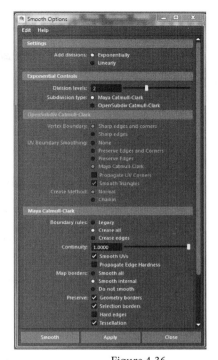

Figure 4.36

Set the options for the Smooth operation.

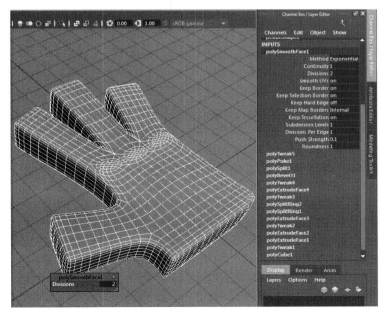

Figure 4.37

The smoothed hand is shown with all its history nodes.

Creating Areas of Detail on a Poly Mesh

As you saw with the cartoon hand, it became necessary to add more faces to parts of the surface to create various details, such as with the knuckles. Maya provides several ways to add surface detail or increase a poly's subdivisions, as you've begun to see in the cartoon hand exercise. Let's take a deeper look at these and more tools for adding detail to a mesh.

The Add Divisions Tool

You can use the Add Divisions tool to increase the number of faces of a poly surface by evenly dividing either all faces or just those selected. Select the poly surface face or faces and choose Edit Mesh → Add Divisions (under the Components section of the menu). You can also click the Add Divisions icon in Modeling Toolkit (![Add Divisions]).

The tool is context sensitive to your current selection, so when you have faces selected, you will add divisions to those faces. When you have edges selected, the tool will split the edges adding vertices. In the option box, you can adjust the number of times the faces are divided by moving the Division Levels slider. With Add Divisions set to Exponentially under the Settings heading, the Mode drop-down menu gives you the choice to subdivide your faces into quads (four-sided faces, as on the left of Figure 4.38) or triangles (three-sided faces, as on the right in Figure 4.38). Quads traditionally make the most sense.

Figure 4.38

The Mode drop-down menu of the Add Divisions tool lets you subdivide faces into quads or triangles.

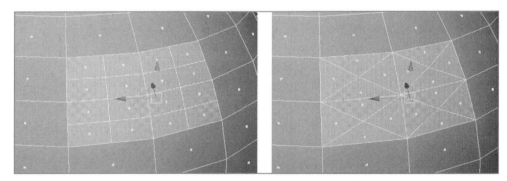

You can also select a poly edge to divide. Running this tool on edges divides the selected edges into separate edges along the same face, giving you more vertices along that edge. It doesn't divide the face; rather, you can use it to change the shape of the face by moving the new vertices or edge segments, as shown in Figure 4.39. Just make sure to select Add Divisions when you have edges selected.

You use the Add Divisions tool to create regions of detail on a poly surface.

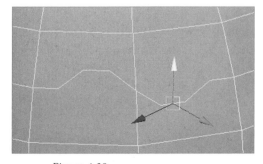

Figure 4.39

Dividing edges

Modeling Toolkit Multi-Cut Tool

As you saw when creating more faces and edges for the hand's knuckles in the previous exercise, Modeling Toolkit's Multi-Cut tool allows you to lay down edges along faces fairly easily. You access the Multi-Cut tool in Modeling Toolkit, under the Tools heading. You can also make multiple cuts on the same face, as shown in Figure 4.40.

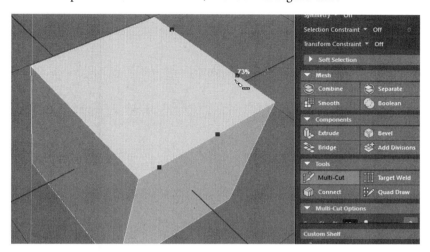

Figure 4.40

The Modeling Toolkit Multi-Cut tool

You can also access the Multi-Cut tool through Mesh Tools → Multi-Cut.

The Insert Edge Loop Tool

This handy tool adds edges to a poly selection, much like the Multi-Cut tool, but it does so more quickly by working along the entire poly surface, along common vertices. The Insert Edge Loop tool automatically runs a new edge along the poly surface perpendicular to the subdivision line you click, without requiring you to click multiple times as with the Modeling Toolkit Multi-Cut tool. You used this tool in the decorative box in Chapter 3, "The Autodesk® Maya® 2016 Interface," and earlier in this chapter on the cartoon hand and will continue using it throughout this book. You'll find it indispensable in creating polygonal models because it creates subdivisions quickly.

For instance, subdividing a polygonal cube is quicker than using the Multi-Cut tool. With a poly cube selected, choose Mesh Tools → Insert Edge Loop. Click an edge, and the tool places an edge running perpendicular from that point to the next edge across the surface and across to the next edge, as shown in Figure 4.41. If you click and drag along an edge, you can interactively position the new split edges.

Figure 4.41

Using the Insert Edge Loop tool

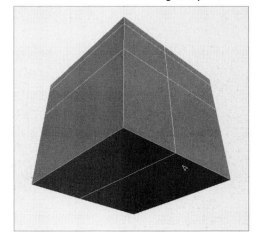

The Offset Edge Loop Tool

Much like the Insert Edge Loop tool, the Offset Edge Loop tool (Mesh Tools → Offset Edge Loop) inserts not one but two edge loop rings of edges across the surface of a poly. Edges are placed on both sides of a selected edge, equally spaced apart. For example, create a polygon sphere and select one of the vertical edges, as shown in Figure 4.42. Maya displays two dashed lines on both sides of the selected edge. Drag the mouse to place the offset edge loops; release the mouse button to create the two new edge loops.

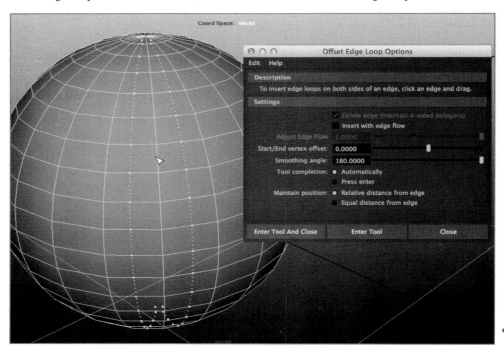

Figure 4.42

The Offset Edge Loop tool and its options

The Offset Edge Loop tool is perfect for adding detail symmetrically on a surface quickly.

Modeling Toolkit Connect Tool

Similar to the Insert Edge Loop tool is the Modeling Toolkit Connect function. Simply select an edge and click the Connect button in the Modeling Toolkit panel. This will create edges going around the object perpendicular to the selected edge. The Slide attribute places the perpendicular cut along the selected edge, which is slightly less interactive than Insert Edge Loop. However, the Segments attribute allows you to insert more than one ring of edges, while Pinch spaces those extra segments evenly (Figure 4.43). You can also select Mesh Tools → Connect in the main menu bar.

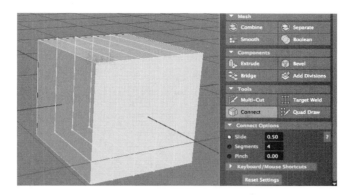

Figure 4.43
The Modeling Toolkit Connect tool creates edges much like Insert Edge Loop.

Modeling Toolkit Drag and Bridge Tool

One of Modeling Toolkit's nicest features is its drag selection mode. This allows you to essentially click and drag your cursor over the components you want selected with your cursor instead of having to click every component, almost like painting.

Try This

1. Create a cube in an empty scene and set Subdivisions Width to **1**, Subdivisions Height to **4**, and Subdivisions Depth to **5**, as shown in Figure 4.44. Figure 4.44 is shown in X-Ray mode (which is enabled in the Perspective panel's menu bar by choosing Shading → X-Ray).

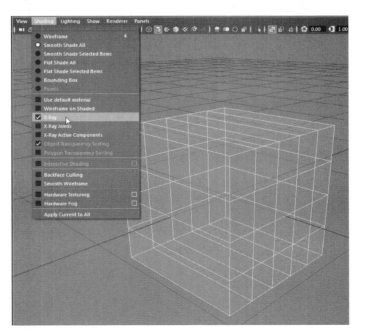

Figure 4.44
Create a subdivided box.

2. You are going to delete a square shape out of the front and back of the box. Exit X-Ray view mode if you are currently in X-Ray (view panel menu: Shading → X-Ray).

3. Make sure the Modeling Toolkit panel is open. Enter into face selection mode through the marking menu.

4. In the Modeling Toolkit panel, select the Drag option under the transformation icons, as shown in Figure 4.45. Your selection cursor changes to a circle. Click one of the inside faces and drag along a six-face square in the middle of the front of the cube, also in Figure 4.45.

Figure 4.45

Drag+select a six-face square on the front of the box.

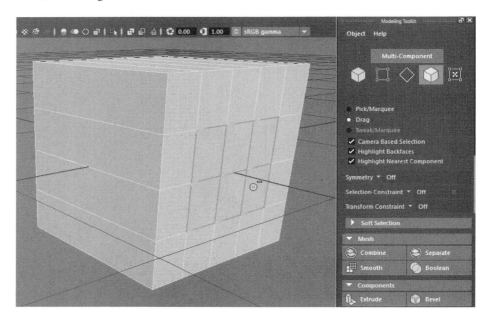

Figure 4.46

Delete the square shapes out of the box.

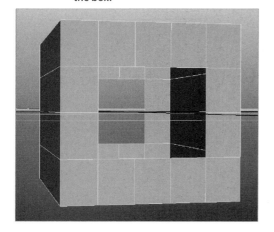

5. Orbit your view to see the back of the box, hold down Shift, and Drag+select the same six-face square on the back of the box.

6. Press Delete on your keyboard to delete the 12 selected faces, leaving you with a hollow box, as shown in Figure 4.46.

7. Now you're going to "fill in" the box to make a square-shaped tube. Switch to edge selection and select the Pick/Marquee option in the Modeling Toolkit panel (it's right above the Drag option). Click to select the two front and back edges shown in Figure 4.47 (left).

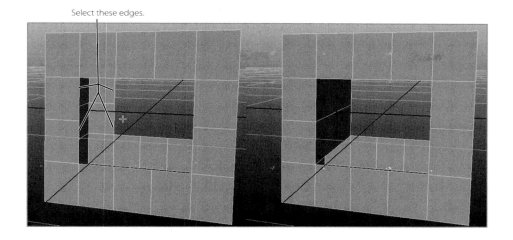

Select these edges.

Figure 4.47

Select these edges (left) and bridge them (right).

8. In the Modeling Toolkit panel, click Bridge, and new faces will appear connecting the selected edges (Figure 4.47, right). In the floating panel, set Divisions to **0**.

9. Repeat steps 7 and 8 on the bottom three edges to connect the bottom, as shown in Figure 4.48.

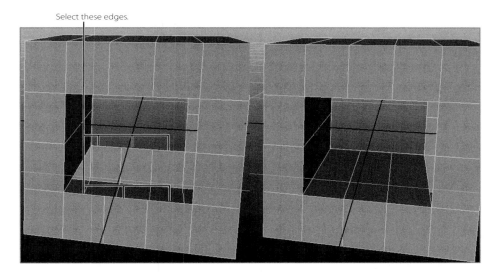

Select these edges.

Figure 4.48

Bridge the bottom faces.

10. Repeat for the remaining edges to fill the holes, making a square pipe that is now solid on the inside.

Experiment with the Divisions attribute for the Modeling Toolkit Bridge tool to get a curvature in the bridged faces.

Modeling Toolkit Symmetry Selections

One of the charms of Modeling Toolkit is its ability to select in symmetry, meaning the components you select on one side of a surface are automatically selected on the other side, making modeling appreciably faster. While Maya has its own Symmetry feature in the transformation tools (Move, Rotate, Scale) covered in Chapter 3, it is limited to simple transforms. Tools such as Extrude or Bevel will not work in Maya's symmetry mode. Let's see how Modeling Toolkit Symmetry works.

Try This

Figure 4.49

Turn on Symmetry mode.

1. Create a polygon sphere in a new scene. Press 5 for Shaded view and make sure Modeling Toolkit is open.

2. Select an edge on the sphere that you want to be the centerline for the symmetry.

3. In the Modeling Toolkit panel, click the word *Symmetry* for a pull-down menu and select Topology, as shown in Figure 4.49. Once you do, the sphere's object name will display next to Symmetry.

4. Now enter face selection. As you move your mouse before you select, it is mirrored, and when you do select a face or faces, that selection will be mirrored on the other side of the mesh (Figure 4.50).

Now if you engage any poly editing function, it will act on the symmetrically selected components, whether they are faces, edges, or vertices.

Keep in mind that for Modeling Toolkit Symmetry to work, your mesh needs to be symmetrical itself. Uneven topology, where one side has a different number of faces than the other, will not work correctly.

Figure 4.50

Selecting faces on one side selects them on the other.

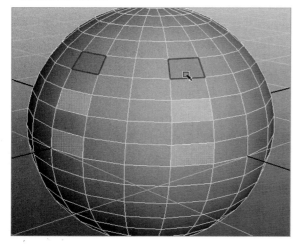

Combine, Merge, and the Target Weld Tool

The Combine function is important in cleaning up your model and creating a unified single mesh out of the many parts that form it. When modeling, you'll sometimes use several different polygon meshes and surfaces to generate your final shape. Using Combine, you can create a single polygonal object out of the pieces.

Frequently, when you're modeling a mesh, you'll need to fold over pieces and weld parts together, especially when you combine meshes into a single mesh. Doing so often leaves you with several vertices occupying the same space. Merging them simplifies the model and makes the mesh much nicer to work with, from rigging to rendering.

The Merge tool fuses multiple vertices at the same point into one vertex on the model. The Target Weld tool from Modeling Toolkit is a more interactive way to fuse vertices together. You'll take a look at both in order to compare the workflows.

In the following simple example, you'll create two boxes that connect to each other along a common edge, and then you'll combine and merge them into one seamless polygonal mesh. To begin, follow these steps:

1. In a new scene, create two poly cubes and place them apart from each other, more or less as shown in Figure 4.51.

Figure 4.51

Place two polygonal cubes close to each other.

2. Select the bottom edge of the cube on the right that faces the other cube and choose Edit Mesh → Extrude (in the Components section of the menu). Pull the edge out a little to create a new face, as shown in Figure 4.52. This will be a flange connecting the two cubes. It isn't important how far you pull the edge out; you'll connect the two cubes by moving the vertices manually.

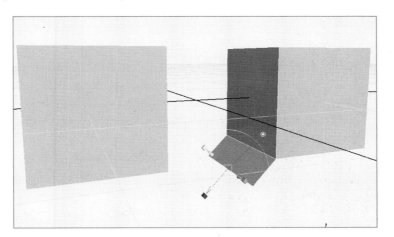

Figure 4.52

Extrude the bottom edge to create a flange.

3. Select the first corner vertex on the newly extruded face and snap it into place on the corner vertex of the other cube, as shown in Figure 4.53 (left). Remember, you can click the Snap To Points icon ( ) to snap the vertex onto the cube's corner.

Figure 4.53

Snap the first corner vertex to the newly extruded face (left) and then the second corner vertex (right).

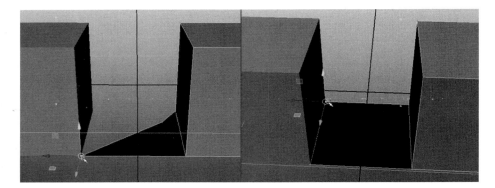

4. Snap the other vertex to the opposite corner so that the cubes are connected with a flange along a common edge, as shown in Figure 4.53 (right).

Even though the cubes seem to be connected at a common edge, they're still two separate polygonal meshes. You can easily select and move just one of the stacked vertices and disconnect the connective face of the two cubes. You need to merge the stacked vertices of the cubes into a single vertex. However, the Merge function won't fuse vertices from two separate meshes together; you must first combine the cubes into a single poly mesh. The following steps continue this task.

5. Select the two cubes (one has the extra flange on the bottom, of course) and choose Mesh → Combine. Doing so makes a single poly mesh out of the two cubes. You can now use the Merge function.

6. Even though the cubes are now one mesh, you still have two vertices at each of the connecting corners of the cube on the left. Click the vertex in the front corner of the newly combined boxes and pull the vertex back as shown in Figure 4.54 (left), which will disconnect the flange at one end. (Click the vertex to select just one. Don't use a marquee selection, which will select both vertices at once.)

7. Let's start at the back corner. To merge the vertices at that corner, select both the vertices that are on top of each other at the far corner by using a marquee selection and then choose Edit Mesh → Merge to fuse the two vertices. As you can see in Figure 4.54 (right), clicking the back corner vertex and moving it reshapes both cubes since the corner is now fused together.

Corner is fused.

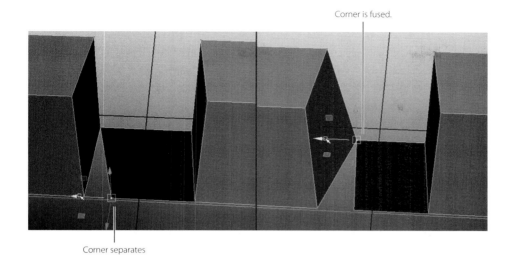

Corner separates

Figure 4.54

There are still two different vertices at the corner, and the boxes aren't really connected (left). The back corner is now connected properly (right).

8. Now, for the front corner where you peeled back the vertex to create a gap in step 6, you'll use the Target Weld tool instead. In this case, you do not need the two vertices sitting on top of each other or even close together as with the Merge tool. Choose Mesh Tools → Target Weld. Click the corner vertex on the flange on the cube on the right and then drag your cursor to highlight the corner vertex on the box on the left, as shown in Figure 4.55. Now the near corner of this mesh is fused into a single vertex.

Figure 4.55

Merge tool in action

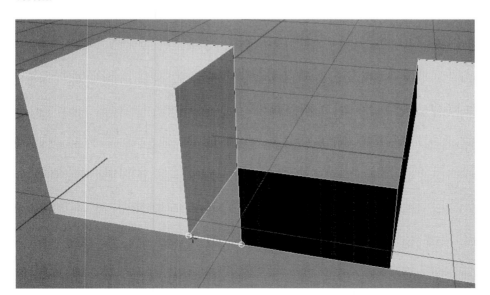

To separate a combined mesh back into its component meshes, choose Mesh → Separate. You can't use Separate if the mesh you've combined has merged vertices.

You'll notice fewer errors and issues with clean models when you animate, light, and render them. Combining meshes makes them easier to deal with, and the Merge function and the Target Weld tool cut down on unwanted vertices.

If the Merge function isn't working on vertices in your model, make sure the model is a single mesh, and if not, use the Combine function.

The Slide Edge Tool

If you need to move an edge on a model, selecting the edge or edges and using the Move tool will change the shape of the mesh. Let's see how this works:

1. Choose Create → Polygon Primitives → Cone ❏ and set Height Divisions to 2, as shown in Figure 4.56 (left).

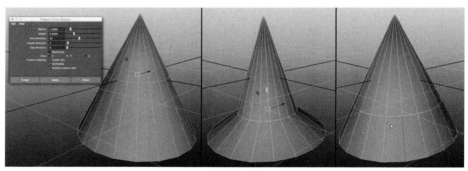

Moving the loop of edges   Sliding the loop of edges

Figure 4.56

Create a cone (left). The middle image shows what happens to the cone when you move the middle loop of edges as opposed to using the Slide Edge tool, as shown on the right.

2. RMB+click and select Edges and then double-click the middle row of horizontal edges to select the entire loop. Move the loop of selected edges down, and the cone turns into a pointy hat, as shown in Figure 4.56 (middle).

3. Press Z for undo to return the object to its original cone shape. Now, with the same loop of edges selected, choose Mesh Tools → Slide Edge and MMB+drag one of the vertical edges (the vertical edge you MMB+click+drag will turn red) of the cone to slide the selected loop of edges up and down the cone without changing its shape, as shown in Figure 4.56 (right).

The Slide Edge tool is perfect for moving edges on a complex mesh surface without altering the shape of that surface.

The Duplicate Face Tool

Select one or more faces and choose Edit Mesh → Duplicate to create a copy of the selected faces. You can use the manipulator that appears to move, scale, or rotate your copied faces, which are now their own object.

The Extract Tool

The Extract tool is similar to the Extrude tool, but it doesn't create any extra faces. Select the faces and choose Mesh → Extract to pull the faces off the surface (see Figure 4.57). If the Separate Extracted Faces option is enabled in the option box, the extracted face will be a separate poly object; otherwise, it will remain part of the original.

Figure 4.57
Pull off the faces.

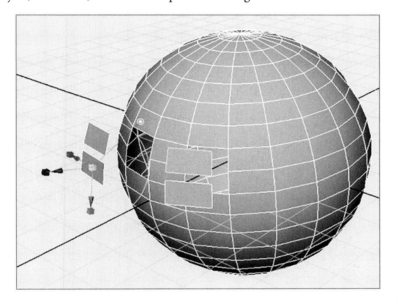

This tool is useful for creating a new mesh from part of the original mesh you are extracting from. You can also use the Extract tool to create a hole in an object and still keep the original faces. When you use this tool with the Multi-Cut tool to make custom edges, you can create cutouts of almost any shape. You'll see this functionality of creating custom-shaped holes with the Split Mesh With Projected Curve function in a moment.

The Smooth Tool

The Smooth tool (choose Mesh → Smooth) evenly subdivides the poly surface or selected faces, creating several more faces to smooth and round out the original poly object, as you saw earlier in this chapter with the cartoon hand model exercise.

Creating a Hole in a Mesh Surface Using Split Mesh With Projected Curve

Sometimes you need to cut a hole in a mesh to create an opening or window of sorts. You can simply select faces on that mesh and delete them to create a simple, face-shaped hole. However, if you need a more intricate, custom-shaped hole, you'll need to first use Split Mesh With Projected Curve to make a custom shape.

1. Create a polygon sphere in a new scene.

2. Now you'll create a curve directly on the sphere to outline the hole's shape. With the sphere selected, click the Make the Selected Object Live icon (▧) in the status bar next to the snapping icons. The text box next to this icon will change from No Live Surface to pSphere1 and will turn blue (▧ pSphere1). Making an object live will enable you to perform some functions directly on that mesh.

3. Choose Create → Curve Tools → EP Curve Tool. Click the sphere and a little *X* appears. Click again, and a line begins to appear on the sphere. Click a number of points to create an interesting shape, and because the sphere is live, these curve points will be placed on top of the sphere, as shown in Figure 4.58 (top). You can simply snap the final EP you draw on top of the first EP you drew with point snaps (▧) to close the curve shape. In the Outliner, the line is called curve1. You can learn more about creating curves in Chapter 5, "Modeling with NURBS Surfaces and Deformers."

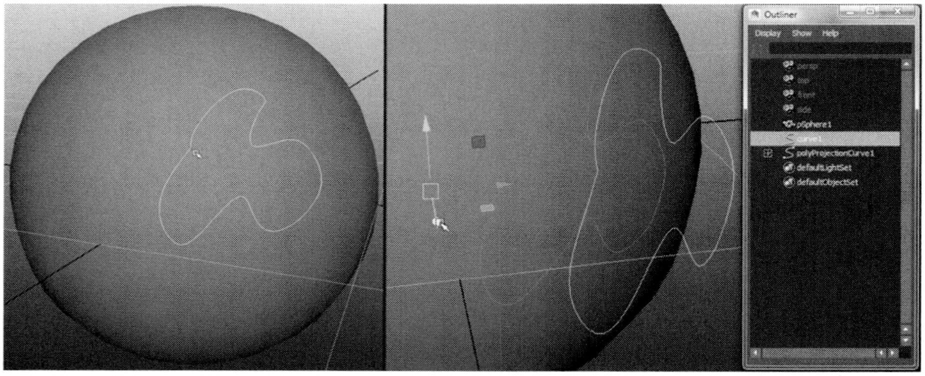

Figure 4.58

Draw an EP curve directly on the sphere (left). The projected curve (shown on the sphere in pink) adjusts if you move the original curve (shown away from the sphere in green).

4. You need to project this curved shape onto the sphere because it is still a separate object despite you creating it on top of the sphere. Disable Make Live by clicking its icon (▧) again.

5. Next, select the sphere and then the curved line. Choose Edit Mesh → Project Curve On Mesh. Now if you select curve1 in the Outliner (Figure 4.58, right) and move it around in your scene, the projected curve on the sphere (shown in your scene as pink) will adjust, staying on the sphere as shown in Figure 4.58 (right).

6. Now you can use this projected curve to outline a new set of edges on your sphere! In the Outliner, select the sphere and the projected curve (`polyProjectionCurve1`) and choose Edit Mesh → Split Mesh With Projected Curve.

7. Maya creates a new sphere that is subdivided with the new edges you drew, as you can see in the Outliner in Figure 4.59 (left). You can delete the original sphere and curve you drew (`pSphere1` and `curve1`), as well as the projected curve (`polyProjection-Curve1`), leaving you with `pSphere2`.

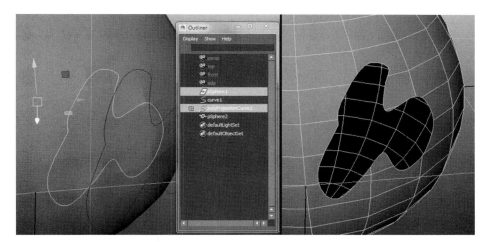

Figure 4.59

Splitting the sphere with its projected curve (left) and then deleting those faces to make a custom hole (right)

8. Now simply delete the faces inside that shape, and you have your custom hole, as shown in Figure 4.59 (right)!

> Keep in mind creating custom holes like this in your mesh will likely create Ngons, which are polygons with more than four sides. Ngons are explained in the "Modeling a Catapult" exercise.

Projecting a line shape onto a mesh surface will allow you to not only cut holes as in this exercise but also easily create custom lengths of edges for modeling use.

Sculpting Tools

With the sculpting tools, you paint on a polygon surface to move the vertices in and out, essentially to mold the surface, as you will see with the candle modeling exercise in Chapter 5. In that chapter, you will use this tool to add detail to a polygon model. Once you have played with the Sculpt Geometry tool in Chapter 5, try loading the `poly_hand_v3.mb` model and sculpting some detail into the cartoon hand.

To access the different sculpting tools, select your poly object, choose Mesh Tools → Sculpting Tools, and select the tool to use. Make sure to click ❏ for the options box so you can adjust each tool setting as you play around. Tear off the Sculpting Tools menu to access each of the different tools; then play around with sculpting a sphere to get a hang of it (see Figure 4.60).

Figure 4.60

**The Sculpt
Geometry tool
deforms the surface.**

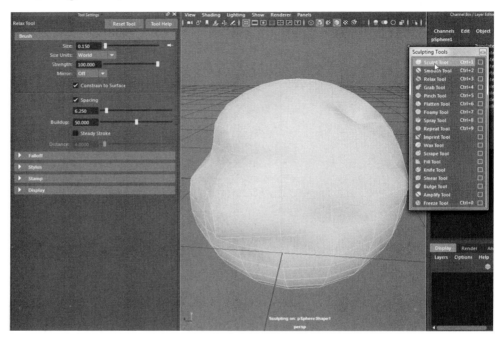

I won't cover all of these tools in great length in this book; however, you will see how some of the sculpting tools work in the next chapter. Create a poly with a large number of subdivisions so you'll have a smoother result when using the sculpting tools.

Modeling a Catapult

You're going to create a catapult in this exercise using nothing but polygons. You'll use some sketches as a reference for the model. Since this is a more involved object than a hand, it's much better to start with good plans. This, of course, involves some research, web surfing, image gathering, or sketching to get a feel for what it truly is you're trying to make.

To begin, create a new project for all the files called Catapult or copy the Catapult project from the companion website (www.sybex.com/go/introducingmaya2016) to your hard drive. If you do not create a new project, set your current project to the copied Catapult project on your drive. Choose File → Set Project and select the Catapult project downloaded from the companion website. Remember that you can enable Incremental Save to make backups at any point in the exercise.

Now, let's use a design already sketched out for reference. To begin, study the design sketches included in the Sourceimages folder of the project. These sketches set up the intent rather easily.

In Chapter 8, "Introduction to Animation," you'll animate the catapult. When building any model, it's important to keep animation in mind, especially for grouping related objects in the scene hierarchy so that they will move as you intend. Creating a good scene hierarchy will be crucial to a smooth animation workflow, so throughout this exercise you'll use the Outliner to keep the catapult's component pieces organized as you create them.

The Production Process

The trick with a complex object model is to approach it part by part. Deconstruct the major elements of the original into distinct shapes that you can approach one by one. The catapult can be broken down to five distinct objects, each with its own subobjects.

- Base
- Wheels
- Fulcrum assembly
- Winch assembly
- Arm assembly

You will model each part separately based on the sketch in Figure 4.61 and the detailed schematic in Figure 4.62.

Figure 4.61

A sketch of the catapult to model

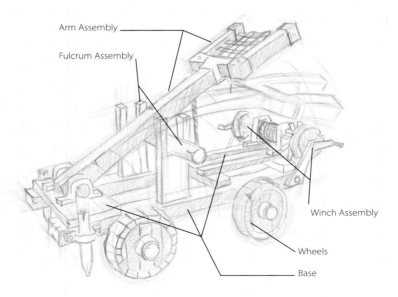

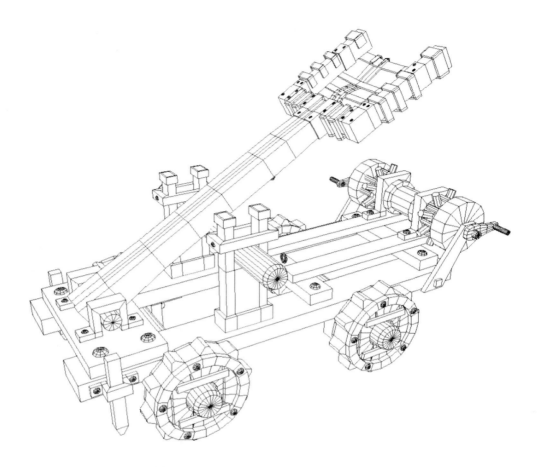

The Base

The base consists of simple polygonal cubes representing timber and arranged to connect to each other. Keep in mind that in this exercise Interactive Creation for primitives is turned off (select Create → Polygon Primitives and make sure Interactive Creation is unchecked). Also, in the Perspective view, choose Shading → Wireframe On Shaded to turn on the wireframe lines while in Shaded mode to match the figures in this exercise.

Creating the Base Objects

To begin the catapult base, follow these steps:

1. Choose Create → Polygon Primitives → Cube to lay down your first cube. This will be for the two long, broad boards running alongside.

2. Scale the cube to 2.0 in X, 0.8 in Y, and 19.5 in Z. Move it off the center of the grid about 2 units to the right.

3. Now you'll add some detail to the simple cube by beveling the sides, using either Modeling Toolkit or the traditional Bevel tool. Select the four edges running on top of the board. In the main menu bar, select Edit Mesh → Bevel. Set Fraction to **0.2** and Segments to **2**. Figure 4.63 shows the resulting board.

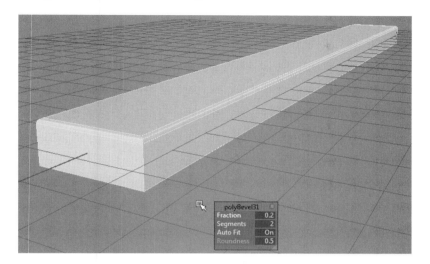

Figure 4.63

Create a bevel for the baseboard object.

4. Select the remaining edges on the board, bevel them to a fraction of **0.3**, and set Segments to **2**. See Figure 4.64.

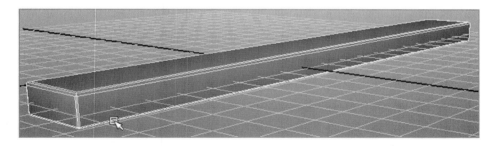

Figure 4.64

Beveling the bottom edges

Beveling the edges of your models can be an important detail. Light will pick up edges much better when they are beveled, even slightly. Perfect 90-degree corners can look too much like CG models and not real objects.

5. Select the board and choose Edit → Duplicate to place a copy of the board exactly where the original is in the scene. The new duplicated board is already selected for you, so just move the copy about 4 units to the left. You should now have something similar to Figure 4.65 (top).

Figure 4.65

The long boards at the base (top) and the platform board in place (bottom)

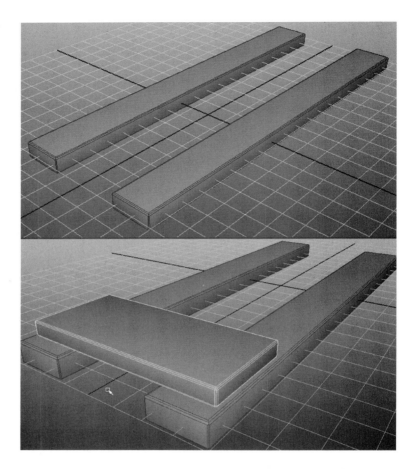

6. Now for the cross braces and platform. Create a poly cube and scale it to 7.25 in X, 0.6 in Y, and 3.25 in Z. Place this platform on top of the two beams, at the end of the catapult's base.

7. With the first board that you beveled, you had a different bevel for the top edges than for the bottom and sides. For this board, you'll have the same bevel width for all its edges. Select the cube in object mode (not the edges as before) and choose Edit Mesh → Bevel or click the Bevel icon in Modeling Toolkit. Set Fraction to **0.2** and Segments to **2**. Figure 4.65 (bottom) shows the platform board in place and beveled.

8. Create a cube for the first of the top two cross braces and scale it 6.5 in X, 0.6 in Y, and 1.2 in Z. Place it on top of the beams at the head of the base and bevel this cube exactly as in the previous step.

9. Duplicate the cube and move the copy about a third of the way down toward the end (Figure 4.66).

Figure 4.66

**Cross bracing
the base**

Using Booleans

You're going to add some detail as you go along, namely, the large screws that hold the timber together. The screws will basically be slotted screw heads placed at the intersection of the pieces. In this section, you will use Booleans to help create the screw heads.

Booleans are impressive operations that allow you to, among other things, cut holes or shapes in a mesh fairly easily. Basically, a Boolean is a geometric operation that creates a shape from the addition of two shapes (Union), the subtraction of one shape from another (Difference), or the common intersection of two shapes (Intersection).

Be forewarned, however, that Boolean operations can be problematic. Sometimes you get a result that is wrong—or, even worse, the entire mesh disappears and you have to undo. Use Booleans sparingly and only on a mesh that is clean and prepared. You've cleaned and prepped your panel mesh, so there should be no problems. (Actually, there will be a problem, but that's half the fun of learning, so let's get on with it.)

First, you need to create the rounded screw head.

1. Create a polygonal sphere (Create → Polygon Primitives → Sphere) and move it from the origin off to the side in the X-axis of the base model. Scale the sphere down to 0.15 in XYZ.

2. With the sphere still selected, switch to the front view and press F to frame. RMB+click the sphere and select Face from the marking menu (Figure 4.67). Select the bottom half of the sphere's faces and press Delete on your keyboard to make a hemisphere (Figure 4.68).

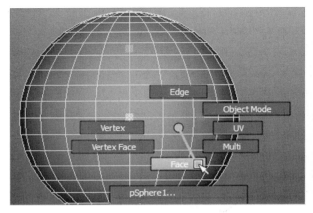

Figure 4.67

Use the marking menu to set the selection to Face.

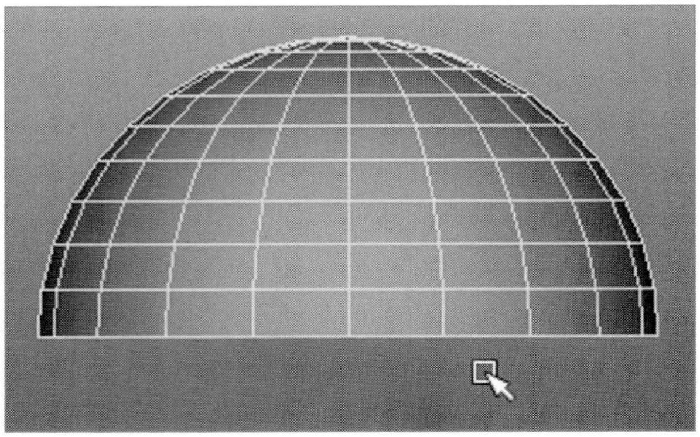

Figure 4.68

Delete the bottom half of the faces.

3.   RMB+click the hemisphere and select Object Mode from the marking menu; this exits face selection mode. Create a poly cube and scale it to 0.4, 0.1, 0.04. Place it over the hemisphere as shown in Figure 4.69.

Figure 4.69

Place the scaled cube over the screw head.

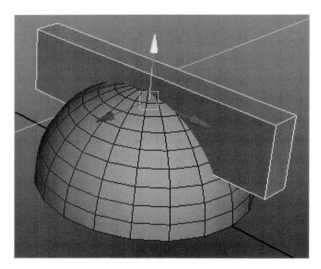

Figure 4.70

Selecting a Difference Boolean

Now you have both objects that you need for a Boolean operation, and they are placed properly to create a slot in the top of the screw head.

4.   Select the hemisphere and then the cube set into it. Select Mesh → Booleans → Difference (Figure 4.70). The cube disappears, and the screw head is left with a slot in the top. However, the screw head appears hollow. In the floating menu of the Boolean operation, set the Classification attribute to Edge from Normal, and your screw head will become solid, as shown in Figure 4.71.

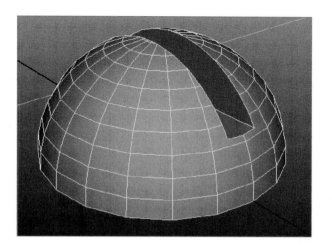

Figure 4.71

The screw head is slotted.

Ngons!

If you take a good close look at the screw head, especially where the slot is, you will notice faces that have more than four sides, which makes them Ngons. As I noted earlier in the chapter, faces that have more than four edges may be problematic with further modeling or rendering. This simple screw head most likely will not pose any problems in the application here, but let's go over how to prevent any problems early on. You will select the potential problem faces (those around the slot) and triangulate them.

1. Select all the faces around the slot, as shown in Figure 4.72 (left). Choose Mesh → Triangulate. This is the easiest and fastest way to subdivide these faces from being Ngons without having to use the Multi-Cut tool to manually fix them. And although it may not look as clean as before (Figure 4.72, right), the geometry is clean and will not be a potential problem like Ngons may be.

Figure 4.72

Select the faces around the slot (left) and triangulate them (right).

2. Select the screw head and choose Edit → Delete By Type → History. This cleans out any history on the object now that you're satisfied with it.

3. Notice that the screw head's pivot point is at the origin. With the object selected, choose Modify → Center Pivot.

4. Name the object **ScrewHead** and position it at one of the intersections of the boards you've built so far.

5. Duplicate that first screw head and place the copies one by one at all the other intersections on the base, as shown in Figure 4.73. These are pretty big screws, huh? For this simple catapult, they'll do fine. The workflow to make more realistic screws is the same if you want to make this again with more realism and scale.

Figure 4.73

Place the screw heads on the base and organize your scene.

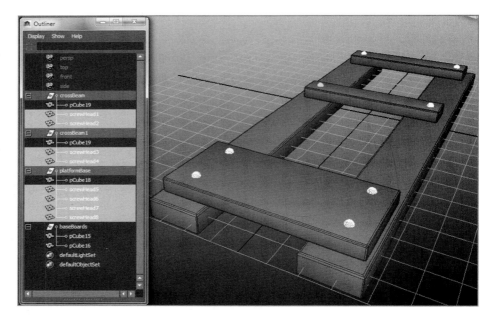

6. Now take the objects in the scene and group them into a logical order, as shown in the Outliner in Figure 4.73.

Save your file and compare it to catapult_v1.mb in the Catapult project from the companion website to see what the completed base should look like.

The time you spend keeping your scene objects organized now will pay off later when you animate the catapult in Chapter 8.

The Winch Baseboards

Next to model for the base are the bars that hold the winch assembly to the base. Refer to the sketch of the catapult (Figure 4.60, earlier) to refresh yourself on the layout of the catapult and its pieces. Follow these steps:

1. Create two long, narrow, beveled poly cubes for the baseboards of the winch and position them across the top two side braces. Put a couple of screws on the middle crossbeam (see Figure 4.74).

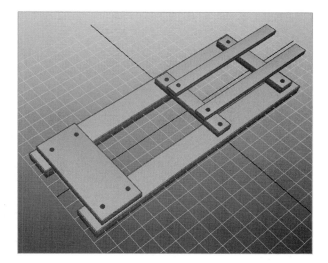

Figure 4.74

Adding the winch baseboards

2. For the brackets that hold down the winch, create a small poly cube and move it off to the side of the base to get it out of the way. Scale the cube to 0.5, 0.3, 0.45. Select the side face and click the Extrude button in the Modeling Toolkit panel. Use **0.8** for the Thickness attribute, as shown in Figure 4.75.

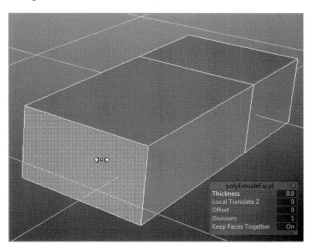

Figure 4.75

Use Modeling Toolkit to extrude the face.

3. Select the top face of the original cube and use Modeling Toolkit to extrude it to a Thickness setting of **1.54** to take it up to an *L* shape. Select the two inside vertices on the top of the *L* and move them up to create about a 45-degree angle at the tip, as shown in Figure 4.76.

Figure 4.76

Extrude the top to create an *L* shape; then move the vertices up to angle the top of the *L*.

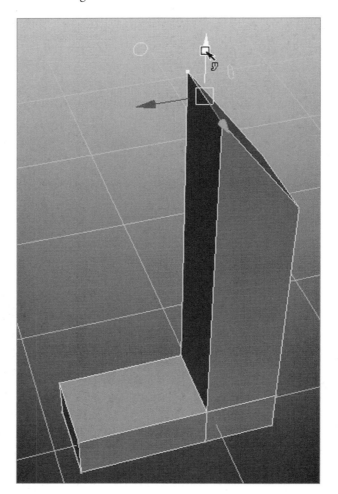

4. Select that angled face and select Extrude in Modeling Toolkit or choose Edit Mesh → Extrude for an extrusion. Click the cyan-colored switch icon above the Extrude manipulator (shown next to the cursor in Figure 4.77, left). This will switch the extrusion axis (Figure 4.77, center) so you can pull the faces out straight and not angled up. Then grab the Z Move manipulator and manually pull the extrusion out about 0.75 units.

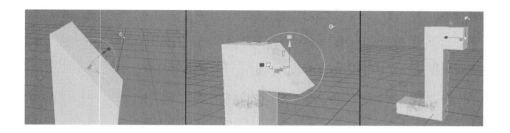

Figure 4.77

Click the switch icon (left) to switch the axis of extrusion (center). Rotate and scale the face to square it (right).

5. Press E to exit the Extrude tool and enter Rotate. Select the end face and rotate it to make it flat vertically and scale it down in Y-axis to prevent it from flaring upward (Figure 4.77, right). It is important to make the face vertical because it affects step 6.

6. This shape forms half of the braces you need. To create the other half, select the face shown in Figure 4.78 (left) and delete it (press Delete). Enter Object mode, select the mesh, and choose Mesh → Mirror Geometry ❑. Set Mirror Direction to -Z, and leave the options as shown in Figure 4.78 (right). Click Mirror, and you will have a full bracket.

   If your face is not rotated to be vertical in the previous step, you may see a gap between the two sides of the bracket. In this case, select the vertices on both sides of this gap and use Edit Mesh → Merge to Center to seal the bracket into one piece.

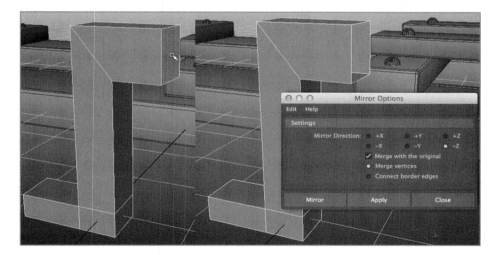

Figure 4.78

Delete the face (left) and set the Mirror Geometry options (right).

7. Name the object **bracket** and move it on top of one of the baseboards for the winch; then place a duplicated screw head on the flanges of the bracket. Group the bracket and screw heads together by selecting them and choosing Edit → Group; call the group **bracketGroup**.

8. Duplicate bracketGroup and move the copy to the other baseboard, as shown in Figure 4.79. Organize your scene as shown in the Outliner in Figure 4.79.

Figure 4.79

The winch's base completed

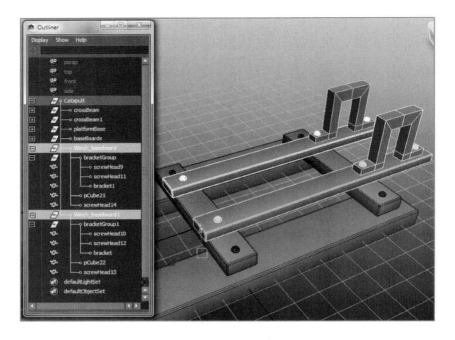

The Ground Spikes

The last items you need for the base are the spikes that secure the base into the ground at the foot of the catapult. Follow these steps:

1. Duplicate a bracket group and name it **bracketGroupCOPY**. Remove the group from its current hierarchy (the baseboard group) by MMB+dragging it to another location in the Outliner (see Figure 4.80). Center its pivot (Modify → Center Pivot).

2. Move the bracket to the other side of the base. Rotate it on its side, scale it to about half its size in all three axes, and place it as shown in Figure 4.81 (left). Select the top vertices and move them closer to the base, as shown in Figure 4.81 (right).

3. Now for the spike itself. Create a poly cube and position and scale it to fit through the bracket. Scale the spike cube to about 3.5 in the Y-axis. Select the bottom face of the spike cube and choose Edit Mesh → Extrude or use Modeling Toolkit. In the floating panel, set Thickness to **0.5** and Offset to **0.15**, as shown in Figure 4.82. You may have to adjust the scale of the cube and or the Offset value of the extrusion to get your spike to resemble the one in the book since the exact scaling of the cube you just created may be different than what I've done here.

Figure 4.80

MMB+dragging the duplicated bracketGroup to another location in the Outliner removes the group from the Winch_baseboard1 group.

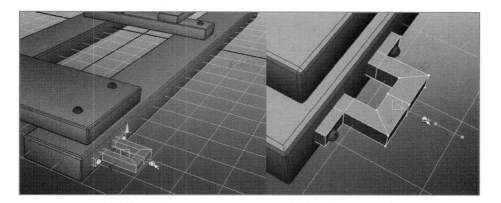

Figure 4.81

Position and scale the bracket assembly for the ground spikes (left). Move the vertices to reduce the depth (right).

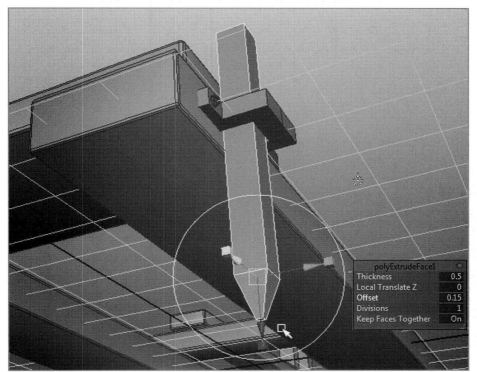

Figure 4.82

Creating the spike

4. Bevel the spike if you'd like. Then select spike and bracketGroupCOPY and group them together, calling the new group **stakeGroup**; center its pivot.

5. Duplicate the stake group and move and rotate it 180 degrees in the Y-axis to fit to the other side of the base. Organize everything into a parent Catapult group (see Figure 4.83) and save your scene as a new version.

Figure 4.83

The completed base

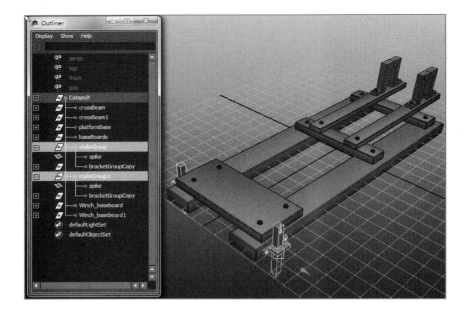

The scene file `catapult_v2.mb` in the Catapult project from the companion website has the completed base for comparison.

The Wheels

What's a catapult if you can't move it around to vanquish your enemies? So now, you will create the wheels. Follow these steps:

1. First is the axle. Create a polygon cylinder (Create → Polygon Primitives → Cylinder) and then scale, rotate, and place it as shown in Figure 4.84 to be the rear axle.

Figure 4.84

Place the rear axle.

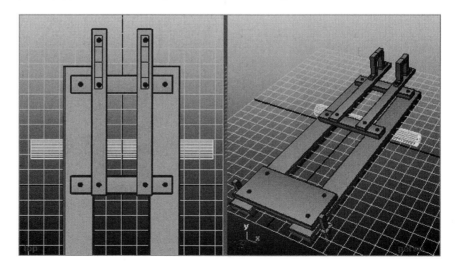

2. Duplicate one of the stake assembly's bracket groups (bracketGroupCOPY) two times; then move and scale each of the two copies to hold the axle on either side. Move down the top vertices of the bracket to make the bracket fit snugly around the axle as needed, as in Figure 4.85. Remember to move the duplicated brackets out of their existing hierarchy in the stakeGroups. Group both the axle brackets together and name the group **Axle_Brackets**. You are not grouping the brackets with the axle cylinder. Keep them separate. You'll organize the hierarchy better a little later.

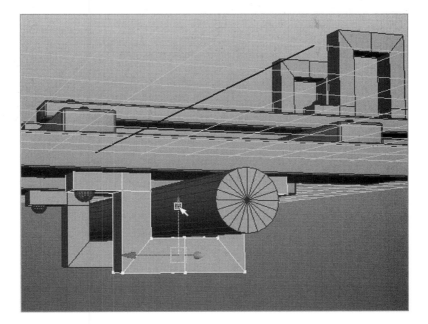

Figure 4.85

Place brackets to hold the rear axle and adjust the vertices to make it fit.

3. To make the axle a little more interesting, let's add a taper at the ends. You will insert new edges around the ends by using Insert Edge Loop, which will be much faster than the Multi-Cut tool in this case. Select the rear axle cylinder and choose Mesh Tools → Insert Edge Loop. Your cursor turns into a triangle. Select one of the horizontal edges on the cylinder toward one end, as shown in Figure 4.86. A dashed line will appear running vertically around the cylinder. Drag the cursor to place the dashed line as shown in Figure 4.86 and release the mouse button to commit the new edges to that location. Repeat the procedure for the other side.

4. Select the end cap faces and scale them down on each side of the axle cylinder, as shown in Figure 4.87, to create tapered ends. Name the cylinder **rearAxle**. Now you're ready for the rear wheels.

Figure 4.86

Insert an edge loop around the end of the cylinder.

Figure 4.86

Insert an edge loop around the end of the cylinder.

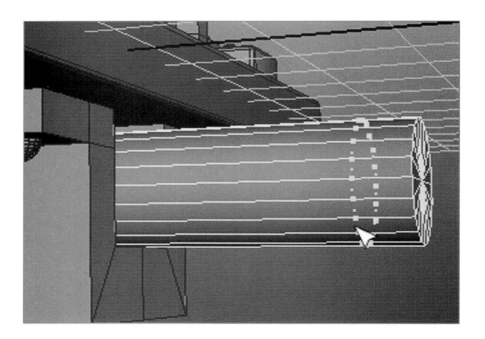

Figure 4.87

Taper the ends of the axle.

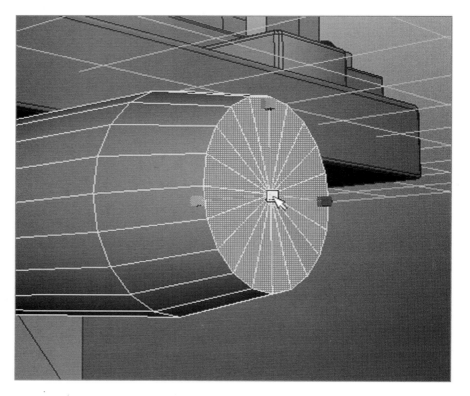

5. To model a wheel, first you'll use NURBS curves to lay out a profile to revolve. Go into the front view. Choose Create → Curve Tools → CV Curve Tool ❐ and select 1 Linear for Curve Degree. Since the wheel's profile will have no smooth curves, you can create a linear CV curve like that in Figure 4.88, laying down CVs clockwise starting in the top-left corner, as shown; otherwise, your wheel may become inside-out and flat black in step 7. This is something that can easily be fixed in step 7 as well. It's important for the design to create three spans for the top part of the curve. Place the pivot point (hold down the D key or press Insert on a PC or Home on a Mac) about three-quarters of a unit below the curve, as shown. This curve will be the profile of the front of the wheel.

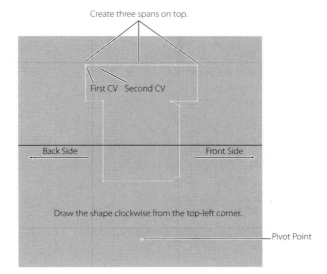

Figure 4.88

The profile curve for the wheel is drawn clockwise in the front view panel.

6. Place the profile above the rear axle. To make sure the pivot point for the profile lines up with the center of the axle, turn on Snap To Points (a.k.a. Point Snap) (⬚) and press and hold down D to move the pivot. Snap the pivot to the center of the axle, as shown in Figure 4.89. Turn off Point Snap.

7. Select the curve and revolve it by choosing Surfaces → Revolve ❐ (Figure 4.90). In the option box, set Axis Preset to X to make it revolve correctly. Change Segments from the default 8 to **20** to give a smoother wheel. Set Output Geometry to Polygons and set Tessellation Method to Control Points. This will create the edges of the faces along the CV points on the curve. Click Revolve, and there it is (Figure 4.91).

   If for some reason your wheel object displays as black, this means the surface is inside out (the normals are reversed). With the wheel object selected, in the Modeling menu set, select Mesh Display → Reverse under the Normals menu heading.

Figure 4.89

**The profile curve is
in place for the
rear wheel.**

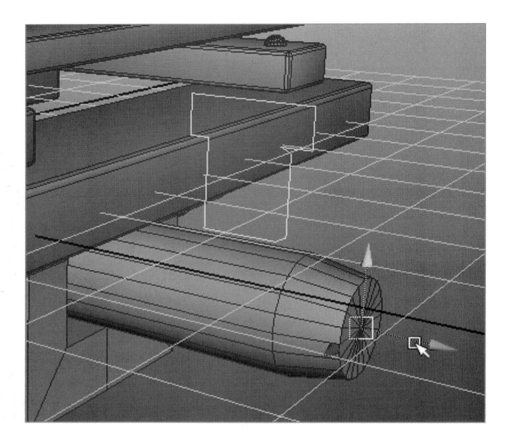

8. Select the wheel object and bevel it. With the wheel still selected, delete the history and the original NURBS curve since you won't need either again.

9. Add some detail to the wheel. Duplicate a screw head and remove the copy from whatever group it was in by MMB+dragging it out of the current group in the Outliner. Arrange a few of the screw heads around the front face of the wheel.

Figure 4.90

**Selecting the
Revolve surface
operation**

10. Add a couple of braces on the front of the wheel above and below the wheel's middle hole with two thin, stretched, and beveled poly cubes, with screws on either side (as shown in Figure 4.92). Again, make sure to remove the duplicated screw heads from whatever group you got them from.

11. Select all the objects of the wheel, group them together by pressing Ctrl+G, and call the group **wheel**. Center the wheel group's pivot point by choosing Modify → Center Pivot.

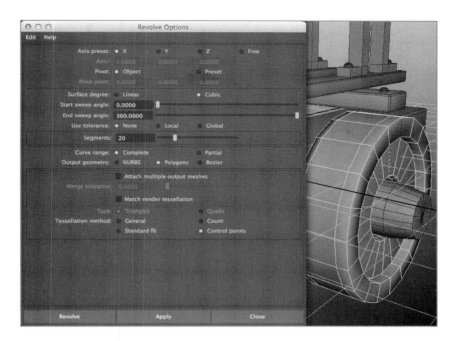

Figure 4.91

The wheel revolved

Figure 4.92

Adding detail to the wheel

12. Adding studs to the wheel makes for better traction when moving the catapult through mud and also for a cooler-looking catapult. To create all the studs at once, grab every other middle face along the outside of the wheel and extrude them with a Thickness of -**0.3** and an Offset of **0.1**, as shown in Figure 4.93. If your studs are extruding inward into the wheel, then simply use a Thickness value of 0.3 instead of -0.3.

Figure 4.93

Extrude studs for the wheel.

13. Copy the wheel group and rotate it 180 degrees in the Y-axis to create the other rear wheel for the other side. Position it on the other side of the rear axle.

14. Group the two wheels with the rear axle and call the new group node **Rear_Wheel**.

15. Select the Rear_Wheel node and the Axle_Brackets group node and duplicate them by choosing Edit → Duplicate or by pressing the hotkey Ctrl+D. Move the objects to the foot of the catapult for the front wheels. Rename the wheel group node **Front_Wheel**.

16. Add the new axle bracket and wheel group nodes to the Catapult top node by MMB+dragging them onto the Catapult node in the Outliner; save your scene. Figure 4.94 shows the positions and Outliner hierarchy of the wheels.

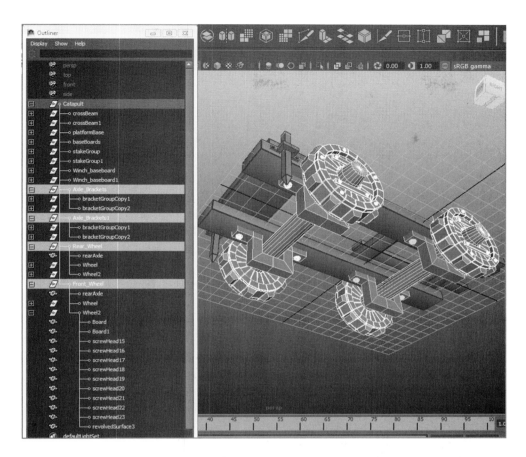

The file catapult_v3.mb in the Catapult project from the companion website reflects the finished wheels and base.

The Winch Assembly

To be able to pull the catapult arm down to cock it to fire a projectile, you'll need the winch assembly to wind a rope that connects to the arm to wind it down into firing position. Since animating a rope can be a rather involved and advanced technique, the catapult will not actually be built with a rope. To build the winch assembly, follow these steps:

1. The first part of the winch is the pulley around which the rope winds. In the front view panel, create a profile curve for extrusion as you did with the wheel that looks more or less like the profile curve in Figure 4.95, drawn clockwise starting with the left side of the profile curve. In this figure, the first CV of the profile curve is on the left end of the curve. Place the pivot point of the curve at that first CV. Revolve the curve around the X-axis with only 12 segments (as opposed to the wheel's 20). Center its pivot, and you have the pulley.

If your pulley object is black, its surface is likely inside out (reversed normals), depending on how you created the profile curve in this step. In this case, select the pulley object and select Mesh Display → Reverse under the Normals menu heading.

Figure 4.95

Create a profile curve and revolve it to create the object shown below the profile curve.

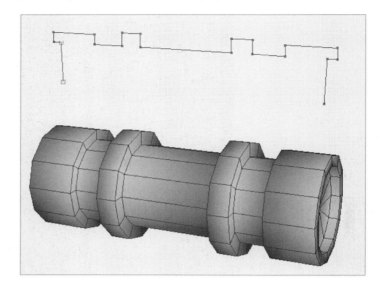

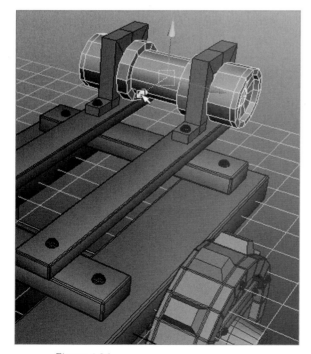

Figure 4.96

Place the pulley.

2. Position the pulley at the rear of the catapult, placing the brackets in the grooves (see Figure 4.96).

3. Now you'll need some sort of geared wheel and handle to crank the pulley. Create a poly cylinder and rotate it so it's on its side like one of the wheels. Scale it to a squat disk with scale values of **1.4** in the X- and Z-axes and **0.4** in the Y-axis. Select the disk and bevel it.

4. Off on the side of your scene, create another poly cylinder, and rotate it to its side as well. Scale it to be a long, thin stick. You'll use this as the first of eight gear teeth for the wheel. Position it at the top of the wheel, as shown in Figure 4.97. Click the Snap To Points icon in the Status line ( ) and snap the pivot point (press D to move the pivot) to the center of the wheel. Turn off Snap To Points.

5. Instead of duplicating the gear tooth and positioning it seven more times individually, you'll use the array capabilities of the Duplicate Special tool. Select the tooth and choose Edit → Duplicate Special ❏. In the option box, set Rotate to **45** in the X-axis, and set Number Of Copies to **7**. Since the pivot for the tooth is at the center of the wheel, as soon as you click the Duplicate Special button, Maya places seven copies around the wheel at 45-degree intervals (Figure 4.98).

Figure 4.97

Making a gear wheel

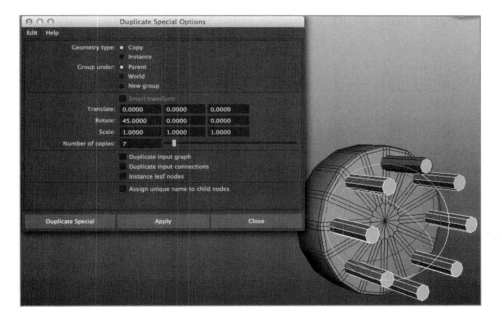

Figure 4.98

Eight gear teeth in place

6. Now for the handle. Create a poly cube with enough segments for you to adjust vertices and faces to match the handle shown in Figure 4.99. Create cylinders for the crank axle and handle and place them as shown. Group all the parts together and snap the pivot point to the center of the gear wheel disk. Name the group **handle**. You can bevel the handle if you want.

Figure 4.99

Use two cylinders and a poly cube to create the handle shapes.

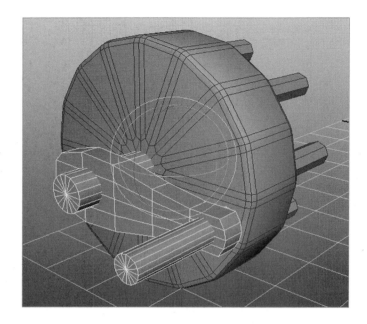

7. Group the geometry together, call the object **Turn_Wheel**, and center its pivot. Place it at the end of the pulley. Place a copy (rotated 180 degrees) on the other side of the pulley. Figure 4.100 shows the placement.

Figure 4.100

Place the turn wheels.

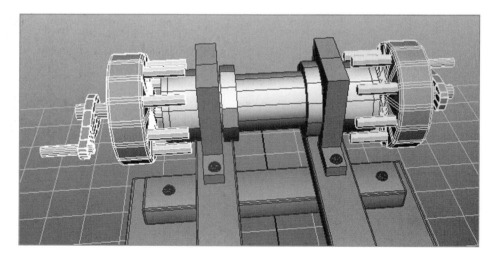

8. Now you'll need gear teeth on the pulley cylinder shape. Create a poly cylinder to be a long, thin tube like the gear teeth and position it at the end of the pulley. Place it so that it is in between two of the turning wheel gear teeth. Place the pivot at the center of the pulley using Snap To Points.

9. Duplicate the new tooth seven times around the pulley at 45-degree intervals with Duplicate Special.

10. Make a copy of each of those eight teeth and move the copies to the other side of the pulley for the other gear. Group the pulley and turning wheels together and name the object **Winch**, as shown in Figure 4.101. Center the pivot.

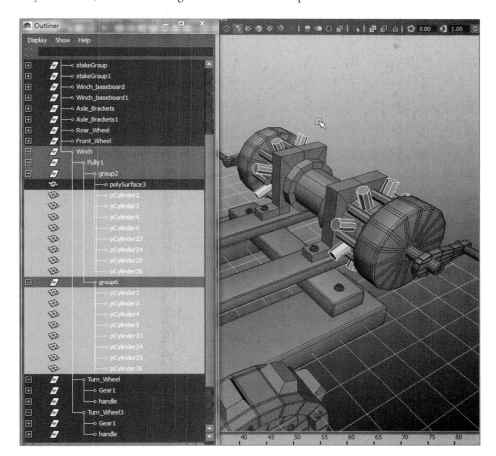

Figure 4.101

The winch gears and handles

11. Using a couple of poly cubes that you shape by moving vertices, make a winch arm on either side to brace the winch to the catapult. Bevel the shapes when you are happy with their shapes. Place the braces between the crank handle and the turning wheel on both sides, and bolt them to the catapult's base, as shown in Figure 4.102. Group them and add them to the hierarchy as shown. Save your scene file.

To verify your work up to this point, compare it to `catapult_v4.mb` in the Catapult project from the companion website.

Figure 4.102

The assembled winch

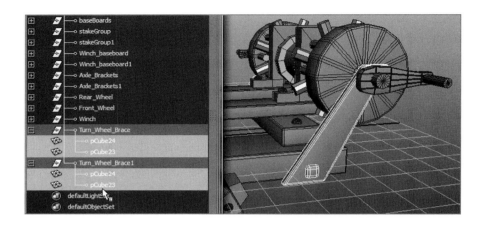

The Arm

OK, now I'm kicking you out of the nest to fly on your own! Try creating the arm (see Figure 4.103), without step-by-step instruction, using all the techniques you've learned and the following hints and diagrams:

- Create the intricate-looking arm with face extrusions. That's all you'll need for the arm geometry. Follow Figure 4.104 for subdivision positions to make the extrusions work correctly.

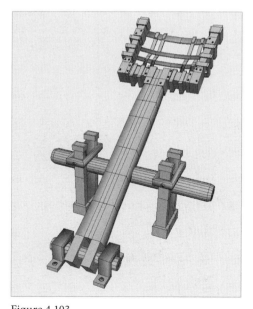

Figure 4.103

The catapult arm assembly

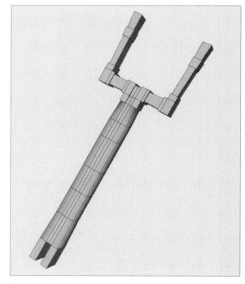

Figure 4.104

Follow the subdivisions on your model.

- Duplicate and place screw heads around the basket assembly, as shown in Figure 4.105.

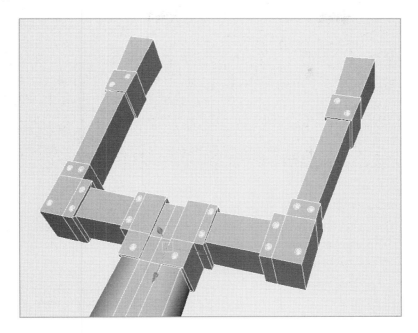

Figure 4.105

Place screw heads around the basket arms.

- Create the straps for the basket with poly cubes. It's easier than it looks. You'll just need to create and extrude the cubes with enough subdivisions to allow you to bend them to weave them together, as shown in Figure 4.106. The ends of the straps wrap around the arm's basket with extrusions.

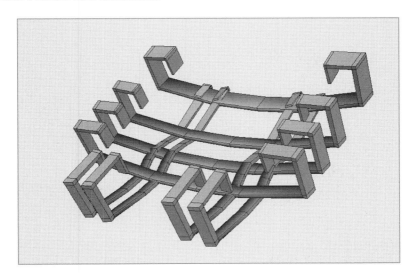

Figure 4.106

Basket straps

- Create the hinge for the arm with a couple of duplicated brackets and a cylinder.
- Create the arm's stand with multiple extrusions from a cube. Follow the subdivisions in Figure 4.107 for reference.

Figure 4.107

Follow the subdivisions on the arm stand.

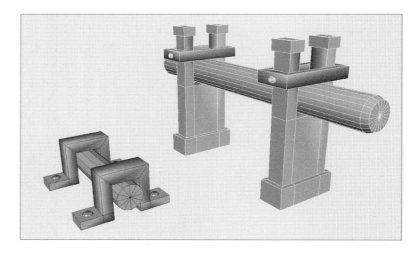

- Bevel the parts you feel could use some nice edging, including the arm and stand pieces.
- Group the objects together and add their groups to the Catapult node.

When you've finished, save your scene file and compare it to catapult_v5.mb in the Catapult project from the companion website. Figure 4.108 shows the finished catapult.

Figure 4.108

The completed catapult

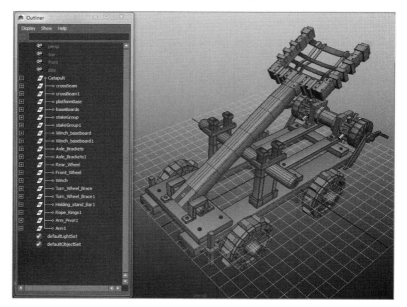

Summary

In this chapter, you learned about the basic modeling workflows with Maya and Modeling Toolkit and how best to approach a model. This chapter dealt with polygon modeling and covered several polygon creation and editing tools, as well as several polygon subdivision tools. You put those tools to good use by building a cartoon hand and smoothing it out, as well as making a model of an old-fashioned catapult using traditional Maya workflows as well as new Modeling Toolkit workflows. The latter exercise stressed the importance of putting a model together step-by-step and understanding how elements join together to form a whole in a proper hierarchy. You'll have a chance to make another model of that kind in Chapter 6, when you create a toy airplane that is used to light and render later in the book.

Complex models become much easier to create when you recognize how to deconstruct them into their base components. You can divide even simple objects into more easily managed segments from which you can create a model.

The art of modeling with polygons is like anything else in Maya: Your technique and workflow will improve with practice and time. It's less important to know all the tricks of the trade than it is to know how to approach a model and fit it into a wireframe mesh.

CHAPTER 5

Modeling with NURBS Surfaces and Deformers

NURBS is based on organic mathematics, which means you can create smooth curves and surfaces. NURBS models can be made of a single surface molded to fit, or they can be a collection of patches connected like a quilt. In any event, NURBS provides ample power for creating smooth surfaces for your models.

Now that you've learned the basics of creating and editing poly meshes, you'll get into creating some organic surfaces using NURBS techniques. This chapter also explains how to use deformers to adjust a model, as opposed to editing the geometry directly as you did with the previous modeling methods.

Learning Outcomes: In this chapter, you will be able to

- Use the surfacing techniques (Loft, Set Planar, and Revolve) to create surfaces

- Convert NURBS geometry into polygons

- Create polygon meshes directly from NURBS techniques

- Model a pair of glass candle holders and convert them to polygons

- Create CV curves and use Revolve to create a poly mesh

- Attach and detach curves

- Use the Sculpt Geometry tool to sculpt a mesh surface

- Use the Soft Deformation Modifier

- Use nonlinear deformers to adjust existing geometry

- Create edits to existing models using lattices

- Animate an object to deform through a lattice

NURBS for Organic Curves

NURBS is an acronym for *Non-Uniform Rational B-Spline*. That's good to know for cocktail parties. NURBS modeling excels at creating curved shapes and lines, so it's most often used for organic forms such as animals and people, as well as highly detailed cars. These organic shapes are typically created with a quilt of NURBS surfaces, called *patches*. Patch modeling can be powerful for creating complex shapes such as characters, but it can also be quite difficult and will not be covered in this book. I will, however, touch on the basics of NURBS surface modeling in this chapter.

In essence, Bézier curves are created with a starting and ending *control vertex* (CV) and usually two or more CVs in between that provide a smooth curvature. As each CV is laid down, the curve or spline tries to go from the previous CV to the next one in the smoothest possible manner.

As shown in Figure 5.1, CVs control the curvature. The *hulls* connect the CVs and are useful for selecting multiple rows of CVs at a time. The starting CV appears in the Autodesk® Maya® software as a closed box. The second CV, which defines the curve's direction, is an open box, so you can easily see the direction in which a curve has been created. The curve ends, of course, on the endpoint CV. The start and end CVs are the only CVs that are always actually on the curve itself.

Figure 5.1

A Bézier curve and its components

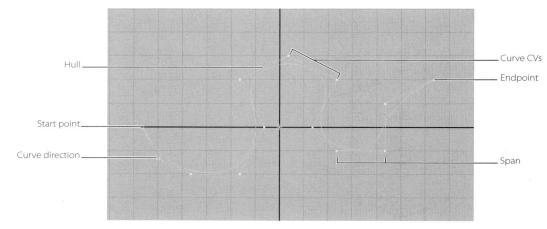

NURBS Modeling

NURBS surfaces are defined by curves called *isoparms*, which are created with CVs. The surface is created between these isoparms to form *spans* that follow the surface curvature defined by the isoparms, as in Figure 5.2. The more spans, the greater the detail and control over the surface.

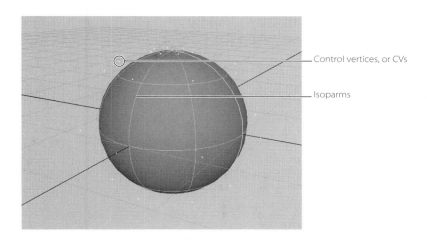

Figure 5.2
NURBS surfaces are created between isoparms. You can sculpt them by moving their CVs.

It's easier to get a smooth deformation on a NURBS surface with few CVs than on a polygon. Achieving the same smooth look on a polygon would take much more surface detail. As you can see in Figure 5.3, NURBS modeling yields a smoother deformation, whereas polygons can become jagged at the edges.

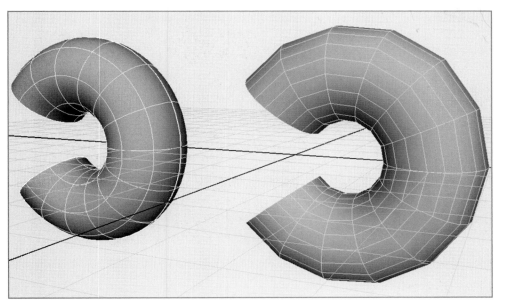

Figure 5.3
A NURBS cylinder (left) and a polygonal cylinder (right) bent into a C shape. The NURBS cylinder remains smooth, and the polygon cylinder shows its edges.

You can convert NURBS to polygons at any time, but converting polygons back to NURBS can be tricky.

Try This   Open a new scene (choose File → New Scene). In the new scene, you'll create a few curves on the ground plane grid in the perspective (persp) panel. Maximize the perspective view by moving your cursor to it and pressing the spacebar. Choose Create → Curve

Tools → CV Curve Tool. Your cursor turns into a cross. Lay down a series of points to define a curved line on the grid. Notice how the Bézier curve is created between the CVs as they're laid down.

Spans are isoparms that run horizontally in a NURBS surface; *sections* are isoparms that run vertically in the object.

NURBS surfaces are created by connecting (or *spanning*) curves. Typical NURBS modeling pipelines first involve creating curves that define the edges, outline, paths, and/ or boundaries of surfaces.

A surface's shape is defined by its isoparms. These surface curves, or curves that reside solely on a surface, show the outline of a shape much as the chicken wire does in a wire mesh sculpture. CVs on the isoparms define and govern the shape of these isoparms just as they would regular curves. Adjusting a NURBS surface involves manipulating the CVs of the object.

Levels of Detail

NURBS is a type of surface in Maya that lets you adjust its detail level at any time to become more or less defined as needed. Pressing 1, 2, or 3 toggles between detail levels for any selected NURBS object from low quality at 1 to high quality at 3.

NURBS Surfacing Techniques

The easiest way to create a NURBS surface is to create a NURBS primitive, and then you can sculpt the primitive surface by moving its CVs. But you can also make surfaces in several ways without using a primitive. All these methods involve using NURBS curves to define a boundary, shape, or path of the surface and then using one of the methods described in the following sections to create the surfaces.

Lofting

The most common surfacing method is *lofting*, which takes at least two curves and creates a surface span between each selected curve in the order in which they're selected. Figure 5.4 shows the result of lofting a few curves together.

To create the loft in Figure 5.4, follow these steps:

1. Switch to the Modeling menu set (press F2).

2. Draw the two curves.

3. Select the curves in the order in which you want the surface to be generated.

4. Choose Surfaces → Loft, or click the Loft icon in the Curves/Surfaces shelf ( ).

When you define more curves for the loft, Maya can create more complex shapes. The more CVs for each curve, the more isoparms you have and the more detail in the surface. Lofting works best when curves are drawn as cross-sectional slices of the object to be modeled.

Lofting is used to make a variety of surfaces, which may be as simple as tabletops or as complex as human faces.

Revolved Surface

A *revolved surface* requires only one curve that is turned around a point in space to create a surface, like a woodworker shaping a table leg on a lathe. First you draw a *profile curve* to create a profile of the desired object, and then you revolve this curve (anywhere from 0 degrees to 360 degrees) around a single point in the scene to sweep a surface.

The profile revolves around the object's pivot point, which is typically placed at the origin but can be easily moved. Figure 5.5 (left) shows the profile curve for a wine glass. The curve is then revolved around the Y-axis a full 360 degrees to create the wine glass. Figure 5.5 (right) is the complete revolved surface with the profile revolved around the Y-axis.

To create a revolved surface, draw and select your profile curve and then choose Surfaces → Revolve.

A revolved surface is useful for creating objects such as bottles, furniture legs, and baseball bats—anything that is symmetrical around an axis.

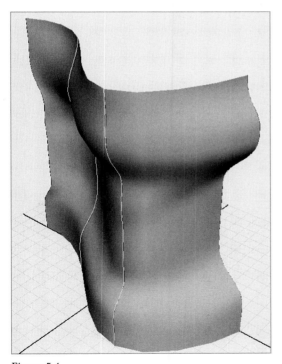

Figure 5.4

A loft created with four curves that are selected in order from left to right

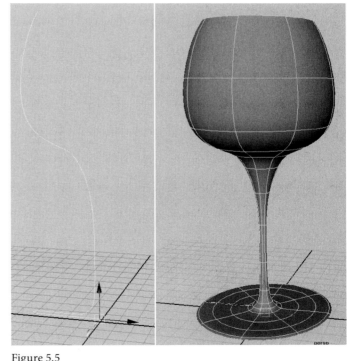

Figure 5.5

A profile curve is drawn in the outline of a wine glass in the Y-axis (left image) and the revolved surface (right image).

Extruded Surface

An *extruded surface* uses two curves: a profile curve and a path curve. First you draw the profile curve to create the profile shape of the desired surface. Then you sweep the curve from one end of the path curve to its other end, creating spans of a surface along its travel. The higher the CV count on each curve, the more detail the surface will have. An extruded surface can also take the profile curve and simply stretch it to a specified distance straight along one direction or axis, doing away with the profile curve. Figure 5.6 shows the profile and path curves, and Figure 5.7 shows the resulting surface after the profile is extruded along the path.

Figure 5.6

The profile curve is drawn in the shape of an *I*, and the path curve comes up and bends toward the camera.

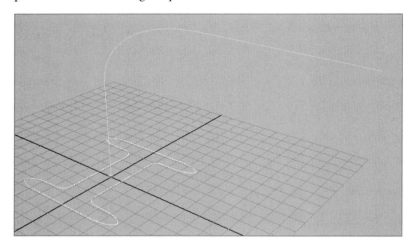

Figure 5.7

After extrusion, the surface becomes a bent I-beam.

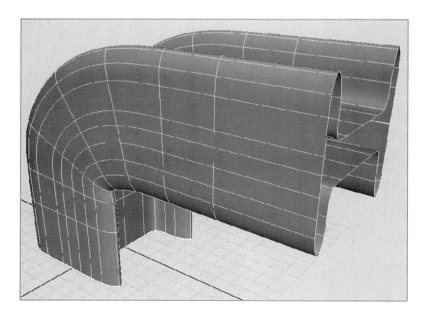

To create an extruded surface, follow these steps:

1. Draw both curves.

2. Select the profile curve.

3. Shift+click the path curve.

4. Choose Surfaces → Extrude.

An extruded surface is used to make items such as winding tunnels, coiled garden hoses, springs, and curtains.

Planar Surface

A *planar surface* uses one perfectly flat curve to make a two-dimensional cap in the shape of that curve. You do this by laying down a NURBS plane (a flat, square NURBS primitive) and carving out the shape of the curve like a cookie cutter. The resulting surface is a perfectly flat, cutout shape.

To create a planar surface, draw and select the curve and then choose Surfaces → Planar.

You can also use multiple curves within each other to create a planar surface with holes in it. A simple planar surface is shown on the left side of Figure 5.8. When a second curve is added inside the original curve and both are selected, the planar surface is created with a hole. On the right side is the result when the outer curve is selected first and then the inner curve is selected before choosing Surfaces → Planar.

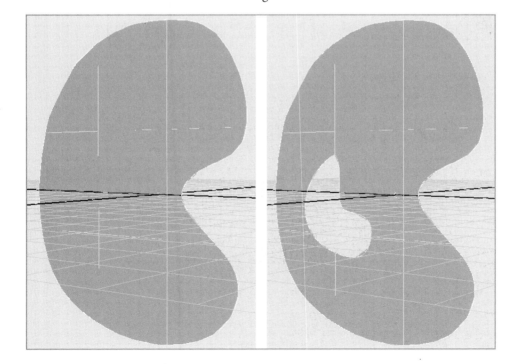

Figure 5.8

A planar surface based on a single curve (left); a planar surface based on a curve within a curve to create the cutout (right)

A planar surface is great for flat lettering, for pieces of a marionette doll or paper cutout, or for capping the ends of a hollow extrusion. It's usually best to create the planar surface as a polygon mesh, a technique you'll see later in this chapter in the "Using NURBS Surfacing to Create Polygons" section.

> If you try creating a planar surface using a curve and notice that Maya doesn't allow it, verify that the curve is perfectly flat. If any of the CVs aren't on the same plane as the others, the planar surface won't work.

Beveled Surface

With the Bevel Surface function you take an open or closed curve and extrude its outline to create a side surface. It creates a bevel on one or both corners of the resulting surface to create an edge that can be made smooth or sharp (see Figure 5.9). The many options in the Bevel tool allow you to control the size of the bevel and depth of extrusion, giving you great flexibility. When a bevel is created, you can easily cap the bevel with planar surfaces.

To create a bevel, draw and select your curve and then choose Surfaces → Bevel.

Maya also offers a Bevel Plus surface, which has more creation options for advanced bevels. A beveled surface is great for creating 3D lettering, for creating items such as bottle caps or buttons, and for rounding out an object's edges.

Figure 5.9

A curve before and after it's beveled. The beveled surface has been given a planar cap.

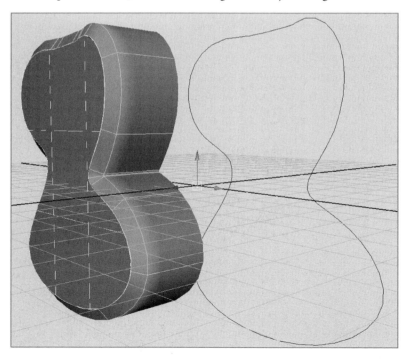

Boundary Surface

A *boundary surface* is so named because it's created within the boundaries of three or four surrounding curves. For example, you draw two vertical curves opposite each other to define the two side edges of the surface. Then you draw two horizontal curves to define the upper and lower edges. These curves can have depth; they need not be flat for the boundary surface to work, unlike a planar surface. Although you can select the curves in any order, it's best to select them in opposing pairs. In Figure 5.10, four curves are created and arranged to form the edges of a surface. First, you would select the vertical pair of curves because they're opposing pairs; then, you would select the second two horizontal curves before choosing Surfaces → Boundary.

A boundary surface is useful for creating shapes such as car hoods, fenders, and other formed panels, especially when created as polygon mesh.

Using NURBS Surfacing to Create Polygons

You can easily create swatches of polygon surfaces instead of NURBS surfaces by using any of these NURBS surfacing tools. To create a polygonal surface instead of a NURBS surface, open the option box for any particular NURBS tool.

Try This   Draw two CV curves as you did at the beginning of this chapter, both with the same number of CVs. Choose Surfaces → Loft □ and click the Polygons option for Output Geometry. Set Type to Quads and leave the Tessellation method as Standard fit. Set the Chord height ratio to 0.95 and the 3D delta to 0.07, as shown in Figure 5.11. Click Apply.

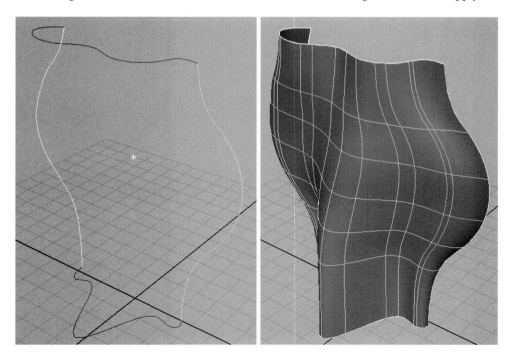

Figure 5.10

Four curves arranged to create the edges for a surface (left); the resulting boundary surface formed from the four curves (right)

Figure 5.11

Create two curves and loft between them to make a polygon mesh.

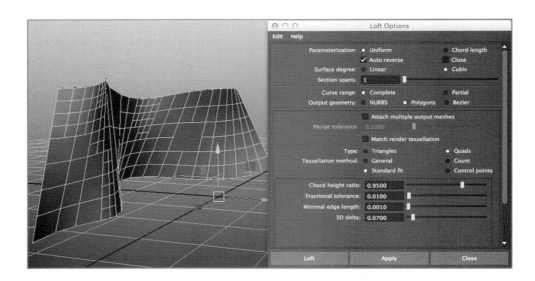

The creation options that appear at the bottom of the option window affect the tessellation of the resulting surface; that is, you use them to specify the level of detail and the number of faces with which the surface is created.

The Standard Fit Tessellation method uses the fewest faces to create the surface without compromising overall integrity. The sliders adjust the resulting number of faces in order to fit the finer curvature of the input curves, particularly Chord Height Ratio and 3D delta.

The Chord Height Ratio determines the amount of curve in a particular region and calculates how many more faces to use to give an adequate representation of that curved area with polygons. Values approaching 1.0 create more faces and better detail with surfaces that have multiple or very intense curves. Lower 3D Delta values will fit smaller faces around tight curves and lower the Fractional Tolerance settings, giving you a smoother surface and a greater number of faces.

Construction History

History has to do with how objects react to change. Leaving History on when creating objects allows you to adjust the original parameters that created that object. For example, the loft you just created will update whenever the curves you used to create the loft move or change shape.

Try This   Select the new poly surface you just lofted in the previous "Try This" and open the Attribute Editor. Select the nurbsTessellate1 tab and open the Advanced Tessellation Options heading. In the Standard Fit Options heading, experiment with changing the Chord Height Ratio and Delta values to see how the poly surface re-creates itself.

Also try selecting the CVs of the original curves (RMB+click one of the two curves you made and select Control Vertex from the marking menu). Adjust the curve, and the surface will re-create itself because of surface history.

> You must toggle History on before you create the objects if you want History to be on for the objects.

In the status line, the History icon (⬛) toggles History on and off. Why wouldn't you want History turned on for everything? After a long day of modeling, having History on for every single object can slow down your scene file, adding unnecessary bloat to your workflow. But it isn't typically a problem on most surface types unless the scene is huge, so you should leave it on while you're still modeling.

If you no longer want a surface or an object to retain its History, you can selectively delete it from the surface. Select the surface and choose Edit → Delete By Type → History. You can also rid the entire scene of History by choosing Edit → Delete All By Type → History. Just don't get them mixed up!

Other Tessellation Methods

Standard Fit will probably do the best job in most situations; however, here are the other tessellation methods you can use:

- The General Tessellation method creates a specific number of lines, evenly dividing the horizontal (U) and vertical (V) into rows of polygon faces.

- The Control Points method tessellates the surface according to the number of points on the input curves. As the number of CVs and spans on the curves increase, so does the number of divisions of polygons.

- The Count method simply relies on how many faces you tell it to make—the higher the count, the higher the tessellation on the surface. Experiment with the options to get the best poly surface results.

Converting a NURBS Model to Polygons

Some people prefer to model on NURBS curves and either create poly surfaces or convert to polygons after the entire model is done with NURBS surfaces. Ultimately, you'll find your own workflow preference, but it helps greatly if you're comfortable using all surfacing methods. In the following section, you'll convert a NURBS model to polygons.

Try This Convert a NURBS-modeled axe into a poly model like one that might be needed in a game.

Open axe_model_v1.mb in the Scenes folder of the Axe project from the companion web page. The toughest part of this simple process is getting the poly model to follow all the curves in the axe with fidelity, so you'll have to convert parts of the axe differently. Follow these steps:

1. Grab the handle and choose Modify → Convert → NURBS To Polygons ☐. Use the default presets. If need be, reestablish your settings by choosing Edit → Reset Settings; the handle converts well to polygons. Click Apply, and a poly version of the axe handle appears on top of the NURBS version. Move it eight units to the right to get it out of the way. You'll move the other parts eight units as well to assemble the poly axe properly.

2. Select the back part of the axe head. All those surfaces are grouped together to make selection easy. The default settings will work for this part as well, so click Apply and move the resulting model eight units to the left.

3. The front of the axe head holds a lot of different arcs, so you'll have to create it with finer controls. Change Fractional Tolerance from 0.01 to 0.0005. This yields more polygons but finer-curved surfaces. Figure 5.12 shows the result.

Figure 5.12

A faithful high-poly conversion (on the right) of a NURBS axe (on the left)

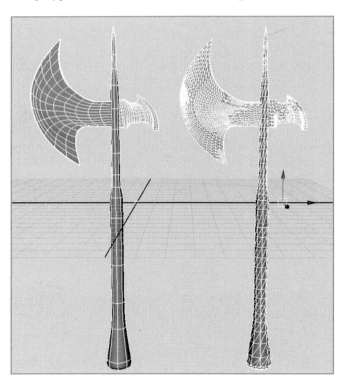

Using Artisan to Sculpt NURBS

Imagine that you can create a NURBS surface and sculpt it using your cursor the way hands mold the surface of wet clay. As you saw with the Sculpt Geometry tool in Chapter 4, you can push and pull vertices easily by virtually painting on the surface. You can sculpt NURBS surfaces much the same way by accessing Surfaces → Sculpt Geometry Tool ❑.

If you plan to sculpt a more detailed surface, be sure to create the surface with plenty of surface spans and sections. You'll try this tool a little bit in the next section.

Creating a Pair of Glass Candle Holders

Let's put some of this information to good use and build a pair of glass candle jars. You will use these glass jars in Chapters 7, 10, and 11 to create shaders (materials), light them, and render them. Copy the project folder candleHolder from the book's companion web page, www.sybex.com/go/introducingmaya2016, and set your project to it.

Figure 5.13

Start with the first four CVs, and then work clockwise to complete your curve to match this shape.

First four CVs

Creating the Objects

You'll start with a profile curve for a Revolve surface:

1. Click Create → Curve Tools → CV Curve tool and turn on grid snaps ( ) in the status bar.

2. In the front view panel, click the origin to snap the first CV to (0,0,0). Snap the second and third CVs to the grid points on the left. Click the fourth CV slightly higher than the third CV to create a sharp curve. Figure 5.13 marks the first four CVs.

   Continue laying down CVs to match the shape shown in Figure 5.13. This will be the profile curve for the body of the jar.

3. In the Modeling menu set, select Surfaces → Revolve ❑. Make sure Axis Preset is Y and set Output Geometry to Polygons. Set Type to Quads. To get smooth curves in the mesh, increase Chord Height Ratio to **0.97** or use **0.935** for a less dense model instead. (See the "Making Less Dense Candle Geometry" sidebar for more information.) Lower 3D Delta to **0.06**. Click Revolve to make the jar's body (Figure 5.14).

MAKING LESS DENSE CANDLE GEOMETRY

The geometry you are now creating for the candle is pretty smooth and therefore will make a larger file and tax your system just a little more. You can create all the revolved surfaces in step 3 and future steps by using a Chord Height Ratio value of 0.935 instead of 0.97. This will create significantly fewer polygons to tax your system if your machine is running slow. However, the candle may not look quite as detailed as you are creating in this and future chapters where you light and render the candle.

Figure 5.14

Revolve the surface with these settings.

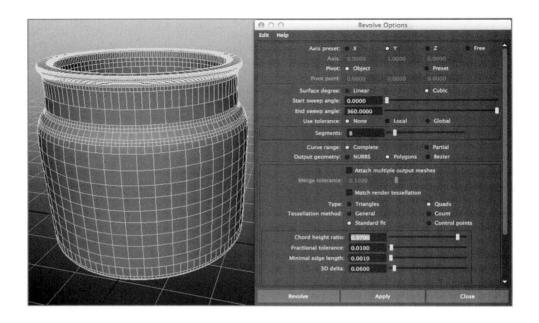

4. Now for the lid. In the front view panel, click the Show menu in the view panel's menu bar and toggle off Polygons, as shown in Figure 5.15. This will disable polygon display in the front view panel to make it easy to work on the next profile curve for the lid.

Figure 5.15

Turn off polygons in the front view panel.

5. The lid will have two parts: the main glass lid and a plastic stopper that goes around the bottom of the glass part where it inserts into the jar. Create a curve to match Figure 5.16. Notice where the first few CVs are created and follow counterclockwise to lay down all the CVs as shown.

6. Now let's make a profile curve for the plastic sealer that goes around the base of the lid. In the front view panel, create another curve to match the shape in Figure 5.17.

7. Now, the plastic sealer is open ended, so you need to close that curve to get a solid geometry when you revolve it. In Object mode, select the curve and choose Curves → Open/Close. The end will close, but it will elongate. Select the end CVs and move them back to line up with the glass lid, as shown in Figure 5.18.

8. Now for the fun part! Go into the persp view panel, select the plastic sealer's profile curve, and choose Surfaces → Revolve just as you did last time, with the same settings originally shown in step 3 and Figure 5.14. Figure 5.19 (left) shows the plastic sealer.

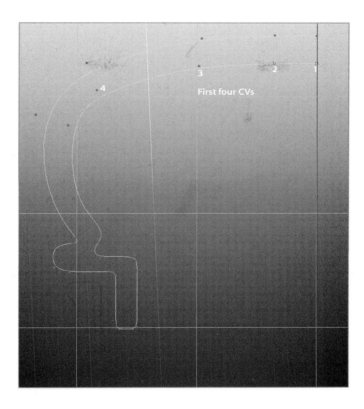

Figure 5.16

Start with the first CVs shown and follow the line counterclockwise to create this profile for the glass lid.

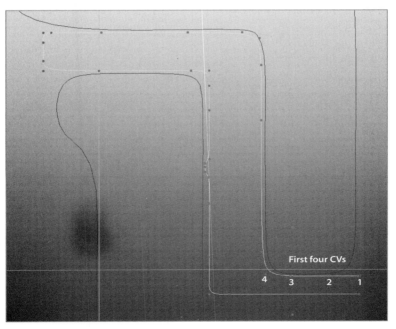

Figure 5.17

Profile curve for the plastic sealer for the lid

Figure 5.18

Close the curve and adjust the CVs to reshape the profile for the plastic stopper.

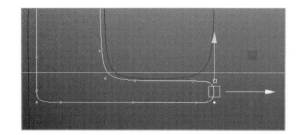

Figure 5.19

The plastic sealer (left) and the completed jar (right)

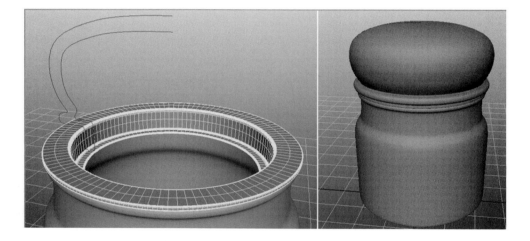

Figure 5.20

Selecting a point on Curve

9. What's a candle jar without a candle? You need the candle in the jar to form right up against the glass, so you'll use part of the same profile curve you used for the jar. Select the original jar body profile curve, and in the Outliner, change its name to **glassProfile**. With it still selected, choose Edit → Duplicate (or press Ctrl+D to copy the curve). Rename that curve from glassProfile to **candleProfile**.

10. Select the glassProfile curve again and press Ctrl+H to hide it from view. Its entry in the Outliner will turn gray. RMB+click the duplicated curve (candleProfile) and select Curve Point from the marking menu. Click the curve and drag the little red point that appears on the curve up the inside wall to right below where it begins to curve in, as shown in Figure 5.20. Release the mouse, and the point turns yellow. You are going to break the curve at this point.

11. Choose Curves → Detach to cut the curve at that point. The top of the curve should be green now and the bottom white. Select just the top part of the curve and press Delete to delete it. Figure 5.21 (left) shows the remaining curve you'll use to create the candle.

12. Draw a straight line curve as shown in the front view panel to match Figure 5.21 (right). It's okay if the first CV isn't exactly on the candle's profile curve; close is good enough.

13. Now select both the straight line curve and the candleProfile curve and choose Curves → Attach ❏. Set Attach Method to Connect, set Multiple Knots to Remove, and uncheck Keep Originals, as shown in Figure 5.22. Click Attach, and the two curves will connect as shown to make the candle's profile curve.

14. With that candle curve selected, choose Surfaces → Revolve with the same settings as in step 3 to create the candle.

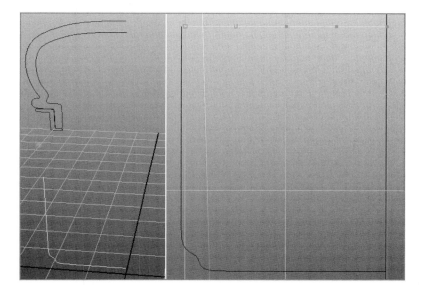

Figure 5.21

The candle's profile curve

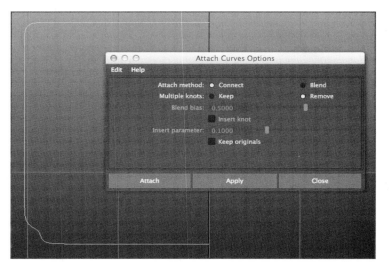

Figure 5.22

Attach the curves to complete the candle's profile.

You can edit the shape of any of these curves you've created, and because of History, the surfaces you created with Revolve will adjust to match the new profiles. To turn the glass profile curve (glassProfile) back on, select it in the Outliner and press Shift+H. You can easily edit the shape of the object to your liking now. Once you are done, simply delete the profile curves if you don't need them anymore.

Once you delete the profile curves, name the objects. Group the lid objects together (name it **jarLid**) and group the glass jar and candle together (name it **jarCandle**), as shown in Figure 5.23. Finally, in the front view panel, select Show → Polygons (in the view panel's menu bar) to turn on the display of polygons in that view panel.

You can find the candle jar in candleModel_v01.mb in the scenes folder of the candleHolder project. This file still retains the original profile curves for you. candleModel_v02.mb has the completed jar without the original profile curves and with the objects properly named and grouped. This file uses the smoother geometry called for in step 3 (with a Chord Height Ratio value of 0.97) and therefore is also a larger file than if you created the jar with a lower Chord Height Ratio value.

Figure 5.23

The final candle's hierarchy

A curve point is a point directly on a curve. You cannot move a curve point like you can a CV to adjust the shape of the curve. Curve points are used mostly for attach and detach functions.

Detailing the Objects

Now let's add a little detail to the candle inside the jar using the Sculpt geometry tool. Continue with your own file, or open candleModel_v02.mb in the scenes folder of the candleHolder project.

1. Select the outer glass jar and press Ctrl+H to hide it. In the Outliner, select the jarLid group and press Ctrl+H to hide the lid and plastic sealer, too.

2. In the Modeling menu set, choose Mesh Tools → Sculpting Tools → Sculpt Tool ☐. It's especially important to open the option box for this tool.

   In the Sculpt Tool options, set Brush Size to 0.25. Your cursor changes to the Artisan brush, a gray circle, as shown in Figure 5.24.

3. If you click the candle with the brush, it will push in the geometry quite a bit. Undo anything you may have done with this tool. If the geometry pulls out instead of pushing in, turn on the Invert check box in the tool options. In the options, set Strength to 0.2, this will limit the amount of influence each brush stroke will have on moving the geometry. This ensures that the sculpting is layered slowly; each successive brush stroke will push the geometry slowly further. Feel free to reduce the Strength value for more finesse in your sculpting. You could also adjust the Buildup value to 3.0 instead of adjusting Strength. This attribute controls the maximum amount you affect the geometry with each stroke. Adjusting Strength, however, allows for more finesse.

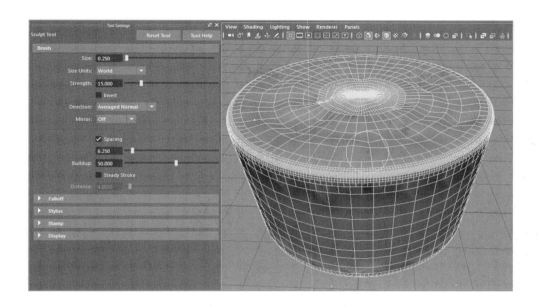

Figure 5.24

The Sculpt tool lets you mold your surface by painting on it. Here, the brush is set to push in the surface of the sphere as you paint.

Sculpt the top of the candle slightly to create an uneven surface. Figure 5.24 shows the resulting uneven candle top. Try not to sculpt the sides of the candle; this may cause the sides to bulge out and then penetrate the glass jar. Try working only on the top of the candle for a melted look.

4. In the options, toggle on the Invert setting to allow the Sculpt tool to pull up the geometry. Slowly raise the middle top of the candle to create a place for the wick, as shown in Figure 5.25.

5. Press W to exit the Sculpt tool and then close Tool Options. With Interactive Creation turned off, create a polygon cylinder with Height Divisions of 8 and Cap Divisions of 4. Scale and place the cylinder to be the wick of the candle, as shown in Figure 5.26 (left).

Figure 5.25

Raise the top center a little for a place to put the candle's wick.

6. Select vertices and move and rotate them around to give the cylinder a more interesting shape. Then use the Sculpt tool to misshape the cylinder as if the wick has already been burned, as shown in Figure 5.26 (right). Press 3 to see a smooth preview of the wick as you work.

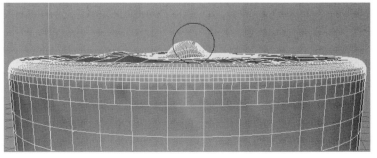

Figure 5.26

Place a cylinder as the candle's wick (left) and use the Sculpt tool and manual vertex manipulation to shape it into an already burned wick as shown (right).

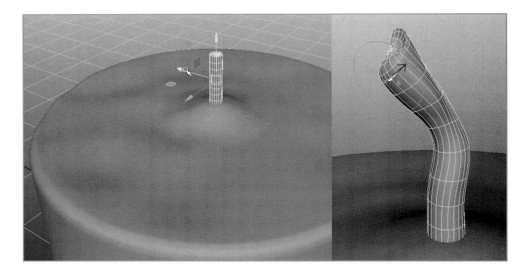

Additionally, the Smooth tool (Mesh Tools → Sculpting Tools → Smooth Tool) blends the pushed-in and pulled-out areas of the surface to yield a smoother result. In general, if you plan to sculpt a detailed surface, be sure to create the mesh with plenty of faces.

7. Once you are happy with the wick, smooth the wick's geometry by choosing Mesh → Smooth ☐. Set Division Levels to **1** and click Smooth.

8. Select the wick and erase the history on it by choosing Edit → Delete By Type → History. Name the object **wick** and place it into the jarCandle group, as shown in Figure 5.27.

9. In the Outliner, select the jarLid group and press Shift+H to unhide it. Also select the glassJar object (under the jarCandle group) to unhide that as well. Then group both jarLid and jarCandle groups together into a new group called **candleGroup**.

You can check your work against the file `candleModel_v02.mb` in the `scenes` folder of the candleHolder project. With the glass candle jar holder complete, you'll be able to use it later to create a glass and candle wax shader in Chapter 7 and then render the object with reflections and refractions in Chapter 11. Nice job! Go grab a cookie.

Figure 5.27

Group the wick into the hierarchy.

Modeling with Simple Deformers

In many ways, deformers are the Swiss Army knives of Maya animation, except that you can't open a bottle with them. *Deformers* are handy for creating and editing modeled shapes in Maya. These tools allow you to change the shape of an object easily. Rather than using CVs or vertices to distort or bend an object manually, you can use a deformer to affect the entire object. Popular deformers, such as Bend and Flare, can be powerful tools for adjusting your models quickly and evenly, as you're about to see.

Nonlinear deformers, such as Bend and Flare, create simple shape adjustments for the attached geometry, such as bending the object. You can also use deformers in animation to create effects or deformations in your objects. You'll explore this later in the book.

Using the Soft Modification Deformer

First, let's try using the Soft Modification tool. Choose Modify → Transformation Tools → Soft Modification Tool, and its icon ( ) appears below the Tool Box. This tool allows you to select an area on a surface or model and make any adjustments in an interesting way. These adjustments taper off away from the initial place of selection, giving you an easy way to soft-modify an area of a model, much like lifting up a tablecloth from the middle.

To try the Soft Modification tool, follow these steps:

1. In a new scene create a Polygon plane by choosing Create → Polygon Primitives → Plane □. Set both the Width Divisions and Height Divisions sliders to 10 and click Create.

2. Click and drag a plane on the grid if Interactive Creation is turned on; otherwise, a plane appears at the origin on your grid. Select the Scale tool and scale the plane up to about the size of the grid.

3. Select Modify → Transformation Tools → Soft Modification Tool and click the plane somewhere just off the middle. Doing so creates an *S* and a special manipulator to allow you to move, rotate, or scale this soft selection (see Figure 5.28). You also see a yellow-to-red-to-black gradient around the S manipulator. This shows you the area and degree of influence, where yellow moves the most and black the least.

4. Grab the cone handle and drag it up to move the soft selection up. Notice that the plane lifts up in that area only, gradually falling off.

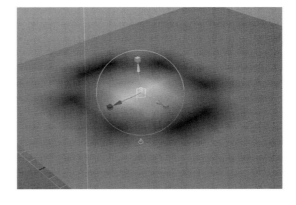

Figure 5.28

Creating and manipulating a soft modification

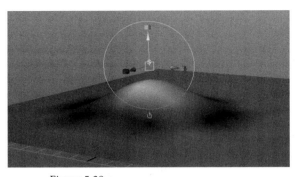

Figure 5.29

Lifting an area of the Polygon plane

5. Grabbing the cube handle scales the soft selection, and dragging the circle rotates it. After you've finished making your soft adjustments, make sure to press W for the Move tool and to exit the Soft Modification tool. Otherwise, you will create new soft modification handles every time you click the mesh.

You can go back to any soft selection by selecting the *S* on the surface for later editing. You can place as many soft selections as you need on a surface. Figure 5.29 shows the soft modification adjusting the plane.

Modeling Using the Bend Deformer

Let's apply a deformer. In a new Maya scene, you'll create a polygonal cylinder and bend it to get a quick idea of how deformers work. Follow these steps:

1. Choose Create → Polygon Primitives and turn on Interactive Creation. Then, choose Create → Polygon Primitives → Cylinder. Click and drag to create the base. Make it a few units in diameter; the exact sizing isn't important here. Click and drag to make the height of the cylinder 7 or 8 units. Make sure your create options are set to the defaults so that they're consistent with these directions.

> To make sure the settings are at their defaults, open the command's option box and click the Reset Settings or Reset Tool button.

2. With the cylinder selected, make sure you're still in the Modeling menu set and choose Deform → Nonlinear → Bend, under the Create section. Your cylinder turns magenta if you are in wireframe display mode, and a thin line appears at the center of the cylinder, running lengthwise. Figure 5.30 shows the deformer and its Channel Box attributes. Depending on your settings, your deformer may be created in a different axis than the one pictured. You can reset the deformer's options as needed. Click bend1 in the Channel Box to expand the deformer's attributes as shown in the figure.

3. Click Curvature and enter a value of **60**. Notice that the cylinder takes on an odd shape, as shown in Figure 5.31. The Bend deformer itself is bending nicely, but the geometry isn't. Also, the geometry is offset and weird-looking because there aren't enough divisions in the geometry to allow for a proper bend.

4. Select the cylinder, and click polyCylinder1 in the Channel Box to expand the shape node's attributes. Enter a value of **12** for the Subdivisions Height attribute (see Figure 5.32), and your cylinder will bend with the deformer properly, as shown in Figure 5.33.

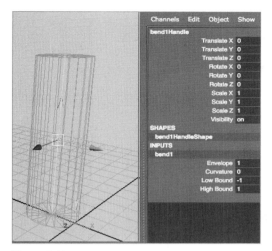

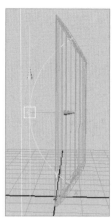

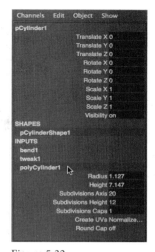

Figure 5.30
Creating the Bend deformer

Figure 5.31
Notice the problem with this cylinder?

Figure 5.32
Increase Subdivisions Height to 12.

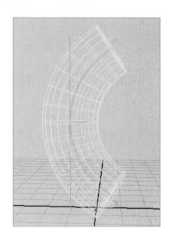

Figure 5.33
The cylinder bends properly now that it has the right number of divisions.

5. Try adjusting the Bend deformer's Low Bound and High Bound attributes. This allows you to bend one part of the cylinder without affecting the other. For example, set the Bend deformer's High Bound option to **0.25** instead of 1. This causes the top half of the cylinder to bend only one-quarter of the way up and continue straight from there.

Experiment with moving the Bend deformer and seeing how doing so affects the geometry of the cylinder. The deformer's position plays an important role in how it shapes an object's geometry.

Adjusting an Existing Axe Model

In this exercise, you'll take a NURBS model of an axe and fine-tune the back end of the axe head. In the existing model, the back end of the axe head is blunt, as you can see in Figure 5.34. You'll need to sharpen the blunt end with a nonlinear deformer. Open the AxeHead_v01.ma file in the scenes folder of the Axe project from the companion web page, and follow these steps:

1. Select the top group of the axe head's back end. To do so, open the Outliner and select axeHead_Back (see Figure 5.35).

Figure 5.34

The axe head is blunt.

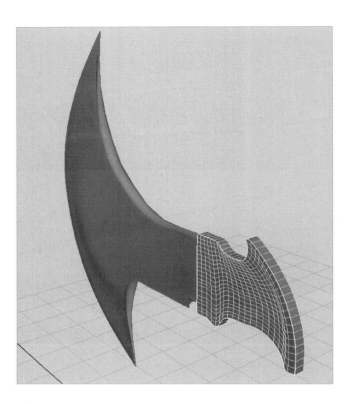

Figure 5.35

Select the back of the axe head.

2. Press F4 to switch to the Modeling menu set, if you're not already.

3. Create a Flare deformer by choosing Deform → Nonlinear → Flare, under the Create section. The Flare deformer appears as a cylindrical object (see Figure 5.36).

4. Rotate the deformer 90 degrees in the Z-axis, as shown in Figure 5.37.

5. Open the Attribute Editor (Ctrl+A), click the flare1 tab to access the Flare controls, and enter the following values:

Attribute	Value
Start Flare Z	0.020
High Bound	0.50

These values taper in the end of that part of the axe head, as shown in Figure 5.38. This is a much easier way of sharpening the blunt end than adjusting the individual CVs of the NURBS surfaces.

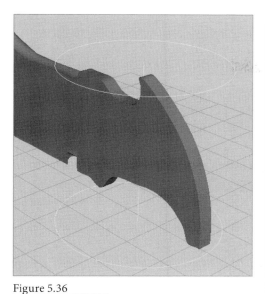

Figure 5.36

The Flare deformer appears as a cylinder.

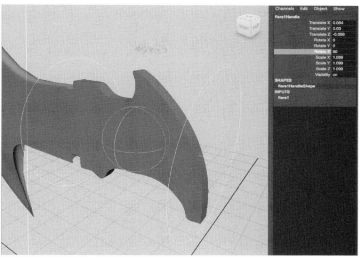

Figure 5.37

Rotate the deformer 90 degrees in the Z-axis.

Figure 5.38

Sharpen the axe's back edge.

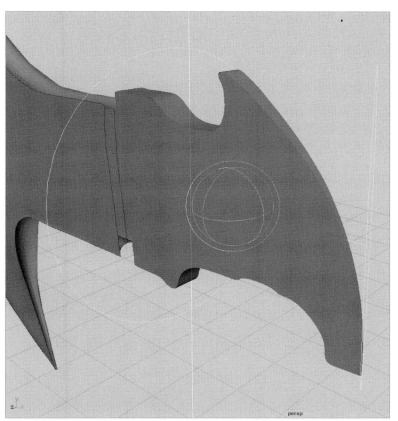

Deformers use History to distort the geometry to which they're attached. You can animate any of the attributes that control the deformer shapes, but in this case you're using the deformer as a means to adjust a model. When you get the desired shape, you can discard the deformer. However, simply selecting and deleting the deformer will reset the geometry to its original blunt shape. You need to pick the axeHead_Back geometry group (not the deformer) and delete its History by choosing Edit → Delete By Type → History.

The Lattice Deformer

When a model requires more intricate editing with a deformer, you'll need to use a lattice. A *lattice* is a scaffold that fits around your geometry. The lattice object controls the shape of the geometry. When a lattice point is moved, the lattice smoothly deforms the underlying geometry. The more lattice points, the greater control you have. The more divisions the geometry has, the more smoothly the geometry will deform.

Lattices are especially useful when you need to edit a relatively complex poly mesh or NURBS surface that is too dense to edit efficiently directly with CVs or vertices. With a lattice, you don't have to move the individual surface points.

Lattices can work on any surface type, and a single lattice can affect multiple surfaces simultaneously. You can also move an object through a lattice (or vice versa) to animate a deformation effect, such as a golf ball sliding through a garden hose.

Creating an Alien Hand

Make sure you're in the Modeling menu set. To adjust an existing model or surface, select the models or applicable groups to deform, and choose Deform → Lattice, under the Create section. Figure 5.39 shows a polygonal hand model with a default lattice applied. The top node of the hand has been selected and the lattice applied.

Figure 5.39

A lattice is applied to the polygonal hand model.

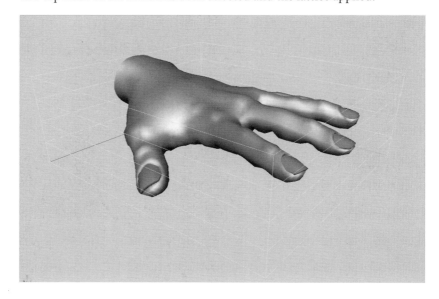

Your objective is to create an alien hand by thinning and elongating the hand and each of the fingers—we all know aliens have long, gawky fingers! Because it would take a lot of time and effort to achieve this by moving the vertices of the poly mesh itself, using lattices here is ideal.

To elongate and thin the entire hand, load the scene file detailed_poly_hand.ma from the Poly_Hand project from the companion web page, and follow these steps:

1. Select the top node of the hand (poly_hand) in the Outliner and choose Deform → Lattice, under the Create section. Doing so creates a default lattice that affects the entire hand, fingernails and all. Although you can change the lattice settings in the option box upon creation, you'll edit the lattice after it's applied to the hand.

2. The lattice is selected after it's created. Open the Attribute Editor and click the ffd-1LatticeShape tab. The three attributes of interest here are S Divisions, T Divisions, and U Divisions. These sliders control how many divisions the lattice uses to deform its geometry. Set S Divisions to **3**, T Divisions to **2**, and U Divisions to **3** for the result shown in Figure 5.40.

A 3×2×3 lattice refers to the number of division lines in the lattice as opposed to the number of sections; otherwise, this would be a 2×1×2 lattice!

Figure 5.40

Changing the number of divisions in the lattice

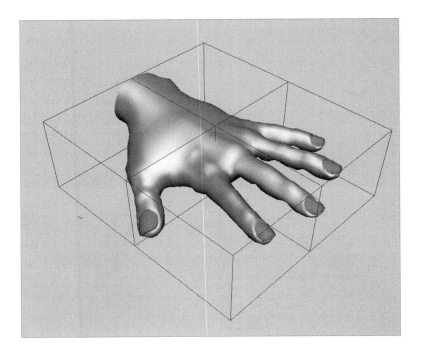

3. With the lattice selected, press F8 to switch to Component mode and display the lattice's points. You'll use these points to change the overall shape of the hand. Select the lattice points on the thumb side of the hand and move them to squeeze in that half of the hand. Notice how only that zone of the model is affected by that part of the lattice.

4. Toggle back to Object mode (press F8 again) and scale the entire lattice to be thinner in the Z-axis and longer in the X-axis. The entire hand is deformed in accordance with how the lattice is scaled (see Figure 5.41).

Figure 5.41

Lengthen the hand using the deformer.

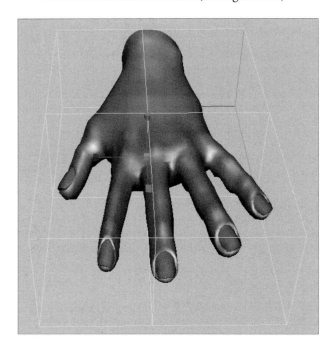

Now that you've altered the hand, you have no need for this lattice. If you delete the lattice, the hand will snap back to its original shape. You need to delete the construction history on the hand to get rid of the lattice, as you did with the axe head exercise earlier in this chapter.

5. Select the top node of the hand and choose Edit → Delete By Type → History.

Creating Alien Fingers

The next step is to elongate the individual fingers and widen the knuckles. Let's begin with the index finger. Follow these steps:

1. Select the top node of the hand and create a new lattice as before. It forms around the entire hand.

Although you can divide the lattice so that its divisions line up with the fingers, it's much easier and more interactive to scale and position the entire lattice so it fits around the index finger only.

Simply moving and scaling the selected lattice will deform the hand geometry. You don't want to do this. Instead, you need to select the lattice and its base node. This lets you change the lattice without affecting the hand.

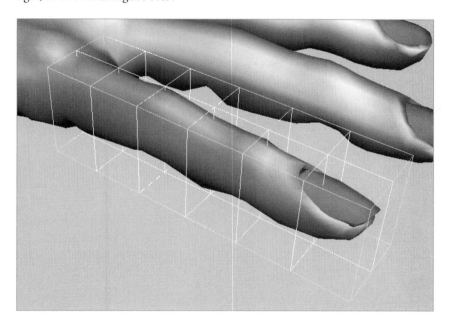

Figure 5.42

Select the lattice and base nodes.

2. In the Outliner, select both the ffd1Lattice and ffd1Base nodes (see Figure 5.42).

3. Scale, rotate, and transform the lattice to fit around the index finger, as shown in Figure 5.43.

Figure 5.43

Position the lattice and its base to fit around the index finger.

4. Deselect the base, and set the lattice S Divisions to **7**, T Divisions to **2**, and U Divisions to **3**.

5. Adjust the lattice to lengthen the finger by pulling the lattice points (see Figure 5.44). Pick the lattice points around each of the knuckles individually and scale them sideways to widen them.

6. To delete the lattice and keep the changes to the finger, select the top node of the hand and delete its History.

Figure 5.44

Flare out the knuckles.

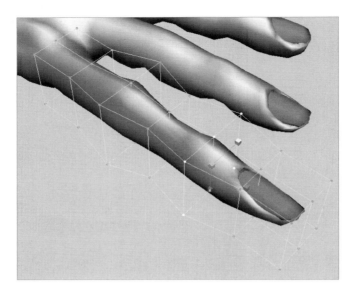

7. Repeat this entire procedure for the rest of the fingers to finish your alien hand. (Try to creep out your younger sister with it.)

8. To get rid of all the lattices and keep the alien shape, select the hand meshes and choose Edit → Delete By Type → History.

The alien hand in Figure 5.45 was created by adjusting the polygonal hand from this exercise using only lattices.

Figure 5.45

The human hand model is transformed into an alien hand by using lattices to deform the geometry.

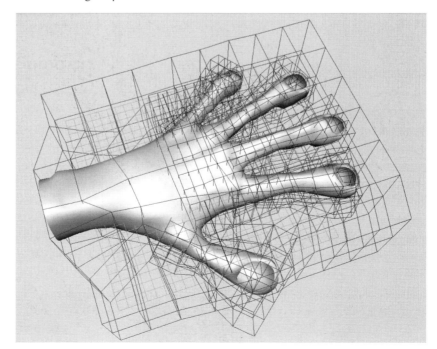

As you can see, lattices give you powerful editing capabilities without the complication of dealing with surface points directly. Lattices can help you reshape an entire complex model quickly or adjust minor details on parts of a larger whole.

In Chapter 8, "Introduction to Animation," you'll animate an object using another type of deformer. You'll also learn how to deform an object along a path.

Animating Through a Lattice

Lattices don't only work on polygons; they can be used on any geometry in Maya and at any stage in your workflow to create or adjust models. You can also use lattices to create animated effects. For example, you can create the effect of a balloon squeezing through a pipe by animating the balloon geometry through a lattice.

In the following exercise, you'll create a NURBS sphere with 8 sections and 16 spans and an open-ended NURBS cylinder that has no end caps:

1. Choose Create → NURBS Primitives → Sphere ❑, set Number Of Sections to **8** and Number Of Spans to **16**, and create the sphere.

2. Choose Create → NURBS Primitives → Cylinder ❑ and check None for the Caps option. Scale and arrange the sphere balloon and cylinder pipe as shown in Figure 5.46.

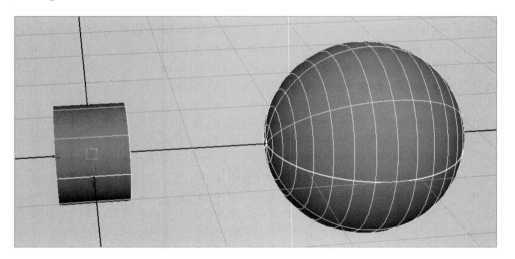

Figure 5.46

Arrange the balloon and pipe.

3. Select the balloon and create a lattice for it (see Figure 5.47). (This time, go into the Animation menu set and choose Anim Deform → Lattice.) Set the S, T, and U Divisions to **4**, **19**, and **4**, respectively. You set this number of lattice divisions to create a smoother deformation when the sphere goes through the pipe.

4. Select the lattice and its base in the Outliner (ffd1Lattice and ffd1Base nodes) and move the middle of the lattice so it fits over the length of the pipe (see Figure 5.48).

Figure 5.47

Create a lattice for the sphere.

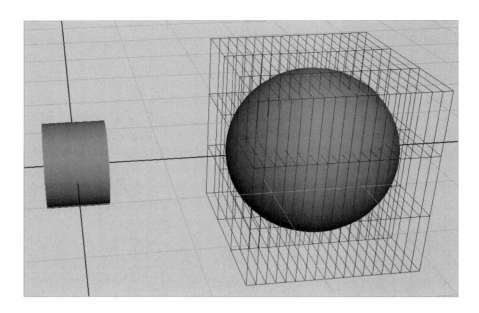

Figure 5.48

Relocate the lattice to the cylinder.

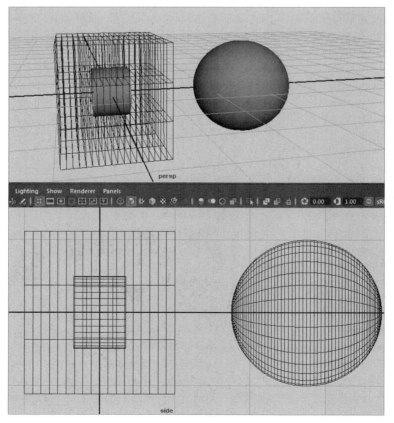

5. Deselect the lattice base and choose Component mode for the lattice. Select the appropriate points and shape the lattice so the middle of the lattice fits into the cylinder (see Figure 5.49).

6. Select the sphere and move it back and forth through the pipe and lattice. Notice how it squeezes to fit through. If you look closely, you'll see that the sphere starts to squeeze a little before it enters the pipe. You'll also see parts of the sphere sticking out of the very ends of the pipe. This effect, in which geometry passes through itself or another surface, is called *interpenetration*. You can avoid this by using a more highly segmented sphere and lattice. If you try this exercise with a lower-segmented sphere and/or lattice, you'll notice the interpenetrations even more. Figure 5.50 shows the balloon squeezing through the pipe.

Figure 5.49

Squeeze in the lattice points to fit the cylinder.

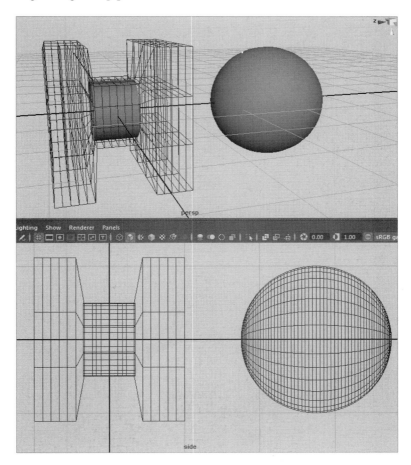

Figure 5.50

**Squeezing the bal-
loon through the
pipe using a lattice
deformer**

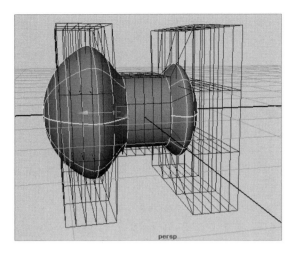

In a similar fashion, you can create a lattice along a curve path and have an object travel through it. You'll try this in Chapter 8.

Summary

In this chapter, you tackled NURBS modeling by going through the usual surfacing tools, from lofting to revolving. Then you explored the implications of surface History and how surfaces adjust to changes when History is enabled. You then put those lessons to work on creating a pair of glass candle holders.

This chapter also covered various modeling techniques to help you break away from typical ways of thinking. You learned how to use a lattice to adjust a polygon hand model into an alien hand, as well as how to animate a balloon pushing through a pipe. Different workflows give you the flexibility to choose your own modeling style. To make good choices, however, you'll need to practice.

Keep at it; model everything you can get your hands and eyes on. As you're doing that, stay on top of how you organize your nodes and keep everything named and organized.

For further practice, use this chapter as a reference to create some of the following models using NURBS surfaces and lattices to aid in shaping polygons:

Bathroom Sink   Snap a few digital stills of your bathroom sink or find some pictures on the Internet. A sink will give you a great chance to explore NURBS surfacing, making pristine curves and smooth surfaces. It may be a bit involved, but it's not overwhelming.

Cartoon Head   Use Maya Artisan and the Sculpt Geometry tool to turn an ordinary sphere into a cartoonish head. It's fun to use Sculpt Geometry to model. Try to make the head using only Artisan.

Computer Mouse   A PC or Mac mouse makes a great simple NURBS model.

CHAPTER 6

Practical Experience!

It's time to put what you've learned so far into action. In this chapter, you'll build a child's airplane toy. The plane project uses poly and NURBS modeling techniques to give you some practical experience with a larger project in the Autodesk® Maya® software.

Learning Outcomes: In this chapter, you will be able to

- Use bevels and extrusions efficiently

- Manipulate curves to create poly meshes with Revolves and Loft Surfaces

- Create a shape with a path extrusion

- Use reference images to shape your models

- See how to set up views with grid lines to align reference images for modeling

- See how images are lined up to make reference images for modeling

- Work in the Hypershade to assign image maps to objects in the scene

- Use a Boolean operation to cut holes in a mesh

Evaluating the Toy Plane

Download the entire Plane project folder structure from the book's companion web page (www.sybex.com/go/introducingmaya2016) to your computer's hard drive and set your project to that location.

Also on the book's website (as well as the author's site www.koosh3d.com) are video tutorials taking you through parts of this exercise.

Figure 6.1 shows a bathtub toy airplane that you'll be modeling first in this chapter. There's certainly enough detail in this object to make it a good exercise, but it won't be difficult to complete. You can always return to this exercise to add more of your own detail or even redesign it for more challenge, which is something I highly recommend.

Figure 6.1

The toy plane is cute!

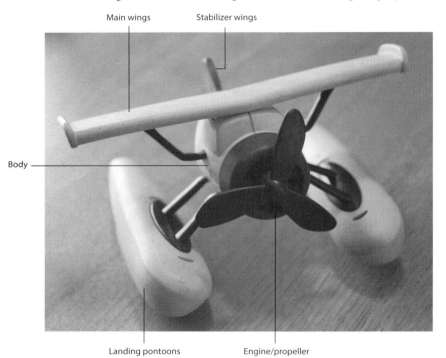

Main wings Stabilizer wings

Body

Landing pontoons Engine/propeller

Study the photos (Figure 6.1, Figure 6.2, and Figure 6.3) carefully to get an understanding of the components that make up this object. You will model the parts individually instead of attacking the entire shape as a single object. This way of thinking helps complex objects become easier to understand and model. The plane consists of the body, landing pontoons, engine/propeller, stabilizer wings, and main wings, as shown in Figure 6.1. In Chapter 3's decorative box exercise, you used reference planes to give you an accurate guide to build the box, and you'll do the same with the individual parts of the plane.

Figure 6.2

**The side photo of
the plane**

Figure 6.3

**The top photo of
the plane**

Building the Landing Pontoons

Let's start with the landing pontoons. You need to model only one and then make a duplicate and mirror it for the other side.

Reference Images

First you need to assemble the reference planes to make the model easier to build. Figure 6.4 shows the top, side, and front views of a pontoon scaled and lined up in Adobe Photoshop. I copied and pasted the individual photos into a larger image and then used grid lines to line up the proportions of the pontoon. Keep in mind that when you take a photo, in most cases there will be *perspective shift*, or *parallax*, in the image. Because of that shift, the different views of the same object will never exactly line up. Once each individual photo is scaled and lined up like in Figure 6.4, you can output each image as its own file to bring into Maya for top, side, and front references.

Figure 6.4

The reference photos of the pontoon are lined up.

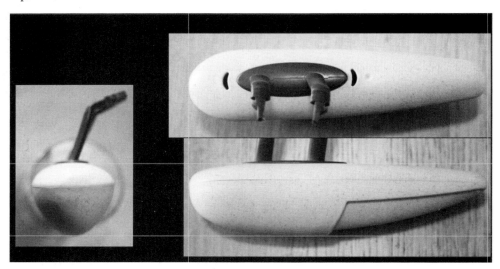

Now, you'll import the images and create the model reference planes on which to work.

Creating Reference Planes for the Images

The reference images of the toy airplane have already been created for you. You can find them in the Sourceimages folder of the Plane project on the companion website. They're shown in Table 6.1.

Table 6.1

Reference views and sizes

FILENAME	VIEW	IMAGE SIZE	ASPECT RATIO
pontoonTopReference.jpg	Top	1600×650	1:0.406
pontoonSideReference.jpg	Side	1600×650	1:0.406
pontoonFrontReference.jpg	Front	1600×650	1:0.406

Why is the image resolution important? Well, it's not so much the resolution of the photos but rather the aspect ratio of each image. To properly map these images onto the planes you'll use in Maya, each plane has to be the same aspect ratio as its image. For example, an image that is 100×50 pixels has an aspect ratio of 2:1 and is, therefore, a wide horizontal rectangle. For it to map properly, the plane on which it's mapped in Maya must have a scale ratio of 2:1 so that it's also a wide horizontal rectangle. Otherwise, the image may distort, causing inaccuracies in your model. Since each of the pontoon references was made the same size, it's a little easier.

You'll need to create three planes for each of the three views. First make sure Interactive Creation is turned off; then follow these steps:

Figure 6.5

Creating a plane for the top view

1. In a new scene, go to the front view panel and create a polygonal plane by choosing Create → Polygon Primitives → Plane ❑. This plane is for the front image, so in the

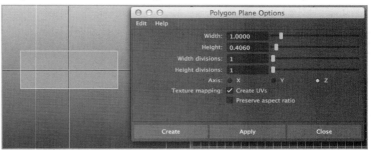

   option box, set Axis to **Z**, Width to **1**, and Height to **0.406**. Set Width Divisions and Height Divisions both to **1**. Make sure the check box for Preserve Aspect Ratio is deselected and Axis is set to **Z** to place the plane properly in the front view, as shown in Figure 6.5; click Apply. Name this plane **frontRefPlane**.

2. Switch to the side view panel. Create a second plane, again with a Width value of **1** and a Height value of **0.406**. Set Axis to **X**, and make sure the Preserve Aspect Ratio check box remains unchecked. Name this plane **sideRefPlane**.

Figure 6.6

The three view planes are ready.

3. Switch to the top view panel. Create a third plane with Width remaining at **1**, Height at **0.406**, but Axis now set to **Y**. Make sure the Preserve Aspect Ratio box is still unchecked. Your perspective panel should look like Figure 6.6. Name this plane **topRefPlane**.

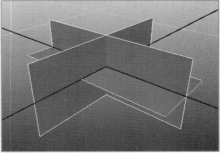

Mapping the Reference Planes

Now that all three image planes have been created with the proper aspect ratio, you're ready to map the photos to them to create the reference for the model.

1. Open the Hypershade (Windows → Rendering Editors → Hypershade) or click the Hypershade icon in the Status Line ( ). Open a file browser in your operating system (OS) and navigate to the Sourceimages folder of the Plane project on your hard drive.

2. Click the pontoonSideReference.jpg file in your file browser and drag it into the Work Area of the Hypershade window to import the file image. Drag the other two images (pontoonFrontReference.jpg and pontoonTopReference.jpg) into the Hypershade one at a time, as shown in Figure 6.7.

If you don't see the image of the pontoon in the icons in the Hypershade like in Figure 6.7, simply right-click the file node icon and select Refresh Swatch from the marking menu.

3. You must create shaders for each of the planes. In the left panel of the Hypershade window, click the Lambert icon three times to create three new Lambert shaders (Lambert2, Lambert3, and Lambert4), which should now display in the top area. For more information about shaders and texturing, see Chapter 7, "Autodesk® Maya® Shading and Texturing." Remember, you can use Alt+MMB to move around the Work Area, and you can use Alt+RMB+click to zoom in and out.

Figure 6.7

Importing the photos into the Hypershade window

4. Select all the new lamberts and MMB drag them from the top area to the Work Area of the Hypershade. On the pontoonFrontReference.jpg node in the Work Area, click the green circle next to Out Color and drag the rubber band line that appears to the red circle next to Color on Lambert2's node. Maya maps the image to the color of the Lambert shader, as shown on the top of in Figure 6.8.

   As an alternate way to attach the image to the shader, double-click the Lambert and then MMB+drag the image to the Lambert shader's Color attribute in the Property Editor in the Hypershade.

5. Click and drag the Out Color rubber band connectors from the other two images onto the red circles of the other two Lambert shaders to connect the images to the shaders as you did in step 4. Name the shaders **lambertSide**, **lambertFront**, and **lambertTop**, respectively, by double-clicking them to open the Attribute Editor and changing their names (see the bottom of Figure 6.8).

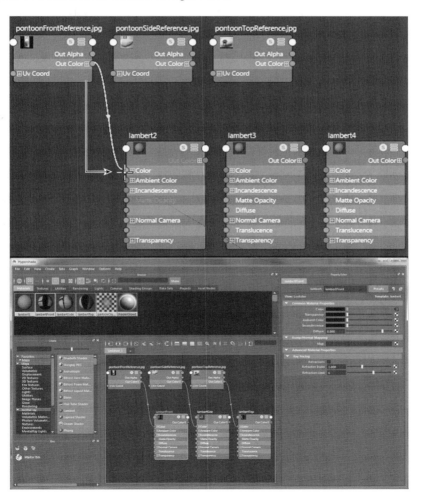

Figure 6.8

Attach the images to the shaders and name them.

6. Assign the shaders to the reference planes. To do so, MMB+drag the Lambert shader that is connected to the side view image (lambertSide) to the side view plane in the perspective panel. Switch the perspective view into Texture display mode by pressing 6 while in that panel.

7. Drag the top view's Lambert shader to the top reference plane and drag the front Lambert shader to the front reference plane to assign the other two views. You should now have the three reference planes laid out as shown in Figure 6.9, although the top view plane needs to be re-oriented.

Figure 6.9

All three reference planes are mapped, though the top view is oriented wrong.

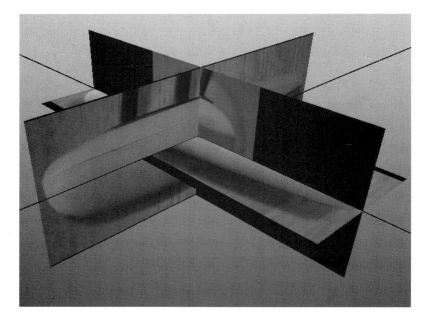

8. All isn't rosy yet! Select the top view plane in the persp view and rotate it 90 degrees in the Y-axis. Take a look around the reference planes, and you'll see that the front reference is slightly larger and a bit to the right of the top view reference plane. Select the front reference plane (frontRefPlane) and scale it to **0.925** in X, Y, and Z; set Translate X to **-0.102** to center it properly (see Figure 6.10).

9. Remember that the scale of these planes is small right now. You don't need to use real-world units for this project. However, you should scale the reference planes so that you have a larger scale with which to work. Select all three reference planes and group them together by pressing Ctrl+G; name the group node **pontoonRefPlanesGroup**.

10. Select the top group node and uniformly scale it to 12 units, as shown in Figure 6.11.

11. To give yourself more room to work, select the front view plane and move it back, as shown in Figure 6.12.

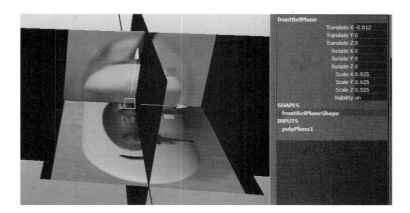

Figure 6.10

Scale and move
the front reference
pontoon to match
the side reference
pontoon. Done!

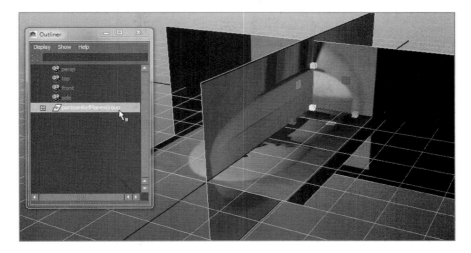

Figure 6.11

Group and then
scale the reference
planes up.

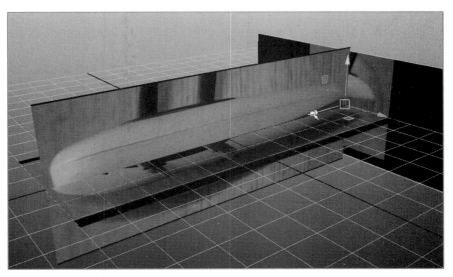

Figure 6.12

Move the front ref-
erence plane back.

12. Create a display layer for the planes to make it easy to manage them later. To do so, select pontoonRefPlanesGroup and, in the Layer Editor below the Channel Box, click the Create A New Layer And Assign Selected Objects icon (▨).

Double-click the new layer and name it **pontoonRefLayer** in the window that pops up (see Figure 6.13). Your Layer Editor should resemble the one shown in Figure 6.14. For more on the Layer Editor, see Chapter 3.

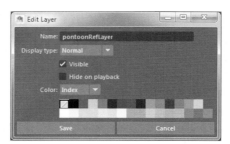

Figure 6.13

Name the new layer.

Figure 6.14

The new layer in Layer Editor

To toggle the display of the reference planes to get them out of the way, you can simply toggle the box to the extreme left of the layer name, currently checked with a *V* for "visible" in Figure 6.14. Keep it visible for now.

Save your work. You can download the scene file pontoonModel_v01.ma from the Scenes folder of the Plane project from the companion website to check your work or skip to this point.

Just be sure to set your project to the Plane project on your hard drive after downloading the entire project from the website. Otherwise, the images for the reference planes may not show up.

> To remain in step with this chapter, make sure Interactive Creation is turned off when you create any new primitives.

Blocking Out the Pontoon

The pontoon will start with a poly cube in the following steps:

Figure 6.15

Set the reference planes layer to Reference to make it unselectable in the view panels.

1. In the top view, press 6 to see Textured mode, if you haven't already. In the Layer Editor, click the empty area to the right of the Visibility toggle box for the pontoonRefLayer layer twice so you see an *R* appear, as shown in Figure 6.15. This action sets that layer as a reference layer and makes the objects in the layer unselectable in the view panels. If you try clicking any of the three reference planes, nothing will happen, making it easier to model on top of. Clicking it once more will return the layer to normal.

2. Create a poly cube. You need to see the cube as a wireframe but still see the reference image as a textured object. In the top view panel's menu (not the main Maya menu bar), select Shading → X-Ray (Figure 6.16) to allow you to see through the box but not lose your reference image display. Place and scale the cube over the pontoon; then RMB+click the mesh and select Vertex from the marking menu

Figure 6.16

Set your view panel shading display to X-Ray.

(to enter vertex mode) to move the corner vertices to roughly match the shape of the pontoon, as shown in Figure 6.17.

3. Switch to the side view panel and enable X-Ray mode (Shading → X-Ray). Move the corner vertices to get a rough shape of the pontoon from the side, as shown in Figure 6.18.

4. Switch to Object mode (RMB+click the cube and select Object Mode from the marking menu, as shown in Figure 6.19). This is the fastest way to switch selection modes.

5. Make sure you are in the Modeling menu set and select the pontoon. Choose Mesh Tools → Insert Edge Loop. Insert nine edge loops along the pontoon, as shown in Figure 6.20 (top).

6. Using the marking menu, RMB+click the mesh to switch back to vertex selection. While in the side view panel, move the vertices of the new edge loops to better match the shape of the pontoon's side, as shown in Figure 6.20 (bottom). Don't worry about the dark gray arms that attach the pontoon to the body of the plane; shape your cube only to the yellow pontoon for now.

Figure 6.17

Shape a cube over the body of the pontoon in the top view panel.

Figure 6.18

Shape the pontoon in the side view.

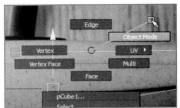

Figure 6.19

Select Object Mode in the marking menu.

Figure 6.20

Insert nine edge loops along the pontoon's side (top) and then move vertices to better match the shape in the side view panel (bottom).

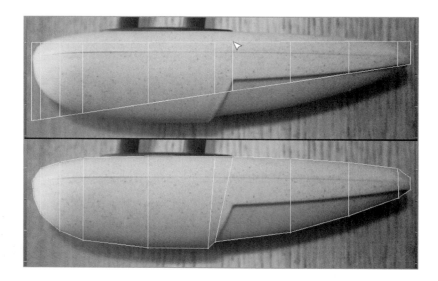

7. Switch to the top view panel and move the vertices to better match the shape from the top, as shown in Figure 6.21.

8. In the side view panel, insert three edge loops (Mesh Tools → Insert Edge Loop), as shown in Figure 6.22. Save your work as the next version to avoid writing over your older work.

Shaping the Pontoon

The scene file pontoonModel_v02.ma in the Scenes folder of the Plane project will bring you to this point. Now, let's shape the pontoon some more.

1. In the persp view, rotate your view (a.k.a. tumble) to see the bottom of the pontoon. Make sure X-Ray is off so you can see the pontoon as a solid object. In the Layer Editor, toggle the shading mode of the pontoonRefLayer by clicking the R toggle until it displays a *T*. The planes turn to a gray wireframe.

Figure 6.21

Move vertices in the top view panel to better match the pontoon's shape.

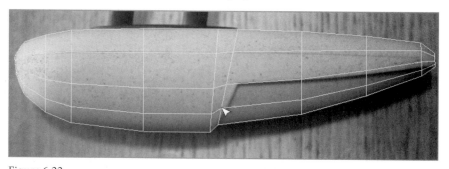

Figure 6.22

Insert three edge loops as shown in the side view panel.

2. Switch to edge selection mode. One by one from front to back, select the bottom row of edges on the pontoon's underside, and scale them in the X-axis *only* to taper the belly of the shape, as shown in Figure 6.23. You can shape it to your liking, without worrying about much accuracy to the photo references. You can refer to Figures 6.2 and 6.3 for a better look at the two pontoons' shapes.

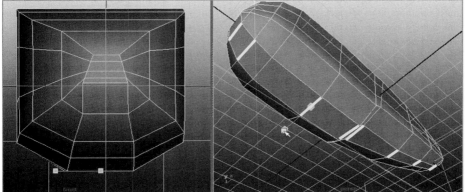

Taper these edges

Figure 6.23

Shape the bottom of the pontoon to your fancy by scaling down the bottom row of edges one at a time in the X-axis.

3. In the persp view panel, select the vertices one at a time on the section up from the very bottom that you just adjusted in the previous step and shape them slightly to continue the taper of the belly to your liking. Figure 6.24 shows the pontoon so far.

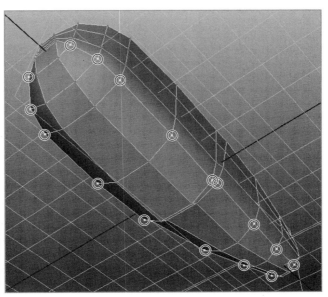

Adjust these vertices

Figure 6.24

Keep shaping the pontoon, now by moving the vertices that are one segment higher than the bottom edges you just adjusted.

4. Now tumble your view in the persp view panel to see the top of the pontoon. Select the top row of edges and scale them in a little bit to taper the top slightly, as shown in Figure 6.25.

Figure 6.25

Taper the top edges to your liking.

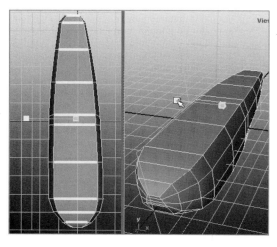

Taper these edges

5. The shape of the pontoon can differ from the reference planes a bit; you're trying to get the overall proportion/shape from the photos. You can continue to shape the pontoon to your liking. Once you are happy with it, select the pontoon and press 3 in the persp view panel to see a smooth preview. It looks much more like the actual pontoon when you see it in Smooth Preview (Figure 6.26). Save your work as a new version number!

Figure 6.26

The base pontoon

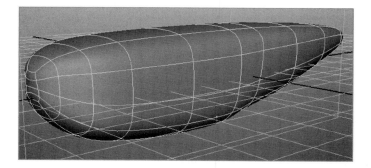

Attaching the Arms

The scene file pontoonModel_v03.ma in the Scenes folder of the Plane project will bring you to this point. Now let's tackle the gray arms that will eventually attach the pontoon to the plane's body. You'll also start using Modeling Toolkit in the following steps:

1. In the top view panel, create a cube. Click the Channel Box/Layer Editor tab on the right of the UI to show the Channel Box if it isn't already displayed (Figure 6.27).

With the new cube selected, click the polyCube2 entry (your cube may have a slightly different number, like polyCube3 or so), which will show you attributes for the cube's subdivisions. Set Subdivisions Width to **2**, Subdivisions Height to **2**, and Subdivisions Depth to **6**, as shown in Figure 6.27.

2. Turn the display toggle of the pontoonRefLayer back to R. Move, rotate and scale the cube to fit the gray base of the attaching arms in the top view panel. Move its vertices to better match the shape, as shown in Figure 6.28. Note that this base shape is purposely not centered on the pontoon. Name the cube pontoonArmBase. Also, select the body of the pontoon and name it **pontoon**.

3. Turn off X-Ray mode if it's on in the persp view panel (Shading → X-Ray). Move the pontoonArmBase cube and scale it down in the Y-axis to have just the top sticking through the pontoon. Adjust the top vertices to curve the top to fit the top of the pontoon, as shown in Figure 6.29.

4. Click the Show/Hide Modeling Toolkit icon in the upper right of the Maya UI, as shown in Figure 6.30, to display Modeling Toolkit where the Channel Box usually is. The right side of the UI now displays the suite of tools in the toolkit, and the Modeling Toolkit tab appears alongside the Channel Box/Layer Editor and Attribute Editor tabs.

Figure 6.27

Create a new cube with these subdivision values.

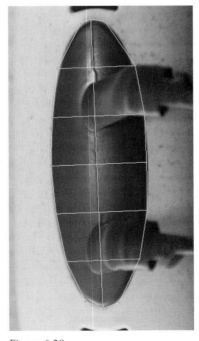

Figure 6.28

Shape the cube to fit the base of the attaching arms.

Figure 6.29

Scale and position the cube. Adjust the top vertices to match the pontoon's curvature.

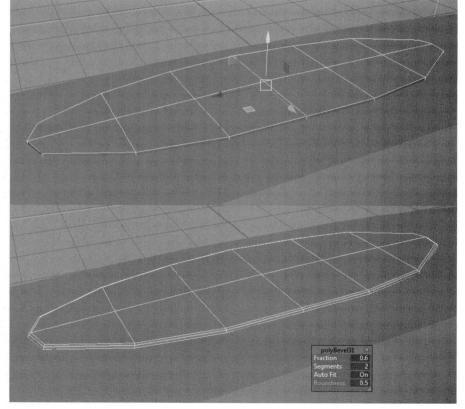

Figure 6.30

Show Modeling Toolkit, if it's not already shown.

Figure 6.31

Select the top outside edges (top) and bevel them.

5. Click the Edge Selection icon at the top of the toolkit (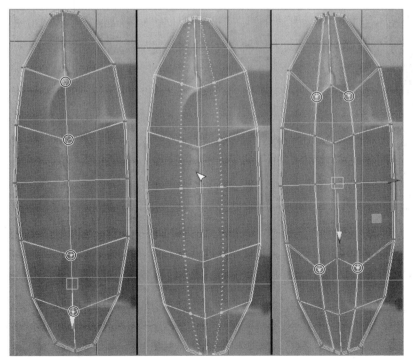). Select the outside row of edges all the way around the top, as shown in Figure 6.31 (top). Then click the Bevel button in Modeling Toolkit. Enter a Segments value of **2** and a Fraction value of **0.60**, as shown in Figure 6.31.

6. In the top view, adjust the shown vertices to align with the arms coming out of the base, as shown in Figure 6.32 (left). Then in the main menu bar, choose Mesh Tools → Offset Edge Loop and select the middle vertical loop of edges on top of the arm base to place two edge loops, as shown in Figure 6.32 (middle). Press W to exit the tool and enter the Move tool. Select the shown vertices and adjust them to fit the base of the arms, as shown in Figure 6.32 (right).

7. In Modeling Toolkit, click the Face Selection icon ( ). Select the faces shown in Figure 6.33 (top) and then click the Extrude button in Modeling Toolkit. First set the Thickness value to **3.50** to extrude the faces up in space, next set Divisions to **6** for extra segments, and finally set Offset to **0.07** for a slight taper, as shown in Figure 6.33 (bottom). Click the W to exit the tool.

Figure 6.32

Line up the vertices to where the arms come out of the base (left) and then use Offset Edge Loop to place edge loops as shown (middle). Finally, adjust the selected vertices to fit around the arm at the base (right).

Adjust these vertices

Figure 6.33

Select these faces (top) and extrude them with Modeling Toolkit (bottom).

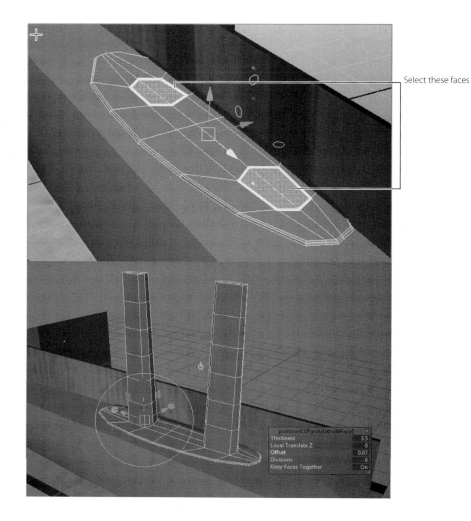

Select these faces

8. In the front view panel, select vertices and move them to create an angle to the right for the arm. At the top of the arm, select the top two rows of vertices and move and rotate them to create a bend, as shown in Figure 6.34.

9. Click the Channel Box/Layer Editor tab to switch out of the Modeling Toolkit view, and in the Layer Editor, turn off the visibility of the pontoonRefLayer. Turn off X-Ray view in your views.

10. Select both the pontoon and the arm base and press Ctrl+G to group them. Name the group **leftPontoonGroup**. Press 3 to see the pontoon in Smooth Preview, as shown in Figure 6.35. Save your work. There's just one detail to add at the back of the pontoon.

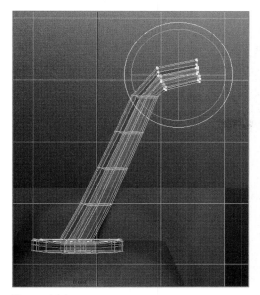

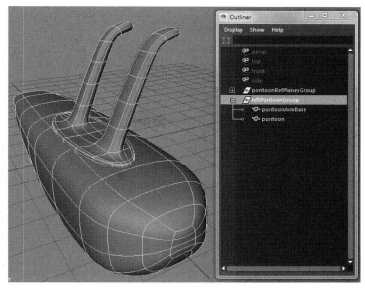

Figure 6.34

Create an angle to the arm and a bend at the tip.

Figure 6.35

The left-side pontoon is almost done and shown here in smooth preview.

11. With the pontoon selected, press 1 to exit smooth preview. Go back into Modeling Toolkit by clicking its tab. Enter Face Selection (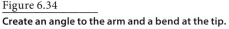) and select the nine faces in the back-bottom part of the pontoon, as shown in Figure 6.36 (left). Click the Extrude button in Modeling Toolkit and set Divisions to **3**, Thickness to **-0.17**, and Offset to **0.11**, as shown in Figure 6.36 (right). Click W to exit the tool. This creates a little indent at the back of the pontoon, and the Divisions value of 3 will keep the edges sharper when you eventually smooth the model.

12. In the Outliner, select the pontoonRefPlanesGroup and delete it. In the Layer Editor, RMB+click the pontoonRefLayer and select Delete Layer. Lastly, open the Hypershade (Windows → Rendering Editors → Hypershade) and select Edit → Delete Unused Nodes. This will get rid of the reference photos on the planes you just deleted. You are doing all this so when you assemble the final plane, you will not import unwanted reference planes, display layers, or shaders along with the pontoon. It's best to keep a clean workflow!

You're done with the pontoon! Go celebrate with some cookies. Save your work! You will undoubtedly adjust this model later when you attach it to the plane's body, as well as smooth the geometry. You can compare your work to the scene file `pontoonModel_v04.ma` in the Scenes folder of the Plane project.

Figure 6.36

Select these nine faces (left) and create an inset in the bottom back of the pontoon using Extrude (right).

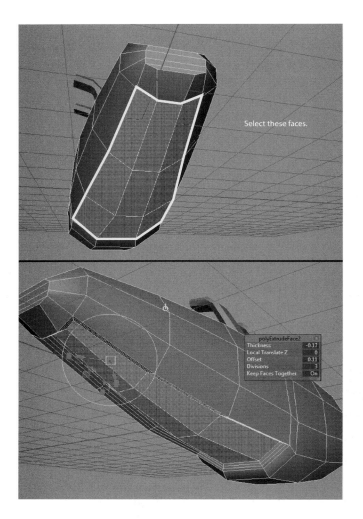

Figure 6.36

Select these nine faces (left) and create an inset in the bottom back of the pontoon using Extrude (right).

Oh, What a Body! Modeling the Body of the Plane

With one of the pontoons finished, you can move on to model the body of the plane in much the same way you modeled the pontoon. If you like a challenge and can use the practice, use the steps at the beginning of the chapter where you created three reference view planes for the pontoon to create three new reference view planes for the body of the plane in a new Maya scene. In the Sourceimages folder of the Plane project, you will find bodyBackReference.jpg, bodyBottomReference.jpg, and bodySideReference.jpg to use as the images. They are all sized 1600×1200 with an aspect ratio of 1:0.750. Just make sure to line up the planes and uniformly scale them as needed. Group them together and make sure the reference planes end up about 14 units in length to better fit the scale of the pontoon you already made.

You can skip creating the reference planes and get right to modeling by loading the scene file bodyModel_v01.ma in the Scenes folder of the Plane project. This file has the reference view planes already set up and ready with the proper grouping and scale. Who loves you?

Blocking Out the Shape

In this section, you'll block out the shape of the body. Follow these steps:

1. Create a cube at the origin. This time instead of using X-Ray shading to see through the model to the reference images, you'll force the body geometry to show as wireframe even in Shaded mode. With the cube selected, open the Attribute Editor, click the pCube1 tab, and then click the Display heading. Click the Drawing Overrides heading, check the box Enable Overrides, and then uncheck the Shading box, as shown in Figure 6.37.

   Your cube should display as a wireframe, even though your reference planes display Textured view.

2. Using the top and side views, scale and place the cube over the body of the plane. You want a little overlap between the body and the gray engine at the front of the plane, as shown in Figure 6.38. In the Channel Box, click the polyCube1 entry to reveal the subdivision values.

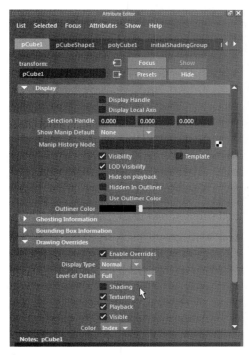

Figure 6.37

Create a drawing override to make the cube display as a wireframe all the time.

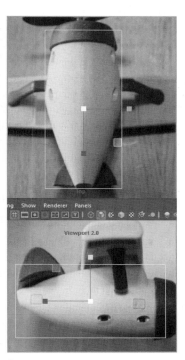

Figure 6.38

Create a cube and place it properly using the top and side views.

3. In the side view panel, insert eight vertical edge loops (Mesh Tools → Insert Edge Loop), as shown in Figure 6.39 (top). Still in the side view, adjust the vertices to shape the cube to the plane, as shown in Figure 6.39 (bottom).

Figure 6.39

Insert these edge loops (top) and then adjust the vertices to shape the cube to the plane (bottom).

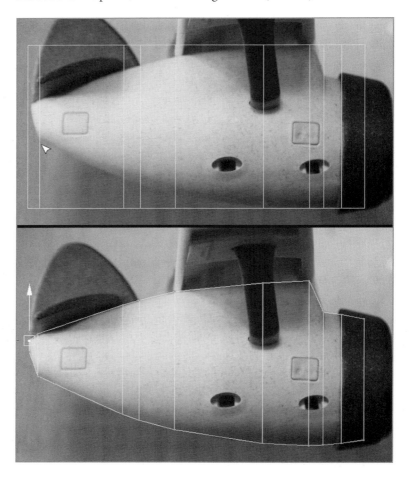

4. In the top view, insert a horizontal edge loop at the widest part of the plane, as shown in Figure 6.40 (left). Then place a vertical edge loop straight up the middle of the plane, as shown in Figure 6.40 (middle). Finally, adjust the vertices to fit the shape of the plane, as shown in Figure 6.40 (right). Name the object **body**.

5. Go into the persp view panel, and with the body selected, press 3 for smooth preview. In the Attribute Editor for the body in the body tab, under Display → Drawing Overrides, turn off Enable Overrides to see the mesh in Shaded mode. It's looking pretty good.

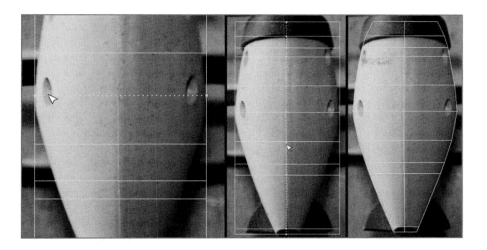

Figure 6.40

Place a horizontal edge loop (left) and then a vertical edge loop up the center (middle). Then move vertices to shape the body in the top view (right).

6. In the side view panel, notice the very back end of the body is too rounded when you compare it to the side of the plane, as in Figure 6.41 (left). Press 1 to exit smooth preview, and it lines back up again. The smoothing rounds that corner too much. To avoid that, you need to add two more edge loops, as shown in Figure 6.41 (middle), to preserve detail when smoothed. Press 3 again, and the back end lines up nicer in smooth preview, as shown in Figure 6.41 (right).

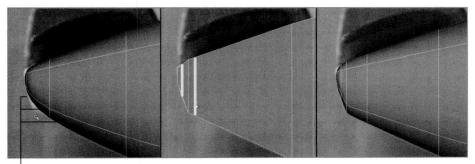

Too rounded here   Insert these edge loops

Figure 6.41

The end of the body gets too smooth (left), so add these two edge loops (middle), and when you smooth preview again, the end fits better (right).

7. Turn off the image reference planes' layer (bodyRefLayer) in the Layer Editor.

8. Press 1 to exit smooth preview. Display the Modeling Toolkit by clicking its tab in the Channel Box area.

    If Modeling Toolkit tab is not present, you need to click the Show Modeling Toolkit icon (▣) in the upper right of the UI (as previously shown in Figure 6.30).

9. Enable Face Selection by clicking its icon (▣) in Modeling Toolkit, and select the six faces at the back of the body, as shown in Figure 6.42 (left). Then click the Extrude

button and set Divisions to **3**, Thickness to **-0.10**, and Offset to **0.20**. This creates a little inset at the back of the plane similar to the toy's back end. Click the Extrude button again to exit the tool.

Figure 6.42

Select these faces (left) and then extrude them to create an inset.

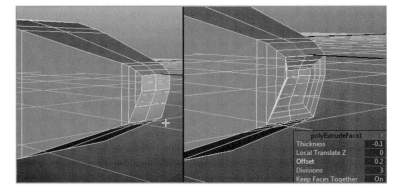

10. With the body selected, press 3 for smooth preview, and you'll likely notice a little bit of pinching around the inset you just created as in Figure 6.43 (left). Stay in smooth preview. Enter Vertex Selection by clicking the [ ] icon in Modeling Toolkit and move a pair of vertices, as shown in Figure 6.43 (right), to alleviate the pinching. Repeat for the other side.

Now you're done with the body of the plane. You can check your work against the scene file bodyModel_v02.ma in the Scenes folder of the Plane project.

Figure 6.43

There is a pinch in the back (left), so adjust a few vertices to fix it (right).

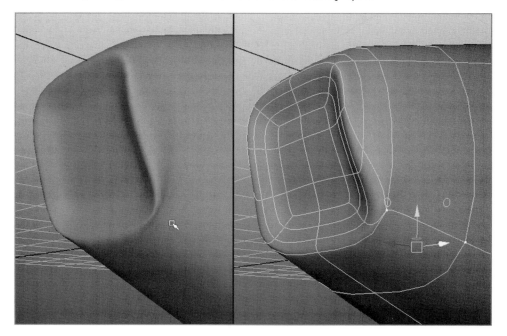

The Rear Stabilizers

You'll create these back stabilizer wings as a new model directly in the body scene. Continue with your file or use bodyModel_v02.ma to start modeling the rear stabilizer wings.

1. Turn visibility on for bodyRefLayer in the Layer Editor (click the toggle to display a V). Select the body geometry and turn on Enable Overrides again to make it display as wireframe (found in the Attribute Editor's body tab under Display → Drawing Overrides) as you did in step 1 of the previous section, "Blocking Out the Shape."

2. Create a poly cube in the side view panel; using the side and front view panels, move, rotate, and scale the cube to roughly fit the vertical stabilizer wing, as shown in Figure 6.44 (top left and top right).

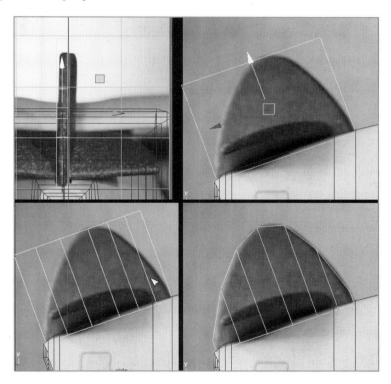

Figure 6.44

Create and place a cube for the vertical wing (top). Insert edge loops (bottom left) and adjust the shape (bottom right).

3. Using the Insert Edge Loop tool, insert five new edge loops vertically, as shown in Figure 6.44 (bottom left), and use the vertices to adjust the shape of the wing, as shown in Figure 6.44 (bottom right).

4. Insert a vertical edge loop, as shown in Figure 6.45 (top left), to align with the side wing that comes out from the vertical wing.

Figure 6.45

Insert a vertical edge loop (left) and then use Multi-Cut to insert a pair of horizontal edges that loop around (middle and right).

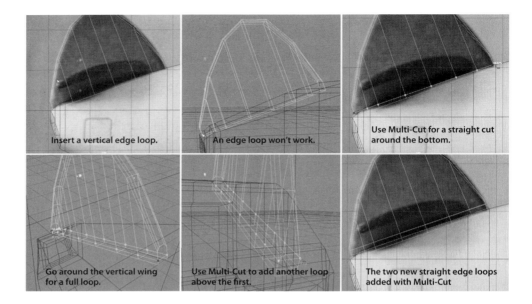

5. Now you need to insert some edge loops to let you extrude the horizontal side wings that come out of the vertical wing to make an upside-down *T* for the stabilizers. If you use the Insert Edge Loop tool, the edge loops will be curved like the arch of the shape so far, as shown in Figure 6.45 (top middle). Instead, select the vertical wing object, and choose Mesh Tools → Multi-Cut.

   In the side view panel, click to place the first vertex of the multi-cut as shown in Figure 6.45 (top right) and then click the opposite side of the vertical wing to insert edges across the bottom of the vertical wing, again as in Figure 6.45 (top right).

   In the perspective panel, swing your view around so you can complete the multi-cut around to the other side of the vertical wing, clicking finally on the original yellow point where you started the multi-cut. The cursor will display the word *close*, as shown in Figure 6.45 (lower left).

6. Use the tool again as in step 5 to place a parallel cut a little further up the vertical wing, as shown in Figure 6.45 (lower middle). Figure 6.45 (lower right) shows a side view of both added rows of edges inserted with the Multi-Cut tool.

7. In Modeling Toolkit, enable Edge Selection (◇). In the persp view panel, if you double-click one of the upper edges on the vertical wing's top arch, it will select an entire edge loop on the top arch of the wing shape. Do this twice to select the edge loops on both sides of the arch of the wing, as shown in Figure 6.46 (left).

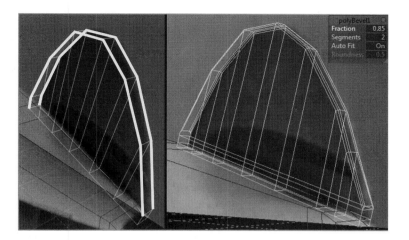

Figure 6.46

Select these edges (left) and bevel them (right).

8. Click the Bevel button in Modeling Toolkit and set Segments to **2** and Fraction to **0.85**, as shown in Figure 6.46 (right). Press W to exit the tool.

9. In the persp view panel, select the five faces shown at the base of the vertical wing where the side wings are. Make sure to select five on each side of the vertical wing, as shown in Figure 6.47.

10. In Modeling Toolkit, click Extrude and set Divisions to **3**, Thickness to **1.5**, and Offset to **0.03** for a slight taper at the end, as shown in Figure 6.48 (left). Press W for the Move tool and then use the top view to adjust vertices to loosely match the shape of these side wings for the stabilizers, as shown in Figure 6.48 (right). As you can see, the image used for reference is not centered well. But you should keep your geometry symmetrical, even though it won't line up well on the right side of the plane in the image.

Figure 6.47

Select these five faces on both sides of the vertical wing.

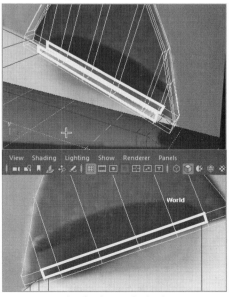

Select five faces on both sides

11. Turn off the visibility of the bodyRefLayer in the Layer Editor. For the stabilizer wings, uncheck Enable Overrides in the Attribute Editor to show the wings in Shaded mode. Also, in the persp view's panel menu bar, select Shading → Wireframe On Shaded to display wireframe on top of the shaded models.

Figure 6.48

Extrude the side wings (left) and shape them to create a nice shape, even though it won't line up on one side (right).

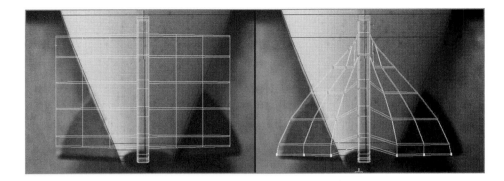

12. Select the outer loop of edges around the side wings, as shown in Figure 6.49 (left), and click Bevel in Modeling Toolkit with a Segments value of **2** and an Fraction value of **1.5**, as shown in Figure 6.49 (right).

Figure 6.49

Select the edges around the side wings (left) and bevel them (right).

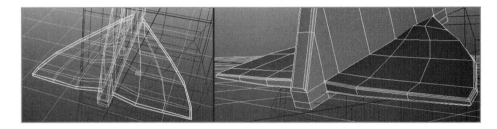

13. At the front of the vertical wing, select the vertices shown in Figure 6.50 and scale them closer together in the X-axis to taper the front blade of that wing a bit. Select the tail wing object and call it **tail**.

Figure 6.50

Select these vertices and squeeze them together in the X-axis.

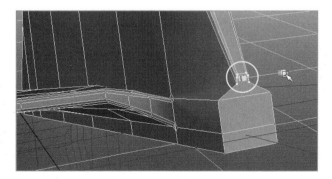

14. Select the plane's body geometry and uncheck Enable Overrides (in the Attribute Editor's body tab under Display ➔ Drawing Overrides) so you can see the entire plane in Shaded mode. Press 3 to see it in smooth preview. Press 1 to get out of smooth preview for the meshes.

Save your work! You can check your work against the scene file bodyModel_v03.ma in the Scenes folder of the Plane project.

You Spin Me Right Round—The Engine and Propeller

Now for the propeller! In the same scene as the body, you'll create the engine and propellers at the front of the plane. Begin with your current scene, or use bodyModel_v03.ma. To begin with the engine, follow along here:

1. In the Layer Editor, make sure the bodyRefLayer is visible and the R toggle is off so you can see and select the plane images. You need only the side reference image now, so select the other two image reference planes and press Ctrl+H to hide them. In the Outliner, their entries (bodyBottomRefPlane and bodyBackRefPlane) show up as gray. To unhide them, you would select them in the Outliner and press Shift+H. Leave them hidden for now.

2. Select the body and press 3 for smooth preview.

3. In the side view, create a CV curve to match the top half profile of the engine, as shown in Figure 6.51. You'll use this curve to revolve a surface.

4. In the persp view, select the profile curve and choose Display → NURBS → CVs to show the CVs of the curve. Click the Snap To Points icon in the status bar (⬚).

5. Press and hold D to engage the Pivot Move tool and move the pivot of the curve to snap to the bottom CV in the middle of the engine, as shown in Figure 6.52. This will ensure a good revolve. Turn off the point snap and then, with the curve selected, choose Display → NURBS → CVs to turn off the CVs on the curve.

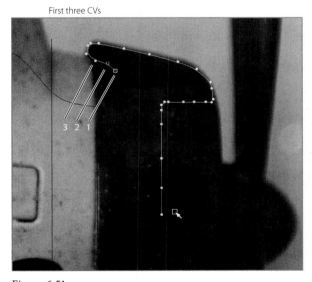

Figure 6.51
Draw a profile curve for the shape of the engine.

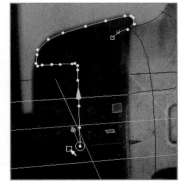

Figure 6.52
Snap the pivot to the bottom CV.

6. Then, with the curve selected, choose Surfaces → Revolve ❑. Set Axis preset to **Z**, Segments to **8**, Output Geometry to Polygons, and Type to Quads; leave the Tessellation method on Standard Fit. Set the Chord Height ratio to **0.925** and the 3D delta to **0.10**. Click Revolve to make the engine fit around the front of the plane, as shown in Figure 6.53.

7. The engine may not be perfectly centered on the plane body, so move it to center it on the body. Then choose Edit → Delete By Type → History to erase the history on that shape. Select the profile curve and delete it. Select the engine geometry you just created and name it **engine**.

Figure 6.53

Revolve the curve to make the engine geometry.

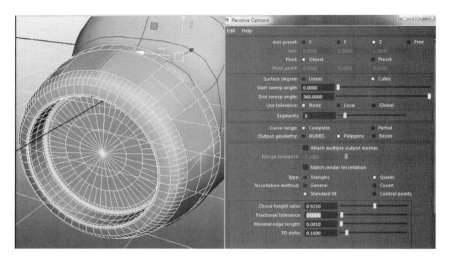

Engine Detail

Now for some detail inside the engine.

1. Choose Create → Polygon Primitives → Cylinder ❑ and set Axis Divisions to **16**, Height Divisions to **11**, and Cap Divisions to **1**. Set Axis to Y and leave the rest at the defaults. Click Create and place the cylinder in front of the engine. Scale it to **0.125** in X and Z, and set the Y-axis scale to **0.4**, as shown in Figure 6.54.

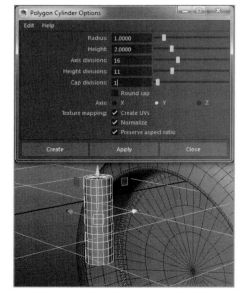

Figure 6.54

Create this cylinder and place it in front of the engine.

2. In Modeling Toolkit, enter Face Selection; in the side view, select every other ring of faces, as shown in Figure 6.55 (left). Click the Extrude button and enter a Thickness value of **0.03** and a Divisions value of **1**, as shown in Figure 6.55 (right).

3. Select the cylinder in Object mode, move it back into the engine, and place it as shown in Figure 6.56.

4. Turn on Snap To Points (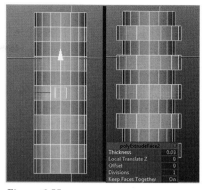) and press and hold D to move the pivot. Snap the pivot point of the cylinder to the center of the engine, as shown in Figure 6.57.

5. Choose Edit → Duplicate Special ❑. Set Rotate to **36** in the Z-axis and Number Of Copies to **9** and click Apply, as shown in Figure 6.58. This creates a ring of these cylinders inside the engine.

Figure 6.55

Select every other ring of faces (left) and extrude them (right).

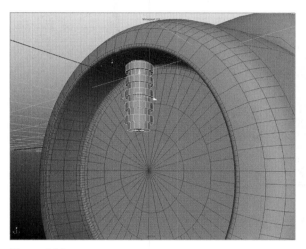

Figure 6.56

Place the cylinder into the engine.

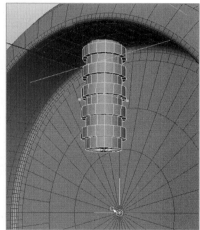

Figure 6.57

Snap the pivot to the engine's center.

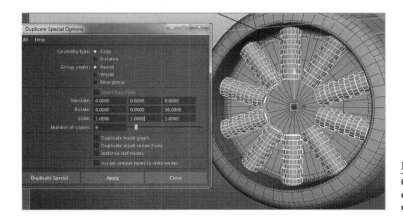

Figure 6.58

Create a ring of cylinders inside the engine.

The Propeller Blades

Follow these steps to create the propeller blades:

1. Create a polygon cone. In the Channel Box, click polyCone1 and set Subdivisions Axis to **6** and Subdivisions Height to **3**. Scale the cone to **0.72** in all three axes and rotate and place it against the inside of the engine. Select the sharp tip's vertex and push it back to make the cone blunt, as shown in Figure 6.59.

2. In the Modeling menu set, insert an edge loop toward the middle of the cone, as shown in Figure 6.60. Select every other of the new faces on the cone and click the Extrude button in Modeling Toolkit. Set Divisions to **1**, Thickness to **3.2**, and Offset to **0** to create the blades of the propeller, as shown in Figure 6.61. Click Extrude to turn off the tool.

3. The blades sure do look weird; they are angled away from the engine. With the three faces at the ends of the blades still selected, move them back in the Y-axis to make them flush with the engine. The blades will go through the engine geometry a little bit, and that's okay for now.

4. On each of the three blades, insert an edge loop about where the blade intersects with the engine geometry, as shown in Figure 6.62 (left), and then scale the new edge loops to be much larger, as in Figure 6.62 (right).

5. If you press 3 for smooth preview, the propellers look pretty good. Select them and move them out so the blades don't penetrate the engine geometry.

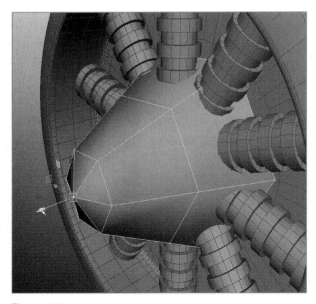

Figure 6.59

Place a cone in the engine and shorten the tip to make it blunt.

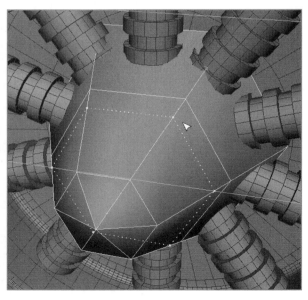

Figure 6.60

Insert an edge loop.

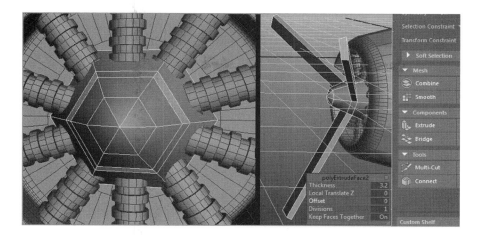

Figure 6.61

Select every other face (left) and extrude them to create the propeller blades (right).

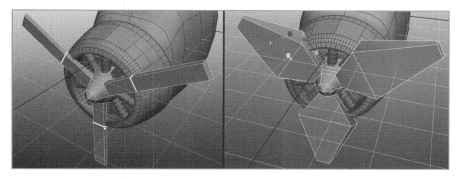

Figure 6.62

Insert an edge loop on each of the three blades (left) and then scale the new edge loops to be much bigger (right).

6. Stay in smooth preview for the body (but not the engine; the engine will not need smoothing later) and work around the body of the plane. Move vertices on the body where it meets the engine to make sure that the body is not penetrating the engine.

Now you're done with the body and need to move to the wings. Save your work and compare it to the scene file bodyModel_v04.ma in the Scenes folder of the Plane project. Note that this file has the plane body and propeller and stabilizer wings already set in smooth preview.

The Plane's Wings

How can you fly without wings? Here you'll create the wings in the existing plane body scene file and get them to attach to the body.

Modeling the Wing

Continue with your own model or use bodyModel_v04.ma to continue.

1. Turn the visibility on for the bodyRefLayer. Then, in the Outliner, select the two hidden gray reference planes grouped under bodyRefPlanesGroup (click the plus sign to reveal them in the Outliner). Press Shift+H to unhide them in your view panels.

2. Select all the parts of the plane you have made so far and press Ctrl+H to hide them.

3. In the persp view, press 6 for Texture mode to see the reference image of the toy plane again. Create a cube and, in the Attribute Editor, in the pCube tab, check Enable Overrides under Display → Drawing Overrides. Turn off Shading as you've done before to make the cube display as wireframe. Using the top views, size and orient the cube to fit over the wing, as shown in Figure 6.63 (top). Since there is some perspective shift in the photos, the placements will be rough and will not line up in the side view at all, and that's okay. Insert edge loops, as shown in Figure 6.63 (bottom), to create more segments.

Figure 6.63

Create a cube and place it as shown to start the left side of the wing (top). Insert the edge loops as shown (bottom).

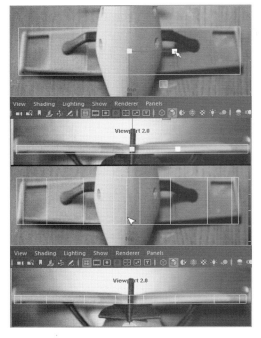

4. Now you'll need to shape the wing. This time, let's use a feature called Symmetry. In the top view, RMB+click the body and enter vertex mode. Then choose Modify → Transformation Tools → Move Tool □ (or double-click the Move tool icon (▦) in the Tool Box).

5. In the option box, toward the bottom under the Symmetry Settings heading, click Symmetry and choose Object X from the pull-down menu. Now, any time you select vertices on one side of the wing, the opposite side's vertices will be selected as well. This way you can shape one side of the wing, and the other side will shape itself to match.

6. Use the top view to shape the left side of the wing, and as you do so, the right side will shape itself. Don't worry if the shape of the wing does not match the image; remember that the image is not perfectly symmetrical. This is okay. Figure 6.64 shows the wing shaped using the Symmetry feature.

7. In the front view and with Symmetry still on, shape the wing on the left to the image, as shown in Figure 6.65 (top).

Figure 6.64

Using Symmetry lets you shape one side of the wing and reflect that shape to the other side automatically.

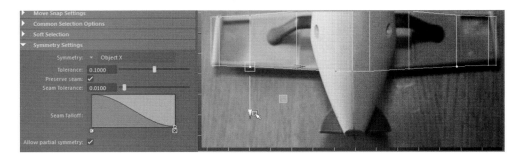

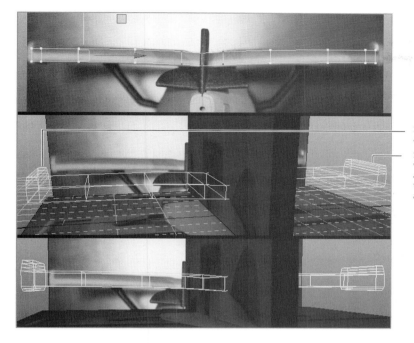

Figure 6.65

Shape the vertices on one side, and Symmetry will shape the other side (top). Extrude the top face (middle). Then select and extrude the bottom end face (bottom).

Select this face and extrude

Symmetry will select and extrude this face automatically

8. RMB+click the body and choose Faces for face selection mode. At the end of the wing on the left, select the top face at the very end. Symmetry will automatically select the other side's top end face as well.

9. Then in Modeling Toolkit, click the Extrude button. Set Divisions to **3**, Thickness to **0.35**, and Offset to **0.05**. Both ends will extrude up, as shown in Figure 6.65 (middle).

10. Select the bottom face at the end of the wing on the left side. Again, in Modeling Toolkit, click the Extrude button. Set Divisions to **2**, Thickness to **0.15**, and Offset to **0.05**. This will extrude the ends of the wings, as shown in Figure 6.65 (bottom).

11. In the Move tool options, turn off Symmetry. Turn off the display of the reference image layer (bodyRefLayer). From here on, you'll shape the plane without the reference images. Select the top back edge that runs across the wing, as shown in Figure 6.66 (top), and move the edges down to taper the back of the wing down.

12. Select the wing and in the Attribute Editor uncheck Enable Overrides to show the wing in Shaded mode again. Press 5 for Shaded mode in the persp view. Insert an edge loop two-thirds of the way up the side of the wing, as shown in Figure 6.66 (bottom). This will help retain the shape of the wing when you smooth the mesh later.

Figure 6.66

Select the topside
back edges of the
wing and move
them down to taper
the wing (top).
Insert an edge loop
two-thirds up the
side of the wing
(bottom).

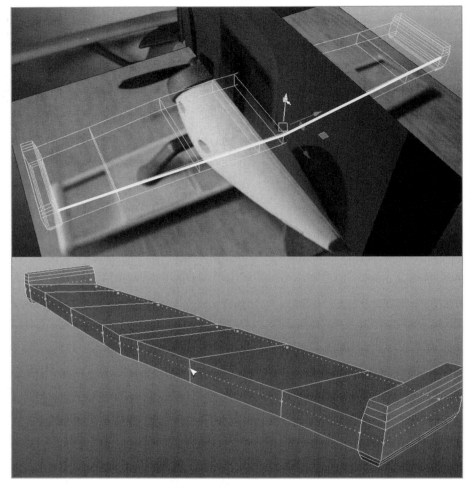

Select the edges on the top back of the wing

13. Open the option box for the Move tool (Modify → Transformation Tools → Move Tool ❑). Turn on Symmetry.

14. RMB+click the wing and enter edge selection. Shape the tip of the wing as shown in Figure 6.67. Symmetry will take care of the opposite side. Then add an edge loop as shown. You will have to add an edge loop to the wing tip on the other side; Symmetry will not work with the Insert Edge Loop tool.

15. Make any personal adjustments you'd like and press 3 to smooth preview the wing. Once you're happy with the shape, press 1 to exit smooth preview and choose Mesh → Smooth ❑. Make sure the settings are at default in the option box by selecting Edit → Reset Settings and then click Smooth.

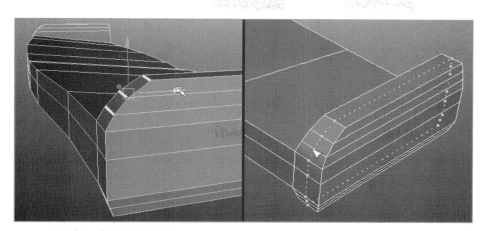

Figure 6.67

Shape the tip of the wing to curve it back a bit (left) and then add an edge loop at the wing tip for both sides of the wing (right).

Move these edges to shape the tip

16. Orbit your camera to look at the underside of the wing. On the underside of the wing, select the faces, as shown in Figure 6.68. In Modeling Toolkit, click the Extrude button. Set Divisions to **2**, Thickness to **-0.16**, and Offset to **0.10**, as in Figure 6.68 (bottom).

Figure 6.68

Select these faces under the wing (top) and extrude to create indents in the wing's underside (bottom).

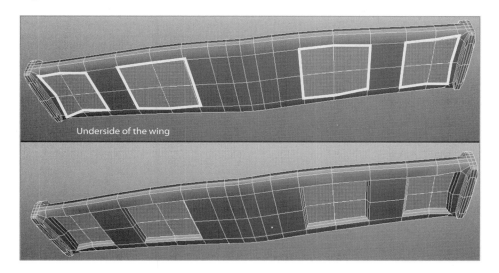

Underside of the wing

17. Now select the outer edges of those four new indents in the underside of the wing, as shown in Figure 6.69 (top). In Modeling Toolkit, bevel them with a Segments value of **2** and a Fraction value of **0.60**, as shown in Figure 6.69 (bottom). Turn off Bevel. Save!

Figure 6.69

Select these edges (top) and bevel them (bottom).

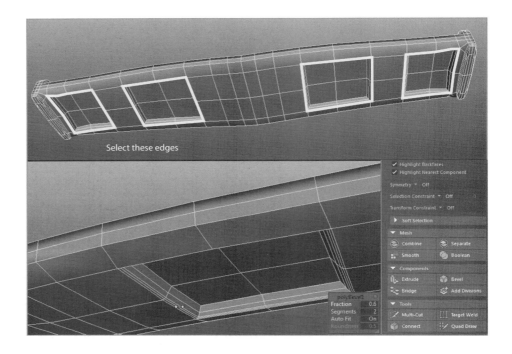

Select these edges

Figure 6.70

The Outliner shows the organized scene.

Organizing the Scene and Smoothing the Geometry

Now let's take a moment to clean up and organize the scene and smooth the rest of the geometry:

1. Open the Outliner and select all the hidden objects that appear in gray text. Press Shift+H to unhide them. You should now see the plane, back stabilizer wings, and propellers in smooth preview.

2. In the Outliner, select all the pCylinder objects you created inside the engine and press Ctrl+G to group them. Call the group **insideEngine**.

3. Select the propeller and name it **props**. Select the wing and call it **wings**. Figure 6.70 shows the Outliner with the proper names.

4. Select all the parts of the plane and press 1 to exit smooth preview for all the objects.

5. Select the body, propellers, and tail wings, as shown in Figure 6.71 (top left), and choose Mesh → Smooth ❑. Check to make sure Add Divisions attribute is set to Exponentially, select Maya Catmull-Clark for Subdivision Type, and set Division Levels to **2**, as shown in Figure 6.71 (right). Click Apply to smooth the plane, as shown in Figure 6.71 (bottom left).

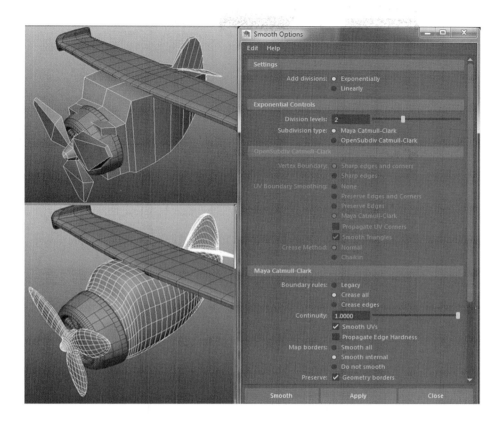

Figure 6.71

The plane before smoothing (left) and after smoothing (right)

6. Select all the geometry and choose Edit → Delete By Type → History to get rid of all the construction history.

7. Since you don't need the reference images anymore, delete the reference plane's top group (bodyRefPlanesGroup). RMB+click the bodyRefLayer in the Layer Editor and select Delete Layer. And in the Hypershade (Windows → Rendering Editors → Hypershade), click Edit → Delete Unused Nodes. Save!

Adding the Wing Supports

Now you just need to connect the wings to the plane using the following steps:

1. The wings sit a little low and penetrate the top of the plane's body a little bit. Select the wing object and move it up to sit on top of the body. Rotate it a bit in the X-axis to align it with the angle of the top of the plane's body better.

2. Let's smooth the wing a little more. With the wing selected, choose Mesh → Smooth, set Division Levels back to **1**, and click Smooth. Select the smoothed wing and delete the history (Edit → Delete By Type → History).

3. Now let's make the support connecting the wing to the sides of the plane. Maximize the front view (press the spacebar). Choose Create → Curve Tools → CV Curve Tool and create a curve starting at the body of the plane up to the underside of the left-side wing, as shown in Figure 6.72.

Figure 6.72
Create this curve for the wing support.

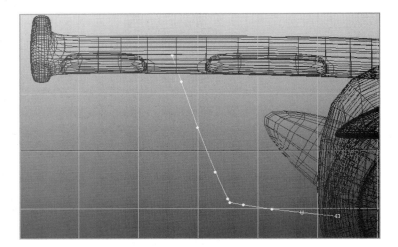

4. In the persp view's menu, select Show and uncheck Polygons to turn off polygon view in the view panel. This shows you the curve you just made by itself. Select the curve and select Display → NURBS → CVs to show the CV points on the curve.

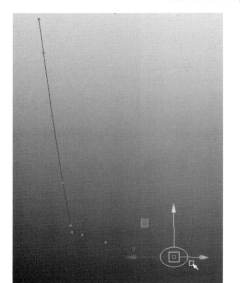

5. Next, create a circle (Create → NURBS Primitives → Circle). Scale it to a small oval and place it at the start of the CV curve line you just made, which is just inside the body of the plane. You can use Snap To Points to place the oval exactly at the start of the curve, as shown in Figure 6.73.

6. In the persp view panel's menu, click Show and check Polygons back on. Stay in wireframe view (press 4).

7. Select the oval and the curve and select Surfaces → Extrude ❐. Set Style to Tube, Result Position to At Path, Output Geometry to Polygons, and Type to Quads; click Extrude, as shown in Figure 6.74. Press 5 to see it in Shaded mode and assess how you like it. You can adjust the shape or size of the oval as well as the shape of the CV curve line to customize the resulting support shape that connects the wing to the body.

Figure 6.73
Create an oval shape and place it at the start of the curve.

8. If you are happy with the shape of the support, select the original oval and the CV curve and delete them. Select the support arm geometry and name it **supportArm** in the Outliner.

9. Now you need another for the other side of the plane. With supportArm selected, press Ctrl+D to duplicate it in place. In the Channel Box, enter an X-Scale value of **-1.0** to create a mirror of the original arm. Since the pivot point of the original supportArm is in the center, scaling it in X-axis to -1 should place it perfectly on the other side of the plane.

10. Move the arms a little toward the back of the plane so the part that meets the wing is centered on the wing, as shown in Figure 6.75.

11. Select both support arms and choose Modify → Freeze Transformations. Name them **wingSupport1** and **wingSupport2**.

12. Select the wing supports and the wing itself, group them together, and call the group **wingGroup**. Move wingGroup a little closer to the front of the plane to line up the wing, as shown in Figure 6.76.

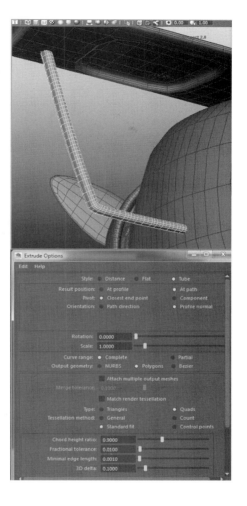

Figure 6.74

Extrude to create the support for the wing.

Figure 6.75

The support arms in place

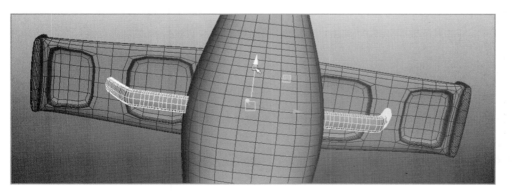

Figure 6.76

Place the wing assembly.

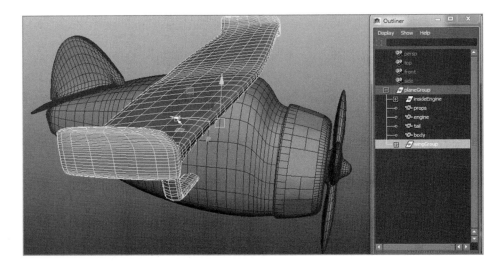

13. Select the insideEngine and wingGroup groups and all the other parts of the plane and group them together. Call the group **planeGroup**.

Save your work and compare it to the scene file bodyModel_v05.ma in the Scenes folder of the Plane project.

Assembling the Plane

You have all the parts finished, so let's assemble the plane into a complete scene and make any finishing touches. In your current body model or the bodyModel_v05.ma scene, you just need to import the pontoons and you're done.

1. Choose File → Import. In the file dialog, on the right side, make sure Use Namespaces is checked. Navigate to the latest pontoon model you created or to the pontoonModel_v04.ma file in the Scenes folder of the Plane project on the website.

2. A single pontoon will appear, unsmoothed, in the middle of the scene. In the Outliner, its name will be something like pontoonModel_v04:leftPontoonGroup. The name before the colon is the filename from which you imported the model. The part of the name on the right is the node name.

3. Select the two pieces of geometry that make up the pontoon (not the top group) and choose Mesh → Smooth ☐. Set Division Levels to **1** and click Smooth.

4. Select the top node of the newly smoothed pontoon assembly (pontoonModel_v04:leftPontoonGroup) and rename it to **leftPontoonGroup** in the Outliner. Then

move it into place (as shown in Figure 6.77) and orient it properly by rotating it 180 degrees in the Y-axis.

5. Duplicate the pontoon group (leftPontoonGroup) by pressing Ctrl+D and set the copy's X-axis scale to **–1.0**. Call the new group **rightPontoonGroup** and move it to the other side of the plane body. Figure 6.77 shows the proper placement for both pontoons.

6. Select the geometry for both pontoons (not the top nodes) and choose Edit → Delete By Type → History.

7. With the geometry still selected, choose Modify → Freeze Transformations.

8. Using the Outliner, place both pontoon groups into the planeGroup by MMB+dragging them onto the planeGroup node.

9. Now you'll adjust how the pontoons look on the plane. In the Outliner, select the two top nodes of the pontoons. Select Deform → Lattice ❏. Set Divisions to **4, 3, 2** and click Create. This places a single lattice box around both the pontoons.

10. You want to spread the pontoons to make a wider base for the plane. RMB+click the lattice itself and choose Lattice Point. Select the eight lattice points shown in Figure 6.78 (left) and move them away from the plane and up closer to the wing, as shown in Figure 6.78 (right).

Figure 6.77

Place the pontoon, duplicate it, and place the duplicate on the other side.

11. Repeat for the other pontoon's lattice points to make the stance of the pontoons wider and closer to the wing. If your pontoon geometry is different from the one shown or the ones in the sample scene file pontoonModel_v04.ma, you may need to adjust your lattice differently. You may also choose to skip this step because it's a minor tweak. The proportions look nicer now!

12. Select the pontoon group nodes (Figure 6.79) and delete their history to get rid of the lattice (Edit → Delete By Type → History).

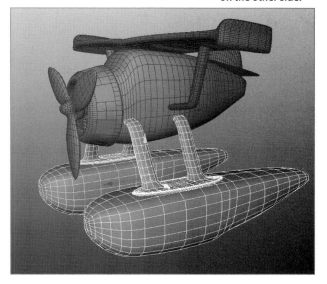

Figure 6.79 shows the completed plane and its hierarchy. You can check your work against the scene file bodyModel_v06.ma in the Scenes folder of the Plane project. In the following chapters, you will add textures and lighting to render the plane as a plastic bathtub toy.

Figure 6.78

Select these eight lattice points and move the pontoon away from the plane body and up closer to the wing (left).

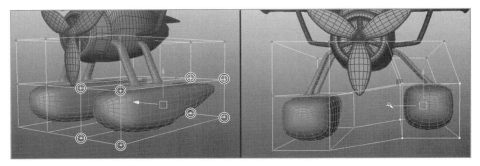

Select these eight lattice points

Figure 6.79

The pontoons are adjusted, and the plane is ready to fly!

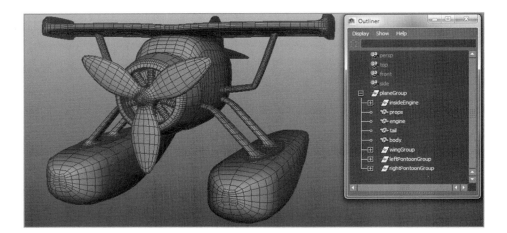

Summary

In this chapter, you flexed your knowledge from the previous chapters and concentrated on creating a model of a child's bathtub toy airplane. You used many of the tools discussed in the previous chapters, from extruding to adding edge loops to using bevels.

Creating a model can be a lot of hard and sometimes tedious work, but when you start seeing it take shape, the excitement begins to build. From the basic shaping of the plane's parts to the detail of assembling the plane, you worked hard in this chapter to create the toy plane.

You can take the procedures you used in this chapter to build your own toy design. The important lesson to take away from this chapter is how in depth you can get with a model and how a lengthy modeling process takes shape. Along the way, don't forget to name your pieces and group everything in a sensible fashion.

CHAPTER 7

Autodesk® Maya® Shading and Texturing

Shading *is the term* for applying colors and textures to create *materials*, also known in the Autodesk® Maya® software as *shaders*. A shader defines an object's look—its color, tactile texture, transparency, luminescence, glow, and so forth.

Learning Outcomes: In this chapter, you will be able to

- Differentiate between different shader types

- Create and edit shader networks in the Hypershade window

- Apply shaders and textures to a model

- Set up UVs on a model for the best texture placement

- Understand the steps to set up texture images to fit a model's UV layout

- Tweak UVs to align texture details

- Use Maya's toon shading to create a cartoon look

Maya Shading

When you create any objects, Maya assigns a default shader to them called Lambert1, which has a neutral gray color. The shader allows your objects to render and display properly. If no shader is attached to a surface, an object can't be seen when rendered. In the Maya viewports, it will appear wireframe all the time, or as flat green, even in Shaded view.

Shading is the proper term for applying a renderable color, surface bumps, transparency, reflection, shine, or similar attributes to an object in Maya. It's closely related to, but distinct from, *texturing*, which is what you do when you apply a map or other node to an *attribute of a shader* to create some sort of surface detail. For example, adding a scanned photo of a brick wall to the Color attribute of a shader is considered applying texture. Adding another scanned photo of the bumps and contours of the same brick wall to the Bump Mapping attribute is also considered applying a texture. Nevertheless, because textures are often applied to shaders, the entire process of shading is sometimes informally referred to as *texturing*. Applying textures to shaders is also called *texture mapping* or simply *mapping*.

Shaders are based on nodes. Each node holds the attributes that define the shader. You create shader networks of interconnected shading nodes, akin to the hierarchies and groups of models.

Figure 7.1

The Maya shading nodes and categories

As you learn about shading in this chapter, you'll deal at length with the Hypershade window. See Chapter 2, "Jumping into Basic Animation Headfirst," and Chapter 3, "The Autodesk® Maya® 2016 Interface," for the layout of this window and for a hands-on introduction. You can access the Hypershade window by choosing Windows → Rendering Editors → Hypershade. Shading in Maya is almost always done hand in hand with lighting. At the least, textures are tweaked and edited in the lighting stage of production.

Shader Types

Open the Hypershade window by choosing Windows → Rendering Editors → Hypershade. In the left column of the Hypershade window, you'll see a listing of Maya shading nodes (Figure 7.1), split into categories. The first category displays surface nodes, a.k.a. material nodes or shader types. Of these shader types, a few are common to other animation packages (Lambert, Phong, and Blinn for example).

The way light bounces off an object defines how you see that object. The surface of the object may have pigments that affect the wavelength of light that reflects off it, giving the surface color. Other features of that object's surface also dictate how light is reflected.

Most light, after it hits a surface, *diffuses* across an area of that surface showing off the object's color. It may also reflect a hot spot called a *specular* highlight (a basic reflection of a light source). The shaders in Maya differ in how they deal with specular and diffuse parameters according to the specific math that drives them. As you learn about the shader types, think of the things around you and what shader type would best fit them. Some Maya shaders, such as the Hair Tube shader and the Use Background shader, are specific to creating special effects. It's important to learn the fundamentals first, so I'll cover the shading types you'll be using right off the bat.

You can adjust the settings for a shader's look either through the Hypershade's Property Editor or through the usual Attribute Editor in the main Maya UI. Next you'll take a quick look at the different types of shaders and what they do.

The Lambert Shader Type

The default shader type is *Lambert*, an evenly diffused shading type found in dull or matte surfaces. A sheet of regular paper, for example, is a Lambert surface.

A Lambert surface diffuses and scatters light evenly across its surface in all directions, as you can see in Figure 7.2.

The Phong Shader Type

Phong shading brings to a surface's rendering the notions of specular highlight and reflectivity. A Phong surface reflects light with a sharp hot spot, creating a specular highlight that drops off sharply, as shown in Figure 7.3. You'll find that glossy objects such as plastics, glass, and most metals take well to Phong shading.

The Blinn Shader Type

The *Blinn* shading method brings to the surface a highly accurate specular lighting model that offers superior control over the specular's appearance (see Figure 7.4). A Blinn surface reflects light with a hot spot, creating a specular that diffuses somewhat more gradually than a Phong. The result is a shader that is good for use on shiny surfaces and metallic surfaces.

Figure 7.2

A Lambert shader

Figure 7.3

A Phong shader

The Phong E Shader Type

The Phong E shader type expands the Phong shading model to include more control over the specular highlight. A Phong E surface reflects light much like a regular Phong does, but it has more detailed control over the specular settings to adjust the glossiness of the surface (see Figure 7.5). This creates a surface with a specular that drops off more gradually and yet remains sharper than a Blinn. Phong E also has greater color control over the specular than do Phong and Blinn, giving you more options for metallic reflections.

The Anisotropic Shader Type

The Anisotropic shader is good to use on surfaces that are deformed, such as a foil wrapper or warped plastic (see Figure 7.6).

Anisotropic refers to something whose properties differ according to direction. An anisotropic surface reflects light unevenly and creates an irregular-shaped specular highlight that is good for representing surfaces with directional grooves, like CDs. This creates a specular highlight that is uneven across the surface, changing according to the direction you specify on the surface, as opposed to a Blinn or Phong where the specular is circular.

The Layered Shader Type

A *Layered* shader allows the stacking of shaders to create complex shading effects, which is useful for creating objects composed of multiple materials (see Figure 7.7). By using the Layered shader to texture different materials on different parts of the object, you can avoid using excess geometry.

You control Layered shaders by using transparency maps to define which areas show which layers of the shader. You drag material nodes into the top area of the Attribute Editor and stack them from left to right, with the leftmost shader being the topmost layer assigned to the surface, like a candy shell around a chocolate.

Layered shaders are valuable resources to control compound and complex shaders. They're also perfect for putting labels on objects or adding dirt to aged surfaces.

Figure 7.4

A Blinn shader

Figure 7.5

A Phong E shader

Figure 7.6
An Anisotropic shader

Figure 7.7
A Layered shader

The Ramp Shader Type

A *ramp texture* is a gradient that can be attached to almost any attribute of a shader as a *texture node*. Ramps can create smooth transitions between colors and can even be used to control particles. (See Chapter 12, "Autodesk® Maya® Dynamics and Effects.") When used as a texture, a ramp can be connected to any attribute of a shader to create graduating color scales, transparency effects, increasing glow effects, and so on.

The *Ramp shader* (as opposed to the ramp texture discussed earlier) is a self-contained shader node that automatically has several ramp texture nodes (a.k.a. gradients) attached to its attributes. This makes for a simplified editing environment for the shader because all the colors and handles are accessible through the Ramp shader's own Property Editor, as shown in Figure 7.8. The Attribute Editor will display much the same information, just slightly differently than the Property Editor.

To create a new color in any of the horizontal ramps, click in the swatch to create a new ramp position. Edit its color through its Selected Color swatch. You can move the position by grabbing the circle right above the ramp and dragging left or right. To delete a color, click the box beneath it.

These ramp textures are automatically attached to the Color, Transparency, Incandescence, Specular Color, Reflectivity, and Environment attributes of a Ramp shader. In addition, a special curve ramp is attached to the Specular Roll Off attribute to give you more precise control over how the specular highlight diminishes over the surface.

Bifrost Materials

You can see three icons marked Bifrost Materials in the Create panel, toward the top. Bifrost is a liquid simulation engine in Maya that typically uses its own materials, found here. Since I do not cover the

Figure 7.8
A Ramp shader in the Property Editor

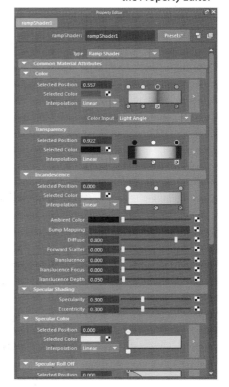

advanced workflow behind Bifrost in this book, I will leave these materials out of this book as well.

Shaderfx and Stingray PBS Shader Types

These shaders sit at the top of the Create panel in the Hypershade. Shaderfx is an editing tool for creating shader networks for game engines. Stingray is Autodesk's own game engine. Because these are advanced shaders specific to games, their functions will not be covered in this introductory book. However, in short, they will allow you to create materials and looks for your game assets in Maya and let you import those looks directly into the appropriate game engine without needing to re-create the materials in the engine itself.

Shader Attributes

Shaders are composed of nodes just like other Maya objects. Within these nodes, attributes define what shaders do. Here is a brief rundown of the common shader attributes with which you'll be working:

Color   An RGB or HSV value defines what color the shader is when it receives a neutral color light. For more on RGB and HSV, see the "RGB and HSV" sidebar in this chapter.

Transparency   The higher the Transparency value, the less opaque and more see-through the object becomes. Although usually expressed in a black-to-white gradient, with black being opaque or solid and white being totally clear, transparency can have color. In a color transparency, the shader's color shifts because only some of its RGB values are transparent, as opposed to the whole.

Ambient Color   This color affects the overall color attribute of a shader because this adds a flat ambient color irrespective of lighting in the scene. The default is black, which keeps the darker areas of a surface dark. The lighter the ambient color, the lighter those areas become. A bright Ambient Color setting flattens out an object, as shown in Figure 7.9.

RGB AND HSV

Computers represent color as sets of numeric values corresponding to the red, green, and blue channels of the image. An 8-bit image ranges from 0 to 255, so for each primary color you have 256 possible levels. With three channels, you have 256×256×256 (16.7 million) possible combinations of each primary color mixed to form the final color. Each RGB channel defines how much of that color is present in the displayed color.

Color value can also be set on the hue, saturation, and value (HSV) channels. The hue value defines the actual tint (from red to green to violet) of the color. The saturation defines *how much* of that tint is present in the color. Finally, value defines the brightness of the color, from black to white. The higher the value, the brighter the color will be.

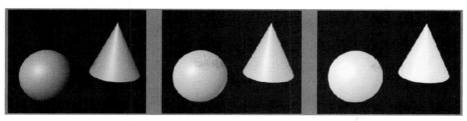

Figure 7.9
Ambient color values flatten an object.

Ambient Color = Black   Ambient Color = Medium Gray   Ambient Color = White

Figure 7.9

Ambient color values flatten an object.

Incandescence   This attribute is the ability to self-illuminate. Objects that seem to give off or have their own light, such as an office's fluorescent light fixture, can be given an Incandescence value. Incandescence doesn't, however, light objects around it in regular renders, nor does it create a glow. Also, it tends to flatten the object into a pure color (see Figure 7.10). As you'll see in Chapter 11, "Autodesk® Maya® Rendering," incandescence can also help light a scene in the mental ray® Final Gather rendering.

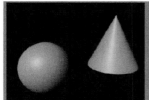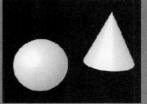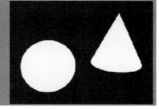

Incandescence = 0   Incandescence = 0.5   Incandescence = 1

Figure 7.10

Incandescence values

Bump Mapping   This attribute creates a textured feel for the surface by adding highlights and shadows to the render. It doesn't alter the surface of the geometry, although it makes the surface appear to have ridges, marks, scratches, and so forth. The more intense the variation in tones of a bump map, the greater the bump. Bump maps are frequently used to make surfaces look more real because nothing in reality has a perfectly smooth surface. Using bumps very close up may create problems; bumps are generally good for adding inexpensive detail to a model that isn't in extreme close-up (see Figure 7.11).

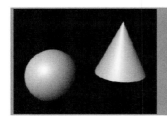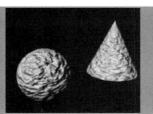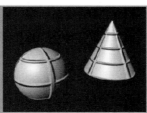

No Bump Map   Fractal Texture Bump Map   Grid Texture Bump Map

Figure 7.11

The effects of a bump map

Bump maps on geometry don't work well when seen up close. Those cases require displacement maps. I'll cover displacement maps in Chapter 11.

Diffuse   This value governs how much light is reflected from the surface in all directions. When light strikes a surface, light disperses across the surface and helps illuminate it. The higher this value, the brighter its object is when lit. The lower the Diffuse value, the more light is "absorbed" into the surface, yielding a darker result (see Figure 7.12).

Figure 7.12

How a Diffuse value affects a shader's look

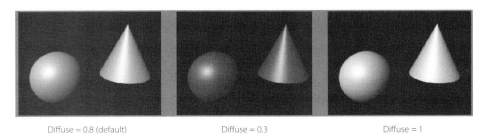

Diffuse = 0.8 (default)   Diffuse = 0.3   Diffuse = 1

Translucence and Translucence Focus   The Translucence and Translucence Focus attributes give the material the ability to transmit light through its surface, like a piece of canvas in front of a light. At a value of 1 for Translucence, all light shines through the object; at 0, none does. The Translucence Focus attribute specifies how much of that light is scattered. A light material such as paper should have a high translucence focus, and thicker surfaces should have low focus rates.

Glow Intensity   Found in the Special Effects section of the Attribute Editor, the Glow Intensity attribute adds a glow to the object, as if it were emitting light into a foggy area (see Figure 7.13). You'll add glow to an object in Chapter 10, "Autodesk® Maya® Lighting."

Figure 7.13

Adding a glow

Glow = 0   Glow = 0.5   Glow = 1

Matte Opacity   Objects rendered through Maya generate a solid *matte*. Where there is a solid object, the matte is white; where there is nothing, the matte is black. In compositing programs, which bring together elements created independently into a single composite scene, mattes help to separate rendered CG from their backgrounds. Turning down the slider decreases the brightness of the object's matte, making it appear more transparent.

For more information about mattes, see the sidebar "Image Mattes" in this chapter, and see Chapter 11.

Raytrace Options   With raytracing, you can achieve true reflections and refractions in your scene. This subset of attributes allows you to set the shader's raytracing abilities. See Chapter 11 for more on raytracing.

Some attributes are available only with certain shader types. The following are the attributes for the Phong, Phong E, and Blinn shaders because they can be shiny and reflective:

Specular Color   This sets the color of the highlights on a shiny surface. Black produces no specular, and white creates a bright one.

Reflectivity   This sets the amount of reflection visible in the surface. The higher the value, the more reflective the object will render. Increasing this value increases the visibility of the Reflected Color attribute or of true reflections in the scene when raytraced.

Reflected Color   This gives the surface a reflection. Texture maps are generally assigned to this attribute to give the object a reflection of whatever is in the image file or texture without having to generate time-consuming true reflections with a raytraced render. Using raytracing to get true reflections, however, is the only way to generate reflections of other objects in the scene.

Cosine Power   Available only with a Phong shader, this attribute changes the size of the shiny highlights (a.k.a. specular) on the surface. The higher the number, the smaller the highlight looks.

Roughness, Highlight Size, Whiteness   These control the specular highlight on a Phong E surface only. They control specular focus, amount of specular, and highlight color, respectively.

mental ray Attributes   Because Autodesk integrates features of the Nvidia mental ray rendering engine into Maya, an object's Attribute Editor usually includes a set of mental ray options. Shaders are no different. If you open the Mental Ray heading in the Attribute Editor for a shader, you'll see attributes such as Reflection Blur and Irradiance, as well as a few ways to override the Maya shading attributes with those of mental ray. You'll work with mental ray in Chapters 10 and 11.

IMAGE MATTES

Image files are stored with a red, a green, and a blue channel that keep the amount of each color in each pixel of the image. Some image formats, including TIFF and TARGA, also have an alpha channel, known as a *matte channel* or *image matte*. This is a grayscale channel that controls the opacity of an image. Completely white parts of the matte make those parts of the image opaque (solid), whereas black parts make those parts of the image fully transparent. Gray in the matte channel makes those parts of the image partly transparent. These mattes are used in *compositing*—bringing together elements created separately into a single composite scene. See Chapter 11 for an example of how an alpha channel works.

Shading and Texturing the Toy Plane

In the following section, you'll add shaders to the toy plane from Chapter 6, "Practical Experience!" This exercise is also available in a video on the book's web page, as well as my YouTube account. The plane is fairly straightforward to shade. Use bodyModel_v06.ma from the plane project from the companion website. You have just two colors on the body of the plane. You'll start by making shaders in the Hypershade.

1. With either your scene file or bodyModel_v06.ma loaded, open the Hypershade (Windows → Rendering Editors → Hypershade). You need to re-create a plastic look for the toy plane. Create two Blinn shaders by clicking Blinn in the Create column in the Hypershade twice, as shown in Figure 7.14. Name the first shader **gray** and the second shader **yellow**.

Figure 7.14

Create two Blinn shaders.

The toy plane is yellow and gray, but it has some flakes of dark gray in both colors. Figure 7.15 is a close-up photo of a yellow pontoon to showcase the dark "noise" in the plastic color. You will mimic that with a texture node called Noise.

2. In the Create Panel of the Hypershade, click 2D Textures to display the 2D texture nodes. Then click Noise to create a new noise texture, though you won't notice that it's been made immediately. Click the Textures tab at the top of the Hypershade to display the noise texture you just created, as shown in Figure 7.16 (left). MMB+drag the noise1 icon from the top of the Hypershade to the work area in the lower right of the Hypershade. The icon here (as shown in Figure 7.16, right) allows you to make shader connections easier. More on this later.

3. It doesn't look like much now, but you will adjust the attributes on this noise texture to simulate the dark flakes in the plastic. With the noise texture node still selected, in the Property Editor (or the Attribute Editor, if you prefer) set the attribute values as shown in Table 7.1, leaving the remaining attributes at their default values.

Table 7.1

Noise texture values

ATTRIBUTE	VALUE
Threshold	0.735
Amplitude	0.56
Ratio	2.02
Frequency Ratio	6.62
Spottyness	1.4

Also in the Color Balance heading, click the white color swatch next to the Color Gain attribute and set that color to a mustard yellow using the HSV values of **46.**, **0.756**, **0.472**, as shown in Figure 7.17. Click in the top of the Property Editor and rename the node from noise1 to **noiseYellow**. This color will give you the yellow you need for that plastic.

Figure 7.15

A close-up of a yellow pontoon shows flakes of dark gray in the plastic color.

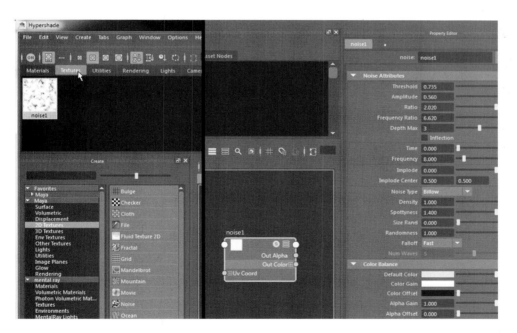

Figure 7.16

Click to create a new noise texture node and find it in the Textures tab (left). The noise1 icon in the Work Area of the Hypershade next to the Property Editor showing its attributes (right).

Figure 7.17

**Setting the noise
texture values**

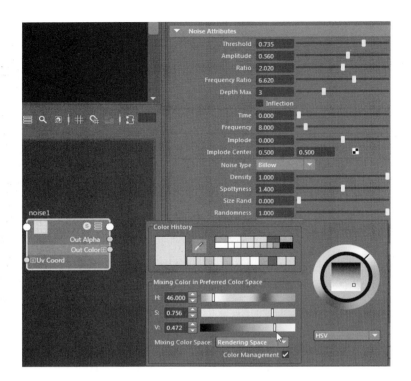

4. You'll duplicate the yellow noise node to make a blue-gray version for the gray plastic parts of the plane. In the Hypershade, select noiseYellow and choose Edit → Duplicate → Shading Network. Name the duplicate texture node **noiseGray**. The duplicated texture will appear on the Textures tab at the top of the Hypershade. MMB+drag the noiseGray texture node down to the Work Area next to the yellow one you've already created.

5. In the Color Balance heading for the noiseGray node, set the Color Gain HSV values to **231**, **0.56**, **0.20**.

6. Switch to the Materials tab and select the gray shader in the Hypershade to display it in the Property Editor. MMB+drag the grayNoise node from the Work Area to the Color attribute of the gray shader in the Attribute Editor, as shown in Figure 7.18. This will set the gray noise texture you just made to be the color of the gray plastic material.

7. Select the yellow Blinn shader and then MMB+drag the noiseYellow node from the Work Area to the Color attribute. This connects the yellow color to the yellow Blinn shader.

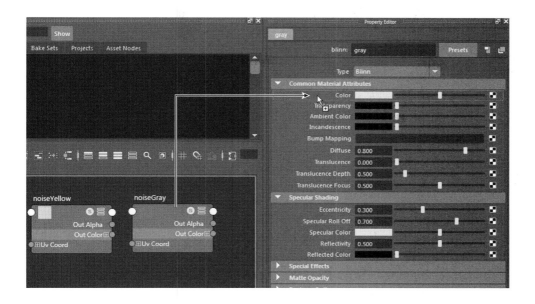

Figure 7.18

Connect the gray noise texture to the Color attribute of the gray Blinn shader.

8. Now let's assign the shaders to the parts of the plane. In the persp viewport, select the wings, body, and two pontoons and assign the yellow Blinn shader to them by RMB+clicking in the Hypershade and selecting Assign Material To Selection, as shown in Figure 7.19.

9. Select the remaining parts of the plane and assign the gray Blinn shader to them, as shown in Figure 7.20.

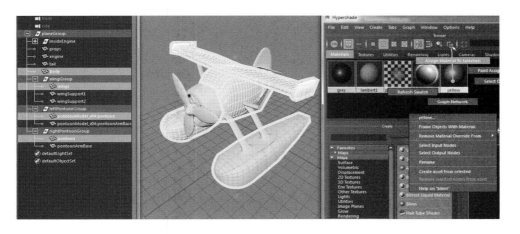

Figure 7.19

Select these parts of the plane and assign the yellow Blinn to them.

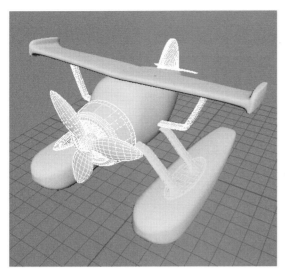

Figure 7.20

Select the remaining parts of the plane and assign the gray Blinn shader to them.

Now let's see what it looks like! In the persp viewport, render a view of your plane by clicking the Render Current frame icon on the Status line (⬛). Since you haven't created any lights in the scene, Maya will use default lights and render an image (Figure 7.21) with the basic shaders you just created. Not bad. Feel free to adjust the colors or the attributes of the noise textures to your liking. Once you start lighting the scene in Chapter 10, you will adjust the shaders to make the toy plane look like better plastic. For now, you're done! You can check your work against the scene file plane-Shading_v01.ma in the Scenes folder of the Plane project.

You can embellish a model a lot at the texturing level. The more you explore and experience shaders and modeling, the better you'll be at juggling modeling with texturing to get the most effective solution. For example, you can use more elaborate noise patterns to mimic the flakes in the plane's plastic, as opposed to using the simple pattern you created with a noise texture. That is a more involved workflow, which you will tackle later in this chapter with UVs and texture maps.

You'll begin UV layout and texturing a child's red wagon later in this chapter and then go into more detailed texturing with the decorative box, which you'll then light and render in mental ray. For even more practice, try loading the catapult model from Chapter 4, "Beginning Polygonal Modeling," and texturing it from top to bottom.

Figure 7.21

The plane renders with yellow and gray Blinn shaders to look a little like plastic.

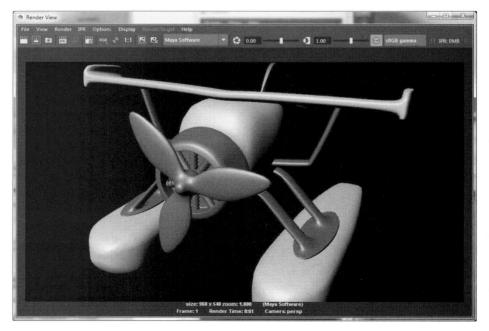

Textures and Surfaces

Texture nodes generate maps to connect to an attribute of a shader. There are two types of textures: procedural and bitmapped (sometimes called maps). *Procedural* textures use Maya attributes to generate an effect, such as a ramp gradient, checkerboard, or fractal noise texture. You can adjust each of these procedural textures by changing their attribute values.

A *map*, on the other hand, is a saved image file that is imported into the scene through a file texture node. These files are pregenerated through whatever imaging programs you have and include digital pictures and scanned photos. You need to place all texture nodes onto their surfaces through the shader. You can map them directly onto the UV values of the surface or project them.

UV Mapping

UV mapping places the texture directly on the surface and uses the surface coordinates (called UVs) for its positioning. In this case, you must do a lot of work to line up the UVs on the surface to make sure the created images line up properly. What follows is a brief summary of how UV mapping works. You'll get hands-on experience with UV layout with the red wagon and decorative box exercises later in this chapter.

Just as 3D space is based on coordinates in XYZ, surfaces have coordinates denoted by U and V values along a 2D coordinate system for width and height. The UV value helps a texture position itself on the surface. The U and V values range from 0 to 1, with (0,0) UV being the origin point of the surface.

Maya creates UVs for primitive surfaces automatically, but frequently you need to edit UVs for proper texture placement, particularly on polygonal meshes after you've edited them. In some instances, placing textures on a poly mesh requires projecting the textures onto the mesh because the poly UVs may not line up as expected after the mesh has been edited. See the next section, "Using Projections."

If the placement of your texture or image isn't quite right, simply use the 2D placement node of the texture node to position it properly. See the section "Texture Nodes" later in this chapter for more information.

Using Projections

You need to place textures on the surface. You can often do so using UV placement, but some textures need to be projected onto the surface. A *projection* is what it sounds like. The file image, ramp, or other texture being used can be *beamed* onto the object in several ways.

You can create any texture node as either a normal UV map or a projected texture. In the Create Render Node window, clicking a texture icon creates it as a normal mapped texture. To create the texture as a projection, you must RMB+click the icon and select Create As Projection (see Figure 7.22).

Figure 7.22

Selecting the type of map layout

When you create a projected texture, a new node is attached to the texture node. This projection node controls the method of projection with an attached 3D placement node, which you saw in the axe exercise. Select the projection node to set the type of projection in the Property Editor or the Attribute Editor (see Figure 7.23).

Setting the projection type will allow you to project an image or a texture without having it warp and distort, depending on the model you're mapping. For example, a planar projection on a sphere will warp the edges of the image as they stretch into infinity on the sides of the sphere.

Try This In a new scene, create a NURBS sphere and a NURBS cone and place them side-by-side. Create a Blinn shader and assign it to both objects. In the Blinn shader's Attribute Editor, set its Color attribute to a checkerboard pattern, as shown in Figure 7.24.

Now, try removing the color map from the Blinn shader you just made. In the Blinn shader's Attribute Editor, RMB+click on the word *Color*; then choose Break Connection from the context menu. Doing so severs the connection to the checker texture map node and resets the color to gray. Now, re-create a new checker texture map for the color, but this time create it as a projection by RMB+clicking the Checker texture icon in the Create Render Node window. In the illustration on the left in Figure 7.25, you see the perspective view in Texture mode (press the 6 key) with the two objects and the planar projection placement node.

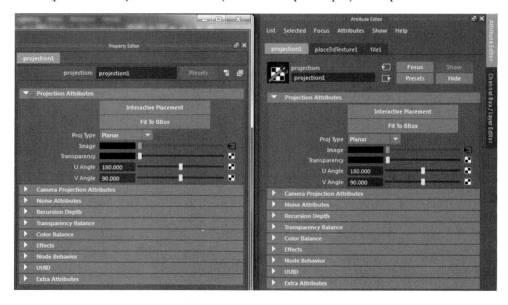

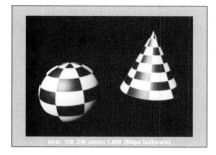

Figure 7.24

Assign a checkerboard pattern to the sphere and cone with Normal checked.

Figure 7.25

A planar projection checkerboard in the viewport (left) and rendered (right)

Try moving the planar placement object around in the scene to see how the texture maps itself to the objects. The illustration on the right of Figure 7.25 shows the rendered objects.

Try the other projection types to see how they affect the texture being mapped.

Projection placement nodes control how the projection maps its image or texture onto the surface. Using a sphere with a spherical projected checker, with U and V wrap turned off on the checkerboard texture, you can see how manipulating the place3dTexture node affects the texture.

In addition to the Move, Rotate, and Scale tools, you can use the special manipulator (press T to activate or click the Show Manipulator Tool icon in the toolbar) to adjust the placement as you watch it update on your object. However, your viewport may not display a projected map properly, so in your viewport, choose Renderer and select Legacy High Quality Viewport, as shown in Figure 7.26, where you will see the special manipulator for the Spherical projection as well.

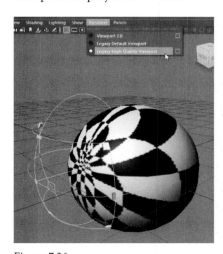

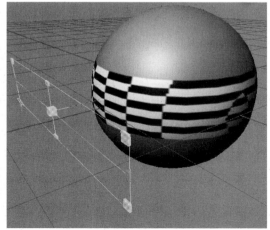

Figure 7.26

The spherical projection's manipulator tool

Figure 7.27

The manipulator wrapping the checkerboard texture around the sphere (left of image, perspective view; right of image, rendered view)

Drag the handles on the special manipulator to change the coverage of the projection, orientation, size, and so forth. All projection types have special manipulators. Figure 7.27 shows the manipulator wrapping the checkerboard pattern in a thin band all the way around the sphere (shown in Legacy High Quality Viewport as shown in Figure 7.26).

To summarize, projection textures depend on a projector node to position the texture onto the geometry. If the object assigned to a projected texture is moving, consider grouping the projection placement node to the object itself in the Outliner.

Texture Nodes

You can create a number of texture nodes in Maya. This section covers the most important. All texture nodes, however, have common attributes that affect their final look. In the Hypershade, click to create any node from the 2D Textures section in the Create panel (in this case, a checker) and take a look at its attributes in the Hypershade's Property Editor (see Figure 7.28). The Color Balance and Effects headings affect the color of the texture (as you saw with the noise textures from the plane exercise).

Color Balance   This set of attributes adjusts the overall brightness and color balance of your texture. Use these attributes to tint or brighten a texture without having to change all the individual attributes of the shader.

Effects   You can invert the texture's color space by clicking the Invert check box. This changes black to white and white to black in addition to inverting the RGB values of colors.

You can map textures to almost any shader attribute for detail. Even the tiniest amount of texture on a surface's bump, specular, or color increases its realism.

Figure 7.28

Some common attributes for all texture nodes

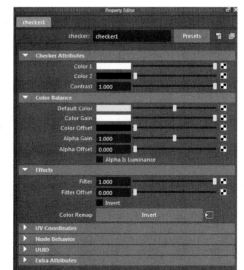

Place2dTexture Nodes

The 2D texture nodes come with a 2D placement node that controls their repetition, rotation, size, offset, and so on. You can immediately access this node in the Attribute Editor by clicking its tab, or in the Hypershade, select the texture node from the Textures tab (in this case a checker) and click the Input And Output Connections icon in the Hypershade. Then click the place2dTexture node and examine its attributes in the Property Editor. Adjust the setting in this node of your 2D texture in the Attribute Editor, or Property Editor as shown in Figure 7.29, to position it within the Shader network.

The Repeat UV setting controls how many times the texture is repeated on whatever shader attribute it's connected to, such as Color. The higher the wrap values, the smaller the texture appears, but the more times it appears on the surface.

The Wrap U and Wrap V check boxes allow the texture to wrap around the edges of their limits to repeat. When these check boxes are turned off, the texture appears only once, and the rest of the surface is the color of the Default Color attribute found in the texture node.

The Mirror U and Mirror V settings allow the texture to mirror itself when it repeats. The Coverage, Translate Frame, and Rotate Frame settings control where the image is mapped. They're useful for positioning a digital image or a scanned picture.

Ramp Texture

A *ramp* is a gradient in which one color transitions into the next color. A ramp is useful for many things, but mostly it's perfect for making color gradients. Initially the ramp texture will show as a simple black-to-white gradient (from left to right), as shown in Figure 7.30.

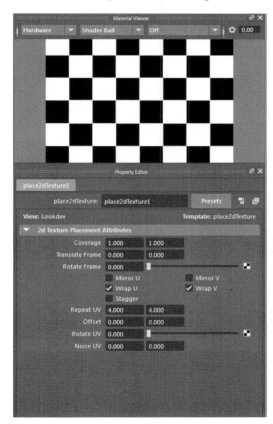

Figure 7.29

A 2D placement node in the Hypershade Property Editor (while in default Lookdev view mode, with the Material Viewer showing the checker pattern)

Figure 7.30

The ramp texture in the Property Editor

But it's easy to create gradients using any colors. Simply use the round handles on top of the ramp to select that color and to move it left and right on the ramp. The square handle at the bottom deletes the color. To create a new color, click inside the ramp. Figure 7.31 shows a multicolored ramp. Clicking the right arrow button to the right of the ramp shown in Figure 7.31 will open a larger ramp window to work with if you need extra precision. Note that Figure 7.31 is from the Attribute Editor and not the Hypershade Property Editor.

Figure 7.31

Adding and changing colors in a ramp is easy!

The ramp *texture* is different from the Ramp *shader*. The Ramp shader automatically has several ramp textures mapped to some of its attributes.

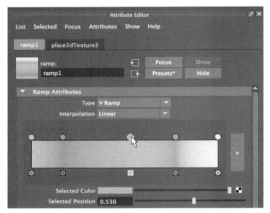

The Type setting allows you to create a gradient running along the U or V direction of the surface, as well as to make circular, radial, diagonal, and other types of gradients. The Interpolation setting controls how the colors grade from one to the next. Experiment with them to see how they work.

The U Wave and V Wave attributes let you add a squiggle to the U or V coordinate of the ramp, and the Noise and Noise Freq (frequency) attributes specify randomness for the placement of the ramp colors throughout the surface.

Using the HSV Color Noise attributes, you can specify random noise patterns of hue, saturation, and value to add some interest to your texture. The HSV Color Noise options are great for making your shader just a bit different to enhance its look.

Fractal, Noise, and Mountain Textures

The Fractal, Noise, and Mountain textures are used to create a random noise pattern to add to an object's color, transparency, or any other shader attribute. For example, when creating a surface, you'll almost always want to add a little dirt or a few surface blemishes to the shader to make the object look less CG. These textures are commonly used for creating bump maps.

Bulge, Cloth, Checker, Grid, and Water Textures

The Bulge, Cloth, Checker, Grid, and Water textures help create surface features when used on a shader's Bump Mapping attribute. Each creates an interesting pattern to add to a surface to create tactile detail, but you can also use them to create color or specular irregularities.

When used as a texture for a bump, Grid is useful for creating the spacing between tiles, Cloth is perfect for clothing, and Checker is good for rubber grips. Placing a Water texture on a slight reflection makes for a nice poolside reflection in patio furniture.

The File Node

You use the file node to import image files into Maya for texturing. For instance, if you want to texture a CG face with a digital picture of your own face, you can use the file node to import a Maya-supported image file.

Importing an Image File as a Texture

To attach an image to the Color attribute of a Lambert shader, for example, follow these steps:

1. Create a Lambert shader in the Hypershade. (Phong, Blinn, or any of the shaders will do.)

2. Click the Map button ( ) next to the Color attribute of the new Lambert shader to map a texture to it. RMB+click the File button in the Create Render Node window that pops up and select Create Texture. The Attribute Editor shows the attributes for the file node (with an image already loaded); see Figure 7.32.

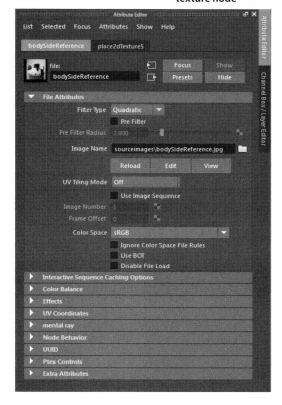

Figure 7.32

The file texture node

3. Next to the Image Name attribute, click the Folder icon to open the file browser to select an image. Find the image file of choice on your computer. (It's best to put images to use as textures in the project's Sourceimages folder. As a matter of fact, the file browser defaults directly to the Sourceimages folder of your current project.) Double-click the file to load it.

4. After you import the image file, it connects to the Color attribute of that shader and also automatically connects the alpha to transparency if there is an alpha channel in the image. You can position it as you please by using its place2dTexture node or by manipulating the projection node if you created the file texture node as a projection.

You can attach an image file to any attribute of a shader that is *mappable*, meaning it's able to accept a texture node. Frequently, image files are used for the color of a shader as well as for bump and transparency maps. You can replace the image file by double-clicking the file texture node in the Hypershade and choosing another image file with the file browser.

ATTRIBUTE EDITOR VS. PROPERTY EDITOR

You can choose to view and edit material (shader) and texture nodes in either the Hypershade's Property Editor or the Attribute Editor in the main UI. I prefer the Attribute Editor as it gives you a small preview icon of your material or texture in the upper-left corner. However using the Property Editor right in the Hypershade is fast and convenient. You can use one or the other as you choose as you continue with the steps in this book.

Using Photoshop Files: The PSD File Node

Maya can also use Adobe Photoshop PSD files as image files in creating shading networks. The advantage of using PSD files is that you can specify the layers within the Photoshop file for different attributes of the shader, as opposed to importing several image files to map onto each shader attribute separately. This, of course, requires a modest knowledge of Photoshop and some experience with Maya shading. As you learn how to shade with Maya, you'll come to appreciate the enhancements inherent in using Photoshop networks.

Try This　You'll create a single Photoshop file that will shade this sphere with color as well as transparency and a bump. Again, you're doing this instead of creating three different image files (such as TIFFs) for each of those shading attributes.

1. Create a poly sphere in a new scene and assign a new Lambert shader to it through the Hypershade. This creates a new shader and assigns it to the selection, in this case your sphere.

2. Select the sphere and in the Rendering menu set (F6), choose Texturing → Create PSD Network. In the option box that opens, select Color, Transparency, and Bump from the list of attributes on the left side and click the right arrow to move them to the Selected Attributes list on the right, as shown in Figure 7.33.

3. Select a location and filename for the PSD image's location. By default, Maya places the PSD file it generates in the Sourceimages folder of your current project, named after the surface to which it applies. Click Create.

4. In Photoshop, open the newly created PSD file. You see three layers grouped under three folders named after the shader attributes you selected when creating the PSD file. There are folders for lambert2.bump, lambert2.transparency, and lambert2.color, as well as a layer called UVSnapShot.

　　The UVSnapShot layer gives you a wireframe layout of the UVs on the sphere as a guideline to paint your textures. Because the sphere is an easy model, you don't need this layer, so turn it off. You'll use UV SnapShot later in this chapter when texturing a toy wagon.

You can now paint whatever image you want into each of the layers to create maps for each of the shader attributes, all in one convenient file. Save the PSD file. You can save over it or create a new filename for the painted file.

5. In Maya, open the Hypershade, and open the Attribute Editor for the Lambert shader assigned to the sphere (in this case, Lambert2). If you graph the connections to the Lambert shader in the Hypershade window's work panel, you see that the PSD file you generated is already connected to the Color, Bump, and Transparency attributes of the shader, with the proper layering set for you, as shown in Figure 7.34. Note however, the icons for the PSD layers (Color, Bump, and Transparency) all display the topmost layer of the PSD, in this case the Bump. This is normal, however irritating.

6. Open the file nodes for the shader and replace the PSD file with your new painted PSD file. If you saved your PSD file with the same name, all you need to do is click the Reload button to update the psdFile node.

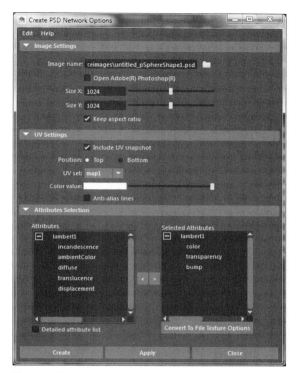

Figure 7.33

The Create PSD Network Options window

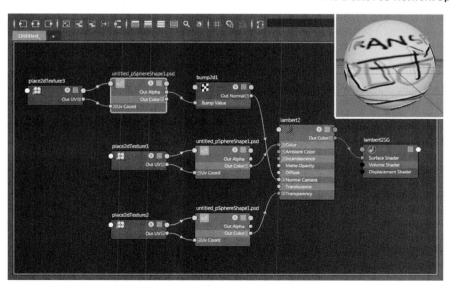

Figure 7.34

The PSD network for the Lambert shader in the Hypershade shows the connections to Color, Bump, and Transparency. The image inset (upper right) shows the sphere with the different PSD layers applied appropriately in Maya's viewport 2.0.

If you decide you need to add another attribute to the PSD file's layering or if you need to remove an attribute, you can edit the PSD network. Select the shader in the Hypershade and choose Edit → Edit PSD Network. In the option box, select new attributes to assign to the PSD file or remove existing attributes and their corresponding Photoshop layer groups. When you click Apply or Edit, Maya saves over the PSD file with the new layout.

3D and Environment Textures

3D textures are projected within a 3D space. These textures are great for objects that need to reflect an environment, for example.

Instead of simply applying the texture to the plane of the surface as 2D textures do, 3D textures create an area in which the shader is affected. As an object moves through a scene with a 3D placement node, its shader looks as if it swims, unless that placement node is parented or constrained to that object. (For more on constraints, see Chapter 9, "More Animation!")

Disconnecting a Texture

Sometimes, the texture you've applied to an object isn't what you want, and you need to remove it from the shader. To do so, double-click the shader in the Hypershade to open its Attribute Editor.

You can then disconnect an image file or any other texture node from the shader's attribute by RMB+clicking the attribute's name in the Attribute Editor and choosing Break Connection from the context menu, as shown in Figure 7.35.

Figure 7.35

RMB+clicking a shader's attribute allows you to disconnect a texture node from the shader.

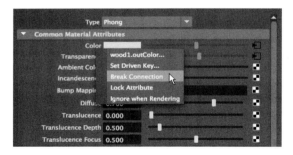

Textures and UVs for the Red Wagon

Now you'll assign shaders to a child's red wagon toy model. Figure 7.36 shows the real wagon. If you are reading a digital copy of this book, you can see the colors in Figure 7.36 easily. Otherwise, you can download the ColorWagon.tif photo from the book's website. The wagon is fairly simple; it will need a few colored shaders (Red, Black, Blue, and White) for the body, along with a few texture maps for the decals—which is where the real fun begins. The wagon will also require some more intricate work on the shaders and textures for the wood railings and silver metal screws, bolts, and handlebar; these will be a good foray into image maps and UVs.

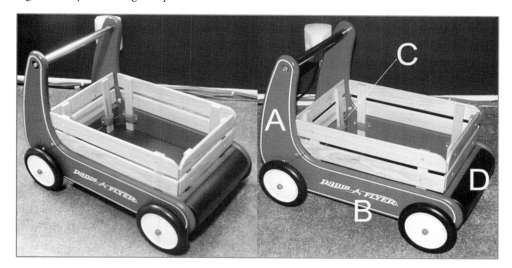

Figure 7.36

The red wagon and its named parts

This exercise is a prime example of how lighting and shading go hand in hand.

Assigning Shaders

Load the file RedWagonModel.ma from the Scenes folder of the RedWagon project to begin shading the model of the wagon.

Shading is the common term for adding shaders to an object.

Study the color images of the wagon and see how light reflects off its plastic, metal, and wood surfaces. Blinn shaders will be perfect for nearly all the parts of the wagon. Follow these steps:

1. Open the Hypershade window and create four Blinn shaders.

2. Assign the following HSV values to the Color attribute of each Blinn shader and name them as shown in Table 7.2 and in Figure 7.37. You'll create the Chrome Metal and Wood shaders later.

WAGON COLOR	SHADER NAME	H VALUE	S VALUE	V VALUE
Red	Red	355	0.910	0.650
Black	Black	0	0	0
White	White	0	0	1
Blue	Blue	220	0.775	0.560

Table 7.2

HSV color values for the wagon's colors

Figure 7.37

Create the four colored Blinn shaders.

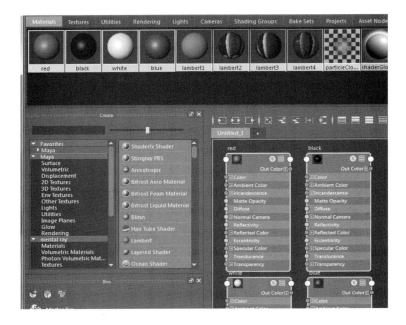

Initial Assignments

Look at the color image of the wagon from the book's web page (or in the e-edition of the book). The bullnose and tires are black, the wheel rims are white, the floor is blue, the screws and bolts and handlebar are chrome metal, the railings are wood, and the main body is red. Assign shaders to the wagon according to the color photo and the following steps:

1. In the viewport, select the side panels (the A and B panels, without the screws and bolts) and the wheel rim caps, as shown in Figure 7.38, and assign the Red Blinn shader to them. Press 6 to enter Texture Display mode.

2. Select the wheelMesh objects for all four wheels and assign them the White shader. The tires also turn white, but you'll fix that shortly; don't worry about it now. See Figure 7.39.

3. Select the bullnose (the rounded cylinder in front of the wagon) and assign it the Black Blinn.

4. Select the wagonFloor object and assign it the Red shader, as shown in Figure 7.40. You'll notice that the front and back bodies of the wagon turn red like they're supposed to, but so does the floor of the wagon, which should be blue according to the photo. If you try to assign the Blue shader to the wagon floor mesh, the floor will be correct, but the front and back of the wagon will be blue and not red. You'll fix this later.

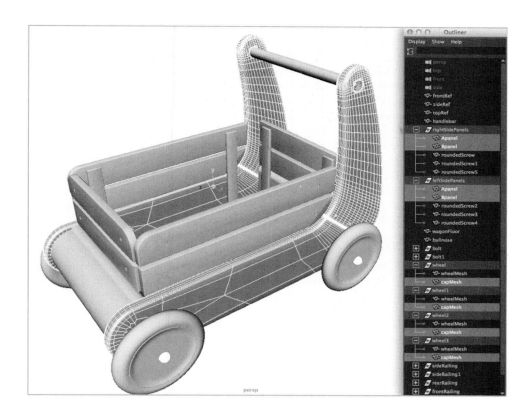

Figure 7.38
Assign the Red shader.

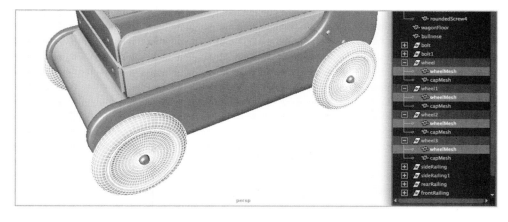

Figure 7.39
Assign the White shader.

Figure 7.40

Assign the Red shader to the wagon floor just for now; you'll change it to blue later.

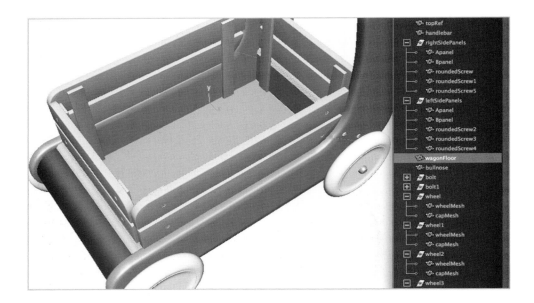

Now you have initial assignments for the basic colors of the wagon's body. Let's tweak these shaders' colors next.

Figure 7.41

The tire on the wagon

Creating a Shading Network for the Wheels

Refer to Figure 7.41 to observe how the materials are different for the rim and the tire of the wheel. The rim is glossier and has a tighter, sharper specular, whereas the tire has a diffuse specular and is quite bumpy. You'll create a Layered shader for the wheels with white feeding into the rim portion and black into the tire portion.

Coloring the Wheel

First you need to determine where the white ends and the black starts on the surface of the wheel mesh.

Figure 7.42

Set the ramp to a U Ramp type.

1. Select the White shader in the Hypershade window. Click the Map icon (■) next to the Color attribute. RMB+click the Ramp Texture icon and select Create Texture. The wheel's color turns to a black-to-white gradient clockwise around the wheel, which is the wrong direction; you need the gradient to run from the center to the edge. In the ramp texture's Property Editor, set Type to U Ramp, as shown in Figure 7.42.

If the ramp doesn't show up in your viewports, make sure you press 6 to enter Texture Display mode. If the colors and ramp texture still don't display, make sure Use Default Material isn't checked in the viewport's Shading menu.

2. Now the gradient is running black from the center to light gray on the outside edge through to white on the reverse side of the wheel. Select the round handle for the black color and change Selected Color to white. Then select the round white handle on the right side of the ramp and change Selected Color to black.

3. Click in the middle of the ramp to create a new color, which will be gray. Set that color to black. Move that new black handle in the ramp until its Selected Position value is about 0.6, as shown in Figure 7.43. Note that I am using the Attribute Editor to adjust the ramp in this figure, though you can use the Property Editor as well.

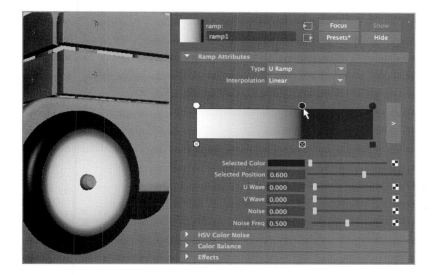

Figure 7.43

Move the new black handle.

4. Set the Interpolation attribute (found above the ramp color) to None so you get clean transitions from white to black, instead of a soft linear gradient where the black slowly grades to white. Name this ramp **wheelPositionRamp**.

5. The backs of the wheels are solid black. In the wheelPositionRamp, move the round handle for the black color all the way at the right of the ramp and set that color to white; set its position to about **0.920** to place white behind the wheels, keeping the black only where the tire is. See Figure 7.44.

Now that you've pinpointed where the white rim ends and the black tire begins, you'll use this ramp as a transparency texture to place the Tire shader on top of the Rim shader in a Layered shader that you'll create later. This will allow you to have two different materials on your tire, a smooth white plastic and a rough black plastic.

Figure 7.44
**Setting the tire loca-
tion using a ramp**

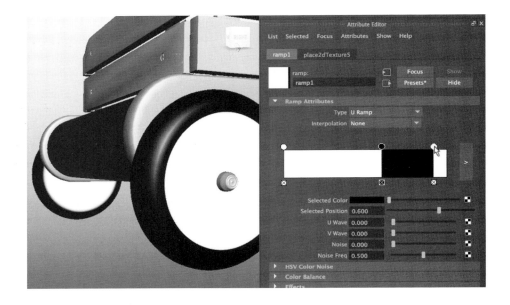

6. You don't need this Ramp shader on the color of the shader anymore—you did this so you could easily see the ramp positions on the wheel in the viewports. In the Hypershade, select the White shader and click the Input And Output Connections icon ( ) to graph the shader in the work area, as shown in Figure 7.45.

Figure 7.45
**The White shader
has the ramp
attached as color.**

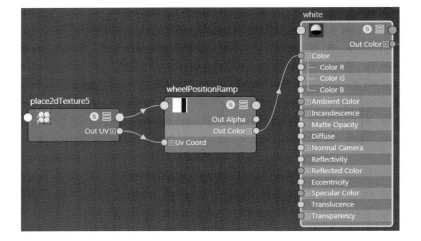

7. In the Property Editor, RMB+click the Color attribute and select Break Connection from the context menu to disconnect the ramp from the color. Set the Color back to white. Notice that the rubber band link connecting the ramp texture node to the White shader node disappears in the Hypershade window.

8. Create a Layered shader. MMB+drag the White shader from the Hypershade to the top of the Layered Shader Attributes window, as shown in Figure 7.46. Delete the default Green shader in the Attribute Editor by clicking the checked box below its swatch.

9. Create a new Blinn shader and set its color to black. Name the shader **tireShader**. Select the Layered shader and then MMB+drag the new tireShader from the Hypershade to the Layered shader's Attribute Editor (or Property Editor in the Hypershade) and then place it to the left of the White shader, as shown in Figure 7.47. Name the Layered shader **wheelShader**.

10. Select the wheels and assign the wheelShader Layered shader to them. The wheels should appear all white (yours may turn all black). This is where the ramp you created earlier (wheelPositionRamp) will come into play in the next steps.

11. Select the wheelShader and click Input And Output Connections to graph the network in the Work Area of the Hypershade window. In the top panel of the Hypershade, click the Texture tab to display the texture nodes in the scene so you can see wheelPositionRamp's node.

12. In the wheelShader's Attribute Editor, click the tireShader swatch on the left. MMB+drag the wheelPositionRamp node to the Transparency attribute, as shown in Figure 7.48.

Figure 7.46

Drag the White shader to the Layered shader and delete the default Green shader from it.

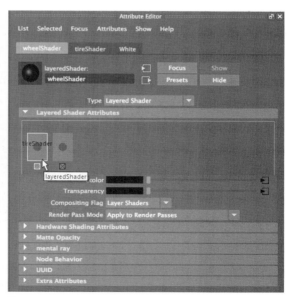

Figure 7.47

MMB drag the black tireShader material to the Layered Shader.

Figure 7.48

Attach the ramp to the Transparency attribute of the tireShader in the wheelShader.

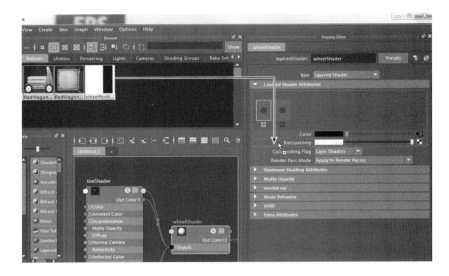

13. When you attach the ramp, the wheelShader icon turns white on top and black on the bottom. Render a frame in the persp viewport to make sure the black tires line up properly, as shown in Figure 7.49. The wheel coloring is complete!

Figure 7.49

The tires are done!

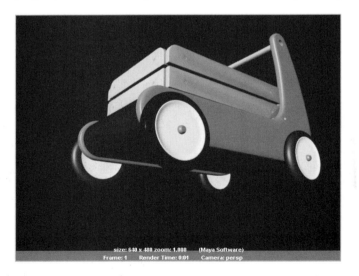

HEY, HOLD ON A MINUTE: WHY TWO SHADERS?

Why did you go through a Layered shader with two different shaders (one white and one black) when you could more easily use one shader and assign the same black-to-white ramp to its color? You did this because the white rim and the black tire are different materials, and you need to use two different shaders to properly show that in renders.

Setting the Feel for the Materials and Adding a Bump Map

Because the material look and feel on the real wheels differs quite a bit between the rim and the tire, you'll further tweak the white rim and the black tire shaders. The rim is a smooth, glossy white, and the tire is a bumpy black with a broad specular. Follow these steps:

1. Let's set up a good angle of view for your test renders. Position your persp viewport to resemble the view in Figure 7.50. Render a frame.

2. Select the White shader and set Eccentricity to **0.05** and Specular Roll Off to **0.5**. Doing so sharpens the specular highlight on the rim.

3. Select the black tireShader and set Eccentricity to **0.375** and Specular Roll Off to **0.6** to make the highlight more diffuse across the tire. Set Reflectivity to **0.05**. Render a frame; refer to Figure 7.51 to see how the specular highlight is broader and less glossy than in Figure 7.50.

4. Open the Attribute Editor for the tireShader and click the Map icon ( ) in the Bump Mapping section. In the Create Render Node window, click to create a fractal texture map. Notice that the entire wheelShader icon becomes bumpy. Render a frame, and you'll see that the entire wheel is bumpy—not just the tire. (See Figure 7.52.) Argh!

5. You have to use the wheelPositionRamp to prevent the bump from showing on the white rim. Select the wheelShader and click the Input And Output Connections icon ( ) in the Hypershade to graph its network (Figure 7.53).

Figure 7.50

Set your view to this angle and render a frame.

Figure 7.51

Setting specular levels

Figure 7.52

The whole wheel becomes bumpy!

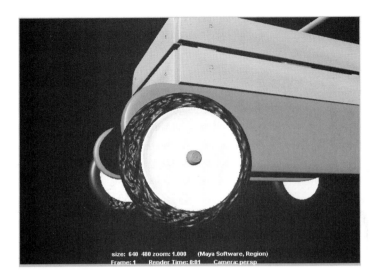

Figure 7.53

Graph the wheel-Shader network.

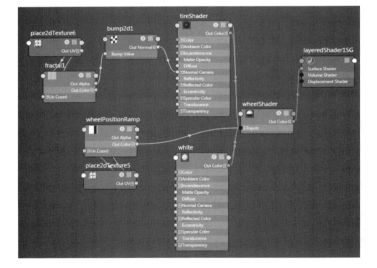

Notice the single green connecting line between the fractal1 node's OutAlpha output socket and the bump2d1 node's BumpValue input socket in the Hypershade. This means the alpha channel of the fractal feeds the amount of bump that is rendered on the tireShader. You have to alter the alpha coming out of the fractal node with the positioning ramp to block the rim from having any bump. The white areas of the ramp allow the bump map from the fractal to show on the tire, whereas the black area of the ramp keeps any bump from appearing. Because you already used this ramp to position the Rim shader and the Tire shader on the wheel, it will work perfectly for the bump position as well.

6. Select the fractal to display it in the Attribute Editor and MMB+drag the wheelPosi-tionRamp from the Hypershade to the Alpha Gain attribute for the fractal, as shown in Figure 7.54.

Figure 7.54

MMB+drag the ramp to the Alpha Gain attribute of the fractal.

7. Render a frame, and you see that now the tire has no bump and the rim is bumpy (Figure 7.55).

Figure 7.55

The tire is smooth, and now the rim is bumpy.

Figure 7.56
Create a reverse node.

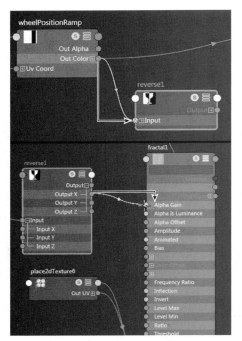

Figure 7.57
First connect the ramp to the Reverse node (top image). Then connect the Reverse node to the Fractal node (bottom image).

8. This is easy enough to fix. All you need to do is reverse the ramp and then feed that reversal into the Alpha Gain attribute of the fractal so that the tire is bumpy and the rim is smooth. In the Hypershade, in the Create pane on the left, click the Maya → Utilities heading and then click the Reverse icon to create a reverse node in the Hypershade window's Utilities tab. See Figure 7.56. MMB+drag this new Reverse node from the top of the Hypershade (in the Utilities tab) down to the work area.

9. In the Hypershade, click+drag the OutColor socket of the wheelPositionRamp node onto the Input socket of the Reverse node and release the mouse button. This connects the output of the ramp into the reverse node, which will then reverse the effect of the ramp on the fractal when you connect it in the next step. Figure 7.57 (left).

10. On the fractal1 node's upper right, click the node display size icon (▤) until the three slots are filled white (▤). This expands the fractal1 icon to display more input and output sockets. In the upper-right corner of the reverse1 node, click the plus symbol next to Output (Output⊞●) to display Output X, Output Y, and Output Z sockets as shown in Figure 7.57 (right).

11. Drag the Output X socket from the reverse1 node to the Alpha Gain input socket on the fractal1 node.

12. Open the Render Settings window by choosing Windows → Rendering Editors → Render Settings (or click the Render Settings icon [▣] in the status bar at the top of the UI). Click the Maya Software tab and set Quality to Production Quality in the pulldown menu. (See Figure 7.58.) Render a frame; you finally have a bump on the tire and a smooth rim. See Figure 7.59.

13. It's not a convincing bump yet, so select the fractal node and set Ratio to **0.85**. In the Hypershade, click the Placement node icon for the fractal (it should be called something like *place2dTexture6*), and in the Property Editor, set the Repeat UV values to **18** and **48**, as shown in Figure 7.60. Doing so makes the fractal pattern finely speckled on the tire.

14. Render a frame; the fractal's scale on the bumpy tire looks too strong. Double-click the bump2d node in the Hypershade, and in the Property Editor, set Bump Depth to **0.04**. Render and check your frame against Figure 7.61. The bump looks much better, if not a little strong from this angle; you can finesse it to taste from here.

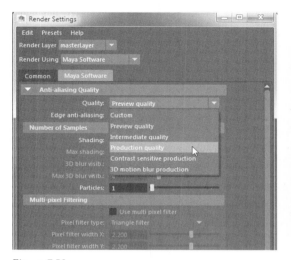

Figure 7.58

Set Quality to Production Quality.

Figure 7.59

Now you have the bump where you need it.

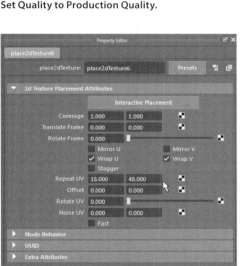

Figure 7.60

Set the Repeat UV values for the fractal map.

Figure 7.61

The wheel looks pretty good.

Tire Summary

Congratulations! You've made your first somewhat complex shading network, as shown in Figure 7.62. By now, you should have a pretty good idea of how to get around the Hypershade and create shading networks. To recap, you're using a ramp to place the two different (Tire and Rim) shaders on the wheel, as well as using it to place the bump map on just the tire part by using a reverse node. The more times you make shading networks, the easier they will become to create.

Figure 7.62

Your first complex shading network

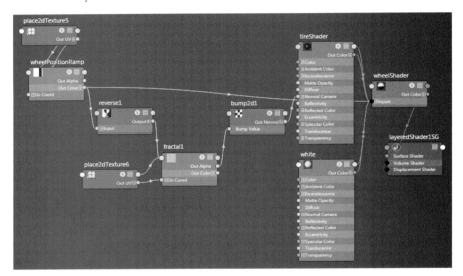

This type of shading is called *procedural shading* because you used nothing but stock Maya texture nodes to accomplish what you needed for the wheels. In the following sections, you'll make good use of image mapping to create the decals for the wagon body as well as the wood for the railings.

You can load the file RedWagonTexture_v01.ma from the Scenes folder of the RedWagon project to check your work or skip to this point.

Figure 7.63

You need to add the body decals.

Putting Decals on the Body

Figure 7.63 shows you the decals that need to go onto the body of the wagon. They include the wagon's logo, which you'll replace with your own graphic design, and the white stripe that lines the side panels.

Instead of trying to make a procedural texture as you did with the wheel, you'll create an image map that will texture the side panels' white stripe. The stripe is far too difficult to create otherwise. You'll create an image file using Photoshop (or another image editor) to make sure the white stripe (and later the red wagon logo) lines up correctly.

Working with UVs

Mapping polygons can involve the task of defining UV coordinates for them so that you can more easily paint an image map for the mesh. When you create a NURBS surface, UV coordinates are inherent to the surface. At the *origin* (or the beginning) of the surface, the UV coordinate is (0,0). When the surface extends all the way to the left and all the way up, the UV coordinate is (1,1). When you paint an 800×600-pixel image in Photoshop, for example, it's safe to assume that the first pixel of the image (at $X = 0$ and $Y = 0$ in Photoshop) will map directly to the UV coordinate (0,0) on the NURBS surface, whereas the top-right pixel in the image will map to the UV (1,1) of the surface. Toward that end, mapping an image to a NURBS surface is fairly straightforward. The bottom of the image will map to the bottom of the surface, the top to the top, and so on. Figure 7.64 shows how an image is mapped onto a NURBS plane and a NURBS sphere.

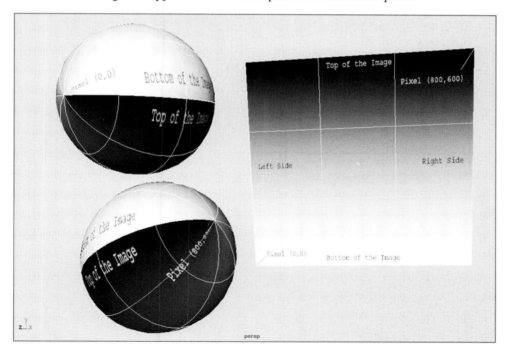

Figure 7.64

An image file is mapped to a NURBS plane and a NURBS sphere. Notice the locations marked in the image and how they map to the locations on the surface, with the pixel coordinates directly corresponding to the surface's UV coordinates.

The locations in the image, marked by text, correspond to the positions on the NURBS plane. The sphere, because it's a surface bent around spherically, shows that the origin of the UV coordinates is at the sphere's pole on the left and that the image wraps itself around it (bowing out in the middle) to meet at the seam along the front edge as shown.

When you're creating polygons, however, this isn't always the case. You must sometimes create your own UV coordinates on a polygonal surface to get a clean layout on which to paint in Photoshop. Although poly UV mapping becomes fairly involved and complicated, it's a concept that is important to grasp early. When poly models are created, they have UV coordinates; however, these coordinates may not be laid out in the best way for texture-image manipulation.

Working with the A Panels

Let's look at how the UVs are laid out for the A panel of the wagon model. Use Figure 7.36 earlier in the chapter to remind yourself where the A panel is.

1. Using the scene file RedWagonTexture_v01.ma from the Scenes folder of the RedWagon project, select the A panel on one side of the wagon and choose Windows → UV Editor, as shown in Figure 7.65.

Figure 7.65

The A panel in the UV Editor

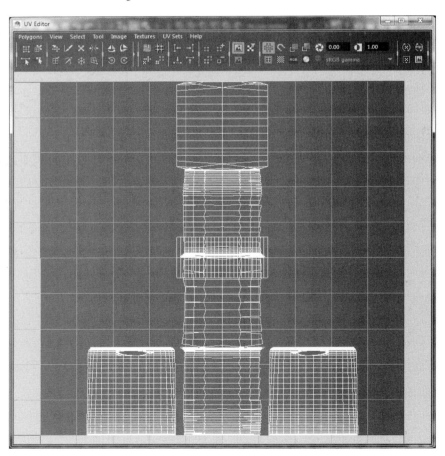

This section assumes you have some working knowledge of Adobe Photoshop. You can skip the creation of the maps and use the maps already on the companion web page, which are called out in the text later in the exercise.

The UV Editor works almost like any other viewport. You may navigate the window and zoom in and out using the familiar Alt+mouse button combinations.

2. RMB+click any part of the wireframe layout in the UV Editor window and select UV to enter the UV selection. Select the entire wireframe mesh at the lower right, as shown in Figure 7.66. Notice that green points are selected—almost as if they were vertices. These are UV points, and they're what define the UV coordinates on that part of the mesh. Look in the perspective viewport; the entire front face of the A panel is selected as well as the green UV points.

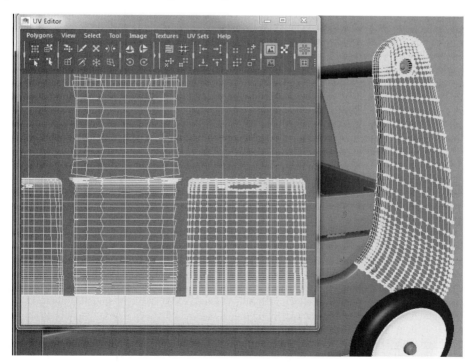

Figure 7.66

Select the UVs on this part of the A panel mesh.

Feel free to select parts of the UV layout in the UV Editor to see what corresponding points appear on the mesh in the persp viewport. This will help orient you as to how the UV layout works on this mesh.

3. You need to again lay out just this area of the mesh's UVs. Because you already have the entire front side of the panel selected in UVs, let's convert that selection to poly faces on the model. In the Modeling menu set and in the Maya main menu bar, choose Select → Convert Selection → To Faces. The front faces of the A panel mesh are now selected, as shown in Figure 7.67. You can always manually select just the front faces of the mesh, but this conversion method is much faster. The UV Editor shows just those faces now.

Figure 7.67

Convert the UVs you just selected to a face selection. This method easily isolates the front faces of the A panel for you to lay out their UVs again.

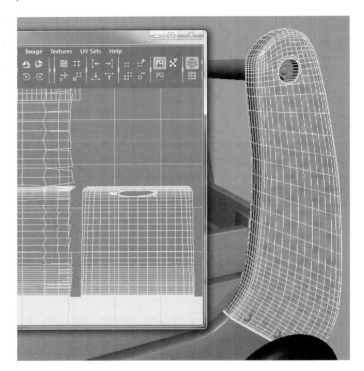

4. With those faces selected, make sure you're in the Modeling menu set. In the main menu bar, choose UV → Planar ❐ from the Create section of the UV menu. In the option box, set the Project From option to X Axis, check the Keep Image Width/ Height Ratio option, and then click Project. (See Figure 7.68.) The UV Editor shows the front A panel face.

5. Now the front face has a much simpler UV layout from which to paint. However, it's centered in the UV Editor and will overlap the other UVs of the same mesh. You should move and size it to fit into its original corner, more or less, to make sure no UVs double up on each other. First, double-click the Move tool icon to open its options and make sure that Symmetry is turned off. If Symmetry is enabled for the Move tool, this and the following steps will not work for you.

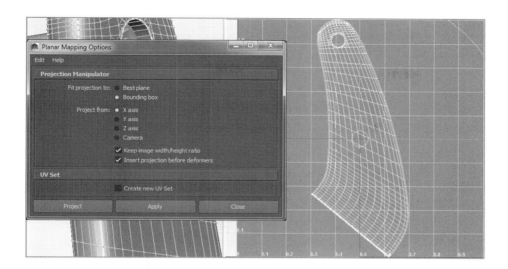

Figure 7.68

Create a planar projection for the UV layout.

6. In the UV Editor, RMB+click the wireframe and select Shell to enter Shell selection. Move your cursor over the new UV shape you just created of the A panel, and the wireframe "shell" appears green in the UV Editor. See Figure 7.69. Click to select that shape, and it turns orange when you move the cursor away (as if it has selected the faces, which is perfect).

7. Press W for the Move tool and move the selected UV shell to the side of the UV Editor. Press R for the Scale tool and scale the shell down a bit to fit into the corner, as shown in Figure 7.70.

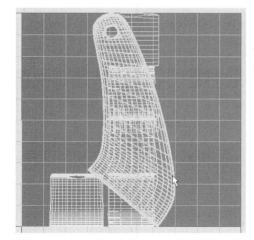

Figure 7.69

The UV shell for the A panel, representing all of the front side's UVs

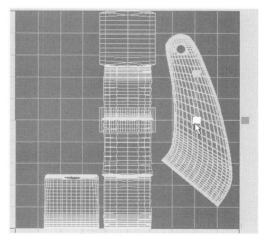

Figure 7.70

Position these UVs to make sure they don't overlap the rest of the A panel mesh's UVs.

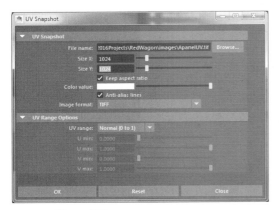

Figure 7.71

Settings for the UV snapshot

8. Earlier in the chapter, you saw how to write out a PSD file with a UV snapshot as one of its layers. You'll use a similar technique to paint the decal for the panel. Click an empty area of the UV Editor to deselect everything. Then, in Object Selection mode (press F8 if you need to exit Component Selection), select the A panel mesh in the persp viewport in the main Maya UI.

9. In the UV Editor window, select Polygons → UV Snapshot to open the option box. Set both Size X and Size Y to **1024**. Change the image format to TIFF, click the Browse button at the top next to the File Name field, and navigate to the RedWagon project's Sourceimages folder on your hard drive. Name the file `ApanelUV_mine.tif`, and click Save. Note that the Sourceimages folder already has a `ApanelUV.tif` for your convenience, which is why you add "_mine" to the filename. Leave UV Range set to Normal (0 to 1), and click OK. See Figure 7.71.

WORKING IN PHOTOSHOP

Next, you'll go into Photoshop to paint your map according to the UV layout you just output.

1. In your OS file browser, navigate to the RedWagon project's Sourceimages folder and open the file `ApanelUV.tif` in Photoshop. Figure 7.72 shows the layout of the UVs that you'll use to create the white stripe for the front of the A panel.

Figure 7.72

Using a UV snapshot makes working with the UV layout for the A panel easy.

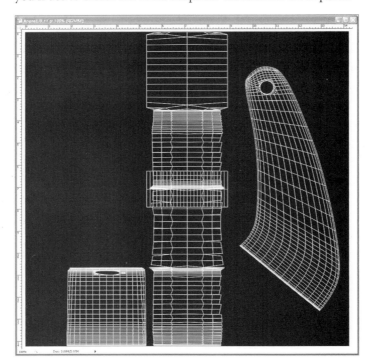

2. In Photoshop, create a new layer on top of the background layer that is the UV layout (white on black, as shown). Using the Paint Bucket tool, fill that new layer with the same red you used on the shader in your scene. To do so, click the foreground color swatch in Photoshop and set H to **355**, S to **91** percent, and B to **65** percent, as shown in Figure 7.73. Click OK.

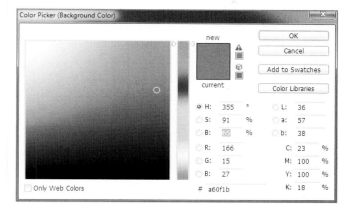

Figure 7.73
In Photoshop's Color Picker, create the same red you used for the wagon.

3. Using the Paint Bucket tool, click to fill the entire image with the red you just created. The trouble is that now you can't see the UV layout. Set the Opacity value of the red layer in Photoshop to **50** percent, as shown in Figure 7.74.

4. Set Photoshop's foreground color to white. Using the Line and Brush tools set to a width of about 6 pixels, draw a stripe following the UV layout lines, as shown in Figure 7.75. Doing so places that white stripe along the A panel's outer edge because the UV lines you're following correspond to that area of the mesh. The rest will be left red.

5. You may have drawn directly on the red layer in Photoshop or created a new layer for the stripe. In either case, set the Opacity value of the red layer back to **100** percent so you can no longer see the UV layout. Your image file should look like the one in Figure 7.76. Save the image as **ApanelStripeMine.tif** in the Sourceimages folder of your RedWagon project. You can keep the layers in the TIFF file, or you can choose to flatten the image or merge the layers. It may be best to keep the stripe and red on separate layers so that you can go back into Photoshop and edit the stripe as needed.

Figure 7.74
Set the opacity for the red layer in Photoshop so you can see the UV layout on the layer below.

You may create your own image using Photoshop (**ApanelStripeMine.tif**) and use the ApanelStripe.tif image file in the Sourceimages folder of the RedWagon project on the companion web page instead.

Figure 7.75

Follow the UV lines to draw the white stripe.

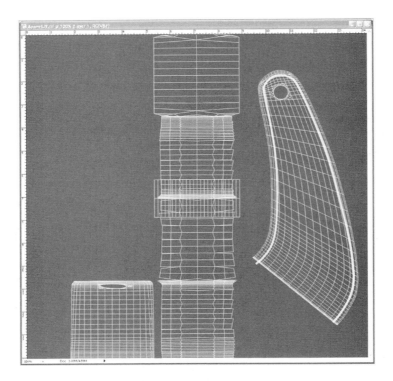

Figure 7.76

The striped image file

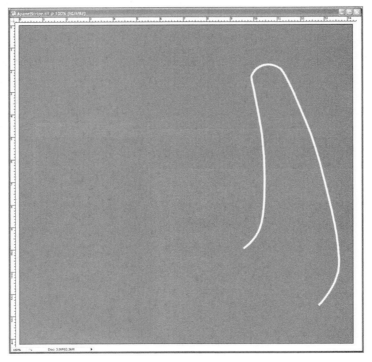

CREATING AND ASSIGNING THE SHADER

Now, let's create the shader and get it assigned to the geometry.

1. In Maya, open the Hypershade and select the Red shader. Duplicate it by choosing Edit → Duplicate → Shading Network in the Hypershade window, as shown in Figure 7.77.

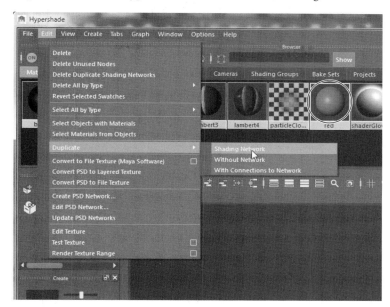

Figure 7.77

Duplicate the original Red shader.

2. Rename the newly duplicated shader (currently called red1) to **ApanelStripe**. In the Property Editor, click the Map icon (◦) next to Color and choose File. In the Attribute Editor, click the Folder icon next to the Image Name field. Navigate to your Sourceimages folder and select ApanelStripeMine.tif (or use the one provided instead—ApanelStripe.tif), as shown in Figure 7.78.

3. In the Hypershade, you may see that the Shader icon may turn somewhat transparent. Maya may automatically map the Transparency attribute of the shader as well as the color since you are using a TIFF (which may contain an alpha channel). In the Property Editor, RMB+click Transparency, and select Break Connection from the context window if there is a connection. Now your shader is set to the same red you used earlier, but now it gives you a stripe along the side A panel.

4. Assign the ApanelStripe shader to the A panel mesh and press 6 for Texture Display mode in the persp viewport. See Figure 7.79. The stripe lines up well.

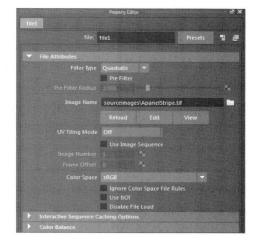

Figure 7.78

Select ApanelStripe.tif or your own ApanelStripeMine.tif **file.**

COPYING UVS

You need to put the stripe on the other side's A panel. Select the other A panel and assign the ApanelStripe shader to it. You'll notice that no stripe appears. (See Figure 7.80.) This is because the UV layout for this A panel hasn't been set up yet. Don't worry; you don't have to redo everything you did for the first A panel. You can essentially copy the UVs from the first A panel mesh to this one.

1. Select the first A panel (with the stripe) and the second panel (without the stripe). In the Modeling menu set, choose Mesh → Transfer Attributes ❐. In the option box, set Sample Space to Topology, as shown in Figure 7.81, and click Transfer.

2. The stripe appears on the inside of the back A panel, not on the outside as you need. Select that A panel and choose Modify → Center Pivot.

3. In the Channel Box, enter a value of **–1.0** for Scale X. The stripe flips to the correct side, as shown in Figure 7.82.

4. With that A panel still selected, choose Modify → Freeze Transformations.

You can load the file RedWagonTexture_v02.ma from the Scenes folder of the RedWagon project to check your work or skip to this point.

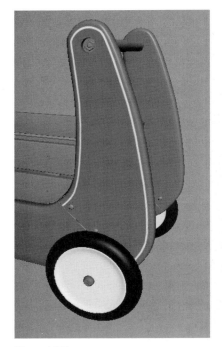

Figure 7.79

The stripe

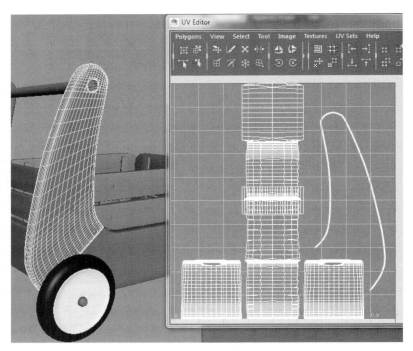

Figure 7.80

Assign the ApanelStripe shader to the other side's A panel.

The file texture you'll use for the panels was painted in Photoshop to place the stripes and logo properly on the wagon using their UV layouts. Study the image file and see how it fits on the mesh of the wagon. Try adjusting the image file with your own artwork to see how your image map affects the placement on the mesh.

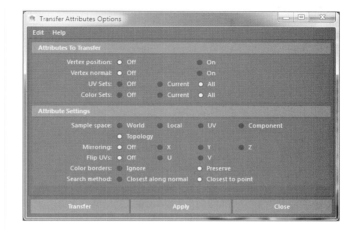

Figure 7.81

The Transfer Attributes settings

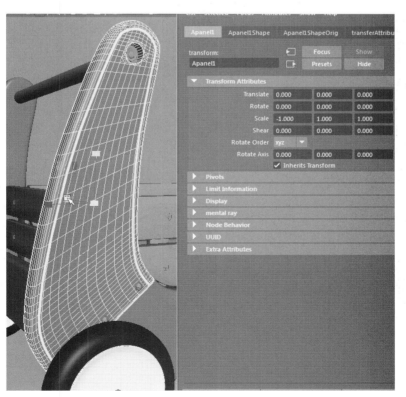

Figure 7.82

The stripe is on the correct side now.

Working with the B Panels

With the A panels done, you'll move on to the B panels (Figure 7.36 earlier in the chapter) and use much the same methodology you did with the A panels. To begin, follow these steps:

1. Select one of the B panels, shown in Figure 7.83, and open the UV Editor window.

Figure 7.83

Starting on the B panels

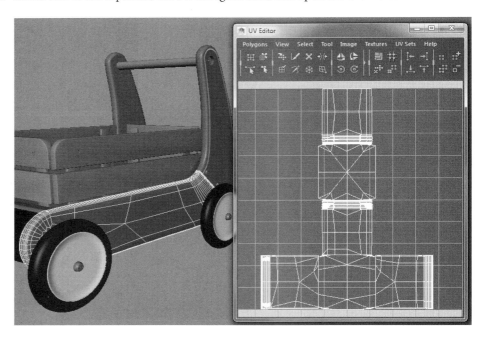

2. The B panel does not have a convenient shell like you had with the A panel before. For the B panel, select the UVs on the lower-right side of the layout in the UV Editor, as shown in Figure 7.84, to isolate the front face of the B panel.

Figure 7.84

Select the front face UVs for the B panel.

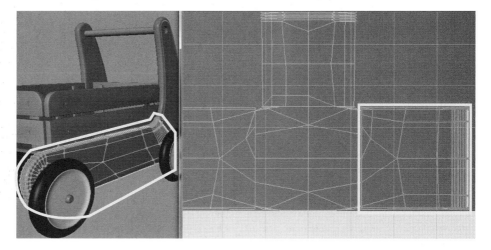

3. In the UV Editor, choose Select → Convert Selection To Faces. You've isolated the front face of the B panel.

4. Choose UV → Planar ☐. In the option box, set the Project From option to X Axis, and make sure the Keep Image Width/Height Ratio option is checked, just as before. Your B panel shows up nicely laid out in the UV Editor. See Figure 7.85.

5. This action has created a shell, making it easier to work with the front side of the B panel. RMB+click the wireframe in the UV Editor and choose Shell. Make sure that Symmetry is not turned on for the Move tool before proceeding. Select the B panel shell shape and use Move (W), Scale (R), and Rotate (E) to position the UV layout for that front face, as shown in Figure 7.86.

6. Press F8, and select the B panel mesh itself in the main Maya UI. In the UV Editor, save a UV snapshot called **BpanelUV.tif** to the Sourceimages folder of the RedWagon project.

7. Open the BpanelUV.tif image in Photoshop and follow the same steps as you did for the A panel to lay down a red layer and paint a stripe along the layout, as shown in Figure 7.87. It's best to save the stripe on its own layer in Photoshop because you'll probably need to edit and reposition the stripe to make sure it lines up with the A panel stripe after you assign the shader.

8. Create your own logo to place in the middle of panel B and place it in the Photoshop image file, as shown in Figure 7.88. Save the image file as **BpanelStripeMine.tif** into the Sourceimages folder.

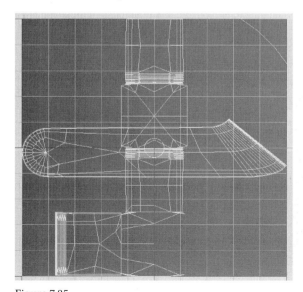

Figure 7.85

The planar projection creates a nice UV layout for the front faces of the B panel.

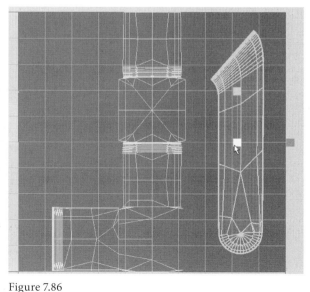

Figure 7.86

Put the front face UV shell on the side.

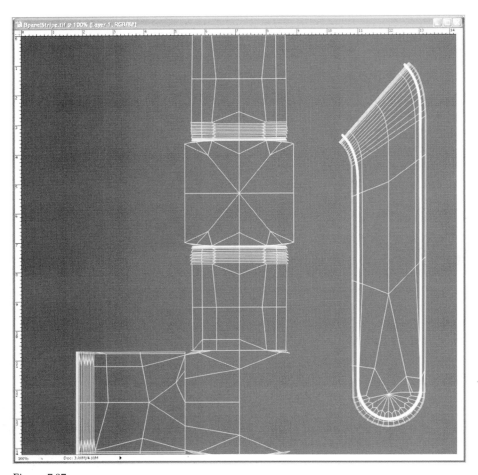

Figure 7.87
Create the B panel's stripe in Photoshop using the UV snapshot.

Figure 7.88
Create the logo in Photoshop.

You can skip the image creation in Photoshop and use the BpanelStripe.tif image file in the Sourceimages folder of the RedWagon project on the companion web page.

9. Duplicate another Red shader and, as you did previously, assign the BpanelStripeMine .tif (or use the file provided, which is BpanelStripe.tif) as its color map. If necessary, disconnect the transparency from the shader as you did with the A panel's shader. Name the shader **BpanelStripe**.

10. Assign the BpanelStripe shader to the B panel, as shown in Figure 7.89.

Figure 7.89

The B panel has its decals.

CREATING THE OTHER B PANEL TEXTURE

Finally, you need to create the shader for the other side's B panel. Assign the BpanelStripe shader to the other B panel. Nothing happens, because the UVs for the second B panel aren't set up yet.

However, because there is a logo with text, setting up its UVs won't be as simple as copying the UVs from the first B panel and then mirroring the mesh, as you did with the A panel with a Scale X value of −1.0. Doing so will make the logo and text read backward. First you'll copy and flip the UVs to the other B panel.

1. Select the first B panel with the correct texture; then select the other side's B panel and choose Mesh → Transfer Attributes ❑. Make sure Sample Space is still set to Topology and set Flip UVs to U. Click Transfer to copy the UVs, flipping them over, as you can see in Figure 7.90.

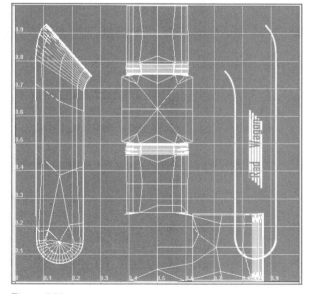

Figure 7.90

Copying and flipping the UVs to the other B panel

2. You have to go back to Photoshop and create a second `BpanelStripe.tif` image file with a mirrored logo. In Photoshop, create a marquee around the logo and mirror or flip the canvas horizontally. See Figure 7.91.

Figure 7.91

Flip the original image horizontally to fit the new UV layout of the second B panel.

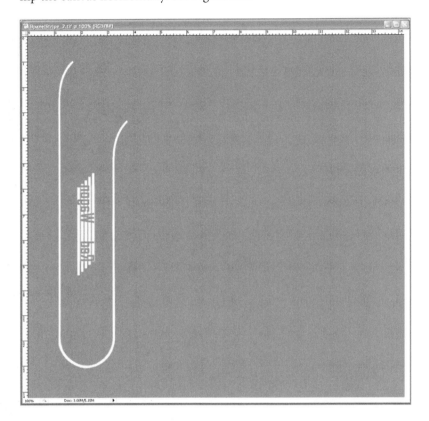

3. Select the logo portion of the image and flip that vertically, as shown in Figure 7.92. Save the image as **BpanelStripeMine_2.tif**. You may instead use the image provided— `BpanelStripe_2.tif`.

4. Duplicate the BpanelStripe shader in the Hypershade by selecting the shader and choosing Edit → Duplicate → Shading Network. The copy is called BpanelStripe1.

5. Select the newly copied BpanelStripe1 shader and graph its input and output connections (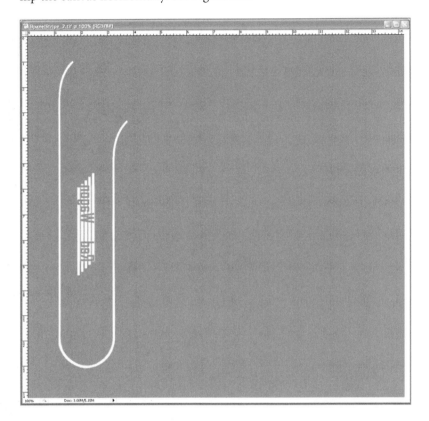) in the Hypershade. Select its file node to view it in the Property Editor. Click the Folder icon to select a new image file and then select the `BpanelStripeMine_2.tif` (or the provided `BpanelStripe_2.tif`) you just created in the Sourceimages folder. See Figure 7.93.

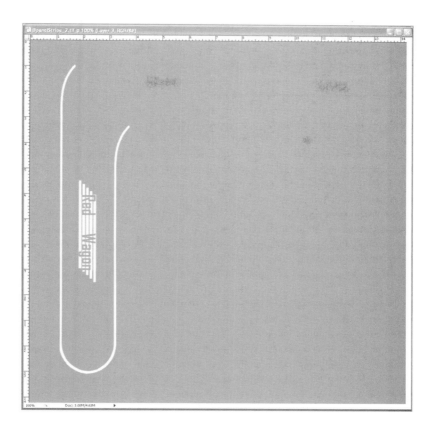

Figure 7.92

**Flip the logo
vertically and save
the image as its
own file.**

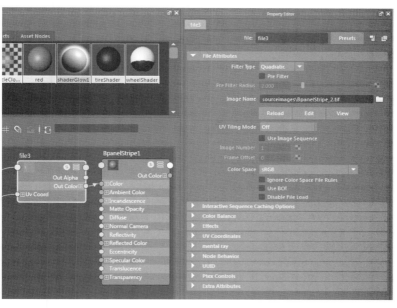

Figure 7.93

**Assign the new
image file to the
new BpanelStripe1
shader.**

6. The stripe and logo display on the wrong side of the B panel. Select the mesh and center its pivot.

7. Set the Scale X attribute for the B panel to **–1.0** to mirror it. The stripe and logo decals now show up on the correct side of the panel. Select the mesh and freeze its transforms. Figure 7.94 shows the wagon so far.

Figure 7.94

The wagon has decals on both sides.

Texturing the Floor

Figure 7.95

Select the floor faces.

Right now, the floor of the wagon is red, like the rest of its body. However, the real wagon has a blue floor, not red. If you select the mesh for the wagon's floor (named wagonFloor) and assign the Blue shader you created, the whole body of the wagon turns blue, and that isn't what you want. You need only the inside and bottom of the floor to be blue, not the front and back sides of the wagon's body.

You'll make a face assignment instead of dealing with UVs and image files. RMB+click the wagon floor mesh and select Face from the marking menu. Select the two faces for the floor, as shown in Figure 7.95.

With the faces selected, assign the Blue shader from the Hypershade window, and you're finished! You have a blue floor. All that remains now are the screws, bolts, handle, and wood railings.

You can load the file RedWagonTexture_v03.ma from the Scenes folder of the RedWagon project to check your work or skip to this point.

Shading the Wood Railings

You'll use procedural shading to use the Wood texture available in Maya to create the wood railings. Begin here:

1. In the Hypershade, create a new Phong material.

2. Click the Color attribute's Map icon ( ) and choose the Wood texture from the 3D Textures heading in the Create pane in the Hypershade.

3. In the Attribute Editor for the Wood texture, set the Filler Color and Vein Color attributes according to Table 7.3.

ATTRIBUTE	H VALUE	S VALUE	V VALUE
Filler Color	43	0.25	1.0
Vein Color	10.7	0.315	0.9

Table 7.3

Filler Color and Vein Color attributes

4. Set Vein Spread to **0.5**, Layer Size to **0.5**, Randomness to **1.0**, Age to **10.0**, and Grain Contrast to **0.33**. In the Noise Attributes heading, set Amplitude X to **0.2** and Amplitude Y to **0.1**, as shown in Figure 7.96. Name the shader **Wood**.

5. Select all the wood railings and posts and assign the Wood shader to them. Render a frame and compare it to Figure 7.97. Notice the green cube place3dTexture node that is now in your scene. See Figure 7.98.

6. The side wood railings look fine; however, the wavy pattern on the front and back wood railings looks a bit odd. In the Hypershade, duplicate the shading network for the Wood shader and call the new shader **woodFront**.

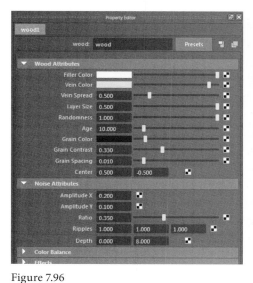

Figure 7.96

Setting the Wood texture

Figure 7.97

Assign the Wood shader.

Figure 7.98

The place3dTexture node for the wood texture

7. Assign that shader to the front and back railings and posts. Graph the network on the woodFront shader in the Hypershade window's work area.

8. In the Hypershade, select the place3dTexture2 node (Figure 7.99) and the green cube in the viewports.

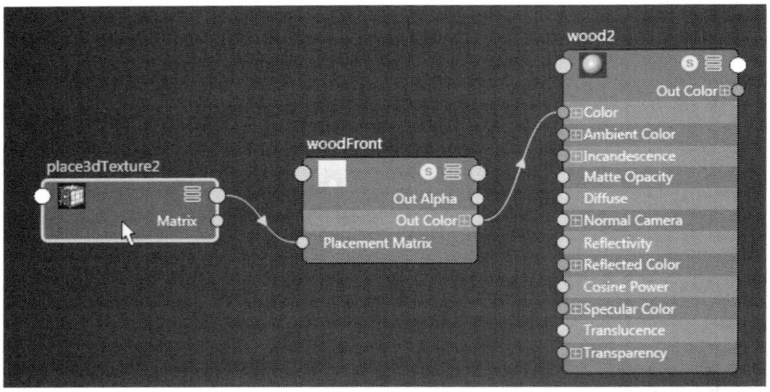

Figure 7.99

Select the placement node for the second wood texture.

9. Rotate that placement node in the persp viewport 90 degrees to the right or left. Render a frame, and compare it to Figure 7.100. The wood should no longer have that awkward wavy pattern.

The wood railings are finished. Now, for some extra challenge, you can use pictures of real wood to map onto the railings for a more detailed look. The procedural Wood texture can give you only so much realism. If you create your own wood maps, use your experience with the side panels to create UV layouts for the railings so you can paint realistic wood textures using Photoshop. You'll use custom photos and texture image maps next to simulate the rich wood in the decorative box later in the chapter.

Figure 7.100

The wood on the front and back railings looks better.

Finishing the Wagon

Now that the railings are done and you have test renders, there are only two parts left to texture: the bullnose front of the wagon and the metal handle and screws. From here, take your time and create a bump map based on a fractal, as you did for the tires, and apply it to the bullnose's black shader. Figure 7.101 shows a nice subtle bump map on the bullnose.

Figure 7.101

A nice bump for the bullnose

And last, you'll need a metal shader for the screws, bolts, and handlebar for the wagon. Use a Phong shader with a blue-gray color and a low diffuse value and assign it to all the metal parts of the wagon, as shown in Figure 7.102. You can then add an

Figure 7.102

Select all the metal screws, the bolts, and the handlebar and assign the Metal shader to them.

environment map to the reflection color like you did for the table lamp stem earlier in this chapter to give the metal a reflective look.

Because metal is a tricky material to render and a lot of a metal's look is derived from reflections, you'll finish setting the Metal shader's attributes in Chapter 11, when you render the wagon as well as the table lamp. You'll enable raytracing to get realistic reflections and gauge how to best set up the Metal shader for a great look.

Figure 7.103 shows the wagon with all its parts assigned to shaders. Figure 7.104 shows a quick render of the wagon as it is now.

You can load the file RedWagonTexture_v04.ma from the Scenes folder of the RedWagon project to check your work or skip to this point.

Figure 7.103

The wagon in the Perspective panel

Figure 7.104

A current render of the wagon

Photo-Real Mapping: The Decorative Box

With all the references you can find to any given object on the Internet, why not use real photos to create the textures for a model? That's exactly what you'll do here, with the decorative box you modeled in Chapter 3, using pictures of the real box.

You'll take this texturing exercise one important step further in Chapter 11 and experience how you can add detail to an object through displacement mapping, after you assign the colors in this chapter. This will allow you to add finer detail to a model without modeling those details.

Setting Up UVs (Blech!)

The UVs on the decorative box aren't too badly laid out by default, as you can see in Figure 7.105. The only parts of the box that are missing in the UV layout are the feet. That is a common issue when extruding polygons: their UVs are rarely laid out automatically as you extrude them. Frequently, they're bunched up together in a flat layout that is difficult, if not impossible, to see in the UV Editor.

Open the file `boxModel07.mb` in the Scenes folder of the Decorative_Box project on the companion web page or continue with your own model.

First you have to make room for the feet UVs.

1. Select all the UVs for the entire box in the UV Editor. Press R for the Scale tool and scale everything down uniformly to gain some space in the normalized UV space, shown in Figure 7.106.

2. Now you have to create new UVs for the four feet and then move them to where they should be in the full box's UV layout. Go into Component mode and select the poly faces for the four feet, as shown in Figure 7.107.

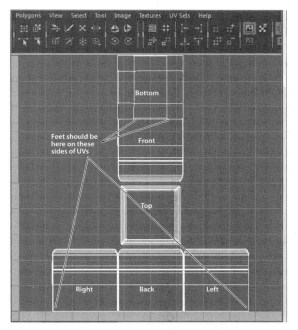

Figure 7.105

The feet UVs are missing from the box model.

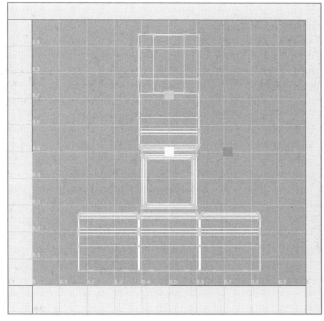

Figure 7.106

Scale all the UVs down a bit.

Figure 7.107

Select the faces for the feet.

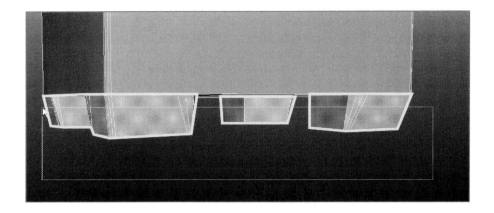

3. With the faces selected, go to the main Maya window. In the Modeling menu set, select UV → Automatic. The feet now have UVs that you can see in Figure 7.108. However, they're all over the place. You have to individually select and move each face of each foot to its appropriate place on the box's overall UV layout.

Figure 7.108

The automatic UV creation puts the UVs everywhere.

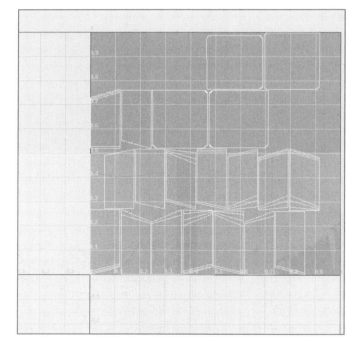

4. Select all the feet UVs in the UV Editor and scale them all down uniformly together. You want to scale them all so that one of the squares fits into the corner of the top shape, as shown in Figure 7.109 (left). Then move them all together off to the side, as shown in Figure 7.109 (right). You'll position and scale them to fit properly soon.

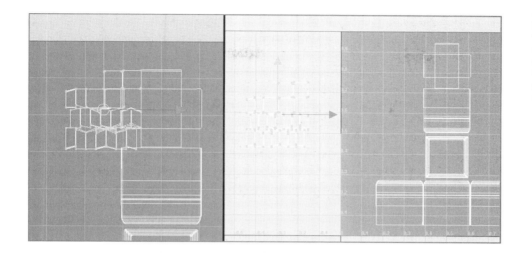

Figure 7.109

Scale the feet UVs to fit the size of the rest of the box's UVs (left). Then move the feet UVs to the side of the UV editor (right).

Laying out UVs can be a time-consuming affair, as you've seen with the wagon. Although it's recommended that you follow along with this exercise to lay out UVs for the box (because doing so will give you more practice and experience with UVs), you can skip straight to color-mapping the box in the next section by downloading the file boxTexture01.mb in the Scenes folder of the Decorative_Box project on the companion web page.

5. Now comes the task of figuring out which UV fits where. In the UV Editor window, select the edges shown in Figure 7.110 by Shift+single-clicking them. Do not use a marquee selection to make sure you select only the single edges you need. Notice that as you select each edge, they become selected in the model as well as the feet UVs off on the side of the UV Editor window. These are the edges where the outside sides of the feet meet the box. If you find it easier, you can select those edges from the model itself instead of the UV Editor.

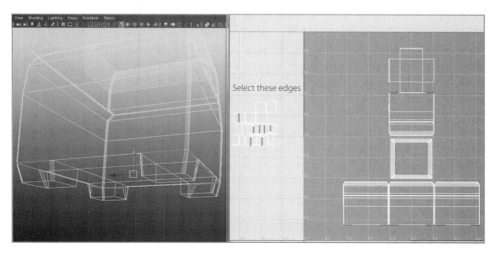

Figure 7.110

Select these individual edges either in the model view or in the UV Editor.

6. With those edges selected, in the UV Editor choose the Move And Sew The Selected Edges icon (Figure 7.111). This will snap the UVs for the outside sides of the feet to their respective sides on the box. If you did not scale the feet UVs in step 4 well enough, you will notice that the feet will stick out from the sides of the box's UVs, as shown in Figure 7.112 (left). If that is the case, it's easier to return to step 4 (press Z for undo until you reach step 4 again) and scale those feet UVs more accurately. This can have a little bit of a back and forth. As long as you are within reasonable size, you will be fine. Figure 7.112 (right) shows a better matching scale of the feet after the UVs are sewn together.

Figure 7.111

The Move And Sew The Selected Edges icon in the UV Editor

Figure 7.112

Sew the feet edges to the box. On the left, the feet UVs are scaled too big in step 4. On the right, the feet UVs are scaled properly.

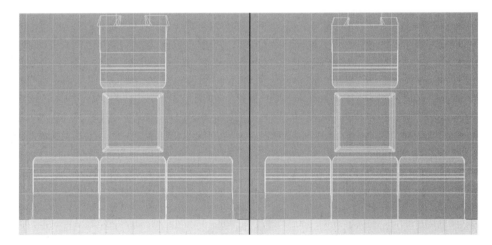

7. RMB+click in the UV Editor and select Shell from the marking menu. Select all the Shells together, including the feet shells on the side, and scale everything slightly smaller to better fit in the UV space allotted, and then move them together to re-center the layout, as shown in Figure 7.113 (left). Then select the shell for the bottom of the box and move it up away from the backside of the box, as shown in Figure 7.113 (right).

8. Figure 7.113 (right) also shows the remaining feet UVs off on the left side of the UV Editor window. The four square shapes are the bottoms of the feet. Select one of the square shells and move it to fit to the bottom UVs of the box, as shown in Figure 7.114 (right).

9. Repeat step 8 to place all the feet bottom shapes around the UVs of the bottom of the box, as shown in Figure 7.115.

10. Individually select the shells of the remaining feet UVs on the side of the UV Editor and line them up to the side of the box bottom also shown in Figure 7.115. Those remaining feet UVs are the inside faces of the feet and share the same generic wood texture as the bottom of the box, so aligning and sewing them together like you did for the outside faces of the feet in steps 5 and 6 is not necessary (Figure 7.116).

> Before you begin trying to move UVs and UV shells, make sure that Symmetry is turned off for the Move tool through its options.

When you've finished, your UV Editor should resemble the one shown in Figure 7.117. Because the box's decorations are seamless from the top of the box down to the four sides, let's lay out the UVs to make painting and editing in Photoshop easier.

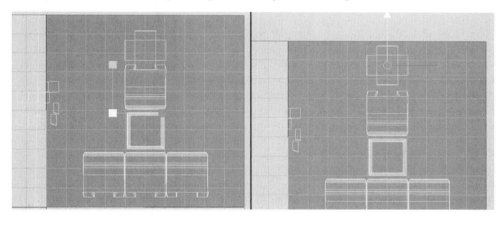

Figure 7.113

Scale down and re-center the UV layout (left); then select the shell and move the bottom UVs up in the UV Editor (right).

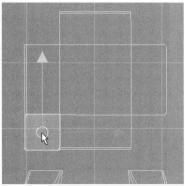

Figure 7.114

Select one square UV shell and move it to fit the box bottom UV shape.

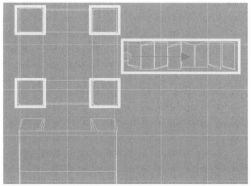

Figure 7.115

Place the feet bottoms to the box bottom and then line up the remaining feet UVs to the side.

Figure 7.116

These faces will have a generic wood texture like the bottom of the box and do not need to be carefully lined up.

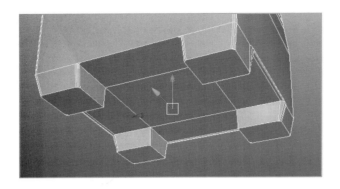

Figure 7.117

Finally, you're finished with the feet UVs.

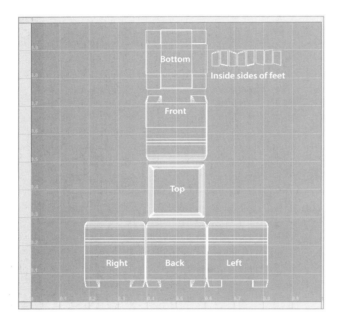

In the UV Editor, select the box top's edges, as shown in Figure 7.118 (left). Then click the Move And Sew The Selected Edges icon (shown earlier in Figure 7.111) in the UV Editor, and your UV layout should match Figure 7.118 (right). The top and sides of the box are all one UV shell now.

UV layout can be an exacting chore, but when it's completed, you're free to lay out your textures. You can check your work against the file boxTexture01.ma in the Scenes folder of the Decorative_Box project on the companion web page. You can also take a much needed breather. I sure hope you've been saving your work!

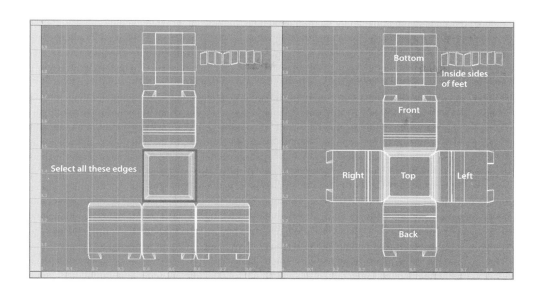

Figure 7.118
Select the box top edges (left) and sew them together (right).

Color Mapping the Box

Now that you have a good UV layout, you can output a UV snapshot and get to work editing your photos of the box to make the color maps. Start with the following steps:

1. Select the box and open the UV Editor window. From the UV Editor menu, select Polygons → UV Snapshot. In the UV Snapshot window, set Size X and Y to **2048**. Change Image Format to TIFF.

   Click the Browse button and select a location for your UV snapshot image. Generally, the project's Sourceimages folder is the best place for it. Make sure you don't write over the UV snapshot already created for you. Type in a name for your UV snapshot and click OK to create the image. Figure 7.119 shows the option box, and Figure 7.120 shows the UV snapshot image.

Figure 7.119

Setting the UV Snapshot options

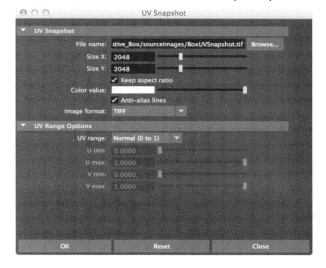

2. Open the UV snapshot image in Photoshop or your favorite image editor and set it as its own layer. Rename the layer to **UV Snapshot**. I've done the heavy lifting for you and have prepared five photos of the decorative box that you can use to

map the model. Figure 7.121 shows the photos of the box. This image file is included as lineup.jpg in the Sourceimages folder in the Decorative_Box project on the companion web page.

Figure 7.120

The UV snapshot for the decorative box, shown as black lines on white. You may see white lines on black in Photoshop.

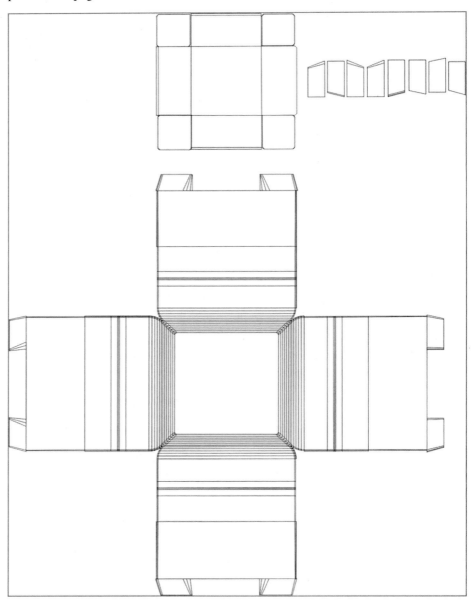

Figure 7.121

Photos of the box

Top   Right   Left   Front   Back

3. As you've probably guessed, you need to copy and paste the photos to their respective views over the UV Snapshot layer. Open the `lineup.jpg` file in Photoshop alongside the UV snapshot. Marquee+select a box around the top image (the one at the left in Figure 7.121) and copy it (Ctrl+C or Edit → Copy in Photoshop).

4. Go to the UV snapshot image in Photoshop and paste the image on top. Rename the new layer to **Box Top** and set the layer's Opacity to 50% so you can still see the UV layout, as shown in Figure 7.122.

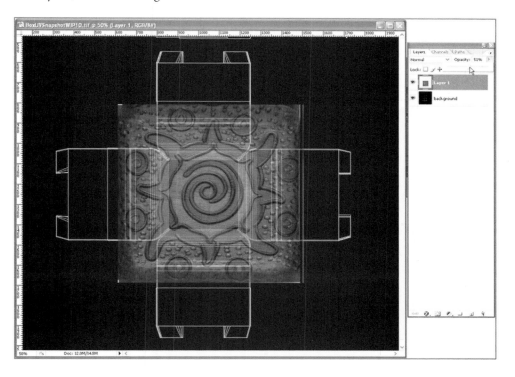

Figure 7.122

Paste the top image onto the UV snapshot image.

5. Use the Scale function in Photoshop (Edit → Transform → Scale) to move and scale the top image to fit over the top of the UV layout, as shown in Figure 7.123. Make sure you scale the box-top image uniformly to keep it from distorting. You can do this by holding the Shift key as you scale the image up or down.

Figure 7.123

Position and scale the top image in Photoshop to line up with the UVs of the top of the model. Notice the overlap of the sides and the top.

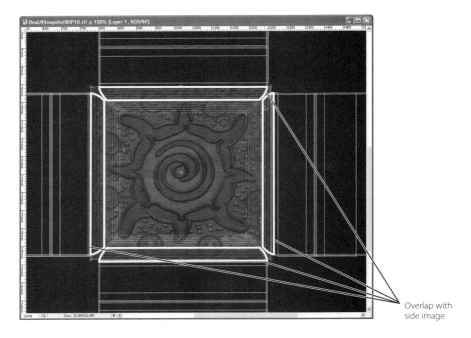

These photo images of the box have been retouched and painted to create an overlap. This means that parts of the sides of the box show in the top image. As you can see in Figure 7.123, the top image extends slightly all around the four sides. This allows the different parts of the texture map (top and four sides) to overlap and blend with each other better when put on the model.

Save your work as **boxColorMap01.psd** in the project's Sourceimages folder. Saving as a Photoshop file will preserve the layers for easier editing.

6. Marquee+select the right-side image of the box (immediately to the right of the top image in lineup.jpg) and copy it. Paste it into boxColorMap01.psd in Photoshop. Do your best to align the right-side image with the top image, using the features of the box to line them up, as you can see in Figure 7.124. You can fix this later by adjusting both the map and the UVs on the box for a tighter fit. For now, be fairly accurate and leave the finesse for later. Save the file.

7. Use the same procedures in Photoshop to line up the other sides of the box, as shown in Figure 7.125. Set the box-top image to be the topmost layer, make sure all the layers are at 100% opacity, and then turn off the UV Snapshot layer so it's not visible.

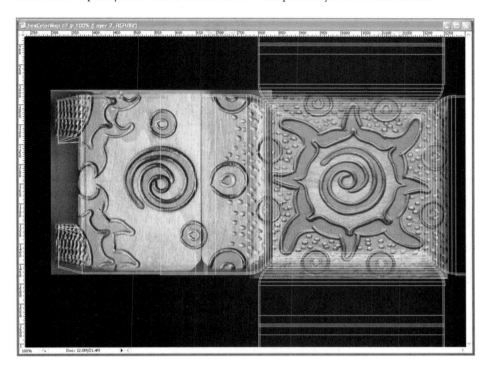

Figure 7.124

Align the right-side image with the right-side UVs.

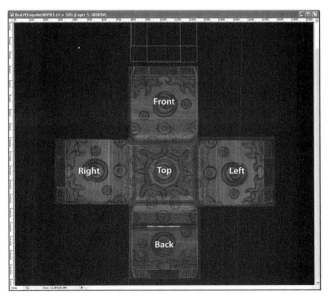

Figure 7.125

Copy, paste, and line up the box sides and the back to their respective UV areas.

8. And finally, open the file `boxBottomAndFeet.jpg` from the Sourceimages folder of the project. Select the entire image and copy and paste into your `boxColorMap01.psd` file. Position and place the image to fit the bottom UVs of the box in your map in Photoshop. Just get close; you will fine-tune the placement of image to UV later.

9. Save the final Photoshop file. Then, resave the file as a JPEG called **boxColorMap01.jpg**. This is the file you'll map. (See Figure 7.126.)

Figure 7.126

The color map layout file boxColor-Map01.jpg

Mapping the Box

Let's map this color image to the box and see how it fits. Based on rendering the box, you can make adjustments to the UVs and the image map to get everything to line up. This, of course, requires more Photoshop and/or image-editing experience, which could be a series of books of its own. If you don't have enough image-editing experience, have no fear: the images have been created for you so you can get the experience of mapping them and learn about the underlying workflow that this sort of texturing requires. Follow these steps:

1. In Maya, open the Hypershade window and create a new Phong shader. In the Property Editor, click the Map icon (⚬) next to the Color attribute and select File.

2. In the Property Editor for the File icon, click the Folder icon next to the Image Name attribute, navigate to the Sourceimages folder for the project, and select the `boxColor-Map01.jpg` file (not the PSD file). Graph the Input and Output Connections on the new Phong into the work area (see Figure 7.127).

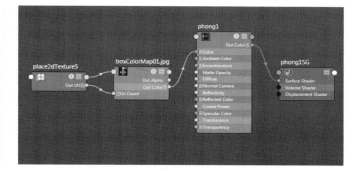

Figure 7.127

The color map's file node

3. Select the file1 node and in the Property Editor rename it to **boxColorMap**. (See Figure 7.128.)

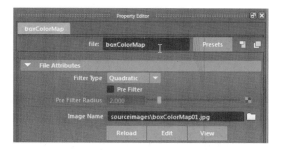

Figure 7.128

The icon is named properly.

4. Select the box and assign the Phong shader to it. Rename the Phong to **boxShader**. In the persp viewport, press 6 for Texture view. The color map is fairly well aligned on the model. Not bad! (See Figure 7.129.)

Figure 7.129

The color map fits pretty well already, but there are a few alignment issues at the edges.

5. Render a frame to see how the box looks. Notice that there are small alignment issues at the edges where the sides meet and where the top meets the sides. Save your Maya scene.

This gives you a pretty good place to work from. You need to adjust the color map image to be more seamless. The scene file boxTexture02.ma in the Scenes folder of the Decorative_ Box project on the companion web page will catch you up to this point.

Photoshop Work

This is where image-editing experience is valuable. Here, it's all about working in Photoshop to further line up the sides to the top and the sides to each other to minimize alignment issues and yield a seamless texture map. Although I won't get into the minutia of photo editing here, I'll show the progression of the images and the general workflow used in Photoshop to make the color map's different sides and top line up or merge better. The images have already been created and are on the companion web page in the Sourceimages folder for this project.

For example, using masking in Photoshop, spend some time feathering the intersection of the box's sides in boxColorMap01.psd so there is no hard line between the different sides and the top. Figure 7.130 shows a smoother transition between the different parts. This image has been created for you; it's boxColorMap02.jpg in the Sourceimages folder. Make sure you don't overwrite that file if you're painting your own.

Figure 7.130

Use masks to feather the transitions between the different parts of the box.

In Maya, double-click the boxColorMap node in the Hypershade and in the Attribute Editor replace the original boxColorMap01.jpg file with the boxColorMap02.jpg file from the Sourceimages folder (or your own retouched image file). Render and compare the difference. The top and front should merge a little better. In the persp viewport, orbit around the box in Texture View mode (press 6) to identify any other alignment issues. In some cases, as you can see in Figure 7.131, gray or black is mapped onto the box on its right side, and there is a warped area. Also, the crease where the lid meets the box is lower than you've modeled.

The blank areas on the box are outside the bounds of the image in the Photoshop image and can be fixed by adjusting the UVs in Maya. The same goes for the distorted areas on the side of the box—you just need to adjust the UVs.

Figure 7.131

There are blank areas on the box as well as a little distortion.

1. Select the box and open the UV Editor window. Figure 7.132 shows some primary areas for you to work on.

2. In the UV Editor, select the UVs (RMB+click and choose UV) shown in Figure 7.133 on the left. Press W for the Move tool and realign the UVs to the seam where the lid meets the box, as shown in Figure 7.133 on the right. As you make the changes in the UV Editor, you should immediately notice them in the Perspective window (as long as you're in Texture View mode).

Figure 7.132

Here are the main problems to fix.

Lineup issues are here

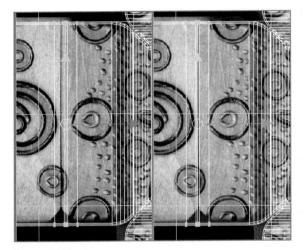

Figure 7.133

Move the UVs.

Figure 7.134

Line up the UVs to the image for the right side of the box.

3. Look at the image on top in Figure 7.134. Move the appropriate UVs to align the edge of the UV layout to the image for the right side of the box, as shown on the bottom of Figure 7.134.

4. The distortion is getting better, and the texture fits nicer. But notice in the image on the left of Figure 7.135 that the right side of the box and the back of the box don't line up well. There are some other instances of the textures not lining up well all around the box. Using the Texture View mode (press 6) in the Perspective window and the UV Editor, go around the box in its entirety and adjust the UVs, point by point as needed, so that they all line up to the image in the UV Editor. Make sure that the sides line up at the edges of the box as well as you can. The image on the right of Figure 7.135 shows correctly aligned UVs for the right side/back side of the box. Don't forget to line up the bottom of the box and feet, too. That part should be much easier.

Figure 7.135

Line up the UVs for the right-side/back-side edge of the box.

This part of tweaking the UVs takes time and patience. The key is to keep looking back and forth between the UV Editor and the persp panel to see how the textures are lining up as you move the UVs. Figure 7.136 shows the UV Editor and a persp view of the box with UVs lined up and reasonably ready to go. You can compare your work to the scene file boxTexture03.ma in the Scenes folder of the Decorative_Box project on the companion web page. Render a few different views to take in all the hard work. In Chapter 10, you'll light the box and prepare it for rendering, and in Chapter 11, you'll use displacement maps created from these photos to detail the indentations and carvings that are in the actual box. You've had enough excitement for one chapter.

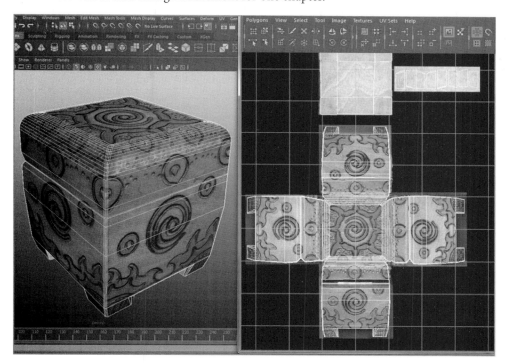

Figure 7.136

The UVs laid out for the decorative box

Toon Shading

Not everything needs to be textured to look real. Maya has a neat shading system that gives you a cartoon look using clever shaders and a powerful feature called Paint Effects, which you will look at a bit more in Chapter 12. The toon-shading system makes your scenes and animations render more like traditional cartoons with flat colors and outlines. Next, you'll take a quick look at how to apply toon shading to the wagon you textured earlier in this chapter to make it render more like a cartoon.

Try This Set your project to the RedWagon project and open the `RedWagonModel.ma` scene file from the Scenes folder.

1. You'll see the wagon in a 3/4 view in the persp viewport. Select all the parts of the body of the wagon without the railings or wheels, as shown in Figure 7.137.

2. Switch to the Rendering menu set (F6) and select Toon → Assign Fill Shader → Shaded Brightness Two Tone. There is a new Ramp shader added to the scene in the Hypershade's Materials tab. Select and graph it into the work area, as shown in Figure 7.138.

3. Under the Color heading, set the color of the gray part of the ramp to a dark red and set the white part of the ramp to a bright red. Your wagon should turn red in the persp viewport if you're in Shaded or Texture view. Render a frame, and you should see the wagon in only two tones of red but with gray railings and wheels (shown in grayscale in Figure 7.139).

4. Select the rail objects and select Toon → Assign Fill Shader → Shaded Brightness Two Tone to create another Toon shader. Set the colors to a dark tan and a bright tan color in the Color ramp.

5. Select the handlebar and all four wheels and create another two-tone fill shader with a gray and white Color ramp (which is the default).

6. The frame, railings, and wheels now have a Toon shader as well. Notice the wheels in Figure 7.140 and how cool they look when toon-shaded. Of course, adjust any of the colors to your liking.

Figure 7.137

Select the main body of the wagon, without the wheels or the rails.

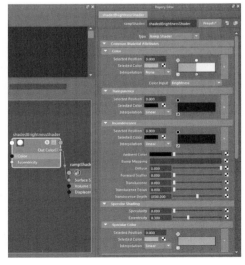

Figure 7.138

A Ramp shader is added to the scene and applied to the wagon's body.

Figure 7.139

The wagon now has a toon-shaded body. The front side of the wagon is a darker red than the front because of the lighting in the scene.

Figure 7.140

The wagon has Toon shaders for the fill color applied.

7. Now for the toon outlines. Select all the parts of the wagon and select Toon → Assign Outline → Add New Toon Outline. A black outline appears around the outside of the wagon's parts, and a new node called pfxToon1 appears in the Outliner or Hypergraph. The outlining is accomplished with Paint Effects.

8. Before you render a frame, set the background to white to make the black toon outlines pop. To do so, select the persp camera and open the Attribute Editor. Under the Environment heading, set Background Color to white.

9. Open the Render Settings window and make sure that the renderer is set to Maya Software. Render a frame and compare your work to Figure 7.141. The outlines are too thick!

> The mental ray renderer doesn't render Paint Effects by default. You have to render with Maya Software rendering to be able to see Paint Effects strokes (that is, your toon outlines). To see Paint Effects with mental ray, you must convert the paint effects to polygons, a procedure only briefly mentioned in this chapter.

10. Select the pfxToon1 node in the Outliner and open the Attribute Editor window. Click the pfxToonShape1 tab to open the attributes for the outlines. Set the Line Width attribute to **0.03** and render a frame. Compare your work to Figure 7.142.

Adjust the toon outline thickness the way you like and have some fun playing with the toon outline's attributes to see how they affect the toon rendering of the wagon. As you can see, there are a lot of attributes for the toon outlines. Paint Effects is quite a complex system, but after you experiment with the toon outlines, it'll make much more sense. You will return to Paint Effects in Chapter 12 for another quick look at that wonderful system.

Figure 7.141

The black outlines are applied, but they're too thick.

Figure 7.142

The cartoon wagon

Feel free to adjust the colors and the ramps of the fill shader to suit your tastes, and you can easily try the other Fill shader types, such as a three-tone shader to get a bit more detail in the coloring of the wagon. This is just a quick primer to get you into toon shading. The rest, as always, is up to you. With some playing and experimenting, you'll be rendering some pretty nifty cartoon scenes in no time.

For Further Study

For a challenge and more experience, create new image maps for the wagon and try your own decal designs with more traditional (non-toon) renders. You can even change the textures for the decorative box and make your own design. As previously suggested, you can try to create more realistic wood maps for the wagon's railings. In Chapter 10, you'll begin to see how shading and rendering go hand in hand; you'll adjust many of the shader attributes you created in this chapter to render the toy plane and decorative box in Chapter 11.

Summary

In this chapter, you learned about the types of shaders and how they work. Each shader has a set of attributes that give material definition, and each attribute has a different effect on how a model looks.

To gain practice, you textured the toy plane scene using a couple of shaders and texture nodes.

Next, you learned about the methods you can use to project textures onto a surface, and you learned about the Maya texture nodes, including PSD networks and the basics of UVs, and how to use them to place images onto your wagon and decorative box models in detailed exercises exposing you to manipulating UVs and using Photoshop to create maps. And finally, you took a quick look at toon shading and created a cartoonish render of the wagon.

Texturing a scene is never an isolated process. Making textures work involves render settings, lighting, and even geometry manipulation and creation. Your work in this chapter will be expanded in Chapters 10 and 11 with discussions of lighting and rendering.

The single best weapon in your texturing arsenal, and indeed in all aspects of CG art, is your eye, specifically, your observations of the world around you and how they relate to the world you're creating in CG.

CHAPTER 8

Introduction to Animation

The best way to learn about animation is to start animating, so you'll begin this chapter with the classic exercise of bouncing a ball. You'll then take a closer look at the animation tools the Autodesk® Maya® software provides and how they work for your scene. You'll do that by throwing an axe. Finally, you'll tackle animating a more complex system of parts when you bring a locomotive to life.

Learning Outcomes: In this chapter, you will be able to

- Set keyframes to establish the movement scheme for an object

- Import objects into a scene

- Create the feeling of weight and mass for an animated object using scale animation

- Read animation curves in the Graph Editor

- Differentiate among different animation principles such as squash, stretch, anticipation, and follow-through

- Set up a hierarchy for better animation control

- Transfer animation between objects

- Create text

- Create motion trails and animate objects along a path

- Set up models for animation

- Use selection handles to speed up workflow

- Animate objects in time with each other

Keyframe Animation: Bouncing a Ball

No matter where you study animation, you'll always find the classic animation exercise of creating a bouncing ball. Although it's a straightforward exercise and you've probably seen it a hundred times on the Web and in other books, the bouncing ball is a perfect exercise with which to begin animating. You can imbue the ball with so much character that the possibilities are almost endless, so try to run this exercise as many times as you can handle. You'll improve with every attempt.

First, you'll create a rubber ball and create a proper animation hierarchy for it. Then, you'll add cartoonish movement to accentuate some principles of the animation techniques discussed at the end of the ultra-fabulous Chapter 1, "Introduction to Computer Graphics and 3D."

Visit the book's web page for a video tutorial on this ball animation exercise.

Creating a Cartoon Ball

First you need to create the ball, as well as the project for this exercise. Follow these steps:

1. In a new scene, make sure you have turned off Interactive Creation. Begin by creating a poly sphere and then create a poly plane. Scale the plane up to be a ground.

2. Press 5 for Shaded mode.

3. Move the sphere 1.0 unit up in the Y-axis so that it's resting on the ground and not halfway through it, as shown in Figure 8.1.

Figure 8.1

Place the ball on the ground.

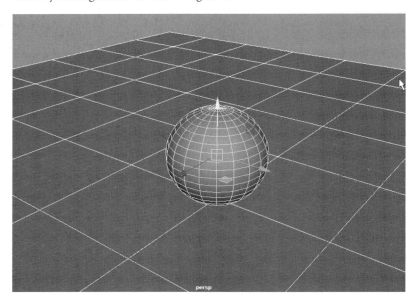

4. Choose Modify → Freeze Transformations to set the ball's resting height to **0**, as opposed to 1. This action sets the ball's Translate attribute to 0, effectively resetting the object's values. This is called *freezing the transforms*. This is useful when you position, scale, and orient an object and need to set its new location, orientation, and size as the beginning state.

5. Choose File → Project Window to create a new project. Call the project `Bouncing_Ball` and place it in the same parent folder as your Solar_System project folder. Choose Edit → Reset Settings to create the necessary folders in your project and then click Accept. Save the scene file into that project.

Setting Up the Hierarchy

First you'll set up the ball with three null nodes above it, listed here from the top parent node down: translate, scale, rotate. All the animation will be placed on these three nodes and not the sphere itself. This will allow you to easily animate the ball bouncing, squashing, stretching, and moving forward in space.

Figure 8.2

The ball's hierarchy

1. Select the sphere and press Ctrl+G to create the first group. In the Outliner, call this new group **rotate**.

2. With the rotate node selected, press Ctrl+G to create the **scale** group and name it accordingly.

3. With the scale group selected, press Ctrl+G one last time to create the **translate** group and name it accordingly. Figure 8.2 shows the hierarchy.

   As you animate, you'll quickly see why you've set up a hierarchy for the ball, instead of just putting keys on the sphere.

Animating the Ball

Your next step is to keyframe the positions of the ball using the nodes above the sphere. You'll start with the *gross animation*, which is the overall movement scheme, aka *blocking*. You'll move the ball up and down to begin its choreography in these steps:

1. Press W to open the Translate tool, select the translate node, and move it up to the top of the frame, say about 10 units up in the Y-axis and 8 units back in the X-axis at (**−8,10,0**). Place the camera so that you'll have some room to work in the frame.

2. Instead of selecting the Translate attributes in the Channel Box and RMB+clicking for the Key Selected command, you'll use hotkeys this time.

   Press Shift+W to set keyframes on Translate X, Translate Y, and Translate Z at frame 1 for the top node of the ball (named translate). To make sure your scene is set up properly, set your animation speed to 30fps by choosing Windows → Settings/Preferences → Preferences to open the Preferences window or by clicking the Animation Preferences button ( ) next to the Auto Keyframe button. In the Settings category of the Preferences window, set Time to NTSC (30fps). A frame range of 1 to 120 is good for now. Figure 8.3 shows the ball's start position.

FRAME RATES

By default, Maya is set to 24fps, which is usually what you'd want to use. For the ball animation, we are using 30fps just to show you how to change the frame rate in Maya. Feel free to change it back to 24fps for other projects. 24fps is pretty much the standard.

3. In the lower-right corner of the UI, click the Auto Keyframe button ( ) to turn it on; it turns blue. Auto Keyframe automatically sets a keyframe at the current time for any attribute that has changed since its last keyframe for the selected object or node.

    For the Auto Keyframe feature to work, you first have to set an initial keyframe manually for each of the attributes you want to animate.

4. Disregarding any specific timing, go to frame 10 and move the ball down in the Y-axis until it's about one-quarter through the ground plane. Because you'll be creating squash and stretch for this cartoon ball (see Chapter 1 for a brief explanation), you need to send the ball through the ground a little bit. Then, move the ball about 3 units to the right, to about (−5,−0.4,0). The Auto Keyframe feature sets a keyframe in the X- and Y-axes at frame 10. Remember, this is all on the translate node, not the sphere.

Figure 8.3

Start the ball here and set a keyframe on the translate node.

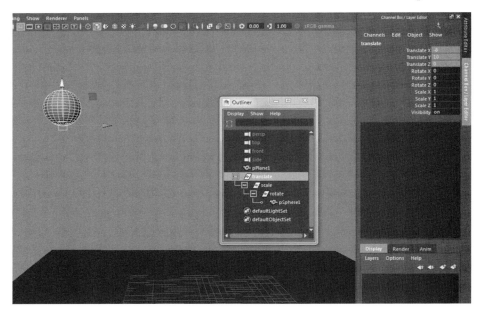

5. Move to frame 20 and raise the ball back up to about half of its original height and to the right about 2.5 units (**–2.5,4,0**). Auto Keyframe sets X and Y Translation keyframes at frame 20 and will continue to set keyframes for the ball as you animate.

6. At frame 30, place the ball back down a little less than one-quarter of the way through the ground and about 2 units to the right, at about (**–0.5,–0.3,0**).

7. At frame 40, place the ball back up in the air in the Y-axis at a fraction of its original height and to the right about 1.5 units, at about (**1.1,1.85,0**).

8. Repeat this procedure every 10 frames to about frame 110 so that you bounce the ball a few more times up and down and to the right (positive in the X-axis). Make sure you're decreasing the ball's height and traveling in X with each successive bounce and decreasing how much the ball passes through the ground with every landing until it rests on top of the ground plane. Open the Graph Editor for a peek into the ball's animation curves (see Figure 8.4). (Choose Windows → Animation Editors → Graph Editor.)

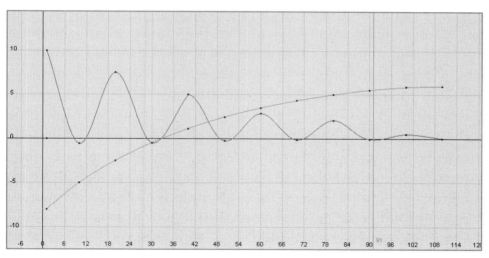

Figure 8.4
The Graph Editor curves for the ball's translate node

By holding down the Shift key as you pressed W in step 2, you set a keyframe for Translate. Likewise, you can keyframe Rotation and Scale with hotkeys. Here's a summary of the keystrokes for setting keyframes:

Shift+W Sets a keyframe for the selection's position in all three axes at the current time

Shift+E Sets a keyframe for the selection's rotation in all three axes at the current time

Shift+R Sets a keyframe for the selection's scale in all three axes at the current time

You'll resume this exercise after a look at the Graph Editor.

Using the Graph Editor

To use the Maya Graph Editor, select Windows → Animation Editors → Graph Editor. It's an unbelievably powerful tool for the animator (see Figure 8.5) to edit keyframes in animation.

Figure 8.5

The Graph Editor

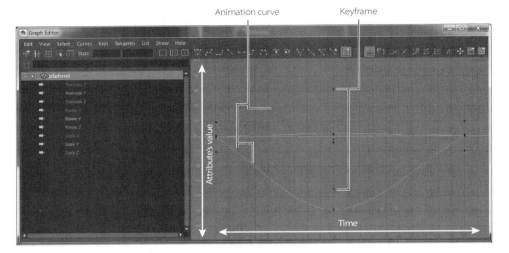

Every movement that is set in Maya generates a graph of value versus time, and the Graph Editor gives you direct access to those curves for fine-tuning your animation. The Graph Editor displays animation curves as value versus time, with value running vertically and time horizontally. Keyframes are represented on the curves as points that can be freely moved to adjust timing or value. This window is truly an animator's best friend. Move a keyframe in time to the right (to be later in the timeline), for example, to slow the action. Move the same keyframe to the left (to be earlier in the timeline) to speed up the action.

The Graph Editor is divided into two sections. The left column, which is much like the Outliner, displays the selected objects and their hierarchy with a listing of their animated channels or attributes. By default, all of an object's keyframed channels are displayed as colored curves in the display to the right of the list. However, by selecting an object or an object's channel in the list, you can isolate only those curves that you want to see.

Reading the Curves in the Graph Editor

Using the Graph Editor to *read animation curves*, you can judge an object's direction, speed, acceleration, and timing. You'll invariably come across problems and issues with your animation that require a careful review of their curves. Here are a couple of key concepts to keep in mind.

First, the curves in the Graph Editor are like the NURBS curves you've modeled with so far. This time, points on an animation curve represent keyframes, and you can control the curvature with their *tangency handles*. By grabbing one end of a key's handle and dragging it up or down, you adjust the curvature.

Second, the graph is a representation of an object attribute's position (vertical) over time (horizontal). So, not only does the placement of the keys on the curve make a big difference, so does the shape of the curve itself. Here is a quick primer on how to read a curve in the Graph Editor and, hence, how to edit it.

In Figure 8.6, the object's Translate X attribute is being animated. At the beginning, the curve quickly begins to move positively (that is, to the right) in the Z-axis. The object shoots off to the right and comes to an *ease-out*, where it decelerates to a stop. The stop is signified by the flat part of the curve at the first keyframe at frame 41. The object then quickly accelerates in the negative X direction (left) and maintains a fairly even speed until it hits frame 62, where it suddenly changes direction and goes back right for about 45 frames. It then slowly decelerates to a full stop in an ease-out.

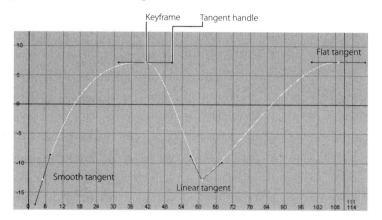

Figure 8.6

An animation curve

Consider a single object in motion. The shape of the curve in the Graph Editor defines how the object moves. The object shown in Figure 8.7 is moving in a steady manner in one direction.

Figure 8.7

Linear movement

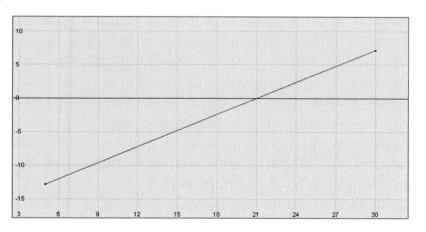

Figure 8.8 shows the object slowly accelerating toward frame 30, where it suddenly comes to a stop. If there is nothing beyond the end of the curve, there is no motion. The one exception deals with the *infinity* of curves, which is discussed shortly.

Figure 8.8

Acceleration (ease-in)

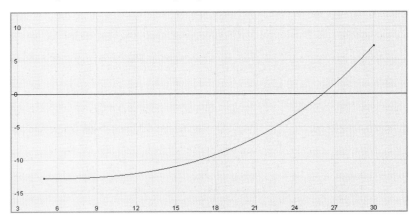

The object in Figure 8.9 begins moving immediately and comes to a slow stop by frame 27, where the curve first becomes flat.

Figure 8.9

Deceleration (ease-out)

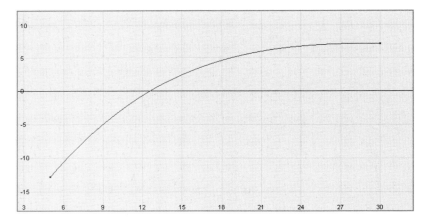

Creating a Cartoon Ball

Now, let's apply what you've learned about the Graph Editor to the bouncing ball. Follow these steps:

1. Open the Graph Editor and look at the ball's animation curves. They should be similar to the curves shown earlier in Figure 8.4.

2. Notice how only the X- and Y-axes' translates have curves, and yet Translate Z has a single keyframe but no curve. It's from the initial position keyframe you set at frame 1. Because you've moved the sphere only in the X- and Y-axes, Auto Keyframe hasn't set any keys in the Z-axis.

3. Play back the animation and see how it feels. Be sure to open the Animation Preferences window. Click the Animation Preferences icon ( ) to set the playback speed to Real-Time (30fps). You'll find this icon in the Playback section in the Time Slider category.

4. Timing is the main issue now, so you want to focus on how fast the ball bounces and then move keyframes to tweak the animation. To move a keyframe, you would select it in the Graph Editor, then press W for the Move tool, and finally MMB+click to move it. But before you move any keys, do the following:

   - Watch the motion, and you'll see that the ball is falling too fast initially, although the second and third bounces should look fine.

   - To fix the timing, move the keyframes in the Graph Editor. For the X- and Y-axes, select the keyframes at frame 10 and all the others beyond on both curves. Move them all back two frames (see Figure 8.10).

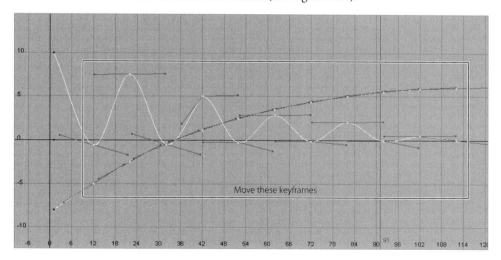

Figure 8.10

Move all the keyframes for both curves to the right to slow the initial fall by two frames, but leave the timing the same for the rest.

As the ball's bounce decays over time, it goes up less but still takes the same amount of time (10 frames) to go up the lesser distance. For better timing, adjust the last few bounces to occur faster. Select the keys on the last three bounces and move them, one by one, a frame or two to the left to decrease the time on the last short bounces (see Figure 8.11).

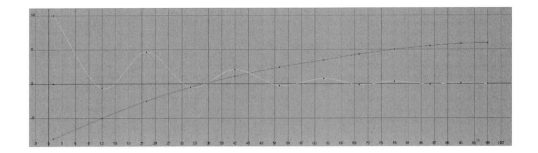

To move a key in the Graph Editor, press W to enter the Move tool, MMB+click, and drag the cursor in the Graph Editor window. Press the Shift key and drag the cursor left and right or up and down to lock the movement to either horizontal or vertical to make it easier to control.

Understanding Timing

In animation, timing is all about getting the keyframes in the proper order. Judging the speed of an object in animation is critical to getting it to look right, and that comes down to timing. Download the file ball_v1.ma from the Bouncing_Ball project on the companion web page, www.sybex.com/go/introducingmaya2016, to get to this point.

When you play back the animation, it seems a bit unrealistic, as though the ball is rising and falling on a wave as opposed to really hitting the ground and bouncing back. The problem with the animation is that the ball eases in and out as it rises and falls. By default, setting a key in Maya sets the keyframes to have an ease-in and ease-out in their curves, meaning their curves are smooth like a NURBS curve. For a more natural motion, you need to accelerate the ball as it falls with a sharp valley in the curve, and you need to decelerate it as it rises with smooth peaks. Follow these steps:

1. In the Graph Editor, select the Translate Y entry in the left panel of the window to isolate your view to just that curve in the editor panel on the right. Select all the landing keyframes (the ones in the valleys of the curve) and change their interpolation from smooth to linear by clicking the Linear Tangents button (▨).

2. Likewise, select all the peak keyframes at the ball's rise and change their tangents to flat by clicking the Flat Tangents icon (▱) to make the animation curve like the one shown in Figure 8.12.

3. When you play back the animation, the ball seems to be moving more realistically. If you need to, adjust the keys a bit more to get the timing to feel right to you, before you move on to squash and stretch and rotation.

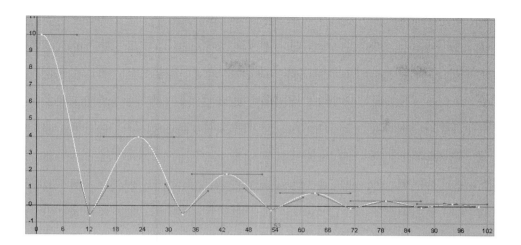

Figure 8.12

The adjusted timing of the bounce

Squashing and Stretching the Ball

The concept of *squash and stretch* has been an animation staple for as long as animation has existed. It's a way to convey the weight of an object by deforming it to react (usually in an exaggerated way) to gravity and motion. You can do this by scaling your object.

Download the file ball_v2.ma from the Bouncing_Ball project on the book's web page and follow these steps:

1. Select the scale node (not the sphere!) and select Modify → Center Pivot. This places the scale pivot point in the middle of the ball.

2. At frame 9, press Shift+R to set initial scale keyframes on the scale node of the ball, a few frames before the ball impacts the ground.

3. To initiate squash and stretch, go to frame 12, where the ball hits the floor the first time. With the scale node selected, press R to open the Scale tool; scale the ball down in the Y-axis until it no longer goes through the floor (about **0.6**), as shown in the image on the top in Figure 8.13. Set a keyframe for scale by pressing Shift+R.

Figure 8.13

Squashing and stretching the ball to react to bouncing on the floor

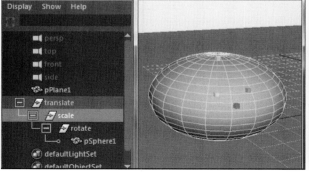
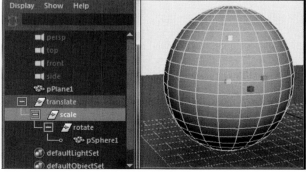

4. Move ahead in the animation about three frames to frame 15. Scale the ball up in the Y-axis slightly past normal to stretch it up (about **1.15**) immediately after its bounce, as shown in the image on the bottom in Figure 8.13. Three frames later, at frame 18, set the Y-axis scale back to **1** to return the ball to its regular shape.

5. Scrub your animation, and you should see the ball begin stretching even before it hits the ground. That's a bit too much exaggeration, so open the Graph Editor and move the Y-axis scale key from 9 to 11. Now, the ball squashes when it hits the floor and stretches as it bounces up.

6. Repeat this procedure for the remaining bounces, squashing the ball as it hits the floor and stretching it as it bounces up. Remember to decay the scale factor as the ball's bouncing decays to a stop; the final bounce or two should have very little squash and stretch, if any.

Download the file `ball_v3.ma` from the `Bouncing_Ball` project on the book's web page to get to this point.

Rotating the Ball

Let's add some roll to the ball in the following steps:

1. Select the ball's rotate node and select Modify → Center Pivot to set that node's pivot at the center of the ball.

2. At frame 1, press Shift+E to set keys for rotation at (**0,0,0**).

3. Scrub to the end of your animation (frame 100 in this example) and set a value of **−480** for Rotate Z in the Channel Box, as shown in Figure 8.14.

4. Open the Graph Editor to see the rotation curve on the ball's rotate node. It's a linear (straight) line angled down from 0 to −480. You need the rotation to slow to a stop at the end of the animation, so select the final keyframe and click ▭ to make it a flat tangent.

Figure 8.14

Setting a roll for the ball

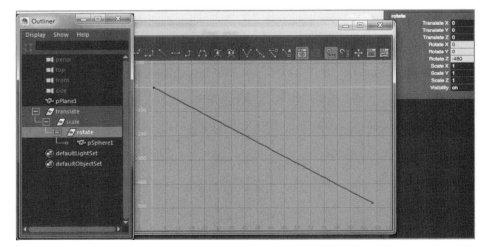

Load the file `ball_v4.ma` from the `Bouncing_Ball` project from the companion web page to see an example of the finished bouncing ball. Although the bouncing of this ball looks okay, it could definitely use some finesse, a little timing change, and so on. Open the file, open the Graph Editor, and edit the file to get a feel for animating it in your own style.

Throwing an Axe

This next project will exercise your use of hierarchies and introduce you to creating and refining motion to achieve proper animation for a more complex scene than the bouncing ball. The workflow is simple but standard for properly setting up a scene for animation, also known as *rigging*. First you'll model an axe and a target, and then you'll set up the grouping and pivots for how you want to animate. Then you'll throw your axe!

Why won't you throw the NURBS axe you've already created and textured? Because later in this chapter, you'll need it for an exercise on importing and replacing an object in Maya while keeping the animation intact. You'll see a video tutorial on the book's website for the axe-throwing exercise.

The Preproduction Process

To begin the animation right away, you'll use a basic axe and bull's-eye target to focus on animation and technique.

Create a new project by choosing File → Project Window and clicking the New button. Place this project in the same folder or drive as your other projects, call it **Axe**, and click Accept. Click the Animation Preferences button and set the frames per second to 30fps.

What separates good animation from bad animation is the feeling of weight that the audience infers from the animation. People instinctively understand how nature works in motion. You see an object in motion, how it moves, and how it affects its surroundings. From that, you can feel the essence of its motion, with its weight making a distinct impression on you. As it pertains to animation, that essence is simply called *weight*. A good feeling of weight in animation depends on timing and follow-through, which require practice.

It's a good idea first to try an action you want to animate. It may upset the cat if you grab a real axe and start throwing it around your house, but you can take a pen, remove its cap, and lob it across the room. Notice how it arcs through the air, how it spins around its center of balance, and how it hits its mark. Just try not to take out anyone's eye with the pen. According to some Internet research, the perfect axe throw should contain as few spins as possible.

Animating the Axe: Keyframing Gross Animation

The first step is to keyframe the positions of the axe, starting with its *gross animation*— that is, the movement from one end of the axe's trajectory to the other.

Setting Initial Keyframes

Load the scene file axe_v1.mb in the Scenes folder of the Axe project from the companion web page and follow these steps:

1. Select the axe's top group node. To make selecting groups such as this easier, display the object's selection handle. To do so, select the axe's top node and choose Display → Transform Display → Selection Handles. Doing this displays a small cross, called a *selection handle* (+), at the axe's pivot point. You need only select this selection handle to select the top node of the axe.

> You can turn on selection handles for practically any object in Maya—no matter where it is in a group's hierarchy—whether it's a child or a parent.

2. With the axe selected, go to frame 1 and set a keyframe for the rotation and translation.

3. Hold down the Shift key, press W for the axe's translation keyframes and then press E for the axe's rotation keyframes for its start position.

Creating Anticipation

Instead of the axe just flying through the air toward the target, you'll animate the axe moving back first to create *anticipation*, as if an invisible arm were pulling the axe back before throwing it. Follow these steps:

1. Go to frame 15.

2. Move the axe back in the X-axis about 8 units and rotate it counterclockwise about 45 degrees.

3. The Auto Keyframe feature sets keyframes for the position and new rotation at frame 15.

    Because you've moved the axe back only in the X-axis and made the rotation only on the Z-axis, Auto Keyframe sets keyframes only for Translate X and Rotate Z. The other position and rotation axes aren't auto-keyframed because their values didn't change. Take note of this fact.

4. Scrub through the animation and notice how the axe moves back in anticipation.

5. Go to frame 40 and move the axe so that its blade cuts into the center of the target.

> Auto Keyframe inserts a keyframe at the current time for the selected object's changed attributes only.

Notice that you have to move the axe in the X- and Y-axes, whereas before you had to move it back only in the X-axis to create anticipation. This is because the axis of motion for the axe rotates along with the axe. This is an example of the *Local axis*. The Local axis for any given object shifts according to the object's orientation. Because you angled the axe back about 45 degrees, its Local axis rotated back the same amount.

The file axe_v2.mb in the Scenes folder of the Axe project from the companion web page will catch you up to this point in the animation.

This last step reveals a problem with the animation. If you scrub your animation now, you'll notice that the axe's movement back is different from before, setting a keyframe at frame 40. Why intentionally create a problem like this? Troubleshooting problems in a scene is vital to getting good as a CG animator, so the more you learn how to diagnose problems, the easier production will become.

The problem is caused by the Auto Keyframe feature. At frame 1, you set an initial keyframe for the X-, Y-, and Z-axes of translation and rotation. Then, at frame 15, you moved the axe back in the X-axis only (in addition to rotating it in the Z-axis only).

Auto Keyframe set a keyframe for Translate X at frame 15. At frame 40, you moved the axe in *both* the X- and Y-axes to strike the target. Auto Keyframe set a keyframe at 40 for Translate X and Translate Y. Because the last keyframe for Translate Y was set at 1 and not at 15, as in the case of Translate X, there is now a bobble in the Y position of the axe between frames 1 and 15.

With the axe selected, open the Graph Editor (choose Windows → Animation Editors → Graph Editor) to see what's happening. You should see red, green, and blue line segments running up and down and left and right. You'll probably have to zoom your view to something more intelligible. By using the Alt key (or the Alt/Option key on a Mac) and mouse-button combinations, you can navigate the Graph Editor much as you can any of the modeling windows.

The hotkeys A and F also work in the Graph Editor. Click anywhere in the Graph Editor window to make sure it's the active window and press A to zoom all your curves into view. Your window should look something like Figure 8.15.

The curves in the Graph Editor represent the values of the axe's position and rotation at any given time. The X-, Y-, and Z-axes are in their representative red, green, or blue color, and the specific attributes are listed much like they are in the Outliner in the left column. Selecting an object or an attribute on the left displays its curves on the right.

You should also notice that the curves are all at different scales. The three rotate curves range in value from about –45 to 45, the Translate Y curve ranges from about 15 to 5, and Translate Z looks flat in the Graph Editor. It's tough to edit a curve with low values and still be able to see the timings of a larger value curve.

Figure 8.15

The Graph Editor displays the axe's animation curves.

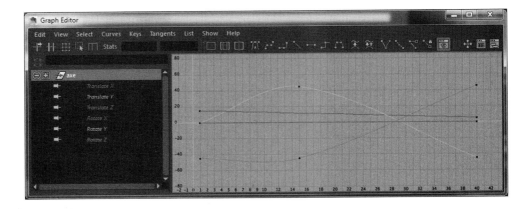

You can select the specific attribute and zoom in on its curve to see it better, or you can *normalize* the curves so that you can see them all in one view. Click the Enable Normalized Curve Display icon in the top icon bar of the Graph Editor (). The values don't change, but the curves now display in a better scale in relation to each other so you can see them all together.

Figure 8.16 shows the Graph Editor from Figure 8.15 after the curves have been normalized. Keep in mind that this doesn't change the animation in the slightest. All it does is allow you to see all the curves and their relative motion. You can denormalize the view by clicking the Disable Normalized Curve Display icon in the Graph Editor ().

Figure 8.16

The normalized view in the Graph Editor lets you see all the curves of an animation together in the same scale.

Notice that the curve for Translate Y has keyframes only at frames 1 and 40. The animation dips in the first 15 frames because there is no keyframe at frame 15 like there is for Translate Z. That dip wasn't there before you set the end keyframe at frame 40.

Continue the exercise by fixing this issue:

1. Move the first keyframe of Translate Y from frame 1 to frame 15 to fix the dip.

   - Press W to activate the Move tool in Maya or click the Move Nearest Picked Key Tool icon () in the Graph Editor.

- Click the Time Snap On/Off icon (![icon]) to toggle it on.
- Select the offending Translate Y keyframe at frame 1 and MMB+click and drag it to the right until it's at frame 15.

  Scrub your animation, and the backward movement looks like it did before.

  The axe now needs an arc on its way to the target.

2. Go to the middle of the axe's flight, frame 27.

3. Move the axe up in the Y-axis a bit using the green handle of the Tool manipulator.

   If the axe is slightly rotated in frame, Auto Keyframe can set a key for both Translate Y and Translate X, although you were perhaps expecting only a key in Translate Y. Because the Move tool is on the axe's Local axis and because the axe was slightly rotated at frame 27, there is a change in the Y and X positions in the World axis, which is the axis represented in the Graph Editor.

4. Select the Translate X key at frame 27 in the Graph Editor, if one was created, and press Delete to delete it.

5. Now you'll add a full spin to the axe to give the animation more reality and life. You can spin it in one of two ways.

   - Go to frame 40, select the axe, and rotate it clockwise a full 360 degrees positive. Auto Keyframe enters a new rotation value at frame 40, overwriting the old value. You should see the Rotate Z curve angle down steeply as soon as you let go of the Rotate manipulator.
   - In the Graph Editor, make sure you're at frame 40, grab the last keyframe on the Rotate Z curve, and MMB+click and drag it down, probably past the lower limit of the window. If you keep the middle mouse button pressed as you move the mouse, the keyframe keeps moving as you move the mouse, even if the keyframe has left the visible bounds of the Graph Editor.

   If you hold down Shift as you MMB+click and drag the keyframe to move it in the Graph Editor, the keyframe will move in only one axis (up or down, left or right).

   By moving the keyframe down, you change the Rotate Z value to a lower number, which spins the axe clockwise. Before you try that, though, move your Graph Editor window so you can see the axe in the Perspective window. As you move the Rotate Z keyframe down in the Graph Editor, you see the axe rotate interactively. Move the keyframe down until the axe does a full spin.

6. Play back the animation by clicking the Play button in the playback controls. If your animation looks blazingly fast, open the Animation Preferences window by clicking its icon (![icon]) and set Playback Speed to Real-Time (30fps).

Now, when you play back the animation, it should look slow. Maya is playing the scene back in real time, but even at 30fps, the scene plays back slowly, which means that the animation of the axe is too slow.

7. All you need to do is tinker in the Graph Editor a bit to get the right timing. For a good result in timing, move the first set of keyframes from 15 to 13. Then, grab the Translate Y keyframe at frame 27 and move it to 19. Finally, grab the keyframes at frame 40 and move them all back to frame 25. Play back the scene.

> Changing the playback speed of an animation through the Animation Preferences window doesn't alter the timing of your animation. It only changes the speed at which Maya plays the animation back to you in its windows. To change the playback speed, choose Windows → Setting/Preferences → Preferences to open the Preferences window, choose Settings → Working Units, and select the proper setting.

Adding Follow-Through

Load the axe_v3.mb file from the Axe project on the book's web page or continue with your own file.

The axe is missing weight. You can add some finesse to the scene using follow-through and secondary motion to give more weight to the scene.

In the axe scene, follow-through motion is the axe blade driving farther into the target a little beyond its initial impact. Secondary motion is the recoil in the target as the momentum of the axe transfers into it. As you increase the amount of follow-through and secondary motion, you increase the axe's implied weight. You must, however, walk a fine line; you don't want to go too far with follow-through or secondary motion. Follow these steps:

1. Select the axe in the scene using its selection handle and open the Graph Editor.

2. Because you'll add three frames to the end of this animation for follow-through, go to frame 28 (25 is the end of the current animation).

3. In the Perspective window, rotate the axe another 1.5 degrees in the Z-axis.

4. Rotating the axe in step 3 moves the axe's blade down a bit in the Y-axis. To bring the axe back up close to where it was before the extra rotation, move the axe up slightly using the Translate Y manipulator handle. This also digs the axe into the target a little more. You'll see a keyframe for Translate Y and most probably for Translate X, as well as for Rotate Z.

If you play back the animation, the follow-through doesn't look good. The axe hits the target and then digs into it as if the action were done in two separate moves by two different animators who never talked to each other. You need to smooth out the transition from the axe strike and its follow-through in the Graph Editor.

5. Highlight the Rotate Z attribute in the Graph Editor to get rid of the other curves in the window. Figure 8.17 shows the Rotate Z curve of the axe after the follow-through animation is added.

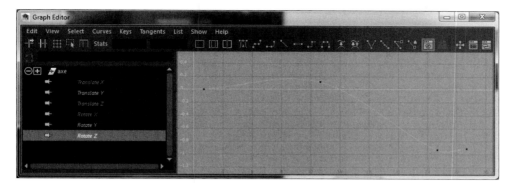

Figure 8.17

The normalized Rotate Z curve of the axe after the follow-through animation

6. Focus on the last three frames of the curve and zoom into that range only. The curve, as it is now, dips down past where it should and recoils back up a small amount.

   When you set keyframes for the axe, you create Bézier splines animation curves in the Graph Editor. These curves stay as smooth as possible from beginning to end. When you set the new keyframe, rotating the axe about 1.5 more degrees for follow-through, the animation curve responds by creating a dip, as shown in Figure 8.17, to keep the whole curve as smooth as possible.

SECONDARY MOTION AND FOLLOW-THROUGH

Secondary motion in animation comprises all the little things in a scene that move because something else in the scene is moving. For example, when a superhero jumps from a tall building and his or her cape flutters in the wind, the cape's undulation is secondary motion.

Follow-through is the action in animation that immediately follows an object's or a character's main action. For example, after the superhero lands from their jump, his or her knees buckle a little, and the superhero bends at the waist, reacting to his or her weight as it settles, creating follow-through.

The axe needs to hit the target with force and dig its way in, slowly coming to a stop. You need to adjust the curvature of the keyframes at frame 25 by using the keyframe's tangents. *Tangents* are handles that change the amount of curvature influence of a point on a b-spline (Bézier spline). Selecting the keyframe in question reveals its tangents, as shown in Figure 8.18.

7. Select the Out tangent (handle on the right side of the key) for the Rotate Z attribute's key at frame 25 and MMB+click and drag it up to get rid of the dip. Notice that the tangency for the In tangent (handle on the left side of the key) also changes.

8. Press Z to undo your change. You need to break the tangent handles so that one doesn't disturb the other.

9. Select the Out handle and click the Break Tangents icon () to break the tangent.

10. Move the handle up to get rid of the dip so that the curve segment from frame 25 to frame 28 is a straight line, angled down. Figure 8.19 is zoomed into this segment of the curve after it's been fixed.

Figure 8.18

The tangent handles of a keyframe. The handle to the left of the keyframe is the In tangent, and the handle to the right is its Out tangent.

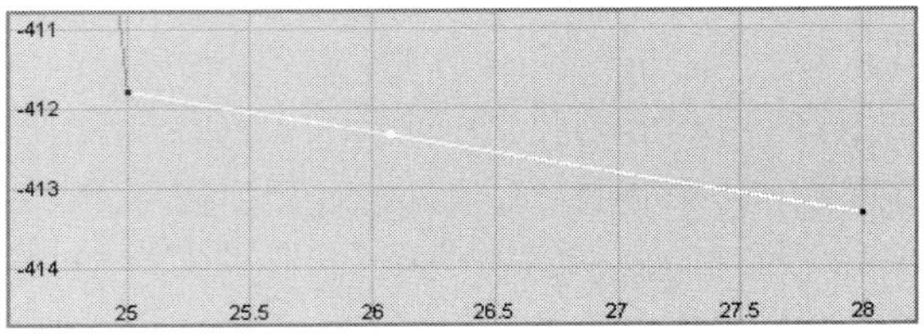

Figure 8.19

Zoomed into the end segment of the Rotate Z animation curve after the dip is fixed

Now, to get the axe to stop slowly as it digs into the target, you need to curve that end segment of the Rotate Z curve to flatten it out.

11. Grab the last frame to reveal its handles. You can manually move the In handle to make it horizontal, or you can click the Flat Tangents icon (▫—▫) on the left side of the icon bar, under the menus in the Graph Editor.

The curve's final segment for Rotate Z should now look like Figure 8.20.

Figure 8.20

Zoomed into the end segment of the Rotate Z animation curve. Notice how the curve now smoothly comes to a stop by flattening out.

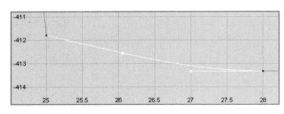

12. Adjust the keyframe tangents similarly for the axe's Translate Y and Translate X curves, as shown in Figure 8.21.

13. Play back the animation, and you should see the axe impact the target and sink into it a bit for its follow-through.

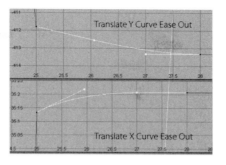

Figure 8.21

Smoothed translate curves to ease out the motion

Now, you need to polish things up more.

Adding Secondary Motion

Load axe_v4.mb from the Axe project from the book's web page or continue with your own scene file. For secondary motion, you'll move the target in reaction to the impact from the axe's momentum.

An object in motion has momentum. Momentum is calculated by multiplying the mass of an object by its velocity. So, the heavier and faster an object is, the more momentum it has. When two objects collide, some or all momentum transfers from one object to the other.

In the axe scene's impact, the axe lodges in the target, and its momentum is almost fully transferred to the target. But because the target is more massive than the axe, the target moves only slightly in reaction. The more you make the target recoil, the heavier the axe will seem.

First, group the axe's parent node under the target's parent node by grouping the axe under the target; when you move the target to recoil, it will keep the axe lodged in it. You will use the Hypergraph instead of the Outliner, so let's take a quick look at its interface first.

The Hypergraph Explained

The Hypergraph: Hierarchy (referred to as just the Hypergraph in this book) displays all the objects in your scene in a graphical layout similar to a flowchart (see Figure 8.22). Select Windows → Hypergraph: Hierarchy to see the relationships between objects in your scene more directly. This window may be somewhat more difficult for a novice to decipher, but it affords you great control over object interconnectivity, hierarchy, and input and output connections. The Hypergraph: Connections window is technically called the Hypergraph window, but it shows you the interconnections of attributes among nodes as opposed to the node hierarchy in the scene.

Navigating the Hypergraph is the same as navigating any Modeling window, using the familiar Alt key and mouse combinations for tracking and zooming.

Figure 8.22

The Hypergraph interface

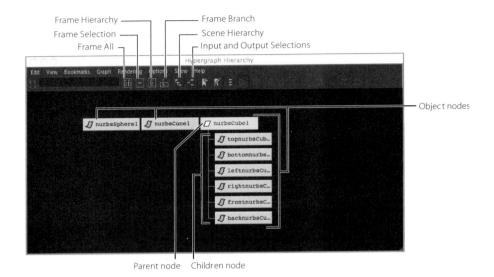

Continuing the Axe

First you need to reset the target node's Translate and Rotate attributes to **0** and its Scale attributes to **1**.

1. To freeze the transforms, select the parent target node and then choose Modify → Freeze Transformations.

2. Select Windows → Hypergraph: Hierarchy. MMB+click and drag the axe node to the target node in the Hypergraph to group the axe node under the target node. This can also be done in the Outliner.

3. Go to frame 25, the moment of impact, and set the position and rotation keyframes on Target.

Figure 8.23

The front-panel display of the target reacting to the impact of the axe

4. Go to frame 28, rotate the target node in the Z-axis about 2.5 degrees, and move it up and back slightly in the Y- and X-axes, as shown in Figure 8.23.

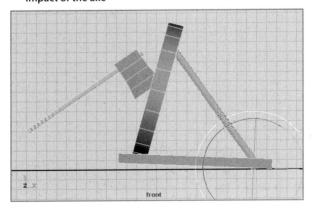

5. Go to frame 31. Rotate the target node back to 0 in the Z-axis, move it down to 0 in the Y-axis, and move it back a bit more in the X-axis.

6. Go to frame 35 and repeat step 4, but move it only half as much in Rotate Z, Translate X, and Translate Y.

7. Go to frame 40 and repeat step 5, but move Target back only slightly in the X-axis.

If you don't freeze the transforms on the target's parent node before grouping the axe under it, the axe's animation will change and yield undesirable results.

The preceding steps should give you an animation similar to axe_v5.mb in the Axe project from the companion web page.

Animating on a Path

As an alternative to keyframing the position of the axe, you can animate it on a path. Path animation allows you to assign an object to move along the course of a curve, called a *path*.

Load axe_v6.mb from the Axe project from the companion web page. This is the finished axe animation, but the translation keys have been deleted, though the rotation keys and everything else are intact. You'll replace the translation keyframes with a motion path instead. There is an arched curve in this scene called pathCurve that was already created for you using the CV curve tool. Look how nice I am to you!

1. Once you open the scene (axe_v6.mb), scrub the animation and you'll see that the axe spins around; it and the target recoil at the moment of impact, but the axe doesn't actually move. There is also a curve in the scene that represents the eventual motion of the axe.

2. Select the axe node in the Outliner (see Figure 8.24) and then Shift+select the path curve. In the Animation menu set, choose Constrain → Motion Paths → Attach To Motion Path ☐.

3. In the option box, turn off the Follow check box.

   The Follow feature orients the object on the path so that its front always points in the direction of travel. This will interfere with the axe's motion, so you'll leave it off. Click Apply, and now the axe will follow the line from end to end between frame 1 and frame 60. Of course, you have to adjust the timing to fit better, as with the original axe animation.

   The file axe_path_v1.mb in the Axe project will bring you up to this point.

4. Select the axe node and open the Graph Editor to see the axe's curves. There is a purple curve called motionPath1.U Value curve that replaces the translation curves. On the left side of the Graph Editor, select any of the motionPath1.U Value curve entries to display only that animation curve on the right of the editor. Zoom into the graph curve by pressing A to view all.

Figure 8.24

Select the Axe project's group node.

5. The curve is an ease-in and ease-out curve from 1 to 60. You need the axe to hit at frame 25, so move the end of that curve to frame 25 from frame 60. Then use the tangent handle to shape the end of the curve to be more like Figure 8.25. This will add acceleration to the end of the curve for more of a punch on the hit.

Figure 8.25

Set the last key to frame 25 and reshape the curve at the end.

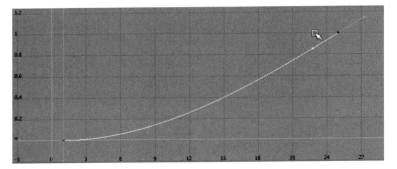

6. Scrub the animation until the axe moves all the way back (frame 4). You'll add a keyframe here to help retime the backward movement. Select the purple U Value animation curve and then select the Insert Keys tool (H) in the top-left corner of the Graph Editor. MMB+click the curve to create a key at frame 4. (You can MMB+click and then drag the cursor to place the key precisely at frame 4 before releasing the mouse button.)

7. Move this new keyframe to frame 7. Scrub the animation, and the timing is just about right. You'll have to adjust the tangents a bit to make the axe move more like before, but the movement is essentially there with path animation.

The file `axe_path_v2.mb` in the Axe project will bring you up to this point.

Path animation is extremely useful, especially for animating an object along a particular course. By adjusting the resulting animation curve in the Graph Editor, you can easily readjust the timing of the path animation, and you can always adjust the shape of the path curve itself to change the motion of the object. A good path animation exercise is to reanimate the Solar_System exercise with paths instead of the keyframes you set on the rotations.

Replacing an Object

It's common practice to animate a *proxy* object—a simple stand-in model that you later replace. The next exercise will show you how to replace the axe you already animated with a fancier NURBS model and how to copy an animation from one object to another.

Replacing the Axe

Load the scene file `axe_v5.mb` from the book's web page. Now, follow these steps:

1. Choose File → Import.

2. Locate and import the `Axe_Replace.ma` scene file from the Scenes folder of the Axe project from the companion web page. The new axe appears at the origin in your scene.

Transferring Animation

Transferring all the properties and actions of the original axe to a new axe requires some setup. Follow these steps:

1. Move the pivot on the new axe's top node (called either new_Axe or Axe_ Replacement:new_Axe) to the same relative position as the pivot on the original animated axe (up toward the top and a little out front of the handle, just under the blade). This ensures that the new axe has the same spin as the old axe. Otherwise, the animation won't look right when transferred to the new axe. Figure 8.26 shows the pivot's location.

2. Use grid snap to place the top node of the new axe at the origin.

3. Choose Display → Transform Display → Selection Handles to turn on the selection handle of the new axe.

4. Go to frame 1. Select the original axe's axe node, open the Graph Editor, and choose Edit → Copy.

5. Select the new axe to display its curves in the Graph Editor. It has no curves to display yet. With the new_Axe node selected in the Graph Editor, choose Edit → Paste. As shown in Figure 8.27, the new axe is slightly offset from the original axe.

> When you copy and paste curves in the Graph Editor, make sure you're on the first frame of the animation. Pasting curves places them at the current frame. Because the animation of the original axe started at frame 1, make sure you're at frame 1 when you paste the curves to the new axe.

6. You have to move the new axe to match the original, but because it's already animated, you'll move it using the curves in the Graph Editor. With the new axe selected, in the Graph Editor select the Translate Y curve; move it down to match the height of the original axe.

7. Scrub the animation to see that the new axe has the same animation except at the end when it hits the target. Remember that you grouped the original axe under the target node for follow-through animation. Place the new axe under this node as well.

   The file `axe_v7.mb` in the Axe project from the book's web page has the new axe imported and all the animation copied to get you caught up to this point.

8. After you scrub the animation and make sure the new axe animates properly, select the original axe's node and delete it.

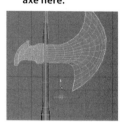

Figure 8.26

Place the pivot point on the new axe here.

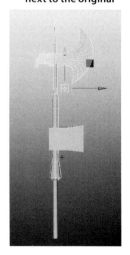

Figure 8.27

The new axe placed next to the original

Animating Flying Text

It's inevitable. Sooner or later, you will need to animate a flying logo or flying text. Animating flying text—at least, the way you'll do it here—can show you how to animate pretty much anything that has to twist, wind, and bend along a path; this technique isn't just for text.

You'll need to create the text, so follow these steps:

1. In a new scene, select Create → Text ❐. In the option box, enter your text and select a font to use (see Figure 8.28). In this case, stick with Times New Roman. Set Type to Bevel.

Figure 8.28

**The Text Curves
Options box**

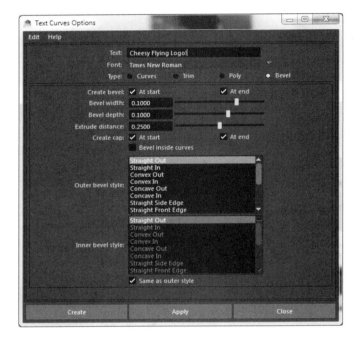

Setting the Type attribute to Poly for your text creates curve outlines for the text and planar faces for the letters, for a flat-text effect. Setting the Type Creation option to Curves gives you just the curve outlines. Finally, using Trim to create your text makes the letters out of flat planar NURBS surfaces. However, no typographical surface history is created with text. To allow you to edit the text, you must re-create the text and/or font as needed.

2. Leave the rest of the creation methods at their defaults. Doing so creates the text as beveled faces to make solid text with thickness.

3. When you have the text, you need to create a curve for it to animate along. Using either the CV or EP Curve tool, create a winding curve like a rollercoaster for the logo, shown with the text in Figure 8.29.

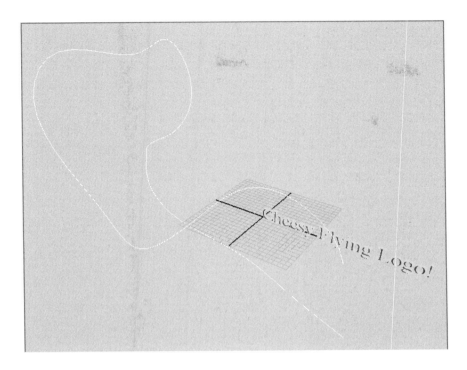

Figure 8.29
**Create a curve
path for the text to
follow.**

4. Just as you did with the axe exercise, you'll assign the text object to this curve.
   Set your frame range to 1–100. Select the text, Shift+select the curve, and, in the
   Animation menu set, choose Constrain → Motion Paths → Attach To Motion Path ❑.
   Check the Follow box to turn it on. Set Front Axis to X and Up Axis to Y and select
   the Bank check box, as shown in Figure 8.30.

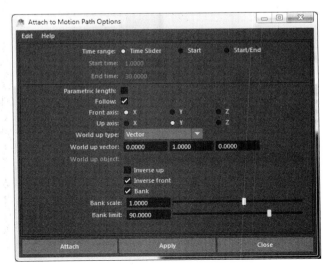

Figure 8.30
**The Attach To
Motion Path
Options box**

Depending on how you create your curve and text, you may need to experiment with the Front Axis and Up Axis attributes to get the text to fly the way you want.

5. Orbit the camera around to the other side, and you can see the text on the path, as shown in Figure 8.31. In the Attribute Editor for the motion path, notice the U Value attribute; this is the position of the text along the curve from 0 to 1. Scrub the animation, and the text should glide along the curve.

6. The text isn't bending along with the curve at all yet. To accomplish this, you need to add a lattice that bends the text to the curvature of the path. Select the text object, and choose Constrain → Motion Paths → Flow Path Object ❑.

7. In the option box for the Flow Path Object, set Divisions: Front to **120**, Up to **2**, and Side to **2**, and select Curve for Lattice Around. Make sure the Local Effect box is unchecked. Doing so creates a lattice that follows the curve, giving it 120 segments along the path. This lattice deforms the text as it travels along the path to the curvature of the path.

8. Scrub your animation, and you see a fairly strange result; parts of the text explode out from the lattice, as shown in Figure 8.32.

9. The geometry is going outside the influence of the lattice. To fix the situation, select the lattice and base node; then scale up the lattice *and* its base node together to create a larger size of influence around the path (see Figure 8.33).

Scrub your animation to check the frame range and how well the text flies through the lattice. When the lattice and its base are large enough to handle the text along all of the path's corners and turns, *voilà*—Cheesy Flying Logo! (See Figure 8.34.)

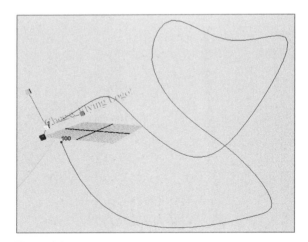

Figure 8.31

The text is on the path.

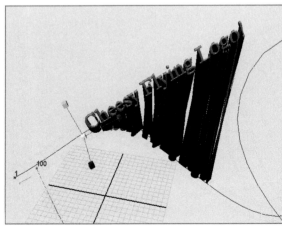

Figure 8.32

The geometry doesn't fit the lattice well. Ouch!

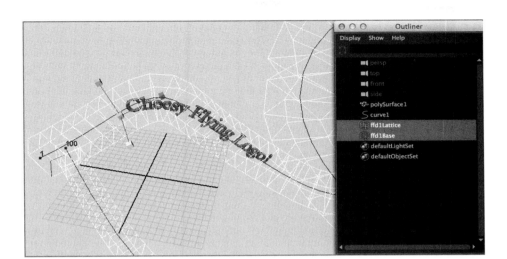

Figure 8.33

Scale the lattice and its base node to accommodate the flying text.

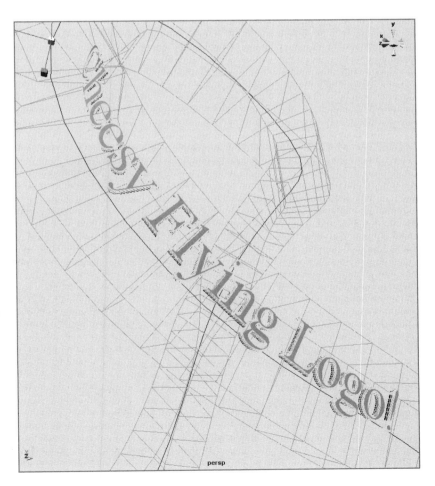

Figure 8.34

Cheesy Flying Logo! makes a nice turn.

Animating the Catapult

As an exercise in animating a system of parts of a model, you'll now animate the catapult from Chapter 4, "Beginning Polygonal Modeling." You'll turn its winch to bend back the catapult arm, which shoots the projectiles, and then you'll fire and watch the arm fly up.

Let's get acquainted with the scene file and make sure its pivots and hierarchies are set up properly. The scene file catapult_anim_v1.mb in the Catapult_Anim project from the companion web page has everything in order, although it's always good to make sure. Figure 8.35 shows the catapult with its winch selected and ready to animate.

Get a sense of timing put down for the winch first and use that to pull back the arm to fire. Follow these steps:

1. Select the Winch group with its selection handle. At frame 1, set a keyframe for rotation. If the selection handle isn't turned on, select Winch from the Outliner and turn on the selection handle by choosing Display → Transform Display → Selection Handles. To keep it clean as you go along, instead of pressing Shift+E to set a key for all three axes of rotation, select only the Rotate X attribute in the Channel Box, right-click to open the context menu, and choose Key Selected. There only needs to be rotation in X for the winch.

2. Jump to frame 60. Rotate the winch backward a few times or enter **–400** or so for the Rotate X attribute.

3. Open the Graph Editor, ease in the curve a bit, and ease out the curve a lot so that the rotation starts casually but grinds to a stop as the arm becomes more difficult to pull back.

Figure 8.35

The catapult's winch is ready to animate.

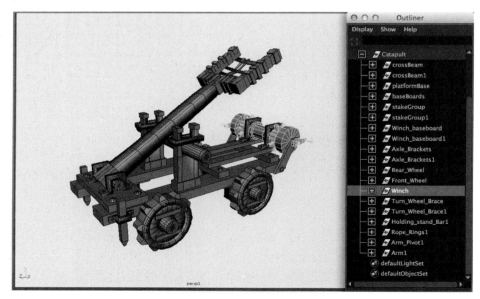

Because animating a rope is a fairly advanced task, the catapult is animated without its rope; however, the principle of an imaginary rope pulling the arm down to create tension in the arm drives the animation.

4. To accentuate the more difficult winding at the end, add a key to the X-axis rotation through the Graph Editor. To do so, select the curve and click the Insert Keys Tool icon (⊞) in the upper-left corner of the Graph Editor.

5. MMB+click and drag to place a new keyframe positioned at frame 42. You can always drag the key back and forth on the curve to place it directly at frame 42. It may help to turn on key snapping first. (See Figure 8.36.)

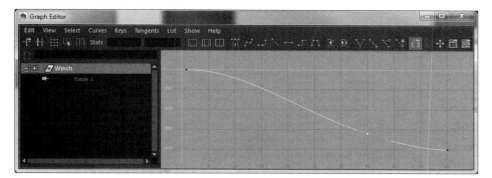

Figure 8.36

Insert a keyframe at frame 42.

6. Move that keyframe down to create a stronger ease-out for the winch. Be careful not to let the curve dip down so that the winch switches directions. Adjust the handles to smooth the curve. You can also add a little recoil to the winch by inserting a new keyframe through the Graph Editor at frame 70. (See Figure 8.37.)

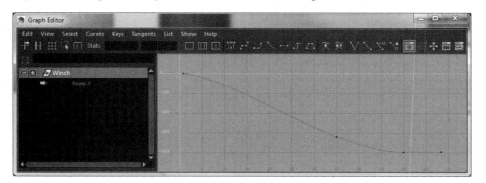

Figure 8.37

Creating a greater ease-out and adding a little recoil at the end

Animating with Deformers

It's time to animate the arm coiling back, using the winch's timing as it's driving the arm. Because the catapult's arm is supported by a brace and the whole idea of a catapult is based on tension, you have to bend the arm back as the winch pulls it.

You'll use a nonlinear deformer, just as you did in the axe head exercise in Chapter 5, but this time, you'll animate the deformer to create the bending of the catapult arm. Follow these steps:

1. Switch to the Modeling menu set. Select the Arm1 group and choose Deform → Nonlinear → Bend to create a Bend deformer perpendicular to the arm. Select the deformer and rotate it to line it up with the arm, as shown in Figure 8.38.

Figure 8.38

Align the Bend deformer with the catapult arm.

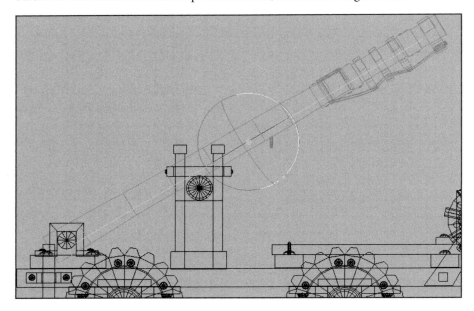

Figure 8.39

Orient the Bend deformer to bend the arm back and down.

2. With the Bend deformer selected, look in the Channel Box for bend1 under the Inputs section, and click it to expand its attributes. Try entering **0.5** for Curvature. More than likely, the catapult arm will bend sideways. Rotate the deformer so that the arm is bending back and down instead, as shown in Figure 8.39.

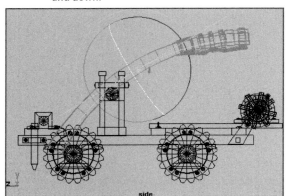

3. You don't want the arm's base to bend back, just the basket side. You want it to bend at the brace point, not in the middle where it is now. Move the deformer down the length of the arm until the middle lines up with the arm's support brace.

4. To prevent the bottom of the arm from bending, change the Low Bound attribute to **0**. To keep the basket from bending, set the High Bound attribute to **0.9**.

5. Instead of trying to match the speed, ease-in, and ease-out of the winch, set the gross keyframes for the arm pulling back first. Reset Curvature to **0** and set

a key for Curvature at frame 1. (Select bend1's Curvature in the Channel Box, right-click, and choose Key Selected from the context menu.)

The Low Bound and High Bound attributes control how far up and down the deformer the object is affected. The Envelope attribute for a deformer governs how much the object is affected overall, with 0 not affecting the geometry at all.

6. Go to frame 60 and set Curvature to **0.8**. If Auto Keyframe is turned on, this sets a keyframe; otherwise, set a key manually. (See Figure 8.40.)

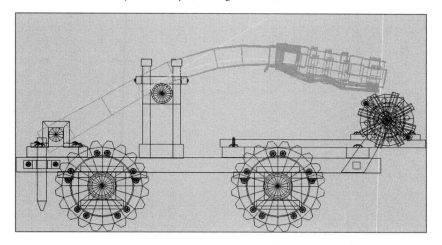

Figure 8.40

Bend the arm back at frame 60 and set a keyframe.

7. If you play back the animation, notice that the way the winch winds back and the way the arm bends don't match. In the Graph Editor, you can adjust the animation curve on the Bend deformer to match the winch's curve.

8. Insert a key on the Curvature curve at frame 42 and move it up to match the curvature you created for the winch.

9. Insert a new key at frame 70 and make the arm bend back up slightly as the winch recoils. Set Curvature to about **0.79** from 0.8. (See Figure 8.41.)

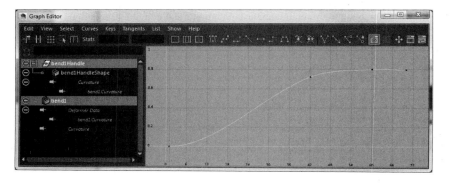

Figure 8.41

Try to match the relative curvature of the winch's animation curve with the Bend deformer's animation curve.

Figure 8.42

Group the deformer node under the Arm1 group node.

10. Go to frame 90 and set a key again for Curvature at **0**. Set a key at 0.82 for frame 97 to create anticipation and then keyframe at frame 103 to release the arm and fire the imaginary payload with a Curvature of **–0.8**.

11. Add some rotation to the arm for dramatic effect. At about frame 100, during the release, the arm is almost straight. Select the Arm1 group and set a rotation key on the X-axis. Go to frame 105 and rotate the arm 45 degrees to the left in the X-axis. If the starting rotation of the arm is at 30 (as it is in the sample file), set an X-axis rotation key of **75** at frame 105.

12. Notice that the arm is bending strangely now that it's being rotated. It's moving off the deformer, so its influence is changing for the worse. To fix this, go back to frame 100 and group the deformer node (called *bend1Handle*) under the Arm1 group, as shown in Figure 8.42. Now it rotates along with the arm, adding its own bending influence.

13. Work on setting keyframes on the deformer and the arm's rotation so that the arm falls back down onto the support brace and quivers until it becomes straight again. The animation curve for the Bend deformer should look like Figure 8.43. The rotation of the arm should look like Figure 8.44. Remember to make the tangents flat on the keys where the arm bounces off the brace and at the peaks, like the ball's bounce from earlier in the chapter.

Figure 8.43

The animation curve for the arm's vibration back and forth as it comes to a rest

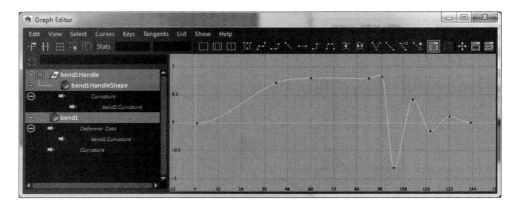

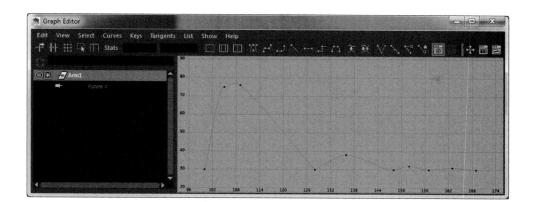

Figure 8.44

The animation curve for the arm's rotation as it heaves up and falls back down, coming to an easy rest on the brace

The file `catapult_anim_v2.mb` will give you a good reference to check out the timing of the arm bend and rotation. Here are some items you can animate to make this a complete animation:

- Spin the winch around as the arm releases, as if its rope is being yanked away from it.
- Animate the entire catapult rocking forward and backward as the arm releases, similar to the way a car rocks when you jump onto the hood.
- Move the catapult forward on a road, spinning its wheels as best you can to match the distance it travels.
- Design and build your own catapult and animate it along the same lines.

Summary

In this chapter, you began to learn the fundamentals of animating a scene. Starting with a bouncing ball, you learned how to work in the Graph Editor to set up and adjust timing as well as how to add squash and stretch to the animation. The next exercise, throwing an axe, expanded on your experience of creating timing in the Graph Editor and showed you how to add anticipation, follow-through, and secondary motion to your scene. You then learned how to animate the axe throw using path animation. You went on to learn how to replace a proxy object that is already animated with a different finished model and how to transfer the animation. Finally, you used the catapult to animate with deformers and further your experience in the Graph Editor.

Animating a "complex" system, such as a catapult, involves creating layers of animation based on facets of the mechanics of the system's movement. With the catapult, you tackled the individual parts separately and then worked to unify the animations. You'll use rigging concepts in the next chapter to automate some of that process for a locomotive. The same is true of the `Bouncing_Ball` and `Axe_Throwing` exercises. The different needs of the animation were addressed one by one, starting with the gross animation and ending with finishing touches to add weight.

Animation is the art of observation, interpretation, and implementation. Learning to see how things move, deciphering why they move as they do, and then applying all that to your Maya scene is what animation is all about.

CHAPTER 9

More Animation!

Now that you have a little more animation experience, you can get into some more involved animation practices and toolsets, exploring the principles covered in this book and its examples. Animation is a long journey, and you should use this book as a stepping-off point. For everything you're being exposed to here, there are many more techniques to discover.

Learning Outcomes: In this chapter, you will be able to

- Use hierarchies in animation tasks

- Create and manipulate a skeleton system for animation and group models to bones

- Create a walk cycle using forward kinematics for pose animation

- Discern the two ways—smooth and interactive—to bind a mesh to a skeleton in Maya

- Use inverse kinematics in a rig of a simple character

- Create a walk cycle using IK animation

- Use constraints to automate animation

- Create set-driven keys for animation rigging

- Rig a locomotive for automated animation

- Rig a simple character for basic character animation

Skeletons and Kinematics

In your body, your muscles move the bones of your skeleton, and as your bones move, parts of your body move. In computer graphics (CG) animation, a *skeleton* is an armature built into a 3D model that drives the geometry when the bones are moved. You insert a skeleton into a CG model and attach or bind it to the geometry. The skeleton's bones are animated, which in turn move the parts of the geometry to which they're attached. By using a skeleton, the Autodesk® Maya® software allows you to bend and deform the attached geometry at the skeleton's *joints*. A skeleton is useful for character work, but skeletons have many other uses. Any time you need to drive the geometry of a model with an internal system, such as a fly-fishing line or a tree bending in the wind, you can use skeletons. You'll use skeletons to drive locomotive wheels and a simple character later in this chapter.

Skeletons and Hierarchy

Skeletons rely on hierarchies (see Figure 9.1). Bones are created in a hierarchical manner, resulting in a *root joint* that is the parent of all the joints beneath it in the hierarchy. For example, a hip joint can be the root joint of a leg skeleton system in which the *knee joint* is the leg's child, the *ankle joint* belongs to the knee, and the five *toe joints* are the ankle's children.

Geometry need not deform to be attached to a bone system; objects can be grouped with or under joints. They move under their parent joint and rotate around that joint's pivot as opposed to their own pivot point.

A skeleton is really just a collection of grouped and properly positioned pivot points called *joints* that you use to move your geometry. A *bone* is the length between each joint; bones show you only the skeletal system and are not actual geometry.

Inverse kinematics (IK) and *forward kinematics* (FK) are the methods you use to animate a skeletal system. FK rotates the bones directly at their top joint to assume poses. This method resembles *stop-motion animation*, in which you pose a puppet, along with its underlying armature, frame by frame. With FK, the animator moves the character into position by rotating the joints that run the geometry.

Rotating a joint affects the position of the bones and joints beneath it in the hierarchy (see Figure 9.2). If you rotate the hip up, the knee and ankle swing up as if the character is kicking.

IK uses a more complex, but often easier, system of *IK handles* that are attached to the tip of a joint system. The corresponding base of the IK system is attached farther up the skeleton hierarchy to a joint determined as the root of that IK segment. It need not be the root joint of the entire skeleton, though.

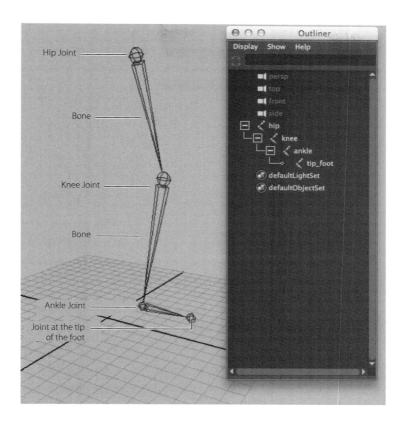

Figure 9.1

**A leg skeleton and
its hierarchy**

Hip Joint

Bone

Knee Joint

Bone

Ankle Joint

Joint at the tip
of the foot

The bones and joints in the IK chain are
affected only by movement of the IK handle.
When the handle moves, an *IK solver* figures
out how to rotate all the joints to accommodate
the new position of the IK handle.

The effect is as if someone grabbed
your hand and moved it. The person holding your hand is similar to an IK handle.
Moving your hand causes the bones in your
arm to rotate around the shoulder, elbow, and
wrist. As you can see in Figure 9.3, the animation flows up the hierarchy and is therefore
called inverse kinematics.

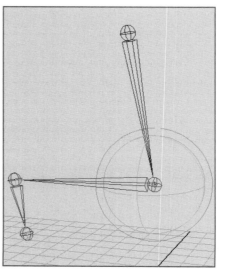

Figure 9.2

**In forward kinemat-
ics, the joints are
rotated directly.**

Figure 9.3

In inverse kinematics, the joints rotate in response to the IK handle's position.

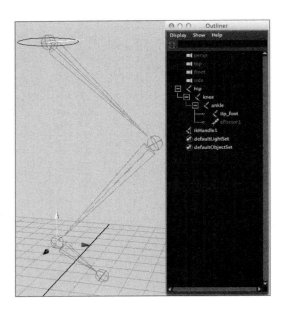

Forward Kinematics: The Block Man

To understand skeletal hierarchy, look at Figure 9.4, which shows a simple biped (two-legged) character made of primitive blocks. He's called the Block Man. (Clever!) Each block represents part of the body, with gaps between the blocks representing points where the body pivots.

The pivot of each block is placed to represent the appropriate joint location. For example, the shin's pivot is located at the knee. Each block is grouped up the chain so that the foot moves with the shin, which moves with the thigh, which moves with the pelvis.

The hands are grouped under the arms, which are grouped under the shoulders, and so forth, down the spine to the pelvis. The head groups under the first neck block and so on down the spine to the pelvis. The pelvis is the center of the body, which is known as the *root* of the figure.

Figure 9.4

The Block Man's cubes arranged

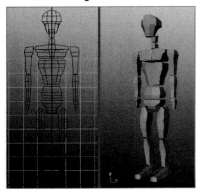

The way this figure is grouped (see Figure 9.5) represents how the hierarchy of a character works for the most part. Each body part is attached and becomes the child of the part above it in the chain.

Load the file block_man_v02.ma from the Block_Man project folder on the book's web page, www.sybex.com/go/introducingmaya2016, for a good reference of the grouping structure. This file shows you what a skeleton hierarchy does.

In the Hypergraph Hierarchy window, choose Options → Layout → Freeform Layout to position the nodes any way you want. To make selections easier, you can arrange the nodes as if they were on a body (see Figure 9.6). You can toggle between freeform and automatic, and your freeform layout will be retained.

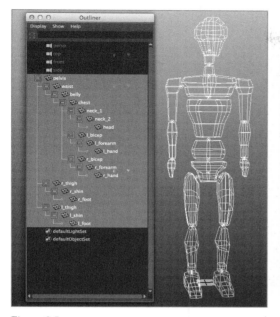

Figure 9.5

Pivot placements and grouping

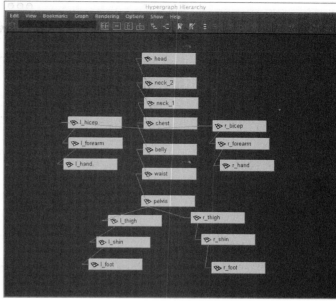

Figure 9.6

A freeform layout in the Hypergraph Hierarchy window

Creating the Skeleton

The basis of how the Block Man is laid out and grouped is what skeletons are all about. Skeletons make character animation easier by automating, at the least, the hierarchy and pivot placement described earlier.

THE PELVIS AS ROOT

Traditionally, the pelvis is the basis of all biped setups. The root of any skeletal system (whether using bones or geometry as the example) is the character's pivot point—the center of balance. Because a biped character centers itself on two feet, its pelvis becomes the root of its skeletal system. In CG, the pelvis becomes the parent node of the whole system and is the node used to move or orient the entire character. In a skeleton system, this would be the root joint.

The root is then the top parent of the system below it and runs the entire chain. Therefore, selecting character parts straight from the Outliner or the Hypergraph is sometimes easier. You can see that a good naming convention is always important with character setups.

You'll use the Block Man to create a simple skeleton. Load block_man_v01.ma from the Block_Man project. This is the same as block_man_v02.ma, but this version isn't grouped.

1. Maximize the front view window. Switch to the Rigging menu set by using the drop-down menu or by pressing F3.

2. Activate the Joint tool by choosing Skeleton → Create Joints. Your cursor turns into a cross.

3. Click in the middle of the pelvis to place the first joint, which is the root joint of the skeleton.

4. Shift+click up to the space between the pelvis and the waist.

> The joint display sizes in your Maya window may not match those shown in the book. This isn't a problem; however, you can change the joint sizes by clicking Display → Animation → Joint Size.

By pressing Shift as you click, you create a joint in a straight line from the last joint placement. A bone is created between the two joints as a visual guide to the skeleton. The placement of the joints depends on the active view.

5. Click more joints up the spine at the gaps between the body parts, as shown in Figure 9.7. Place the second-to-last joint at the base of the skull, as shown in the side view in Figure 9.7. Place the last joint at the top of the head. Then press Enter to exit Create Joints. Select the top joint at the head and, in a side view, move that joint toward the forehead as shown to make the angle in Figure 9.7.

Figure 9.7

Place spine joints straight up the middle of the body and offset the last joint in the head.

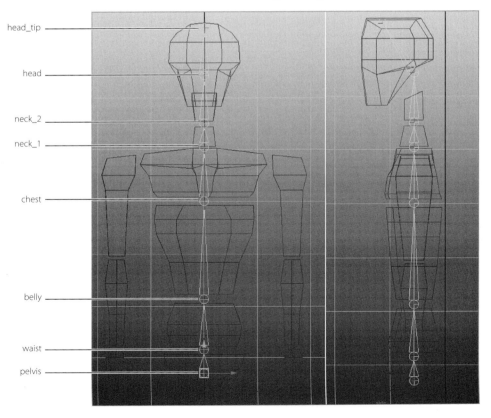

6. Use Figure 9.7 as a guide to name all your joints. Now you need to start a new branch of joints leading into the legs and arms. Begin with the arms.

> Pressing the Up arrow key takes you up one node in a hierarchy (a.k.a. *pick-walking*). Pressing the Down arrow key takes you down one node in a hierarchy. This approach also applies to skeletons because they're hierarchies.

7. Activate Create Joints (Skeleton → Create Joints). In the front view, click to place a new joint at the top-left side of the upper chest just to the side of the joints you've already placed (see Figure 9.8, left); then click to place a second connected joint in the bicep at the shoulder. Click down to create joints at the elbow, the wrist, and the tip of the character's right hand (which is on the left side of your screen). Press Enter to complete that part of the skeleton.

8. Reenter Create Joints and repeat the previous step to create joints for the other arm, as shown in Figure 9.8 (right). Name your joints!

9. You'll notice that the arms are not part of the main skeleton yet. You need to connect them to the main skeleton. Open the Outliner and select the lt_clavicle joint. MMB+drag it to the chest node to group it to the chest (see Figure 9.9). Notice that a new bone appears between these two joints. Group the rt_clavicle to the chest as well. Figure 9.10 shows the arms are now part of the main skeleton.

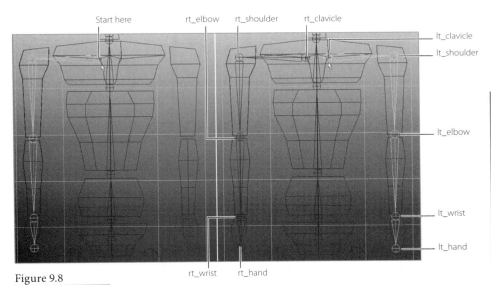

Figure 9.8

Place joints for the arm.

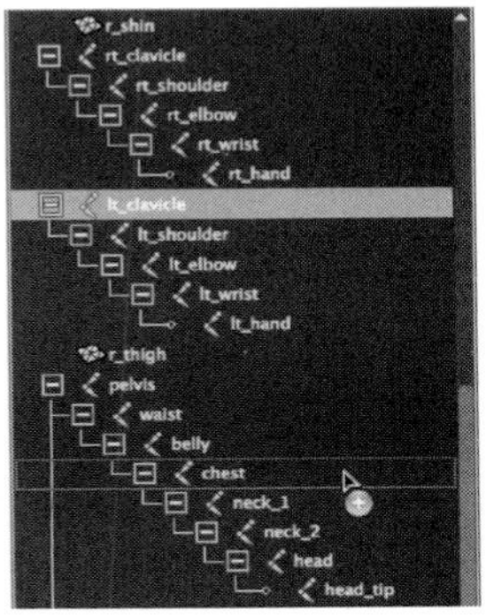

Figure 9.9

Group the lt_clavicle to the chest.

Figure 9.10

The arms are grouped to the chest, and the joints are connected with new bones.

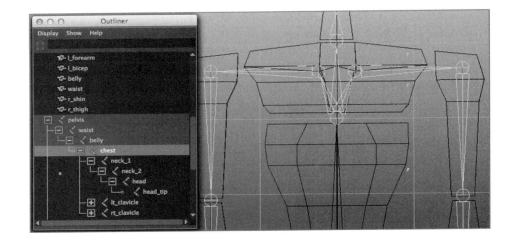

10. To start another string of joints in the first leg, enter Create Joints. Then click the pelvis joint, selecting it. In the front view, place the first leg joint at the top of the screen-left thigh (the character's right thigh). Place the next joint between the thigh and knee and then another at the top of the foot where it meets the ankle. Do not exit Create Joints yet!

11. Switch to the side view and place another joint at the ankle, another in the middle bottom of the foot, and the last joint at the tip of the foot. Press Enter to exit Create Joints, and you'll see that your leg is already attached to the pelvis; there's no need to group in the Outliner this time like with the clavicles.

Figure 9.11

Place the leg joints and name them.

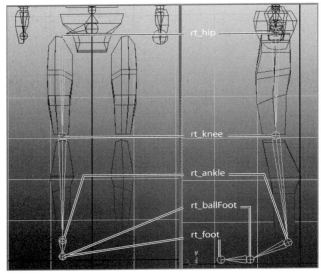

12. In the side view, select the knee joint, and enter Pivot mode by pressing and holding the D key. Very slightly move the knee joint away from the front of the character, out toward the toe. This slight bend will be needed later when you continue the character rig. Using Pivot mode, make sure your joints are placed properly for the leg and foot using Figure 9.11 as a guide. Name your joints!

13. Select the rt_hip joint and press Ctrl+D to duplicate the hip and the joints beneath it. In the front view, move the new rt_hip1 joint to the other leg and place it as shown in Figure 9.12 (left). Rename those new joints as shown.

You're all done! You'll be adding to this later in the chapter as you create a more well-rounded rig for the character, but for now, check your work against Figure 9.12 (right) and the `block_man_skeleton_v01.ma` file from the Block_Man project.

Attaching to the Skeleton

You now have a full skeleton for your character. To attach the geometry, all you need to do is parent the body parts under their appropriate joints. Before you get to that, take a few minutes and make sure all your joints are named in the Outliner to make the scene easier to manage. You can use Figure 9.13 as a naming reference.

You can also load the `block_man_skeleton_v01.ma` file from the Block_Man project to get to this point.

To parent the Block Man's geometry to the skeleton, follow these steps:

1. Starting with the pelvis, parent it under the pelvis joint by MMB+clicking and dragging it to the pelvis joint. Once it's in the group, MMB+drag the pelvis_geom again and place it between the pelvis and waist joints, as shown in Figure 9.13.

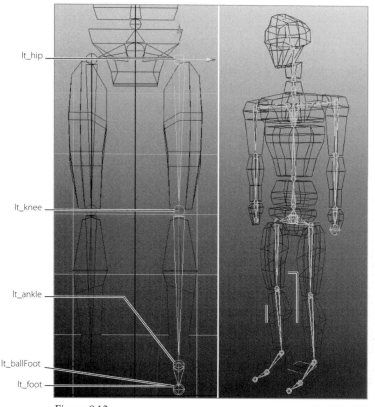

Figure 9.12

Duplicate the leg joints, move them to the other leg, and name the new joints (left). The skeleton is complete (right).

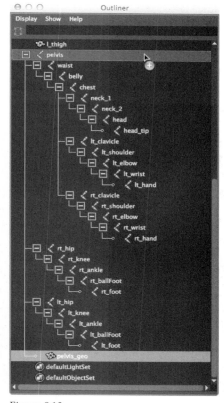

Figure 9.13

After you check your naming, you'll parent the pelvis geometry under the pelvis joint.

2. Continue the MMB+dragging process in the Outliner to place everything but the feet geometry in its proper place in the skeleton using the following list and Figure 9.14 as guides. You will deal with the feet a little differently. Figure 9.14 shows the finished hierarchy in the Outliner and Hypergraph.

   - Shins under the knees; thighs under the hips
   - Hands under the wrists; forearms under the elbows
   - Biceps under the shoulder joints
   - Head under the head joint (not the head_tip joint)
   - Top neck geometry (neck_2) under neck_2 joint
   - Bottom neck geometry (neck_1) under the neck_1 joint
   - Chest under the chest joint
   - Belly under the belly joint
   - Waist under the waist joint

3. Now you'll bind the feet to the foot joints, instead of grouping them. Since there is a joint in the middle of the foot, you'll want to bend the foot. You will explore binding in more detail later in the chapter, but for now, select the l_foot geometry in the Outliner; then press Ctrl and select all three foot joints (lt_ankle, lt_ballFoot, and lt_foot) in the Outliner as well (see Figure 9.15, left).

4. Select Skin → Bind Skin ☐, set Bind To to Selected Joints and Bind Method to Heat Map, and click the Bind Skin button. This will bind (a.k.a. skin) the foot geometry to the joints so you can then bend, or deform, the foot.

5. To test the bind, select the middle foot joint (lt_ballFoot) and rotate it; the tip of the foot should move. Select the ankle and rotate it, and the whole foot should move. Undo your rotations or set the rotations back to 0 so that the foot is at its rest pose (a.k.a. *bind pose*) again. Just don't undo the binding unless you need to redo steps 3 and 4. (See Figure 9.15, right.)

6. Repeat steps 3 and 4 for the other foot to bind the geometry and test its movement. Just remember to undo your rotations to return to the bind pose.

The Block Man is now set up with a skeleton that you'll use to make a simple walk cycle. This exercise will help get you more familiar and comfortable with animating a character. You will do more to this setup to make a better animation rig for the Block Man character later in the chapter.

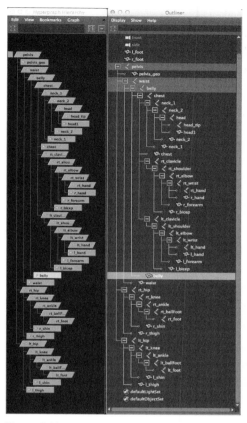

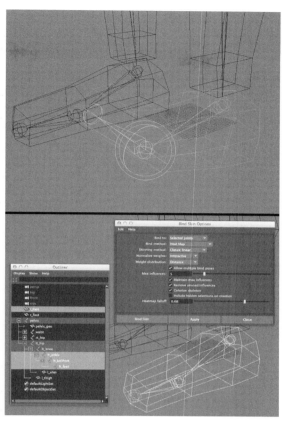

Figure 9.14

Parent all the geometry except the feet into its proper place in the skeleton. The finished hierarchy is shown in the Hypergraph and Outliner side-by-side.

Figure 9.15

Bind Skin Options: the left foot geometry and the left foot joints selected (top). Bind and test the left foot (bottom).

The Block Man: FK Walk Cycle

A *walk cycle* is an animation that takes the character through a few steps that can be repeated many times so that the character seems to be taking numerous steps. In a cycle, make sure the position of the first frame matches the position of the last frame so that when the animation sequence is cycled, no "pop" occurs in the motion at that point.

Now, try animating this character's walk cycle using FK on the skeleton. You'll find the workflow straightforward, as if you were adjusting positions on a doll.

Load the block_man_skeleton_v02.ma file from the Block_Man project from the companion web page for the properly grouped and bound model and skeleton. In this file, the right arm and leg have drawing overrides enabled; this makes their wireframe display white to make it easier to distinguish between the right and left sides while working.

Use the key poses in the following figures to guide you in animating the body as it walks. You'll key at five-frame intervals to lay down the gross animation. You can go back and adjust the timing of the joint rotations in the Graph Editor to make the animation better later. The white leg and arm are behind the body, farther from the camera.

This type of animation is also called *pose animation* because you're posing the character from keyframe to keyframe.

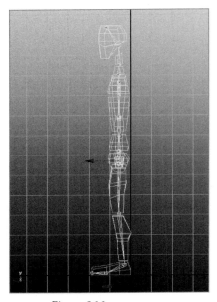

Figure 9.16

The character's starting position

Starting Out: Frames 1 and 5

Figure 9.16 shows the character's starting position. Here, you'll set a key for this position and then begin the walk cycle by moving the joints into their second position and keyframing that.

1. At frame 1, set a key for the rotation of all the joints. The easiest way is to select all the joints (and only the joints) in the Outliner or the Hypergraph. With pose animation, you have to make sure that all the joints are keyframed at every step, even if Auto Keyframe is turned on. Also set a position keyframe for just the pelvis joint.

2. Go to frame 5. Rotate the back leg back (the Block Man's right, white leg), rotate the rt_ballFoot joint to bend the foot, and bend the ankle to make the ball of the foot level again. Lower the body (select and move the pelvis joint) to line up the back heel with the ground. This will keep the man on the ground as he goes through the walk cycle, although he won't actually move forward yet.

3. Rotate the near leg (the man's left blue wireframe leg) forward, bend the knee, and pivot the foot up a bit.

SELECTING ONLY JOINTS IN THE OUTLINER

A quick way to select all the joints, and only the joints, is to filter the Outliner view to show only joints. In the Outliner, choose Show → Objects → Joints. To reset the Outliner, choose Show → Show All.

4. Rotate the back white wireframe arm forward and rotate the near arm back (opposite from the legs). Bend the arms at the elbows.

5. Bend the man forward at the waist, bend neck_1 forward, and tilt the head back up to compensate a little. Figure 9.17 shows the pose at this point.

6. Select all the joints in the Outliner and set a rotation key. You're setting a pose for all the joints, which will ensure that all the body parts are in sync.

If you don't key everything every step of the way, some parts of the body won't key with Auto Keyframe properly because the last time they moved may have been two steps previous. This may cause confusion, so it's best to key every joint at every step until you feel more comfortable editing character animation.

Frame 10

Figure 9.18 shows the position you'll keyframe at frame 10; it's approximately midstride for the first leg.

1. Go to frame 10. Rotate the back leg out further and level the foot. Lower the body to place the man on the ground.

2. Rotate the front leg out, straighten the knee, and flatten the foot to place it on the ground. This is midstride. Swing the arms in their current direction a touch more. Bend the torso forward some more. Make sure you set a key for all the joints.

Frame 15

Figure 9.19 shows the position you'll keyframe at frame 15. At this point, the character begins to shift his weight to the front leg as it plants on the ground, and the character also begins lifting the back leg.

1. Go to frame 15. Rotate the front leg back toward the body and raise the body as the man steps to keep the front foot flat on the ground. Rotate the back knee up to lift the foot and rotate the foot down to make him push off the toe.

2. Start swinging the arms in the opposite direction. Start straightening the torso back up, but bend the head forward a bit.

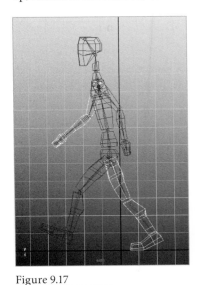

Figure 9.17
The second pose (frame 5)

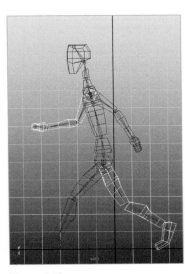

Figure 9.18
The third pose (frame 10)

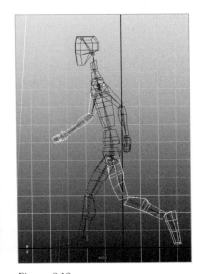

Figure 9.19
The fourth pose (frame 15)

Frame 20

At frame 20, the man will shift all his weight onto the front leg and move his body over that leg, lifting his rear leg to begin its swing out front to finish the stride. Figure 9.20 shows the pose.

Follow these steps:

1. Rotate the front leg almost straight under the man and lift up the body to keep the front foot on the ground. Lift the rear leg and swing it forward.

2. Straighten the torso and keep the arms swinging in their new direction. Key all the joints.

Frame 25

Now, the man will swing his whole body forward, pivoting on the left leg (the dark one) to put himself off center and ready to fall forward into the next step. Figure 9.21 shows the pose.

Here are the steps:

1. Go to frame 25.

2. Rotate the front (dark) leg back behind the man and swing the white leg up and ready to take the next step. Lower the body to keep the now rear foot (the dark one) on the ground.

Frame 30

Use Figure 9.22 as a guide for creating the next pose. Notice that it's similar to the pose at frame 10. As a matter of fact, the only major differences are which leg and arm are in front. Everything else should be about the same. You'll want some variety in the exact positions to make the animation more interesting, but the poses are similar.

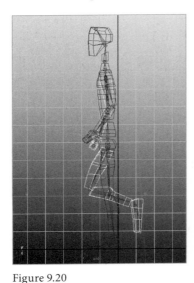
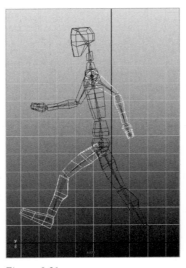
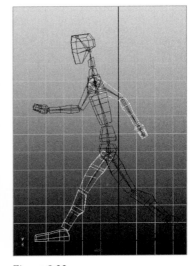

Figure 9.20
The fifth pose (frame 20)

Figure 9.21
The sixth pose (frame 25)

Figure 9.22
The seventh pose (frame 30)

Completing the First Steps

You've finished a set of poses for the character's first step. You animated the left leg taking a step forward in the first series of poses. The next series of poses has to do with the right leg. The pose at frame 35 corresponds to the pose at frame 15. Frame 40 matches frame 20. You will copy keyframes in the Graph Editor to make more steps, but first let's retime these initial keys before continuing.

When a 30-frame section is complete, you need to return to the animation through the Graph Editor. Adjust all the keyframes that you initially set at these five-frame intervals to make the animation more realistic. Right now, you have only the gross keyframes in place, so the timing is off. Timing the frames properly is ultimately a matter of how the animation looks to you.

Logistically speaking, some poses take a little less time to achieve than the evenly spaced five frames you used. For example, achieving the second pose from the start position should take four frames. The third pose (see Figure 9.18, earlier in the chapter) from frame 5 to frame 10 should take four frames. The next frame section, originally from frame 10 to 15 (the fourth pose; see Figure 9.19, earlier in the chapter), should take only three frames. To accomplish this easily, follow these steps:

1. Select the top node of the skeleton (the pelvis) and open the Graph Editor. On the pelvis node in the left side of the Graph Editor, Shift+click the plus sign to open the entire tree of nodes beneath the pelvis. All the animated channels show their curves, as shown in Figure 9.23 (top).

2. Marquee-select all the keyframes on the curves beyond frame 1, not including those at frame 1. Press the W key to activate the Translate tool. Shift+MMB+click in the Graph Editor (so you can move in only one axis) and drag the keys horizontally to move them all 1 unit (frame) to the left. All the keyframes move, and the second pose now goes from frame 5 to frame 4.

3. Deselect the keys now at frame 4 by holding down the Ctrl key (you also use the Ctrl key on a Mac) and marquee-deselecting all those keys at frame 4. Shift+MMB+click and drag the remaining selected keys 1 unit to the left again. The third pose goes from being at frame 9 to frame 8.

4. Deselect the keys now at frame 8 and Shift+click and drag the other selected keys to the left two frames so that the fourth pose animates between frame 8 and frame 11. Deselect the frame 11 keys and move the rest over two frames to the left again so that the next section runs from frame 11 to frame 14. The following section should go from frame 14 to frame 18. The final section should go from frame 18 to frame 22. Figure 9.23 (bottom) shows the new layout for the curves.

The Graph Editor shows the walk animation curves (top). The curves are retimed (bottom).

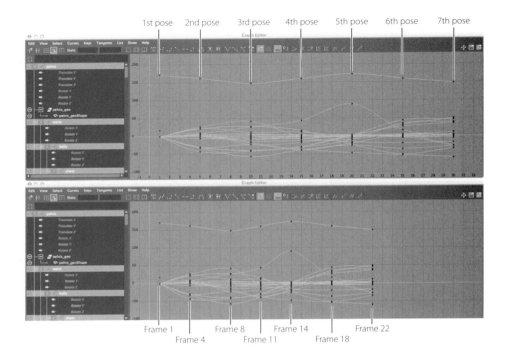

5. Continue to set and adjust keys for another cycle or two of the walk. The majority of time spent in animating something like this involves using the Graph Editor to time out the keyframes to make the animation look believable. Also, try offsetting some of the arm rotations a frame to the left or right to break up the monotony that arises from having everything keyed on the same frame.

    Load the file `block_walk_v01.mov` or `block_walk_v01.avi` of this walk cycle from the Images folder of the Block_Man project on the companion web page to see the animation in motion. It's a rough cycle, and you have to keep adjusting the character's height to keep the feet on the ground. This is where IK comes in handy, as you'll see later in this chapter. Also, the file `block_man_skeleton_walk_v01.ma` in the Block_Man project has the keyframed steps for you to play with and continue animating.

Copy and Paste Keyframes

Now that you have a base to work with, you'll copy and paste keyframes to extend the animation. This process can get a little tricky, so take it slow if you're not comfortable with the Graph Editor yet. Open the file `block_man_skeleton_walk_v01.ma` to follow along with these steps:

1. Extend the Time Range slider to 18 frames and open the Graph Editor. Select the back (white) leg at the `rt_hip` joint.

2. In the Graph Editor, Shift+click the plus sign next to the rt_hip entry to see all the joints and all their curves beneath it in the hierarchy.

3. Marquee-select all the keys from frame 4 to frame 22. In the Graph Editor window, select Edit → Copy.

4. Move the Time slider to frame 30 and, in the Graph Editor window, select Edit → Paste □. In the option box, set the Paste method to Merge. This setting is important; otherwise, the curves will not paste properly for your use! Click Apply to paste the keys at frame 30. Figure 9.24 shows the pasted frames in the Graph Editor and the Paste options.

Figure 9.24

Copy and paste keys for the white leg.

5. Select the other leg (lt_hip) and repeat steps 2 through 4 to copy all the keys from frames 4 through 22. Go to frame 30 and paste (with the Merge option as in step 3) the keys for this leg. Don't forget to Shift+click to expand all the joints beneath the hip joint in the Graph Editor to see, copy, and paste all the joints' keys as you did in step 1.

6. Repeat steps 2 through 4 for each of the two arms (rt_shoulder and lt_shoulder) to copy and paste their keys as well (copying keys from frame 4 through 22 and pasting at frame 30). Again, don't forget to Shift+click them in the Graph Editor (step 2)!

7. If you scrub your animation in the Timeline all the way to frame 48, you can verify that the animation copied properly for the arms and legs.

8. The body is not moving yet, so let's copy and paste those keys now. In the Outliner, Ctrl+select the waist, belly, chest, neck_1, neck_2, and head joints.

9. Repeat steps 3 and 4 to copy and paste keys from frames 4 through 22 to frame 30 as you did with the legs and arms. There is no need to Shift+click any of the joints in the Graph Editor (step 2) this time since you individually selected each of the joints you need. Figure 9.25 shows the pasted frames for the body movement.

10. Scrub your animation, and you'll see you need to copy and paste keys for the pelvis next. Select the pelvis joint.

11. In the Graph Editor, select all the keys from frame 1 to frame 22. This time, go to frame 27 and paste (with the Merge option as before!) the keys.

12. Scrub your animation, and everything should be working great! But around frame 25, you should see the character dip down too far. Simply raise him up and key the pelvis position at frame 25 to compensate, and you're done! The Block Man is walking for a full 48-frame clip now.

Figure 9.25

Copy and paste keys for the body movement.

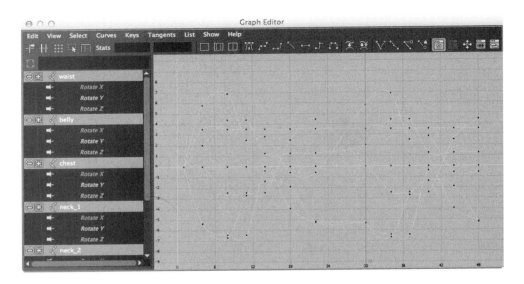

Open the file `block_man_skeleton_walk_v02.ma` from the Block_Man project to check your work to this point.

Walk Cycle Wrap-Up

This walk cycle animation is more about getting comfortable with keyframing and skeletons than it is about creating great walk animation, so take some time to practice and get better. Character animation takes a lot of time and patience, and I encourage you to keep tweaking this animation and even create different walks of your own. Animating walk cycles is a good way to hone your skills. Several great books are devoted to character rigging and animation alone, and you can research the field for ways to become more proficient. But keep in mind that movement and timing are what make animation good, not the setup or the model.

Skeletons: The Hand

For another foray into a skeletal system, you can give yourself a hand—literally. You'll use a skeleton to deform the geometry and animate it as a hand would move.

Load the file `poly_hand_skeleton_v01.ma` from the Poly_Hand_Anim project from the companion web page. The hand is shown in Figure 9.26 (top).

You'll use it to create a bone structure to make the hand animate. This process is called *rigging*.

Rigging the Hand

To create the first bones of the hand, follow these steps:

1. Maximize the top view window. Switch to the Rigging menu set by using the drop-down menu or by pressing F4.

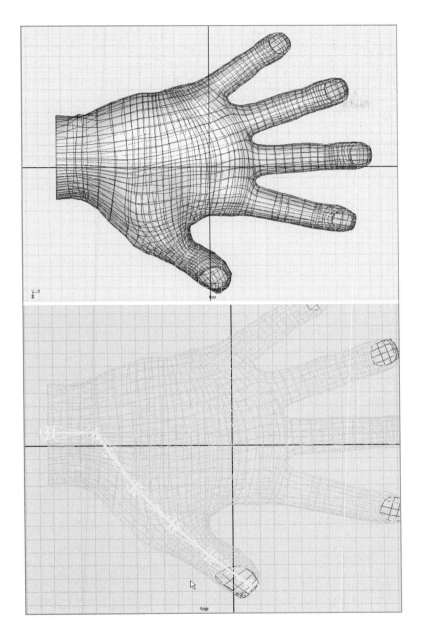

Figure 9.26

The hand mesh (top); placing joints in the hand (bottom)

2. Activate Create Joints by choosing Skeleton → Create Joints. Your cursor turns into a cross.

3. Click at the base of the wrist to place the first joint. This will be the root joint of the hand.

4. Shift+click the bottom part of the palm.

5. Place joints down through the thumb from this second joint, according to the corresponding bones in Figure 9.26 (bottom).

6. To start another string of joints into the palm, press the Up arrow key four times until you're at the second joint at the base of the palm.

7. The next joint you place will be a branch from this joint. Place that joint in the middle of the palm. Place another joint up further along the palm and then branch it out to the index finger. Press the Up arrow key to return to that upper palm joint and start a new branch into the middle finger.

Repeat this procedure to place joints for the remaining fingers, as shown in Figure 9.27. With these joints placed, you have a simple skeleton rig for the hand. This rig allows you quite a bit of hand and finger movement.

Figure 9.27

The joints in the hand

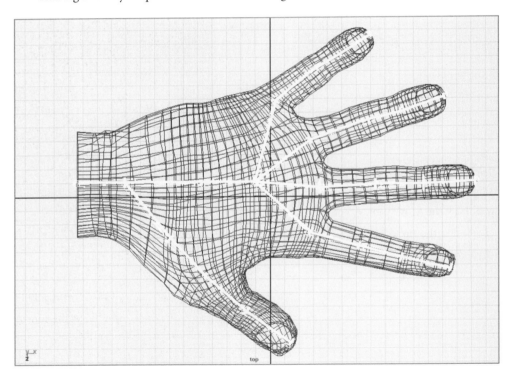

Check the other views (see Figure 9.28) to see where you need to tweak your joint positions to fit the hand. Ideally, you want the joints to be set inside your intended geometry in the same way that real bones are laid out.

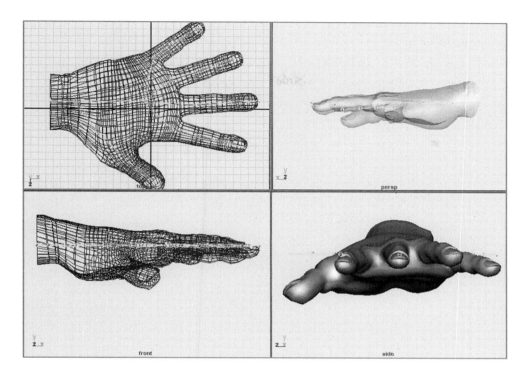

Figure 9.28

Four views of the hand with initial placement of the joints

Positioning the Joints

To position the joints, you can use either of two Maya tools: Move or Move Pivot. First you'll try the Move tool.

1. Select the tip joint for the pinky. It needs to be lowered into the pinky itself.

2. Select the Move tool (press W) and move it down into the tip of the pinky.

3. Now, move on to the top pinky knuckle. Notice that if you move the knuckle, the tip moves as well. That's not such a great idea.

Instead, it's best to move joints as pivots. Because joints are nothing more than pivots, go into Move Pivot mode (hold down the D key to activate Move Pivot or press the Ins key on Windows or the fn+Home key on a Mac) to move joints.

1. Select the top pinky-knuckle joint, and move it with Move Pivot instead. Only the joint moves, and the bones adjust to the new position.

2. Set the positions on the remaining joints to be inside the hand properly, as shown in Figure 9.29 and Figure 9.30.

Figure 9.29

The joints of the hand placed properly in the geometry

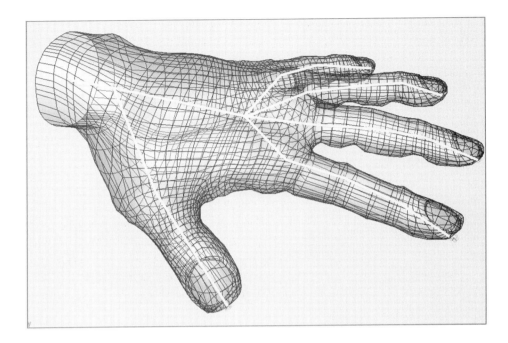

Figure 9.30

Second view of the hand's skeleton

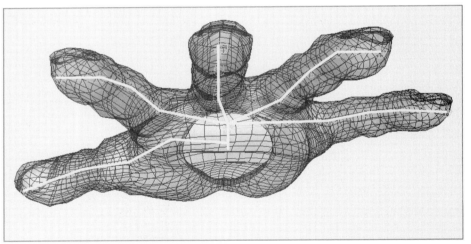

Binding to Geometry

An integral part of rigging a character or an object with a skeleton is *binding*, also known as *skinning*. Binding is another way to attach geometry to a skeletal system. With the Block Man, you directly attached the whole pieces of geometry to the bones through parenting, whereas binding involves attaching *clusters*, or groups of vertices or CVs, of the geometry to the skeleton to allow the skeleton to deform the model. This is typically how skeletons are used in character animation work. (For more on grouping and parenting, refer to the solar system exercise in Chapter 2, "Jumping into Basic Animation Headfirst.")

The basic technique of binding a character is easy. However, Maya gives you tremendous control over how your geometry deforms.

Binding Overview

Binding is, in theory, identical to the Lattice deformer you saw in Chapter 5, "Modeling with NURBS Surfaces and Deformers." A lattice attached to an object exerts influence over parts of the model according to the sections of the lattice. Each section affects the CVs of a NURBS surface or the vertices of a polygon surface within its borders—and as a section of the lattice moves, it takes those points of the model with it.

Skeletal binding does much the same thing. It attaches the model's points to the bones, and as the bones pivot around their joints, the section of the model that is attached follows.

By attaching vertices or CVs (depending on your geometry) to a skeleton, you can bend or distort the geometry. When a bone moves or rotates about its joint, it pulls with it the points that are attached to it. The geometry then deforms to fit the new configuration of the bones bound to it.

You can bind geometry to a skeleton in two ways: using Bind Skin and using Interactive Bind Skin. Figure 9.31 shows a cylinder with a Bind Skin. An Interactive Bind Skin will yield similar results to the regular bind. The only real difference between the two methods is the editing capabilities while you are binding the skin. You'll take a look at these differences later in the chapter.

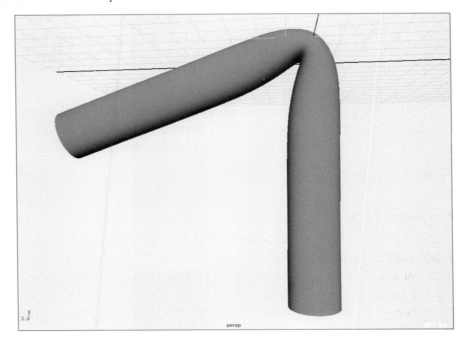

Figure 9.31

Bind Skin with a cylinder. The crease is fairly smooth. You may expect this result from the interactive Bind Skin as well.

persp

With a Bind Skin, there are two common binding methods that I'll compare here: Closest Distance and Heat Map. Create a polygon cylinder, with Height Divisions of 16. The more spans you have in the deformable model, the better it will bend. Scale the cylinder in Y to a scale of 5 to make it tall. Duplicate the cylinder and move it over in your window in the X-axis. Now, in the front view, create a four-bone (five-joint) skeleton that starts at the bottom of the first cylinder and goes straight up the middle, ending at the tip. Duplicate the skeleton and move it to the center of the second cylinder (see Figure 9.32). Check in your different viewports to make sure the skeleton is in the middle of the cylinders.

CREATING A SMOOTH BIND WITH CLOSEST DISTANCE

To create a smooth bind, select the root of the first skeleton and its cylinder and choose Skin → Bind Skin ❒.

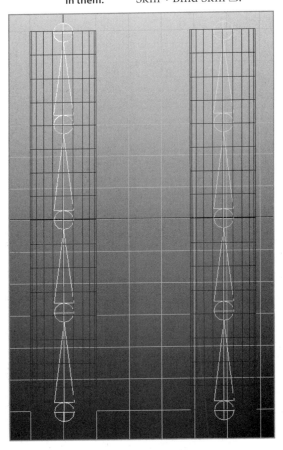

Figure 9.32

Make two cylinders with skeletons in them.

In the option box, you'll find the Bind To parameter at the top, set to the default of Joint Hierarchy (set it to Joint Hierarchy if it is different). You'll also find, under the Bind Method drop-down menu, the options Closest Distance, Closest In Hierarchy, Heat Map, and Geodesic Voxel. Closest Distance disregards a joint's position in the hierarchy of the skeleton and assigns influences according to how far the point is from the joint. The Heat Map method uses a "heat diffusion" technique to create influence falloff radiating out from the joint and is arguably the most commonly used for character work because it assigns skin weights best suited for character movement, giving you creases at bending areas that are more believable than with the Closest Distance method.

Max Influences sets a limit on how many joints can affect a single point. Dropoff Rate determines how a joint's influence diminishes on points farther from it. For example, with Smooth Bind, one shoulder joint can influence, to varying degrees, points stretching down the arm and into the chest and belly. By limiting these two parameters, you can control how much of your model is pulled along by a particular joint.

Set Bind Method to Closest Distance and click Bind Skin in the option box window to bind your first cylinder to the bones using Closest Distance (the default).

CREATING A SMOOTH BIND WITH HEAT MAP

Now select the root of the second skeleton and the second cylinder and choose Skin →
Bind Skin ❑. This time, set the Bind Method to Heat Map.

Bend both cylinders to get a feel for how each creases at the bending joints. Figure 9.33
shows the difference. The Heat Map binding on the right shows more defined creases
at the joints, much like fingers, while the Closest Distance binding on the left creates a
smoother arc over the entire cylinder.

Interactive Skin Bind is practically the same as Smooth Bind and yields similar results
to the smooth binding using Closest Distance shown in Figure 9.33, but the editing of the
influences is slightly different than for Smooth Bind. You will explore Interactive Skin
Bind with the hand model later in this chapter.

DETACHING A SKELETON

If you want to do away with your binding, select the skeleton and its geometry, and
choose Skin → Unbind Skin. The model will snap to the shape it had before the bind was
applied and the joints were rotated. It's common to bind and detach skeletons several
times on the same model as you try to figure out the exact configuration that works best
for you and your animation.

If you need to go back to the initial position of the skeleton at the point of binding it to
the model, you can automatically set the skeleton back to the bind pose after any rotations
have been applied to any of its joints. Simply select the skeleton and choose Skin → Go To
Bind Pose to snap the skeleton and model into the position they were when you bound
them together. It's also best to set your skeleton to the bind pose whenever you edit your
binding weights.

Figure 9.33

Closest Distance
and Heat Map-
Smooth-bound cyl-
inders. The cylinder
on the left is Closest
Distance bound,
and the one on the
right is Heat Map
bound.

Binding the Hand: Closest Distance Method

Try skinning the hand with Bind Skin.

Load your own hand or the `poly_hand_skeleton_v02.ma` file from the Poly_Hand_
Anim project from the web page. You can
also access a video tutorial to help you with
this exercise from the author's website (`www.koosh3d.com`). Now, follow these steps to
smooth-bind the hand:

1. Select the skeleton's root at the wrist
   and Shift+click the hand as shown in
   Figure 9.34. Choose Skin → Bind Skin
   ❑. Make sure Bind Method is set to
   Closest Distance and click Bind Skin.

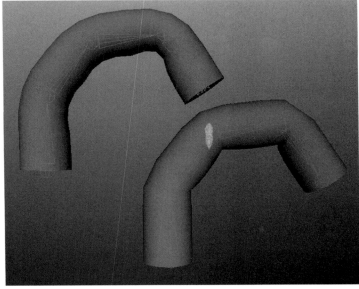

Figure 9.34

Select the root joint as well as the top node of the hand.

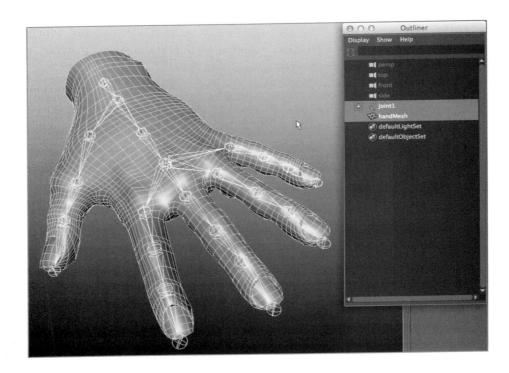

2. Try rotating some of the knuckle joints to see how the fingers respond. Go back to the bind pose when you're finished.

3. Rotate the middle knuckle of the index finger down. Notice how the knuckle gets thinner the more you bend the finger there. Go to the top knuckle of the index finger and rotate that joint. Notice that part of the hand moves with the finger. Figure 9.35 shows the result of bending at the index finger.

Figure 9.35

Bending at the index finger causes some unwanted deformation.

Editing a Bind

You usually edit a bind by *painting skin weights*. Because points on the model are influenced by multiple joints in a smooth bind, you need to adjust just how much influence is exerted by these joints on the same points.

1. Make sure you're in Shaded mode (press 5). Select the hand and then choose Skin → Paint Skin Weights ❑.

> You paint skin weights on the affected geometry and not on the joints themselves, so you need to select the model and not the skeleton before invoking this tool.

2. Your hand should turn black, with a bit of light gray at the wrist (or perhaps at the index finger if that joint is selected). The option box appears, listing the joints that are connected to the hand, as shown in Figure 9.36.

3. The color value (between white and black) determines how much binding influence the selected joint in the option box is exerting on that part of the geometry. It's best to name your joints properly so that selecting from this window is easier and more intuitive. If you loaded the file from the web page, you need to name the joints yourself to organize the scene and make working with it easier.

4. In the option box, select joint 9, the index finger's top knuckle, and make sure the Paint Operation button under the Influence section is set to Replace. Change the Value slider to 0. In the Stroke section, Radius(U) and Radius(L) govern the size of your brush. In the Influence section, make sure the Opacity slider is set to 1.

> To change the size of your Artisan Brush while you're painting weights, you can hold down the B key and drag the mouse left or right to adjust the radius of the brush interactively.

5. Click and paint a black color around parts of the hand and palm that shouldn't be affected by the index finger bending at its top knuckle (joint 9), as shown in Figure 9.37.

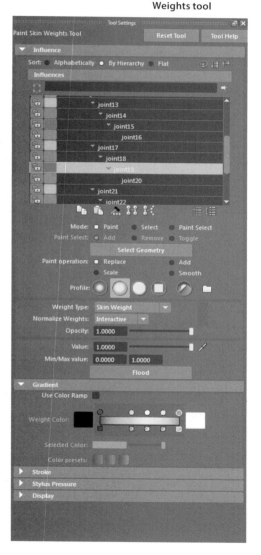

Figure 9.36

The option box for the Paint Skin Weights tool

Figure 9.37

Paint the new weights to avoid unwanted deformations in the hand.

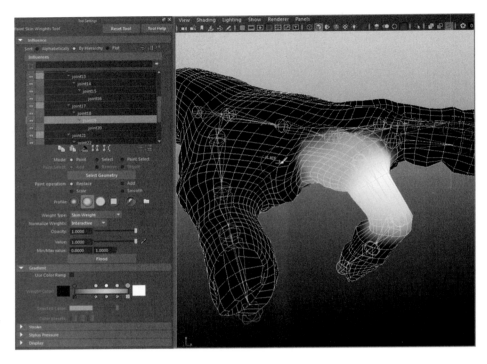

6. Smooth out the area where it goes from white to black. In the option box, in the Influence section, set Paint Operation to Smooth. Right-click to smooth the area around the knuckle for a cleaner deformation, as shown in Figure 9.38. Your index knuckle should now bend beautifully.

Figure 9.38

Smoothing out the bend at the index finger

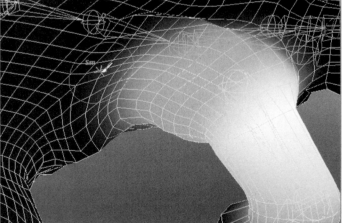

Skin weights must always be normalized in a smooth bind, meaning the values have to add up to 1. When you reduce the influence of a joint on an area of the surface, the influence amount is automatically shifted to other joints in the hierarchy that have influence over that area; those joints are now more responsible for its movement.

You can exit the Paint Skin Weights tool by selecting another tool (press W for Translate, for example), and your view will return to regular Shaded mode. Try bending the rest of the fingers and painting their influences; then, animate the hand, making gestures or grabbing an object using FK animation to set keys on the rotations.

When you paint weights on polygons, keep in mind that you're painting using the UVs. You may need to re-create the UVs of a polygonal mesh with a UV projection map for the Paint Weights tool to function properly, especially when you're importing and exporting the weight maps from one mesh to another (a procedure you won't encounter until later in your Maya experience).

The scene `poly_hand_skeleton_v03.ma` from the Poly_Hand_Anim project from the companion web page has the hand smooth-bound with painted weights on just the index finger for your reference. Try painting the other knuckles as needed for your animation.

Rigging work is essential for getting a good animation from your model. In a professional shop, it usually falls under the domain of a technical director (TD) who oversees the setup of characters and may also model their geometry. The more time I spent rigging scenes for the animators when I was a TD on the television show *South Park*, the easier and faster they were able to accomplish their animations.

Binding the Hand: Heat Map Method

Now let's try the same exercise using a Heat Map binding method instead of Closest Distance.

Load your own hand model before it was bound or the `poly_hand_skeleton_v02.ma` file from the Poly_Hand_Anim project from the web page. Now, follow these steps to smooth-bind the hand with the Heat Map method to compare to the previous method you tried:

1. Select the skeleton's root at the wrist and the hand mesh and choose Skin → Bind Skin ❑. Change Bind Method to Heat Map and click Bind Skin.

2. Rotate the middle knuckle of the index finger down. Go to the top knuckle of the index finger and rotate that joint as well. Notice that the bending is cleaner than before. Not much of the hand moves when you bend the index finger joints as it did in the previous exercise using the Closest Method. Figure 9.39 shows the result of bending at the index finger having used the Heat Map method of the Smooth Bind.

Figure 9.39

The index finger seems to bend more cleanly than before.

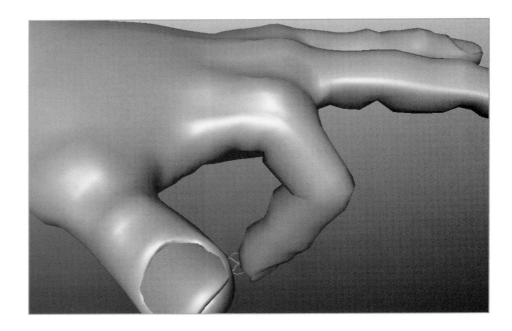

3. Select the hand mesh and choose Skin → Paint Skin Weights ☐. Just as before, the hand turns black except for white areas on the mesh corresponding to the selected joint (shown in Figure 9.40 with the index finger's joint9 selected).

4. Paint weights on this hand, and you'll notice that it is a little easier now that you've used Heat Map instead of Closest Distance.

Figure 9.40

Painting skin weights on the Heat Map method bound hand

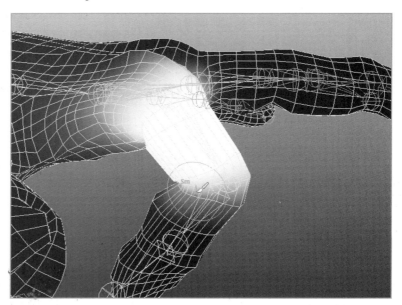

The Heat Map method gives you cleaner creases and bends at the knuckles, where Closest Point was a bit more soft, often deforming parts of the hand that shouldn't be affected much by a bending finger. There's still some painting to be done to make the fingers bend perfectly even when using the Heat Map method. The poly_hand_skeleton_v04.ma file from the Poly_Hand_Anim project has the hand with the index finger with painted weights as a reference for you.

Binding the Hand: Interactive Bind

Now, try skinning the hand with Interactive Bind.

Load your own hand or the poly_hand_skeleton_v02.ma file from the Poly_Hand_Anim project from the web page.

The Interactive Bind method is a bit easier to control when compared to the painting of the Smooth Bind weights.

1. Select the root joint at the wrist and the handMesh object and choose Skin → Interactive Bind Skin. Figure 9.41 shows the color scheme of a Volume manipulator that allows you to set the initial skin weights of the hand easily.

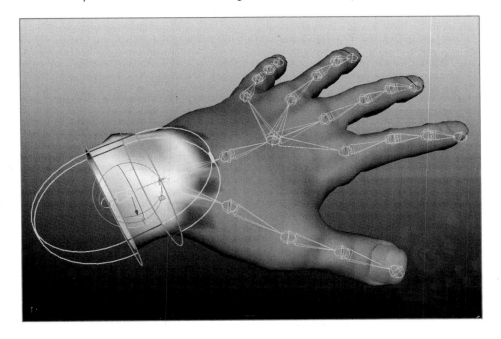

Figure 9.41

The Volume manipulator shows the influence of the selected joint at the wrist.

2. In the Outliner, select the different joints of the hand to see how the interactive binding shows the volume influences. Then select the top knuckle of the index finger (joint9). Figure 9.42 shows the influence. Select the red circle at the end of the Volume manipulator and size it down to reduce the influence on the middle finger, as shown in Figure 9.43.

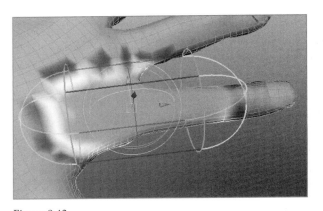

Figure 9.42

The index finger's first knuckle influences the middle finger, too.

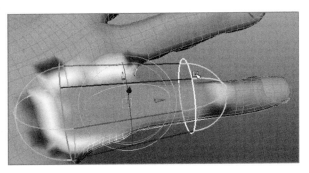

Figure 9.43

Use the Volume manipulator to reduce the influence on the middle finger.

3. Grab the green spherical end, and you can see that you can move that in or out to lengthen or shorten the Volume manipulator. You can use the move or rotate handles to move the volume as well. Make adjustments to the finger to remove influences on the middle finger and other undesired areas of the hand, as shown in Figure 9.44.

Editing the interactive skin bind, as you can see, is easy using the Volume manipulators. If you exited the tool when you first created the bind and no longer see the Volume manipulators, you can access them by choosing Skin → Interactive Bind Skin Tool. When you access this tool, the Volume manipulators appear again, and you're able to adjust your skin's influences.

Figure 9.44

Set the influences by adjusting the Volume manipulator.

When you are happy with the proper level of influence, keep picking the other joints in the index finger to make sure your binding is proper. Then continue to the other fingers to set up the binding on the hand properly. Though this method is easier than painting weights as we did before, it is not as easy to control. Test the bind by bending the joints. Here you are using a more interactive way to bind a mesh than Smooth Bind, which may be more or less effective depending on the model you are binding. It does, however, use the Closest Distance method by default, and the Heat Map method is not available for the Interactive Bind. In addition, you can paint skin weights when you use Interactive Bind, just as you did with the regular Bind Skin.

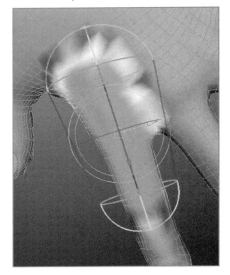

In the case of this hand and skeleton setup, the most effective binding has been using a Smooth Bind with the Heat Map method, with some subsequent skin weight painting.

This process is pretty handy. Now, try your hand at creating a skeleton and binding it to your cartoon hand model from earlier in the book. When you're done, congratulations, give yourself a hand!

Inverse Kinematics

With IK, you have tools that let you plant a foot where it needs to be so you're not always moving the skeleton or model to compensate and keep the heel in place.

For legs, IK is nothing short of a blessing. There is no clearly preferable workflow to suggest for dealing with rigging arms and hands, however. Many people use IK on hands as well, but it can be better to animate the legs with IK and animate every other part of the body with FK. IK is best used when parts of the body (such as the feet) need to be planted at times. Planting the hands isn't necessary for a walk cycle, and having IK handles on the arms may create additional work while you are animating them. You will create a more well-rounded character rig that uses IK and easy-to-use character controls at the end of the chapter. First, let's get familiar with how IK works.

Rigging IK Legs

Let's go back to the Block Man. Switch to that project and load your version or the `block_man_skeleton_v02.ma` file from the Block_Man project from the companion web page.

You'll create an IK chain from the hip to the ankle on each foot. Creating the IK from the hip to the toe won't work.

Because IK automatically bends the joints in its chain according to where its end effector, or IK handle, is located, it has to choose which way to bend at a particular joint. This is why you created the legs slightly bent in the Block Man rig earlier in the chapter.

If you did not do this or your setup has straight legs for whatever reason, select the two knee joints and, in Pivot mode (hold down the D key), move the knees forward a bit over the feet to create a slight crook in the legs. Don't go too far; a slight amount is enough. This lets the IK solver know which way those joints are supposed to go.

Now, on to creating the IK:

1. In the Rigging menu set, open the IK Handle tool by choosing Skeleton → Create IK Handle. Your cursor changes to a cross.

2. Select the start joint for the IK chain. This will be the root of this chain. Click the left thigh joint and then pick your end effector at the ankle joint. The bones in the IK chain turn brown. Repeat this procedure for the other leg. Figure 9.45 shows handles on both ankles.

   If for some reason you can't manage to pick a joint for the IK tool, make sure Show → Pivots is turned on in your view panel. Also, if you have difficulty seeing the handles, you can increase their size by choosing Display → Animation → IK Handle Size.

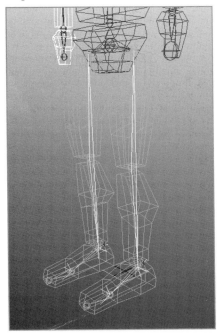

Figure 9.45

IK handles on both ankles with the roots at the hip joints

3. Move the IK handles around to see how the legs react. When you're finished, reset the IK handle positions.

4. Grab the top joint of the skeleton, which is the pelvis joint. Move the joint, and the entire body moves with it. Deselect the pelvis and then select the two ankle IK handles and set a translation key for them (press Shift+W). Grab the pelvis joint again and move it. The feet stick to their positions on the ground. Move the pelvis down, and the legs bend at the knees. Notice how the feet bend into the ground, though (see Figure 9.46, left).

Figure 9.46

Creating another IK chain from the ankle to the tip of the foot and setting keyframes makes the feet stay on the ground (right) and not rotate into the ground (left).

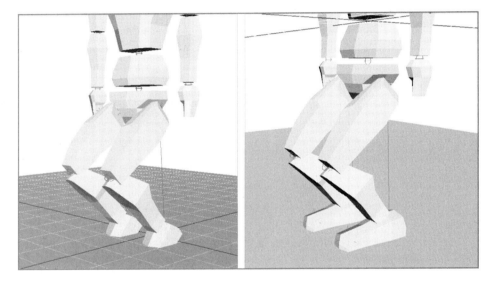

5. Move the pelvis back to the origin. You can create an IK handle for the foot so that the foot stays flat on the ground. Open the IK Handle tool. For the start joint, select the first ankle; for the end effector, select the joint in the middle of that foot (lt_ballFoot or rt_ballFoot). Repeat for the other foot.

You can invoke the last tool you used by pressing Y.

6. Set a translate key for the foot IK handles. Move the pelvis down; the legs bend at the knees and the ankle, keeping the feet flush on the ground (see Figure 9.46, right).

Creating an IK Walk Animation

Because the Block Man's feet will stick to the ground, creating a walk cycle with IK animation is far easier than using FK ("Why didn't you tell me that before?"). Making the animation look good is still a tough job that requires a lot of practice, though.

Load the scene file `block_man_IK_v01.ma` from the Block_Man project from the companion web page or use your own IK-rigged Block Man with handles at the ankles and feet. The white leg and arm are, again, on the far side of the character. You'll set keys every five frames again for the gross animation. To keep this short, I'll just discuss setting poses with the feet. You can always return to the scene to add animation to the upper body with FK, as you did earlier in this chapter. Follow these steps:

1. On frame 1, set translate keys on the pelvis joint and all four IK handles for their start position.

2. Go to frame 5 and move the pelvis forward about 1 unit. The legs and feet lift off the ground a bit and strain to keep their position, but they stay back. Lower the pelvis to get the feet flat on the ground again. Set a key for the pelvis. Because Auto Keyframe is turned on, all keys are set for this animation. (With the FK animation, you set keys for everything at every pose.)

3. Grab both near IK handles for the ankle and foot (blue leg) and move them forward and up to match the pose shown in Figure 9.47.

4. Go to frame 10. Move the front foot forward and plant it on the ground. Move the pelvis another three-fourths of a unit. Set translation keys for the rear ankle and foot handles where they are. Be sure to place the pelvis so that the rear foot is almost flat on the ground. Match the pose shown in Figure 9.48.

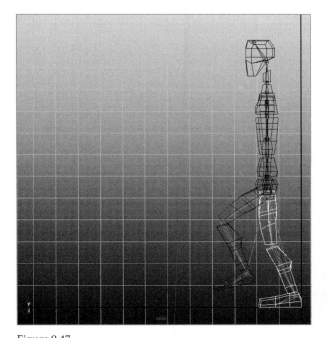

Figure 9.47

Step 3's pose (frame 5)

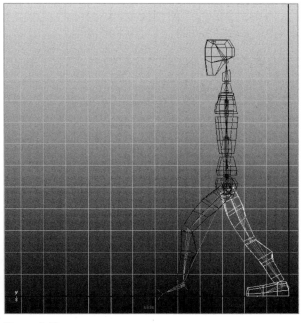

Figure 9.48

Step 4's pose (frame 10)

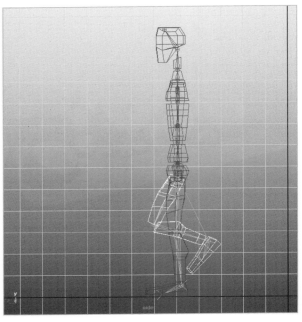

Figure 9.49
Step 5's pose (frame 15)

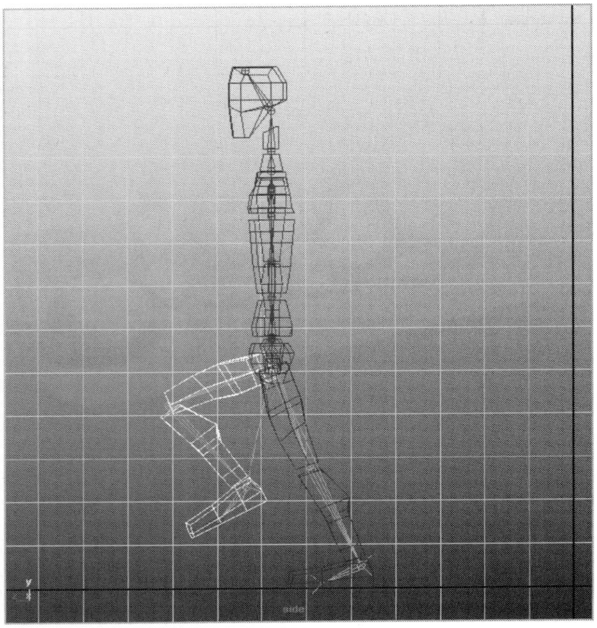

Figure 9.50
Step 6's pose (frame 20)

5. Go to frame 15. Move the pelvis another 2 units to center the body over the front foot. Lift the rear ankle and foot IK handles up to bend the knee and bring the knee up a bit. Match the pose shown in Figure 9.49.

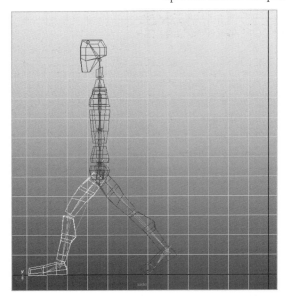

6. Go to frame 20. Move the pelvis forward 1 unit and swing the white leg forward as in the pose shown in Figure 9.50.

7. Move the pelvis three-fourths of a unit forward and plant the front leg down. Set keys for the rear leg and foot where they stand. Match the pose shown in Figure 9.51.

The next pose should match the pose in frame 10, although with the other leg. Continue the cycle, with each successive pose matching the one 15 frames before it on the opposite side.

At the end of this chapter, you'll take this process one step further and create a simple character animation rig for the entire Block Man so you can have a nicely functioning character for animation.

Figure 9.51
Step 7's pose (frame 25)

Further Uses for IK Chains

Many animators use IK chains more often in effects animation than in character work. IK chains can drive whips and ropes, flutter flags, bounce ponytails, and pump pistons as well as move legs and arms. For example, you can use a different type of IK chain, the *spline* IK chain, to control the shape of your bone chain with a NURBS spline. This IK chain is great for snakes and other long, deforming objects.

To create a spline IK chain, choose Skeleton → Create IK Spline Handle and then select your top joint and end effector. Maya creates a spline running the length of the bone chain. Adjusting the curvature of the spline in turn drives the bones, which in turn drive the geometry bound to them. Figure 9.52 shows a spline curve affecting the curvature of the bones in its spline IK chain.

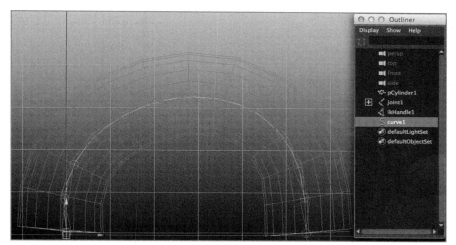

Figure 9.52

A spline IK chain is driven by the curvature of a NURBS spline. Adjusting the curve's CVs moves the joints.

Basic Relationships: Constraints

As you know, Maya is all about the relationships between object nodes. You can create animation on one object based on the animation of another object by setting up a relationship between the objects. The simplest way to do that (outside of grouping) is to create a *constraint*. For example, you can "glue" one object to another's position or rotation through a constraint.

A constraint creates a direct relationship between the source and the target object's Translate, Rotate, or Scale attributes. This section explores six types of constraints: point, orient, scale, aim, geometry, and normal.

The Point Constraint

To attach a source object to a target object but have the source follow only the position of the target, use a *point constraint*. A point constraint connects only the Translate attributes of the source to the target. To use this method, select the target objects and then Shift+click the source object. In either the Animation menu set (F4) or the Rigging menu set (F3), choose Constrain → Point ☐.

Figure 9.53

A cone point that is constrained to a sphere follows that sphere's position.

Constraints are based on the pivots of the objects, so a point constraint snaps the source at its pivot point to the pivot point of the target and keeps it there, even in animation. But the options allow you to set an offset that creates a gap between the source and the target.

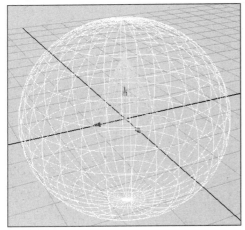

You can constrain the same source to more than one target object. The source then takes up the average position between the multiple targets. By setting the Weight slider in the option box, you can create more of an influence on the source by any of the targets.

In Figure 9.53, a cone has been point-constrained to a sphere. Wherever the sphere goes, the cone follows. This is different from parenting the cone to the sphere in that only its translations are affected by the sphere. If you rotate or scale the sphere, the cone won't rotate or scale with it.

Although you can blend keyframe animation with constraint animation, as a beginner to Maya, consider that after you set a point constraint like that shown in Figure 9.53, you're unable to control the cone's Translate attributes because they're being driven by the sphere's translations.

Point constraints are perfect to animate a character carrying a cane or a sword, for example. The rotations on the sword are still free to animate, but the sword is attached to the character's belt and follows the character throughout the scene.

The Orient Constraint

An *orient constraint* attaches the source's Rotation attributes to the target's Rotation attributes. Select the target object or objects first, then Shift+click the source object, and then choose Constrain → Orient ☐.

The Offset parameter allows you to set an offset in any axis. Otherwise, the source assumes the exact orientation of the target. In the case of multiple targets, the source uses the average of their orientations. Figure 9.54 shows the cone's orientation following an elongated sphere (the target).

A rotation constraint saves a lot of hassle when you have to animate an object to keep rotating in the same direction as another object. For example, you can use the rotation of one wheel of a locomotive to drive the rotation of all the other wheels.

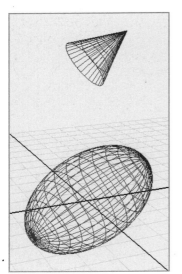

Figure 9.54

The cone's rotations match the sphere's rotations.

The Point on Poly Constraint

A *point on poly constraint* attaches a source object to a vertex of a mesh. Select the target object's vertex first and then Shift+click the object you want to place at that point (see Figure 9.55, left). In the Animation or Rigging menu set, choose Constrain → Point On Poly ❐.

Selected vertex

Figure 9.55

The red ball is placed on the tree branch like a fruit with a point on poly constraint.

The object is snapped to the vertex of the target at its pivot point. Even if the target object is animated and deforming, like a character, the object will stay on that vertex. Figure 9.55 (right) shows the sphere pinned to the branch at the selected vertex location.

The point on poly constraint is good for pinning objects together, such as leaves on a branch.

The Aim Constraint

The *aim constraint* adjusts the source's rotations so that the source always points to the target object. Select the target objects first and then Shift+click the source object. In the Animation or Rigging menu set, choose Constrain → Aim ❐.

The aim constraint has more options than the other constraints because you need to specify which axis of the source is to point to the target. You do so using the Aim Vector and Up Vector settings.

The Aim Vector setting specifies which axis of the source is the "front" and points to the target. In the cone and sphere examples, you set the Aim Vector option of the cone to (**0,1,0**) to make the Y-axis the front so that the cone's point aims at the sphere. If Aim Vector is set to (**1,0,0**), for example, the cone's side points to the sphere. Figure 9.56 shows the cone pointing to the sphere with an Aim Vector setting of (0,1,0).

Figure 9.56

**The cone aiming at
the sphere**

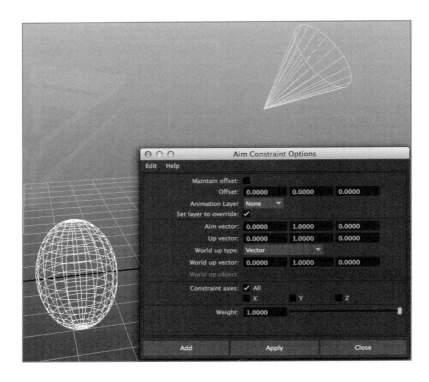

The Offset values create an offset on the source's Rotation attributes, tilting it one way or another. The Up Vector setting specifies which way the cone faces when it's pointing to the sphere.

Aim constraints are perfect for animating cameras to follow a subject, such as a car at a racetrack.

Geometry and Normal Constraints

The *geometry* and *normal constraints* constrain the source object to the surface of the target object (as long as it's a NURBS or poly mesh).

With a geometry constraint, the source object attaches, at its pivot point, to the surface of the target. It tries to keep its own position as best it can, shifting as its target surface changes beneath it. Again, select the target, select the source object, and choose Constrain → Geometry.

A geometry constraint is useful when you want to keep an object on a deforming surface, such as a floating boat on a lake. Figure 9.57 shows the cone after it has been geometry-constrained to a NURBS plane that is being deformed by a Wave deformer (in the Rigging menu, set choose Deform → Nonlinear → Wave). The cone sits on the surface as the waves ripple through, but it doesn't rock back and forth to stay oriented with the surface.

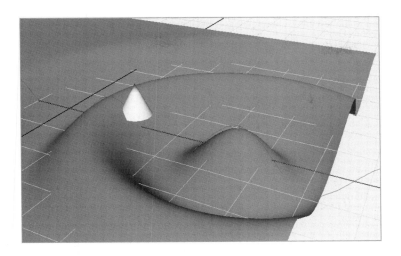

Figure 9.57

With a geometry constraint, the cone sits on the deforming surface.

To get the cone to orient itself so that it truly floats on the surface, you need to use a normal constraint. Using a normal constraint rotates the cone to follow the surface's normals, keeping it perpendicular to the surface.

A *surface normal* is an imaginary perpendicular tangent line that emanates from all surfaces to give the surface direction.

The normal constraint is similar to the aim constraint, and its options are similar. Using the Aim Vector setting, you specify which way is up for the object to define the orientation that the source should maintain. However, this setting doesn't constrain the location of the source to the target. If you want a floating effect, use geometry and a normal constraint to get the cone to bob up and down and roll back and forth as the waves ripple along (see Figure 9.58).

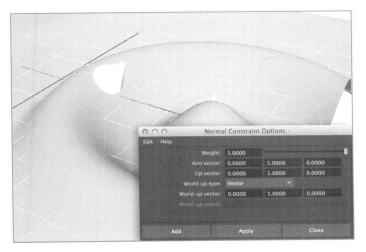

Figure 9.58

The cone now animates to float on the water surface, using both geometry and normal constraints.

Scale, Parent, Tangent, and Pole Vector Constraints

Four more constraints are possible in Maya: the scale, parent, tangent, and pole vector constraints. Simply, a *scale constraint* attaches the source's Scale attributes to the target's Scale attributes. A *parent constraint* constrains an object's translation and rotation to another object by mimicking a parent-child relationship without actually parenting the objects. This keeps objects aligned without worrying about any grouping issues. You'll have a firsthand look at this in the exercise where you rig the locomotive later in this chapter. Lucky you!

A *tangent constraint* keeps an object's orientation so that the object always points along a curve's direction. This constraint is usually used with a geometry constraint or path animation to keep the object traveling along a curve pointed in the right direction, no matter the direction of the curve. A point on poly constraint allows you to select a vertex on a poly mesh and constrain an object to that vertex. *Pole vector constraints* are used extensively in character animation rigs to keep IK joints from flipping beyond 180 degrees of motion.

Basic Relationships: Set-Driven Keys

A favorite feature for animation riggers is the *set-driven key* (SDK). An SDK establishes a relationship for objects that lets you create controls that drive certain features of a character or an object in a scene.

Before you can use an SDK, you must create extra attributes and attach them to a character's top node. These new attributes drive part of the character's animation. The term *character* is used broadly here. For example, you can set up a vehicle so that an SDK turns its wheels.

Let's start with a simple SDK relationship between two objects. You'll create a relationship between a ball and a cone. As the ball moves up in the Y-axis, the cone spins in the X-axis. As the ball descends, the cone spins back. You'll then revisit the hand and set up an SDK on the skeleton that animates the model.

Creating a Set-Driven Key

Figure 9.59
Lay out a cone and a sphere.

To create a simple SDK to make a sphere control the animation of a cone's rotation, follow these steps:

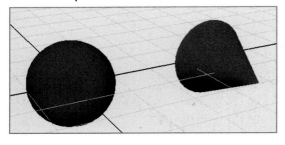

1. Create a Poly sphere and a poly cone in a new scene. Move the cone to the side of the sphere and lay it on its side, as shown in Figure 9.59.

2. Select the sphere and, in the Animation menu set, choose Key → Set Driven Key → Set. The Set Driven Key window opens with the pSphere1 object selected in the

lower half of the window (the Driven section). Its attributes are listed on the right, as shown in Figure 9.60.

3. You want the sphere to drive the animation of the cone, so you need to switch the sphere to be the driver and not what's driven. Click the Load Driver button to list the sphere in the top half of the window.

4. Select the cone and click the Load Driven button to display the cone's attributes in the bottom half of the window.

5. In the Driver section, select the sphere's Translate Y attribute. In the Driven section, select the cone's Rotate X attribute. Click the Key button to set an SDK that essentially says that when the sphere is on the ground (Y = 0), the cone's X rotation is 0 because both attributes are currently 0. The cone's Rotate X attribute turns orange in the Channel Box, meaning a driven key has been set.

6. Select the sphere and raise it in Y to a height of **5**. Select the cone and rotate it in X to **1800** to make it spin properly. Click the Key button in the Set Driven Key window to specify that when the sphere is at a height of **5**, the cone's Rotate X attribute is **1800** degrees. As the sphere's height increases from 0 to 5, the cone spins from 0 to 1800 in X.

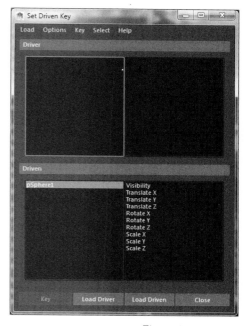

Figure 9.60

The Set Driven Key window

An Advanced Set-Driven Key: The Hand

Automating some animations on a character is indispensable to an animator. This can't be truer than when setting up an SDK for hand control. After you model and bind a hand to a skeleton, you're ready for an SDK.

Open the scene poly_hand_skeleton_v05.ma from the Poly_Hand_Anim project from the companion web page or use your own file that has the hand and its skeleton and is bound to the skin. Your file shouldn't have animation, though. Set your hand to the bind pose before you begin.

Creating a New Attribute

First you'll create a new attribute called index_pull to control a contracting finger.

1. Select the hand. In the handMesh tab of the Attribute Editor, click the Extra Attributes section. For now, at least, this section is empty.

2. In the Attribute Editor's menu bar, choose Attributes → Add Attributes to open the Add Attribute window, which is shown in Figure 9.61. In the Long Name field, enter **index_pull**. Maya will automatically display that attribute as Index Pull in the UI.

Make sure the Make Attribute Keyable option is selected and that the Float option is selected in the Data Type section. In the Numeric Attribute Properties section, set Minimum to **0**, Maximum to **10**, and Default to **0**. Click OK.

After you click OK, the Index_Pull slider appears in the Attribute Editor and the Channel Box when you select the handMesh object. This attribute alone will control the entire index finger.

Assigning the Set-Driven Key

To set up the relationships with the SDK, follow these steps:

1. With the handMesh selected, open the Set Driven Key window (choose Key → Set Driven Key → Set). Click Load Driver to specify that the hand should drive the animation.

2. Because you're animating the index finger pulling back, you want to drive the rotations of the top three knuckles. Deselect the hand, and then Shift+click all three knuckles on the index finger to select them. Click the Load Driven button. All three knuckles appear on the bottom.

3. Select the hand's Index Pull attribute (although you named the attribute index_pull, Maya will display it as Index Pull in the Set Driven Key window and a few other places like the Channel Box) and the three knuckles' Rotate Y attributes, as shown in Figure 9.62.

Figure 9.61
The Add Attribute window

Figure 9.62
The Set Driven Key window for the hand

4. With the rotations of the knuckles at 0 and the Index Pull attribute at 0 as well, click the Key button to set the first relationship. When Index Pull is at 0, the finger is extended.

5. Select the handMesh node and set the Index Pull attribute to **5**.

6. Select the fingertip's knuckle (joint11 in the web page file) and rotate it in Y to **20**. Select the next joint up the chain (the middle knuckle, joint10) and rotate it to **35** in the Y-axis. Select the final index knuckle (joint9) and rotate it in the Y-axis to **5**.

7. In the Set Driven Key window, select the three joints' Rotate Y and the handMesh Index Pull attribute and click the Key button. When the Index Pull attribute is at 5, the finger assumes this bent position.

8. Select the handMesh and set Index Pull to **10**.

9. Set the tip knuckle (joint11) to rotate to **65** in Y. Set the middle knuckle (joint10) to **60**. Set the last knuckle (joint9) to **50**. Click the Key button to see the result shown in Figure 9.63.

Select the handMesh node and change the value of the Index Pull attribute to curl your index finger. All you need to do to animate the finger is to set keys on that one attribute! Furthermore, you can set up a single SDK to control the bending of all the fingers at once, or you can set up one SDK for each finger for more control.

Open the scene poly_hand_skeleton_v06.ma from the Poly_Hand_Anim project available on the companion web page to see the hand with the SDK set up on the index finger.

Figure 9.63

The bent index finger

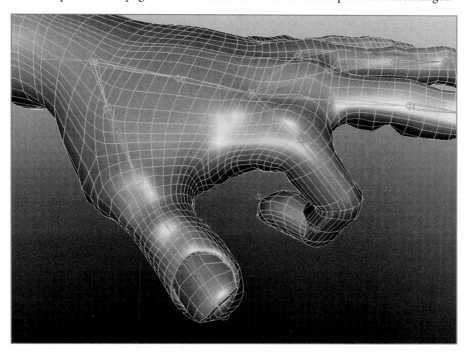

Rigging the Locomotive

In this section, you'll use a locomotive to put your new animation skills to use. Download the file fancy_locomotive_anim_v1.mb from the Scenes folder of the Locomotive project from the book's web page; this scene is shown in Figure 9.64. Notice in this scene there are small plus signs near the wheels. These are selection handles, allowing you to more easily select objects or groups of objects. They have been enabled for some of the objects on the locomotive to make it easier to work with. To toggle selection handles on or off for any node in Maya, select Display → Transform Display → Selection Handles.

Figure 9.64

The fancier locomotive model

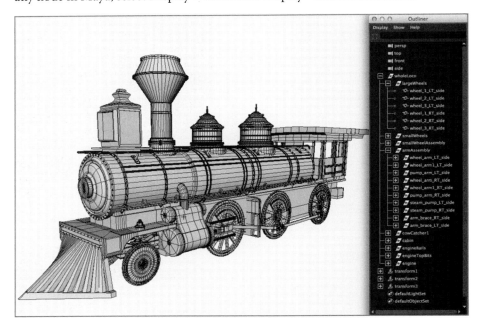

After selection handles for the locomotive's wheels and drive arms are turned on, only the objects that have selection handles will be selected when you make a marquee selection that covers the entire locomotive.

Setting Up Wheel Control

Your goal here is to rig the scene to animate all the secondary movements automatically based on some simple controls, like you did for the hand earlier this chapter. In reality, the locomotive's steam pump drives the arms that then turn the wheels on the locomotive. You'll work backward, however, and use one wheel to drive the animation of everything else.

As a challenge, you can also try this exercise of rigging the locomotive wheel's to rotate in unison by using rotation constraints instead of the Connection Editor.

Because all the large wheels have the same diameter, they rotate the same as the locomotive moves. In this case, you'll use the Connection Editor to attach the X Rotation on all the wheels to your main control wheel. You'll pick the middle wheel to be the control. To set up the locomotive, follow these steps:

1. Select the middle wheel on the left side of the locomotive (node wheel_2_LT_side), as shown in Figure 9.65. Open the Connection Editor (choose Windows → General Editors → Connection Editor). Click the Reload Left button to load the attributes of the selected middle wheel. Now, select the front wheel on the left side and click the Reload Right button.

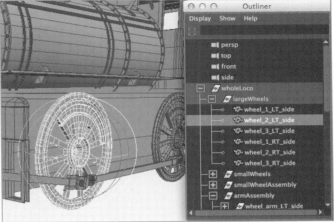

Figure 9.65

Select the middle wheel.

2. Scroll down in the Connection Editor until you find Rotate in both columns. Click to highlight Rotate in the left column and then click to highlight Rotate in the right column. Doing so connects the two rotations so that they both rotate at the same time, effectively letting you drive the animation of both wheels from just the center wheel. Figure 9.66 shows the Connection Editor.

3. Select the back wheel on the left side (wheel_3_LT_side). Click the Reload Right button in the Connection Editor. Connect the Rotate attribute for the middle and back wheels. Close the Connection Editor and select just the middle wheel. When you rotate the wheel, all three wheels rotate together.

4. Repeat this procedure to connect the rotations of the three wheels on the other side to this middle wheel as well. Now all six wheels rotate in sync with the one control wheel. When you select that left-side middle wheel (the control wheel), the other five wheels turn magenta, signifying a connection between these objects.

> If you get strange results when you connect the rotations of objects (for example, if the wheels flip over or rotate the opposite direction of the control wheel), try disconnecting all the connections, freezing transforms, and reconnecting the attributes.

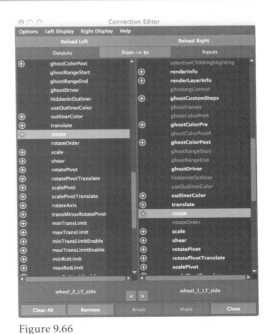

Figure 9.66

Connect the rotations of the two wheels.

Controlling the Wheel Arms

You've now automated the animation of the wheels. Next, you'll figure out how to connect the wheel arms to the wheels and drive their motion as well. To do so, follow these steps:

1. Create a single joint that lines up with the first wheel arm. The root joint is placed where the wheel arm meets the middle wheel (control wheel), and the end joint is placed where the wheel arm meets the pump arm, as shown in Figure 9.67. The pump arm has been templated in this graphic (displays in light gray wireframe) to show you the entire wheel arm and joint.

Figure 9.67

Create a joint from the middle wheel to the pump arm at the first wheel.

2. Group the joint under the control wheel's node, as shown in the Outliner, earlier in Figure 9.65. Then, group the wheel arm under the top joint. This way, the joint rotates with the control wheel, also shown in Figure 9.68, albeit incorrectly for the pump arm.

3. As you saw in Figure 9.68, the joint isn't rotating properly to make the pump arm work right. The other end of it needs to attach to the pump arm in front of the front wheel, not fly up in space. You can use an IK handle for this. Make sure the rotation of the control wheel and the joint/wheel arm are set back to **0** to place them in the original position. In the Rigging menu set, choose Skeleton → Create IK Handle. Make sure the settings are reset for the tool. Select the root joint as the start joint for the IK handle. Select the other tip of the bone as the end effector. You now have an IK handle at the tip where the wheel arm connects to the pump arm, as shown in Figure 9.69.

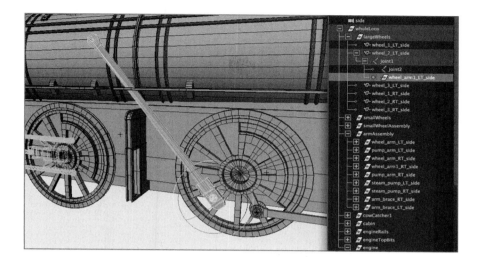

Figure 9.68

Group the top joint under the wheel and then group the wheel arm under the top joint.

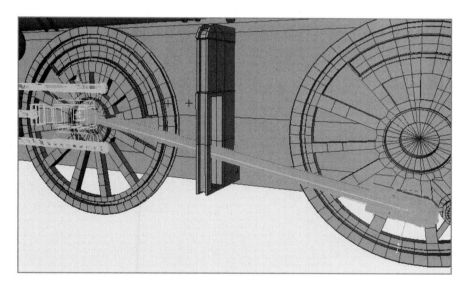

Figure 9.69

Place the end effector where the pump arm and the first wheel connect.

4. If you rotate the control wheel now, the wheel arm still separates from the pump arm. This is because the IK handle you just created needs a keyframe to keep it in position—that is, attached to the pump arm. Select the IK handle and, at frame 1, set a position keyframe. Now, if you rotate the control wheel, the joint and wheel arm pump back and forth.

5. Group the IK handle (ikHandle1) under the top node of the locomotive (wholeLoco), as shown in Figure 9.70.

Figure 9.70

Group the IK handle under the locomotive's top node.

Controlling the Pump Arm

Next, you need to attach the pump arm to the wheel arm so that it pumps back and forth as the control wheel turns. If you simply group the pump arm with the end joint of the wheel arm's bone, the pump arm will float up and down as it pumps back and forth. You need to use a constraint to force the pump arm to move back and forth only in the Z-axis.

1. Make sure the control wheel is set back to 0 rotation. Select the pump arm, templated in Figure 9.71 so that you can see through to the wheel arm and joint, and line up its pivot with the end joint of the wheel arm bone.

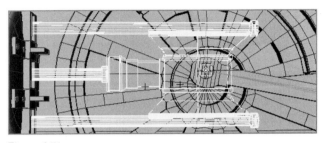

Figure 9.71

Line up the pivot of the pump arm with the end joint of the wheel arm joint.

2. Select the end joint (called joint2), Ctrl+click (or Cmd+click on a Mac) the pump arm group in the Outliner (called pump_arm_LT_side), and in the Rigging menu set choose Constrain → Point ❏. In the option box, under Constraint Axes, select only Z to constrain the pump arm only in the Z-axis and click the Add button. Now if you rotate the control wheel, you see the pump arm and wheel arm connected. The pump arm pumps back and forth, although you'll immediately notice a need to adjust the model to make the piece fit when it animates. Figure 9.72 shows that the pump arm's geometry isn't yet quite right for animation. This is normal for this process and luckily needs only a quick fix.

3. To fix the pump arm, select the vertices on the ends of the cylinders and extend them to make them longer, as shown in Figure 9.73. Now the pump arm won't pull out of the steam pump assembly.

4. Adjust the pump arm so that the geometry fits when the pump pushes in as well.

The scene file fancy_locomotive_anim_v2.mb will catch you up to this point. Compare it to your work.

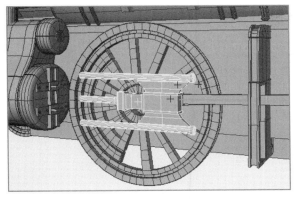

Figure 9.72

The pump arm is too short!

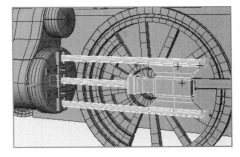

Figure 9.73

Use vertices to extend the pump arm.

Controlling the Back Wheel

All that remains is to control the animation of the back wheel and its wheel arm. To set up the wheel arm animation, follow these steps:

1. Using the methods described in the steps in the "Controlling the Wheel Arms" section, create a joint to follow along the wheel arm between the middle control wheel and the back wheel. The root of the joint is set at the control wheel, as shown in Figure 9.74.

Figure 9.74

Create a joint to control the back wheel arm.

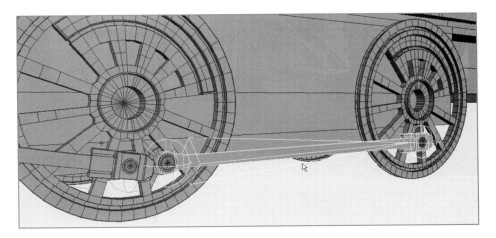

2. As before, create an IK handle for the end joint of this new bone, where it meets the back wheel, as shown in Figure 9.75. Make sure the handle is at the back wheel, not the middle control wheel.

Figure 9.75

Create an IK handle to attach the wheel arm and the back wheel to the control wheel.

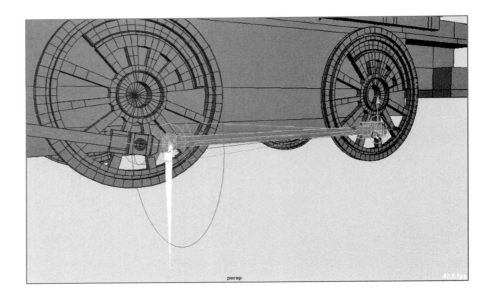

3. Group the new joint under the master wheel and then group the wheel arm under this new joint. If you rotate the control wheel, the wheel arm rotates with the joint and wheel but doesn't connect to the back wheel yet. You need to attach the IK handle you just created for that joint to the back wheel.

If you group the IK handle, as shown earlier in Figure 9.70, you'll run into a problem when you animate. Let's try it. Group the IK handle (ikHandle2) under the end back wheel, as shown in Figure 9.76, and then rotate the control wheel. The wheel arm pumps back and forth along with the back wheel, but every now and then the wheel arm geometry flips over backward. This isn't good.

Figure 9.76

The wheel arm geometry flips over if you group the IK handle under the back wheel.

Fixing this is easy. The grouping of the IK handle to the back wheel is causing the issue. Although that is pretty much what you want to do, parenting the IK handle under the wheel is problematic. Here is where the parent constraint becomes extremely helpful. It gives you the desired result without the geometry flipping.

4. Make sure your control wheel is back to **0** rotation first. MMB+click in the Outliner and place the IK handle outside the hierarchy of the locomotive to remove the IK handle from under the back wheel's node. You may also undo your past actions to the point before you grouped the IK handle (ikHandle2) under the back wheel. (You have to love Undo!)

5. Select the back wheel, Shift+click the IK handle (ikHandle2), and choose Constrain → Parent. Now, if you rotate the control wheel, everything works great.

6. Group the IK handle (ikHandle2) under the top node of the locomotive (wholeLoco).

    You can use `fancy_locomotive_anim_v3.mb` to compare your work.

> Again, seeing procedures go slightly awry, like when the wheel arm flipped over, is important. Doing so gives you a taste of trouble and a chance to fix it. Troubleshooting is an integral skill for a good CG artist.

Finishing the Rig

You're almost home free with the locomotive wheel rigging. Everything works great when you rotate the control wheel. If you select the top node of the locomotive and translate the train back and forth, everything should work perfectly. Repeat the steps in the previous few sections to connect the wheel arms and wheels on the other side of the locomotive, and you're finished! Figure 9.77 shows the completed and rigged locomotive.

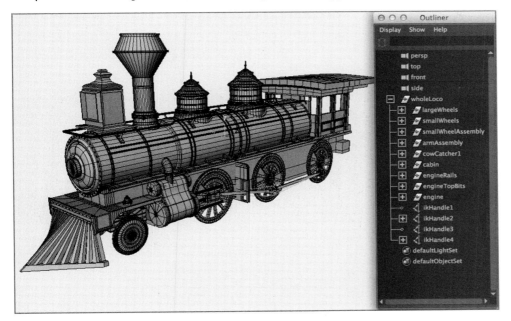

Figure 9.77

The rigged fancy locomotive

Creating a Simple Character Rig

In this section, you will revisit the Block Man setup to create a more well-rounded character rig with controls like professional animators use. This rig was created by Maks Naporowski, a fellow instructor at USC and CG animator/rigger, as a fairly simple biped rig for animation. Bear in mind that character rigging is an involved process, and you are starting to scratch the surface here. When you are done with this rig, you will have a simple two-legged character that you can easily animate using the controls you will set up based on what you've already accomplished throughout this chapter.

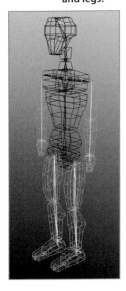

Figure 9.78

Create IK handles for the arms and legs.

Creating Control Shapes

Animators hardly ever manipulate and keyframe IK handles or joints directly when a good rig is available to them, and that's what you should keep in mind for the following rig:

1. Open the scene file `block_man_skeleton_v02.ma` from the Block_Man project.

2. In the Rigging menu set, choose Skeleton → Create IK Handle ❑. In the option box, set the Current solver attribute to Rotate-Plane Solver. Click one of the hip joints and then click the ankle joint. This makes an IK chain for the leg. Repeat for the other leg. Name them **lt_ikHandle** and **rt_ikHandle**.

3. Create an IK chain for the arms, from the shoulder to the wrist, also making sure to use the Rotate-Plane Solver. Name them as well. Figure 9.78 shows all four IK handles created.

4. Create a circle (Create → NURBS Primitives → Circle). Scale it up and center it around the left wrist. Name this circle **lt_arm_CNTRL**. Duplicate the circle, move the copy to center on the right wrist, and name it **rt_arm_CNTRL**. Refer to Figure 9.79 for placement.

Figure 9.79

Create circles for the wrists, place them, and assign them to their own display layers.

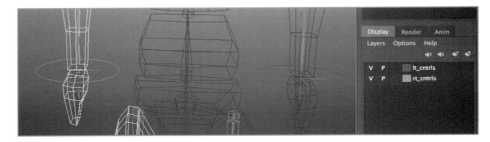

5. In the Channel Box/Layer Editor, click the Display tab in the Layer Editor and create two new layers: **lt_cntrls** (make it blue) and **rt_cntrls** (make it red). Assign the left wrist circle to lt_cntrls and the right wrist circle to rt_cntrls. This makes it easier to visualize and control. (See Figure 9.79.)

6. Select both circles and select Modify → Freeze Transformations. This will zero out their positions. Name the left wrist circle **lt_arm_CNTRL** and the right wrist circle **rt_arm_CNTRL.**

7. Create two more circles and adjust their CVs to make them oval to fit around the feet. Size and place them around the feet as shown in Figure 9.80. Assign each foot oval to the appropriate lt_cntrls or rt_cntrls display layers and name the ovals **lt_foot_CNTRL** and **rt_foot_CNTRL**, respectively.

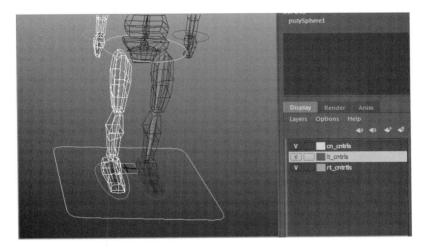

Figure 9.80

Create control shapes for the feet, pelvis, and body.

8. Create a large circle and center it around the pelvis joint (name it **body_CNTRL**). Make another large square shape and place it on the floor around the feet (name it **main_CNTRL**). Assign these two shapes to a new display layer called **cn_cntrls** and make it green.

These shapes will be the primary controllers for the animation of the character. They are easy to select and manipulate and make animation much easier.

Setting Up the Controls

Now comes the tough part of rigging it all to work! You'll group the shapes and create relationships to the skeleton here:

1. Parent the body_CNTRL under the main_CNTRL shape.

2. Parent the two arm controllers (rt_arm_CNTRL and lt_arm_CNTRL) under the main_CNTRL shape as well.

3. Parent each of the two wrist IK handles under each respective circle shape, as shown in Figure 9.81.

Figure 9.81

Grouping the controllers and IK handles

4. Select the left wrist circle and the lt_wrist joint and choose Constrain → Orient ❒. In the option box, turn on Maintain Offset and click Add.

This allows you to control the hand's rotation with the circle, as well as the hand's position. Select the wrist circle and move and rotate it around to see how the arm reacts. The elbow can swing around a little much, so you'll add a control for the twist of the arm.

5. Select the left wrist circle and open the Attribute Editor. Choose Attributes → Add Attribute. Enter the name **twist** to the wrist circle and keep the options at their default (Data Type: Float).

6. Now you'll connect it to the IK handle. Select the left wrists' IK handle and also its circle controller and choose Windows → Node Editor. You will see two nodes in the Node Editor (see Figure 9.82, top). Click once on the View Mode icon (▤) on the right of each node to expand its view, as shown in Figure 9.82 (bottom).The white and colored circles on either side of the nodes are input and output sockets.

Figure 9.82

The Node Editor displays the IK handle and the circle control shape in compact display (top). The nodes with expanded display show attributes (bottom).

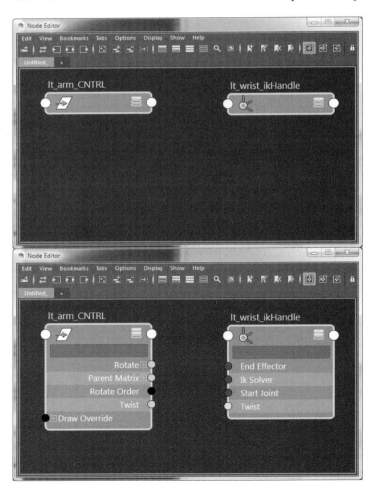

THE NODE EDITOR

The Node Editor gives you an easy way to create and manage connections between objects or nodes. You can navigate in it easily with Alt+mouse combinations like other Maya windows, and you can arrange the display of nodes however you want.

7. Click the output socket of the lt_arm_CNTRL node (the green circle on the right) next to the Twist attribute and drag the cursor to reveal a yellow rubber band attached to your cursor. Drag the mouse to the input socket of the lt_wrist_ikHandle node's Twist attribute (the light blue circle on the left) and release the mouse button. This connects these two attributes; however, the Node Editor doesn't show the connection immediately. To see the actual connection, click the lt_arm_CNTRL node in the Node Editor and click the Input And Output Connections icon (▣) at the top of the window. You'll now see the connection is made through an intermediate node (unitConversion1), as in Figure 9.83.

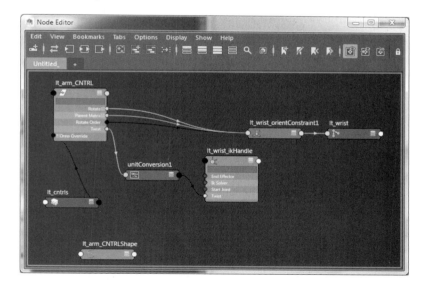

Figure 9.83

You've connected the Twist attributes, though you can't see it until you click Input And Output Connections icon, which is kind of silly.

You can ignore this extra node, but rest assured that the connection is made. Clicking the Input And Output Connections icon (▣) is always a good idea to check your connections in the Node Editor.

8. Now if you select the wrist circle and adjust the twist value, the arm will twist. If nothing happens, check your node connection and make sure you used the ikRP-solver when you created the IK handles in the previous section.

9. Repeat steps 4 through 8 for the right hand.

10. Now let's do the same for the feet for the Twist attribute. Select the left foot's control oval and add a new attribute called **twist**. Select the oval and the ankle joint (lt_ikHandle1) and open the Node Editor and connect the Twist attributes as you did in step 7 for the arm. Repeat for the right leg.

11. Select the pelvis joint and parent that under the body_CNTRL circle.

Setting Up Heel Controls

Now let's move on to creating some nice foot controls to allow the character to stand on his tiptoes or his heels easily. For that you will need to build a reverse joint chain to control the foot from the heel to supplement the existing leg joints.

1. In the side view, choose Skeleton → Create Joints and place a joint at the back of the left heel, as shown in Figure 9.84. Place the second joint exactly on the existing toe joint (lt_foot). Hold down V for point snaps when you create the joint so you can snap it exactly to that toe joint. Snap the third joint to the existing lt_ballFoot joint; finally, snap the fourth joint to the existing lt_ankle joint.

Figure 9.84

Create a reverse joint chain for the left foot.

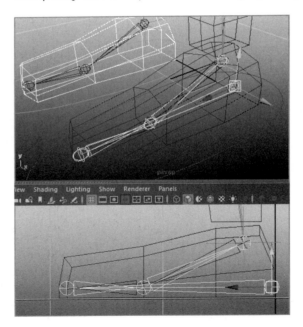

2. Grab the top joint of this reverse chain and parent it under the lt_foot_CNTRL oval. Name the joints as noted in Figure 9.85. Finally, parent the left ankle's IK handle (lt_ihHandle1) under the lt_rev_ankle joint as shown. Repeat for the other foot.

Figure 9.85

Parent the heel joints and ankle IK handles.

3. Next, parent both the foot control ovals under the main_CNTRL square. (See Figure 9.86.)

4. Select the main_CNTRL square and move the rig around. The character moves along with it. Select the body_CNTRL circle. When you move the body control, the feet and hands stay because of IK (see Figure 9.87), and that's how you want it. Undo your moves.

5. Create a display layer called **rigging**. Select the lt_rev_heel and rt_rev_heel joints you just created and parented and assign them to the new rigging display layer. This will make it easy to hide these extra reverse joints to keep them out of the way later.

6. Select the lt_rev_toes joint first and then the lt_ballfoot joint (see Figure 9.88 for the selections) and choose Constrain → Orient □. Make sure Maintain Offset is checked and click Apply. The constraint node should appear under the lt_ballFoot node, as shown in the Outliner in Figure 9.88 (left image).

7. Select the lt_rev_ballFoot joint and then the lt_ankle joint and create an aim constraint like in the previous step.

8. Repeat steps 6 and 7 for the right foot.

9. When you're done, your Outliner should be similar to the one shown in Figure 9.88 (right image). If your constraint nodes are not in the right places, check to make sure you selected the nodes in order in steps 6 and 7 when you made the aim constraint.

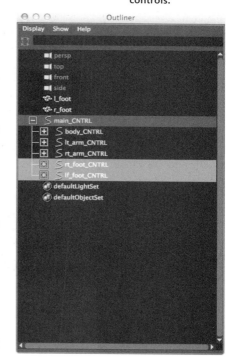

Figure 9.86

Parent the foot controls.

Figure 9.87

Moving the body control and the main control works perfectly.

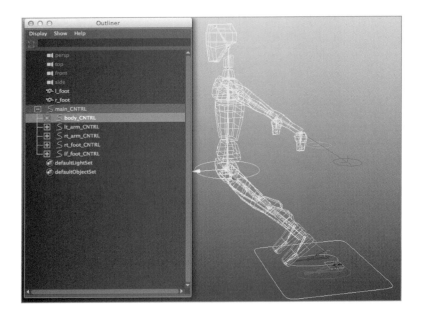

Figure 9.88

Aim constrain the two joints together.

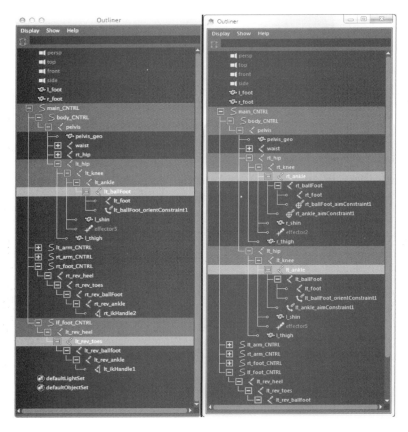

Set-Driven Keys: Heel Controls

Now let's set up some fancy heel controls.

1. Select the left foot control oval and add a new attribute to it called **heel**. In the options, change Data Type to Float, but give it a Minimum of –5 and a Maximum of **10** (see Figure 9.89). Repeat for the right foot.

    You need to set up a set-driven key to raise or lower the heel based on the value of the Heel attribute.

2. Select the left foot control oval and choose Key → Set Driven Key → Set from the Animation menu set. Click Load Driver to load the control oval as the driver of this SDK.

3. Select lt_rev_heel and click Load Driven in the SDK window.

4. In the SDK window, select Heel as the driver attribute on the oval and the RotateZ attribute on the driven joint (see Figure 9.90).

5. Make sure the Heel attribute is set to **0** and the Rotate Z for the lt_rev_heel joint is also **0**. Click Key in the SDK window.

6. Set the Heel attribute to –**5** and rotate the lt_rev_heel **45** degrees up in Z. Click Key in the SDK window. If you now select the foot control oval and change the Heel attribute to between –**5** and **0**, the heel will raise and lower. Make sure to set it back to **0** when you're done testing.

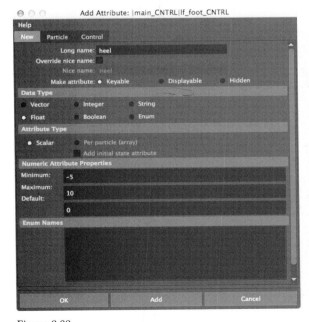

Figure 9.89

Create a new attribute for the foot control oval.

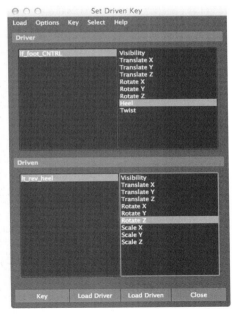

Figure 9.90

The first SDK relationship for the reverse heel joint

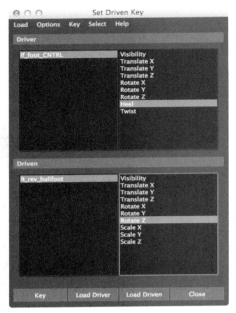

Figure 9.91

The next SDK relationship for the reverse ballFoot joint

Figure 9.92

When the Heel attribute is at 5, the heel should raise up like shown.

7. Select the lt_rev_ballFoot joint and click Load Driven in the SDK window. Keep lf_foot_CNTRL's Heel as the driver. Select the RotateZ attribute for the driven joint (see Figure 9.91.)

8. Set Heel to **0** and rotate in Z for the rev_ballFoot to **0**. Click Key in the SDK window.

9. Set Heel to **5** and rotate in Z for the rev_ballFoot to **45** degrees. Click Key in the SDK window.

10. Set Heel to **10** and rotate in Z for the rev_ballFoot back to **0**. Click Key in the SDK window.

11. Test the Heel slider by sliding it to a value of 5, and you should see the back of the foot moving up, as shown in Figure 9.92. Set Heel to **10**, and the heel comes back down.

12. Finally, select lt_rev_toes and click Load Driven in the SDK window. Keep lf_foot_CNTRL's Heel as the driver. Select Rotate Z as the driven channel for the lt_rev_toes joint in the SDK window. Figure 9.93 shows the SDK relationship.

13. Set Heel to **5** and make sure the lt_rev_toes joint's Rotate Z is **0**. Click Key in the SDK window.

14. Set Heel to **10** and rotate in Z the lt_rev_toes joint to **45** degrees. Click Key in the SDK window.

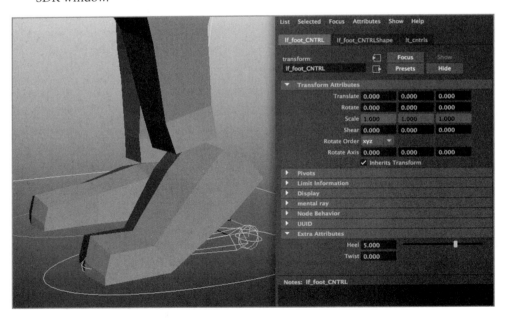

15. Test the Heel slider, and you'll see at a value of 10 that the foot is up and the toes are on the ground (see Figure 9.94).

16. Repeat steps 1 through 15 for the right foot. This time, you will use the rt_ nodes in place of the lt_ nodes you used earlier.

Make sure you're saving your progress as you go! When you're done, your rig should have some pretty handy controls. You will move the entire character using the main_CNTRL node. You can move the body itself while keeping sticky IK hands and feet by using the body_CNTRL node. And, of course, you control the arms/hands and legs/feet using the respective arm_CNTRL and foot_CNTRL nodes. All keyframes and animation should happen on these nodes only; you should not have to manipulate the joints or the IK handles directly at all. And that, in a somewhat long-winded nutshell, is the purpose of a character rig.

You can load the file `character_rig_v01.ma` from the Block_Man project to check your work or just to use as a rigged character for some animation fun!

For Further Study

Animation is as much a sport as it is an art, meaning practice makes you better. Use the rigged character from the end of this chapter to redo the walk animations from the beginning of the chapter. Also try different types and moods of walk.

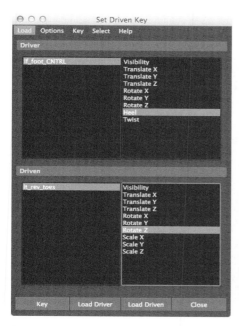

Figure 9.93

The final SDK relationship for the reverse toe joint

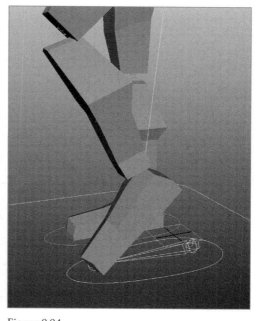

Figure 9.94

The foot position when Heel is set to 10

Can you animate a simple walk that looks happy and enthusiastic? Can you make that walk sad and lonely? Being able to convey emotion in your movement is key, and the more you try, the better you get.

Summary

In this chapter, you extended your experience with animation and learned about rigging techniques and automation. Starting with the simple Block Man, you learned how to set up a hierarchy for forward kinematics animation to create a walk cycle. Then, you used a skeleton to rig a hand for animation. Next, you learned how to bind the geometry of the hand to the skeleton using two different methods of smooth bind and also the interactive bind, as well as how to edit the binding. You also learned how to create an IK system to drive the joints in the Block Man for an IK walk cycle animation. After that, you learned how constraints can be used in rigging and how to set up set-driven keys to create easy controls to animate the hand. Then, you put all these rigging tricks together to rig the wheels of the locomotive to automate the animation of that complex system with a single control based on the middle wheel. And finally, you tackled a pretty tough rigging assignment in rigging the Block Man even further to have some nice options for movement using controllers.

The true work in animation comes from recognizing what to do in the face of certain challenges and how to approach their solutions. Maya offers a large animation toolset, and the more familiar you become with the tools, the better you'll be able to judge which tools to use in your work. Don't stop with this chapter; experiment with the features not covered here to see what happens.

Animation is about observation and interpretation. The animator's duty is to understand how and why something moves and to translate that into their medium without losing the movement's fidelity, tenacity, or honesty.

CHAPTER 10

Lighting®

Light shapes the world by showing us what we see. It creates a sense of depth, it initiates the perception of color, and it allows us to distinguish shape and form. For a scene to be successful in computer graphics (CG), these realities of light need to be reproduced as faithfully as possible. The trick is learning to see light and its astonishing effects on the world around us.

Learning Outcomes: In this chapter, you will be able to

- Understand basic concepts for setting up CG lighting

- Choose the appropriate Autodesk® Maya® light for a scene based on light attributes

- Control which lights illuminate certain objects through light linking

- Create mood and realism with raytraced shadows

- Illuminate and render a scene with mental ray® Physical Sun and Sky

- Produce special lighting effects with volumetric lighting, lens flare, and shader glow

- Practice setting up a basic lighting solution for the toy airplane, glass candle holder, and decorative box

- Use raytracing to cast shadows in your scene and use refractions to create a glass look

- Animate the attributes of a light and aim lights with the special manipulator

Basic Lighting Concepts

It's no surprise that lighting in Maya resembles direct-lighting techniques used in photography and filmmaking. Lights of various types are placed around a scene to illuminate the subjects as they would be for a still life or a portrait. Your scene and what's in it dictate, to some degree at least, which lights you put where.

Although it's easy to insert and configure lights, it's *how* you light that will make or break your scene. Knowing how to do that really comes only with a good deal of experience and experimentation, as well as a good eye and patience.

This chapter will familiarize you with the basic techniques of lighting a scene in Maya and start you on the road to finding out more.

What Your Scene Needs

Ideally, your scene needs areas of highlight and shadow. *Overlighting* a scene flattens everything and diminishes details. Figure 10.1 shows a still life with too many bright lights.

Similarly, *underlighting* your scene makes it muddy and lifeless, and it flattens the entire frame. Figure 10.2 shows the still life underlit. The bumps and curves of the mesh are hardly noticeable.

Like a good photographer, you want your image to have the full range of exposure. As in Figure 10.3, light and shadow complement each other and work to show the features of your surface.

Figure 10.1

An overlit still life

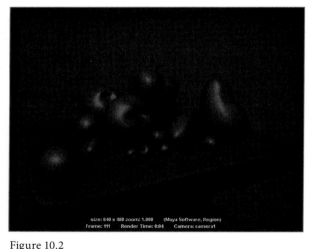

Figure 10.2

An underlit still life

Figure 10.3

Balanced lighting creates a more interesting picture.

Three-Point Lighting

The traditional filmmaking and television approach to lighting is called *three-point lighting*. Three distinct roles are used to light the subject of a shot. More than one light can be used for each of the three roles, but the scene should seem to have only one primary (or *key*) light, a softer light to fill the scene, and a back light to pop the subject out from the background.

Three-point lighting ensures that the primary subject's features aren't just illuminated but featured with highlights and shadow. Using three directions and qualities of light creates the best level of depth. Figure 10.4 shows a schematic of a basic three-point setup.

Figure 10.4

A three-point lighting schematic

Key Light

A *key light* is placed in front of the subject and off to the side of the camera to provide the principal light on the subject. Because it's usually off-center, the key light creates one side of brighter light, increasing the depth of the shot. This light also provides the primary shadows and gives the important sense of lighting direction in the shot.

Although it's possible for several lights to fulfill the role of key light in a scene—for example, three ceiling lights overhead—one light should dominate, creating a definitive direction. Figure 10.5 (left) shows the subject being lit by only a key light, although it's physically composed of two lights.

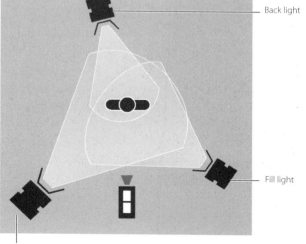

Back light

Fill light

Key light

Figure 10.5

Key light only

The direction of the two lights remains the same, and one takes intensity precedence over the other and casts shadows. The effect creates a single key light, which produces a moody still life.

Try This   Set your project to the Lighting project downloaded from the book's website. Open the scene file still_life_v01.ma from the Scenes folder.

1. Set your project to the Lighting project downloaded from the book's website. Open the scene file still_life_v01.ma from the Scenes folder.

2. In the camera1 viewport panel, press 7 for lighting mode. It should turn black; there are no lights.

3. Click Create → Lights → Point Light and, in the persp window, place it as your key light (Figure 10.5, right). Use the camera1 viewport to gauge how the lighting composition is working for optimum placement of the Point light.

Fill Light

A more diffused light than the key light, the *fill light* seems directionless and evenly spread across the subject's dark side. This fills the rest of the subject with light and decreases the dark area caused by the key light.

The fill light isn't usually meant to cast any shadows onto the subject or background itself and is actually used to help soften the shadows created by the key light. Figure 10.6 shows the still life with an added fill light. Notice how it softens the shadows and illuminates the dark areas the key light misses.

Typically, you place the fill light in front of the subject and aim it so that it comes from the opposite side of the key light to target the dark side of the subject. Even though the still life in Figure 10.6 is still a fairly moody composition, much more is visible than with only the key light in the previous figure.

Figure 10.6

A fill light is now included.

Try This   In the existing scene that you started with a single Point light:

1. Choose Create → Lights → Directional Light. Where you place the light doesn't matter, but how you rotate it does.

2. Rotate the light so you get a lighting direction opposite to the direction of the key light from the Point light already in the scene.

3. With the Directional light selected, change its Intensity attribute in the Channel Box or the Attribute Editor from 1.0 to **0.5**. Use the camera1 viewport to see how the fill light is working.

Back Light

The *back light*, or rim light, is placed behind the subject to create a bit of a halo, which helps pop the subject out in the shot. Therefore, the subject has more presence against its background. Figure 10.7 shows how helpful a back light can be.

Figure 10.7

A back light makes the subject pop right out.

The back light brings the fruit in this still life out from the background and adds some highlights to the edges, giving the composition more focus on the fruit.

Don't confuse the back light with the background light, which is used to light the environment itself.

Try This   In your current scene with the two lights:

1. Create a third light to be a Spot light.

2. You can use Move and Rotate to position the light to shine from behind the fruit, or you can use the special manipulator. To use that, press T with the Spot light selected. You will see two Move manipulators, one for the source of the light and one for the target.

3. Move the target to the front of the column stand and move the target behind and slightly above the fruit (Figure 10.7, right). Use the camera1 viewport to see how the back light should be placed.

Using Three-Point Lighting

The three-point lighting system is used for the primary subject of the scene. Because it's based on position and angle of the subject to the camera, a new setup is needed when the camera is moved for a different shot in the same scene. Three-point lighting is, therefore, not scene specific but shot specific, as long as it does not break the overall continuity of the scene.

After the lighting is set up for the subject of a shot, the background must be lit. Use a directed primary light source that matches the direction of the key light for the main light, and use a softer fill light to illuminate the rest of the scene and soften the primary shadows.

Maya Lights

Six types of light are available in Maya: Ambient, Directional, Point, Spot, Area, and Volume. These lights are also used when rendering in mental ray. How you use each dictates whether they become key, fill, or rim lights. Each light can fill any of those roles, although some are better for certain jobs than others. The most commonly used light types for most scenes are Spot, Directional, and Ambient. All of these Maya lights render in Maya software as well as mental ray.

To create each light, choose Create → Lights and click the light type; that light will appear at the origin of your scene.

Common Light Attributes

Lights in Maya are treated like any other object node. They can be transformed, rotated, scaled, duplicated, deleted, and so forth, and they are visible as nodes in the Hypergraph and Outliner alongside other objects in the scene. Like any other node, lights have attributes that govern how they function. Figure 10.8 shows the Attribute Editor for a typical light.

When you select any light type and then open the Attribute Editor, you'll see the following attributes and options:

Type This drop-down menu sets the type of light. You can change from one light type to another (for instance, from Spot to Point) at any time; however, you may not keyframe changing a light's Type attribute.

Color This attribute controls the color cast by the light. The darker the color, the dimmer the light will be. You can use Color in conjunction with Intensity to govern brightness, although it's best to set the brightness of a light to Intensity only. You can keyframe Color easily by simply RMB+clicking the attribute name Color in the Attribute Editor and choosing Set Key. Alternately, you may RMB+click Color in the Channel Box and choose Key Selected from the context menu.

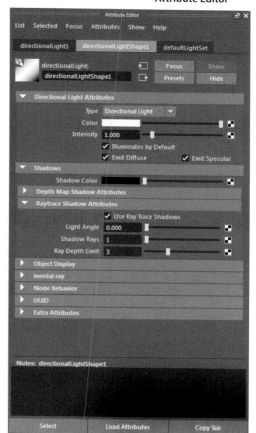

Figure 10.8

A typical light's Attribute Editor

Intensity This attribute specifies how much light is cast. The higher the intensity, the brighter the illumination will be. You can also keyframe intensity by RMB+clicking the attribute just as with Color.

Illuminates By Default check box This check box deals with *light linking*, or the ability to illuminate specific objects with specific lights. Clearing this check box causes the light not to illuminate all objects by default, requiring you to link the light to objects you do want it to light. Keep this check box checked unless you're linking lights to specific objects. This chapter will briefly touch on light linking later.

Emit Diffuse and Emit Specular check boxes For all light types except the Ambient light type, these check boxes toggle on or off the ability to cast diffuse lighting or specular highlights on an object (see Figure 10.9). This is useful for creating specific lighting effects. For example, if lighting an object makes it too shiny, you can disable the specular emission from one or more of the lights on that object to reduce the glare.

Figure 10.9

Lights can render diffuse or specular components if needed.

Full render   Diffuse only render   Specular only render

Light Types

Beyond the common light attributes, each light type carries its own attributes that govern its particular settings. In the following section, open the scene file still_life_v01.ma from the Lighting project and create the light being described to see firsthand how that particular light affects the scene.

Ambient Lights

Ambient lights cast an even light across the entire scene. These lights are used for creating a quick, even illumination in a scene; but, as you can see in Figure 10.10, they run the risk of flattening the composition. They're perhaps best used sparingly and at low intensities as fill lights or background lights, though I personally don't recommend using them at all.

The Ambient Shade slider in the Attribute Editor governs how flat the lighting is. The lower the value, the flatter the lighting. Figure 10.11 shows the effect of two contrasting Ambient Shade settings.

Figure 10.10

Ambient light

Directional Lights

Directional lights cast a light in a general direction evenly across the scene (see Figure 10.12). These lights are perhaps second to Spot lights as the most commonly used light type. They're perfect for sunlight or general indoor lighting, for key lights, and for fill and back lights. They give an accurate sense of direction without having to emanate from a specific source.

Point Lights

A *Point light* casts light from a single specific point in space, similar to a bare lightbulb. Its light is spread evenly from the emission point (see Figure 10.13).

Figure 10.11

A low Ambient Shade setting flattens the image.

Ambient Shade = 0.1

Ambient Shade = 1.0

Using the Decay Rate drop-down menu in the Attribute Editor, you can set how a Point light's intensity diminishes over distance. With No Decay, the Point light illuminates an object far away as evenly as it does up close. This is the most common setting for most applications.

Setting Decay Rate to Linear, Quadratic, or Cubic requires you to increase the intensity level exponentially to compensate for the decay. You can use Decay Rate settings to illuminate nearby objects and to leave distant ones unaffected. In reality, lights have decay rates, so using them in CG creates a more natural falloff for light, as shown in Figure 10.14.

Point lights are good for effects such as candlelight or setting a mood.

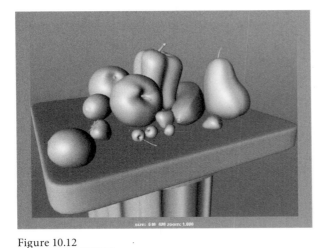

Figure 10.12

Directional light

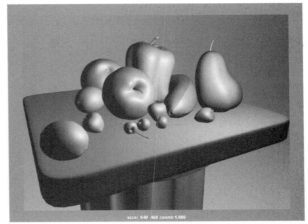

Figure 10.13

A Point light placed in the front right of frame

Spot Lights

Spot lights are arguably the most used lights in Maya because they can be used for keys, fills, or rims, and they're efficient.

Similar to Directional lights, Spot lights emphasize direction. But these lights emit from a specific point and radiate out in a cone shape, whereas Directional lights emit from an infinite source from a certain direction. As such, Spot lights can create a circular focus of light on the geometry much like a flashlight on a wall; Directional lights spread the light evenly. Figure 10.15 shows a Spot light on the still life.

The following attributes govern the behavior of Spot lights:

Decay Rate   Specifies the rate at which the light's intensity falls off with distance, as with the Point light. Again, the intensity needs to increase exponentially to account for any decay.

Cone Angle   Sets the width of the cone of light emitted by the Spot light. The wider a cone, the more calculation intensive it becomes.

Penumbra Angle   Specifies how much the intensity at the edges of the cone and hence the circular focus dissipate. (See Figure 10.16.) A negative value softens the light into the width of the cone, decreasing the size of the focus; a positive value softens away from the cone.

Dropoff   Specifies how much light is decayed along the distance of the cone. The higher the drop-off, the dimmer the light gets farther along the length of the cone. This effect is much better to use than a decay rate, and it gives similar results.

Practical lights are easily created with Spot lights. For example, a desk lamp's light is best simulated with a Spot light. Remember, with a Spot light, you can press T for the special manipulator, allowing you to move the source and target of the Spot light easily to orient and place the light in your scene.

Figure 10.14
A Point light with a Decay Rate set

Figure 10.15
Using a Spot light

Penumbra = 0   Penumbra = –10   Penumbra = 10

Area Lights

Area lights emit light from a flat rectangular shape only (see Figure 10.17). They behave similarly to Point lights, except they emit from an area and not from a single point. You can still set a decay rate, just as you can with Point lights. Area lights are the only lights whose scale affects their intensity. The larger an Area light, the brighter the light.

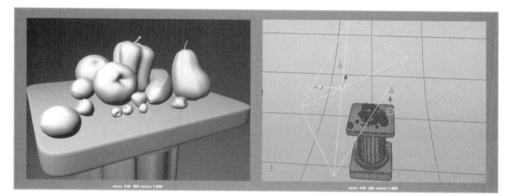

Figure 10.17

An Area light and its placement

Because you can control the size of the area of light being emitted, these lights are also very good for creating effects such as a sliver of light falling onto an object from a crack in a door (as in Figure 10.18), overhead skylights, or the simulation of large, diffused lighting fixtures such as overhead office lights. Use Area lights when you need to light a specific area of an object.

Additionally, Area lights give off a softer feel the larger they are. Often area lights give the best photographic light quality compared to the other light types, and I personally prefer using them the most, especially when used with mental ray rendering. They create the most accurate-looking shadows, though at the expense of slightly longer render times.

Figure 10.18

**An Area light as
a sliver and its
placement**

Volume Lights

Volume lights emit light from a specific 3D volumetric area as opposed to an Area light's flat rectangle (see Figure 10.19). Proximity is important for a Volume light, as is its scale.

A Volume light can have the following attributes:

Light Shape   A Volume light can be in the shape of a sphere, a box, a cylinder, or a cone. You select a shape from the Light Shape drop-down menu.

Color Range   This section of attributes sets the color of the light using a built-in ramp. The ramp (from right to left) specifies the color from inside to outside. For instance, a white-to-black ramp from right to left creates a white light at the center of the Volume light that grades down to black toward the outer edge.

Volume Light Dir   This attribute sets the direction for the light's color range: Outward lights from inside out, Inward lights from the volume's edge into the center, and Down Axis lights as a gradient in an axis of the light.

Arc And Cone End Radius   This attribute defines the shape for the volume.

Penumbra   For cylinder and cone shapes, this attribute adjusts how much the light dims along the edge of its length.

Figure 10.19

**A Volume light and
placement**

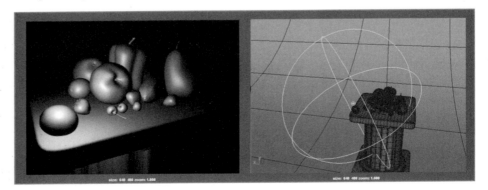

Use Volume lights when you need to control the specific area in which light is cast or when you need an object to move into and out of a particular area of light. Volume lights are not to be confused with *volumetric lighting*, such as the effect of a flashlight in smoke or headlights driving through fog. For volumetric effects, see the section "Volumetric Lighting" later in this chapter.

Lighting a Scene

Any of these aforementioned lights will work with Maya Software rendering and mental ray rendering. It's also best to start with just a couple types of light, such as Directional and Spot no matter which renderer you use, before turning to the more sophisticated types, such as Area and Volume.

Getting the essence of lighting is far more important in the beginning than understanding the nuances of all the attributes of a light. At first, limit yourself to Spots and Directional lights and try to avoid any Ambient light use.

Light Linking

You can control which lights illuminate which objects by using Maya *light linking*. However, by default, lights created in your scene illuminate all objects in the scene. The easiest way to create an exclusive lighting relationship is first to create a light and then to turn off the attribute Illuminates By Default in the light's Attribute Editor. This ensures that this light won't cast light on any object unless specifically made to do so through light linking.

1. Open the scene file `still_life_linking_v01.ma` from the Lighting project or use your own scene that already has at least three lights. Click the Render button (▦) in the Status line to render a frame (Figure 10.20). There are no shadows; you'll deal with that in the next section.

2. Create a new Directional light and, in the Attribute Editor, turn off the check box Illuminates By Default (it's right below the Intensity slider). Set Intensity to **1** or more. You can see the placement of the light in Figure 10.21.

3. Render a frame, and you won't see any change. Adding a new light with Illuminates By Default disabled won't increase the light level in the scene.

4. To assign your new light to the objects you want to illuminate exclusively, choose Windows → Relationship Editors → Light Linking → Light-Centric. This opens the Relationship Editor and sets it for light linking. Light-Centric means the lights are featured in the left side of the panel, as shown in Figure 10.21, and the objects in your scene that will be lit are on the right.

Figure 10.20

All of the scene's lights illuminate the scene.

size: 640 x 480 zoom: 1.000   (Maya Software)
Frame: 111   Render Time: 0:02   Camera: camera1

Figure 10.21

The Light Linking window and the newly added Directional light

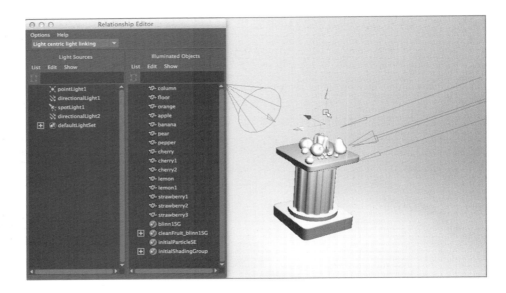

Figure 10.21

The Light Linking window and the newly added Directional light

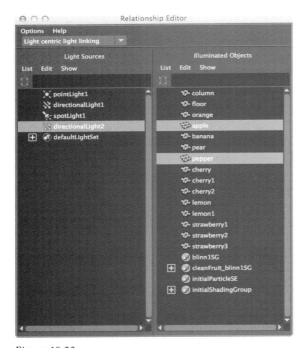

Figure 10.22

Select the scene objects to link to the Directional light.

5. Now, select the light you want to link (in this case, the directionalLight2 you just created) and the objects in the scene you'd like to link to (in this case, the apple and the pepper, as shown in Figure 10.22). Notice that no other objects on the right side of the Relationship Editor are selected; this means they will receive no illumination from this light source.

6. Render a frame, and you'll see that the objects you linked are lit by the new light. In this case, the apple and the pepper are brighter than the other fruit in the still life. (See Figure 10.23.)

When you're in Lighted mode (press 7 in the viewport) and using the default Viewport 2.0 renderer, linked lights aren't taken into account in that display. However, if you switch the viewport renderer from Viewport 2.0 to High Quality Rendering (in the viewport's menu bar, choose Renderer → Legacy High Quality Viewport), you will be able to see light linking work. Linked lights work with both Maya Software rendering and mental ray rendering.

Adding Shadows

Don't be too quick to create an abundance of light in your scene to show off your models and textures. Shrouding objects in darkness and shadow is just as important as revealing them in light. A careful balance of light and dark is important for a composition. As Figure 10.24 shows, the realism of a scene is greatly increased with the simple addition of well-placed shadows. Don't be afraid of the dark. Use it liberally but in balance.

Creating Shadows in Maya

Lights can cast shadows in one of two ways, depending on how the scene is rendered: *depth map shadows* and *raytraced shadows*. Depth map shadows are faster; however, with computing being as fast as it is now, it's usually just best to use raytraced shadows because they are more accurate and usually look much nicer. You will use raytraced shadows throughout this book.

When you create a light in Maya, raytraced shadows are enabled by default for the light. However, since Maya Software rendering does not have raytracing enabled by default, your renders will not have any shadows at first. You will need to turn on raytracing or switch to mental ray rendering to see your raytraced shadows. You will explore raytracing and mental ray further in Chapter 11, "Autodesk® Maya® Rendering."

If you do not want to raytrace your shadows for whatever reason, you will need to enable *shadow maps* for your lights by clicking the Use Depth Map Shadows check box in the Shadows area of the light's Attribute Editor. Maya will then generate *shadow maps* that locate where shadows fall by following the path of the light backward from the lighted object to the light itself. Shadow maps are generally fast because they do not need raytracing, but they are not very accurate.

On the other hand, *raytracing* involves tracing a ray of light from every light source in all directions and tracing the reflection to the camera lens. Therefore, you can create more accurate shadows in your renders.

As you can see, depth map shadows are not as nice as raytraced shadows when you compare Figure 10.25 and Figure 10.26. Raytracing shadows is pretty much the norm now.

Figure 10.23

A linked light creates extra light for only the apple and the pepper behind it. The other objects aren't illuminated by that light.

Figure 10.24

Darkness and shadow help add a sense of realism, depth, and mood to an otherwise simple still life.

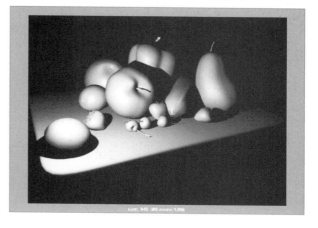

Figure 10.25

A light with depth map shadows renders faster, though not as detailed as raytracing.

Figure 10.26

A light with raytraced shadows produces more detailed shadows.

Raytraced Shadows

When you create a light, the light's Use Ray Trace Shadows setting in the Attribute Editor (see Figure 10.27, toward the bottom of the Attribute Editor window) is turned on by default. If you are rendering with Maya Software, open the Render Settings window by choosing Windows → Rendering Editors → Render Settings or by clicking the Render Settings icon (⌗) in the Status line; then enable the Raytracing check box under the Raytracing Quality heading. Let's add shadows to the scene using Maya Software rendering first.

1. In the file still_life_linking_v01.mb from the Lighting project, select the Point light. In the Attribute Editor, turn on Use Ray Trace Shadows under the Shadows → Raytrace Shadow Attributes heading (Figure 10.27, right). In this scene, raytrace shadows have been disabled on purpose. All new lights you create will automatically have raytraced shadows enabled.

2. Select the Directional light and turn on Use Ray Trace Shadows.

3. Open the Render Settings window and enable Raytracing (Figure 10.27, left).

4. Render a frame, and you'll see the scene looks more natural now with shadows (Figure 10.28). Turning on raytracing has also enabled reflections, which you'll look at later this chapter. Notice how the brighter key light (Point light) casts darker shadows than the darker fill light (Directional). As a general rule, you don't want too many lights in the scene all casting shadows; that may confuse the composition.

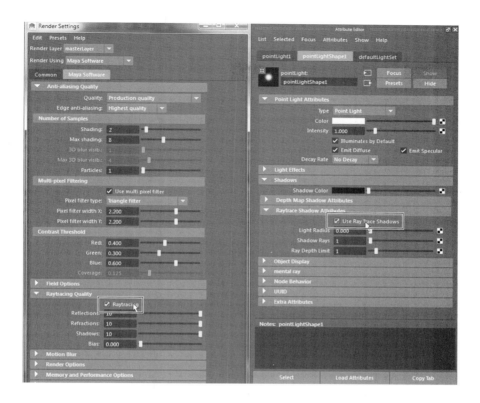

Figure 10.27

Make sure Use Ray Trace Shadows is checked on for the light (right) and enable Raytracing for the Maya Software renderer in the Render Settings window (left).

Figure 10.28

Raytraced shadows add a lot to the scene.

For an object that has a transparency map applied to its shader, however, only ray-traced shadows can cast proper shadows. On the left of Figure 10.29 is a plane with a mapped checkerboard transparency casting a raytraced shadow over the still life. On the right is the same light using shadow maps instead of raytraced shadows.

Figure 10.29

Only raytraced
shadows work with
transparencies.

Raytraced shadow   Shadow map shadow

Controlling Shadows per Object

To better control your lighting, you can specify whether an object can cast and receive shadows in Maya. For example, if you have geometry casting light in front of a shadow but you don't want it to cast a shadow, you can manually turn off that feature for that object only.

To turn off shadow casting for an object, follow these steps:

1. Select the foreground lemon in the `still_life_linking_v01.ma` scene and open the Attribute Editor.

2. In the Render Stats section is a group of check boxes that control the render properties of the object, as shown in Figure 10.30 (left). Clear the Casts Shadows check box. If you don't want the object to receive shadows, clear the Receive Shadows check box.

3. Render a frame, and you'll see the lemon has no shadows on the column's tabletop; compare the render in Figure 10.30 (right) with Figure 10.28.

Figure 10.30

You easily can set
whether an object
casts or receives
shadows in the
Attribute Editor
(left). The lemon
does not cast a
shadow anymore
(compare with
Figure 10.28).

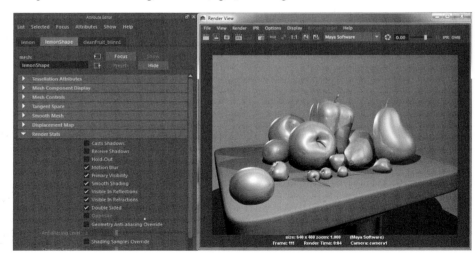

Raytracing Soft Shadows

One interesting feature of shadows is that they can diffuse or soften as the shadow falls farther away from the object casting the shadow. For example, hold a pen on its end on your desk and notice how the pen's shadow gets softer or fuzzier the farther it is from where the pen meets the table. This small detail can greatly enhance the reality of any render. To use soft shadows, follow these steps:

Figure 10.31

Regular raytraced shadows

1. Open the `still_life_shadows_v01.mb` scene from the Lighting project. Check out the render settings. Raytracing is already enabled for the key and fill lights as well as for the renderer.

2. Render a frame and notice that the shadows are sharp. Save that image into the render buffer by clicking the Keep Image () icon in the Render View settings. In Figure 10.31, you can see the still life rendered with sharp, raytraced shadows.

3. Select the Point light and open the Attribute Editor. Under the Shadows → Raytrace Shadow Attributes heading, set Light Radius to **0.2**, as shown in Figure 10.32.

4. Select the visible Directional light (not the hidden directionalLight2 in the Outliner) and set its Light Angle option to **4.0**. A Directional light's attribute is called Light Angle instead of Light Radius, but it does the same thing. Now render a frame and compare it to the previous frame you rendered. The shadows are soft but noisy, especially on the background (Figure 10.33). Save your image in the render buffer.

   The Directional light had a much higher light radius than the Point light because its shadows react differently. The Point light's distance from the subject plays a big part in how the light affects the shadows from the subject, so it is more sensitive to Light Radius values than is the non-position-dependent Directional light.

Figure 10.32

Setting the Light Radius value

5. Now you'll mitigate the noise. Select the Point light and in the Shadows → Raytrace Shadow Attributes heading, set Shadow Rays to **16**. Select the Directional light and set its Shadow Rays value to **12**.

6. Render the frame, and your shadows should resemble the ones in Figure 10.34. The higher your Light Radius value, the higher you need to set your Shadow Rays setting to compensate for noise.

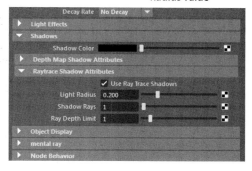

Figure 10.33

Soft but noisy shadows

Figure 10.34

A higher Shadow Rays setting makes for cleaner soft shadows.

Notice how the shadows soften more toward the edge of the shadow; the shadow is still sharp at the point of contact. This gives a much nicer feeling of depth to the scene. There is an increase in render time—it's important to evaluate how much softening you need so you don't overdo the look or increase the render time too much.

Using soft shadows was easy! Make sure you enable raytracing in Render Settings, of course. These soft raytraced shadows work both in Maya Software rendering and in mental ray rendering.

mental ray Lighting

mental ray lighting and rendering open up a large range of possibilities within Maya. As with all rendering, lighting plays a primary role. I'll cover mental ray rendering more in the next chapter; however, because rendering and lighting go hand in hand, it's tough to ignore it in this chapter. This section is a primer on mental ray light functionality.

> Open the Render Settings window by choosing Windows → Rendering Editors → Render Settings. If you don't see the mental ray option in the Render Using drop-down menu, you need to load the plug-in. Choose Windows → Settings/Preferences → Plug-in Manager to open the Plug-in Manager. Make sure Mayatomr.mll (or Mayatomr.bundle on a Mac) is checked for Loaded as well as for Auto Load to ensure that it loads by default.

Two additional functions that mental ray brings to the Maya table are caustics and global illumination (GI). *Caustics* is the scattering of light reflections off and through semitransparent objects, such as the light that shines on the ceiling above an indoor pool or the sunshine at the bottom of an outdoor pool. *Global illumination* is the effect of light reflected from one object to another. For example, if you place colored spheres inside a gray box and shine a light into the box, the walls and floor of that box pick up the color of the spheres. The light from the spheres reflects onto the walls and tints them with the spheres' color. Furthermore, the light from the floor of the box bounces and helps illuminate the undersides of the balls.

For example, Figure 10.35 shows a scene file that has a dozen or so glass spheres inside an enclosed box. The box has four holes in the top, and two Spot lights with shadows turned on are positioned outside the box, shining in through the holes. Figure 10.35 shows a typical Maya Software render. The spheres are visible and reflect the environment, but overall they are dark, with the rest of the box in shadow and no bounced light.

However, when rendering through mental ray for Maya (see Figure 10.36), the light that enters the box bounces around the scene and illuminates the other spheres. The color of the spheres also colors the area immediately around them because of GI and/or Final Gather (which are lighting methods that allow light to bounce around in the scene giving a greater sense of realism to the render). Additionally, the light shines through the semi-transparent spheres and casts caustic highlights on the floor. If you are reading a digital version of this book, you can see the color bouncing around in Figure 10.36.

Figure 10.35
The Maya Software render of the box of spheres scene

Figure 10.36
The mental ray for Maya render of the scene

Image-Based Lighting

mental ray also gives you image-based lighting (IBL) in Maya. This method of lighting uses an image, typically a high dynamic range image (HDRI), to illuminate the scene using Final Gather or GI. Final Gather is a form of global illumination that relies on direct as well as indirect illumination. Direct illumination calculates the amount of light coming directly from lights in the scene and renders the result. However, it misses an important aspect of real-life lighting: diffuse reflections of light. Indirect illumination happens when light bounces off objects in a scene in order to reach and therefore light the rest of the scene—that is, diffuse reflections. Final Gather is typically a faster way than GI to get indirect illumination in a scene.

I'll briefly touch on Final Gather here as you explore Physical Sun and Sky lighting in the next section. However, I'll cover both IBL and Final Gather in depth in Chapter 11, when you light the toy plane and decorative box model (with displacement maps for box details as well).

Figure 10.37

Enable mental ray
rendering in Render
Settings.

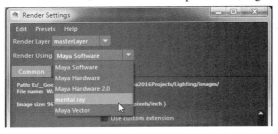

Figure 10.37

Enable mental ray
rendering in Render
Settings.

mental ray Physical Sun and Sky

In Physical Sun and Sky lighting, mental ray for Maya creates nodes in your scene to simulate an open-air sunlight effect for your scene lighting. It's a quick way to create a nice-looking render. You'll place the textured red wagon into an open scene and apply a Physical Sun and Sky (PSAS) in the following exercise.

Make sure your project is set to the Lighting project from the web page and use the scene file WagonSunlight_v01.ma from the Scenes folder to follow along with these steps:

1. The perspective camera for this scene is already set up in the persp viewport. Open the Render Settings window and switch to mental ray rendering in the Render Using pull-down menu at the top of the window, as shown in Figure 10.37.

2. In the Render Settings window, click the Scene tab. Under the Cameras → Environment heading, click the Create button next to Physical Sun And Sky. The Attribute Editor opens for the mia_physicalsky1 node you just created, as shown in Figure 10.38.

Figure 10.38

The mia_physical-
sky1 node

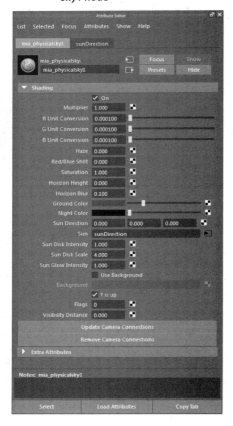

3. Render a frame in the Perspective window and compare it to Figure 10.39. It's a bit bright, but there's something very nice about this render. Notice that the metal handlebar takes on a good look right off the bat.

   The render is too bright, and the wood slats for the railings shouldn't be reflective. Your render should also show that the fire-engine red of the wagon is a bit washed out.

4. Let's first address the wood railings. Open the Hypershade, and double-click the first Wood shader. Change Reflectivity to **0.1** from 0.5. Repeat for the second Wood shader.

5. In the Render View window, click and drag a box region around the wood railings, as shown in Figure 10.40. Click the Render Region button (▣) to render that part of the frame only.

6. The wood looks much better now, so let's move on to the brightness of the scene. Open the Render Settings window, and go to the Scene tab. Click the Input arrow next to the Physical Sun And Sky attribute's button (Figure 10.41). Doing so opens the Attribute Editor for the Physical Sun and Sky.

7. Change Multiplier to **0.5** from 1.0, and re-render the frame. The brightness comes down nicely, and the wagon is less blown out than in your previous renders. See Figure 10.42.

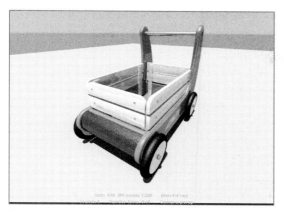

Figure 10.39

The first PSAS render doesn't look too shabby.

Figure 10.40

Render this region to check the reflection in the wood railings.

8. Let's play with the direction of the sun. Look in your persp viewport, and you see a Directional light sitting smack in the middle of the scene. Maya uses this light to set the direction of the sunlight, and it doesn't contribute to the lighting of the scene in any other way. Only its rotation is important to PSAS. Its intensity, color, and other attributes are irrelevant. In this scene, the Directional light is called sunDirection and is in the wagon behind the third texture placement node, as you can see in Figure 10.43. This light represents the sunlight and is currently pointing almost straight down, as if the sun is high in the sky. It seems as if it's about noon. RotateX for the sunDirection light is –75.

Figure 10.41

Click to open the attributes for the daylight system.

Figure 10.42

Bringing down the brightness of the sun

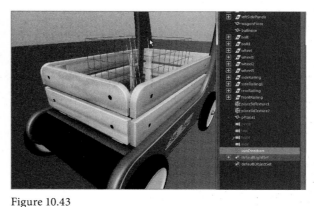

Figure 10.43

The sunDirection light adjusts only the direction of the sun-light in the scene.

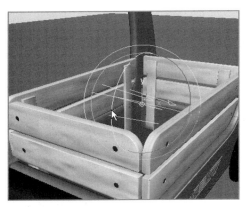

Figure 10.44

Angle the sun farther away from the camera.

9. That third texture placement node is getting in the way. To turn off its display easily, in the persp viewport, click Show → Texture Placements to uncheck it. The green box disappears in this view until you turn it back on through the Show menu. Now that you can see the Directional light better, you see that the sun is pointed slightly toward the back of the wagon. Rotate the light so that it's angled away from the camera even more, as shown in Figure 10.44. The sunDirection's RotateX should be about **–25**.

10. Render the frame, and you'll see quite a difference in the scene. Maya automatically adjusts PSAS settings to make the render appear as if the sun is about to set. This is because of the new angle. The scene (shown in Figure 10.45) not only shows a new lighting direction (the shadows fall toward the back and are longer) but also is a darker and warmer light, as if it were mid-to-late afternoon.

11. Angle the sunDirection light even more (so RotateX is at about **–2.5**), almost parallel with the ground plane, and render a frame. Now the sun has all but set, and it's dark dusk, just before night falls on the scene. See Figure 10.46.

12. Rotate the sunDirection even more so that it's at a RotateX of about **15**. It's now dark, and you can barely make out the wagon. (See Figure 10.47.) It's time to go home before your mom gets mad. Remember, you can adjust the overall brightness of the scene by adjusting the mia_physicalsky1 node attributes, as you did in steps 6 and 7.

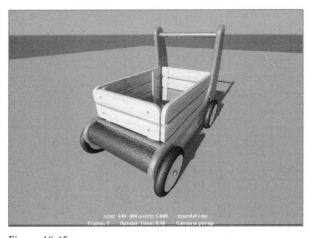

Figure 10.45

Now it's late afternoon.

Figure 10.46

It's getting late; you should get home before nightfall.

Figure 10.47

Ooh, it's dark—Mom is gonna be mad.

Figure 10.48

The sun also rises!

You can add lights to the scene as well; you aren't limited to the system's results. For example, Figure 10.48 shows a render of the wagon with the sun beginning to rise behind it, making the foreground a bit dark. Figure 10.49 shows the same render but with an added Directional light (with an Intensity of just **0.25**) pointing toward the front of the wagon. This helps define the front of the wagon, hinting that there is another light source, perhaps a porch light behind the camera.

The PSAS system can get you some fairly nice results quickly. Keep experimenting with different sunDirection angles as well as the attributes for the system to see what results you can get for your scene. Add lights to create areas of detail in your model.

Unbeknownst to you, when you invoked the PSAS system, Maya turned on Final Gather in the mental ray settings, as well as added a few nodes to the scene including a sky environment that surrounds your scene. This enabled indirect lighting to work in the scene. To get rid of the PSAS, you must go to the Render Settings window, and in the Indirect Lighting tab where you first turned on PSAS, you must click the Delete bar.

Figure 10.49

Adding a light to illuminate the front of the wagon in this sunrise scene

You'll explore Final Gather in the next chapter. At the end of that chapter, though, I'll introduce HDRI and image-based lighting for a fairly photoreal rendering of the toy plane and decorative box.

This is the perfect time for a break, so save your work (as if I have to tell you that at this point!), go grab some iced tea, and rest your eyes for a bit. In the next section, I'll go over various special lighting effects before returning to the wagon.

Lighting Effects

In CG, you must fake certain traits of light in the real world. Using certain methods, you can create smoky light beams, glowing lights, and lens flares. Although some of these effects fall under the domain of rendering and shader tricks, they're best explored in the context of lighting because they're created by light in the real world.

Volumetric Lighting

How do you create an effect such as a flashlight beam shining through fog? This lighting effect is called *volumetric lighting*, and you can use it to create some stunning results that can sometimes be time-consuming to render.

You can't apply volumetric effects to Ambient and Directional light types. To add a volumetric effect to any of the other types of lights, select the light and, in the Attribute Editor under the Light Effects section, click the checkered Map button to the right of the Light Fog attribute. This creates a new render node that appears in the Hypershade window. After you click the Map button, the Attribute Editor takes you to the lightFog node.

Maya handles volumetric lights by attaching a lightFog node to some lights such as a Spot light. The Color and Density attributes under this node control the brightness, thickness, and color of the fog attached to that light. Furthermore, in the light's Attribute Editor, you can control the fog with the Fog Spread and Fog Intensity settings. Fog Intensity increases the brightness of the fog, and Fog Spread controls how well the fog is defined within its confines. For example, a Spot light with fog shows the fog in its cone. Figure 10.50 shows how Fog Spread affects the conical fog shape. You'll see that some lights do not have the same fog controls mentioned earlier. The Spot light is perhaps the easiest light with which to create a fog effect.

To remove a fog effect, RMB+click the Light Fog label in the light's Attribute Editor and choose Break Connection from the context menu.

Figure 10.50

Fog Spread affects how the fog dissipates to the edges of the cone.

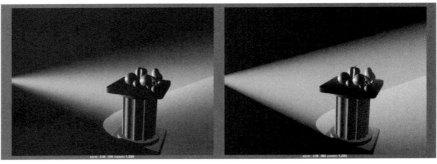

Fog Spread = 0.5   Fog Spread = 2.0

If you want the rays of light within the fog to cast shadows, check Use Depth Map Shadows for the light. You'll have to increase the depth map resolution for a higher-quality image.

Lens Flare

Lens flare and *light glow*, as illustrated in Figure 10.51, mimic the real-world effect created when light strikes a lens or when the light source is visible in the frame. The flare is created when the light hits the lens at a particular angle and causes a reflection of itself in the optics of the lens.

Figure 10.51

Light glow and lens flare turned on for the back light

To enable a light glow, under the Light Effects section in the light's Attribute Editor, click the checkered Map button next to the Light Glow attribute to create an OpticalFX node that appears in the Hypershade. The Attribute Editor shifts focus to that new node, which controls the behavior of the light glow and lens flare. The OpticalFX node contains the following attributes and settings:

Glow Type   Setting this attribute specifies the kind of glow: Linear, Exponential, Ball, Lens Flare, and Rim Halo. These define the size and shape of the glow from the light.

Halo Type   Specifying a halo creates a foggy halo around the light in addition to the glow. You can find controls for the halo in the Halo section in the Attribute Editor.

Star Points   Setting this attribute specifies the number of star points the glow generates.

Rotation   Setting this attribute rotates the orientation of the star points.

Radial Frequency   Used in conjunction with the Glow Radial Noise attribute (see the next item) in the Glow Attributes section, this attribute defines the smoothness of any added glow noise.

Glow Radial Noise   Setting this attribute adds noise to the glow effect, creating light and dark patches within the glow for a more random look, as shown in Figure 10.52.

Glow Color   Setting this attribute specifies the color of the glow.

Glow Intensity and Spread   Setting these attributes specifies the brightness and thickness of the glow and how well it fades away.

To turn on a lens flare along with the light glow, click the Lens Flare check box at the upper right in the Attribute Editor for OpticalFX. The attributes in the Lens Flare section control the look of the flare.

Figure 10.52

Glow Radial Noise attribute

Glow Radial Noise = 0   Glow Radial Noise = 0.5

Light glows and flares can be highly effective in scenes, adding credibility to the lighting, but they're often misused or, worse, overused in CG. Used sparingly and with subtlety, lens flares can go a long way toward adding a nice touch to your scene.

Shader Glow Effects

To create a glowing effect, it's sometimes better to place a glow on a geometry's shader instead of the light. Because a light must be seen in the shot and pointed at the camera to see any light glow and flare, a shader glow is sometimes more desirable. This process will composite a glow on the object that is assigned the Glow shader to simulate a volumetric light, such as a street lamp on a foggy night. Shader glows have far less render cost than true volumetric lights.

Try This To light a still-life scene, follow these steps:

1. Open the still_life_v03.ma file in the Lighting project on the web page. Create a Spot light, place it over the still life, and aim it directly down onto the fruit, as shown in Figure 10.53. Turn on Use Depth Map Shadows for the light and set Resolution to **1024**. Set Penumbra Angle to **10** and Intensity to **1.5**. Press 7 for Lighted mode in the Camera1 viewport to see how the light is being cast.

2. The Spot light provides the practical light in the scene. You'll place a bare bulb on a wire directly above the fruit. Create a NURBS sphere, and position it right over the fruit but in the frame for camera1 to see. In the Render Stats section of the Attribute Editor for the sphere, turn off Casts Shadows.

3. Create a long, thin cylinder for the lightbulb's wire and position it as if the bulb were hanging from it, as shown in Figure 10.54. Turn off Casts Shadows for the cylinder as well.

Figure 10.53

Aim a Spot light down toward the fruit.

Figure 10.54

Place a bulb on a wire over the fruit pedestal.

4. Create a black Phong E shader to assign to the cylinder.

5. Create a Phong shader for the bulb and assign it to the NURBS sphere. Set its Color to a pale, light yellow, and make it about 50 percent transparent.

6. Select the Spot light and set its Color to the same yellow. You can do this easily through the Color Chooser. With the shader for the bulb selected, open the Color Chooser by clicking the pale yellow color you just made. Click the right arrow to place the yellow color in the swatches to the right of the main color swatch, or RMB+click any of the swatches.

7. Pick the Spot light and click its Color attribute to set the Color Chooser to that color. Click the yellow swatch you created to get the same color on the light. For detail's sake, make the light's color less saturated.

8. To make the shader glow for the bulb, open the Hypershade and select the bulb's Phong material. In the Attribute Editor's Special Effects section, drag the Glow Intensity slider from 0 to **1.0**. If you render the frame, you'll see that the glow isn't quite enough to make a convincing lightbulb. In the Hypershade, select the shader-Glow1 node; this node controls all the glows in the scene.

9. Set Quality to **0.1**. In the Glow Attributes section, set Glow Intensity to **6.0**, set Glow Spread to **0.5**, and set Glow Radial Noise to **0.2**.

The scene file still_life_v04.mb from the web page contains the full scene for your reference. See Figure 10.55 for the final result.

Figure 10.55

The bare lightbulb over the still life is created with a shader glow.

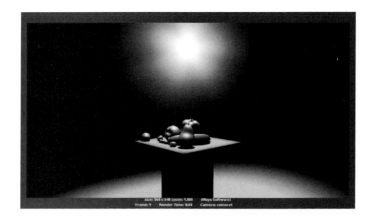

Assembling and Lighting a Scene

In this section, you'll set up and light a simple scene with the toy plane and the decorative box so that you can render them together. Furthermore, in the next chapter, you'll start using displacement maps for detail on the box, and you'll use HDRI, mental ray, and Final Gather to get the most from lighting and rendering. The lighting you'll start with will be basic for now. In the following exercise, you'll create a basic lighting setup for the scene and get a direct lighting solution first. In the next chapter, you'll expand on this lighting using mental ray and HDRI.

Set your current project to the Plane project, which you should have already downloaded from the book's web page. This is important to make sure Maya finds all the project files it needs, so it bears repeating: Set your project to Plane! Did you set your project yet?

How about now?

Assembling the Scene

To begin lighting, open the `planeLightingScene_v01.ma` scene file from the Scenes folder of the project. This is a simple scene with a camera in place and a corner made up of a redwood tabletop and two white walls:

1. Import the assets you need, starting with the toy plane. Select File → Import and, in the Options section on the right of the Import dialog window, turn off Use Namespaces, set Resolve to Clashing Nodes, and leave With set to the file name. This makes sure that Maya doesn't append any additional names to original objects being imported from this file. Next choose `planeShading_v01.ma` from the Scenes folder.

2. Open the Outliner and select the top node of the toy plane (planeGroup). Go into the four-view layout so you can see all four viewports. Select one of the viewports and

select Panels → Perspective → renderCam. This way you can work in the persp viewport and see how it affects the camera view from which you'll be rendering.

Next you will bring in the decorative box from the previous chapters. This time, instead of importing, you will use referencing. This allows you to import a file into your current scene. However, with a reference, any time you adjust the original file, it will automatically update that model in the scene it has been referenced in. You'll see this in action in the next chapter.

3. Choose File → Create Reference. On the right side of the Reference dialog window, check the Use Namespaces box to turn it on. This will place the filename you are referencing in front of the object names in the Outliner.

4. Navigate to your Plane project. In the Scenes folder, select boxDetail01.mb to bring in the latest decorative box scene from Chapter 7, "Autodesk® Maya® Shading and Texturing," as a reference. This is actually the same scene file as boxTextures03.mb in the Decorative_Box project that you completed in Chapter 7, but cleaned up a bit and placed in the Plane project folders for simplicity's sake. The texture files you need are also copied into the Plane project's Sourceimages folder.

5. Rotate the box to 200 degrees in the Y-axis and position the box next to the toy plane to match Figure 10.56.

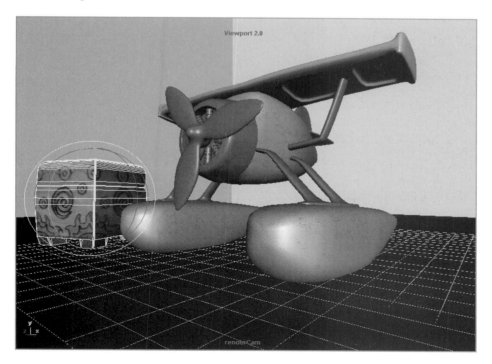

Figure 10.56

Orient and place the decorative box next to the plane to match this position.

6. You'll now import the glass candle holder you created in Chapter 5 using NURBS techniques. There's no need to use a reference like you did with the decorative box, so select File → Import and turn off Use Namespaces, set Resolve to Clashing Nodes, and leave With set to the filename, just like in step 1.

7. Navigate to the candleholder project and, in the Scenes folder, select and import the candleModel_v03.mb file.

8. In the Outliner, select the candle's top node (candleGroup) and move it to the front side of the toy plane, near to the camera. You will also have to scale the candleGroup to **0.65** to match the position and size in Figure 10.57. Don't worry, the candle holder is all gray for now. Save!

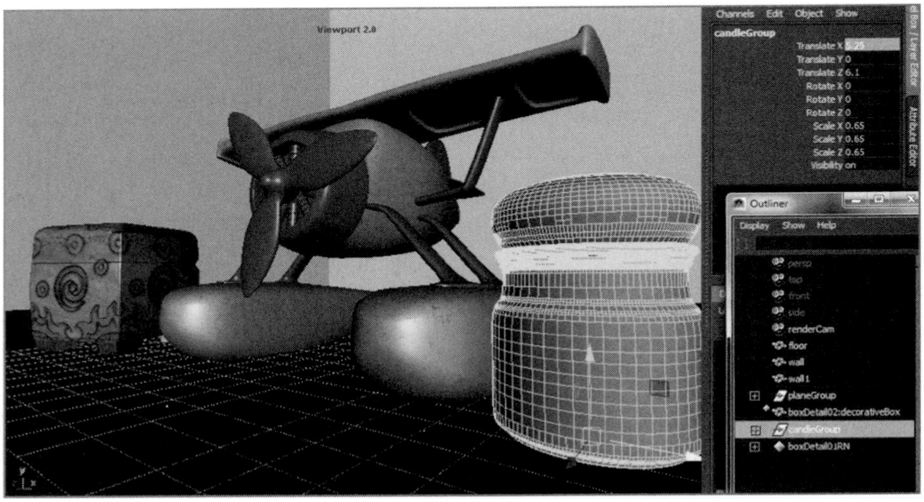

Figure 10.57

Import and place the candle to match this layout.

Creating the Lights

Save your file and compare it to planeLightingScene_v02.ma or skip to the following section. Here you will lay out lighting using the three-point lighting system discussed earlier.

1. In the renderCam viewport, press 6 for Texture mode and then 7 for lighted display mode. Using the persp viewport, create a Spot light; in the Attribute Editor, set Cone Angle to **70.0** and Penumbra Angle to **10.0**. Place and orient the Spot light to be the key light, matching the position and orientation shown in Figure 10.58.

2. Create a Directional light and place that as shown in Figure 10.59. Set Intensity to **0.6**.

3. Create a rim light with a Spot light with an Intensity value set to **0.7**; place it as shown in Figure 10.60. Set Penumbra Angle to **10.0**. Try using the special manipulator for the Spot light by pressing T. This way you can place the source and the target of the light to more easily position it.

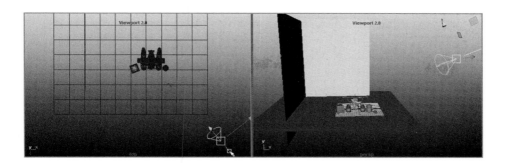

Figure 10.58

Create a Spot light and place it as shown.

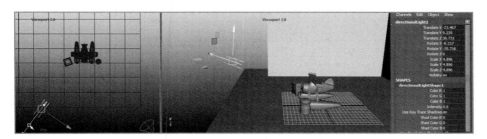

Figure 10.59

Create and place a Directional light as shown here.

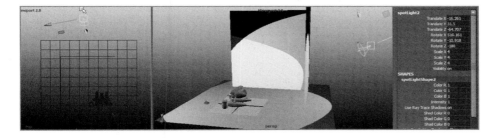

Figure 10.60

Create a Spot light for a rim light and place it as shown here.

4. In the renderCam viewport, render a frame (by clicking the 📷 icon in the Status line); you should see something like what is shown in Figure 10.61. You need to create a simple glass shader for the candle, and there are no shadows or reflections yet, but it's a start. You'll enable raytracing in the next section to make a glass shader and render shadows.

Reflection and Shadows

Save your file and compare it to `planeLightingScene_v03.ma` or skip to the following section. Here you will make rendering reflections and shadows possible.

1. Open the Render Settings window (📷) and click the Maya Software tab. In the Raytracing Quality section, click to enable Raytracing. If you render your scene now, you'll notice shadows in the image; however, the rim light has disappeared. That is because it is behind the back wall and is being blocked. You need to turn off shadows for that rim light in the next step.

Figure 10.61

A simple render of the plane

2. Select the Spot light that is your rim light (behind the back wall). In the Attribute Editor, under Shadows → Raytrace Shadow Attributes, uncheck the Use Ray Trace Shadows box to turn off those shadows.

3. If you render the frame now, it should resemble the image in Figure 10.62. It's a basic look, but it's getting nicer now that you see reflections in the objects (except the candle holder) and shadows.

4. Now let's soften the shadows. Select the first Spot light you created (the key light) and, in the Shadows → Raytrace Shadow Attributes section, set Light Radius to **9.0** and Shadow Rays to **12**.

Figure 10.62

Render with the rim light shadows turned off.

5. Render a frame, and the shadows look nicer and more real. You can experiment with the light's Light Radius and Shadow Rays values to dial in the shadows to your liking. The sharper the shadow, the smaller and the closer the source of the light will appear.

6. However, the reflections in the toy plane make the plastic look too shiny. Select the body of the plane in the persp viewport and open the Hypershade window. In the Hypershade, click the Graph Materials On Selected Objects icon () to bring up the plane's yellow Blinn shader in the Work Area.

7. Click the yellow shader and, in the Property Editor, under the Specular Shading section, set Eccentricity to **0.425**, Specular Roll Off to **0.525**, and Reflectivity to **0.25**.

8. Select the gray Blinn shader and repeat the same attribute values as step 7.

9. In the Hypershade, click the phongFloor shader and set its Cosine Power to **30** and Reflectivity to **0.15**. Render, and your frame should look more like Figure 10.63.

You can see that simple additions of shadow and reflections helped this render look nicer.

Figure 10.63

Reducing the glossy look of the plastic toy plane and the wooden tabletop

Making Glass

Now turn your attention to the glass candle holder and the candle inside. You can continue with your own scene or load the scene file `planeLightingScene_v04.ma` to skip to this point. You will create a glass shader and a simple shader for the candle in the following steps:

1. In the Hypershade, create a new Phong shader and name it **candleGlass**.

2. Open the Outliner. Shift+click the plus sign to the left of the candleGroup node to expand all the child nodes beneath it. Select the glassJar and glassLid objects; in the Hypershade, RMB+click the new candleGlass Phong shader and choose Assign Material To Selection.

3. In the candleGlass shader, move the Transparency slider so that the black color swatch turns almost pure white. This will make the shader almost entirely transparent.

4. Set Cosine Power to **60** to make the specular highlights tighter and more glossy looking. Render a frame, and you'll notice the jar is now clear glass with a gray candle inside. You may also notice some strange vertical bars between the glass and the gray candle (Figure 10.64).

   This phenomenon occurs when two surfaces penetrate each other. Since Maya is interpreting the geometry of the glass and the candle inside slightly differently during render time, this penetration may occur. You can simply reduce the size of the candle inside ever so slightly. However, you will address this issue when you render this scene with mental ray in the next chapter, so you can leave it be for now.

5. There is a gray ring inside the lid of the jar that should be white plastic. In the Hypershade, create a new Blinn and give it a white color. Set Reflectivity to **0.1**. Call this shader **whitePlastic**.

6. In the Outliner, select the plasticSealer object under the jarLid group and assign it to the whitePlastic shader.

7. Make another Blinn shader and give it a dark red color. Set Eccentricity to **0.125**, Specular Roll Off to **0.85**, and Reflectivity to **0.1**. Name it **candleWax**.

Figure 10.64

Rendering a glass look for the candle jar shows a little bit of penetration with the gray candle inside. That's okay for now.

8. In the Outliner, select the candle object grouped under the jarCandle group and assign it to the candleWax shader.

9. Finally, create a dark gray Lambert called blackWick and assign it to the wick object in the Outliner.

10. Render your scene and have a look. The candle is looking nicer, but the glass is missing something still. You need to create refractions in the glass of the candle holder.

11. Select the candleGlass Shader and, in the Property Editor, scroll down to and open the Ray Tracing section. Check the Refractions box to turn on refractions and set Refractive Index to **1.1**. For refractions to show up, you will need to have a Refraction Index value other than 1. The lower or the higher than 1.0 that you set this value, the more distorted the refraction will be. Small deviations from 1.0 give you the best results; going too high or too low may look super weird.

12. Before you render, go to the Render View window first (if you closed Render View after your last render, choose Windows → Rendering Editors → Render View). Click and drag a box around the candle in the image of your last render and then click the Render Region icon (▣) to just render that part of the frame to save time. Your glass render should look much more like glass now (Figure 10.65).

The render is not looking too shabby, but when you tackle this scene again with mental ray in the next chapter, you will see how powerful mental ray rendering can be. In Chapter 11, you'll add more texture maps to add carving detail to the decorative box, create mental ray specific shaders for the objects in the scene, and enable Final Gather to use an HDR image to light the scene to take it to a new level. Woo!

You can check your work against the scene file planeLightingScene_v05.ma in the Scenes folder of the Plane project.

Figure 10.65

The glass looks much nicer with refractions enabled.

Further Lighting Practice

Lighting professionals in the CG field are called on to find the most efficient way to light a scene and bring it to the peak of its beauty. Again, this comes only from experience. The best way to become a crackerjack lighting artist is to spend years honing your eye and practicing the latest procedures, such as HDR lighting.

The file still_life_v01.ma in the Lighting project on the web page contains the scene of the still life with no lights, so you can play with lighting and shadow methods as well as light linking to create some extra focus on some parts of the frame. The file still_life_v02.mb contains the same scene but with three-point lighting already set up.

Notice in the still_life_v02.ma file that two lights make up the key light (spotLight1 and spotLight2). One light makes up the fill light (directionalLight1), and two lights (spotLight3 and spotLight4) make up the back light.

For practice, download some models from the Internet and arrange them into your own still-life scenes to gain more lighting experience. Set up scenes, time the rendering process, and try to achieve the same lighting look using faster lighting setups that may not be as taxing on the renderer. Also, try taking pictures of situations and trying to match the lighting in the photo.

Try setting up simple scenes. Start with an indoor location that is lit by a single lightbulb. Then, try the same scene in the following locations to expand your lighting repertoire:

- A photography studio
- Outside in the morning on a bright summer day
- Outside at dusk in the fall
- Outside at night under a street lamp
- Inside on a window ledge
- At the bottom of a closet lit by a nearby hallway light

Tips for Using and Animating Lights

When you're lighting a scene, invoking a lighting mode in your perspective or camera viewport will give you great feedback regarding the relative brightness and direction of your lights. Most consumer graphics cards can handle a maximum of eight lights in Lighted mode; some professional cards can handle more.

As you've seen, you invoke Lighted mode by pressing 7 on your keyboard (not through the number pad on the side). You must first be in Shaded mode (press 5) or Texture mode (press 6) to be able to press 7 for Lighted mode. Remember that Lighted mode displays linked lights as if they're lighting the entire scene. This can cause some confusion, so it's wise to take notes on any light linking in your scene.

The Maya IPR renderer is also useful when lighting a scene. This almost-real-time updating renderer will give you a high-quality render of your scene as you adjust your lights. Chapter 11 will explore the IPR renderer.

Animating a Light

Any attribute of a light can be animated in the same way that you animate any other object attribute. You can't, however, animate a light's type. To edit a light's animation, you need only select the light and open the Graph Editor to access its keyframes. You can set keyframes on Intensity, Penumbra Angle, Color, and so on, within the Channel Box or the Attribute Editor. RMB+click the name of the attribute and choose Key Selected from the context menu.

> By animating a light's intensity, you can simulate the real-world appearance of a light turning on or off. To turn on a light, create a quickly increasing curve so that its brightness arcs up slowly at first before climbing to full brightness. This animation mimics the way real lights turn on and off better than simply enabling or disabling them in your scene.

When you animate the color of a light or a shader, you set keyframes for the color's RGB values as three separate keyframes. The Graph Editor shows a separate curve for the red, green, and blue channels of color when you animate a light's color. You can set all three keys at once by RMB+clicking the Color attribute in the Attribute Editor and choosing Set Key from the context menu, as shown in Figure 10.66.

In addition, lights can be animated to be moved, scaled, and rotated like any other object. For further study, try animating the lighting for the simple scenes you set up to practice lighting from the previous section. Try creating animated lights to simulate a candle illuminating your scene, a campfire, or the flashing emergency lights you would find in your average space-station airlock.

Figure 10.66

Set a key for the light.

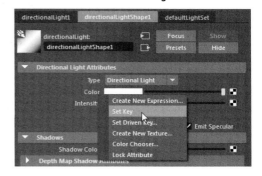

Using the Show Manipulator Tool for Lights

As you saw earlier in the chapter, an easy way to manipulate lights is to use their special manipulator. For example, pressing T or choosing Modify → Transformation Tools → Show Manipulator tool with a Spot light selected gives you two Translate manipulators in the viewport, as shown in Figure 10.67, and displays the icon ( ) below the Tool Box.

This allows you to move the source or target of the light to aim it better. By clicking the cyan circle that appears below the source's Translate manipulator, you can toggle through a number of manipulators to adjust the Spot light's settings, such as cone angle (two clicks clockwise) and penumbra angle (three clicks clockwise). Figure 10.68 shows the manipulator for cone angle.

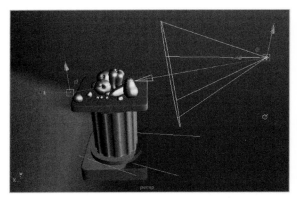

Figure 10.67

Using special manipulators to place and orient the Spot light

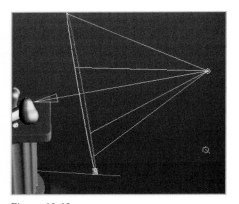

Figure 10.68

Adjusting the cone angle interactively with the special manipulator

Source and Target Translate manipulators are available for all light types through the Show Manipulator tool as well.

Summary

This chapter explored lighting in Maya, beginning with basic concepts that included the three-point lighting technique. You then learned about the different lights in Maya, how they work, and how you can use light linking to control your scene better. Shadows are an important part of lighting and were covered in this chapter, followed by a quick exploration of the Physical Sun and Sky system with mental ray and then lighting effects such as lens flare and light glows. You then created simple lighting for the toy plane, candle holder, and decorative box for a still rendering. You used raytracing to enable reflections and shadows as well as to create a glass look with refractions. Finally, you learned how to begin animating lights for your scenes.

Lighting is truly the linchpin of CG; it can make or break a scene. As you'll see in the next chapter, lighting goes hand in hand with rendering and shading, and the more you understand about all three functions, the better your scenes will look. Don't be afraid to experiment with lighting and shading schemes on all your projects.

CHAPTER 11

Autodesk® Maya® Rendering

Rendering is the last step in creating your CG work. It's the process by which the computer calculates the surface properties, lighting, shadows, movement, and shape of objects, and it saves a sequence of images. Although the computer does all the thinking at this point, you still need to set up your cameras and the render to get exactly what you want.

This chapter will show you how to render your scene using the Autodesk® Maya® Software renderer and mental ray® for Maya, as well as how to create reflections and refractions. In this chapter, you'll use a wine bottle and a still life from previous chapters, and you'll animate a camera to render a sequence.

Learning Outcomes: In this chapter, you will be able to

- Set up your scenes for output through rendering

- Choose resolutions, image formats, and other settings for rendering

- Create and edit cameras

- Render with motion blur and differentiate between the types of motion blur

- Set up and use mental ray

- Render in layers and compose them back together

- Set render layer overrides settings for specific needs

- Use Final Gather in mental ray renders for indirect lighting workflows

- Use Ambient Occlusion to create detail in crevices and for contact shadows

- Apply an HDRI map as a lighting source

- Apply a displacement map to create finer detail in a model

Rendering Setup

When your lighting scene from the previous chapter is complete, you've had a celebration smoothie for your hard work, and you're ready to start a render, you'll need to set up how you want it rendered. Although this is the last part of the CG process, from now on you should be thinking about rendering throughout your production. When you create models and textures with the final image in mind and you gear the lighting toward showing off the scene elegantly, the final touches are relatively easy to set up.

Decide which of the render engines included with Maya you'll use: Maya Software, Maya Hardware (or Hardware 2.0), mental ray for Maya (the most popular of the renderers standard with Maya 2016), or Maya Vector. Each engine has its own particular workflow and can yield entirely different results, although mental ray and Maya Software are close in appearance if you don't use the special features of mental ray. The choice of a rendering method depends on the final look you want and sometimes on the number of machines and licenses with which you can render. Maya Software rendering comes with an unlimited number of licenses, which means you can render on any machine you have (with Maya installed), although you can work with the Maya application only on as many machines for which you have licenses. There are also third-party developers in the CG field that have created other render engines that plug right into Maya, such as V-Ray® for Maya, Maxwell®, and Pixar's RenderMan® for Maya.

No matter which renderer you use, the lighting and general setup are fairly common across the board. Even then, it's a good idea to choose your render engine as you begin creating your scene. It's best to begin with basic mental ray to pick up the fundamentals of lighting, texturing, and rendering before you venture into mental ray special features or try other renderers.

Regardless of the type of render, you need to specify a set of common attributes in the Render Settings window. Choose Windows → Rendering Editors → Render Settings to open the Render Settings window. Figure 11.1 shows the Render Settings window for the Maya Software renderer and its tabs: the Common tab and the Maya Software tab. You use the options in this window's Common tab to set up all your rendering preferences, including the resolution, file type, frame range, and so forth.

Figure 11.1

The Render Settings window

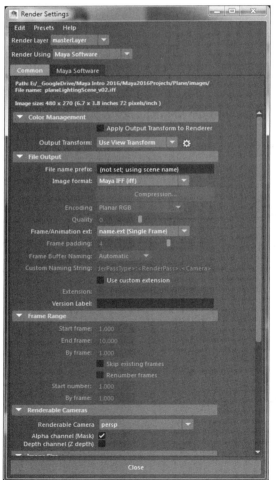

The Common tab contains the settings common to all the rendering methods, such as image size. The Maya Software tab gives you access to render-specific attributes, such as quality settings, raytracing settings, motion blur, and so on.

If you switch the Render Using pull-down menu from the default Maya Software setting to mental ray, you'll notice several tabs: Common, Quality, Scene, Configuration, and Diagnostics. These tabs give you access to all the settings for the powerful mental ray renderer.

You may notice that some of the render engines like mental ray may not show up in the Render Settings window right away. In this case, the renderers' respective plug-ins must be loaded first. I'll discuss this further in the section "mental ray for Maya" later in this chapter.

Choosing a Filename

Rendered images are identified by a filename, a frame number, and an extension, in the form *name.#.ext*. This is an example: `stillife.0234.tif`.

In the File Name Prefix text box, enter the image sequence name. If you don't enter anything in this text box, Maya automatically names your rendered images after your scene file (`stillife` in the example). This is the preferred naming convention; using it, you can immediately identify the scene file from which a particular image file was rendered.

In the Frame/Animation Ext drop-down list box, select *name.#.ext* to render out a sequence of files. If you leave this setting at the default of *name.ext*, only a single frame will render, no matter what the animation range is in the Time slider.

> *Name.#.ext* is perhaps the most commonly used convention, as opposed to *name.ext.#* or *name.#*, because it allows you to identify the file type easily in Windows. Although Mac OS X isn't as picky about the order of the number and extension, most Mac compositing software applications (such as After Effects and Shake) want filenames that end in the three-letter extension. Therefore, it's best for both Mac and Windows users to employ the *name.#.ext* format.

The extension portion of the image name is a three-letter abbreviation for the type of file you're writing to disk to ensure that you can identify the file type.

Image Format

In the Image Format drop-down list box, select the type of image file you want to render. Maya will add the appropriate extension to the filename.

The image format you choose depends on your own preference and your output needs. For example, JPEG files may be great for the small file sizes preferred on the Internet, but their color compression and lack of alpha channel (a feature discussed later in this chapter) make them undesirable for most professional CG work beyond test renders.

It's best to render a sequence of images rather than a movie file for two reasons. First, you want your renders to be their best quality with little or no image compression.

Second, if a render fails during a movie render, you must re-render the entire sequence. With an image sequence, however, you can pick up where the last frame left off.

The best file type format to render to is TIFF. This format enjoys universal support, has little to no compression, and supports an alpha channel. Almost all image-editing and compositing packages can read Targa- and TIFF-formatted files, so either is a safe choice most of the time. For more on image formats, see Chapter 1, "Introduction to Computer Graphics and 3D."

Frame Range

Maya defaults to the frame range 1–10, which you may likely need to change to render your entire sequence. You must choose a naming convention other than Name (Single Frame) to access the frame range. Enter the Start Frame and End Frame attributes for part of the sequence or the entire sequence.

The By Frame attribute specifies the intervals at which the sequence will render. For example, if you want to render only the odd-numbered frames, set the Start Frame attribute to 1, and set the By Frame attribute to 2. If you want to render only even-numbered frames, set Start Frame to 2, set By Frame to 2, and so on. Typically, you leave By Frame set to 1 so that Maya renders each frame.

The Frame Padding attribute and slider deal with how an operating system, such as Windows or Mac OS X, orders its files by inserting leading zeros in the frame number. For example, if Frame Padding is set to 4, the filename contains three leading zeros; therefore, frame 8 is `name.0008.tif` as opposed to `name.8.tif` (which is set to a padding of 1).

Large sequences of files are easier to organize if they all have a frame padding of at least 3. Figure 11.2 shows an image sequence without padding and with padding. The files without padding aren't shown in numeric order.

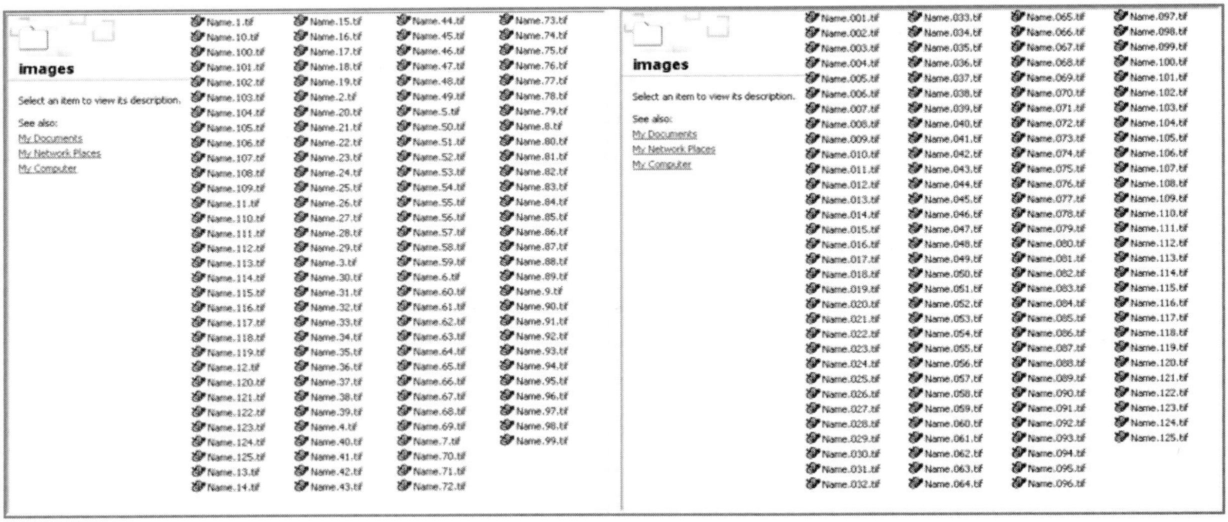

Figure 11.2

Images rendered without frame padding (left). Frame padding makes file sequences easier to organize (right).

Camera and Channels

Under the Renderable Cameras heading, you choose the camera to render and enable the Alpha and Depth channels.

Image files are composed of red, green, and blue channels. Each channel specifies the amount of the primary additive color (red, green, or blue, respectively) in the image. (See Chapter 1 for more on how computers define color.) Some file formats save a fourth channel, called the *alpha channel*. This channel defines the image's transparency level. Just as the red channel defines how much red is in an area of the image, the alpha channel defines how transparent the image is when layered or composited on another image. If the alpha channel is black, the image is perfectly see-through. If the alpha channel is white, the image is solid and opaque. The alpha channel is also known as the *matte*. An object with some transparency like tinted glass will render with a gray alpha channel, as shown in Figure 11.3.

size: 640 480 zoom: 1.000 (Maya Software)

Figure 11.3

This wine bottle's transparency renders with a gray alpha channel.

The alpha channel can be displayed in the Render View window. As discussed later in this chapter, your test renders also display in this window.

To view an image's alpha channel in the Render View window, click the Display Alpha Channel icon ( ). To reset the view to RGB (full-color view), click the Display RGB Channels icon (RGB).

Figure 11.4

Output an alpha channel.

Most renders have the alpha channels selected in the Render Settings window, so leave the Alpha Channel (Mask) check box selected at all times, as shown in Figure 11.4. Note, however, that JPEG, Graphics Interchange Format (GIF), and Windows bitmap files don't support alpha channels, regardless of whether the Alpha Channel (Mask) check box is selected.

Setting Resolution

The Width and Height attributes set the pixel size of the image to be rendered, a.k.a. the image *resolution*. In the Image Size section of the Render Settings window, you can select a resolution from the Presets drop-down list. The commonly used resolution for professional broadcast is 1920×1080 High Definition, which appears as HD 1080 in the Presets list. To composite Maya CG into a standard definition (SD) home-shot digital video (DV) movie, you use the standard DV resolution of 720×480 to render your scene, but you must enter that resolution manually in the Width and Height fields. (For more on resolutions, see Chapter 1.)

The Device Aspect Ratio and Pixel Aspect Ratio attributes adjust the width of the image to accommodate certain professional output needs; you do not need to adjust them here.

> Make sure your Pixel Aspect Ratio attribute is set to 1 before you render, especially HD resolutions, unless you need to render CCIR 601/Quantel NTSC or DV for television needs; otherwise, your image may look squeezed or widened compared to any live-action footage you use to composite.

The higher your resolution, the longer the scene will take to render. With large frame sequences, it's advisable to render tests at half the resolution of the final output or less to save time. In addition to turning down the resolution for a test, you can use a lower-quality render.

Selecting a Render Engine

Maya allows you to select a render engine in the Render Settings window. Although mental ray for Maya is most commonly used, the other rendering methods give you flexibility in choosing a final look for your project.

Maya Software

Maya Software, the default software rendering method, can capture just about everything you want in your scene, from reflections to motion blur and transparencies. You can use the software rendering method in a couple of ways.

USING RAYTRACING

Raytracing, a topic introduced in Chapter 10, "Autodesk® Maya® Lighting," is used to incorporate two optical effects into a rendering that the default software rendering method can't handle. *Raytracing* traces rays of light from each light source to every object in the shot and then traces the light's reflection from the object to the camera's lens. This allows true *reflections* and *refractions* to appear in the render as well as highly defined shadows (for more on shadows, see Chapter 10).

True Reflections   True reflections occur when every object in the scene is viewed in a reflective surface, as a reflection, of course. You can also have objects with reflections explicitly turned off through the Render Stats section in the Attribute Editor in case you don't want a particular reflection, which is common. Although it's possible to simulate reflections in Maya Software using reflection maps, true reflections can be generated only through raytracing.

Refractions   *Refractions* occur when light bends as it passes through one medium into another medium of different density. For example, a pencil in a glass of water appears to be broken. Refraction can also be turned on or off explicitly through Render Stats for objects that you don't want to see refracting through another clear object.

You saw in the previous chapter that raytracing is also a vital component of mental ray for Maya as well as the Maya Software renderer.

As soon as raytracing is enabled, any reflective surface receives a true reflection of the objects and environment in the scene. Even objects with reflection maps reflect other objects in addition to their reflection maps. For more on reflection maps, see the section "Reflections and Refractions" later in this chapter.

RENDER QUALITY

With software rendering, the render quality depends most noticeably on *anti-aliasing*. Anti-aliasing is the effect produced when pixels appear to blur together to soften a jagged edge on an angled line. Increasing the anti-aliasing level of a render produces an image that has smoother angles and curves. The Render Settings window contains presets that specify this level and a few others to set the quality of your render. Follow these steps:

1. In the Render Settings window, make sure Maya Software is selected in the Render Using drop-down list and click the Maya Software tab.

2. In the Anti-aliasing Quality section, select either Preview Quality or Production Quality from the Quality preset drop-down list.

Figure 11.5 shows the fruit still life from Chapter 10 rendered with the Preview Quality preset and the same image with the Production Quality preset. Of course, the higher the quality, the longer the render will take.

Maya Hardware and Hardware 2.0

The hardware rendering method uses your graphic card's processor to render the scene. Hardware renders are similar to what you may see when you play a 3D video game.

This method results in faster render times, but it lacks some of the features and quality you get from a software render. In Figure 11.6, the first image shows a wine bottle as rendered through hardware. The render time is blazingly fast, but the quality suffers. The second image shows the software render of the same frame. Hardware rendering becomes a good way to test-render a scene, although only certain video cards fully support Maya Hardware rendering.

To use the Maya Hardware renderer, in the Render Settings window, make sure Maya Hardware is selected in the Render Using drop-down list. To specify hardware quality, select a level from the Number Of Samples drop-down list on the Maya Hardware tab.

mental ray for Maya

mental ray for Maya has become a standard for rendering through Maya, supplanting the Maya Software renderer because of its stability and quality results. The mental ray for

Maya rendering method can also let you emulate the behavior of light even more realistically than the other rendering methods, as you saw in the previous chapter's Physical Sun and Sky exercise. Based on raytracing, mental ray takes the concept further by adding photon maps to the light traces. That is, it projects photon particles from lights and records their behavior and trajectory. The end result allows the phenomena of light *caustics* and *bounce*, also known as *global illumination.*

The mental ray for Maya renderer can be an advanced and intricate rendering language with shaders and procedures all its own. This chapter briefly covers one of the popular mental ray methods called Final Gather using HDR image-based lighting. To use mental ray, you still need to be experienced with the basics of lighting and rendering. At its base, mental ray will give you results similar to those of Maya Software when all of the bells and whistles of mental ray are not enabled. So it's often best to just use mental ray throughout.

Maya Vector

Vector rendering lets you render your objects with an illustrated or cartoon look. You can render "ink" outlines of your characters to composite over flat-color passes. Figure 11.7 shows the fruit still life rendered with Maya Vector. This rendering method is different from the Maya toon-shading feature, which is briefly covered in Chapter 12, "Autodesk® Maya® Dynamics and Effects."

Figure 11.7

The fruit still life as a vector render

Maya Vector can output animated files in Adobe Flash format for direct use in web pages and animations, as well as Adobe Illustrator files and the usual list of image formats. To specify the attribute settings for Maya Vector, you use the Maya Vector tab in the Render Settings window (see Figure 11.8).

Figure 11.8

The Maya Vector rendering settings

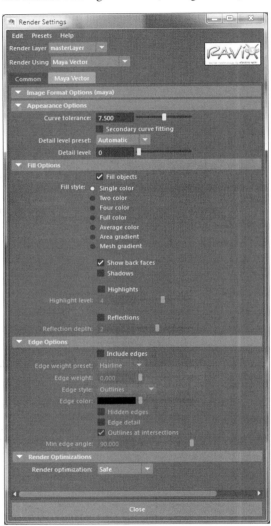

In the Fill Options section, click the Fill Objects check box, and select the number of colors for each object to set the look of the render. If you want the renderer to include an outline of the edges of your geometry, in the Edge Options section, click the Include Edges check box and set the line weights.

Previewing Your Render: The Render View Window

The Render View window automatically opens when you test-render a frame, as you've already seen in your work through this book. To open it manually, choose Windows → Rendering Editors → Render View. Your current scene renders in the Render View window. Figure 11.9 shows the names of the icons in this window, and the following list highlights what the more important ones do.

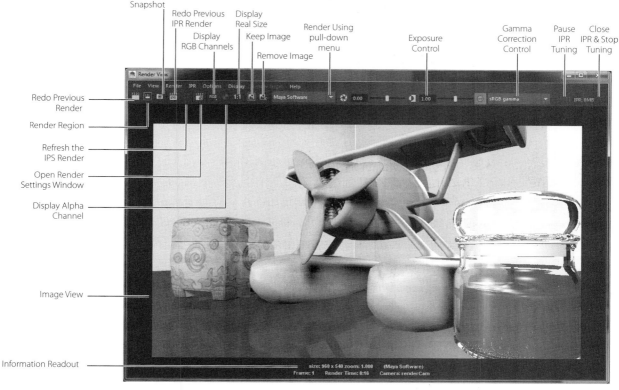

Figure 11.9

The Render View window

Redo Previous Render Renders the last-rendered viewport.

Render Region Renders only the selected portion of an image. To select a portion of an image, click within the image in the Render View window and drag a red box around a region.

Snapshot Grabs a snapshot of the currently selected modeling panel and inserts it as a background in the Render View. You can more easily do a render region this way.

Open Render Settings Window Opens the Render Settings window (also known as the Render Globals window in previous versions of Maya).

Display RGB Channels   Displays the full color of the image.

Display Alpha Channel   Displays only the alpha matte of the render as a black-and-white image.

Display Real Size   Resets the image size to 100 percent to make sure the image displays properly. When the Render View window is resized or when you select a new render resolution, the image renders to fit the window, and the image is resized if needed. If your render looks blocky, make sure the Render View window is displaying at real size before adjusting the options in the Render Settings window.

Render Using Pull Down Menu   Lets you select the rendering method. This is the same as selecting it in the Render Settings window.

Exposure and Gamma Correction Controls   These sliders allow you to adjust the brightness of the rendered image for viewing purposes. The first slider controls the overall brightness of the image while the second slider (Gamma Control) effectively runs the relative brightness of the lights and darks in the image, which in essence controls the contrast.

Information Readout   At the bottom of the Render View window is a readout of information about the frame rendered. This information tells you the resolution, renderer used, frame number, render time, and camera used to render. This readout is a huge help in comparing different render settings and different frames as you progress in your work, especially when you keep images in the buffer (as explained later).

Saving/Loading an Image

Although you typically use the Render View window to test a scene, you can also use it to save single frames by choosing File → Save Image to save in any image formats supported in Maya. Likewise, choose File → Open Image to display any previously rendered image file in this window. If your task in Maya is to create a single frame, this is the best way to render and save it.

Keep/Remove Image

The Render View window is a prime place to see adjustments to various parts of your scene. You can store images in its buffer by clicking the Keep Image icon. When you do, a scroll bar appears at the bottom of the window, and you can scroll through any saved images. This is handy for making a change, rendering it, and scrolling back and forth between the old saved image and the new render to make sure the change is to your liking. You can store a number of images in the buffer. For a faster way to preview changes, use IPR rendering, as discussed next.

IPR Rendering

As you saw in Chapter 7, a fast way to preview changes to your scene is to use Maya Interactive Photorealistic Rendering (IPR). After you IPR-render a viewport, specify the region you want to tune by dragging a box around that area of the image in the Render View window. Maya updates that region every time you make a shader or lighting change to the scene. Figure 11.10 shows the decorative box as an IPR mental ray render as the color and specular levels are being fine-tuned against a wireframe snapshot of the model.

Figure 11.10

IPR rendering lets you fine-tune your textures and lighting with near-real-time feedback.

IPR is perfect for finding just the right lighting and specular levels. It will, however, register raytracing elements such as refractions and true reflections only if the scene is set to render through mental ray for Maya. Overall, IPR quality is fairly close to that of a full render while still allowing you to watch your tuning in near real time.

Setting the Default Renderer

By default, whenever you launch Maya, it sets Maya Software as the renderer of choice. To change this to mental ray, for example, in the main menu bar select Windows → Settings/ Preferences → Preferences. In the Preferences window, select Rendering in the list on the left side, and set the Preferred renderer drop-down menu to mental ray and click Save. From here on, new scenes will default to using mental ray.

Reflections and Refractions

As you saw in Chapter 7, creating a "faked" reflection with a map for an object is pretty simple. To generate true reflections without the use of maps, however, you'll need to manually enable raytracing in Maya Software or use mental ray for Maya, which has raytracing enabled by default. With raytracing, Maya or mental ray reflects any objects in the scene that fall in the proper line of sight. All you need to do is use shaders that have reflection attributes such as Phong or Blinn. Note that Lambert shader does not reflect.

Raytraced Reflections

Figure 11.11

Enabling raytracing in Maya Software rendering

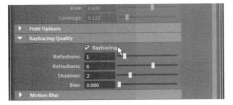

Rendering reflections using mental ray is simple. Just assign shaders to your objects that have a Reflection attribute such as Phong or Blinn. If you prefer not to use mental ray, however, you must enable raytraced reflections with Maya Software rendering. First, make sure to use a material that has a Reflections attribute (for example, Phong or Blinn). Then, open the Render Settings window and choose Maya Software as your renderer. On the Maya Software tab, click the Raytracing check box in the Raytracing Quality section. (See Figure 11.11.)

The sliders control the quality of the render by specifying how many times to reflect or refract for any given object. Setting Reflections to 2, for example, enables an object's reflection in a second object to appear as part of its reflection in a third object.

The first image in Figure 11.12 shows the still life reflecting onto the surface of its table. In this case, Reflections is set to 1. If you increase Reflections to 2, however, you'll see the reflections of the pieces of fruit in each other also reflecting in the surface of the table.

Figure 11.12

Reflections set to 1 (left); Reflections set to 2 (right)

Notice the difference in the reflections of the fruit in the table between the two renders. Raytraced reflections can consume valuable render resources and time, so it's a good idea to make your scene efficient.

You can control the number of reflections on a per-object basis through its shader as opposed to setting limits on the entire scene through the Render Settings window. To access a shader's reflection limits, select the shader in the Hypershade. In the Raytrace Options section of the Property Editor or the Attribute Editor, drag the Reflection Limit slider to set the maximum number of reflections for that shader. The lower value (either this value or the Reflections value in the Render Settings window) dictates how many reflections are rendered for every object attached to that shader. The default shader reflection limit is 1, so make sure you change the Reflections value as well as each shader's value if you want more than one level of reflection.

Furthermore, you may not want some objects to cast reflections in a scene with raytraced reflections. To specify that an object doesn't cast reflections, select the object in a Maya panel and open the Attribute Editor. In the Render Stats section, clear the Visible In Reflections check box.

Rendering Refractions

Refractions are also a raytraced-only ability. Refractions require that an object be semi-transparent so that you can see through it to the object (or objects) behind it being refracted. To control refractions, use the shader.

To enable refractions in either Maya Software or mental ray rendering, select an appropriate shader in the Hypershade. In the Raytrace Options section of the Property Editor (or Attribute Editor), click the Refractions check box. Now you need to set a refractive index for the shader and a refraction limit, similar to the reflection limit.

The refractive index must be greater or less than 1 to cause a visible refraction. Typically, a number within 0.2 of 1 is perfect for most refractive effects. The first image in Figure 11.13 is raytraced with a refractive index of 1.2 on the wine bottle and glasses; the second image has a refractive index of 0.8 on both bottle and glasses.

You can specify whether an object is visible in a refracting object by clicking or clearing the Visible In Refractions check box in the Render Stats section of the object's Attribute Editor.

When rendering refractions, make sure the Refractions attribute under Raytracing Quality in the Maya Software tab of the Render Settings is set to at least 2 or higher; otherwise, your refraction may not appear properly. For mental ray, it is the Transmission attribute found under the Trace Depth heading on the Quality tab, as shown in Figure 11.13 (bottom right).

Figure 11.13

Refractive index of 1.2 (left top render); refractive index of 0.8 (left bottom render); setting the refraction quality in the shader's Property Editor (top right) and the Render Settings (bottom right)

Using Cameras

Cameras capture all the animation fun in the scene. The more you know about photography, the easier these concepts are to understand.

The term *camera*, in essence, refers to any perspective view. You can have as many cameras in the scene as you want, but it's wise to have a camera you're planning to render with placed to frame the shot and a different camera acting as the perspective work view so you can move around your scene as you work. The original persp viewport fits that latter role well, although it can be used as a render camera just as easily.

You can also render any of your work windows to test-render orthogonal views of your model the same way you render a perspective view.

Creating a Camera

The simplest way to create a new camera is to choose Panels → Perspective → New, as you've seen in a previous exercise. This creates a new camera node in Maya and sets that active panel to its view. Cameras will work in any renderer, though some renderers such as VRay may provide their own specialized cameras or camera attributes.

You can select a camera in a viewport and transform it (move it, rotate it, scale it) just as you would select and transform any other object in Maya to be animated or positioned. Furthermore, you can move a camera and rotate it using the Alt/Option key and mouse button combinations.

For example, click inside a new Maya Scene Perspective window to make it active. Select that view's camera by choosing View → Select Camera. The camera's attributes appear in the Channel Box. Try moving the view around using the Alt/Option key and mouse button combinations. Notice how the attributes change to reflect the new position and rotation of the camera. You can animate the camera—for example, zoom in or out or pan across the scene—by setting keyframes on any of these attributes.

Camera Types

You can create three types of nonstereo cameras for your scene: Camera; Camera And Aim; and Camera, Aim, And Up (also known as single-node, two-node, and three-node cameras, respectively). To create any of these cameras, choose Create → Cameras. You can also change the type of these cameras at any time through the Attribute Editor. The other two options for creating cameras are Stereo Camera and Multi Stereo Rig to allow for a stereoscopic effect, although they aren't covered in this book.

The single-node camera (Camera) is the most common (see Figure 11.14). This camera consists of a single camera node that you move and rotate as you would any other object for proper positioning. The persp viewport's camera is a single-node camera.

The two-node camera (Camera And Aim) consists of the camera node and an aim node. You use the aim node to point the camera as opposed to rotating it to orient it properly. This is useful for animating a camera following an object. You animate the move-

Figure 11.14

A single-node camera

ment of the aim node to follow your object much as you'd follow a car around a racetrack. The camera pivots to follow its aim point and, hence, the object. (See Figure 11.15.)

The three-node camera (Camera, Aim, And Up) has a camera node, an aim node, and an up node. The additional up node is to orient the camera's up direction. This gives you the ability to animate the side-to-side rotation of the camera as well as its aim direction. (See Figure 11.16.)

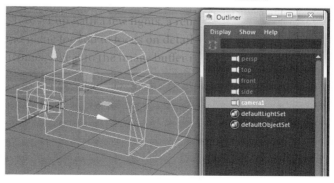

Figure 11.15

A two-node camera

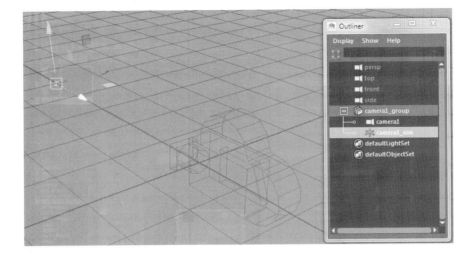

Figure 11.16

A three-node camera

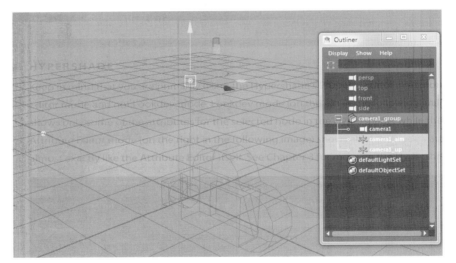

Camera Attributes

As an example, download the still_life_render_v02.ma scene from the Lighting project on the book's web page, www.sybex.com/go/introducingmaya2016, and set your project to Lighting. You'll see a green box in the persp viewport that displays the resolution (set to 960×540, which is half HD resolution) and the name of the camera (camera1).

Special attributes control the function of camera nodes. To set these attributes, follow these steps:

1. Select the camera through the Outliner and open the Attribute Editor (Ctrl+A), or click the Camera Attributes icon (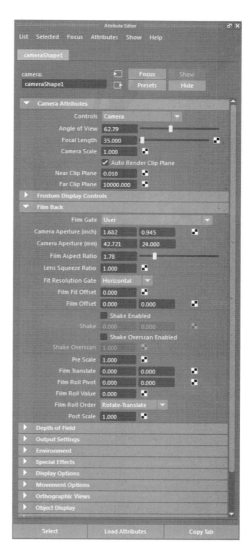) at the top of the camera's viewport.

2. At the top of the window, select the type of camera controls you want. The Controls attribute sets the type of camera from single- to two- to three-control nodes. Figure 11.17 shows the Attribute Editor for the camera1 camera.

Focal Length

The Focal Length attribute specifies the length of the lens. The lower the focal length (a.k.a. short lens), the wider the view. At very low numbers, however, the image is distorted, as you can see in the comparison in Figure 11.18. The higher the focal length, the closer the subject seems to the camera.

Although adjusting the Focal Length attribute of a camera zooms in and out, it isn't the same as moving the camera closer to your subject using the Alt+RMB+click procedure to zoom in viewports (which is called *trucking* the camera). Focal-length zooming can create optical distortions, such as can be created with a fish-eye lens.

If you need to match some CG element in Maya to a photograph or video that you've imported as an image plane, set your camera's focal length to match that of the real camera used for the background photo. Some photos will contain that information in the metadata of the image file, though it's always a good idea to write it down at the time of shooting the photos.

Figure 11.17

The Attribute Editor for the persp camera

Focal Length = 35   Focal Length = 8   Focal Length = 60

Figure 11.18

Different focal lengths

Clipping Planes

All cameras in Maya have clipping planes that restrict the amount of information that can be seen through them. The clipping plane is defined by the Near Clip Plane and Far Clip Plane attributes. These set the minimum and maximum distances, respectively, of the clipping plane. Any object or portion of an object that passes beyond these distances won't show in the window and should not render.

If you notice objects disappearing as you move your camera and create a scene, it may be because of the clipping plane. Increase the Far Clip Plane attribute, and the objects should reappear in the view. You can display the near and far clipping planes of any camera with the check boxes in the Frustum Display Controls section, as well as view your angle of view by turning on Display Frustum.

Film Back

The Film Back attributes concern the type of output you'll be dealing with after your renders are finished and you're ready to put your animation on tape, DVD, film, or what have you.

Film Gate Defines the aspect ratio of your camera's view. Images that are output to HD television have an aspect ratio of 1:1.78, which aggravatingly enough does not have a preset in the Film Gate drop-down list. For a generic HD camera output, simply set Film Aspect Ratio to **1.78**. For standard-definition TV output, simply select 35mm TV Projection from the Film Gate drop-down list. (For more on aspect ratios, see Chapter 1.)

Fit Resolution Gate Allows you to align footage you may have imported as an image plane to match up CG properly to live action.

Overscan

Found in the Display Options section for the camera's Attribute Editor, Overscan lets you resize the view without changing the film gate that will render. For example, the scene on the top in Figure 11.19 is set up with an Overscan setting of 1.3, allowing you to see more than what will render, which is defined by the outline box. The scene on the bottom in

Figure 11.19 is set up with an Overscan setting of 2, which increases even more how much you see in the camera1 panel but doesn't change the view when rendered.

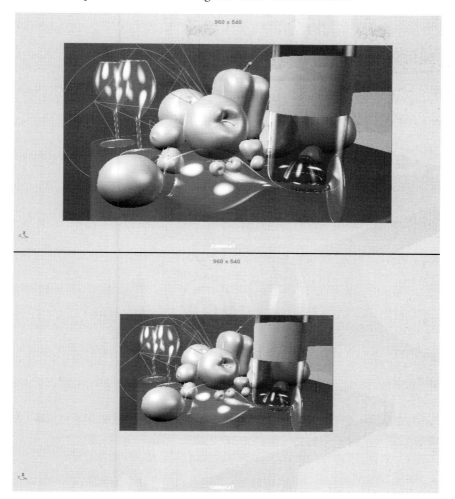

Figure 11.19

Overscan settings define how much you can see of your scene in the camera but not how much renders in the image.

You can turn the green box in the camera's viewport on and off through the camera's Attribute Editor. Also in the Display Options section are Display Film Gate and Display Resolution check boxes, shown in Figure 11.20. Ideally, these two green boxes should align perfectly in the view pane. If the resolution box (the solid green line) doesn't line up with the film gate box (the dashed green line), change your

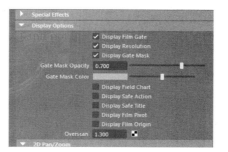

Figure 11.20

Camera display options

film gate selection to match the resolution's aspect ratio in the Render Settings window. A resolution of 960×540, for example, has an aspect ratio of 1.78, the same as the user-defined film gate currently set with a Film Aspect Ratio of 1.78 for this scene.

Environment

In the Environment section, you'll find attributes to adjust the background color that renders and to create an image plane, as shown in Figure 11.21.

If you want to use a solid color as the camera's background when you render, click the color swatch next to Background Color to change the background color in your renders

using the Color Chooser. The slider allows you to control the value, or brightness, of the current color. Neither changes the background color of your viewports, however.

CAMERA IMAGE PLANES

A camera image plane isn't like the reference planes you used for modeling the red wagon in Chapter 6, "Practical Experience!" In this case, an image plane is created to be a background specific for that particular camera or viewport, but it's typically also used as a reference, much like the planes you created and mapped in Chapter 6. Camera image planes are useful when you're matching your scene to existing footage or an image. For example, if you need to animate a flying saucer into a home video of a family gathering, you would import the video as an image sequence into Maya through a perspective camera to be able to line up your UFO properly to zap your cousins.

You can import an image plane by clicking the Create button in the Environment section of the Attribute Editor (see Figure 11.21) or directly through a viewport's menu, as you'll see in the next exercise.

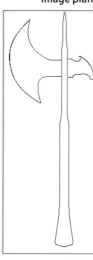

In this exercise, you'll learn how to import a sketch of an axe into the front viewport for a modeling assignment. (You won't actually model the axe, however.) The image, a sketch of a simple axe design, is to be used as a template for outlining the model. You can find the file `Axe_outline_1.tif` in the Sourceimages folder of the Axe project on the companion web page; it's shown in Figure 11.22.

Follow these steps:

1. Choose File → New Scene.

2. Import the sketch of the axe into Maya as a camera image plane for the front viewport. In your front window, choose View → Image Plane → Import Image.

3. Point to `Axe_outline_1.tif` in the Axe project's sourceimages folder and load it. The sketch displays in your front window and as a selected plane in the Perspective window (see Figure 11.23). You should see the image plane's attributes in the Attribute Editor. At first, the plane looks a little small in your viewports, but you can adjust the size of the image plane in the Attribute Editor under the Placement Extras heading using the Width and Height attributes as you did in the top image. In the Attribute

Editor, make sure that the Maintain Pic Aspect Ratio box is checked and set Width and Height to 25.0×17.325, as in the bottom image.

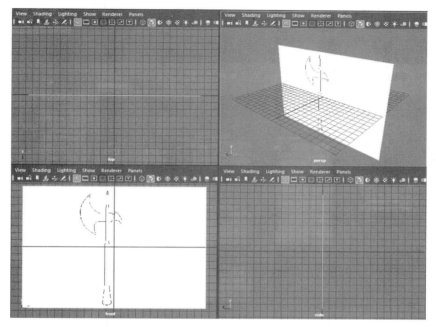

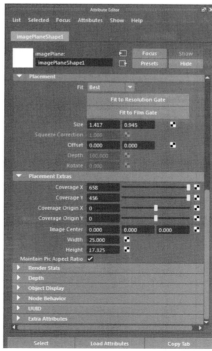

Figure 11.23

Importing a camera image plane into the front viewport (top) and setting the Image plane attributes (bottom)

Now you'd be ready to trace the outline of the axe easily in the front viewport, if you were going to model the axe.

> If you can't see the image plane, click Show in the viewport and make sure Image Planes is checked.

IMAGE PLANE SEQUENCE

A movie file or a sequence of files can also be brought in to animate or to track motion (a.k.a. *matchmoving*) as a camera image plane. It's generally best to use a frame sequence, however. When you bring in an image for an image plane, check the Use Image Sequence box in the image plane's Attribute Editor window, as shown in Figure 11.24. Maya will automatically load the image to correspond to the frame number in the scene. For example, at frame 29 in your Maya animation, Maya loads frame 29 of your image sequence. But your image file sequence must be numbered correctly (such as `filename.###.tif`). You can import an image plane into any perspective view in the same way.

> If the clutter of seeing a camera image plane in the other windows bothers you, under Image Plane Attributes in the Attribute Editor, change the radio button selection next to Display from In All Views to Looking Through Camera. This setting removes the image plane from the other windows.

Figure 11.24

Importing a sequence of image files as a camera image plane

Motion Blur

Motion blur is an optical phenomenon that occurs when an object moves quickly in front of a camera; the object looks blurred as it crosses the frame. Maya Software rendering renders motion blur in two ways—2D blur or 3D blur—although neither will render as reflections.

- In the 2D blur process, Maya calculates after the frame is rendered. Any objects moving in the frame are blurred with a 2D filter effect. The 2D blur is effective for most applications and faster than 3D blur.

- The 3D blur process is calculated while a frame of the sequence is rendering. Every motion blur–enabled object is blurred with typically better results than 2D blur but at a cost of a much longer render time.

I'll briefly cover motion blur in mental ray for Maya later in the chapter.

To enable motion blur for the Maya Software renderer, open the Render Settings window. In the Motion Blur section on the Maya Software tab, click the Motion Blur check box. Then, choose 2D or 3D blur.

Typically, you control the amount of blur rendered for 2D and 3D by setting the Blur By Frame attribute—the higher the number, the greater the blur. Using additional controls, however, you can increase or decrease the 2D blur effect in the render. The Blur Length attribute affects the streakiness of the blur to further increase or decrease the amount of motion blur set with the Blur By Frame attribute.

> Setting a camera's Shutter Angle attribute (in the camera's Attribute Editor in the Special Effects section) also affects the amount of blur rendered—the higher the number, the greater the blur.

Batch Rendering

So far, you've used single-frame rendering numerous times to see a scene in the Render View window. But how do you start rendering an animation sequence to disk? This is called *batch rendering* in Maya, whichever renderer you use. To batch-render an entire scene, follow these steps:

1. Open the Render Settings window and choose Maya Software to use to render. On the Common tab, in the File Output section, set Frame/Animation Ext to *name*.#.ext to enable rendering an animation. Otherwise, Maya will render only a single frame.

2. Next, enter the start and end frames of your animation and select your image format. Select your quality and resolution settings. Finally, set the camera you want to render in the Renderable Camera attribute.

> Be sure to select *name*.#.ext in the Frame/Animation Ext drop-down list to render a sequence of files. Remember, if you leave the default setting, which is name.ext, only a single frame renders.

3. In the main Maya window under the Rendering menu set, choose Render → Batch Render ❐ to open the Batch Render Animation dialog box (or the Batch Render Frame box when rendering a single image). Figure 11.25 shows the Maya Software rendering batch options on top, and the bottom image shows the batch options for mental ray rendering.

Figure 11.25

The Batch Render Frame dialog box for Maya Software (top) and mental ray rendering (bottom)

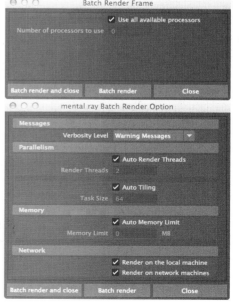

4. If you have a multiprocessor, hyperthreading, or dual-core machine, select how many CPUs you would like to use to render your scene. A value of 0 will use all processors on the machine.

5. Click Batch Render to render the frame range you specified in the Render Settings window. The render occurs in the background, and you see progress updates in the Command line at the bottom of your Maya screen and in the Script Editor window if you open it.

Figure 11.26

The Render Settings window shows you where the images will be rendered.

To see a frame as the batch render progresses, choose Render → Show Batch Render. To cancel a batch render, choose Render → Cancel Batch Render.

When you batch render, your image files are written to the images folder of the current project. Make sure your project is properly set; otherwise, your files will end up in an unexpected folder. You can always see the render path and the image name at the top of the Render Settings window, as shown in Figure 11.26.

Rendering the Wine Bottle

In this section, you'll set up and render an animated camera to move over 25 frames of a wine bottle still life using Maya Software rendering at first.

Set your current project to the Lighting project downloaded from the book's web page and then load still_life_render_v01.ma. You'll also adjust your render settings and some shader properties to make the wine bottle look more like glass.

Selecting Render Settings Options

Set your resolution and quality settings in the Render Settings window.

1. Open the Render Settings window and select Maya Software. Click the Maya Software tab.

2. From the Quality drop-down list, select Production Quality. Doing so presets the appropriate settings to produce a high-quality render.

3. Click the Common tab. Set Frame/Animation Ext to *name*.#.ext, set Start Frame to **1**, set End Frame to **25**, and set Frame Padding to **2**.

4. From the Image Format drop-down list, select TIFF.

5. Make sure Renderable Camera is set to camera1. In the Image Size section, set Presets to HD 540.

Setting Up the Scene

Now, set up some of the objects in the scene. The wine bottle has been imported into the still life scene, and three wine glasses have been added. All the lights are in place, as is the camera.

Start by setting up this scene to raytrace to get true reflections and refractions.

1. Turn on refractions for the Glass shaders. In the Hypershade, select the Glasses material and in the Property Editor or the Attribute Editor, under the Raytrace Options section, click the Refractions check box and set Refractive Index to **1.2**. Set Reflection Limit to **2**. Select the Wine_Bottle material and repeat the previous steps.

2. You need to change your lights' shadows to raytraced shadows. Remember that semi-transparent objects cast solid shadows unless shadows are raytraced, so the glasses and wine bottle will cast shadows as if they were solid and not glass. In the Outliner, select spotLight1. In the Attribute Editor, in the Shadows section, enable Use Ray Trace Shadows. Repeat these steps for the remaining two shadow-casting lights: spotLight4 and spotLight3. Figure 11.27 shows the three shadow-casting lights in the scene in white.

3. Open the Render Settings window and turn on raytracing in the Raytracing Quality section. Set Reflections to **2**.

Figure 11.27
Shadow lights

You can't select all three lights at once to turn on raytraced shadows in the Attribute Editor. Any adjustments you make in the Attribute Editor affect only the most recently selected object, not multiple selections.

Setting Up the Camera

Next, you'll set up the camera to render the scene.

1. Make sure you are looking through the camera1 camera. Open the camera's Attribute Editor through the camera1 viewport menu (choose View → Camera Attribute Editor or click the Camera Attributes icon [ ]).

2. Select the Display Film Gate option in the Display Options section to turn on a dashed green box in the camera1 viewport. Enable the Display Resolution option. Notice that the two boxes aren't aligned.

3. Because the resolution is 960×540, you'll need a 1.78 aspect ratio. Enter **1.78** for the Film Aspect Ratio under the Film Back section of the Render Settings. The two green boxes now align. Although it's not absolutely necessary to match the resolution with the film gate, it's definitely good practice to do so, especially if you'll later insert CG in live-action videos.

4. As soon as you change the film gate, the framing of the scene changes. You may need to move the camera out to frame the entire still life. If you try to use the Alt key and mouse button combinations to zoom out, you'll notice that you can't move the camera in this scene; the movement attributes for the camera have been locked to prevent accidental movement that would disrupt the shot.

5. To unlock the camera, choose View → Select Camera. The camera's attributes appear in the Channel Box. Some are grayed out, signifying that they're locked and can't be changed. Highlight the locked attributes and RMB+click Unlock Selected in the Channel Box.

6. Create an animated camera move to pull out and reveal the still life slowly over 25 frames. Set your Range slider to 1 to 25 frames. Go to frame 1. The camera1 view should be similar to that shown in Figure 11.28. Select all three Translate and Rotate channels in the Channel Box and RMB+click Key Selected to set keyframes for the first camera position.

7. Move (actually, truck) the camera out by pressing Alt+RMB+click to a wider framing to reveal the entire still life. Highlight the Translate and Rotate channels again in the Channel Box and set keyframes for them. (See Figure 11.29.)

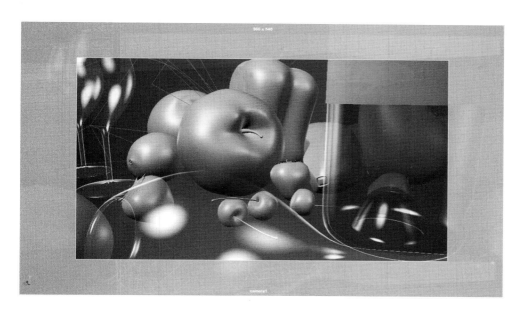

Figure 11.28

The camera view at the beginning of the animation

Figure 11.29

Pull out the camera.

Scrub your animation, and you'll see a pullout revealing the full scene.

You can lock the camera to prevent accidentally moving the view after you set your keyframes, especially if Auto Keyframe is on. Select the Translate and Rotate attributes in the Channel Box, RMB+click, and choose Lock Selected.

Batch Rendering and Playing Back the Sequence

Now, you're ready to render the 25-frame sequence. Choose Render → Batch Render.

Because you're raytracing this scene at full resolution, this render could take 20 minutes or longer. To chart the progress of the render, open the Script Editor by clicking its icon on the Help line or by choosing Windows → General Editors → Script Editor.

To see the frames play back, you'll need a program that can load the images in sequence and play them back for you. You can also import the image sequence into a compositing or editing program, such as Adobe After Effects or Premiere, to play back as a clip and edit as you like.

You can also use FCheck, a frame viewer that is included with Maya. This small and surprisingly powerful program plays back your images in real time so that you can judge your finished animation. To use FCheck, follow these steps:

1. In Windows, choose Start → All Programs → Autodesk → Autodesk Maya 2016 → FCheck to open the FCheck window, as shown in Figure 11.30.

Figure 11.30

FCheck, shown here with a sample image, plays back your rendered sequence.

2. Choose File → Open Animation.

3. In the file browser, find your images folder in your project and click the first frame of the sequence you want to play back. FCheck loads the images frame by frame into RAM and then plays them back in real time. Just set your playback speed and use the DVD controls to play back your sequence.

mental ray for Maya

You had some experience with mental ray rendering in the previous chapter as you lighted using Physical Sun and Sky, which automatically used Final Gather to render. In this part of the chapter, I'll discuss mental ray options to begin to scratch the surface of this powerful renderer.

First, if you haven't done so already, be sure that mental ray is loaded. When you first start up, mental ray for Maya may not load because it's considered a plug-in. Choose Windows → Settings/Preferences → Plug-in Manager to open the Plug-in Manager, shown in Figure 11.31. Make sure both the Loaded and Auto Load check boxes for `Mayatomr.mll` (or `Mayatomr.bundle` for Mac users) are checked so that mental ray for Maya loads by default.

To render with mental ray, open the Render Settings window and change the Render Using drop-down menu selection to mental ray, as shown in Figure 11.32 (shown with the Quality tab selected). The Render Settings window now has the Common tab along with four other mental ray–specific tabs: Quality, Scene, Configuration, and Diagnostics.

mental ray Quality Settings

As with the Maya Software renderer, the primary quality settings for the mental ray renderer center on anti-aliasing. However, mental ray for Maya offers you finer control over how you set the

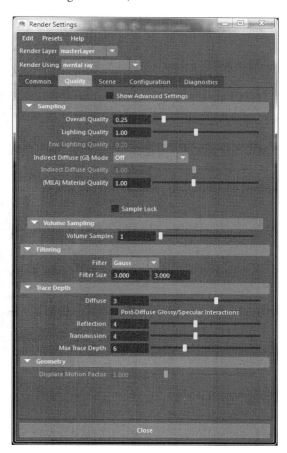

Figure 11.31

Use the Plug-in Manager to load mental ray for Maya.

Figure 11.32

The Render Settings window for mental ray, showing the Quality tab

quality levels through the Render Settings window. In the Quality tab, you'll find a check box for Show Advanced Settings. This is off by default and is perfectly fine being left off, unless you need access to the finer controls mental ray has to offer.

In the Sampling section, the primary value to deal with for image quality is the Overall Quality slider. This slider will increase the quality of your renders and anti-aliasing. A value of 0.25 will give you fast, adequate results, while moving up to 0.5 will make most renders look quite good. A value of 1.0 should be the highest you'll need for very clean renders (though it will take longer to calculate, the higher you set this slider). The Lighting Quality slider should usually be left at 1.0, unless you are using textures on area lights, a technique not covered in this book.

The Indirect Diffuse (GI) Mode drop-down menu allows you to enable Global Illumination techniques, which are covered later in this chapter.

Lastly, the Trace Depth section on the Quality tab gives you access to raytracing quality settings for the entire scene. The Reflection value sets the number of recursive reflections (reflections of reflections) you can see in your scene. Transmission value sets how far refractions will occur in your scene (seeing refractions of refractions). These numbers will override the Reflection and Refraction Limits you set on your individual shaders, as you did with the wine glasses in the example earlier in this chapter.

As a rule of thumb, the Max Trace Depth value should usually be set to the sum of the Reflection and Transmission values. So for example, if you have set Reflection to 4 and Transmission to 3, your Max Trace Depth should be 7.

Figure 11.33
mental ray batch render options

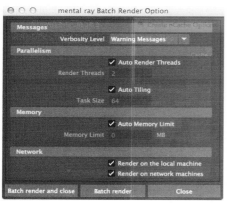

With this version of Maya, mental ray's UI has become much more easy to use, by basically hiding a lot of the intricate controls that used to be available in the Render Settings. By turning on the Show Advanced Settings check box at the top of the Quality tab, you can access these fine-tuning controls, but as a beginner, your focus should stay on the Overall Quality slider as well as the Trace Depth values if you are rendering reflective and or refractive objects like glass.

When you're ready to render your scene to disk, you still use batch rendering; however, the options in the Batch Render Option window are different (Figure 11.33) than they are for Maya Software.

Render Settings in Action!

In this section, you'll look at how the Overall Quality slider works to determine the quality of the render of a toy wagon. You can find the scene (RedWagonRenderSettings.ma) to render in the RedWagon project on the book's web page. Make sure to set your project to RedWagon.

Open the Render Settings window, making sure you are set to mental ray, and open the Quality tab. The Overall Quality should be set to **0.10** in this file already.

This render setting is low at first and will yield the render (of the persp camera) shown in Figure 11.34, which took just less than twenty seconds. You can see jagged highlights on the wagon, especially the white lines on the side body, the reflections in the front black nose, and the edge of the white rims on the back wheel, as well as a lot of jagged pixel noise in the wagon's black plastic front and tires.

Figure 11.34

A toy wagon rendered with low sampling values. Notice the jagged highlights on the white decal lines. Also a close-up of the wooden rails shows jagged edges.

If you increase the Overall Quality slider to **1.0**, you'll see an immediate increase in quality (especially in the reflections of the wagon and the white decal lines) and a noticeable increase in render time (now the frame takes more than 90 seconds), as shown in Figure 11.35.

Figure 11.35

Better Overall Quality improves the wagon's appearance, especially in the close-up of the wooden rails and the shadow beneath the wagon.

You can get an even cleaner render. If you crank up the Overall Quality value to the heavens, such as 2.0, you get only a slightly cleaner render than before but with a much longer render time. Figure 11.36 shows the same render but with an Overall Quality setting of 2.0. This rendered in just under three minutes and gives you only marginal improvement in quality.

Figure 11.36

The wagon has barely any better quality with a Overall Quality value of 2.0 but with twice the render time.

You have to decide in your own images how far to set Overall Quality for the best result in the shortest render times. Simply cranking up the quality slider will result in only small improvements but much longer render times. Your results as you render the scene on your own computer will be more noticeable than the images shown here.

Motion Blur with mental ray

Now that you have a primer on quality settings in mental ray for Maya, you'll learn how motion blur works.

1. Load the `Planets_motionBlur.ma` scene file from the Solar_System project on the web page. This is an animated scene of the solar system with just the first few planets and moons, as shown in Figure 11.37. A blast from the past!

2. Open the Render Settings window. The scene should already be set to render with mental ray. If your scene isn't, make sure the mental ray for Maya plug-in is loaded and set the scene to render with mental ray.

3. On the Common tab, set Frame/Animation Ext to *name*.*#*.ext, Frame Padding to **3**, Start Frame to **1**, and End Frame to **100**.

4. Set Image Size to HD 540 and leave the renderable camera to persp.

5. Go to frame 75 and render a frame from the persp viewport. Figure 11.38 shows the result.

6. In Render Settings, click to open the Scene tab. In the Cameras heading, open the Shutter subheading. In the Motion Blur drop-down menu, select No Deformation, as shown in Figure 11.39. This setting is the faster of two motion blur methods and works for objects that move in the scene without deformation. *Deformations* occur when the mesh or surface of an object changes, such as when you use a lattice or a skeleton rig like IK to drive a character. For deforming objects, you need to use Full as the Motion Blur setting.

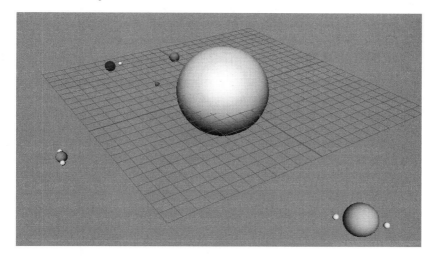

Figure 11.37

The Solar_System project is back!

Figure 11.38

A render of frame 75 shows the planets in motion without any motion blur.

Figure 11.39

Turn on motion blur.

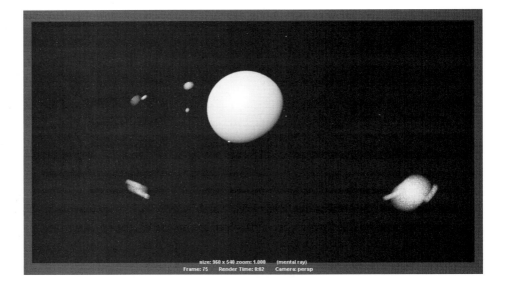

7. Click to open the Quality tab in the Render Settings. Set Overall Quality to **0.1**. On the Scene tab, under the Cameras → Shutter heading, set the Motion Blur By attribute from 1.0 to **3.0** for quite a bit of blur. Render a frame at frame 75. (See Figure 11.40.)

Figure 11.40

Render a frame with motion blur turned on.

8. The render is very fast and shows quite a bit of blur; however, the quality is low. You see a lot of graininess in your render, especially with the yellow and red planets at the bottom of the screen. On the Quality tab of the Render Settings window, change Overall Quality to **0.50**. This render should be fast but cleaner, with a smoother but still-grainy motion blur for the planets. Notice, however, that the render time increases by more than 50 percent! Now try Overall Quality at **2.0** (Figure 11.41

shows this much cleaner render). You control the amount of motion blur in your scene with the Motion Blur By attribute (step 7) for your scene.

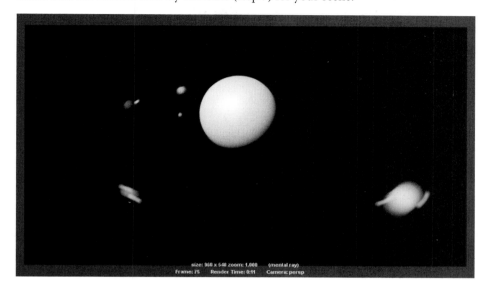

Figure 11.41
Motion blur looks much better with higher sampling levels.

Render Layers

Most of the time, it's best to composite different elements together to form a final CG image. Professional CG workflow almost always requires multiple render passes that are composited together later for the maximum in efficiency and quality.

Maya does a great job of making rendering in layers much easier with render layers. As you saw earlier in this book, using display layers helps a lot in keeping your scene organized. Render layers operate in basically the same way, although they function by separating different elements of the scene into separate renders.

I'll address the most basic and commonly utilized render layer functionality here: separating objects into different renders. You'll select elements in a scene and assign them to different render layers. When you batch-render the scene, Maya will render each of the layers separately and save the files into their own subfolders in the images folder of your current project. You'll then need to load all the different rendered layers into a compositing program, such as The Foundry's NUKE or Adobe After Effects, and composite the layers together.

Render Passes in mental ray

A powerful feature in mental ray rendering, Render Passes, makes rendering in passes and elements much more efficient. Passes allow you to separate shadows, reflections, diffuse color, and so on, from the render to give the most control in compositing over the image. This mental ray–specific workflow is fairly advanced and requires an existing knowledge of rendering and compositing render passes (such as you will do with render layers) to fully grasp. Thus, I won't cover these features in this book; however, you should be aware of this mental ray rendering pipeline as you move beyond this introduction and continue rendering with mental ray in your own work.

Rendering the Still Life in Layers

In this example, you'll separate a scene into different layers for rendering with mental ray, though the render layer workflow here applies to Maya Software rendering as well.

To separate a scene into different layers, follow these steps:

1. Set your project to the Lighting project downloaded from the book's web page and open the still life scene (still_life_renderLayers_v01.ma from the Scenes folder to start there). The lights and a camera are already set up in this scene. Set your camera view to camera1. Open Render Settings and make sure mental ray is the current renderer. Set Overall Quality to **0.5** in the Quality tab.

2. To separate the scene into different renders, in the Layer Editor (below the Channel Box), click the Render tab to switch to the Render Layers view. Select the foreground lemon and click the Create New Layer And Assign Selected Objects icon ( ). Doing so creates a new render layer called layer1 and assigns the lemon to it. (See Figure 11.42, top.)

Figure 11.42

The newly created render layer with the foreground lemon assigned

3. Click layer1, and everything but the lemon disappears from the scene (bottom Figure 11.42). Double-click layer1 in the Layer Editor and rename it **lemonPass**, as shown in Figure 11.43.

4. If you test-render a frame, the frame should turn black. You need to assign your lights to the render layer as well. Select all the lights in the scene using the Outliner, as shown in Figure 11.44. RMB+click the lemonPass layer in the Layer Editor and select Add Selected Objects from the context menu. If you render a test frame now, the lemon renders as shown in Figure 11.45.

Figure 11.43
Rename the render layer to lemonPass.

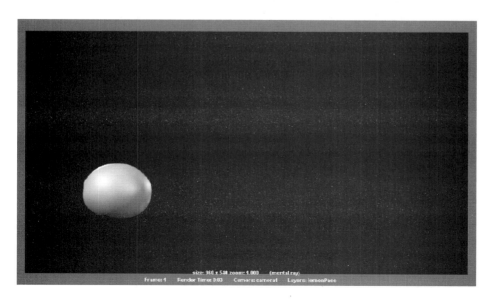

Figure 11.44
Add the lights to the lemonPass render layer.

Figure 11.45
The lemon rendered on its very own layer

5. Create a render layer for the column and floor: click the masterLayer render layer and then select the column, the floor, and all the lights in the scene. As you did with the lemon, click the Create New Layer And Assign Selected Objects icon (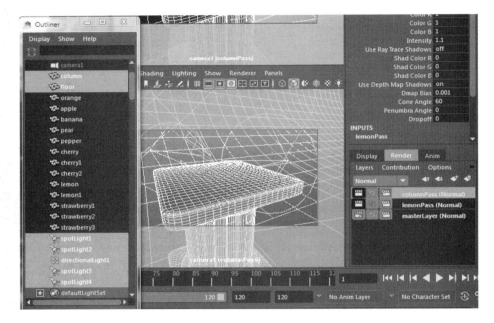) and then click the newly created layer to select and display it. Double-click the layer name to rename the render layer **columnPass** (see Figure 11.46).

Figure 11.46
The floor and col-
umn are assigned
to their own render
layer, along with
the lights.

6. Click back to the masterLayer; then select all the rest of the pieces of fruit as well as all the lights, as shown in Figure 11.47, and create their render layer called **fruitPass**. You should now have three render layers and the default masterLayer. The master-Layer is always present to house all the elements of the scene. It switches to being not renderable as soon as you create a new render layer, as evidenced by the little yellow *X* in its now grayed-out Renderable icon (⬛).

7. Using the first icon on each of the render layer entries in the Layer Editor, you can toggle whether that layer will render. Make sure all your render layers are renderable and leave the masterLayer off. Because all the elements of the scene are assigned to one render layer or another, the whole scene is covered. The masterLayer nonetheless is always present because it represents all the objects in the scene, assigned to layers or not.

8. With the fruitPass render layer selected, test-render a frame, as shown in Figure 11.48. You should see just the fruit and not the background, column, or foreground lemon. Notice the reflections in the fruit.

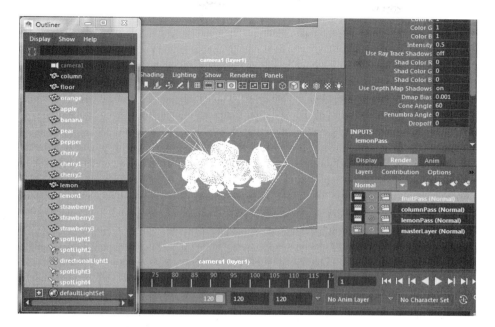

Figure 11.47
The newly created fruitPass render layer

Figure 11.48
Rendering the rest of the fruit

Test-Rendering Everything Together

By default, Maya renders only the selected render layer. You can, however, tell Maya to test-render and show you all the layers composited together to give you a preview of what you'll end up with when you composite all the layers together after batch-rendering the scene.

To test-render all the layers together, click the Options menu in the Layer Editor, as shown in Figure 11.49, and toggle on Render All Layers by clicking the check box if it isn't

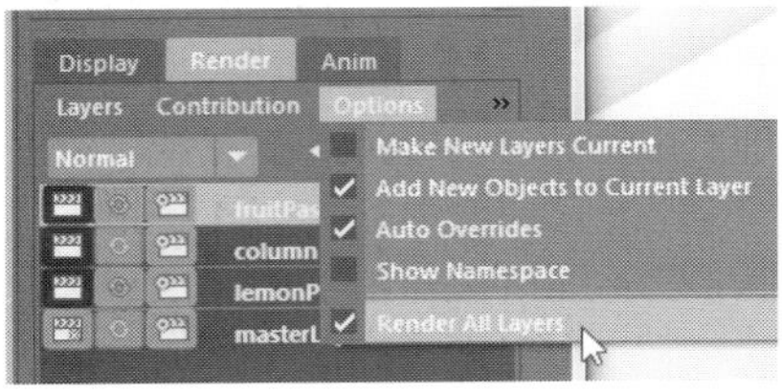

Figure 11.49

Turn on Render All Layers.

already selected.

Now if you test-render a frame, Maya will render each layer separately and then composite them together. Test-render a frame with Render All Layers enabled, and you should notice that the foreground lemon is missing, as in Figure 11.50.

Figure 11.50

Rendering all the layers together

This is because the render layers in the Layer Editor need to be reordered so that columnPass is on the bottom, fruitPass is in the middle, and lemonPass is on top. This is the layer ordering for the composite. You can reorder the render layers by MMB+clicking a layer and dragging it up or down to its new location in the Layer Editor, as in Figure 11.51.

Now if you render the frame with Render All Layers enabled, you see the scene properly placed, as shown in Figure 11.52. Notice that shadows and reflections on the column's tabletop are missing, however. For that, you will need to create render layer overrides to allow reflections and shadows of an object to render, but without the object itself rendering.

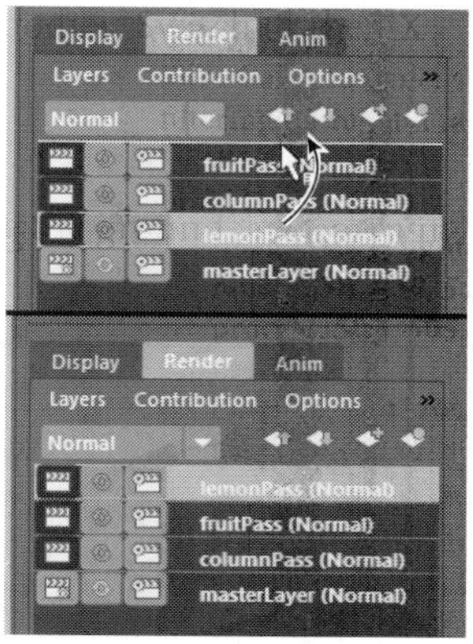

Render Layer Overrides

Where are the shadows and reflections? If you recall from earlier in this chapter, this scene renders with shadows, and this scene should have reflections as well. However, the reflections and shadow-casting objects are on different layers than the column. Shadows and reflections can't be cast from one layer onto another. In the following steps, you'll use render layer overrides to set up your columnPass layer to have shadows and reflections from the fruit but not render the fruit on top of the column.

1. Click to the columnPass render layer. In the Outliner, select all the fruit objects and add them to the layer (Figure 11.53).

Figure 11.51

MMB+click and drag the lemonPass layer to the top of the Layer Editor (top). This will reorder the render layers (bottom).

Figure 11.52

Now the lemon appears in the render, but shadows and reflections on the table are missing!

Render layers and overrides are powerful workflow tools in Maya. Because there can be an obscene number of overrides in any given render layer, it's important to follow through this workflow carefully. Practice it to gain a comfort level before getting too fancy with render layers and overrides. Also, it helps to keep notes beside your keyboard to help you stay organized with render layers and overrides. And lastly, there are occasional problems when assigning shaders to the faces of a mesh (as opposed to the entire mesh) when using render layers. Try to always assign shaders to the entire mesh and not to faces in those cases. If you need multiple shaders on a single mesh, instead use Layered shaders and UV maps.

Figure 11.53

Add the fruit back into the layer.

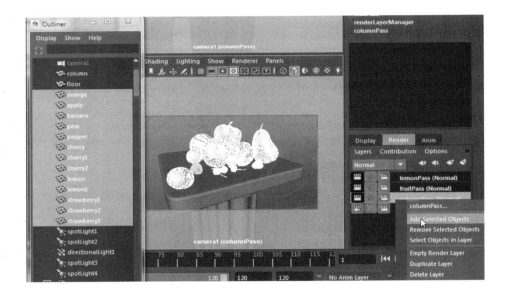

2. If you render the layer now, it will render the fruit. To turn them off without removing them from the layer (and hence lose shadows and reflections), you'll set render layer overrides for each of the fruit objects. Select the orange, and open the Attribute Editor.

3. On the orangeShape tab in the Attribute Editor, click to open the Render Stats heading. Here you see switches allowing for different ways to render the object. You want the orange to cast reflections and shadows in the scene, without rendering itself, so uncheck the Primary Visibility box. It will turn orange to signify that there is now a render layer override on that attribute for the current render layer (columnPass) only (Figure 11.54).

   As a matter of fact, if you click the other render layers with the orange still selected, you will notice that the Primary Visibility setting for the orange turns back on and loses its orange color in the Attribute Editor on the other render layers. Render layer overrides work only on the layers in which they were created.

4. Now select each fruit model down the list in the Outliner individually and turn off Primary Visibility one by one. You cannot select all the objects at once and turn off Primary Visibility in the Attribute Editor; it will register the action only for the last selected object and not them all.

> To change attribute values on multiple objects at once, such as Primary Visibility, you can use Windows → General Editors → Attribute Spread Sheet. Be careful, though!

5. Turn off Render All Layers (in the Layer Editor, uncheck Options → Render All Layers). Render the columnPass layer, and you'll see the top of the column is rendering with shadows and reflections but not the fruit! (See Figure 11.55.)

6. Finally, you make the shadows look nicer by using raytrace shadows. Select spotLight1, and in the Attribute Editor, under the Shadows → Depth Map Shadow Attributes heading, turn off Use Depth Map Shadows. Scroll down a bit until you see the Raytrace Shadow Attributes heading; open it, and turn on Use Ray Trace Shadows.

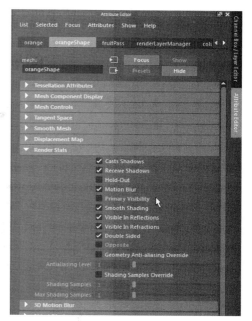

Figure 11.54

Turn off Primary Visibility to set a render layer override for the orange on the columnPass layer.

Figure 11.55

The column is rendering with depth map shadows and reflections.

7. Repeat step 6 for spotLight3 and spotLight4. Render, and you'll see sharp shadows now on the column (Figure 11.56).

Figure 11.56

The raytraced shadows are clean but too sharp.

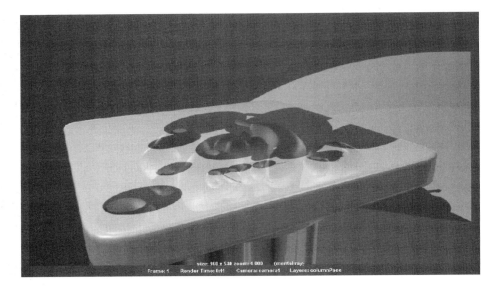

8. Let's enable soft shadows now for those three spotlights. Select spotLight1, and in the Raytrace Shadow Attributes, set Light Radius to **0.4** and Shadow Rays to **16**. Repeat the procedure for spotLight3 and spotLight4. The shadows will look much more believable now.

9. Turn on Render All Layers (Option menu of the Layer Editor) and render a frame to see the entire composition (Figure 11.57). Once you verify everything is working and looking good, you can now render your scene into separate layers for better control in compositing.

You can check your work against the file still_life_renderLayers_v02.ma from the scenes folder of the Lighting project on the book's web page.

Batch Rendering with Render Layers

Now that you have everything separated into render layers, let's talk about batch-rendering the scene to composite later. Make your selected render layers renderable by making sure the Renderable icon next to each render layer is enabled, as shown in Figure 11.58. Disabled render layers are grayed out and have a little yellow X.

Figure 11.57

The layers all rendered together with soft shadows and reflections

In the Render Settings window, make sure Renderable Camera is set to camera1, as shown in Figure 11.59. Select your image file type and anything else you need to set in the Render Settings window. Then, in the main Maya window, choose Render → Batch Render to render the scene. Because render layers are enabled here, Maya renders the scene into different subfolders under the images folder of your current project. Each render layer gets its own folder in the images folder, as shown in Figure 11.60.

I have only begun to scratch the surface here. When you get the hang of rendering and as your CG needs begin to grow, you'll find a plethora of options when rendering with layers and rendering with passes through mental ray. This section and the "Ambient Occlusion" section later in this chapter are here only to familiarize you with the basic workflow of render layers. You can find a wealth of information about rendering in layers and passes in the Maya online documentation under the Help menu.

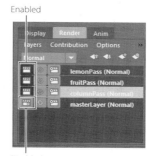

Enabled

Disabled

Figure 11.58

Check to make sure the layers you want to render are enabled.

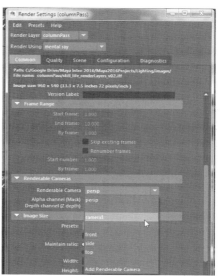

Figure 11.59

Select camera1 as your renderable camera in the Render Settings window.

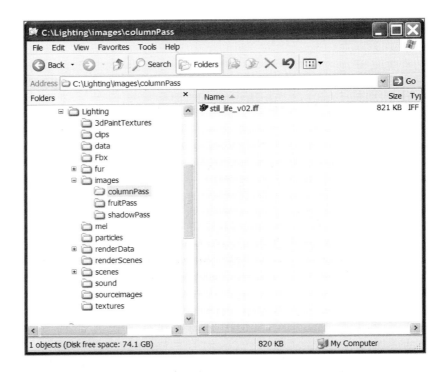

Final Gather

Final Gather (FG) is a type of rendering with mental ray that includes a simple light bounce within the scene. Final Gather traces light as it reflects off surfaces to illuminate the scene for a nicely realistic render that takes into account color bleed of light from one surface to another. For example, a red wall casts a red hue on the surface right next to it. FG is an intricate dance of settings and numbers that lets you get perfect renders. It's tough to cover in an introductory book such as this; however, this section will give you a primer to start using FG. In a follow-up section, you'll use a combination of lights and HDRI with Final Gather to render the decorative box.

The basic premise is that FG uses the illumination in the scene from lights as well as objects with color and incandescence set in their shaders to create a soft natural light. Its base settings will give you nice results right from the start.

To render the still life fruit scene with FG, begin by creating a dome light, which evenly illuminates a scene from a dome around the scene. (The term *dome light* is a bit of a misnomer because a dome light isn't itself a light.) You'll construct a simple sphere, cut it in half to create a dome, and give it an Incandescent shader to provide the light for the scene. This type of quick FG setup is extremely useful for rendering out soft lighting and shadows to show off a model or a composition.

To light and render with FG, follow these steps:

1. Ensure that mental ray for Maya is loaded.

2. Load the still life scene file `still_life_mentalray_v01.ma` from the Lighting project from the book's web page. In the persp viewport (not the camera1 panel), create a polygonal sphere and scale it up to enclose the entire scene. Select the bottom half faces of the sphere, delete them to cut the sphere in half, and name the object **light-Dome**. Place the dome to fit over the scene, as shown in Figure 11.61.

3. Add an Incandescent shader to the dome to give the scene some illumination through FG. To do so, in the Hypershade create a new Lambert shader. Turn up its incandescence to a medium light gray. Assign the new shader to the dome.

4. Maya automatically creates a general default light in a scene that has no lights when you try to render it. This is so you can test-render your scene quickly. However, because this incandescent dome light should be the only light source in the FG render, you have to turn off the default light feature before you render. Open the Render Settings window and, under the Common tab's Render Options heading (at the bottom of the Attribute Editor), turn off the Enable Default Light check box. For Final Gather rendering, this is very important. Always turn off the default light.

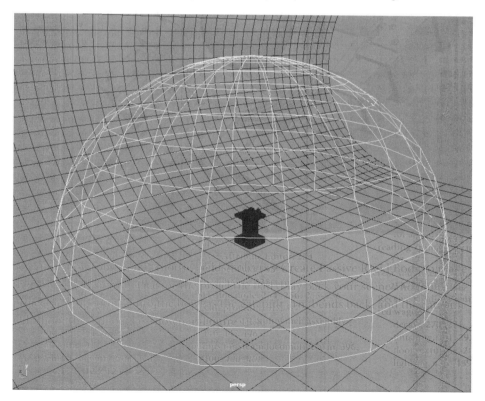

Figure 11.61

Create a hemisphere to act as a light dome.

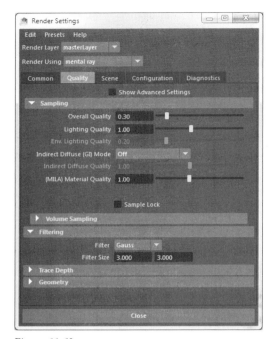

Figure 11.62
The Quality tab

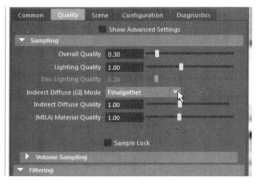

Figure 11.63
Final Gather is turned on.

Don't forget to turn Enable Default Light back on when you're finished with this FG exercise.

5. At the top of the Render Settings window, switch the Render Using attribute to mental ray. You can keep the settings on the Common tab to render at HD 540. Choose the Quality tab to access its settings. Set Overall Quality to **0.3**. Figure 11.62 shows the Quality tab of the Render Settings window.

6. Still in the Quality tab, set the Indirect Diffuse (GI) Mode drop-down menu to Final Gather. This turns on Final Gather. You can leave the settings at their defaults for your first render. Figure 11.63 shows the Indirect Lighting tab for the Render Settings window with Final Gather turned on.

7. You need to make sure the sphere you're using as a dome light doesn't render out in the scene. Select the sphere and, in its Attribute Editor under the Render Stats heading, turn off Primary Visibility. Since there are no render layers in the scene, it doesn't turn orange like with the previous section's exercise. Highlight the camera1 viewport and render the frame. Maya makes two passes at the scene and shows you something like Figure 11.64. You can control the brightness of the scene with the Incandescence attribute value of the dome's shader.

You adjust the level of lighting by increasing or decreasing the amount of incandescence on the light dome's shader. The proximity of the sphere also affects the light amount, so moving the sphere closer or farther away will change the lighting level as well. You can also insert lights into the scene as you see fit.

Again here with Maya 2016, mental ray settings have been greatly simplified. You can access more fine-tuning settings by clicking the Show Advanced Settings check box at the top of the Quality tab. If you are familiar with previous versions of mental ray for Maya, you can also access the old methods of controlling Final Gather by enabling Show Advanced Settings and opening the Legacy Options heading at the bottom of the Quality tab.

Figure 11.64

The Final Gather render of the still life

For you to improve the quality of the Final Gather in your scene, you can simply adjust the Indirect Diffuse Quality slider, which is set to 1.0 by default. In the top image of Figure 11.65, the Indirect Diffuse Quality setting is set to 0.1, which is rather low. Notice the splotchy noise all over the frame. However, this frame took a mere 8 seconds to render, compared to a render time of 35 seconds for Figure 11.64. In the bottom image of Figure 11.65, the Indirect Diffuse Quality value was set to 2.5, which is rather high. Compare the bottom render of Figure 11.65 to Figure 11.64, and you won't notice much of a quality difference in the Final Gather; however, the render with a 2.5 Indirect Diffuse Quality took 2 minutes and 30 seconds compared to just 35 seconds of the original render.

High Indirect Diffuse Quality settings are typically for detailed scenes and animations. If you render this scene yourself with these different settings, you'll be able to notice the shadows become cleaner with the higher Indirect Diffuse Quality, though this subtle change is not possible to see in the printed images in this book.

Load the still life scene file `still_life_mentalray_v02.ma` from the Lighting project from the book's web page to compare to your own work. Final Gather is a tough nut to crack; it will take you some time to become proficient at rendering with FG in scene files and especially with animated scenes. Later in this chapter, you'll try your hand at using FG, HDRI, and regular lights to render the decorative box from the previous chapters.

Figure 11.65

Top: Indirect Diffuse
Quality set to 0.1
is fast but noisy.
Bottom: Indirect
Diffuse Quality set
at 2.5 increases
the smoothness
of the soft shad-
ows compared to
Figure 11.64. It's
hard to see here,
but you'll notice it in
your own render.

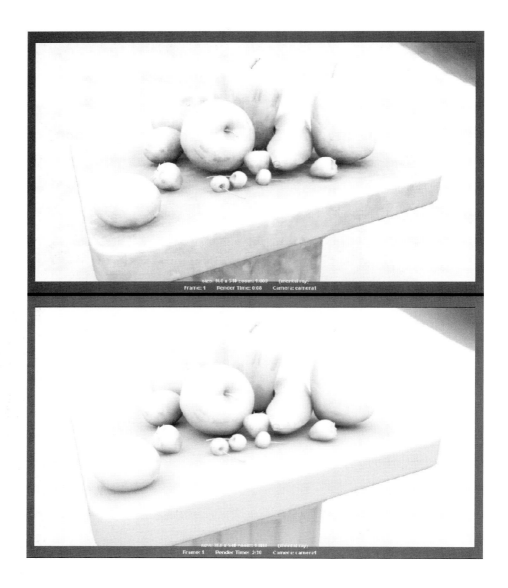

Figure 11.65

Top: Indirect Diffuse
Quality set to 0.1
is fast but noisy.
Bottom: Indirect
Diffuse Quality set
at 2.5 increases
the smoothness
of the soft shad-
ows compared to
Figure 11.64. It's
hard to see here,
but you'll notice it in
your own render.

Ambient Occlusion

Ambient Occlusion is a special render pass that helps add depth and reality to a render. Ambient Occlusion goes by the premise that when two objects or surfaces are close to each other, they reduce the amount of light at the intersection. Ambient Occlusion passes make for great contact shadows and bring out the definition in surface creases and corners nicely. Figure 11.66 shows an Ambient Occlusion pass for the living room scene from the PDF Global Illumination exercise included on the book's web page.

Figure 11.66

The Ambient Occlusion pass is black and white and is used to darken areas of the original color render.

How the composite works is simple. Ambient Occlusion gives you a black-and-white pass of the same geometry you've already rendered. This pass is then multiplied over the color render. That means a brightness value of white (a value of 1) in the Ambient Occlusion pass won't change the color of the original render (when the original color of the render is multiplied by 1, it stays the same color). The black areas of the ambient occlusion image (with a brightness value of 0) turn the same areas of the original render black (when the original color of the render is multiplied by 0, it goes to black). The gray points of the multiplying image darken the original render. It sounds confusing, but when you see it, it makes much better sense.

The Living Room

You'll now take an existing render of a living room and add an Ambient Occlusion pass using render layers. Set your current project to the Livingroom project you copied from the web page, open the livingRoom_v1.ma file from the scenes folder, and follow these steps:

Figure 11.67

Select the scene objects for your Ambient Occlusion pass.

1. Make sure mental ray is loaded, of course, and that Render Settings is set to Render Using mental ray. You need to create a new render layer for the Ambient Occlusion. This layer requires all the objects in the scene but the lights to be assigned to it. In this scene, the only light is a single Directional light. In the Outliner, select all the top nodes of the scene, but leave out the light, as shown in Figure 11.67.

2. Click the Render tab in the Layer Editor to switch to Render and then click the Create New Layer And Assign Selected Objects icon (). Doing so creates a new layer (layer1) along with the preexisting masterLayer, as shown in Figure 11.68.

Figure 11.68

Create a new render layer.

3. Click the new layer (layer1) to activate it. Everything in the scene should display as it did before, although the light disappears from view. Double-click layer1 and rename it **ambientOcclusion**. Click in a blank spot in the scene to unselect the objects in the scene.

4. You're going to use a preset to create a material override. This takes all the objects in the scene and assigns a single material to them, in this case an Ambient Occlusion shader that generates the Ambient Occlusion pass for the entire scene. RMB+click the ambientOcclusion layer and select Attributes. In the Attribute Editor, click and hold down the Presets button. From the menu that appears, select Occlusion, as shown in Figure 11.69.

Figure 11.69

Setting an Occlusion preset for the layer

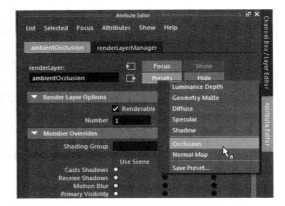

If you're in Shaded mode, everything should turn black in the viewports. This is normal because everything now has the Ambient Occlusion Surface shader assigned, and that shader displays black in Maya panels. If you click the masterLayer, everything pops back into place.

5. When you select Occlusion from the Presets menu, your Attribute Editor window should display a new shader called surfaceShader1. Figure 11.70 shows the new Ambient Occlusion shader in the Hypershade's Browser panel. Select the shader and click Input And Output Connections icon in the Hypershade ( ) to display it in the work area as shown. Rename that shader to **ambOccShader**. Don't worry if you don't see the surfaceShader1 in your Attribute Editor; you'll come back to it in later steps.

6. While still in the ambientOcclusion layer, render a frame. You should see something like Figure 11.71. You needn't worry about most of the settings in the Render Settings window; the layer preset takes care of it all.

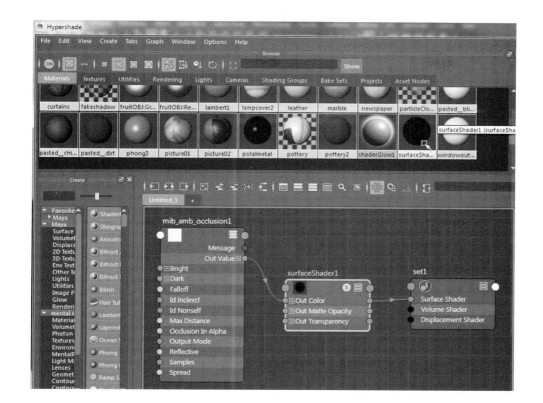

Figure 11.70

The Ambient Occlusion shader in the Hypershade

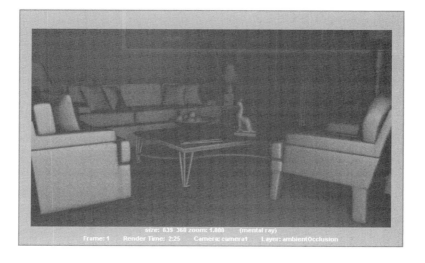

Figure 11.71

The first render from the Ambient Occlusion pass doesn't look great— it's too dark.

7. The render is mostly black, which darkens the original color render to black almost everywhere. You need the Ambient Occlusion shader to render mostly white with some darkening at the corners and where objects contact each other. You can adjust the Ambient Occlusion shader to fix this. Open the Hypershade window and click ambOccShader (or surfaceShader1, if you didn't rename it earlier in step 5—rename it now).

8. Notice that the Out Color attribute has a texture connection to it (signified by the ![icon] icon). Click this button or select the mib_amb_occlusion1 node in the Hypershade Work Area to display the mib_amb_occlusion1 texture node in the Property Editor, as shown in Figure 11.72.

Figure 11.72

The Ambient Occlusion shader attributes

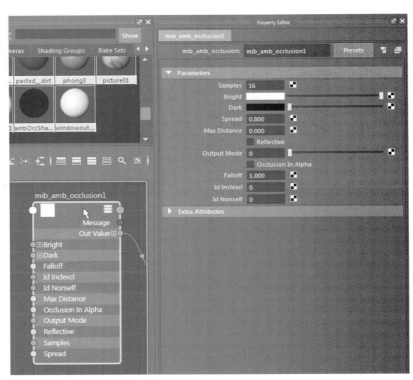

9. Set the Max Distance attribute to **4.0**, as shown in Figure 11.73, and render the frame again. Your Ambient Occlusion layer should look like Figure 11.74. It should have also taken less than half as long to render as the darker render from step 6.

10. Notice that the glass in the window and the glass on the coffee table have shadows on them. Because glass is clear, they shouldn't have any Ambient Occlusion applied to them; it would look odd

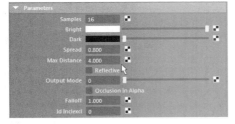

Figure 11.73

Set Max Distance to 4.

in the final composite. Select those pieces of geometry (Figure 11.75 shows the Outliner view for those pieces).

Figure 11.74

The Ambient Occlusion layer pass looks much better, but you aren't finished yet!

11. With the glass geometry selected, select Display → Hide → Hide Selection. Now the glass won't render in the Ambient Occlusion pass. But because you hid the objects only in this render layer, they still appear in the master-Layer; they will still render as glass in the color pass.

12. Render the frame, and you should have something similar to Figure 11.76. This is the Ambient Occlusion pass you need to composite.

Figure 11.76

The Ambient Occlusion pass

Figure 11.75

The Outliner view of the glass geometry in the scene

Rendering the Results

You could save the image you just rendered in the Render View window to use in the composite and then render the masterLayer for the color pass in the Render View and save that frame as well. Instead, let's batch-render the scene to show how Maya handles rendering with layers enabled. To batch-render the scene, follow these steps:

1. Turn on the Renderable icon box ( ) for the masterLayer and make sure it's on for the ambientOcclusion layer as well.

2. Click the masterLayer. Open the Render Settings window, and on the Common tab, verify all the settings to render a single frame (*name*.#.ext in the Frame/Animation Ext field) at 640×360 (which is half 720p HD resolution). Also, set Image Format to TIFF and select camera1 as the renderable camera.

3. If you batch-render (by choosing Render → Batch Render), Maya renders both render layers into the images folder of your project in separate folders, as shown in Figure 11.77.

Figure 11.77

Maya renders the layers into their own folders by default.

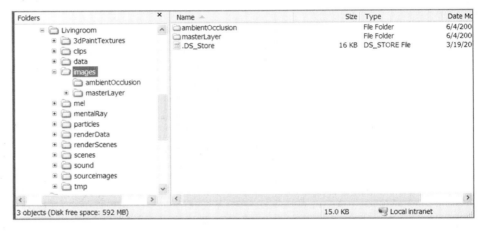

If for some reason your renders don't show up in your project's images folder, open the Script Editor window and look at the batch-render report. The render feedback shows you where the rendered images were saved, as shown in Figure 11.78. You may also want to make sure you set your project to the Livingroom project from the web page.

Compositing the Results

Now that the two layers are rendered in their respective folders, load them into your favorite compositing package. You'll layer the Ambient Occlusion pass over the color render using a Multiply Transfer mode. This exercise uses Adobe After Effects CS4 to demonstrate how the Ambient Occlusion pass is composited over the original color render.

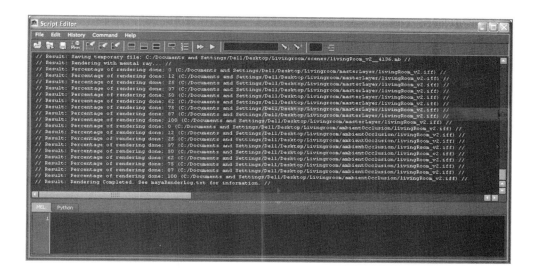

Figure 11.78

The Script Editor gives you feedback on the progress of the batch render.

Figure 11.79 shows After Effects with the masterLayer color pass loaded. Figure 11.80 shows the ambientOcclusion pass layered on top of the color layer. Finally, Figure 11.81 shows the ambientOcclusion pass changed to a Multiply Transfer mode (as it's called in After Effects). Notice how the dark areas of the Ambient Occlusion pass help give contact shadows and depth to the color pass. *Voilà!*

Figure 11.79

The masterLayer render pass is loaded into After Effects.

Figure 11.80

The ambientOcclusion render pass is loaded into After Effects.

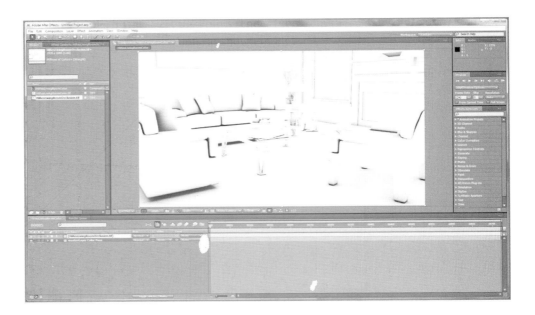

Figure 11.81

The ambientOcclusion pass is multiplied over the color pass and creates a more realistic image.

This is a prime example of rendering different passes to achieve a more realistic result. Use different layers to put your final images together in composite.

You can see the difference Ambient Occlusion made to the living-room image in the Color Section of this book and on the web page.

HDRI

As you saw in the Final Gather section, FG rendering is based on the illumination in the scene from lights as well as the brightness of objects in the scene, such as a light dome. In a previous section, you used an incandescent dome to light the still-life scene. But what if you were to use an image instead of just white for the light dome?

Furthermore, what if the image you used was a high dynamic range image (HDRI)? Several photos at varying exposures are taken of the same subject; they range from very dark (low exposure), highlighting only the brightest parts of the scene, and go all the way up to very bright (overexposure), capturing the absolute darkest parts of the scene. When these images (usually five or seven images) are compiled into an HDR image, you get a fantastic range of bright to dark for that one subject.

How does this help you light? With image-based lighting (IBL), mental ray creates an environment sphere in your scene to which you assign an image, usually an HDRI. That environment sphere, much like the white dome in the Final Gather exercise earlier in the chapter, uses the brightness of its image to cast light in your Maya scene.

The best type of image to capture for an IBL is sometimes called a *light probe*. This is a picture of an environment, such as the office reflected in a chrome ball shown on the left of Figure 11.82 or the stitched-together panoramic stills compiled into a map shown on the right of Figure 11.82. The stitched panoramic on the right of Figure 11.82 was photographed at four 90-degree angles using a fish-eye camera lens capable of capturing a field of view of close to 180 degrees using a panoramic tripod attachment.

Figure 11.82 shows the middle exposure of five exposures taken of the office and one of the four angles of the living room. Figure 11.83 shows five images in the range from underexposed (dark) to overexposed (bright) photos that were used to compile the HDRIs shown here. You will use an HDRI made from the living-room panoramic photos to light the decorative box in the next section.

The living-room photos are taken at 90-degree intervals inside the living room and then stitched and compiled in an HDRI file using a photographic software package (shown in Figure 11.84). The HDRI file is called `livingRoomPanoramic.hdr` and is in the sourceimages folder of the Plane project on the web page for the next section's IBL lighting exercise. You won't be able to see the extensive range of the HDR image because the great majority of computer displays are limited to a display of 8-bit color.

Figure 11.82

A light-probe photo of a desk is taken with a chrome ball (left) and a panoramic stitch (right).

Figure 11.83

Five exposures make up the HDRI of a desk using a chrome ball (left); and a living room using a panoramic stitch (right), which is to be used in the next section.

Figure 11.84

Fish-eye photos are taken at four angles of the living room, each with several exposures from light to dark (above). The fish-eye photos are then warped and stitched together using the handy software package PTGui and merged into an HDR image file (bottom).

The HDRI will eventually be mapped onto an IBL sphere. This is a large sphere that surrounds the environment in your Maya scene. The individual photos first need to be stitched together and converted to a rectangular image file, as shown in Figure 11.84. The full spherical panorama space captured in these photos and stitched together is laid out into a rectangular format that is suitable to project onto a sphere in Maya, just as if a geographic map on a school room globe was unwrapped into a rectangular sheet of paper.

Software such as HDRShop, available online for free, allows you to combine multiple images into an HDRI. One useful program, PTGui from the Netherlands (available for a demo online at www.ptgui.com), allows you to stitch panoramas as well as merge HDR images, which makes it a fantastic tool for CG lighters and photographers. As long as the photos to be stitched were taken with enough overlap at the edges, PTGui is able to turn them into a large panoramic photo. And if the proper exposure ranges were also taken, PTGui creates a solid HDRI as well. I won't get into the details of creating the HDRI because it's an advanced topic using Adobe Photoshop, PTGui, and/or other software; however, it's good to know the origins of HDR images and how they come to be used in an IBL.

You will use an HDRI to light a scene later in the chapter.

Displacement Mapping the Decorative Box

Before continuing with the lighting and rendering for the lamp and decorative box, let's first address a need for detailing just the box by itself. Look at the actual photo of the box in Chapter 3 (Figure 3.21) and compare it to the renders of the box in Chapter 10 (Figure 10.65); you'll see that the carved details in the CG box need more detail. Let's start by taking a closer look at the box by itself.

1. Make sure your project is set to the Plane project. Open the file planeLightingScene_ v05.ma from the Plane project. An error may come up saying that the reference file cannot be found (if so, it will look like Figure 11.85). If that is the case, simply click Browse and navigate to where you have saved the Decorative_Box project's scenes folder, where you will find the scene file boxDetail01.ma. Otherwise, the scene should open with no issues. There is a copy of the boxDetail01.ma file in the scenes folder for the plane project as well.

Figure 11.85

Oh no! Reference file not found!

2. Select the top node of the toy plane (planeGroup) and create a new display layer called **planeLayer**. Turn off visibility for the planeLayer.

3. In the Render Settings window, change the renderer to mental ray.

4. Use the persp camera (not the renderCam) and line up a view of the box to match the box render shown in Figure 11.86.

Figure 11.86

The decorative box's current look when you finished the lighting in Chapter 10

5. Render a frame, and you should notice more closely the lack of definition in the box when compared to the real photo of the box (Figure 3.21 in Chapter 3).

6. Save your work!

In the current render, the grooves are flat and shiny, whereas in the real box, they're carved into the wood and aren't glossy like the rest of the box. You will add definition to the model through textures next.

You can use the scene file `planeLightingScene_v06.ma` to catch up to this point or compare your camera angles.

Reflection Map

Just as you use a map to put color on the box, you can use similar maps to specify where and how much the box will reflect. Figure 11.87 shows the color map you used to texture the box in Chapter 7 side-by-side with a black-and-white map that shows only the carved regions of the box. This map was created with elbow grease and hard work to manually isolate just the carved areas of the box in Photoshop. See how much I do for you?

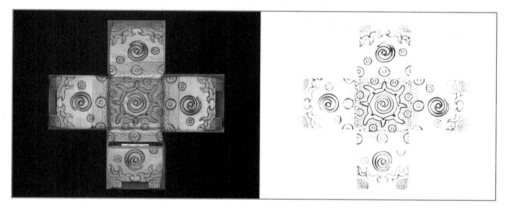

Figure 11.87

The black-and-white map on the right shows only the carved areas of the box.

You'll first take the reflections out of the carved areas in the following steps:

1. Set your project to the Decorative_Box project from the companion website.

2. Open the `boxDetail02.ma` scene. This scene has the box set up with a few lights, a render camera and render settings preset, and a ground plane for you to focus on detailing just the box. Render a frame and study the outcome. Save it to the image buffer in the Render View window.

3. Open the Hypershade. In the Create panel, click 2D Textures under the Maya heading and choose File to open a new image file node (called file1). Go into the Browser panel's Textures tab, and MMB+drag file1 to show it in the Work Area and Property Editor. See Figure 11.88.

Figure 11.88

**Create a new
file node.**

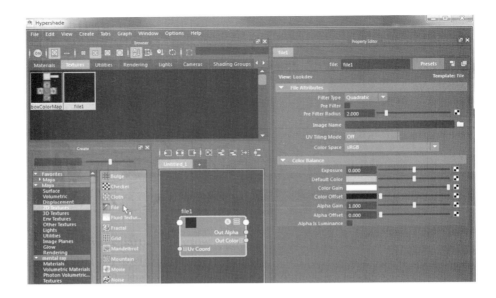

HYPERSHADE

Keep in mind that you are primarily using the Hypershade's Property Editor in Attribute
Editor mode and not Lookdev mode. Lookdev mode (on the left in the following image)
shows only some of the attributes for the selected node in the Hypershade, while the
Attribute Editor mode (on the right in the following image) shows all of the node's attributes
almost exactly like the Attribute Editor itself. See Chapter 3 for more on the Hypershade.

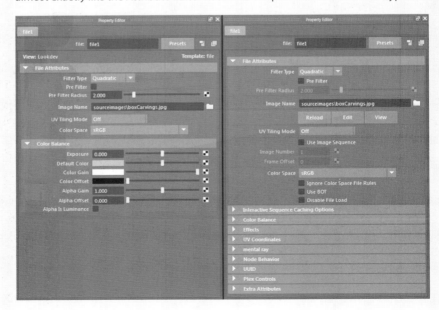

4. Double-click the file node to open its attributes in the Attribute Editor and then navigate to find and choose the boxCarvings.jpg file in the sourceimages folder of the Decorative_Box project. See Figure 11.89, which shows the Attribute Editor view of the loaded image file.

5. If the sample swatch at the top of the Attribute Editor for the file1 node doesn't show the image you just selected, it is because the image is too large for Maya to create a thumbnail swatch automatically. RMB+click the file node in the Hypershade and choose Refresh Swatch from the marking menu. Of course, the only way to see the image in the Hypershade is to have the Material Viewer panel on (which you usually do not throughout this book). Figure 11.90 shows the swatch with the black-and-white image in the Material Viewer above the Property Editor. This isn't necessary, but it makes it easier for you to identify what file map is where.

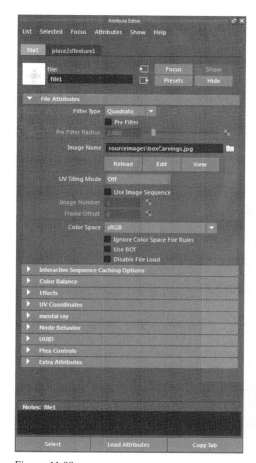

Figure 11.89

Select the proper image file.

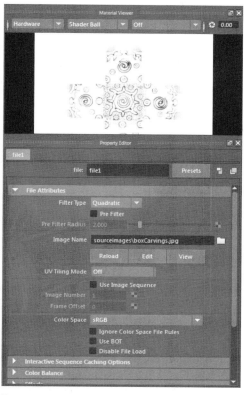

Figure 11.90

The Material Viewer shows a preview of the image you're using.

6. MMB+drag the phong1 node from the Browser's Materials tab of the Hypershade window down to the Work Area, alongside the file1 node.

7. Click the phong1 node to view its attributes in the Property Editor. Drag the Out Alpha output socket to the Reflectivity input socket for the Phong1 shader, as shown in Figure 11.91.

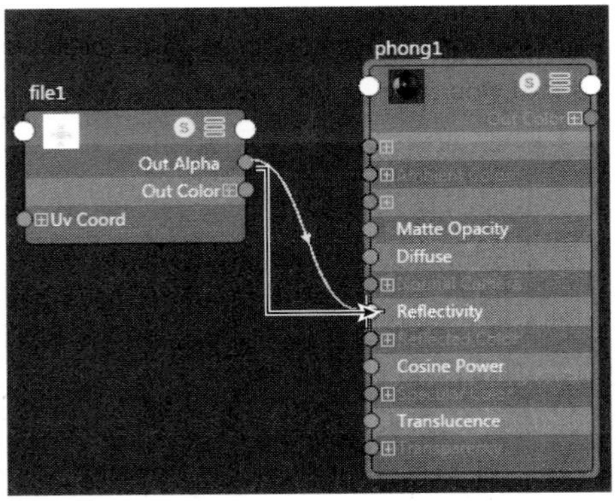

Figure 11.91

Map the new image file to the Reflectivity attribute.

8. Notice the connection line in the Hypershade between the file1 and phong1 nodes. The white areas of the map tell the phong1 shader to have a reflectivity of 1, whereas the black areas have zero reflectivity. This effectively removes reflections from the box's carvings. Render a frame of the box in the renderCam view and compare it to Figure 11.92.

Figure 11.92

The reflections are stronger; the entire box looks like a mirror.

9. In the Render View window, click the Keep Image icon () to store this render in the render buffer. Doing so allows you to easily compare renders to see the changes you make as you continue.

10. The box's reflections are now stronger all over, and the carvings still reflect. You need to turn on one switch. Select the file1 node and open the Color Balance heading in the Property Editor. Check the box for the Alpha Is Luminance attribute. This instructs Maya to use the luminance values (basically the brightness) of the image to output to the reflectivity attribute of the phong1 shader. The box renders properly, and the carvings have no reflections, as shown in Figure 11.93. Save this render into the render buffer with the Keep Image icon ( ).

Figure 11.93

The carvings don't reflect, but the rest of the box's reflections are still too strong.

11. You need to reduce the reflections on the rest of the box. Double-click the file1 node to open the Attribute Editor. In the Color Balance heading, set Alpha Gain to **0.4**, as shown in Figure 11.94. You may also do this in the Hypershade's Property Editor, of course. This sets the brightest part of the reflections to be capped at 0.4 and not the previous 1.0. Render, and you see a much better reflection in the box and no reflections in the carvings. (See Figure 11.95.) Save this to the render buffer.

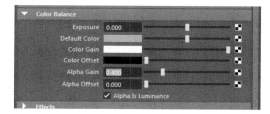

12. Rename the file1 node to **reflectionMap** and the phong1 node to **boxShader** and save your work to a new version.

Figure 11.94

Set Alpha Gain to 0.4.

Figure 11.95

The reflections look much better now.

You can open the scene file boxDetail03.ma from the scenes folder in the Decorative_ Box project to catch up to this point or to check your work so far.

Displacement Mapping

Now that the reflections are set up, you'll use the same image map to create displacements in the box to sink the carvings into the box. Isn't that convenient?

1. In the Hypershade, clear the Work Area by clicking the Clear Graph icon (![icon]). Then create a new file node, and in the Property Editor, navigate to and select the boxCarvings.jpg file in the sourceimages folder again. You don't want to reuse the same file node as you did for the reflections (reflectionMap node) before because you need to change some of its attributes for use as a displacement map. Name the new file node **displacementMap**.

2. In the Materials tab, click the boxShader node to show it in the Property Editor and MMB+drag the shader to the Work Area of the Hypershade. Click the boxShader node and graph its input and output connections (![icon]). This displays the shader network. Note the phong1SG node that appears in the Work Area connected to the boxShader node.

3. In the Textures tab of the Browser panel of the Hypershade, drag the displacement-Map node to the Work Area. Notice the file node displays its name (displacement-Map) in the Browser panel but displays the filename (boxCarvings.jpg) in the Work Area as shown in Figure 11.96. This can be a little confusing.

4. Click the phong1SG to display it in the Property Editor. Then, MMB+drag the displacementMap node from the Work Area to the boxShader's Displacement Mat attribute in the Property Editor, as shown in Figure 11.97. Make sure you MMB+click and drag; a regular click on the displacementMap node will change the Property Editor's display from the boxShader to the displacementMap node.

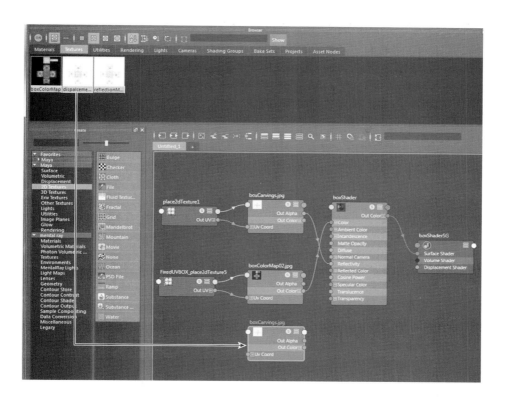

Figure 11.96

The shader network for the box

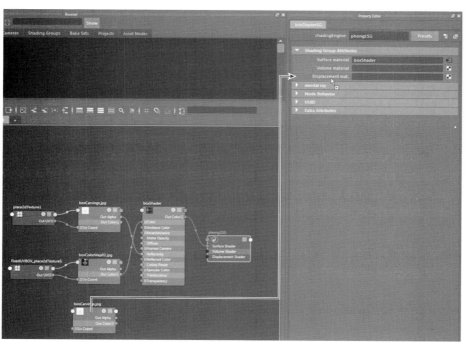

Figure 11.97

Add the new image map to the boxShader's Displacement Mat attribute in the Property Editor.

5. Notice in the Work Area that there is no rubber band connecting the displacement-Map node to the phong1SG node as you may expect. Select the phong1SG node and click (▨) to see the input and output connections. A new node appears called displacementShader1 connecting the displacementMap to the phong1SG node. The Hypershade shows you the entire shader network, including the displacement map connection, as shown in the top image in Figure 11.97. Notice that the displacement connects to the phong1SG node and not directly to the boxShader node. This is normal and how it's always done.

6. Render the box and see what happens now that you have a displacement map applied. Figure 11.98 shows how the box seems to have exploded!

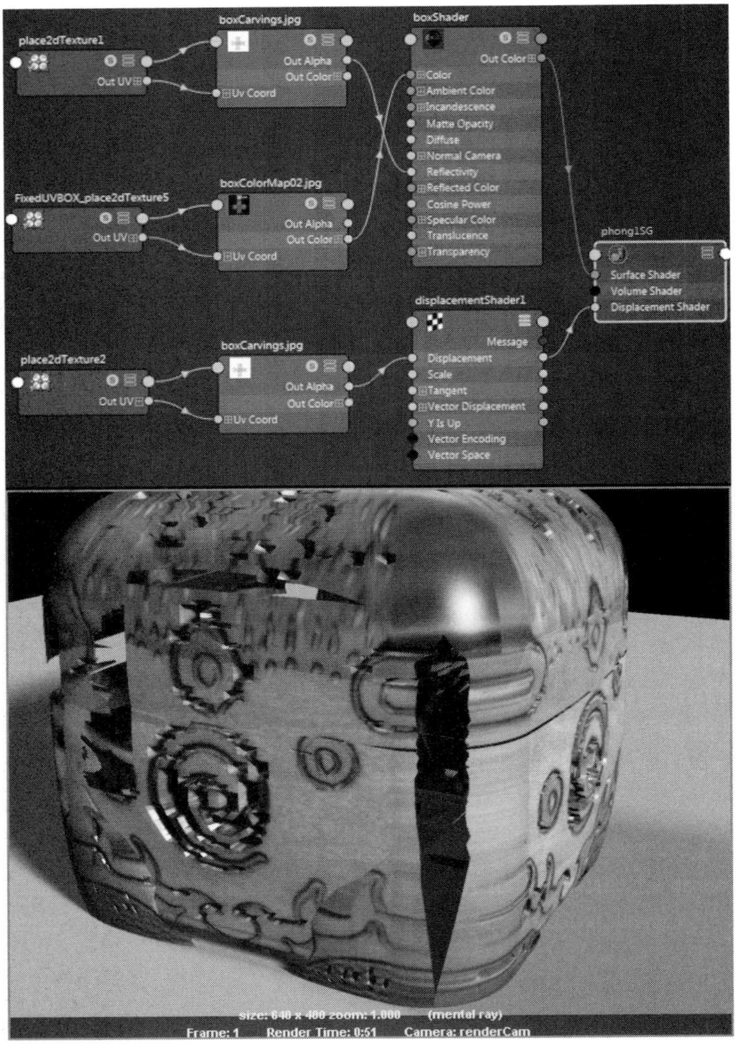

Figure 11.98

The complete shader network (top). But the displacements seem to be wrong when rendered (bottom)!

Not to worry—this is to be expected. The values coming from the black-and-white map dictate how much of the geometry is displaced (moved). Obviously, you don't have an image that works well for the amount of displacement, although it does look like the displacements are in the proper place to correspond to where the carvings are on the box.

Occasionally when you click to view the input and output of a shader as you did in step 3, the Hypershade will put some nodes on top of others. If you don't see any of the nodes, try clicking and dragging some of the nodes around in the Hypershade to see whether there are any accidentally hidden nodes. These little touches make Maya extra fun!

7. Click the displacementMap node in the Hypershade (it's called boxCarvings.jpg in the Work Area but properly named in the Browser panel). In the Property Editor, open the Effects heading and click the Invert check box. This turns the background to black and the carvings to white. Set Alpha Gain to **0.03** in the Color Balance heading and make sure Alpha Is Luminance is also checked. (See Figure 11.99.) The Alpha Gain value reduces the amount of displacement, and inverting the image lets the rest of the box outside of the carvings not be displaced.

8. Render a frame and compare it to Figure 11.100. It's not looking very good. The box isn't exploding anymore, and only the carvings are displacing, which is good. However, the carvings are sticking out, instead of in.

9. Set the Alpha Gain attribute to **–0.015** to push the carvings in a little instead of out. Render and compare to Figure 11.101. The carvings are set into the wood as they should be, but the render looks bad. The displacements are very jagged and ill-defined.

10. The jagged look of the carvings has to do with the tessellation of the box—that is, the detail of the box's polygonal mesh. There are advanced ways to address how mental ray deals with displacements; however, the most basic method is to adjust the detail of the box's mesh. Figure 11.102 shows the current box's mesh. Notice that the sides of the box are simply detailed. To increase the box's faces to add detail, select the box, and then, in the Modeling menu set, choose Edit Mesh → Add Divisions ❑. Set the options to Exponentially and Division Levels to **3**, as shown in Figure 11.103. Click Add Divisions to execute.

Figure 11.99

Set the attributes for the displacement image.

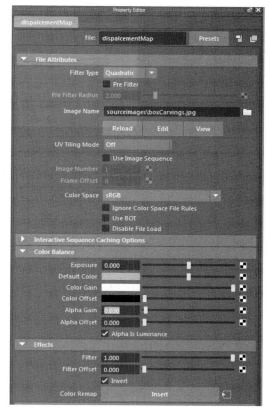

Figure 11.100
The carvings are displacing outward.

Figure 11.101
The carvings are inset into the wood, but they don't look good yet.

USING SCALE ATTRIBUTE FOR THE DISPLACEMENTSHADER NODE INSTEAD OF ALPHA GAIN

In this exercise you are using the Alpha Gain attribute on the file node to control the amount of the displacement created by the carvings in the box. With mental ray, you can use the Scale attribute in the displacementShader1 node created instead. For example, in this exercise, instead of setting Alpha Gain to -0.015 as in step 7, leave Alpha Gain at 1.0 (default). Click the displacementShader1 node and set the Scale attribute to **-0.015** and render. Compare the two results, and they should be the same. This attribute may not work all the time (especially with Maya Software rendering), however, so getting used to using Alpha Gain to control the amount of displacement is the sure-fire way to do it.

Figure 11.102
The current box's mesh isn't detailed enough.

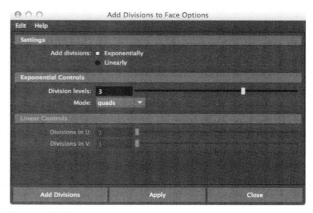

Figure 11.103
Set the Add Divisions values.

11. Figure 11.104 shows the newly tessellated box. It's far more detailed in the mesh. When you render, it gives a result similar to Figure 11.105. You can compare your work to the scene file boxDetail04.ma in the scenes folder of the Decorative_Box project.

12. Now that you have the detail you want in the box, you need to prepare the box's scene file to be referenced back into your lamp lighting scene. Select the ground plane, the renderCam camera, and the three lights in the scene and delete them. Save your work to a new version.

Compare your work to the scene file boxDetail05.ma in the scenes folder of the Decorative_Box project.

Notice that the render times increased because you increased the detail on the mesh in step 8. This increase is normal, but it can become a problem if the mesh is too divided and has more faces than you need. This box has fairly detailed carvings, so the level to which you set Add Divisions in step 8 gives a good result without being too detailed. As your experience increases in Maya and mental ray rendering, you'll learn how to use functions such as the mental ray Approximation Editor to keep the overall detail low on the mesh but with smooth displacement results when you render. This is an advanced technique, so I won't cover it in this book. You've taken in quite a lot by this point already.

The next time you select the box and open the Attribute Editor, you'll see a new tab called polySubdFace1. This is the node added with the Add Divisions function in step 8. Feel free to adjust the Subdivision Levels setting on that tab and render to see how the detail levels affect the final render. Also, try better quality settings in Render Settings, as you did with the red wagon earlier in this chapter, to clean up the render to your satisfaction.

You'll next add an IBL sphere and use the HDR image you saw earlier in the chapter.

Figure 11.104
Added divisions

Figure 11.105
The displacements render much better now.

Rendering the Scene with mental ray

You're all grown up and ready to light a full scene using Final Gather, IBL with an HDRI, and regular lights to get the best bang for your buck out of mental ray rendering. In the previous chapter, you quickly lit the plane, candle, and decorative box with key, fill, and rim lights (the three-point lighting system) and set it to render with Maya Software ray-tracing. In this exercise, you'll take this concept a few steps further and change the scene to best use mental ray, so take a deep breath, call your mother and tell her you love her, and let's get started!

Set your project to the Plane project. Open the `planeLightingScene_v06.ma` file in the scenes folder. Remember that you turned off the plane's display layer earlier, so the plane will not be seen when you load this file. This scene has the lights and soft shadows created in Chapter 10 and is set to render through mental ray with raytracing enabled already. Let's take a critical look at the render from the earlier Figure 11.86.

Now that you have created a more detailed box, let's update the reference in this scene. Choose File → Reference Editor. You are currently reading in `boxDetail01.ma`. Click `boxDetail01.ma` to select the entry and choose Reference → Replace Reference. Navigate to the Decorative_Box project's scene folder and select `boxDetail05.ma`.

All your work detailing the box will now pop into the lamp lighting scene. Render a frame from the persp camera view. Figure 11.106 shows a comparison of the render from before (top) and the newly detailed box in the lamp lighting scene (bottom). The detailed box looks much nicer now, although you have to tweak the render quality settings in this scene later.

Adding an IBL

Here's where things get fun. You'll add an IBL node to the scene and add the living room HDR image to that IBL. First make sure you have mental ray selected as your renderer in the Render Settings window and then follow along with these steps:

1. In your already open `planeLightingScene_v06.ma` scene, turn on the planeLayer visibility. Render a frame in the renderCam view and save it to the buffer in the Render View window. You can also start moving around with your persp camera view again, since you're no longer focusing on the box.

2. In the Render Settings window, click the Scene tab. At the top, in the Cameras → Environment heading, click the Create button for Image Based Lighting, as shown in Figure 11.107.

3. The Attribute Editor opens a view of the newly created IBL (named mentalray-IblShape1), as shown in Figure 11.108.

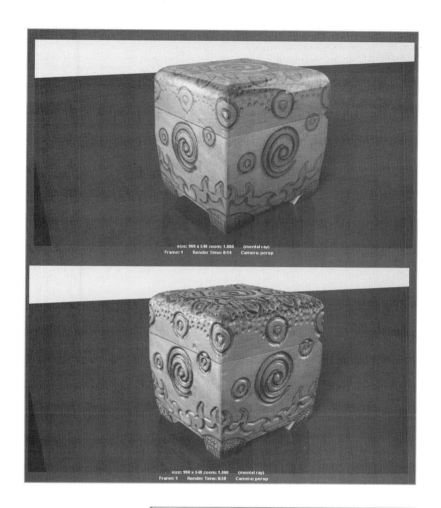

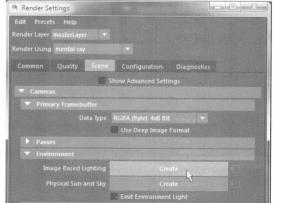

Figure 11.107

Click to create an IBL.

Figure 11.108

The Attribute Editor for the IBL node

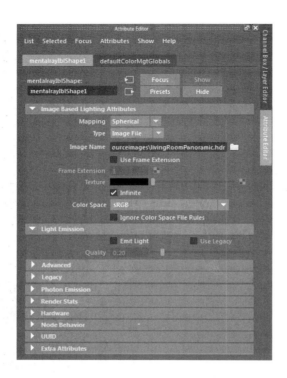

4. Click the folder icon (![folder icon]) next to the Image Name attribute. Navigate to the sourceimages folder of the Plane project on your system and select the file livingRoomPanoramic.hdr. You see in your view panes that a large yellow sphere is created in your scene. In the Hardware section in the Attribute Editor, set Hardware Exposure to **3** to lighten up the view of the HDR image in the viewports. The living-room panoramic HDR image is mapped. (See Figure 11.109.)

5. Use your persp camera to take a good look at the placement of the IBL sphere and the HDR image mapped to it. Select the IBL (you can click the IBL's yellow wireframe lines or select mentalrayIbl1 in the Outliner) and rotate the IBL sphere to 80 in the Y-axis so that the bright sun in the window is behind the renderCam and the window faces the wing of the plane on the right side of the frame. Figure 11.110 shows the orientation of the IBL.

6. In the renderCam view, render a frame, and you'll see that the lighting is largely unchanged from your earlier renders in step 1, though you should see more reflections in the plane and the candle's glass. Next you need to enable Final Gather to take better advantage of the IBL and the HDRI mapped to it.

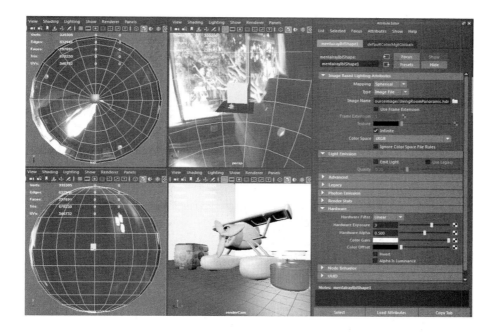

Figure 11.109

The IBL is in place and mapped to the living room panoramic HDRI.

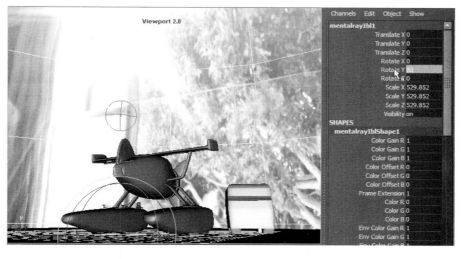

Figure 11.110

Rotate the IBL sphere in the Y-axis to 80.

7. On the Render Settings window's Quality tab, set Indirect Diffuse (GI) Mode to Final Gather. Render a frame, and it should appear extremely bright now; it's way too bright!

8. In the Attribute Editor for the IBL, click the Color Space pulldown menu and select Raw (Figure 11.111). This will use the proper color space for the HDRI file so its color values are read and interpreted properly. The default sRGB made the image far too bright, blowing out the Final Gather rendering.

9. Render a frame and compare it to the image in Figure 11.112. Save the image by clicking the Keep Image icon (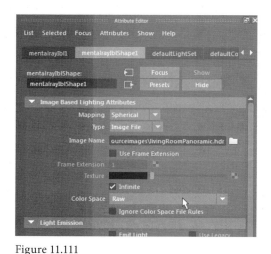) and compare it to your earlier render before the IBL and before Final Gather. Also notice the bounced light on the redwood tabletop, which is a nice touch, albeit splotchy right now.

> If you need to prevent the HDR image from showing up in the background of your renders, select the IBL sphere, and, in the Attribute Editor under the Render Stats heading, turn off Primary Visibility. The background will then render black without the IBL.

The render is a little bright and quite noisy. You have three lights in the scene already and now an HDRI. Let's get rid of all the lights and start fresh to convert this to an entire mental ray scene, shaders and all.

10. In the Outliner select the three lights in the scene, spotLight1, spotLight2, and directionalLight1. Press Ctrl+H to hide them, which will effectively turn them off in the scene. There's no need to delete the lights; hiding them will do.

11. Re-render the scene, and you'll see only the HDRI contribution to the scene (bottom image in Figure 11.112). The render will get more noisy, but you'll tackle that noise a little later. You will now add some direct light with an Area light, which gives a much nicer lighting than the other lights you've used.

Figure 11.111

Setting the proper Raw color space for the HDR image.

Figure 11.112

It's noisy and a bit too bright of a render (top). Seeing only the HDRI lighting the scene (bottom).

12. In the persp viewport, create an area light (Create → Lights → Area Light). Scale it to 3 in XYZ, set Intensity to 2, and place it to face the toy plane, as shown in Figure 11.113.

13. Render the scene (it will take a few minutes), and you'll see it's brighter, of course, but the toy plane looks a little bright, like the light is too close as shown in Figure 11.114. Before you change the lighting, let's re-create the materials with mental ray shaders. This will illustrate how shaders can affect lighting, and vice versa.

14. Open the Hypershade and MMB+drag the yellow Blinn shader to the Work Area. You'll start with changing this yellow Blinn to a yellow mia_material, a versatile mental ray shader. With the yellow Blinn selected, click the Input And Output Connections icon ( ) to see the connections for the yellow Blinn shader.

15. In the left side of the Hypershade, in the Create panel, click Mental Ray Materials; then click to create a mia_material_x shader and drag it to the Work Area from the Materials tab, as shown in Figure 11.115.

16. In the Work Area of the Hypershade, drag the noiseYellow's Out Color output socket to the new mia_material_x1 shader's Diffuse input socket, as shown in Figure 11.116. This will connect the yellow noise pattern you created earlier to be the color of the new mia material. Name the new material **yellowMia**.

17. Now, let's assign the new mia material yellow to the yellow parts of the plane. This is pretty easily done through the Hypershade (either the Browser panel or the Work Area). RMB+click the old yellow Blinn shader and select Select Objects With Material from the marking menu. This will select all the yellow parts of the plane. Next, RMB+click the yellowMia shader and select Assign Material To Selection. That's it. See Figure 11.117.

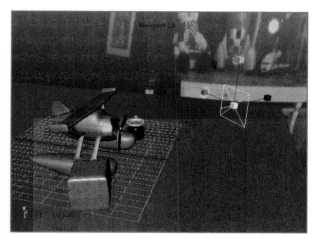

Figure 11.113
Create an Area light and place it as shown here.

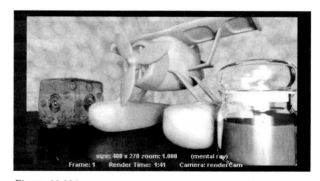

Figure 11.114
Adding an Area light makes the toy airplane look a little too bright but not too shabby.

Figure 11.115

Create an mia_
material_x shader
and bring it down to
the Work Area.

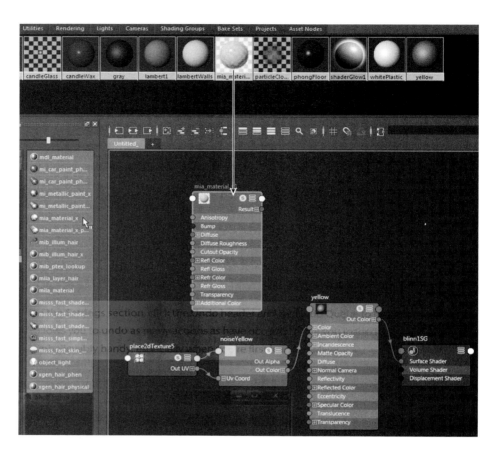

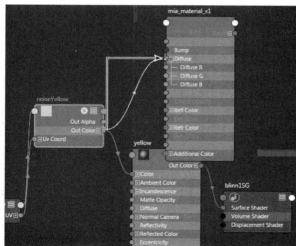

Figure 11.116

Connect the yellow texture to the new mia shader.

Figure 11.117

Assign the new yellowMia shader to the yellow parts of the plane.

18. Select the yellowMia shader and notice that the attributes are a bit different from the shaders you've seen like Blinn or Phong. The Color attribute in the Diffuse section is the basic color of the shader; that's where the yellow noise pattern is connected. You need to adjust the specular highlight to make the shader less glossy. Notice there are no specular controls. Instead, with this shader, the specular highlights are controlled in the Reflection section with the Reflectivity and Glossiness attributes. Set Glossiness to **0.35** to lessen the gloss on the yellow plastic and reduce Reflectivity to **0.20** to reduce the shine and reflection you'll get once you render.

19. Repeat steps 13–17 for the old gray Blinn shader to make a new gray mia_material_x (call it **greyMia**). This way you can replace the gray parts of the plane with greyMia.

20. Now that the toy plane has been converted to mental ray mia shaders, render the frame and compare it to your previous render with the Blinn shaders. Figure 11.118 shows the mia shader render of the plane. You can notice some subtle differences in how the mia_material is affected by light when compared to the Blinn render from Figure 11.114.

21. Repeat steps 13–17 again to change the shader of the redwood tabletop to a mia material as well (call it **floorMia**). Except for the floor's mia material, set Reflectivity to **0.4** and Glossiness to **0.70** to make it a bit shiny.

22. Lastly, make another mia material. This time, set the Diffuse section's Color to a medium gray and set Reflectivity to **0**. This will be a matte material for the walls. Assign this new shader (call it **wallsMia**).

23. Finally, select the Area light and set Intensity to **1.0** from 2 to bring down the brightness in the scene. Render and compare your render to the previous renders and to Figure 11.119.

Lighting, rendering, and shading all go hand in hand, and as you can see from the previous exercise, you have to go back and forth to best achieve the look you want. Now

Figure 11.118

The mia material creates a more subtle look for the plane, though the scene is still too bright!

Figure 11.119

Rendering the mia materials on the plane, table top, and walls

you're not done yet, there is quite a bit of noise in the renders. I'll address that next. You can check your work (or skip to this point) against the scene file `planeLightingScene_v07.ma` from the scenes folder in the Plane project.

> **ORIENTING THE IBL**
>
> Play around with the rotations of the IBL to see how the lighting differs until you settle on a look you like.

Fixing Final Gather Noise

The render from the previous section looks nice, except that it's noisy. Notice the blotches of light all over the walls and floor. This is from having low-quality settings for FG. On the Render Settings' Quality tab, increase Indirect Diffuse Quality to **2.0**. Doing so dramatically increases the render time for the frame (more than tripling the previous time); however, it makes the scene look much better—practically eradicating the blotchy nature of the previous renders. (See Figure 11.120.) Save the image to your Render View buffer.

If your renders are running just too long to tolerate, feel free to reduce the Indirect Diffuse Quality lower as you see fit; 1.5 gives a good result as well.

Figure 11.120

Using a higher setting for Indirect Diffuse Quality makes a big difference.

You can open the scene file `planeLighting-Scene_v08.ma` from the scenes folder in the Plane project to catch up to this point or to check your work so far.

FG is a difficult beast to tame, especially with an IBL. It takes a lot of experience, patience, and practice to be able to use this powerful feature of mental ray successfully in scenes. Experiment with different HDR images that you can download from the Internet as well as adjusting the lights in the scene.

Fixing General Render Noise

You may have gotten rid of the blotchy Final Gather noise (mostly, at least), but if you take a close look at Figure 11.120, you can see there is some noise on the back wall. This is coming from the shadow being cast by the Area light in the scene. At first blush you may think to increase the overall Render Settings Overall Quality slider above the current 0.25. And that is not a bad instinct, but this noise is all in that back shadow. If the edges of the plane or decorative box or candle were jagged, then yes, the Quality slider would be your solution. This is all about the area light and its shadow, and for that there is a focused solution.

To fix the noisy shadow, go to the `planeLightingScene_v08.ma` scene and select the Area light. Since this is an Area light and it inherently has soft shadows, there is no Light Radius attribute to set the shadow softness. The softness of an Area light shadow corresponds to the size of the Area light. The larger the light, the softer its shadows will render. Our shadow seems too soft, so let's make the Area light smaller first to sharpen the shadow a bit.

Select the Area light and reduce its scale to 1.75 in X, Y, and Z. Next, change Shadow Rays (in the Attribute Editor, under the Shadows → Raytrace Shadow Attributes section) to **12** from 1 and render to see the shadow render much cleaner than before. Compare the render in Figure 11.121 to Figure 11.120 where Shadow Rays was set to the default of **1** and the Area light was bigger. The shadow is a bit sharper, more defined, and much cleaner.

> For a nice challenge, you could re-create the shaders for the candle and decorative box using mia_materials to see the difference they can make in your renders. Many different materials could be simulated with the mia_materials shader.

Adding Depth of Field

One last item of interest is adding a depth of field (DOF) to the image. This effect adds blur to the render for the areas of the image that may be out of the lens's focal depth. It can greatly add to the photorealism of a rendered image.

Select the renderCam and open the Attribute Editor. In the Depth Of Field heading, check the Depth Of Field attribute. Set Focus Distance to **11** and set F Stop to **6**. The F Stop setting, like a real lens, sets how much is in focus around the focal distance. With a higher F Stop value, the focus runs deeper than with a low F Stop value. As you adjust your Focus Distance attribute, you can see the blurriness in the camera's viewport—as long as you have Viewport 2.0 enabled, which it is by default. If not, in the viewport, choose Renderer → Viewport 2.0.

Figure 11.122 shows the final render of the scene with DOF enabled. Your render times will be longer, and if you want a better render than this one, which has some grain especially in the glass candle holder, you'll likely need to increase your Overall Quality value. This render can take quite some time, though. Figure 11.122 took 25 minutes to render on a workstation laptop.

size: 480 x 270 zoom: 1.000   (mental ray)
Frame: 1   Render Time: 24:53   Camera: renderCam

Figure 11.122

The propeller is in focus! You're finished!

The scene `planeLightingScene_v09.ma` from the scenes folder in the Plane project will take you to this point.

Notice from the render that the back of the toy plane is thrown out of focus, along with the candle, decorative box, and back walls. Experiment with varying focus distance and F Stop values to try different looks for your scene.

Depending on the need and the size of the render, you'll have to set the sampling levels to suit your needs—but be warned that your rendering times will dramatically increase, easily tripling depending on the quality settings. There are several ways to create DOF in a render that are faster or more controllable than what I've covered here. You can render out a depth pass to use with a lens filter in a compositing package such as Nuke to keep render times down. There are also more accurate DOF methods in mental ray and its lens shaders that you can experiment with when you've comfortably grasped the overall workflow presented here.

Try also experimenting with the different sampling modes to see whether you can shave time off the render. Finally, adding an Ambient Occlusion pass isn't absolutely necessary for this render, although it may enhance the look of the contact shadows.

Wrapping Up

When you've learned a lot more about lighting and gained confidence with the processes of lighting, rendering, and compositing, you'll find a wealth of options when you render in several different layers. For example, if this plane, candle, and decorative box scene was a professional job, its render would most likely be split into a flat-color pass, a reflection pass, a specular highlight pass, a shadow pass, an Ambient Occlusion pass, a depth pass, and several different matte passes that separate parts of the scene to give the compositor the ultimate control in adjusting the image to taste.

You may not know what all those passes do right now, but understanding will come with time as long as you continue practicing your CG Kung Fu. Rendering your own color passes and Ambient Occlusions will give you some beautiful renders even without all the other passes. Keep in mind that small changes and additions can take you a long way toward a truly rich image.

> For an interesting challenge, take a photo in your house; render the plane, candle, and box to match the lighting in the photo; and then composite the render against your photo.

Summary

In this chapter, you learned how to set up your scene for rendering. Starting with the Render Settings window and moving on to the different render engines available, you learned how to render your scene for a particular look. Then, I covered how to preview your render and how to use IPR for fast scene feedback. I moved on to cover how to render reflections and refractions, how to create and use cameras, and how to render with motion blur. You tested your skill on a wine bottle scene, and to batch-render it out into a sequence of images, you checked it in a program like FCheck. You also used Maya render layers, overrides, and rendering an Ambient Occlusion pass to make your renders more realistic. Finally, you applied this knowledge to rendering the toy plane, a glass candle holder, and the decorative box using Final Gather and an HDRI of a living room.

Getting to this point in a scene can take some work, but when you see the results playing back on your screen, all the work seems more than worth it. Always allow enough time to ensure that your animations render properly and at their best quality. Most beginners seriously underestimate the time needed to complete this step properly in CG production.

After you create numerous scenes and render them, you'll begin to understand how to construct your next scenes so that they render better and faster. Be sure to keep on top of your file management—rendering can produce an awful lot of files, and you don't want to have them scattered all over the place.

CHAPTER 12

Autodesk® Maya® Dynamics and Effects

Special effects animations simulate not only physical phenomena, such as smoke and fire, but also the natural movements of colliding bodies. Behind the latter type of animation is the Autodesk® Maya® dynamics engine, which is the sophisticated software that creates realistic-looking motion based on the principles of physics.

Another Maya animation tool, Paint Effects, can create dynamic fields of grass and flowers, a head full of hair, and other such systems in a matter of minutes. Maya also offers dynamic simulations for hair, fur, and cloth. In this chapter, I'll cover the basics of dynamics in Maya and let you practice working with particles by making steam.

Learning Outcomes: In this chapter, you will be able to

- Create rigid body dynamic objects and create forces to act upon them

- Keyframe animated passive rigid bodies to act on active rigid bodies

- Bake out simulations to keyframes and simplify animation curves

- Understand nParticle workflow

- Emit nParticles and have them move and render to simulate steam

- Draw Paint Effects strokes

- Create and manipulate an nCloth object

- Collide nObjects and add forces and dynamic constraints

- Cache your nDynamics to disk

- Customize the Maya interface

An Overview of Maya Dynamics

Dynamics is simulating motion by applying the principles of physics. Rather than assigning keyframes to objects to animate them, with Maya dynamics you assign physical characteristics that define how an object behaves in a simulated world. You create the objects as usual in Maya, and then you convert them to *nCloth* objects, which can be rigid objects or soft objects like cloth. Rigid dynamics, where the surface of a dynamic object does not deform, are fairly easy to set up and play around with in Maya, especially when using the Legacy Rigid Body Dynamics system that Maya 2016 retains. You will take a quick look into that later in the chapter.

Dynamic objects, whether particles or objects that are rigid or deforming (like cloth), are affected by external forces called *fields*, which exert a force on them to create motion. Fields can range from wind forces to gravity and can have their own specific effects on dynamic bodies.

In Maya, dynamic objects are categorized as nCloth, nParticles, nHair, Legacy Rigid Bodies, Maya Fluids, and Bifrost liquid simulation. nCloth are meshes created in Maya that have varying degrees of rigidity, so you can create solid objects (and hence avoid using Legacy Rigid Bodies) as well as cloth objects. *nParticles* are points in space that have renderable properties and are used for numerous effects, such as fire and smoke. I'll cover nParticle basics in the latter half of this chapter. *nHair* consists of curves that behave dynamically, such as strings. *Fluids* are, in essence, volumetric particles that can exhibit surface properties. You can use fluid dynamics for natural effects such as billowing clouds or plumes of smoke. Bifrost is a liquid simulation allowing you to create animations such as pouring water.

Nucleus is a stable and interactive engine for calculating dynamic simulations in Maya and is the basis for all the nDynamic objects mentioned earlier (except for Bifrost).

I'll introduce nCloth and nParticles later in this chapter; however, soft bodies, nHair, Bifrost, and fluid dynamics are advanced topics and won't be covered in this book.

Rigid Bodies

Rigid bodies are now a legacy feature in Maya that deal with the dynamics of solid objects, such as a pair of dice or a baseball. Fields and collisions affect the entire object and move it accordingly. I will provide a brief look into them because this legacy system is still a little simpler to implement than using nCloth for rigid objects, at least in my view.

Creating Active and Passive Rigid Body Objects

Any surface geometry in Maya can be converted to a rigid body. After it's converted, that surface can respond to the effects of fields and take part in collisions. Sounds like fun, eh?

The two types of legacy rigid bodies are active and passive. An *active rigid body* is affected by collisions and fields. A *passive rigid body* isn't affected by fields and remains still when it collides with another object. A passive rigid body is used as a surface against which active rigid bodies collide.

As an example, let's create a bouncing ball using Maya rigid bodies. Switch to the FX menu set and follow these steps:

1. Create a polygonal plane and scale it to be a ground surface.

2. Create a poly sphere and position it a number of units above the ground, as shown in Figure 12.1.

3. Make sure you're in the FX menu set (choose FX from the Status line's drop-down bar). Select the poly sphere and choose Fields/Solvers → Create Active Rigid Body. The sphere's Translate and Rotate attributes turn yellow. There will be a dynamic input for those attributes, so you can't set keyframes on any of them.

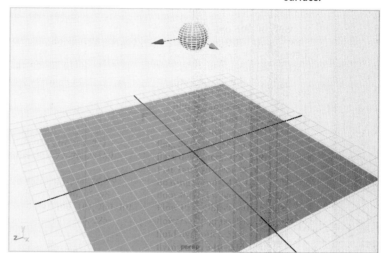

Figure 12.1

Place a poly sphere a few units above a poly plane ground surface.

4. Select the ground plane and choose Fields/Solvers → Create Passive Rigid Body. Doing so sets the poly plane as the floor. For this exercise, stick with the default settings and ignore the various creation options and Rigid Body attributes.

5. To put the ball into motion, you need to create a field to affect it. Select the sphere and choose Fields/Solvers → Gravity. By selecting the active rigid objects while you create the field, you connect that field to the objects automatically. Fields affect only the active rigid bodies to which they're connected. If you hadn't established this connection initially, you could still do so later, through the Dynamic Relationships Editor. You'll find out more about this process later in this chapter.

If you try to scrub the timeline, you'll notice that the animation doesn't run properly. Because dynamics simulates physics, no keyframes are set. You must play the scene from start to finish for the calculations to execute properly. You must also play the scene using the Play Every Frame option. Click the Animation Preferences button to the right of the Range slider, or choose Windows → Settings/Preferences → Preferences. In the Preferences window, choose Time Slider under the Settings header. Choose Play Every Frame from the Playback Speed menu. You can also set the maximum frames per second that your scene will play back by setting the Max Playback Speed attribute.

To play back the simulation, set your frame range from 1 to at least 240. Go to frame 1 and click Play. Make sure you have the proper Playback Speed settings in your Preferences window; otherwise, the simulation won't play properly.

When the simulation plays, you'll notice that the sphere begins to fall after a few frames and collides with the ground plane, bouncing back up.

As an experiment, try turning the passive body plane into an active body using the following steps:

1. Select the plane and open the Attribute Editor.

2. In the rigidBody2 tab, select the Active check box. This switches the plane from a passive body to an active body.

3. Play the simulation. The ball falls to hit the plane and knock it away. Because the plane is now an active body, it's moved by collisions. But because it isn't connected to the gravity field, it doesn't fall with the ball.

To connect the now-active body plane to the gravity field, open the Dynamic Relationships Editor window, shown in Figure 12.2 (choose Windows → Relationship Editors → Dynamic Relationships).

Figure 12.2

The Dynamic Relationships Editor window

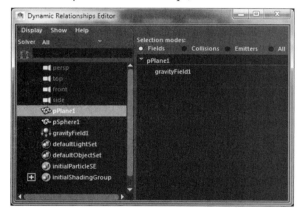

On the left is an Outliner list of the objects in your scene. On the right is a list from which you can choose a category of objects to list: Fields (default), Collisions, Emitters, or All. Select the geometry (pPlane1) on the left side and then connect it to the gravity field by selecting the gravityField1 node on the right.

When you connect the gravity field to the plane and run the simulation, you'll see the plane fall away with the ball. Because the two fall at the same rate (the rate set by the single gravity field), they don't collide. To disconnect the plane from the gravity field, deselect the gravity field in the right panel.

> You can also connect a dynamic object to a field by selecting the dynamic object or objects and then the desired field and choosing Fields/Solvers → Assign To Selected. This method is more useful for connecting multiple dynamic objects to a field.

Turning the active body plane back to a passive floor is as simple as returning to frame 1, the beginning of the simulation, and clearing the Active attribute in the Attribute Editor. By turning the active body back to a passive body, you regain an immovable floor upon which the ball can collide and bounce.

RELATIONSHIP EDITORS

The relationship editors, such as the Dynamic Relationships Editor window, let you connect two nodes to create a special relationship. With the Dynamic Relationships Editor window you connect dynamic attributes so that fields, particles, and rigid bodies can interact in a simulation. Another example of a relationship editor is the Light Linking window mentioned in Chapter 10, "Autodesk® Maya® Lighting," which allows you to connect lights to geometry so that they light only a specific object or objects. These are fairly advanced topics; however, as you learn more about Maya, their use will become integral in your workflow.

Moving a Rigid Body

Because the Maya dynamics engine controls the movement of any active rigid bodies, you can't set keyframes on their translation or rotation. With a passive object, however, you can set keyframes on translation and rotation as you can with any other Maya object. You also can easily keyframe an object to turn either active or passive. For instance, in the earlier bouncing ball example, you could animate the rotation of the passive body ground plane to roll the ball around on it.

Any movement that the passive body has through regular keyframe animation is translated into momentum, which is passed on to any active rigid bodies with which the passive body collides. Think of a baseball bat that strikes a baseball. The bat is a passive rigid body that you have keyframed to swing. The baseball is an active rigid body that is hit by (collides with) the bat as it swings. The momentum of the bat is transferred to the ball, and the ball is sent flying into the stadium stands. You'll see an example of this in action in the next exercise.

Rigid Body Attributes

Here is a rundown of the more important attributes for both passive and active rigid bodies as they pertain to collisions:

Mass Sets the relative mass of the rigid body. Set on active or passive rigid bodies, *mass* is a factor in how much momentum is transferred from one object to another. A more massive object pushes a less massive one with less effort and is itself less prone to movement when hit. Mass is relative, so if all rigid bodies have the same mass value, there is no difference in the simulation.

Static and Dynamic Friction Sliders Set how much friction the rigid body has while at rest (static) and while in motion (dynamic). *Friction* specifies how much the object resists moving or being moved. A friction of 0 makes the rigid body move freely, as if on ice.

Bounciness Specifies how resilient the body is upon collision. The higher the *bounciness* value, the more bounce the object has upon collision.

Damping Creates a drag on the object in dynamic motion so that it slows down over time. The higher the *damping*, the more the body's motion diminishes.

Initial Velocity Gives the rigid body an initial push to move it in the corresponding axis.

Initial Spin Gives the rigid body object an initial twist to start the rotation of the object in that axis.

Impulse Position Gives the object a constant push in that axis. The effect is cumulative; the object will accelerate if the impulse isn't turned off.

Spin Impulse Rotates the object constantly in the desired axis. The spin will accelerate if the impulse isn't turned off.

Center of Mass (0,0,0) Places the center of the object's mass at its pivot point, typically at its geometric center. This value offsets the center of mass, so the rigid body object behaves as if its center of balance is offset, like trick dice or a top-weighted ball.

Creating animation with legacy rigid bodies is straightforward and can go a long way toward creating natural-looking motion for your scene. Integrating such animation into a final project can become fairly complicated, though, so it's prudent to become familiar with the workings of rigid body dynamics before relying on that sort of workflow for an animated project.

Here are a few suggestions for scenes using rigid body dynamics:

Bowling Lane The bowling ball is keyframed as a passive object until it hits the active rigid pins at the end of the lane. This scene is simple to create and manipulate.

Dice Active rigid dice are thrown into a passive rigid craps table. This exercise challenges your dynamics abilities as well as your modeling skills if you create an accurate craps table.

Game of Marbles This scene challenges your texturing and rendering abilities as well as your dynamics abilities as you animate marbles rolling into each other.

Rigid Body Dynamics: Shoot the Catapult!

Now for a fun exercise—you'll use rigid body dynamics to shoot a projectile with the already animated catapult from Chapter 8. Open the scene file catapult_anim_v2.mb from the Catapult_Anim project downloaded from the companion website.

1. For the projectile, create a polygon sphere and place it above the basket, as shown in Figure 12.3.

Since dynamics takes a lot of calculations, to make things easier you will create
an invisible object to be the passive rigid
body collider instead of the existing geometry of the basket itself. This is a frequent
workflow in dynamics, where proxy geometry (often hidden) is used to alleviate calculations and speed up the scene.

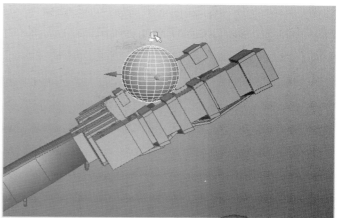

2. Create another poly sphere with Axis
   Divisions and Height Divisions both set
   to **40**.

3. Select the top-half faces of the sphere and
   delete them to create a bowl and place it

Figure 12.3

**Place a sphere over
the basket.**

over the catapult basket, as shown in Figure 12.4. Use the D key along with Point
Snaps to place the bowl's pivot point on the top rim of the bowl, also shown in
Figure 12.4.

Figure 12.4

**It puts the sphere in
the basket, or else it
gets the hose again.**

The animation of the catapult arm is driven by a Bend deformer, so simply placing and grouping the bowl to the basket will not work. You will use a point on poly constraint to rivet the bowl to a vertex on the arm.

4. Select the vertex shown in Figure 12.5; then Shift+select the bowl object. In the Animation menu set, choose Constrain → Point On Poly. The bowl will snap to the arm, as shown in Figure 12.6.

Figure 12.5

Select the vertex.

5. Select the bowl and, in the Channel Box, click the pSphere2_pointOnPolyConstraint1 node. Set Offset Rotate Y to **-90** and Offset Rotate X to **8** to place the bowl in the basket better (Figure 12.7).

6. Go into the FX menu set. Select the projectile sphere and at frame 1 of the animation choose Fields/Solvers → Gravity. The ball will instantly become an active rigid body and will have a gravity attached. If you play back your scene, the ball will simply fall through the bowl and catapult.

Figure 12.6

The bowl snaps to the arm at a weird angle.

Figure 12.7

Set offsets to place the bowl properly in the basket.

7. Select the bowl object and choose Fields/Solvers → Create Passive Rigid Body to make the bowl a collision surface for the projectile ball. Play back your scene and *bam!* The projectile will bounce into the bowl as the catapult arm bends back, and the catapult will shoot the ball out, as shown in Figure 12.8.

8. Select the bowl object and press Ctrl+H to hide it. Now when you play back your scene, the ball looks like it rests inside the catapult basket. The scene file `catapult_dynamics_v1.mb` will catch you up to this point.

If you play back the scene frame by frame, you'll notice that the arm and basket will briefly pass through the projectile ball for a few frames as the arm shoots back up around frames 102–104. Increasing the subdivisions of the ball and the bowl before making them rigid bodies will help the collisions, but for a fun exercise, this works great. Play with the placement of the ball at the start of the scene, as well as the gravity and any other fields you care to experiment with, to try to land the projectile in different places in the scene.

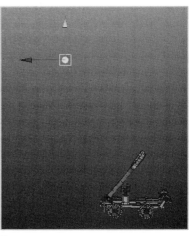

Baking Out a Simulation

Frequently, you create a dynamic simulation to fit into another scene, perhaps to interact with other

Figure 12.8
The ball shoots!

objects. In such cases, you want to exchange the dynamic properties of the dynamic body you have set up in a simulation for regular, old-fashioned animation curves that you can more easily edit. You can easily take a simulation that you've created and bake it out to curves. As much fun as it is to think of cupcakes, *baking* is a somewhat catchall term used to describe converting one type of action or procedure into another; in this case, you're baking dynamics into keyframes.

You'll take the simulation you set up earlier with the catapult and turn it into keyframes. Keep in mind that you can use this introduction as a foundation for your own explorations.

To bake out the rigid body simulation of the catapult projectile, follow these steps:

1. Open the scene file `catapult_dynamics_v1.mb` from the Catapult_Anim project on the web page, or if you prefer, open your own scene from the previous exercise.

2. Select the projectile ball (pSphere1) and choose Edit → Keys → Bake Simulation ❑. In the option box, shown in Figure 12.9, set Time Range to Time Slider (which should be set to 1 to 240). This, of course, sets the range you would like to bake into curves.

3. Set Hierarchy to Selected and set Channels to From Channel Box. This ensures you have control over which keys are created. Make sure Keep Unbaked Keys and Disable Implicit Control are checked and that Sparse Curve Bake is turned off. Before clicking the Bake or Apply button, select the Translate and Rotate channels in the Channel Box. Click Bake.

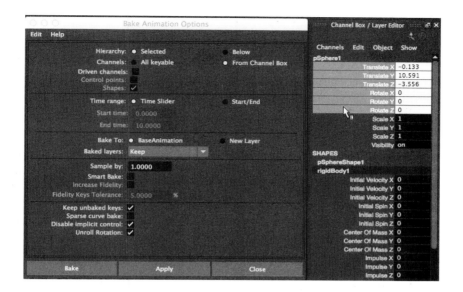

Figure 12.9

The Bake Simulation Options window

4. Maya runs through the simulation. Scrub the timeline back and forth. Notice how the projectile shoots as if the dynamic simulation were running—except that you can scrub in the timeline, which you can't do with a dynamics simulation. With the projectile selected, open the Graph Editor; you'll see something similar to Figure 12.10.

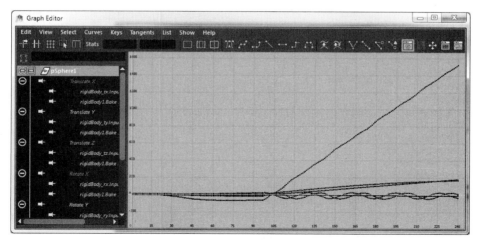

Figure 12.10

The projectile has animation curves.

The curves are crowded; they have keyframes at every frame. A typical dynamics bake gives results like this. But you can set the Bake command to sparse the curves for you; that is, it can take out keyframes at frames that have values within a certain tolerance so that a minor change in the ball's position or rotation need not have a keyframe on the curve.

5. Let's go back in time and try this again. Press Z (Undo) until you back up to right before you baked out the simulation to curves. You can also close this scene and reopen it from the original project, if necessary. This time, select the projectile sphere and choose Edit → Keys → Bake Simulation ❑. In the option box, turn on the Sparse Curve Bake setting and set Sample By to **5**. Select the Translate and Rotate channels in the Channel Box and click Bake.

Maya runs through the simulation again and bakes everything out to curves. This time it makes a sparser animation curve for each channel because it's setting keyframes only at five-frame intervals, as shown in Figure 12.11. If you open the Graph Editor, you'll notice that the curves are much friendlier to look at and edit.

Figure 12.11

Sampling by fives
makes a cleaner
curve.

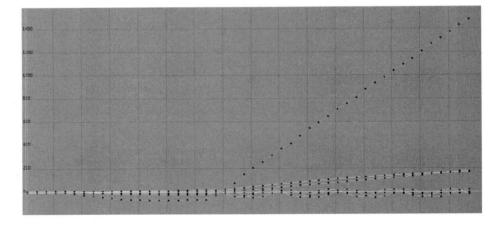

Sampling by fives may give you an easier curve to edit, but it may also oversimplify the animation of your objects; make sure you use the best Sampling setting for your simulation when you need to convert it to curves for editing.

Simplifying Animation Curves

Despite a higher Sampling setting when you bake out the simulation, you can still be left with a lot of keyframes to deal with, especially if you have to modify the animation extensively from here. One last trick you can use is to simplify the curve further through the Graph Editor. You have to work with curves of the same relative size, so you'll start with the rotation curves because they have larger values. To simplify the curve in the Graph Editor, follow these steps:

1. Select the projectile and open the Graph Editor. In the left Outliner side, select Rotate X, Rotate Y, and Rotate Z to display only these curves in the graph view. Figure 12.12 shows the curves.

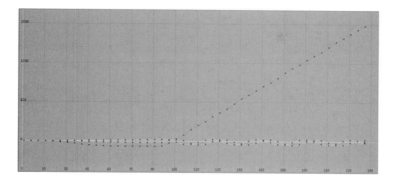

Figure 12.12

The Graph Editor displays the rotation curves of the projectile ball.

2. In the left panel of the Graph Editor, select the rigidBody_rx.Input[1], rigidBodyry.Input[1], and rigidBody rz.Input[1] nodes displayed under the Rotate X, Y, and Z entries for all three curves, as shown in Figure 12.13. In the Graph Editor menu, choose Curves → Simplify Curve □. In the option box, set Time Range to All, set Simplify Method to Classic, set Time Tolerance to **10**, and set Value Tolerance to **1.0**. These are fairly high values, but because you're dealing with rotation of the projectile, the degree values are high enough. For more intricate values such as Translation, you would use much lower tolerances when simplifying a curve.

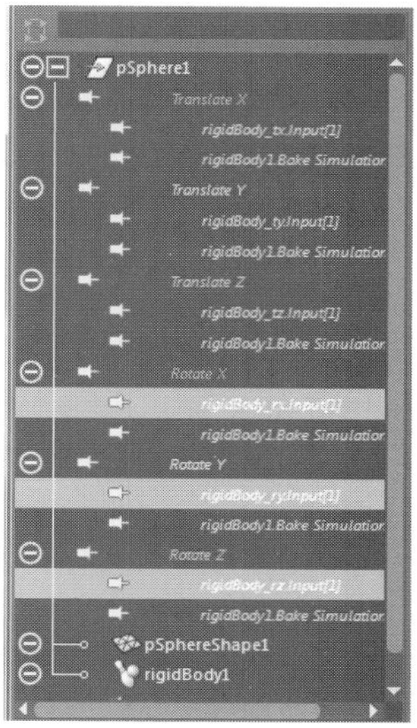

Figure 12.13

Select the curves to simplify them.

3. Click Simplify, and you see that the curves retain their basic shapes but lose some of their keyframes. Figure 12.14 shows the simplified curves, which differ perhaps a little from the original curve that had keys at every five frames.

Simplifying curves is a handy way to convert a dynamic simulation to curves. Keep in mind that you may lose fidelity to the original animation after you simplify a curve, so use this technique with care. The curve simplification works with good old-fashioned keyframed curves as well; if you inherit a scene from another animator and need to simplify the curves, do it just as you did here.

Figure 12.14

**A simplified curve
for the rotations of
the eight ball**

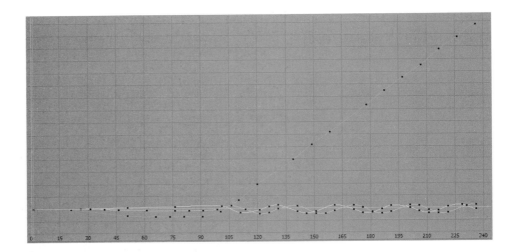

nParticle Dynamics

Like legacy rigid body objects, particles are moved dynamically using collisions and
fields. In short, a *particle* is a point in space that is given renderable properties—that is, it
can render out. When particles are used en masse, they can create effects such as smoke,
a swarm of insects, fireworks, and so on. nParticles implement particles through the
Maya Nucleus solver, which provides better and easier simulations than traditional Maya
particles.

Although nParticles can be an advanced and involved aspect of Maya, it's important to
have some exposure to them as you begin to learn Maya.

It's important to think of particle animation as manipulating a larger system rather
than as controlling every single particle. nParticles are most often used together in large
numbers so that the entirety is rendered out to create an effect. You control fields and
dynamic attributes to govern the motion of the system as a whole.

Emitting nParticles

A typical workflow for creating an nParticle effect in Maya breaks out into two parts:
motion and rendering. First, you create and define the behavior of particles through
emission. An *emitter* is a Maya object that creates the particles. After you create fields and
adjust particle behavior within a dynamic simulation, much as you would do with rigid
body motion, you give the particles renderable qualities to define how they look. This second aspect of the workflow defines how the particles come together to create the desired
effect, such as steam. You'll make a locomotive pump emit steam later in this chapter.

To create an nParticle system, follow these steps:

1. Make sure you're in the FX menu set, choose nParticles → Create Options, and select Cloud. Then choose nParticles → Create Emitter ☐. The option box gives you various creation options for the nParticle emitter, as shown in Figure 12.15.

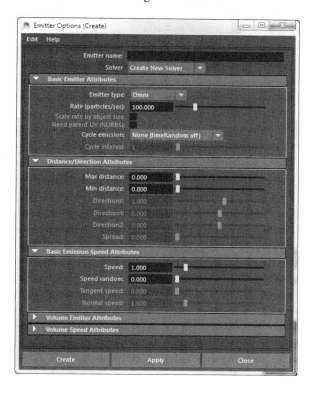

Figure 12.15

Creation options for an nParticle emitter

The default settings create an Omni emitter with a rate of 100 particles per second and a speed of 1.0. Click Create. A small round object (the emitter) appears at the origin.

2. Set your time range to 1–240 frames. Click the Play button to play the scene. As with rigid body dynamics, you must also play back the scene using the Play Every Frame option. You can't scrub or reverse-play particles unless you create a cache file. You'll learn how to create a particle disk cache later in this chapter.

You'll notice a mass of circles streaming out of the emitter in all directions (see Figure 12.16). These are the nParticles.

Figure 12.16

An Omni emitter emits a swarm of cloud particles in all directions.

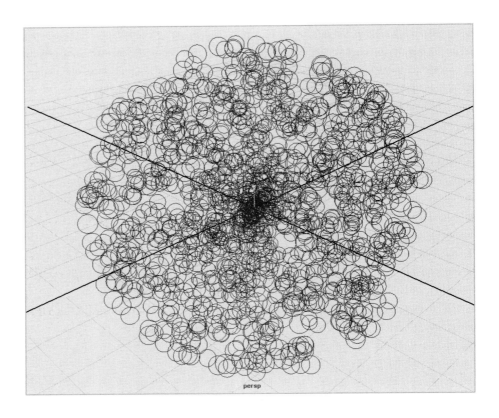

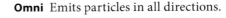

Figure 12.17

Cloud nParticles are sprayed in a specific direction.

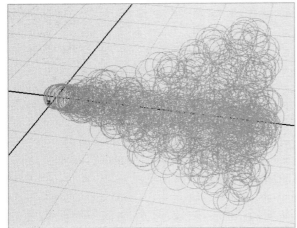

Emitter Attributes

You can control how particles are created and behave by changing the type of emitter and adjusting its attributes. Here are the most often used emitters:

Omni Emits particles in all directions.

Directional Emits a spray of particles in a specific direction, as shown in Figure 12.17.

Volume Emits particles from within a specified volume, as shown in Figure 12.18. The volume can be a cube, a sphere, a cylinder, a cone, or a torus. By default, the particles can leave the perimeter of the volume.

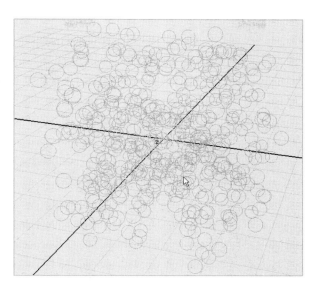

Figure 12.18

Cloud nParticles emit from anywhere inside the emitter's volume.

After you create an emitter, its attributes govern how the particles are released into the scene. Every emitter has the following attributes to control the emission:

Rate Governs how many particles are emitted per second.

Speed Specifies how fast the particles move out from the emitter.

Speed Random Randomizes the speed of the particles as they're emitted, for a more natural look.

Min and Max Distance Emits particles within an offset distance from the emitter. You enter values for the Min and Max Distance settings. Figure 12.19 shows a Directional emitter with Min Distance and Max Distance settings of 3.

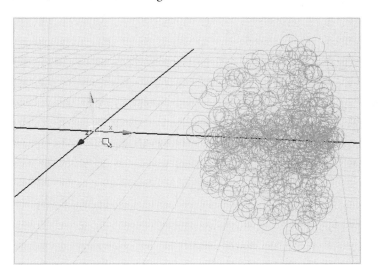

Figure 12.19

An emitter with Min Distance and Max Distance settings of 3 emits cloud nParticles 3 units from itself.

nParticle Attributes

After being created, or born, and set into motion by an emitter, nParticles rely on their own attributes and any fields or collisions in the scene to govern their motion, just like rigid body objects.

Figure 12.20

nParticle attributes

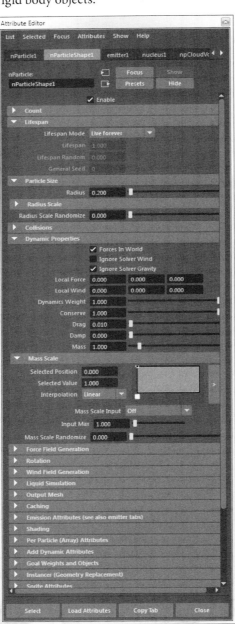

In Figure 12.20, the Attribute Editor shows a number of tabs for the selected particle object. nParticle1 is the particle object node. This has the familiar Translate, Rotate, and Scale attributes, like most other object nodes. But the shape node, nParticleShape1, is where all the important attributes are for a particle, and it's displayed by default when you select a particle object. The third tab in the Attribute Editor is the emitter1 node that belongs to the particle's emitter. This makes it easier to toggle back and forth to adjust emitter and particle settings.

The Lifespan Attributes

When any particle is born, you can give it a *lifespan*, which allows the particle to die when it reaches a certain point in time. As you'll see with the steam locomotive later in the chapter, a particle that has a lifespan can change over that lifespan. For example, a particle may start out as white and fade away at the end of its life. A lifespan also helps keep the total number of particles in a scene to a minimum, which helps the scene run more efficiently.

You use the Lifespan mode to select the type of lifespan for the nParticle.

Live Forever The particles in the scene can exist indefinitely.

Constant All particles die when their Lifespan value is reached. Lifespan is measured in seconds, so upon emission, a particle with a Lifespan of 1.0 will exist for 30 frames (in a scene set up at 30fps) before it disappears.

Random Range This type sets a lifespan in Constant mode but assigns a range value via the Lifespan Random attribute to allow some particles to live longer than others for a more natural effect.

LifespanPP Only This mode is used in conjunction with expressions that are programmed into the particle with Maya Embedded Language (MEL). Expressions are an advanced Maya concept and aren't used in this book.

The Shading Attributes

The Shading attributes determine how your particles look and how they will render. Two types of particle rendering are used in Maya: software and hardware. *Hardware particles* are typically rendered out separately from anything else in the scene and are then composited with the rest of the scene. Because of the compound workflow for hardware particles, this book will introduce you to a software particle type called *Cloud*. Cloud, like other *software particles*, can be rendered with the rest of a scene through the software renderer.

With your particles selected, open the Attribute Editor. In the Shading section, you'll find the Particle Render Type drop-down menu (see Figure 12.21).

The three render types listed with the (s/w) suffix are software-rendered particles. All the other types can be rendered only through the Maya Hardware renderer. Select your render type, and Maya adds the proper attributes you'll need for the render type you selected.

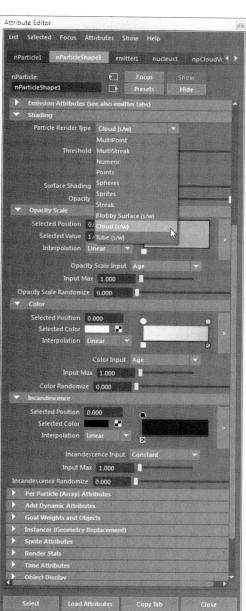

Figure 12.21

The Particle Render Type drop-down menu

For example, if you select the Points render type from the menu, your particles change from circles on the screen to dots, as shown in Figure 12.22.

Figure 12.22

Dots on the screen represent point particles.

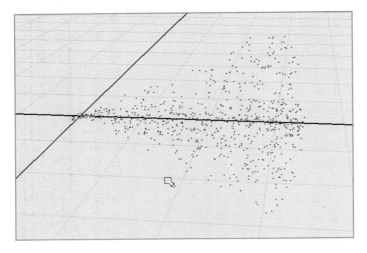

Several new attributes that control the look of the particles appear when you switch the Particle Render Type setting. Each Particle Render Type setting has its own set of render attributes. Set your nParticles back to the Cloud type. The Cloud particle type attributes are Threshold, Surface Shading, and Opacity. (See Figure 12.23.)

Figure 12.23

Each Particle Render Type setting displays its own set of attributes.

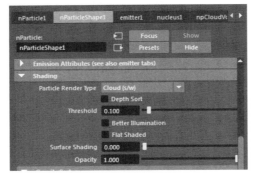

In the Shading heading for the cloud nParticles, shown in Figure 12.24, are controls for the Opacity Scale, Color, and Incandescence attributes. They control how the particles look when simulated and rendered. Notice how each of these controls is based on ramps.

nParticles are already set up to allow you to control the color, opacity, and incandescence during the life of the particle. For example, by default, the Color attribute is set up with a white to cyan ramp. This means that each of the particles will begin life white in color and will gradually turn cyan toward the end of its lifespan, or Age setting.

Likewise, the Particle Size heading in the Attribute Editor contains a ramp for Radius Scale that works much the same way as the Color attribute just described. In this case, you use the Radius Scale ramp to increase or decrease the size of the particle along its Age setting.

nCaching Particles

It would be nice to turn particles into money cash, but I can show you only how to turn your particles into a disk cache. You can cache the motion of your particles to memory or to disk to make playback and editing of your particle animation easier. To cache particles to your system's fast RAM memory, select the nParticle object you want to cache, and open the Attribute Editor. In the Caching section, under Memory Caching, select the Cache Data check box. Play back your scene, and the particles cache into your memory for faster playback. You can also scrub your timeline to see your particle animation. If you make changes to your animation, the scene won't reflect the changes until you delete the cache from memory by selecting the particle object and unchecking the Memory Cache check box in the Attribute Editor. The amount of information the memory cache can hold depends on your machine's RAM.

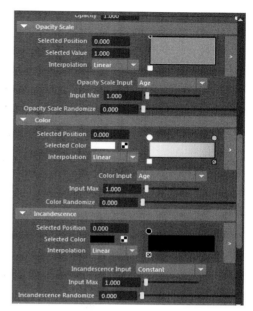

Figure 12.24

Controls for the Opacity Scale, Color, and Incandescence attributes

Although memory caching is generally faster than disk caching, creating a disk cache lets you cache all the particles as they exist throughout their duration in your scene and ensures that the particles are rendered correctly, especially if you're rendering on multiple computers or across a network. You usually create a particle disk cache before rendering.

> If you make changes to your particle simulation but you don't see the changes reflected when you play back the scene, make sure you've turned off any memory or deleted any disk cache from previous versions of the simulation.

Creating an nCache on Disk

After you've created a particle scene and you want to be able to scrub the timeline back and forth to see your particle motion and how it acts in the scene, you can create a particle nCache to disk. This lets you play back the entire scene as you like, without running the simulation from the start and by every frame.

To create an nCache, make sure to be in the FX menu set, select the nParticle object in your view panel or Outliner, and choose nCache → Create New Cache → nObject. Maya will run the simulation according to the timeline and save the position of all the particle systems in the scene to cache files in your current project's Data/Cache folder. You can then play or even scrub your animation back and forth, and the particles will run properly.

If you make any dynamics changes to the particles, such as emission rate or speed, you'll need to detach the cache file from the scene for the changes to take effect. Choose nCache → Delete Cache. You can open the option box to select whether you want to delete the cache files physically or merely detach them from the current nParticles.

Now that you understand the basics of particle dynamics, it's time to see for yourself how they work.

Animating a Particle Effect: Locomotive Steam

You'll create a spray of steam puffing out of a pump on the side of a locomotive that drives the wheels that you rigged previously. You'll use the scene fancy_locomotive_anim_v3.ma from Chapter 9, "More Animation!"

Emitting the nParticles

The first step is to create an emitter to spray from the steam pump and to set up the motion and behavior of the nParticles.

1. In the FX menu set, make sure nParticles → Create Options → Cloud is still checked and then choose nParticles → Create Emitter ❑. Make sure you select the first entry of Create Emitter in the menu under the Emit section, and not the second listing of Create Emitter under the Legacy Particles section of the menu at the bottom. Set Emitter Type to Directional and click Create. Place the emitter at the end of the pump, as shown in Figure 12.25.

2. To set up the emission in the proper direction, adjust the attributes of the emitter. In the Distance/Direction Attributes section, set Direction Y to **0**, Direction X to **0**, and Direction Z to **1**. This emits the particles straight out of the pump over the first large wheel and toward the back of the engine.

> The Direction attributes are relative. Entering a value of **1** for Direction X and a value of **2** for Direction Y makes the particles spray at twice the height (Y) of their lateral distance (X).

3. Play back your scene. The cloud nParticles emit in a straight line from the engine, as shown in Figure 12.26.

    You can load the file locomotive_steam_v1.ma from the Locomotive project on the web page to check your work.

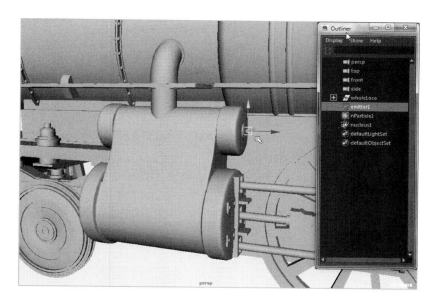

Figure 12.25

Place the emitter at the end of the pump.

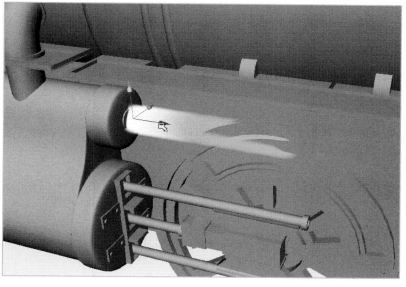

Figure 12.26

Cloud nParticles emit in a straight line from the pump.

4. To change the particle emission to more of a spray, adjust the Spread attribute for the emitter. Click the emitter1 tab in the particle's Attribute Editor (or select the emitter to focus the Attribute Editor on it instead) and change Spread from 0 to **0.30**. Figure 12.27 shows the new cloud spray.

> The Spread attribute sets the cone angle for a directional emission. A value of 0 results in a thin line of particles. A value of 1 emits particles in a 180-degree arc.

Figure 12.27

The emitter's Spread attribute widens the spray of particles.

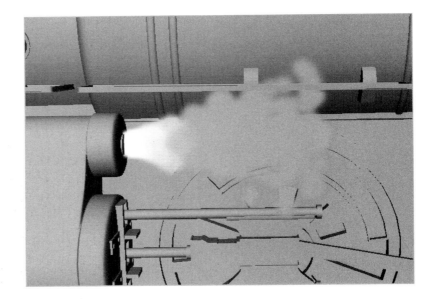

5. The emission is rather slow for hot steam being pumped out as the locomotive drives the wheels, so change the Speed setting for the emitter from 1 to **2.0** and change Speed Random from 0 to **1**. Doing so creates a random speed range between 1 and 3 for each particle. These two attributes are found in the emitter's Attribute Editor in the Basic Emission Speed Attributes section.

6. So that all the steam doesn't emit from the same point, keep the emitter's Min Distance at 0, but set its Max Distance to **0.3**. This creates a range of offset between 0 and 0.3 units for the particles to emit from, as shown in Figure 12.28.

Figure 12.28

A range of offset between 0 and 0.3 units creates a more believable emission.

Setting nParticle Attributes

It's always good to get the particles moving as closely to what you need as possible before you tend to their look. Now that you have the particles emitting properly from the steam pump, you'll adjust the nParticle attributes. Start by setting a lifespan for them and then add rendering attributes.

1. Select the nParticle object and open the Attribute Editor. In the Lifespan section, set Lifespan Mode to Random Range. Set Lifespan to **2** and Lifespan Random to **1**. This creates a range of 1 to 3 for each particle's lifespan. (This is based on a lifespan of 2, plus or minus a random value from 0 to 1.)

2. You can control the radius of the particles as they're emitted from the pump. Under the Particle Size heading in the Attribute Editor, set a Radius attribute of **0.50**. Set the Radius Scale Randomize attribute to **0.25**. This allows you to have particles that emit with a radius range between 0.25 and 0.75. Figure 12.29 shows the attributes.

3. If you play back the simulation, you'll see the particles are quite large initially. Because steam expands as it travels, you need to adjust the size (radius) of your nParticles to make them smaller at birth; they will grow larger over their lifespan and produce a good look for your steam.

4. In the Radius Scale heading in the Attribute Editor, click the arrow to the right of the ramp to open a larger view of the ramp, as shown in Figure 12.30.

5. Click and drag the ramp's first and only handle (an open circle at the upper-left corner of the Ramp window) down to a value of about 0.25, as shown in Figure 12.31. The particles get smaller as you adjust the ramp value.

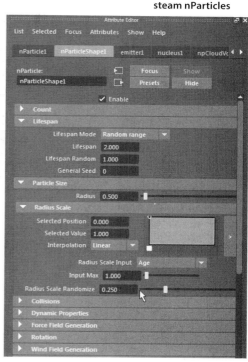

Figure 12.29

The initial radius settings for the steam nParticles

Click here.

Figure 12.30

Open the Radius Scale ramp.

Figure 12.31

**Decrease the radius
of the nParticles
using the Radius
Scale ramp.**

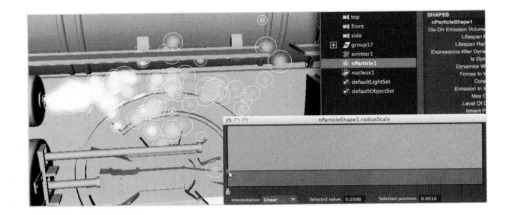

6. To allow the particles to grow in size, add a second handle to the scale curve by clicking anywhere on that line and drag to a value of 1.0 and the position shown in Figure 12.32. The particles toward the end of the spray get larger.

Figure 12.32

**Adjust the Radius
Scale ramp to grow
the particles.**

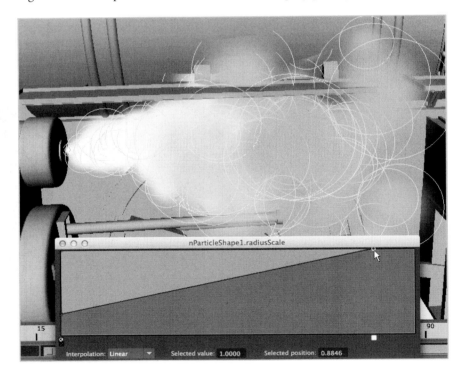

7. You can set up collisions so the nParticle steam doesn't travel right through the mesh of the locomotive. Select the meshes shown in Figure 12.33 and choose nCloth → Create Passive Collider.

8. In the Outliner, select the three nRigid nodes that were just created and set the Friction attribute in the Channel Box to **0.0** from the default of 0.10. Play back your scene, and your particles now collide with the surface of the locomotive. (See Figure 12.34.)

Figure 12.34

The particles now react nicely against the side of the locomotive.

If you want to check your work, download the file `locomotive_steam_v2.ma` from the Locomotive project on the web page.

Setting Rendering Attributes

After you define the nParticle movement to your liking, you can create the proper look for the nParticles. This means setting and adjusting their rendering parameters.

PARTICLE TYPE

Because Maya has several types of particles, the particles are set up according to their type; the workflow in this section applies only to the Cloud particle type.

1. Select the nParticle object and open the Attribute Editor. Expand the Shading heading and look at the Color ramp. By default, the particles go from white to light blue in color. Click the cyan color's circle handle on top of the ramp. The Selected Color attribute next to the ramp shows the cyan color. Click in the swatch to open the Color Chooser and change the color to a light gray.

2. Click the arrow bar to the right of the Opacity Scale ramp to open a larger ramp view. Grab the first handle in the upper-left corner and drag it down to a value of **0.12**.

3. The steam needs to be less opaque at its birth, grow more opaque toward the middle of its life, and fade completely away at the end of the particle's life. Click to create new handles to create a curve for the ramp, as shown in Figure 12.35. The values for the five ramp handles shown from left to right are 0.12, 0.30, 0.20, 0.08, and 0.

Figure 12.35

Creating an Opacity ramp for the steam

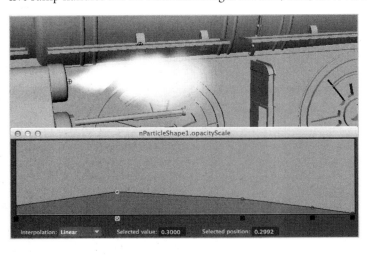

4. In the Render Settings window, set Image Size to **640×480**. On the Maya Software tab, set Quality to Intermediate Quality. Run the animation, and stop it when some steam has been emitted. Render a frame. It should look like Figure 12.36. The steam doesn't travel far enough along the engine; it disappears too soon.

Figure 12.36
**The steam seems
too short and small.**

With the steam nParticles selected, open the Attribute Editor; in the Radius Scale, under the Particle Size heading, change the first handle's value from 0.25 to **0.35** to make the steam particles a bit larger. Below the Opacity Scale ramp is the Input Max slider; set that value to **1.6**.

5. Select the emitter1 tab, and change the Spread value for the emitter to **0.2**. Change Rate (Particles/Sec) to **200** and Speed to **3.0**. Play back the simulation, and render a frame to compare to Figure 12.37.

Figure 12.37
**A better emission
but a bit too solid**

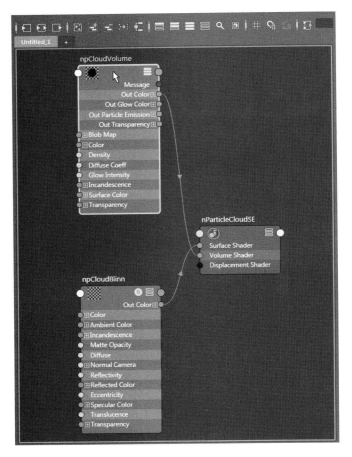

6. The Color ramp in the nParticle's Attribute Editor controls the color of the steam, and a shader is assigned to the particles. In the view panel, select the steam nParticle object and open the Hypershade window. In the Hypershade, click the Graph Materials On Selected Objects icon (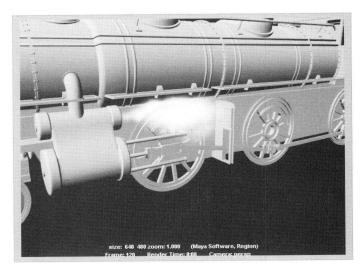) to show the particle's shader, as shown in Figure 12.38.

7. In the Hypershade, select the npCloudVolume shader. Notice in the Hypershade's Property Editor (or in the Attribute Editor) that the attributes in the Common Material Attributes section all have connections (they display this icon:). The ramp controls in the nParticle Attribute Editor are controlling the attributes in this Particle Cloud shader.

8. Under the Transparency heading in the Attribute Editor for the shader, set Density to **0.35**. Try a render; the steam should look better. (See Figure 12.39.)

Figure 12.38

The shaders assigned to the cloud nParticle

Figure 12.39

The steam is less flat and solid.

Batch-render a 200-frame sequence of the scene at a lower resolution, such as 320×240, to see how the particles look as they animate. (Check the frames with FCheck. Refer to Chapter 11, "Autodesk® Maya® Rendering," for more on FCheck.)

Open the file `locomotive_steam_v3.ma` from the Locomotive project on the web page to check your work.

Experiment with the steam by animating the Rate attribute of the emitter to make the steam pump out in time with the wheel arm. Also, try animating the Speed values and playing with different values in the Radius and Opacity ramps. The steam you'll get in this tutorial looks pretty good, but it isn't as lifelike as it could be. Particle animators are always learning new tricks and expanding their skills, and that comes from always trying new things and retrying the same effects with different methods.

When you feel comfortable with the steam exercise, try using the cloud nParticle to create steam for a mug of coffee. That steam moves much more slowly and is less defined than the blowing steam of the locomotive, and it should pose a new challenge. Also try your hand at creating a smoke trail for a rocket ship, a wafting stream of cigarette smoke, or even the billowing smoke coming from the engine's chimney.

Cloud nParticles are the perfect particle type with which to begin. As you feel more comfortable animating with clouds, experiment with the other render types. The more you experiment with all the types of nParticles, the easier they will be to harness.

Introduction to Paint Effects

One tool in the Maya effects arsenal, Paint Effects, lets you create results such as a field of grass rippling in the wind, a head of hair or feathers, or even a colorful aurora in the sky. Paint Effects is a rendering effect found in the Modeling menu set under the Generate menu. It has incredible dynamic properties that can make leaves rustle or trees sway in a storm. Paint Effects uses its own dynamics calculations to create natural motion. It's one of the most powerful tools in Maya, with features that go far beyond the scope of this introductory book. Here you'll learn how to create a Paint Effects scene and how to access all the preset brushes to create your own effects.

Paint Effects uses brushes to paint effects into your 3D scene. The brushes create strokes on a surface or in the Maya modeling views that produce tubes, which render out through the Maya Software renderer. These Paint Effects tubes have dynamic properties, which means they can move according to their own forces. Therefore, you can easily create a field of blowing grass.

Try This Create a field of blowing grass and flowers; it will take you all of five minutes.

1. Start with a new scene file. Maximize the perspective view. (Press the spacebar with the Perspective window active.)

2. Switch to the Modeling menu set (press F2). Choose Generate → Get Brush under the Paint Effects section of the menu to open the Visor window. The Visor window displays all the preset Paint Effects brushes that automatically create certain effects. Select the Grasses folder in the Visor's left panel to display the grass brushes available (see Figure 12.40). You can navigate the Visor window as you would navigate any other Maya window, using the Alt key and the mouse buttons.

Figure 12.40

The preset grass brushes in the Visor window

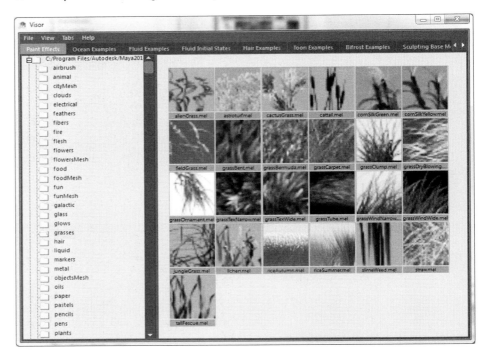

3. Click the grassWindWide.mel brush to activate the Paint Effects tool and set it to this grass brush. Your cursor changes to a Pencil icon.

4. In the Perspective window, click and drag two lines across the grid, as shown in Figure 12.41, to create two Paint Effects strokes of blowing grass. If you can't see the grass in your view panel, increase Global Scale in the Paint Effects Brush Settings in either the Attribute Editor or the Channel Box to see the grass being drawn onto the screen.

5. To change your brush so you can add some flowers between the grass, choose Generate → Get Brush and select the Flowers folder. Select the dandelion_Yellow.mel brush. Your Paint Effects tool is now set to paint yellow flowers.

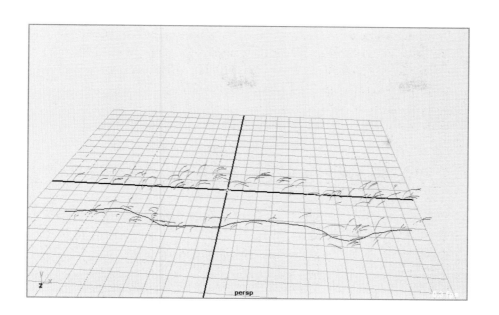

Figure 12.41

Click and drag two lines across the grid.

6. Click and drag a new stroke between the strokes of grass, as shown in Figure 12.42.

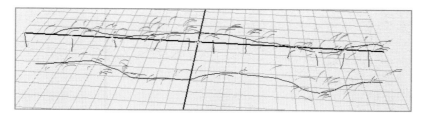

Figure 12.42

Add new strokes to add flowers to the grass.

7. Position your camera, and render a frame. Make sure you're using Maya Software and not mental ray® to render through the Render Settings window and that you use a large enough resolution, such as 640×480, so that you can see the details. Render out a 120-frame sequence to see how the grass animates in the wind. Figure 12.43 shows a scene filled with grass strokes as well as a number of different flowers.

After you create a Paint Effects stroke, you can edit the look and movement of the effect through the Attribute Editor. You'll notice, however, that there are a large number of attributes to edit with Paint Effects. The next section introduces the attributes that are most useful to the beginning Maya user.

Figure 12.43

Paint Effects can add flowers and grass to any scene.

Paint Effects Attributes

It's best to create a single stroke of Paint Effects in a blank scene and experiment with adjusting the various attributes to see how they affect the strokes. Select the stroke and open the Attribute Editor. Switch to the stroke's tab to access the attributes. For example, for an African Lily Paint Effects stroke, the Attribute Editor tab is called africanLily1.

Each Paint Effects stroke produces tubes that render to create the desired effect. Each tube (you can think of a tube as a stalk) can grow to have branches, twigs, leaves, flowers, and buds. Each section of a tube has its own controls to give you the greatest flexibility in creating your effect. As you experiment with Paint Effects, you'll begin to understand how each attribute contributes to the final look of the effect.

Here is a summary of some Paint Effects attributes:

Brush Profile Gives you control over how the tubes are generated from the stroke; this is done with the Brush Width attribute. This attribute makes tubes emit from a wider breadth from the stroke to cover more of an area.

Shading and Tube Shading Gives you access to the color controls for the tubes on a stroke.

Color 1 and Color 2 From bottom to top, graduates from Color 1 to Color 2 along the stalk only. The leaves and branches have their own color attributes, which you can display by choosing Tubes → Growth.

Incandescence 1 and 2 Adds a gradient self-illumination to the tubes.

Transparency 1 and 2 Adds a gradient transparency to each tube.

Hue/Sat/Value Rand Adds some randomness to the color of the tubes.

In the Tubes section, you'll find all the attributes to control the growth of the Paint Effects effect. In the Creation subsection, you can access the following:

Tubes Per Step Controls the number of tubes along the stroke. For example, this setting increases or decreases the number of flowers for the africanLily1 stroke.

Length Min/Max Controls the height of the tubes to make taller flowers or grass (or other effects).

Tube Width 1 and Width2 Controls the width of the tubes (the stalks of the flowers).

In the Growth subsection, you can access controls for branches, twigs, leaves, flowers, and buds for the Paint Effects strokes. Each attribute in these sections controls the number, size, and shape of those elements. Although not all strokes in Paint Effects create flowers, all strokes contain these headings.

The Behavior subsection contains the controls for the dynamic forces affecting the tubes in a Paint Effects stroke. Adjust these attributes if you want your flowers to blow more in the wind.

Paint Effects are rendered as a *postprocess*, which means they won't render in reflections or refractions as is and they will not render in mental ray without conversion to polygons. They're processed and rendered after every other object in the scene is rendered out in Maya Software rendering only.

To render Paint Effects in mental ray, you can convert Paint Effects to polygonal surfaces. They will then render in the scene along with any other objects so that they can take part in reflections and refractions. To convert a Paint Effects stroke to polygons, select the stroke and choose Modify → Convert → Paint Effects To Polygons. The polygon Paint Effects tubes can still be edited by most of the Paint Effects attributes mentioned so far; however, some, such as color, don't affect the poly tubes. Instead, the color information is converted into a shader that is assigned to the polygons. It's best to finalize your Paint Effects strokes before converting to polygons to avoid any confusion.

Paint Effects is a strong Maya tool, and you can use it to create complex effects such as a field of blowing flowers. A large number of controls to create a variety of effects come with that complexity. Fortunately, Maya comes with a generous sampling of preset brushes. Experiment with a few brushes and their attributes to see what kinds of effects and strange plants you can create.

Getting Started with nCloth

nCloth, part of the nucleus dynamics in Autodesk Maya, is a simple yet powerful way to create cloth simulations in your scene. From complex clothing on a moving character to a simple flag, nCloth dynamics can create stunning movement, albeit with some serious setup. I will briefly touch on the nCloth workflow here to give you a taste for it and familiarize you with the basics of getting started.

Making a Tablecloth

Switch to the FX menu set. The nCloth menu is where you need to start to drape a simple tablecloth on a round table in the following steps:

1. Create a flat disc with a poly cylinder to make the basic table. Set the Y scale to **0.175** and the X and Z scales to **5.25**. Set Subdivisions Axis to **36** for more segments to make the cylinder smoother.

2. Create a poly plane with a scale of **20** to be larger than the cylinder. Set both Subdivisions Width and Subdivisions Height to **40** for extra detail in the mesh. Place the square a few units above the cylinder, as shown in Figure 12.44.

Figure 12.44

Place a square plane above a flat cylinder.

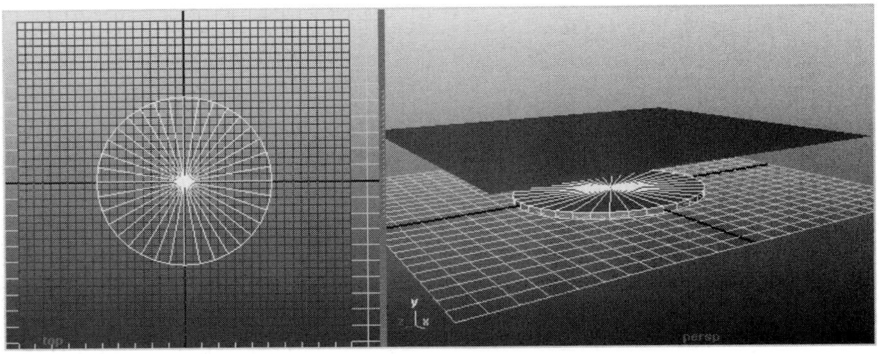

3. Now you'll set the plane to be a cloth object. Select the plane and choose nCloth → Create nCloth. The plane will turn purple, and a pair of new nodes is added to the scene: nucleus1 and nCloth1.

4. Set your frame range to **1-240** and click Play. The plane falls down and through the cylinder object. The nucleus engine has already set up the nCloth plane to have gravity.

5. Now let's define the cylinder as a collision object to make it the tabletop for the table-cloth. Select the cylinder and choose nCloth → Create Passive Collider. That's it! Click Play, and watch the cloth fall onto the table and take shape around it. (See Figure 12.45.)

Well, as easy as that was, there's a lot more to it to achieve the specific effect you may need. But you're on the road already. The first thing to understand is that the higher the resolution of the poly mesh, the better the look and movement of the cloth, at the cost of speed. At 40 subdivisions on the plane, the simulation runs pretty well, but you can see jagged areas of the tablecloth, so you would need to start with a much higher mesh for a smoother result.

Select the tablecloth and open the Attribute Editor. A wide range of attributes can be adjusted for different cloth settings; however, you can choose from a number of built-in presets to make life easier. In the Attribute Editor, choose Presets*, as shown in

Figure 12.46. Select Silk → Replace. As you can see, several Blend options appear in the submenu, allowing you to blend your current settings with the preset settings.

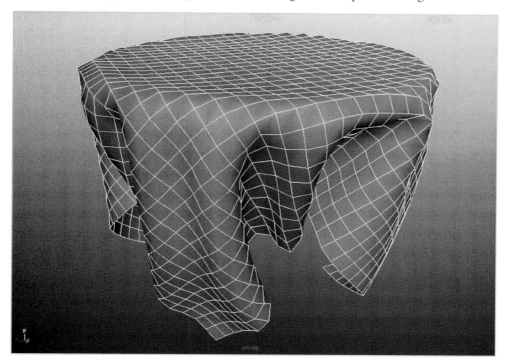

Figure 12.45

The cloth is working already!

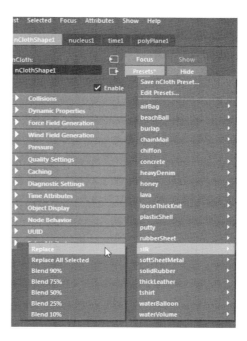

Figure 12.46

The built-in nCloth presets

In this case, you've chosen Replace to set the tablecloth object to simulate silk. It will be lighter and airier than before. Figure 12.47 (left) shows the tablecloth at frame 200 with the silk preset. Now, in the Attribute Editor, choose Presets → thickLeather → Replace for a heavier cloth simulation (Figure 12.47, right). Notice the playback for the heavy leather was slower as well.

Figure 12.47

The silk cloth simulation is lighter (left); the leather simulation is heavier and runs slower.

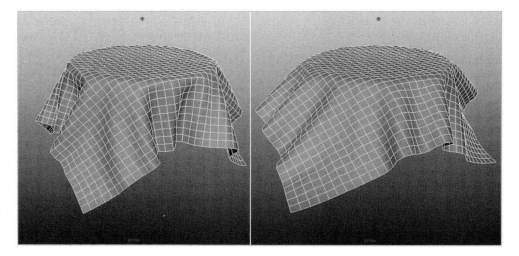

As a beginner to Maya, you may find it most helpful to go through the range of presets and see how the attributes for the nCloth change. Here is a preliminary rundown of some of the nCloth attributes found under the Dynamic Properties heading in the Attribute Editor. Try changing some of these values to see how your tablecloth reacts, and you'll gain a finer appreciation for the mechanics of nCloth.

Stretch Resistance Controls how easily the nCloth will stretch. The lower this value, the more rubbery and elastic the cloth will behave.

Bend Resistance Controls how well the mesh will bend in reaction to external dynamic forces and collisions. The higher this value, the stiffer the cloth.

Rigidity Sets the stiffness of the cloth object. Even a small value will have a stiffening impact on the simulation.

Input Mesh Attract Compels the cloth mesh to reassume its original shape before the cloth simulation, which in this case is a flat square plane. At a value of 1, the cloth may not move at all. Using some Input Mesh Attract will also give the cloth object a stiffer and more resilient/rubbery appearance.

Making a Flag

Now let's make a quick flag simulation to get familiar with nConstraints.

1. Make a rectangular polygon plane that is scaled to (20, 14, 14) and with subdivisions of **40** in width and height. Orient and place it above the home grid, as shown in Figure 12.48.

2. With the flag selected, choose nCloth → Create nCloth. Set your frame range to **1-240** and click Play. The flag falls straight down. You need to keep one end from falling to simulate the flag being attached to a pole.

3. Select the edge vertices on the left side of the flag, as shown in Figure 12.49, and choose nConstraint → Transform Constraint. The vertices you selected turn green, and a locator appears at the side of the flag. Now click Play, and the flag falls, while one end is tethered as if on a pole (see Figure 12.50).

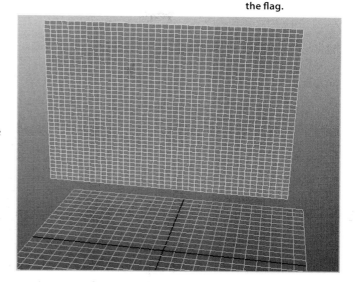

Figure 12.48
Create the mesh for the flag.

Select these vertices

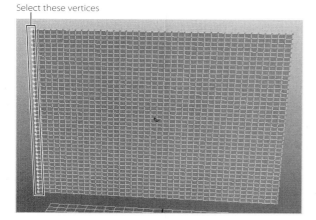

Figure 12.49
Select the vertices for the nConstraint.

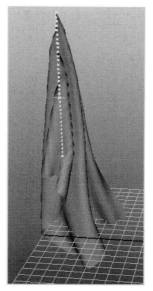

Figure 12.50
The flag is tethered to an imaginary pole now.

4. Now you'll add wind to make the flag wave. Select the flag and open the Attribute Editor. Click the nucleus1 tab, and under the Gravity and Wind heading, set the Wind Speed attribute to **16**. Figure 12.51 shows the flag flapping in the wind.

Adjust the Air Density, Wind Speed, Wind Direction, and Wind Noise attributes to adjust how the flag waves. You can use a similar workflow to create drapes blowing in an open window, for instance.

Caching an nCloth

Making a disk cache for a cloth simulation is important for better playback in your scene. Also, if you are rendering, it's always a good idea to cache your simulation to avoid any issues. Caching an nCloth is simple. Select the cloth object, such as the flag from the previous example, and in the main menu bar, choose nCache → Create New Cache → nObject ❐.

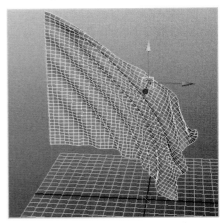

Figure 12.51
Wave the flag.

Figure 12.52 shows the options for the nCache. Here you can specify where the cache files are saved as well as the frame range for the cache. Once you create the cache, you will be able to scrub your playback back and forth.

Figure 12.52
Create nCache Options dialog box

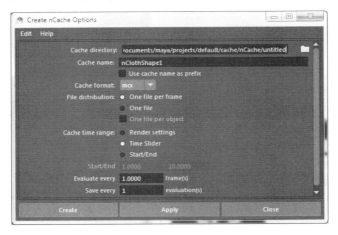

If you need to change your simulation, you must first remove the cache before changing nCloth or nucleus attributes. To do so, select the cloth object and choose nCache → Delete Cache ❐. In the option box, you can select whether you want to delete the cache files or just disconnect them from the nCloth object.

You can reattach an existing cache file by selecting the nCloth object and choosing nCache → Attach Cache. The existing cache must be from that object or one with the same topology.

Customizing Maya

One of the most endearing features of Maya is its almost infinite customizability. Everyone has different tastes, and everyone works in their own way. Simply put, for everything you can do in Maya, you have several ways of doing it. There are always a couple ways to access the Maya tools, features, and functions as well.

This flexibility may be confusing at first, but you'll discover that in the long run it's advantageous. The ability to customize enables the greatest flexibility in individual workflow.

It's best to use Maya at its defaults as you first learn. However, when you feel comfortable enough with your progress, you can use this section to change some of the interface elements in Maya to better suit how you like to work.

Figure 12.53

The Settings/Preferences menu

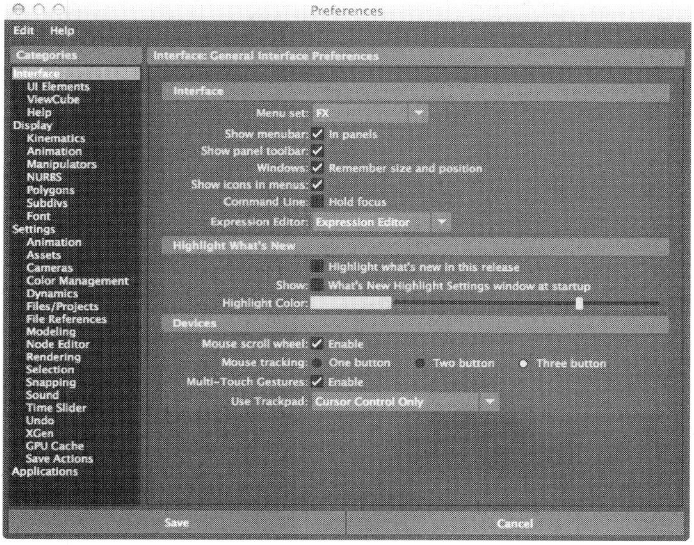

User Preferences

All the customization features are found under Windows → Settings/Preferences, which displays the window shown in Figure 12.53.

The Preferences window (see Figure 12.54) lets you make changes to the look of the program as well as to toolset defaults by selecting from the categories listed in the left pane of the window.

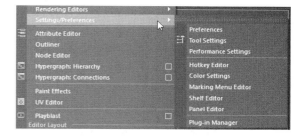

Figure 12.54

The Preferences window

The Preferences window is separated into categories that define different aspects of the program. Interface and Display deal with options to change the look of the program. Interface affects the main user interface, whereas Display affects how objects are displayed in the workspace.

The Settings category lets you change the default values of several tools and their general operation. An essential aspect of this category is Working Units; these options set the working parameters of your scene (in particular, the Time setting).

By adjusting the Time setting, you tell Maya your frame rate of animation. If you're working in film, you use a frame rate of 24 frames per second (fps). If you're working in NTSC video (the standard video/television format in the Americas), you use the frame rate of 30fps.

The Applications category lets you specify which applications you want Maya to start automatically when a function is called. For example, while looking at the Attribute Editor for a texture image, you can click a single button to open that image in your favorite image editor, which you specify here.

> In the Settings section, click the Undo header and set Undo Queue to Infinite. Doing so allows you to undo as many actions as have occurred since you loaded the file. This feature is unbelievably handy, especially when you're first learning Maya.

Figure 12.55
The Shelf Editor

Shelves

Under the Shelf Editor command (Windows → Settings/Preferences → Shelf Editor) lurks a window that manages your shelves (see Figure 12.55). You can create or delete shelves or manage the items on the Shelf with this function. This is handy when you create your own workflow for a project. Simply click the Shelves tab to display the icons on that Shelf in the Shelf Editor window. Click in the Shelf Contents section to edit the icons and where they reside on that selected Shelf. Clicking the Command tab gives you access to the MEL command for that icon when it is single-clicked in the Shelf. Click the Double Click Command tab for the MEL command for the icon when it is double-clicked in the Shelf.

You can also edit Shelf icons from within the UI without the Shelf Editor window. To add a menu command to the current Shelf, hold down Ctrl+Alt+Shift and click the function or command directly from its menu. Items from the Tool Box, pull-down menus, or the Script Editor can be added to any Shelf.

- To add an item from the Tool Box, MMB+drag its icon from the Tool Box into the appropriate Shelf.

- To add an item from a menu to the current Shelf, hold down the Ctrl+Alt+Shift keys while selecting the item from the menu.

- To add an item (a MEL command) from the Script Editor, highlight the text of the MEL command in the Script Editor and MMB+drag it onto the Shelf. A MEL icon will be created that will run the command when you click it.

- To remove an item from a Shelf, MMB+drag its icon to the Garbage Can icon at the end of the Shelf or use Windows → Settings/Preferences → Shelf Editor.

Hotkeys

Hotkeys are keyboard shortcuts that can access almost any Maya tool or command. You've already encountered a few in your exploration of the interface and in the solar system exercise in Chapter 2, "Jumping into Basic Animation Headfirst." What fun! You can create even more hotkeys, as well as reassign existing hotkeys, through the Hotkey Editor, shown in Figure 12.56 (Windows → Settings/Preferences → Hotkey Editor).

Figure 12.56

The Hotkey Editor

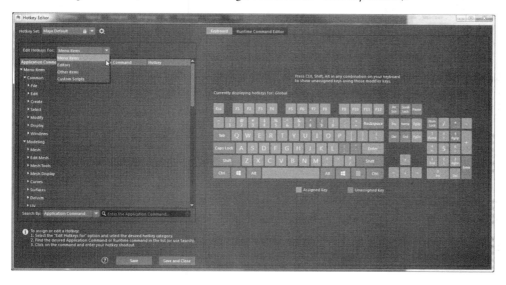

Through this monolith of a window, you can set a key combination to be used as a shortcut to virtually any command in Maya. This is the last customization you want to touch. Because so many tools have hotkeys assigned by default, it's important to get to know them first before you start changing things to suit how you work.

Every menu command is represented on the left of the window when you select menu items from the drop-down menu, as shown in Figure 12.56. Menu categories are on the left, and as you select each command, its current hotkey (if any) appears in the Hotkey column. Simply enter the key combination you want to assign to the selected command under the Hotkey column. The keyboard on the right side of the window simply shows the existing assigned keys; it's not used to assign keys.

Keep in mind that Maya is *case sensitive*, meaning that it differentiates between upper-case and lowercase letters. For example, one of my personal hotkeys is Ctrl+H to hide the selected object from view; pressing Shift+Ctrl+H unhides it.

> The important things to focus on right now are discovering how to use the tools to accomplish the tasks you need to perform and establishing a basic workflow. Toward that end, I strongly suggest learning Maya in its default configuration and using only the menu structure and default shelves to access all your commands at first, with the exception of the most basic hotkeys.

Color Settings

You can set the colors for almost any part of the interface to your liking through the Colors window shown in Figure 12.57 (Windows → Settings/Preferences → Color Settings).

The window is separated into different aspects of the Maya interface by headings. The 3D Views heading lets you change the color of all the panels' backgrounds. For example, color settings give you a chance to set the interface to complement your office's decor as well as make certain items easier to read.

Customizing Maya is important. However—and this can't be stressed enough—it's important to get your bearings with default Maya settings before you venture out and change hotkeys and such. When you're ready, this chapter will still be here for your reference.

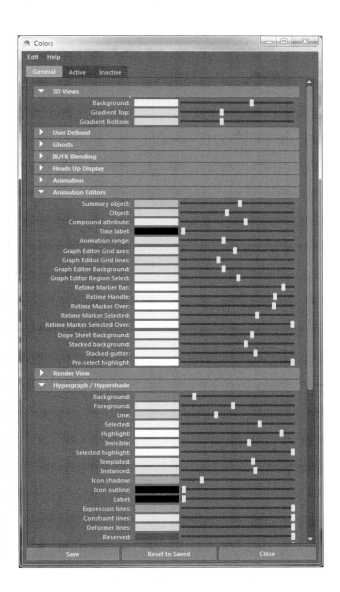

Figure 12.57

Changing the interface colors is simple.

Summary

In this chapter, you learned how to create dynamic objects and create simulations. Beginning with rigid body dynamics, you had a quick, fun exercise where you shot a projectile with the catapult, and then you learned how to bake that simulation into animation curves for fine-tuning. Next, you learned about particle effects by creating a steam effect for a locomotive using nParticles. Then, you learned a little about the Maya Paint Effects tool and how you can easily use it to create various effects such as grass and flowers. Then you learned how to create cloth effects using nCloth to make a tablecloth and a flag, and finally, you learned how to customize Maya to suit your own preferences.

To further your learning, try creating a scene on a grassy hillside with train tracks running through. Animate the locomotive, steam and all, driving through the scene and blowing the grass as it passes. You can also create a train whistle and a steam effect when the whistle blows, and you can create various other trails of smoke and steam as the locomotive drives through.

The best way to be exposed to Maya dynamics is simply to experiment once you're familiar with the general workflow in Maya. You'll find that the workflow in dynamics is more iterative than other Maya workflows because you're required to experiment frequently with different values to see how they affect the final simulation. With time, you'll develop a strong intuition, and you'll accomplish more complex simulations faster and with greater effect.

Where Do You Go from Here?

It's so hard to say goodbye! But this is really a "hello" to learning more about animation and 3D!

Please explore other resources and tutorials to expand your working knowledge of Maya. Several websites contain numerous tips, tricks, and tutorials for all aspects of Maya; my own resources and instructional videos and links are online at http://koosh3d.com/ and on Facebook at facebook.com/IntroMaya, and you can contact or follow me through Twitter at @Koosh3d.

Of course, www.autodesk.com/maya has a wide range of learning tools. Now that you've gained your all-important first exposure, you'll be better equipped to forge ahead confidently.

The most important thing you should have learned from this book is that proficiency and competence with Maya come with practice, but even more so from your own artistic exploration. Treat this text and your experience with its information as a formal introduction to a new language and way of working for yourself; doing so is imperative. The rest of it—the gorgeous still frames and eloquent animations—come with furthering your study of your own art, working diligently to achieve your vision, and having fun along the way. Enjoy, and good luck.

Index

Note to the Reader: Throughout this index **boldfaced** page numbers indicate primary discussions of a topic. *Italicized* page numbers indicate illustrations.

N

INTRODUCTION TO ECONOMIC REASONING

The Addison-Wesley Series in Economics

Abel/Bernanke
Macroeconomics

Berndt
The Practice of Econometrics

Bierman/Fernandez
Game Theory with Economic Applications

Binger/Hoffman
Microeconomics with Calculus

Boyer
Principles of Transportation Economics

Branson
Macroeconomic Theory and Policy

Browning/Zupan
Microeconomic Theory and Applications

Bruce
Public Finance and the American Economy

Burgess
The Economics of Regulation and Antitrust

Byrns/Stone
Economics

Carlton/Perloff
Modern Industrial Organization

Caves/Frankel/Jones
World Trade and Payments: An Introduction

Chapman
Environmental Economics: Introduction to Theory, Application, and Policy

Cooter/Ulen
Law and Economics

Eaton/Mishkin
Readings to accompany The Economics of Money, Banking, and Financial Markets

Ehrenberg/Smith
Modern Labor Economics

Ekelund/Tollison
Economics: Private Markets and Public Choice

Filer/Hamermesh/Rees
The Economics of Work and Pay

Fusfeld
The Age of the Economist

Gerber
International Economics

Ghiara
Learning Economics: A Practical Workbook

Gibson
International Finance

Gordon
Macroeconomics

Gregory
Essentials of Economics

Gregory/Ruffin
Economics

Gregory/Stuart
Russian and Soviet Economic Structure and Performance

Griffiths/Wall
Intermediate Microeconomics

Gros/Steinherr
Winds of Change: Economic Transition in Central and Eastern Europe

Hartwick/Olewiler
The Economics of Natural Resource Use

Hogendorn
Economic Development

Hoy/Livernois/McKenna/Rees/Stengos
Mathematics for Economics

Hubbard
Money, the Financial System, and the Economy

Hughes/Cain
American Economic History

Husted/Melvin
International Economics

Jehle/Reny
Advanced Microeconomic Theory

Klein
Mathematical Methods for Economics

Krugman/Obstfeld
International Economics: Theory and Policy

Laidler
The Demand for Money: Theories, Evidence, and Problems

Lesser/Dodds/Zerbe
Environmental Economics and Policy

Lipsey/Courant/Ragan
Economics

McCarty
Dollars and Sense

Melvin
International Money and Finance

Miller
Economics Today

Miller/Benjamin/North
The Economics of Public Issues

Miller/VanHoose
Essentials of Money, Banking, and Financial Markets

Mills/Hamilton
Urban Economics

Mishkin
The Economics of Money, Banking, and Financial Markets

Parkin
Economics

Parkin/Bade
Economics in Action Software

Perloff
Microeconomics

Phelps
Health Economics

Riddell/Shackelford/Stamos
Economics: A Tool for Critically Understanding Society

Ritter/Silber/Udell
Principles of Money, Banking, and Financial Markets

Rohlf
Introduction to Economic Reasoning

Ruffin/Gregory
Principles of Economics

Salvatore
Microeconomics

Sargent
Rational Expectations and Inflation

Scherer
Industry Structure, Strategy, and Public Policy

Schotter
Microeconomics

Sherman/Kolk
Business Cycles and Forecasting

Smith
Case Studies in Economic Development

Studenmund
Using Econometrics

Su
Economic Fluctuations and Forecasting

Tietenberg
Environmental and Natural Resource Economics

Tietenberg
Environmental Economics and Policy

Todaro
Economic Development

Waldman/Jensen
Industrial Organization: Theory and Practice

Zerbe/Dively/Lesser
Benefit-Cost Analysis

Introduction to Economic Reasoning

FOURTH EDITION

WILLIAM D. ROHLF, JR.
Drury College

ADDISON-WESLEY

An imprint of Addison Wesley Longman, Inc.

Reading, Massachusetts • Menlo Park, California • New York • Harlow, England
Don Mills, Ontario • Sydney • Mexico City • Madrid • Amsterdam

Executive Editor: Denise Clinton
Development Editor: Rebecca Ferris
Supplements Editor: Deb Kiernan
Production Supervisor: Heather Bingham
Project Coordination: Electronic Publishing Services Inc., NYC
Text Designer: Electronic Publishing Services Inc., NYC
Electronic Page Makeup: Electronic Publishing Services Inc., NYC
Cover Designer: Diana C. Coe/Regina Hagen
Marketing Manager: Jennifer Chapelle
Design Manager: Regina Hagen
Photo Researcher: Billie Porter

For permission to use copyrighted material, grateful acknowledgment is made to the copyright holders on p. 555, which are hereby made part of this copyright page.

Reprinted with corrections, December 1998

Library of Congress Cataloging-in-Publication Data

Rohlf, William D.
        Introduction to economic reasoning / William D. Rohlf, Jr. —4th
    ed.
            p.   cm.
        Includes index.
        ISBN 0-201-18558-X
        1. Economics, 2. United States—Economic conditions. I. Title.
    HB171.5.R73   1998
    330—dc21   98-15488
                                                                CIP

ISBN 0-201-18558-X
  2 3 4 5 6 7 8 9 10–CRW–02 01 00 99 98

To my parents, who helped me learn the value of persistence.

Preface

Almost one hundred years ago, Alfred Marshall defined economics as "the study of mankind in the ordinary business of life." Today, the ordinary business of life has become incredibly complex. The purpose of this textbook is to help prepare students for that life.

Introduction to Economic Reasoning is intended for students taking the one-term course in introductory economics. Many of these students, perhaps a majority, will take only one course in economics. They have a variety of interests and educational objectives. Some are enrolled in pre-professional programs; others will pursue majors in areas such as business, psychology, or the liberal arts. At a number of institutions, the one-term course also enrolls first-year students in MBA programs and other graduate business programs. Many of these students pursued nonbusiness majors as undergraduates and did not elect to take an economics course. Others desire to review economics before entering the graduate program. Although the students enrolling in the one-term course have diverse objectives and interests, they can all benefit from a course that prepares them to understand economic issues better and helps them to become better decision makers.

THE FOCUS OF THE BOOK

How do we prepare students to understand economic issues and help them become better decision makers? I am convinced that we cannot accomplish these objectives by focusing solely on economic issues and short-cutting a discussion of economic concepts. This approach might provide students with ready answers to existing problems, but it would do little to prepare students for coping with new social problems and little to refine their decision-making skills. To accomplish those objectives, we must teach students something about economic reasoning.

Economists are fond of saying that economics is a way of thinking, or a way of reasoning about problems. The essence of economic reasoning is the ability to use theories or models to make sense out of the real world and devise policy solutions to economic problems. If we want students to use economic reasoning, we have to help them to learn and understand the basic economic theories. Without an understanding of economic theory, a course in economics can leave the student with little more than memorized solutions to current economic problems.

THE NEED TO MAKE CHOICES

Obviously, we can't do everything in a one-term course in introductory economics. And unless we can keep the student's interest and show the relevance of economics, we can't accomplish anything. So the instructor in a one-term course (and the author of a one-term text) must make choices. He or she must decide what to include and what to exclude, how to balance theory with application, and how to motivate the students without sounding too much like a cheerleader. This textbook attempts to bridge these extremes.

Because economists use theories or models in problem solving, the core of this text is economic theory. No essential micro or macro concept is omitted. Many refinements are omitted, however, so that more time can be devoted to the careful development of the most important concepts. This is one of the distinctive features of the text: a very careful development of the core ideas in economic theory.

MAKING ECONOMICS RELEVANT

Today's student wants to know why he or she should be studying economics. What problems or issues will it help to clarify? What decisions will it help to improve? In *Introduction to Economic Reasoning,* the relevance of economics is illustrated by the use of examples in the text and through special features entitled "Use Your Economic Reasoning." These features, which are listed in a separate table of contents on pages xxv-xxvi, contain current news articles that have been carefully selected to illustrate the relevance of the economic principles being discussed and to provide the student with an opportunity to test his or her knowledge of those principles. Each article is accompanied by a set of questions to ensure that the student gains the maximum benefit from the article, and the features themselves have been designed to make them easy to locate.

WRITING STYLE

In writing this text, my overriding objective has been to make economics accessible to the average student. I have been careful to avoid unnecessarily sophisticated vocabulary and needlessly long sentences. Most important, I have worked to ensure that my explanations of economic concepts are carefully and clearly developed. While professors may adopt a text for a wide variety of reasons, I am convinced that the most common reason for discontinuing its use is because students can't understand it. Your students will be able to read this text and understand it.

AIDS IN LEARNING

In addition to a clear writing style, the text contains a number of other learning aids:

1. Learning objectives are stated at the beginning of each chapter.
2. New terms are presented in boldface italic type and are always defined when they are introduced.
3. "Use Your Economic Reasoning" news article selections not only generate student interest but also give the student an opportunity to apply the concepts that have been presented and thereby reinforce learning.
4. Careful summaries highlight the contents of each chapter.
5. A glossary of new terms appears at the end of each chapter so that a student can easily review definitions.
6. A study guide including fill-in-the-blank and multiple choice questions (with answers) and problems and questions for discussion appears at the end of each chapter. This increases the likelihood that the study guide will be used, and encourages the student to review the chapter to correct deficiencies.

ADDITIONAL FEATURES

1. The demand and supply model (the core of micro theory) is more fully developed than in other one-semester texts, and the student is given numerous opportunities to test his or her understanding of the model.
2. The organization of the text provides for maximum flexibility in use. Instructors can choose how detailed they want to make their coverage of a given topic.
3. Modern developments in macroeconomic theory, such as the theory of rational expectations, are presented in a manner that is accessible to the beginning student.
4. The student is exposed to important areas of debate among economists (the activist-nonactivist debate in macroeconomics, for example) without being left with the impression that economic analysis is solely a matter of opinion.

FOURTH EDITION CHANGES

The fourth edition contains an all-new Chapter 5, "Marginal Reasoning and Profit Maximization." This chapter is intended to more fully demonstrate the power of marginal reasoning to improve personal and business decision making. The chapter begins with numerous illustrations of the value of marginal reasoning in our personal lives, and then shows how the same principle can be applied in the business world. Introduced in Chapter 5, the marginal principle serves as the unifying theme throughout the remaining micro chapters.

Additional changes in the fourth edition include an expanded discussion of game theory, new coverage of economies and diseconomies of scale, and substantially revised coverage of fiscal policy. In addition, the macro chapters have been reorganized to provide instructors with enhanced flexibility. The aggregate demand-aggregate supply model now serves as the framework for all of the core macro chapters. Optional coverage of the Keynesian aggregate expenditures model is self-contained in Chapter 13, "An Alternative View: The Keynesian Total Expenditures Model." The fourth edition also contains almost thirty new "Use Your Economic Reasoning" selections drawn from such publications as the *Wall Street Journal, Business Week,* and the *New York Times.*

STRATEGIES FOR USING THE TEXT

Introduction to Economic Reasoning provides balanced coverage of microeconomics and macroeconomics. The book is divided into four parts. A two-chapter introduction (Part 1) examines the basic economic problem and economic systems. This is followed by seven chapters on microeconomics (Part 2), seven chapters on macroeconomics (Part 3), and two chapters on international economics (Part 4).

The chapters in the text are arranged in micro-macro sequence, but an instructor could easily reverse this order by covering Chapters 1, 2, and 3 and then moving directly to Part 3. The remaining micro chapters and Part 4 could then be covered in sequence.

If an instructor desires to shorten the micro portion of the course, numerous options exist. Chapter 4 ("The Elasticity of Demand and Supply") can be omitted with no loss of continuity. And the discussion of market models can be tailored to provide varying degrees of coverage. For instance, instructors who do not want to emphasize the marginal principle can omit Chapter 5 ("Marginal Reasoning and Profit Maximization"). Instructors desiring still briefer coverage of market models can also omit Chapter 8 ("Industry Structure and Public Policy"). An instructor following these suggestions would be left with the core of micro theory: the model of supply and demand, the distinction between price takers and price searchers, and a discussion of market failure.

The macro coverage can also be reduced. For instance, instructors may omit Chapter 11 ("Keynes and the Classical Economists...") and Chapter 16 ("The Modern Activist Nonactivist Debate..."). The remaining macro chapters will identify measures of aggregate performance, introduce students to the aggregate demand-aggregate supply model, and discuss fiscal and monetary policies. Alternatively, an instructor might choose to downplay the full development of the AD-AS model by covering Chapter 11 ("Keynes and the Classical Economists") instead of Chapter 12 ("Aggregate Demand and Supply...").

International economics is the last part of the book. This material has traditionally been the first to be omitted whenever an instructor found it necessary to shorten his or her course. Today, the growing importance of this subject matter may call for a different strategy. As a compromise course of action, an instructor might cover Chapter 16 ("International Trade") and omit Chapter 17 ("International Finance").

SUPPLEMENTARY MATERIALS

The instructor's manual that accompanies this book is intended to make the instructor's job easier. New instructors may benefit from the teaching tips provided for each chapter. The manual also contains answers to the "Use Your Economic Reasoning" questions and "Problems and Questions for Discussion." For the fourth edition, we have expanded the number of questions in the text bank. Transparency masters of all the text images are located in the back of the instructor's manual.

The test bank is also available in Test Generator Software (TestGen-EQ with QuizMaster-EQ for Windows). Fully networkable, this software is available for Windows and Macintosh. TestGen-EQ's friendly graphical interface enables instructors to easily view, edit, and add questions; transfer questions to tests; and print tests in a variety of fonts and forms. Search and sort features let the instructor quickly locate questions and arrange them in a preferred order. QuizMaster-EQ automatically grades the exams, stores results on disk, and allows the instructor to view or print a variety of reports.

To facilitate classroom presentation, PowerPoint slides of all the text images are available for Macintosh and Windows. A PowerPoint viewer is provided for use by those who do not have the full software program.

ACKNOWLEDGMENTS

One author is listed on the cover of this textbook, but there are many people who have helped in its preparation and to whom I owe my thanks.

First I would like to thank those who reviewed the fourth edition proposal and/or manuscript:

James Clark
Wichita State University

Abhay Ghiara
Devry Institute of Technology

Timothy Goodspeed
Hunter College

Andrew Hanssen
Montana State University

Barry Kotlove
Edmonds Community College

Muhammad Mustafa
South Carolina State University

Costas Nicolaou
University of Manitoba

Charles Roberts
Western Kentucky University

Geoffrey Schneider
Bucknell University

Joe Swaffar
Pima Community College

Douglas Walker
Louisiana State University

Maurice Weinrobe
Clark University

Donald Wells
University of Arizona

Michael White
St. Cloud State University

John Young
Riverside Community College

Their comments and suggestions have been immensely helpful to me and are reflected in the content of this revision.

As with the previous editions, I owe a particular debt of thanks to Steve Mullins, my colleague at Drury College. He was often called upon to help me interpret reviewer comments and decide between conflicting opinions. His good judgment and ready assistance have made a major difference in the quality of this edition.

I would also like to thank those with whom I have worked at Addison-Wesley: Denise Clinton, Rebecca Ferris, Sylvia Mallory, Deb Kiernan, Heather Bingham, and Mary Dyer. Their attention to detail and their personal encouragement have been very much appreciated.

Finally, I would like to thank my wife, Bev. Without her patience and support this edition would never have been completed.

W.D.R.
Springfield, MO

Brief Contents

Contents

Use Your Economic Reasoning News Articles

"Use Your Economic Reasoning" is a news article spread that builds critical thinking skills by illustrating and reinforcing the economic concepts of each chapter.

PART ONE

Introduction: Scarcity and the Economic System

Chapter 1 explains what the study of economics is about and how the knowledge you gain from this course may affect your thinking in many ways. Here you will be introduced to the concept of "opportunity cost"—one of the most important concepts in economics and in everyday living. You will learn about the role of economic theory in helping us make sense out of the things we observe in the world around us. In Chapter 2 you will discover what an economic system is and how economic systems differ from country to country.

With that introductory material behind you, you can begin exploring economics in more detail. Part 2 of the text examines microeconomics: the study of individual markets and individual business firms. Part 3 explores macroeconomics: the study of the economy as a whole and the factors that influence the economy's overall performance. Part 4 considers international economics: the study of economic exchanges between nations.

The Study of Economics

Beginning a subject you haven't explored before is something like starting out on a blind date: You always hope for the best but anticipate the worst. This time, be reassured. No course you take in college is likely to be more relevant to your future—whatever your interests—than this one. An understanding of economic principles is valuable because so many of the questions and decisions that touch our lives have an economic aspect. This is true whether you are evaluating something as personal as your decision to attend college or attempting to grapple with one of today's fundamental social issues: the debate about how to improve elementary and secondary education in the United States, for example, or how to provide adequate retirement incomes for older Americans without overburdening younger Americans, or the advisability of protecting U.S. businesses and workers from foreign competition. Each of these issues has important implications for your welfare and mine, yet they are just a few of the many complex questions that confront us as consumers, workers, and citizens. To understand and evaluate what economists, politicians, and others are saying about these issues, we need a knowledge of economics. Then we can do a better job of separating the "sense" from the "nonsense" and forming intelligent opinions.

Obviously you won't learn all there is to know about economics from one short textbook. But here is your opportunity to build a solid understanding of basic economic principles and discover how economists interpret data and analyze economic problems. That is especially important because economics is as much a way of reasoning as it is a body of knowledge. Once you have learned what it means to "consider the opportunity costs," to "compare the costs and benefits," and to "think marginally," nothing will ever look quite the same again. You'll find yourself making better decisions about everything from how to use your time more effectively to whom to support in the next presidential election. Watching the TV news and reading newspapers and magazines will become more meaningful and enjoyable. You will begin to notice the economic dimension of virtually every problem confronting society—pollution, crime, health care, higher education, and so on. Your knowledge of economics will help you understand and deal better with all these problems.

The Economic Problem

The fundamental economic problem facing individuals and societies alike is the fact that our wants exceed our capacity for satisfying those wants. Consider, for example, one of your personal economic problems: how to use your limited income—your limited financial resources. With the possible exception of the very rich, none of us can afford to buy everything we'd like to have. Each of us can think of a virtually limitless number of products we want or "need": food, shelter, clothing, membership at a health club, new tires for the car, a personal computer. Economist and social critic John Kenneth Galbraith has suggested that the satisfaction of a want through the purchase of a product not only fails to reduce our wants but in fact creates new ones. Purchase an audio system, for instance, and soon you will want compact discs, headphones, storage cabinets, and the like.

Societies face essentially the same dilemma: The wants of their members exceed the societies' capacities for satisfying those wants. In order to satisfy human wants, societies or nations require the use of **economic resources,** the scarce inputs that are used in the process of creating a good or providing a service. Traditionally economists divide these resources into four categories: land, labor, capital, and entrepreneurship. **Land** signifies more than earth or acreage; it includes all raw materials—timber, water, minerals, and other production inputs—that are created by nature. **Labor** denotes the work—

both physical and mental—that goes into the production process. **Capital** refers to human-made aids to production, such as factories, machinery, and tools. **Entrepreneurship** is the managerial function that combines all these economic resources in an effective way and uncovers new opportunities to earn a profit—for example, through new products or processes. Entrepreneurship is characterized by a willingness to take the risks associated with a business venture.

Every society's stock of economic resources is limited, or *scarce*, in relation to the infinite wants of its members. At any given time, even the world's richest economies have available only so much raw material, labor, equipment, and managerial talent to use in producing goods and services. Consequently, an economy's ability to produce goods and services is limited, just as an individual's ability to satisfy his or her personal wants is limited.

The inability to satisfy all our wants forces us to make choices about how we can best use our limited resources. That is what economics is all about: making wise choices about how to use scarce resources. Therefore, we define **economics** as the study of how to use our limited resources to satisfy our unlimited wants as fully as possible. When individuals, businesses, or nations try to make the most of what they have, they are "economizing."

Cost-Benefit Analysis and Opportunity Cost

In order to make wise choices, we must compare the costs and benefits associated with each alternative or option we consider. A particular decision or choice will improve our well-being only if the benefits associated with that decision exceed the costs, if what we gain is worth more to us than what we lose. Individuals, businesses, and even governments engage in **cost-benefit analysis**—a systematic comparison of costs and benefits—before deciding on a course of action.

Comparing costs and benefits probably seems like a relatively straightforward process. Sometimes that's the case, but not always. In some instances, the costs and benefits may be very subjective and hard to compare. In other instances, there may be hidden costs or benefits that are easily ignored.

One of the fundamental lessons of economics is that all our choices entail costs: There is no "free lunch." Whenever you make a decision to do or have one thing, you sacrifice the opportunity to do or have some other thing. The best, or *most valued*, alternative you must sacrifice in order to take a particular action is the **opportunity cost** of that action. What opportunity are you sacrificing by reading this chapter? Perhaps you could be studying for another class or watching your favorite TV show. The opportunity cost of reading this chapter is whatever you wanted to do most. When your city council or town meeting allocates tax dollars to install sidewalks, it may sacrifice books for the public library, streetlights for a residential area, or tennis courts for a local park. Whatever that body would have chosen to do if it hadn't installed sidewalks is the opportunity cost of the sidewalks.

When Congress debates the size of the defense budget, the outcome of that debate affects each of us. If a nation's resources are fully employed, an increase in the output of military goods and services requires a reduction in the output of something else. An increase in military spending may mean a cut in funding for job training, road construction, or aid to education; it may mean an increase in taxes which, in turn, will lead to a reduction in private consumer spending and the output of consumer goods.

Either way, more military output means less civilian output because, at any given time, there is a limit to the amount of total output the economy can produce. This doesn't necessarily mean that we shouldn't spend more on military goods if there are sound reasons for doing so. It does mean that we should be aware of what that spending costs us in terms of private goods and services or other government programs. The economist's point here is that we can't make the best decisions about how to use our scarce resources unless we know the true costs and benefits of our decisions. (See "Army Recruiting Is Hurt by Economy," on page 8, to learn why fewer high school students are deciding that the benefits of joining the Army outweigh the costs.)

The Production Possibilities Curve

We can illustrate the concept of opportunity cost with a simple graph called a production possibilities curve. (The appendix at the end of this chapter explains how graphs are constructed and interpreted.) A **production possibilities curve** shows the combinations of goods that the economy is capable of producing with its present stock of economic resources and its existing techniques of production. Because it outlines the boundaries, or limits, of the economy's ability to produce output, it is sometimes called a *production possibilities frontier*. Any point along or inside the frontier represents a combination of goods that the economy can produce; any point above the curve is beyond the economy's present production capacity.

Exhibit 1.1 shows the production capabilities of a hypothetical economy. The economy's output of civilian goods is measured on the vertical axis and

EXHIBIT 1.1

The Production Possibilities Curve

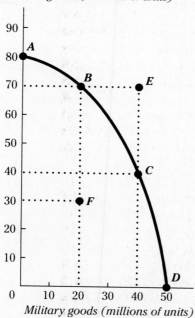

Civilian goods (millions of units)

Military goods (millions of units)

The production possibilities curve, *ABCD*, shows the combinations of civilian goods and military goods that the economy is capable of producing with its present stock of economic resources and the existing techniques of production. Any point on or below the curve is possible. Any point above the curve is ruled out (impossible).

its output of military goods on the horizontal axis. According to this exhibit, if all the economy's resources were used to produce civilian goods, 80 million units of civilian goods could be produced each year (point *A*). On the other hand, if the economy were to use all its economic resources to produce military goods, 50 million units of military goods could be produced each year (point *D*). Between these extremes lie other production possibilities—combined outputs of military and civilian goods that the economy is capable of producing. For example, the economy might choose to produce 70 million units of civilian goods and 20 million units of military goods (point *B*). Or it might choose to produce 40 million units of civilian goods and 40 million units of military goods (point *C*). We can see, then, that the curve *ABCD* outlines the boundaries of our hypothetical economy's production abilities. Point *E*, which lies above the curve, represents a combination of products that is beyond the economy's present capacity.

Use Your Economic Reasoning

Army Recruiting Is Hurt By Economy

Number of New Enlistees Could Fall Short of Goal

By Thomas E. Ricks
Staff Reporter of the Wall Street Journal

WASHINGTON—The strongest economy in the history of the all-volunteer military is hurting the Army's recruiting efforts and could result in the service falling short of its enlistment goal for the first time since 1979.

The current goal for enlistees in the federal fiscal year ending Sept. 30 is 89,700, and officially the Army hasn't given up on coming close. But some Army officers predict they'll fail to meet that target by at least 4,000 people, and perhaps by 10,000. Indeed, Army insiders say re-

cruiters may be lucky to fill just half of September's unusually large quota of 12,000.

This year's recruitment goal has risen following recent cutbacks designed to bring total manpower down to 495,000. Now that the Army has reached that planned figure, officials find they need a bigger inflow of young people to maintain that level.

Underscoring the problem, the shortfall comes even though the Army has increased enlistment bonuses and lowered its standards. New recruits can receive up to $12,000 in cash bonuses (compared with a previous $8,000 ceiling), while only about 92% of them now have high school diplomas, down

from about 95% last fiscal year. "Fiscal year 1997 is a very challenging recruiting year," the Army Recruiting Command said in a statement in response to a query from this newspaper. This recruiting shortfall hadn't been previously disclosed.

The Army and the other armed services have relied on recruiting volunteers since 1973, when the draft was ended. That's also the last time the unemployment rate was as low as it is now—about 4.8%. Labor economists said it's not surprising that the strong economy is causing problems for the Army. "Recruitment to the military is particularly sensitive to three things," said Harvard's

Unfortunately, economies do not always live up to their production capabilities. Whenever an economy is operating at a point inside its production possibilities curve, we know that economic resources are not being fully employed. For example, at point *F* in Exh. 1.1, our hypothetical economy is producing 30 million units of civilian goods and 20 million units of military goods each year. But according to the production possibilities curve, the economy could do much better. For example, it could increase its output of civilian goods to 70 million units a year without sacrificing any military goods (point *B*). Or it could expand its output of civilian goods to 40 million units while also expanding its production of military goods to 40 million

Lawrence Katz, "the state of the civilian economy, compensation in the military and the educational benefits" offered to veterans. The Army problems have arisen even though recruits are now eligible for up to $40,000 in college education benefits, a $10,000 increase from last year.

Surprisingly, recruits say their efforts haven't been hampered by the Army's sexual-abuse scandal at its base at Aberdeen, MD. In fact, woman are continuing to enlist at about the same proportion—roughly 20%—as before that scandal broke. Rather, recruiters say they get the cold shoulder from all groups of potential soldiers. "It's rough across the board," said Sgt. First Class Henri Nance, an Army recruiter in Baltimore. "I think it's the economy...."

Adding to the Army's problem, observed Alan Krueger, a labor economist at Princeton University, is that college enrollments are increasing nowadays. Because the economic

payoff for having a college degree is at an all-time high, he said, "The right strategy for most individuals in that cohort (of 18- to 21-year-olds) would be to go to college...."

Alarms aren't ringing yet at the Army, primarily because more soldiers than expected are staying in the

service, said Col. John Warren, an Army reenlistment manager. However, Sgt. First Class Terry Graves, an Army recruiter in New York City, said "pickings are getting slimmer" because he can no longer enlist high school dropouts, while those who do graduate increasingly go to college.

USE YOUR ECONOMIC REASONING

1. What is the opportunity cost of joining the Army?
2. Is the opportunity cost of joining the Army higher when the economy is strong (and the unemployment rate is low) or when the economy is weak (and the unemployment rate is high)? Defend your answer.
3. According to Lawrence Katz, "Recruitment to the military is particularly sensitive to three things." List the three factors and

explain how each of them influences the cost-benefit comparison by which individuals decide whether to join the Army.
4. How would you explain the increase in the Army's recruitment problems, given that it now provides larger enlistment bonuses and more college education benefits than a year ago? (Hint: Use the cost-benefit framework to answer this question.)

units (point C). In short, when an economy has unemployed resources, it is not satisfying as many of the society's unlimited wants as it could if it used its full potential.

OPPORTUNITY COSTS ALONG THE CURVE

We have seen that the production possibilities curve graphically represents the concept of opportunity cost. When an economy's resources are fully employed—that is, when an economy is operating on the production possibilities curve rather than inside it—larger amounts of one product can be obtained only by producing smaller amounts of the other product. The production possibilities curve slopes downward to the right to illustrate opportunity cost: More of one thing means less of the other thing. We can see opportunity costs changing as we move from one point on the production possibilities curve to another. For example, suppose that the society is operating at point *A* on the production possibilities curve in Exh. 1.1, producing 80 million units of civilian goods and no military goods. If the society decides that it would prefer to operate at point *B*, the opportunity cost of acquiring the first 20 million units of military goods would be the loss of 10 million units of civilian goods. The economy can move from point *A* to point *B* only by transferring resources from the production of civilian goods to the production of military goods.

Suppose that the society would like to have even more military goods— for example, 40 million units of military goods produced each year. According to the production possibilities curve, the opportunity cost of acquiring the next 20 million units of military goods (and moving from point *B* to point *C*) would be a loss of 30 million units of civilian goods—three times what it cost the society to acquire the first 20 million units of military goods. Moving from point *C* to point *D* would be even more expensive. In order to acquire the last 10 million units of military goods, the society would have to sacrifice 40 million units of civilian goods.

THE LAW OF INCREASING COSTS

Our hypothetical production possibilities curve illustrates an important principle known as the **law of increasing costs:** As more of a particular product is produced, its opportunity cost per unit will increase. How do we explain the law of increasing costs? Why does our hypothetical society have to sacrifice larger and larger amounts of civilian output in order to obtain each additional increment of military output?

The explanation is fairly simple. Not all resources are alike; some economic resources—skilled labor and specialized machinery, for instance— are better suited to the production of one product than another. In our example some resources are better suited to the production of civilian goods and services, others to the production of military products. Consequently when the society attempts to expand its output of military goods and services, it must eventually use resources that are not well suited to producing those military products.

To illustrate that problem, let's examine the process of transferring resources from the production of civilian products to the production of military products. Suppose that initially our hypothetical economy is not producing any military output. At first, it will not be difficult for the economy to increase its military output. Some of the existing capital resources, including factories, can be converted to the production of military products with relative ease, and many members of the labor force will have skills that are readily transferable to the production of military products. For example, it would be fairly simple to convert a clothing factory to the production of uniforms or to convert an awning factory to the production of tents. Since these conversions are relatively easy, the society will gain just about as much in military output as it will lose in civilian output.

But to continue expanding the output of military products, it will be necessary to use resources that are increasingly less suitable. For instance, consider the difficulty that might be encountered in converting an amusement park to a missile-manufacturing facility, or a toy factory to an explosives plant. Much of the equipment that was useful in producing civilian output will be of no use in producing military output. Therefore, although the conversion of these facilities will require society to give up a large quantity of civilian output (many rides at the amusement park and thousands of toys), it will not result in very many additional units of military output.

The point is that because some resources are better suited to the production of civilian goods than to the production of military products, increasing amounts of civilian goods and services will have to be sacrificed to obtain each additional increment of military output. It is this principle (the law of increasing costs) that causes the production possibilities frontier to have the curved shape depicted in Exhs. 1.1 and 1.2.

ECONOMIC GROWTH AND THE BENEFITS OF TRADE

As we have seen, it is important for economies to operate on, rather than inside, their production possibilities curves. But even when an economy fully employs its resources, it cannot satisfy all of a society's wants. Any point *above* the production possibilities frontier exceeds the economy's current production capabilities. For instance, point *E* in Exh. 1.2, which combines 70 million units of civilian goods and 40 million units of military goods, is beyond the inside production possibilities curve representing the existing capacity of this hypothetical economy. Society clearly would prefer that combination of products to the combination represented by, say, point *C*, but it can't obtain it.

Of course, the economy's production capacity is not permanently fixed. If the quantity of economic resources were to increase or if better production methods were discovered, the economy could produce more goods and services. Such an increase in production capacity is usually described as *economic growth* and is illustrated by shifting the production possibilities

EXHIBIT 1.2

Illustrating Economic Growth

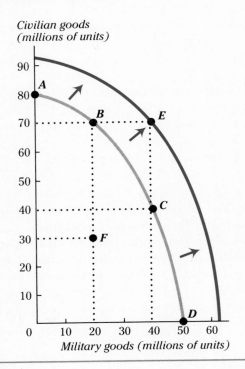

If the quantity of economic resources were to increase or better production methods were discovered, the economy's ability to produce goods and services would expand. Such economic growth can be illustrated by shifting the production possibilities curve to the right.

curve to the right. The outside curve in Exh. 1.2 represents economic growth sufficient to take point *E* within the economy's production possibilities frontier.

Trade between nations can provide benefits that are very similar to those that result from economic growth—increased amounts of goods and services. To illustrate, suppose that our hypothetical economy is operating at point *A* on the inside production possibilities curve in Exh. 1.2, producing 80 units of civilian goods and no military goods. According to the production possibilities curve, the economy could acquire 40 million units of military goods (and move to point *C*) only if it was willing to give up 40 million units of civilian goods; the cost of acquiring each additional unit of military goods would be the sacrifice of one unit of civilian goods. But suppose that through trade with other nations, this economy could acquire a unit of military goods by sacrificing only one-fourth of a unit of civilian

Like economic growth, free trade can increase the goods and services available for consumption.

goods. That would permit the economy to acquire the 40 million units of military goods it desires by giving up (trading) only 10 million units of civilian goods. The economy could move to point *E,* a point well beyond its own production capabilities.[1]

The ability to acquire goods at a lower opportunity cost (and thereby increase the total amount of goods and services available for consumption) is why **free trade**—trade that is not hindered by artificial restrictions or trade barriers—is generally supported by economists. Chapter 17 explores the theoretical basis for trade in much greater detail.

As you can see, the production possibilities curve is a useful tool for thinking about our economy. It shows that an economy with fully employed resources cannot produce more of one thing without sacrificing something else. Equally important, the production possibilities model can be used to illustrate the benefits of economic growth and free trade. Of course, neither economic growth nor free trade eliminates the need to make choices about how to use our scarce resources. The next section explores the nature of those choices in more detail.

---

[1] Unlike economic growth, trade does not shift an economy's production possibilities curve but instead merely permits a nation to consume a combination of products beyond its own production capabilities.

The Three Fundamental Questions

The choice between military goods and civilian goods is only one of the broad decisions that the United States and other nations face. The dilemma of unlimited wants and limited economic resources forces each society to make three basic choices, to answer the "three fundamental questions" of economics: (1) What goods and services will we produce and in what quantities? (2) How will these goods and services be produced? (3) For whom will these products be produced—that is, how will the output be distributed?

WHAT TO PRODUCE

Because no society can produce everything its members desire, each society must sort through and assess its various wants and then decide which goods and services to produce in what quantities. Deciding the relative value of military products against civilian goods is only one part of the picture, because each society must determine precisely which civilian and military products it will produce. For example, it must decide whether to produce clothing or to conserve its scarce resources for some other use. Next, it must decide what types of clothing to produce—how many shirts, dresses, pairs of slacks, overcoats, and so on. Finally, it must decide in what sizes to produce these items of clothing and determine the quantities of each size. Only after considering all such alternatives can a society decide which goods and services to produce.

HOW TO PRODUCE

After deciding which products to produce, each society must also decide what materials and methods to use in their production. In most cases, a given good or service can be produced in more than one way. For instance, a shirt can be made of cotton, wool, or acrylic fibers. It can be sewn entirely by hand, partly by hand, or entirely by machine. It can be packaged in paper, cardboard, plastic, or some combination of materials. It can be shipped by truck, train, boat, or plane. In short, the producer must choose among many options with regard to materials, production methods, and means of shipment.

FOR WHOM TO PRODUCE

Finally, each society must decide how to distribute or divide up its limited output among those who desire to receive it. Should everyone receive equal shares of society's output? Should those who produce more receive more? What about those who don't produce at all, either because they can't work or because they don't want to work? How much of society's output should *they* receive? In deciding how to distribute output—how output will be shared—different societies are influenced by their traditions and cultural values.

Whether a society is rich or poor, simple or complex, democratic or authoritarian, it must have some *economic system* through which it addresses the three fundamental questions. Chapter 2 examines a variety of economic systems and discusses how each responds to these questions.

Five Economic Goals

A given economic system's answers to the three fundamental questions are not always satisfactory to either the nation's citizens or its leaders. For example, if an economy is operating inside its production possibilities curve, it is not using all its production capabilities and is therefore not satisfying as many human wants as possible. A society with unemployed resources may want to take steps to improve the economy's performance so that it does a better job of fulfilling citizens' expectations or, in some cases, the expectations of those in power.

What should a society expect from its economic system? Before a society can attempt to improve its economic performance, it must have a set of goals, objectives, or standards by which to judge that performance. Although there is room for debate about precisely what constitutes "good performance" from an economic system, many societies recognize five essential goals:

1. *Full employment of economic resources.* If a society is to obtain maximum benefit from its scarce resources, it must utilize them fully. Whenever resources are unemployed—when factories stand idle, laborers lack work, or farmland lies untilled—the society is sacrificing the goods and services that those resources could have produced. Therefore, it is doing a less than optimal job of satisfying the unlimited wants of its members.

2. *Efficiency.* Economic efficiency means getting the most benefit out of limited resources. This goal has two separate elements: (a) production of the goods and services that consumers desire the most and (b) realization of this production at the lowest cost in terms of scarce resources. Economic efficiency is the very essence of economics. If an economic system fully employs its resources but uses them to produce relatively unwanted products, the society cannot hope to achieve maximum satisfaction from its resources. By the same token, if an economy does not minimize the amount

When labor or other economic resources are unemployed, society must do without the goods and services those resources could have produced.

of resources used in producing *each* product, it will not be able to produce as many products; consequently, fewer wants will be satisfied.

3. *Economic growth.* Because most people want and expect their standard of living to improve continually, economic growth—expansion in the economy's output of goods and services—is an important objective. If population is increasing, some economic growth is necessary just to maintain the existing standard of material welfare. When a nation's population is stable or is increasing less rapidly than output, economic growth results in more goods and services per person, contributing to a higher standard of living.

4. *A fair distribution of income.* Distribution of income means the way income is divided among the members of a society. In modern economies the income distribution is the primary factor determining how output will be shared. (In primitive economies, such as Ethiopia or Burundi, custom or tradition plays a major role in deciding how output is divided.) People with larger incomes receive larger shares of their economy's output. Is this a fair distribution of output? Some contend that it is. Others call for redistribution of income to eliminate poverty in the society. Still others argue that nothing less than an equal distribution is truly fair.

5. *A stable price level.* A major goal of most economies is a stable price level. Societies fear inflation—that is, a rise in the general level of prices. Inflation redistributes income arbitrarily: Some people's incomes rise more rapidly than inflation, whereas other people find that their incomes can't keep pace. The former group emerges with a larger share of the economy's output, while the latter group must make do with less than before. The demoralizing effect of this redistribution can lead to social unrest.

In pursuing the five economic goals, societies strive to maintain compatibility with their noneconomic, or sociopolitical, objectives. Americans, for example, want to achieve these economic goals without harming the environment or sacrificing the rights of people to select their occupations, own property, and spend their incomes as they choose. Societies that place high value on tradition, such as Japan, may strive to pursue these economic goals without violating the customs of the past. Insofar as the cultural, political, religious, and other noneconomic values of societies differ, the relative importance of each of the five economic goals and the methods of meeting those goals will also differ.

Conflicts and Trade-offs

Defining economic goals is only the first step in attempting to improve our economy's performance. The next step is to decide how to achieve these goals. Often the pursuit of one goal forces us to sacrifice at least part of some other economic or noneconomic goal. That is what economists call a *trade-off*—society gets more of one thing only by giving up, or trading off, something else. This is another way of stating the problem of opportunity cost. The opportunity cost of achieving a particular goal is whatever other goal has to be sacrificed or compromised. Let's consider three problems societies face in pursuing economic goals.

FULL EMPLOYMENT VERSUS STABLE PRICES

The goal of achieving full employment may conflict with the goal of maintaining a stable price level. Experience has taught us that attempting to reduce unemployment generally results in a higher rate of inflation. By the same token, attempts to reduce the rate of inflation often lead to higher unemployment. Frequently it becomes necessary to sacrifice part of one goal in favor of the other. For instance, society may accept some unemployment to maintain a lower inflation rate. The trade-off each society makes depends partly on economic analysis but is also influenced by societal values.[2]

---

[2] Most economists agree that there is a short-run trade-off between unemployment and inflation that may not exist in the long run. This issue is discussed in Chapter 12.

ECONOMIC GROWTH VERSUS ENVIRONMENTAL PROTECTION

Conflict frequently occurs between the goals of economic growth and a clean environment. Although most Americans support these two goals, it has become apparent that expansion of the economy's output takes a toll on the environment. For instance, our attempts to expand agricultural output by using pesticides and chemical fertilizers have been partially responsible for the pollution of our rivers and streams. We make trade-offs between economic growth and environmental preservation, trade-offs that reflect prevailing national values.

EQUALITY VERSUS EFFICIENCY

Consider now the potential conflict between income equality and economic efficiency. Suppose that a society decided that fair income distribution demanded greater equality of income than currently exists. Many economists would point out that efforts to achieve greater equality tend to have a negative impact on economic efficiency. Remember, efficiency means producing the most-wanted products in the least costly way. To accomplish this, the economy must be able to direct labor to the areas where it is most needed, often by making wages and salaries in these areas more attractive than those in other areas. For example, if a society needs to increase its number of computer programmers more rapidly than its number of teachers or nurses, it can encourage people to become computer programmers by making that occupation more rewarding financially than teaching or nursing.[3] If pay differentials are reduced in order to meet the goal of equality, a society will sacrifice economic efficiency because it will be more difficult to direct the flow of labor.

CHOOSING BETWEEN OBJECTIVES

When our society's goals conflict and demand that we choose between them, it is not the function of economists to decide which is the more important. The choice between objectives such as more rapid economic growth and a cleaner environment, or between greater equality and enhanced efficiency, is not solely a matter of objective cost-benefit analysis. Rather, it involves "normative judgments"—judgments about what *should be* rather than what *is*. This is a realm in which economists have no more expertise than anyone else. Setting goals is the job of the society or its representatives. The function of the economist is to make sure that those in charge of setting goals (or devising policies to achieve goals) are aware of the alternatives available to them and the sacrifices

---

[3] In some economic systems these adjustments in wages and salaries would occur automatically; in others deliberate action would be required. Chapter 2 has more to say about how specific economic systems direct or allocate labor.

each alternative requires—in other words, the costs and benefits of their actions. (See "Expense Means Many Can't Get AIDS Drugs," on pages 20–21 for an example of a policy debate that clearly involves normative judgments.)

Economic Theory and Policy

Before economists can recommend policies for dealing with economic problems or achieving goals, they must understand thoroughly how the economic system operates. This is where economic theory comes into play.

Theories are generalizations about causal relationships between facts, or variables; they help us to understand how events are connected or what causes what in the world around us. Theories are also referred to as laws, principles, and models. When in later chapters you encounter the *law* of demand, the *principle* of comparative advantage, and the *model* of command socialism, bear in mind that each of these tools is a theory.

THEORY IN EVERDAY LIFE

You probably think of theory as something exotic; something you would not normally encounter or use. But nothing could be farther from the truth. We each use theory in our daily life. If you don't recognize the role of theory in your life, it's because many of the theories you use were learned informally and are applied unconsciously. To illustrate, consider the following problem. You roll out of bed in the morning and crawl to the TV to turn it on. But instead of seeing your favorite morning program, all you see is a black screen—no picture, no sound, nothing. What is the *first* thing you will do to try to get the TV to work? You won't call the cable company, not at first anyway, and you won't throw the TV out the window—yet. Take some time to think about what you would do before reading further.

In response to this question, a common answer is "I'd check to see if it's plugged in." Most people agree that that's a sensible response, but why do we agree on this sensible answer? Why don't people say, "I'd look outside to see if it's snowing," or "I'd run to my car to see if it has gas in it." They don't select these answers because we all know they have nothing to do with getting a picture on our TV. And, more importantly, we know that electricity *does* have something to do with getting a picture. In short, we all have theories about how TVs work, and all those theories involve electricity. Your theory may be fairly elaborate—if you've had a physics course—or it may be fairly simple, if you've learned it informally by repeated observations. Here's a simple theory of how TVs work:

$$\text{electricity} \rightarrow \text{causes} \rightarrow \text{pictures.}$$

Use Your Economic Reasoning

Expense Means Many Can't Get AIDS Drugs

By Robert Pear

WASHINGTON, Feb 15— Even though new drugs show great promise in combating AIDS, many patients are finding that they cannot easily get the costly medicines because of restrictions imposed by health maintenance organizations and by state programs set up to assist people with low incomes.

Some H.M.O.s say they limit pharmacy benefits to a specified amount—$3,000 a year a patient is typical.

That is far less than the cost of the drug combinations often recommended by doctors. These regimens, some of which combine new protease inhibitor drugs with older antiviral medications, can easily cost $10,000 to $15,000 a year, and doctors say AIDS patients may need to take the drugs indefinitely.

In research reported in the last year, the drug combinations appear to be highly effective in suppressing H.I.V., the virus that causes AIDS, and in improving patients' health. These reports have raised hopes and generated a huge increase in demand for the drugs, surpassing the expectations of drug manufacturers, private health plans and AIDS drug assistance programs financed by Federal and state authorities.

Experience with the new AIDS drugs may foreshadow the difficult trade-offs that await taxpayers and policy makers as scientists develop costly treatments for other diseases like cancer or Alzheimer's.

"You try to ration things as ethically as possible," said Paul G. Loberti, administrator of the AIDS office in the Rhode Island Health Department.

Each state has a drug assistance program to provide prescription drugs to low-income people who are not covered by private health insurance or Medicaid. At President Clinton's insistence, the Federal Government has sharply increased its contribution to these programs and will provide 85 percent of the $300 million they spend in the coming year. But in interviews, officials in several states said the money was still not enough to meet the demand for the new drugs.

In Missouri, John K. Hubbs, chief of the AIDS bureau of the state Health Department, said: "We have established a limit on the number of patients to whom we can provide protease inhibitors: 132. And we have imposed a cap of $10,000 on what we will pay for a patient's combination drug therapy."

The AIDS drug assistance programs in Arkansas, Nevada, South Dakota and Oregon do not cover any of the protease inhibitors, which block reproduction of the AIDS virus. Covering such drugs "would blow our budget out of the water," said Lisa McAuliffe, coordinator of the Oregon program . . .

The limits imposed by H.M.O.s on pharmacy benefits are not explicitly directed at people with AIDS but affect them more than others.

Ronald D. Wackett, the pharmacy director at Mid Atlantic Medical Services, a managed care company in the Washington area, said its health plans often set annual limits on drug coverage at $2,000 or $3,000 a person.

Michael H. Savage, a spokesman for Mid Atlantic, said that if people with AIDS needed drugs beyond that limit, "they are pretty much on their own." Moreover, he said: "It is not the H.M.O. imposing the limit. The employer purchasing the health plan chooses the benefit levels that he or she wishes to offer employees...."

Dr. Richard O'Connor, a medical director at Physicians Health Services, an H.M.O. based in Trumbull, Conn., said: "We are seeing a proliferation of very expensive drugs not only for AIDS, but also for cancer, multiple sclerosis, depression, hypertension and other conditions."

Several studies suggest that the protease inhibitors, though expensive, may cut the cost of treating AIDS by reducing the need for hospital care, home health care and other services. "The studies suggest that overall costs will come down, but we don't have enough information to document that in our plan," said Mohan Vodoor, a vice president of the Health Insurance Plan of Greater New York, an H.M.O. . . .

In his new budget, President Clinton proposed per-capita limits on Federal Medicaid spending. People with AIDS and state officials strenuously oppose such limits, saying they would threaten access to promising AIDS drug therapies.

USE YOUR ECONOMIC REASONING

1. What is the opportunity cost of using Medicaid dollars to pay for AIDS drugs?
2. Health maintenance organizations impose limits on drug coverage based on what employers are willing to pay. What is the opportunity cost to an employer of spending more money for health coverage?
3. President Clinton has proposed per-capita limits on federal Medicaid spending. Do you oppose or support such limits? Does your position involve normative judgments? Explain.
4. What does the author mean by "difficult trade-offs...await... policy makers as scientists develop costly treatments for other diseases like cancer or Alzheimer's?"

Note that this theory does not fully describe the way TVs work; theories never do. Theories help us understand the real world by simplifying reality. In fact, theories or models are sometimes described as simplified pictures of the real world. By leaving out extraneous details and complexities, theories help us see the essential relationships more clearly, much as a map clarifies the shape and layout of a city by excluding unnecesary detail.

LESSONS FROM THE PRODUCTION POSSIBILITIES MODEL

The production possibilities curve introduced earlier in the chapter is a simple model of an economy. It certainly doesn't tell us everything we would like to know about an economy; in fact, it leaves out a host of details. But it points out very clearly that every economy's production capacity is limited, so that attempts to produce more of one thing mean producing less of something else.

The production possibilities model also points out another important feature of models or theories: They are based on assumptions. The production possibilities model assumes that resources are limited and that some resources are better suited to producing one product than another.[4] Those assumptions give us a production possibilities curve that slopes downward and is concave. If we make different assumptions, we end up with a different model and different conclusions. For example, if an economy had *unlimited* resources, its production possibilities curve would slope upward because it could produce more of both products simultaneously; that is, it would not be necessary to give up some military products to produce more civilian products. (What would the production possibilities curve look like if resources were fixed but were equally well suited to producing either product?)[5] The objective is to start with assumptions that are sufficiently realistic so that the resulting model allows us to explain and predict the real world. Otherwise, we end up with a model of little or no practical value.

A THEORY OF CIGARETTE CONSUMPTION

Theories are absolutely essential to solving problems and making sense out of the world we live in. Without a theory of how the TV works, we don't know what to do when it doesn't work; we don't know how to solve the problem. The same is true of economic problems. When you read the evening newspaper or tune in the evening news on television, you are exposed to a deluge of

---

[4] The production possibilities model also assumes the existing techniques of production. In other words, it assumes that technology does not change.

[5] Under these assumptions, the production possibilities curve would slope downward (since producing more of one thing would still require the sacrifice of some of the other thing), but it would be a straight line rather than curving outward.

facts and figures about everything from housing construction to foreign trade. Without theories to help you interpret them, however, these data are of little value because you don't know what facts are relevant to the problem at hand.

In the early 1990s, researchers noted that cigarette consumption in the United States was no longer declining as rapidly as it had in the previous decade. In other words, smokers were not "kicking the habit" as readily as before. Health experts wanted to understand why the trend toward quitting smoking was slowing down. Without a theory explaining cigarette consumption, researchers wouldn't know where to begin looking for an explanation because they wouldn't know what facts were relevant.

On the other hand, suppose that over time we have developed a tentative theory, a hypothesis, that lower cigarette prices cause higher cigarette consumption. That would pinpoint certain relevant facts that might explain the increase in cigarette consumption. We could test our theory by gathering data for a number of different time periods to see if, in fact, cigarette consumption has increased and decreased consistently in accordance with changes in price.

Testing economic theories is more difficult than it might seem. For example, to determine whether cigarette consumption is, in fact, related to the price of cigarettes, economists have to be able to eliminate the impact of changes in personal income and other nonprice factors that might affect the quantity of cigarettes consumed. After all, even if the price of cigarettes is a major factor influencing the amount consumed, it is clearly not the only factor.[6] Unfortunately, economists cannot control these factors as precisely as chemists or physicists can control variables in their experiments. So economists do the next best thing; that is, they assume that other factors, such as personal incomes, remain constant. This is the assumption of **ceteris paribus**, which literally means "other things being equal." In a sense, what economists are doing is stating the conditions under which they expect a theory to be valid. To illustrate, our theory about cigarette consumption might be restated this way: "Consumers will buy more cigarettes at lower prices than at higher prices, ceteris paribus—other things being equal or held constant." Economists then compare what actually happens to what, on the basis of theory, they expected. If the facts are not consistant with the theory, we must determine whether it is because the theory is invalid or because the assumption of ceteris paribus has been violated (that is, because something other than the price of cigarettes has changed). Of course, if the theory is found to be invalid—if its predictions are not consistent with reality—it's back to the drawing board; more work will be required to devise a better theory.

---

[6] For example, it seems likely that over a given period, personal income also affects cigarette consumption. If the incomes of smokers remain constant while cigarette prices fall, cigarette consumption may well increase. But if incomes fall during the same period, offsetting the rise in cigarette prices, cigarette consumption will probably remain the same or may even decrease.

POLICIES AND PREDICTIONS

Once a theory has been tested and accepted, it can be used as a basis for making predictions and as a guide for formulating economic policy. On the basis of our cigarette-price theory, for example, we would predict that if cigarette prices go up, consumption will decline and if prices fall, consumption will increase. We could also use this theory as the basis for devising policies for influencing the level of cigarette consumption. In order to reduce cigarette consumption, for instance, we might recommend an increase in the federal tax on cigarettes. This higher tax would make the retail price to consumers higher and therby reduce consumption.

Economists and Conclusions

The formulation of policies for dealing with economic problems is the most important use of economic theory and the most important function of economists. But if you listen to TV news or read the newspaper, you know that economists do not always agree on matters of economic policy. Laypersons may therefore be skeptical about the contribution that economics can make to solving society's problems. Because you are going to spend that next few months studying economics, it seems appropriate to take a few minutes now to consider the two reasons why economists disagree. Economists may disagree either because they have different views of what *should be* or because they have different views about what *is*.

We've already explained that economists possess no special expertise in choosing goals, in deciding how things ought to be. Yet like all thinking people, economists have individual values and opinions about which of society's economic goals are most important. Consider the issue of smoking. Many economists support higher taxes on cigarettes in an effort to deter smoking, particularly among young smokers who have yet to become addicted. But others argue that such a policy would impose a financial hardship on older smokers who are, on average, poorer than nonsmokers and who are unlikely to change their behavior because of the higher taxes. Here the disagreement is about goals. Which is more important, reducing smoking by young people or protecting the living standards of older smokers? Obviously, economists with different philosophies about what the society should be attempting to achieve will have different recommendations with regard to economic policy.

Economists may also disagree about economic policies because they disagree about how how things are—about how the economy works or how a particular policy would work. For example, even economists who support higher cigarette taxes to stem teenage smoking may disagree about the amount of the tax hike. Here the source of disagreement is likely to be conflicting statistical evidence regarding the responsiveness of consumers to changes in cigarette prices.

For instance, some studies suggest that a tax hike of $.70 per pack would be sufficient to cut teenage smoking in half, while other studies suggest that the tax increase would need to be $1 or more to accomplish that objective.[7] Because of these conflicting results, economists may make different recommendations about how much to increase cigarette taxes—recommendations that reflect their different conclusions about how teens would respond to the tax hike.

In summary, economists can disagree either bercause they have different views about what should be or because they have different views about how the economy works. Of course , these areas of dispute are more likely to be reported than areas of agreement. But the fact that economists, like all social scientists, are intensely interested in exploring and debating issues on which they disagree does not mean that they can never reach a conclusion. There are many issues and answers on which economists are in general agreement, so don't let the disagreements about particular policy questions mislead you. The study of economics has a great deal to contribute to your understanding of the world and its many social problems. Approach that study with an open mind, and it will help you to make sense out of facts and events you never before understood.

The Organization of the Text

Now that you have some sense of what the study of economics is about, let's take a brief look at the organization of this book. It is composed of four major parts. Part 1 forms the introduction and lays the conceptual groundwork for the rest of the text. Part 2 takes up **microeconomics,** the study of the individual units of the economy. These chapters examine how the prices of particular goods and services are determined and how individual consumers and businesses function. True to its name, microeconomics looks at the small units that make up the whole economy. Part 3 examines **macroeconomics,** the study of the economy's overall performance and the factors influencing that performance. These chapters address such problems as unemployment and inflation and examine the role of government in combating these economic ills. Through macroeconomics you will begin to view the economy in terms of the big picture. Part 4 turns to **international economics,** the study of international trade and finance. These chapters explore the reasons for trade and how transactions between nations are financed.

As you can see, economics embraces several specialized areas. Because these areas are interrelated, what you learn in Part 1 will help you understand problems taken up in Part 4. In fact, to a large extent, the chapters in this text build on one another. So please take the time to understand each one thoroughly for an easier and more rewarding trip through economic theory and practice.

---

[7] Studies suggest that each 1 percent increase in the price of a pack of cigarettes will reduce teenage consumption by 1 to 1.4 percent. If the current selling price of a pack of cigarettes is $2, its price would need to be raised to between $2.70 and $3 to reduce teen consumption by 50 percent.

Summary

The fundamental economic problem facing both individuals and societies is that our wants exceed our capacity for satisfying those wants. No society has enough *economic resources* (*land*, *labor*, *capital*, and *entrepreneurship*) to satisfy its members fully. Consequently, individuals and societies must make choices about how best to use their limited resources. *Economics* is the study of how to use our limited resources to satisfy our unlimited wants as fully as possible.

Making wise choices requires *cost-benefit analysis*—a systematic comparison of costs and benefits. A decision will only improve our well-being if the benefits associated with that decision exceed the costs.

One of the principal lessons of economics is that all choices entail costs, that there is no "free lunch." Whenever you make a decision to do or have one thing, you are sacrificing the opportunity to do or have some other thing. The most valued alternative you must sacrifice in order to take a given action is the *opportunity cost* of that action.

A *production possibilities curve* illustrates the concept of opportunity cost by showing the combinations of goods that an economy is capable of producing with its present stock of economic resources and existing techniques of production. It shows that unless there are unemployed resources, producing more of one thing means producing less of something else.

The dilemma of unlimited wants and limited resources forces each society to make three basic choices, to answer the three fundamental questions of economics: (1) What goods and services will the society produce and in what quantities? (2) How will these goods and services be produced? (3) For whom will these products be produced?

In order to determine how well it is answering the three fundamental questions, a society must establish goals or objectives against which it compares its performance. Full employment, economic efficiency, economic growth, a fair distribution of income, and a stable price level are widely accepted goals. When these goals are in conflict, as they often are, the pursuit of one goal commonly requires a trade-off, some sacrifice in terms of fulfilling another goal.

Before economists can recommend policies for dealing with economic problems or achieving specific objectives, they must develop *economic theories*, generalizations about causal relationships between economic facts, or variables. Testing economic theories can be tricky because the assumption of *ceteris paribus* ("other things being equal") is often violated. This makes it difficult to determine when a theory is flawed, since the results of an experiment could be biased by changes in uncontrolled factors.

Once a theory has been tested and accepted, it can be used as a basis for making predictions and as a guide to formulating economic policy. When it comes to making policy recommendations, economists do not always agree. They may disagree for one or both of two distinct reasons: because they have different views about what *should be* or because they have have different views about what *is*.

GLOSSARY

Capital. Human-made aids to the production process; for example, factories, machinery, and tools.

Ceteris paribus. "Other things being equal"; the assumption that other variables remain constant.

Cost-benefit analysis. A systematic comparison of costs and benefits.

Economics. The study of how to use our limited resources to satisfy our unlimited wants as fully as possible.

Economic resources. The scarce inputs used in the process of creating a good or providing a service; specifically, land, labor, capital, and entrepreneurship.

Economic theories. Generalizations about causal relationships between economic facts, or variables.

Entrepreneurship. The managerial function that combines land, labor, and capital in a cost-effective way and uncovers new opportunities to earn profit; includes willingness to take the risks associated with a business venture.

Free trade. Trade that is not hindered by artificial restrictions or trade barriers of any type.

International economics. The study of international trade and finance: why nations trade and how their transactions are financed.

Labor. The mental and physical work of those employed in the production process.

Land. All the natural resources or raw materials used in production; for example, acreage, timber, water, iron ore.

Law of increasing costs. As more of a particular product is produced, the opportunity cost per unit will increase.

Macroeconomics. The study of the economy's overall performance and the factors influencing that performance.

Microeconomics. The study of the behavior of individual economic units.

Normative issue. A question that calls for a value judgment about how things ought to be.

Opportunity cost. The best, or most valued, alternative that is sacrificed when a particular action is taken.

Production possibilities curve. A curve that shows the combinations of goods that an economy is capable of producing with its present stock of economic resources and existing techniques of production.

Theories. Generalizations about causal relationships between facts, or variables.

STUDY QUESTIONS

Fill in the Blanks

1. Land, labor, and capital are examples of ___economic resources___

2. The dilemma of ___unlimited,___ wants and ___limited___ resources is referred to as the economic problem.

3. ___Entrepreneurship___ are combiners, innovators, and risk takers.

4. The term ___land___ is used by economists to describe the economic resources created by nature.

5. When we sacrifice one alternative for another, the alternative forgone is called the _opportunity cost_ of that action.

6. A _production possibilities curve_ shows the combinations of goods that an economy is capable of producing.

7. Economists use economic _theories (models)_ to make sense out of the facts they observe.

8. When the pursuit of one objective forces society to sacrifice or compromise some other objective, economists say that a _trade-off_ exists.

9. Issues involving what "should be" rather than what "is" are referred to as _normative_ issues.

10. Because economists cannot conduct controlled experiments, they often make the assumption of _ceteris paribus_ to state the conditions under which they expect their theory to hold.

Multiple Choice

1. Economics is the study of how to
   a) distribute output fairly.
   b) do the best we can with what we have.
   c) reduce our unlimited wants.
   d) expand our stock of economic resources.

2. The opportunity cost of attending summer school is
   a) whatever you could have purchased with the money spent for tuition and books.
   b) negative, because you will finish college more rapidly by attending summer school.
   c) the income you could have earned over the summer.
   d) the products, income, and recreational opportunities that must be forgone.

3. If something has an opportunity cost, we should
   a) avoid that action.
   b) take that action.
   c) be sure that the benefit of the action exceeds the cost.
   d) be sure that the cost of the action exceeds the benefit.

4. Producing the most-wanted products in the least costly way is
   a) full employment.
   b) economic growth.
   c) a fair income distribution.
   d) economic efficiency.

5. Economists have trouble testing their theories because
   a) people are unpredictable.
   b) the real world is too complicated to be explained.
   c) they can't hold constant the "other factors" that might influence the outcome of the experiment.
   d) the necessary economic data are almost never available.

6. Economists should not be permitted to
   a) devise policies to achieve economic goals.
   b) determine society's economic goals.
   c) explain how the economy works.
   d) explain how particular economic goals conflict.

7. Economists sometimes reach different conclusions on a given issue because
   a) they disagree about goals.
   b) they disagree about the way the economy works.
   c) a and b
   d) neither a nor b

8. Macroeconomics deals with the study of
   a) international trade.
   b) individual economic units.
   c) production possibilities.
   d) the economy's overall performance.

9. Of the three fundamental questions, the "distribution" question has to do with
   a) who will receive the output.
   b) how the output will be shipped from the place of production to the consumer.
   c) how economic resources are distributed to producers.
   d) what products will be produced.

10. Suppose that you have just found $10 on the street and are thinking of using it to buy a ticket to the movies. The opportunity cost of going to the show would be
    a) nothing—since you found the money, you are sacrificing nothing to spend it.
    b) whatever you would have bought with the money if you hadn't used it to go to the show.
    c) the other activities you would have to sacrifice to attend the show.
    d) b and c

11. The production possibilities curve slopes downward because
    a) some resources are better suited to the production of one product than another.
    b) economic resources are limited.
    c) economic wants are unlimited.
    d) All of the above

Use the production possibilities curve at the end of this section in answering questions 12 through 14.

12. If the economy is operating at point *C*, the opportunity cost of producing an additional 10,000 automobiles will be
    a) 10 million bushels of wheat.
    b) 20 million bushels of wheat.
    c) 30 million bushels of wheat.
    d) 40 million bushels of wheat.

13. Point *G* on the diagram represents
    a) an optimal use of the society's resources.
    b) a combination of outputs beyond the economy's productive capacity.
    c) a situation in which some of the economy's resources are unemployed.
    d) the same output combination as point *B*.

14. The production possibilities curve might shift outward to include *G* if
    a) the economy put all unemployed resources to work.
    b) the economy experienced more rapid price inflation.
    c) improved training increased the productivity of workers.
    d) the nation's population declined

15. Foreign trade permits an economy to
    a) eliminate the problem of scarcity.
    b) operate inside its production possibilities curve.
    c) shift its production possibilities curve outward.
    d) consume a combination of products beyond its own production possibilities.

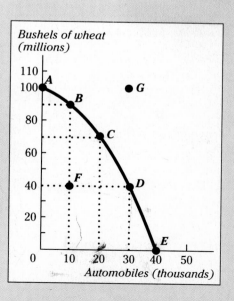

Problems and Questions for Discussion

1. List the four categories of economic resources and explain each.

2. Define *economics*. Why is economics sometimes called the "study of choice"?

3. List and explain the three fundamental choices that each society is forced to make.

4. What is meant when we say that a secretary is efficient? What about a salesclerk? Why is economic efficiency an important performance objective for an economy?

5. Airline personnel are often allowed to make a certain number of free flights each year. How would you compute the opportunity cost to the airlines of these free trips? Might this cost vary from route to route? Might the cost be different at different times of the year? Explain.

6. List and briefly explain the economic objectives recognized as worthwhile by many societies.

7. What are trade-offs? Give some examples.

8. A theory that has been around for quite some time says, "Better-educated people earn higher incomes than less-educated people, ceteris paribus." If we know a high school dropout who earns $200,000 a year, does this mean that we should discard the theory? Explain.

9. Suppose that we accept the theory given in problem 8 and decide to use it to formulate policies for reducing poverty. Apply this theory by suggesting three policies to reduce poverty.

10. Why is it important to separate the process of setting economic goals from the process of devising policies for achieving these goals? In which process is the economist more expert? Explain.

11. How would you go about using cost-benefit analysis to decide whether or not to attend college? What factors would complicate this analysis?

12. Foreign immigration into the United States normally shifts the U.S. production possibilities curve to the right. Why? If it has this impact, why do some citizens oppose immigration? Is foreign immigration a normative issue?

ANSWER KEY

Fill in the Blanks

1. economic resources
2. unlimited, limited
3. Entrepreneurs
4. land

5. opportunity cost
6. production possibilities curve
7. theories (or models)

8. trade-off
9. normative
10. ceteris paribus

Multiple Choice

1. b	4. d	7. c	10. d	13. b
2. d	5. c	8. d	11. b	14. c
3. c	6. b	9. a	12. c	15. d

APPENDIX: Working with Graphs

Economists frequently use graphs to illustrate economic concepts. This appendix provides a brief review of graphing and offers some practice problems to help you become more comfortable working with graphs.

The Purpose of Graphs

The basic purpose of a graph is to represent the relationship between two variables. A *variable* is any quantity that can take on different numeric values. Suppose, for example, that a university has conducted a survey to determine the relationship between two variables: the number of hours its students study and their grade-point averages. The results of that hypothetical survey could be shown in table, or schedule, form, as in panel a of Exh. A.1, or they could be represented graphically, as in panel b of Exh. A.1. Notice the difference: The graph reveals the relationship between the variables at a glance; you don't have to compare data as you do when reading the table.

Constructing a Graph

The first step in constructing a graph is to draw two perpendicular lines. These lines are called *axes*. In our example the vertical axis is used to measure the first variable, the grade-point average; the horizontal axis is used to measure the second variable, hours of study. The place where the two axes meet is called the *origin* because it is the starting point for measuring each of the variables; in our example the origin is zero. Once the axes are in place, we are ready to draw, or *plot*, the points that represent the relationship between the variables. Let's begin with the students who study 32 hours a week. According to the table in panel a, these students typically earn a grade-point average of 4.0. To show this relationship graphically, we find the point on the horizontal axis that represents 32 hours of study per week. Next, we move directly upward from that point until we reach a height of 4.0 grade points. This point, which we will label *A*, represents a combination of two values; it tells us at a glance that the typical student who studies 32 hours a week will earn a 4.0 grade-point average.

We plot the rest of the information found in panel a in the same way. To represent the typical, or average, grade of the student who studies 24 hours a week, all we need to do is locate the number 24 on the horizontal axis and then move up vertically from that point to a distance of 3.0 grade points (point *B*). We plot all the remaining points on the graph in the same way.

Once we have plotted all the points, we can connect them to form a curve. Economists use the term *curve* to describe any graphical relationship between two variables, so don't be surprised when you discover a straight line referred to as a curve. You can see that the resulting curve slopes upward and to the right. This indicates that there is a positive, or *direct*, relationship between the two variables—as one variable (study time) increases, the other (grade-point average) also increases. If the resulting curve had sloped downward and to the right, it would have indicated a negative, or *inverse*, relationship between the two variables—as one variable increased, the other would decrease. We would be surprised to find an inverse relationship between these particular variables; that would

EXHIBIT A.1

The Hypothetical Relationship between Grades and Study Time

HOURS OF STUDY (PER WEEK)	GRADE-POINT AVERAGE
32	4.0
28	3.5
24	3.0
20	2.5
16	2.0
12	1.5
8	1.0
4	0.4
0	0.0

(a) Relationship with Table

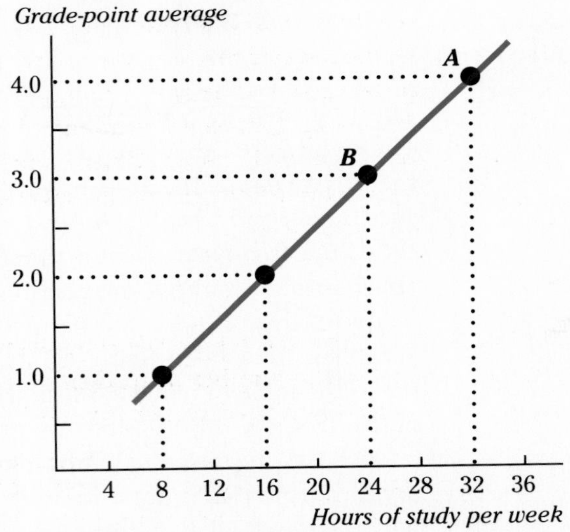

(b) Relationship with Graph

Both panels a and b illustrate the relationship between hours of study and grades. Panel a uses a table to show this relationship; panel b, a graph. Both illustrations show that the relationship between the two variables is direct; more hours of study tend to be associated with a higher grade-point average.

suggest the unlikely possibility that increased study time lowers the grade-point average!

Practice in Graphing

All graphs are basically the same, so if you understand the one we just considered, you should be able to master all the graphs in this textbook and in library sources. If you want some practice, take a few minutes to graph the three sets of data at the end of this appendix.

The first step is to draw and label the vertical and horizontal axes and mark them off in units that are convenient to work with. As you probably know, mathematicians always measure the *independent* variable (the variable that causes the other to change) along the horizontal axis and the *dependent* variable (the variable that responds to changes) along the vertical axis. Economists are less strict in deciding which variable to place on which axis, so don't be alarmed if occasionally you see the dependent variable on the horizontal axis.

Once you have decided which variable to place on which axis, the next step is to plot the information from the table as points and connect them. Then see if you can interpret your graph. What does it tell you about the relationship between the two variables? Are they directly or inversely related? (It's possible that they are not related at all. For example, there is probably no relationship between a student's weight and his or her grade-point average.) Does the relationship change somewhere along the graph? The way to become comfortable with graphs is to work with them. Try drawing these graphs to see how easy it is.

1. Graph the relationship between the hourly wage rate paid by the school and the number of students desiring to work in the school cafeteria. Is the relationship direct or inverse?

POINT	WAGE RATE (PER HOUR)	NUMBER OF STUDENT WORKERS
A	$5.50	5
B	6.00	10
C	6.50	15
D	7.00	20
E	7.50	25
F	8.00	30

2. Graph the relationship between the average daily temperature and the average number of students playing tennis on the school tennis courts. How does this relationship change?

POINT	TEMPERATURE (IN DEGREES FAHRENHEIT)	NUMBER OF TENNIS PLAYERS
A	60	20
B	70	30
C	80	40
D	90	30
E	100	20

3. Graph the relationship between the price of gasoline and the quantity of gasoline purchased by consumers. Is the relationship direct or inverse?

POINT	PRICE (PER GALLON)	QUANTITY PURCHASED (IN GALLONS)
A	$ .50	15 million
B	1.00	12 million
C	1.50	9 million
D	2.00	6 million
E	2.50	3 million

Economic Systems

Every nation, from the richest to the poorest, faces the same economic dilemma: how to satisfy people's unlimited wants with its limited economic resources. Each society must decide which products and services to produce, how to produce them, and for whom to produce them; in other words, it must establish an economic system. An **economic system** is a set of procedures for answering the three fundamental questions of economics—what, how, and for whom to produce. We will identify different economic systems according to the following criteria:

Who owns the means of production?

Who makes the economic choices that determine what, how, and for whom to produce?

What mechanism is used to ensure that these decisions are carried out?[1]

---

[1] This is the classification system adopted by Gary M. and Joyce E. Pickersgill in *Contemporary Economic Systems* (Englewood Cliffs, N.J.: Prentice-Hall, 1974), p. 10.

The variety of real-world economic systems is probably as great as the number of world nations, but all economic systems lie somewhere between two divergent models. At one extreme the means of production are privately owned, economic choices are made by individuals, and implementation occurs through markets. At the other extreme the means of production are owned publicly, by the state; economic choices are made collectively, and implementation occurs through commands from a central authority.

The purpose of this chapter is to give you an overview of how economic systems function. First, we examine the two divergent models—pure capitalism and pure command socialism. Recall from Chapter 1 that models simplify reality, making it possible for us to see more clearly how the parts of a system function and interact. Once we have become familiar with these theoretical models, we can compare the economies of the United States and the former Soviet Union against them to discover how they conform and how they deviate from the models.

The Model of Pure Capitalism

Our model of pure capitalism describes a hypothetical economy. As you work through the following sections, remember that you are learning about a theoretical model, not an existing system. As you will see later in the chapter, the United States and other real-world economies don't conform perfectly to either of the two divergent models. Here we will examine the elements of pure capitalism, diagram the operation (or functioning) of the system, see how it answers the three fundamental questions, and conclude by assessing its strengths and weaknesses.

ELEMENTS OF CAPITALISM

By definition **capitalism** is an economic system in which the means of production are privately owned, and fundamental economic choices are made by individuals and implemented through the market mechanism—the interaction of buyers and sellers. The model of pure capitalism is entirely consistent with our definition and contains five basic elements, which we will describe briefly.

Private Property and Freedom of Choice. One of the principal features of capitalism is private property. In a capitalist economy, private individuals and groups are the owners of the **means of production:** the raw materials, factories, farms, and other economic resources used to produce goods and services. These resource owners may sell or use their resources, including their own labor, as they see fit. Businesses are free to decide what products they will produce and to purchase the necessary economic resources from whomever they choose. Consumers, in turn, are free to spend their incomes any way they like. They can purchase whatever products they choose, and they can decide what fraction of their incomes to save and what fraction to spend.

Self-Interest. The driving force of capitalism is self-interest. In 1776 Adam Smith, the founder of economics, described a capitalist economy as one in which the primary concern of each player—of each producer, worker, and consumer—was to promote his or her own welfare.[2]

Smith introduced the **invisible hand** doctrine, which held that as individuals pursued their own interests, they would be led as if by an invisible hand to promote the good of the society as a whole. In order to earn the highest profits, predicted Smith, producers would generate the products consumers wanted most. Workers would offer their services where they were most needed because wages would be highest in those sectors. Consumers would favor producers who offered superior products and/or lower prices because they would seek the best value for their money. The result would be an economy that produced the goods and services desired by the society without the need for any central direction by government.

Markets and Prices. Capitalism is often described as a market system. This is because a capitalist economy contains numerous interdependent markets through which the functioning of the economy is coordinated and directed. A **market** consists of all actual or potential buyers and sellers of a particular item and can be local, regional, national, or international. For example, there are numerous local and regional markets for used automobiles, each consisting of all buyers and sellers of such vehicles in that particular area. Similar markets exist for all other goods and services and for all economic resources as well.

Market prices are determined by the interaction of buyers and sellers and serve two important functions. First, prices help to divide up, or ration, the society's limited output of goods and services among those who desire to receive it. Only those who are willing and able to pay the market price receive the product. Second, prices motivate businesses to produce more of some products and less of others. Businesses generally want to supply products that yield the highest profits, the ones with the highest prices in relation to their costs of production. These products tend to be those most desired by consumers. So, by motivating suppliers, price changes help to

---

[2] Adam Smith's description of the functioning of a capitalist economy appeared in *An Inquiry into the Nature and Causes of the Wealth of Nations,* published in 1776.

ensure that society's scarce resources are used to produce the goods and services most highly valued by consumers.

Competition. Adam Smith recognized that for the invisible hand to work—for individuals seeking their own interests to promote the good of all—the pursuit of self-interest had to be guided and restrained by competition. Competition ensures that producers remain responsive to consumers and that prices remain reasonable.

Pure capitalism requires **pure competition,** a situation in which a large number of relatively small buyers and sellers interact to determine prices.[3] Under conditions of pure competition, no individual buyer or seller can set—or even significantly influence—the prevailing price of a product or resource. Prices are thus determined by market forces, not by powerful buyers or sellers, and change only when market conditions change.

Limited Government Intervention. Pure capitalism is above all a **laissez-faire economy.** (*Laissez-faire* is a French phrase that in this context means "let the people do as they choose.") The model describes no role for government in making economic decisions. Through pricing, the market makes all production and distribution decisions—what, how, and for whom to produce—and competition ensures that consumers will be charged reasonable prices. The only role of government is to provide the kind of environment in which a market economy can function well. For example, government must define and enforce the private-property rights that enable individuals to own and use property.

THE CIRCULAR-FLOW MODEL

We can represent the operation of a capitalist economy in a diagram called the circular-flow model. Exhibit 2.1 models an economy composed of only two sectors: households and businesses. You can see that these two sectors are connected through transactions, or flows, that occur continuously between them. We'll examine how each sector processes the flow it receives and returns it to the other sector.

The Household and Business Sectors. The household sector is shown at the right in Exh. 2.1. A **household** is both a living unit and an economic unit. Whether it consists of a single person or many people, each household will have a source of income and will spend that income. The household sector is composed of all the individual households in the economy. Because households own the land, labor, capital, and entrepreneurship that businesses need

---

[3] Further assumptions relating to pure competition are described in Chapter 6.

EXHIBIT 2.1

The Circular Flow of Pure Capitalism

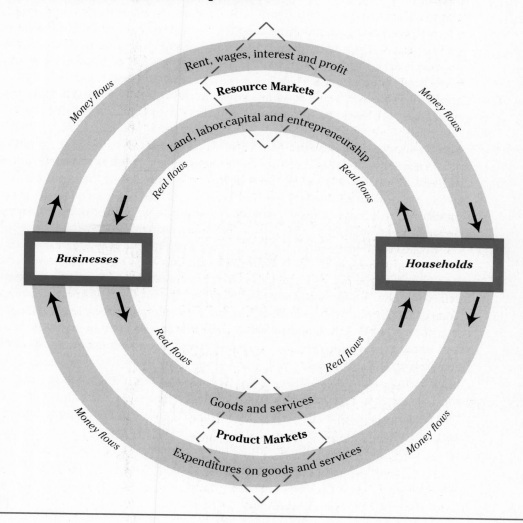

to produce goods and services, this sector is the source of all economic resources in the model of pure capitalism. It is also the source of consumer spending for the goods and services produced.

The business sector, on the left, is composed of all the businesses in the economy. The business sector purchases economic resources from households, converts those resources into products, and sells the products to the households.

Real Flows and Money Flows. You can see in the diagram that two types of flows circle in opposite directions. In the outside circle *money flows*, in the form of rent, wages, interest, and profit, go from businesses to households to pay for economic resources. These flows return to businesses as households pay for products. *Real flows* involve the physical movement of the resources and products. The inner flow in the diagram shows economic resources in the form of land, labor, capital, and entrepreneurship flowing from the household sector to the business sector, where they are used to produce goods and services. The unbroken arrows in the diagram show that these circular flows are endless.

The Resource and Product Markets. Markets are the key to the operation of a capitalist system because they hold together its decentralized economy of millions of individual buyers and sellers. The interaction of these buyers and sellers ensures that the right products (the ones desired by consumers) are produced and that economic resources flow to the right producers (the ones producing the most-wanted products at the lowest prices).

In the resource markets, depicted in the upper portion of Exh. 2.1, the interaction of buyers and sellers determines the prices of the various economic resources. For example, in the labor market for accountants, an accountant's salary is determined by the interaction of employers seeking to hire accountants (the buyers) and accountants seeking employment (the sellers). Changes in resource prices guide and motivate resource suppliers to provide the type and quantity of resources producers need most. Using our example of labor, suppose that the number of businesses desiring accountants is expanding more rapidly than new accountants are being trained. What will happen to the salaries of accountants? They will tend to increase. As a result, we can expect more people in the household sector to invest the time and money necessary to become accountants. You can see how the price mechanism ensures that (1) the types of labor, equipment, and other resources most needed by businesses will be supplied and (2) these resources will be supplied in the proper quantities.

In the product markets, depicted in the lower portion of Exh. 2.1, the prices of all products—from eggs and overcoats to haircuts and airline tickets—again are determined by the interaction of buyers and sellers. Prices serve the same function here as they do in the resource market: They make it possible to divide up, or ration, the limited amount of output among all those who wish to receive it. Only those consumers who are willing and able to pay the market price can obtain the product. When prices change, this informs producers about desired changes in the amount they are producing and motivates them to supply the new quantity. For example, when consumers want more of a product than is available, they tend to bid up its price. Producers, getting a clear signal that consumers like that item, thus have an incentive to supply more of it.

HOW CAPITALISM ANSWERS THE THREE FUNDAMENTAL QUESTIONS

Now that we have discussed the elements of pure capitalism and have a general idea of the role of markets in such an economy, we can determine more easily how this system answers the three fundamental questions.

What to Produce. One feature of pure capitalism is **consumer sovereignty,** an economic condition in which consumers dictate which goods and services businesses will produce. Because producers are motivated by profits and because the most profitable products tend to be the ones consumers desire most, producers must be responsive to consumer preferences. To illustrate consumer sovereignty in action, let's consider how automobile manufacturers in a pure capitalist economy would respond if consumer preferences suddenly took a dramatic turn away from standard-sized cars in favor of small ones. If people began to buy more compacts or subcompacts and fewer full-sized cars, the price of small cars would rise and they would become more profitable, whereas full-sized cars would decline in price and become less profitable. Therefore, automobile manufacturers would produce more compacts and fewer full-sized cars: just what consumers want.

Because consumers are free to spend their incomes as they choose, producers who wish to earn profits must be responsive to consumers' desires. As a result, pure capitalism might be described as a system in which the consumer is the ruler and the producer an obedient servant.

How to Produce. Automobile producers have a number of options available for manufacturing compact cars and other vehicles that consumers desire. They can produce these automobiles through highly mechanized techniques, or they can rely primarily on skilled labor and simpler tools. They can manufacture car bodies from steel, aluminum, fiberglass, or some combination of the three. In selecting which production technique and combination of resources to use, capitalist manufacturers will minimize the cost of production; they will adopt the *least-cost* approach because lower costs contribute to higher profits.

The search for the least-cost approach is guided by the market prices of the various economic resources. Because the scarcest resources cost the most,

In a capitalist economy, highly mechanized production methods—such as those utilizing robots—may be selected if labor is expensive.

producers use them only when they cannot substitute less expensive resources. For example, if steel is very expensive, automobile makers will tend to use it only where other materials would be inadequate, perhaps in the frame or in other parts of the car that require great strength. Thus, the prices of resources help to ensure that resources are used to their best advantage in a capitalist economy. Abundant, cheaper resources are used when they will suffice; scarcer, more costly resources are conserved.

For Whom to Produce. Finally, we consider the task of distributing our hypothetical economy's output of automobiles. We know that only those who can afford to buy automobiles will receive them. The ability to pay, however, is only half the picture; the other half is willingness to purchase, which takes into account consumer preferences. Some of those who can afford a new car will prefer to spend their money elsewhere: remodeling their homes perhaps or sending their children to college. Some who seemingly cannot afford a new car may be able to purchase one by doing without other things—new clothes or a larger apartment, for example. Of course, consumers with low incomes will face less attractive choices than those earning high incomes. A low-income consumer may sacrifice basic necessities in order to afford an automobile, whereas a wealthy consumer need choose only between the new car and some luxury item, such as a sailboat or a winter vacation. In the final analysis those with higher incomes will always have more choices than those with lower incomes and will receive a larger share of the economy's total output.

CAPITALISM: STRENGTHS AND WEAKNESSES

Before moving on from our discussion of pure capitalism, we will describe briefly some of the strengths and weaknesses inherent in such a system. One of the major strengths of pure capitalism is *economic efficiency*. In a market economy, businesses are encouraged to produce the products that consumers want most and to produce those products at the lowest cost in terms of scarce resources. A system that accomplishes those objectives goes a long way toward ensuring that a society achieves the maximum benefit possible from its limited resources.

A second positive feature of capitalism is *economic freedom*. Under pure capitalism, consumers, workers, and producers are free to make decisions based on self-interest. To many people this economic freedom is the overwhelming virtue of the capitalist model.

Economist Milton Friedman, a vocal advocate of competitive capitalism, notes a third strength of the system: It promotes *political freedom* by separating economic and political power. The existence of private ownership of the means of production ensures that government officials are not in a position to deny jobs or goods and services to individuals whose political views conflict with their own.[4]

Pure capitalism also has some shortcomings. First, people are not uniformly equal in ability, and some will succeed to a greater extent than others. In a capitalist system the result is the unequal distribution of income and output. This inequality tends to be perpetuated because the children of the rich usually have access to better educational opportunities and often inherit the income-producing assets of their parents. Such inequality weakens capitalism's claim that it produces the goods and services that the *society* wants the most. It is more the case that capitalism produces the products that the *consumers who have the money* want most.

A second, closely related criticism was voiced by the late Arthur Okun, chairman of the Council of Economic Advisors during the Johnson administration. In a capitalist economy, observed Okun, money can buy a great many things that are not supposed to be for sale:

> Money buys legal services that can obtain preferred treatment before the law; it buys platforms that give extra weight to the owner's freedom of speech; it buys influence with elected officials and thus compromises the principle of one person, one vote. . . . Even though money generally cannot buy extra helpings of rights directly, it can buy services that, in effect, produce more or better rights.[5]

Third, pure capitalism may be criticized for encouraging the destruction of the environment. Because air, rivers, lakes, and streams are **common-**

---

[4] Milton Friedman, *Capitalism and Freedom* (Chicago: The University of Chicago Press, 1962), p. 9.
[5] Arthur M. Okun, *Equality and Efficiency: The Big Tradeoff* (Washington: The Brookings Institution, 1975), p. 22.

property resources belonging to the society as a whole, they tend to be seen as free—available to be used or abused without charge or concern. The pursuit of self-interest would cause producers to dump their wastes into nearby rivers to avoid the cost of disposing of those wastes in an environmentally acceptable manner. Farmers would select pesticides according to their favorable impact on output and without regard to their undesirable effects on wildlife and water supplies. In this case, Adam Smith's invisible hand fails. The pursuit of self-interest by individuals may not promote the good of all but may instead lead to environmental destruction.

The Model of Pure Command Socialism

The opposite of the model of pure capitalism is the model of pure command socialism. The socialist command economy described in this section represents no existing economic system. Like the model of pure capitalism, the model of pure command socialism is simply a tool to help us understand how command economies operate. Again, we will examine the basic elements of the model, diagram how the hypothetical economy operates, and see how the system decides what, how, and for whom to produce. Then we will examine the strengths and weaknesses of pure command socialism.

ELEMENTS OF COMMAND SOCIALISM

We define **command socialism** as an economic system in which the means of production are publicly owned, the fundamental economic choices are made by a central authority, and commands are used to ensure that these decisions are implemented. Four basic elements of pure command socialism support this definition.

Public Ownership. A socialist economy is characterized by state, or public, ownership of the means of production. In the model of pure command socialism, state ownership is complete. The factories, farms, mines, hospitals, and other forms of capital are publicly owned. Even labor is publicly owned in the sense that workers and managers do not select their own employment but are assigned their jobs by the state.

Centralized Decision Making. One of the most distinctive features of command socialism is that economic choices are made by a central authority. This central authority may be either responsive to the feelings of the people (democratic socialism) or unresponsive to their wishes (authoritarian socialism or communism). In either case, this authority makes the fundamental production and distribution decisions and then takes the necessary actions to see that these decisions are carried out.

Economic Planning. In the model of command socialism, economic planning replaces the market as the method for coordinating economic decisions. The central authority, or central planning board, gathers information about existing production capacities, supplies of raw materials, and labor force capabilities. It then draws up a master plan specifying production objectives for each sector or industry in the economy. Industrywide objectives are translated into specific production targets for each factory, farm, mine, or other kind of producing unit. Central planning ensures that specific production objectives agree so that automobile manufacturers will not produce 1 million cars, for example, while tire manufacturers produce only 2 million tires.

Allocation by Command. In command socialism, resources and products are allocated by directive, or command, and the central authority uses its power to enforce these decisions. Once it determines production and distribution objectives, the central planning board dictates to each producing unit the quantity and assortment of goods the unit is to produce and the combination of resources it is to use. Commands are also issued to producers of raw materials and other production inputs to supply these inputs to the producing units that need them. Further commands direct individuals to places of employment—wherever the central planning board determines that their services are needed—and dictate distribution of the economy's output of goods and services. All the allocative functions that a capitalist economy leaves to the market and the pursuit of self-interest are accomplished in pure command socialism through planning and allocation by directive.

THE PYRAMID MODEL

Exhibit 2.2 represents a socialist command economy as a pyramid, with the central planning board at the top and the various producing and consuming units below it. This diagram emphasizes the primary feature of a command economy: centralization of economic decision making.

The outer arrow at the right in Exh. 2.2 shows how information about production capacities, raw materials supplies, and labor capabilities flows up from the producing units in the middle of the pyramid to the central planning board at the top. Information, if requested, about which goods and services consumers desire also flows up from the consuming units at the base of the pyramid (outer left arrow). Production objectives, or targets, are transmitted back to the individual producing units, which then supply the targeted quantity and

EXHIBIT 2.2

The Command Pyramid

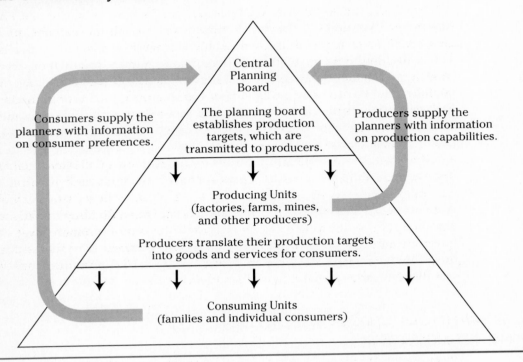

Central
Planning
Board

Consumers supply the
planners with information
on consumer preferences.

The planning board
establishes production
targets, which are
transmitted to producers.

Producers supply the
planners with information
on production capabilities.

Producing Units
(factories, farms, mines,
and other producers)

Producers translate their production targets
into goods and services for consumers.

Consuming Units
(families and individual consumers)

assortment of products and produce them as specified. Finally, the output is distributed to consumers in accordance with the plan.

HOW COMMAND SOCIALISM ANSWERS THE THREE FUNDAMENTAL QUESTIONS

In many respects the operation of a socialist command economy is easier to understand than the functioning of a capitalist economy. The answers to the three fundamental questions are decided by the central planning board, which then uses its authority to ensure that all directives are carried out.

The central planners can select any output targets, any mix of products within the limits set by the economy's production capacity. Of course, the planners will have to gather an abundance of information before they have a good picture of the economy's capabilities. They must determine the size of the labor force and the skills it possesses, for example, as well as how many factories exist and what they are capable of producing. Until the central planners have this kind of information, they cannot establish realistic output targets. And, even then, they will face some tough decisions because, as you already know, more of one thing means less of something else. So if they decide to produce more automobiles, they won't be able to manufacture as many refrigerators and military weapons and other products.

In deciding how to produce each product, central planners must try to stretch the economy's limited resources as far as possible. This requires that each resource be used efficiently—where it makes the greatest contribution to the economy's output. If some resource is particularly scarce, planners must be careful to use it only where no other input will suffice; otherwise they won't be able to maximize the economy's output.

Even with the best planning, an economy's resources will stretch only so far. The central planning board can allocate the economy's limited output in accordance with any objective it has set. If the planning board's primary objective is equality, it can develop a method of rationing, dividing up the society's output in equal shares to each member. If it wants to promote loyalty to the government, the central authority can give supporters extra shares while penalizing dissenters. Whatever its objectives, the central planning board can use distribution as a method to further them.

COMMAND SOCIALISM: STRENGTHS AND WEAKNESSES

Like pure capitalism, the economy of pure command socialism has certain strengths and certain weaknesses. Some people argue that a major strength of command socialism is its ability to promote a high degree of equality in the distribution of income and output. Because the central planners control the distribution of goods and services, they can elect to distribute output in ways that achieve whatever degree of equality in living standard they consider appropriate. Thus, it is theoretically possible for command socialism to avoid the extremely unequal income and output distribution that characterizes pure capitalism.

Another major strength of command socialism is its potential for achieving economic objectives in a relatively short period of time. As an example, consider the power of the planners to foster more rapid economic growth. If a society wants to increase its capacity for producing goods and services, it must devote more of its resources to producing capital goods (factories and equipment) and fewer resources to producing consumer goods. In other words, society must consume less *now* in order to be able to produce and consume more *later*. Because the central authority has the power to dictate the fraction of the society's resources that will be devoted to capital goods production, in effect, it can force the society to make the sacrifices necessary to increase the rate of economic growth.

You probably recognize that the power to bring about rapid economic changes is not necessarily a good thing. The major shortcoming of command socialism, in fact, is the possibility that the central planning board may pursue goals that do not reflect the needs or desires of the majority. If the socialist government is not democratically elected, its goals may bear no relationship to the needs of the general population.

A second weakness in the model of command socialism is its inefficient information network. The system we have described needs more information than it can reasonably expect to acquire and process to ensure efficient use of the economy's resources. The system must not only have a substantial organizational network to acquire information about consumer preferences and production capabilities but must also use that network to transmit the decisions of central planners to millions of economic units. Moreover, the central planners have to be able to process all the acquired information and return it in the form of a consistent plan—a staggering task, considering that the output of one industry is often the production input required by some other industry. Finally, they must see that each product is produced efficiently. This complex and cumbersome process is bound to result in breakdowns in communication and decision making. When these occur, the wrong products may be produced or the right ones produced using the wrong combinations of resources. In either case, inefficiency means that the society does not achieve maximum benefit from its limited resources.

Mixed Economies: The Real-World Solution

No existing economic system adheres strictly to either pure capitalism or pure command socialism. All real-world economies are **mixed economies;** they represent a blending of the two models. To illustrate the diversity among economic systems, we will consider two distinctly different economies: the United States and the former Soviet Union. Our discussion will begin with the U.S. economy, the system that will occupy most of our attention throughout this text.

THE U.S. ECONOMIC SYSTEM

Because the U.S. economic system is marked by such a high degree of private ownership and individual decision making, American children learn early from their teachers, the news media, and others that they live in a capitalist economy. And certainly there is ample evidence to support that viewpoint. Most U.S. businesses, from industrial giants like General Motors and IBM to small firms like your neighborhood barbershop or hair salon, are private operations, not government-owned enterprises. The U.S. economy is coordinated and directed largely by the market mechanism, the interaction of buyers and sellers in thousands of interdependent markets. Each of those buyers and sellers is guided by self-interest, which among producers takes the form of profit seeking. Fortunately for consumers, the drive for profits is usually kept in check by another feature of pure capitalism: competition. In most American industries, competition, though not pure, is adequate to keep prices reasonable and to ensure that consumers receive fair treatment.

Given these elements of pure capitalism, why do we call the United States a *mixed economy*? There are several reasons. First, let us consider the degree of public ownership in our economic system. Although most American businesses are privately owned, some very important and visible producers are publicly owned enterprises. For example, the electricity on which we rely to heat and cool our homes and run our appliances is supplied in part by municipal, state, or county power companies. With few exceptions, we attend public elementary and secondary schools. When we apply for admission to college, we mail those applications via the U.S. Postal Service, often to state universities. If we ride the bus in the morning, that bus is probably the property of a public transit system. In short, although public ownership is by no means the dominant feature of the American economy, it cannot be ignored.

Nor is public ownership the lone feature that our predominantly capitalist economy "borrows" from command socialism. Many of our basic economic choices are made or influenced by powerful economic units—government, labor, and business—rather than by individuals, and often these decisions are implemented by commands rather than through markets.

Regulations and restrictions are two means through which the government exerts influence on businesses and consumers. Think of the regulations imposed on automobile manufacturers, for example. They must produce cars that (1) meet specified mileage requirements; (2) conform to certain exhaust-emission standards; (3) can sustain a front- or rear-end crash of a specified force without serious injury to passengers; and (4) include air bags, seat belts, and other safety features. In addition to complying with these directives or commands, automobile producers must conform to the plant health and safety regulations set by the Occupational Safety and Health Administration, and their factories must operate within the various pollution-control standards set by the Environmental Protection Agency. To a greater or lesser extent, most American industries are subject to government regulations.

Government spending and taxing decisions constitute another significant influence on the mixture of goods and services that the economy produces and the distribution of those goods and services among the members of the society. Through its tax policies, for example, the federal government encourages investment in certain industries and discourages investment in others. Our tax system requires that people who earn higher incomes pay a greater fraction of their incomes in taxes, thus altering the distribution of output. Government expenditures for education, national defense, and aid to the poor also have a significant impact on what our economy produces and who will receive that output.

Government is not the only powerful economic unit in our economy. Labor organizations and large businesses have a substantial impact on the way our economy operates. In many industries, labor unions influence market forces and use their bargaining power to force wage increases and negotiate work rules that maximize employment and reduce the likelihood of layoffs. Unions use their political clout and considerable financial resources to lobby for government policies—minimum wage laws and import bans, for example—that enhance their own economic position. Indeed, it is the business of the labor union to attempt to influence to its advantage any market force that has an impact on wages and working conditions.

Powerful businesses exert their own influence on market forces. Under pure capitalism all businesses would respond to prices dictated by the market, but businesses in our economy often use their size to influence the prices of both the resources they buy and the products they sell. They use advertising in an attempt to influence consumer spending patterns and convince prospective buyers that their product is worth more than the ones offered by competitors. They also use their financial resources and their status as major employers to influence government policies. Like labor unions, powerful businesses use every tool at their disposal to try to alter the economic environment to their advantage.

In summary, the U.S. economy diverges from the model of pure capitalism in a variety of ways. Publicly owned enterprises make an important contribution to the economy; laws and government regulations significantly influence economic decisions; and powerful labor unions and businesses are able to influence the economic environment rather than simply respond to it. Whether these modifications of pure capitalism are good or bad is a matter for debate. What is clear is that the U.S. economic system is really a mixed economy. Rather than adhering strictly to the capitalist model, it combines elements of capitalism and command socialism.

THE SOVIET ECONOMIC SYSTEM

The Soviet Union was dissolved in 1991 and was replaced by the Commonwealth of Independent States, a federation of former Soviet republics.

The changes that are occurring in the Russian economy are benefiting some and harming others.

Although the Soviet Union has passed into history, much can be learned from examining the Soviet economic system. For decades the Soviet economy was the economic system that most closely approximated the model of pure command socialism. By studying the Soviet system, we will see just how different an economic system can be from our own and still share the designation *mixed economy*. We will also gain insights into the economies of China and Cuba, since these systems, although changing, duplicate in many ways the old Soviet system. Finally, an understanding of the Soviet system is essential if we are to appreciate the problems confronting the new Commonwealth states as they attempt to construct their own economic systems from the ruins of the Soviet economy. Although the Soviet Union has been declared dead, the ghost of the Soviet economic system will haunt the Commonwealth states for a long time to come.

The Soviet economic system had much in common with the model of pure command socialism. Most factories, farms, and other enterprises were owned and operated by the state rather than by private citizens. The fundamental choices about what, how, and for whom to produce were made by the State Planning Committee (GOSPLAN), and GOSPLAN's decisions were implemented mainly by command.

However, even prior to market reforms (which will be discussed later), the Soviet economy deviated significantly from the model of command socialism; distinct strands of capitalism were woven into the economy's socialist fabric. Consider Soviet agriculture, for example, which operated at three levels: state farms, collective farms, and private plots. Soviet state farms were run the same as other state enterprises; they received commands from the planning authority and were expected to meet their production objectives. But collective farms, at least in theory, operated by and for the benefit of their members. (In practice, however, a significant portion of a collective farm's output had to be sold to the state at prices dictated by the state.) The private sector was made up of small plots that peasants farmed in addition to the work they did on collective farms. Although these small plots occupied less than 2 percent of the nation's farmland, they were cultivated intensively and produced roughly one-third of the nation's agricultural output. Part of this output was consumed by the owners, but the major portion was sold in open markets at prices dictated by market forces.

Further elements of capitalism were evident in the labor sector of the Soviet economy; planners attempted to duplicate some of the wage adjustments that would occur naturally in a free market. Although Soviet planners dictated production goals, they did not adhere to the model of command socialism by issuing directives about who would work at which occupations. Instead, they manipulated wages to bring about the changes they desired. For example, if too few people wanted to become electricians, wages for electricians were increased in order to attract more individuals to this occupation. If there were too many electricians, wages were either reduced or simply not increased when other wage increases were ordered.

Consumer prices were managed in a similar fashion. Rather than command which consumer goods each household would receive, central planners set the prices for each consumer good and allowed households to make their own choices based on their reactions to those prices. Although planners kept some prices artificially low as a matter of policy—the prices of basic food items, for example—they manipulated most prices in an attempt to equalize the amounts available and the amounts consumers desired. Whereas free competitive markets automatically produce this result, Soviet pricing was never flexible enough to duplicate the market process precisely. That is, Soviet prices never changed quickly enough or often enough to ensure that the amounts desired by consumers would exactly duplicate the amounts available.

In addition to manipulating wages and prices, Soviet planners used market-related incentives to achieve their goals. Successful managers, for example, were rewarded with bonuses that might amount to a substantial fraction of their annual income. Payments in kind—a chance for a better apartment or a nice vacation, for instance—also provided incentive for good performance.

As you can see, the economy of the Soviet Union combined elements of capitalism and command socialism. The capitalist elements began to take on even greater weight when Mikhail Gorbachev became supreme leader of the Soviet Union in 1985. Calling the Soviet economic system rigid and inefficient, he introduced measures to correct these problems. State-owned enterprises were given more freedom in pricing their products and were given permission to buy inputs and sell their products abroad, without going through the planning board. Individuals were allowed to sell services (house painting and home and auto repair, for example), and some private enterprises, such as restaurants, were permitted. Political reforms were also undertaken when Gorbachev became convinced that economic reform could be accomplished only if accompanied by democratization of the political system.

Although Gorbachev's moves to reform the economy were accorded much attention in the press, they were in fact modest and piecemeal changes. Gorbachev clearly recognized the failures of the Soviet Union, but he was unwilling to accept some basic tenets of capitalism—the concept of private property, for instance. This ambivalence led to conflicting policy moves. Measures to promote free markets were passed one day, only to be revoked or somehow neutralized the next. This resulted in chaos for producers and a substantial disruption in the supplies of goods and services. In short, Gorbachev succeeded in discrediting and disrupting the Soviet economic system without really moving the economy closer to capitalism.

As the Soviet economy disintegrated, the Communist party collapsed and most of the Soviet republics declared their independence. Gorbachev's power waned and Russian president Boris Yeltsin, who had advocated more rapid economic reform, moved to center stage. In December 1991 the Soviet Union was offically dissolved and replaced with the Commonwealth of Independent States, a loose federation of former Soviet republics.

Economic reform has occurred since the disintegration, but it has not been smooth or easy. Consider the situation in Russia, for example. By 1996 approximately 60 percent of Russia's output was produced by privately owned enterprises, a statistic that underscores the rapid changes occurring in the economy.[6] But while the share of output coming from the private sector has been rising, the total output of the Russian economy has fallen in every year since the breakup of the Soviet Union.[7] In short, the growth of the private sector has not been rapid enough to offset the decline in output resulting from the closing of state enterprises. As a consequence, unemployment has become a major social problem.

---

[6] "Privatization Is Not the Key to Successful Transition," by Martin C. Spechler, *Challenge*, January–February 1996.
[7] Based on estimates by the International Monetary Fund, *Economic Report of the President*, 1996.

Making a Million Isn't What It Used to Be

Life in Russia's fast lane—with quick riches and extravagant spending—hits a few speed bumps

By Marshall Ingwerson
Staff Writer of THE CHRISTIAN SCIENCE MONITOR

MOSCOW

On a Paris corner, a New Russian compliments another on his tie.

"I paid $1,000 for it in that shop right there," says the fellow with the tie.

"You're a fool," scoffs the other New Russian, "I saw the same tie just around the corner for $2,000."

This is one of the dozens of popular jokes in Russia these days on New Russians—the flashy, Mercedes-driving, Rolex-wearing, Riviera-sunning, casino-playing, gold-chained, nouveaux riches of the post-Soviet years who never ask the price—unless to make a show of paying more.

But in another sign of creeping economic stability, the age of the flamboyant Russian nouveaux riches is doing a fast fade. It shows at art auctions and at Rolls Royce dealerships in Moscow. It shows in a slight narrowing of the income gap between rich and poor in official Russian statistics. And it shows in a shift in the culture of prosperous Muscovites.

While the ultra-rich are still ultra-rich in their guarded suburban compounds, much of the fast money that bought German cars and Italian clothes in post-Soviet Russia has been lost.

They have left a growing group of affluent but not-rich Russians that are finally settling down and getting to work.

Nikolai Leonov, answering his own telephone behind a spartan desk in a small but modern office, is by no means poor today as he pours his time and money into his catalog sales business. But two years ago he was rich. He drove a top-of-the-line Audi sedan and spent little time running this business, because he and some friends were making big money in investing and banking.

"But we were not professionals," he acknowledges.

They lost their money when two banks they had invested in went bankrupt.

They are not alone. "Those who became suddenly rich were not professionals in any field," says Mr. Leonov, who himself had a doctorate in geophysics but knew little about banking. "Mostly, they have lost their money."

"Now you have to know something about your business."

This is a story heard in many tony Moscow circles these days.

Still Wealthy, Less Flamboyant

There is still plenty of serious money in the hands of wealthy Russians. Limousines with tinted windows and four-wheel-drive chase cars for security still careen around town. Supermarkets and athletic clubs that once catered to foreigners with hard currency are now frequented by prosperous Russians. And at art and antique auctions in Western Europe, Russian buyers are still major players.

SOURCE: *The Christian Science Monitor*, Feb. 26,1997, p.1. Reprinted with permission from *The Christian Science Monitor.* Copyright 1997, The Christian Science Publishing Society. All Rights Reserved.

But the culture of wealth is changing—Mercedes-Benz and BMW are out of fashion, says Leonov. Instead, Russians with money prefer the lower profile of a Volvo. "It's a nice car but it doesn't stand out too much."

In the Klondike years of primitive Russian capitalism, roughly 1992 through 1994, thousands became rich overnight. They struck export deals. Friends called friends who called friends about selling a barge load of scrap copper or an oil shipment. They were in the right places when state property was privatized. They opened banks and won deposits from state agencies and large export firms.

The key to wealth was seldom clever business skills, but rather the right connections inherited from the Soviet years. Many of the nouveaux riches were the sons and daughters of the late-Communist nomenklatura, the party and bureaucratic elite. The line between what was respectable and disreputable was gray, but many of the nouveaux riches were—and are—outright criminals. No one can say with certainty how many.

In the heady years, says Anatoly Zaitsev, assistant director of the Gelos Antiquarian Association, an auction house and gallery,

he recalls one buyer who gestured at an entire wall of rare, 19th-century paintings and antiques and said, "Pack it up by 2 p.m. tomorrow," without asking the price.

"There were plenty of people with buckets of money," he says, "but they got it through some big [stroke of] chance. They never learned how to earn it." So they spent it they same way they got it, in big careless chunks. "They threw it on the wind...."

"In the past two years, those who learned to earn money started businesses and are running them," says Mr. Zaitsev. "Those who didn't are no longer wealthy."

The wealth of many of the newly rich Russians rests on just one, two, or three very successful deals, says Olga

Kryshtanovskaya, director of elite studies at the Sociology Institute for the Russian Academy of Sciences. "If they get half a million or a million dollars, they keep spending it for the rest of their lives," she says, without ever establishing a regular income. But in the past couple of years, she says, such people have been pushed almost entirely out of big businesses, and the opportunities for hyper-profitable deals have dried up considerably....

The emerging class of wealthy Russians looks more like an upper-middle class in the West. Most of them are much like Leonov at his catalog business.

They are working harder for their money and thinking more about planning for the years ahead....

USE YOUR ECONOMIC REASONING

1. Why were 1992 through 1994 described as the "Klondike years" of primitive Russian capitalism? What was the key to becoming rich during this period?
2. Do you think the Klondike years have contributed to a positive attitude toward Russian entrepreneurs and the pursuit of profit or to a negative attitude? Will this cause Russians to support or oppose additional reforms?
3. How has the pursuit of wealth in Russia changed since 1994? What factors might be responsible for this new approach to achieving wealth?

Even those workers who are fortunate enough to have their state enterprises privatized (converted to private businesses) or who find jobs in newly created private firms have not been immune to unemployment. The old planned economy—which guaranteed everyone a job—left state enterprises overstaffed, with high production costs. As privatization has occurred, the pursuit of profit, coupled with intense competition from imported products, has forced the managers of these enterprises to downsize their workforce, retaining only the best employees. In addition, many new and privatized firms have failed because their products were inferior to those imported from the West and elsewhere. As a consequence, their workers have also joined the ranks of the unemployed.

The high unemployment, coupled with the virtual elimination of any sort of compensation for the unemployed, has impoverished a significant fraction of the Russian population. Economist Martin Spechler, an associate of the Russian and East European Institute at Indiana University, reports that 30 percent of the Russian population is existing at less than a subsistence level. At the same time, entrepreneurs and some skilled workers have seen their incomes dramatically increased. (The path to Russian riches may be different now than it was shortly after the breakup. See "Making a Million Isn't What It Used to Be," on pages 54–55.) In short, the changes that are sweeping the Russian economy are benefiting some and harming others. Those who have benefited are able to choose from store shelves that are stocked with products never before available, many imported from the West. At the same time, unemployed Russians find that they cannot afford even the modest lifestyle they enjoyed under the old planned system.

In addition to unemployment and poverty, a variety of other problems exist in Russia and throughout the Commonwealth states. Some big industries—particularly those related to the military—continue to receive government subsidies or loans that permit them to stay in business even though they are unprofitable. These subsidies contribute to inflation, which is now a major problem throughout the commonwealth. In addition, both the banking and legal systems are primitive. The poorly developed banking system makes it difficult to channel funds to promising businesses, while the crude legal system makes it difficult to enforce the contracts that underlie market transactions. A still more fundamental problem is that there is little understanding of the profit motive or the value of competition, two essential ingredients of capitalism. As a consequence, successful entrepreneurs are often likened to criminals rather than being respected for the jobs they create.

Can Russia and the other Commonwealth states overcome these problems and move closer to the capitalist model, or will the citizens become frustrated and demand a return to something like the old command system? Will the new independent states cooperate, or will economic or ethnic rivalries cause the Commonwealth to fail? No one can answer these questions. Reformers throughout the Commonwealth believe that market reforms can raise living standards, but the transition to a more market-oriented economy will be slow and painful, and success is by no means guaranteed.

THE DIVERSITY OF REAL-WORLD ECONOMIES

Compared to the United States and the former Soviet Union, most of the world's economies are characterized by a more thorough blending of capitalism and command socialism. Few, if any, approximate the model of pure capitalism better than the United States, and none matches the model of command socialism better than the Soviet Union did. Exhibit 2.3 summarizes the characteristics of nine national economies. Although this summary is by no means a refined analysis of the cited economies, it captures the diversity of organization of these real-world systems. As you can see, a high degree of public ownership usually corresponds with a high degree of central direction and command implementation. But there is no hard-and-fast rule. The nations appear to mix and match these three features as if they were experimenting to find the best combination for their particular situations.

In recent years many countries that we have come to think of as socialist have shown an increased interest in the market mechanism. We have already mentioned the changes in the Soviet Union, but there are other examples. Hungary, Czechoslovakia, Poland, and China are among the nations experimenting with a greater role for markets.

EXHIBIT 2.3

Characteristics of Some Selected Economies

COUNTRY	DEGREE OF PUBLIC OWNERSHIP	DEGREE OF CENTRAL DIRECTION	DEGREE OF COMMAND IMPLEMENTATION
Brazil	Moderate	Moderate	Minimal
China	Extensive	Extensive	Extensive
France	Moderate	Moderate	Minimal
Germany	Moderate	Minimal	Minimal
Great Britain	Moderate	Minimal	Minimal
Japan	Minimal	Moderate	Minimal
former Soviet Union	Extensive	Extensive	Extensive
Sweden	Moderate	Moderate	Moderate
United States	Minimal	Minimal	Minimal

Even if the market mechanism continues to win converts, we should not expect to see a world populated by precise copies of the model of pure capitalism. Each national economic system will remain unique, its own blend of public and private ownership, individual and collective decision making, and command and market implementation. The principles we have explored in this chapter provide a framework for understanding the more than 150 unique economies in the world.

In the remaining chapters of this text, we will examine the operation of the U.S. economy in more detail. To better understand our economy, however, we need to know more about how markets work and how government influences economic choices in our system. In Chapter 3 we begin to broaden our understanding of markets.

Summary

An *economic system* is a set of established procedures by which a society answers the three fundamental questions of what, how, and for whom to produce. Although economic systems differ significantly, all can be described according to three criteria: Who owns the *means of production*? Who makes the economic choices about what, how, and for whom to produce? What method is used to ensure that these economic choices are carried out?

Economists commonly use theoretical models to explain the operation of economic systems. At one extreme the model of *pure capitalism* describes an economic system in which the means of production are privately owned and fundamental economic choices are made by individuals and implemented through markets. The principal features of pure capitalism include private property and freedom of choice, with self-interest as the driving force (held in check by *pure competition*); price determination through markets; and a *laissez-faire* condition of minimum government intervention.

In a capitalist economy *consumer sovereignty* dictates which goods and services will be produced. If consumers want more of a particular product, its price will tend to rise, encouraging profit-seeking businesses to produce more of it. To produce these products, businesses buy economic resources (e.g., labor) from households, thereby providing households with the money needed to purchase the output of businesses. The circular-flow model of capitalism diagrams this process by showing how the flows of money (money flows) and of resources and products (real flows) circulate between the household and business sectors and operate through product and resource markets.

At the other extreme the model of *command socialism* describes an economic system in which the means of production are owned by the public or the state, decisions on the three fundamental questions are made by a central authority, and implementation of these decisions occurs through command.

The principal features of command socialism include public ownership, centralized decision making, economic planning, and allocation by command.

In command socialism the central planning authority gathers information on production capabilities and consumer preference (if the latter is a concern) and establishes production targets for the producing units, such as factories and farms. These units are required to produce the products dictated by the central authority in the manner specified. Output is then distributed according to the central authority's goals. Command socialism is depicted as a pyramid, with the central planning board at the top and the producing and consuming units below. The producing and consuming units supply information to the central planners, who use this information to develop production targets and decide how the limited output will be distributed among the potential consumers.

No existing economic system fits neatly into either model. All real-world economies are *mixed* because they represent some blending of the two models. For example, the U.S. economy, commonly described as a capitalist system, contains some elements of a socialist command economy. Public ownership is not uncommon in the United States, and powerful economic units—government, business, and labor—influence many of the fundamental economic choices. And the Soviet economy, the system thought to exemplify command socialism, contained some elements of capitalism. Free markets existed for certain products, and market-related incentives were sometimes used instead of commands. Most of the world's economies represent more complete blendings of capitalism and command socialism.

GLOSSARY

Capitalism. An economic system in which the means of production are privately owned and fundamental economic choices are made by individuals and implemented through the market mechanism—the interaction of buyers and sellers.

Command socialism. An economic system in which the means of production are publicly owned, the fundamental economic choices are made by a central authority, and commands are used to ensure that these decisions are implemented.

Common-property resources. Resources that belong to society as a whole rather than to particular individuals.

Consumer sovereignty. An economic condition in which consumers dictate which goods and services will be produced by businesses.

Economic system. The set of established procedures by which a society provides answers to the three fundamental questions.

Household. A living unit that also functions as an economic unit. Whether it consists of a single person or a large family, each household has a source of income and responsibility for spending that income.

Invisible hand. A doctrine introduced by Adam Smith in 1776 holding that individuals pursuing their self-interest will be guided (as if by an invisible hand) to achieve objectives that are also in the best interest of society as a whole.

Laissez-faire economy. An economy in which the degree of government intervention is minimal.

Market. All actual or potential buyers and sellers of a particular item. Markets can be international, national, regional, or local.

Means of production. The raw materials, factories, farms, and other economic resources used to produce goods and services.

Mixed economies. Economies that represent a blending of capitalism and command socialism. All real-world economies are mixed economies.

Pure competition. A situation in which a large number of relatively small buyers and sellers interact.

STUDY QUESTIONS

Fill in the Blanks

1. The driving force or engine of capitalism is ___Self - interest___

2. The functioning of a capitalist economy is coordinated and directed through ___Markets___ in which ___prices___ are determined by the interaction of buyers and sellers.

3. In the model of pure capitalism, the pursuit of self-interest by producers is kept in check by ___Competition___. The model of pure capitalism requires ___pure competition___, a situation in which there are a large number of buyers and sellers of each product.

4. Because businesspeople in a capitalist economy are motivated by self-interest, they want to produce the goods and services that will allow them to earn the highest ___profits___. Those products tend to be the ones that are most desired by ___consumers___.

5. According to Milton Friedman, competitive capitalism promotes ___political freedom___ by separating economic and political power.

6. In pure command socialism the fundamental economic decisions are made by the ___Central authority___ and implemented through ___commands___.

7. In pure command socialism ___economic planning___ replaces the market as the method of coordinating the various economic decisions.

8. It is possible to represent a socialist command economy as a ___pyramid___ with the ___planning board___ at the top and producing and consuming units at the bottom.

9. One weakness of command socialism is its inefficient ___information___ network.

10. The United States and the former Soviet Union are both examples of ___mixed___ economies.

Multiple Choice

1. Which of the following is *not* a characteristic of pure capitalism?
   a) Public ownership of the means of production
   b) The pursuit of self-interest
   c) Markets and prices
   d) Pure competition
   e) Limited government

2. In a market economy the scarcest resources will be used very conservatively because
   a) central planners will allocate such resources only where they are most needed.
   b) the scarcest resources will tend to have the highest prices.
   c) government officials will not permit their use.
   d) the scarcest resources will tend to have the lowest prices.

3. In a capitalist economy
   a) businesses are free to produce whatever products they choose.
   b) consumers are free to utilize their incomes as they see fit.
   c) resource owners have the freedom to sell their resources to whomever they choose.
   d) All of the above
   e) None of the above

4. Consumer sovereignty means that
   a) consumers dictate which goods and services will be produced by the way they spend their money.
   b) central planners allocate a major share of society's resources to the production of consumer goods.
   c) the role of government in the economy is very limited.
   d) all economic resources are used efficiently.

5. According to the "invisible hand" doctrine,
   a) as individuals pursue their own interests, they tend to promote the interests of society as a whole.
   b) the actions of individuals often have unanticipated and undesirable effects on society.
   c) individuals should put the interests of society first.
   d) when individuals attempt to promote the best interests of the entire society, they also further their own personal interests.

6. Adam Smith recognized that the "invisible hand" would function as he envisioned only if
   a) individuals unconsciously considered the welfare of others in making their decisions.
   b) government regulations forced businesses to behave in an ethical manner.
   c) a high degree of competition existed in the economy.
   d) individuals lived in accordance with the golden rule.

7. In a market economy, if consumers suddenly stop buying 10-speed bikes and start buying 21-speed bikes,
   a) the price of 10-speeds will tend to fall and more of them will be produced.
   b) the price of 21-speeds will tend to rise, making them less profitable to produce and encouraging producers to supply more of them.
   c) resources will tend to be shifted from the production of 10-speeds to the production of 21-speeds.
   d) the price of 10-speeds will tend to rise, making them more profitable to produce and encouraging producers to supply more of them.

8. Which of the following best describes command socialism?
   a) An economic system characterized by private ownership of the means of production, centralized decision making, and command implementation.
   b) An economic system characterized by public ownership of the means of

production, centralized decision making, and market implementation.

c) An economic system characterized by public ownership of the means of production, individual decision making, and command implementation.

d) An economic system characterized by public ownership of the means of production, centralized decision making, and command implementation.

9. Which of the following is correct?

a) In command socialism, the basic economic choices are made by individuals.

b) In pure capitalism, powerful economic units have a substantial impact on the way economic choices are made.

c) In command socialism, producers are required to produce whatever products central planners dictate.

d) In pure capitalism, economic planning ensures that the various production decisions will be consistent with one another.

10. In deciding what products to produce, the central planners in a socialist command economy need not consider

a) the size of the economy's labor force.

b) the production capabilities of the economy's factories.

c) consumer preferences.

d) the economy's stock of raw materials.

11. In order to get the most output from society's limited resources, the scarcest resources must be used only where no other input will suffice.

a) In command socialism this function is performed by planners; in pure capitalism it is performed by the central government.

b) In pure capitalism this function is performed by input prices; in command socialism it is performed by planners.

c) In command socialism this function is performed by the producing units; in pure capitalism it is performed by planners.

d) In pure capitalism this function is performed by government regulations, in command socialism it is performed by output targets.

12. In a comparison of command socialism and pure capitalism, which of the following is true?

a) Prices play a larger role in command socialism than in pure capitalism.

b) Resources are likely to be used more efficiently in command socialism than in pure capitalism.

c) Economic planning plays a larger role in pure capitalism than in command socialism.

d) Decision making is more decentralized in pure capitalism than in command socialism.

13. Which of the following is a true statement about the economic system of the former Soviet Union?

a) All prices were set by market forces.

b) Workers were free to make their own choices about jobs, based on their reactions to wages set by central planners.

c) Bonuses of all forms were illegal.

d) All agricultural output was produced on state farms.

14. One reason the United States is not an example of pure capitalism is that

a) most producing units are publicly owned.

b) commands are used to implement some economic decisions.

c) the pursuit of self-interest is a powerful force.

d) markets are used to coordinate most economic decisions.

15. Which of the following was *not* an accomplishment of Mikhail Gorbachev?

a) Discrediting the Soviet economic system.

b) Introducing greater political freedom.

c) Eliminating most price regulation.

d) Permitting some small private enterprises.

Problems and Questions for Discussion

1. What is an economic system? Why is it valid to say that no two real-world economic systems are exactly alike?

2. List the characteristics or elements of pure capitalism and explain each. Are any of these elements absent from the U.S. economy? Explain.

3. How would a socialist command economy answer the three fundamental questions? What elements of command socialism exist in the U.S. economy?

4. Explain the role of economic planning in command socialism. Who is in charge of economic planning in a capitalist economy?

5. Try to draw the circular-flow diagram without looking back at the diagram in the text. Now, label all the parts of the diagram, and indicate which flows are money flows and which are real flows. Use the diagram to explain how a capitalist economy works.

6. Draw the command pyramid and label the parts. What does the command pyramid tell us about the way a socialist command economy functions?

7. If all real-world economies are mixed economies, why is the U.S. economy commonly described as a market economy and the former Soviet economy as a command system?

8. Why might a centrally planned economy, such as the Soviet economy, use economic incentives rather than commands to accomplish some objectives? If the leadership is willing to rely on incentives and markets to some extent, why does it restrict their use?

9. Soviet factory managers were known to deliberately understate their factories' production capabilities when reporting to central planners. How was such understatement to their advantage?

10. The development of high-speed computers might be a more important breakthrough for a socialist command economy than for a capitalist economy. Why?

ANSWER KEY

Fill in the Blanks

1. self-interest
2. markets, prices
3. competition, pure competition
4. profits, consumers
5. political freedom
6. central authority, commands
7. economic planning
8. pyramid, planning board
9. information
10. mixed

Multiple Choice

1. a	4. a	7. c	10. c	13. b
2. b	5. a	8. d	11. b	14. b
3. d	6. c	9. c	12. d	15. c

PART TWO

Microeconomics: Markets, Prices, and the Role of Competition

In Chapter 3 we begin our study of microeconomics by investigating how prices are determined in competitive markets. You will learn the precise meaning of "supply" and "demand" and how the interaction of these forces determines prices. You will examine how prices can change and will learn the functions that price changes perform in a market economy. In Chapter 4 you will investigate the degree of consumer and producer responsiveness to price changes.

Chapter 5 explores the idea that human beings are rational decision makers who are motivated by self-interest. You will find that rational decision making involves a careful comparison of costs and benefits and that the relevant costs and benefits are always "marginal." Chapter 6 examines the behavior of the purely competitive firm and explores how firms use marginal reasoning to determine the profit-maximizing output. You will discover the characteristics of a competitive industry and see why competition is beneficial for consumers. Chapter 7 examines how firms acquire pricing discretion, or market power, and how the behavior of firms that possess market power differs from that of purely competitive firms. An appendix to the chapter examines the pricing techniques actually employed by businesses and compares them to the theoretical techniques suggested by economists. Chapter 8 considers the "degrees" of competition that exist in different industry structures and explores the impact of those different industry structures on the well-being of consumers. Chapter 9 looks at some of the inherent limitations of a market economy by examining the origin of problems such as pollution.

Demand and Supply: Price Determination in Competitive Markets

1. Define demand and supply and represent these concepts graphically.
2. State the "laws" of demand and supply.
3. Identify the determinants of demand and supply.
4. Recognize the difference between a change in demand (supply) and a change in the quantity demanded (supplied).
5. Explain and illustrate graphically how the equilibrium price and quantity are determined.
6. Describe the rationing, signaling, and motivating functions of prices.
7. Identify the factors that can cause the equilibrium price to change.
8. Use demand and supply curves to predict changes in the equilibrium price and quantity.
9. Discuss the impact of government-established maximum and minimum prices.

How do markets work? A market economy is governed by the interaction of buyers and sellers in thousands of different product and resource markets. This interaction—what you might describe as bargaining or negotiating—determines prices. The prevailing prices of goods and services tell producers which products consumers want the most. Resource prices tell producers which resources to use to produce those products profitably. Because resource prices affect consumers' incomes, they also influence the distribution of goods and services. For example, workers whose skills are particularly scarce can command higher salaries and thereby claim a larger share of the society's limited output. In short, prices play a very important role in the functioning of all mixed economies.

This chapter introduces the model of demand and supply, the model intended to illustrate how buyers and sellers interact to determine prices in competitive markets. Competitive markets are composed of many independent buyers and sellers, each too small to be able to influence the market price significantly. We'll explore the meaning of competitive markets in greater detail later in the text. For now, just remember that in competitive markets, prices are determined by the impersonal forces of demand and supply, not by manipulations of powerful buyers or sellers.

After you study this chapter, you will have a better understanding of how prices are determined and a greater appreciation of the role that prices play in a market economy. You'll understand why the price of gold fluctuates and why salaries are higher in some occupations than in others. You'll understand why antique cars often command higher prices than this year's models and why a poor wheat harvest in Canada or Ukraine can mean higher bread prices in the United States. You will also understand how prices both direct the actions of producers and determine the distribution of society's limited output of goods and services. In summary, the material in this chapter will give you a clearer comprehension of the role of markets and prices in our economy.

Demand

In a market economy, consumers are sovereign; that is, consumers dictate which goods and services will be produced. But it is consumer *demand* rather than consumer wants or desires that actually directs the market. We have already noted that human wants are unlimited. Wanting an item, however, and being willing and able to pay for it are two distinctly different things. If the item we want carries a price tag, we may do without it: We may lack the money to pay or we may prefer to spend that money on something else.

People who are both *willing and able* to make purchases are the consumers who determine which products a market economy will produce. When consumers lack either the willingness or the ability to spend their dollars, producers do not respond. Thus, the concept of demand includes the willingness and ability of potential buyers to purchase a product. We define **demand** as a schedule (or table) showing the quantities of a good or service that consumers are willing and able to purchase at various prices during a given time period, when all factors other than the product's price remain unchanged.

Exhibit 3.1 illustrates the concept of demand through a simple example. The schedule shows the yearly demand for jogging shoes of a given quality in the hypothetical community of Hometown, U.S.A. You can see that the number of pairs of jogging shoes that Hometown consumers are willing and able to purchase each year depends on the selling price. If jogging shoes sell for $100 a pair, Hometowners will purchase 2,000 pairs a year, assuming that other factors remain the same—their incomes, for example, and their present jogging routines.

EXHIBIT 3.1

Hometown Demand for Jogging Shoes

PRICE (per pair)	QUANTITY (pairs per year)
$100	2,000
$ 80	4,000
$ 60	6,000
$ 40	8,000
$ 20	10,000

DEMAND CURVES

Economists usually represent schedules in the form of graphs. To graph the demand for jogging shoes, we first plot the information in Exh. 3.1 and then connect the points to form a demand curve, as shown in Exh. 3.2. A **demand curve** is simply a graphical representation of demand. By convention we measure price on the vertical axis and quantity on the horizontal axis. Each point on the curve represents a price and the quantity that consumers would

EXHIBIT 3.2

The Demand Curve for Jogging Shoes in Hometown, U.S.A.

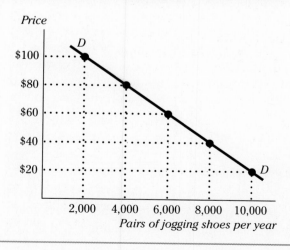

A demand curve is a graphical representation of demand. It demonstrates the inverse relationship between price and quantity demanded.

demand per year at that price. For example, we can see in Exh. 3.2 that at a price of $80, Hometown joggers would demand 4,000 pairs; at a price of $60, the quantity demanded would increase to 6,000 pairs.

The Law of Demand

Our hypothetical demand schedule and demand curve for jogging shoes demonstrate clearly what economists call the **law of demand,** which holds that the quantity demanded of a product is *negatively, or inversely, related* to its price. This simply means that consumers will purchase more of a product at lower prices than at higher prices. That's why demand curves always slope downward and to the right.

Economists believe that two factors explain the inverse relationship between price and quantity demanded:

1. When prices are lower, consumers can afford to purchase a larger quantity of the product out of any given income. Economists refer to this *ability* to purchase more as the **income effect** of a price reduction.
2. At lower prices the product becomes more attractive relative to other items serving the same function. This **substitution effect** explains the *willingness* of consumers to substitute for other products the product that has declined in price.

To illustrate the income and substitution effects, let's return to our Hometown consumers. Why will they purchase more jogging shoes at $20 than at $100? Because of the income effect, their incomes will now buy more: If the price of jogging shoes declines and other prices don't change, consumers will be able to buy more goods and services with their fixed incomes. It's almost as though each consumer had received a raise. And because of the substitution effect, consumers will buy jogging shoes instead of tennis shoes, sandals, or moccasins because jogging shoes have become a better footwear buy. Because of both the income effect and the substitution effect, we all, like these hypothetical consumers, tend to purchase more of a product at a lower price than at a higher price.

Determinants of Demand

The demand curve and the law of demand emphasize the relationship between the price of a product and the quantity demanded. But price is not the only factor that determines how much of a product consumers will buy. A variety of other factors underlie the demand schedule and determine the precise position of the demand curve. These **determinants of demand** include income, tastes and preferences, expectations regarding future prices, the price of related goods, and the number of buyers in the market. Any demand curve is based on the assumption that these factors are held constant. Changes in one or more of these determinants cause the entire demand curve to shift to a new position.

INCOME

The most obvious determinant of demand is income. Consumers' incomes influence their *ability* to purchase goods and services. For what economists call **normal goods,** an increase in income will cause consumers to purchase more of a product than before at each possible price. For example, an increase in per capita income (income per person) will probably cause consumers to buy more steak than before at whatever price exists. We would show this by shifting the demand curve to the right, as illustrated in Exh. 3.3.

Not all products are normal goods, however. An increase in income will cause consumers to purchase less of an **inferior good,** thus shifting the demand curve to the left. Powdered milk, generic macaroni and cheese, and

---

EXHIBIT 3.3

Income as a Determinant of Demand

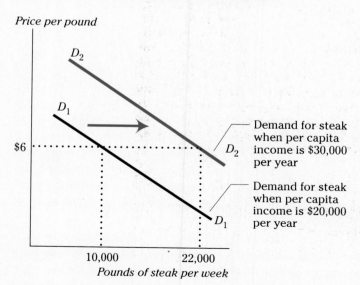

Price per pound

D_2

D_1

$6

D_2 — Demand for steak when per capita income is $30,000 per year

D_1 — Demand for steak when per capita income is $20,000 per year

10,000   22,000

Pounds of steak per week

An increase in per capita income will shift the demand curve for a normal good to the right. Consumers will purchase more of the product at each price.

cheap wine are examples of products that might be inferior goods. When consumers' incomes increase, they may choose to buy less of these products in favor of more appetizing grocery items.

TASTES AND PREFERENCES

Consumers' tastes and preferences—how well they like the product relative to other products—are also important determinants of demand. A change in tastes and preferences will affect the demand for products. For example, the desire to limit cholesterol intake has altered consumer tastes and preferences for various food products. Today consumers demand less red meat and fewer eggs than in times past but demand more fish and chicken. In other words, this change in tastes and preferences has caused the demand curves for red meat and eggs to shift to the left and the demand curves for fish and chicken to shift to the right.

EXPECTATIONS ABOUT PRICES

Expectations may also influence consumer behavior. For example, the expectation that the price of an item will rise in the future usually encourages consumers to buy it now. We would represent this by shifting the entire demand curve to the right to show that more would be demanded now at whatever price prevailed. Similarly, the expectation that a product will decline in price is a good incentive to postpone buying it; the present demand curve for the product would shift to the left.

PRICE OF RELATED GOODS

A somewhat less obvious determinant of demand is the price of related goods. Although all goods compete for a consumer's income, the price of substitutes and complements may be particularly important in explaining consumer behavior. **Substitutes** are simply products that can be used in place of other products because, to a greater or lesser extent, they satisfy the same consumer wants. Hot dogs are a typical substitute for hamburgers, and tennis shoes may substitute for jogging shoes unless one is a serious jogger. **Complements** are products normally purchased along with or in conjunction with another product. For example, pickle relish and hot dogs are complements, as are lettuce and salad dressing.

If the price of hamburgers increased and the price of hot dogs remained unchanged, consumers might be expected to buy fewer hamburgers and more hot dogs. The demand curve for hot dogs would shift to the right. By the same token, an increase in the price of lettuce is likely to have an adverse effect on the sale of salad dressing. Because people buy salad dressing as a complement to salad vegetables, anything that causes consumers to eat fewer salads causes them to demand less salad dressing. The demand curve for salad dressing would shift to the left.

THE NUMBER OF CONSUMERS IN THE MARKET

The final determinant of demand is the number of consumers in the market. The more consumers who demand a particular product, the greater the total demand for the product. When the number of consumers increases, the demand curve for the product shifts to the right to show that a greater quantity is now demanded at each price. If the number of consumers declines, the demand curve shifts to the left.

As we think about the demand for a particular product, we need to remember the five determinants we have listed and how changes in these factors will affect the demand curve. We also need to recognize that more and more U.S. firms are selling their products to consumers in Mexico, Europe, and other locations outside the United States. As a consequence, the position of the demand curve for many products is determined not solely by local or national factors but by international factors as well. For instance, rising incomes in Mexico are certain to shift the demand curve for U.S. automobiles to the right, whereas the increased availability of cheap Chilean wines will probably shift the demand curve for many California wines to the left. The point is that markets are often international in scope, so that we need to look beyond national boundaries to determine the level of demand.

Change in Quantity Demanded Versus Change in Demand

In analyzing the factors that cause consumers to increase or decrease their purchases of a particular product, it is helpful to distinguish between the impact of a change (1) in the price of the product and (2) in one or more of the determinants of demand.

A change in the price of the product results in a **change in quantity demanded** and is represented graphically by movement along a stationary demand curve. For example, if the price of steak declines from $6 a pound to $4 a pound, consumers will move from point A to point B on demand curve D_1 in Exh. 3.4. Note that the consumers will now choose to purchase a greater quantity of the product because its price is lower. This is an increase in the quantity demanded. If, on the other hand, the price rises from $2 a pound to $4 a pound, the consumers will move from point C to point B on the demand curve. Here a price increase will cause a reduction in the quantity demanded.

EXHIBIT 3.4

Distinguishing Change in Demand from Change in Quantity Demanded

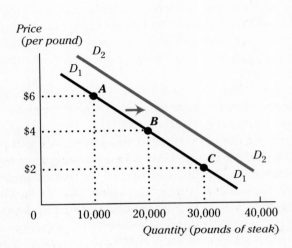

A change in the price of steak will cause a *change in the quantity demanded*. When the price of steak declines from $6 to $2 a pound, the quantity demanded increases from 10,000 to 30,000 pounds; consumers move from *A* to *C* along demand curve D_1.

A change in a determinant of demand will cause a *change in demand*: the entire curve will shift. The movement from D_1 to D_2 is an increase in demand.

When any determinant of demand changes, the result is a **change in demand**—an entirely new demand schedule represented graphically by a shift of the demand curve to a new position. If consumers develop a stronger preference for steak, for instance, or if the prices of substitutes for steak rise, the entire demand curve for steak will shift to the right—an increase in demand. This shift is depicted in Exh. 3.4. An entire demand curve shift to the left would denote a decrease in demand. See "Used-Car Prices Cool, Chilling Detriot," on pages 76–77, to test your understanding of the difference between a change in demand and a change in the quantity demanded.

Supply

A knowledge of demand is essential to an understanding of how prices are determined, but it is only half the picture. Now we turn to the supply side of the market.

When we use the term "supply" in our everyday language, we are usually referring to a fixed quantity. That's what the owner of the local sporting-goods store means when advertising a *limited supply* of Fleet Feet tennis shoes or SuperFit swimsuits. But that's not what economists mean when they talk about supply. To economists, supply is a schedule—just as demand is. **Supply** is a

EXHIBIT 3.5

Hometown Supply of Jogging Shoes

PRICE (per pair)	QUANTITY (pairs per year)
$100	10,000
$ 80	8,000
$ 60	6,000
$ 40	4,000
$ 10	2,000

schedule (or table) showing the quantities of a good or service that producers are willing and able to offer for sale at various prices during a given time period, when all factors other than the product's price remain unchanged.

Exhibit 3.5 represents the annual supply of jogging shoes in the Hometown market area. As the schedule shows, the number of pairs of jogging shoes that suppliers will make available for sale depends on the price of jogging shoes. At a price of $100 a pair, suppliers are willing to produce 10,000 pairs of jogging shoes a year; at a price of $60, they would offer only 6,000 pairs. Because supply is a schedule, we can't determine the quantity supplied unless we know the selling price.

THE SUPPLY CURVE

To transform our supply schedule into a supply curve, we follow the same procedure we used in constructing a demand curve. Here we graph the information in Exh. 3.5, measuring price on the vertical axis and quantity on the horizontal axis. When we've finished graphing the points from the schedule, we connect them to get a **supply curve**—a graphical representation of supply (Exh. 3.6 on page 78).

Interpreting a supply curve is basically the same as interpreting a demand curve. Each point on the curve represents a price and the quantity of jogging shoes that producers will supply at that price. You can see, for example, that producers will supply 4,000 pairs of shoes at a price of $40 per pair or 8,000 pairs at a price of $80 per pair.

The Law of Supply

You've probably noticed that the supply curve slopes upward and to the right. The supply curve slopes upward because the **law of supply** holds that price and quantity supplied are *positively, or directly, related*. Producers will supply a larger quantity at higher prices than at lower prices.

Use Your Economic Reasoning

Used-Car Prices Cool, Chilling Detroit. Drop Since Spring Is Bad Omen for New-Vehicle Sales

By Oscar Suris
Staff reporter of the Wall Street Journal

DETROIT-Retail prices for used cars and light trucks have been on a downward spiral in recent months, a trend that auto-industry experts say usually spells trouble for sales of new vehicles.

With used vehicles fetching less, consumers have less credit from their trade-ins to spend on new vehicles. Softer used-car prices also suggest that consumers are more willing to put off big-ticket purchases, a trend that usu-

ally spreads to those contemplating visits to new-car dealerships.

The U.S. Commerce Department's monthly index of used-car prices has been registering year-to-year declines since May, following shrinking price rises since January. U.S. sales of new vehicles have reflected the trend, registering a year-to-year drop of 2.2% in ^

profit margins. For one thing, lower prices for older vehicles force auto makers to offer more generous cash rebates and discounted financing terms to ensure that new vehicles remain price-competitive. Lower used-vehicle values also make automobile leases, one of Detroit's favorite marketing tools, inherently more expensive to underwrite, since much of the profit from leasing comes from the resale leased vehicles....

However, used-car prices n't the only thing behind recent softening in

Why would producers supply more jogging shoes at a higher price than at a lower price? The major reason is that the higher price allows them to cover the higher unit costs associated with producing the additional output. It probably costs more to produce the thousandth pair of jogging shoes than it did to produce the five hundredth pair. It's also likely that it would cost even more to produce the two thousandth pair, and so on. Producers are willing to supply a greater quantity at a higher price because the higher price enables businesses to cover the higher cost of producing the additional units—units that would not have been profitable at lower prices.

new-car sales. Economists and industry experts say burgeoning consumer debt loads are a problem. Higher interest rates have also made a tax-friendly source of credit, the home equity loan, less affordable for many. Add slow growth in real incomes, and it becomes clearer why auto makers like Ford Motor Co. and Toyota Motor Corp. have spent much of this year offering fat rebates and deeply discounted lease deals on bread-and-butter products such as the Taurus and Camry sedans.

"This is an attempt to create one's own wind to keep the kite sailing," says [economist David] Littman, who observes that new-car sales predictably went south in the late '80s following a decline in used-car prices in 1985....

Another factor that could further deflate used-car prices: the growing number of two- to three-year-old

vehicles returning to dealerships from lease deals.

Scott Merlis of Merlis Automotive International Inc., a consulting group, estimates that expiring automotive leases will return 4.6 million cars and light trucks to the used-car market this year, up

from 3.9 million in 1995. Mr. Merlis says the impact from that wave will be lower prices for used cars and more competition for new vehicles.

"We are getting to the point where supply is beginning to overtake demand," he says.

USE YOUR ECONOMIC REASONING

1. Why might falling used-car prices lead to lower sales of new cars? Should the lower sales of new cars be described as a reduction in demand or a reduction in the quantity demanded? How would you represent this graphically?

2. What factors in addition to lower used-car prices are depressing new-car sales? Are these factors shifting the demand curve for new cars or causing movement along the curve?

3. Ford and Toyota are offering rebates in an attempt to sell more cars. Are they attempting to increase demand or the quantity demanded? Suppose that, instead of offering rebates, they initiated a new advertising campaign touting the superiority of their automobiles; would that tend to increase demand or the quantity demanded?

Costs per unit tend to increase with output because some of a business's resources, such as its production plant and equipment, cannot be expanded in a short period of time. Therefore, as the business increases output by hiring more labor and employing more raw materials, it eventually begins to overutilize its factory and equipment. This leads to congestion, workers waiting to use equipment, more frequent breakdowns of equipment, and production bottlenecks—situations in which one stage of the production process is slowing down the entire operation. These problems increase the cost of producing additional units. Producers will supply the additional units only if

EXHIBIT 3.6

The Supply Curve of Jogging Shoes in Hometown, U.S.A.

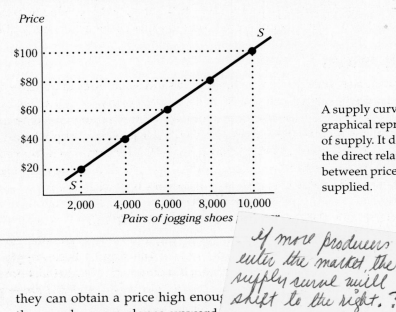

A supply curve is a graphical representation of supply. It demonstrates the direct relationship between price and quantity supplied.

[handwritten note: If more producers enter the market, the supply curve will shift to the right. ?]

they can obtain a price high enou̶ ̶ ̶ ̶ ̶ ̶ osts. Thus, the supply curve slopes upward ̶ ̶ ̶ ̶ ̶ ̶ ̶ ̶ ̶ ̶ ary to call forth additional output from supp ̶ ̶ ̶ ̶

Determinants of Supply

The supply curve shows the relationship between the price of a product and the quantity supplied when other factors remain unchanged. However, price is not the only factor that influences the amount producers will offer for sale. Three major **determinants of supply** underlie the supply schedule and determine the position of the supply curve: technology, prices of the resources used in producing the product, and the number of producers in the market. Each supply curve is based on the assumption that these factors are held constant. Changes in any of the determinants will shift the entire supply curve to a new position.

TECHNOLOGY

Each supply curve is based on the existing technology. **Technology** is our state of knowledge about how to produce products. It influences the types of machines we use and the combinations of other resources we select to produce goods and services. A **technological advance** is the discovery of a better way to produce a product—a method that uses fewer resources to produce each unit of output or

that produces more output from a given amount of resources. Because a technological advance allows producers to supply a higher quantity at any given price,
it is represented by shifting the supply curve to the right, as depicted in Exh. 3.7.
As you can see, the development of a better method for producing personal computers will allow computer producers to supply a higher quantity at each price.

RESOURCE PRICES

Businesses must purchase economic resources in order to produce their products. Each supply curve assumes that the prices of resources remain unchanged. An increase in the price of labor, materials, or some other production
input will increase producers' costs and cause them to supply less at any given
price. The supply curve will shift to the left. A reduction in resource prices will
have the opposite effect; the supply curve will shift to the right because producers will be able to supply a higher quantity at each price.

THE NUMBER OF PRODUCERS IN THE MARKET

A third determinant of supply is the number of producers in the particular
market: the more producers, the greater the supply. Each supply curve assumes that the number of producers is unchanged. If additional producers enter the market, the supply curve will shift to the right; if some producers
leave, the supply curve will shift left.

EXHIBIT 3.7

The Impact of a Technological Advance
on the Supply of Personal Computers

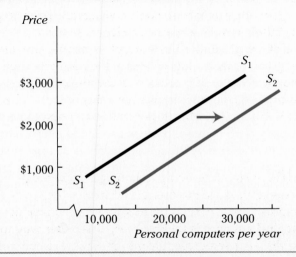

A technological advance
will allow producers to
supply a higher quantity at
any given price.

Many other changes have essentially the same impact on supply as an increase or decrease in the number of producers. A severe frost destroys half the orange crop, decreasing supply; a good growing season enlarges the wheat harvest, increasing supply; trade barriers are lowered and additional beef enters the United States, increasing supply. With each of these changes, the supply curve shifts as it would if the number of suppliers had increased or decreased.

As with demand, we need to recognize that the three determinants of supply—technology, resource prices, and the number of producers in the market—may be subject to international influences. For instance, the need to compete with foreign rivals has been a major factor spurring U.S. producers to search for and implement cost-reducing technological advances. In the furniture industry, for example, pressure from foreign producers has resulted in innovations that increase the amount of furniture produced from a given amount of wood. These innovations will cause the supply curve for furniture to shift to the right. At the same time, the supply curve of aluminum has shifted to the right for a very different reason. In the wake of the collapse of the Soviet Union, Russia has been supplying the world with massive amounts of aluminum—aluminum that once would have gone to military uses in the USSR. As you can see, we cannot ignore international factors as we attempt to determine the level of supply.

Change in Supply versus Change in Quantity Supplied

Earlier in this chapter you learned the difference between a change in demand and a change in *quantity* demanded. Economists make the same distinction for supply. A **change in the quantity supplied** results from a change in the price of the product, with factors other than price held constant. It is represented graphically by movement along a stationary supply curve. According to Exh. 3.8, if the price of personal computers declines from $2,000 to $1,000, the quantity supplied will decrease from 20,000 units to only 10,000 units a year, as suppliers move from point *B* to point *A* along supply curve S_1. But if the price of computers increases from $2,000 to $3,000, producers will move from point *B* to point *C*, and the quantity supplied will expand from 20,000 to 30,000 computers a year.

A **change in supply** is an increase or decrease in the amount of a product supplied at each and every price. A change in supply is caused by a change in one of the determinants of supply and is represented graphically by a shift of the entire supply curve, as depicted in Exh. 3.8. If the supply curve shifts to the right (from S_1 to S_2), it denotes an increase in supply; a shift to the left indicates a decrease in supply. (To test your ability to distinguish between a change in supply and a change in the quantity supplied, read the article "Business of Mining Gets a Lot Less Basic," on pages 82–83, and answer the questions.)

EXHIBIT 3.8

Distinguishing Change in Supply from Change in Quantity Supplied

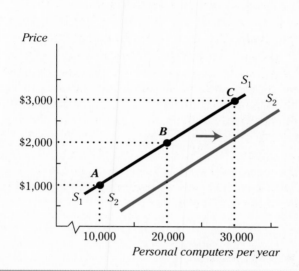

A change in the price of computers will cause a *change in the quantity supplied.* When price increases from $1,000 to $3,000, the quantity supplied increases from 10,000 to 30,000 computers per year; we move from *A* to *C* along supply curve S_1.

A change in a determinant of supply will cause a *change in supply:* the entire curve will shift. The movement from S_1 to S_2 is an increase in supply.

The Process of Price Determination

Now that you understand the basics of demand and supply, let's put those two pieces of the puzzle together and examine how prices are determined. To do that, we'll consider again the market for jogging shoes. Exhibit 3.9 (on page 84) displays hypothetical demand and supply schedules for that product. As you already know, the demand schedule shows the quantities of jogging shoes that will be demanded at various prices, and the supply schedule reveals the quantities that will be supplied at those prices. But which of these possible prices will prevail in the market? And what quantity of jogging shoes will be exchanged between buyers and sellers? To answer those questions, let's compare the reactions of buyers and sellers to each possible price.

What would happen in the market if jogging shoes were selling for $20 a pair? Because the $20 price would be attractive to consumers but not to producers, 10,000 pairs of jogging shoes would be demanded, but only 2,000 pairs would be supplied. At the $20 price there would be a **shortage**—an excess of quantity demanded over quantity supplied—of 8,000 pairs of jogging

Business of Mining Gets a Lot Less Basic

By *Michael M. Phillips*
Staff Reporter of the Wall Street
Journal

Mining, that most basic of industries, is increasingly throwing down its old tools and picking up new technology.

It's a matter of survival. "We essentially keep…afloat by using as much technology as we can," says Jim Hesketh, superintendent of mine engineering at the Sierrita copper and molybdenum mine in Green Valley, Ariz.

At Sierrita, a property of Cyprus Amax Minerals Co. of Englewood, Colo., satellites, computers, lasers and a host of other advances are cutting costs, making it economically feasible to continue digging low-grade ore and selling it for a profit.

"The general public views mining as a bunch of Neanderthal-type guys trying to chip away at some face with picks and shovels—clearly that's not the state of the industry," says Ed Dowling, director of process management and engineering at Cyprus Amax.

Most high-quality, accessible pockets of natural resources in the U.S. have been tapped out, leaving oil, gas and mining companies with deposits that are low-grade or buried in hard-to-reach places. That makes it tough to compete against foreign producers with lower labor costs and richer reserves, especially when commodity prices fluctuate.

Some companies haven't been up to the challenge. But those who have pulled through—from Colorado coal mines to Minnesota taconite pits—have done so by investing in technology that lets fewer workers produce more from less.

The numbers speak for themselves. In 1987, 717,000 Americans worked in extractive industries. Since then, 21% of those jobs have disappeared, but the workers who remain have become much more productive. In copper mining, the average worker in 1994 produced 20% more per hour than in 1990; in coal mining, productivity grew 27%.

In underground coal mines the most significant innovation has been long-wall mining, in which two whirling drills race along a face of coal hundreds of feet long, chewing out chunks as big as desks and depositing them on a conveyor belt to the surface.

Cyprus Amax installed a new long wall at its Twenty-mile coal mine in Colorado last year. Now a handful of miners can crack off more than a thousand tons of coal each hour, pacing back and forth in the grimy darkness 1,000 feet below the Rocky Mountains—with electronic control pads in their hands. As the drills scrape away the coal face, 148 computer-controlled hydraulic roof supports creep forward as well, protecting the miners from cave-ins.

After the supports move forward, the roof falls loudly, but safely, in their wake. A controlled collapse, miners figure, is better than a surprise one, and the procedure allows them to pull out massive quantities of coal without leaving rock

SOURCE: *Wall Street Journal*, March 18,1997, p. B1. Reprinted by permission of the *Wall Street Journal*, ©1997 Dow Jones & Company Inc. All Rights Reserved Worldwide.

support pillars. The Twenty-mile machine recently finished extracting a rectangular coal bed some 8 feet high, 840 feet wide and 18,000 feet long. The operation set a new one-month long-wall world record, 893,108 tons, and almost doubled labor productivity.

While Twentymile's coal reserve remains rich, the Homestake Gold Mine in Lead, S.D., has seen ore quality sink. The underground mine, discovered in 1876, was losing money fast in the early 1990s, and its parent, Homestake Mining Co. of San Francisco, was questioning its economic viability. The mine has since turned profitable again, in part because the company installed a computer system that allows one operator to control ventilation, pumping, fire detection, and seismic monitoring—critical functions that let miners more safely exploit otherwise dangerous areas. "It helped to make the mine cost-effective again," says Steve Orr, Homestake's vice president of U.S. operations.

In Minnesota taconite pits, which produce low-grade iron ore, the biggest cost saver has been large-capacity haul trucks, which allow one driver to carry 240 tons of rock in a single trip from pit to crusher. Caterpillar Inc., in Peoria, IL., is now working on a vehicle with a 340-ton capacity, an improvement made possible in part by Groupe Michelin's new tire technologies designed to support the 1.2 million-pound vehicles. Even blasting, which breaks ore into scoopable chunks, has seen tremendous advances. One device being tested is an electronic ignitor, which could time a sequential blast of a million pounds of explosives down to a few microseconds, lower processing costs....

The next big industry money saver could be the automated mine. Caterpillar is developing a driverless haul truck controlled via satellite.

Mr. Hesketh estimates that within a decade every major piece of open-pit mining equipment will be un-manned—drilling, blasting, scooping and hauling when the computer tells it to do so. Should problems crop up, an off-site operator could correct the problem using virtual-reality controls.

"In effect, [the mining industry] is tackling process control in exactly the same manner that the U.S. manufacturing industry was forced to do in the 1980s in order to stay globally competitive," says David J. Everhart, director of Caterpillar's corporate mining group. "The mining houses in the '90s are faced with the same challenge."

USE YOUR ECONOMIC REASONING

1. Why are U.S. mining firms finding it difficult to compete with foreign mining firms: What advantages do the foreign firms possess?
2. How are technological advances helping U.S. firms to lower costs and compete with foreign firms? Be specific; what costs are being reduced through these technological advances?
3. Will technological advances in the mining industry increase the supply of coal (iron ore, etc.) or the quantity supplied? How should we represent this graphically?

EXHIBIT 3.9

The Demand and Supply of Jogging Shoes in Hometown, U.S.A.

PRICE (per pair)	QUANTITY DEMANDED (pairs per year)	QUANTITY SUPPLIED (pairs per year)
$100	2,000	10,000
$ 80	4,000	8,000
$ 60	6,000	6,000
$ 40	8,000	4,000
$ 20	10,000	2,000

shoes. Therefore, some potential buyers would offer to pay a higher price in order to obtain the product. Competition among these buyers would tend to push the price to a higher level, and the higher price of jogging shoes would tend to reduce the quantity demanded while encouraging producers to expand the quantity supplied. In this way price increases would tend to reduce the shortage of jogging shoes.

Suppose that the price of jogging shoes rose to $40 a pair. At that price 8,000 pairs of jogging shoes would be demanded and 4,000 pairs supplied. Once again there would be a shortage, but this time it would amount to only 4,000 pairs of jogging shoes (8,000 pairs demanded minus 4,000 pairs supplied). Competition among potential buyers again would bid up the price of jogging shoes. The higher price would lead to a reduction in the quantity demanded and an increase in the quantity supplied, which would reduce the shortage still further.

You can probably see what happens as we move from lower to higher prices. Now let's reverse the process, beginning with the highest price in Exh. 3.9. A price of $100 would tend to encourage production and discourage consumption. Producers would be willing to supply 10,000 pairs of jogging shoes a year, but consumers would demand only 2,000 pairs. The result would be a **surplus**—an excess of quantity supplied over quantity demanded—of 8,000 pairs of jogging shoes a year. How do producers react to a surplus? They begin to cut the price of the product in order to compete for existing customers and lure additional customers into the market. The lower price of jogging shoes tends to increase the quantity demanded and decrease the quantity supplied, thus reducing the surplus. If the price fell to $80, there would still be a surplus of 4,000 pairs of jogging shoes (8,000 pairs supplied minus the 4,000 pairs demanded). Price cutting would then continue, and the surplus would continue to shrink.

EQUILIBRIUM PRICE AND QUANTITY

In our example $60 is the market-clearing, or equilibrium, price, and 6,000 units is the equilibrium quantity. The **equilibrium price** is the price that brings about an equality between the quantity demanded and the quantity supplied. The **equilibrium quantity** is the quantity demanded and supplied at the equilibrium price. Equilibrium essentially means stability; once established, the equilibrium price will be maintained so long as the basic supply and demand conditions remain unchanged.

In a competitive market the actual, or prevailing, price will tend toward equilibrium. As you saw in Exh. 3.9, when the price of jogging shoes is above or below equilibrium, market pressures tend to push it down or up toward the equilibrium level. Only when the existing price is at the equilibrium level will there be neither a shortage nor a surplus and no pressure for price to change.

We use supply and demand curves to represent the process of price determination. By graphing the demand and supply schedules in Exh. 3.9, we can construct the demand and supply curves found in Exh. 3.10 on page 86. These curves intersect at the equilibrium price ($60) and the equilibrium quantity (6,000 pairs of jogging shoes). At any price *above* equilibrium (say, $80), we can measure the amount of the surplus as the horizontal distance between the demand curve and the supply curve. For any price *below* equilibrium ($20, for example), the horizontal distance between the curves tells us the amount of the shortage. As we noted earlier, the shortage or surplus tends to shrink as price approaches the equilibrium level. The graph visually represents these shrinking amounts in the diminishing distance between the demand curve and the supply curve. When price finally achieves equilibrium, the curves intersect. At that point quantity demanded equals quantity supplied, and there is neither shortage nor surplus.

THE RATIONING, AND MOTIVATING FUNCTIONS OF PRICES

In the preceding example the equilibrium price succeeds in matching up the quantity supplied and the quantity demanded because it performs two important functions. First, the equilibrium price rations jogging shoes perfectly among the various users; at a price of $60, 6,000 pairs of jogging shoes are demanded—exactly the quantity made available by producers. Second, the $60 price motivates producers to supply the correct quantity, the quantity consumers are willing to purchase at $60. Let's consider these important functions in greater detail.

You may recall from Chapter 2 that because every society faces the basic economic problem of unlimited wants and limited resources, some system must exist for **rationing**—that is, dividing up or allocating the scarce items among those who want them. In the United States and other economies that rely heavily on markets, price is the dominant rationing device. Rationing in a

EXHIBIT 3.10

Demand and Supply Curves for Jogging Shoes in Hometown, U.S.A.

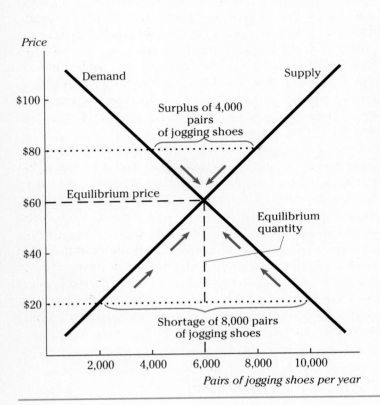

The equilibrium price is the price that equates the quantity supplied and the quantity demanded. In our example the equilibrium price is $60. Whenever the existing price is above or below equilibrium, pressure exists to push it toward the equilibrium level. For example, at a price of $80, there would be a surplus, and price cutting would take place. At a price of $20, there would be a shortage, and the price would tend to rise in order to eliminate the shortage. The arrows indicate the direction of the adjustments in price and quantity.

market economy works hand in hand with **motivating**—providing incentives to produce the desired output. Let's use Exh. 3.10 to examine this process further, first from the perspective of the consumers demanding jogging shoes and then from the perspective of the producers supplying them.

    How does the price of a product ration the supply of it among users? Prices ration because they influence our ability and willingness to purchase the product. The higher the price of jogging shoes, the more of our income it takes to buy them (which means a greater sacrifice in terms of other goods and services we must do without), and the less attractive jogging shoes become in relation to substitute products (tennis shoes, for instance).

    To illustrate how price rations, let's begin with a relatively low price for jogging shoes—$20. If jogging shoes were selling for $20 (a price well below equilibrium), consumers would be willing and able to purchase a relatively high quantity—10,000 pairs. But as we learned earlier, producers are willing to supply only 2,000 pairs at that price, and so there will be a shortage, and price will tend to rise. As the price of jogging shoes rises toward its equilibrium level, the quantity demanded is reduced—fewer consumers are willing and able to pay the higher price. By discouraging consumers from purchasing the product, the higher price of jogging shoes helps to bring the quantity demanded into line with the number of jogging shoes available; it *rations* jogging shoes. By the same token, at a price initially above equilibrium—for example, $80—the quantity demanded would be too low. But price will tend to decline, and the falling price will encourage consumers to purchase more of the product. Thus, higher prices ration by reducing the quantity demanded, and lower prices ration by increasing it.

But changing prices do more than reduce or increase the quantity demanded: They also motivate producers to expand or contract production. We know from the law of supply that more will be supplied at higher prices than at lower prices. Thus, when the price of jogging shoes increases from $20 to $60, the quantity of jogging shoes supplied will increase from 2,000 pairs to 6,000 pairs. At the same time, the quantity of jogging shoes is being rationed among consumers; the quantity demanded is declining from 10,000 pairs to 6,000 pairs. This is how the rationing and motivating functions of price work together to balance the desires of consumers and producers and prevent a shortage or surplus. Every consumer who values jogging shoes enough to pay $60 will have them, and every producer that is willing to supply jogging shoes at that price will be able to sell its entire output.

Changes in the Equilibrium Price

You have seen that in the absence of artificial restrictions, prices in competitive markets tend toward equilibrium. Once established, the equilibrium price will hold as long as the underlying demand and supply conditions remain unchanged. Of course, such conditions don't remain unchanged forever, often not even for a short time. Anything that causes a change in either demand or supply will bring about a new equilibrium price.

THE IMPACT OF A CHANGE IN DEMAND

Recall from earlier in this chapter that the determinants of demand are all the factors that underlie the demand schedule and determine the precise position of the demand curve. These include consumer tastes and preferences, consumer income, the prices of substitutes and complements, expectations regarding future prices, and the number of buyers in the market. Changes in any of these factors will cause a change in demand—a shift of the entire demand curve.

The housing market provides a good example. Increased demand for new houses in your city or town could result from any of several factors: heightened desire for single-family dwellings instead of apartments, an increase in residents' incomes, rent hikes in the area, expectations of higher housing prices in the near future, or a local population expansion. Any of these changes will cause the demand curve for new homes to shift to the right, as depicted in Exh. 3.11.

You can see that 8,000 new houses are demanded and supplied at the initial equilibrium price of $120,000. However, as demand increases from D_1 to D_2, perhaps because of an increased number of buyers in the market, there is a shortage of 4,000 houses (12,000 minus 8,000) at the $120,000 price. This shortage will lead to competition among prospective home buyers, which in turn will push the average price upward toward the new equilibrium level of $130,000. The higher price will ration new houses by reducing the quantity demanded and will motivate builders to increase the quantity supplied from 8,000 to 10,000. Note here that the increase in demand (the shift of the entire demand curve) causes an increase in the *quantity* supplied (movement along the stationary supply curve). In other words, a *shift* in one curve causes movement *along* the other curve. Thus, an increase in demand leads to a higher equilibrium in both price ($130,000) and quantity (10,000 new homes per year).

Now, suppose that any of the conditions that might have increased the demand for new houses is reversed, causing demand to decline. As shown in

---

EXHIBIT 3.11

The Effect of an Increase in Demand on the Equilibrium Price

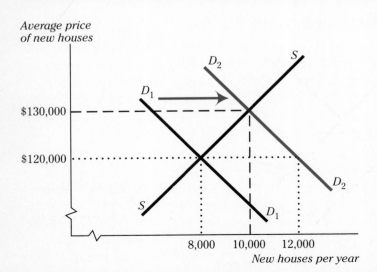

An increase in the demand for new houses will cause the equilibrium price of new homes to rise.

Exh. 3.12, the demand curve will shift to the left, from D_1 to D_2. As demand declines, a surplus of houses develops at the old price of $120,000 (only 4,000 homes will be demanded, but 8,000 will be supplied). This surplus will lead to price cutting as builders compete for buyers and as customers shop around for the best buys. Once again, the price change performs two functions. The falling price convinces home buyers to purchase more than 4,000 homes per year, and it motivates builders to supply fewer than 8,000 homes. Price will continue to decline until the quantity of new houses demanded is exactly equal to the quantity supplied at that price. In our example the new equilibrium price is $110,000, and the new equilibrium quantity is 6,000 new homes per year.

THE IMPACT OF A CHANGE IN SUPPLY

Price changes also can be initiated on the supply side. Recall the three determinants of supply: technology, prices of economic resources, and the number of suppliers in the market. Changes in any of these factors that underlie the supply schedule will cause a change in supply. In our example the supply of housing might be increased by any of the following: (1) the development of new construction methods that enable builders to produce more houses from a given amount of resources; (2) decreases in the cost of land,

---

EXHIBIT 3.12

The Effect of a Decrease in Demand on the Equilibrium Price

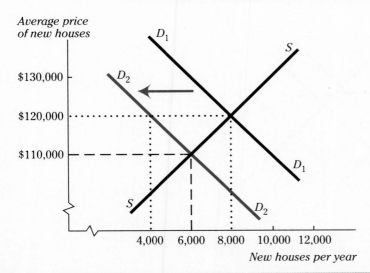

A decrease in the demand for new houses will cause the equilibrium price of new homes to fall.

labor, or materials used in home construction; (3) an increase in the number of builders, enabling the market to produce more houses than before at each possible price.

An increase in the supply of new houses is represented by shifting the supply curve to the right, as shown in Exh. 3.13. When the supply of housing increases from S_1 to S_2, 12,000 new homes will be supplied at a price of $120,000, but only 8,000 will be demanded. As before, the surplus will lead to price cutting downward toward the new equilibrium level of $110,000. Note that here the increase in supply (the shift of the entire supply curve) causes an increase in the *quantity* demanded (movement along the stationary demand curve). As we saw earlier, a shift in one curve causes movement *along* the other. This is the process that results in the lower price and the higher equilibrium quantity. A *decrease* in the supply of housing would have the opposite effect; it would raise the equilibrium price and lower the equilibrium quantity.

THE IMPACT OF SIMULTANEOUS CHANGES IN DEMAND AND SUPPLY

All the price changes we have explored so far have resulted from a single cause: either a change in demand while supply remained constant or a change in supply while demand remained constant. But in many real-world

---

EXHIBIT 3.13

Effect of an Increase in Supply on Equilibrium Price

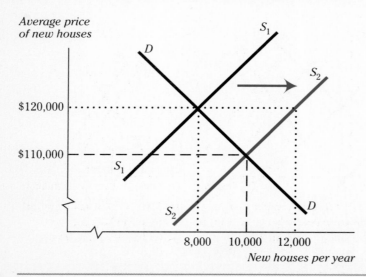

An increase in the supply of new houses will cause the equilibrium price of new homes to fall.

situations simultaneous changes occur in demand and supply. Let's consider two examples in the housing market. In the first case we find an area undergoing a population expansion (a source of increased demand for new houses) at the same time that building-material costs are rising (causing a decrease in supply). In the second case a period of high unemployment is causing the incomes of area residents to decline (less demand for new houses) while new production methods are reducing the cost of new-home construction (increased supply).

In these two examples the forces of demand and supply are pulling in opposite directions—the demand curve is shifting one way while the supply curve is shifting the other way. Under these conditions it is relatively easy to determine what will happen to the equilibrium price. In the first example demand increases while supply decreases, so that the equilibrium price tends to rise. In the second example demand decreases while supply increases, so that the equilibrium price tends to fall. Take a minute to draw the diagrams and convince yourself of these results.

Predicting the impact of simultaneous changes in demand and supply becomes a little trickier when both the demand curve and the supply curve are shifting in the same direction. As you can see from Exh. 3.14, when demand and supply are both increasing, we can be certain that the equilibrium quantity will also increase. But the impact on the equilibrium price is

EXHIBIT 3.14

Effect of Simultaneous Increases in Demand and Supply on Equilibrium Price

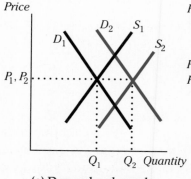

(a) Demand and supply increase by equal amounts; quantity increases but price does not change.

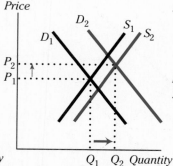

(b) Demand increases by more than supply; both price and quantity increase.

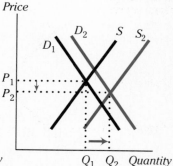

(c) Supply increases by more than demand; quantity increases, but price falls.

High-School Diplomas Prompt Job Offers

Work Is Plentiful for '97 Graduates With Basic Skills

By Michael M. Phillips
Staff Reporter of the Wall Street Journal

The prom may be over, but for the high-school class of 1997, the good times are just starting. Graduating seniors looking for full-time work are facing the best job market in years.

Nationally, the unemployment rate is a low 5%. Freshly minted high-school graduates don't have it nearly that good—16.8% of 16-19-year-olds were jobless in June. But for teens, that's not a bad figure; 23% of them were jobless in June 1992.

National prosperity, it appears, is trickling down to the nation's youngest workers, with employers increasingly desperate to fill the kind of entry-level slots that new, non-college-bound grads traditionally seek.

"I'd say the high-school class of '97—if they have good basic skills and a good work ethic—ought to be in a great position," says Ron Bullock, president of Bison Gear & Engineering Corp., a St. Charles, IL., manufacturer of gear motors for industrial equipment.

The wage gap between high-school grads and college grads began to widen rapidly during the late 1970s, with a degree bringing ever-greater wages and opportunities. In recent years, however, that wage gap has leveled off. And economists say high-school graduates could see their prospects improve as demand for their services expands with the economy and their numbers shrink because more of their classmates are going on to college.

Interim Services Inc., a Fort Lauderdale, Fla.-based temporary-help firm that annually places some 40,000 recent high-school grads, has seen wages for the young workers rise between 6% and 8% in the past year, compared with 4.5% for all Interim workers. Manpower Inc., the Milwaukee-based

uncertain; it depends on how much demand increases relative to supply. If demand and supply increase by the same amounts, the equilibrium price will not change. If demand increases more than supply, the equilibrium price will rise. If supply increases more than demand, the equilibrium price will fall. (If demand and supply both *decrease*, the equilibrium price is certain to decrease. But in this instance the impact on equilibrium *quantity* will be indeterminate. See if you can predict what will happen to the equilibrium temp agency that placed 780,000 employees last year, also reports a rise in wages for entry-level positions.

Job openings for new grads are plentiful in many, but not all, cities and industries. Sacramento, Calif., for one, is hot; Syracuse, N.Y., is not. "This year has looked really good," says Robert G. Lose, area coordinator for the Sacramento County Office of Education's regional occupational program. "We've had a pretty significant increase in placements. I would say primarily in the last five to six months," he adds....

Employers are especially inclined to hire grads with math and science backgrounds, as well as computer skills, auto-repair expertise or other technical abilities. Many school districts, aware that even factory jobs now require technical knowledge, have rejiggered their courses to arm job-bound students with appropriate skills. "Employers are more attracted to the kids because they know

they don't have to keep going over the basics," says Henri Cepero, a specialist in cooperative education at the Dade County, Fla., public schools.

But many managers say that with labor markets this tight, they are willing to settle for any grad with a strong work ethic and a solid grounding in the basics. "We

aren't looking for Rhodes scholars," says Bucky Pope, director of human resources at Philadelphia's Sandmeyer Steel Co. "We're looking for kids who want to come to work. If they come to work and have basic math skills and basic English verbal skills—we'll do the rest. We're willing to train them."

USE YOUR ECONOMIC REASONING

1. According to the article, the wage gap between high school graduates and college graduates began to widen in the late 1970s. Draw a supply and demand graph for high school graduates, and label the equilibrium wage rate $4 per hour. Draw another supply and demand graph for college graduates, and label the equilibrium wage something higher, say, $6. Now, try to explain the forces that might

have caused the wage gap (the differential between the wage rate paid high school grads and the wage paid college grads) to widen.

2. Some economists believe that the wage gap may begin shrinking in the near future in part because more students are opting to attend college. Use your supply and demand graphs to explain how this change would tend to reduce the wage gap.

quantity if demand and supply both decrease by the same amount, if demand decreases more than supply, and if supply decreases more than demand.)

In summary the price of a product can change because of a change in demand, a change in supply, or simultaneous changes in demand and supply. In all cases the basic principle is the same: Whenever demand increases in relation to supply, the equilibrium price will rise; whenever supply increases relative to demand, the equilibrium price will fall. By keeping that principle in mind, we can predict what is going to happen to the price of cattle or wheat or any other product whose price is determined in a competitive market. Read "High-School Diplomas Prompt Job Offer," on pages 92–93, and see if you can explain why the wage gap between college and high school graduates may soon start to fall.

Intervention in Price Determination: Supports and Ceilings

Sometimes the prices that result from the interaction of demand and supply may cause hardship for producers or consumers and may therefore be perceived as "unfair" by the injured group. Producers may feel that prevailing market prices are too low to provide them with adequate incomes. Consumers may believe that market prices are too high and thus place an unreasonable burden on households—particularly low-income households. To protect their various interests, both consumers and producers form pressure groups and lobby the government to intervene in the process of price determination. Agricultural price supports, minimum-wage laws, interest rate ceilings, and rent controls are just a few examples that illustrate the success of these campaigns.

PRICE SUPPORTS

Government usually intervenes in pricing by establishing maximum or minimum prices. A **price support** is a legally established minimum price above the equilibrium price.[1] In the 1930s, for example, the federal government initiated a program of agricultural price supports designed to raise the income of farmers. Under this program the government "supported" the price of the product by agreeing to purchase, at the legally established price, whatever output the farmer was unable to sell at that price.

Exhibit 3.15 shows a hypothetical situation in which the government has established a price support (or support price) for corn at $4, which is $1 above the equilibrium price of $3 per bushel. At $4 a bushel, customers are willing to purchase only 10 billion bushels a year, but producers are eager to supply 20 billion bushels. We know that in a free or unregulated market, sellers of corn would deal with the surplus of 10 billion bushels by cutting prices down to the equilibrium level of $3, at which the equilibrium quantity of 15 billion bushels

---

[1] When established, price supports are usually above the equilibrium price. Over time, however, the equilibrium price may rise above the support level, causing the price support to be ineffective. For example, in 1995 the minimum wage (a form of support price) of $4.25 was probably below the equilibrium wage for unskilled labor in most parts of the country.

would be supplied. Once the government establishes a price support of $4, however, the market remains in disequilibrium, with surpluses continuing to accumulate. The government is then required to buy the surplus corn, store it, and dispose of it (through donations to poor nations, for example), all at the expense of taxpayers. In April of 1996, this expense caused Congress to pass the Federal Agricultural Improvement and Reform Act (FAIR), legislation ending price supports for wheat, feed grains, cotton, and rice. To ease the transition to a free market, the bill replaces traditional price supports with fixed but declining payments every year until 2002, regardless of market prices or how much is planted. While some are hailing this legislation (also known as the Freedom to Farm Act) as the end of government intervention in farming, that assessment is probably premature. In the first place, FAIR legislation expires in 2002, and it is unclear what will happen after that. A return to price supports is a real possibility. In addition, the Reform Act did nothing to eliminate a variety of indirect subsidies that have the same effect as price supports. For instance, the federal government still regulates the price of milk at an artificially high level, and it continues to tax imported peanuts and sugar in an effort to restrict

EXHIBIT 3.15

Price Supports and Surpluses

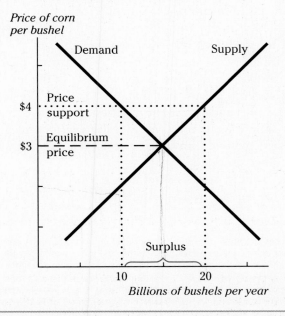

supply and prop up the domestic price of those products. In short, even if agricultural price supports are a thing of the past, other government efforts to prop up agricultural prices remain in effect.[2]

When we look beyond agricultural markets, the minimum wage provides another example of a price support. By law most employers are required to pay their employees at least the government-established minimum wage ($5.15 an hour in 1997). Because this wage is generally above the equilibrium wage for unskilled labor, there are more people willing to work at that wage than employers are willing to hire at that wage. Of course, those who can find jobs are better off because of the minimum wage. But some unskilled workers who would have been able to find jobs at the equilibrium wage will be unemployed at the minimum wage. This occurs because employers simply do not believe that these workers will be able to contribute enough to the production process to justify that high a wage. Just as the price support for corn created a surplus of that product, the minimum wage creates a surplus of workers. To the extent that the minimum wage increases unemployment, it conflicts with our objective of raising the incomes of low-income Americans.

PRICE CEILINGS

Government may also intervene in the pricing process when it is convinced that prevailing prices are either too high or are increasing too rapidly. In such cases the government will set **price ceilings,** maximum prices that are established below the equilibrium price. During World War II, for example, price ceilings were placed on most nonfarm prices in order to prevent them from being pushed to exorbitant levels by the demands of the war effort. Price ceilings (or ceiling prices) also have been used during peacetime as a technique both for combating inflation (a general rise in the level of prices) and for controlling specific prices. For instance, in 1971 President Nixon "froze" virtually all wages and prices for a period of 90 days in an attempt to slow the rate of inflation. In the same decade the federal government used price ceilings selectively to limit the prices of beef, pork, gasoline, and natural gas, among other products.

One form of price ceiling that was initiated in World War II still survives today. **Rent ceilings** (or rent controls) are maximum rents that are established

---

[2] While Exhibit 3.15 captures the most important elements of the price support program, it is not completely accurate. Under federal price support legislation, customers would pay the market price, not the support price, as depicted in the graph. The difference is made up by the federal government in a **deficiency payment** ($1 a bushel, in this example) paid directly to the farmer. As a result, the actual shortage will be somewhat smaller than that depicted in the exhibit. Because consumers are responding to the market price, they will want to purchase 15 million bushels. On the other hand, since suppliers are responding to the support price, they will want to supply 20 million bushels. The result will be a surplus of 5 billion bushels, which must be purchased by the government (at $4 a bushel).

below the equilibrium level. They were initially instituted in World War II to prevent transient wartime workers (who were typically well paid) from outbidding local residents for apartments in industrial cities. After the war, these ceilings were abolished everywhere except in New York. Then in the inflationary 1970s, rent-control laws spread to cities in Massachusetts, to much of suburban Long Island and New Jersey, to Washington, and to about half the population of California.

Although rent ceilings may seem to be in the best interest of consumers, they frequently create problems for prospective renters. Because the rent is fixed at an artificially low level, more people will want to rent in that city (or the rent-controlled portions of the city) than would desire to do so at the equilibrium rent. In addition, the low rent will make renting apartments less attractive to owners, who consequently will make fewer apartments available than would be provided at the equilibrium rent. The result will be a shortage of apartments and a number of unsatisfied customers.

Exhibit 3.16 represents the plight of consumers in a rent-controlled city. As you can see from the exhibit, $600 is the equilibrium rent, the rent at which the number of apartments consumers desire to rent is equal to the number that apartment owners want to make available. At the $400 rent ceiling (or ceiling rent), consumers want to rent 20,000 apartments, but owners are willing to supply only 14,000 units. There is a shortage of 6,000 apartments. We know that in unregulated markets a shortage of apartments or any other item, will lead to a price increase, which motivates businesses to supply more of the item and which rations some consumers out of the market. A ceiling prevents the rent from rising to its equilibrium level, so that landlords are faced with more potential renters than they can satisfy. Consequently, they must use some secondary rationing device to decide which consumers will get apartments.

A **secondary rationing device** is a nonprice condition that supplements the primary rationing device, price. The prospective apartment renter in our example must not only be willing to pay the $400 rent but must also be able to satisfy some supplementary requirement imposed by landlords. Perhaps landlords will grant apartments only on the basis of first-come-first-served. Or perhaps they will choose to rent only to applicants without children and pets or only to those with the best jobs (and therefore the greatest likelihood of making timely rent payments). Perhaps they will rent only to retired persons or to those with verifiable references. Whether the use of a secondary, nonprice rationing device is preferable to higher rents is a matter for you to decide. It is clear, however, that rent ceilings do not eliminate the need to ration; they simply force sellers to use secondary rationing devices.

In New York City, where 70,000 units are under strict rent controls and an additional 900,000 units are subject to more modest rent regulations, finding an apartment is a major problem. Because rents are kept below their equilibrium level, New Yorkers face a perpetual housing shortage. To some extent, existing

EXHIBIT 3.16

Price Ceilings and Shortages

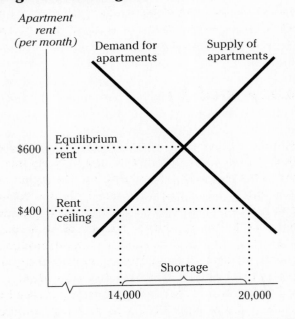

A price ceiling will tend to produce a shortage since price is legally fixed below the equilibrium level. In this example a rent ceiling of $400 leads to a shortage of 6,000 apartments.

housing is rationed on a first-come-first-serve basis, and would-be renters spend countless hours in a vain attempt to find a vacant apartment. Some frustrated searchers resort to checking obituaries in hope of zeroing in on a newly available rental before anyone else hears of it; others make secret payments to landlords for the privilege of a new lease. Of course, landlords know how to play the system too. In 1996 a New York real estate executive was found guilty of requiring tenants to make political contributions in order to obtain leases on rent-regulated apartments.[3]

Low rents not only produce a shortage but also prevent the supply of housing from expanding. In fact, landlords may allow some rental units to deteriorate. If rental income cannot rise, owners cannot profit from money spent on improvements or even break even on money invested in maintenance. In summary, although rent ceilings succeed in maintaining low rents for those lucky enough to find apartments, they create shortages and prevent expansion, problems that would be eliminated if rents were allowed to rise to their equilibrium level.

---

[3] "Landlord Guilty of Asking Tenants for Political Gifts," by John Sullivan, *New York Times*, Nov. 23, 1996, page 23.

Recent initiatives have abolished or weakened rent-control ordinances in a number of U.S. cities. For example, in 1994, Massachusetts voters abolished rent controls, and in 1995 the California legislature made it illegal as of 1999 for cities to limit the rent that landlords can charge for vacant apartments. New York rent-control ordinances, however, survived the challenge; in 1997 they were renewed for another six years.

Economic Efficiency and the Role of Prices

The automatic response of price changes to changes in demand and supply conditions is an important feature of a market economy. As increasing consumer demand pushes the price of a product upward, the higher price rations some consumers out of the market and simultaneously motivates producers to expand their production of the product. Because these producers are receiving a higher price for their product, they will be able to outbid producers of less-valued items for the resources needed to expand production. In this way price changes help to ensure that businesses produce the goods and services that consumers value the most, in the quantities they desire.

Price changes also help ensure that each product is produced with as few of society's scarce resources as possible. As a particular resource becomes scarcer (because of increased demand or reduced supply), its price tends to rise. This higher cost encourages producers to economize on its use by substituting cheaper resources whenever possible. The end result is the efficient use of society's scarce resources: Producers supply the most-wanted products in the least-costly way in terms of scarce resources.[4] The way competitive markets promote the efficient use of resources is explored in greater detail in Chapter 5. Later chapters examine how such factors as inadequate competition and the ability of firms to ignore the "cost" of the pollution they create can interfere with the ability of markets to achieve this optimal result.

Summary

In a competitive market, prices are determined by the interaction of demand and supply. *Demand* is a schedule showing the quantities of a good or service that consumers are willing and able to purchase at various prices during some given time period, when all factors other than the product's price remain unchanged.

---

[4] Note that the fewer the resources an economy needs to produce each product, the more goods and services it can produce with its limited resource stock. Thus, an economy that is operating efficiently is producing the goods and services that consumers value the most *and* producing as many of those goods and services as possible from the society's scarce resources.

Demand may be represented graphically in a *demand curve,* which slopes downward and to the right because the *law of demand* holds that consumers will purchase more of a product at a lower price than at a higher price. *Supply* is a schedule showing the quantities of a good or service that producers are willing and able to offer for sale at various prices during a given time period, when all factors other than the product's price remain unchanged. Supply may be represented graphically as a *supply curve.* The supply curve slopes upward and to the right because the *law of supply* states that price and quantity supplied are positively related; that is, a greater quantity will be supplied at higher prices than at lower prices.

The demand curve will shift to a new position if there is a change in any of the *determinants of demand:* consumer income, tastes and preferences, expectations regarding future prices, the prices of substitute and complementary goods, and the number of consumers in the market. By the same token, the supply curve will shift if there is a change in one or more of the *determinants of supply:* technology, the prices of resources, or the number of producers in the market.

Economists are careful to distinguish between a change in the quantity demanded and a change in demand. A change in the amount purchased as a result of a change in the price of the product while other factors are held constant is a *change in the quantity demanded* and is represented by movement up or down a stationary demand curve. A change in any of the determinants of demand while price is held constant will cause consumers to purchase more or less of a product at each possible price. This is described as a *change in demand* and is represented by a shift of the entire demand curve to the right (in the case of increased demand) or to the left (in the case of decreased demand).

A similar distinction is necessary on the supply side of the market. A *change in the quantity supplied* results from a change in the price of the product and is represented graphically by a movement along a stationary supply curve. A *change in supply* results from a change in one of the determinants of supply and is represented by a shift of the entire supply curve to a new position.

The *equilibrium price* is the price that brings about an equality between the quantity demanded and the quantity supplied, which we call the *equilibrium quantity.* The equilibrium price can be identified by the intersection of the demand and supply curves. If the prevailing price is above equilibrium, a *surplus*—an excess of quantity supplied over quantity demanded—will occur, and sellers will be forced to reduce price to eliminate the surplus. If the prevailing price is below equilibrium, a *shortage*—an excess of quantity demanded over quantity supplied—occurs, and buyers will bid up the price as they compete for the product. Only when the existing price is at the equilibrium level will there be neither a shortage nor a surplus and no pressure for price to change.

Prices perform two important functions: They (1) *ration,* or divide, the limited amount of available output among possible buyers; and (2) *motivate* producers to supply the desired quantity. Higher prices ration by discouraging consumers from purchasing a product; they also motivate producers to increase the quantity supplied. Lower prices have the opposite effect. They encourage consumers to purchase more of the product and simultaneously motivate producers to reduce the quantity supplied. The equilibrium price succeeds in matching the quantity demanded with the quantity supplied because it balances the desires of consumers and producers. Every consumer who values the product enough to pay the equilibrium price will have it, and every producer that is willing to supply the product at that price will be able to sell its entire output.

In the absence of artificial restrictions, prices will rise and fall in response to changes in demand and supply. Whenever demand increases in relation to supply, the equilibrium price will tend to rise; whenever supply increases in relation to demand, the equilibrium price will fall. These price changes help to ensure that producers not only supply the goods and services consumers value the most but also use as few scarce resources as possible in the production of those goods and services.

Price supports (minimum prices above the equilibrium price) and *price ceilings* (maximum prices below the equilibrium price) prevent price from reaching its equilibrium level in the market. Because these restrictions interfere with the rationing and motivating functions of price, they give rise to surpluses (supports) and shortages (ceilings). Price ceilings also create the need for *secondary rationing devices*—nonprice conditions that supplement the primary rationing device, which is price.

GLOSSARY

Change in demand. An increase or decrease in the quantity demanded at each possible price, caused by a change in the determinants of demand; represented graphically by a shift of the entire demand curve to a new position.

Change in quantity demanded. An increase or decrease in the amount of a product demanded as a result of a change in its price, with factors other than price held constant; represented graphically by movement along a stationary demand curve.

Change in quantity supplied. An increase or decrease in the amount of a product supplied as a result of a change in its price, with factors other than price held constant; represented graphically by movement along a stationary supply curve.

Change in supply. An increase or decrease in the amount of a product supplied at each and every price, caused by a change in the determinants of supply; represented graphically by a shift of the entire supply curve.

Complement. A product that is normally purchased along with another good or in conjunction with another good.

Deficiency payment. A payment made to farmers on a price-support program; equal to the difference between the market price and the support price times the number of bushels sold.

Demand. A schedule showing the quantities of a good or service that consumers are willing and able to purchase at various prices during a given time period, when all factors other than the product's price remain unchanged.

Demand curve. A graphical representation of demand, showing the quantities of a good or service that consumers are willing and able to purchase at various prices during a given time period, ceteris paribus.

Determinants of demand. The factors that underlie the demand schedule and determine the precise position of the demand curve: income, tastes and preferences, expectations regarding prices, the prices of related goods, and the number of consumers in the market.

Determinants of supply. The factors that underlie the supply schedule and determine the precise position of the supply curve: technology, resource prices, and number of producers in the market.

Equilibrium price. The price that brings about an equality between the quantity demanded and the quantity supplied.

Equilibrium quantity. The quantity demanded and supplied at the equilibrium price.

Income effect. Consumer ability to purchase greater quantities of a product that has declined in price.

Inferior good. A product for which demand decreases as income increases and increases as income decreases.

Law of demand. The quantity demanded of a product is negatively, or inversely, related to its price. Consumers will purchase more of a product at lower prices than at higher prices.

Law of supply. The quantity supplied of a product is positively, or directly, related to its price. Producers will supply a larger quantity at higher prices than at lower prices.

Motivating. The function of providing incentives to supply the proper quantities of demanded products.

Normal good. A product for which demand either increases as income increases or decreases as income decreases.

Price ceiling. A legally established maximum price below the equilibrium price.

Price support. A legally established minimum price above the equilibrium price.

Rationing. The function of dividing up or allocating a society's scarce items among those who want them.

Rent ceiling. A legally established maximum rent below the equilibrium rent.

Rent control. A legally established maximum rent below the equilibrium rent.

Secondary rationing device. A nonprice condition that supplements the primary rationing device, which is price.

Shortage. An excess of quantity demanded over quantity supplied.

Substitute. A product that can be used in place of some other product because, to a greater or lesser extent, it satisfies the same consumer wants.

Substitution effect. Consumers' willingness to substitute for other products the product that has declined in price.

Supply. A schedule showing the quantities of a good or service that producers are willing and able to offer for sale at various prices during a given time period, when all factors other than the product's price remain unchanged.

Supply curve. A graphical representation of supply.

Surplus. An excess of quantity supplied over quantity demanded.

Technology. The state of knowledge about how to produce products.

Technological advance. The discovery of a better way to produce a product; a method that uses fewer resources to produce each unit of output or that produces more output from a given amount of resources.

STUDY QUESTIONS

Fill in the Blanks

1. If the entire demand curve shifts to a new position, we describe this as a change in

   <u>demand</u> .

2. If a product is a normal good, an increase in income will cause the demand curve for

   the product to shift to the <u>right</u> .

3. Movement along a stationary supply curve due to a change in price is called a

   change in <u>quantity supplied</u>

4. The function of dividing up or allocating scarce items among those who desire to

   receive them is called <u>rationing</u> .

5. The price that exactly clears the market is called the _equilibrium_ price.

6. Whenever the prevailing price is above equilibrium, a _Surplus_ will exist.

7. Prices perform two important functions: They ration scarce items among the consumers who desire to receive them; and they _motivate_ producers to supply that quantity.

8. If supply rises and demand declines, we would expect the equilibrium price to _fall_ .

9. If supply increases more than demand, the equilibrium price will _fall_ .

10. We would expect a price ceiling to lead to a _Shortage_ .

Multiple Choice

1. If the price of automobiles increases and all other factors remain unchanged, it will be reasonable to expect
   a) an increase in the demand for automobiles.
   b) a decrease in the demand for automobiles.
   c) an increase in the quantity of automobiles demanded.
   d) a decrease in the quantity of automobiles demanded.

2. If the demand curve for Brock's Heavy Beer shifts to the left, this could be due to
   a) an increase in the price of Brock's Heavy Beer.
   b) an increase in consumer income.
   c) an increase in the price of other beers.
   d) a shift in tastes and preferences to light beers.

3. An increase in the price of apples is likely to cause
   a) a decrease in the demand for apples.
   b) an increase in the quantity demanded of apples.
   c) an increase in the demand for other types of fruit.
   d) an increase in the quantity demanded of other types of fruit.

4. If the price of black walnuts increases and other factors remain unchanged, it is reasonable to expect
   a) a decrease in the demand for black walnuts.
   b) an increase in the supply of black walnuts.
   c) an increase in the quantity of black walnuts supplied.
   d) a decrease in the demand for pecans and other walnut substitutes.

5. A new labor settlement that increases the cost of producing computers will probably cause
   a) a decrease in supply of computers.
   b) a reduction in the demand for computers.
   c) a reduction in the quantity of computers supplied.
   d) the supply curve of computers to shift to the right.

6. If grasshoppers destroy half of the wheat crop, the result will be
   a) an increase in the demand for wheat.
   b) a decrease in the demand for wheat.
   c) a decrease in the quantity of wheat supplied.
   d) a leftward shift of the supply curve for wheat.

7. If demand increases and supply declines,
   a) the equilibrium price and quantity will both increase.
   b) the equilibrium price will rise, but the quantity will fall.
   c) the equilibrium price will fall, but the quantity will rise.
   d) the equilibrium price and quantity will both fall.
   e) the equilibrium price will rise; quantity will be indeterminate.

8. If the U.S. government were to artificially restrict the price of beef below the equilibrium level, the result would be
   a) a shortage.
   b) a surplus.
   c) an excess of quantity supplied over quantity demanded.
   d) none of the above

9. If the demand for used cars declines, the likely result will be
   a) an increase in the supply of used cars.
   b) a reduction in the equilibrium price of used cars
   c) an increase in the equilibrium price of used cars.
   d) a temporary shortage of used cars at the old price.

10. If the price of cattle feed increases, the result will probably be
    a) an increase in the supply of cattle and lower cattle prices.
    b) a decrease in the supply of cattle and higher cattle prices.
    c) an increase in the demand for cattle and higher cattle prices.
    d) a decrease in the demand for cattle and lower cattle prices.

11. If a shortage exists, it indicates that the existing price is
    a) the equilibrium price.
    b) below the equilibrium price.
    c) above the equilibrium price.

12. Consider the market for mobile homes. If personal incomes in the United States rise, we would expect to see
    a) a decline in mobile home prices if mobile homes are a normal good.
    b) an increase in the demand for mobile homes if mobile homes are an inferior good.
    c) a decrease in mobile home prices if mobile homes are an inferior good.
    d) a decrease in the demand for mobile homes if mobile homes are a normal good.

13. If the price of coffee increases, the probable result will be
    a) a decrease in the demand for coffee.
    b) a decrease in the price of substitutes for coffee.
    c) an increase in the price of substitutes for coffee.
    d) a decrease in the supply of coffee.

14. Which of the following statements is *incorrect*?
    a) If demand increases and supply remains constant, the equilibrium price will rise.
    b) If supply rises and demand remains constant, the equilibrium price will fall.
    c) If demand rises and supply falls, the equilibrium price will rise.
    d) If supply increases and demand decreases, the equilibrium price will rise.

15. If additional farmers enter the hog-producing industry, the result will be
    a) lower prices but a higher equilibrium quantity.
    b) higher prices but a lower equilibrium quantity.
    c) lower prices but the same equilibrium quantity.
    d) lower prices and a lower equilibrium quantity.

16. If the supply of cattle is increasing more rapidly than the demand,
    a) cattle prices will rise.
    b) cattle prices will fall.
    c) cattle prices will not change.
    d) each of the above is possible.

Problems and Questions for Discussion

1. My eldest daughter says that she really "needs" a new sweatshirt, but she won't use her allowance to buy it. ("I don't need it *that* badly.") How can a "need" evaporate like that? What is the difference between *need* and *demand*?

2. Podunk College experienced a substantial drop in enrollment last year. What possible

explanations can you, as an economist, offer for what happened? Try to list all possibilities.

3. Why does the supply curve slope upward and to the right? In other words, why will producers supply a higher quantity at higher prices?

4. Which of the following events would cause movement along a stationary supply curve for wheat, and which would cause the supply curve to shift? Explain each situation from the producer's point of view.
   a) The price of wheat declines.
   b) The cost of fertilizer rises.
   c) Wheat blight destroys half the wheat crop.
   d) New combines make it possible for one person to do the work of three.

5. Explain the economic reasoning behind the following newspaper headlines:
   a) "Weather Slows Fishing: Seafood Prices Double"
   b) "Sugar: Crisis of Plenty"
   c) "Minimum Wage Costs Jobs"
   d) "Bountiful Wheat Crop Is Hurting Growers"

6. If the supply of oranges in a competitive market decreases as a result of severe weather, will there be a shortage of oranges? Why or why not? (*Hint:* Use graphs to help answer this question.)

7. Suppose that your local tennis courts are very crowded and your city is considering charging a fee to ration their use. Who would like to have a fee charged? Would only wealthy individuals feel this way? Why might someone be in favor of a fee?

8. People, including news reporters, often use the terms *supply* and *demand* incorrectly. For example, you will often read "Supply exceeds demand" or "Demand exceeds supply." What is wrong with these statements? What does the writer probably mean to say?

9. Why is it important that prices in a market economy be allowed to change in response to changing demand and supply conditions? What functions do these changing prices perform?

10. Assume that consumers are buying equal numbers of hamburgers and hot dogs when these products are selling at the same price. If the supply of hamburger declines, what will happen to the price of hamburgers? What about the price of hot dogs? Graph your conclusions.

ANSWER KEY

Fill in the Blanks

1. demand
2. right
3. quantity supplied
4. rationing

5. equilibrium
6. surplus
7. motivate
8. fall

9. fall
10. shortage

Multiple Choice

1. d
2. d
3. c
4. c

5. a
6. d
7. e

8. a
9. b
10. b

11. b
12. c
13. c

14. d
15. a
16. b

4

The Elasticity of Demand and Supply

In Chapter 3 we considered how demand and supply interact to determine prices, and we discovered how changes in demand or supply cause prices to change. In this chapter we investigate the degree of consumer and producer responsiveness to increases or decreases in prices. Economists refer to this degree of responsiveness as the price "elasticity." As you will see, the concept of price elasticity is extremely important and has many applications in the world around you.

Elasticity of Demand

The law of demand tells producers that if they raise their prices, consumers will buy less and that if producers lower their prices, consumers will buy more. But the law of demand doesn't tell them anything about the size of the response to a given change in price. If a professional football team decides to raise the price of season tickets by $50, how many fewer tickets will fans buy? If a local health club doubles its rates, how many customers will it lose? To answer these questions, we need some knowledge of how responsive consumers are to changes in the price of a particular product—we need to know something about the price elasticity of demand.

The **price elasticity of demand** is a measure of the responsiveness of the quantity demanded of a product to a change in its price. If the quantity demanded expands or contracts a great deal in response to a price change, demand is said to be very responsive, or *elastic*; if the quantity demanded doesn't change very much, demand is described as not very responsive, or *inelastic*.

As a gauge of the responsiveness of consumers, the absolute size of the changes in price and quantity means very little. Suppose that a $5 price reduction causes consumers to demand an additional 1,000 units of some product. Should we describe the demand for this product as elastic or inelastic? We can't tell unless we know the starting point, the initial price and quantity. To illustrate, suppose the firm had cut price from $10 to $5 and this price reduction caused the quantity demanded to increase from 100,000 units to 101,000 units. Would you describe demand as elastic (very responsive to the price change) under those conditions? Probably not; a 50 percent price reduction led to only a 1 percent increase in the quantity demanded! But if the price had been reduced from $100 to $95 (the same $5 but in this case only 5 percent of the original price) and the quantity demanded had increased from 1,000 to 2,000 units (100 percent), you would probably agree that consumers were quite responsive to the change in price; demand is elastic.

The point is that when we describe the responsiveness of consumers, we need to think in terms of percentages—the percent change in price and the percent change in the quantity demanded. This approach adjusts for the initial prices and quantities and gives us a much more meaningful comparison.

THE COEFFICIENT OF DEMAND ELASTICITY

We can measure the degree of elasticity or inelasticity by calculating a value called the **coefficient of demand elasticity.** We compute the coefficient of elasticity by dividing the percentage change in quantity demanded by the percentage change in price:

$$\text{Coefficient of elasticity} = \frac{\dfrac{\Delta Q}{Q}}{\dfrac{\Delta P}{P}} = \frac{\text{Percentage change in quantity demanded}}{\text{Percentage change in price}}$$

In this formula for the coefficient, Q stands for quantity, P for price, and the Greek letter delta (Δ) for "change in." $\Delta Q/Q$ is the percentage change in quantity demanded, and $\Delta P/P$ is the percentage change in price.

Let's apply this formula to the elasticity of demand for Fantastic Cola after a price hike. We'll say that after the price per six-pack rises from $2.50 to $3, weekly sales decline from 1,000 six-packs to 900. What is the price elasticity of demand for Fantastic Cola? If the change in quantity demanded (ΔQ) is 100 fewer six-packs per week and the original quantity demanded (Q) is 1,000 six-packs, the percentage change in quantity demanded (–100/1,000) is –10 percent. And if the change in price (ΔP) is $.50 and the original price (P) is $2.50, the percentage change in price ($.50/$2.50) is 20 percent. If we divide the 10 percent reduction in quantity by the 20 percent increase in price, we arrive at an elasticity coefficient of –.5.[1]

$$\text{Coefficient of elasticity} = \frac{\dfrac{-100}{1000}}{\dfrac{\$.50}{\$2.50}} = \frac{-10\%}{20\%} = -.5$$

An elasticity coefficient of .5 means that for every 1 percent change in price, the quantity demanded will change by 0.5 percent. Thus, if the price of Fantastic Cola goes up by 10 percent, we would expect a 5 percent reduction in the quantity demanded. If it increases by 20 percent, we would expect a 10 percent reduction in quantity demanded. However, if the elasticity coefficient were 2.0 instead of .5, each 1 percent change in price would cause a 2 percent change in quantity demanded. For example, a 10 percent increase in price would cause a 20 percent decrease in quantity demanded.

You will note that in our formula the elasticity coefficient (–.5) carries a negative sign. We know from the law of demand that changes in price normally cause the quantity demanded to change in the opposite direction. Thus, price increases cause reductions in the quantity demanded, whereas price reductions cause increases in the quantity demanded. In either case the sign is negative and is usually ignored in referring to price elasticity values.

---

[1] The simple formula we are using to compute the elasticity coefficient produces somewhat ambiguous results. If the sellers of Fantastic Cola raise the price from $2.50 to $3, the value of the elasticity coefficient is .5. But if the sellers lower their price from $3 to $2.50, the coefficient will be .67 because the initial price and quantity are different.

Economic theory does not suggest any reason why these two coefficients should be different, so we might argue that they should be the same. This can be accomplished by using the average of the two prices and the average of the two quantities as the base values for computing percentages. When this approach is used, the value of the coefficient will be the same regardless of whether the initial price is the higher price or the lower price. In the Fantastic Cola example the value of the elasticity coefficient would be .58. In the modified formula below, we add the two quantities Q_1 and Q_2 and divide by 2 to arrive at the average quantity. Average price is determined the same way.

$$\frac{\Delta Q/[(Q_1 + Q_2)/2]}{\Delta P/[(P_1 + P_2)/2]} = \frac{100/(1,900/2)}{\$.50/(\$5.50/2)} = \frac{100/950}{\$.50/\$2.75} = \frac{10.5\%}{18.2\%} = .58$$

DEGREES OF ELASTICITY

Economists use the coefficient of elasticity to define precisely the terms *elastic* and *inelastic*. Elastic demand exists when the coefficient of elasticity is greater than 1, when a given percentage change in price brings about a larger percentage change in the quantity demanded. When the elasticity coefficient is less than 1, demand is inelastic; a given percentage change in price brings about a smaller percentage change in the quantity demanded. If the coefficient is exactly 1, *unitary elasticity* prevails; a given percentage change in price results in an identical percentage change in quantity demanded. The elasticity coefficient can vary from zero to infinity, where zero represents the least elastic demand imaginable and infinity represents the most elastic demand imaginable.

If the coefficient of elasticity is zero, a change in price brings no change at all in the quantity demanded. Demand is described as *perfectly inelastic,* and the demand curve is a vertical straight line. For example, over some range of prices, the demand for lifesaving drugs, such as insulin, may be perfectly inelastic. Another example is the demand for dialysis treatment by those suffering from kidney failure.

If the coefficient of elasticity approaches infinity, a very small change in price leads to an enormous change in the quantity demanded. Demand is said to be *perfectly elastic* and is graphed as a horizontal straight line. Perfectly inelastic and perfectly elastic demand curves are depicted in Exh. 4.1. The individual apple farmer faces a situation that illustrates perfectly elastic demand. If the market price of apples is $10 a bushel, the farmer can sell as much as desired at that price. But a farmer who attempts to charge more than $10 will sell nothing; consumers will simply buy their apples from someone else. This is the type of situation we represent with a perfectly elastic demand curve. In Chapter 6 we will have much more to say about perfectly elastic demand curves.

ELASTICITY ALONG A STRAIGHT-LINE DEMAND CURVE

In most instances demand curves do not show just one degree of elasticity; they show several. All linear, downward-sloping demand curves show unitary elasticity midway on the curve, with elastic demand above the midpoint and inelastic demand below it. Exhibit 4.2 depicts such a demand curve.

In Exh. 4.2, note that because the demand curve is a straight line, it has a constant inclination, or "slope." Therefore, a price change of a given size will always bring the same quantity change. In this hypothetical example each $.60 drop in price brings an increase of 60 million gallons in the quantity demanded, regardless of whether we are at the upper or the lower end of the curve. (Look, for example, at what happens to the quantity demanded when price declines from $2.40 to $1.80 or from $1.80 to $1.20; in both instances

EXHIBIT 4.1

Perfectly Inelastic and Perfectly Elastic Demand Curves

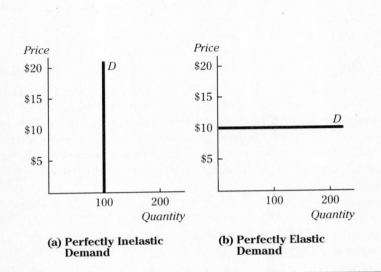

(a) Perfectly Inelastic Demand

(b) Perfectly Elastic Demand

(a) Despite an increase or decrease in price, consumers buy exactly the same quantity. The demand curve for insulin may look like this over some price range. (b) A very small increase in price would cause consumers to reduce their purchases to zero. The individual apple farmer may face a demand curve like this one.

quantity increases by 60 million gallons.) That would seem to suggest that consumers are equally responsive to price changes at either end of the curve. But that's not true! We have to remember that the responsiveness, or elasticity of demand, deals with percentage changes, not with absolute quantities.

If you remember that fact, you will recognize that the responsiveness of consumers changes quite dramatically as we move along this demand curve. For instance, when price drops from $3 to $2.40 (a 20 percent decline), quantity demanded increases from 60 million to 120 million gallons (a 100 percent increase). Since the percentage change in quantity is greater than the percentage change in price, demand is elastic at this upper end of the curve. At the other end the same *absolute* changes in price and quantity represent different percentage changes and consequently produce different elasticities. For instance, when price declines from $1.20 to $.60 (a 50 percent change), the quantity demanded increases from 240 million to 300 million gallons (a 25 percent change). The coefficient of elasticity is .5; demand is inelastic. We want to remember, then, that the slope of a demand curve is not the same as its elasticity. A linear demand curve has a constant slope, but it displays many different degrees of elasticity.

EXHIBIT 4.2

How Elasticity Changes along a Hypothetical Demand Curve for Gasoline

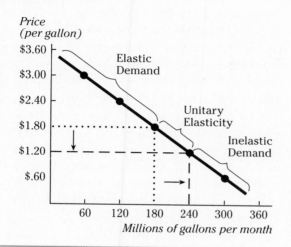

Every straight-line demand curve that is downward sloping displays unitary elasticity at its midpoint, elastic demand above it, and inelastic demand below it.

ELASTICITY AND TOTAL REVENUE

Knowing how responsive consumers will be to price changes is of vital interest to businesses. The elasticity of demand determines what happens to a business's **total revenue**—the total receipts from the sale of its product—when it alters the price of the product it is selling. (Total revenue is equal to the price of the product multiplied by the quantity sold: $TR = P \times Q$.)

To better understand total revenue and the importance of the degree of elasticity, put yourself in the place of the seller making a pricing decision. Suppose that you're a college president contemplating an increase in tuition from, say, $2,500 to $2,700 a semester. The basic question you face is whether the gain in revenue due to the higher tuition per student will be offset by the loss in revenue due to the smaller number of students who are willing and able to pay that higher tuition. To answer that question, you must know how responsive students will be to changes in tuition. In other words, you must have some estimate of the elasticity of demand for an education at your college.[2]

---

[2] In reality the question faced by a college president or a businessperson would be somewhat more complicated because any pricing decision may also have an indirect impact on the firm's costs. For example, because a higher price will cause a firm to sell less of its product, the firm may also incur lower costs since it will not need to produce as much output. Before making any pricing decision, a wise entrepreneur considers its impact on costs as well as on revenues. (The nature and behavior of a firm's costs are discussed in Chapter 6.)

Case 1: Elastic Demand. Suppose that demand is highly elastic, that is, very responsive to price changes. If tuition is increased, the college will receive more money from each student, but it will enroll considerably fewer students; the percentage change downward in quantity demanded will be greater than the percentage change upward in price. As a result, the college will take in less total revenue than it did before the tuition hike. In the face of elastic demand, the logical action for the college to take—assuming there are vacant dormitory rooms and unfilled classes—would be to lower, not raise, tuition. The college will receive less from each student who enrolls, but it will enroll many more students, and total revenue will increase.

Case 2: Inelastic Demand. Suppose that demand for an education at your college is inelastic, that is, not very responsive to price changes. If the college increases tuition, it will lose some students but not very many, and the percentage change in quantity demanded will be less than the percentage change in price. Because each student will pay more than before, the result will be an increase in total revenue. If you decided to reduce tuition under these inelastic conditions, you would probably be fired. The tuition reduction wouldn't attract many new students, and all the students would pay a lower rate than before. As a result, total revenue would be lower than it was before the tuition reduction.

Case 3: Unitary Elasticity. If the demand for an education at your college is of unitary elasticity, any change in price will be offset exactly by a proportional change in the quantity demanded (enrollment). If you institute a 10 percent tuition increase, 10 percent fewer students will enroll, and total revenue will be unchanged. If you put into effect a 5 percent tuition reduction, 5 percent more students will enroll, and total revenue will be unchanged. As long as demand is of unitary elasticity, total revenue is unaffected by the seller's pricing decision.

The relationship among price changes, elasticity, and total revenue (*TR*) for each of the three cases is summarized in Exh. 4.3. Before continuing, take the time to work through the exhibit. You will see that if demand is inelastic, a price reduction will lead to a decline in total revenue, and a price increase will cause total revenue to increase. If demand is elastic, a price reduction will lead to an increase in total revenue, and a price increase will cause total revenue to decline. With unitary elasticity, a price change up or down is offset by a proportional change in quantity demanded, and total revenue remains unchanged.

EXHIBIT 4.3

Elasticity and Total Revenue

DEGREE OF ELASTICITY	PRICE INCREASE			PRICE DECREASE		
Case 1: Elastic demand. (The coefficient of elasticity is greater than 1.)	↑ P	↓ × Q =	↓ TR	↓ P	↑ × Q =	↑ TR
Case 2: Inelastic demand. (The coefficient of elasticity is less than 1.)	↑ P	↓ × Q =	↑ TR	↓ P	↑ × Q =	↓ TR
Case 3: Unitary elasticity (The coefficient of elasticity is equal to 1.)	↑ P	↓ × Q =	No change TR	↓ P	↑ × Q =	No change TR

Symbols: ↑ increase, ↓ decrease

The elasticity of demand for a firm's product dictates what will happen to total revenue (price × quantity) when the firm alters price. When demand is elastic, a price increase results in a *significantly lower* quantity demanded and, therefore, in lower total revenue, whereas a price decrease leads to a *significantly higher* quantity demanded and, therefore, results in higher total revenue. When demand is inelastic, a price increase results in a lower quantity demanded *but not much lower,* so that total revenue increases; a price decrease results in a higher quantity demanded *but not much higher,* so that total revenue decreases. If demand is of unitary elasticity, any change in price will be exactly offset by the change in quantity demanded, so that total revenue will not change.

THE DETERMINANTS OF ELASTICITY

As you saw in the preceding discussion, producers need to know whether the demand for their services and products is elastic or inelastic before they can make intelligent pricing decisions. But how can sellers know? Often they can gain insight into the elasticity of demand by considering two major factors that dictate the degree of elasticity: the number of good substitutes available and the importance of the product in consumers' budgets. As you examine these factors, recall our earlier discussion of the *income* and *substitution effects* that underlie the law of demand.

The Number of Available Substitutes for the Product. The primary factor in determining the price elasticity of demand is the number of good substitutes available. Recall that a substitute is a product that can be used in place of another product because, to a greater or lesser extent, it satisfies the same consumer wants. Some people consider chicken a good substitute for fish, for example; many people would acknowledge that a Ford automobile is an acceptable substitute for a Chevrolet with the same features.

When a large number of good substitutes exist, demand for a product tends to be elastic because consumers have alternatives—they can buy something else if the price of the product becomes too high. But if a product has few good substitutes, demand tends to be inelastic because consumers have few options; they must buy the product even at the higher price. Movie tickets, pond-raised catfish, and women's hats have elastic demand because there are a large number of substitutes for each of these items. Cigarettes, electricity, local telephone service, and gasoline tend to have relatively inelastic demand because of the limited options available to consumers.[3]

The Importance of the Product in Consumers' Budgets. The second factor influencing the elasticity of demand for a product is the importance of the product in consumers' budgets. If consumers are spending a significant portion of their income on a particular item (rent or long-distance phone service, for example), a price hike for that item will force a vigorous search for less-expensive substitutes. Demand will tend to be elastic. But if expenditures on the product are relatively small (the average family's annual outlay for lemon juice or soy sauce, for instance), consumers are more likely to ignore the price increase. Demand will tend to be inelastic.

Some major budget items persist in having relatively inelastic demand. For example, even though many smokers spend a significant fraction of their incomes on cigarettes, statistical research shows that the demand for cigarettes by adults is quite inelastic. In this case demand is inelastic because the more important determinant of elasticity is the number of good substitutes. If, like cigarettes, a product has few good substitutes, the fact that it is a major expense item is generally less important to consumers. The article on pages 116–117, "Anti-Tobacco Groups Push for Higher Cigarette Taxes," looks at efforts to deter smoking by teenagers. Read the article to discover the role of the elasticity of demand in determining the success of these efforts.

---

[3] The elasticity of demand for a product tends to increase over time. When the price of a product increases, consumers may not be aware of substitutes for that product, and so demand initially may be inelastic. But the more time that elapses after the price change, the more opportunities consumers have to discover substitutes and to develop new tastes and new habits. As consumers discover more substitutes, demand tends to become more elastic.

Elasticity of Supply

Thus far we have considered only how the quantity demanded responds to price changes. Now we explore the supply side of the market. The price elasticity of supply describes the responsiveness of producers to price changes. More precisely, the **price elasticity of supply** is a measure of the responsiveness of the quantity supplied of a product to a change in its price.

THE COEFFICIENT OF SUPPLY ELASTICITY

Individual producers of goods and services display varying degrees of response when the price of a product changes. Some are able to expand or contract their supply of the product significantly in a short period of time; others are able to make only minimal adjustments. The more responsive producers are to a change in price, the more elastic their supply.

We measure the elasticity of supply by calculating the **coefficient of supply elasticity,** a value that indicates the degree to which the quantity supplied will change in response to a price change. The coefficient of supply elasticity is computed by dividing the percentage change in quantity supplied by the percentage change in price:

$$\text{Coefficient of elasticity} = \frac{\dfrac{\Delta Q}{Q}}{\dfrac{\Delta P}{P}} = \frac{\text{Percentage change in quantity supplied}}{\text{Percentage change in price}}$$

Suppose that the price of coal rises from $40 to $50 a ton and that coal production in the United States therefore increases from 600 to 900 million tons a year. To compute the coefficient of supply elasticity, we first determine the percentage change in quantity supplied: If the change in quantity supplied (ΔQ) is 300 million tons and the original quantity supplied (Q) is 600 million tons, the percentage change in quantity supplied (300/600) is 50 percent. Next, we take the percentage change in price: If the change in price (ΔP) is $10 and the original price is $40, the percentage change in price ($10/$40) is 25 percent. When we divide the 50 percent increase in quantity supplied by the 25 percent increase in price, we arrive at an elasticity coefficient of 2.[4]

$$\text{Coefficient of elasticity} = \frac{\dfrac{300}{600}}{\dfrac{\$10}{\$40}} = \frac{50\%}{25\%} = 2$$

---

[4] As with the elasticity of demand, the more precise formula for calculating the elasticity of supply involves using the average of the two prices and the average of the two quantities as the base values for computing percentages.

Use Your Economic Reasoning

Anti-Tobacco Groups Push for Higher Cigarette Taxes

By David Cay Johnston

In a drive to reverse a recent surge in teen-age smoking, anti-tobacco forces are pushing for a combination of state and Federal tax increases that could raise the cost of a pack of cigarettes by more than $1.

Buoyed by public revulsion at disclosures that tobacco companies have been aiming at teen-agers for years with sophisticated advertising and marketing techniques, advocates are lobbying for tax increases in 19 states and hope to have campaigns going in all 50 by next year.

Also, Congress is considering a bill introduced last month by Senators Orrin G. Hatch, Republican of Utah, and Edward M. Kennedy, Democrat of Massachusetts, to nearly triple the Federal excise tax on cigarettes, to 67 cents a pack from 24 cents....

"Raising tobacco taxes is our No. 1 strategy to damage the tobacco industry," says John D. Giglio, manager of tobacco-control advocacy for the American Cancer Society. "The tobacco industry has found ways around everything else we have done to reduce smoking by teenagers, but they can't repeal the laws of economics."

The anti-tobacco lobby's goal is to raise state cigarette taxes to a uniform $2 a pack nationwide in the next several years, from the current range of 2.5 cents in Virginia to 82.5 cents in Washington State.

If the Federal Government increases its tax to 67 cents as well, the average cost of a pack of cigarettes would rise to $4.23, from $1.80, as the result of the tax increases alone. That, opponents of smoking believe, would be enough to drive millions of smokers, adults and teen-agers alike, to kick the habit and dissuade hundreds of thousands of young people from taking it up....

The two main groups behind the current drive are the Robert Wood Johnson Foundation in Princeton, N.J., which has committed $100 million to anti-smoking efforts, and the American Cancer Society, which has committed $10 million.

The money is being used to hire organizers, distribute voter education materials, hold conferences and take surveys. The two organizations are also the main financial backers of the Campaign for Tobacco-Free Kids, a national tobacco-control advocate.

"Legislators read polls," said Dr. Steven Schroeder, the foundation president, "and the polls tell them that this is probably the only tax that has widespread appeal. People know it is a deterrent and that the longer you can delay kids from starting smoking, the less likely they are to become smokers."

That is a truism that the tobacco industry has long understood—and worried about. An internal memorandum at the Phillip Morris Companies from 1981 said the company should "take seriously" a statement by the National Bureau of Economic Research in Cambridge, Mass., that higher Federal excise taxes could be used to reduce smoking by young people.

SOURCE: *New York Times*, April 3, 1997, p. 18A. Copyright © 1997-96 by The New York Times Co. Reprinted by Permission.

"It is clear that price has a pronounced effect on the smoking prevalence of teen-agers," the memorandum said, adding that the bureau's estimate that a 10 percent increase in cigarette prices would lead to a 12 percent decline in the number of teen-agers taking up smoking was "of greatest significance to the company...."

Even William F. Shughart, who has served as an expert witness for the cigarette industry, said that raising cigarette taxes would reduce teen-age smoking. "[Teens] are more price-sensitive than adults," said Mr. Shughart, a senior fellow with the Independent Institute, a libertarian research center in Oakland, Calif., and the Self Professor of Economics at the University of Mississippi. He added, though, that higher taxes could not be justified because the costs to society of smoking were more than covered by existing cigarette taxes....

Most teen-agers do not smoke, and some are vocal in their distaste for tobacco. Joe Lewis, 17, a senior at Wootton High School in Rockville, Md., and a member of a local group, Students Opposed to Smoking, says bumping up taxes by a nickel or a dime would have little effect. He advocates the full shock treatment.

"If cigarette prices went up by a dollar, a lot of kids would still try cigarettes once, like I did," he said. "But the younger ones, the seventh and eighth graders, couldn't afford it and wouldn't become addicted."

USE YOUR ECONOMIC REASONING

1. Giglio believes that raising tobacco taxes will damage the tobacco industry because it can't "repeal the laws of economics." What specific law or theory does he have in mind?
2. The article suggests that a 10% increase in cigarette prices would lead to a 12% decline in the number of teens taking up smoking (or quitting before they've really become addicted). Use this information to calculate the coefficient of demand elasticity.
2. How much will the price of cigarettes need to be raised (through taxes) to reduce teen consumption by 60%? Show your work.
3. Some economists criticize efforts to raise taxes because they will harm low-income adults while doing little to deter adult smoking. Explain this criticism.

Note that whereas the coefficient of demand elasticity is negative, the co-efficient of supply elasticity usually is positive: Because of the law of supply, an increase in price leads to an increase in the quantity supplied.

INTERPRETING THE ELASTICITY COEFFICIENT

We interpret coefficients of supply elasticity in essentially the same way we interpret coefficients of demand elasticity. A supply elasticity of 2 means that for every 1 percent change in price, the quantity supplied will change by 2 percent. For example, a 10 percent increase in price would lead to a 20 percent increase in the quantity supplied, and a 20 percent increase in price would lead to a 40 percent increase in the quantity supplied. Of course, reductions in price will have the opposite effect. A 10 percent decrease in price would lead to a 20 percent reduction in the quantity supplied.

An elasticity coefficient greater than 1 means that supply is elastic, or very responsive to price changes; a given percentage change in price results in a larger percentage change in quantity supplied. When the elasticity coefficient is less than 1, supply is inelastic; a given percentage change in price results in a smaller percentage change in quantity supplied. If the coefficient is exactly 1, supply is of unitary elasticity; a given percentage change in price results in an identical percentage change in the quantity supplied.

USING SUPPLY ELASTICITY IN POLICY DECISIONS

An understanding of the elasticity of supply can be useful to government pol-icymakers and others seeking solutions to economic problems. Consider, for example, the energy-policy debate that occurred in the late 1970s, a time when the United States was heavily dependent on foreign oil to meet its energy needs. During this period the price of domestically produced oil was regu-lated; it could not rise above the government-dictated price. Imported oil was beyond government control, however, and in the mid-1970s it skyrocketed in price. To reduce dependence on foreign oil, some politicians and policy-makers began to argue for the deregulation of domestic oil prices so that U.S. producers would have incentives for increased exploration and production. Deregulation began in 1978–1979 and, in conjunction with consumer conser-vation (brought about by higher prices), helped to reduce substantially our dependence on foreign oil.

Suppose that the United States would like to increase domestic oil pro-duction by 50 percent to reduce its dependence on foreign oil. How much would the price of domestic oil have to rise to make that possible? Since the supply elasticity of oil is about 1 (actually it's slightly less than 1), the price of oil would have to rise by 50 percent. (Remember, when the coefficient is 1, each 1 percent change in price brings a 1 percent change in quantity supplied.) Of course, if supply were more elastic—if producers were more sensitive to price changes—a smaller price hike would accomplish the same result. For example, if the coefficient were 2, the price of oil would have to rise by only 25 percent in order to increase the quantity supplied by 50 percent.

As you can see, the elasticity of supply allows us to determine how much price has to rise to convince suppliers to increase their output by a given amount. That kind of information is very important in making sound decisions about energy policy and addressing a host of other questions.

TIME AND THE ELASTICITY OF SUPPLY

The responsiveness of suppliers to a change in the price of their product depends on the amount of time they are given to adjust their output to the new price. As a general rule, the longer producers are given to adapt to a price change, the greater the elasticity of supply. We can see the importance of time as a determinant of elasticity by comparing the kinds of adjustments suppliers facing a price change can make in the short run with the changes they can make in the long run.

The Short Run. In economics the **short run** is defined as the period of time during which at least one of a business's inputs (usually plant and equipment) is fixed—that is, incapable of being changed. Therefore, short-run adjustments to a change in price are limited. Producers must use their existing plants and equipment more or less intensively, adding or eliminating a work shift or using a larger or smaller workforce on existing shifts.

The short-run supply curve in Exh. 4.4 shows an increase in the price of oil from $20 to $25 a barrel ($5 equals a 25 percent increase) bringing an increase in the quantity of oil supplied from 800 to 900 million barrels (100 million barrels equals an increase of 12.5 percent). Thus, the coefficient of supply elasticity is .50 (12.5%/25%); supply is quite inelastic in the short run.

The Long Run. The **long run** is defined as the period of time during which all a business's inputs, including plant and equipment, can be changed. The long run provides sufficient time for firms to build new production facilities and to expand or contract existing facilities. New firms can enter the industry and existing firms can leave. These kinds of adjustments make it possible to alter output significantly in response to a price change.

Note that the long-run response to an increase in the price of oil from $20 to $25 a barrel (a 25 percent increase) is an increase in the quantity of oil supplied from 800 million to 1 billion barrels (200 million barrels equals a 25 percent increase). The coefficient of supply elasticity in this case is 1.0 (25%/25%), and so supply is of unitary elasticity in the long run.

As you can see from our example, the elasticity of supply may vary substantially from the short run to the long run for a given product. Both the

EXHIBIT 4.4

The Effect of Time on the Elasticity of Supply

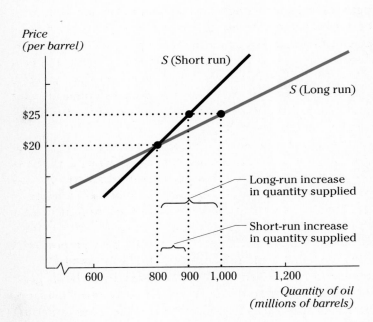

The more time a firm or industry is given to respond to a change in price, the larger the increase or decrease in the quantity supplied and the greater the elasticity of supply. Suppose, for example, that the price of oil rises from $20 to $25 a barrel. In the short run the quantity supplied can be increased from 800 million barrels per year to 900 million barrels; in the long run it is possible to increase the quantity supplied from 800 million barrels to 1 billion barrels per year.

short-run and the long-run elasticities of supply also vary from industry to industry and even from firm to firm. What is certain for any particular firm or industry, however, is that the elasticity of supply will increase directly in relation to the length of time that a firm or an industry is given to adjust to the price change. The response of petroleum producers to higher oil prices illustrates the important role that price changes can play in motivating producers.

Summary

To know how much more consumers will purchase at lower prices or how much less they will purchase at higher prices, we need to know how responsive consumers are to price changes. The *price elasticity of demand* is a measure of the responsiveness of the quantity demanded to a change in price. If a given percentage change in price brings about a larger percentage change in quantity demanded (a coefficient of elasticity greater than 1), demand is described as *elastic*. If a given percentage change in price brings about a smaller percentage change in quantity demanded (a coefficient less than 1), demand is said to be *inelastic*. If a given percentage change in price brings an equal percentage change in quantity demanded (a coefficient equal to 1), *unitary elasticity* prevails.

If demand is perfectly inelastic (the coefficient of elasticity is zero), a very large change in price will bring no change in the quantity demanded; the demand curve will be a vertical straight line. If demand is perfectly elastic (the coefficient approaches infinity), a very small change in price will bring an extremely large change in the quantity demanded; the demand curve will be a horizontal straight line. Most demand curves, however, do not show just one degree of elasticity; they show several. All linear, downward-sloping demand curves will show unitary elasticity in the middle, elastic demand at the upper end, and inelastic demand at the lower end.

The degree of elasticity is important to businesses because it determines what happens to *total revenue,* or total receipts from sales, when a business alters the price of its product. If demand is elastic, a price reduction will lead to an increase in total revenue, and a price increase will cause total revenue to decline. If demand is inelastic, a price reduction will lead to a decline in total revenue, and a price hike will cause total revenue to increase. With unitary elastic demand, any change in price will be offset exactly by a proportional change in the quantity demanded, and total revenue will be unchanged.

The major determinants of the elasticity of demand are the number of good substitutes that exist and the importance of the product in consumers' budgets. The greater the number of substitutes for a product and the more important the item in the budgets of consumers, the greater the elasticity of demand for the product.

Suppliers as well as consumers respond to price changes. The measure of suppliers' responsiveness to a change in the price of their product is called the *price elasticity of supply*. Economists use the *coefficient of supply elasticity* to determine the degree of responsiveness. The formula for the coefficient is the percentage change in quantity supplied divided by the percentage change in price. Supply is elastic if the coefficient is greater than 1, inelastic if it is less than 1, and unitary if it is equal to 1.

As a general rule, the more time a firm or industry is given to adapt to a specified price change, the larger the change in quantity supplied and the greater the elasticity of supply. The *short run* is a time during which at least one input is fixed. In the short run, output can be expanded by employing additional units of labor and raw materials, but time does not permit plant and equipment expansion. Producers have additional options in the *long run,* a period of time sufficient to change all inputs. In the long run, new production facilities can be built and existing facilities can be expanded. As a consequence, output can be increased much more in the long run than in the short run.

GLOSSARY

Coefficient of demand elasticity. A value that indicates the degree to which quantity demanded will change in response to a price change.

Coefficient of supply elasticity. A value that indicates the degree to which the quantity supplied will change in response to a price change.

Long run. The period of time during which all a business's inputs, including plant and equipment, can be changed.

Price elasticity of demand. A measure of the responsiveness of the quantity demanded

of a product to a change in its price.

Price elasticity of supply. A measure of the responsiveness of the quantity supplied of a product to a change in its price.

Short run. The period of time during which at least one of a business's inputs (usually plant and equipment) is fixed—that is, incapable of being changed.

Total revenue. The total receipts of a business from the sale of its product. Total revenue is determined by multiplying the selling price of the product by the number of units sold.

STUDY QUESTIONS

Fill in the Blanks

1. If a decrease in the price of the product leads to a decrease in total revenue, demand must be (elastic/inelastic/unitary) *inelastic* .

2. If a 10 percent reduction in price leads to a 20 percent increase in quantity demanded, the coefficient of elasticity would be equal to *2.0* .

3. If the coefficient of elasticity is greater than 1, demand is *elastic* ; if it is less than 1, demand is *inelastic* ; if it is equal to 1, demand is *unitary* .

4. The major determinant of the elasticity of demand for a product is the number of good *substitutes* that exist for the product.

5. The greater the fraction of the family budget spent for a particular product, the (greater/smaller) *Greater* the elasticity of demand for that product.

6. A perfectly inelastic demand curve would be a (vertical/horizontal) *Vertical* straight line.

7. Along a downward-sloping linear demand curve, the elasticity of demand is the greatest at the (upper/lower) *Upper* end of the curve.

8. The degree of responsiveness of suppliers to a price change depends in part on the amount of *time* they are given to adapt to the change.

9. The time period during which all resources or inputs are variable is called the *long run* .

10. In general, the greater the period of time producers are given to adjust to a change in price, the (greater/smaller) *Greater* the elasticity of supply.

Multiple Choice

1. If a seller reduces the price of a product and this leads to an increase in the quantity sold, what can be concluded?
   a) Demand is elastic.
   b) Demand is inelastic.
   c) Demand is of unitary elasticity.
   d) Nothing can be concluded about the degree of elasticity.

2. If the demand curve for a product is a vertical straight line, the coefficient of elasticity would be
   a) zero.
   b) 1.
   c) infinity.
   d) different between any two points on the curve.

3. If an increase in price causes total revenue to fall, what can be concluded?
   a) Demand is elastic.
   b) Demand is inelastic.
   c) Unitary elasticity prevails.

4. On a downward-sloping demand curve, demand is more elastic
   a) at the upper end.
   b) at the lower end.
   c) in the middle.

5. In general, demand for a product is more elastic
   a) the fewer the substitutes and the larger the fraction of the family budget spent on that product.
   b) the greater the number of substitutes and the larger the fraction of the family budget spent on that product.
   c) the fewer the substitutes and the smaller the fraction of the family budget spent on that product.
   d) the greater the number of substitutes and the smaller the fraction of the family budget spent on that product.

6. The local transit company is contemplating an increase in bus fares in order to expand revenues. A local senior-citizens group, Seniors for Fair Fares, argues that a rate increase would lead to lower revenues. This disagreement suggests that
   a) the transit company does not believe that the rate increase would reduce the number of riders, but the SFF believes that it would.
   b) the transit company believes that the demand for bus service is elastic, but the SFF believes that it is inelastic.
   c) the transit company believes that the demand for bus service is inelastic, but the SFF believes that it is elastic.

7. If the supply curve for a product was a vertical straight line,
   a) the quantity supplied would not depend on price.
   b) supply would be a fixed quantity.
   c) supply would be perfectly inelastic; that is, the elasticity coefficient would be equal to zero.
   d) All of the above

8. Which of the following is *not* a short-run adjustment?
   a) The purchase of additional raw materials
   b) The construction of a new factory building
   c) The hiring of additional workers
   d) The addition of a second production shift

9. If the coefficient of supply elasticity for widgets is equal to 4, a 20 percent increase in the price of widgets would cause the quantity supplied to expand by
   a) 80 percent.
   b) 5 percent.
   c) 40 percent.
   d) 4 percent.

10. In general, we can say that supply is more elastic
    a) in the short run than in the long run.
    b) in the long run than in the short run.

#2 is 5

n as a method
what assump-
e elasticity of
you think that
college? Why

2. If the price of Wrinkled jeans is reduced from $10 to $8 a pair and the quantity demanded increases from 5,000 to 10,000 pairs a month, what is the coefficient of demand elasticity?

3. According to Mark Moore, of Harvard's Kennedy School of Government, the ideal demand-side drug policy would make illegal drugs cheap for addicts and expensive for neophytes. What logic can you see for such a policy, and how would it relate to the elasticity of demand for illegal drugs?

4. Which would tend to be more elastic, the demand for automobiles or the demand for Ford automobiles? Why?

5. Suppose that the price elasticity of demand for water is 2.0 and that the government wants to reduce the quantity of water demanded by 40 percent. By how much must the price of water be raised to

accomplish this objective?

6. Sales taxes are a major source of revenue for many state governments. But higher taxes mean higher prices, which mean lower quantities sold by merchants. If the government wants to expand its tax revenue yet inflict minimum damage on the sales of merchants, should it tax products with elastic demand or inelastic demand? Why? Can you see any drawbacks to focusing taxes on these products?

7. Suppose that the coefficient of supply elasticity is equal to 2.5 for a particular product. If the price of that product increases by 10 percent, how much will the quantity supplied increase?

8. If price declines by 5 percent and quantity supplied declines by 20 percent, what is the coefficient of supply elasticity?

9. Why do we expect supply to be more elastic in the long run than in the short run?

10. Suppose that the coefficient of supply elasticity for housing was equal to 1.5. How much would the price of housing need to rise in order to expand the quantity of housing supplied by 30 percent?

ANSWER KEY

Fill in the Blanks

1. inelastic
2. 2.0
3. elastic, inelastic, unitary
4. substitutes
5. greater
6. vertical
7. upper
8. time
9. long run
10. greater

Multiple Choice

1. d
2. a
3. a
4. a
5. b
6. c
7. d
8. b
9. a
10. b

CHAPTER 5

Marginal Reasoning and Profit Maximization

LEARNING OBJECTIVES

1. State the assumptions that economists make about human beings.
2. Describe how individuals and businesses use cost-benefit analysis to guide their decision making.
3. Discuss some of the pitfalls in decision-making.
4. Explain what is meant by marginal reasoning.
5. Explain how marginal reasoning can improve both personal and business decision-making.
6. Describe how a business selects the profit-maximizing level of output.

As we learned in Chapter 1, we all use models to help us understand the world around us. The past four chapters have introduced you to some economic models: the production possibilities model, the model of supply and demand, and the model of elasticity, for example. You will be introduced to many more theories or models in this book because, as we've already discovered, it is only through models that we can begin to explain the real world and solve real-world problems. But economics is more than a haphazard collection of theories or models with no unifying theme. Underlying all the models in economics is the assumption that human beings are motivated by self-interest and that they make rational decisions based on self-interest. We begin this chapter by examining those assumptions. We'll see that rational decision making involves a comparison of costs and benefits and that the appropriate costs and benefits for comparison are marginal costs and benefits. After that we examine some of the pitfalls in decision making and see how they can be avoided. The chapter concludes by exploring the similarity between individual and business decision making, and by examining how businesses select the profit-maximizing level of output.

Explaining Human Behavior: The Role of Assumptions

As we noted in Chapter 1, models are always based on assumptions; the more realistic the assumptions, the greater the likelihood that the resulting model will be useful in understanding the real world. In attempting to explain and predict the behavior of individuals, economists make the assumption that men and women are motivated primarily by self-interest and pursue self-interest through a rational comparison of costs and benefits.

THE PURSUIT OF SELF-INTEREST

Assuming that people are motivated by self-interest is clearly an over-simplification. The factors that motivate human beings are very complex and include empathy, a sense of duty or obligation, and many others. But following the lead of Adam Smith, the father of economics, economists argue that foremost among these motivations is the pursuit of self-interest.

The role of self-interest in motivating men and women may seem self-evident to you. But the fact is that we sometimes forget this fundamental characteristic of human nature. And forgetting it may cause us to make errors in judgment. Consider, for example, the automobile salesman who promises to be your friend and "give you a good deal." If self-interest is the primary factor motivating salespeople, your first response when confronted by such a pledge should be to question it. After all, a salesperson who is motivated by self-interest won't be concerned about promoting yours—at least no more than the competition demands. And when an advertisement offers "free" products or "unbelievable bargains," don't rush down to the store. Read the fine print; that's where you will generally discover the true cost.

Remembering that people are driven by self-interest will do more than help you make good decisions; it will also help you understand behavior that may seem strange if you forget this fundamental motivation. For example, why is it that college students make it a point to call their distant grandmother while they are visiting their parents but never manage a call from the pay phone in their dormitory. And why is it that there is always overcrowding on the Internet, where we pay one fee for unlimited access, but there is seldom overcrowding on long-distance phone lines, where customers are charged by the minute. And how is it that some people leave large tips in restaurants they visit regularly and smaller ones when they are out of town. Economists will argue that none of this behavior is random or accidental; it simply results from the pursuit of self-interest.

COMPARING COSTS AND BENEFITS

How do individuals pursue their self-interest; how do they make certain that their decisions improve their own well-being? They do so by always comparing the costs and benefits of a contemplated action rather than acting impulsively. Consider, for example, the decision that confronts you in the morning when your alarm goes off. Do you get out of bed and go to class or stay in bed and get a couple more hours of sleep? Economists assume that rather than just hitting the alarm and going back to sleep (an impulsive reaction), you weigh the costs and benefits of getting up. In other words, you consider what you would learn in class and the likelihood of a quiz (the benefits of getting up) against the lost sleep (the cost of getting up) and make a decision. If the value of going to class exceeds the cost, you get up. If not, you make the rational decision and stay in bed.

There are several important things to note about this decision-making process. First, self-interest seeking individuals consider only the costs and benefits that affect them personally. They don't consider the benefits that their presence might convey to others in the class—better class discussion, for example—or the costs that their absence might impose on others, provoking a quiz from the professor, for instance. Second, this cost-benefit comparison may be performed unconsciously, without any real deliberation. Through experience you may know that there are substantial costs associated with missing class, and so you get up automatically, without much consideration of alternatives. It's only on mornings following a particularly short night that the cost-benefit comparison really kicks in.[1] Third, this comparison is based on expected costs and benefits; you won't know the true costs and benefits until after the fact. You may jump out of bed expecting an exhilarating class period—and not get it. Or you may stay in bed expecting to miss very little, only to find out that Brad Pitt and Melanie Griffith were team-teaching class that day, or—perhaps more realistically—you missed a 20-point quiz.

The Importance of Marginal Analysis

When costs and benefits are compared, the relevant costs and benefits for comparison are the *marginal* costs and benefits. **Marginal** means extra, or additional; the marginal costs and benefits are the additional costs and benefits

---

[1] Many cost-benefit comparisons are performed instinctively or unconsciously because you've performed them many times before. For instance, do the additional benefits provided by designer jeans justify the premium prices they generally command? You probably had to reflect on that question the first few times you went shopping. But after that, the decision became much simpler. Now, all you have to hear is the price differential and you know what you want to buy.

resulting from the decision. It may appear obvious that it's marginal costs and benefits that matter, but it's easy to confuse marginal and total values if you're not careful. And that can result in poor decision making (or in good decisions that are misunderstood).

To illustrate, consider once again that morning debate, "Do I stay in bed or get up and go to class?" Suppose that, one morning, you decide to skip class and sleep in. The next day, you tell the prof the truth—"I needed the sleep." What response might you expect from the prof? There are a number of possibilities, but one is something like this: "You mean you value sleep more than my class?" Hearing that reaction might cause you to regret missing class, but your morning's decision has actually been misrepresented. If you had to choose between sleep and, say, accounting, accounting would lose hands down. So would literature and physics and probably even the psychology of human sexuality! But that's not really the choice that most of us have to make, and it's not the choice you were trying to communicate to the prof. The choice is really not between accounting and sleep; it is between an *additional* or marginal hour of accounting and an *additional* or marginal hour of sleep. That's where decisions are always made, on the margin, between a little more of this and a little more of that.

As you can see, failing to recognize the difference between total and marginal values can lead to poor decisions, or it can get you into trouble for making good decisions that you can't defend. Consider the following additional examples:

1. Your boss asks you to work late in order to finish an important job. Your husband (wife) calls at work to find out why you're not home. He asks, "Is your job more important to you than I am?"

2. You have an 85 average in accounting and a 79 average in literature. Each course requires 80 percent to earn a B grade. Final exam week finds you spending most of your time studying literature. Is literature more important to you than accounting?

3. At the family picnic you've had three helpings of Mom's potato salad, and one helping of Aunt Mildred's cole slaw. Mom sees you reach for the cole slaw and says, "Do you like the cole slaw better than my potato salad?"

In each of these instances, the failure to recognize the difference between total and marginal values is the source of the misunderstanding. Even though you value your husband more than your job, there may be situations in which an additional evening at work is more important to you than an additional evening with him. And even if you love accounting and loathe literature, you still may value an additional weekend studying literature more highly than an additional weekend studying accounting. Finally, even if you prefer Mom's potato salad to Aunt Mildred's cole slaw and virtually every other food on the face of the earth, there is nothing irrational about preferring one more scoop of cole slaw, especially after already having three scoops of potato salad.

The Improper Estimation of Costs

Even people who understand the difference between marginal and total values sometimes make bad decisions. More often than not, these poor decisions are the result of a mistaken estimate of the cost of the decision in question. Sometimes people forget to consider important costs, and sometimes they see costs where there are none. Let's consider these problems in turn.

IGNORING OPPORTUNITY COSTS

Economists are fond of telling us that all decisions have costs, that there is no such thing as a "free lunch." This was part of the message of Chapter 1. Any time we make a decision to do or to have one thing, we sacrifice the opportunity to do or to have some other thing. The most-valued alternative we sacrifice to take an action is the opportunity cost of that action.

The opportunity cost concept holds that costs exist whether or not money changes hands. In fact, the money you pay for a product is just a veil; the true cost of that product is the other things you could have purchased with the same money. If you spend $200 on a CD player, the real cost of the CD player is the pizzas, movie tickets, and jeans you could have bought with the same money.

Otto's Garage, Inc. Sometimes we forget that the true cost of any decision is the opportunity cost, and that can lead to poor decisions. Consider the case of Otto Run, a recent graduate of Smalltown Technical College. Otto and his brother, Will, decided to start their own auto-repair business. So they visited their banker to arrange financing for the building they want to construct. When the banker asked them where the new business would be located, Otto reported that the location would be the corner of Main and First Streets, a longtime vacant lot in a prime location. That seemed to the banker like an expensive piece of real estate for an auto-repair shop; so she asked the brothers why they had chosen that location. Otto's response was, "Because we own the land and it won't cost us anything to use it." His answer illustrates a common problem in making decisions—failing to consider opportunity costs. Because these budding entrepreneurs were not required to make a dollar payment to buy or lease the land, they assumed that it was free; they ignored the opportunity cost.

In this instance the piece of land that was going to be used for the auto-repair business was in a good location and quite valuable. It could easily have been sold to a land developer as a building site for a bank or some other facility requiring good customer access. The true cost of using that land was whatever money the brothers sacrificed by using the land themselves.

Professor Noslack and the New York Yankees. The message of opportunity cost can also be helpful in reminding us that costs exist even if they are not easily reducible to money. To illustrate: A student walked into Professor Noslack's office to discuss his plans to attend an upcoming New York Yankees baseball game instead of his chemistry class. "My brother said he'll pick me up, drive me to the game, and pay for everything. I can't pass up this opportunity; it won't cost me anything." When Professor Noslack asked the student his average in the course, there was a moment's pause; he wasn't doing very well. And the class he was planning to miss was scheduled to be a review for the upcoming exam—an exam he really needed to pass. The point here is not that the student made a poor decision by deciding to skip class; rather, it is that the student failed to consider all the relevant costs, including the (nonmonetary) opportunity costs of missing class. (The failure to consider opportunity costs may help to explain why patients request unneeded antibiotics. Read the article on pages 132–133 to discover the opportunity cost of this behavior, and learn how economic reasoning may ultimately save the day.)

FAILING TO IGNORE FIXED COSTS

Ignoring opportunity costs is not the only source of poor decision making. Another problem is mistaking fixed costs for marginal costs.

All the costs that confront us in our personal lives and in business can be categorized as either *fixed costs* or *variable costs*. **Fixed costs** are costs that do not vary with the level of the activity engaged in, whether that activity is driving a car, owning a home, or (in the case of a business) producing output. **Variable costs,** as the name implies, vary with the level of activity. They go up when you engage in more of the activity (drive more, spend more time at home, produce more output) and down when you engage in less. Fixed costs and variable costs can also be thought of as unavoidable and avoidable costs, respectively. Because fixed costs don't vary with the level of activity, they can't be avoided by doing less of the activity. Variable costs, on the other hand, are avoidable; do less of an activity and you reduce your variable costs.

Consider, for example, the costs of driving a car. Some of those costs are fixed—the monthly payment, for example, and the cost of insurance. Whether you drive one mile or a thousand, the amount of your fixed costs will be unchanged. Other costs, the cost of gasoline and oil, for example, vary with the amount you drive; the more you drive, the more you spend for gas and oil.

The Flying Smiths. The distinction between fixed and variable costs is an important one for decision making. To illustrate, consider the following problem. Bob Smith and his wife, Robin, are planning a two-week ski trip. They've been given free use of a condo once they arrive, so the major expense of the ski holiday is the transportation to and from the resort. They're trying to decide whether to take a plane or drive their car. They realize that driving will use up some of their skiing time, but they think the beauty of the drive will compensate for that loss. The round-trip plane fare for the couple is $400. Robin, who is an accountant, has estimated the cost of making the trip by car as follows:

$150	gas
160	one night's motel lodging each way
200	half a month's car payment
20	half a month's car insurance
10	estimated wear on tires
$540	Total Cost of transportation

Because the cost of taking the car exceeds the cost of taking the plane, the Smiths decide to take the plane. Do you agree with their decision?

As you may have noticed, the problem with Robin's estimate of the driving costs is that it fails to distinguish between fixed and variable costs. More precisely, this estimate fails to isolate the *marginal cost* of taking the trip. The car payment and the monthly payment for insurance are fixed costs; those payments have to be made whether the Smiths drive or fly. The true cost of driving to Colorado is only $320—the extra or additional variable cost of operating the automobile and the added cost of lodging. If the Smiths compare that cost to the cost of airfare, driving is the clear choice.

Note that the decision-making process used to decide between taking a plane and driving a car is really no different than the cost-benefit analysis discussed earlier. The benefit of driving the car is the $400 you save by not having to take the plane. If the cost of driving the car is less than the benefit, you drive the car; otherwise, you take the plane. But if you get your estimate of costs wrong—if you include fixed costs that don't belong— you make the wrong decision and spend money needlessly.

One more note before we proceed. Even though the car payment and the insurance payment are fixed costs in this instance, they might be marginal costs under other circumstances. Suppose, for example, that you've just

Use Your Economic Reasoning

This Winter, Try to Avoid Taking Unneeded Antibiotics

September brings the promise of another cold and flu season. When a cold strikes on the eve of a business trip, or a school-age child contracts a sore throat, how many of us phone for the quick fix of an antibiotic?

This year should be different.

After failed attempts to curb antibiotics abuse, the U.S. Centers for Disease Control and Prevention and its allies are switching tactics this month. Backed by the American Academy of Pediatrics, the American Society of Microbiology and others, CDCP is warning that misuse of the drugs isn't just a problem in hospitals but a personal threat to everyone who takes unnecessary drugs.

Thousands of doctors and clinics will receive pamphlets from the CDCP asking them to return to classic practices: Get cultures, prescribe antibiotics only for confirmed bacterial infections and treat viral cold symptoms with comfort care.

"We estimate that 50 million prescriptions for oral antibiotics are written unnecessarily every year," says Benjamin Schwartz, epidemiologist at the CDCP in Atlanta. "That's a third of the total."

Using antibiotics doesn't hasten recovery from viral colds. Instead, it wipes out all stray sensitive bacteria, leaving behind superstrains that are impervious to drugs. When these take hold in the throat, the ear, or on the skin, the next infection may be drug-resistant.

Rampant antibiotics abuse happens through the collusion of lazy physicians writing prescriptions against good medical judgment, with patients who are too busy to come in for a throat swab but desirous that the doctor "do something."

Doctors too often cave in to time pressures, or attempts to save patients the cost of a lab test. All are potential accomplices in a process that fosters superbugs and depletes the medical tool kit.

The result: pneumococcus—the leading cause of bacterial meningitis, bloodstream infections and ear infections—is already resistant to penicillin in 20% of cases, and resistant to certain sulfa drugs in 25% of cases nationwide. Since last month, researchers have reported the first two cases of vancomycin-resistant *Istaphylococcus aureus* in Michigan and New Jersey.

But the summer has brought hopeful medical news on resistance. In Finland, where drug-resistant group A streptococcus had risen alarmingly, researchers imposed restricted antibiotic use. After the curbs, the incidence of resistance dropped sharply. The Finnish study gives U.S. researchers hope that they can emulate this success.

To tighten U.S. doctors' prescribing antibiotics on demand, CDCP and its partners are promoting "a new paradigm" from common-cold care. If your doctor diagnoses a viral cold that needs no antibiotic, you won't be sent away empty-handed. You'll get a pamphlet detailing how and why unneeded antibiotics hurt you, plus a written "prescription" with suggestions for over-the-counter medicine and symptomatic

SOURCE: *Wall Street Journal*, Sept. 15, 1997. p. B1. Reprinted by permission of the *Wall Street Journal*, © 1997 Dow Jones & Company, Inc. All Rights Reserved Worldwide.

relief while your immune system fights off the virus.

Patients would forgo antibiotics if they had better communication, Dr. Schwartz believes. But these days, pressured patients and over-scheduled physicians find the illusory quick fix of a prescription easier than sweating out the cycle of a virus. CDCP's educational materials could help, but the transition will make demands on everyone's time and patience if it's to succeed....

The key is convincing consumers of their personal stakes in this battle. "Our big mistake was telling people they were screwing up the globe," says Michael Marcy of Kaiser Permanente California Healthcare Program in Panorama City, Calif. "Now we're saying you're harming yourself and you're harming your child."

Kaiser, he says, aims to educate cold-sufferers that it's normal for a virus to last more than a week, and for coughs to persist two weeks (longer in smokers). Fevers are a natural defense mechanism treatable with acetaminophen or ibuprofen, he adds....

If CDCP's campaign can break the cycle of overuse, more powerful bacteria-fighting drugs, now hurtling toward obsolescence, may get a new lease on life. "If you are circumspect about use, you'll without a doubt prolong the useful life of an antibiotic," predicts Anthony Fauci, director of the National Institute of Allergy and Infectious diseases.

The CDCP brochure offers a primer on antibiotics, stressing that viral infections run their course in time. Until you're well, it offers a "prescription" for relief: drink lots of fluids, use a cool-mist vaporizer and soothe sore throats with sprays and lozenges.

USE YOUR ECONOMIC REASONING

1. Patients often request antibiotics inappropriately because they overestimate the benefits and underestimate the costs of doing so. Discuss.
2. What is the opportunity cost (to patients) of taking antibiotics when they don't really need them?
3. Use cost-benefit analysis to explain why doctors might find it in their self-interest to overprescribe antibiotics.
4. Health officials initially tried to stem inappropriate antibiotic use by "telling people they were screwing up the globe." Why was that a "big mistake?" What was wrong with their model of human behavior?
5. How have health officials modified their message to patients in order to gain greater support for reducing unnecessary antibiotic use? Is this new approach more or less consistent with the economist's model of what motivates human beings?

moved to New York City and you're trying to decide whether to buy a car or rely on mass transit to get to work and travel about the city. Under those circumstances, the car and insurance payments are marginal costs of owning an automobile. They need to be considered along with the cost of gas, parking fees, and so forth, in deciding whether it's cheaper to travel by mass transit or purchase a car. But if you decide to purchase the car and have it insured, the insurance and car payments immediately become fixed costs in determining the cost of any trip you intend to make. The point is that insurance and car payments become fixed costs only after you've made a commitment to pay them; up to that point, they are avoidable and need to be considered along with any other marginal costs and benefits. If you're confused, read on; the case of Peggy and Sue should shed additional light on the distinction between fixed and marginal costs.

Peggy, Sue, and the One-Year Lease.   Peggy and Sue live in an apartment near Ivy College. They've both decided to return home for the summer and would like to sublet their apartment for the three months of summer vacation. Peggy and Sue signed a one-year lease that obligates them to pay $500 a month, including utilities. They have been advertising their apartment for the past three weeks but have found no takers. Several new apartments have been erected in the city, and apartment rents have fallen dramatically since they have signed their lease. Two friends have hinted that they might be willing to rent the apartment if Peggy and Sue would accept substantially less than $500. Peggy and Sue would like to be able to cover their $500 monthly payment, and they're reluctant to accept less than that amount. What advice would you offer them?

Peggy and Sue need to seriously consider any offer that is made. Obviously they want to rent the apartment for as much as possible; $600 would be great if they could get it. But if the best offer they get is $300, or even $200, they should take it. After all, the $500 rent they are obliged to pay is a fixed cost; they have to pay it whether they sublet the apartment or not. If they can get $300 by subletting, they have to come up with only another $200 on their own. If they reject that offer, they have to pay the entire $500 themselves.

Of course, there are some intangibles here. There is always some risk that the people who sublet the apartment may damage it or destroy Peggy and Sue's relationship with the landlord or in some other way impose costs on them. These intangibles are worth something and may establish a "floor" or minimum rent that Peggy and Sue are willing to accept. That's fine; there's nothing wrong with that logic. The important point is that the $500 rent is a fixed cost and is irrelevant in deciding how much to accept when subletting.

The Travels of Bonnie and Claude. As we've seen, the irrelevance of fixed costs doesn't prevent them from creeping into all kinds of decisions. As a final example, consider the trials of a young married couple, Bonnie and Claude Jones, who have been shopping for a new sofa. The couple recently found a sofa they like at a local furniture store, but it is selling for $800, somewhat more than they want to pay. A neighbor has suggested that they drive to Furnitureville—a 100 mile trip—because she's heard that the prices there are 25 percent lower. If they make the trip, Susan will have to miss half a day's work at a cost of about $50 in forgone income. In addition, Claude estimates that they will spend another $25 for gas. After discussion, the couple decides that the expected benefits of the trip (the $200 they anticipate saving on the sofa) justify the expense.

When they arrive, they discover that furniture prices are indeed lower than at home—but not much lower. The sofa that sold at home for $800 sells there for $775 (including delivery). Mr. Jones is very disappointed. He wants to turn around and head back home. "If we include the money we've lost because of the trip, these sofas cost $850; that's even more than the $800 they're asking back home." Mrs. Jones isn't so sure. "I don't think we should count the cost of the trip; we've already lost that money. I think we should go ahead and buy the sofa here since it's $25 less than back home." Who do you think is correct?

If you sided with Mrs. Jones, you're on the right track. The cost of the trip is a fixed cost; it can't be avoided after the trip is made and shouldn't

A trip to a baseball game isn't free, even if someone else agrees to buy the tickets and pay for the snacks.

affect the sofa-buying decision in any way. If the Joneses had known the sofa prices in Furnitureville before they made the trip, they would have stayed home. But once they've made the trip, they have to pay for it whether or not they buy the sofa. The correct decision is to buy the sofa in Furnitureville because the additional cost of the sofa there ($775) is less than the additional cost of the sofa back home ($800). The cost of the trip is fixed or "sunk" and irrelevant; it's water under the bridge or spilt milk. (Fixed costs are sometimes referred to as **sunk costs**, a label that conveys the notion that fixed costs are unavoidable.)

Before moving on to the next example, let's consider another possible outcome from the trip to Furnitureville. Suppose that on arrival, the Joneses had discovered that the sofa they were interested in was selling for $850, $50 more than back home. Under those circumstances, the correct decision would be to buy the sofa in their hometown. But the Joneses may fall into the trap of believing that it is necessary to buy the sofa in Furnitureville to justify the cost of the trip. In other words, "We've paid for this trip and we need to have something to show for it." But as we've already noted, the cost of the trip is sunk; it cannot be avoided. If the Joneses insist on buying the sofa in Furnitureville, all they will have to show for the trip is thinner wallets.

As the foregoing examples illustrate, there are many pitfalls in wise decision making. It's easy to ignore some relevant costs and equally easy to see costs where there are none. The key to avoiding these pitfalls is remembering to think marginally and to consider the opportunity costs. By applying these rules you can make better personal decisions about everything from how to spend your money to what to do next Saturday night. (Many Internet users *do* understand what it means to "think marginally." Read the article on pages 138–139 to learn how marginal reasoning is clogging the Internet.)

Business Decision Making and Profit Maximization

Now that we have introduced the marginal principle and have seen how it can improve personal decision making, we shift the emphasis to business decision making. Much of this text focuses on the behavior of businesses rather than that of individuals. That's because businesses are at the center of the productive activity in our economy. They not only produce the goods and services that consumers demand, they also provide the employment opportunities that make it possible for consumers to purchase those goods and services. Business decision making is really no different than personal decision making; it involves a comparison of costs and benefits. The only real distinction between business and personal decision making is the goals involved. Economists generally assume that self-interest–seeking individuals attempt to maximize personal satisfaction, or **utility**. Businesses, on the other hand, are generally assumed to be **profit maximizers;** they are attempting to make decisions that will allow them to earn as much profit as possible.

Profit is the excess of a business firm's total revenue over its total costs. Businesses pursue profits by producing and selling products. **Total revenue** represents the total receipts of the business, that is, the amount of money it takes in from the sale of its product. Total revenue is calculated by multiplying the selling price of the product by the number of units sold. **Total cost** refers to the sum of all the fixed and variable costs incurred by a business in producing its product and making it available for sale. As long as a business's total revenue exceeds its total costs, it is earning a profit. When total costs exceed total revenue, the business is incurring a **loss**. (Profit and loss are simple accounting terms; we'll see later why economists need special terms for different kinds of profits.)

Selecting the Profit-Maximizing Level of Output

The most fundamental decision that a business makes is selecting the optimal level of output, the output that will maximize its profits or minimize its losses. Managers attempt to locate that output by repeatedly asking themselves the same question: "Will the marginal benefit from producing this additional unit of output exceed the marginal cost?" As long as the answer is yes, they continue to expand production. When the answer is no, they stop; they've found the optimal level of output.

MARGINAL REVENUE IS THE MARGINAL BENEFIT

The benefit that a firm receives from producing and selling its product is the money it takes in—the revenue it receives. As we've already noted, the amount of revenue the firm generates depends on two things: the selling price of the product and the quantity of the product sold. For the sake of illustration, imagine that you own a small sawmill producing pine lumber for home building. Suppose, also, that the prevailing price of pine lumber is $270 per thousand

Use Your Economic Reasoning

An "All You Can Eat" Price Is Clogging Internet Access

By Peter H. Lewis

The most popular number for computer users... has become $19.95, which is emerging as the standard monthly price for unlimited access to the Internet. But this "all you can eat" price is rapidly causing indigestion among network-access providers, phone companies, and many customers.

Freed from the constraints of hourly rates, millions of computer users are spending hours every day connected to the Internet and on-line information services. That in turn is causing a surge in busy signals, a slowdown of service, and frustration in cyberspace.

The network traffic jams have been increasing in recent months, as more Internet access companies switched to $19.95 price plans. But the real tie-ups began on Dec. 1, when the largest Internet service provider, America Online, with seven million customers, shifted to flat-rate pricing. Not only did the company's number of daily on-line sessions increase by one-third, to 9 million—totalling 3.1 million hours of connection time—but the average America Online subscriber is staying on line 20 percent longer than before.

And because some customers are having so much trouble getting on line, once they do get a connection many deliberately keep the line tied up—in some cases using special software to hang onto their connection as they work or even sleep....

The rising popularity of these freely available programs, with names like Keep Alive, Rascal, Stay

feet and that this price is set by market forces and is largely beyond your control. (The next chapter will examine this assumption in some detail.) Under these circumstances, what is the marginal benefit to your sawmill of selling an additional thousand feet of lumber? If you answered $270, you've got the right idea. That $270 is the price the firm receives for each unit of output (each thousand feet of lumber) it sells. It also represents the mill's marginal revenue—the additional revenue from selling one more unit of output.

Exhibit 5.1 illustrates how the sawmill's total revenue and marginal revenue change as the mill expands production. As you can see from column 2,

Connected, and Ponger, mean that thousands of dial-in connections are being commandeered and made unavailable to others....

Jim Diestel, director of advanced services for Pacific Bell in San Francisco, said that the average Internet data call earlier this fall lasted one hour, compared to three to four minutes for a voice call, and that was before both America Online and AT&T expanded their flat-rate programs.

For the telephone companies, the longer data calls play havoc with their ability to forecast network loads and manage capacity....

The trend towards flat-rate pricing has also been especially damaging to the hundreds of small Internet service providers who once had the market to themselves but who now must compete with flat-rate giants like America Online....

Even among customers, the flat-rate pricing plan is not universally popular. People who do not use the Internet more than a few hours a month probably preferred paying $2.95 an hour.

But for Internet enthusiasts, the all-you-can-eat price plans are prompting residential phone customers to add second and third phone lines....

"Business is booming," said Jeff Ward, vice president for federal policy for the Nynex Corporation, the regional Bell company for New York and New England.

Ward noted that the number of additional lines was up 14 percent in the last year, while the overall increase in phone lines grew just 2 percent. "The number of teens has remained relatively constant, so the surge in demand is computer driven," he said....

USE YOUR ECONOMIC REASONING

1. Under the flat-rate pricing scheme, what is the marginal cost of an additional hour of Internet time, once you've become a subscriber?
2. How much benefit (in monetary terms) must users anticipate receiving from an additional hour of Internet use in order to justify staying connected for that hour?
3. Use cost-benefit analysis to explain why flat-rate pricing has led to a "clogging" of Internet access.

total revenue (the result of multiplying the selling price times the number of units sold) climbs steadily upward as output is increased. On the other hand, the marginal revenue values in column 3 remain constant. Because marginal revenue represents the additional revenue from selling another unit of output, we compute marginal revenue by finding the change in total revenue from one output level to the next. For example, we can see from the exhibit that the mill's total revenue is $540 if it sells two units of output and $810 if it sells three units. The $270 difference between these values ($810 − $540 = $270) represents the marginal revenue from selling the third unit of output. Because

EXHIBIT 5.1

Marginal Revenue from Selling Pine Lumber

OUTPUT PER DAY	TOTAL REVENUE	MARGINAL REVENUE
0	0	—
1	$ 270	$270
2	540	270
3	810	270
4	1,080	270
5	1,350	270
6	1,620	270
7	1,890	270
8	2,160	270
9	2,430	270
10	2,700	270

the mill receives an additional $270 each time it sells another unit, total revenue rises by an additional $270 with each unit sold, and marginal revenue remains constant at that amount.

If each additional unit produced and sold adds $270 to the firm's revenue, how many units should the firm produce? That depends on marginal cost. Remember the decision-making rule: Engage in an activity as long as the marginal benefit (marginal revenue) exceeds the marginal cost.

COMPUTING MARGINAL COST

Marginal cost is the cost of producing an additional unit of output; so it is the change in total cost from one unit of output to another. Consider, for example, the marginal cost of the first unit of output in Exh. 5.2. If it costs the firm $180 to produce zero output (remember fixed costs) and $445 to produce one unit of output, the marginal cost of the first unit of lumber is $265. The marginal cost of the second thousand feet of lumber is $240, the difference between the total cost of $445 and the total cost of $685. Take a few moments to compute the marginal costs for the remaining units of output, using the total cost column in Exh. 5.2. Then, check your answers against the marginal cost column in that exhibit.

EXHIBIT 5.2

The Marginal Cost of Manufacturing Pine Lumber

OUTPUT PER DAY	TOTAL COST	MARGINAL COST
0	$ 180	—
1	445	$265
2	685	240
3	895	210
4	1,075	180
5	1,285	210
6	1,525	240
7	1,795	270
8	2,125	330
9	2,515	390
10	2,965	450

If you examine the marginal cost column closely, you will notice that marginal cost declines initially and then increases as output expands further. Why does it behave this way? The behavior of marginal cost is related to the productivity of the factors of production (or economic resources) used in producing the product.

When inputs are more productive, they produce more—they add more to the firm's output. This, in turn, means lower costs for the business. In small sawmills, for example, labor costs can be a major cost of doing business. The labor cost of producing an additional unit of output depends on the amount of labor time it takes to produce that unit. If our mill is paying its workers $10 an hour and it takes eight hours to produce the additional unit, the labor cost of that unit is $80. If the additional unit could be produced in only six hours, the labor cost of that unit could be reduced to $60.

The amount of labor time it takes to produce each additional unit of output is not constant. It depends on the degree of *specialization* of labor: the extent to which workers perform a single task rather than several. Workers who specialize tend to do their jobs better and more quickly, which means lower marginal cost.

When a firm is producing relatively little output, the labor cost of producing an additional unit tends to be high because the low volume permits little specialization. To illustrate, think about the variety of tasks you would need to perform if you wanted to run our hypothetical sawmill alone. You would be required to roll the logs onto the saws and cut them into lumber. Then, to smooth the rough surfaces of the boards, you would have to set up and operate the planer. Next, you would need to stack the lumber for drying. And, of course, you'd be the one who cleaned and serviced the equipment so that it continued to operate properly.

Many additional tasks would be required, but by now you probably get the point. If you were trying to run the mill by yourself, you would spend a great deal of time moving from one task to the next, and it's likely that you wouldn't become very proficient at any of them. As a consequence, more hours would be required to accomplish each task than would be needed if you were allowed to specialize in one job (or a few jobs) and become more skilled. This is why the marginal cost of producing the first unit of lumber is relatively high ($265.)

As output expands, opportunities for specialization increase. For example, if the lumber mill needs to hire two workers to keep up with demand, one of them might do all the sawing while the other planes the boards and stacks them for drying. This greater specialization permits workers to become better at their jobs and reduces the time wasted in moving from one task to another. The result is a lower marginal cost for the second unit of output ($240) and an even lower cost for the third ($210) and fourth ($180) because the amount of labor time required to produce these additional units of output is reduced. Remember, this is a hypothetical example; the numbers are not precise but are meant only to illustrate a principle. In some businesses, specialization can result in significant reductions in marginal cost; in others, the savings may be minimal.

Marginal cost will not decline indefinitely. If the firm continues to expand output, it will eventually start to overutilize its plant and equipment, causing marginal cost to rise. In the short run, each business firm must operate with a fixed amount of plant and equipment. If the firm continues to hire additional workers in order to increase output, at some point it will experience congestion and workers waiting to use equipment. Of course, if workers are standing idle, they are not producing output but they are being paid. This causes the marginal cost of producing an additional unit of output to rise, as it does in our example when the output is expanded from four to five units of lumber.

In summary, if a firm continues to expand output in the short run, it will eventually overutilize its fixed plant and equipment, causing marginal cost to rise. This principle is simply an extension of the law of increasing costs introduced in Chapter 1.

USING THE DECISION RULE

Once we've computed marginal revenue (*MR*) and marginal cost (*MC*) at each level of output, selecting the optimal level of output is a relatively simple matter. We just apply the decision rule we've been using throughout the chapter: *Continue to produce as long as the marginal benefit exceeds the marginal cost.*

A note of caution before we proceed. Even if businesses consistently apply the decision rule, they are not assured of profits. Sometimes weak demand or high costs make it impossible for them to earn a profit. But even under these conditions, marginal reasoning is important. By comparing marginal costs and marginal benefits, the firm can minimize its loss and perhaps survive until business conditions improve. In short, while marginal reasoning doesn't ensure profits, it does ensure that you will do as well as possible under the existing circumstances.

Having noted that point of clarification, let's return to the hypothetical sawmill. The first three columns of Exh. 5.3 summarize the relationship between output, marginal revenue, and marginal cost that we discovered earlier. The fourth column adds another interesting bit of information, the mill's profit (or loss) at each level of output. As we've already discovered, profit is the difference between total revenue and total cost; this column

---

EXHIBIT 5.3

Selecting the Profit-Maximizing Level of Output

OUTPUT PER DAY	MARGINAL REVENUE	MARGINAL COST	PROFIT
0	—	—	−180
1	$270	$265	−175
2	270	240	−145
3	270	210	− 85
4	270	180	+ 5
5	270	210	+ 65
6	270	240	+ 95
7	270	270	+ 95
8	270	330	+ 35
9	270	390	− 85
10	270	450	−265

simply performs that comparison for each level of output. If the $180 loss at zero output mystifies you, remember fixed costs. Even if production ceases and revenue drops to zero, some costs will remain to be paid.

Even without column 4, the information contained in Exh. 5.3 can be used to determine the optimal (profit-maximizing/loss-minimizing) level of output. As we noted earlier, production managers attempt to locate the optimal output by repeatedly asking themselves the same question: "Will the marginal revenue from producing this additional unit of output exceed the marginal cost?" As long as the answer is yes, they continue to expand production.

Let's start with the first unit of output and ask that question. As you can see from the exhibit, the marginal revenue from the sale of the first unit of output ($270) exceeds the marginal cost of producing that unit ($265). The first unit of output should be produced because it makes the mill $5 better off than it would be if it produced nothing. (Note that the mill's loss drops from $180 to $175.) What about the second unit of output; should it be produced? According to the exhibit, the answer is yes. That unit adds another $270 to the firm's revenue but only $240 to the mill's costs; it makes the business $30 better off (the mill's loss declines from $175 to $145).

How long should the mill continue expanding production? Marginal reasoning tells us to produce each unit for which *MR* exceeds *MC* but no units for which *MC* exceeds *MR*. If the mill's manager follows that logic, he or she will expand production right up to the point at which marginal revenue is equal to marginal cost, at seven units of output. Note that the mill's profit is maximized at that point. By employing marginal reasoning, we have located the profit-maximizing output.

You may have noted that the mill's profit is actually maximized at either six or seven units of output. To eliminate any ambiguity, we will assume that businesses go ahead and produce the unit where *MC* = *MR*. As we will see in a moment, that makes it a relatively easy matter to locate the profit-maximizing output graphically. In some situations, there will be no (nonfractional) level of output at which *MR* and *MC* are exactly equal. In such instances the firm should continue to produce each unit of output whose *MR* exceeds its *MC*. Our complete rule for profit maximization, then, is to expand production as long as marginal revenue is greater than or equal to marginal cost.

GRAPHING AND PROFIT MAXIMIZATION

Graphing the marginal revenue and marginal cost curves is an alternate method of determining the optimal level of output. This approach is represented in Exh. 5.4. Since the mill receives an additional $270 for each and every unit of lumber it sells, its marginal revenue curve is a horizontal

EXHIBIT 5.4

Finding the Profit-Maximizing Output Graphically

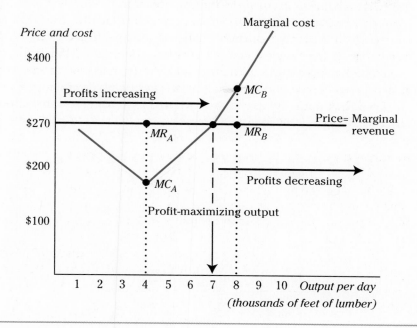

straight line at a height of $270. On the other hand, the mill's marginal cost curve is U-shaped; it dips and then rises. As noted earlier, this shape stems from the changing productivity of the mill's inputs. At low output levels, few opportunities for specialization lead to high marginal costs. As output expands, increased opportunities for specialization bring lower marginal costs. Ultimately, the overutilization of the mill forces workers to wait to use the equipment, driving marginal cost back up and explaining the U-shaped marginal cost curve in the exhibit.

As long as the marginal revenue curve is above the marginal cost curve, MR exceeds MC, and it makes sense for the firm to expand output. For example, the marginal revenue from the sale of the fourth unit of output (represented by the point labeled MR_A on the marginal revenue curve) exceeds the marginal cost of producing it (represented by point MC_A on the marginal cost curve); so the mill will be better off producing that unit. The same is true of all additional units up to the seventh. At that point the marginal revenue curve intersects the marginal curve, so that $MR = MC$; the additional cost of producing the unit is exactly equal to the additional revenue derived from its sale. If the mill produced more than seven units of output, the marginal cost of producing those units would exceed the marginal revenue, making the firm worse off. For example, the marginal cost of producing the eighth unit of output (represented by MC_B on the marginal cost curve) is $330, well in excess of the $270 marginal revenue derived from that unit (point MR_B on the marginal revenue curve). It stands to reason, then, that output should be expanded right up to the point at which marginal revenue equals marginal cost but not beyond. That gives us a simple way of isolating the profit-maximizing rate of output graphically: Produce at the output for which the marginal cost curve intersects the marginal revenue curve (where $MR = MC$).

WISE DECISIONS DON'T ALWAYS LEAD TO PROFITS

As we noted earlier, the best decision making in the world can't guarantee profits. Sometimes market conditions are depressed, and the very best a firm can do is to minimize its loss. Consider, for example, a situation in which the demand for pine lumber has declined, reducing its market price from $270 to only $250. What should the mill do under these circumstances? It should use marginal reasoning, just as before. Look at Exh. 5.5 and see if you can find the loss-minimizing output without using column 4. (For simplicity, the table has been slightly abbreviated.)

Note that in this instance there is no output for which marginal revenue is exactly equal to marginal cost. Therefore, the mill should expand production, as long as $MR > MC$, to six units per day. Column 4 confirms that six units is indeed the loss-minimizing output; once again, marginal reasoning has served us well.

There are rare but realistic circumstances in which the business will not find it desirable to expand production up to the output at which $MR = MC$. Suppose, for example, that the price of lumber became really depressed and the mill could predict that, at the output at which $MR = MC$, it would incur a loss of, say, $225. What would it do? Under these circumstances the mill would minimize its loss by shutting down or ceasing operations until market conditions improve and it can get a better price for its product. If a mill shuts down, the loss it incurs is equal to its fixed costs—the costs that continue even at zero production. Recall that in our example the mill's fixed costs total $180 a day, substantially less than the $225 a day the business would lose by continuing to operate. The next chapter will discuss in greater detail the possibility of shutting down. For now, focus your attention on the profit-maximization rule (expand production up to the point at which $MR = MC$); it's the rule that guides business decision making in the vast majority of cases.

Review this exhibit

EXHIBIT 5.5

Selecting the Loss-Minimizing Level

OUTPUT PER DAY	MARGINAL REVENUE	MARGINAL COST	PROFIT
:	:	:	:
2	250	240	−190
3	250	210	−150
4	250	180	− 80
5	250	210	− 40
6	250	240	− 30
7	250	270	− 50
8	250	330	−130

Gas Stations, Fast Food, and the All-Night Grocery Store

Thus far we've concentrated on the role of marginal reasoning in helping businesses select the optimal level of output. But the role of marginal reasoning is much broader than that. It permeates every aspect of business. And knowing what it means to "think marginally" can help you understand business decisions that baffle others.

WHATEVER HAPPENED TO GAS STATIONS?

There are plenty of mysteries in life, and economics won't help you to unravel all of them. But it can help to clarify one that may bug your parents: Whatever happened to gas stations? At one time there were thousands of genuine gas stations in the United States, stations that sold almost nothing but gas. And convenience stores sold quick groceries but not gas. Now, in many areas, gasoline stations are rarities, and every convenience store has gas pumps. What happened? Part of the story is the introduction of self-service gasoline; that made it possible for convenience stores to sell gas. And the increase in the number of working mothers made a difference, too; that change put greater emphasis on convenience—the ability to buy a carton of milk without trudging to the grocery store. But much of the answer lies in the marginal principle, and that's what we want to discuss here.

Imagine yourself as the owner of one of the few remaining genuine, honest-to-goodness gas stations in the United States. On the way home from work, you need a carton of milk and a few other groceries, and so you run into a convenience store and pick them up. You notice that the price you pay is somewhat higher than what you'd pay in a grocery store, but you don't complain; the convenience is worth it. But that starts you thinking. Why can't you sell those items and make that money? (Notice competition rearing its head; more about that in the next chapter.) So you sit down with a pad of paper and a calculator and do some figuring. How much would it cost to rent a cooler for milk and soda pop, and a display rack for bread and snack items? Not much. What about the extra electrical cost of running the cooler? Not much. And how many extra people would you have to hire to collect money from customers buying groceries? None. Pretty soon you've cleared the junk out of your gas station, installed the cooler and display racks, and another gas station has given way to a mini convenience store; the marginal principle rides again.

Owners of early convenience stores also understood marginal reasoning, and they tended to view gasoline as a marginal item. But adding gas pumps to a convenience store probably required more thought than adding coolers to gas stations. Although the additional cost of pumping gas is minimal once the pumps are in place (and that cost is fixed, or "sunk"), the cost of adding the pumps is not trivial. So, before that decision was made, the convenience store owners needed to determine whether the additional revenue that the pumps would generate would pay for the cost of the pumps, the additional electricity to run them, and the wholesale cost of the gasoline.

The answer must generally be yes because gas pumps are everywhere. The difference between gas stations and convenience stores has largely disappeared. (Note that once some convenience stores begin adding gas pumps, it puts pressure on other convenience stores in the area to do the same. If you can buy gas *and* groceries at Bob's Quick Mart, you won't stop at Joan's Fast Stop if it sells only groceries. So the option of not selling gasoline has now been largely eliminated for convenience store owners.)

WHY IS BREAKFAST EVERYWHERE?

If you want more evidence that businesses understand marginal reasoning, consider the ease with which you can find a cheap, quick breakfast. Even though lunch is clearly the main meal at McDonald's and Burger King, managers at these franchises understand that they can enlarge their profits by serving breakfast. That's because once the restaurant is in place, there is little added cost to serving the morning meal. The big expense items, rent and the cost of the franchise, are fixed costs; they have to be paid whether or not breakfast is served. So the restaurants do a quick cost-benefit analysis and compare the additional revenue they can generate by offering breakfast to the additional cost of serving breakfast (the cost of the food items, the additional labor time, the higher electric bill, etc.). On that basis, it appears that the breakfast meal must generally pay for itself. That's why there are so many places where you can grab a quick breakfast as you dash to class or to work.

SALE! BUY BELOW COST!

Marginal reasoning even helps to explain those end-of-season sales. If you've ever found yourself looking through the sale merchandise, you've probably noticed that you can save quite a bit on the normal retail price. In fact, if you're patient and wait for the final reductions, those prices can be below even the wholesale prices paid by the stores. Does that make sense? Does it make sense to sell a designer sweater for $25 if it cost the store $50? Sure it does! Remember the rules: Sunk costs are sunk; compare marginal costs and marginal benefits.

The amount the store paid for the sweater is irrelevant in the decision about how much to sell it for. The question is: Does the marginal benefit of selling it to you for $25 exceed the marginal cost? But what's the marginal cost of selling it to you? If the sweater hasn't sold all season, the store's next course of action will be selling it to one of those chains that sell close-out merchandise. That may net the store only $5 or $10. If that's the case, the marginal revenue from selling that sweater to you ($25) exceeds the marginal cost (the $5–$10 it could get elsewhere). The store's not being silly; it's using marginal reasoning.

LATE-NIGHT MOVIES AND EMPTY AIRPLANES

Before we close our discussion of marginal reasoning, consider the following examples for just a moment. Have you ever attended one of those late-night movies or flown home on a nearly empty airplane or visited an all-night grocery store at 2 a.m.? If you have, the limited number of customers may have had you wondering, "How can they afford to do this?" Before you feel too much sympathy for the businesses involved, remember the marginal principle; it provides the answer.

What a store paid for an item is irrelevant when it comes to determining closeout prices.

Let's take a closer look at the example of the movie theater. Once the rent on the building and the movie has been paid (both fixed costs), the marginal cost of showing the film one more time can be very low, the wages of a ticket taker and someone to run the concession stand (sometimes the same person), and a little more for utilities. So the movie theater doesn't have to attract many customers to its late-night showing to make it profitable. That's why you may find yourself attending a showing with only a dozen other people. The same thing is true of the late-night grocery store, perhaps to an even greater extent. Grocery stores tend to restock their shelves in the evening, so that the lights are still on and there are still personnel in the stores. If those employees can take a moment to check out customers, the marginal cost of serving those customers is very low. So the stores can advertise 24-hour service at very little added cost.

Even airlines find themselves in this situation, though not to the same extent. A major cost of running an airline is renting or buying the airplane. Once that expense is paid, the marginal cost of additional flights can be low enough to justify flying planes that are less than one-third full.

Of course, there are factors that can complicate marginal decision making. For instance, the movie theaters are not always able to rent films for a fixed fee; sometimes they are required to pay the film company a certain percentage

of the ticket price. That would increase the theater's marginal cost and make it more difficult to justify late-night movies that might be sparsely attended. Another factor is the possibility of the theater's stealing its own customers. If the theater customers who decide to attend the midnight movie would have attended an earlier show (if the midnight show were not available), all the theater has done by offering the additional showing is to increase its costs and reduce its profits. The same is true of the airline. There is no point in offering additional flights if there is space on the earlier flights and the airline is convinced that the customers will have to fly with it anyway.

One more thought before closing this chapter. Although marginal costs (and revenues) are the key to good decision making in the preceding examples, firms must *ultimately* cover all their costs—including fixed costs—to remain in business. Consider the movie theater example once again. As we've seen, the theater owner should ignore fixed costs such as rent and insurance in deciding whether to remain open for an additional late-night showing. Those costs already exist, once the decision had been made to open a movie theater. But if the theater's total operations (afternoon, evening, and late-night showings) are unable to generate enough revenue to cover all costs, including those fixed costs, it will eventually be forced to close its doors. After all, landlords and insurance companies expect to be paid. If they aren't, they will stop providing their services, and the theater will be history. We'll have much more to say about this in the next chapter. But as you can see, there is more to running a business than understanding marginal reasoning. And there's more to economics as well. In the next chapter we will take a closer look at the behavior of business firms and explore the meaning of competitive markets.

Summary

Economic models assume that men and women are motivated by self-interest and that they pursue self-interest through a rational comparison of costs and benefits. The relevant costs and benefits for comparison are marginal costs and benefits. The *marginal* costs and benefits are the extra or additional costs and benefits resulting from a decision. A decision will improve one's well-being only if the marginal benefits from that decision exceed the marginal costs.

Even rational people sometimes make bad decisions. Poor decisions stem from mistaking marginal and total values and from improperly estimating the costs of a decision. It is important to remember that all decisions have opportunity costs. In some instances these opportunity costs can easily be stated in monetary terms; in other instances they cannot. In either case failure to consider all opportunity costs can lead to poor decisions. Poor decisions can also result from mistaking relevant and irrelevant costs. The only costs that are relevant for decision making are *marginal costs*, the additional costs that result from making a decision. Costs are irrelevant if they are unaffected by a decision. Irrelevant costs include fixed, or "sunk," costs. *Fixed costs* are costs that do not vary with the level of activity engaged in and that cannot be avoided.

Business decision making also involves a comparison of costs and benefits. The only major difference between business decision making and personal decision making is the goals involved. According to economic theory, individuals attempt to maximize personal satisfaction or *utility*, while businesses attempt to maximize profits.

Profit is the excess of a business's total revenue over its total costs. Total revenue represents the total receipts of a business and can be calculated by multiplying the selling price of the product times the number of units sold. *Total cost* represents the sum of all the business's fixed costs (those costs that do not vary with the level of output) and *variable costs* (those costs that do vary with the level of output). As long as a business's total revenue exceeds its total costs, it will earn a profit. When total costs exceed total revenue, the business will incur a *loss*.

The fundamental decision that a business makes is selecting the level of output that maximizes its profits or minimizes its loss. In order to select this output, businesses compare marginal revenue and marginal cost. Output should be expanded up to the point at which marginal revenue is equal to marginal cost ($MR=MC$) but not beyond. Graphically, the profit-maximizing output can be determined by locating the output at which the marginal revenue curve intersects the marginal cost curve. Although producing where $MR = MC$ does not ensure a profit, it generally allows the firm to do as well as possible under existing market conditions. In other words, producing at the output where $MR = MC$ will generally allow the firm either to maximize its profit or to minimize its loss.

In addition to using marginal reasoning to select the profit-maximizing/loss-minimizing level of output, firms use marginal reasoning in making other business decisions. For instance, fast-food restaurants use marginal reasoning in deciding whether to serve breakfast, and airlines use marginal reasoning in deciding whether to run an additional flight between two cities. While fixed costs are irrelevant in such decisions, firms must ultimately generate enough revenue to cover all costs if they are to remain in business.

GLOSSARY

Fixed costs. Costs that do not vary with the level of the activity in which the individual or business is engaged and that cannot be avoided; for businesses, costs that do not change with the level of output.

Loss. The excess of total cost over total revenue.

Marginal. Additional or extra.

Profit. The excess of a business's total revenue over its total cost.

Profit maximizer. A business that attempts to earn as much profit as possible.

Sunk cost. Costs that cannot be avoided. See *Fixed costs.*

Total cost. Total fixed cost plus total variable cost.

Total revenue. The total receipts of a business from the sale of its product. Total revenue is calculated by multiplying the selling price of the product times the number of units sold.

Utility. Personal satisfaction.

Variable costs. Costs that vary with the level of activity in which the individual or business is engaged; for businesses, costs that change with the level of output.

STUDY QUESTIONS

Fill in the Blanks

1. Economists argue that individuals are motivated primarily by the pursuit of _Self-interest_.

2. Rational people make decisions by comparing _marginal costs_ and _marginal benefits_.

3. _Fixed_ costs are costs that do not vary with output and cannot be avoided.

4. Total cost is the sum of _total fixed_ cost and _total variable_ cost.

5. _Marginal_ means extra or additional.

6. Economists generally assume that individuals seek to maximize _utility_ and that businesses seek to maximize _profit_.

7. Economists argue that profits are generally maximized (or losses minimized) at the output for which _MR_ is equal to _MR, MC_.

8. A business would be better off shutting down (producing no output) than producing, if the loss it would incur by operating would be greater than its _fixed_ costs.

9. Marginal costs may initially decline as output is expanded and more workers are hired because higher levels of production permit greater _specialization_.

10. The statement "There's no such thing as a free lunch" means that every decision has an _opportunity cost_.

Multiple Choice

1. Economists assume that individuals
   a) are motivated primarily by concern for others.
   b) act impulsively.
   c) pursue their own self-interest.
   d) use their intuition to make wise decisions.

2. According to economists, when people make decisions, they
   a) are primarily concerned about the costs and benefits that their decisions impose on others.
   b) base their decisions on expected costs and benefits rather than true costs and benefits.
   c) must consciously weigh costs and marginal benefits in order to make wise decisions.
   d) must carefully compare sunk costs and marginal benefits in order to make wise choices.

3. Economic models may not accurately predict the behavior of individuals if those individuals
   a) fail to consider the interests of others.
   b) act selfishly.
   c) behave in an impulsive manner.
   d) always consider the opportunity costs of their decisions.

4. Bob walked into the clothing store and, without a moment's hesitation, bought the first shirt he saw that was his size. His behavior
   a) is clearly consistent with the assumption of rationality.
   b) might be rational if he has very little time to shop.
   c) is clearly impulsive and is therefore inconsistent with the assumption of rationality.
   d) might be impulsive if he had previously considered the alternative shirts in the store and their prices.

5. Which of the following behaviors is inconsistent with the way economists assume individuals will act?
   a) Susie selected her car by reading reports, test-driving several models, and comparing their features and prices.
   b) Alex wanted to go to the concert but considered the likely impact on his calculus grade and decided to study instead.
   c) Fran really wanted the red dress but thought it was too expensive; so she bought the green one instead.
   d) The salesman offered to let John use the store phone, but because John didn't want to interfere with business calls, he used the pay phone.

6. If we use the cost-benefit model, which of the following high school students is most likely to attend college?
   a) A student with an aptitude for auto mechanics
   b) A student with a decent job and opportunities for advancement
   c) A student who values present income much more highly than future income
   d) A student who qualifies for several scholarships

7. Suppose that a rational person decides to spend an evening watching TV instead of studying. That person must
   a) be a poor student.
   b) have ignored the opportunity cost of studying.
   c) value TV more highly than studying.
   d) value a marginal evening of TV more highly than an marginal evening of studying.

8. Julie is 25 years old and living in an apartment. She is thinking about quitting her job and returning to college. Which of the following is least likely to be relevant to that decision?
   a) The salary she is currently earning
   b) Tuition at the college she is considering
   c) The cost of meals while she attends college
   d) The cost of books and supplies

9. Profits are maximized (or losses minimized) at the output level where
   a) marginal revenue exceeds marginal cost by the largest amount.
   b) fixed costs are minimized.
   c) marginal revenue is equal to marginal cost.
   d) marginal cost is at a minimum.

10. If the marginal cost of producing an additional unit of output is $50 and the marginal revenue from selling that unit is $60,

    a) the unit should not be produced since it will make the business worse off.
    b) the unit should be produced since it will make the business $60 better off.
    c) the unit should not be produced since the business is already maximizing its profit.
    d) the unit should be produced since it will make the business $10 better off.

    Use the following information in answering questions 11–13.

    Data for John's Cabinet Company

OUTPUT PER WEEK	MARGINAL REVENUE	MARGINAL COST
0	—	—
1	$440	$350
2	440	325
3	440	350
4	440	375
5	440	400
6	440	450
7	440	525
8	440	625
9	440	750
10	440	900

11. John's Cabinet Company will maximize its profit (or minimize its loss) by producing
    a) 2 cabinets a week.
    b) 5 cabinets a week.
    c) 7 cabinets a week.
    d) 10 cabinets a week.

12. If John's Cabinet Company could sell each cabinet for $525 instead of $440, the profit-maximizing level of output would be
    a) 2 cabinets a week.
    b) 5 cabinets a week.
    c) 7 cabinets a week.
    d) 10 cabinets a week.

13. John's Cabinet Company is
    a) earning a profit.
    b) incurring a loss.
    c) cannot determine profit or loss from the information given.

    Use the following information in answering questions 14–18.

    Data for Apex Golf Cart Company

OUTPUT PER DAY	TOTAL COST
0	$ 200
1	500
2	700
3	1,000
4	1,400
5	1,900
6	2,500
7	3,300
8	4,300
9	5,500
10	7,000

14. The Apex Golf Cart Company faces fixed costs
    a) of $200 per day.
    b) of $300 per day.
    c) of $7,000 per day.
    d) that cannot be determined from the information given.

15. The marginal cost of producing the fourth golf cart each day is
    a) $1,400.
    b) $300.
    c) $400.
    d) $350.

16. If Apex can sell additional golf carts for $800 each, the profit-maximizing (loss-minimizing) level of output is
a) 2 carts per day.
b) 5 carts per day.
c) 7 carts per day.
d) 8 carts per day

17. If the price Apex can get for its carts increases to $950, the profit-maximizing (loss-minimizing) output will be
a) 2 carts per day.
b) 5 carts per day.

c) 7 carts per day.
d) 8 carts per day

18. Assume that the price Apex can get for its carts remains at $950 but that the company's fixed costs increase to $500 a day. Under those conditions, the profit-maximizing (loss-minimizing) output will be
a) 2 carts per day.
b) 5 carts per day.
c) 7 carts per day.
d) 8 carts per day.

Problems and Questions for Discussion

1. Bobby Goodguy volunteers for several local charities and is a member of several service organizations. Is it possible that such behavior is in his (financial) self-interest?

2. Why do individuals base their decisions on expected costs and benefits rather than true costs and benefits?

3. Studies tell us that students who have a difficult time in high school are less likely to attend college than students who find high school easy. Use the cost-benefit model to explain this finding.

4. Edith decided that her $100,000 a year job at Gord Motors wasn't fulfilling. So she invested savings of $20,000 (which had been earning 10% a year) in starting her own travel agency. At the end of the year, the accountants gave her the following report. After examining the report, explain why economists might criticize it and how they would be likely to amend it.

Total Revenue
From Customers $225,000
Salaries of John, Joan, and Bob.............$ 75,000
Salary of Edith. 35,000
Rent...60,000
Office supplies..10,000
Phone and utilities 15,000
Total costs...$195,000
Profit...$ 35,000

5. Susie absolutely must drive home for Christmas. She would like a rider to share the cost of the two-day trip. Her monthly car payment is $210, and car insurance costs her another $30 monthly. In addition, she estimates that gas will cost her $100. The only student who has responded to her advertisement for a rider is willing to pay $40. Should she take the rider? Defend your answer.

6. Consider your answer to question 5. Suppose that Susie could take the bus home at a cost of $120. Should she take the bus or drive? Defend your answer.

7. *(Warning: Extra tough question; uses ideas not fully discussed in the chapter. Try it only if you like a challenge.)* Highflyer Corporation manufactures kites, which are being sold throughout the United States. It is currently producing 100,000 kites a year and operating its factory at 70 percent of capacity. At that output the average cost of manufacturing a kite is about $2 (average cost is computed by dividing total cost by the number of units sold). Experience has shown that average cost drops somewhat as output is expanded beyond 100,000 units but rises again if output is increased above 125,000 units.

The Highflyer Corporation normally sells its kites for $2.50 each. It recently received an order for an additional 10,000 kites from a foreign buyer, but the buyer specified that it would pay no more then $1.50 a kite. Highflyer executives want to accept the order, but the firm's accountants estimate that at 110,000 units a year, the average cost of producing a kite would be $1.90, more than the $1.50 price being offered. Should Highflyer accept the offer?

8. Bill paid $50 for an old record album at an estate sale because he thought it was a rare Elvis recording. He was wrong; the album is worth only about $10. Bill won't sell at that price because he can't stand the thought of losing $40. What's wrong with his reasoning?

9. *(Another toughie; Proceed at your own risk.)* Bonnie believes that it is possible to calculate the total cost of producing x units of output by summing (adding up) the marginal cost of producing all units of output from 1 through x. Is she correct? Why or why not?

10. The amount of money that a firm loses by shutting down and producing no output is its fixed costs. Why? Under what circumstances would it make more sense to shut down than to produce at the output at which $MR = MC$?

ANSWER KEY

Fill in the Blanks

1. self-interest
2. marginal costs and marginal benefits
3. fixed
4. total fixed, total variable
5. Marginal
6. utility, profit
7. *MR, MC*
8. fixed
9. specialization
10. opportunity cost

Multiple Choice

1. c
2. b
3. c
4. b
5. d
6. d
7. d
8. c
9. c
10. d
11. b
12. c
13. c
14. a
15. c
16. c
17. c
18. c

Price Taking: The Purely Competitive Firm

1. Identify the characteristics of a purely competitive industry.
2. Explain why a purely competitive firm is described as a "price taker."
3. Describe the demand and marginal revenue curves of the price taker.
4. Describe how a price taker determines the profit-maximizing level of output.
5. Distinguish between the long run and the short run.
6. Identify the different types of production costs: fixed, variable, total, average, and marginal.
7. Describe how each type of production cost is related to changes in the level of output.
8. Distinguish between an economic profit and a normal profit.
9. Evaluate graphically the extent of a price taker's profit or loss.
10. Discuss the distinction between production efficiency and allocative efficiency.
11. Explain how long-run price, profitability, and efficiency are related to the absence of barriers to entry.

In Chapter 3 we discussed how demand and supply interact to determine prices in competitive markets. To fully understand the operation of competitive markets, we need to step behind the scenes and examine the decision-making processes of the individual supplier, commonly known as the *firm.*

The **firm** is the basic producing unit in a market economy. It buys economic resources—land, labor, capital, and entrepreneurship—and combines them to produce goods and services. A group of firms that produce identical or similar products is called an **industry.** Exxon, Phillips Petroleum, and Texaco are firms in the petroleum industry; McDonald's, KFC (Kentucky Fried Chicken), and your local pizzeria are firms in the fast-food industry.

Economists argue that the performance of firms—how effectively they serve consumers—depends on the degree of competition within the industry;

the greater the competition, the better the performance. As we have seen in earlier chapters, performing well in a market economy means producing the goods and services that consumers desire most and selling those goods and services at the lowest possible prices. We begin this chapter by examining the assumptions that underlie the model of pure competition. Then we investigate the types of production costs the firm incurs and discover how it decides on the level of output that will maximize its profits. Finally, we examine the factors that cause firms to enter or leave an industry, explaining why this behavior is thought to be in the best interest of consumers.

The Nature of Pure Competition

Since the time of Adam Smith, economists have recognized that a market economy will serve consumers well only if competition exists to protect their interests. The competition economists have in mind, however, is more than mere rivalry among a few sellers. By definition, pure competition must satisfy three basic assumptions:

1. *There must be a large number of sellers, each producing a relatively small fraction of the total industry supply.* This rules out the possibility that a single firm could affect price by altering its level of output.
2. *The firms in the industry must sell identical products.* This condition excludes the possibility of any product differences, including those created through advertising, and ensures that consumers will view the products of different firms as perfect substitutes.
3. *There can be no substantial barriers (obstacles) to entering or leaving the industry.* Examples of barriers to entry include patent restrictions, large investment requirements, and restrictive licensing regulations.

If you find these conditions somewhat unrealistic, don't be alarmed. No industries in the United States or any other economy meet all those conditions perfectly. Pure competition is not an attempt to describe any existing industry; rather, it is an economic *model* that will allow us to see how an industry would function if it conformed to certain assumptions. In later chapters we will relax these assumptions and see how the performance of industries will change when these conditions are no longer satisfied.

By using the benefits of pure competition as our standard, or yardstick, we can better understand the problems that may emerge when industries are less competitive. The competitive model also will offer insights into the behavior of industries that come reasonably close to meeting the assumptions of pure competition. These highly competitive industries include building construction, lumber manufacturing, limestone and gravel mining, and the agricultural industries, such as hog and dairy-product production.[1]

The Firm under Pure Competition

In a purely competitive industry the individual firm is best described as a **price taker;** it must accept price as a given that is beyond its control. This description follows from two of the basic assumptions of our model. First, because each firm produces such a small fraction of the total industry's supply, no single firm can influence the market price by altering its level of production. Even if a firm withheld its entire output from the market, the industry supply curve would not shift significantly to the left, and the equilibrium price would be essentially unchanged. Second, because all firms sell identical products, no one firm can charge a higher price for its product without losing all its customers; consumers would simply buy cheaper identical products from other firms. As a consequence of both these conditions, the firm must accept, or *take*, the price that is determined by the impersonal forces of supply and demand.

To illustrate how a firm operates under pure competition, we'll return to an example introduced in Chapter 5, a hypothetical producer of pine lumber. (Readers who skipped the preceding chapter need not be concerned. This chapter complements Chapter 5 but is not dependent on it.) Pine lumber is an important component in the construction of new homes. It is produced by several thousand sawmills in the United States, and the lumber produced by one mill is virtually identical to the lumber produced by another. We will assume that the individual lumber producer is such a small part of the total industry that it cannot influence the market price. Whether that price means a profit or a loss, the firm can do nothing to alter it. The firm can't charge more than the prevailing price because its product is identical to that of all other producers. Withholding the firm's output from the market in an attempt to drive up prices would be fruitless because its output is just a drop in the bucket and would never be missed.

The price the firm receives for its product can change, of course, but price changes under pure competition are due to changes in *industry* demand and supply conditions, not to any actions the firm may take. Price is a

---

[1] Although most agricultural industries conform reasonably well to the competitive model, price supports and other forms of government intervention in agriculture limit the usefulness of the model in describing the performance of agricultural producers. To the extent that the Federal Agricultural Improvement and Reform Act (1996) reduces that intervention, the model's usefulness is enhanced.

EXHIBIT 6.1

The Firm as a Price Taker

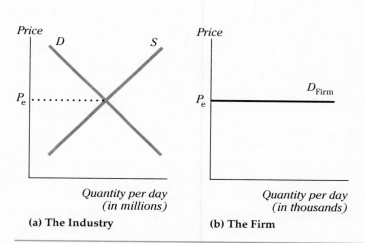

In a purely competitive industry, market forces determine the equilibrium price, and the individual firm is unable to influence that price. The demand curve facing the firm is a horizontal line at the height of the market price because the firm can sell as much output as it desires at the prevailing price but nothing at a higher price. Note that the industry's quantity is measured in millions, whereas the firm's is measured in thousands.

(a) The Industry

(b) The Firm

given, and the demand curve facing the individual firm is therefore a horizontal line at the equilibrium price. A horizontal demand curve in Exh. 6.1 indicates that the firm can sell as much output as it wishes at the market price but no output at a higher price. Under conditions of pure competition, a firm's demand curve is perfectly, or infinitely, elastic. Recall from Chapter 4 that a high degree of elasticity means that a small change in price will lead to a large change in the quantity demanded. Here a very small change in price leads to an infinitely large change in the quantity demanded because our lumber mill would lose *all* its customers if it raised its price even slightly.

Profit Maximization and Price Takers

The model of pure competition assumes that firms are *profit maximizers;* that is, they are always attempting to earn the most profit possible. *Profit* is the excess of a firm's total revenue over its total costs. When a firm's total costs exceed its total revenue, the firm is incurring a *loss.* (Profit and loss are simple accounting terms; the next section explains why economists need special terms for different kinds of profits.)

A firm's ***total revenue (TR)*** is the amount of money it takes in from the sale of its product; *TR* is calculated by multiplying the selling price of the product by the number of units sold. ***Total cost (TC)*** refers to the sum of all the costs incurred by a business in producing its product and making it available for sale. The behavior of total cost—how rapidly it increases when output is expanded—helps to determine which level of output will maximize a firm's profit. If producing an additional unit of output adds more to a firm's revenue than it adds to cost, the additional unit should be produced. If the unit adds more to cost than it adds to revenue, it should not be produced. In other words, if an extra unit of output is profitable, it should be produced. We'll explore this profit-maximizing rule in greater detail after we discuss the types of costs a firm incurs and how they vary with output.

Short-Run Costs of Production

All firms must incur costs in order to produce the goods or services that they offer in the marketplace. Although this chapter concentrates on the purely competitive firm, the discussion of production costs that is presented here applies to all firms, regardless of the competitive setting in which they operate.

Our discussion of production costs will focus on the short run. The short run, as you learned in Chapter 4, is a time period during which at least one of a business's inputs (usually its plant and equipment) is incapable of being changed. In the short run a business must expand output by using its fixed production plant more intensively, since it does not have sufficient time to build a new plant or expand its existing facilities. In the long run, you will recall, all inputs can be varied, including plant and equipment. Firms have sufficient time to build new production facilities and to expand or contract existing ones. We'll have more to say about the firm's long-run adjustments later in the chapter.

TOTAL COSTS: FIXED AND VARIABLE

Short-run production costs can be classified as either fixed or variable. Total cost *(TC)* is simply the sum of the fixed and variable costs incurred by the firm.

Fixed Costs. Costs that do not vary with the level of output are called **fixed costs**. They neither increase when the firm produces more nor decrease when the firm produces less. Fixed costs are often referred to as *overhead* and include such expenditures as insurance payments, rent on the production plant, fees for business licenses, salaries of managers, and property taxes.

The salaries of security guards
are fixed costs because they must
be paid even if a firm decides
not to produce any output.

The distinguishing feature of fixed costs is that they have to be paid whether or not the firm is producing anything. If our hypothetical sawmill was forced to shut down because of a strike, the firm would still have to pay the salaries of its managers in order to avoid losing them to other companies. It would still have to make interest payments on loans it had taken to purchase the production plant and equipment. It would continue making payments for damage and accident insurance, and it would still require the services of security guards (an expense that might even increase).

Economists also include a normal profit as a fixed cost. **Normal profit** is the amount that the owners of a business could have earned if the money, time, and other resources they have invested in the business were invested elsewhere, in the next-best alternative. In other words, normal profit is the opportunity cost of owner-supplied resources. As an example, suppose that the owner of our sawmill had been earning $30,000 a year working for another lumber producer before he decided to buy his own mill. When he quit his job, he withdrew $20,000 from his savings account, which had been earning 10 percent interest per year, and used the money as a down payment to buy the sawmill. Since the earnings he gave up to launch this venture are his $30,000 supervisor's salary plus $2,000 interest (10 percent of $20,000) on his savings, he would have to make $32,000 in his business (after subtracting all other costs) in order to earn a normal profit.

A normal profit is a fixed cost of keeping a business going. In fact, a firm that is earning a normal profit is said to be *breaking even*. Although some individuals may be willing to work for less than normal profit—perhaps because of the sense of independence they gain by being their own bosses—most owners will keep their resources employed only where they can expect at least a normal return.

Any profit above a normal profit is called an **economic profit.** If, for example, our lumber mill has total revenues of $75,000 and total costs of $57,000 (including $32,000 normal profit), the remaining $18,000 is economic profit. Economic profit is not considered a cost because the owners would remain in the business even at zero economic profit, where the firm would be breaking even.

Variable Costs. Costs that change with the level of output are termed **variable costs**. They tend to increase when the level of output increases and to decline when output declines. Many of a business's costs are variable costs: payments for raw materials, such as timber, iron ore, and crude oil, and the manufactured inputs transformed from such materials (lumber, sheet steel, paint); wages and salaries of production workers; payments for electricity and water; and shipping expenses.

In many instances a specific element of cost may be partly a fixed cost and partly a variable cost. For example, although a firm's electricity bill increases as production expands, some fraction of that bill should be considered a fixed cost because it relates to security lights, running the air conditioners in administrative offices, and other functions that are independent of the rate of output.

Total Cost. Each firm's total cost *(TC)* of production is the sum of its total fixed cost *(TFC)* and its total variable cost *(TVC)*. The first four columns of Exh. 6.2 illustrate how these costs respond to changes in the level of output. The figures in column 2 show that the firm's total fixed cost (the sum of its expenditures for insurance payments, management salaries, and other fixed expenses) is constant, whereas column 3 shows the firm's total variable cost (total expenditures for gasoline, oil, labor, and other variable expenses) increasing as the level of output increases. Because total cost (column 4) includes this variable cost component, it also increases with the level of production.

AVERAGE COSTS: FIXED, VARIABLE, AND TOTAL

Producers are often more interested in the average cost of producing a unit of output than they are in any of the total cost concepts we've examined. By comparing average, or per unit, costs with those of other firms in the industry, a producer can judge how efficient (or inefficient) its own operation is.

Average cost functions are of three types: average fixed cost, average variable cost, and average total cost. **Average fixed cost *(AFC)*** is computed by dividing total fixed cost by the firm's output. For example, if the firm was

EXHIBIT 6.2

Daily Costs of Manufacturing Pine Lumber

OUTPUT (thousands of feet of lumber)*	TOTAL FIXED COST (TFC)	TOTAL VARIABLE COST (TVC)	TOTAL COST (TC)	AVERAGE FIXED COST (AFC)	AVERAGE VARIABLE COST (AVC)	AVERAGE TOTAL COST (ATC)
0	$180	$ 0	$ 180	—	—	—
1	180	270	450	$180.00	$270.00	$450.00
2	180	510	690	90.00	255.00	345.00
3	180	720	900	60.00	240.00	300.00
4	180	900	1080	45.00	225.00	270.00
5	180	1110	1290	36.00	222.00	258.00
6	180	1350	1530	30.00	225.00	255.00
7	180	1620	1800	25.71	231.43	257.14
8	180	1950	2130	22.50	243.75	266.25
9	180	2340	2520	20.00	260.00	280.00
10	180	2790	2970	18.00	279.00	297.00

*Large quantities of lumber are generally sold in increments of 1000 *board feet*; a board foot measures 12 × 12 × 1 inches.

producing seven units of output, the *AFC* would be $180/7 = $25.71. As you can see in column 5 of Exh. 6.2, average fixed cost declines as output expands. This must be true because we are dividing a constant—total fixed cost—by larger and larger amounts of output. The decline in *AFC* is what a business means when it talks about "spreading its overhead" over more units of output.

The figures in column 6 describe the behavior of the firm's average variable cost. **Average variable cost (AVC)** is calculated by dividing the total variable cost at a given output level by the amount of output produced. For instance, if our lumber mill was producing six units of output (6,000 feet of lumber), its *AVC* would be $1,350/6 = $225. As you can see from the table, average variable cost declines initially and then rises as output continues to expand. The reason for this behavior will be provided a little later.

Average total cost (ATC) is always equal to average fixed cost plus average variable cost. For instance, the average total cost of producing four units of output is equal to the average fixed cost of $45 *plus* the average variable cost of $225; that means that *ATC* is equal to $270. Average total cost can also be computed by dividing the total cost at a particular level of output by the number of units of output. Using that technique, we find that the average total cost of producing four units of output is $1,080/4 = $270, the same answer as before. As you can see from column 7, average total cost declines initially and then rises.

MARGINAL COST

Average total cost is useful in gauging a firm's efficiency in production, but the concept of marginal cost plays the more important role in guiding production decisions. As we learned in Chapter 5, the term *marginal* means "extra" or "additional." Thus, **marginal cost (MC)** is the additional cost of producing one more unit of output. It is equal to the change in total cost from one unit of output to the next. Consider, for example, the marginal cost of the first unit of output—the first thousand feet of lumber—in Exh. 6.3. If it costs the firm $180 to produce zero output (remember fixed costs) and $450 to produce one unit of output, the marginal cost of the first unit of lumber is $270. The *MC* of the

EXHIBIT 6.3

The Marginal Cost of Manufacturing Pine Lumber

OUTPUT PER DAY (thousands of feet of lumber)	TOTAL COST (*TC*)	MARGINAL COST (*MC*)
0	$ 180	—
1	450	$270
2	690	240
3	900	210
4	1,080	180
5	1,290	210
6	1,530	240
7	1,800	270
8	2,130	330
9	2,520	390
10	2,970	450

Marginal cost is the additional cost of producing one more unit of output. For example, if it costs the firm $1,290 to produce five units of lumber and $1,530 to produce six units of lumber, the marginal cost of the sixth unit of lumber is $240.

second unit of output is $240, the difference between TC $450 and TC $690. Take a few moments to compute the marginal costs for the remaining units of output, using the total cost column in Exh. 6.3. Then, check your answers against the marginal cost column in that exhibit.

The Cost Curves

The information scheduled in Exhs. 6.2 and 6.3 is depicted as cost curves in Exh. 6.4. We read cost curves in much the same way we read the demand and supply curves presented in Chapter 3. If we are interested in knowing the average total cost of producing three units of output, for example, we find three units on the horizontal axis, move directly up from that quantity to the ATC curve (point A), move across to the vertical axis, and read $300. The ATC of producing three units of output is $300 per unit. To determine the AVC when six units are being produced, we find that quantity on the horizontal axis, move directly up to the AVC curve (point B), move across to the vertical axis, and read $225. The AVC of producing six units of output is $225. The other cost curves are read in the same way.

Cost curves help us see how a particular cost behaves as the level of output changes. Note that AFC declines as output increases, reflecting the spreading of fixed costs over more units of output. The marginal cost curve and the average cost curves (AVC and ATC) decline initially and then begin to increase as output expands, giving them a U shape. As you read the following sections, you will see why the curves behave this way.

THE MARGINAL COST CURVE

Why does marginal cost first decline and then increase? As you've already learned, marginal cost is the additional cost of producing one more unit of output. It is a variable cost because it changes as output changes. The shape of the marginal cost curve, therefore, must be related to some specific variable cost—often the cost of labor.

Let's see how changing labor costs can account for the U-shaped curve in Exh. 6.4. The labor cost of producing an additional unit of output depends on the amount of labor time it takes to produce that unit. If our firm is paying its workers $10 per hour and it takes eight hours of labor to produce the additional unit, the labor cost of that unit is $80. Keep in mind that the amount of labor time it takes to produce each additional unit of output is not constant. It depends on the degree of *specialization* of labor, the extent to which workers perform a single task rather than several. Workers who specialize do their jobs better, which means lower MC.

EXHIBIT 6.4

A Graphic Look at Costs

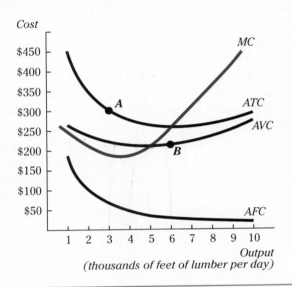

Cost curves show the way a particular type of cost is related to the level of output. Average fixed cost (*AFC*) declines as output increases. Marginal cost (*MC*), average variable cost (*AVC*), and average total cost (*ATC*) graph as U-shaped curves; that is, these types of costs decline initially and then rise.

When a firm is producing relatively little output, the labor cost of producing an additional unit tends to be high. Because output is low, the few workers employed are required to perform a variety of diverse tasks. But the diversity of the tasks prevents workers from becoming proficient at any of them, and so a substantial amount of labor time is required to complete each task, and the cost of producing additional units is high. For instance, if you were attempting to run our hypothetical sawmill alone, you would be required to saw the logs, plane the boards to smooth them, stack the lumber for drying, and clean and service the equipment. With all these tasks to perform, you probably wouldn't become very proficient at any of them. As a consequence, the time required to accomplish each task would be relatively high. In addition, time would be wasted in moving from task to task. These factors result in a high marginal cost ($270) for the first unit of lumber.

As output expands and more workers are hired, workers can specialize in one or a few jobs and thereby become better at them. For instance, if the lumber mill needs to hire two workers to keep up with demand, one of them might do all the sawing while the other planes the boards and stacks them for drying. This greater specialization permits workers to become more proficient at their jobs and reduces the time wasted in moving between jobs. The result is a lower marginal cost for the second unit of output ($240) and an even lower cost for the third ($210) and fourth ($180) because the amount of labor time required to produce these additional units of output is reduced.

As long as the advantages of increased specialization allow our mill to expand output more rapidly than employment (and labor cost), marginal cost will continue to fall. But that won't happen indefinitely. Remember: In the short run the mill must operate with a fixed amount of plant and equipment. This restriction limits the degree of specialization possible. At some point the mill's equipment will be fully utilized, and the major advantages of specialization will be exhausted. Once the sawmill has someone working full-time on the sawing machine, the planing machine, and the forklift, further gains from specialization may be difficult to achieve. Additional workers will still allow the firm to expand output (by bringing materials to the saw operator, for example, or filling in while she takes lunch breaks), but the gain in output will be smaller than before. Workers will sometimes find themselves idle because they are waiting to use equipment. And the space limitations of a fixed plant may ultimately lead to congestion and reduce output gains even further. For these reasons the marginal cost of producing an additional unit of output will ultimately rise, as it does in our example when output is expanded from four to five units of lumber.[2]

In summary, if a firm continues to expand output in the short run, eventually it will overutilize its fixed plant and equipment, causing marginal cost to rise. This principle is simply an extension of the law of increasing costs introduced in Chapter 1.

THE RELATIONSHIP BETWEEN MARGINAL AND AVERAGE COSTS

Marginal cost is related to average variable cost and average total cost in a very precise way. In Exh. 6.4 you'll notice that the *MC* curve intersects the *AVC* curve at the lowest point, or minimum, of the *AVC* curve. This point is not a chance intersection but is due to the relationship between marginal and average cost values. A simple example will help clarify this relationship.

---

[2] The fixed factor need not be plant and equipment; in agriculture it might be land. As a farmer adds units of fertilizer (or some other variable input such as labor, irrigation water, or insecticide) to a fixed plot of land, the second unit of fertilizer may increase the output of corn by more than the first unit, and the third unit of fertilizer may increase output by more than the second. Thus, the cost of producing each additional bushel of corn declines initially because it takes less fertilizer (and therefore less expenditure on fertilizer) to produce it.

Again, this process can't continue indefinitely. Eventually it will reach the point at which the fixed land is being overutilized, the point at which the next unit of fertilizer applied to the land will yield less additional output than the unit before it. When that happens, the marginal cost of producing the next bushel of corn will rise. In other words, the marginal cost curve will turn upward.

Let's assume that you want to know the average weight of the students in your class. To determine the class average, you coax each student onto the scales, add up the individual weights, and then divide by the number of students in the class. If an additional (marginal) student who weighs more than the average joins the class, the average will be pulled up. If the additional student weighs less than the previous class average, the average will be pulled down. As you can see, the marginal value determines what happens to the average.

Essentially the same logic applies to the cost curves. Notice that so long as the *MC* curve is below the *AVC* curve, the *AVC* is falling; the marginal value is pulling down the average just as the thin student pulled down the class average. However, when *MC* is above *AVC*, *AVC* is rising; the marginal value is pulling the average up. When *MC* = *AVC*—that is, when *MC* and *AVC* intersect—the average will remain unchanged. As you can see, the shape of the *AVC* curve depends largely on the behavior of marginal cost. Thus, if *MC* declines initially and then increases as output continues to expand, *AVC* must display the same general behavior.

The shape of the *ATC* curve is also influenced by marginal cost but in a somewhat more complex manner. Recall that average total cost is the sum of average fixed cost and average variable cost. Initially both *AVC* and *AFC* decline, and so *ATC* declines as well. But note that *ATC* continues to decline after *AVC* has turned upward. This occurs because *AFC* is continuing to decline, and for a while the downward pull of *AFC* outweighs the upward pull of *AVC*. Eventually the increase in *AVC* will more than offset the decrease in *AFC*, and *ATC* will begin to rise. Thus, *ATC* will have the same basic shape as *AVC*, but the minimum point on the curve will occur at a somewhat higher output. (An increase in the cost of inputs—higher wage rates or raw materials prices, for instance—would shift the cost curves upward without altering the basic relationship between the curves. A reduction in input costs would have the opposite effect; it would shift the curves downward.)

In summary, the marginal cost curve plays a major role in determining the shape of both the average variable and average total cost curves. As you will see in a moment, marginal cost also plays a major role in guiding the production decisions of the competitive firm.

Profit Maximization in the Short Run

Because the purely competitive firm is a price taker, in effect bound to the price determined by the market, the only variable it can control to maximize its profit (when market conditions permit a profit) or minimize its loss (when a loss is unavoidable) is the level of output.

In the short run the purely competitive firm can produce any level of output within the capacity of its existing plant and equipment. It adjusts its output by altering the amount of variable resources (labor and raw materials, for example) that it employs in conjunction with its fixed plant and equipment. In the long run, of course, the firm has additional options for expanding or contracting production.

DETERMINING THE PROFIT-MAXIMIZING OUTPUT

How do firms go about selecting the profit-maximizing level of output? They behave as you and I do when making a decision about how to spend our time and money: They compare costs and benefits. In fact, the process of selecting the profit-maximizing (loss-minimizing) level of output can be likened to a series of cost-benefit comparisons. Imagine a production manager repeatedly asking the same question: Does the benefit from producing one more unit of output exceed the cost? As long as the answer is yes, it is sensible for the firm to continue expanding output. When the answer is no, the firm should go no further.

For a business the benefit from producing and selling output is the revenue it takes in. Marginal revenue (*MR*) is the additional revenue to be gained by selling one more unit of output. When firms are price takers, *MR* is always equal to price because the additional revenue to be gained by selling one more unit is exactly the market price (*MR=P*). This price must be compared with marginal cost, the cost of producing one more unit of output. A firm seeking to achieve the profit-maximizing output will continue to increase production as long as price or marginal revenue exceeds marginal cost. When price exceeds marginal cost (*P>MC*), each additional unit produced makes the firm better off because it adds more to the firm's revenue than to its cost.

Exhibit 6.5 illustrates this decision-making process in action. The market price in this example is $270, so that each additional unit produced will add $270 to revenue. If we begin our cost-benefit comparison with the fifth unit of output, we can see that the $270 the firm gains from producing this unit is more than the $210 marginal cost of that unit. In short, the firm will be $60 better off for producing that unit. The firm should produce the sixth unit as well. Although marginal cost rises to $240 for that unit, it is still less than the $270 selling price, leaving the firm $30 better off. (It is important to recognize that although the sixth unit adds less to profit than the fifth unit, it continues to enlarge the firm's total profit, and so it should be produced.)[3]

The seventh unit of output is a little trickier to evaluate. It brings in no more revenue ($270) than it costs to produce ($270), so the firm should be neutral or indifferent toward its production. Economists generally assume, however, that

---

[3] With the information provided thus far, we cannot determine whether this firm is earning a profit or incurring a loss. But we can say that by producing the sixth unit, the firm will either enlarge its total profit *or* reduce its total loss. You'll see how to determine the profit or loss in just a moment.

EXHIBIT 6.5

The Profit-Maximizing Output

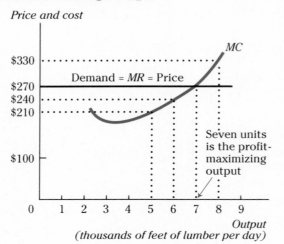

The profit-maximizing firm should continue to expand output until *MR* = *MC*. In this case profit maximization (or loss minimization) occurs at an output of seven units (7,000 feet) of lumber per day.

the firm will go ahead and produce that unit. As we noted in Chapter 5, this assumption provides us with a simple rule for selecting the profit-maximizing output: Produce the level of output at which *MR* = *MC*, the output that corresponds to the point where the *MR* and *MC* curves intersect. In instances when there is no whole-number unit of output for which *MR* is exactly equal to *MC*, the firm should produce all the units for which *MR* > *MC* but no unit for which *MC* > *MR*.

MARGINAL COST AND FIRM SUPPLY

Because the purely competitive firm determines the profit-maximizing output by equating price and marginal cost, any change in the prevailing market price will alter the amount of output it will choose to produce. Suppose, for example, that the existing market price was $330 instead of $270. You can see from Exh. 6.5 that if the firm's demand curve was horizontal at that price, the firm would expand output to eight units per day (the output at which the demand curve would intersect the *MC* curve). Alternatively, a price of $240 would cause the firm to produce less; the demand curve would intersect the *MC* curve at six units. As you can see, the competitive firm always operates along its marginal cost curve, supplying whatever output is dictated by its intersection with the prevailing market price (the firm's demand curve). For that reason, the marginal cost curve can be thought of as the firm's supply curve because it indicates how much the firm will produce or "supply" at any given price. (Actually, the firm's supply curve is only the portion of the marginal cost curve lying above the average variable cost curve—look back at Exh. 6.4 to see what that means. That's because if price falls below average variable cost, the firm won't produce any output. More about that in a moment.)

EVALUATING PROFIT OR LOSS

By producing where marginal revenue is equal to marginal cost, the purely competitive firm is doing the best it can; it is either maximizing its profit or minimizing its loss. Marginal values alone, however, will not tell us exactly how well the firm is doing; they will not tell us whether the firm is earning a profit or incurring a loss, and they will not tell us the amount of the profit or loss. To answer those questions, we need to calculate and compare the firm's total revenue and total cost. You already know that total revenue is computed by multiplying the selling price of the product by the number of units sold. To compute total cost, we need the information provided by the average total cost curve. Multiplying the *ATC* by the number of units of output produced gives us the total cost of producing the output level. (Recall that we get our per unit cost, or *ATC*, by performing the reverse operation: dividing *TC* at a particular level of output by the number of units.) By comparing total revenue with total cost, we can determine the profit or loss of the firm. Some examples should help clarify this procedure.

Profits, Losses, and Breaking Even. Exhibit 6.6 shows a purely competitive firm in three different short-run situations. As you study the three cases, keep in mind that market price equals *MR* under conditions of pure competition. And the *MR* = *P* curve is the demand curve for the purely competitive firm. In each case the firm is producing where the *MC* curve intersects the demand curve, where *MC* = *MR*, but it is experiencing different degrees of success in these three situations. In part (a), the firm is enjoying an above-normal, or economic, profit. The amount of this profit can be determined by comparing total revenue with total cost. Total revenue is equal to $1,890 (the $270 selling price × 7 units), whereas total cost is only $1,799 (*ATC* of $257 × 7 units). Therefore, the firm is earning an economic profit of $91. (Alternatively, we could determine the firm's profit by multiplying the average, or per-unit, profit by the number of units sold. Here the firm is earning a profit of $13 per unit ($270 − $257 = $13) and selling seven units; total profit is $13 × 7 = $91.)

In part (b) the firm isn't doing as well. Its total revenue of $1,530 ($255 × 6 units) exactly matches its total cost, so that the firm is breaking even; it is earning zero economic profit. Remember, zero economic profit is the same as normal profit, the amount the owners of the business could expect to earn if they invested their resources elsewhere. In part (c) the firm has fallen on hard times. Price is now so low that it will no longer cover average total

EXHIBIT 6.6

Finding the Profit or Loss

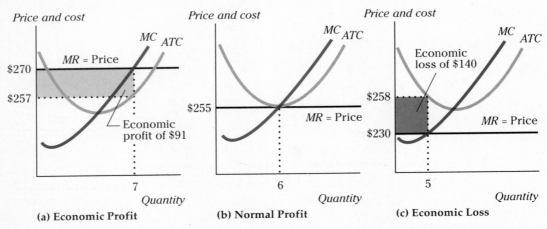

(a) Economic Profit   **(b) Normal Profit**   **(c) Economic Loss**

All firms maximize their profits or minimize their losses by producing the level
of output at which marginal revenue is equal to marginal cost. In some instances a
firm will be able to earn an above-normal, or *economic*, profit. In other instances
only a normal profit—zero economic profit—will be possible. Finally, in some cases
an economic loss—less than a normal profit—will be the best the firm can do.

cost. Indeed, the firm will be earning less than a normal profit and therefore
facing an *economic loss:* total cost, including all opportunity cost, will exceed
total revenue. In our example the total cost is $1,290 ($258 × 5 units), whereas
its total revenue is only $1,150 (*ATC* of $230 × 5 units), a loss of $140. (Note
that if we multiply the per-unit loss of $28 × 5 units, we arrive at the same
$140 figure for the firm's total loss.)

Operating with a Loss. Why would the company continue to produce in
part (c)? Why not simply close down the business and not reopen until conditions improve? The answer has to do with fixed costs, or overhead, which
must be paid whether or not any output is produced. If a firm shuts down
temporarily—if it stays in the industry but stops producing output—its loss
will equal its total fixed costs. But if the price the firm can get for its product is
high enough to allow the firm to cover its variable costs (costs that would not
exist if the firm shut down) and pay *some* of its fixed costs, the firm will be better off if it continues to operate. This is why U.S. wheat farmers continued to
produce in the mid-1980s despite substantial losses, and why cattle ranchers
kept raising cattle in 1996, even though prices were at a ten-year low and well

EXHIBIT 6.7

Minimizing a Loss

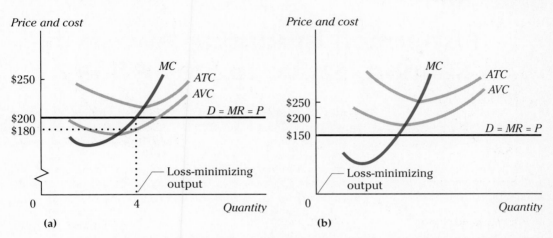

Whenever price exceeds average variable cost *(P > AVC)*, the firm will minimize its loss by continuing to operate. This is the situation represented in part (a), where the firm will continue to produce despite an economic loss. When price is less than average variable cost *(P < AVC)*, the firm will minimize its loss by shutting down. This situation is represented in part (b).

below average total cost. In both cases, continuing to operate resulted in smaller losses than would have been incurred by shutting down. When price dips so low that the firm can no longer recover even the variable cost of production, it will shut down and wait for better times.

Exhibit 6.7 illustrates these two situations. In part (a) the selling price of $200 is greater than the average variable cost of $180, so that each unit the firm produces (up to the point at which *MR = MC*) provides it with $20 ($200 − $180 = $20) to help pay its fixed costs. Although the firm will still incur a loss, continued operation will make the loss smaller than it would be if the firm shut down and paid its fixed costs. In part (b) the $150 price is less than the *AVC* of $175, and so each unit the firm produces increases its total loss by $25. This firm would be better off to shut down, accept its fixed-cost loss, and wait for business conditions to improve. Of course, if losses continue for an extended period, eventually the firm will be forced out of business. In summary, when *P > AVC*, the firm will minimize its loss by continuing to operate; when *P < AVC*, the firm should shut down. (The article on pages 176–177, "Fisherman in Alaska...Strive to Stay Afloat," illustrates how market conditions can lead to losses and how firms attempt to make the best of the situation.)

Use Your Economic Reasoning

Fishermen in Alaska, Awash in Salmon, Strive to Stay Afloat

By Bill Richards
Staff reporter of The Wall Street Journal

ROCKY POINT, Alaska- Hundreds of silvery salmon thrash and flash as they pour out of the net and into the hold of Michael Meint's 42-foot fishing boat, Jimani. In the background, clouds boil against steep, rocky hillsides and chunks of blue glacial ice drift across Prince William Sound.

It is a picture-postcard scene of a dying industry.

Alaska is awash in salmon. Huge fish runs have been building here. Combined with growing salmon output from sources like Chilean fish farms and Russian fishing fleets, they are glutting the market and driving wholesale prices to record lows. As a result, the fishing industry— Alaska's biggest employer and second-largest revenue producer, after oil—is choking on its own bounty...

Anywhere else that would be an elementary lesson in supply and demand. But Alaska's $1 billion salmon industry is different. In an era of computer-run corporate farms and genetically engineered crops, salmon fishing here still operates on romance as much as on economics. Fisherman sneer at foreign fish farms and boast they are "the last hunter-gatherers." In the small salmon-fishing ports tucked along Prince William Sound's serrated shoreline, pickup trucks bear bumper stickers that say, "Real salmon don't eat pellets."

"If you're in the beef or chicken business, you set up to produce according to market demand," says Kenneth Roemhildt, who manages a cannery in Cordova for North Pacific Processors Inc., one of four salmon processors on the city's waterfront. "In the

Profit Maximization in the Long Run

In the short run the purely competitive firm must do the best it can with fixed plant and equipment, but in the long run the firm has many more options; all costs are variable in the long run. If the industry has been profitable, the firm may decide to expand the size of its production plant or otherwise increase its productive capacity. If losses have been common, it can sell out and invest in another industry, one in which the prospects for profits appear brighter. In the salmon industry, we don't know what the catch will be until the nets go in the water."

That strategy worked fine in the past, when Alaska's salmon had no real competition...But Alaska can't control fish farms springing up in Norway, Chile, Canada and states like Washington and Maine. Farm-raised fish account for about half the world's salmon sales, up from 7% a decade ago. Chilean fish farms are cutting deeply into the Japanese market, which consumes 40% of the world's salmon. Last year, sales of farmed salmon for the first time exceeded sales of Alaska's wild salmon.

"The hunter-gatherers are trying to compete with the farmers, and, just like everywhere else, the hunter-gatherers are losing," says William Gilbert, who operates Norquest Seafoods Inc.'s cannery in Cordova...

At the Fishermen United storefront headquarters in Cordova, posters on the wall tout salmon cheeseburgers, salmon sandwiches and other salmon dishes. But Executive Director Dorne Hawxhurst says many of her group's 300 members have given up fishing for pinks. "The ones that haven't are fishing their brains out and going broke," she says.

Mr. Meints falls in the latter category. On a recent three-day trip, he and his crew spent 20-hour days pulling a total of 80,000 pounds of pinks out of Prince William Sound. That kind of catch would have grossed nearly $64,000 for the Jimani and its crew in the past. But this year, Mr. Meints says, watching another load of fish come up over the side of the boat, "at five cents a pound, its hardly worth the effort." Mr Meints says that even though he is losing money, he needs to keep fishing to generate cash flow to pay bills. But if he hits his million-pound target this summer, the boat will gross only $80,000, even after he gets an additional three cents a pound for storing his catch in freezing brine....

USE YOUR ECONOMIC REASONING

1. Why has the market price of salmon fallen so low?
2. How do you explain the fact that some fishermen have stopped fishing but others continue even though they are losing money? Represent each situation graphically.

short run the number of firms in an industry remains constant—time is inadequate for firms to enter or leave. But in the long run there is time for these adjustments to occur, and the industry can expand or contract. In this section we examine how firms in a purely competitive industry adjust to the presence or absence of short-run profits and how this adjustment process eventually leads to long-run equilibrium for the industry. **Long-run equilibrium** is a situation in which the size of an industry is stable: There is no incentive for additional firms to enter the industry and no pressure for existing firms to leave.

EXHIBIT 6.8

The Long-Run Adjustment Process

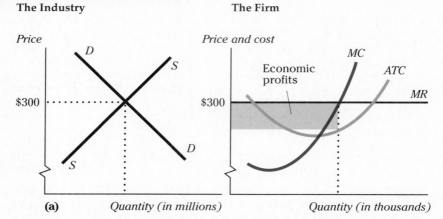

(a) At a price of $300, the firms in the industry will be able to earn an economic profit. Since above-normal profits are being earned, additional firms will be attracted to the industry. This development is reflected in (b).

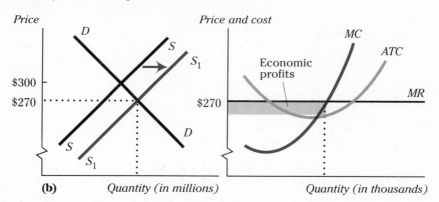

(b) As additional firms enter the industry, the industry supply curve will shift from S to S₁ and price will be forced down to $270. However, since that price still permits an economic profit to be earned, additional firms will enter the industry, as revealed in (c), on the next page.

SETTING THE STAGE:
THE SHORT-RUN PICTURE

In Exh. 6.8 we follow the path by which a purely competitive firm and industry arrive at long-run equilibrium. Each panel shows the demand and supply curves for the industry on the left and the diagram for a representative firm on the right. In part (a) the industry demand and supply curves establish a price

EXHIBIT 6.8 (Cont.)

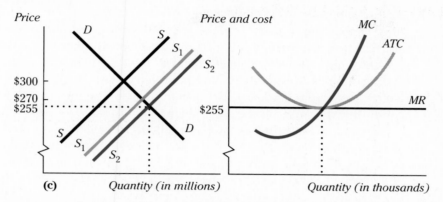

(c) The entrance of additional firms will shift the supply curve to S_2 and depress market price to $255. At that price the firms in the industry will be able to earn only a normal profit. There will be no incentive for additional firms to enter the industry, and the industry will be in long-run equilibrium.

---

of $300. The representative firm takes that price as a given and maximizes its profit by producing where $MC = MR$. Because the representative firm is earning an economic profit in the short run, additional firms will be attracted to this industry in the long run.

THE ENTRANCE OF FIRMS: ATTRACTION OF PROFITS

The entrance of additional firms is made possible by one of the assumptions of the purely competitive model—the absence of significant barriers to entry. As additional firms enter the industry, they will increase industry supply and depress the market price. The increase in industry supply occurs because the industry supply curve is the sum of all the firms' supply curves and is found by adding together those curves.[4] If additional firms enter the industry, the curves of those firms must be added, shifting the industry curve to the right. This adjustment is represented in the left-hand graph of Exh. 6.8 (b), where supply

---

[4] Summing the supply curves of all the firms is relatively easy (remember, each firm's supply curve is its marginal cost curve above average variable cost). We simply add up the quantities that the firms will supply at each market price. For simplicity, suppose that there are only two firms in our industry. If firm A supplies 5 units at $300 and firm B supplies 7 units at the same price, the industry supply curve would show 12 units being supplied at $300. The amount supplied by the industry at other prices would be determined in the same manner.

has increased to S_1 and intersects the demand curve to establish a new price of $270. Note that at the new price the firms in the industry are still able to earn economic profits; *ATC* is still below *MR* = *P*. As a consequence, firms will continue to enter the industry until the price falls to $255, where the demand curve and S_2 intersect in part (c), and price is consistent with normal profits.

Once the price of $255 is established, both the firm and the industry are in long-run equilibrium: they have achieved a state of balance, a situation in which there is no tendency for further change. The industry is in long-run equilibrium because at zero profit there is no incentive for additional firms to enter it and no incentive for established firms to leave it. The individual firms are in equilibrium because they have no incentive to alter their level of output so long as the market price remains at $255. (Cranberry growers were earning high profits in 1997, but some were worried that the profit bubble might soon burst. Read "…Let's Bet the Farm on Cranberry Crops," on pages 182–183, and decide if you'd be willing to place that bet.)

THE EXIT OF FIRMS: LOOKING FOR GREENER PASTURES

If a purely competitive industry undergoes short-run economic losses, a similar adjustment process is likely to result. In the long run some firms will respond to the short-run losses (less than normal profits) by leaving the industry to search for a better opportunity elsewhere. As these firms exit, industry supply decreases and the market price rises. Firms will continue to leave the industry until the market price has risen sufficiently to afford the remaining firms exactly a normal profit. When that happens, the exodus will cease; the firms and the industry will be in long-run equilibrium.

The Benefits of Pure Competition

As we noted at the beginning of this chapter, economists often use the model of pure competition as an ideal by which to judge other, less competitive industry structures. Economists hold pure competition in such high esteem primarily because it would lead to an efficient use of our scarce resources.

PRODUCTION EFFICIENCY

One of the most important features of pure competition is its tendency to promote **production efficiency**: production at the lowest possible average total cost, or minimum *ATC*. As you look at Exh. 6.9, you'll see that the purely competitive firm is in long-run equilibrium when it is producing at the output level where its *ATC* curve is tangent to, or barely touching, its demand curve. This tangency occurs at the lowest point on the firm's *ATC* curve, showing

EXHIBIT 6.9

The Competitive Firm in Long-Run Equilibrium

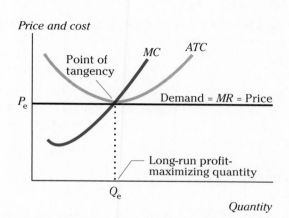

In long-run equilibrium the competitive firm will earn only a normal profit. This is indicated in the graph by the tangency between the demand curve, or price line, and the *ATC* curve at the profit-maximizing output (where $MR(P) = MC$). The equality of price and minimum *ATC* indicates that the firm is achieving *production efficiency*.

that the firm is producing at the lowest possible average cost. In essence, this means that the product is being produced with as few scarce resources as possible. Production efficiency is a benefit of pure competition; it allows us to spread our scarce resources across more products, and in so doing it enables us to satisfy more of society's unlimited wants.

Note also that in long-run equilibrium, consumers are able to purchase the product at a price equal to this minimum *ATC*. This must be true because at the tangency point in Exh. 6.9, Price $(MR) = ATC$. Thus, we can see that the benefits of production efficiency are passed on to consumers. They receive the lowest possible price, given the cost conditions that exist in the industry.

ALLOCATIVE EFFICIENCY

If pure competition resulted in the efficient production of millions of buggy whips or other products not in much demand, consumers obviously would not be pleased. However, pure competition also leads to **allocative efficiency:** Producers use society's scarce resources to provide consumers with the proper quantities of the goods and services they desire most. Economists argue that if pure competition prevailed throughout the economy, all our scarce resources would be allocated or distributed so as to produce the precise mix of products that consumers desire most.

Use Your Economic Reasoning

Forget Cattle and Corn; Let's Bet the Farm On Cranberry Crops

Surge in Fruit's Price Brings A Gold-Rush Mentality; Will Cran-Bubble Burst?

By Barbara Carton
Staff reporter of the Wall Street Journal

GLADSTONE, Mich.—Bob Barron, a red-bearded dairy farmer, bounces through a rutted hayfield in his old blue Ford truck and points out the windshield to where he believes his future lies.

After more than 20 years earning a modest living raising dairy cows, Mr. Barron is betting on cranberries, spending $3 million to transform 100 acres here into a cranberry bog.

If this seems an odd choice for a dairy farmer, guess again. These are boom times for cranberries. Two mediocre harvests have left the industry short about 40 million pounds of fruit. Cranberry prices have soared to as high as $110 per 100-pound barrel, nearly 50% more than growers were paid two years ago....

Fueling the demand is a hugely successful marketing effort by Ocean Spray Cranberries Inc., the $1.4 billion growers cooperative in Lakeville, Mass.... It has managed to convince many Americans that the intensely tart cranberry, if drenched in enough sugar, goes great [in] everything from muffins to vodka. Ocean Spray went as far as to employ Sarah Ferguson, the Duchess of York, to hawk cran-libations earlier this year; its promotion efforts have also gotten a boost from recent medical research showing that drinking lots of cranberry juice can reduce bladder infections by 42%....

Land Prices Soar

Heightened demand has sparked something of a stampede mentality. From Oregon to Maine, new cranberry bogs are sprouting in places where no one has ever bogged before. Traditionally, most U.S. cranberry farming has been done in only five states: Wisconsin, Massachusetts, New Jersey, Oregon and Washington.

Meanwhile, prices of existing bogland around the country have climbed as much as 75% in the past five years to $35,000 an acre, says bog appraiser Arthur E. Clapp of Tolland, Conn. Others are paying plenty more: Northland says it has shelled out as much as $70,000 an acre. Total cranberry plantings in North America have jumped nearly 23% since 1990, to 37,500 acres. An acre usually yields between 130 and 170 100-pound barrels of cranberries....

Chilean Crops

Other entrepreneurs are furiously scouting bog potential in Canada, Ireland, Poland, Latvia, Lithuania and the Ukraine. In Chile, where most folks have never tasted cranberries, Warren Simmons of California has planted 750 acres and hopes to boost that to as many as 2,000. Mr Simmons, founder of Chevy's, a West Coast chain of Mexican restaurants, says he turned to cranberries for his latest venture five years ago after ordering a large quantity for holiday margaritas at his retaurants—and being dumbfounded to learn his supplier couldn't deliver.

In the U.S., the bog frenzy has prompted worry among some environmental groups, including Trout Unlimited, which already blames berry farming for the destruction of sensitive wetlands and wildlife habitat.

In New Jersey, a proposal by the state's Department of Environmental Protection to allow the cranberry industry to use as many as 300 acres of protected wetlands over a five-year period has been stalled because of environmentalists' objections....

Bogging Schools

If cranberry farmers don't like the treatment they are getting in New Jersey, they can always try Michigan: Among the incentives it is offering are tax breaks, a streamlined environmental permitting process, and state-subsidized "cranberry schools" that teach the A-to-Z of bogging. Though Michigan only has 150 acres of cranberries now, it hopes to double that by December and aims to plant 5,000 acres within the next decade.

So aggresive has the state been that it was recently "disinvited" from a Massachusetts cranberry trade meeting, says Robert Craig, director of Michigan's Office of Agricultural Development. "I think they thought we were a raiding party," he says.

For many growers, the boom *has* been a party. Sipping a bottle of cranberry juice in the cranberry-colored office of the 200-acre Carver, Mass., farm that his grandfather started in 1919, grower Gary Garretson says he has always made a decent enough living. But recent high returns have allowed him to reinvest $350,000 to develop 10 new acres of bog, $100,000-a-year to rejuvenate unproductive bogs and $5,000 for a new computerized soil-mapping system to boost yields....

The Crash of '59

There is a chance that the cranberry bubble may suddenly burst, leaving speculators with nothing but a bunch of soggy land. Old-timers remember 1959, when an unwarranted pesticide scare crushed the cranberry market. While analysts like to point out that the international market for cranberry products is largely untapped, skeptics wonder if foreign palates will take to the obscure North American fruit.

Mr. Kennedy, the Minnesota semiconductor executive turned cranberry farmer, is undeterred. Although he expects his initial return-on-investment will be "terribly ugly" (it can cost $30,000 or more to develop and plant one acre of cranberries) Mr. Kennedy expects to reap $1.7 million of annual revenue and at least $425,000 of net profit from 132 acrs. That is only one-third of the acreage he hopes to plant.

"I intend to make a very, very good living," he says....

USE YOUR ECONOMIC REASONING

1. Why have cranberry prices "soared" in recent years? What have those higher prices done to the profits of cranberry growers?
2. Draw firm and industry diagrams representing the present situation.
3. If cranberry farming is a competitve industry, how would you expect growers to respond to the situation depicted in your answer to question 2? Are they responding in that manner? Cite passages from the article to support your conclusion.
4. According to the article, "There is a chance that the cranberry [profit] bubble may suddenly burst." The article warns of a pesticide scare. The competitve model warns of a more predictable danger. What is it? How would it be represented graphically?
5. Can you think of any factors that might delay the bursting of the cranberry bubble, anything that might allow cranberry farmers to enjoy economic profits for some time?

Allocative efficiency requires that each product be produced up to the point at which the benefit its consumption provides to society *(marginal social benefit)* is exactly equal to the cost its production imposes on society *(marginal social cost).* In most instances, the benefits that a product provides to society are simply the benefits received by those who purchase the product. The value of these benefits is reflected in the price that consumers are willing to pay; the greater the benefit, the higher the price. This, in turn, can be determined from the industry demand curve. For instance, if consumers are willing to purchase 1,000 units of lumber at $300 and 1,001 units of lumber at $299, then the maximum price that consumers are willing to pay for the 1,001st unit of output must be $299 (since they were unwilling to purchase that unit at $300).[5]

Marginal social cost represents what society must give up to produce an additional unit of the product; in other words, it represents opportunity cost. Opportunity cost is generally reflected in the costs that the businesses incur to produce the product. In the case of pure competition, this can be determined from the industry supply curve. Because the industry supply curve is the sum of the firms' supply curves, it can be thought of as the marginal cost curve of the industry. (Remember: Under conditions of pure competition, the individual firm's supply curve is its marginal cost curve; so the industry supply curve is simply the sum of those curves.) By turning to the marginal cost curve (the industry supply curve), we can determine the sacrifice that society must make to produce an additional unit of the product in question. For instance, if the marginal cost of an additional unit of lumber is $200, that means that society must do without $200 worth of alternative goods—whatever products the same amount of raw materials, labor, and capital could have produced—in order to obtain this unit of lumber.[6]

As long as the marginal social benefit from an additional unit of output exceeds the marginal social cost, it is in society's interest to continue expanding production. This point is illustrated in Exh.6.10. Suppose the industry chose to produce Q_A units of output. As you can see from the diagram, the marginal social benefit of the last unit of output is $300, while the marginal social cost is only $270; clearly, output should be expanded since consumers value additional units of lumber more than the alternative products they could receive instead. If the industry chose to produce Q_B units, it would have carried production too far. The marginal social benefit of the last unit produced is equal to only $270, while the marginal social cost is equal to $300. Society

---

[5] In some instances the consumption of a product conveys benefits to individuals in addition to those who purchased the product. For instance, when you purchase a flu shot, you benefit, but so do others (who will not get the flu from you). These *external benefits* are not reflected in the industry demand curve. Chapter 9 will discuss the impact of external benefits on the efficient allocation of resources.
[6] In some instances the costs incurred by a business do not reflect all the costs associated with the production of a product. For instance, if a firm disposes of wastes by dumping them into a river in order to minimize its disposal costs, that action may kill fish and impose cleanup costs on other parties. These *external costs* are not reflected in the firm's cost curves. Chapter 9 will examine the impact of external costs on the allocation of scarce resources.

EXHIBIT 6.10

Pure Competition and Allocation Efficiency

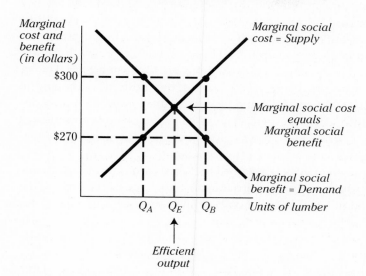

Allocative efficiency requires that each product be produced up to the point at which the marginal social benefit of the last unit produced is equal to the marginal social cost. That output is found where the demand and supply curves intersect, at Q_e in this example.

would be better off if more resources were allocated to the production of other things and fewer to the production of lumber.

The optimal, or allocatively efficient, level of production occurs where the marginal social benefit and marginal social cost intersect, Q_E in our example. At that output the value of the benefit consumers receive from the last unit produced is exactly equal to the value of the alternative goods that must be sacrificed for its production. Pure competition ensures this outcome. Purely competitive industries always produce at the output level where the demand (marginal social benefit) and supply (marginal social cost) curves intersect. Therefore, pure competition ensures the efficient allocation of society's scarce resources.[7]

Let's synthesize what we have just discussed: Under conditions of pure competition, self-interest-seeking producers are guided by the presence or absence of profits to produce the right amounts of the products that consumers desire most. The forces of competition also lead to long-run equilibrium, whereby all firms in the industry operate at the lowest possible average cost (minimum *ATC*) and receive a price just equal to that cost. Thus, in the long run, consumers are able to purchase their most-desired products at the lowest possible prices.

---

[7] This conclusion assumes that there are no external costs or benefits associated with the production or consumption of the product. (See footnotes 5 and 6 for examples of external costs and benefits.) When *externalities* (external costs or benefits) exist, the industry supply and demand curves will not fully reflect social costs and benefits, and resources will be allocated inefficiently. This possibility will be considered in Chapter 9.

Summary

A *firm* is the basic producing unit in a market economy, and an *industry* is a group of firms that produce similar or identical products. A purely competitive industry is one in which (1) a large number of sellers (firms) each produce a small fraction of the total industry supply; (2) the products offered by the different sellers are identical in the minds of consumers; and (3) no substantial barriers exist to prevent firms from entering or leaving the industry. Although no industries meet these conditions fully, the model of pure competition provides a standard by which to judge the performance of less competitive industries and helps us to predict price and output behavior in industries that come reasonably close to meeting the assumptions of the model.

The model of pure competition assumes that firms are profit maximizers; that is, they are always attempting to earn the most profit possible. *Profit* is the excess of a firm's total revenue over its total cost. When a firm's total costs exceed its total revenue, the firm is incurring a *loss*.

All costs can be classified as either fixed or variable. *Fixed costs* are costs that do not vary with the level of output. *Variable costs* are costs that change with the level of output. *Total cost* is simply the sum of the fixed and variable costs incurred by the firm.

The purely competitive firm may be described as a *price taker*; it accepts the price determined by market forces. The only variable that a purely competitive firm can control in order to influence its profit position is the level of output. In order to reach its profit-maximizing level of output, a firm should produce at the point where marginal revenue equals marginal cost. For the purely competitive firm, the price taker, *marginal revenue (MR)* is equal to price, or average revenue per unit sold; *MR* is the revenue earned from selling one more unit of output. *Marginal cost (MC)* is the additional cost of producing one more unit and is a more important concept than *average total cost (ATC)* because it determines the level of output that earns maximum profit.

In the long run, firms in a purely competitive industry tend to earn a *normal profit*, the amount that the owners' resources could earn elsewhere; earning normal profit means breaking even. Above-normal profits are called *economic profits*, and below-normal profits are called *economic losses*. If economic profits exist in the short run, the entrance of additional firms will cause an increase in supply and drive down the market price to the level of zero economic profits, where all firms are breaking even at normal profit. If losses exist, firms will exit the industry until price has risen to a level consistent with normal profits.

When *long-run equilibrium* is finally established, the purely competitive firm will be producing at minimum *ATC*, the point at which its *ATC* curve is tangent to its demand curve. When firms operate at minimum *ATC*, *production efficiency* exists. This is a desirable outcome because it indicates that the fewest possible scarce resources are being used to produce the product and that, therefore, more of society's unlimited wants are being met. In addition to production efficiency, pure competition leads to *allocative efficiency:* the production of the goods and services consumers want most in the quantities they desire. An efficient allocation of resources requires that each product be produced up to the point at which the *marginal social benefit* is equal to the *marginal social cost.* Pure competition ensures this outcome. Thus, we can say that pure competition achieves both production efficiency and allocative efficiency in long-run equilibrium.

GLOSSARY

Allocative efficiency. Using society's scarce resources to produce in the proper quantities the products that consumers value most.

Average fixed cost (AFC). Total fixed cost divided by the number of units being produced.

Average total cost (ATC). Total cost divided by the number of units being produced.

Average variable cost (AVC). Total variable cost divided by the number of units being produced.

Barriers to entry. Obstacles that discourage or prevent firms from entering an industry; examples include patent restrictions, large investment requirements, and restrictive licensing regulations.

Economic loss. The amount by which total cost, including all opportunity costs, exceeds total revenue.

Economic profit. The amount by which total revenue exceeds total cost, including the opportunity cost of owner-supplied resources; also called an *above-normal profit.*

Firm. The basic producing unit in a market economy. Firms buy economic resources and combine them to produce goods and services.

Fixed costs. Costs that do not vary with the level of output.

Industry. A group of firms that produce identical or similar products.

Long-run equilibrium. A situation in which the size of an industry is stable: There is no incentive for additional firms to enter the industry and no pressure for established firms to leave it.

Marginal cost (MC). The additional cost of producing one more unit of output.

Marginal revenue (MR). The additional revenue to be gained by selling one more unit of output.

Marginal social benefit. The benefit that the consumption of another unit of output conveys to society.

Marginal social cost. The cost that the production of another unit of output imposes on society.

Normal profit. An amount equal to what the owners of a business could have earned if their resources had been employed elsewhere; the opportunity cost of owner-supplied resources.

Price taker. A firm that must accept price as a given that is beyond its control.

Production efficiency. Producing a product at the lowest possible average total cost. The essence of production efficiency is that each product is produced with the fewest possible scarce resources .

Total cost (TC). Total fixed cost plus total variable cost.

Total revenue (TR). The total receipts of a business from the sale of its product. Total revenue is calculated by multiplying the selling price of the product times the number of units sold.

Variable costs. Costs that change with the level of output, tending to increase when output increases and to decrease when output declines.

STUDY QUESTIONS

Fill in the Blanks

1. A purely competitive firm is sometimes described as a _Price taker_ because it must accept the price dictated by the market.

2. The demand curve of the purely competitive firm is a _horizontal_ line at the price determined in the market.

3. Costs that don't vary with output are called _fixed_ costs; costs that vary with output are called _Variable_ costs.

4. A business that has no output must still pay its _fixed_ costs.

5. _Marginal_ cost is the additional cost of producing one more unit of output.

6. Average total cost, _average variable_ cost, and _marginal_ cost all graph as U-shaped curves.

7. If a competitive firm wants to maximize its profits, it should continue to produce additional units so long as _marginal revenue_ is greater than or equal to _Marginal Cost_.

8. If economic profits exist in the short run, they will tend to be _eliminated_ in the long run as firms _enter_ the industry and depress market price.

9. If losses exist in the short run, firms will tend to _exit_ the industry in the long run. This will reduce market _Supply_ and help to push price back up.

10. When $P = MC$, _allocative_ efficiency exists; when a firm produces its product at minimum ATC, _production_ efficiency exists.

Multiple Choice

1. Which of the following is not characteristic of a purely competitive industry?
   a) A large number of sellers
   b) Identical products
   (c) Substantial barriers to entry
   d) Relatively small firms

2. Which of the following is the best example of a price taker?
   a) General Motors
   b) Big Bob's Burger Barn
   c) IBM
   (d) An average wheat farmer

Answer questions 3–5 on the basis of the following information:

QUANTITY	TOTAL COST
0	$10
1	18
2	23
3	30
4	42

3. The firm's fixed cost is
   a) $5.
   b) $42.

c) $23.
d) $10.

4. The marginal cost of the third unit would be
a) $30.
b) $7.
c) $10.
d) $5.

5. If the firm produced three units, average total cost would be
a) $10.
b) $30.
c) $7.
d) None of the above

6. Which of the following is least likely to be a variable cost?
a) The cost of raw materials
b) Insurance payments
c) The wages of production workers
d) Shipping expenses

7.

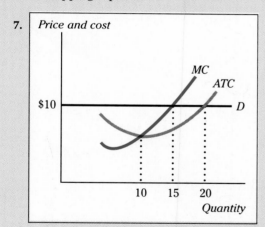

The firm depicted should
a) produce 10 units and maximize its profits.
b) produce 15 units and maximize its profits.
c) produce 10 units and minimize its losses.
d) produce 15 units and minimize its losses.
e) shut down.

8.

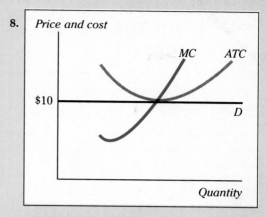

The firm depicted is
a) facing a loss.
b) making an economic profit.
c) making a normal profit.
d) about to go out of business.

9.

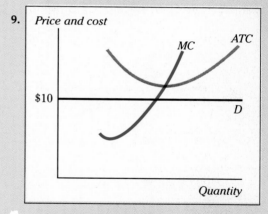

The firm represented is
a) earning a profit.
b) facing a loss.
c) not a competitive firm.
d) breaking even.

10. If the firms in an industry are earning economic profits,
a) additional firms will enter the industry, and the supply curve will shift to the left.
some firms will decide to leave the industry, and the supply curve will shift to the left.

c) additional firms will enter the industry, and the supply curve will shift to the right.

d) some firms will leave the industry, and the supply curve will shift to the right.

11. The Lazy Z Ranch is a purely competitive firm producing hogs. Its owner anticipates that at the output where $MR = MC$, the firm's total costs will be $500,000, its total variable costs will be $300,000, and the firm will earn $250,000 in revenue. This firm should
   a) raise the price of its hogs.
   b) shut down to minimize its loss.
   c) continue to produce the present output to minimize its loss.
   d) expand its output.

12. Suppose the firms in a purely competitive industry are in a long-run equilibrium when the industry experiences a reduction in demand. Which of the following will occur?
   a) In the short run, firms will earn profits and will expand output; in the long run, additional firms will enter the industry until only a normal profit is earned.
   b) In the short run, firms will incur losses but will continue to produce the same output; in the long run, firms will leave the industry until only a normal profit is earned.
   c) In the short run, firms will earn profits and will contract output; in the long run, firms will leave the industry until the remaining firms can earn an economic profit.
   d) In the short run, firms will incur losses and will contract output; in the long

run, firms will leave the industry until the remaining firms can earn a normal profit.

13. If the firms in an industry are experiencing short-run losses, they should
   a) leave the industry and enter a different, more profitable industry.
   b) continue to operate provided that the prevailing market price is higher than the firm's average variable cost.
   c) shut down and wait for market conditions to improve.
   d) shut down provided that the prevailing market price is less than the firm's average total cost.

14. Suppose that a firm experienced a doubling of its total fixed costs while prevailing market price did not change. Under those conditions the firm would
   a) produce less output and experience lower profits or larger losses.
   b) produce more output and experience higher profits or smaller losses.
   c) produce the same output but experience higher profits or smaller losses.
   d) produce the same output but experience lower profits or larger losses.

15. Which of the following would not cause a competitive firm to increase its output?
   a) An increase in industry demand
   b) A downward shift of the marginal cost curve
   c) An increase in the market price
   d) A wage hike that shifted the marginal cost curve upward

Problems and Questions for Discussion

1. Even when an industry does not meet the first two requirements of pure competition, consumers will still benefit if barriers to entry are low. Why?

2. Complete the following:

QUANTITY	TC	TVC	TFC	MC	ATC
0	$ 50				
1	100				
2	130				
3	180				
4	260				
5	380				

3. One reason for the declining prices of hand-held calculators may be the fat profits earned by early producers. Explain.

4. Can you think of any undesirable aspects of pure competition? From the consumer's standpoint? From the producer's standpoint?

5. Why would a firm continue to operate even though it is incurring a loss? When should it decide to shut down?

6.
QUANTITY	TOTAL COST
0	$ 50
1	100
2	130
3	180
4	260
5	380

If the prevailing price of this firm's product is $50, how many units of output should it produce? Would it earn a profit or incur a loss? How much profit or loss?

7.
QUANTITY	MARGINAL COST
1	$20
2	10
3	30
4	40
5	50

If the prevailing price of our product is $35 and our total fixed costs are $15, how many units of output should we produce? What will be the amount of our profit or loss?

8. Draw the diagrams necessary to show a purely competitive firm and industry in long-run equilibrium.

9. In long-run equilibrium the purely competitive firm is forced to produce where price equals minimum *ATC*. Why is that good news for consumers?

10. What is meant by allocative efficiency? Why must an industry produce at the output where supply is equal to demand for resources to be allocated efficiently.

ANSWER KEY
Fill in the Blanks
1. price taker
2. horizontal
3. fixed, variable
4. fixed
5. Marginal
6. average variable, marginal
7. marginal revenue, marginal cost
8. eliminated, enter
9. exit, supply
10. allocative, production

Multiple Choice
1. c	4. b	7. b	10. c	13. b
2. d	5. a	8. c	11. b	14. d
3. d	6. b	9. b	12. d	15. d

Price Searching: The Firm with Market Power

1. Define market power and discuss its sources.
2. Distinguish between a price searcher and a price taker.
3. Describe a price searcher's demand and marginal revenue curves.
4. Describe how a price searcher determines the profit-maximizing price and output.
5. Define price discrimination, and explain why some firms employ the practice while others do not.
6. Evaluate graphically the extent of a price searcher's profit or loss.
7. Discuss the impact of barriers to entry on the long-run profitability of price searchers.
8. Explain why price searchers distort the allocation of scarce resources.
9. Explain what is meant by economies/diseconomies of scale and how they may influence the number of sellers that survive in a particular industry.

In the world of pure competition the individual firm is a price taker—it has no pricing discretion of its own because price is determined by the impersonal forces of supply and demand. The individual seller manipulates only production output, deciding how much or how little to offer for sale at the given price.

We saw in Chapter 6 that lumber manufacturers, wheat farmers, cattle ranchers, and some other agricultural producers are price takers. However, most sellers in the U.S. economy possess a degree of pricing discretion or **market power**, some ability to influence the market price of their products. In Chapter 7, we examine how firms acquire market power and how these firms select the prices they will charge for their products. We'll explore the circumstances under which firms find it profitable to charge different prices to different customers and discuss why this practice is not universal. We'll discover why some firms with market power are able to earn long-run profits while others are not, and we'll consider how the existence of market power can distort the allocation of scarce resources. The appendix to this chapter goes on to explore some pricing techniques employed by businesses and to evaluate the extent to which these techniques make use of economic theory.

The Acquisition of Market Power

Recalling the plight of the purely competitive firm can help us understand the sources of market power. Consider the situation facing a Kansas wheat farmer. If farmer Brown wants a higher price for wheat, there is little he can do. If he attempts to charge more than the market price, he will sell nothing because his wheat is identical to that offered by other sellers. And he can't drive up wheat prices by planting less (and thereby reducing supply) because his output is only a drop in the bucket and would never be missed.

Most firms are not like Kansas wheat farmers; most firms *are* able to influence price in one or both of these ways. A firm may acquire market power (1) through **product differentiation**, distinguishing its product from similar products offered by other sellers, and/or (2) by gaining control of a significant fraction of total industry output. Sellers with either or both of these abilities can exert some influence on the market price of their product; sellers that possess neither ability are powerless to influence price.

PRODUCT DIFFERENTIATION AS A SOURCE OF MARKET POWER

Product differentiation promotes market power by convincing buyers that a particular firm's product is unique or superior and therefore worth a higher price than the products offered by competitors. By claiming superiority, manufacturers of brand-name aspirin tablets manage to obtain prices that are substantially higher than those charged by sellers of generic and store-brand analgesics. By associating uniqueness with status, the makers of designer-label jeans are able to sell their product at prices much higher than nameless jeans can command.

Sellers can differentiate their products in a wide variety of ways. Some product differentiation is based on real, albeit sometimes slight, product differences; in other cases the essential differentiation is created by advertising and promotional efforts. Both types of product differentiation allow the seller to distinguish its product from the competition and thereby acquire pricing discretion that is not available to the purely competitive firm.

CONTROL OVER SUPPLY AS A SOURCE OF MARKET POWER

Firms that cannot differentiate their products successfully must turn elsewhere to acquire market power. Sellers of standardized commodities such as oil and steel can gain pricing discretion by controlling a significant share of the industry output of that product. As you already know, whenever supply is reduced, price tends to rise. When a firm produces a significant share of the total industry output, it may be able to restrict supply and thereby drive up price.

Controlling supply is a relatively easy matter when an industry is made up of a single firm, **a monopoly**. Under these circumstances, the monopolist's decision alone determines the amount of output for sale. That's the situation, for example, in the case of AZT, the primary drug used in combating AIDS; Glaxo Wellcome's patent on that product gives it a monopoly and the sole right to determine the level of output. But most industries contain more than a single firm, and that makes the task of controlling output more difficult. One firm's decision to supply less (and thereby drive up price) can be offset by another firm's decision to supply more.

Firms that are determined to restrict supply can sometimes avoid these off-setting output decisions through an arrangement known as a *cartel*. A **cartel** is a group of producers acting together to control output (supply) and the price of their product. Although cartels are illegal in the United States (and therefore must be kept secret to avoid prosecution), several international cartels exist and operate in a relatively open manner. Perhaps the best known of these is the Organization of Petroleum Exporting Countries (OPEC). This group of primarily Middle Eastern oil-producing nations attempts to control the output of its members in order to influence the price of oil and maximize their joint profits.[1] In the 1970s the cartel controlled a substantial fraction of the world's oil production and was able to increase prices substantially (from about $2 a barrel to more than $30) by simply cutting back on production. In the early 1980s the cartel's control over price began to slip as conservation reduced the demand for oil and additional supplies were discovered. This, in turn, led to a breakdown in cooperation among OPEC members, a breakdown that has resulted in additional supplies of oil and still lower oil prices. Although OPEC would like to regain the degree of pricing control it enjoyed in the early 1970s, most experts see little chance of this happening. The article on pages 196–197 ,"OPEC's Two Top Exporters Plan to Prod Other Members to Cut Oil Production," looks at some of the problems OPEC faces in attempting to gain greater control over oil prices.[2]

Cartels are not the only method by which groups of firms attempt to limit supply and maintain high prices. In fact, when an industry is

---

[1] OPEC was established in 1960 by Iran, Iraq, Kuwait, Saudi Arabia, and Venezuela. Six more countries have joined the cartel since then: Qatar, Indonesia, Libya, Algeria, Nigeria, and the United Arab Emirates.

[2] While OPEC is probably the best-known example of a cartel, there are others. For instance, the DeBeers diamond cartel controls more than 75% of the world's rough (uncut) diamonds and has used that control to limit supply and maintain high diamond prices. And the Trans-Atlantic Conference—a little-known shipping cartel—sets rates on the tens of billions of dollars of cargo transported by ships. While these cartels have lasted for decades, they are now threatened by new suppliers and defections by the membership. It remains to be seen how they will withstand these pressures.

The local utility company possesses substantial market power, since it is generally the only source of electricity.

composed of just a few firms, an **oligopoly**, the mere recognition that the firms have a joint interest in limiting output may be all that is necessary to promote that behavior. (This possibility is discussed in Chapter 8.) When cartels and voluntary cooperation fail, firms can sometimes elicit government help to control the supply of a product. For instance, U.S. automakers successfully lobbied Congress for restrictions limiting the number of new foreign automobiles permitted into the United States. By limiting supply, these restrictions help domestic producers maintain high prices. Similar campaigns have been responsible for limiting the imports of shoes, peanuts, lumber, and numerous other products, all leading to higher prices for U.S. consumers.

DEGREES OF MARKET POWER

It stands to reason that all firms would like to possess as much market power as possible. But some firms succeed to a greater extent than others. The local telephone company and the local producer of electric power are obvious examples of firms with substantial market power. Here a single firm is the entire industry and has complete control over the industry's output, giving it substantial pricing discretion. Because of the potentially exploitive market power these firms possess, their rates are commonly regulated by state or

Use Your Economic Reasoning

OPEC's Two Top Exporters Plan to Prod Other Members to Cut Oil Production

By Bhushan Bahree and Peter Fritsch

VIENNA—Saudi Arabia and Iran, OPEC's two largest oil exporters, agreed to work together to prod other members to curtail crude production with the goal of raising world oil prices by as much as $4 a barrel.

The unusual alliance resulted from a meeting yesterday between Saudi oil minister Ali Naimi and his Iranian counterpart, Gholamreza Aghazadeh. The two agreed to push other members of the Organization of Petroleum Exporting Countries to cut crude output in response to a nearly 25% drop in world oil prices so far this year, according to OPEC delegates.

Although Kuwait and the United Arab Emirates are expected to support the Saudi-Iranian initiative, a number of other OPEC members have long ignored the group's output restraints and show no signs of changing.

Saudi Arabia and Iran, which together represent about 45% of the group's production, are often at loggerheads on OPEC policy but can be a strong force when they ally themselves. They are expected to argue their case when ministers begin their semiannual meeting today....

Nevertheless, the Saudi-Iranian strategy may not win enough additional converts to succeed.

"Quotas have no real

SOURCE: *Wall Street Journal,* June 27, 1997, Sec. C, p.12. Reprinted by permission of the *Wall Street Journal* © 1997 Dow Jones & Company, Inc. All Rights Reserved Worldwide.

local government agencies in an attempt to protect the public from unreasonable prices.

Few firms possess the potential market power enjoyed by the local phone company. The neighborhood dry-cleaning establishment and the nearby pizzeria also have market power, but not very much. These establishments can charge somewhat higher prices than their competitors because they offer convenient locations and/or slightly different products; but their prices cannot be much higher because their products are very similar. In Chapter 8 we'll take a closer look at the degrees of market power that exist in different types of industries. For now, the important thing to remember is that most firms possess at least some pricing discretion; they are not price takers.

meaning today," a senior Venezuelan official said..., explaining Venezuela's preference for maximizing its share of a fast-growing world oil market....

Venezuela isn't alone in busting its OPEC quota. Other members, such as Nigeria, Qatar and Algeria, also are exceeding their production quotas and pumping flat out. Saudi Arabia and Kuwait are the only two OPEC members that have throttled back their output to adhere to their quotas and prop up world oil prices....

OPEC officials said the Saudi-Iranian initiative, while publicly seeking a full return to quota levels, is based on thinking that even a small reduction in the group's oil output of some 27 million barrels a day will push prices strongly higher in the high-demand second half of the year....

USE YOUR ECONOMIC REASONING

1. Why do Saudi Arabia and Iran want OPEC to curtail crude oil production? Illustrate graphically how their actions might produce the intended result.
2. In order to restrict output to a given level, OPEC member countries are given output quotas (limits), which they are expected to honor. But because the capacity output of the member nations is almost twice the sum of the quotas, the potential for cheating (producing more than the assigned amount) is great. What impact does this cheating have on oil prices?
3. According to the article, Saudi Arabia and Kuwait are the only two OPEC members that have adhered to their quotas. What would happen to oil prices if other OPEC countries could also be convinced to adhere to their quotas?
4. Why do OPEC officials believe that even a small reduction in OPEC oil production will push prices "strongly higher" in the second half of the year? Represent this outcome graphically.

Price Searching

Firms with pricing discretion are sometimes described as **price searchers,** which means that although they have some freedom in setting prices, they still must search for the profit-maximizing price. A price searcher may possess substantial market power (as does the local telephone company) or very little (as does the local pizzeria), but all price searchers have one thing in common: Unlike price takers, which will lose all their customers if they raise their prices, price searchers can charge more and still retain some customers. Conversely, although price takers can sell any quantity they desire at the market price, price searchers must reduce price to sell more.

Consider as a hypothetical example High Tech Inc., a small manufacturer of computer desks. Although a number of firms produce such furniture, we can be sure that if High Tech raises the price of its desks, it won't lose all its customers so long as it keeps its price within reason. Some customers will prefer the quality or design of the High Tech desks to those offered by other sellers. Other customers may be swayed by the firm's product warranty or by its record for prompt delivery. Still others may be influenced by the firm's policy of accepting old desks in trade or by the variety of payment plans it offers. For all these reasons and others, High Tech will still sell some desks despite the price increase. But it won't be able to sell the same quantity; it will have to choose between selling more desks at a lower price or fewer desks at a higher price. That's the fundamental dilemma faced by all price searchers.

THE PRICE SEARCHER'S DEMAND CURVE

Since price searchers have to reduce their prices in order to sell a higher quantity, they must face downward-sloping demand curves, not the horizontal demand curves confronting price takers. Exhibit 7.1 depicts the demand curve facing our hypothetical desk manufacturer. It shows that at $900 a desk, High Tech will sell only three desks each week. At $600 it will sell nine desks a week. Of course, at $200 a desk, sales will be even higher—seventeen desks a week. Although the price searcher can select any price it wants, it cannot choose a high price ($900 a desk) and expect to sell a high quantity (such as seventeen desks a week) because that's not a point on the

---

EXHIBIT 7.1

The Price Searcher's Demand Curve

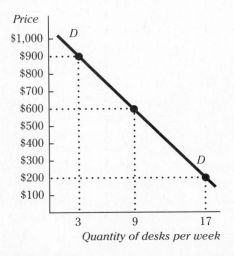

A price searcher can select any price it wants, but it must accept the quantity that results from that price. For example, High Tech can charge $900 per desk and sell three desks each week; it can charge $600 per desk and sell nine desks a week; or it can charge $200 and sell seventeen desks a week.

demand curve. Thus, even a price searcher finds that its actions are con-strained by its demand curve; it cannot choose a price without being locked into a quantity. The firm's task, then, is to decide which of the price-quantity combinations it prefers in order to maximize its profit.

The Profit-Maximization Rule

For a price searcher the profit-maximization rule is essentially the same as it is for a price taker: Produce where marginal revenue equals marginal cost. The difference between a price searcher and a price taker is not in the logic used to maximize profits but in the environment confronting the seller. The price taker has no control over price, and so it uses the profit-maximization rule solely to determine the optimal level of output. The price searcher, on the other hand, uses this rule to determine both output and price.

CALCULATING MARGINAL REVENUE

The first step in determining the profit-maximizing price and quantity is find-ing the price searcher's marginal revenue curve. Because a price searcher faces a downward-sloping demand curve, it must reduce price to sell more. Consequently, the marginal revenue that the price searcher gains by selling an additional unit of output will always be *less* than the selling price of the prod-uct (not equal to the price, as under pure competition), and the firm's mar-ginal revenue curve will lie inside its demand curve. Since this idea is conveyed best with an example, let's consider Exh. 7.2.

The first two columns of Exh. 7.2 represent the demand schedule for desks that was graphed in Exh. 7.1. You can see that at a price of $1,000, only one desk will be sold each week. At a price of $950, two desks will be sold each week, and total revenue would increase to $1,900. What will be the mar-ginal revenue from selling a second desk? (Remember, marginal revenue is the additional revenue gained by selling one more unit.) The correct answer is $900 ($1,900 − $1,000 = $900), $50 less than the $950 selling price. This rela-tionship—marginal revenue being less than price—holds at all price levels.[3] To understand why, we need to consider the price reduction in more detail.

When High Tech reduces the price of executive desks from $1,000 to $950, it allows the first customer—the one who would have paid $1,000—to acquire the product for $950. In return the seller manages to attract an additional cus-tomer who is willing to pay $950 but wouldn't pay $1,000. The marginal rev-enue from the second desk is $900—the $950 the firm gains by selling one more unit *minus* the $50 lost by having to reduce the price on the first unit. Because

---

[3] Note that marginal revenue will always be equal to price for the first unit of output. For all sub-sequent units, marginal revenue will be less than price.

EXHIBIT 7.2

Marginal Revenue for a Price Searcher

PRICE PER UNIT	QUANTITY DEMANDED	TOTAL REVENUE	MARGINAL REVENUE
$1,050	0	$ 0	
1,000	1	1,000	$1,000
950	2	1,900	900
900	3	2,700	800
850	4	3,400	700
800	5	4,000	600
750	6	4,500	500
700	7	4,900	400
650	8	5,200	300
600	9	5,400	200
550	10	5,500	100
500	11	5,500	0
450	12	5,400	−100

marginal revenue is less than price, a price searcher's marginal revenue curve will always lie inside, or below, its demand curve (Exh. 7.3).

THE PROFIT-MAXIMIZING PRICE AND QUANTITY

To maximize its profit (or minimize its loss), High Tech must produce at the output where marginal revenue is equal to marginal cost. This rule permits the firm to continue producing additional units only so long as those units add more to revenue than to costs. Exhibit 7.3 graphs High Tech's demand and marginal revenue curves along with its marginal cost curve. Note that the marginal cost curve has the U-shape introduced in Chapter 6; marginal cost declines initially and then rises as output is increased.

How many desks should High Tech produce and sell in order to maximize its profits? You can tell by studying the graph (or the table accompanying it) that the profit-maximizing (loss-minimizing) output is seven units per week. When output is less than seven units a week, marginal revenue exceeds marginal cost. For instance, the marginal revenue from the fifth unit of output is $600, and the marginal cost of that unit is only $300. Thus, High Tech will be $300 better off if it produces and sells that unit. The sixth unit doesn't make as great a contribution to the firm, but the marginal revenue of $500 still exceeds the marginal cost of

EXHIBIT 7.3

Determining the Profit-Maximizing Price

PRICE PER UNIT	QUANTITY OF DESKS	MARGINAL REVENUE	MARGINAL COST
$800	5	$600	$300
750	6	500	340
700	7	400	400
650	8	300	480
600	9	200	580

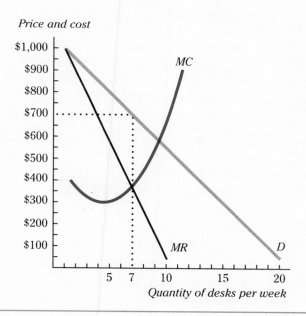

Quantity of desks per week

All firms maximize their profits (or minimize their losses) by producing the output at which marginal revenue is equal to marginal cost. In this example the profit-maximizing output is seven units. Once the profit-maximizing output has been determined, the profit-maximizing price can be discovered by drawing a line directly up to the firm's demand curve and over to the vertical axis. In our example the profit-maximizing price is $700 per desk.

$340, and so the unit should be produced. The seventh unit adds $400 to revenue and $400 to cost; thus, seven units represents the profit-maximizing (loss-minimizing) output: the output at which *MR* = *MC*. Because all subsequent units would add more to cost than to revenue, their sale would either reduce the firm's profit or increase its loss.[4]

---

[4] In this example the firm will earn the same profit (or incur the same loss) whether it sells six or seven units of output. The firm wants to operate where *MR* = *MC*, not because it benefits from the last unit sold but because it benefits from each unit up to that point.

Once the profit-maximizing output has been determined, the profit-maximizing price can be discovered by drawing a line directly up to the firm's demand curve and over to the vertical axis. Remember, the demand curve shows the amount that consumers are willing to purchase at various prices. If we know the price, we can tell how much will be purchased. Conversely, if we know the quantity (output), we can use the demand curve to determine the maximum price the firm can charge and still sell that amount of output. In our example High Tech should charge a price of $700 per desk; that's the firm's profit-maximizing price.[5]

A DIGRESSION ON PRICE DISCRIMINATION

In the preceding example we have assumed that there is a single profit-maximizing price, and we'll return to that assumption in just a moment. But in some instances there is more than one profit-maximizing price. *Price discrimination* exists when firms charge different consumers different prices for the same product.

Surgeons and lawyers and car dealers often practice "individual" price discrimination. They charge virtually every customer a different price, a price based largely on the customer's ability to pay (but limited, at least in the case of automobiles, by how much that customer has "shopped around" and become informed about the prices charged elsewhere). To illustrate, suppose that Honest John's Autos is selling the Rampage automobile. Assume also that the following represents a portion of the demand schedule for Honest John's automobiles.

PRICE	QUANTITY
$20,000	1
19,000	2
18,000	3
17,000	4
16,000	5

As you can see, only one consumer is willing to pay Honest John $20,000 for a Rampage. A second consumer won't pay $20,000 but is willing to pay $19,000. (Note that two consumers are willing to buy automobiles at a price of $19,000; one is the first consumer, who would pay $20,000.[6]) A third consumer won't pay $19,000 but will pay $18,000.

Car dealers that practice price discrimination want their sales personnel to obtain the highest price that each consumer will pay. So the salesperson would

---

[5] In many real-world situations, firms do not possess precise information about their demand and marginal cost curves, and so they find it difficult to employ the $MC = MR$ pricing rule in precisely the manner described here. The appendix to this chapter, "Pricing in Practice," examines the pricing techniques employed by these firms.
[6] This assumes that each consumer buys only one automobile.

try to extract $20,000 from the first customer, $19,000 from the second, $18,000 from the third, and so on. Honest John would be willing to continue selling additional units as long as the price he could obtain was at least equal to the marginal cost of an additional vehicle. (Notice that when firms discriminate, the marginal revenue the firm receives from the sale of an additional unit is *equal* to its selling price, not less than its selling price as it was for the nondiscriminating price searcher.) For instance, if the marginal cost of an additional Rampage is $16,500, Honest John would be willing to sell the fourth vehicle (which adds $17,000 to his revenue) but not the fifth (which contributes only $16,000).

It is unlikely that the salesperson would actually be able to obtain the maximum price a consumer would be willing to pay. But effective sales personnel may come close. Sales reps who started at the sticker price on the vehicle and then haggle, giving in only when necessary, might approximate this solution. And, of course, that would mean more profit for the dealer than could be obtained by selling all four of these vehicles at a price low enough to convince the fourth buyer to participate.

Another form of price discrimination is "group" price discrimination. This is a situation in which a firm charges different prices to different *categories* of consumers. For example, movie theaters commonly charge different ticket prices to adults, students, and senior citizens. And we'd all like to order from the children's menu when we're short on cash. Even telephone companies practice price discrimination, charging one price for long-distance service during the day (when most calls are business-related) and a lower price in the evening (when we make our personal calls).

The purpose of group price discrimination is similar to the purpose of individual price discrimination—to obtain the highest price possible from each category of consumer. Consider, for instance, the different ticket prices that airlines charge business and vacation travelers. The airlines recognize that business travelers usually *must* travel by air; they cannot afford the time involved in a lengthy automobile trip. In addition, many of these trips arise on short notice, so the business executive has no other alternative. These factors mean that the business traveler's demand curve for plane travel is less elastic—less price-sensitive—than the vacation traveler, who usually has a more flexible time schedule. By charging business travelers higher fares, the airlines maximize their profits from that group without discouraging travel by vacationers.[7] (Some colleges and universities are emulating the pricing practices of the airlines. Read "Colleges Manipulate Financial Aid Offers...," on pages 204–206, to learn how price discrimination is being used to determine financial aid and the tuition you are required to pay.)

---

[7] Airlines separate business and vacation travelers by requiring that the lower-priced tickets (intended for vacationers) be purchased well in advance and/or that the traveler stay over at least one Saturday night before returning. These are requirements that most business travelers are unable or unwilling to meet.

Use Your Economic Reasoning

Colleges Manipulate Financial-Aid Offers, Shortchanging Many

Early Admittees and Others Are Eager, So Schools Figure They'll Pay More

By Steve Stecklow
Staff Reporter of the Wall Street Journal

Peter Anderson, a freshman at Johns Hopkins University in Baltimore, may have made a costly mistake: He told the school that he planned to be a premed major.

The problem is, Johns Hopkins already has plenty of premed majors. It wanted more humanities majors. And so in an experiment last spring, it quietly offered fatter financial-aid grants to incoming humanities majors than to most of their premed counterparts. While Peter is getting $14,000 a year, he might have snared about $3,000 more if he planned to major in, say, art history....

The Anxiety Factor

Johns Hopkins's bold experiment is being tried out at colleges all over the country. At these schools, grants no longer are based overwhelmingly on a student's demonstrated financial need, but also on his or her "price sensitivity" to college costs, calculated from dozens of factors that all add up to one thing: how anxious the student is to attend. The more eager the student—and Hopkins is high on the list for premed majors like Peter—the less aid they can expect to get. Although students and families awaiting word of college admissions this week aren't being told, these colleges are employing some of the same "yield management" techniques used to price and fill airline seats and hotel rooms.

The statistical models, which have become widespread only in the past few years, go by innocuous names like "financial aid leveraging." But they are quietly transforming the size and shape of student bodies in all sorts of ways, some of which are alarming educators. A sampling:

• The Johns Hopkins model—which the school isn't currently using but may try again in the future—suggested slashing aid to some prospects who came for on-campus interviews. The reason: Those students are statistically more likely to enroll, so need less aid to entice them. A school official now denies putting that part of the model into practice.

At Pittsburgh's Carnegie Mellon University and other schools, eager freshmen accepted through the early-admissions program can end up with less financial aid than comparable students who apply later. "If finances are a concern, you shouldn't be applying any place for an early decision," says William F. Elliott, vice president for enrollment....

A New Buzzword

The schools argue that the new financial-aid engineering is necessary at a time when tuitions are high and many private schools don't have enough aid to go around. The complex computer modeling, they say, is designed to help them get the kind of students they want without giving away too much of their own money—since aid grants are, after all, a form of price discounting.

About 60% of the nation's 1,500 private four-year college now use statistical analysis "in some form" to dole out aid, estimates Steven T. Syverson, dean of admissions and financial aid at Lawrence University in Appleton, Wis. "Maximizing revenue is the buzzword of educational administrators these days," explains Jon Boeckenstedt, St. Bonaventure's dean of enrollment management. He concedes "there are some inequities certainly operating" at his school, but adds, "I would challenge anyone to come up with a system that's always fair and always equitable...."

Colleges, of course, have always offered their most attractive aid packages to their hottest prospects, such as athletes or especially gifted students. But the sophisticated computer analyses that so many schools use now didn't start until about 15 years ago, and didn't become widespread until 1992.

That year, Congress liberalized the federal formula for calculating financial need, making most families eligible for more aid. Unfortunately, the government didn't provide extra federal funds to pay for all that extra aid. Colleges were forced either to boost their own financial-aid budgets, or to offer aid more selectively. Many chose the latter path, out of necessity.

Beyond Pure Need

To achieve their ends, these schools still start by calculating a student's demonstrated "need"—determined by family income, assets and debt. Instead of stopping there, though, some schools then factor in dozens of variables that affect a student's propensity to attend the college once he or she is accepted. The higher the propensity, the less financial aid the student may expect. Factors can include a student's home state, ethnic background and area of study, and who initiated the first contact with the school.

"Those who have the most interest in the school are going to be less price sensitive," explains Stephen H. Brooks, a Waltham, Mass., consultant who has performed statistical analyses for about two dozen schools, including Johns Hopkins, New York University, Rochester Institute of Technology, and Hobart and William Smith colleges....

Dr. Brooks offers this advice to families: "If you go into the showroom and say you want to have that red Corvette, they're not going to cut the price much. I would say being a little cagey would be helpful."

Johns Hopkins turned to Dr. Brooks last year when it wanted to increase its humanities enrollment by 20% and reduce its overcrowded premed program. At a Nasfaa conference in San Antonio last summer, a Hopkins official explained how the school achieved its goal by using an econometric model, a mathematical analysis that tries to predict down to the dollar what it will cost to persuade a student to enroll.

The model suggested that Hopkins should offer $3,000 more to prospective humanities students with Scholastic Assessment Test scores over 1,200 and relatively low financial-aid needs; the extra money would increase enrollment probability by nine percentage points. One group of students, the model suggested, shouldn't get the extra cash: those who had had campus interviews, a step Hopkins itself "strongly" recommends. Campus interviewees already were about 9% more likely to enroll at Hopkins than other prospects, so the cash incentive wasn't necessary,

(continued on next page)

(continued from previous page)

concluded the analysis, which was based on two years of past enrollment data.

The model also suggested cutting by $1,000 the aid offers to most premed campus interviewees with SAT scores below 1,300. Those students were already hooked, so "it wouldn't knock that many students out. But it would increase the net revenue from this group," explained Robert J. Massa, the school's dean of enrollment management.

Parents in the Dark

"So let's look at the results," said Dr. Massa, as he displayed a bar chart on an overhead projector. "In fact, what we wanted to happen

did happen." Humanities students increased "by exactly 20%" while the premed group dropped "by about 10"

students, he said. He stressed, however, that the analysis was "just one tool," not "the sole path."...

USE YOUR ECONOMIC REASONING

1. Are these colleges practicing individual or group price discrimination? Defend your conclusion.
2. Airlines charge higher prices to the travelers with the less elastic demand. Is that the approach being used by colleges; are college students with less elastic demand being charged higher tuition (receiving less financial aid)?
3. Dr. Brooks advises students to be "a little cagey" in applying to colleges. Why is he making this suggestion?

Why doesn't everyone practice price discrimination? There are two primary reasons. First, it takes time, and time is money. Think about our car dealer again. It can take hours for the salesperson to negotiate with a customer and arrive at the price that particular customer will pay. That time expenditure makes sense in the case of big-ticket items such as cars and motor homes and boats. But it doesn't make sense for milk and clothing and most of the items we buy every day.

A second reason why firms may not practice price discrimination is that they may be unable to prevent consumers from reselling items that they can buy more cheaply than other customers. For instance, suppose that the Ajax TV Center was charging regular customers $300 for a TV set but allowing senior citizens to buy the same set for $250. Under these circumstances we might expect to see some seniors buying TV sets in large quantities and reselling them at a profit. That would be a nice way for those senior citizens to earn extra cash, but it would make it very difficult for Ajax to sell any television sets at the higher price. The point is that when we can't prevent a product's resale, we generally offer that product at the same price to everyone. Because most markets are characterized by uniform pricing, we will now return to our single-price model.

Evaluating the Short-Run Profit or Loss

As we discovered in Chapter 6, producing where $MR = MC$ does not ensure a profit. It ensures only that the firm will do as well as possible in any short-run situation. Recall that we find profits by subtracting total costs from total revenue. In our present example we can't tell whether High Tech Inc. is earning a profit or incurring a loss because we've focused entirely on marginal values.

To compute High Tech's short-run profit or loss, we need to know the firm's total revenue and its total costs. Exhibit 7.4 shows our hypothetical price searcher in three different situations. In case (a) the firm is earning a profit. As in the previous chapter, the amount of the profit can be determined by comparing total revenue with total cost. Total revenue is equal to $4,900 (the $700 selling price $\times$ 7 units—the profit-maximizing output). Total cost is equal to $4,200 (the *ATC* of $600 $\times$ 7 units). This leaves the firm with an economic profit of $700 ($4,900 $-$ $4,200 = $700).

Case (b) finds our price searcher earning only a normal profit. You can see in the diagram that the *MC* curve intersects the *MR* curve at an output of six desks. At that output the profit-maximizing price would be $600, so that total revenue would be $3,600 ($600 $\times$ 6 units). Since the *ATC* curve is tangent to the demand curve at $600, *ATC* must also be $600 when the firm is producing six desks. Therefore, the firm's total cost is $3,600 (the *ATC* of $600 $\times$ 6 units). This means that the firm is earning zero economic profit ($3,600 $-$ $3,600 = $0), or a normal profit. Recall that a normal profit is acceptable; the owners of the business are earning as much as they could expect to earn if they invested their time and money elsewhere.

Case (c) depicts the price searcher facing a short-run economic loss (earning less than a normal profit). At the profit-maximizing (loss-minimizing) output of five desks, the firm's total cost of $3,250 (*ATC* of $650 $\times$ 5 units) exceeds its total revenue of $2,750 (the $550 selling price $\times$ 5 units). This results in a loss of $500 ($3,250 $-$ $2,750 = $500). Note, however, that the selling price of $550 exceeds the firm's average variable cost of approximately $500, and so the firm should continue to operate rather than shut down. Since P exceeds *AVC* by $50, each of the five units produced will contribute $50 toward paying the firm's fixed costs. Through continued operation, the firm reduces its loss by $250. Of course, if *AVC* exceeded price (for example, if the average variable cost curve were positioned where the *ATC* curve is located at present), the firm would minimize its loss by shutting down.

EXHIBIT 7.4

Calculating the Short-Run Profit or Loss

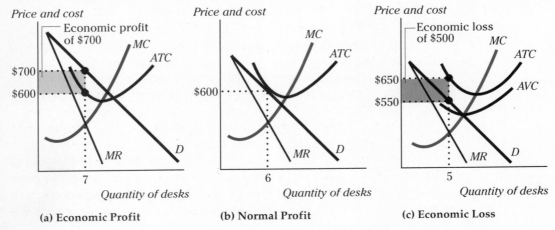

(a) Economic Profit   (b) Normal Profit   (c) Economic Loss

Case (a): When the profit-maximizing price is above *ATC*, the price searcher will earn an economic profit. Case (b): When the price is exactly equal to *ATC*, the price searcher will earn a zero economic profit, or a normal profit. Case (c): When the price is less than *ATC*, the firm will incur an economic loss—it will earn less than a normal profit.

Barriers to Entry and Long-Run Profits

We've seen that in the short run, price searchers may gain economic profits, may earn a normal profit, may even sustain a loss. But how do they do in the long run? Is it possible for price searchers to earn economic profits in the long run, or is a normal profit the best that can be expected? (All firms, whether price searchers or price takers, must earn at least a normal profit in the long run, or the owners will sell out and reinvest their money where a normal return is possible.)

If a price searcher is earning an economic profit in the short run, its ability to continue earning that profit in the long run depends on the extent of the barriers to entering that industry. Recall from Chapter 6 that barriers to entry are obstacles that discourage or prevent firms from entering an industry. These obstacles include patent restrictions, large investments requirements, and restrictive licensing regulations.

Some price searchers exist in industries with substantial entry barriers—prescription medicine and aircraft manufacturing, for example. Others exist in industries with very modest barriers—shoe retailing, fast photo processing, and dry-cleaning establishments, to cite a few. Because entry barriers differ from industry to industry, we can't generalize about the long-run fate of price searchers as we could about the fate of price takers. (Recall that a normal profit is the *best* that a price taker can expect in the long run. Because there are no significant barriers to entering purely competitive industries, any short-run profits will be eliminated in the long run, as additional firms enter and drive down prices.)

If price searchers are protected by substantial barriers to entry, short-run profits can turn into long-run profits. For instance, it is estimated that Hoffman-La Roche of Switzerland earned multi*billion* dollar profits from the world-wide sale of its Valium and Librium tranquilizers, drugs that were protected by patents and therefore could not be duplicated by competitors.[8] Although profits of this magnitude are clearly exceptional, they indicate the impact of entry barriers. In the absence of substantial barriers, we expect economic profits to attract additional sellers into the market. This leads to price cutting and other forms of competition that have the potential to eliminate economic profits in the long run.

Thus, the fact that a price searcher earns above-normal profits in the short run is no assurance that it will be able to do so in the long run. Unless entry barriers exist, the entrance of additional firms will result in added competition for consumers' dollars and subsequent elimination of all economic profits.

Price Searchers and Resource Allocation

Consumers are obviously better off when low entry barriers ensure low prices and low profits. But the profits earned by Hoffman-La Roche and other price searchers are not the primary social concern of economists. After all, high prices harm consumers, but they benefit stockholders and others who own businesses. So, we can't say that the entire society is harmed by barriers to entry. A more serious concern is the inefficient allocation of resources that results from the presence of market power.

Recall from Chapter 6 that an efficient allocation of resources requires that each product be produced up to the point at which the marginal social benefit that the product provides is exactly equal to its marginal social cost. Marginal social benefit can be determined from the industry demand curve, and marginal social cost from the marginal cost curve. If all production is

[8] F. M. Scherer, *Industrial Market Structure and Economic Performance*, 2d ed. (Chicago: Rand McNally, 1980), p. 449.

continued up to the point at which the demand curve is intersected by the marginal cost curve, we can be assured that society's scarce resources are being used to produce the mix of products that consumers value most.[9]

When pure competition exists, production is automatically expanded to the allocatively efficient level. But that's not the case when firms possess market power. Price searchers distort the allocation of scarce resources because they do not allow production to continue up to the point at which the marginal social benefit (*MSB*) is equal to the marginal social cost (*MSC*). To do so would cause these firms to earn a smaller profit. Consider Exh. 7.5. The profit-maximizing price searcher will produce where *MR* intersects *MC*, at seven units in this example. At that output, marginal revenue and marginal cost are equal. But if you move upward in the exhibit from seven units of output to the demand (or marginal benefit) curve, you find that price is equal to $700. This tells us that consumers derive $700 worth of benefit from the seventh unit of output, even though its marginal cost is only $400. In short, consumers

---

[9]As we noted in Chapter 6, this conclusion assumes no spillover costs or benefits associated with the production or consumption of the products in question.

EXHIBIT 7.5

Price Searchers and Resource Misallocation

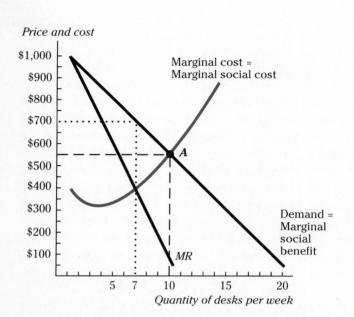

Allocative efficiency requires that production take place at the output where the demand curve intersects the marginal cost curve, an output of ten units in this example. But the profit-maximizing price searcher will produce where *MR* = *MC*, an output of seven units. By restricting output, price searchers fail to provide consumers with the optimal quantity of this product and misdirect resources to the production of less-valued goods and services.

value this unit of output more highly than the alternative products that could be produced with the same resources. The same is true of the eighth and ninth units of output; marginal benefit exceeds marginal cost for each of those units.

An efficient allocation of resources would require the price searcher to produce at the output where the marginal cost curve intersects the demand (marginal benefit) curve (see point A in Exh. 7.5). If our hypothetical price searcher produced ten units of output and charged a price of $550 (so that $P = MC$), resources would be allocated efficiently. But that won't happen because expanding output in this manner would cause the firm to earn a smaller profit. Note that for each unit beyond seven (the profit-maximizing output), marginal cost *exceeds* marginal revenue. Production of these additional units would be allocatively efficient but would lower the firm's total profit. And since it is the pursuit of profits that drives businesses (and not the goal of allocative efficiency), we can be sure that output will be expanded only to the profit-maximizing level.

In summary, price searchers distort the allocation of scarce resources by producing too little output and thereby forcing resources to be used in the production of less-valued products. In response to this resource misallocation, the federal government has employed a variety of means to encourage competition or correct for the negative impact of market power.

Price Searchers and Economies of Scale

Although price searchers do not achieve allocative efficiency, there may be instances in which this shortcoming is counterbalanced by lower production costs than could be achieved by price takers. This possibility exists when *economies of scale* occur in the production process

Economies of scale are reductions in the average cost of production that occur as a firm expands its size of plant and scale output. As you learned in Chapter 4, all inputs are variable in the long run; firms can build larger (or smaller) production facilities and can enter or leave an industry. In some instances the construction of larger production facilities can lead to lower average production cost (average total cost). When this is the case, the long-run average total cost ($LRATC$) curve of the firm slopes downward as in Exh. 7.6. Under these circumstances "bigger is better." Larger firms, producing larger quantities of output per period, will be able to achieve lower average costs than smaller firms.

Larger firms may be able to achieve lower costs for a variety of reasons. As firms build larger facilities and expand output, they can justify specialized equipment and personnel that would not make sense for a smaller firm producing less output. For instance, large manufacturers of men's shirts can justify million dollar pieces of equipment that do nothing but sew collars. They can justify this expense because the machine sews collars very quickly

EXHIBIT 7.6

Economies of Scale

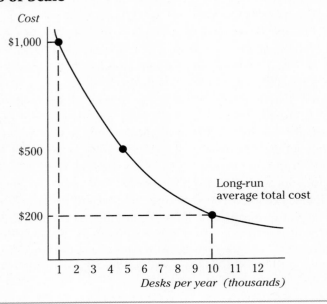

Economies of scale cause the firm's long-run total cost curve to slope downward.

and with few errors. This saves on the labor cost of performing this operation when compared to the less-sophisticated equipment and more labor-intensive technique that would be employed by a smaller firm. Of course, this saving occurs only if the machine can be kept busy so that its cost can be spread over millions of shirts. That's why only larger firms opt for this approach. Smaller firms are forced to stick with more labor-intensive processes that generally mean higher average costs. High volume also allows firms to achieve greater specialization of labor than firms producing less output. For example, our large shirt manufacturer may be able to justify employing a crew of workers whose sole job is the maintenance of equipment, and a different crew whose sole task is stocking the factory with supplies. By allowing these workers to concentrate on a single task, the firm enables them to become better at their jobs, which results in fewer errors and reduces the time necessary to perform each task. In short, more specialized equipment and greater specialization of labor may allow larger firms to produce their products at lower average costs than smaller firms, whose size makes these options uneconomical.

The importance of economies of scale varies from industry to industry. In some industries large firms have substantially lower average costs than small firms; in others the difference is insignificant. Similarly, there are industries in which the advantages of size continue indefinitely and others in which they are quickly exhausted. When the long-run average total cost curve declines indefinitely, as it does in Exh. 7.6, it is always cheaper for a single firm (a monopolist) to serve the industry. Note that a single firm can produce an industry output of 10,000 desks at an average cost of $200, whereas if there were ten firms sharing the same market, average cost would rise to $1,000. When a market is most cheaply served by a single firm, it is described as a **natural monopoly**. This is a situation in which the benefits to society of lower production costs may outweigh the harm caused by a price searcher's tendency to restrict output below the allocatively efficient level.

If the cost curve depicted in Exh. 7.6 were commonplace, the U.S. economy would be largely populated by monopolies. But that's not the case; monopoly is relatively rare in our economy. That's because most long-run average cost curves don't decline indefinitely; they eventually turn up. The cost curve depicted in Exh 7.7 displays economies of scale up to point *A* (an output of 1,000 units) and *diseconomies of scale* beyond that point. **Diseconomies of scale** are increases in the average cost of production stemming from larger plant size and scale of output; they cause the long-run average total cost curve to turn upward, as it does to the right of point *A*. The major source of diseconomies of scale is the difficulty of managing a large enterprise. When organizations become very large, it becomes difficult to maintain the communication and information flows necessary to coordinate such enterprises. This results in long delays and inappropriate decisions, which raise the

EXHIBIT 7.7

Economies of Scale

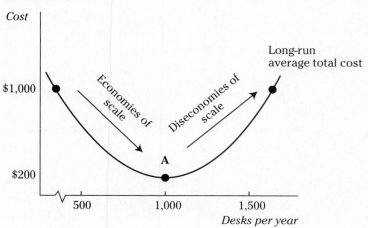

Long-run average costs decline as a result of economies of scale and increase as a result of diseconomies of scale.

average cost of production, causing the long-run average total cost curve to turn upward.

When a firm experiences both economies and diseconomies of scale, bigger is better but only up to a point. The firm's *LRATC* curve will have the U shape depicted in Exh. 7.7. Under these conditions the degree of competition that is likely to emerge in the industry depends on both the optimal size of the firm (the output at which the *LRATC* curve is at a minimum) and the total demand for the industry's product. In our hypothetical example, for instance, if consumers are willing to purchase 100,000 desks at $200 (a price that would provide a normal profit), this industry could support 100 optimal-sized firms (100,000/1,000 = 100), and so it would tend to be highly competitive. But if consumers were willing to purchase only 3,000 desks at that price, the industry could supply only three optimal-sized firms and would be likely to develop into an oligopoly. Although more competition is generally preferred to less, under these circumstances oligopoly would probably be preferable to a more competitive industry structure because insisting on a large number of firms would require each firm to be too small to achieve significant scale economies.[10]

In summary, when firms must be relatively large in order to achieve economies of scale, consumers may be better off with one firm or a few large firms, even though this means an absence of competition. Under these circumstances the advantages of lower production costs (and lower prices) may more than compensate for any allocative inefficiency resulting from the limited number of competitors.

Summary

In most U.S. industries, individual firms have some pricing discretion, or *market power*. A firm may acquire market power either through *product differentiation*—distinguishing its product from similar products offered by other sellers—or by gaining control of a significant fraction of total industry output. Firms with either or both of these abilities can exert some influence on the market price of their product.

Sellers with pricing discretion are described as *price searchers* because they must search for the profit-maximizing price. All price searchers face demand curves that slope downward and to the right. Unlike the price taker, which can sell as much as it desires at the market price, the price searcher has to reduce price to sell more. Therefore, the price searcher is forced to choose between selling a lower quantity at a higher price or selling a higher quantity at a lower price.

---

[10] If the oligopolists enjoy substantial economies of scale, they may be able to earn economic profits and still charge a lower price than would prevail if the industry were composed of a large number of firms, each too small to achieve significant economies of scale.

Because price must be reduced to sell more, the marginal revenue the price searcher obtains from selling an additional unit of output is always less than the unit's selling price, and the price searcher's marginal revenue curve lies inside its demand curve. The price searcher can determine the profit-maximizing (loss-minimizing) level of output by equating marginal revenue and marginal cost. The profit-maximizing price can then be discovered by drawing a line directly up from the quantity to the firm's demand curve and over to the vertical (price) axis.

Some price searchers are able to enlarge their profits by practicing price discrimination. *Price discrimination* is charging different consumers different prices for the same product. When firms engage in individual price discrimination, they attempt to charge each consumer the maximum price he or she will pay. Group price discrimination results when firms charge different prices to different categories of consumers.

Like price takers, price searchers must determine the amount of their profit or loss by comparing total revenue and total cost. If total revenue exceeds total cost, the price searcher is earning an economic profit; if total cost exceeds total revenue, the firm is incurring an economic loss. When total revenue is exactly equal to total cost, the firm is earning a normal profit.

Although a normal profit is the most a price taker can hope to earn in the long run, a price searcher may be able to do better. When price searchers are protected by substantial barriers to entry, they may continue to earn long-run economic profits.

The possibility of long-run profits is not the only outcome that distinguishes price searchers from price takers. In addition, price searchers fail to achieve allocative efficiency. Allocative efficiency requires that producers expand output up to the point at which the marginal social benefit of the last unit produced is exactly equal to its marginal social cost. Price searchers stop short of that point; that is, they produce less output than is socially desirable.

Although price searchers fail to achieve allocative efficiency, there may be instances in which this shortcoming is counterbalanced by the ability to achieve *economies of scale. Economies* of scale are reductions in the average cost of production that occur when a firm expands its plant size and the scale of its output. When economies of scale continue indefinitely, the market will always be most cheaply served by a single firm. This situation is termed a *natural monopoly.* Natural monopolies are rare. In most instances, long-run costs decline initially but eventually turn up as a result of *diseconomies of scale.*

When a production process exhibits both economies and diseconomies of scale, the firm's long-run average total cost curve will be U-shaped; it will decline initially but will eventually turn upward. Under these circumstances the degree of competition that is likely to emerge in the industry depends on both the optimal size of the firm and the total demand for the industry's product. When the optimal size of the firm is relatively large, consumers may be better off with a few large firms that are able to achieve all economies of scale, even though this means less competition.

GLOSSARY

Cartel. A group of producers acting together to control output and the price of their product.

Diseconomies of scale. Increases in the average cost of production caused by larger plant size and scale of output.

Economies of scale. Reductions in the average cost of production caused by larger plant size and scale of output.

Market power. Pricing discretion; the ability of a firm to influence the market price of its product.

Monopoly. An industry characterized by a single firm selling a product for which there are no close substitutes and by substantial barriers to entry.

Natural monopoly. A situation in which a single firm can supply the entire market at a lower average cost than two or more firms could.

Oligopoly. An industry characterized by relatively few large sellers and substantial barriers to entry.

Price discrimination. The practice of charging different consumers different prices for the same product.

Price searcher. A firm that possesses pricing discretion.

Product differentiation. Distinguishing a product from similar products offered by other sellers in the industry through advertising, packaging, or physical product differences.

STUDY QUESTIONS
Fill in the Blanks

1. Firms that possess pricing discretion are sometimes described as _price searchers_.

2. _Product differentiation_ creates market power by convincing buyers that a particular product is unique and superior.

3. A price searcher maximizes profit by equating _marginal cost_ and _marginal revenue_.

4. For a price searcher, marginal revenue is (greater/less) _less_ than price.

5. In the short run, a price searcher that is incurring a loss will continue to operate rather than shut down, provided that price is greater than _average variable_ cost.

6. A price searcher will not be able to earn economic profits in the long run unless _barriers to entry_ exist.

7. A price searcher would achieve allocative efficiency if it produced at the output where the _demand_ curve intersects the marginal cost curve.

8. Price searchers will not choose to produce the allocatively efficient level of output because doing so would reduce their _profit_.

9. A _natural monopoly_ is a situation in which a market is most cheaply served by a single firm.

10. If the long-run average cost curve of a firm is U-shaped, we know that the firm initially experiences _economies_ of scale, and ultimately experiences _diseconomies_ of scale.

Multiple Choice

1. Which of the following would probably *not* be a price searcher?
   a) The local utility company
   b) A Kansas wheat farmer
   c) General Motors
   d) A local movie theater

2. All price searchers
   a) face downward-sloping demand curves.
   b) must reduce price to sell more.
   c) can raise their prices without losing all their customers.
   d) possess some pricing discretion.
   e) All of the above

3. Both price searchers and price takers
   a) must produce homogeneous products.
   b) produce where $MR = MC$ to maximize profits.
   c) face horizontal demand curves.
   d) must earn normal profits in the long run.

4. If a price searcher is operating where MR exceeds MC,
   a) it is producing the profit-maximizing output.
   b) it is producing too much to maximize profits.
   c) it is producing too little to maximize profits.
   d) None of the above is true.

   Use the exhibit following question 7 to answer questions 5–7.

5. To maximize its profit or minimize its loss, this price searcher should
   a) produce six units and charge a price of $50.
   b) produce six units and charge a price of $110.
   c) produce eight units and charge a price of $90.
   d) produce nine units and charge a price of $80.

6. This price searcher is
   a) incurring a loss of $180.
   b) earning a normal profit.

   c) earning a profit of $360.
   d) earning a profit of $180.

7. Allocative efficiency would require this firm to
   a) produce seven and one-half units of output and charge a price of $78.
   b) produce eight units and charge a price of $90.
   c) produce six units and charge a price of $50.
   d) None of the above

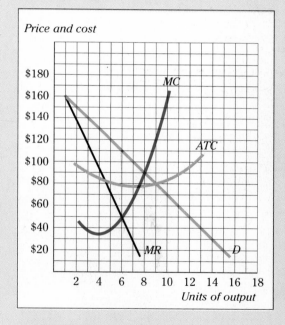

8. If a price searcher's fixed costs have increased,
   a) the firm's profit-maximizing quantity will increase.
   b) the firm's profit-maximizing quantity will not change.
   c) the firm's profit-maximizing quantity will decline.
   d) the firm will operate at a loss.

9. Sonic Waterbeds faces a traditional downward-sloping demand curve (included below), but its marginal cost curve is a

horizontal straight line at a height of $600. In other words, marginal costs are constant at $600. How many units should Sonic sell, and what price should it charge to maximize profit?

PRICE (per bed)	QUANTITY (per day)
$1,000	1
900	2
800	3
700	4
600	5
500	6

a) One unit at $1,000
b) Two units at $900
c) Three units at $800
d) Four units at $700
e) Five units at $600

10. If the waterbed retailer described in question 9 was able to practice individual price discrimination, it would sell _____ waterbeds and earn a profit of _____ dollars on the last waterbed sold.
   a) 3, 200
   b) 4, 200
   c) 5, 0
   d) 6, 0

11. When firms practice group price discrimination, they tend to charge higher prices to consumers
   a) whose demand is more elastic.
   b) who are more price-sensitive.
   c) whose demand is less elastic.
   d) who do comparison shopping.

12. When a price searcher produces the output level at which marginal revenue is equal to marginal cost, it is
   a) maximizing its profit and producing the allocatively efficient level of output.
   b) maximizing its profit but producing more than the allocatively efficient level of output.
   c) maximizing its profit but producing less than the allocatively efficient level of output.

   d) producing less than the profit-maximizing output.

13. Imagine a situation in which a firm experienced diseconomies of scale immediately. The long-run average total cost curve would be
   a) U-shaped.
   b) downward-sloping.
   c) upward-sloping.
   d) a horizontal straight line.

14. Imagine a long-run average cost curve that is U-shaped and has its minimum at 5,000 units of output and an average cost of $10. Under those conditions this industry would be
   a) a natural monopoly if only 5,000 units were demanded at $10 but highly competitive if 10,000 units were demanded at that price.
   b) an oligopoly if only 5,000 units were demanded at $10 but highly competitive if 10,000 units were demanded at that price.
   c) highly competitive if 10,000 units were demanded at $10.
   d) a natural monopoly if only 5,000 units were demanded at $10 but highly competitive if 500,000 units were demanded at that price.

Problems and Questions for Discussion

1. The price searcher's price and output decisions are one and the same. Explain.

2. Explain how product differentiation conveys market power.

3. Why is marginal revenue less than price for a price searcher? Illustrate with an example.

4. From time to time, farmers have attempted to form organizations to restrict the amount of corn and other grains being planted. What is the real intent of these organizations, and why do you think they have been largely ineffective in achieving their objective?

5. Why do cartels need cooperation of their members to ensure high prices? How can cheating—selling more output than permitted, for example—undermine a cartel?

6. Why should consumers be concerned about barriers to entry?

7. Both price searchers and price takers produce at the output where $MR = MC$. Yet price takers achieve allocative efficiency, whereas price searchers do not. Explain.

8. Suppose that a price searcher finds itself incurring a short-run loss. How should it decide whether to shut down or continue to operate? What would the price searcher's graph look like if it was in a shut-down situation?

9. If the long-run average total cost curve always slopes downward, bigger is better and the industry will probably develop into a monopoly. What do you suppose it would mean if the firm's long-run cost curve was horizontal? Would big firms be able to drive the small ones out of business? Would large firms be at a disadvantage?

10. If the firm's long-run average total cost curve is U-shaped the industry could be a monopoly or purely competitive or even an oligopoly. We can't tell from the information given. What additional information is needed, and how would we use it to determine the degree of competition in this industry?

ANSWER KEY

Fill in the Blanks

1. price searchers
2. Product differentiation
3. marginal cost, marginal revenue
4. less
5. average variable
6. barriers to entry
7. demand
8. profit
9. natural monopoly
10. economies, diseconomies

Multiple Choice

1. b
2. e
3. b
4. c
5. b
6. d
7. b
8. b
9. c
10. c
11. c
12. c
13. c
14. d

APPENDIX: Pricing in Practice

Pricing in Practice

A firm's day-to-day pricing techniques may differ somewhat from the theoretically correct-pricing practices that we have discussed thus far. This difference stems in part from the fact that firms are frequently guided by motives other than profit maximization. Ethical considerations, for example, may result in the pursuit of a "satisfactory" profit rather than a maximum profit. The quest for prestige is another motive that may cause the firm or its managers to maximize sales or market share, subject to some minimum profit constraint.[11] Firms pursuing objectives such as these will not select the price at which *MR=MC*. For instance, if a firm wants to maximize sales, it will choose a lower price than the one that maximizes profit to encourage additional customers to buy the product.

Even those firms motivated by the pursuit of maximum profit may find it difficult to employ the *MR=MC* rule in precisely the manner we've described. In most real-world situations, pricing takes place in an environment beset with uncertainty. Firms seldom possess precise information about their demand and cost curves. These deficiencies force sellers to rely on other methods for determining price.

COST-PLUS PRICING

The most common technique for determining selling price is probably **cost-plus pricing** (or full-cost pricing, as it is sometimes called). In its simplest form the cost-plus method involves adding some percentage, or markup, to the cost of the goods acquired for sale. For example, a furniture store may pay $100 for a chair, mark it up 150 percent, and attempt to sell it for $250.

Firms using this method do not consider all their costs in arriving at the selling price. They assume that the markup on the **cost of goods sold** (the cost of the items they buy for resale) will be sufficient to cover all other costs—rent, utilities, wages, and salaries—and leave something for profit.

A more sophisticated version of the cost-plus technique attempts to ensure that *all* costs are recovered by building them into the price. Here the seller arrives at a price by determining first the average total cost *(ATC)* of producing the product or offering the service and then adding some margin for profit.

---

[11] Although firms may choose to pursue objectives other than profit maximization, they must strive to achieve at least a normal profit in the long run. Otherwise they won't be able to attract the economic resources they need in order to remain in business. Thus, although some firms may not choose to pursue profit *maximization,* no firm can ignore profitability entirely.

A Cost-Plus Example: Building a Boat. Let's assume that we have just purchased a boat-manufacturing facility for $200,000. It has an expected useful life of 20 years and was designed with a production capacity of 1,000 boats per year. The estimated cost of materials is $150 per boat, and estimated direct labor cost (the cost of the labor directly involved in the manufacture of the boat) is $200 per boat. Besides these variable costs, we have a variety of fixed costs—everything from utility payments to the salaries of security guards—which amount to $125,000 per year. Since our factory cost $200,000 and has a useful life of 20 years, we must also add $10,000 per year ($200,000/20 years) for **depreciation**—the reduction in the value of the production plant due to wear and tear and obsolescence.

Assuming that we expect to sell 1,000 boats this year, which would mean that we would be able to operate the plant at its designed capacity, we arrive at the following costs per boat:

Direct labor	$200.00
Materials	150.00
Depreciation on plant and equipment ($10,000 per year, or $10 per boat—i.e., $10,000 divided by 1,000 boats)	10.00
Fixed costs ($125,000 per year, or $125 per boat—i.e., $125,000 divided by 1,000 boats)	125.00
Total cost per boat (average total cost)	**$485.00**

Now that we have the average total cost of producing a boat, the final step in determining the selling price is adding on the markup that provides our profit margin. A number of factors seem to influence the size of the markup that firms strive to achieve. For instance, executives commonly mention the firm's assessment of what is a "fair" or "reasonable" profit margin.

Custom is another factor that seems to play a major role in some industries. Retailers, for example, often use a particular percentage markup simply because they have always used it or because it is the accepted, therefore "normal," markup in the industry. Obviously a markup that endures long enough to become customary must be somewhat successful in allowing firms to meet their profit objectives. In fact, it may indicate that these firms have discovered through informal means the price and output levels that would have emerged if they had applied the theoretical $MR = MC$ rule.

A final factor influencing the size of the markup is the impact of competition. Although a firm may desire high profit margins, ultimately the degree of actual and potential competition determines what margins the firm will be able to achieve. The more competitive the industry, the lower the profit margin.

Let's assume that we've considered all these factors and have decided to use a 10 percent markup on cost in determining our selling price. Our final step, then, is to add the 10 percent markup to the average total cost calculated earlier. The resulting value is the firm's selling price as determined by the cost-plus technique:

Total cost per boat (average total cost)	$485.00
Markup on cost (10 percent × $485)	48.50
Selling price	**$533.50**

Cost-Plus Pricing in Action. Cost-plus pricing has been criticized by economists as a naive pricing technique that ignores demand and competition and bases price solely on cost considerations. When the cost-plus technique is used in a mechanical or unthinking way, these criticisms are certainly valid. But that's seldom the case. Most businesses consider carefully the strength of demand and the degree of competition before selecting their markup or profit margin. In addition, the cost-plus price generally is viewed as a preliminary estimate, or starting point, rather than as the final price. Since demand and competition can seldom be measured precisely, the firm must be willing to adjust its price if it has misjudged market conditions. It is through these subjective adjustments that the firm gropes its way closer to the profit-maximizing price. A few examples may help to illustrate this point.

Example 1: The Department Store. A local department store receives its shipment of Nifty Popcorn Poppers just in time for the Christmas gift-buying season. It prices the item at $19.50 in order to earn a 30 percent markup on the popper's cost.

Two weeks later the store has sold 50 percent of the shipment, and Christmas is still six weeks away. The manager realizes that he has a "hot" selling item and that he won't be able to get any more from the manufacturer in time for Christmas. He decides to increase his markup (and consequently the product's selling price) in order to take advantage of the product's strong demand.

Example 2: The Car Dealer. A car dealer in a large metropolitan area has found that in the past several years she has been able to average a 15 percent profit margin on the cost of the automobiles she sells. Her experience has taught her that it is much easier to sell a car at a high markup early in the season, when people will pay to be among the first to own the new model, than later, when the next year's model is about to be announced. So the dealer instructs her sales personnel to strive for a 20–25 percent markup early in the year and to settle for a 5–10 percent margin toward the end of the season.

Example 3: The Appliance Manufacturer. Acme Appliance manufactures refrigerators for sale to a regional market. In response to consumers' different budgets and "needs" in terms of optional features, the company offers two models: a basic model that is available only in white and a deluxe model that offers additional features and comes in a variety of colors.

In pricing its product, Acme feels that a 10 percent markup on average cost will produce the desired rate of return on its investment. Rather than use a single markup percentage, however, Acme has decided to apply a 5 percent markup to the basic model and a 15 percent markup to the deluxe model, for an average markup of 10 percent. This decision was made because previous sales experience indicated that low-income customers are substantially more sensitive to price than are intermediate- and high-income customers.

Although the cost-plus technique is essentially straightforward, its application requires management personnel to make subjective judgments about the strength of demand and the degree of competition, as these examples illustrate. Both factors are difficult to evaluate and impossible to quantify. As a consequence, pricing remains more an art than a science.

MARGINAL ANALYSIS AND MANAGERIAL DECISIONS

As the foregoing examples indicate, firms that desire to maximize profits must adjust their cost-plus prices to reflect market conditions; they cannot use the technique mechanically. Learning to "think marginally" can also lead to better decisions and greater profits.

The major limitation of the cost-plus technique is that it doesn't rely on the *marginal analysis* introduced in Chapter 5. It concentrates instead on average values, stressing the need to recover all costs plus some markup. That can lead to smaller profits (or larger losses) than necessary since (as we discovered in Chapter 5) marginal costs are the only relevant costs for many business decisions.

Although firms commonly lack the information required to use the *MR* = *MC* approach to price determination, they generally have some knowledge of marginal values. For instance, even though a firm probably does not know the marginal cost of producing the 200,000th unit of output, it can usually determine the additional cost of producing some block of units—another 10,000 cars, for example. And it can probably discover the additional cost of some contemplated course of action, such as adding or discontinuing a product line. This information will allow a firm to improve the quality of its decisions.

To illustrate, suppose that you own a chain of fast-food restaurants that has traditionally opened for business at 11 A.M. What costs would you consider in deciding whether it would be profitable to open earlier in order to serve breakfast?

The cost-plus approach implies that the decision should be based on the full cost (or *fully allocated cost,* as it is sometimes called) of the new project—on the project's share of the firm's total costs. In other words, the breakfast meal would be expected to generate enough revenue to pay for the labor, utilities, and food used in the morning meal, plus a share of the firm's overhead costs (rent, insurance, equipment depreciation) and some profit margin. If you anticipate enough business to achieve that objective, you should open for business. Otherwise you would remain closed.

Marginal analysis yields a different conclusion. According to marginal analysis, the only costs relevant to a decision are those that are influenced by the decision. In deciding whether to open for breakfast, you should *ignore* such costs as rent and insurance because these fixed costs will have to be paid whether or not the restaurants are open for breakfast. The only true cost of serving breakfast is the marginal cost: the increase in the restaurant's total cost that results from the breakfast meal. If the marginal revenue derived from serving breakfast is expected to exceed the marginal cost, you should open earlier. If not, you should continue to serve only the noon and evening meals.

Marginal analysis can often improve the quality of managerial decisions. Many projects that don't appear to be profitable when evaluated on the basis of their fully allocated costs look quite appealing when analyzed in terms of their marginal costs and revenues. By using marginal analysis and applying judgment to cost-plus prices, firms may be able to approximate the profit levels that would be achieved by using the $MR = MC$ rule.

Test your understanding of the material contained in this appendix by answering the following questions:

1. Explain the cost-plus pricing technique.
2. Why is it often necessary to modify the result determined by the cost-plus method?
3. If a firm includes all its costs in its price by using the cost-plus method, will it ever show a loss? Explain.
4. What determines the markup used in the cost-plus pricing technique?
5. A major limitation of the cost-plus technique is that it does not utilize marginal analysis. Discuss.
6 The Springfield Bouncers, a new professional basketball team, want to rent the high school gymnasium on Sunday afternoons. How would you determine an appropriate rent? If they reject your first offer, how would you determine the *minimum* acceptable rate?

7. Bland manufacturing Company manufactures men's suits for sale throughout the Midwest. For the past five years Bland has operated with about 20 percent unused capacity. Last month a retailer on the West Coast offered to buy as many suits as Bland could supply as long as the price did not exceed $45 per suit. This price is substantially below the price Bland charges its regular customers. Given the information presented below, should Bland accept the offer? Why or why not?

   ATC at present output level (80,000 units) = $55

   ATC at capacity output (100,000 units) = $50

   Normal markup = 40% on *ATC*

Industry Structure and Public Policy

Nearly all the firms in our economy enjoy some pricing discretion, or market power. In Chapter 7 we saw how these firms determine their prices, and we considered the impact of market power on the allocation of scarce resources. Chapter 8 takes a closer look at the degrees of market power that exist in different industries and considers how the makeup, or structure, of an industry influences the amount of pricing discretion enjoyed by its individual firms. This chapter also explores the impact of market power on consumer welfare and examines the role of antitrust enforcement and government regulation in limiting that power.

Industry Structure and Market Power

You have learned that a firm may acquire market power either through product differentiation—distinguishing its product from similar products offered by other sellers—or by gaining control of a significant fraction of total industry output. The degree of product differentiation and the extent to which a firm is able to control industry output are related to the structure of the industry in which the firm operates. **Industry structure** is the makeup of an industry as determined by certain factors: (1) the number of sellers and their size distribution (all sellers approximately the same size as opposed to some much larger than others); (2) the nature of the product; (3) the extent of barriers to entering or leaving the industry. Note that these factors correspond to the three assumptions of the competitive model discussed early in Chapter 6.

There are four basic industry structures: pure competition, monopolistic competition, oligopoly, and pure monopoly. Their characteristics are summarized in Exh. 8.1. You are already familiar with pure competition, so we will use that model to open our discussion of the relationship between industry structure and market power.

Pure Competition

As you learned in Chapter 6, firms that operate in a purely competitive industry are price takers and lack market power for two reasons. First, because they produce and sell identical products, no one firm can expect consumers to pay a higher price than they would pay elsewhere. Such firms must be content with the price dictated by the market. Second, because the purely competitive firm is quite small in relation to the industry, it cannot affect the total industry supply enough to alter the market price. It cannot, for instance, push up prices the way the OPEC oil cartel did in the 1970s or the way the De Beers diamond cartel does today.

That cannot happen in wheat or corn production or any other industry that approximates pure competition. In these industries the individual seller supplies such a small fraction of total industry output that the firm is not in a position to alter the market price by reducing production. Once again, the purely competitive firm has no choice but to accept the price that is dictated by the market.

EXHIBIT 8.1

Industry Structure: A Preview

PURE COMPETITION (No pricing discretion)	MONOPOLISTIC COMPETITION (Modest pricing discretion)	OLIGOPOLY (Modest to substantial pricing discretion)	PURE MONOPOLY (Substantial pricing discretion)
1. Many sellers, each small in relation to the industry	1. Many sellers, each small in relation to the industry	1. Few sellers, large in relation to the industry	1. One firm the sole supplier
2. Identical products	2. Somewhat differentiated products	2. Identical or differentiated products	2. Unique product; no close substitutes
3. No substantial barriers to entry	3. No substantial barriers to entry	3. Substantial barriers to entry	3. Substantial barriers to entry
Examples: Many agricultural industries and a few manufacturing industries (cotton weaving) come close.	*Examples:* Retail trade (hair salons, restaurants, gas stations) and a few manufacturing industries (men's suits and women's dresses)	*Examples:* Steel and aluminum manufacturing (identical products); automobile and cigarette manufacturing (differentiated products)	*Examples:* Local telephone and utility companies

Monopolistic Competition

Few industries in the U.S. economy approximate pure competition. Monopolistic competition is a much more common industry structure. Most of the retailers with which you do business regularly are firms in monopolistically competitive industries: restaurants, day-care centers, grocery stores, hair salons, and photo processors, to name just a few examples. In addition, some manufacturers, such as those making wooden furniture, women's dresses, and men's suits, operate in monopolistically competitive industries.

Like pure competition, **monopolistic competition** is characterized by a large number of relatively small sellers and by modest barriers to entering the industry. The feature that distinguishes monopolistic competition from pure competition is product differentiation. Each monopolistically competitive firm sells a product that is slightly different from those of other firms in the industry. Firms compete on price *and* through product differentiation. Products are differentiated by style, quality, packaging, the location of the seller, advertising, the services offered by the firm (free delivery, for example), and other real or imagined characteristics.

As the term suggests, a monopolistically competitive firm is part monopolist and part competitor. It is a monopolist because it is the only firm selling its unique product; it is competitive because of the large number of firms selling products that are close substitutes. We all have a favorite pizza parlor. It is a monopolist in the limited sense that no other restaurant offers exactly the same food, service, atmosphere, and location. On the other hand, our pizza parlor is in competition with dozens, perhaps hundreds, of other restaurants that sell pizza and substitutes for pizza as well. Your neighborhood hardware store and clothing retailer are in a similar situation. They may have convenient locations and offer some brand names that are not available elsewhere, but they face substantial competition from other sellers of similar products.

MONOPOLISTIC COMPETITION AND MARKET POWER

Insofar as it sells a unique product, each monopolistically competitive firm has some pricing discretion. In other words, it is a price searcher rather than a price taker. If a monopolistic competitor raises the price of its product, it will lose some customers but not all of them. Some will still prefer the product because they believe it to be superior to that of competitors. We can infer, then, that the firm faces a downward-sloping demand curve, not the horizontal or perfectly elastic demand curve facing competitive firms. However, with many substitute products available, the demand for the monopolistically competitive firm's product will be quite elastic, so that consumers will be very responsive to price changes. As a consequence, the market power of the firm is limited; no monopolistically competitive firm can raise its price very much without losing an injuriously large number of customers.

The low entry barriers also function as a check on market power. Additional firms can easily enter a monopolistically competitive industry to take advantage of short-run economic profits. Consider the monopolistically competitive firm represented in Exh. 8.2. In case (a) the firm is earning a short-run profit (price exceeds ATC at the output where $MR = MC$). In the long run, however, this profit will be eliminated by the entrance of additional firms selling similar but slightly differentiated products. As the new firms enter the industry, the demand curve facing our hypothetical firm will begin to shift to the left because each firm's share of total industry demand will become smaller. If there are now 20 pizza restaurants instead of 10, the typical restaurant will have fewer customers than before. Additional firms will continue to enter the industry (and the individual firm's demand curve will continue to shift leftward) until the typical firm is earning just a normal

EXHIBIT 8.2

The Long-Run Adjustment Process in Monopolistic Competition

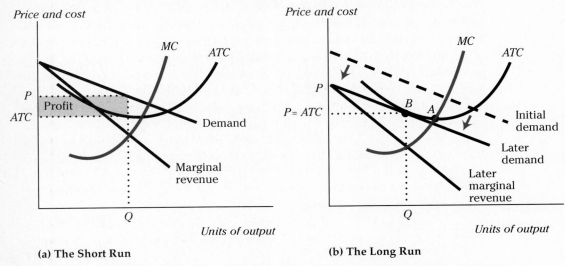

(a) The Short Run

(b) The Long Run

In the short run a monopolistically competitive firm may earn an economic profit, as represented in case (a). In the long run, however, the presence of the above-normal profit will cause additional firms to enter the industry, reducing each firm's share of the industry demand and eventually eliminating all economic profit, as in case (b). In long-run equilibrium the typical monopolistically competitive firm will earn just a normal profit.

profit. This situation is depicted in case (b). In long-run equilibrium, then, the monopolistically competitive firm will do no better than a purely competitive firm; it will just break even. (The article on pages 232–233, "Popular Pizza Chain's Gimmick Is Taste," discusses one firm's quest for lasting profits in an already crowded industry. Read this article and decide if you'd be willing to bet on its long-run success.)

EVALUATING MONOPOLISTIC COMPETITION

We discovered in Chapter 6 that price searchers misallocate resources because they fail to expand output up to the point at which the marginal social benefit equals the marginal social cost. An examination of Exh. 8.2 confirms that monopolistically competitive firms behave this way. Note that in long-run equilibrium, as shown in case (b), the firm maximizes profit at an output of Q. But at that output the price (which reflects the marginal benefit from consuming that unit) exceeds marginal cost. This tells us that society values the last unit of *this* product more highly than the other products that could be produced with the same resources. Allocative efficiency would require the firm to expand output until the marginal social benefit equals the marginal social cost, until the demand curve intersects the marginal cost curve. (Why won't the firm be willing to do that?[1]) If output must be increased to achieve allocative efficiency, we know that at present the firm must be producing less than the efficient level. In summary, monopolistically competitive firms produce less output than is socially desirable.

In addition to distorting the allocation of resources, monopolistically competitive firms are somewhat less efficient at producing their products and charge slightly higher prices than purely competitive firms with the same costs. These outcomes are at least in part the result of the overcrowding that characterizes most monopolistically competitive industries.

The crowded nature of monopolistically competitive industries is illustrated by the large number of clothing stores, video-rental establishments, convenience groceries, and fast-food restaurants in your city or town. By differentiating its product, each of these firms is able to capture a small share of the market. But often so many firms share that market that it is difficult for any one of them to attract enough customers to use its facilities efficiently—to permit it to operate at minimum *ATC*.

Because the monopolistically competitive firm underutilizes its production facilities, its average cost of production will be higher than the *ATC* of a purely competitive firm with identical cost curves.[2] For example, consider the *ATC* curve in case (b) of Exh. 8.2. In long-run equilibrium a purely competitive firm would earn zero economic profit and produce its product at minimum *ATC* (point *A*), whereas we've seen that monopolistically competitive firms will operate at a somewhat higher *ATC* (point *B*). As a consequence, the monopolistically competitive firm must charge a higher price than the purely competitive firm in order to earn a normal profit in the long run.

---

[1] The firm won't be willing to expand output because that behavior is not consistent with profit maximization; *MC* exceeds *MR* for each unit beyond Q. In fact, if the firm chose to produce at the output where the demand curve intersects the *MC* curve, it would incur a loss since the *ATC* curve is above the demand curve at that point

[2] This analysis assumes that the monopolistic competitor has cost curves that are identical to those of the pure competitor. In fact, the monopolistic competitor probably has higher costs due to advertising expense and other product differentiation efforts. Thus, there are two reasons to expect its selling price to be higher: It does not operate at the minimum on its *ATC* curve (whereas a pure competitor does), *and* its *ATC* curve is higher than that of a pure competitor.

Use Your Economic Reasoning

Popular Pizza Chain's Gimmick Is Taste

By Richard Gibson

Pizza from Papa John's costs more than Little Caesar's and arrives no faster than Domino's. And Papa John's offers none of the salads, sandwiches or sit-down service available at Pizza Hut.

Yet Papa John's International Inc. is outperforming those competitors and the entire fast-food industry. Sales last year at company-owned restaurants open more than a year grew nearly 12%—twice the industry average. Profits? Up 66% last year. The price of its stock has quadrupled since a 1993 initial public offering. Already the nation's fourth-largest pizza chain, it is adding dozens of new stores every month to the 1,200 or so it operates in 32 states.

Its secret? Posted on conference-room walls at company headquarters in Louisville, Ky., are awards from publications declaring Papa John's the best-tasting pizza in markets around the country. This year, Papa John's unseated Pizza Hut as the best pizza chain overall in the U.S., according to

Restaurants and Institutions magazine.

As titans like McDonald's Corp. struggled to regain momentum, and as PepsiCo Inc. flees the fast-food business altogether by jettisoning its Pizza Hut, Taco Bell and KFC chains, Papa John's is on a tear. Experts say that's because it isn't trying to sell convenience, low cost or variety. It is selling taste.

The company's slogan is "better ingredients, better pizza." While much of the competition uses sauce made from concentrate, Papa John's touts sauce from vine-ripened tomatoes. It buys only premium mozzarella. As for dough, while competitors either make it at each site or use frozen dough, Papa John's establishes a dough kitchen in each region to serve nearby restaurants. It is picky about dough ingredients right down to the water —purified only. Other chains sometimes use tap water, but Papa John's founder and chief executive John Schnatter insists he can taste the

difference. "It's hard to carve rotten wood," says Mr. Schnatter, who is given to folksy phrases.

Last year, Domino's Pizza Inc. challenged Papa John's claim of "fresher and higher-quality ingredients," but the Better Business Bureau's national advertising division investigated and found the claim accurate.

Pizza preparation matters, too. Driving home from a University of Louisville basketball game late one night, Mr. Schnatter, who is 35 years old, stops by one of his company's stores and opens two ready-to-go pizza boxes. He doesn't like what he sees. The crusts are puffy—"inner-tube edges," he calls them— so Mr. Schnatter tells the embarrassed store manager to make replacements.

Customers do notice. "The cheese has more flavor to it," says Ryan Gillen, a 19-year-old Northwestern University freshman, as he picks up a pizza at a Papa John's in Evansville, Ill. "This is the place most

SOURCE: *Wall Street Journal*, April 28, 1997, p.1. Reprinted by permission of the *Wall Street Journal*, © 1997 Dow Jones & Company, Inc. All Rights Reserved Worldwide.

students in my dorm get pizza," he says.

Rivals are scrambling to stunt Papa John's growth. Pizza Hut has launched a counterattack—the details of which are secret—called "Stopa the Papa." Domino's, after years of touting delivery speed, is concocting a campaign that emphasizes quality. Papa John's claims that before it enters a market, competitors often try to reserve the phone number the chain likes to use; anything ending in "7272" (PAPA).

Papa John's plans to step up its attack. By year's end, it expects to be in 37 states, making television advertising—a major marketing tool of its three larger competitors—an efficient buy.

Some observers say that novelty is a bigger factor than taste, and that time will hurt Papa John's. In a market as mature as pizza, "being the new guy" means people will try you, says industry consultant John Correll. "But," he adds, "eventually there's a very good chance they will have to do something different to avoid flaming out like the other guys...."

Much of Papa John's success stems from what it doesn't do. It doesn't serve food on its premises. No pizza by the slice. It sells just two

kinds of pie, traditional and thin-crust. Its only other offerings are bread sticks and cheese sticks, plus soft drinks in bottles and cans. The company rarely discounts, yet seeks to be competitively priced; a 14-inch cheese pie costs about $8.60; one with everything on it, called "the works" is $11.95.

Papa John's stripped-down menu is intended to ensure that even the newest employee can make a top-notch pizza. A "keep it simple, stupid" approach

pervades operations, from a goof-proof kitchen layout to dough mix that comes to regional commissaries preblended.

"For every one person who says we should do something different, there are 10 who say, no, we shouldn't," says Barry Barron, who oversees the U.S. Southwest for Papa John's. From observing or working for rivals, "they've seen what can go wrong," says Mr. Baron. Indeed, he used to be a Pizza Hut regional manager.

USE YOUR ECONOMIC REASONING

1. Do you think it is accurate to describe the pizza restaurants in your town as a monopolistically competitive industry? Why or why not?
2. As a monopolistically competitive industry matures, it becomes increasingly necessary for firms to differentiate themselves from their rivals. Why? How has Papa John's attempted to differentiate itself?
3. Let's assume that the local pizza industry is mo-

nopolistically competitive and that the Papa John's in your community is earning an economic profit. Represent this situation graphically.
4. Imagine a situation in which there are dozens of pizza restaurants in a community, but the Papa John's restaurants are the only ones earning economic profits. What would you expect to happen in the long run? Represent this adjustment process graphically.

Fortunately for consumers, the difference in price is probably not substantial. Furthermore, consumers gain something for the additional dollars they pay. Remember, purely competitive firms sell products that are identical in the minds of consumers, whereas monopolistic competitors aim for product differentiation. Many of us are willing to pay a little more to obtain the product variety that monopolistic competition provides.

Oligopoly

Millions of firms in hundreds of U.S. retail industries match the model of monopolistic competition reasonably well. However, most manufacturing industries—steel, aluminum, automobiles, and prescription drugs, for example—are more accurately described as oligopolistic. An **oligopoly** is an industry dominated by a few relatively large sellers that are protected by substantial barriers to entry. The distinguishing feature of all oligopolistic industries is the high degree of interdependence among the sellers and the very personal nature of the rivalry that results from that interdependence.

OLIGOPOLISTS AND MARKET POWER

Because oligopolistic firms enjoy a large share of their market, their production decisions have a significant impact on market price. A substantial increase in production by any one of them would cause downward pressure on price; a significant decrease would tend to push price upward. Suppose, for instance, that the Aluminum Company of America (Alcoa) decided to increase production by 50 percent. Since Alcoa is a major producer, this increase in output would expand industry supply significantly and thereby depress the industry price. A substantial reduction in Alcoa's output would tend to have the opposite effect; it would push price upward.

We have seen that soybean farmers, hog producers, and others in purely competitive industries cannot influence price by manipulating industry output: They're not big enough; that is, they don't control a large enough share of the market. In addition, the large number of firms in these competitive industries makes it virtually impossible for them to coordinate their actions— to agree to limit production, for example. As a consequence, changes in the output of a competitive industry are always the unplanned result of independent actions by thousands of producers. Output in an oligopolistic industry, on the other hand, is often carefully controlled by the few large firms that dominate production. This control is one of the keys to the pricing discretion of the oligopolists.

Some oligopolists also acquire market power through product differentiation. Although producers of such commodities as aluminum ingots, steel sheet, and heating oil sell virtually identical products, many oligopolists sell differentiated products. Producers of automobiles, pet food, greeting cards, cigarettes, breakfast cereals, and washers and dryers belong in this category. Oligopolistic sellers of differentiated products possess market power both because they are large in relation to the total industry *and* because their product is in some way unique.

MUTUAL INTERDEPENDENCE AND GAME THEORY

Since oligopolistic firms have pricing discretion, they are price searchers rather than price takers. But the high degree of interdependence among oligopolists tends to restrict the pricing discretion of the individual firm and complicate its search for the profit-maximizing price.

Because there are only a few large sellers, each firm must consider the reactions of its rivals before taking any action. For instance, before altering the price of its product, Ford Motor Company must consider the reactions of General Motors, Toyota, and the other firms in the industry. And Coca-Cola must weigh the likely reactions of Pepsi-Cola and other soft-drink suppliers before contemplating any price change. In both instances, raising prices may be ill-advised unless the other firms can be counted on to match the price hike. Price reductions may be an equally poor strategy if rivals respond with matching price cuts or with deeper cuts that lead to continuing price warfare.

One tool that economists use to understand and predict the behavior of oligopolists such as Ford and Coca-Cola is *game theory*. **Game theory** is the study of the strategies employed by interdependent players involved in some form of competition, or game. The "players" can be individuals, sport teams, nations, or business firms.. And the "games" involved can be true games of chance or sporting events or struggles between armies on a battlefield or business rivalries.

All games involve strategy and a payoff matrix. A strategy is simply a plan for accomplishing an objective: winning a battle or earning as much profit as possible, for example. And a payoff matrix is a grid showing the outcomes for the various combinations of strategies employed by the players. The following examples will help to illustrate these terms and will also reveal some of the important conclusions of the game theory model.

Games with Dominant Strategies. Consider the rivalry between Coca-Cola and Pepsi-Cola, the most important firms in the soft-drink industry.

Let's assume that these two firms are trying to decide whether to charge $10 or $12 for each case of their soft drinks; these are the alternative strategies under consideration. In making this decision, each firm recognizes that its profit (the payoff from its strategy) depends not only on the price its selects but also on the price selected by its rival. The different possible outcomes are contained in the payoff matrix presented in Exh. 8.3.

According to the matrix, if Coke charges $12 a case and Pepsi chooses the same price, each firm will earn a profit of $300 million (see the cell in the upper left-hand corner of the matrix). The problem with this strategy is that neither firm can be certain that its rival will decide to charge $12. In fact, as the matrix reveals, each firm has incentive to undercut its rival. For example, if Coke selects the $12 price and Pepsi counters with a $10 price, Pepsi will earn a profit of $400 million (see the lower left-hand cell), while Coke will earn only $100 million. If Pepsi charges $12 and Coke opts to charge $10, the outcome will be reversed; Coke will earn a $400 million profit, and Pepsi will earn only $100 million (see the upper right-hand cell).

EXHIBIT 8.3

A Game with Two Dominant Strategies

Coke's price strategies

		$12	$10
Pepsi's price strategies	$12	Each firm earns a profit of $300 million.	Coke earns $400 million. Pepsi earns $100 million.
	$10	Coke earns $100 million. Pepsi earns $400 million.	Each firm earns a profit of $200 million.

The payoffs matrix shows that each firm's profits depend not only on its actions but also on the actions of its rival. For instance, if Coke charges $12, it will earn a profit of $300 million if Pepsi matches that price but only $100 million if Pepsi opts to charge $10.

In this example each firm has a *dominant strategy,* a strategy that should be pursued regardless of the strategy selected by its rival. The dominant strategy for both Coke and Pepsi is to charge $10; that strategy leads to higher profits regardless of the strategy selected by the other firm.

The remaining possibility is that both firms will decide to charge $10. In that case each firm will earn a profit of $200 million. While this is not the best the firms could do, it is not the worst either since it avoids the possibility of earning a profit of only $100 million. According to game theorists, both oligopolists will see the $10 price as particularly attractive. There are two reasons for this attraction: First, if one firm decides to charge $10 and its rival opts to charge $12, the firm charging the lower ($10) price will earn a $400 profit, the highest amount possible. Second, charging $10 eliminates the possibility that a firm will be undercut by its rival and find itself able to earn a profit of only $100 million (the lowest outcome in the matrix).

In the preceding example the decision to select the $10 price is the *dominant strategy* for both firms. A **dominant strategy** is one that should be pursued regardless of the strategy selected by the rival. In our example, for instance, Coke is better off charging the $10 price regardless of whether Pepsi opts to match that price or to charge $12 instead. The same is true for Pepsi. As a result the equilibrium solution occurs in the lower right-hand cell, with both firms charging $10. As long as these firms act independently, neither firm has any incentive to modify its strategy.

Games without Dominant Strategies. Not all games have dominant strategies. Others have dominant strategies for one rival but not the other. To illustrate, suppose that Coke and Pepsi are trying to decide whether to utilize both television and newspaper advertising or to limit their campaigns to newspaper advertising. As in the earlier example, the payoff for each strategy depends on the reaction of the rival. These payoffs are represented in Exh. 8.4. Take a moment to examine the matrix before reading further. Can you determine the strategy that will be selected by each firm? Does each firm have a dominant strategy?

In this case Pepsi does *not* have a dominant strategy; its optimal strategy depends on the strategy adopted by Coke. If Coke decides to pursue both TV and newspaper advertising, Pepsi's optimal strategy is to use both TV and newspaper advertising as well (a profit of $200 million rather than $100 million). On the other hand, if Coke decides to limit its advertising to newspapers, Pepsi's best strategy is to do the same (a profit of $350 million rather than $300 million). As you can see, Pepsi does not have a dominant strategy; its best strategy depends on what Coke does.

Before Pepsi can decide on a strategy, it must predict what Coke is likely to do. In this instance that's not too difficult because Coke *does* have a dominant strategy. Here Coke's dominant strategy is to engage in both TV and newspaper advertising; that yields the most profit regardless of the strategy

EXHIBIT 8.4

A Game with Only One Dominant Strategy

Coke's advertising strategies

		TV and newspaper	Newspaper only
Pepsi's advertising strategies	TV and newspaper	Coke earns $300 million. Pepsi earns $200 million.	Coke earns $200 million. Pepsi earns $300 million.
	Newspaper only	Coke earns $500 million. Pepsi earns $100 million.	Coke earns $400 million. Pepsi earns $350 million.

In this example Coke's dominant strategy is to engage in both TV and newspaper advertising. Pepsi does not have a dominant strategy; its optimal strategy depends on the strategy adopted by Coke.

pursued by Pepsi.[3] Once Pepsi recognizes that Coke's dominant strategy is to advertise in both media, it knows that its own best strategy is to follow suit. The equilibrium solution, then, is in the upper left-hand cell, with both firms advertising in both media.[4]

One interesting point about the equilibrium solution is that neither firm earns as much profit as it could if both firms decided to avoid TV advertising. But each firm is reluctant to select this strategy for fear that the other firm *will* run TV ads. A similar problem existed in the initial example. (See Exh. 8.3 to refresh your memory.) Even though the dominant strategy was to select the $10 price, each firm could earn more profit if both firms decided

---

[3] Note that if Pepsi engages in TV and newspaper advertising and Coke does the same, Coke earns a profit of $300 million rather than the $200 million it would earn if it chose only newspaper advertising. On the other hand, if Pepsi limits its campaign to newspaper advertising, Coke will earn a profit of $400 million if it matches that strategy or $500 million if it uses both media. As you can see, Coke is always better off to pursue a strategy of both TV and newspaper advertising.

[4] If both firms decide to advertise they will have reached a "Nash equilibrium" (named for John Nash, the 1997 Nobel prize–winning economist who discovered the concept). A Nash equilibrium exists when each firm's strategy is the best it can choose, given the strategy chosen by the other firm. There is more than one way to achieve a Nash equilibrium. For example, when both firms have a dominant strategy, the result is a Nash equilibrium. But, as this example illustrates, a Nash equilibrium does not *require* that both players have dominant strategies.

to charge $12. But, as in the advertising example, neither firm was willing to pursue that strategy for fear of being undercut by its rival. This points to the incentive that oligopolists have to cooperate (rather than compete). We turn next to the methods that they might employ to facilitate cooperation.

TACTICS FOR COOPERATING

Oligopolists may respond to their interdependence by employing tactics that allow them to cooperate and make mutually advantageous decisions. One tactic is **collusion**, agreement among sellers to fix prices, divide up the market, or in some other way limit competition. For instance, in our earlier example (see Exh. 8.3), suppose that Pepsi and Coke secretly agreed to charge $12 (rather than $10). That action would allow each firm to earn more profit. An agreement to avoid TV advertising (see Exh. 8.4) would have a similar impact.

Collusive agreements result in cartels, such as the OPEC oil cartel and the De Beers diamond cartel. Although collusive agreements are legal in some countries, they are illegal in the United States and are punishable by fine and imprisonment. (As a consequence, firms attempt to keep them secret.) In spite of the penalties, some U.S. firms continue to engage in collusion. Dozens of violators are prosecuted each year, and many others probably go undetected. That business executives are willing to risk prison sentences to engage in collusion is testimony both to the potential financial gains and to the problems posed by interdependence.

A more subtle form of cooperation (and communication) is price leadership. **Price leadership** is much like a game of follow-the-leader. One firm— perhaps the biggest, the most efficient, or simply the most trusted—initiates all increases or decreases in prices. The remaining firms in the industry follow the leader. This leader-follower behavior is generally reinforced by indirect forms of communication (rather than the direct communication involved in collusion). For example, price leaders usually signal their intent to raise prices through press releases or through public speeches. This lets the follower firms know that a price increase is coming so that they will not be taken by surprise. (If the price leader hikes its price and no one follows, it will probably have to back down, creating confusion for the industry.) This tactic allows the firms in the industry to accomplish price changes legally, without collusion.

Neither collusive agreements nor price leadership may be necessary when an industry is dominated by firms that recognize their interdependence. **Conscious parallelism** occurs when, without any communication whatsoever, firms adopt similar policies. For instance, even without meeting or signaling each other, firms may come to recognize that price cutting, because it invites retaliation, leaves all firms worse off. They may therefore shun this practice as long as their rivals reciprocate. Conscious parallelism may also explain why all firms in an industry provide the same discounts to larger buyers and why they all raise prices at the same time of year.

Collusion, price leadership, and conscious parallelism all tend to result in an avoidance of price competition. Instead, oligopolists channel their competitive drive into *nonprice competition*—advertising, packaging, and new product development. This form of rivalry has two significant advantages over price competition. First, a new product or a successful advertising campaign is more difficult for a competitor to match than a price cut is, and so an oligopolist may gain a more permanent advantage over its rivals. Second, rivalry through product differentiation or new product development is less likely than price competition to get out of control and severely damage the profits of all firms in the industry. Thus, nonprice competition is seen as a more promising strategy than price competition.

FACTORS LIMITING COOPERATION

Although oligopolists strive to avoid price warfare and confine their rivalry to nonprice competition, these efforts are not always successful. Collusion and price leadership often break down because of the strong temptation to cheat (price-cut) in order to win customers. Even conscious parallelism can give way to price cutting if firms believe their actions may be undetected. To understand this temptation, look back at Exh. 8.3 for a moment. Suppose that Coke and Pepsi have agreed, either informally or through collusion, to charge a price of $12. Each firm recognizes that if it undercuts the other firm by charging $10, it can expand its profits. And if the firm is not too greedy—if the price cutting is limited to a small fraction of industry sales, for example—the practice may go undiscovered and the rival may not retaliate.

The likelihood of cheating is greatest in markets in which prices tend to be secret (so that price cutting may go undetected) and in which long contracts may delay the impact of retaliation. Cheating also becomes more commonplace as the number of firms in the industry increases since it becomes more difficult for the firms to agree on the best price. In addition, the state of the economy clearly influences the likelihood of cheating. History shows that price cutting is particularly common in periods of weak demand, when firms have substantial excess capacity that they would like to put to work. During such periods, firms will be tempted to undercut their rivals in order to expand sales.

In truth, the success of oligopolists in avoiding price competition varies significantly from industry to industry. Some industries—the breakfast cereal and cigarette manufacturing industries, for example—have demonstrated a marked ability to avoid price competition; others—steel manufacturing, for

Oligopolists often channel their competitive instincts into nonprice competition: advertising, packaging, and new product development.

instance—experience recurring bouts of price warfare.[5] Because the behavior of oligopolists is so varied, it is difficult to generalize about the impact of oligopoly on social welfare. We will attempt some cautious observations after discussing the final industry structure, pure monopoly.

Monopoly

Although both monopolistic competitors and oligopolists have some pricing discretion, the classic example of a firm with market power is the monopolist.

Monopoly is an industry structure in which a single firm sells a product for which there are no close substitutes. (Monopoly is sometimes called *pure monopoly* to emphasize that it is the industry structure farthest removed from pure competition.) A firm can become a monopolist in a variety of ways but can remain a monopolist only if barriers prevent other firms from entering the industry. One barrier to entry is exclusive control of some critical input— a basic raw material needed in the production process, for instance. A second way a firm may enjoy a monopoly is through sheer size, when larger size brings with it greater efficiency and lower production costs. Entry into the

---

[5] Although cereal producers have a long history of avoiding price warfare, recent price cutting shows that even their discipline can break down. In 1996 Kellogg and Philip Morris (which owns Post and Nabisco cereals) announced price cuts averaging about 20 percent. This led to price cutting by other manufacturers.

industry is effectively blocked by the large capital investment a rival would require to begin operating at competitive size. A possible third source of monopoly is government policies. For instance, the U.S. government issues patents that provide a firm with the exclusive right to control a new product for a period of seventeen years. The government franchise is another example of government policies promoting monopoly. A **government franchise** is an exclusive license to provide a product or service. Government franchises account for the presence of only one restaurant chain on the interstate highway and the single boat-rental establishment in a state park. National governments can also create or preserve monopolies through their trade policies. By erecting trade barriers, governments can prevent foreign products from entering their countries, thereby reserving the market for domestic firms.

MONOPOLY AND MARKET POWER

Monopolists enjoy substantial pricing discretion because they are the sole suppliers of their products. This enables the monopolist to manipulate industry output and thereby alter the market price. The monopolist's control over output does not provide it with complete or unlimited pricing discretion, however. Complete pricing discretion would result in a vertical, perfectly inelastic demand curve, signifying the ability to increase price without losing *any* customers. This condition would represent the true opposite of the purely competitive firm, which possesses no market power and faces a horizontal, perfectly elastic demand curve.

But a monopolist does stand to lose some customers when it raises its price, because monopolists face a certain amount of competition from rivals in *other* industries. Think about your local telephone and utility companies, for example. These sellers continue to fit the description of a monopolist fairly well, though much has been written about new forms of competition that are on the horizon and may ultimately destroy their monopoly status.[6] But even today neither is without competition. If the telephone company charges exorbitant rates for its service, we can communicate by letter or by CB radio or by personal visit. If the utility company effects a drastic rate increase for electricity, we can begin by reducing our use of electricity. We can insulate our homes and install

---

[6] Technological advances and regulatory changes threaten to ultimately undermine the pricing discretion of both the local phone company and the local power company. Someday in the not-to-distant future, people living in New York City or Detroit may be able to buy their electricity from producers in Wyoming or elsewhere in the United States. And local phone customers may be able to choose from several phone companies. But, for now, most local customers remain wedded to monopolist providers of these services.

energy-saving appliances; ultimately we can even purchase our own electricity generator.

In the face of increasing fuel and electricity costs, many U.S. consumers have already insulated their homes, installed passive solar heat, and demanded energy-saving devices. And although none of us wants to resort to a CB radio as a substitute for local telephone service, some customers might choose to do just that if rates become high enough. The availability of substitutes, however imperfect, constrains the monopolist's pricing discretion.

MONOPOLY AND PROFIT MAXIMIZATION

Because a monopolist stands to lose some customers when it raises its price, the demand curve it faces must slope downward just as those of other price searchers do. This tells us that the monopolist must restrict output to charge a high price; conversely, it must reduce price to sell more. The monopolist will select the profit-maximizing output and price in exactly the same way other price searchers do; it will produce the output at which $MR = MC$ and find its price by going up to the demand curve. The difference between a monopolist and other price searchers is found not in the rules used to determine their price but in the competitive situation. Monopolistically competitive firms and oligopolists face some degree of competition from other firms in the industry. The monopolist *is* the industry, and so its only competition comes from firms in other industries.

Because monopolists enjoy substantial pricing discretion, it is commonly believed that they must earn economic profits. But that need not be the case. In the short run, monopolists, like other producers, may experience economic profits, normal profits, or even losses. How well a monopolist will fare depends on the demand and cost conditions that it faces. Imagine, for instance, a firm that has patented a medicine for a very rare disease—with an average diagnosis of ten cases a year. This monopolist has substantial pricing discretion with these unfortunate victims, but the demand is so limited that the product probably will be unprofitable to produce. Or consider the boat-rental concession at an isolated state park. The owner enjoys a government-granted monopoly, but if few vacationers frequent the lake, it won't be a very profitable monopoly. The point is that even a monopolist can't earn a profit if the demand for its product is very limited. High production costs can signal a similar problem. Exhibit 8.5 depicts a monopolist incurring a short-run economic loss.

When monopolists are able to earn short-run profits, substantial entry barriers help them to continue earning those profits in the long run. But the long run does not mean forever! Ultimately the development of new products, the introduction of new technologies, and/or the elimination of legal

EXHIBIT 8.5

A Monopolist Incurring a Loss

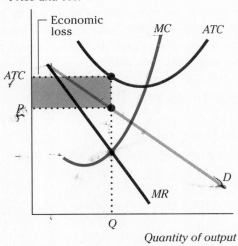

Even a monopolist can incur a loss if there is little demand for its product or if its costs are high.

barriers to entry tend to undermine the monopolist's position. For example, at one time Atlantic Telephone and Telegraph (AT&T) enjoyed a monopoly in providing long-distance telephone service. But new technology ultimately destroyed its monopoly status (this will be discussed in greater detail in a moment). Or consider the monopoly currently enjoyed by Glaxo Wellcome in the manufacture of AZT, the drug used to treat AIDS patients. Glaxo Wellcome obtained a monopoly in AZT by developing the drug and then obtaining a patent to prevent other firms from duplicating it. But the substantial profits the firm is earning from the drug ensure that other companies will go to great lengths to develop a substitute. And even if they are not successful, patent protection will ultimately expire and consumers will be flooded with generic forms of AZT, which will substantially lower its price and Glaxo Wellcome's profits. (Analysts have been forecasting the demise of local cable monopolies for some time. But most are still alive and kicking consumers. Read "Cable TV Lacks Competition..." on pages 246–247 to discover why.)

None of this is intended to make you feel sorry for monopolists. Technological progress is hard to predict and generally occurs slowly. And patent protection is currently granted for a period of seventeen years. The point is that change is inevitable and eventually most monopolists find their status eroded by forces that are largely beyond their control.

The Consequences of Monopoly or Oligopoly

The presence of monopolies can have a significant effect on consumer well-being. Monopolists tend to produce too little output and sometimes charge prices that are inflated by economic profits. These negative effects may be partially offset by lower production costs or greater innovation. Oligopoly can have a similar impact on consumer welfare, though it is much more difficult to generalize about the consequences of this industry structure.

THE PROBLEMS OF MISALLOCATION OF RESOURCES AND REDISTRIBUTION OF INCOME

Economists generally agree that monopolists distort the allocation of scarce resources. Like monopolistically competitive firms, monopolists fail to produce up to the point where marginal social benefit equals marginal social cost—the point at which resources would be allocated efficiently. As a consequence, too few resources are devoted to the production of the goods and services produced by monopolists, and too many resources are left over to be used in the more competitive sectors of the economy. For example, if there were only two industries in the economy, a monopolized computer industry and a purely competitive farming industry, society probably would receive too few computers and too many agricultural products.

The redistribution of income is another problem caused by monopolies. Because entrance into these industries is blocked, consumers may be required to pay higher prices than necessary, prices that include economic profits on top of the normal profits that are necessary to convince firms to continue operation. These higher prices redistribute income from consumers (who will be worse off) to monopolists (who will be better off).

Although economists are fairly confident in generalizing about the consequences of monopoly, they find it more difficult to make blanket statements regarding the impact of oligopoly. This is primarily because the behavior of oligopolists is so varied. To the extent that oligopolists cooperate and avoid price competition, the welfare effects of oligopoly probably are very similar to the effects of pure monopoly. When cooperation breaks down, consumer welfare is enhanced and the negative effects of oligopoly are reduced. Since it is clear that oligopolists do not always succeed in avoiding price competition, the impact of oligopoly on consumer well-being probably lies somewhere between the impacts of monopoly and pure competition.

Use Your Economic Reasoning

Cable TV Lacks Competition, F.C.C. Notes

By Seth Schiesel

The Federal Communications Commission confirmed in a report yesterday what most cable television subscribers already knew; that the information revolution has failed to create serious competition to standard cable television and that the public is paying higher cable rates as a result…

Cable television rates increased by 8.5 percent last year, the commission report said, bringing the average monthly bill for standard service to $28.83. That far outstrips the 1.7 percent increase in overall consumer prices last year.

The commission attributed the increase to the virtual absence of competition among cable operators. Of the 73.6 million households that subscribe to some sort of advanced television service as of last June, 64.2 million, or 87.2 percent, used cable, the commission reported. A vast majority of the remainder used some sort of satellite system.

The 87 percent market share for cable represented a slight decrease from its 89 percent share of the advanced television arena in September 1996. But Mr. Kennard said the current pace of competition would not be enough to insure reasonable prices in the future.

The Telecommunications Act of 1996 says that almost all restrictions on cable rates are to be lifted in March 1999. Many members of Congress who voted for the act said they believed that by then there would be widespread competition to standard cable. Big local telephone companies, for example, had indicated that they would try to use their extensive networks of copper and fiber optic cables to enter the $30 billion market for advanced television services.

But most of those plans collapsed as large local phone companies like the Bell Atlantic Corporation directed much of their energy and resources to their high-stakes battle against the major long-distance carriers, including the AT&T Corporation, for domination of the $200 billion market for everyday phone calls.

New types of direct-broadcast satellite services, like DirecTV and Primestar, now serve about 7.2 million customers. But the F.C.C. and consumer advocates say that direct-broadcast satellite is not a full-fledged competitor to cable because of the higher initial costs of satellite services and because the satellite services are not allowed to carry signals from local stations.

Cable subscribers incur a first-year cost of about $400, said Mark Cooper, director of research for the Consumer

SOURCE: *New York Times*, Jan. 14, 1998, p. D6. Copyright © 1997/96 by The New York Times Co. Reprinted by Permission.

Federation of America, while first-year satellite users spend about $1,100, including the cost of equipment and installation.

Representative W.J. Tauzin, the Louisiana Republican who leads the House subcommittee on telecommunications, said through a spokesman that satellite services could be nurtured into more serious competition to cable if Congress passed legislation reducing the fees that satellite operators pay to program developers and if satellites were allowed to carry local programming.

Representative Edward J. Markey, a Democrat from Massachusetts who is the ranking minority member of the telecommunications panel, said in an interview that he would support legislation to delay the deregulation of cable rates.

"There is already a rising cable-rate El Nino hitting consumers all across America," he said. "Should the cable consumer have to pay outrageous rates because the telephone companies' theory has collapsed? No...."

Current F.C.C. regulations allow cable operators to raise prices if they add new channels, if existing channels begin to cost more or to help pay the cost of upgrading a cable network to carry new services like the Internet.

But consumer advocates say the rules cannot insure reasonable prices. "These regulations are a joke," said Gene Kimmelman, co-director of the Washington office of Consumers Union. "They are a sham, and they do nothing but allow monopolistic pricing."

Large cable operators say the increasing prices mostly reflect the rising cost of programming. "We feel strongly that competition is increasing, and we definitely are considering ourselves in a competitive environment," said Lela Cocoros, a spokeswoman for Telecommunications, Inc., the No. 1 cable company. "The programming rates are getting higher all the time, especially when you get into the sports arena."

Mr. Kennard said he would direct F.C.C. staff members to study how closely rises in the cost of programming were linked to increases in subscribers' bills.

USE YOUR ECONOMIC REASONING

1. Analysts expected local telephone companies to provide competition for local cable TV operators. Why hasn't that happened?
2. How does the higher initial cost of establishing service prevent satellite TV from being a "full-fledged competitor" to cable?
3. Under existing law, cable companies are required to carry local stations, but satellite operators can legally beam local programs only to households that can't otherwise get signals clearly. How do these laws affect competition between those rivals?
4. How does Representative Tauzin propose to "nurture" satellite services into more serious competition for cable.

247

THE POSSIBLE BENEFITS OF SIZE

Although monopoly and oligopoly often have undesirable effects on consumer welfare, this is not always the case. Under certain conditions these structures may benefit society. For example, if a monopolist's/oligopolist's greater size leads to economies of scale (lower long-run average costs), it may be able to charge a lower price than a competitive firm even as it earns an economic profit. And because monopolists and oligopolists are often able to earn economic profits in the long run, they can afford the investment necessary to develop new products and cost-reducing production techniques. Thus, in the long run, society may receive better products and lower prices from monopolists and oligopolists than from competitive firms.

Studies of the U.S. economy provide limited support for these arguments. For example, in the refrigerator-manufacturing industry a firm needs 15–20 percent of the market in order to achieve production efficiency, or minimum *ATC*. This means that for optimal efficiency, room exists for only five or six firms in that industry. The efficient manufacture and distribution of beer requires a somewhat smaller but nevertheless substantial market share: 10–14 percent.(Plant economies of scale appeared to become more important in the 1970s and early 80s, but the emergence of many microbreweries shows that small firms can still survive—albeit with higher average costs—if they are successful in differentiating their products and charging premium prices.) But in the majority of the manufacturing industries surveyed, firms with 3 percent of the market or less were large enough to operate at minimum *ATC*. Thus, it is not generally necessary for industries to be dominated by one or a few firms in order to achieve efficiency in production and distribution.[7]

Evidence on business research and development efforts leads to a similar conclusion. Firms in highly competitive industries are not particularly innovative, perhaps because they are unable to earn the profits necessary to finance research and development efforts. But firms in "tightly" oligopolistic industries (in which a very few firms closely coordinate their actions) don't tend to be innovative either. These firms often have the money but seem to lack the incentive, which stems from competitive pressure, to invest in research and development. The most innovative tend to be medium-sized firms in "loosely" oligopolistic industries—industries composed of several firms (perhaps ten or twenty) with no single dominant firm. Because some competitive pressure exists, it may be harder for the firms in these industries to coordinate their actions, but because they have some pricing discretion, such firms often earn the economic profits necessary to support research and development efforts.[8]

---

[7] F. M. Scherer and David Ross, *Industrial Market Structure and Economic Performance*, 3rd Edition (Houghton Mifflin, 1990), p. 140.

[8] Douglas F. Greer, *Industrial Organization and Public Policy* (New York: Macmillan, 1980), p. 598.

In summary, economies of scale and greater innovation may sometimes compensate for the resource misallocation and income redistribution caused by oligopolists and monopolists. In some cases we may even be able to justify a "natural" monopoly on the basis of greater production efficiency or technical considerations, a possibility that was discussed in the last chapter. Even when we take these benefits into consideration, however, we find that manufacturing industries have fewer and larger firms than necessary to achieve the advantages of production efficiency and increased innovation. In general, U.S. consumers would be better off if the existing industry structure were more, not less, competitive.

Antitrust and Regulation

Because the exercise of market power by monopolists and oligopolists can distort the allocation of scarce resources and redistribute income, the federal government pursues policies designed to promote competition and restrict the actions of firms with market power. The primary weapons used in the battle against market power are antitrust laws and industry regulation. As you will see, these two approaches to the problem differ significantly in both their philosophies and the remedies they propose.

ANTITRUST ENFORCEMENT

Antitrust laws have as their objective the maintenance and promotion of competition. These laws (1) outlaw collusion, (2) make it illegal for a firm to attempt to achieve a monopoly, and (3) ban **mergers,** the union of two or more companies into a single firm, when such mergers are likely to result in substantially less competition.

Virtually all antitrust enforcement in the United States is based on three fundamental statutes: the Sherman Antitrust Act of 1890, the Clayton Antitrust Act of 1914, and the Federal Trade Commission Act, also passed in 1914. Exhibit 8.6 offers a brief comparison of these laws.

The Sherman Antitrust Act. The Sherman Act, the first of the big three, was a response to the monopolistic exploitation that occurred in the latter half of the nineteenth century, when trusts had become commonplace. **Trusts** are combinations of firms organized for the purpose of restraining price competition and thereby gaining economic profit. (For our purposes, a trust is the same thing as a cartel.) So many companies were merging at this time that competitors were disappearing at an alarming rate. Du Pont, for example, achieved a near monopoly in the manufacture of explosives by either merging

250   *PART 2*   MICROECONOMICS: MARKETS, PRICES, AND THE ROLE OF COMPETITION

EXHIBIT 8.6

The Antitrust Laws and What They Do

The Sherman Antitrust Act (1890)	Outlawed agreements to fix prices, limit output, or share the market. Also declared that monopolies and attempts to monopolize are illegal.
The Clayton Antitrust Act (1914)	Forbade competitors to merge if the impact of merger would be to lessen competition substantially. Also outlawed certain practices, such as tying contracts.
The Federal Trade Commission Act (1914)	Created the Federal Trade Commission and empowered it to initiate and decide cases involving "unfair competition." Also declared that deceptive practices and unfair methods of competition are illegal.

with or acquiring some 100 rival firms between 1872 and 1912.[9] Monopolies and monopolistic practices translated into higher prices for consumers and inspired a strong political movement that led to the passage of the Sherman Antitrust Act in 1890.

The Sherman Act declared illegal all agreements between competing firms to fix prices, limit output, or otherwise restrict the forces of competition. It also declared illegal all monopolies or "attempts to monopolize any part of trade or commerce among the several states, or with foreign nations." The law was not applied with much force until 1904, when it was used to dissolve the Northern Securities Company, a firm that had been formed to monopolize railroad transportation in certain northern states. Later, in 1911, the law became the basis for the antitrust suit that resulted in the breakup of Standard Oil, a trust that controlled some 90 percent of the petroleum industry.

As a result of the limits laid down by the courts in the Standard Oil case, businesses became somewhat less aggressive in their monopolistic practices.

[9] F. M. Scherer, *Industrial Market Structure and Economic Performance,* 2nd Edition (Chicago: Rand McNally, 1980), p. 121.

Rather than strive for monopoly, they were content to become the dominant firms in their respective oligopolistic industries. However, many firms gained dominion not by abandoning such practices but by pursuing them in disguised and subtle ways. This led Congress in 1914 to pass two more bills aimed at curbing anticompetitive practices: the Clayton Antitrust Act and the Federal Trade Commission Act.

The Clayton Antitrust Act. The Clayton Act was designed primarily to stem the tide of mergers that had already reduced competition significantly in a number of important industries, such as steel production, petroleum refining, and electrical equipment manufacture. The act prohibited mergers between competing firms if the impact of their union would be to "substantially lessen competition or to tend to create a monopoly." The act also outlawed other practices if they lessened competition. "Other practices" included **tying contracts**—agreements specifying that the purchaser would, as a condition of sale for a given product, also buy some other product offered by the seller. Once again, enforcement was a problem because the courts interpreted this law in ways that permitted mergers between competing firms to continue. Finally, in 1950, the Cellar-Kefauver Act amended the Clayton Act by closing a major loophole, thus effectively eliminating the possibility of mergers involving major competitors.

During the Reagan-Bush administration, the government relaxed its restrictions against mergers involving major competitors. This more permissive attitude was at least partially responsible for a wave of merger activity in the 1980s. The Clinton administration has, with a few exceptions, also tended to be relatively consenting in its attitude toward such mergers.

The Federal Trade Commission Act. The last of the three major antitrust statutes, the Federal Trade Commission Act, was also passed in 1914. Its primary purpose was to establish a special agency, the Federal Trade Commission (FTC), empowered to investigate allegations of "unfair methods of competition" and to command businesses in violation of FTC regulations to cease those practices. Although the FTC Act did not specify the precise meaning of "unfair methods of competition," the phrase has been interpreted by the commission to include practices prohibited under the Sherman and Clayton Acts—price fixing and tying contracts, for example—and any other practices that can be shown to limit competition or damage the consuming public. For instance, the FTC has deemed it unfair for a funeral home to fail to provide, in advance, an itemized price list for funeral services and merchandise or to furnish embalming without first informing customers about alternatives.

The Federal Trade Commission is one of the two federal agencies charged with the enforcement of the antitrust statutes. The other agency is the Antitrust

Under the leadership of John D. Rockefeller, the Standard Oil trust acquired a virtual monopoly in petroleum refining.

Division of the Justice Department. The Antitrust Division is responsible for enforcing the Sherman and Clayton Acts and lesser pieces of antitrust legislation. The FTC is also charged with antitrust enforcement, including civil actions against violators of either the Sherman or Clayton Acts, but its responsibilities are somewhat broader. About half its resources are devoted to combating deception and misrepresentation: improper labeling and misleading advertisements, for example. The overlapping responsibilities of the FTC and the Antitrust Division have posed some problems of coordination, but these are at least partially offset by the likelihood that one agency's oversights may be picked up by the other.

Criticisms of Antitrust. Some economists argue that antitrust should be discarded because it is based on the outmoded perception that bigness (being large in relation to the size of the market) is bad. These economists believe that the ability of large firms to achieve economies of scale and rapid development of new products more than compensates for any reduction in competition. This is particularly true, they argue, in an era of increased foreign competition. Lester Thurow of MIT points out that firms that seem large relative to the U. S. economy are not so large when viewed in the context of the world economy; therefore, they possess less market power than is commonly assumed. According to Thurow, even some of the largest U. S. firms are now in danger of being driven out of business by foreign rivals: "Think, for example, about General Motors. For many years it was the largest industrial firm in the world. Today, even if it were the only American auto manufacturer, it would still be in a competitive fight for its life."[10]

According to these economists, U.S. antitrust laws handicap domestic producers in this competitive struggle. Consider, for example, the Japanese *keiretsu*, or "group of companies." This arrangement joins together rival producers, along with their suppliers, banks, and government agencies, in order to share knowledge and gain efficiency. These structures, although legal in Japan, would probably be illegal in the United States under present antitrust laws. Antitrust critics argue that by prohibiting such joint ventures, we tie the hands of our domestic producers and put them at a competitive disadvantage relative to their foreign rivals.[11]

Supporters of antitrust laws point out that while bigness is not always bad, it is not always good either. So, they argue, the correct response is not to discard antitrust enforcement but to apply it on a case-by-case basis. For example, some mergers and cooperative ventures may be in the best interests of consumers because they lower costs or create more effective competitors. But others may reduce competition without achieving offsetting efficiencies. And while competition from foreign firms has changed the economic environment for many U.S. businesses, other industries do not face significant competitive pressure from abroad. Furthermore, statistical evidence suggests that most U.S. firms are large enough to compete effectively with foreign rivals. And while there may be exceptions to this generalization—the *keiretsu* and similar foreign alliances may require that similar alliances be permitted in the United States—the existence of these exceptions does not justify abandoning our antitrust statutes.

INDUSTRY REGULATION

Government regulation of industry approaches the problem of market power from a different perspective and therefore provides a different solution.[12] The basic assumption is that certain industries cannot or should not be made competitive. Hence, the role of government is to provide a framework whereby the actions of these less than competitive firms can be constrained in a manner consistent with the public interest. This is accomplished by establishing regulatory

---

[10] Lester C. Thurow, "An Era of New Competition," *Newsweek,* Jan. 18, 1982, p.63.
[11] Patrick M. Boarman, "Antitrust Laws in a Global Market," *Challenge,* Jan.–Feb. 1993, p.30–36.
[12] Regulation designed to deal with the problems posed by market power is sometimes described as "price and entry regulation" to distinguish it from "health and safety regulation."

agencies empowered to control the prices such firms can charge, the quality of service they must provide, and the conditions under which additional firms will be allowed to enter the industry.

The reason that certain industries should not be made competitive is that they are *natural monopolies*. As we learned in the last chapter, a natural monopoly exists when a single firm can supply the entire market at a lower average cost than two or more firms could. In essence, natural monopolies are situations in which we don't want to permit competition between firms because it would interfere with our ability to achieve the lowest possible production costs. The provision of local phone service is widely thought to be a natural monopoly, as is the provision of electric power. Consider your local phone company, for example. Providing local phone service requires a very large initial investment in switching equipment, telephone poles, wires, and other hardware. These fixed costs are major costs of doing business as a phone company; the variable costs of providing phone service are relatively low. Of course, the more customers the phone company serves, the lower the firm's average fixed costs. And since most of the phone company's costs are fixed costs, as average fixed costs fall, so do average total costs, giving us the declining average costs associated with natural monopoly.

At one time, long-distance phone service was also regarded as a natural monopoly because it was necessary to string expensive copper wire from city to city. Today, microwave communications make it possible to avoid that expense, thus opening the way for competition and eliminating the justification for natural monopoly status. (Similar changes may be undermining the natural monopoly status of the local phone company, but it's probably too early to make that prediction.)[13] The Federal Communications Commission (FCC) continues to regulate the rates charged by AT&T (the former monopolist provider of long-distance service), but it is clear that rates will be fully deregulated after AT&T's new rivals have established themselves.

The major criticism of federal industry regulation is that it has not been confined to natural monopolies. Over the years, numerous industries—including airlines, trucking, radio and television, and water carriers (ships and barges)—have been thought to be sufficiently "clothed with the public interest" to justify regulation. In recent years, that justification has been questioned and virtually all federal regulatory agencies have seen their rate-setting powers either eliminated or substantially reduced.

---

[13] The Telecommunications Act of 1996 was expected to bring a flood of new competitors into the local phone market. That hasn't happened. There is increased competition for business customers in some large urban areas, but residential customers have been stuck with the local monopolist. For a discussion, see "Instead of Flood of Competition, the Communications Act Brought a Trickle," *New York Times*, Feb. 10, 1997, p. D7.

Summary

In the U.S. economy, most firms have some market power, or pricing discretion. Market power is exercised through product differentiation or by altering total industry output. The extent of the firm's market power depends on the structure, or makeup, of the industry in which it operates. The definitive characteristics of *industry structure* are the number of sellers in the industry and their size distribution, the nature of the product, and the extent of barriers to entry. The four basic industry structures are pure competition, monopolistic competition, oligopoly, and pure monopoly.

At one end of the spectrum lie purely competitive firms, which are totally without market power. Because the competitive industry is characterized by a large number of relatively small firms selling undifferentiated products, each firm is powerless to influence price. The absence of significant barriers to entry prevents purely competitive firms from earning economic profits in the long run.

Monopolistic competition is the market structure most closely resembling pure competition; the difference is that monopolistically competitive firms sell differentiated products. The ability to differentiate its product allows the monopolistically competitive firm some pricing discretion although that discretion is limited by the availability of close substitutes offered by competing firms. Monopolistically competitive firms misallocate resources because they fail to produce up to the point at which marginal social benefits equal marginal social costs. They also are somewhat less efficient at producing their products than are purely competitive firms with identical cost curves. These disadvantages are at least partially offset by the product variety offered by these sellers.

The third market structure, *oligopoly,* is characterized by a small number of relatively large firms that are protected by significant barriers to entry. Although these firms may enjoy substantial pricing discretion, their market power is constrained by the high degree of interdependence that exists among oligopolistic firms. *Game theory* is one of the tools used to understand and predict the behavior of these interdependent rivals.

Oligopolists sometime use *collusion,* secret agreements to fix prices, and *price leadership,* informal agreements to follow the price changes of one firm, as tactics to reduce competition. Even in the absence of collusion or price leadership, oligopolists may choose to avoid price competition because it tends to invite retaliation. Instead these firms tend to channel their competitive instincts into *nonprice competition*—advertising, packaging, and new product development.

The market structure farthest removed from pure competition is monopoly, or *pure monopoly.* The monopolist enjoys substantial pricing discretion and dictates the level of output. The monopoly *is* the industry because it is the sole seller of a product for which there are no close substitutes. Unlike that of the purely competitive firm, the monopolist's position is protected by substantial barriers to entry, which may enable monopolistic firms to earn economic profits in the long run.

Like monopolistically competitive firms, monopolists tend to distort the allocation of resources by halting production short of the point at which marginal social benefit equals marginal social cost. Monopolists may charge higher prices than necessary—prices that include economic profits. These higher prices redistribute income from consumers to the monopolists. Oligopoly can have a similar impact on consumer welfare, but it is more difficult to generalize about the consequences of that market structure. In some industries the negative consequences of monopoly or oligopoly may be offset by the lower production costs that result from their greater size or by greater innovation due to their ability to invest economic profits in research and development.

Because monopolists and oligopolists may misallocate resources and redistribute income, the U.S. Congress has passed antitrust laws and created regulatory agencies. Enacted in response to the formation of *trusts* (combinations of firms organized to restrain competition), *antitrust laws* prohibit certain kinds of behavior: price fixing, tying contracts, and *mergers* entered into for the purpose of limiting competition. The major antitrust statutes are the Sherman Antitrust Act of 1890, the Clayton Antitrust Act of 1914, and the Federal Trade Commission Act, also passed in 1914.

Critics of antitrust argue that it should be discarded because it is based on the misperception that bigness is bad. According to this view, the ability of large firms to achieve economies of scale and more rapid new-product development more than compensates for any reduction in competition. Moreover, in an era of increased foreign competition, even relatively large U.S. firms may be small in comparison to the world market. In fact, cooperative ventures between U.S. firms may be necessary in order to compete effectively with foreign rivals.

Supporters of antitrust respond by pointing out that size does not always confer advantages such as economies of scale or more rapid new product development. In addition, available evidence suggests that most U.S. firms are large enough to compete effectively with their foreign rivals.

Industry regulation, the other approach to dealing with potentially exploitive market power, is designed to establish and police rules of behavior for *natural monopolies,* industries in which competition cannot or should not develop because of technical or cost considerations. Unfortunately regulation has been extended to some industries in which there is little evidence of natural monopoly status—transportation, for example. In recent years many of those industries have been deregulated.

GLOSSARY

Antitrust laws. Laws that have as their objective the maintenance and promotion of competition.

Collusion. Agreement among sellers to fix prices or in some other way restrict competition.

Conscious parallelism. A situation in which firms adopt similar policies even though they have had no communication whatsoever.

Dominant strategy. A strategy that should be pursued regardless of the strategy selected by a firm's rivals..

Game theory. The study of the strategies employed by interdependent firms.

Government franchise. An exclusive license to provide some product or service.

Industry structure. The makeup of an industry: its number of sellers and their size distribution, the nature of the product, and the extent of barriers to entry.

Merger. The union of two or more companies into a single firm.

Monopolistic competition. An industry structure characterized by a large number of small sellers of slightly differentiated products and by modest barriers to entry.

Monopoly. An industry structure characterized by a single firm selling a product for which there are no close substitutes and by substantial barriers to entry.

Nash equilibrium. A situation in which each firm's strategy is the best it can choose, given the strategies chosen by the other firms in the industry.

Oligopoly. An industry structure characterized by a few relatively large sellers and substantial barriers to entry.

Price leadership. An informal arrangement whereby a single firm takes the lead in all price changes in the industry.

Trusts. Combinations of firms organized for the purpose of restraining competition and thereby gaining economic profit.

Tying contract. An agreement specifying that the purchaser will, as a condition of sale for some product, also buy some other product offered by the seller.

STUDY QUESTIONS

Fill in the Blanks

1. Firms that can influence the price of their product are said to possess

   Market power

2. An industry dominated by a few relatively large sellers is an _Oligopoly_.

3. The closest market structure to pure competition is _monopolistic competition_.

4. In long-run equilibrium, purely competitive firms and _monopolistically competitive_ firms can earn only a normal profit.

5. The distinguishing feature of oligopoly is the high degree of _interdependence_ that exists among sellers.

6. A _monopoly_ is the sole seller of a product for which there are no good substitutes.

7. _Collusion_ is agreement between sellers to fix prices or limit competition.

8. Monopolists distort the allocation of scarce resources because they produce (more/less) _less_ of their product than is socially desirable.

9. The first major antitrust law, the _Sherman_ Act, was passed in 1890.

10. Both oligopolists and monopolists may earn economic profits in the long run because they are protected by substantial _barriers to entry_ .

11. The study of the strategies employed by interdependent firms is known as _game theory_ .

12. _Conscious parallelism_ refers to oligopolists adopting similar policies without any communication whatsoever.

Multiple Choice

1. Which of the following is *not* an element of industry structure?
   a) The number of sellers in the industry
   b) The extent of barriers to entry
   c) The existence of economic profits
   d) The size distribution of sellers

2. Which of the following statements about unregulated monopolists is *false?*
   a) They may incur an economic loss in the short run.
   b) They maximize their profit (or minimize their loss) by producing the output at which MR = MC.
   c) They sell their product at a price equal to marginal cost.
   d) They face competition from rivals in other industries.

3. Which of the following is *not* a characteristic of monopolistic competition?
   a) Substantial barriers to entry
   b) Differentiated products
   c) A large number of sellers
   d) Small firms

4. Which of the following is probably *not* a monopolistically competitive firm?
   a) A barber shop
   b) A wheat farm
   c) A hardware store
   d) A furniture store

5. American Airlines will not raise prices without first considering how United will behave. This is probably evidence of their
   a) cutthroat competition.
   b) collusion.
   c) interdependence.
   d) price fixing.

6. Which of the following is *not* a characteristic of oligopolistic industries?
   a) Mutual interdependence
   b) Substantial barriers to entry
   c) Relatively large sellers
   d) Fierce price competition

7. Which of the following do monopolistically competitive firms, oligopolists, and monopolists have in common?
   a) All are relatively large.
   b) All have some market power.
   c) All are protected by substantial barriers to entry.
   d) All are concerned about the reactions of rivals to any actions they take.

8. Which of the following statutes outlawed mergers that would substantially lessen competition?
   a) The Sherman Act
   b) The Clayton Act
   c) The Merger Act
   d) The Federal Trade Commission Act

9. What is the primary difference between antitrust enforcement and industry regulation?
   a) Antitrust enforcement attempts to promote competition; industry regulation does not.
   b) Antitrust enforcement has some critics; industry regulation does not.
   c) Antitrust enforcement is concerned about the public interest; industry regulation attempts to protect the regulated firms.
   d) Industry regulation deals only with natural monopolies; antitrust does not.

10. The concept of conscious parallelism suggests that oligopolists
    a) will always collude.
    b) can adopt similar policies without any communication.
    c) use price leadership to coordinate their pricing policies.
    d) prefer price competition to nonprice competition.

Use the payoff matrix at the bottom of this page in answering questions 11 and 12.

11. Which of the following is true?
    a) X's dominant strategy is to charge $15; Y doesn't have a dominant strategy.
    b) The dominant strategy for both X and Y is to charge $15.
    c) Y's dominant strategy is to charge $20; X doesn't have a dominant strategy.
    d) The dominant strategy for both X and Y is to charge $20.

12. If both firms charge $15,
    a) each firm will earn a profit of $30,000.
    b) there will be incentive to collude and raise the price to $20.
    c) firm X will earn $40,000.
    d) firm Y will earn $40,000.

13. Cheating on collusive agreements is more likely when
    a) there are very few firms in the industry.
    b) the economy is weak and firms have excess capacity.
    c) each firm's prices are readily known.
    d) cheaters can expect swift retaliation.

14. Which of the following is *not* an example of a barrier to entry?
    a) A government franchise
    b) Exclusive control of a critical input
    c) The presence of a small number of firms in the industry
    d) The requirement of a large investment to begin production

15. Firms that are monopolists
    a) always earn economic profits in the short run.
    b) always earn economic profits in the long run.
    c) can see their monopoly status eroded by technological progress.
    d) All of the above

16. When a monopolistically competitive firm is in long-run equilibriums,
    a) price equals marginal cost.
    b) the demand curve is tangent to the marginal cost curve.
    c) price equals average total cost.
    d) the firm earns an economic profit.

17. If the firms in a monopolistically competitive industry are earning economic profits,
    a) additional firms will enter the industry, shifting each firm's demand curve to the right.
    b) firms will tend to leave the industry until a normal profit is earned.
    c) firms will enter the industry, reducing the demand for each firm's product.
    d) firms will enter the industry until each firm's demand curve is tangent to its marginal cost curve.

Firm X's price strategies

		$15	$20
Firm Y's price strategies	$15	Each firm earns a $20,000 profit.	X earns $10,000. Y earns $40,000.
	$20	X earns $40,000. Y earns $10,000.	Each firm earns a $30,000 profit.

Firm A's advertising strategies

		Don't advertise	*Advertise*
Firm B's advertising strategies	*Don't advertise*	A earns $100,000. B earns $ 80,000.	A earns $150,000. B earns $0 profit.
	Advertise	A earns $0 profit. B earns $60,000.	A earns $60,000. B earns $40,000.

Use the payoff matrix above in answering questions 18–20.

18. Which if the following is true?
    a) A's dominant strategy is to advertise.
    b) B's dominant strategy is to not to advertise.
    c) A does not have a dominant strategy.
    d) B's dominant strategy is to advertise.

19. If A decides not to advertise, B's best strategy is
    a) not to advertise, in which case it will earn $40,000.
    b) to advertise, in which case it will earn $40,000.

c) not to advertise, in which case it will earn $80,000.
d) to advertise, in which case it will earn $80,000.

20. Because B knows that A's dominant strategy is
    a) to advertise, B's best strategy is to advertise also.
    b) not to advertise, B will also opt not to advertise.
    c) to advertise, B's best strategy is not to advertise.
    d) not to advertise, B's best strategy is to advertise.

Problems and Questions for Discussion

1. What constrains a monopolist's pricing discretion?

2. What problems might be associated with monopolistic or oligopolistic market structures? That is, how might they harm consumer well-being?

3. How do firms acquire market power? What impact do barriers to entry have on a firm's market power?

4. Why would we expect prices to be somewhat higher under monopolistic competition than under pure competition?

5. Suppose that there is only one grocery store in your neighborhood. What limits its market power? If your neighborhood were more isolated, would that increase or decrease the grocery store's market power?

6. In some communities, grocery stores may act as oligopolists, whereas in other communities, they may act as monopolistically competitive firms. How is this possible? How would you distinguish the first situation from the second?

7. Under what circumstances might consumers be better off with monopoly or oligopoly than with a competitive structure?

8. What is meant by a *natural monopoly,* and how can its existence justify regulation?

9. Some economists argue that antitrust is an outmoded policy that should be discarded. Discuss the basis for this conclusion, and summarize the opposing view.

10. Explain what is meant by a dominant strategy.

ANSWER KEY

Fill in the Blanks

1. market power
2. oligopoly
3. monopolistic competition
4. monopolistically competitive
5. interdependence
6. monopoly
7. Collusion
8. less
9. Sherman
10. barriers to entry
11. game theory
12. Conscious parallelism

Multiple Choice

1. c
2. c
3. a
4. b
5. c
6. d
7. b
8. b
9. a
10. b
11. b
12. b
13. b
14. c
15. c
16. c
17. c
18. a
19. c
20. a

CHAPTER 9

Market Failure

LEARNING OBJECTIVES

1. Define market failure and identify its sources.
2. Distinguish between internal and external costs (and benefits).
3. Describe how externalities distort the allocation of scarce resources.
4. Explain pollution as the result of poorly defined property rights.
5. Discuss why pollution taxes are superior to emissions standards.
6. Explain why government should encourage the production of products yielding significant external benefits.
7. Distinguish between private and public goods.
8. Explain the free-rider problem and its consequences.
9. Describe the income distribution and the extent of poverty in the U.S. economy.
10. Discuss the views of public choice economists and the concept of government failure.

At times a market economy may produce too much or too little of certain products and thus fail to make the most efficient use of society's limited resources. This, as you might expect, is referred to as **market failure.** In *The Affluent Society,* John Kenneth Galbraith describes numerous instances of market failure:

> …The family which takes its mauve and cerise, air-conditioned, power-steered, and power-braked automobile out for a tour passes through cities that are badly paved, made hideous by litter, blighted buildings, billboards, and posts for wires that should long since have been put underground. They pass on into a countryside that has been rendered largely invisible by commercial art….They picnic on exquisitely packaged food from a portable icebox by a polluted stream and go on to spend the night at a park which is a menace to public health and morals. Just before dozing off on an air mattress, beneath a nylon tent, amid the stench of decaying refuse, they may reflect vaguely on the curious unevenness of their blessings. Is this, indeed, the American genius?[1]

---

[1] John Kenneth Galbraith, *The Affluent Society* (New York: New American Library, 1958), pp. 199–200.

In Galbraith's view the American economy has produced an abundance of consumer goods—automobiles, appliances, sporting goods, and numerous other items—but far too little of other goods that Americans desire: clean air and water, parks, and well-paved roads, for example. Why do such market failures occur? As you will learn in this chapter, there are three major sources of market failure: market power, externalities, and public goods. The passage from Professor Galbraith's book points at two of these: externalities and public goods. In this chapter we explore those two sources of market failure in some detail. Because the impact of market power has been examined at length in Chapters 7 and 8, we will review it only briefly here.

Market Power Revisited

As you've already discovered, resources are allocated efficiently when they are used to produce the goods and services that consumers value most. This, in turn, requires that each product be produced up to the point at which the benefit its consumption provides to society (the marginal social benefit) is exactly equal to the cost its production imposes on society (the marginal social cost). This occurs under pure competition, but it doesn't happen when firms possess market power.[2] Consequently, the existence of market power constitutes the first source of market failure.

Firms with market power tend to restrict output in order to force up prices. As a consequence they halt production short of the output at which marginal social benefit equals marginal social cost, causing too few of society's resources to be allocated to the goods and services they produce. In simplified terms this means that because firms such as IBM and General Electric have market power, fewer of society's resources are devoted to producing computers and appliances, and too few Americans will be able to own these products. Instead, these resources will flow to the production of products that consumers value less. Markets are "failing" in the sense that they are not allocating resources in the most efficient way, that is, to the production of the goods and services that consumers value most.

Although virtually all economists agree that this form of market failure exists, clearly it is not what Galbraith was describing when he wrote the words we quoted. Galbraith seems to believe that Americans have done quite well in the area of consumer goods. How, then, do we explain his criticism of our economy's performance? The answer lies beyond the problems caused by market power, in some shortcomings of the market mechanism itself.

---

[2] The conclusion that pure competition leads to an efficient allocation of resources rests on the assumption that there are no externalities. *Externalities* are costs or benefits that are not borne by either buyers or sellers but that spill over onto third parties. They are the next topic in this chapter.

Externalities as a Source of Market Failure

A second source of resource misallocation is the failure of markets to take into account all the costs and benefits associated with the production and consumption of a good or service.

Consider for a moment the information that guides producers and consumers in their decision making. When businesses are deciding what production techniques to use and what resources to purchase, they consider only **private costs**, or **internal costs**—the costs borne by the firm. They do not take into account any external costs that are borne by (or spill over onto) other parties. Consumers behave in a similar manner: They tend to consider only **private benefits**, or **internal benefits**—the benefits that accrue to the person or persons purchasing the product—and to ignore any external benefits that might be received by others.

If businesses and consumers are permitted to ignore these external costs and benefits, or **externalities,** the result will be an inefficient use of our scarce resources. We will produce too much of some items because we do not consider the full costs; we will produce too little of others because we do not consider the full benefits.

EXTERNALITIES: THE CASE OF EXTERNAL COSTS

It's not difficult to think of personal situations in which external costs have come into play. Perhaps you've planned to savor a quiet dinner at your favorite restaurant, only to have a shrieking baby seated with its harried parents at the next table. Think about the movie you might have enjoyed if that rambunctious five-year-old hadn't been using the back of your seat as a bongo drum. Why do parents bring young children to these places, knowing that they will probably disturb the people around them? According to the teachings of Adam Smith, they are pursuing their own self-interest—in this case by minimizing the monetary cost of an evening's entertainment. But their actions are imposing different kinds of costs on everyone around them. The frazzled nerves, poorly digested meals, and generally spoiled evenings experienced by you and your fellow diners or moviegoers are examples of **external costs:** the costs created by one party or group and imposed on, or *spilled over onto* some other (nonconsenting) party or group.

Pollution as an External Cost. The classic example of external costs is pollution: the contamination of our land, air, and water caused by the litter that lines our streets and highways, the noxious fumes emitted into our atmosphere, and the wastes dumped into our rivers, lakes, and streams. Why does pollution exist? The answer is really quite obvious. It's less expensive for a manufacturer to dispose of its wastes in a nearby river, for example, than to haul that material to a so-called safe area. But it is a low-cost method of disposal only in terms of the private costs borne by the manufacturing firm. If we consider the social cost, there may well be a cheaper method of disposal.

Social cost refers to the full cost to society of producing a product. It represents the sum of private costs plus external costs. In situations where there are no external costs, private costs and social costs will be the same. But when external costs are present, social costs will be higher than private costs. That's the case in our example of the polluting manufacturing firm. The private cost of manufacturing the firm's product includes the payments made for materials, labor, rent, and everything else it takes to run a business. But it does not include a payment for the damage done when the river is used for waste disposal. Because the firm is able to ignore this cost, it is described as an external cost; it is external to the firm's decision making.

To understand why pollution is a cost, think of the damage it does. Polluted water means fewer fish and fewer people enjoying water sports. It

Dumping wastes into a river may minimize private costs, but it can create substantial external costs.

also means less income for people who rent boats and cottages and sell fishing bait, for example. It further affects the people living downstream, who need water for drinking and bathing; they will have to pay—through taxes—to purify the water. Finally, it may have a deadly effect on the birds and animals that live off the fish and other creatures in the water. Thus, water pollution may create numerous costs for society, costs that are ignored by polluters.

External Costs and Resource Misallocation. When the act of producing or consuming a product creates external costs, an exclusive reliance on private markets and the pursuit of self-interest will result in a misallocation of society's resources. We can illustrate why this is so by investigating a single, hypothetical, purely competitive industry.

For the purpose of our investigation, let's assume that the paint industry is purely competitive. Under those circumstances, the equilibrium price and quantity will be determined by the interaction of the industry demand and supply curves. In Exh. 9.1, demand curve *D* shows the quantity of paint that would be demanded at each possible price. Recall from Chapter 6 that the demand curve is a product's marginal benefit curve because it tells us the value that consumers place on an additional unit of the product. For example, the 100,000th can of paint provides benefits worth $10, and the 120,000th can of paint provides benefits worth $8.

The other important element in the diagram is the supply curve. As you already know, when an industry is purely competitive, the supply curve can be thought of as the marginal cost curve for the industry because it is found by summing the marginal cost curves of the firms in the industry. The first supply curve, S_1, shows the quantity of paint the industry would supply if each firm in the industry considered only its private costs and disposed of its wastes by dumping them into local rivers. As you can see, under these conditions the demand and supply curves reveal an equilibrium price of $8 per can of paint and an equilibrium quantity of 120,000 cans per year.

The equilibrium output of 120,000 cans is labeled the "market output" because that is the output that will be produced in the absence of government intervention. Remember, businesses respond only to private costs; they tend to ignore external costs unless they are required to take them into consideration.

Suppose that we find a way to require the firms in the industry to consider the external costs they have been ignoring. Under those conditions the supply curve would shift to S_2, the curve reflecting the full social cost of production. (Recall that whenever there is an increase in resource prices or anything else that increases the cost of production, the supply curve will shift left, or upward.) As you can see from the diagram, the result of this reduction supply is

EXHIBIT 9.1

The Impact of External Costs

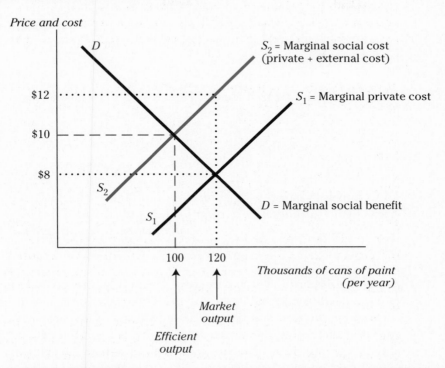

Because paint producers consider only private costs, they produce 120,000 units, more than the optimal, or allocatively efficient, output of 100,000 units.

an increase in the price of paint to $10 a can and a reduction in the equilibrium quantity to 100,000 cans. Note that 100,000 cans is the allocatively efficient level of output, the output for which the marginal social benefit equals the marginal social cost. Consumers receive $10 worth of benefits from the 100,000th can of paint, exactly enough to justify the $10 marginal cost of producing that can.

If 100,000 units is the optimal or efficient level of output, 120,000 must have been too much! So long as paint producers were allowed to shift some of their production costs to society as a whole (or to some portion of society), the price of paint was artificially low; that is, it did not reflect the true social cost of producing paint. Consumers responded to this low price by purchasing an artificially high quantity of paint—more than they would have purchased if the price reflected the true social cost of production. As a consequence more of society's scarce resources were allocated to the production of paint than was socially optimal. (Note that consumers receive marginal benefits worth $8 from the 120,000th can of paint, but the marginal social cost of producing that unit is $12; production has been carried too far.) In summary, when businesses fail to consider external costs, they produce too much of their product from society's point of view.

Correcting for External Costs. How do we force businesses and individuals to consider all the costs of their actions, to treat external costs as if they were private or internal costs? (This process is sometimes referred to as forcing firms to **internalize** all costs.) One possibility is for government to assign property rights to unowned resources such as lakes and rivers so that some individual will be in a position to charge for their use. Another possibility is for Congress to pass laws that forbid (or limit) activities that impose external costs (such as dumping wastes into lakes and streams). A third possibility is for government agencies to harness market incentives in an effort to compensate for external costs. Let's consider those alternatives.

Assigning property rights. Our paint example points out that when manufacturers create external costs, the private market does not record the true costs of production and thereby fails to provide the proper signals to ensure that our resources are used optimally. Why is the private market unable to communicate the true cost of production? In many instances the problem is poorly defined property rights. **Property rights** are the legal rights to use goods, services, or resources. For example, you have the right to use your car and lawnmower and barbeque grill; your neighbor does not. But who owns the Mississippi River and the Atlantic Ocean and the air we breathe? Of course, no one owns these natural resources. And that's the problem. Because no one owns these resources, no one has the right to charge for their use. And because no one has the right to charge for their use, individuals assume that they are available to be used (and abused) for free. Remember, individuals and businesses respond to private costs and benefits; if private markets don't register the cost, people may act as if there is none.

Because the source of the pollution problem is poorly defined property rights, one possible solution is for government to clarify the ownership of the resources being abused. Think about our hypothetical example involving the polluting paint company. Suppose that the state legislature gives the legal ownership of the river to the paint company. Suppose also that the only use of the river has been as the water supply for a small city downstream. Once the ownership of the river is established, we might expect the city to attempt to bargain with the paint company to stop dumping its wastes into the river. Assume, for example, that the next-cheapest disposal technique would cost the company $100,000 a year. Suppose also that it would cost the city $200,000 a year to purchase water from a neighboring community. Since the river is worth more as a source of drinking water than as a method of waste disposal, the city should be able to negotiate with the paint company to stop dumping its wastes in the river. For example, if the city offers the paint company $150,000 to stop discharging its wastes, the paint company would probably agree. The paint company would stop dumping its wastes into the river because it would no longer see the use of the river as free. If it dumps its wastes into the river, it would have to forgo the $150,000 payment from the city. Since the cost of alternative disposal is only $100,000, the firm would choose the alternative method and pocket the $50,000 difference.

Suppose that the legislature assigns the ownership of the river to the city. Would the outcome be different? This time the company would need to approach the city to get permission to dump into the river. The company would be willing to pay up to $100,000 a year to use the river since that is the cost of alternative disposal. But since an alternative water supply would cost the city $200,000, it would not be willing to deal; the river would again be used as a water supply.

The preceding example illustrates two important points. First, when property rights are clearly defined, resources are put to their most valued use; that is, they are used efficiently. In this case the river will be used as a water supply, but in some instances its most valued use might be for waste disposal.[3] Second, the resources will be used efficiently regardless of who is assigned their ownership. (Note that, either way, the river is used as a water supply.) The idea of solving externality problems by assigning property rights and encouraging negotiation is based on the work of Nobel prize-winning economist Ronald Coase. In our society many cases involving externalities are resolved by negotiation after the courts have clarified property rights. However, as Professor Coase has recognized, this solution works only in situations in which the transactions costs—the costs of striking a bargain between the parties—are relatively low and in which the number of people involved is relatively small. When the assignment of

---

[3] Suppose, for example, that alternative disposal would cost the paint company $250,000 a year. In that case the paint company would be willing to bid up to $250,000 to use the river for waste disposal. If it offered the city $225,000, the city would probably agree (since it can purchase water for $200,000 a year), and the river would be used for waste disposal.

property rights does not work, another method must be sought to solve the problem.

Emissions Standards. The U.S. government has attempted to limit pollution by establishing *emissions standards*—laws that specify the maximum amounts of various wastes that each firm will be allowed to emit into the air or water. To meet these emissions standards, firms have to install pollution-control devices, hire additional personnel to monitor these devices, and take other steps that tend to increase the cost of production and lead to higher product prices. When consumers are required to pay a price that more fully reflects the true cost of production, they purchase fewer units of the formerly underpriced items. Therefore, resources can be reallocated to the production of other items whose prices more accurately reflect the full social costs of production.

Although government emissions standards have helped reduce pollution, fulfilling the requirements and limiting the discharge of industrial waste to less than some permitted maximum amount can be very costly. Since the polluting firms come from a wide range of industries and employ vastly different production methods, some firms find it much more expensive than others to reduce their discharges. As a consequence, some firms are able to meet their standards at relatively low cost, whereas others face severe financial burdens. The total cost to society of achieving any given level of environmental quality is the sum of the costs incurred by the various firms.

Pollution Taxes. Many economists contend that it would be less expensive to create a *pollution tax*, which firms would be required to pay on any waste they discharge into the air or water. Under a system of pollution taxes, firms could discharge as much waste into the environment as they chose, but they would have to pay a specified levy—say, $50—for each unit emitted. Ideally this tax would bring about the desired reduction in pollution. If not, it would be raised to whatever dollar amount would convince firms to reduce pollution to acceptable levels.

A major advantage of a pollution tax is that it would allow the firms themselves to decide which ones could cut back on emissions (the discharges of wastes) at the lowest cost. For example, given a fee of $50 for each ton of wastes emitted into the environment, those firms that could reduce their emissions for less than $50 per ton would do so; other firms would continue to pollute and pay the tax. As a result, pollution would be reduced by the firms that could do so most easily and at the lowest cost. Society would then have achieved a given level of environmental quality at the lowest cost in terms of its scarce resources.

A simple example may help to illustrate why the pollution tax is a less expensive approach. Assume that the economy is made up of firms A and B and that each firm is discharging 4 tons of waste a year. Assume also that it costs firm A $30 per ton to reduce emissions and firm B $160 per ton.

Suppose that society wants to reduce the discharge of wastes by 4 tons a year. An emissions standard that required each firm to limit its emissions to 2 tons a year would cost society $380 ($60 for firm A and $320 for firm B). A pollution tax of $50 a ton would accomplish the same objective at a cost of $120 since it would cause firm A to reduce its emissions from 4 tons to zero. (Firm A would opt to reduce its emissions because this approach is less costly than paying the pollution tax. If the firm pays the pollution tax, it will be billed $50 × 4 tons = $200. But it can reduce emissions at a cost of $30 × 4 tons = $120. Thus, it would prefer to reduce its emissions rather than pay the pollution tax.) Note that firm B will prefer to pay the tax; thus, government will receive $200 in pollution tax revenue. This $200 should not be considered a cost of reducing pollution, since it can be used to build roads or schools or be spent in any other way society chooses.

As we noted earlier, the United States has relied on emissions standards to reduce pollution; pollution taxes have been used very sparingly and primarily in an experimental way. But the Clean Air Act of 1990 contains provisions that, like pollution taxes, encourage businesses to reduce pollution in the least costly way. The Clean Air Act encourages businesses to reduce emissions by more than the law requires; businesses are given the right to sell pollution "credits" to other businesses that find it very costly to reduce their emissions. By giving firms the option of buying credits or reducing emissions, the act hopes to achieve its air quality standards at the lowest possible cost. The article on pages 272–274, "Clear Skies Are Goal as Pollution Is Turned Into a Commodity," takes a closer look at how this system works, and discusses how the business community is reacting to this new approach to combating pollution.

The Optimal Level of Pollution. Although emissions standards and pollution taxes are both designed to reduce pollution, neither system is designed to eliminate pollution entirely. The total elimination of pollution would not be in society's best interest since it requires the use of scarce resources that have alternative uses. Economists support reducing pollution only so long as the benefits of added pollution controls exceed their costs. For example, it makes no sense to force firms to pay an additional $30 million to reduce pollution if the added benefits to society amount to only $10 million. For that reason, any rational system of pollution control—whether based on emissions standards or pollution taxes—will permit some level of pollution. Unfortunately, because it is difficult to measure the costs and benefits of pollution control in an exact manner, it is also difficult to determine whether efforts to control pollution have been carried too far or not far enough.

Use Your Economic Reasoning

Clear Skies Are Goal as Pollution Is Turned Into a Commodity

U.S. Promotes the Trading of Emissions Certificates in Global-Warming Pact

By John J. Fialka
Staff Reporter of the Wall Street Journal

WASHINGTON—As part of a sixth-grade science project, Rod Johnson's students in Glens Falls, N.Y., removed 330 tons of sulfur dioxide from the air.

Holding raffles, bake sales and auctions over a three-year period, they raised $25,000 to buy 330 certifications in the U.S. Environmental Protection Agency's acid-rain-emissions trading program—one of the nation's hottest new commodity markets. Each certificate allows the owner to emit one ton of the noxious gas.

Utilities trade the certificates—some selling them for profit, others buying them to comply with air-quality standards. But the students at Glens Falls Middle School are going to sit on theirs. The way the EPA program works, that means the nation's air will be that much cleaner.

Proposed by the Bush administration in 1990 as a novel, market-oriented solution to the problem of acid rain, the trading of what amounts to sulfur-dioxide-pollution permits has led to results that have exceeded expectations. Since its 1994 inception, the trading program, administered by the EPA, has contributed to a 30% drop in sulfur-dioxide emissions from major polluters, the agency says.

Cheap Alternative

President Clinton hopes to sell a version of the trading program to other nations meeting in Kyoto, Japan, in December to conclude a treaty that curbs global warming. Though some environmentalists don't like this approach, and government agencies are finding it hard to explain the complex system to local citizens, businessmen are warming to it. And Mr. Johnson says his students like trading because, "We can identify a problem and then participate in a solution...."

Trading appears to be a cheap way to help curb pollution. Industry had complained that removing sulfur dioxide from the air would cost as much as $1,500 a ton. But the price of about 7.2 million certificates being traded this year reflects a cost of $90 a ton. After years of hand-ringing, acid rain is being reduced by a market that lets individual companies make their own antipollution strategies.

"This program turns companies into pollution minders," says Daniel J. Dudek, a senior economist for the Environmental Defense Fund in New York, who sold the idea to the Bush administration and has become a kind of Johnny Appleseed, spawning other trading plans. "When they [polluters] think about it, they say, 'Hey! That's money going up the stacks.'..."

Basic Idea

The basic idea for the sulfur-dioxide program is relatively simple. The government set a cap that reduced the number of tons of the pollutant it would allow in the air, starting in 1995 and declining thereafter. Then it issued to 110 of the nation's dirtiest power plants tradable certificates that matched their share of the cap. Companies that cut emissions below their cap had extra certificates to sell. Companies that didn't had to buy them from the cleaner companies. Companies can save certificates from year to year, but federal clean-air standards still limit the amount of pollution that can be released.

For Milwaukee-based Wisconsin Electric Power Co., a unit of Wisconsin Energy Corp., the cap meant it had to cut sulfur-dioxide emissions from its five power plants by about 30,000 tons. Daniel L. Chartier, the company's emissions manager, figured he could remove 20,000 tons relatively cheaply by switching to low-sulfur coal. To get the remaining 10,000 tons, he learned, would be tough. He would have to buy two house-size, $130 million machines called "scrubbers."

But because other companies had reduced their emissions well below the cap, the market was flooded with cheap allowances. And since buyers can approach sellers in any part of the country, prices tend to even out. Mr. Chartier bought 10,000 of them, estimating he saved his company more than $100

million. This year he formed the Emissions Marketing Association, and 63 companies, mostly large utilities, have joined it. "We found growing enthusiasm as the knowledge of emissions trading increased," he says.

More markets are coming. Twelve northeastern states are adopting a version of the federal sulfur-dioxide trading program to reduce ozone levels, starting in 1999. Some of them have also joined a group of 37 states considering a larger smog-reduction plan. California has hatched a variety of such programs.

Big Business

While some may find it hard to envision pollution rights as a commodity, trading is already a big business. The EPA expects sulfur-dioxide trading to reach $648 million this year. The utility industry estimates actual volume is probably double that—or equal to the $1.2 billion cash market for U.S. soft red winter wheat. "Trades have basically doubled every year," says Brian McLean, head of EPA's acid-rain division, which tracks trades.

The Environmental Defense Fund's Mr. Dudek says this is only the beginning. He is consulting with traders at British Petroleum Co., helping them determine how a world-wide market in carbon-dioxide-emission allowances would work.

The Clinton administration has made trading a main part of its negotiating position on the treaty to prevent global warming. The treaty would impose a global limit on man-made sources of carbon dioxide, created by burning petroleum products, coal and natural gas. Since the 1850's, concentrations of carbon dioxide have increased in the atmosphere, and many scientists say that is artificially warming the Earth by trapping more of the sun's heat.

Draft versions of the U.S. plan would give each industrial nation an "emissions budget" that would be its pro rata share of the global limit. (A program for developing nations would be negotiated at a later time.) Industrial nations that curb emissions below 1990 levels would have allowances to sell. Countries that can't curb it, or won't, must buy them.

Adapting the U.S. acid-rain program to do that means stretching a trading program designed to cover hundreds of emitters to one that would cover millions and allowing international transactions. This will compound the complexity of trading, but Mr. Dudek insists it will also create many more cheap opportunities to reduce global carbon-dioxide levels....

Meanwhile traders continue to push the envelope.

(continued on next page)

(continued from previous page)

As the result of a modernization program, New York state's Niagara Mohawk Power Corp. cut its carbon-dioxide emissions by 2.5 million tons. It traded emission rights for that amount to an Arizona utility for 20,000 tons of sulfur-dioxide allowances. Then Niagara donated the sulfur-dioxide allowances to local environmental groups, which are retiring them. And $125,000 of the tax benefits Niagara received from the deal are being used to convert a Mexican fishing village to nonpolluting solar power.

Martin A. Smith, chief environmental scientist at Niagara, says the reductions and the experience in trading were worth it. "Do we just stand by and let these gases accumulate?"

USE YOUR ECONOMIC REASONING

1. Imagine two utilities, each discharging 20,000 tons of sulfur dioxide into the atmosphere each year. Utility A can reduce its emissions at a cost of $200 a ton; utility B can reduce its emissions at a cost of $50 a ton. Answer the following questions.
   a. If society wants to reduce sulfur dioxide emissions by 20,000 tons, why would it be preferable to have utility B reduce its emissions to zero rather than have each utility reduce its emissions by 10,000 tons?
   b. Suppose that each utility is given an "emissions certificate" permitting it to discharge 10,000 tons of sulfur dioxide a year. Under what circumstances might utility B be willing to reduce its emissions to zero?
2. How does the trading of emissions certificates help to ensure that our environment standards are achieved at the lowest possible cost? Why is that an important goal?
3. Some environmentalists want to establish a world-wide market in emissions certificates. Under such a system, industrialized nations like the United States might find themselves buying certificates from less developed countries (LDCs). Why is it likely that LDCs can reduce emissions at a lower cost than developed nations?

EXTERNALITIES: THE CASE OF EXTERNAL BENEFITS

Not all externalities are harmful. Sometimes the actions of individuals or businesses create **external benefits**—benefits that are paid for by one party but spill over to other parties. One example is the flowers your neighbors plant in their yard each year. You can enjoy their beauty without contributing to the cost of their planting and upkeep. Another example is flu shots. You pay for them, and they help protect you from the flu. But they also help protect everyone else; if you don't come down with the flu, you can't pass it on to others.

Businesses also can create external benefits. For example, most firms put their workers—particularly their young and/or inexperienced workers—through some sort of training program. Of course, the sponsoring firm gains a more productive, more valuable employee. But most people do not stay with one employer for their entire working careers; when trained employees decide to move on, other employers will benefit from the training they have received.

External Benefits and Resource Allocation. In a pure market economy, individuals would tend to demand too small a quantity of those products that generate external benefits. To understand why this is so, consider your own consumption decisions for a moment. When you are deciding whether to purchase a product (or how much of a product to purchase), you compare the product's benefits with its price. If you value a unit of the product more than the other items you could purchase with the same money, you buy it. If not, you spend your money on the product you value more highly. In effect, you are deciding which product delivers the most benefits for the money. But whose benefits are you considering? Your own, of course! In other words, you respond to private rather than external benefits. Most consumption decisions are made this way. As a result, consumers purchase too small a quantity of the products that create external benefits, and our scarce resources are misallocated. That is to say, fewer resources are devoted to producing these products than are justified by their **social benefits**—the sum of the private benefits received by those who purchase the product and the external benefits received by others.[4]

Adjusting for External Benefits. To illustrate the underproduction of products that carry external benefits, let's examine what would happen if elementary education were left to the discretion of the private market. Reading, writing, and arithmetic are basic skills that have obvious benefits for the individual, but they also benefit society as a whole. In his prize-winning book *Capitalism and Freedom*, economist Milton Friedman makes the case as follows:

> A stable and democratic society is impossible without a minimum amount of literacy and knowledge on the part of most citizens and without widespread acceptance of some common set of values. Education can contribute to both. In consequence, the gain from the education of a child accrues not only to the child or to his parents but also to other members of the society. . . .[5]

---

[4] As we learned earlier, when property rights are clearly defined, the existence of external benefits need not lead to resource misallocation. To illustrate, suppose that a restaurant owner notices higher sales on weekends when a neighboring pub has live entertainment. The restaurant owner may entice the pub into more frequent entertainment by agreeing to share its cost. This bargaining solution can lead to an optimal level of entertainment.

[5] Milton Friedman, *Capitalism and Freedom* (Chicago: University of Chicago Press, 1962), p. 86.

For the sake of our example, let's suppose that all elementary education in the United States is provided through private schools on a voluntary basis. In such a situation the number of children enrolled in these schools would be determined by the forces of demand and supply. As shown in Exh. 9.2 the market would establish a price of $500 per student, and at that price 3 million students would attend elementary school each year. The market demand curve (D_1) provides an incomplete picture, however. It considers marginal private benefits—the benefits received by the students and their parents—but ignores external benefits. If we include the external benefits of education, society would want even more children educated. Demand curve D_2 shows that society would choose to educate 5 million students a year if it considered the full social benefits (private plus external benefits) of education, leading to an equilibrium price of $700 per student.

EXHIBIT 9.2

The Impact of External Benefits

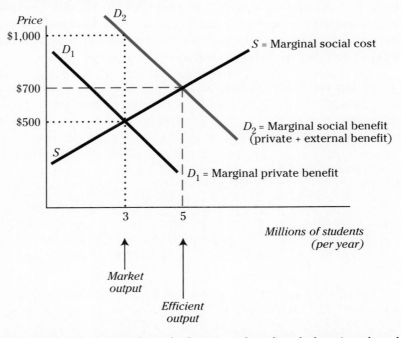

When individuals consider only the private benefits of education, they choose to educate only 3 million students per year, less than the optimal, or allocatively efficient, level of 5 million students per year.

As you can see from Exh. 9.2, individuals pursuing their own self-interest would choose to purchase less education than is justified on the basis of the full social benefits. (To confirm this conclusion, note that the marginal *social* benefit derived from the education of the 3 millionth student is $1,000, well in excess of the $500 marginal social cost of providing that education. Too few students are being educated, from society's point of view.) An obvious solution to this problem would be to require that each child attend school for some minimum number of years, allowing the family to select the school and find the money to pay for it. The U.S. government has taken a different approach, however. That is, most elementary and secondary schools are operated by local governments and financed through taxes rather than through fees charged to parents. This spreads the financial burden for education among all taxpayers rather than just the parents of school-age children. In effect, taxpayers without children "subsidize" taxpayers with children. The rationale for this approach is fairly clear-cut. Since all taxpayers share in the benefits of education (the external benefits, at least), they should share in the costs as well.

In a variety of circumstances, subsidies can be used to encourage the consumption of products that carry external benefits. Consider the flu shots again. They protect not only the people inoculated but also those in contact with them. Still, many people will not pay to receive a flu shot. So if we want more people to get flu shots (but we don't want to pass laws requiring such shots), we could have the government subsidize all or part of the cost. The lower the price of flu shots, the more people who will agree to get them.

There is no reason why subsidized flu shots would have to be provided by government doctors; the government could simply agree to pay private doctors for each flu shot administered. It is precisely this approach that Milton Friedman would like to see implemented in education. Rather than continuing to subsidize public schools, Friedman would prefer a system that permitted students to select their own privately run schools.

> Government could require a minimum level of schooling financed by giving parents vouchers redeemable for a specified maximum sum per child per year if spent on "approved" educational services. Parents would then be free to spend this sum and any additional sum they themselves provided on purchasing educational services from an "approved" institution of their own choice. . . . The role of government would be limited to insuring that the schools met certain minimum standards. . . .[6]

Whether or not you agree with Friedman's particular approach, it should be clear to you by now that subsidies can be useful in correcting for market failure. By encouraging the production and consumption of products yielding external benefits, subsidies help ensure that society's resources are used to

[6] Milton Friedman, *Capitalism and Freedom* (Chicago: University of Chicago Press, 1962), p. 86.

Use Your Economic Reasoning

The Greatest Good For the Greatest Number? Try Lojack.

Peter Passell

If you wire your home and put a warning decal on the window, you're less likely to be burglarized. But frustrated thieves are more likely to break into the house next door. What would happen, though, if you carefully concealed a silent alarm linked to a security service?

Burglars wouldn't be deterred from entering your house but they would be more likely to be caught in the act. And you'd be doing your neighbors a favor by reducing the number of bad guys on the street. In the language of Econ 101, there would be a "positive externality" to your choice of alarms.

In fact, deterrence is most of the point of having a house alarm: nobody wants to confront a thief in the kitchen. But auto theft is another matter. And a company based in Massachusetts, called Lojack, is trying to revolutionize protection against car thefts with its own version of the silent alarm.

It apparently works better than anyone anticipated. Two researchers, Ian Ayes of Yale and Steven Levitt of the University of Chicago, estimate that adding the Lojack system to three cars in a high-crime area reduces auto theft by one car a year. The only catch: individual car owners must pay for the installation even though the biggest share of the benefits goes to others....

Lojack retrieval is built around a small homing beacon. Hidden in the car, the beacon waits passively until the vehicle is reported stolen and is remotely activated from a radio signal tower. Then, police cruisers equipped with tracking receivers can identify the stolen vehicle by a five-digit code.

Since the company was founded in 1986, it has marketed the system in 12 metropolitan areas with serious auto-theft problems—Boston; Miami; Newark; Los Angeles; Chicago; Atlanta; Detroit; New York; Washington; Providence, R.I.; Tampa, Fla., and Norfolk, Va. The company would not disclose how many cars had been protected in each city. But it did provide the data to the two researchers for the year 1994, and they used it to isolate Lojack's impact from other statistical factors influencing rates of car theft.

The results, published by the National Bureau of Research, were remarkable. Boston experienced a 50 percent decline in thefts, transforming it from an auto-theft capital to a city with a theft rate only slightly higher than average. According to Mr. Ayers and Mr. Levitt's estimates, going from no hidden protection to Lojack in 2 percent of cars—roughly the company's average market penetration—reduces theft losses by 40 percent in central cities and about 13 percent within the range of Lojack's metropolitan coverage.

These numbers sound too good to be true, and in one sense they are. For while Lojack installation triples the

SOURCE: *New York Times*, Aug. 21, 1997, p. D2. Copyright © 1997/96 by The New York Times Co. Reprinted by Permission.

probability of arresting a thief, it isn't much of a direct deterrent because relatively few cars are protected even in the high-penetration areas. Indeed, in Boston, the city with the most cars equipped with Lojack systems, the chance of being caught in a randomly selected stolen car has risen by less than one percentage point.

What the Lojack beacon apparently does do very effectively, though, is to disrupt recidivism. Career criminals account for a disproportionate share of auto thefts, stealing dozens or even hundreds of cars a year. So even a small rise in the probability of getting caught during each theft can have a large impact on the number of professionals in prison.

More important, most cars are stolen for their parts rather than resold intact. Theft rings typically operate centralized stripping centers. Hence, putting a "chop shop" out of business can lead to the recovery of dozens of cars, along with arrests of professional thieves.

According to the company, Lojack has led to raids on 53 chop shops in the Los Angeles area alone. That helps to explain why auto thefts fell 20 percent there in the four years after the company entered the market in 1990....

If Lojack is such a blessing, what is stopping people from buying its system? According to the researchers, 90 percent of the benefits go to nonbuyers in the form of lower community-wide theft rates.

Having a Lojack system in your own car does increase the probability of it being recovered quickly, reducing the average loss from about $5,000 to $1,000. But since insurance usually covers all but a small deductible, paying $595 for Lojack amounts to an act of good citizenship rather than self-interest.

The key to making the market for Lojack work efficiently, the researchers suggest, is to require insurers to pass on the benefits in the form of premium discounts. Massachusetts, New York, New Jersey and Rhode Island do mandate discounts, but they are only loosely linked to the neighborhood benefits. And until 1996, Illinois actually banned insurance discounts, a fact that likely explains Lojack's poor sales in Chicago.

USE YOUR ECONOMIC REASONING

1. How would an individual decide whether to install a Lojack system in his or her car; what costs and benefits would he or she consider?
2. The article suggests that there are external benefits associated with the installation of a Lojack system. What are those external benefits?
3. If the external benefits conferred by Lojack are not taken into consideration, will consumers tend to install too many or too few Lojack systems, from a societal point of view?
4. If insurance companies recognize the true benefits of having cars protected by the Lojack system, they might correct the market failure described in question 3, even without government intervention. Please explain how this might occur. Can you think of any reasons why insurance companies might be unwilling or unable to correct this market failure?
5. If insurance companies do not correct this market failure, should government policymakers intervene? If so, what policy would you suggest they pursue?

produce the optimal assortment of goods and services. (Should government subsidize the purchase of silent auto alarms? Read "The Greatest Good for the Greatest Number?…" on pages 278–279, and decide for yourself.)

Market Failure and the Provision of Public Goods

Market power and the existence of externalities are not the only sources of market failure. Markets may also fail to produce optimal results because some products are simply not well suited to sale by private firms. These products must be provided by government or they will not be provided at all.

PRIVATE GOODS VERSUS PUBLIC GOODS

In order to understand this problem, we must think first about the types of goods and services our economy produces. Those goods and services fall into three categories: pure private goods, private goods that yield external benefits, and public goods.

Pure private goods are products that convey their benefits only to the purchaser.[7] The hamburger you had for lunch falls in that category, as does the jacket you wore to class. Most of the products we purchase in the marketplace are pure private goods.

Some products convey most of their benefits to the person making the purchase but also create substantial external benefits for others. These are **private goods that yield significant external benefits.** We have talked about education and flu shots, but there are numerous other examples—fire protection, police protection, and driver's training, to name just a few.

The third category, **public goods,** consists of products that convey their benefits equally to paying and nonpaying members of society. National defense is probably the best example of a public good. If a business attempted to sell "units" of national defense through the marketplace, what problems would arise? The major problem would be that nonpayers would receive virtually the same protection from foreign invasion as those who paid for the protection. There's no way to protect your house from foreign invasion without simultaneously protecting your neighbor's. The inability to exclude nonpayers from receiving the same benefits as those who have paid for the product is what economists call the *free-rider problem.*

---

[7] Note that although pure private goods convey their benefits only to the purchaser, the purchaser may *choose* to share those benefits with others. For instance, you may decide to share your hamburger with another person or allow someone else to wear your jacket. But if others share in the benefits of a pure private good, it is because the purchaser allows them to share those benefits, not because the benefits automatically spilled over onto them.

THE FREE-RIDER PROBLEM

Why does the inability to exclude certain individuals from receiving benefits constitute a problem? Think about national defense for just a moment. How would you feel if you were paying for national defense and your neighbor received exactly the same protection for nothing? Very likely, you would decide to become a free rider yourself, as would many other people. Products such as national defense, flood-control dams, and tornado warning systems cannot be offered so as to restrict their benefits to payers alone. Therefore, no private business can expect to earn a profit by offering such goods and services, and private markets cannot be relied on to produce these products, no matter how important they are for the well-being of the society. Unless the government intervenes, they simply will not be provided at all.

Of course, we're not willing to let that happen. That's why a substantial amount of our tax money pays for national defense and other public goods. (Not all publicly *provided* goods are public goods. Our tax dollars are used to pay for education and public swimming pools and a host of other goods and services that do not meet the characteristics of public goods.) As we have emphasized, the ultimate objective of government intervention is to improve the allocation of society's scarce resources so that the economy will do a better job of satisfying our unlimited wants. To the extent that government intervention contributes to that result, it succeeds in correcting for market failure and in improving our social welfare.

Poverty, Equality, and Trends in the Income Distribution

As we've seen, market failure results when a market economy fails to use its scarce resources in an optimal way; when it produces too much or too little of certain products. But even if a market system were able to achieve an optimal allocation of resources, if it distributed income in a way that a majority of the population saw as inequitable or unfair, we might judge that to be a shortcoming of the system.

In a market system, a person's income depends on what he or she has to sell. Those with greater innate abilities and more assets (land and capital) earn higher incomes; those with fewer abilities and fewer assets earn lower incomes. These differences are often compounded by differences in training and education and by differences in the levels of inherited wealth. As a consequence, a total reliance on the market mechanism can produce substantial inequality in the income distribution. Some people have less while others have much more.

EXHIBIT 9.3

Percent of Aggregate Income Received by Each Fifth of Households in the United States*

	1976	1986	1996
Lowest fifth	4.4%	3.9%	3.7%
Second fifth	10.4	9.7	9.0
Third fifth	17.1	16.2	15.1
Fourth fifth	24.8	24.5	23.3
Highest fifth	43.3	45.7	49.0

*Source: U.S. Bureau of the Census, Current Population Reports, p. 60–197, *Money Income in the United States, 1996,* U.S. Government Printing Office, Washington, D.C., 1997.

How unequal is the income distribution in the United States? As you can see from Exhibit 9.3, there is a significant amount of inequality. In 1996 the households in the lowest quintile (the lowest fifth) of the income distribution received less than 4 percent of total money income in the United States, while the households in the upper fifth received 49 percent of total income. In fact, the households in the upper fifth of the income distribution received almost as much total income as all the households in the bottom four-fifths of the distribution. Moreover, the income distribution in the United States seems to be growing somewhat less equal. As you can see in the exhibit, the fraction of aggregate income going to the richest fifth of U.S. households has increased over the last 20 years, while the share going to the remaining four-fifths of households has declined.

The existence of inequality may not concern us very much if everyone—including the households in the bottom fifth of the income distribution—is earning enough income to live comfortably. What most of us are really concerned about is households that are living in poverty—those with incomes that are insufficient to provide for their basic needs (according to some standard established by society).

In the United States we have adopted income standards by which we judge the extent of poverty. For example, in 1996 a family of four was classified as "poor" if it had an annual income of less than $16,036. By that definition there were 36.5 million poor people in the United States in 1996—a little less than 14 percent of the population.

Most people would probably agree that if 14 percent of our population—one person out of every seven—is living in poverty, we have some cause for concern. The U.S. government has attempted to address the problem of poverty in a variety of ways, primarily by enacting programs designed to address the source of poverty: the inability of the family to earn an adequate income. Examples include government-subsidized training programs for unemployed workers and policies designed to reduce discrimination in hiring. In addition, the minimum wage is intended to lift the earnings of unskilled workers.

Other government programs are designed to reduce the misery of the poor, even if they do not address the cause of poverty. Social Security, for example, provides financial assistance to the old, the disabled, the unemployed, and families that are experiencing financial difficulty because of the death of a breadwinner. Temporary Assistance for Needy Families (TANF) is a federal program that provides money to the states that may be used to aid poor families.[8] In addition to these cash-assistance programs, there are a variety of in-kind assistance programs that provide the poor with some type of good or service. Food stamps and subsidized public housing are two examples. All of these programs are designed to improve the status of the poor and in this way moderate the income distribution dictated by the market.

While there is widespread agreement with the objective of helping the poor, economists are quick to point out that government intervention does not always achieve the intended effects. For instance, many economists believe that the minimum wage does more harm than good, since it tends to reduce employment (at the higher wage, employers hire fewer workers). And attempts to aid poor families can have unintended effect of discouraging work. As these examples suggest, government intervention may not always improve market outcomes. The next section explores that possibility.

Government Failure: The Theory of Public Choice

The existence of market failures and poverty suggests that market economies do not always use resources efficiently or distribute income fairly. But whether government can be relied upon to improve either the allocation of scarce resources or the income distribution is open to debate. In fact, public-choice economists point out that **government failure**—the enactment of government policies that produce inefficient or inequitable results, or both—is also a possibility.

---

[8] The TANF program replaces Aid to Families with Dependent Children (AFDC), the old "welfare" program that was widely criticized for discouraging work. Under program guidelines, adult family members must begin doing some work (or community service) within two years of beginning the program. In addition, benefits are limited to five years. Both the work requirement and the limitation on benefits are intended to encourage work.

Public choice is the study of how government makes economic decisions. This area of economics was developed by James Buchanan, a professor at Virginia Polytechnic Institute and the 1986 recipient of the Nobel Prize in economics. Although many of us would like to think of government as an altruistic body concerned with the public interest, public choice economists advise us to think of government as a collection of individuals each pursuing his or her own self-interest. Just as business executives are interested in maximizing profits, politicians are interested in maximizing their ability to get votes. And government bureaucrats are interested in maximizing their income, power, and longevity. In short, the people who make up government are no different than the rest of us, and we need to remember that if we want to understand their behavior.

Recognizing that politicians are merely "vote maximizers" can help us to understand why special-interest groups exert a disproportionate influence on political outcomes. Consider, for example, the efforts of farmers to maintain price supports. The farm lobby represents a relatively small group of people who are intensely interested in the fate of this program. If price supports are repealed, each of these individuals will be significantly harmed. So farm lobbyists make it clear that their primary interest in selecting a senator or representative is his or her position on this one issue. And they reward those who support their position with significant financial contributions. The rewards for opposing price supports are likely to be nonexistent! Because the cost of price supports to any one consumer is relatively small, few voters are likely to choose their next senator or representative on the basis of how they voted on this issue. As a consequence, public choice theory predicts that members of Congress will vote in favor of price supports even though this program leads to the overproduction of agricultural products (is inefficient) and benefits people with incomes greater than the national average (is inequitable).

It is not just special-interest groups that can distort the spending decisions of government. The voting mechanism itself may lead to inefficient outcomes. One problem is that there is no way for voters to reflect the strength of their preferences. They can vote in favor of an issue, or against it, but they cannot indicate the strength of their favor or opposition. Consider, for example, a vote regarding the building of a flood-control dam. Even if the benefits of the dam vastly outweigh its costs, majority voting may prevent its construction. While voters living near the dam stand to benefit in a major way from its construction, most voters will see little reason to help pay for it. As a consequence, the project is likely to be rejected even though it represents an efficient use of society's resources.

Another problem stems from the logrolling efforts that are commonplace in Congress. **Logrolling** is trading votes to gain support for a proposal; politicians agree to vote for a project they oppose in order to gain votes for a project they support. For example, a senator from Missouri might agree to vote in favor of a bill that would expand the federal highway system in Florida in return for a Florida senator's favorable vote on a bill appropriating more money for

Missouri's military bases. In many instances, logrolling can lead to efficient outcomes. But in others, it can lead to the approval of projects or programs whose costs exceed their benefits.

In addition to the problems posed by special-interest groups and the voting process itself, public choice economists point to the problems posed by government bureaucrats. Many of the spending decisions that are made by our local, state, and federal governments are not made by elected officials; they are made by the bureaucrats who run our various government agencies. Public choice economists argue that these individuals, like the rest of us, pursue their own self-interest. In other words, they seek to increase their salaries, their longevity, and their influence. Rather than attempting to run lean, efficient agencies, their goal is to expand their power and resist all efforts to restrict their agencies' growth or influence. As a consequence, these agencies may become unjustifiably larger and require tax support in excess of the benefits they provide to citizens.

As you can see, public choice economists are not optimistic that government will make decisions that improve either efficiency or equity. Instead, they see politicians and bureaucrats making decisions intended largely to benefit themselves. While public choice economists make important observations, they may overstate their case. In recent years significant strides have been made in reducing trade barriers and some agricultural subsidies, despite howls of protest from those adversely affected. These reforms indicate that government action can lead to a more efficient use of society's scarce resources. In addition, while majority voting can lead to inefficient results, it can also lead to outcomes that are more efficient than those produced by private markets. This is likely to be true, for example, in the case of public goods, where private markets may fail to provide the product at all.

The real message of public choice economics is not that government action always leads to inefficiency or inequity. Rather, it is that we need to be just as alert to the possibility of government failure as we are to the possibility of market failure.

Summary

Market failure occurs when a market economy produces too much or too little of certain products and thus fails to make the most efficient use of society's limited resources.

There are three major sources of market failure: market power, externalities, and public goods. The exercise of market power can lead to a misuse of society's resources because firms with market power tend to restrict output in order to force up prices. Consequently, too few of society's resources will be allocated to the production of the goods and services provided by firms with market power.

Another source of market failure is the market's inability to reflect all costs and benefits. In some instances the act of producing or consuming a product creates *externalities*—costs or benefits that are not borne by either buyers or sellers but that spill over onto third parties. When this happens, the market has no way of taking those costs and benefits into account and adjusting production and consumption decisions accordingly. As a consequence, the market fails to give us optimal results; our resources are not used as well as they could be. We produce too much of some things because we do not consider all costs; we produce too little of other things because we do not consider all benefits. To correct these problems, government must pursue policies that force firms to pay the full social cost of the products they create and encourage the production and consumption of products with external benefits.

Markets may also fail to produce optimal results simply because some products are not well suited for sale by private firms. Public goods fall into that category. *Public goods* are products that convey their benefits equally to all members of society, whether or not all members have paid for those products. National defense is probably the best example. It is virtually impossible to sell national defense through markets because there is no way to exclude nonpayers from receiving the same benefits as payers. Since there is no way for a private businessperson to earn a profit by selling such products, private markets cannot be relied on to produce these goods or services, no matter how important they are to the well-being of the society.

Even if a market system uses its resources efficiently, if income is distributed unfairly, we may judge that to be a shortcoming of the system. There is significant income inequality in the U.S. economy. In 1996 the lowest quintile of the income distribution received less than 4 percent of total money income, while the highest quintile received 49 percent of total income. In addition, almost 14 percent of the population were living in poverty. A variety of programs have been adopted to attack the problem of poverty and moderate the income distribution. These include training programs for the unemployed and programs to provide direct financial assistance to the poor: Temporary Assistance for Needy Families, for example.

Although market economies may fail to use resources efficiently and distribute income fairly, public choice economists are not convinced that government can be counted on to improve either of these outcomes. *Public choice* is the study of how government makes economic decisions. According to public choice economists, government is a collection of individuals each pursuing his or her own self-interest. Because politicians and government bureaucrats make decisions largely to benefit themselves, we cannot count on them to pursue policies that further the public interest. In fact, *government failure*—the enactment of government policies that produce inefficient or inequitable results, or both—is also a possible consequence.

GLOSSARY

External benefits. Benefits paid for by one party or group that spill over to other parties or groups; also referred to as *spillover benefits*.

External costs. Costs created by one party or group and imposed on other (unconsenting) parties or groups; also referred to as *spillover costs*.

Externalities. Costs or benefits that are not borne by either buyers or sellers but that spill over onto third parties.

Government failure. The enactment of government policies that produce inefficient and/or inequitable results.

Internal benefits. The benefits accruing to the person or persons purchasing a good or service; also referred to as *private benefits*.

Internal costs. The costs borne by the firm that produces the good or service; also referred to as *private costs*.

Internalize costs. Consider external costs as if they were private costs.

Logrolling. The trading of votes to gain support for a proposal.

Market failure. Situations in which a market economy produces too much or too little of certain products and thus does not make the most efficient use of society's limited resources.

Private benefits. The benefits accruing to the person or persons purchasing a good or service; also referred to as *internal benefits*.

Private costs. The costs borne by the firm that produces the good or service; also referred to as *internal costs*.

Private goods that yield significant external benefits. Products that convey most of their benefits to the person making the purchase but also create substantial external benefits for other individuals or groups.

Property rights. The legal rights to use goods, services, or resources.

Public choice. The study of how government makes economic decisions.

Public goods. Products that convey their benefits equally to paying and nonpaying members of society.

Pure private goods. Products that convey their benefits only to the purchaser.

Social benefit. The full benefit received by all the members of society; the sum of private benefits and external benefits.

Social cost. The full cost to a society of the production and/or consumption of a product; the sum of private, or internal, costs and external costs.

STUDY QUESTIONS

Fill in the Blanks

1. _Market failures_ are instances in which a market economy fails to make the most efficient use of society's limited resources.

2. The term _externalities or spillovers_ is used to describe costs borne or benefits received by parties other than those involved in the transaction.

3. Social costs are the sum of _private costs_ and _external costs_.

4. One way to encourage the consumption of products with external benefits would be to _subsidize_ their purchase.

5. _Private goods_ are products that convey their benefits only to the buyer.

6. National defense is an example of a _Public good_ .

7. Another word for private costs and benefits is _internal_ costs and benefits.

8. _External benefits_ are benefits that are paid for by one party but that spill over to other parties.

9. The major reason our rivers and streams have been used as disposal sites is

that this approach minimized the firm's _Private or internal_ costs of production.

10. If an action creates no external costs or benefits, private costs will equal _Social_ costs.

11. _Public choice_ is the study of how government makes economic decisions.

12. When politicians trade votes to gain support for a proposal, they are engaging in _logrolling_ .

Multiple Choice

1. A market economy will tend to underproduce products that create
   a) social benefits.
   b) social costs.
   c) external benefits.
   d) external costs.

2. Which of the following is an example of a pure private good?
   a) A desk
   b) Education
   c) A fence between neighbors
   d) A park

3. Which of the following is most likely to produce external costs?
   a) Liquor
   b) A steak
   c) A flower garden
   d) A storm warning system

4. Suppose that chicken-processing plants create external costs. Then, in the absence of government intervention, it is likely that
   a) too few chickens will be processed, from a social point of view, and the price of a processed chicken will be artificially low.
   b) too many chickens will be processed, from a social point of view, and the

   price of a processed chicken will be artificially high.
   c) too few chickens will be processed, from a social point of view, and the price of a processed chicken will be artificially high.
   d) too many chickens will be processed, from a social point of view, and the price of a processed chicken will be artificially low.

5. If the firms in an industry have been creating pollution and are forced to find a method of waste disposal that does not damage the environment, the result will probably be
   a) a lower price for the product offered by the firms.
   b) a higher product price and a higher equilibrium quantity.
   c) a lower product price and a higher equilibrium quantity.
   d) a higher product price and a lower equilibrium quantity.

6. Which of the following is the best example of a pure public good?
   a) A cigarette
   b) A bus
   c) A lighthouse
   d) An automobile

7. Suppose that an AIDS vaccine is developed. In the absence of government intervention, it is likely that
   a) too few AIDS shots will be administered because individuals will fail to consider the private benefits provided by the shots.
   b) too many AIDS shots will be administered because individuals will consider only the private cost of the shots.
   c) too few AIDS shots will be administered because individuals will consider only the private benefits provided by the shots.
   d) too many AIDS shots will be administered because individuals will ignore the external benefits associated with the shots.

8. If a product creates external benefits, the demand curve that reflects all social benefits
   a) will be to the left of the demand curve that reflects only private benefits
   b) will be to the right of the demand curve that reflects only private benefits.
   c) will not slope downward .
   d) will be the same as the demand curve that reflects private benefits.

9. Public goods can lead to market failure because they
   a) create external costs.
   b) create social costs.
   c) cannot be sold easily in markets.
   d) cannot be paid for through taxes.

10. Banning all pollution may not be the optimal strategy, because
   a) the costs may exceed the benefits.
   b) the benefits of this approach are probably limited.
   c) the harm caused by pollution is generally overestimated.
   d) the benefits of a clean environment are generally overestimated.

11. Which of the following is *not* true?
   a) If social costs exceed private costs, external costs are present.

   b) If a product creates external costs, society should devote fewer resources to its production.
   c) If a society fails to consider externalities, it will not use its resources optimally.
   d) Consumers tend to purchase too much of products that create external benefits.

12. Which of the following best describes the free-rider problem?
   a) Your brother always rides home with you but never pays for the gas.
   b) Some private goods create external benefits for those who have not paid.
   c) Some people think that the environment is a free resource and therefore abuse it.
   d) Some goods cannot be sold in markets because the benefits they confer are available to all—whether they have paid or not.

13. Public choice economists argue that
   a) majority voting always leads to efficient outcomes.
   b) government bureaucrats tend to act in the public interest.
   c) politicians generally find it in their self-interest to oppose special-interest groups.
   d) self-interest is the motivation of both business executives and politicians.

14. Suppose that a proposed government project would cost $50,000 and convey benefits worth $100 to 1,000 people, and benefits worth $5 to the remaining 9,000 people in the community. If each person was assessed a $50 tax to pay for this project, the theory of public choice predicts that it would be
   a) rejected because the project's total costs exceed its total benefits.
   b) approved because the project's total benefits exceed its total costs.
   c) rejected because voters are unable to reflect the strength of their preferences.
   d) approved because voters recognize that it is an efficient use of society's limited resources.

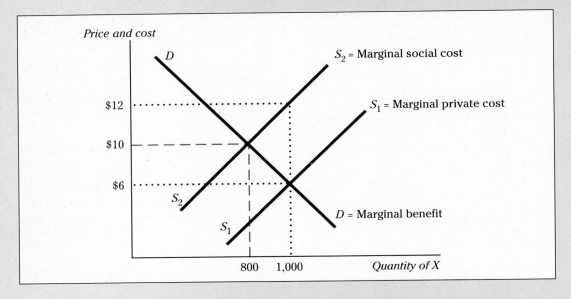

Use the diagram above in answering questions 15 and 16.

15. Suppose that production of product X creates external costs. In the absence of government intervention, this industry would tend to produce

a) 800 units of output, which is less than the allocatively efficient output of 1,000 units.

b) 1,000 units of output, which is more than the allocatively efficient output of 800 units.

c) 800 units, which is the allocatively efficient output.

d) 1,000 units, which is the allocatively efficient output.

16. At 1,000 units of output, the marginal benefit from consuming the last unit of X is equal to

a) $6, but the marginal social cost is equal to about $12, and so, from a social point of view, too little output is being produced.

b) $12, but the marginal social cost is equal to about $6, and so, from a social point of view, too little output is being produced.

c) $6, but the marginal social cost is equal to about $12, and so, from a social point of view, too much output is being produced.

d) $12, but the marginal social cost is equal to about $6, and so, from a social point of view, too much output is being produced.

Problems and Questions for Discussion

1. Why should you and I be concerned about whether our society's resources are used optimally?

2. What is market failure, and what are the sources of this problem?

3. How can fines and subsidies be used to correct market failure?

4. Most businesses are concerned about our environment, but they may be reluctant to stop polluting unless all other firms in their industry are also forced to stop. Why?

5. If we force firms to stop polluting, the result will probably be higher product prices. Is that good or bad? Why?

6. Why is it important (from society's viewpoint) to encourage the production and consumption of products that yield external benefits?

7. If we're really concerned about external costs, there would be some logic in fining any spectator who insisted on standing up to cheer at football games. What would be the logic? What practical considerations make this an impractical solution?

8. Why is a tornado warning system a public good? What about a flood-control dam? Why does it fall into that category?

9. Milton Friedman suggests that although it makes sense to subsidize a general education in the liberal arts, it makes much less sense to subsidize purely vocational training. What do you suppose is the logic behind that distinction?

10. Explain how the free-rider problem leads to market failure.

11. How can the absence of clearly defined property rights lead to the abuse or misuse of a resource?

12. According to Ronald Coase, the assignment of property rights can help to resolve externality problems if the number of parties involved is relatively small. Why is this solution unworkable when a large number of people are involved, as when a firm's pollution affects thousands of people?

ANSWER KEY

Fill in the Blanks

1. Market failures
2. externalities or spillovers
3. private costs, external costs
4. subsidize
5. Private goods
6. public good
7. internal
8. External benefits
9. private or internal
10. social
11. Public choice
12. logrolling

Multiple Choice

1. c	5. d	8. b	11. d	14. c
2. a	6. c	9. c	12. d	15. b
3. a	7. c	10. a	13. d	16. c
4. d				

PART THREE

Macroeconomics: The Economy as a Whole

Macroeconomics is the study of the economy as a whole and the factors that influence the economy's overall performance. (If you have a hard time remembering the difference between microeconomics and macroeconomics, just remember that *micro* means "small"—microcomputer, microfilm, microsurgery—whereas *macro* means "large.") Macroeconomics addresses a number of important questions: What determines the level of total output and total employment in the economy? What causes unemployment? What causes inflation? What can be done to eliminate these problems or at least to reduce their severity? These and many other considerations relating to the economy's overall performance are the domain of macroeconomics.

In Chapter 10 we begin our study of macroeconomics by examining some indicators, or measures, that economists watch to gauge how well the economy is performing. Chapter 11 introduces aggregate demand and aggregate supply and considers how these twin forces interact to determine the overall price level and the levels of output and employment in the economy. The chapter then uses the aggregate demand and supply framework to examine the views of the classical economists—the earliest macroeconomists—and explain why their views were challenged by British economist John Maynard Keynes.

Chapter 12 takes a detailed look at the concepts of aggregate demand and supply that were briefly introduced in Chapter 11 and uses the *AD-AS* framework to examine the possibility that the economy is self-correcting in the long run. Chapter 13 detours from the *AD-AS* model to consider the Keynesian model of income and output determination, a model that emphasizes the short-run and the possibility of an "unemployment equilibrium." Chapter 14 deals with fiscal policy—government spending and taxation policy designed to combat unemployment or inflation. It also considers the limitations of fiscal policy and examines the sources and consequences of federal budget deficits and the public debt.

Chapter 15 explains how depository institutions, such as commercial banks and savings and loan associations, "create" money and how the Federal Reserve attempts to control the money supply in order to guide the economy's performance. Chapter 16 concludes the macroeconomics section of the textbook by exploring the debate between modern "activists," who believe that government should attempt to manage the economy's overall performance, and "nonactivists," who believe that such attempts are ill-advised.

Measuring Aggregate Performance

Of the economic problems we've talked about so far, which one do you think Americans are most concerned about: The market power of large corporations and labor unions? The distortions caused by agricultural price supports or minimum-wage laws? Environmental pollution?

According to national surveys, none of these problems are foremost in the minds of Americans. Throughout most of the last decade, the major concerns voiced by Americans have been two macroeconomic problems: unemployment and inflation. In the next few chapters we'll be examining the factors that influence the economy's *aggregate*, or overall, performance and how problems such as unemployment and inflation arise. We will also consider policies to combat unemployment and inflation and the difficulties that may be encountered in applying these policies.

This chapter sets the stage for that discussion by examining some **economic indicators**—signals, or measures, that tell us how well the economy is performing. After all, policymakers can't take actions that lead to better performance unless they know when problems exist. Economic indicators provide that information. The economic indicators we will discuss in this chapter include the unemployment rate, the Consumer Price Index, and the gross domestic product (GDP)—the indicator that many economists believe is the most important single measure of the economy's performance.

Measuring Unemployment

One dimension of our economy's performance is its ability to provide jobs for those who want to work. For most of us, that's an extremely important aspect of the economy's performance because we value work not only as a source of income but also as a basis for our sense of personal worth. The most highly publicized indicator of performance in this area is the unemployment rate. The **unemployment rate** traditionally reported is the percentage of the civilian labor force that is unemployed. The **civilian labor force** is made up of all persons over the age of sixteen who are not in the armed forces and who are either employed or actively seeking employment. The Bureau of Labor Statistics (BLS), the agency responsible for gathering and analyzing labor force and employment data, surveys some 60,000 households throughout the United States monthly to determine the employment status of the residents. It uses the statistics gathered from this sample (which is scientifically designed to be representative of the entire U.S. population) to estimate the total size of the labor force and the rate of unemployment.

COUNTING THE UNEMPLOYED

How does the Bureau of Labor Statistics decide whether a person should be classified as unemployed? First, it determines whether the person has a job. As far as the BLS is concerned, you are employed if you did *any* work for pay in the week of the survey. It doesn't matter how long you worked, provided that you worked for pay. You are also counted as employed if you worked fifteen hours or more (during the survey week) as an unpaid worker in a family-operated business.

Even if you didn't have a job during the survey week, you are not recognized as unemployed unless you were actively seeking employment. To be "actively seeking employment," you must have done something to try to find a job—filled out applications, responded to want ads, or at least registered at an employment agency. If you did any of those things and failed to find a job, you are officially unemployed. If you didn't look for work, you're considered as "not participating" in the civilian labor force, and consequently you won't be counted as unemployed.

The purpose of the BLS monthly survey is to estimate the size of the civilian labor force (the number employed plus those actively seeking employment) and the number of unemployed. Then the bureau computes the unemployment rate by dividing the total number of unemployed persons by the total number of people in the civilian labor force. In 1997, for example, there were 136 million people in the civilian labor force; 6.7 million were unemployed. These figures represent averages—the average number of people in the civilian labor force and the average number of people unemployed—for 1997. This means that the average **civilian unemployment rate** for 1997 was 4.9 percent.

$$\text{Unemployment rate} = \frac{\text{Total number of unemployed persons}}{\substack{\text{Total number of persons} \\ \text{in the civilian labor force}}}$$

$$\text{Unemployment rate (1997)} = \frac{6.7 \text{ million unemployed persons}}{\substack{136 \text{ million persons in} \\ \text{the civilian labor force}}}$$

$$= 4.9 \text{ percent}$$

As you can see from Exh. 10.1, our unemployment rate compares quite favorably with those of other industrialized nations. In 1997 the average unemployment rate in the seven nations surveyed was 8.2 percent, well above our 4.9 percent. When we look at the figures for the last decade, our performance still looks relatively good; the seven-nation average was 7.6 percent, whereas our average unemployment rate was 6 percent. But is 6 percent the best the U.S. economy can hope to achieve, or can we do better still? Let's turn to that question.

EXHIBIT 10.1

Unemployment Rates in Major Industrialized Countries

	UNITED STATES	CANADA	JAPAN	FRANCE	GERMANY	ITALY	UNITED KINGDOM	7-NATION AVERAGE
Unemployment rate 1997	4.9%	9.2%	3.4%	12.7%	7.8%	12.3%	7.1%	8.2%
Average unemployment rate 1988–1997	6.0%	9.5%	2.7%	11.0%	6.0%	9.5%	8.6%	7.6%

Source: Bureau of Labor Statistics, U.S. Department of Labor, March, 1998.

TYPES OF UNEMPLOYMENT

In general, a high unemployment rate is interpreted as a sign of a weak economy, whereas a low rate is seen as a sign of strength. But in order to recognize a low rate of unemployment when we see it, we have to know what we are aiming for, what is possible or realistic. That, in turn, requires knowledge of the three basic types of unemployment—frictional, cyclical, and structural—and the extent to which these types of unemployment are unavoidable.

Frictional Unemployment. Even when plenty of jobs are available, there are always some people out of work because they are changing jobs or searching for their first job. Economists call this **frictional unemployment** to distinguish a type of labor-market adjustment involving time lags, or "friction." A certain amount of frictional unemployment is unavoidable and probably even desirable. It is a sign that employers are looking for the most-qualified workers and that workers are searching for the best jobs. Neither party is willing to settle for the first thing that comes along. That's good for the economy because it means that the right people are more likely to be matched to the right jobs. But it takes time for workers and employers to find each other, and meanwhile the job seekers are adding to the nation's unemployment rate.

Cyclical Unemployment. Joblessness caused by a reduction in the economy's total demand for goods and services is termed **cyclical unemployment**. When such a reduction occurs, perhaps because consumers have decided to save more and spend less, businesses that are not able to sell as much output as before usually must cut back on production. This means that some of their workers will become unemployed. We call this unemployment cyclical because we recognize that the economy goes through cycles of economic activity. For awhile the economy expands and unemployment declines; then economic activity slows and unemployment rises. You can see this pattern clearly in Exh. 10.2.

When people are cyclically unemployed, the economy is losing the output these workers could have produced, and, of course, the workers are losing the income they could have earned. Many economists argue that it is possible to reduce the amount of cyclical unemployment by using government policies to stimulate the total demand for goods and services.

Structural Unemployment. Changes in the makeup, or structure, of the economy that render certain skills obsolete or in less demand result in **structural unemployment**. The economy is always changing. New prod-

EXHIBIT 10.2

The Unemployment Rate: 1929–1994

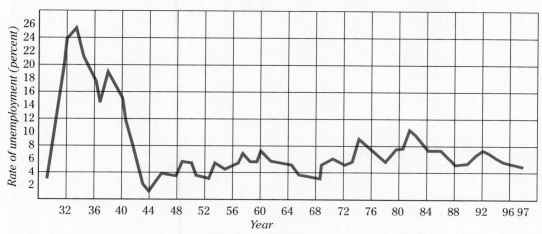

This exhibit shows that the unemployment rate varies significantly from year to year. But even though the unemployment rate is not a constant, there is a pattern to that variation, an up-and-down cycle that keeps repeating itself. For example, we can see that the unemployment rate dropped from a high of about 25 percent in 1933 to approximately 14 percent in 1937. Then the unemployment rate jumped back up to 19 percent in 1938 and started a steady decline that continued until 1944. The same sort of pattern is evident over other time periods although the magnitude of the changes certainly is not as great.

The rate reported is the civilian unemployment rate. Sources for these statistics were *Historical Statistics of the United States* (Bureau of the Census) and *Economic Report of the President*, 1998.

ucts are introduced and old ones are dropped; businesses continually develop new production methods. These kinds of changes can have a profound effect on the demand for labor. Skills that were very much in demand ten or twenty years ago may be virtually obsolete today. Computerized photocomposition machines have virtually eliminated the need for newspaper typesetters, for example, and robots have begun to replace semiskilled workers in automobile manufacturing plants. Further automation will signal a similar fate for workers in many other manufacturing industries.

The Bureau of Labor Statistics predicts that by the year 2000, the number of jobs in manufacturing will decrease to 18.2 million from about 19 million

Structurally unemployed workers may need to be retrained before they can find jobs.

in 1990. Moreover, the nature of manufacturing work will change so that many of today's manufacturing workers will find themselves unqualified for the jobs of the future—jobs that will require more education and the ability to work with programmable machines.[1]

The changing skill requirements for the workplace are not the only source of structural unemployment. Some people cannot hold a job in the modern economy because they never received much education or training in the first place. This is the case with many members of inner-city minorities, who often are educated in second-rate school systems that have a high dropout rate. It is also possible for people to be structurally unemployed even though they have marketable skills. For example, unemployed construction workers in New York State (which has been experiencing the highest unemployment in the nation) may have skills that are very much in demand. But if the available construction jobs are in Midwest, the New York workers remain structurally unemployed.

All structurally unemployed workers have one thing in common: If they are to find jobs, they must make drastic changes. They will have to acquire

---

[1] Doron P. Levin, "Smart Machines, Smart Workers," *New York Times*, Oct. 17, 1988, p. D1.

new skills or move to a different part of the country. They may even find it necessary to do both. Since such changes cannot be made overnight, economists see structural unemployment as a longer-term problem than frictional or cyclical unemployment. This is also the reason why some social scientists view structural unemployment as one of the most serious problems of our time. (A rapidly growing economy increases the employment prospects of all workers, even the structurally unemployed. Read "Low Unemployment Brings Lasting Gains . . . ," on pages 302–303, to learn how.)

FULL EMPLOYMENT VERSUS ZERO UNEMPLOYMENT

Since a certain amount of frictional and structural unemployment is unavoidable, economists consider zero unemployment an unattainable goal. Although no one knows precisely how much unemployment is of the frictional and structural varieties, a common estimate is 5.5 percent. This is considered to be the **natural rate of unemployment**—the minimum level of unemployment that our economy can achieve in normal times.[2] (Note that this is the rate that would exist in the absence of cyclical unemployment.) When the actual rate of unemployment is equal to the natural rate, the economy has achieved **full employment.**

A CLOSER LOOK AT UNEMPLOYMENT RATES

Recognizing that full employment doesn't mean zero unemployment is an important step in learning how to interpret unemployment statistics. The next step is learning to look beyond the overall unemployment rate to see how various groups in our society are being affected. Although we all talk about "the" unemployment rate, in reality the rate of unemployment varies substantially among the different subcategories of the American labor force. Historically, blacks have been about twice as likely to be unemployed as whites, in part because, on the whole, they have lower levels of education and training. For the last decade, women have enjoyed slightly lower unemployment rates than men, largely because a higher proportion of women are employed in the service sector—the fastest-growing sector of the economy. Teenagers, who are

---

[2] The natural rate can change over time in response to such factors as changes in labor markets. Joseph Stiglitz, former chairman of President Clinton's Council of Economic Advisers, estimates that the natural rate has fallen 1.5 percent since the 1980s. According to Stiglitz, "The single most important demographic change is the aging of baby boomers—we now have a more mature labor force, with greater representation of age groups that have traditionally low unemployment rates." (Joseph Stiglitz, "Reflections on the Natural Rate Hypothesis," *Journal of Economics Perspectives*, Winter 1997, p. 66.)

Use Your Economic Reasoning

Low Unemployment Brings Lasting Gains To Town in Michigan

Grand Rapids Firms Try Hard To Train the Unskilled, And People Hunt for Jobs

By David Wiesel
Staff Reporter of the Wall Street Journal

GRAND RAPIDS, Mich.— Good things happen when a community's unemployment rate drops and stays down.

At Davidson Plyforms Inc., which shapes plywood into office-furniture parts, supervisor Randy Williams makes sure that promising new hires are promptly trained to run as many machines as possible. "I try to move them along real quick, or they'll leave," he says. "They've got choices."

At Goodwill Industries, the charity best known for recycling clothes, Willie Mae Hill, a 25-year-old single mother of four who is on welfare and has never had a steady job, sports pink safety glasses while learning to operate an injection-molding machine. The three-week course stresses the need to show up on time as much as the operation of machinery.

At Lacks Enterprises Inc., a maker of plastic auto parts that hired 26 Goodwill graduates last year, the human-resources chief can't be choosy when he suddenly needs 30 or 40 more workers. "Under the circumstances," Roger Andrzejewski says, "you're going to take chances."

And at Faith Inc., a non-profit outfit that tries to make desirable employees of people who haven't worked regularly for years, if ever, a dozen would-be workers showed up in just the first hour one recent morning. Another eight phoned. "When they see people in their peer group getting jobs and getting somewhere, it becomes infectious," says Verne Barry, Faith's founder and president.

Many Benefits

The immediate benefits of low unemployment are obvious; less wasted human potential; higher wages for the low-skilled, who haven't kept up with inflation in recent years; and more money in local cash registers. But this riverside factory town—home of Amway Corp., furniture maker Steelcase Inc. and the Gerald R. Ford Museum—also illustrates the long-term benefits. If the national jobless rate remains near its current 24-year low of 4.8% without sparking inflation, all of America may enjoy them as well:

- Businesses try harder to train workers, precisely what the economic doctors prescribe to spur the slow growth of productivity and living standards.

- They also hire people with checkered pasts and few skills, people they wouldn't consider hiring if they had a choice.

- And people who have been on the sidelines, figuring no one would hire them anyhow, look for work—and sometimes find it. In the Grand Rapids area, the labor force has grown more than 18,000 in the past year, a 3.5% increase. Nationally, nearly 2.1 million people have entered the labor force since May 1996, and a record 63.9% of U.S. adults are working.

Tight labor markets hit western Michigan earlier than most places. After peaking at 8.8% in 1992, the unemployment rate in this area stayed near 4% for the past two years before plunging to 3.1% in April, the latest month for which data are available. Wages for entry-level jobs are climbing at a 4% to 5% annual clip, the local Employers Association says. And 62 temporary-help firms are competing to find office and factory workers for area employers, some of which commission three temp firms to fill the same jobs.

"The average industrial employer in western Michigan says, 'I just need some very basic skills, things like showing up on time, a good track record, people showing some good work ethic. I'll train these people,'" says Dan Barcheski, owner of Staffing Inc., a local temp firm….

Few Attractive Candidates

Few people who come through Goodwill or Faith Inc. are attractive job candidates. They have prison records or drug addictions. They can't list a home phone number because they live in a shelter. They can't give references because they haven't much work history. But with prodding from Mr. Barry or John Hausig, who runs the Goodwill program, a few employers give them a shot at work. In the past four years, 60% of those who finished Goodwill's three-week course have landed jobs and held them at least 90 days, Mr. Hausig says.

"We have to get creative in hiring people here," says Ron Jimmerson, a senior

human-resources specialist at Cascade Engineering Inc., a maker of plastic parts with 500 workers in five plants here. "That's why you start looking at Goodwill, Heartside and places like that."

In one creative experiment, Cascade's chief executive, Fred Keller, and Stuart Ray, who owns 40 Burger Kings in western Michigan, are about to begin offering vocational counseling and factory jobs to young Burger King workers—and Burger King jobs to Cascade job applicants who don't make the cut. Mr. Ray tells his skeptical managers, who want less turnover at their units, that the prospect of better-paying jobs down the road will help them recruit workers. "Kids aren't supposed to be here forever," he says.

Though sparked by socially conscious executives, such programs are far more likely to succeed if workers are in short supply. In a soft labor market, Mr. Ray acknowledges, the chances fade.

But the tight labor market here drives employers to "get creative" regardless of social conscience. Master Finish Co., a small chrome-plating shop with 86 employees, turned to Goodwill almost in desperation when it grew unhappy with workers sent by a temporary-help service. "When you think of Goodwill, what do you think of? Used clothing. You don't think of employees," says John Frody, the quality-control manager. "I never realized they do put a lot of people to work...."

USE YOUR ECONOMIC REASONING

1. How would you classify the people being trained by Goodwill Industries and Faith Inc.? Are they frictionally, cyclically, or structurally unemployed? Explain.
2. When the economy becomes stronger and businesses need additional workers, who do they hire first—those who have been structurally unemployed or those who have been cyclically unemployed?
3. According to the article, "people who have been on the sidelines" have started looking for work. Why have they been on the sidelines? When they start looking, what does that do to the unemployment rate? How could this change send a false signal about the state of the economy?
4. Training workers is expensive. Why are businesses in Michigan willing to invest money in people with "checkered pasts" and few basic skills?

EXHIBIT 10.3

Unemployment Rates for 1997

WORKER CATEGORY	RATE	WORKER CATEGORY	RATE	WORKER CATEGORY	RATE
All civilian workers	4.9%	*White*	4.2%	*Black*	10.0%
Men (20 and over)	4.2	Men (20 and over)	3.6	Men (20 and over)	8.5
Women (20 and over)	4.4	Women (20 and over)	3.7	Women (20 and over)	8.8
Teenagers (16–19)	16.0	Teenagers (16–19)	13.6	Teenagers (16–19)	32.4

Source: *Economic Report of the President*, 1998.

often unskilled and lacking in good work habits, have unemployment rates about two and a half to three times the overall rate for their racial group.

Exhibit 10.3 shows the unemployment rates for 1997. Note that in 1997 the overall unemployment rate for all civilian workers—that is "the" unemployment rate—was 4.9 percent. During the same period the overall rate for blacks (10 percent) was more than twice the rate for white workers (4.2 percent), and this relationship held for each of the subcategories: men, women, and teenagers. The rates for teens were also within the expected range: black and white teens had unemployment rates about three times the overall rate for their racial group. Adult women, however, had *higher* unemployment rates than their male counterparts, not the slightly lower rates anticipated. This was due, at least in part, to the unusually rapid rate at which women entered the labor force in the period from 1994–1997.

As you can see, the overall unemployment rate conceals a great deal of variation across particular groups. Even when the overall rate is low, the unemployment rate among certain subcategories of our population may be unacceptably high. For that reason, those who rely on unemployment statistics for devising policies to combat unemployment or for helping the unemployed in other ways must be willing to look beyond the overall rate to gain a clearer picture of the nature and severity of the unemployment problem.

UNEMPLOYMENT RATES: A WORD OF CAUTION

Before we leave this section on unemployment statistics, a few words of caution are appropriate. Watching the unemployment rate can help you understand whether the economy is growing weaker or stronger. But changes in the unemployment rate from one month to the next may not be very meaningful and, in fact, can sometimes send misleading signals about the state of the economy.

To illustrate that point, suppose that the economy is in the midst of a deep *recession*—a period of reduced economic activity and relatively high unemployment—when the Bureau of Labor Statistics reports a small drop in the unemployment rate. Should that drop be taken as a sign that the economy is growing stronger? Not necessarily. When the economy has been in a recession for quite a while, some unemployed workers become discouraged in their search for jobs and stop looking. Since these "discouraged workers" are no longer actively seeking employment, they are no longer counted as unemployed. That makes the unemployment rate look better, but it's really not a sign that the economy has improved. In fact, it may be a sign that labor-market conditions have become even worse.

Of course, we can be misled in the other direction just as easily. Suppose that the economy has begun to recover from a recession and that the unemployment rate is falling. Suddenly the monthly survey shows an increase. Does that mean that the economy is headed back toward recession? It may, but a more likely interpretation is that the economy's improved condition has attracted a lot of additional job seekers who have swelled the labor force and pushed up the unemployment rate. Here the unemployment rate has risen not because the economy is worse but because it is better: People are more confident about their prospects for finding jobs.

Because changes in the unemployment rate can send misleading signals about the strength of the economy, they should be interpreted with caution. But even when the unemployment rate seems to be sending clear signals (for instance, when it has risen for several consecutive months), we must be careful not to base our evaluation of the economy's health solely on this statistic. After all, the unemployment rate looks at only one dimension of the economy's performance—its ability to provide jobs for the growing labor force. Other dimensions are equally important. To obtain an accurate picture of our economy's performance, we must consider each of these dimensions by examining several different economic indicators.

Measuring Inflation

Another important dimension of our economy's performance is its success or failure in avoiding inflation. **Inflation** is defined as a rise in the general level of prices. (The existence of inflation does not necessarily mean that *all* prices are rising but rather that *more* prices are going up than are coming down.) Inflation means that our dollars won't buy as much as they used to. In general, this means that it will take more money to pay the grocery bill, buy clothes, go out for an evening, or do almost anything else.

UNANTICIPATED INFLATION AND INCOME REDISTRIBUTION

Each of us tends to believe that we are being hurt by inflation, but that is not necessarily the case. We forget that at the same time that prices are rising, our money incomes are also likely to be rising, sometimes at a faster rate than the increase in prices. Instead of focusing solely on prices, then, we ought to be concerned about what economists call real income. **Real income** is the purchasing power of your income—the amount of goods and services it will buy. Economists argue that unanticipated inflation is essentially an income redistribution problem: It takes real income away from some people and gives it to others. (As you will see later, when people anticipate inflation, they tend to prepare for it and thereby reduce its redistributive effects.)

Keeping Pace with Inflation. The people hurt by unanticipated inflation are those whose money incomes (the number of *dollars* they earn) don't keep pace with rising prices. If prices rise by 10 percent but your money income increases by only 5 percent, your real income will have fallen. The amount of goods and services that you can buy with your income will be 5 percent less than before.

Whether your money keeps pace with inflation depends on a variety of factors. The most important is how flexible your income is, that is, how easily it can be adjusted. Professional people—doctors, lawyers, dentists, and so on—often can adjust the prices they charge their customers and thereby stay abreast (or ahead) of inflation. People who own their own businesses—their own hardware store or motel or janitorial service—may be able to adjust their prices similarly. Of course, whether professional people and businesses can successfully increase prices and stay abreast of inflation depends on the degree of the market power they possess. If a seller faces very little competition and therefore has significant market power, it may be able to increase its prices to offset inflation. If it operates in a highly competitive environment, it may not be able to do so.

Workers who are represented by strong unions also may do reasonably well during periods of inflation. Often these unions are able to negotiate cost-of-living adjustment (COLA) clauses, which provide for automatic wage and salary adjustments to compensate for inflation. Other workers may have the forces of demand and supply operating to their advantage. When the demand for workers with a particular skill is strong relative to their supply, those workers often are able to obtain wage or salary increases that more than offset the impact of inflation. Unskilled workers and others in oversupplied fields—those in which there are several prospective employees for each job opening—usually find it more difficult to gain wage increases that match the rate of inflation.

Savers and People on Fixed Incomes. Hardest hit by inflation are people on fixed incomes, whose incomes are by definition inflexible. The classic example is a retired person living on a fixed pension or perhaps on his or her accumulated savings. (Of course, many retired persons are not dependent on fixed pensions. For example, Social Security payments are automatically adjusted for increases in the cost of living.)

Savers can also be hurt by inflation. Whether you are relying on your savings to provide retirement income, to make a down payment on a home someday, or to buy a car next summer, inflation can eat away at the value of your savings account and make your objective more difficult to achieve. For example, if your savings account is paying 6 percent interest and the inflation rate is 10 percent, the purchasing power of your savings is declining by 4 percent a year. After you pay taxes on the interest, you're even further behind.

Creditors versus Debtors. Unanticipated inflation can also hurt banks and other creditors since borrowers will be able to repay their loans with dollars that are worth less than those that were borrowed. As the largest debtor of all, the federal government is probably the biggest gainer from such inflation. Other gainers include families with home mortgages and businesses that borrowed money to purchase factories or equipment.

WHEN INFLATION IS ANTICIPATED

The redistributive effects of inflation occur because inflation is unforeseen or unanticipated. To the extent that inflation is anticipated, the redistributive effects will tend to be reduced because individuals and businesses will take actions to protect themselves from inflation.

COLA clauses are one way in which we attempt to insulate ourselves from inflation, but there are others. For example, banks try to protect themselves from anticipated inflation by working the inflation rate into the interest rates they set for loans. If a bank wants to earn 5 percent interest on a loan and expects the inflation rate to be 4 percent, the bank will charge 9 percent interest to get the desired return. If the inflation rate turns out to be 4 percent, neither the bank nor the customer will be harmed by inflation. Of course, the bank's inflation forecast won't always be correct. Forecasting inflation has proved very difficult, and bankers and others will make mistakes. As a consequence, inflation is likely to benefit some and hurt others.

Consequences of inflation extend beyond its effect on the income distribution. When inflation is anticipated, individuals and businesses waste resources in their attempts to protect themselves from its impact. Labor time and energy are expended shopping around and shifting money from one financial institution to another in pursuit of the highest interest rate. Restaurant menus and business price lists must be continually revised, and sales person-nel must be kept informed of the most recent price information. In short, ef-forts to stay ahead of inflation use up resources that could be used to produce other things.

In addition to wasting resources, inflation (whether anticipated or unan-ticipated) can lead to inefficiency through its tendency to distort the informa-tion provided by the price system. To illustrate, suppose that the price of laptop computers increases. Does the higher price indicate greater demand for the product, or does it merely reflect an increase in the overall price level? Because computer manufacturers are uncertain, they may be reluctant to in-vest in new production capacity. Thus, inflation may slow investment spend-ing and retard the economy's rate of growth.

In summary, inflation, both anticipated and unanticipated, imposes costs on society. Unanticipated inflation causes income redistribution; anticipated inflation causes scarce resources to be wasted and used inefficiently.

CALCULATING A PRICE INDEX

Bankers, union leaders, business executives, and most other people in our society are keenly interested in changes in the general level of prices because they want to try to compensate for those changes; they'd like to build them into the prices they charge their customers and the wages they negotiate with their employers. Government policymakers also want to know what is hap-pening to the price level in order to know when inflation-fighting policies may be necessary.

Economists attempt to measure inflation by using a **price index.** A price index is really nothing more than a ratio of two prices: the price of an item in a base period that serves as a reference point divided into the price of that item in a period we wish to compare to the base period. For example, if the price of steak was $3.75 a pound in 1992 and $6.00 a pound in 1997, the price index for steak in 1997 would be 160 if 1992 was used as the base year:

$$\text{Price index} = \frac{\text{Price in any given period}}{\text{Price in the base period}}$$

$$= \frac{\$6.00}{\$3.75}$$

$$= 1.60 \text{ or } 160 \text{ percent or } 160$$

(Note that although the price index is in fact a percentage, by convention it is written without the percent sign.)

The price index tells us how much the price of the item in question has increased or decreased since the base period. Since the price index in the base period is always 100, an index of 160 means that a price has increased by 60 percent since the base period.[2] By the same logic, an index of 75 would indicate that a price had decreased by 25 percent since the base period. Although price indexes can be used to determine how much prices have risen or fallen since the base period, their most common use is to determine the annual rate of inflation for a particular product or group of products. The **annual inflation rate** is the percent change in a price index from one year to the next. For example, if the price index for steak increased from 160 in 1997 to 170 in 1998, the rate of inflation for steak between 1997 and 1998 would be 6.3 percent (10/160 = 0.063). Exhibit 10.4 provides another example of how to compute the annual inflation rate.

Three basic price indexes are used in the United States: the Consumer Price Index, the Producer Price Index, and the Implicit Price Deflator. Each index surveys a particular range of goods and services in order to determine the rate of inflation among those items. Each computes an overall index showing the average rate of price change for its assortment (or "basket") of commodities and presents individual price indexes for each major class of items in the survey. This makes it possible to determine which products are most responsible for any change in the overall index.

---

[2] The price index in the base period is always 100 because the numbers in the numerator and denominator of the price-index formula must be the same. For example, if we want to calculate the price index for steak in 1992 using 1992 as the base period, we would have $3.75/$3.75 = 1.00 or 100 percent.

EXHIBIT 10.4

Computing the Annual Rate of Inflation for Medical Care

The price index for medical care was 228.2 in 1996 and 234.6 in 1997, using 1984 as the base year. Thus, the price of medical care increased by 128.2 percent between 1984 and 1996. But what was the rate of inflation in medical care between 1996 and 1997?

$$\text{Annual rate of inflation} = \frac{\text{Change in the price index from one year to the next}}{\text{Price index in the initial year}}$$

$$= \frac{234.6 - 228.2}{228.2}$$

$$= \frac{6.4}{228.2}$$

$$= 0.028 \text{ or } 2.8 \text{ percent}$$

THE CONSUMER PRICE INDEX

The best-known index is the Consumer Price Index (CPI). The CPI looks at the prices of some 400 goods and services that have been chosen to represent the kinds of products typically purchased by urban consumers. The CPI measures the purchasing power of consumers' dollars by comparing the current cost of this so-called basket of goods and services to the cost of the same basket at an earlier date.

Exhibit 10.5 shows the kinds of items that are included in the Consumer Price Index survey. You can see how the rate of inflation differs from one class of items to another. The top line—the all-items index—is the CPI usually referred to by economists and the media. It tells us the average rate of price increase for all the items in the market basket. According to the exhibit, the all-items index stood at 160.5 in 1997. Because the most recent CPI uses the average level of prices between 1982 and 1984 as the base, prices increased approximately 60 percent between the period 1982–1984 and 1997. More precisely, in 1997 it cost $160.50 to purchase a basket of goods and services that sold for $100 in 1982–1984. As you can see, some items increased even more than that. For example, medical care rose to an index of 234.6; the cost of medical care increased more than 100 percent (more than doubled) between 1982–1984 and 1997.

Because consumers spend greater percentages of their incomes on certain index items—more, say, on food and beverages than on entertainment—merely averaging all the indexes at face value to arrive at the all-items index would be misleading. Therefore, the all-items index is computed as a *weighted average* of the individual indexes. That is, the things for which consumers spend more of their

---

EXHIBIT 10.5

Consumer Price Indexes, 1997 (1982–1984=100)

ALL ITEMS	**160.5**		
Food and beverages	157.7	Apparel and upkeep	132.9
Housing	156.8	Transportation	144.3
Shelter	176.3	Medical care	234.6
Fuel & other utilities	130.8	Entertainment	162.5
Household furnishings		Other goods and services	224.8
& operation	125.4		

Source: *Economic Report of the President*, 1998.

incomes are counted more heavily in determining the all-items index. For example, if consumers spend twice as much on food and beverages as they do on entertainment, food and beverage prices will be twice as important in computing the all-items index.

By comparing the 1996 and 1997 consumer price indexes, we can compute the annual rate of inflation for consumer goods. Recall that the annual inflation rate is the percent change in a price index from one year to the next. The CPI was 156.9 in 1996 and 160.5 in 1997, so the inflation rate between 1996 and 1997 was 2.3 percent (3.6/156.9 = 0.023). (Although 2.3 percent is a relatively low rate of inflation, many economists argue that the true inflation rate was even lower. In fact, they argue that the CPI regularly overstates the rate of inflation. Read "Imperfect Vision," on pages 312–313, to discover the source of the problem and why politicians want someone else to fix it.)

How does our 2.3% inflation rate compare with the rates experienced by other major industrialized nations? As you can see from Exh. 10.6, our 1997 inflation rate was somewhat higher than most of the other nations surveyed. When we look at inflation over the last decade, a similar picture emerges. Only Italy and the United Kingdom had higher average inflation rates than the U.S.

The rates of inflation reported in this table reflect inflation on consumer goods; the U.S. rates are based on the CPI, and the foreign rates are based on similar indexes. But in some instances we may be more interested in inflation at the wholesale level, or the rate of inflation in government services or capital goods (factories and equipment). For these purposes we need to turn to other price indexes.

EXHIBIT 10.6

Inflation Rates in Major Industrialized Countries

	UNITED STATES	CANADA	JAPAN	FRANCE	GERMANY	ITALY	UNITED KINGDOM	7-NATION AVERAGE
Inflation rate, 1997	2.3%	1.6%	1.7%	1.1%	1.7%	1.7%	3.2%	1.9%
Average inflation rate, 1988–1997	3.5%	2.8%	1.5%	2.4%	2.8%	4.9%	4.5%	3.2%

Source: *Economic Report of the President,* 1998.

Use Your Economic Reasoning

Imperfect Vision

A flawed CPI makes it harder for us to read the past and plan for the future

By Robert J. Samuelson

It's a mark of our progress against inflation that the greatest need now is measuring it. Once in double digits, it's so low that we're not sure what it is. The Boskin Commission—named after its chairman, Michael Boskin—brings us closer to a better reading. The commission of five economists says that the consumer price index (CPI) overstates inflation by 1.1 percentage points a year. The precise size of the overstatement is less important than the fact that it is large and persistent. It burdens the federal budget, distorts our economic record and creates uncertainty about the future.

The reaction to the report has predictably focused on the budget. Social Security and some other programs are indexed to the CPI. If Congress cuts the adjustment (as it should), future benefit increases will be smaller. Similarly, tax brackets and the personal exemption rise automatically with the CPI. This holds down taxes by making less income taxable or taxing at lower rates. A lower CPI adjustment would mean slightly higher taxes. All told, a cut of 1 percentage point (say, from 3 percent to 2) in the adjustment would shave the budget deficits cumulatively by an estimated $628 billion between 1997 and 2006.

But the Boskin report's larger significance is that it demolishes the theory that living standards have stagnated. No longer should it be possible for some economists and politicians to contend that average families have simply run in place in recent decades. The stagnation theory has always been a statistical illusion. If your income rises 3 percent and prices rise 3 percent, then you've got no "real" income gain. But if inflation has actually risen 2 percent, then income is up 1 percent. This is what's happened.

Consider: By the official statistics, the income of the median household—the one exactly in the middle—rose a meager 6.5 percent between 1975 and 1995. That's close to stagnation. But the gain would have been 17 percent if actual inflation was 0.5 percentage points less annually than the official rate; and the gain would have been 29 percent if inflation were 1 percentage point lower a year....

The main reason that the CPI overstates inflation is that it inadequately accounts for new and improved products. Some products that rise in price provide more value for money. Appliances (refrigerators, washers, TVs) last longer and require less repair. So do cars. Since 1980, the average age of a car has risen from 6.6 to 8.4 years. New products (VCRs, microwaves) expand customer convenience but are added into the CPI with a delay—often after big price drops have occurred. And the CPI misses some price cuts—for example, discount air fares before 1982 and frequent-flier miles and grocery coupons today.

The result is that the CPI understates purchasing power. One reason people may not feel the gains is that their wants are rising even faster. In 1987, the median family judged that it needed $20,000 "just to get by," reports one survey; by 1996, that was $30,000—a 50 percent gain that outstripped inflation or real-income gains....

The fact that the CPI isn't perfect doesn't mean that it can be instantly improved. No single statistic will ever exactly measure inflation, because there are too many products whose prices change too often and whose quality variations—for worse as well as better—can never be completely counted. The Bureau of Labor Statistics (BLS), which complies the CPI, disputes some of the commission estimates; there's room for disagreement. The worst response to the report would be for the White House and Congress to pressure the BLS to alter the CPI. The BLS is studying improvements, but if it's stampeded into adopting only those that lower inflation, we could end up with a less useful indicator—one, for example, that masks some price increases.

It's no secret why Democrats and Republicans alike want a quick change. They prefer that the BLS do their dirty work, to relieve them of the responsibility of altering the legislative indexing of Social Security and taxes. Gosh, won't these guys do anything? Indexing is supposed to prevent the automatic erosion of government benefits (through reducing purchasing power) or automatic tax increases (by pushing people into higher brackets). When inflation was high, adopting indexing was right. But it was never supposed to provide automatic benefit increases or tax cuts; and that's what today's over-indexing does.

Although we may not know exactly how much the CPI overstates inflation, we know that it does. Ignoring this mortgages our future.

Politicians get paid to make judgments based on limited evidence. That's what they should do here. Slashing the adjustment at least 0.5 percentage points (say, from 3 percent to 2.5) is justified for five years until we see how the BLS alters the CPI. This wouldn't impose hardships. The rise in average Social Security benefits in the first year would be only about $36 less; tax increases would also be small. If the White House and Congress can't do this, political cowardice would be the only explanation.

USE YOUR ECONOMIC REASONING

1. According to the Boskin Commission, by how much does the CPI overstate the rate of inflation?
2. Suppose that the CPI registered a 5% increase in computer prices last year. Why might that overstate the reduction in purchasing power experienced by computer buyers?
3. Samuelson and others have argued that Social Security benefits (which are indexed to inflation through COLA clauses) should be increased by less than the full change reflected in the CPI. For example, when the CPI registers 3 percent inflation, benefits might be increased by 0.5 percent less, or 2.5 percent. What is the logic behind this recommendation, and why is Congress reluctant to make the change?

THE PRODUCER PRICE INDEX AND
THE IMPLICIT PRICE DEFLATOR

The Producer Price Index (PPI) and the Implicit Price Deflator (IPD) don't receive as much publicity as the Consumer Price Index, which is closely watched because it is used for cost-of-living adjustments in labor contracts and Social Security payments. Nevertheless, they have their particular uses and advantages. The PPI and the IPD are interpreted in precisely the same way as the CPI; that is, an index of 170 means that prices have risen by 70 percent since the base period.

The Producer Price Index is sometimes called the Wholesale Price Index.[3] It reflects the rate of inflation in the wholesale prices of finished products—both consumer goods and capital goods. Economists pay particular attention to the PPI because they think that it provides an indication of what will happen to consumer prices in the months to come. The logic here is fairly simple. Any increases in wholesale prices are eventually going to be passed on to consumers.

The broadest measure of inflation is the Implicit Price Deflator. This index examines the rate of increase in prices for all the different items included in the gross domestic product (GDP). This includes the prices of consumer goods, but it also includes the prices of items produced for business and government use and for export to foreign buyers. The range of products covered by the Implicit Price Deflator will be more apparent after you have completed the next section.

Measuring Total Output

The fundamental purpose of every economic system is to produce output in order to satisfy human wants. Therefore, many economists argue that gross domestic product (GDP) is the most important single indicator of our economy's performance. **Gross domestic product** is the total monetary value of all final goods and services produced within a nation in one year. In other words, it is a measure of the economy's annual production or output.[4]

---

[3] Actually, there are three separate Producer Price Indexes: one for finished goods, one for semi-finished goods, and one for raw materials. The index for finished goods is the one referred to as the Wholesale Price Index. It's also the one commonly referred to in the news.

[4] Until recently, the most commonly reported measure of the U.S. economy's aggregate output was gross national product (GNP). However, in 1991 the Department of Commerce began to use GDP as its basic measure, primarily for comparability with other nations.

Gross national product, by contrast, is the monetary value of all final goods and services produced by domestically owned factors of production in one year. U.S. GNP includes the value of final output produced by the resources owned by U.S. citizens, wherever those resources are located. (GDP includes the value of output produced in the United States by foreign-owned factories and foreign workers but excludes the value of output produced in other countries by U.S. workers and factories owned by U.S. companies.) For the United States, GDP and GNP are virtually identical; for other countries the difference can be quite large.

CALCULATING GDP: A SNEAK PREVIEW

Because GDP is measured in monetary units rather than units of output, we can add apples and oranges, so to speak; we can sum the economy's output of eggs, stereos, houses, tractors, and other products to produce a meaningful statistic. The procedure is quite simple: The output of each product is valued at its selling price, and these values are added to arrive at a figure for GDP.

Although GDP is a measure of output, you should note that only the output of final goods and services is permitted to enter the GDP calculation. *Final goods* are those that are purchased for final use rather than for further processing or resale. For example, a new pair of jeans is a final good, but the thread, cloth, zippers, and snaps that are used in manufacturing the jeans are *intermediate goods.* Since the value of the jeans already includes the value of the thread and other intermediate goods, only the value of the jeans should count in GDP. If the value of intermediate goods were to be included in the calculation, the result would be double counting, which would overstate the value of the economy's annual production.

The cloth and thread used in manufacturing clothing are intermediate goods, whereas the finished garment is a final good.

GDP AND THE CIRCULAR FLOW

There are two ways to measure gross domestic product: the expenditures approach and the income approach. The *expenditures approach* measures how much money is spent in purchasing final goods and services; the *income approach* measures the income that is created in producing these goods and services. Since one person's expenditure becomes another person's income, the two approaches must arrive at the same amount. In dollar terms, total output *must* equal total income.

The equality between total output and total income is reflected in the circular-flow diagram in Exh. 10.7, which is simplified to show the interaction of only the household and business sectors. The expenditures approach measures GDP by summing the various expenditures that make up the flow depicted at the bottom of the diagram. The income approach computes GDP by adding the various categories of income contained in the flow at the top of the diagram. The circular nature of the diagram indicates that all income spent on

---

EXHIBIT 10.7

Total Output = GDP = Total Income

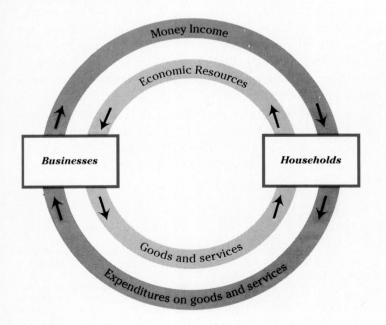

This simplified model of the economy (which ignores government and foreign trade) illustrates that there are two ways to calculate gross domestic product. The total expenditures made by households on final goods and services (the bottom flow) must equal the sum of the income received by the various economic resources (rent + wages + interest + profits)—the uppermost flow in the diagram. Both the total income received by the economic resources and the total household expenditures must equal GDP.

final goods and services must be received by someone as income; thus, total output must equal total income.

THE EXPENDITURES APPROACH

As you know, the U.S. economy is much more complex than the system depicted in Exh. 10.7. In our economy it's not only households that make expenditures for goods and services but also businesses, various levels of government, and foreign consumers. The categories of expenditures made by these groups are as follows:

1. *Personal consumption expenditures.* The total amount spent by consumers for goods and services includes both the purchase of consumer *durables,* such as automobiles, refrigerators, and stereos, and the purchase of *nondurables,* such as food, clothing, and entertainment. This is the largest category of expenditures, accounting for approximately two-thirds of GDP.

2. *Gross private domestic investment.*[5] This category includes all types of expenditures on capital goods, including business expenditures for new factories and equipment and household expenditures for new homes and major home improvements. (For accounting purposes, new homes are classified as an investment.) This category also includes changes in firms' inventories.[6]

3. *Government purchases.* This category covers federal, state, and local governments' purchases of all kinds of goods and services—for example, purchases of government vehicles, office supplies, weapons, concrete for roads, and even the consulting services of private firms hired to advise various government departments. This category excludes transfer payments such as welfare and Social Security, which do not represent the purchase of newly produced goods and services.

4. *Net exports.* Some of the output of American businesses is sold in foreign countries, and so it doesn't show up in our domestic sales. At the same time, some of the final goods and services sold in the United States were produced in foreign countries. To adjust for this situation, we subtract the

---

[5] The term *domestic* means "limited to our own country"; for example, domestic investment takes place within the boundaries of the United States.

[6] Counting changes in inventories as part of investment also ensures that total expenditures will equal the value of total output. If a business produces something this year but doesn't sell it this year, that production goes into inventory and is not recorded in total expenditures. So if we just add up the various types of expenditures, we'll miss the portion of GDP that was not sold. To adjust for this problem, we add any additions to inventory that occur from one year to the next in order to make sure that all production is counted. (Decreases in inventories represent the sale of items produced in previous years. Since those items were included in GDP figures for previous years, they must be subtracted from this year's total expenditures if GDP is to reflect current production accurately.)

value of imported goods from the value of our exports. The resulting figure, called *net exports*, is then added to our domestic sales. The formula for net exports is

Net exports = Total exports − total imports

The net exports total will be positive when exports exceed imports and negative when imports exceed exports.

To calculate gross domestic product by the expenditure approach, we add these four categories of expenditures. This procedure is illustrated in Exh. 10.8, which shows the U.S. GDP for 1997 as measured by both the expenditures approach and the income approach.

THE INCOME APPROACH

Calculating GDP by the income approach is somewhat more complicated than the circular-flow diagram would make it appear. In addition to the various forms of income that are created in the process of producing final goods and services (wages and salaries, rent, interest, and profits), two *nonincome payments* (indirect business taxes and capital consumption allowances) account for a portion of the money received by businesses. The categories of

---

EXHIBIT 10.8

Gross Domestic Product in 1997 (in billions)

EXPENDITURES APPROACH		INCOME APPROACH	
Personal consumption expenditures	$5,485.8	Employee compensation	$4,703.6
		Rental income	147.9
Gross private domestic investment	1,242.5	Net interest	448.7
		Corporate profits	805.0
Government purchases of goods and services	1,452.7	Proprietors' income	544.5
		Indirect business taxes	562.3
Net exports of goods and services	−101.1	Capital consumption allowances	867.9
Gross domestic product	**$8,079.9**	**Gross domestic product**	**$8,079.9**

Source: Developed from the April, 1998 edition of the *Survey of Current Business*, published by the U.S. Department of Commerce.

income received by the economic resources and the types of nonincome payments are as follows:

1. *Compensation of employees.* In addition to wages and salaries, this income category includes such things as payroll taxes and employer contributions to health plans.

2. *Rental income.* This is the income earned by households from the rental of property, such as buildings and land.

3. *Net interest.* This category includes the interest earned by households on the money they lend to businesses to finance inventories, build plant additions, and purchase new machinery.

4. *Corporate profits.* The before-tax profit of corporations, this category has three components, representing the three things that corporations can do with their profits: (a) *corporate profits tax liability*—profits used to pay federal and state taxes, (b) *dividends*—profits paid out to stockholders, and (c) *retained earnings*—profits kept by businesses for reinvestment (also called *undistributed corporate profits*).

5. *Proprietors' income.* This category includes the income earned by unincorporated businesses, such as proprietorships, partnerships, and cooperatives.

6. *Indirect business taxes.* Indirect business taxes include sales taxes and excise taxes. The important thing about such taxes is that they are collected *by* businesses *for* government. Therefore, a portion of the money received by businesses must be passed on directly to government; it is not available as a payment to the owners of economic resources. Such taxes are described as *nonincome payments.*

7. *Capital consumption allowances.* Also called *allowances for depreciation,* these are funds set aside for the eventual replacement of worn-out factories and equipment. Like indirect business taxes, they represent a nonincome payment.

To measure gross domestic product by the income approach, we add the five types of income and the two nonincome payments. As you can see in Exh. 10.8, the answer we get is the same as the one generated earlier by the expenditures approach.[7] Again, that result is necessary because every dollar spent on output must be received by someone as income or as a nonincome payment.

---

[7] In fact, the GDP calculated by the income approach never turns out to be exactly the same as the GDP calculated by the expenditures approach. The difference is what the Department of Commerce calls the *statistical discrepancy.* In Exh. 10.8 the entry for indirect business taxes has been adjusted to incorporate the statistical discrepancy.

INTERPRETING GDP STATISTICS

Now that we know what gross domestic product means and how it is measured, we need to note two facts before interpreting GDP statistics. An increase in GDP does not always mean that we're better off. Similarly, a decrease in GDP is not always a cause for concern and corrective action.

Real GDP versus Money GDP. From 1987 to 1997, gross domestic product in the United States increased from $4,692.3 billion to $8,079.9 billion (from $4½ trillion to $8 trillion), an increase of 72 percent in 10 years. On the surface that seems like a pretty good performance, particularly when you realize that our population increased only about 10 percent in that period. It looks as though the average American had a lot more goods and services at his or her disposal in 1997 than in 1987.

But numbers can be misleading. Because GDP is the physical output of a given year valued at the prices that prevailed in that year, it can increase from one year to another because of increased output, increased prices, or a combination of the two. (To underscore that GDP can change simply in response to a change in prices, economists often refer to GDP as *money* GDP or *nominal* GDP.) Therefore, if we want to know how much *physical* output has increased, we have to calculate the **real gross domestic product**—that is, the GDP that has been adjusted to eliminate the impact of changes in the price level.

To eliminate the impact of changing prices from our GDP comparison, we need to value the output produced in these two different time periods at some common sets of prices. For example, we could value both the 1997 output and the 1987 output at 1987 prices or at 1997 prices or at the prices that prevailed in some intermediate time period. The Bureau of Economic Analysis (BEA) uses the third approach; it values both years' outputs at the prices that prevailed in some base year, currently 1992. According to the BEA, when 1987 and 1997 outputs are valued at 1992 prices, we find that real GDP increased from $5,649.5 billion in 1987 to $7,191.4 in 1997, an increase of 27 percent.

As you can see, the increase in the real GDP (27%) was much smaller than the increase in nominal GDP(72%); much of the increase in money GDP was due to inflation. This is why economists insist on comparing real GDPs rather than nominal GDPs. Comparison of real GDPs gives us a much better picture of what's actually happening to the economy's output and the population's standard of living.

What GDP Does Not Measure. Even real GDP figures should be interpreted with caution. They don't measure all of our society's production, and they certainly don't provide a perfect measure of welfare, or well-being. Some of the things that GDP does not consider are as follows:

1. *Nonmarketed goods and services.* GDP does not measure all production or output but only production that is intended to be sold through markets. This means that GDP excludes the production of homemakers and do-it-yourselfers, as well as all barter transactions, in which one person directly exchanges goods or services with another.

2. *Illegal activities.* GDP does not include illegal goods and services, such as illicit drugs, illegal gambling, and prostitution. It also excludes otherwise legal transactions that are unreported in order to avoid paying taxes—the sale of firewood for cash, for example.

3. *Leisure.* GDP does not measure increases in leisure, but such increases clearly have an impact on our well-being. Even if real gross domestic product didn't increase, if we could produce a constant real GDP with shorter and shorter workweeks, most of us would agree that our lives had improved.

4. *Population.* GDP statistics tell us nothing about the size of the population that must share a given output. A GDP of $2 trillion means one thing in an economy of 100 million people and something completely different in an economy of 500 million people. (It's like the difference between an income of $20,000 for a single person and an income of $20,000 for a family of five.) Economists generally attempt to adjust for this problem by talking about GDP per capita, or per person—that is, GDP divided by the population of the country.

5. *Externalities.* We have a very sophisticated accounting system to keep track of all the goods and services we produce, but we have not established a method of subtracting from GDP when the production process yields negative externalities—air and water pollution, for example. (See Chapter 9 for a review of this concept.)

In response to concerns about our environment, in 1994 the Commerce Department began publishing supplementary, or "satellite," GDP accounts to record changes in our stocks of natural resources. These satellite accounts are still in the experimental state and will not replace the regular GDP reports. The addition of these accounts should help to address concerns about ignoring externalities in our GDP reporting. But the other limitations remain. For now, we'll have to be satisfied with imperfect GDP statistics and an understanding of their limitations.

Summary

To keep track of the economy's performance, people watch *economic indicators*—signals or measures that tell us how well the economy is performing. Three major economic indicators are the unemployment rate, price indexes (the Consumer Price Index, the Producer Price Index, and the Implicit Price Deflator), and the gross domestic product. Each of these indicators looks at a different dimension of the economy's performance.

The *civilian unemployment rate* is the percentage of the civilian labor force that is unemployed. (The civilian labor force is made up of all persons over the age of sixteen who are not in the armed forces and who are either employed or actively seeking employment.) Each month, the Bureau of Labor Statistics surveys some 60,000 households to determine the employment status of the residents. It then uses the results from this sample to estimate the size of the labor force and the rate of unemployment for the nation as a whole.

We attempt to measure inflation with something called a *price index*. A price index is a ratio of two prices: a price in some base period that serves as a reference point divided into the price in whatever period we wish to compare to the base period. For example, if tennis shoes sold for $50 in 1990 and $80 in 1997, the price index for tennis shoes would be 160 if 1990 were used as the base year:

$$
\text{Price index} = \frac{\text{Price in a given period}}{\text{Price in the base period}}
$$

$$
= \frac{\$80.00}{\$50.00}
$$

$$
= 1.60 \text{ or } 160 \text{ percent}
$$

Since the price index in the base period is always 100, an index of 160 means that price has increased by 60 percent since the base period. By the same logic, an index of 75 would indicate that price has decreased by 25 percent since the base period.

The other major indicator, the *gross domestic product* (GDP), is the total monetary value of all final goods and services produced in one year. In other words, it is a measure of the economy's annual production or output. GDP can be estimated by the expenditures approach or by the income approach. The expenditures approach sums the categories of expenditures made for final goods and services. The income approach looks at the forms of income that are created when final goods are produced and adds to those income figures certain nonincome payments.

Since GDP is measured in monetary units (dollars), it is possible to add apples and oranges (that is, to sum the economy's output of eggs, stereos, houses, tractors, and so on) and arrive at a meaningful measure of the economy's total output. GDP figures must be interpreted with caution, however. When we compare the GDPs for two different years, we must be sure to correct for the impact of changing prices—to compare real GDPs, not money GDPs. We must also recognize that GDP is not a complete measure of our economy's production because it excludes the work of homemakers and do-it-yourselfers as well as other nonmarket transactions. Nor is it a complete measure of welfare, or well-being; it doesn't take into account the value of leisure, for example, or the negative externalities associated with the production of some goods and services.

GLOSSARY

Annual inflation rate. The percent change in a price index from one year to the next.

Civilian labor force. All persons over the age of sixteen who are not in the armed forces and who are either employed or actively seeking employment.

Civilian unemployment rate. The percentage of the civilian labor force that is unemployed.

Cyclical unemployment. Joblessness caused by a reduction in the economy's total demand for goods and services.

Economic indicators. Signals or measures that tell us how well the economy is performing.

Frictional unemployment. People who are out of work because they are in the process of changing jobs or are searching for their first job.

Full employment. When the actual rate of unemployment is equal to the natural rate of unemployment.

Gross domestic product. The total monetary value of all final goods and services produced within a nation in one year.

Gross national product. The total monetary value of all final goods and services produced by domestically owned factors of production in one year.

Inflation. A rise in the general level of prices.

Macroeconomics. The study of the economy as a whole and the factors that influence the economy's overall performance.

Natural rate of unemployment. The minimum level of unemployment that an economy can achieve in normal times. The rate of unemployment that would exist in the absence of cyclical unemployment.

Price index. A measure of changes in the general level of prices. Three basic price indexes are used in the United States: the Consumer Price Index, the Producer Price Index, and the Implicit Price Deflator.

Real gross domestic product. Gross domestic product that has been adjusted to eliminate the impact of changes in the price level.

Real income. The purchasing power of your income; the amount of goods and services it will buy.

Structural unemployment. Unemployment caused by changes in the makeup, or structure, of the economy, whereby some skills become obsolete or in less demand.

Unemployment rate. See *Civilian unemployment rate.*

STUDY QUESTIONS

Fill in the Blanks

1. The study of the economy's overall performance and the factors that influence that performance is called *Macroeconomics*

2. Clauses that provide for automatic wage and salary adjustments to compensate for inflation are called *cost of living adjustment (COLA)* clauses.

3. *Economic indicators* are signals, or measures, that tell us how well the economy is performing.

4. The price index that is used to adjust union wage contracts and Social Security payments for inflation is the *Consumer Price Index*

5. Unemployment caused by a reduction in the economy's total demand for goods and services is called *cyclical* unemployment.

6. A common estimate for the natural rate of unemployment is *5.5* percent.

7. People who stop looking for jobs because they are convinced that none are available are called *discouraged workers*

8. The two approaches to measuring GDP are the *expenditures* approach and the *income* approach.

9. GDP that has been adjusted to eliminate the impact of changes in the price level is called *real* GDP.

10. The largest component of spending in GDP is *Consumption* spending.

Multiple Choice

1. The civilian labor force is made up of
   a) all persons over the age of sixteen.
   b) all persons over the age of eighteen who are not in the armed forces.
   c) all persons over the age of sixteen who are not in the armed forces and who are either employed or actively seeking employment.
   d) all persons over the age of eighteen who are not in the armed forces and who are either employed or actively seeking employment.

2. If you are out of work because you are in the process of looking for a better job, economists would say that you are

   a) frictionally unemployed.
   b) cyclically unemployed.
   c) structurally unemployed.
   d) None of the above

3. People who are unemployed because they have no marketable skills are said to be
   a) frictionally unemployed.
   b) cyclically unemployed.
   c) structurally unemployed.
   d) None of the above

4. The unemployment rate for blacks is about
   a) three times the rate for whites.
   b) twice the rate for whites.

c) 2 percent higher than the rate for whites.
d) the same as the rate for whites.

5. Which of the following is false?
   a) Inflation tends to redistribute income.
   b) Inflation is particularly hard on people with fixed incomes.
   c) No one benefits from inflation.
   d) COLA clauses help protect workers from inflation.

6. If the Consumer Price Index is 250, that means that
   a) the average price of a product is $2.50.
   b) prices are two times as high as they were in the base year.
   c) prices have risen 150 percent since the base year.
   d) Both b and c are correct.

7. The natural rate of unemployment is the rate that would exist in the absence of
   a) frictional unemployment.
   b) structural unemployment.
   c) cyclical unemployment.
   d) frictional and structural unemployment.

8. Which of the following items would be counted in GDP?
   a) The work of a homemaker
   b) The sale of a used car
   c) A soda you buy at your local drive-in
   d) The firewood you cut for your home last winter

9. Suppose that Susan received a 3 percent raise last year, but her rent and the other prices she had to pay rose 5 percent. An economist would say that Susan's
   a) real income rose, but her nominal income fell.
   b) nominal income rose, but her money income fell.
   c) money income rose, but her nominal income fell.
   d) nominal income rose, but her real income fell.

10. If both output and prices are higher in year 2 than they were in year 1, which of the following is true?

a) Real GDP declined from year 1 to year 2.
b) GDP declined from year 1 to year 2.
c) GDP increased from year 1 to year 2, but real GDP declined.
d) Both GDP and real GDP increased from year 1 to year 2.

11. The Consumer Price Index was 130.7 in 1990 and 136.2 in 1991. Therefore, the rate of inflation between 1990 and 1991 was
    a) 30.7 percent.
    b) 5.5 percent.
    c) 4.2 percent.
    d) about 136 percent.

12. In comparison to other major industrialized nations,
    a) the U.S. unemployment rate is higher than average.
    b) the U.S. inflation rate is lower than average.
    c) the U.S. inflation rate has been higher than average over the past decade.
    d) the U.S. unemployment rate has been about average over the past decade.

13. Which of the following would *not* be considered in computing GDP by the *expenditures approach*?
    a) Personal consumption expenditures
    b) Gross private domestic investment
    c) Compensation of employees
    d) Net exports

14. Which of the following would *not* be considered in computing GDP by the *income approach*?
    a) Rental income
    b) Corporate profits
    c) Indirect business taxes
    d) Government purchases of goods and services

15. If nominal GDP is increasing but real GDP is not, then,
    a) the economy must be experiencing inflation.
    b) output must be falling.
    c) the price level must be falling.
    d) population must be increasing.

Problems and Questions for Discussion

1. What is the purpose of economic indicators? Can they be of any value to you?

2. A student could be counted as employed, unemployed, or "not participating" in the labor market. Explain.

3. An increase in the unemployment rate is not always a sign of growing weakness in the economy. Explain.

4. Some frictional and structural unemployment is probably a sign of a healthy economy. Why is that true?

5. How does inflation redistribute income?

6. How can savers be hurt by inflation?

7. Why is it true that "the people who are most hurt by inflation are those who have the least bargaining power in the marketplace?"

8. Some workers are convinced that they are worse off today than they were ten years ago, even though they have received annual raises. Is this possible, or must their perceptions be incorrect?

9. Use the following information to compute GDP by the income approach. (Some figures are not required for solving the problem.)

Employee compensation	$400
Proprietor's income	70
Rental income	25
Indirect business taxes	20
Personal consumption	450
Gross investment	250
Net interest	40
Capital consumption allowance	75
Corporate profits	55

10. Use the following information to compute GDP by the expenditures approach. (Some figures are not required for solving the problem.)

Personal consumption	$500
Exports	10
Gross investment	200
Imports	12
Proprietors' income	450
Government purchases	250
Corporate profits	50

11. Why must total income always equal total output?

ANSWER KEY

Fill in the Blanks

1. macroeconomics
2. cost-of-living adjustment (COLA)
3. Economic indicators
4. Consumer Price Index
5. cyclical
6. 5.5
7. discouraged workers
8. expenditures, income
9. real
10. consumption

Multiple Choice

1. c	4. b	7. c	10. d	13. c
2. a	5. c	8. c	11. c	14. d
3. c	6. c	9. d	12. c	15. a

CHAPTER 11

Keynes and the Classical Economists: The Early Debate on Policy Activism

LEARNING OBJECTIVES

1. Define aggregate demand and aggregate supply.
2. Illustrate how an economy's equilibrium GDP and price level are determined and how they can change.
3. Use aggregate demand and supply curves to illustrate the possibility of unemployment or inflation.
4. Explain the difference between activist and nonactivist economists.
5 Discuss why the classical economists believed that a market economy would automatically tend toward full employment.
6. Explain why Keynes rejected the views of the classical economists.
7. Compare the views of Keynes and the classical economists with regard to the proper role of government.

Chapter 10 identified some important dimensions of the economy's overall performance and examined techniques used to measure performance in those areas. Now, in Chapter 11, we will begin to explore why the aggregate economy behaves as it does and how its performance changes. We will also examine the origin of an ongoing debate in macroeconomics—the debate about the appropriateness of government attempts to influence or manage the performance of our overall economy.

First, we introduce the concepts of aggregate demand and aggregate supply. Just as demand and supply are important tools in microeconomics, aggregate demand and aggregate supply are important in macroeconomics. We examine how aggregate demand and aggregate supply interact to determine the levels of output, employment, and prices, and how unemployment and inflation arise.

As you discovered in Chapter 10, unemployment and inflation impose costs on our society. Today, many Americans assume that it is the federal government's responsibility to reduce those costs by combating unemployment and inflation when they occur. But the issue of government intervention to combat macroeconomic problems provokes sharp disagreement among economists. Economists known as "activists" support a significant role for government. "Nonactivists" are economists who believe that government intervention should be avoided.

We will use the framework of aggregate demand–aggregate supply to explore the origin of the activist-nonactivist controversy. This controversy originated more than 50 years ago with a debate between John Maynard Keynes and the then-dominant classical economists. Our examination of this debate sets the stage for Chapter 12, which develops the modern model of a self-adjusting economy, a model that borrows from both Keynes and the classical economists. The historical debate also provides an important backdrop for understanding the ongoing controversy about policy activism.

An Introduction to Aggregate Demand and Aggregate Supply

Chapter 3 showed how demand and supply interact to determine the prices and quantities of products in particular markets. In macroeconomics, aggregate demand and aggregate supply determine the general price level and the level of domestic output, or real GDP. This section presents an overview of the aggregate demand–aggregate supply framework. Chapter 12 will consider these concepts in more detail.

AGGREGATE DEMAND

One of the forces that determines the economy's level of output, employment, and prices is aggregate demand. **Aggregate demand** is the total quantity of output demanded by all sectors in the economy together (households, businesses, governments, and foreigners) at various price levels in a given period of time.

Because the quantity of output demanded by these sectors depends in part on the price level, the *AD* curve slopes downward and to the right like the demand curve for a single product (see Exh. 11.1). But the demand curve and the aggregate demand curve are very different concepts. The demand curve shows the relationship between the price of a particular product and the quantity of that product demanded. The aggregate demand curve relates

...and and Supply Curves

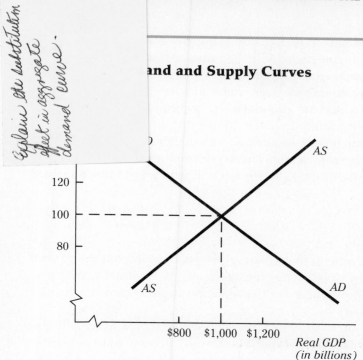

Explain the substitution effect in aggregate demand curve.

The aggregate demand curve shows the quantity of real output demanded at each price level. The aggregate supply curve shows the amount of real output supplied at each price level.

The intersection of the aggregate demand and supply curves determines the equilibrium level of real GDP and the equilibrium price level in the economy.

the overall price level in the economy (as measured by a price index, such as the CPI) to the total quantity of real output that consumers, businesses, governments, and foreigners want to buy.

The demand curve and the aggregate demand curve slope downward for different reasons. When we are considering the demand curve for a single product, we assume that the prices of all other products remain constant as we reduce the price of the product in question. Consumers, of course, respond by buying (substituting) more of this relatively cheaper product. This *substitution effect* cannot, however, explain the downward slope of the aggregate demand curve. The aggregate demand curve is constructed with the price level for the *entire economy* measured on the vertical axis. A reduction in the overall price level means that the average price of *all* goods and services has fallen. Since all prices are falling, the substitution effect cannot explain the increase in the quantity of real GDP demanded.

The downward slope of the aggregate demand curve is due in part to the **real balance effect** (additional reasons will be introduced in Chapter 12). According to the real balance effect, a reduction in the overall price level will increase the quantity of real output demanded because the lower overall price level will enable people to buy more with their cash and other financial assets. If the prices of goods and services fall, the real value or purchasing power of your financial assets—the cash in your wallet, the balance in your savings account, the wealth you have accumulated in government bonds—will increase. In other words, the same amount of money will stretch farther than before—will buy more than before. As a result, a reduction in the price level will cause people to purchase more goods and services. Of course, an increase in the price level will have the opposite effect; it will reduce spending on goods and services.

AGGREGATE SUPPLY

The second force determining the economy's overall output and the general price level is aggregate supply. **Aggregate supply** is the total quantity of output supplied by all producers in the economy together at various price levels in a given time period.

Economists have suggested several possible shapes for the aggregate supply curve. For now, we'll assume that it is upward sloping, like the supply curve for a single product. An upward-sloping aggregate supply curve implies that producers will supply more real output at higher price levels than at lower price levels. Why might producers respond to higher prices by expanding output? One reason is that certain input costs—wage rates, for instance—tend to be fixed by contracts in the short run. As a consequence, when prices rise, producers can profit by expanding output and pocketing the difference between the higher product prices they receive and the fixed input prices they must pay. We'll have more to say about the shape of the *AS* curve later in the text. For now the important point is that higher prices induce producers to supply more output. The aggregate supply curve labeled *AS* in Exh. 11.1 depicts this relationship.

THE EQUILIBRIUM PRICE LEVEL AND REAL GDP

The interaction of aggregate demand and aggregate supply simultaneously determines the equilibrium price level and the equilibrium level of real GDP. This process is illustrated in Exh. 11.1, which shows the intersection of *AS* and *AD* resulting in an equilibrium price level of 100 and an equilibrium real GDP of $1,000 billion. The level of employment in the economy is directly related to the level of output; the greater the economy's real GDP, the more workers are needed (ceteris paribus) and the higher the level of employment. Thus, we can say that the interaction of aggregate demand and aggregate supply determines the level of prices, output, and employment in the economy.

FULL EMPLOYMENT AND POTENTIAL GDP

An important question in macroeconomics is whether the economy will achieve full employment. In other words, will the aggregate demand and supply curves intersect at a level of GDP sufficient to provide full employment? You will recall that full employment does not mean zero unemployment. As we saw in Chapter 10, some frictional and structural unemployment is unavoidable, perhaps even desirable. Today, an unemployment rate in the vicinity of 5.5 percent is regarded as the natural rate of unemployment because that is the best we can hope to attain in normal times. When the actual unemployment rate in the economy is equal to the natural rate, the economy has achieved full employment.

The level of output the economy produces when it operates at full employment, at the natural rate of unemployment, is called potential GDP. **Potential GDP** represents the economy's maximum sustainable level of production; output can expand beyond potential, but it cannot be sustained.

THE POSSIBILITY OF UNEMPLOYMENT OR INFLATION

Even if the economy begins at full employment and potential GDP, it may not remain there. Exh. 11.2 represents a hypothetical economy that is initially in equilibrium at full employment. As you can see, AD_1 and AS_1 intersect at a real GDP of $1,000 billion (the economy's potential GDP) and a price level of 100. Given this starting point, how would the economy react to a change in aggregate demand? Suppose, for example, that business executives become pessimistic about the future and reduce their spending for buildings and equipment. Ceteris paribus, this will cause the aggregate demand curve to shift to the left since less output will now be demanded at any given price level. This is represented in Exh. 11.2 by the movement from AD_1 to AD_2. The reduction in aggregate demand causes the equilibrium price level to fall from 100 to 80 and reduces real GDP from $1,000 billion to $800 billion. Note that the economy's equilibrium real GDP is now below potential, so that the society is no longer enjoying full employment; the reduction in aggregate demand has led to unemployment.

It is also possible for the equilibrium level of GDP to *exceed* potential GDP. To see how, suppose that the federal government decides to spend several billion additional dollars rebuilding the nation's roads and bridges. This added government spending will shift the aggregate demand curve to the right, from AD_1 to AD_3 in Exh. 11.2.

EXHIBIT 11.2

The Impact of a Change in Aggregate Demand

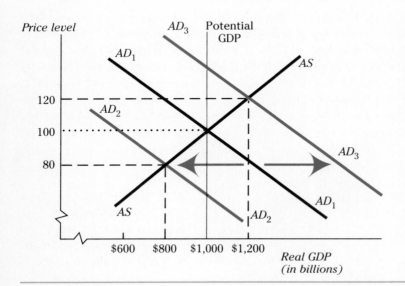

Reductions in aggregate demand, like the shift from AD_1 to AD_2, lead to a lower price level, but they also cause real GDP to fall, and they result in unemployment.

Increases in aggregate demand, like the shift from AD_1 to AD_2, have the beneficial effect of raising output and employment, but they also push up the price level; they cause inflation.

As you can see from the exhibit, this increase in aggregate demand causes the equilibrium level of real GDP to rise from $1,000 billion to $1,200 billion—more than the economy's potential. Unfortunately, the price level in the economy has also risen, from 100 to 120 in this example. In short, the increase in aggregate demand has propelled the economy to a higher level of real GDP, but it has also resulted in inflation.[1]

How will the economy respond to these situations—to equilibrium outputs that are greater or less than potential GDP? How can the economy operate beyond its potential, and how long can it maintain such production? If the economy is experiencing unemployment, will it ever return to the full-employment (potential) GDP? If the economy is experiencing unemployment or inflation, should government attempt to improve the economy's performance by influencing aggregate demand or supply? These important questions of theory and policy are the subject matter of subsequent chapters. Many of these questions first emerged in the debate between the classical economists and John Maynard Keynes. The remainder of this chapter is devoted to that debate.

---

[1] Equilibrium GDP can also deviate from potential GDP because of changes in aggregate supply. The next chapter will consider that possibility as it explores the aggregate demand–aggregate supply model in greater detail.

The Classical Model:
The Case for Laissez-Faire

We will begin our exploration of the activist-nonactivist debate by considering the views of the classical economists. The term **classical economist** describes the mainstream economists who wrote from about 1776 through the early 1930s. For our purposes the most important element of classical economic thought was the belief that a market economy would automatically tend toward full employment. Virtually all the major classical economists held that belief, and apparently people were satisfied with this description of the real world until the Great Depression caused them to question its validity.

SAY'S LAW

The classical economists based their predictions about full employment on a principle known as **Say's Law,** the creation of French economist J. B. Say (1776–1832). According to Say's Law, "Supply creates its own demand." In other words, in the process of producing output, businesses also create enough income to ensure that all the output will be sold. Because this theory occupies such an important place in classical economics, we will examine it in more detail, beginning with a simple circular-flow diagram, Exh. 11.3.

Exhibit 11.3 shows that when businesses produce output, they create *income*, payments that must be made to the providers of the various economic resources. Assume, for example, that businesses want to produce $100 worth of output to sell to households. To do that, businesses must first acquire the economic resources necessary to produce those goods and services. The owners of the economic resources are households, and they expect to be paid—in wages, rent, interest, and profits (remember, profits are the *payment* for entrepreneurship). Therefore, $100 in income payments flows to the household sector. If households spend all the income they receive, everything that was produced will be sold. Supply will have created its own demand.

Because the classical economists accepted Say's Law, they believed that there was nothing to prevent the economy from expanding to full employment. As long as job seekers were willing to work for a wage that was no more than their productivity (their contribution to the output of the firm), profit-seeking businesses would desire to hire everyone who wanted a job. There would always be adequate demand for the output of these additional workers, because "supply creates its own demand."

Many students will immediately recognize that saving could disrupt that simple process. If households decided to save a portion of their earnings, not

EXHIBIT 11.3

Say's Law: Supply Creates Its Own Demand

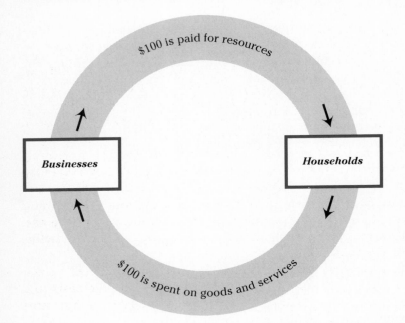

If all the income created in the act of producing output is spent by households, supply will have created its own demand, and all the output will be sold.

all of the income created by businesses would return in the form of spending. Thus, the demand for goods and services would be too small for the supply, and some output would remain unsold. Businesses would then react by cutting back on production and laying off workers, thus causing unemployment.

But the classical economists did not see saving as a problem. Saving would *not* cause a reduction in spending because businesses would borrow all the saved money for investment—the purchase of capital goods, such as factories and machinery. Why were the classical economists so sure that the amount households wished to save would equal the amount businesses wanted to invest? Because of interest rates. In the classical model the interest rate is determined by the demand for and supply of **loanable funds,** money available to be borrowed. If households desired to save more than investors wanted to borrow, the surplus of funds would drive down the interest rate. Because the interest rate is both the reward households receive for saving *and* the price businesses pay to finance investment, a declining interest rate would both discourage saving and encourage investment. The interest rate would continue to fall until the amount that households wanted to save once again equaled the amount businesses desired to invest. At this equilibrium interest rate there would be no uninvested savings. Businesses would be able to sell all their output either to consumers or to investors, and full employment would prevail.

THE ROLE OF FLEXIBLE WAGES AND PRICES

The classical economists believed that Say's Law and the flexibility of interest rates would ensure that spending would be adequate to maintain full employment. But some critics were unconvinced. Suppose that households chose to "hoard" some of their income. (Hoarding money is the act of hiding it or storing it.) When people are concerned about the future, they may choose to hide money in a mattress or in a cookie jar so that they will have something to tide them over during hard times. (Households may prefer this form of saving if they lack confidence in the banking system—a situation that existed in the 1920s, when there were numerous bank failures.) This method of saving creates problems for Say's Law because it removes money from circulation. If households choose to hoard money in cookie jars, that money can't be borrowed by businesses and invested. As a consequence, spending may decline and unemployment may appear.

Although the classical economists admitted that hoarding could cause spending to decline, they did not believe that it would lead to unemployment. Full employment would be maintained because wage and price adjustments would compensate for any deficiency in total spending.

The existence of flexible wages and prices implies an *AS* curve that is vertical, not upward-sloping as in the initial section of this chapter. Recall that the upward slope of the earlier *AS* curve resulted from the assumption that wage rates and some other input prices remain fixed in the short run. Given these rigidities, an increase in the price level would allow businesses to profit by expanding output, thus producing the upward-sloping *AS* curve. But the classical economists believed that *all* prices—including wage rates (the price of labor) and other input prices—were highly flexible. An increase in product prices would therefore be quickly matched by higher costs, which would eliminate any incentive to expand output.

Thus, the existence of highly flexible wages and prices implies an *AS* curve that is vertical at the full-employment level of output (potential GDP), as represented in Exh. 11.4.

To illustrate how flexible wages and prices guarantee full employment, let us assume that the economy is operating at a price level of 100 and a real GDP of $1,000 billion, the intersection of *AS* and AD_1. Now, suppose that consumers become pessimistic about the future and hide some of their income in cookie jars rather than spend it. What will happen? Aggregate demand will fall—the *AD* curve will shift from AD_1 to AD_2—because households are

EXHIBIT 11.4

The Classical Aggregate Supply Curve

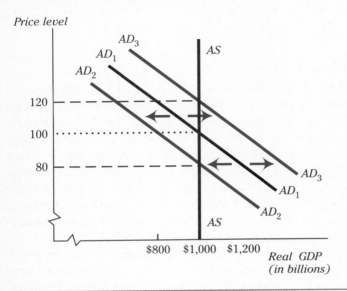

In the classical model a reduction in aggregate demand would immediately lead to falling prices and wages, so that real GDP would be maintained and employment would not fall. Higher aggregate demand would lead to inflation, with no change in output.

spending less and thus demanding less real output at any given price level. Reasoning from the assumptions of the classical economists, a reduction in aggregate demand leads quickly to falling prices. In our example the price level will not be maintained at 100; it will fall to 80. If that occurs, businesses will be able to sell the same amount of real output as before but at lower prices. Wages will also decline because reductions in the demand for goods and services will be accompanied by falling demand for labor, which will lead to labor surpluses and wage reductions. Thus, employers will still be able to make a profit at the lower price level.

If *AD* were to increase (due to dishoarding—spending the money that had been hoarded—for example), this entire process would work in reverse. An increase in aggregate demand from AD_1 to AD_3 would quickly push up product prices. On the surface this would seem to make it attractive for businesses to increase output; if product prices rise while input prices remain stable, producers can make a profit by expanding output to satisfy the higher level of demand. But in the classical model, wage rates and other input prices are also highly flexible, and they would tend to rise because increases in the demand for goods and services would be accompanied by rising demand for labor and other inputs. Thus, businesses would have no incentive to expand output. The higher level of aggregate demand would lead to inflation, leaving output and employment unchanged.

In summary, the classical economists did not believe that changes in aggregate demand would have any impact on real GDP or employment; they maintained that only the price level would be affected.

FULL EMPLOYMENT AND LAISSEZ-FAIRE

As a consequence of their faith in Say's Law and the flexibility of wages and prices, the classical economists viewed full employment as the normal situation. They held this belief in spite of recurring periods of observed unemployment. By the mid-1800s, economists recognized that capitalist economies tend to expand over time but not at a steady rate. Instead, output and employment fluctuate up and down, growing rapidly in some periods and more slowly, or even declining, in others. Today we call these recurring ups and downs in the level of economic activity the **business cycle.** A period of rising output and employment is called an *expansion*; a period of declining output and employment is called a *recession*.

The occasional bouts of unemployment that accompanied the recession stage of the business cycle were not, however, viewed with alarm or seen as contradicting the classical model. Instead, such unemployment was attributed to external shocks (wars and natural disasters, for example) or to changes in consumer preferences.[2] Because the economy required time to adjust to these events, there might be some unemployment in the interim. But such unemployment would be very short-term; it could not persist. Prolonged unemployment would result only if workers' unreasonable wage demands made it unprofitable for firms to hire them. Such unemployment was considered "voluntary"; that is, at the prevailing wage, the people preferred leisure to work. Because prolonged unemployment was regarded as an impossibility and short-term unemployment not deemed a significant social problem, the classical economists focused their energies elsewhere, on studying microeconomic issues and attempting to understand the forces underlying an economy's long-term rate of economic growth (the growth rate of potential GDP).

---

[2] Because the classical economists believed that supply created its own demand, they did not believe that it was possible to have a *general* surplus of goods and services throughout the economy. They recognized, however, that there could be an oversupply of individual products. For example, automobile manufacturers might miscalculate and produce too many automobiles for the prevailing market. In the short run this would result in unsold inventories and unemployment: The current number of workers could no longer be profitably employed by the automobile industry. In the long run, however, both problems would be eliminated. The surplus of automobiles would cause their prices to fall, which would shift labor and other economic resources out of the automobile industry and into some other industry, one characterized by shortages and rising prices.

The classical theorists' belief in the economy's ability to maintain full employment through its own internal mechanisms caused them to favor a policy of laissez-faire, or government by nonintervention. Society was advised to rely on the market mechanism to take care of the economy and to limit the role of government to the areas where it could make a positive contribution—maintaining law and order and providing for the national defense, for example.

The Keynesian Revolution:
The Case for Policy Activism

The classical doctrine and its laissez-faire policy prescriptions were almost universally accepted by economists and policymakers until the time of the Great Depression. Then the massive and prolonged unemployment that characterized the industrialized world challenged the predictions of the classical model.

The term "depression" was coined to describe a severe recession. The Great Depression lived up to its name. In 1929, when it began, unemployment stood at 3.2 percent. By 1933, when the economy hit bottom, the unemployment rate had risen to almost 25 percent. During the same period, the economy's output of goods and services (real GDP) fell by more than 25 percent. Moreover, in 1939, ten years after the depression began, unemployment still exceeded 17 percent, and GDP had barely edged back to the levels achieved a decade earlier. Clearly, the classical belief that any unemployment would be moderate and short-lived seemed in direct conflict with reality.

The most forceful critic of the classical model was John Maynard Keynes, a British economist. His major work, entitled *The General Theory of Employment, Interest, and Money,* was first published in 1936. In a sense, Keynes stood classical economics on its head. Whereas the classical economists believed that supply created its own demand, Keynes argued that causation ran the other way—from demand to supply. In Keynes's view, businesses base their production decisions on the level of expected demand, or expected total spending. The more that consumers, investors, and others plan to spend, the more output businesses will expect to sell and the more they will produce. In other words, supply (or output) responds to demand—not the converse, as the classical economists suggested. Most important, Keynes argued that the level of total spending in the economy could be inadequate to provide full employment, that the classical economists were wrong in believing that interest rate adjustments and wage/price flexibility would prevent unemployment. According to Keynes, full employment is possible only when the level of total spending is adequate. If spending is inadequate, unemployment will result.

John Maynard Keynes contended that the classical economists were wrong in their belief that a market economy automatically tends toward full employment.

In summary, Keynes rejected the classical contention that market economies automatically tend toward full employment; he focused attention on the level of demand or total spending as the critical determinant of an economy's health. We now turn to a more detailed look at his model and the errors he detected in the classical theory.

THE MEANING OF EQUILIBRIUM OUTPUT

To understand the Keynesian model, you need to become more familiar with the concept of **equilibrium output.** As you know, equilibrium means stability: a state of balance or rest. In microeconomics an equilibrium price is a stable price, one that won't change unless there are changes in the underlying supply and demand conditions. In macroeconomics an equilibrium output is a stable output, one that is neither expanding nor contracting.

We can illustrate the concept of equilibrium output with the circular-flow diagram in Exh. 11.5. This diagram depicts a very simplified economy; there is no government sector (hence, there will be no government spending and no taxation) and no foreign sector (so there will be no imports and exports). These simplifications will make it easier for us to grasp the concept of equilibrium. A more complex economy will be introduced in later chapters.

EXHIBIT 11.5

Equilibrium Output with Saving and Investment

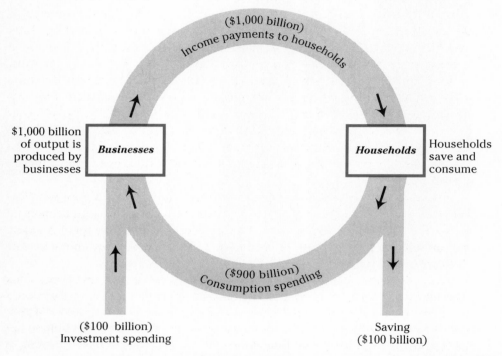

In a simple private economy we can identify the equilibrium output in either of two ways: (1) total spending equals total output, or (2) investment equals saving. In our example, when $1,000 billion worth of output is produced, it creates $1,000 billion worth of spending (consumption of $900 billion plus investment of $100 billion). At the same time, the amount that households desire to save is equal to the amount that businesses want to invest. Hence, $1,000 billion is equilibrium output.

We assume here that businesses expect to sell $1,000 billion worth of output, and so they produce that amount. Of course, that sends to households $1,000 billion in income, which they can either spend or save. In this example we imagine that they choose to save $100 billion. Economists refer to saving as a **leakage,** a subtraction from the flow of spending. Leakages mean that less money returns to businesses, unless the economy can somehow compensate for the loss. In our example the $100 billion leakage means that only $900 billion will be spent on consumption goods. That $900 billion is what we called *personal consumption expenditures* when we showed you how to calculate gross domestic product in Chapter 10.

Consumption spending is not the only form of spending for goods and services, even in the simple private economy we are analyzing. Business investors also purchase a substantial amount of our economy's output (GDP). To keep it simple, let's assume that businesses coincidentally desire to purchase $100 billion worth of output. That investment spending is described as an **injection** since it adds to the basic flow of consumption spending. Total spending for goods and services (consumption spending plus investment spending) amounts to $1,000 billion. As you can see from Exh. 11.5, that is just enough to purchase everything that was produced—the entire $1,000 billion. That means that the producers' expectations have been fulfilled; they expected to sell $1,000 billion of output, and they have sold precisely that amount. Because producers are usually guided by their successes and failures, this would be an important finding. It would be a signal to produce the same amount next year, a response that would mean that the economy was in equilibrium.

As you can see from this example, the economy will be in equilibrium whenever the amount of total spending is exactly sufficient to purchase the economy's entire output (when total spending = total output). When that happens, producers can sell exactly what they've produced, and they have no incentive to alter the level of production.

Note that when the economy is in equilibrium, the amount that households want to save is equal to the amount that businesses desire to invest. The reason for that may be apparent to you. When the amount that is being injected into the spending flow in the form of investment is equal to the amount that is leaking out in the form of saving, the size of the flow is unchanged. The amount returning to businesses will be equal to the amount they paid out; therefore, they will be able to sell exactly what they produced, and the economy will be in equilibrium.

THE PROBLEM OF AN UNEMPLOYMENT EQUILIBRIUM

Keynes and the classical economists agreed that the economy would always tend toward equilibrium, but they disagreed about whether the level of output at which the economy stabilized would permit full employment. In the classical model the economy tends to stabilize at a full-employment equilibrium (at potential GDP). In the Keynesian model the economy tends toward equilibrium but not necessarily at full employment. When the economy is in equilibrium at less than full employment, an **unemployment equilibrium** exists.

We can illustrate why Keynes and the classical economists reached different conclusions about the likelihood of full employment by returning to the circular-flow diagram in Exh. 11.5. Recall that, in this example, households are saving $100 billion, businesses are investing $100 billion, and $1,000 billion is the economy's equilibrium output. To facilitate our comparison between the classical and Keynesian models, let's assume that $1,000 billion is the economy's potential GDP, and so the economy is operating at full employment.

Now, suppose that households decide to increase their saving from $100 billion to $200 billion. What will happen? Obviously, more money is leaking out of the circular flow, in the form of saving. But as we noted earlier, the classical economists did not believe saving would invalidate Say's Law. According to the classical model, this increased saving would simply increase the supply of loanable funds, which would drive down the interest rate and stimulate investment spending. Investment spending would rise from $100 billion to $200 billion, thus maintaining the equilibrium output at $1,000 billion—full employment.

Keynes found fault with this optimistic scenario. According to Keynes, interest rate adjustments cannot be relied on to make saving equal to investment because the interest rate is not the major motivating force in either the saving or the investment decision. In his view the level of *income* is the primary factor influencing the amount that households plan to save; the higher the income, the greater the level of saving. Changes in interest rates have a relatively minor impact on saving decisions. Investment decisions, said Keynes, are governed by profit expectations. The interest rate is only one factor influencing the profitability of an investment, and not the most important factor. If sales are poor and the future looks bleak, businesses are unlikely to undertake new investment, even if the prevailing interest rate is low. Since the interest rate is not the major force guiding saving and investment decisions, it cannot "match up" the plans of savers and investors. As a consequence, when households want to save more than businesses desire to invest, the level of output and employment in the economy will tend to fall. In short, increased saving (reduced spending) can lead to unemployment.

REJECTING THE WAGE FLEXIBILITY ARGUMENT

By itself, Keynes's discrediting of the link between saving and investment was not sufficient to refute the classical claim of a full-employment equilibrium. Remember, the classical economists described *two* forces that ensure full employment in a market economy: interest rate adjustments and wage/price flexibility. If interest rate adjustments fail to synchronize the plans of savers and investors and if this results in too little spending, wage and price flexibility can still ensure full employment. In competitive labor and product markets, inadequate demand would lead to falling wages and prices, which, in turn, would guarantee that all output was sold and would thus prevent involuntary unemployment.

Again Keynes disagreed. He argued that the classical assumption of highly flexible wages and prices was not consistent with the real world. According to Keynes, a variety of forces prevent prices and wages from adjusting quickly, particularly in a downward direction. First, markets are less competitive than the classical theory assumed. Keynes saw that many product markets were monopolistic or oligopolistic. When sellers in these markets noted that demand was declining, they often chose to reduce output rather than lower prices. And in labor markets, particularly those dominated by strong labor unions, workers tended to resist wage cuts. As a consequence, wages and prices did not adjust quickly; they tended to be rigid or "sticky."

The consequences of rigid prices can be seen in Exh. 11.6, which uses the aggregate demand–aggregate supply framework. Let's consider the same scenario outlined in our discussion of the classical model. Assume that consumers become pessimistic about the future and decide to hoard some of their income. Aggregate demand will fall—the AD curve will shift from AD_1 to AD_2—because households demand fewer goods and services at any given price level. This time we will make the assumption that the price level remains stuck at 100 because labor and other contracts prohibit reductions in input

EXHIBIT 11.6

The Keynesian Aggregate Supply Curve

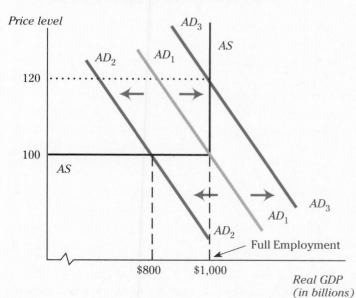

According to Keynes, prices and wages tend to be rigid in the face of falling demand. Thus, a reduction in aggregate demand is quickly translated into lower real GDP and reduced employment (greater unemployment). Attempts to purchase more than the full employment output will lead to inflation without increasing real GDP.

costs, which means that firms cannot afford to reduce prices. The assumption of rigid prices and wages implies a flat, or horizontal, *AS* curve since any reduction in aggregate demand leads to a reduced level of real GDP but no change in the price level. In this example the level of equilibrium GDP would decline from $1,000 billion to $800 billion. Businesses still want to produce $1,000 billion of output, but since they can sell only $800 billion, they must cut production back to that level. Of course, employment would also decline; if employers produce less real output, they require fewer workers. This is essentially the manner in which Keynes explained the Great Depression—as a problem caused by too little aggregate demand, combined with wage and price rigidity.

Although Keynes was concerned primarily with the problem of unemployment, he agreed with the classical economists that inflation would result if consumers, investors, and others attempted to purchase more than the economy was capable of producing.[3] As you can see, the Keynesian *AS* curve becomes vertical at full employment. If aggregate demand was increased from AD_1 to AD_3, the price level would be pushed up, without any increase in real output or employment.

THE CASE FOR GOVERNMENT INTERVENTION

Because Keynes did not believe that a market economy could be relied on to automatically preserve full employment and avoid inflation, he argued that the central government must manage the level of aggregate demand to achieve those objectives. How could this be accomplished? One approach was through **fiscal policy**—the manipulation of government spending and taxation in order to guide the economy's performance. When unemployment exists, the federal government should increase its spending on goods and services (without increasing taxes). This will shift the aggregate demand curve to the right and increase the equilibrium level of real GDP and employment. A reduction in income taxes (without a reduction in government spending) will accomplish the same thing because it will cause households to spend more at any given price level. When inflation exists, government spending should be reduced or taxes increased. These policies will reduce aggregate demand and thus reduce inflationary pressures.

Another approach would be to use **monetary policy:** policy intended to alter the supply of money in order to influence the level of economic activity. When unemployment exists, the Federal Reserve—the governmental agency that regulates the money supply—should increase the amount of money in

---

[3] Keynes viewed the economy's full employment, or potential GDP, as the maximum output the economy was capable of producing rather than as the maximum *sustainable* level of production.

circulation so that households and businesses will find it easier to borrow funds. This will tend to increase spending for goods and services, which will shift the *AD* curve to the right and raise the level of equilibrium output and employment. Inflation calls for a reduction in the money supply. By making it more difficult to borrow funds, the Federal Reserve can reduce spending and thereby combat inflation. We'll have more to say about fiscal and monetary policy later in the text.

THE 1990S: THE DEBATE CONTINUES

Keynesian theory held sway through the 1960s, and many economists remain Keynesians today. But Keynesian thinking began to lose influence in the 1970s, when the Keynesian model seemed unable to explain the stagflation—simultaneous unemployment and inflation—that characterized that period. Since then, Keynesians have been rethinking and modifying their views, and new schools of thought have emerged to challenge their position.

Interestingly, some of these challengers—monetarists and rational expectations theorists—bear a striking resemblance to the classical economists of old. In particular, they generally argue that the economy tends toward full employment and that government intervention is unnecessary and even counterproductive. Thus, the debate about economic policy has come full circle. Economists are once again arguing about the proper role of government in economic policy: Should government actively attempt to stabilize the economy to prevent unemployment or inflation, or should its position be hands off? We will consider the current activist-nonactivist debate later in the text. But the next order of business is to examine the modern self-correcting model of the economy, a model that reflects a blending of the views of Keynes and the classical economists.

Summary

In market economies the interaction of aggregate demand and aggregate supply determines the equilibrium level of real GDP and the overall price level. *Aggregate demand* is the total quantity of output demanded by all sectors in the economy at various price levels in a given period of time. The aggregate demand curve slopes downward, reflecting the fact that more aggregate output is demanded at lower price levels than at higher price levels. *Aggregate supply* is the total quantity of output supplied by all producers in the economy together at various price levels in a given period of time. The aggregate supply curve may be horizontal, vertical, or upward-sloping; its shape depends on the behavior of wages and prices.

The level of output the economy produces when it operates at full employment is called *potential GDP*. The interaction of aggregate demand and supply may give rise to an equilibrium output that is less than potential GDP. When this occurs, unemployment will exist. Economists are in disagreement about the desirability of government efforts to combat such macroeconomic problems as unemployment. Some economists are "activists," supporting a significant role for government; others are "nonactivists," believing that government intervention should be avoided.

The activist-nonactivist controversy originated more than 50 years ago with a debate between John Maynard Keynes and the classical economists who dominated that period. The classical economists felt that a market economy allowed to function without artificial restrictions would provide members of a society with the goods and services they desired while simultaneously maintaining full employment.

The foundation of the classical theory of employment was Say's Law: Supply creates its own demand. More precisely, the act of producing output creates the income that will take that output off the market. Because everything that businesses produce will be sold, there should be nothing to prevent the economy from expanding to full employment.

Even an increase in saving was not considered a problem. The increased availability of loanable funds would cause the interest rate to fall, thereby encouraging businesses to borrow those funds and invest them. If the interest rate somehow failed to equate the plans of savers and investors, wage and price adjustments would compensate for any deficiency in spending. Prolonged unemployment would result only if workers made unreasonable wage demands.

The massive and prolonged unemployment that accompanied the Great Depression cast doubt on the predictions of the classical economists and subjected their model to criticism. The most devastating attack came from John Maynard Keynes. Keynes argued that a market economy does not contain any internal mechanism to ensure full employment. In his view the primary determinant of an economy's health is the level of total spending, or total demand for goods and services. If spending is inadequate, unemployment will result; if it is excessive, inflation will occur.

Keynes believed that it was the responsibility of the federal government to combat unemployment or inflation. This could be accomplished through *fiscal policy*—the manipulation of government spending and taxation in order to guide the economy's performance—or through *monetary policy*—policy intended to alter the money supply as a method of influencing total spending and the economy's performance.

GLOSSARY

Aggregate demand. The total quantity of output demanded by all sectors in the economy together at various price levels in a given time period.

Aggregate supply. The total quantity of output supplied by all producers in the economy together at various price levels in a given time period.

Business cycle. The recurring ups and downs in the level of economic activity.

Classical economists. The mainstream economists who wrote from 1776 through the early 1930s. They believed that a market economy would automatically tend to maintain full employment.

Equilibrium output. A stable output, one that is neither expanding nor contracting.

Fiscal policy. The manipulation of government spending and taxation in order to guide the economy's performance.

Injection. An addition to the circular flow of spending; e.g., investment spending.

Leakage. A subtraction from the circular flow of spending; e.g., saving.

Loanable funds. Money available to be borrowed.

Monetary policy. Policy intended to alter the money supply in order to influence the level of economic activity.

Potential GDP. The level of output produced when the economy is operating at full employment; the maximum sustainable level of production.

Real balance effect. The increase in the amount of aggregate output demanded that results from an increase in the real value of the public's financial assets.

Say's Law. The theory that supply creates its own demand. In the process of producing output, businesses create enough income to ensure that all the output will be sold.

Unemployment equilibrium. A stable level of output that is not large enough to permit full employment.

STUDY QUESTIONS

Fill in the Blanks

1. The level of output the economy produces when it operates at full employment is called ___potential GDP___

2. Economists who support a significant role for government in combating macroeconomic problems are called ___activists___ ; those who believe that government intervention should be avoided are called ___non activists___

3. The theory that supply creates its own demand is called ___Say's Law___.

4. According to Keynes, the primary cause of unemployment is ___too little spending___.

5. The classical economists did not believe that saving would lead to too little spending because they felt that all saving would be ___invested___.

6. In the classical model any long-term unemployment must be _voluntary_.

7. In terms of the circular-flow diagram, saving is often described as a _leakage_, whereas investment is an _injection_.

8. According to Keynes, the level of output and employment is determined primarily by the level of _total spending_.

9. In the classical model the flexibility of interest rates was not the only factor ensuring full employment; flexible _wages_ and _prices_ provided an additional safeguard.

10. The classical economists argued that the proper role for government in the economy was a very _limited_ one.

11. According to Keynes, one way to combat unemployment is for the federal government to increase its spending or reduce _taxes_.

12. If there is no tendency for the level of output to expand or contract, the economy must be producing the _equilibrium_ level of output.

13. Manipulating the level of government spending in order to guide the economy's performance is one form of _fiscal_ policy.

14. Keynes believed that a reduction in aggregate demand would lead to lower output and employment rather than to lower _prices_, as the classical economists suggested.

15. Altering the money supply in an attempt to influence the economy's performance is termed _monetary_ policy.

Multiple Choice

1. The aggregate demand curve slopes downward because
   a) when the price of a product falls, consumers tend to substitute that product for other things.
   b) certain input prices tend to be fixed by contracts in the short run.
   c) as the price level falls, the real value of financial assets increases.
   d) as the price level increases, the purchasing power of consumers' paychecks rises, and they tend to buy more.

2. The aggregate supply curve will slope upward if
   a) all product and input prices (including wage rates) are highly flexible.
   b) higher prices lead to more spending for goods and services.
   c) certain input prices tend to be fixed in the short run.
   d) all product and input prices are inflexible due to long-term contracts.

3. Given an upward-sloping aggregate supply curve, a reduction in aggregate demand would tend to
   a) increase the level of equilibrium real GDP and the overall price level.
   b) decrease the level of equilibrium real GDP and the overall price level.
   c) increase the level of equilibrium real GDP and decrease the overall price level.
   d) decrease the level of equilibrium real GDP and increase the overall price level.

4. Keynesians are considered _____ economists, whereas the classical economists are considered _____ economists.
   a) nonactivist, activist.
   b) laissez-faire, activist.
   c) activist, nonactivist.
   d) nonactivist, laissez-faire

5. According to the classical economists,
   a) unemployment is caused by too little spending.
   b) the interest rate will ensure that the amount households plan to save will equal the amount businesses desire to invest.
   c) increasing government spending is the most reliable method of restoring full employment.
   d) the amount households plan to save is determined primarily by their income.

6. Keynes would suggest that during a period of unemployment, government should
   a) do nothing.
   b) reduce its spending to stimulate the economy.
   c) increase its spending to stimulate the economy.
   d) take legal action against unions in order to make wages more flexible.

7. The aggregate supply curve implied by the classical model is _____ so that a reduction in aggregate demand will mean a lower overall level of _____.
   a) vertical, prices
   b) vertical, output
   c) horizontal, prices
   d) horizontal, output

8. In the Keynesian model, if leakages exceed injections,
   a) the economy is producing the equilibrium output.
   b) the level of output will tend to fall.
   c) the level of output will tend to rise.
   d) the economy must be at full employment.

9. According to the classical model, even when all saving is not invested, full employment will be maintained because
   a) the government will step in and stimulate spending.
   b) the equilibrium wage rate will rise to stimulate spending.
   c) wages and prices will fall to permit businesses to continue hiring everyone who wants to work.
   d) the government will establish special work programs.

10. According to Keynes, the amount that households desire to save is determined primarily by
    a) the rate of interest.
    b) the investment plans of businesses.
    c) the incomes of the households.
    d) None of the above

11. In the Keynesian model the economy is producing the equilibrium output when
    a) total spending equals total output.
    b) total income equals total output.
    c) total saving exceeds total investment.
    d) surplus inventories are maximized.

12. Perhaps the most important implication of Keynesian economics is that
    a) the economy automatically tends toward full employment.
    b) government should not interfere in the operation of the economy.
    c) the economy always tends toward the equilibrium output.
    d) the economy can come to rest at an unemployment equilibrium.

13. According to the classical economists, prolonged unemployment could be caused only by
    a) too little spending.
    b) workers making unreasonable wage demands.
    c) external shocks.
    d) changes in consumer preferences.

14. In the Keynesian model of a private economy, the equilibrium output exists when
    a) total spending equals total demand.
    b) consumption plus investment equals total spending.
    c) the amount that households want to save equals the amount that businesses want to invest.
    d) All of the above

15. Which of the following is an example of the fiscal policy Keynes would find appropriate for a period of unemployment?
    a) Decrease government spending
    b) Increase the money supply
    c) Reduce personal income taxes
    d) Reduce the money supply

Problems and Questions for Discussion

1. What do you believe determines the level of potential GDP in an economy?

2. Why did the classical economists believe that any long-term unemployment had to be voluntary?

3. What flaws did Keynes find in the classical theory's wage-flexibility argument?

4. In what sense did Keynes "stand classical economics on its head"?

5. Explain the concept of equilibrium output, and describe how to identify equilibrium in the Keynesian model.

6. In the Keynesian model, why is a private economy in equilibrium when the amount that households plan to save is equal to the amount that businesses plan to invest?

7. Why did Keynes believe that the proper response to a period of unemployment was for government to increase its spending? How could this policy help to combat unemployment?

8. How did the classical economists explain the existence of short-term unemployment?

9. Explain the role of interest rates in the classical model.

10. Many economists argue that the Great Depression was brought to an end by World War II. In Keynesian terms, how could a war contribute to combating unemployment?

ANSWER KEY

Fill in the Blanks

1. potential GDP
2. activists, nonactivists
3. Say's Law
4. too little spending
5. invested
6. voluntary
7. leakage, injection
8. total spending
9. wages, prices
10. limited
11. taxes
12. equilibrium
13. fiscal
14. prices
15. monetary

Multiple Choice

1. c
2. c
3. b
4. c
5. b
6. c
7. a
8. b
9. c
10. c
11. a
12. d
13. b
14. c
15. c

CHAPTER 12

Aggregate Demand and Supply: The Model of the Self-Correcting Economy

LEARNING OBJECTIVES

1. Identify three factors that are responsible for the downward slope of the aggregate demand curve.
2. Understand more fully why the aggregate supply curve slopes upward.
3. Review how the economy's equilibrium output and price level are determined and how this process is represented graphically.
4. Discuss the factors that will shift the aggregate demand and supply curves to new positions.
5. Predict the impact of changes in aggregate demand or supply on the economy's equilibrium output and the price level.
6. Explain how the economy will tend to automatically eliminate unemployment in the long run.

Chapter 11 introduced the model of aggregate demand and aggregate supply and used that model to examine the views of the classical economists and their critic John Maynard Keynes. As you will recall, the classical economists contended that the economy would automatically tend toward full employment; Keynes disagreed. According to Keynes, the inflexibility of wages and prices meant that reductions in spending could lead to unemployment, which had to be attacked by government policy. But while Keynes totally dismissed the classical contention that the economy is self-correcting, modern economists (including modern Keynesians) agree that wages and prices will eventually decline in the face of falling demand. This possibility implies that the economy will be self-correcting. This chapter examines that possibility by developing the modern model of a self-correcting economy, a model that borrows from both Keynes and the classical economists.

An Overview of the Model

As we discovered in Chapter 11, the intersection of the aggregate demand and aggregate supply curves determines the economy's equilibrium level of real GDP and the overall price level. This is represented in Exh. 12.1, which shows the intersection of *AD* and *AS* determining an overall price level of 100 and an equilibrium real GDP of $1,000 billion.

Chapter 11 provided a brief introduction to aggregate demand and aggregate supply. Our first task in this chapter is to examine these concepts in greater detail. Then we review the process by which the equilibrium output and price level are determined and consider the economy's response to changes in aggregate demand and supply. We begin by reviewing and extending our analysis of aggregate demand.

Aggregate Demand

Aggregate demand is the total quantity of output demanded by all sectors in the economy together at various price levels in a given period of time. Thus, aggregate demand is the sum of consumption spending by households (*C*), investment spending by businesses (*I*), government purchases of goods and services (*G*), and net exports (*NX*) to foreign countries. In short, *AD=C+I+G+NX*.

As you can see from Exh. 12.1, the *aggregate demand curve* slopes downward and to the right, indicating that more real output will be demanded at a lower price level than at a higher price level. There are three reasons for the aggregate demand curve's downward slope: the real balance effect (which was introduced in the last chapter), the interest rate effect, and the international trade effect. Let's consider each of these reasons in turn, beginning with a review of the real balance effect.

THE REAL BALANCE EFFECT

When the price level falls, the real value, or purchasing power, of the public's financial assets—savings accounts, retirement funds, and other financial assets with fixed money values—tends to increase. This makes people feel wealthier, and they tend to demand more goods and services—more real output. The **real balance effect** is the increase in the amount of aggregate output demanded that results from the increased real value of the public's financial assets.

As an example, suppose that you work each summer to help pay for college. This summer you managed to save $2,000, your share of the year's anticipated expenses. Now, assume that the overall price level falls to half of what it was when you established your $2,000 objective. In essence, that means that all prices

EXHIBIT 12.1

An Overview of Aggregate Demand and Supply

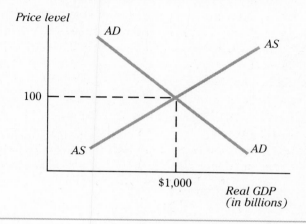

The intersection of the aggregate demand and supply curves determines the equilibrium level of real GDP and the equilibrium price level in the economy.

have been cut in half; so your $2,000 will now stretch twice as far as before. How will you react? You will probably start buying things you don't normally purchase because you have $1,000 in your savings account that won't be needed for anticipated college expenses. That's the real balance effect in action; the real value, or purchasing power, of the money balance in your savings account has increased, and this increase in wealth is spurring you to purchase more goods and services. Of course, if the price level increases, everything will work in reverse; your savings will be worth less, so that you feel less wealthy and demand fewer goods and services than before. Either way we describe it, the price level and spending on real output are moving in opposite directions, and so the aggregate demand curve must slope downward. Exhibit 12.2 depicts the aggregate demand curve for a hypothetical economy.

THE INTEREST RATE EFFECT

In addition to its impact on real balances, a change in the price level also has an effect on the prevailing interest rate. The interest rate is determined by the demand and supply of money. When the price level falls, consumers and businesses will require less money for their day-to-day transactions because a given amount of money will buy more goods and services than before. In other words, a reduction in the price level will reduce the demand for money. Since each aggregate demand curve assumes a fixed supply of money in the economy, a reduction in the demand for money will tend to reduce the price of money—the interest rate. When the interest rate falls, the lower cost of

EXHIBIT 12.2

The Aggregate Demand Curve

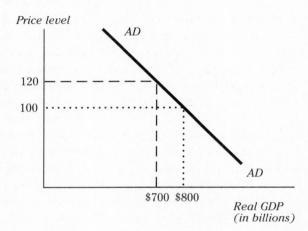

The aggregate demand curve shows an inverse relationship between the overall price level and the quantity of real output demanded. For instance, when the price level decreases from 120 to 100, the quantity of real GDP demanded increases from $700 billion to $800 billion.

borrowing money tends to stimulate investment spending and some types of consumer spending. The **interest rate effect** is the increase in the amount of aggregate output demanded that results when a reduction in the overall price level causes interest rates to fall.[1]

To illustrate, let's suppose that the price level—the average price of goods and services—fell to half of what it is today. Homes that had been selling for $200,000 would cost $100,000; automobiles that had been priced at $20,000 would be available for $10,000. As a consequence, consumers would need to borrow only half as much money as before to finance their new homes and automobiles and other credit purchases. This reduced demand for money would tend to lower interest rates and stimulate spending. Thus, more real output would be demanded at the lower price level. Of course, if the price level increased (which may seem a more realistic possibility), the demand for money would tend to increase, pushing up interest rates and depressing spending on real GDP.

---

[1] The interest rate effect actually has to do with the impact of a price level change on the "real" interest rate—the interest rate after adjustment for inflation. If the nominal interest rate (the interest rate before adjustment) is 15 percent a year and the expected rate of inflation is 5 percent, the real interest rate is 10 percent.

Business investment decisions are influenced by real interest rates, not nominal rates. A higher nominal interest rate (resulting from a higher expected rate of inflation) would not necessarily discourage businesses from borrowing since they would also anticipate receiving higher prices for their products (and thus a higher nominal rate of return). The proof that a higher price level causes a higher real interest rate is beyond the scope of this text.

THE INTERNATIONAL TRADE EFFECT

The third way in which price level changes can affect the amount of aggregate output demanded is through international trade. The two basic transactions in international trade are the importing and exporting of products. **Imports** are goods and services that are purchased from foreign producers. Americans' purchases of German automobiles, French wines, and Japanese electronics are examples of U. S. imports. **Exports** are goods and services that are produced domestically and sold to customers in other countries. The Ford automobiles, California wines, and IBM computers that are sold to customers in Germany, France, and elsewhere are examples of U.S. exports.

How would U.S. imports and exports be affected if the overall price level in the United States fell by, say, 10 percent and everything else (including prices in other countries)[2] remained constant? Since U.S. products would become more attractive in price, we'd expect fewer Americans to buy imported products (because they'd buy domestic products instead) and more foreigners to buy U.S. exports. To illustrate, suppose that the prices of U.S. automobiles fell by 10 percent and the prices of comparable foreign cars remained unchanged. Under these conditions, we'd expect to see more Americans buying cars made in the United States (and fewer buying imports) and increased auto exports as well. In short, at the lower U.S. price level, a larger quantity of U.S. automobiles would be demanded. The **international trade effect** is the increase in the amount of aggregate output demanded that results when a reduction in the price level makes domestic products less expensive relative to foreign products. It provides us with a third reason for the downward slope of the aggregate demand curve.

Changes in Aggregate Demand

As with the demand curve for a single product, we need to distinguish between *movement along* an *AD* curve and a *shift* of the *AD* curve. We've seen that changes in the price level will cause movement up or down along a stationary curve. *Any change in the spending plans of households, businesses, governments, or foreigners that results from something other than a change in the price level will shift the AD curve.* Factors that will shift the aggregate demand curve include changes in the expectations of households and businesses, changes in aggregate wealth, changes in government policies, and changes in foreign income and price levels.

---

[2] Another factor that is assumed constant is the foreign exchange rate, the rate at which one country's currency exchanges for that of another.

HOUSEHOLD AND BUSINESS EXPECTATIONS

Suppose that households and businesses become more upbeat about the future, perhaps because the unemployment rate has been dropping and business has been strong. What impact will these optimistic expectations have on aggregate demand? Households may be expected to increase their consumption spending (since they are more confident of continued employment in the future), whereas businesses may increase their investment spending for factories and machinery in anticipation of future business. Because total spending at any price level is greater the AD curve will shift to the right (from AD_1 to AD_2 in Exh. 12.3), an increase in aggregate demand. More pessimistic expectations have the opposite effect: The AD curve will shift to the left, reflecting a reduction in aggregate demand.

AGGREGATE WEALTH

An increase in the overall wealth of the society also tends to shift the aggregate demand curve to the right. Consider, for example, the impact of a stock market boom that increases the value of households' stock holdings. Since households can finance spending by selling shares of stock and other forms of wealth, this increase in stock values tends to spur consumption spending; households may be expected to demand more real output than before at any price level. A reduction in wealth—due, perhaps, to a decline in the stock market—will shift the AD curve to the left.

EXHIBIT 12.3

Shifts of the Aggregate Demand Curve

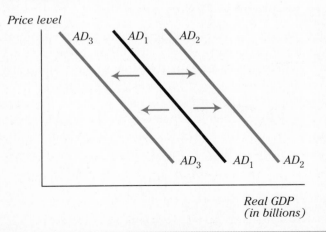

Any change in the spending plans of households, businesses, or government that results from something other than a change in the price level will shift the AD curve. A shift to the right is an increase in aggregate demand; a shift to the left is a decrease.

GOVERNMENT POLICY

Government can also influence aggregate demand through its policies. For instance, a reduction in government spending for goods and services will cause the *AD* curve to shift to the left, as will an increase in personal income taxes (since consumers have less to spend at each price level). A reduction in the money supply will also cause aggregate demand to fall. The size of the economy's money supply is determined by the Federal Reserve, or Fed. If the Fed decreases the money supply, the interest rate that businesses and others have to pay to borrow money will tend to increase. This, in turn, will tend to depress investment spending by businesses and some forms of consumption spending by households, shifting the aggregate demand curve to the left.

Consider an increase in military spending by the federal government. What impact will that have on aggregate demand? It will increase the amount of real GDP demanded at any price level, and so it will shift the *AD* curve to the right (from AD_1 to AD_2 in Exh. 12.3). A tax reduction or an increase in the money supply also tends to increase aggregate demand.

FOREIGN INCOMES AND PRICES

When foreign incomes grow, foreign households increase their consumption spending. Some of this increased spending will be for U.S. products, causing U.S. exports to increase and shifting the aggregate demand curve to the right. Increased foreign prices would also stimulate spending for U.S. products. An increase in foreign price levels would, ceteris paribus, cause U.S. products to appear more attractive and cause foreign consumers to substitute them for those produced domestically. At the same time, Americans would find foreign products less attractive in price, decreasing our imports. Thus, an increase in foreign incomes or price levels would stimulate the demand for U.S. products and shift the *AD* curve to the right.[3] Reductions in foreign incomes or price levels would shift the aggregate demand curve for U.S. products to the left.

In summary, the aggregate demand curve will shift in response to changes in the expectations of households or businesses, wealth, government policy, foreign incomes, or foreign price levels. These are the major causes of shifts in aggregate demand, but the list is not exhaustive; other changes may have a similar impact. The important point is that any change in spending plans that stems from something other than a change in the price level will shift the *AD* curve; changes in the price level will cause movement *along* a stationary curve. The article, "Consumer Still the Big Spender" on pages 358–359, examines the impact on the economy of strong consumer spending. Take a moment to read the article and test what you've learned.

---

[3] This assumes that the foreign exchange rate does not change. Chapter 18 will discuss exchange rates in some detail.

Use Your Economic Reasoning

Consumer Still the Big Spender

Buying Powered the
First Quarter's Exuberant
Performance

By Louis Uchitelle

The national economy has just turned in its best performance in nine years, and the American consumer's surprisingly exuberant spending is the main reason. In no other six-month period in this decade have increases in consumer spending been as large as they were in the six months through March.

Consumer spending grew at an annual rate of 4.9 percent from September through March. The last time the six-month rate climbed higher was in 1988, the height of the last expansion, when it reached 5 percent. Consumers, always big players in the economy, have assumed a bigger role than usual in the robust economic growth of the last two quarters. They spent particularly for computers, clothing and health care, but without cutting back on autos, housing, dining out, airline travel, furniture, appliances and recreation.

Economists, somewhat surprised, are trying to explain why Americans have been so free with their money. The reasons they come up with suggest that the spending rate will slow.

A mild winter and early Easter encouraged more shopping than usual. Big income tax refunds have helped; many people found they could go to a bank, or to H & R Block, the tax preparer, show their tax returns and borrow against their anticipated refunds. A strong dollar helped, by keeping down import prices. The finance arms of auto companies cut car loan rates by two or three percentage points, to encourage sales. Mortgage rates, having declined last year, are only recently beginning to rise. Sharply rising stock prices made people feel wealthier. And consumer borrowing is at very high levels, having risen particularly among lower-income households.

Computers accounted for the biggest rise in consumer spending in the second quarter, nearly 15 percent of the increase, and apparel was uncharacteristically close behind, at 12 percent.

"There was a long period when people did not purchase apparel, so there was some pent-up demand, and this has now been released and satisfied," said Jay Meltzer, director of LJR Redbook Research, which tracks apparel purchases. "Apparel is a deferrable expenditure, and people felt squeezed and worried about downsizing. But finally they spent the money, and I doubt apparel expenditures will continue this strong."

Layoff announcements are still at high levels. And for most middle-income Americans, wages have not risen by more than the inflation rate in this decade. But those at the upper end of the pay scale are gaining ground, and now, for the first time in this six-year-old expansion—one of the longest on record—people at the low end, earning less than $30,000 a year, are getting wage increases that on average exceed the inflation rate. A rise in the minimum wage is a factor, but so is the expanding economy.

"Our most recent surveys show that these workers at the low end have more favorable views of their employment situation," said Richard T. Curtin, director of the University of Michigan's Consumer Surveys. "And feeling a little better, they are spending more."

This is not unusual in an expansion. As the unemployment rate falls and labor shortages develop, employers traditionally turn to low-end workers, hiring a waiter earning $6 an hour, for example, into an $8-an-hour job operating office or factory equipment, training the person for the work....

Job growth has also encouraged spending, particularly among those who had not worked before or for a long time. "You get more spending from people getting a salary for the first time than from people only getting a raise," said Joel Prakken, a partner at Macroeconomic Advisers Inc., an economic consulting and forecasting firm.

But Mr. Prakken and most other forecasters expect the current second quarter to be weaker than the first, partly because consumers will spend less. Debt levels, they reason, are too high, and already some statistics show consumers pulling back. Higher mortgage rates are likely to take their toll on home construction and sales, as well as home furnishings, another strong item over the winter months. Auto sales are also beginning to weaken a bit.

Stock prices, which rose so much in the first quarter, are not likely to keep up the pace, diluting the wealth effect. Income tax refunds are winding down now, of course, and advanced payment of this year's estimated tax is now under way, cutting into disposable income. And job growth had to level off, in Mr. Prakken's view.

"It can't keep growing like this," he said....

USE YOUR ECONOMIC REASONING

1. How would you represent an increase in consumer spending graphically? What impact would it have on the economy, ceteris paribus.
2. What factor has helped to keep auto and housing sales strong?
3. At the time this article was written, the stock market was booming (the value of the stocks owned by households was rising rapidly). What impact was this having on consumer spending?
4. According to the article, "workers at the low end have more favorable views..." More favorable views of what? How are these views affecting their behavior?
5. What factors might ultimately cause consumers to start spending less? Would a decline in the stock market be among those factors? (On October 27, 1997 the Dow Jones Industrial Average declined 554 points, the largest point decline ever recorded.) How would a decline in consumer spending be represented graphically, and what impact would it have on the economy?

Aggregate Supply

Aggregate demand is only half of the model; the other half is aggregate supply. **Aggregate supply** refers to the total quantity of output supplied by all producers in the economy together at various price levels in a given time period.

As we saw in Chapter 11, the shape we assign to the *aggregate supply curve* depends on the assumptions we make about the behavior of wages and prices. If we believe that wages and prices are highly flexible, the *AS* curve will be vertical. If we assume that wages and prices are rigid, the *AS* curve will be horizontal. Most modern economists take a position in the middle; they argue that all wages and prices are flexible in the long run but that at least some wages and input prices are rigid in the short run. This belief results in an *AS* curve that slopes upward in the short run.

An upward-sloping aggregate supply curve indicates that businesses tend to supply more aggregate output at higher price levels than at lower price levels. Businesses behave in this manner because the wage and input price rigidities we have described cause certain costs to be fixed in the short run. This makes it profitable for businesses to expand output if aggregate demand increases and pushes up the prices they can charge for their products.

The major reason for the rigidity of costs is long-term contracts. Contracts with labor unions, for example, are commonly renegotiated every three years. During the term of the agreement, wage rates are at least partially fixed. The prices paid for raw materials and manufactured inputs may also be governed

EXHIBIT 12.4

The Aggregate Supply Curve

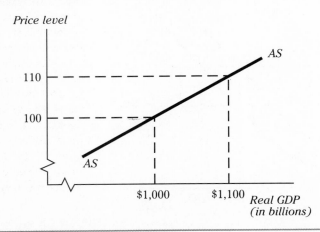

The aggregate supply curve slopes upward because businesses tend to supply more real output at higher price levels than at lower price levels.

by long-term contracts. Because wage rates and other input prices are commonly fixed in the short run, businesses find it profitable to expand output when the selling prices of their products rise. This positive relationship between the overall price level and the economy's real GDP is reflected in the upward slope of the *AS* curve depicted in Exh. 12.4.

THE AGGREGATE SUPPLY CURVE: A CLOSER LOOK

An example from microeconomics may help to illustrate why the *AS* curve slopes upward. Consider the behavior of the competitive firm. Recall that in the model of pure competition, the individual firm is a price taker; it must charge the price dictated by the market. But the firm can sell as much output as it chooses at that price. The firm will continue to expand output so long as the additional (marginal) revenue it will receive from selling an additional unit of output is greater than the additional (marginal) cost of producing that unit. When marginal cost is exactly equal to marginal revenue, the firm will be maximizing its profit (or minimizing its loss). This situation is represented in Exh. 12.5, which shows a firm that is initially maximizing its profit by producing an output of 1,000 units, the output dictated by the intersection of MR_1 and MC_1.

Now, suppose that the market price of the firm's product increases from $10 to $14. This would be represented by shifting the demand curve upward

---

EXHIBIT 12.5

Price Level Adjustments and the Individual Firm

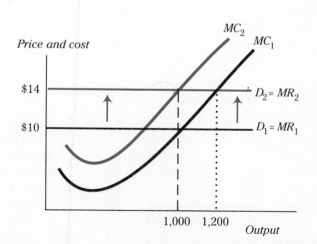

When the price of its product rises and input prices remain unchanged, the competitive firm responds by expanding output. Here output is increased from 1,000 to 1,200 units when the selling price rises from $10 to $14. However, if input prices rise by the same percent as the product price, *MC* will shift up from MC_1 to MC_2, and the profit-maximizing output will be unchanged.

from D_1 to D_2. Note what happens to the firm's profit-maximizing output: It increases from 1,000 units to 1,200 units! The higher price provides incentive for the firm to expand output because the firm can earn a marginal profit on the additional units.

Note that it is not profitable for the firm to expand output indefinitely. Because the marginal cost curve slopes upward, marginal cost will eventually increase enough to match the new price. Of course, production beyond that point will not be profitable. Why does MC increase as the firm expands its output? Why does the MC curve slope upward? Think back to Chapter 6. In the short run, if the firm wants to produce more output, it has to squeeze that production from its fixed factory. It does this by hiring more labor and using its factory and equipment more intensively. But this leads to more and more crowding of the fixed facility. Workers have to wait to use equipment; machines are subject to more frequent breakdowns; workers begin to get in one another's way, and so on. As a consequence, successive units of output become more costly to produce; that is, marginal cost rises. Eventually the cost of producing another unit will have increased enough to match the new product price. At that point the output expansion will cease; the firm will have achieved its new profit-maximizing level of production.

It is essential to note that the firm would not have expanded output if wage rates and other input prices had increased along with the price of the firm's product. Proportionally higher wages and other input prices would have shifted the marginal cost curve up from MC_1 to MC_2. Note that MC_2 intersects MR_2 (the new, higher product price) at 1,000 units of output, the original profit-maximizing output. The higher input prices have completely offset the higher product price, eliminating any incentive to expand output. In the long run, this is precisely what we expect to happen since contracts eventually expire and wage rates and other input prices are able to adjust upward. But in the short run, wage contracts and other rigidities provide a gap between product prices and production costs that makes it profitable for firms to expand output.

Changes in Aggregate Supply

The aggregate supply curve slopes upward because there is a positive relationship between the general price level and the quantity of aggregate output supplied. This relationship assumes that the other factors that influence the amount of real GDP supplied are held constant. Changes in these other factors will cause a change in aggregate supply; the entire AS curve will shift to a new position. The factors that will shift the AS curve include changes in wage rates, the prices of nonlabor inputs, labor productivity, labor supplies, and the capital stock.

THE WAGE RATE

Suppose that the average wage rate paid by firms in the economy increases. What will that do to the AS curve? If it costs more to produce a given level of output, firms will require higher prices in order to produce that output; thus, the AS curve must shift upward (to the left). This is represented in Exh. 12.6 by the movement of the aggregate supply curve from AS_1 to AS_2. Lower wages would have the opposite effect; they would tend to shift the AS curve downward (to the right), from AS_1 to AS_3. Remember that wage rates tend to be fixed by contract in the short term. But when these labor contracts expire, wage rates may be renegotiated up or down, causing the AS curve to shift.

THE PRICES OF NONLABOR INPUTS

Labor is only one of the resources required to produce output. Businesses also need capital equipment, raw materials, manufactured inputs, and managerial talent. Changes in the price of any of these inputs will tend to shift the position of the AS curve; increases will shift it upward, and decreases will shift it downward.

Consider, for instance, the impact of the increase in the price of petroleum products resulting from Iraq's invasion of Kuwait in 1990. When crude oil prices increased, the cost of producing a given level of output rose; thus, the AS curve shifted upward. Bad weather that reduces agricultural output may have a similar impact since it tends to increase the price of wheat, corn, and other agricultural products that are inputs in the production of breakfast cereals and other food items.

EXHIBIT 12.6

Shifts of the Aggregate Supply Curve

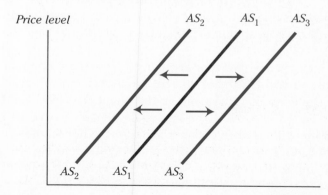

The AS curve will shift upward (to the left) if there is a hike in wage rates, an increase in the prices of nonlabor inputs, or a reduction in labor productivity. It will shift downward (to the right) if wages or other input prices fall or if labor productivity rises.

THE PRODUCTIVITY OF LABOR

The cost of producing output is influenced not only by wage rates and other input prices but also by the productivity of labor—by how efficient labor is at transforming inputs into finished products. If the productivity of labor increases, the cost of producing the finished product tends to fall. Suppose that labor is paid $8 per hour and that the average worker is able to produce ten units of output per hour. The average labor cost of producing each unit of output is $.80 ($8 per hour divided by ten units per hour). Now, suppose that because of improved training or new technology, the average worker could produce twenty units of output per hour. The labor cost per unit of output would fall to $.40 ($8 per hour divided by twenty units of output per hour). As you can see, an increase in labor productivity reduces the cost of producing a given level of output.

A variety of factors can influence the productivity of labor. For example, if the labor force became more highly educated, we would expect its productivity to rise. A technological change that improved the quality of the capital equipment used by labor could also raise productivity. For instance, a faster computer would allow more work to be done per hour. Regardless of the source of higher productivity, its impact is to reduce the cost of producing the goods and services that make up GDP. We represent this impact by shifting the *AS* curve down and to the right, because producers can now offer a given level of output at a lower price than before (or more output than before at the prevailing price).

SUPPLIES OF LABOR AND CAPITAL

Finally, the position of the economy's aggregate supply curve is influenced by the economy's supplies of labor and capital. The larger the labor supply and the stock of capital equipment, the more output the economy is capable of supplying at any price level. Increases in either the labor force or the capital stock will cause the aggregate supply curve to shift to the right. Decreases would have the opposite effect.

Before continuing, let's review. We've seen that the aggregate demand curve shows the quantity of real GDP that will be demanded at each price level, whereas the aggregate supply curve shows the quantity of real GDP that will be supplied at each price level. The aggregate demand curve will shift to a new position if there is a change in the expectations of households or businesses, the level of aggregate wealth, government policy, foreign incomes, or foreign price levels. The aggregate supply curve will shift in response to a change in the wage rate, the prices of nonlabor inputs, labor productivity, or the supplies of labor or capital.

The Equilibrium Output and Price Level

The interaction of aggregate demand and aggregate supply simultaneously determines the equilibrium price level and real GDP in the economy. This process is illustrated in Exh. 12.7, which shows the intersection of *AS* and *AD* resulting in an equilibrium price level of 100 and an equilibrium real GDP of $1,000 billion.

As you can see in the graph, if the price level was initially above equilibrium (120, for example), the amount of real GDP supplied would exceed the amount of real GDP demanded. This would mean unsold merchandise and pressure to cut prices. The price level would decline until the amount of aggregate output demanded was equal to the amount supplied. If the price level was initially below equilibrium (80, for instance), the result would be a shortage that would put upward pressure on prices until the equilibrium price level was achieved and the shortage eliminated.

In summary, only at the equilibrium price level is the amount of real GDP demanded equal to the amount supplied. At any other price level, there will be an overall surplus or shortage, which will tend to alter the prevailing price level.

EXHIBIT 12.7

Equilibrium GDP and Price Level

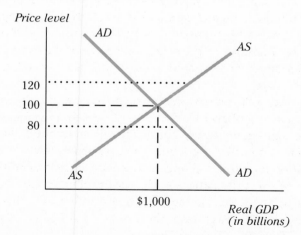

The intersection of the aggregate demand and supply curves determines the price level and the level of output in the economy. Here the equilibrium real GDP is $1,000 billion, and the equilibrium price level is 100.

The Impact of Changes in Aggregate Demand or Supply

In a dynamic economy, aggregate demand and supply change frequently. As these changes occur, the equilibrium price and output levels are disturbed and new levels are established. Suppose, for example, that less optimistic expectations caused businesses to cut back on investment spending. Since this would result in less output being demanded at any given price level, the aggregate demand curve would shift to the left. What impact would this have on the economy? As you can see in Exh. 12.8, when aggregate demand declines from AD_1 to AD_2, the level of real GDP in the economy contracts from $1,000 billion to $850 billion, and the overall price level falls from 100 to 90. Since the economy's ability to provide jobs is tied to the level of production, employment in the economy will also tend to fall (which means that, ceteris paribus, unemployment will rise).

If aggregate demand increased as a result of increased government spending, a tax cut, or some other spur to aggregate demand, the *AD* curve would shift to the right, from AD_1 to AD_3. This would result in higher output and employment, but would also push the price level upward; that is, it

EXHIBIT 12.8

The Effects of Changes in Aggregate Demand on Real Output and Prices

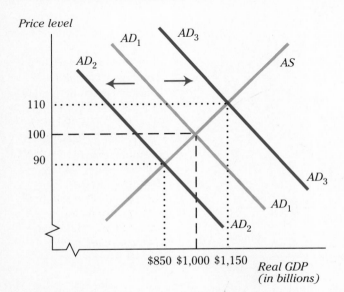

Decreases in aggregate demand will tend to lower the levels of output and employment in the economy while also reducing the overall price level. Increases in aggregate demand will tend to raise output and employment while raising the level of prices.

would generate inflation. Economists describe this as **demand pull inflation** because it is caused by increased aggregate demand.

The economy's equilibrium can also be disturbed by changes in aggregate supply. Suppose that aggregate supply decreased as a result of a supply shock, such as an increase in the price of imported oil or a drought that raised grain prices. Exhibit 12.9 shows that when aggregate supply falls from AS_1 to AS_2, the overall price level is driven up and the equilibrium level of real GDP is reduced.

In this instance the economy is experiencing supply-side, or **cost-push inflation**; higher production costs are pushing up prices. Although both demand-pull and cost-push inflation mean higher prices for consumers, cost-push inflation is doubly destructive because it is associated with falling real output. As you can see from Exh. 12.9, when the aggregate supply curve shifts to the left, the level of equilibrium real GDP falls from $1,000 billion to $850 billion. In short, cost-push inflation raises prices while lowering output and employment. This provides us with one possible explanation for the problem of **stagflation,** high unemployment combined with high inflation.

If reductions in aggregate supply are particularly harmful, increases in aggregate supply appear most beneficial. Suppose that aggregate supply expands in response to an increase in labor productivity. As the AS curve shifts to the right (from AS_1 to AS_3 in Exh. 12.9), the price level is driven down *and* output

EXHIBIT 12.9

The Effects of Changes in Aggregate Supply on Real Output and Prices

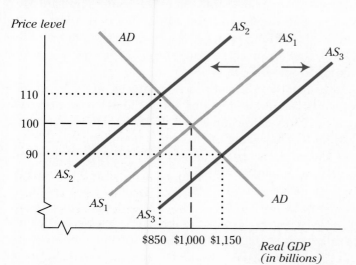

Decreases in aggregate supply will tend to lower the levels of output and employment in the economy while raising the overall price level. Increases in aggregate supply will tend to raise output and employment while lowering the level of prices.

and employment are expanded. It is these obviously desirable outcomes that led to a surge of interest in supply-side economics in the 1980s. Supply-siders promoted a variety of policies designed to enhance labor productivity and otherwise lower production costs in an attempt to increase aggregate supply. Chapter 16 will take a closer look at supply-side problems and remedies.

As the preceding discussion indicates, changes in aggregate demand or supply can lead to unemployment, inflation, or even stagflation. The next section examines the economy's response to these problems and considers the possibility that the economy contains a self-correcting mechanism. (Before proceeding, take a moment to read "Labor Force Kept Expanding . . . ," on pages 370–371. It will test your understanding of the *AD-AS* framework.)

The Model of the Self-Correcting Economy

As you will recall from Chapter 11, the classical economists believed in a self-correcting economy that always tended to operate at full employment. According to the classical model, Say's Law and interest rate flexibility would ensure that aggregate demand was always sufficient to maintain full employment. If these defenses somehow failed, reductions in aggregate demand would be quickly met by falling prices and wages, which would keep the economy operating at potential GDP.

When the Great Depression called the classical model into question, Keynes provided an alternative model to explain the widespread unemployment. According to Keynes, interest rate adjustments cannot be relied on to match up saving and investment plans and ensure adequate aggregate demand. Perhaps most important, Keynes did not believe that reductions in aggregate demand would lead to falling prices and wages. Instead, the rigidity of prices and wages would transform these downturns in aggregate demand into lower real GDP and unemployment.

Many economists argue that the crucial distinction between the classical and Keynesian models is their different assumptions about the behavior of prices and wages. Price-wage flexibility is the final line of defense in the classical model; without that assumption, hoarding can result in unemployment. The assumption of rigid prices and wages is equally important to Keynes; if prices and wages are highly flexible, falling demand does not pose a threat to the economy.

Given the importance of these assumptions, it is interesting to note that most modern economists see some validity in *both* the classical and Keynesian positions. In the short run, at least some prices and wages are inflexible, as Keynes suggested, so that reductions in aggregate demand can cause unemployment. But in the long run, all prices and wages become flexible. Thus, reductions in aggregate demand must ultimately result in falling prices and wages, which return the economy to potential GDP and full employment.

The important conclusion of the foregoing discussion is that the economy does contain a self-correcting mechanism. To illustrate that mechanism, let's consider an economy that is currently operating at potential GDP and examine its short-run and long-run reactions to a change in aggregate demand. We will begin with an increase in aggregate demand and then consider a decrease.

ADJUSTMENTS TO AN INCREASE IN AGGREGATE DEMAND

Suppose that aggregate demand expands because the federal government reduces personal income taxes. Households now have more to spend, and so they tend to demand more goods and services at each price level—the aggregate demand curve shifts to the right, from AD_1 to AD_2 in Exh. 12.10.

When aggregate demand increases, the resulting higher price level creates incentive for businesses to expand output. This incentive is provided by the fact that many of a business's costs—particularly wage rates—are fixed by long-term contracts. When product prices rise, these costs do not; thus, firms stand to profit by expanding output. In our example, output will be increased up to the point at which AS_1 is intersected by AD_2 (point B in Exh. 12.10), well beyond potential GDP.

It may seem contradictory to suggest that the economy can operate beyond its potential. The term "potential" is commonly interpreted to mean "maximum." But the meaning of potential is somewhat different in this context. Potential GDP is not the maximum output the economy is capable of producing but rather the maximum *sustainable* level of production. Businesses can run factories beyond

EXHIBIT 12.10

Adjusting to Higher Aggregate Demand

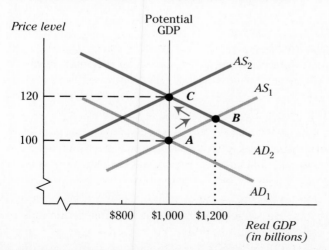

When aggregate demand increases, businesses initially find it profitable to expand output because wage rates and certain other costs are fixed by long-term contracts. Thus, equilibrium real GDP expands beyond potential. But when these contracts expire and costs rise, the AS curve shifts upward and eventually reduces equilibrium output to the level of potential GDP.

Use Your Economic Reasoning

Labor Force Kept Expanding In March

Jobless Rate Fell as Potential Workers Left the Sidelines

By Jacob M. Schlesinger
Staff Reporter of the Wall Street Journal

WASHINGTON—More and more Americans are willing to work, and that's one explanation of why the economy has been able to grow so much with barely a hint of inflation.

The civilian labor force, the number of Americans working or looking for work, continued to grow in March and is up 1.3 million so far this year, the Labor Department said Friday. Last month, 67.3% of all adults were in the labor force, up from 67% in February, and from 66.8% a year earlier. Meanwhile, the employment-to-population ratio—the proportion of adults with jobs—hit a record 63.8%.

The growth in the labor force reverses a perplexing trend from earlier in the current expansion, when millions of potential workers remained on the sidelines despite the economy's growth. Now six years old, with no signs of slowing, the expansion finally appears to be offering incentives to once-excluded segments of the population. In addition, economists said, there are signs that welfare overhaul may be pushing women into the job market out of fear of losing government income.

"These are astounding increases in the labor force," said Ed Yardeni, an economist with Deutsche Morgan Grenfell Inc. "It looks as though lots of people who might have dropped out for a long time—because they heard that even if they could get a job they couldn't keep it, so what's the point—are coming back."

Unemployment Rate Slips

The unemployment rate in March edged down to 5.2% from 5.3% in February, the Labor Department reported. Since last June, the rate has been within the relatively narrow band of 5.2% to 5.4%. Nonfarm employers added 175,000 workers to their payrolls in March. While that was down from the 293,000 in February, it was consistent with reports of continuing solid economic growth. So far in 1997, the economy is creating an average of 242,000 jobs a month, compared with a monthly rate of 216,000 last year.

The March report provided some signs that the strong labor market may now be fueling inflation, but the signals weren't that alarming to economists. The average hourly wage rose by five cents in March, or 0.4%, to $12.15, the same pace of increase as in February. Compared with a year earlier, wages in March were up 4%, the largest jump since 1990.

But many economists believe this report doesn't provide as accurate a picture of employment costs as other government statistics, which do not show such clear-cut increases. In another sign of labor-market tightness, factory overtime rose by 12 minutes to 4.9 hours per week, the highest level since the department started tracking the figure 41 years ago....

Janet Yellen, the chief White House economist, noted in an interview that "historically, this qualifies as a tight labor market." She said that when unemployment rates reached this level in the 1980s, wages and inflation accelerated. "On the other hand," she added, "we've had seemingly quite tight labor markets for quite a long period, and we've not yet seen any evidence of inflationary pressures. Views of the labor market and the forces that are operative in it have changed as a consequence of this experience."

Definitions May Change
One of the most noteworthy changes in recent months has been the large increase in the number of people seeking jobs, a jump that has roughly matched the large number of jobs created. And with more and more people looking for work, traditional definitions of tightness may have been altered.

During recessions, the labor force usually shrinks, as people simply stop looking because they are discouraged about their job prospects. The labor force usually swells again during growth periods. But from 1992 through 1995, the rate of participation in the labor force rose only slowly and erratically, despite solid economic growth. It wasn't until September 1996 that the participation rate began its current path of clear, steady ascent....

The increase in the labor force has been stronger among women than men. For men over 16 years old, the participation rate has grown to 75.2% from 75% over the past year, but for women it has risen to 60% from 59.1%. While that disparity tracks long-time postwar standards, the rise has been particularly sharp recently in the category of "women who maintain families...."

Role of Welfare Changes
Economists speculate that this jump stems from recent and pending cuts in welfare. "Some women are being motivated by welfare reform to eventually find steady employment; others are sincerely looking for work, but may lack required job skills or motivation for steady employment," Morgan Guaranty Trust Co. economist Robert E. Mellman wrote in a report Friday.

He noted that the unemployment rate for women heading households has shot up in the past year, to 9.1% last month from 7.7%, indicating that the new job seekers are still having a relatively difficult time actually finding jobs.

Those trends show that the current high-growth economy may be well-suited for the welfare-overhaul experiment, said Harvard University labor economist Lawrence Katz. And, he added, it makes prospects that the Fed may now try to stem job growth worrisome. "Slowing down the economy at this juncture of historic welfare reform, when there's a need to increase labor-participation rates at the bottom of the market, would be worrisome," said Mr. Katz.

But Princeton University economist Alan Blinder, a former Fed vice chairman, said that policy makers had to worry about how long the growing labor force could keep inflationary pressures in check. "The normal pattern shows a cyclical rebound in labor-force participation, but this can't go on forever," he said. "How much further can it go? I don't know."

USE YOUR ECONOMIC REASONING

1. How would you graphically represent the impact of an increase in the civilian labor force? What impact would this event, by itself, have on the economy?
2. What explains these "astounding increases" in the labor force?
3. How is the growth of the labor force helping to prevent inflation? Support your answer with a graph.
4. What would happen if aggregate demand continued to expand but the growth of the labor force slowed? How would this situation be depicted graphically? What comments in the article point to this concern?

their designed or intended capacities for some period of time, and workers may be willing to work overtime. However, neither of these practices is sustainable; ultimately equipment breaks down and employees become disgruntled and unproductive. But in the short run, these actions permit the economy to operate beyond its potential; that is, they allow actual GDP to exceed potential GDP.

As we've seen, businesses expand output beyond potential GDP because higher prices make it profitable for them to do so. But the higher prices that are attractive to businesses are bad news for employees. Workers find that they must pay more for the goods and services they buy, even though their wage rates are unchanged; thus, their *real* wages—the purchasing power of their money wages—have declined.

Eventually firms will have to renegotiate their labor contracts. When that happens, workers will demand higher wages. Other input suppliers, also pressed by higher prices, will demand more for their resources. The result of the higher renegotiated input prices will be an upward shift of the aggregate supply curve. (Remember that a change in input prices will shift the *AS* curve.) Tight markets for labor and other inputs will put continuing upward pressure on wages and other input prices. The *AS* curve will continue to shift upward until workers and other input suppliers have regained their original purchasing power. This is represented in Exh. 12.10 by the shift from AS_1 to AS_2. Note that when contracts have been renegotiated, the incentive that originally motivated businesses to expand real output to $1,200 billion will have evaporated. Equilibrium real GDP will return to $1,000 billion (point *C* in the exhibit), the level of GDP consistent with the economy's potential output. The self-correcting forces have returned the economy to its potential GDP. As you can see, the long-run impact of the increase in aggregate demand is simply a higher price level since the increase in production cannot be sustained.

ADJUSTMENTS TO A DECREASE IN AGGREGATE DEMAND

The economy's response to a reduction in aggregate demand is similar to its adjustments to an increase, but in the opposite direction. To illustrate, let's again assume that the economy is operating at its potential GDP (at point *A* in Exh. 12.11). If aggregate demand fell from AD_1 to AD_2, firms would initially find their prices falling while some of their costs were fixed by long-term contracts. This would cause them to cut back on output (since output levels that had been profitable at a higher price level are no longer profitable) and to reduce equilibrium GDP below potential. This is represented in Exh. 12.11 by the movement along AS_1 from *A* to *B*. Of course, when actual GDP falls below potential, the rate of unemployment rises above the full employment level.

Eventually labor and other contracts will be renegotiated. At that point, the high unemployment rates and unused productive capacity of input

EXHIBIT 12.11

Adjusting to Lower Aggregate Demand

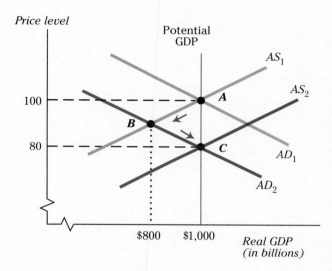

When aggregate demand declines, businesses initially find it necessary to reduce output because wage rates and certain other costs are fixed by long-term contracts. Thus equilibrium real GDP drops below potential. But when these contracts expire and costs fall, the *AS* curve shifts downward and eventually increases equilibrium output to the level of potential GDP.

suppliers will cause wages and other resource prices to fall. As that occurs, the *AS* curve will begin shifting to the right, eventually shifting from AS_1 to AS_2 (from *B* to *C*) and returning the economy to potential GDP and full employment. The long-run impact of the reduction in aggregate demand is a lower price level; output and employment have returned to their initial levels.

The preceding examples suggest that although the economy can deviate from potential GDP in the short run, these deviations are ultimately corrected. In the long run, the economy tends to operate at potential GDP and full employment.[4] If the economy always returns to full employment, is there any justification for government intervention to alter the economy's performance? Chapter 14, "Fiscal Policy, Debt and the Deficit," will begin by examining this issue. Chapter 13, the intervening optional chapter, is entitled "An Alternative View: The Keynesian Total Expenditures Model." It examines an alternative model of equilibrium output, a model that emphasizes aggregate demand. It may be omitted with no loss in continuity.

---

[4] This implies that in the long run the economy's aggregate supply curve is a vertical line at potential GDP. Although a change in aggregate demand can alter output in the short run, in the long run only the price level is affected.

Summary

Economists use the concepts of aggregate demand and aggregate supply to represent the forces that determine the economy's equilibrium GDP and price level. *Aggregate demand* (*AD*) is the total quantity of output demanded by all sectors in the economy together at various price levels in a given period of time. The *aggregate demand curve* slopes downward and to the right, indicating that more real output will be demanded at a lower price level than at a higher price level. There are three reasons for the downward slope of the aggregate demand curve: the real balance effect, the interest rate effect, and the international trade effect. The factors that will shift the aggregate demand curve include changes in the expectations of households and businesses, aggregate wealth, government policy, foreign incomes, and foreign price levels.

Aggregate supply (*AS*) refers to the quantity of output supplied by all producers in the economy together at various price levels in a given period of time. The *aggregate supply curve* slopes upward because higher price levels stimulate businesses to expand output. Since wage rates and some other input prices are commonly fixed by contracts, an increase in the price level provides incentive for firms to increase output. A given aggregate supply curve assumes the prevailing wage rates and prices of nonlabor inputs, the current level of productivity, and the existing supplies of labor and capital. If one or more of these factors change, the *AS* curve will shift to a new position.

The intersection of the aggregate demand and supply curves simultaneously determines the level of equilibrium real GDP and the equilibrium price level in the economy. Shifts in aggregate demand or supply will tend to alter these equilibrium values. If aggregate demand increases, both real GDP and the price level will tend to increase. The economy enjoys higher levels of output and employment, but it experiences *demand-pull inflation*. If aggregate demand declines, the levels of output, employment, and prices decline.

Changes in equilibrium can also be caused by changes in aggregate supply. A supply shock, such as an increase in the price of imported oil, will tend to reduce aggregate supply. This will cause *cost-push inflation* since the higher cost of oil pushes up prices. When aggregate supply is reduced, the levels of output and employment in the economy also decline. Supply shocks provide one possible explanation for *stagflation,* high unemployment combined with high inflation. If aggregate supply increases, the results will be doubly beneficial; the levels of output and employment in the economy will tend to increase, whereas the overall price level will decline.

Most modern economists agree that, to some extent, the economy contains a self-correcting mechanism. In the short run, the economy can deviate from potential GDP because certain wages and prices are rigid. In the long run, however, all wages and prices become flexible. As a consequence, reductions in aggregate demand are ultimately met by falling wages and input prices, which cause aggregate supply to expand and return the economy to potential GDP. Increases in aggregate demand eventually lead to higher wages and input prices, which cause aggregate supply to contract and output and employment to fall. Thus, wage and price adjustments ultimately return the economy to potential GDP and full employment.

GLOSSARY

Aggregate demand. The total quantity of output demanded by all sectors in the economy together at various price levels in a given time period.

Aggregate supply. The total quantity of output supplied by all producers in the economy together at various price levels in a given time period.

Cost-push inflation. Inflation caused by rising costs of production.

Demand-pull inflation. Inflation caused by increases in aggregate demand.

Exports. Goods and services that are produced domestically and sold to customers in other countries.

Imports. Goods and services that are purchased from foreign producers.

Interest rate effect. The increase in the amount of aggregate output demanded that results from the lower interest rates that accompany a reduction in the overall price level.

International trade effect. The increase in the amount of aggregate output demanded that results when a reduction in the price level makes domestic products less expensive in relation to foreign products.

Real balance effect. The increase in the amount of aggregate output demanded that results from an increase in the real value of the public's financial assets.

Stagflation. High unemployment combined with high inflation.

STUDY QUESTIONS

Fill in the Blanks

1. The _aggregate demand_ curve shows the amount of real output that will be demanded at various price levels.

2. According to the _real balance_ effect, an increase in the price level will reduce the purchasing power of financial assets and cause society to demand less real output.

3. Any change in the spending plans of consumers, businesses, or government that results from something other than a change in the _price level_ will shift the aggregate demand curve.

4. A broad-based technological advance will tend to shift the aggregate _supply_ curve to the _right_.

5. According to the interest rate effect, a reduction in the price level will tend to (increase/decrease)

   ___decrease___ the demand for money, which in turn will (increase/

   decrease) ___decrease___ the rate of interest and lead to (an increase/

   a reduction) ___an increase___ in the quantity of real output demanded.

6. Increases in the price level cause businesses to expand output because

   ___Wages rates___ and other

   ___input___ prices are commonly fixed in the short run.

7. An increase in government spending will

   tend to shift the aggregate ___demand___

   curve to the ___right___ .

8. Cost-push inflation is caused by the aggregate ___supply___ curve shifting to the

   (right/left) ___left___ .

9. The term ___stagflation___ is used to describe high inflation combined with high unemployment.

10. If the aggregate supply curve remains stationary, policymakers can reduce inflation if they are willing to accept higher

    ___unemployment___ .

Multiple Choice

1. The type of inflation caused by increased spending for goods and services is
   a) demand-pull inflation.
   b) cost-push inflation.
   c) structural inflation.
   d) expenditure inflation.

2. If a reduction in the price level causes more real output to be demanded,
   a) the aggregate demand curve will shift to the right.
   b) the aggregate demand curve is downward sloping.
   c) the aggregate supply curve will shift to the right.
   d) the aggregate supply curve is downward sloping.

3. Which of the following will shift the aggregate demand curve to the left?
   a) An increase in government spending
   b) A reduction in labor productivity
   c) An increase in personal income taxes
   d) An increase in society's aggregate wealth

4. Which of the following will increase both the price level and real GDP?
   a) A nationwide drought that drives up the prices of agricultural products
   b) A reduction in government spending for goods and services
   c) A reduction in the money supply
   d) Greater optimism among business executives

5. In 1974 disease killed many anchovies and raised anchovy prices. Anchovies are used in cattle feed as a source of protein. The likely impact of this event would be to
   a) raise both the price level and real GDP.
   b) lower both the price level and real GDP.
   c) raise the price level but lower real GDP.
   d) lower the price level but raise real GDP.

6. According to the real balance effect,
   a) a reduction in the price level stimulates spending by lowering interest rates.
   b) an increase in the money supply will shift the aggregate demand curve to the right.
   c) an increase in the price level reduces spending by lowering the real value of society's financial assets.
   d) an increase in society's aggregate wealth will shift the aggregate demand curve to the right.

7. An increase in the productivity of the labor force would be likely to shift
   a) the aggregate supply curve to the right.
   b) the aggregate supply curve to the left.
   c) the aggregate demand curve to the right.
   d) the aggregate demand curve to the left.

8. A decrease in foreign income levels would, ceteris paribus, tend to shift the aggregate _____ curve for U.S. products to the _____.
   a) demand, right
   b) demand, left
   c) supply, right
   d) supply, left

9. The international trade effect provides a rationale for
   a) shifts in the aggregate demand curve.
   b) shifts in the aggregate supply curve.
   c) the slope of the aggregate demand curve.
   d) the slope of the aggregate supply curve.

10. In the short run, an increase in the money supply will
    a) reduce both real GDP and the price level.
    b) reduce real GDP and increase the price level.
    c) increase both real GDP and the price level.
    d) increase real GDP and reduce the price level.

11. If the prevailing price level was initially below equilibrium,
    a) there would be a surplus of output.
    b) the price level would tend to fall.

c) the amount of real GDP supplied would exceed the amount demanded.
    d) there would be a shortage of output.

12. Suppose that Congress increased government spending at the same time that the price of imported oil (which is used to manufacture gasoline and heating oil) increased. In the short run, this would clearly
    a) increase both the price level and real GDP.
    b) reduce both the price level and real GDP.
    c) increase the price level, but the impact on real GDP is uncertain.
    d) increase real GDP, but the impact on the price level is uncertain.

13. The aggregate supply curve slopes upward
    a) as a result of the real balance effect and the interest rate effect.
    b) if all wages and input prices are flexible in the short run.
    c) because increases in the overall price level result in enhanced labor productivity and higher real output.
    d) because input price rigidities make it profitable for firms to expand output when product prices rise.

14. Suppose that the economy is operating below potential GDP. According to the self-correcting model, the economy will ultimately return to potential because
    a) the Fed will expand the money supply.
    b) wages and resource prices will fall as contracts expire and are renegotiated.
    c) workers will eventually demand higher wages, and resource suppliers will demand higher input prices.
    d) aggregate demand will automatically increase enough to push the economy back to potential GDP.

15. When the overall price level rises,
    a) businesses tend to reduce output because production becomes less profitable.
    b) wage rates and other input prices tend to increase immediately, forcing businesses to cut back on production.

c) businesses have incentive to expand output because many costs are fixed by long-term contracts.

d) businesses may either increase or decrease output, depending on the magnitude of the hike in the price level.

16. According to the self-correcting model, if the economy is producing a level of output in excess of potential GDP,
    a) potential GDP will automatically expand to match the actual level of production.
    b) workers and input suppliers will eventually negotiate higher wages and prices, which will return the economy to potential GDP.

c) wages and input prices will ultimately fall, which will return the economy to potential GDP.

d) None of the above; the economy cannot operate beyond potential GDP.

17. According to the self-correcting model,
    a) unemployment can exist indefinitely.
    b) the economy can never operate beyond potential GDP.
    c) unemployment is eventually eliminated by falling wages and prices.
    d) the economy always operates at potential GDP.

Problems and Questions for Discussion

1. Explain in detail why the aggregate demand curve slopes downward .

2. Given a stationary aggregate supply curve, policymakers should be able to reduce unemployment if they are willing to accept higher inflation. Explain and supplement your explanation with a graph.

3. What role do contracts play in explaining the upward slope of the aggregate supply curve?

4. Suppose that, on average, wage rates increase less than the increase in labor productivity. What will happen to the overall price level and real GDP? Explain how you arrived at your conclusion.

5. Whenever the stock market threatens to tumble (bringing down stock prices), economy watchers worry about its potential impact on the economy. Is there any justification for this concern—could a large decline in the stock market harm the economy? Defend your answer.

6. Explain the difference between demand-pull and cost-push inflation. Use aggregate demand and supply curves to show how each problem would be represented graphically.

7. Suppose that the economy is in equilibrium at potential GDP and that policymakers increase aggregate demand (perhaps because they do not recognize that the economy is operating at potential). Discuss the short-run and long-run impact of this change. Supplement your answer with graphs.

8. Consider the short-run impact of the changes listed below. Which changes would cause the economy's price level and real GDP to move in the same direction (both increase, both decrease), and which would cause the price level and real GDP to move in opposite directions (increasing the price level but reducing real output, for example)? After you have worked through the list, see if you can draw any general conclusions.
    a) An increase in government spending
    b) A severe frost that destroys crops
    c) A large decline in the stock market
    d) An increase in labor productivity
    e) An increase in consumer optimism
    f) Higher prices for imported raw materials

9. Suppose that government spending in support of education was increased.

Would this action shift the aggregate demand curve, the aggregate supply curve, or both curves? What would happen to the price level and real GDP?

10. Assume that the economy is in short-run equilibrium at less than full employment. Describe the forces that will ultimately return the economy to potential GDP.

ANSWER KEY

Fill in the Blanks

1. aggregate demand
2. real balance
3. price level
4. supply, right

5. decrease, decrease, an increase
6. wage rates, input
7. demand, right

8. supply, left
9. stagflation
10. unemployment

Multiple Choice

1. a
2. b
3. c
4. d

5. c
6. c
7. a
8. b

9. c
10. c
11. d

12. c
13. d
14. b

15. c
16. b
17. c

CHAPTER 13

An Alternative View: The Keynesian Total Expenditures Model

LEARNING OBJECTIVES

1. Draw the consumption function and explain its appearance.
2. Discuss the factors that will shift the consumption function to a new position.
3. Identify the determinants of investment spending, and be able to explain why investment spending is more volatile than consumption spending.
4. Define and identify an economy's equilibrium output.
5. Explain what is meant by the multiplier effect, and be able to calculate the size of an economy's multiplier.
6. Explain the difference between equilibrium output and full-employment output.
7. Distinguish between inflationary and deflationary gaps.
8. **Appendix.** Describe the fiscal policy measures that Keynesians would take to combat unemployment or inflation.
9. **Appendix.** Describe the impact of government spending and taxation on the economy's equilibrium GDP.

What determines how much output our economy will produce and how many people will be employed? For Keynes, the answer was *total spending—total demand for goods and services*. When total spending increases, businesses produce more output and hire more people. As you learned in Chapter 11, that's the central idea in Keynesian macroeconomic theory: *Total spending is the critical determinant of the overall level of economic activity.*

Today, we know that Keynes ignored an important determinant of the economy's performance—aggregate supply. But there is much to be learned by examining the Keynesian total expenditures model. It will allow us to take a closer look at the factors that influence total spending (aggregate demand) and to consider why total spending tends to fluctuate. It also allows us to introduce an important concept known a the *multiplier*, which will be useful in understanding how changes in spending can have a magnified impact on the overall level of spending and output in the economy.

We begin this chapter by confining our analysis to a two-sector economy—households and businesses. We assume that there is no government and no foreign trade. We also assume that all saving is done by households and all investment by businesses. Further, we assume that the price level remains constant until full employment is reached. (Remember, Keynes believed that prices and wages tend to be rigid, not flexible as the classical economists assumed.)

Our first step is to explore the determinants of consumption and investment spending. Then we consider the way in which consumption, investment, and saving interact to determine the level of equilibrium income and output. Finally, we investigate the possibility of an unemployment or an inflationary equilibrium. The appendix to the chapter introduces government spending and taxation and examines the appropriate Keynesian fiscal policy for combating unemployment or inflation.

Consumption Spending

The largest component of total spending is consumption spending—spending by households for food, clothing, automobiles, education, and all the other goods and services that consumers buy. The most important factor influencing the amount of consumer spending is the level of disposable income. **Disposable income** is your take-home pay, the amount you have left after taxes have been deducted. Because there is no government sector in this chapter's hypothetical economy, no taxes are collected, which means that disposable income will equal total income, or GDP. For both individual households and society as a whole, a positive relationship exists between the amount of disposable income and the amount of consumption spending: The more people earn, the more they spend.

THE CONSUMPTION FUNCTION

The relationship between disposable income and consumption spending is called the **consumption function.** A consumption function shows the amounts that households plan to spend at different levels of disposable income. Exhibit 13.1 shows a hypothetical consumption function that is consistent with Keynesian theory. Note that the amount households plan to spend increases with income but by a smaller amount than the increase in income. In other words, households will spend part of any increase in income and save

EXHIBIT 13.1

A Hypothetical Consumption Function (in billions)

TOTAL INCOME* AND OUTPUT (GDP)	PLANNED CONSUMPTION EXPENDITURES	PLANNED SAVING
$300	$325	$−25
400	400	0
500	475	25
600	550	50
700	625	75
800	700	100

*In our simplified economy total income = total disposable income = GDP.

the rest. Whatever disposable income is not spent by households is saved. **Saving** is the act of not spending; putting money in a savings account, buying stocks and bonds, and stashing cash in a cookie jar are all acts of saving.

According to Exh. 13.1, when income is $300 billion, households desire to spend $325 billion. At that income they are **dissaving** $25 billion; that is, they are dipping into their savings accounts or borrowing to help finance some minimum standard of living. Higher levels of income involve more consumption spending and more saving, or less dissaving. In our example $400 billion represents the income level at which every dollar earned is spent; there is neither saving nor dissaving. At higher incomes, households wish to save a portion of their income. For instance, at an income of $500 billion, households plan to save $25 billion; at an income of $600 billion, they desire to save $50 billion.

Exhibit 13.2 plots the consumption function depicted in Exh. 13.1. The consumption function slopes upward and to the right because consumption spending increases with income. We determine the income level where every dollar is spent by using the 45-degree line drawn in the diagram. Because the vertical and horizontal axes meet at a 90-degree angle, the 45-degree line represents a series of points that are equidistant from the horizontal axis (income) and the vertical axis (consumption). Therefore, *at every point along the 45-degree line, consumption expenditures equal income.* Where the consumption function crosses the 45-degree line, consumers plan to spend everything they earn and save nothing. In our example that happens at an income of $400 billion.

At incomes less than $400 billion, there is dissaving, or negative saving. You can see that when income is $300 billion, consumers plan to dissave

EXHIBIT 13.2

Graphing a Consumption Function

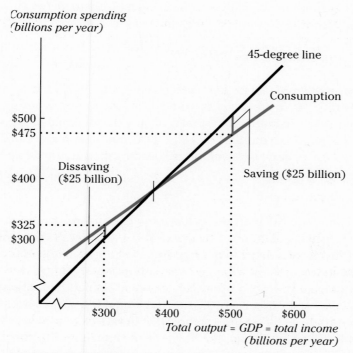

A *consumption function* shows the amounts that households desire to spend at different income levels. According to this hypothetical function, households would spend $325 billion per year if the total income in the economy was $300 billion. Thus, they would be dissaving—dipping into their savings accounts or borrowing— $25 billion at that income level.

Note that the amount of consumption spending rises with the level of income. At an income of $400 billion, households desire to spend exactly what they earn. There would be no saving and no dissaving. At an income of $500 billion, households would spend $475 billion each year and save $25 billion.

$25 billion. The vertical distance between the 45-degree line and the consumption function represents the amount of dissaving at that income. At incomes in excess of $400 billion, there is positive saving. When income is $500 billion, saving is equal to $25 billion. The distance between the 45-degree line and the consumption function gets wider as income increases because the amount of saving increases with income.

THE MARGINAL PROPENSITY TO CONSUME

The way households react to changes in income depends on their **marginal propensity to consume (MPC).** The *MPC* is the fraction of each additional earned dollar that households spend on consumption, or the change in consumption spending divided by the change in income:

$$\text{Marginal propensity to consume } (MPC) = \frac{\text{Change in consumption spending}}{\text{Change in income}}$$

If you receive a $1,000 raise and you plan to spend $900 of that increase, your *MPC* is 9/10, or .90. In other words, you'll spend 90 percent of any additional income you receive. In our hypothetical economy the marginal propensity to consume is 3/4, or .75. Note that in Exhs. 13.1 and 13.2, for every $100 billion increase in GDP (income), consumption spending increases by $75 billion:

$$MPC = \frac{\$\ 75 \text{ billion}}{\$100 \text{ billion}} = \frac{3}{4} = .75$$

You can relate the marginal propensity to consume to the consumption function easily if you know that the slope of any line is, by definition, the vertical change divided by the horizontal change. The slope of the consumption function is the change in consumption spending divided by the change in income, which is precisely how we define the marginal propensity to consume. In other words, the slope of the consumption function is equal to the economy's *MPC*. If the *MPC* in our example were higher (.90 instead of .75, for example), the slope of the consumption function would be steeper; if the *MPC* were lower (perhaps .50), the consumption function would be flatter.

According to our consumption function, only part of an increase in income is spent; the rest is saved. The **marginal propensity to save (MPS)** is the fraction of each additional earned dollar that is saved, or the change in saving divided by the change in income:

$$\text{Marginal propensity to save } (MPS) = \frac{\text{Change in saving}}{\text{Change in income}}$$

Calculating *MPS* is no problem once you know *MPC*. The marginal propensity to consume and the marginal propensity to save have to add up to 1.00, or 100 percent: If *MPC* is .75, you know that *MPS* must be .25. That is, 75 cents from each additional dollar is spent, and 25 cents is saved.

As you study Exhs. 13.1 and 13.2, keep in mind that the consumption function indicates the desired—or planned—levels of consumption, not necessarily the actual levels. Just as the demand curves we encountered in Chapter 3 showed the amount of a product consumers are "willing and able to buy at various prices," the consumption function shows the amounts that households *desire* to consume at various income levels. How much of a product people actually buy depends on the prices that actually prevail. Similarly, the actual level of consumption depends on the actual level of income in the economy.

THE NONINCOME DETERMINANTS OF CONSUMPTION SPENDING

Although consumption spending is determined primarily by the level of disposable income, nonincome factors also play a role. These nonincome factors include (1) people's expectations about what will happen to prices and to their incomes, (2) the cost and availability of consumer credit, and (3) the overall wealth of households.

It is easy to see why consumer expectations can have an impact on spending behavior. If people expect prices to be higher next month or next year, they tend to buy now. Why wait to pay $14,000 for a car next year if you can buy it for $13,000 today? Buying now to avoid higher prices later creates a greater amount of current consumption spending than would normally be expected at each level of income. Similarly, if people expect an increase in income, they will probably spend more from their current income. If you're convinced that you're going to be earning more next year, you'll probably be a little bit freer in your spending habits this year.

The cost and availability of consumer credit also influence the level of consumption spending. Most of us don't limit our spending to our current income. If we really want something, we borrow the money to buy it. But the cost of borrowing money and the ability to get consumer credit can change with the state of the economy. In general, the higher the interest rate and the more difficult it is to get consumer loans, the less consumption spending there will be at any level of total income (GDP).

The third nonincome determinant of consumption spending is the overall wealth of households. A household's wealth includes cash, bank accounts, stocks and bonds, real estate, and other physical assets. Since households can finance consumption spending by depleting bank accounts or selling other forms of wealth, an increase in wealth will permit households to spend more at any given income level. For this reason, an increase in wealth will tend to shift the consumption function upward; a decrease will have the opposite effect.

The consumption function assumes that these nonincome determinants of consumption spending remain unchanged. If that assumption is violated, the entire consumption function shifts. Exhibit 13.3 shows how changing expectations about prices result in different levels of planned consumption spending at each level of income.

EXHIBIT 13.3

Changes in the Nonincome Determinants of Consumption

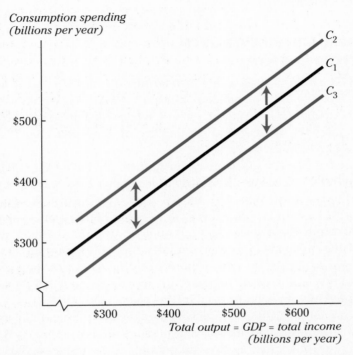

The consumption function assumes that the nonincome determinants of consumption spending remain unchanged. If that assumption is violated, the consumption function will shift to a new position. For example, if consumers expect prices to be higher next year, they will probably choose to purchase more consumer goods this year. The consumption function will shift upward (from C_1 to C_2). If consumers lower their expectations regarding future prices, they will probably choose to purchase fewer consumer goods this year. The consumption function will shift downward (from C_1 to C_3).

Except under extreme conditions, such as those that prevailed during the Great Depression or World War II, the consumption function has been relatively stable; it hasn't shifted up or down very much. Knowing that planned consumption has been stable, how do we explain the fluctuations in total spending that occur in our economy? According to Keynes, the major cause of fluctuations in total spending is the ever-changing rate of investment spending.

Investment Spending

The term *investment*, as you saw in Chapter 10, refers to spending by businesses on capital goods—factories, machinery, and other aids to production. Investment spending has a dual influence on the economy. First, as a major component of total spending, investment spending helps determine the economy's level of total output and total employment. Second, investment is a critical determinant of the economy's rate of growth. We define economic growth as an increase in the economy's productive capacity or potential GDP. Investment spending contributes to economic growth because it enlarges the economy's stock of capital goods and thereby helps increase the economy's capacity to produce goods and services.

THE DETERMINANTS OF INVESTMENT

As you discovered in Chapter 10, profit expectations are the overriding motivation of all investment-spending plans in a market economy. Those expectations are based on a comparison of costs and revenues.

Suppose you are considering investing in a soft-drink machine for the lobby of the student union. How do you decide whether to make the investment? Like any other businessperson, you compare costs and revenues. On the cost side, you consider the price of the machine and the interest charges on the money you would have to borrow to buy it. If you would be using your own money, you consider the opportunity cost of those funds—the amount of interest you will sacrifice if you withdraw that money from your savings to purchase the machine. On the revenue side, you would include the expected income from selling the soft drinks minus the cost of the drinks. If you expect the machine to generate revenues exceeding all your anticipated costs, you have incentive to make the investment. If not, the investment should not be made. All investment decisions involve a similar comparison.

Interest Rates: The Cost of Money. The rate of interest can be an important factor in determining whether an investment will be profitable. A project that does not appear profitable when the interest rate is 20 percent, for example, may be attractive if the interest rate drops to 15 percent or 12 percent. To illustrate, suppose that you can purchase a soft-drink vending machine (which has a useful life of one year) for $1,000 and can borrow the money at 20 percent interest. Assume, also, that you expect to sell 5,000 cans of soft drink a year at 60¢ a can and plan to pay $36\frac{1}{2}$¢ for each can you buy. Would your investment be profitable? A few calculations show that it wouldn't be.

Anticipated revenue (5,000 cans sold at $.60 per can)		$3,000
Anticipated costs		
Cost of the vending machine	$1,000	
Cost of the soft drinks (5,000 cans at $.365)	$1,825	
Cost of borrowed funds ($1,000 at 20 percent)	$ 200	
Total cost		$3,025
Anticipated loss		**$ 25**

According to these calculations, you could expect to lose $25 on your investment if you had to pay 20 percent interest to borrow the money. So, of course, you wouldn't make the investment under those conditions. But if the interest rate declined to 15 percent, the cost of borrowing $1,000 for a year would drop to $150, and the investment would earn a profit of $25. If the interest rate declined further, the profit would be even greater. The point we are making is that lower interest rates encourage businesses to undertake investments that would be unattractive at higher rates. Thus, we have a negative, or inverse, relationship between the rate of interest and the level of investment spending; the lower the interest rate, the higher the level of investment spending. This relationship is illustrated in Exh. 13.4.

Expectations about Revenues and Costs. Although the interest rate influences investment spending plans, it should be clear from our example that it is not the only factor to take into consideration. Businesses will continue to borrow and invest in spite of high interest rates if they are optimistic about future revenues (and costs) and the likelihood of earning a profit. For example, even a 20 or 25 percent interest rate would not discourage you from investing in the vending machine if you were convinced that you could sell 6,000 cans of the soft drink a year. On the other hand, an interest rate as low as 6 percent would be prohibitive if you were forecasting sales of only 4,500 cans. (Take the time to make some calculations and convince yourself of these conclusions.) In short, it is not interest rates themselves that determine the attractiveness of investment projects and the level of investment spending in the economy but rather the interaction of interest rates and expectations about future revenues and costs.

THE INSTABILITY OF INVESTMENT

The preceding discussion shows why investment spending is much less stable than consumption spending. There are several reasons. First, the interest rate tends to change over time, and these changes cause businesses to alter their investment plans.

EXHIBIT 13.4

Investment and the Rate of Interest

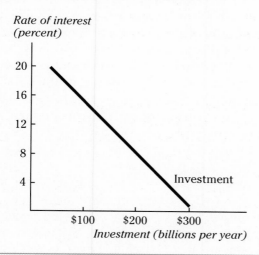

The rate of interest and the level of investment spending are negatively, or inversely, related; the lower the interest rate, the higher the level of investment spending.

Second, businesses' expectations are quite volatile, or changeable. They are influenced by everything from current economic conditions to headlines in the newspaper. If a wave of optimism hits the country, planned investment may skyrocket. When pessimism strikes, investment plunges.

A third source of instability is the simple fact that plans to invest can be postponed. A business may want to build a more modern production plant to improve its competitive position. But if economic conditions suggest that this may not be the best time to build, the business can decide to make the old plant last a little longer.

Finally, investment opportunities occur irregularly, in spurts. New products and new production processes provide businesses with investment opportunities, but these developments do not occur in predictable patterns. A business may encounter several profitable investment opportunities one year and none the next.

Changing interest rates, the volatility of expectations, the ability to postpone investment spending, and the ups and downs of investment opportunities all lead to fluctuations and instability in the level of investment spending. Because investment spending accounts for more than 15 percent of the GDP, these changes can have a major impact on total output and employment in the economy. We'll have more to say about that impact later in this chapter.

The Equilibrium Level of Output

Now that we have analyzed the individual components of spending in our hypothetical economy, we are ready to combine them to see how total spending determines the level of output and employment. Remember, according to Keynesian theory, the level of demand—that is, total spending—determines the amount of output that will be produced and the number of jobs that will be made available. To see how the spending plans of consumers and investors determine the level of output and employment, we turn to Exh. 13.5.

Column 1 in Exh. 13.5 shows several possible levels of output (GDP) that our hypothetical economy could produce. Which level will be chosen by businesses depends on how much they expect to sell. Let's assume that businesses believe they can sell $600 billion worth of output. To produce this output, they hire economic resources: land, labor, capital, and entrepreneurship. This transaction provides households with $600 billion of income, an amount exactly equal to the value of total output. Recall that total income *must* equal total output because all the money received by businesses must be paid to someone.

Column 2 shows the amount that households plan to consume for each level of income (GDP) given in column 1. If the tabular data in column 2 were plotted on a graph, you would recognize the consumption function (Exh. 13.1). You can see that when GDP is $600 billion, households desire to consume $550 billion. Moving to column 3, you see that households want to save $50 billion when GDP is $600 billion.

EXHIBIT 13.5

Determination of Equilibrium Income and Output (data in billions)

(1) TOTAL OUTPUT AND INCOME* (GDP)	(2) PLANNED CONSUMPTION EXPENDITURES	(3) PLANNED SAVING (1–2)	(4) PLANNED INVESTMENT EXPENDITURES	(5) TOTAL PLANNED EXPENDITURES (2 + 4)	(6) TENDENCY OF OUTPUT
$300	$325	$−25	$50	$375	Increase
400	400	0	50	450	Increase
500	475	25	50	525	Increase
600	550	50	50	600	Equilibrium
700	625	75	50	675	Decrease
800	700	100	50	750	Decrease

*In our simplified economy, total income = total disposable income = GDP.

The next category of spending is investment spending (column 4). Our example assumes that investment spending is autonomous, or independent of the level of current output. Unlike consumption spending, investment spending is determined by the factors described earlier: the rate of interest and expectations regarding future revenues and costs. The level of investment spending changes only if those determinants change. Here we've set the level of investment spending at $50 billion. (Later we'll allow the level of investment to change so that we can trace the impact of that change on the level of output and employment.)

In our simplified economy, total spending (column 5) is the sum of consumption spending and investment spending. Note that the amount of total spending rises with the economy's GDP; higher levels of GDP signal higher levels of total spending because consumption spending increases with income. If the business sector produces $600 billion of output, the result will be the creation of $550 billion of consumption spending and $50 billion of investment spending, or a total of $600 billion. This amount will be precisely enough to clear the market of that period's production. Most important, because businesses can sell exactly what they have produced, they will have no incentive to increase or decrease their rate of output. As you learned in Chapter 11, this means that the economy has arrived at its equilibrium output, the output that it will tend to maintain. Businesses can be expected to produce the same amount every year until they have reason to believe that the spending plans of consumers or investors have changed.

INVENTORY ADJUSTMENTS AND EQUILIBRIUM OUTPUT

The preceding example demonstrates that the economy will be in equilibrium only when *total spending is exactly equal to total output.*[1] In other words, an economy has arrived at its equilibrium output when the production of that output level gives rise to precisely enough spending, or demand, to purchase everything that was produced. In our example, $600 billion is the only output that satisfies this requirement. At any other output level, there will be either too much or too little demand, and producers will have incentive to alter their level of production.

Consider, for example, an output of $700 billion. As you have seen, producing $700 billion of output means creating $700 billion of income. Note, however, that not all this income will find its way back to businesses

---

[1] You may remember from Chapter 11 that there is another way to identify the equilibrium output—by finding the output at which planned saving is equal to planned investment. You can see in Exh. 13.5 that planned saving is equal to planned investment at an output of $600 billion, the output already identified as equilibrium.

in the form of spending. Column 5 in Exh. 13.5 shows that only $675 billion of spending will be created—too little to absorb the period's production. Inventories of unsold merchandise will grow, signaling businesses to reduce the rate of output; this move will take the economy closer to equilibrium.

If spending initially exceeded output, the reaction of businesses would be exactly the opposite. For example, if $500 billion of output were produced, it would generate $525 billion of total spending. Because the amount that consumers and investors desire to spend exceeds the level of output, businesses can meet demand only if they supplement their current production with merchandise from their inventories. This unintended reduction in inventories is a signal to increase the rate of output, which, in turn, will push the economy closer to the equilibrium GDP.

As you can see, whenever spending is greater or less than output, producers have incentive to alter production levels; there is a natural tendency to move toward equilibrium. The only output that can be maintained is the output at which total spending is exactly equal to total output; this is the equilibrium output.

EQUILIBRIUM OUTPUT: A GRAPHIC PRESENTATION

The data in Exh. 13.5 are graphed in Exh. 13.6. The line labeled *C + I* (consumption plus investment) is the total expenditure (or total spending) function. This function is simply a graphic representation of column 5 from Exh. 13.5, showing the total amount of planned spending at each level of GDP. It is easy to understand why the total expenditure function looks so much like the consumption function. Because we have assumed investment spending to be an autonomous constant—$50 billion per year—the total spending function can be constructed simply by drawing a line parallel to line *C* (consumption) and exactly $50 billion above it. The other element of the output-expenditure diagram is the 45-degree line. At every point on this line, total spending equals total output. We locate the equilibrium output where the total spending function intersects the 45-degree line ($600 billion).

Changes in Spending and the Multiplier Effect

Changes in the spending plans of either consumers or investors will alter the equilibrium level of income and output in our hypothetical economy. At any given level of income (GDP), consumers may decide to spend more if they believe that prices are going to rise in the near future or if they expect wage and salary increases. Such a change in consumer expectations would be represented

EXHIBIT 13.6

Determination of Equilibrium Income and Output

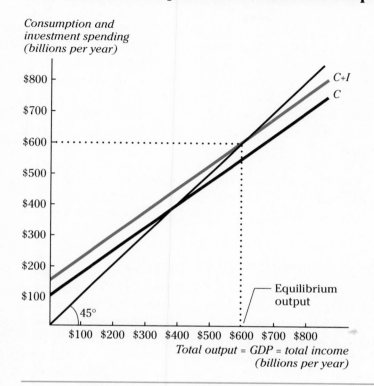

Consumption and investment spending (billions per year)

We can identify the equilibrium output by locating the output at which the total expenditure function crosses the 45-degree line.

Total output = GDP = total income (billions per year)

graphically by an upward shift of the consumption function. Similarly, investors may increase their rate of investment spending if they become more optimistic about the future or if interest rates decline. This change in the level of planned investment would be depicted by an upward shift of the investment function.

Because the economy's total expenditure function is nothing more than the sum of the consumption and investment functions, an upward shift of either one would cause an upward shift of the total expenditure function, which, in turn, would increase the equilibrium level of output. Any change resulting in a downward shift of the consumption or investment functions would reduce the equilibrium output.

To illustrate the impact of a change in the level of planned expenditures, let's assume that the rate of autonomous investment increases by $50 billion per year. This change is represented in Exh. 13.7 by a shift of the total expenditure

EXHIBIT 13.7

The Multiplier Effect

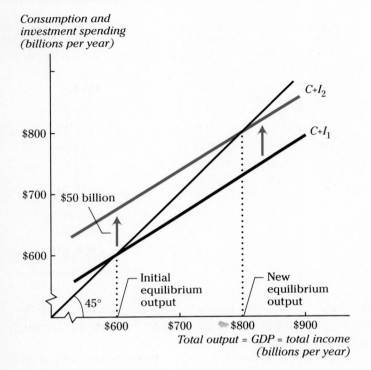

Consumption and investment spending (billions per year)

Because of the multiplier effect, an initial $50 billion increase in spending leads to a $200 billion increase in GDP.

function from $C + I_1$ to $C + I_2$. The most important thing to notice about this example is the relationship between the initial change in investment spending and the resulting change in total output. When investment spending increases by $50 billion, total output increases by much more than that—by $200 billion, to be exact. This phenomenon—that small changes in spending are magnified into larger changes in income and output—is called the **multiplier effect.**

THE MULTIPLIER EFFECT

In order to understand how the multiplier effect operates, let's trace the impact of this increase in investment spending as it works its way through the economy. Exhibit 13.8 illustrates the process. Period one shows the original equilibrium situation from Exh. 13.7 (note that total output equals total spending at $600 billion). In period two, output and consumption spending remain unchanged, but investment spending increases from $50 billion to $100 billion. That pushes total

EXHIBIT 13.8

Tracing the Impact of a Spending Increase (hypothetical data in billions)

PERIOD	TOTAL OUTPUT AND INCOME (GDP)	PLANNED CONSUMPTION EXPENDITURES	PLANNED INVESTMENT EXPENDITURES	TOTAL PLANNED EXPENDITURES
One	**$600.00**	$550.00	$ 50.00	**$600.00**
Two	600.00	550.00	100.00	650.00
Three	650.00	587.50	100.00	687.50
Four	687.50	615.63	100.00	715.63
Five	715.63	636.73	100.00	736.73
Six	736.73	652.56	100.00	752.56
—	—	—	—	—
—	—	—	—	—
Ultimately	**800.00**	700.00	100.00	**800.00**

spending up to $650 billion and disturbs the economy's equilibrium. Since the level of total spending in period two exceeds the economy's output, the demand can be met only by drawing inventories below their desired levels.

In period three, producers increase their output to $650 billion in an attempt to catch up with demand. But when producers expand their output by $50 billion, they create an additional $50 billion of new income—the money that is paid to the owners of economic resources. Recall that our hypothetical economy was constructed with an MPC of 0.75. Therefore, this $50 billion increase in income leads to an additional $37.5 billion of consumption spending (75 percent of $50 billion). As a result, total spending rises by an additional $37.5 billion in period three, and output again fails to keep pace with demand.

In period four, businesses expand their production to $687.5 billion, the level of demand in period three. This $37.5 billion increase in income (output) causes consumption spending to increase by $28.13 billion (75 percent of $37.5 billion). As a consequence, total spending in period four will rise by $28.13 billion, and since total spending continues to exceed total output, inventories again will fall.

As you can see, once equilibrium is disrupted, income and consumption spending continue to feed each other. Any change in income causes consumption spending to expand, which, in turn, causes income and output to expand still further. In theory, the new equilibrium would be reached only after an infinite number of time periods. However, the increases in income and consumption become smaller as equilibrium is approached, so that most of the expansionary effect is felt after the first half-dozen or so periods. In our example, equilibrium is finally attained when output is equal to total spending at $800 billion. (Note that this is the output level at which the total expenditure function crosses the 45-degree line in Exh. 13.7.)

CALCULATING THE MULTIPLIER

In the preceding example, a $50 billion increase in investment spending led to a $200 billion increase in income and output. Thus, the *multiplier* is 4. The **multiplier (M)** is the number by which any initial change in spending is multiplied to find the ultimate change in income and output.

If we know the marginal propensity to consume in our economy, we can estimate the size of the multiplier before the change in spending has run its course. Either of two simple formulas can be used:

$$M = \frac{1}{1 - MPC}$$

or, since $1 - MPC = MPS$,

$$M = \frac{1}{MPS}$$

Applying the formula to our hypothetical economy (with an *MPC* of 0.75), we can verify that the multiplier is indeed 4:

$$M = \frac{1}{1 - MPC}$$

$$M = \frac{1}{1 - 0.75}$$

$$M = 4$$

As we've already seen, a multiplier of 4 tells us that any increase in spending will generate an increase in equilibrium output that is four times as large. (The multiplier also works in reverse; if spending drops, we can expect equilibrium output to decline by four times as much.) Of course, the multiplier can take on different values, depending on the economy's *MPC*. If the *MPC* is 0.5, the multiplier will be 2; if the *MPC* is 0.8, the multiplier will be 5. As you can see, the size of the multiplier is related directly to the size of the economy's marginal propensity to consume: The larger the *MPC*, the larger the multiplier. This relationship exists because when the *MPC* is larger, a greater fraction of any increase in income is spent—meaning that more income is passed on to the next round of consumers, and the ultimate increase in GDP is larger. Studies of the U.S. economy show that the actual U.S. value of the multiplier in this country is about 2. (The U.S. economy's multiplier is significantly smaller than our hypothetical multiplier because taxes and spending for imports reduce the amount of income remaining to be passed on to the next household. When households pay taxes, they have less money to spend for products. Similarly, the money that goes to purchase Japanese autos and French wines leaves the country and is not available to be passed on to other U.S. consumers. The impact of taxation is discussed in the appendix to this chapter.)

Equilibrium with Unemployment or Inflation

Now that we know how the equilibrium output is determined, we want to consider the desirability—from the standpoint of full employment and price stability—of a particular equilibrium GDP. We want to know whether a particular equilibrium is consistent with full employment, unemployment, or inflation.

THE RECESSIONARY GAP

Chapter 11 explained that a major conclusion of the Keynesian revolution is that a capitalist economy can be in equilibrium at less than full employment. Consider the economy represented in Exh. 13.9. Let's assume that $(C + I)_1$ represents the economy's total expenditure function and that the existing level of equilibrium GDP is $600 billion. Let's make the additional assumption that $700 billion is the full-employment output—the level of output that allows us to achieve our target rate of unemployment. (Recall that our target rate of unemployment is higher than zero because a certain amount of frictional and structural unemployment is unavoidable, even in the best of times.) Given these assumptions, it is obvious that our hypothetical economy is in equilibrium at less than full employment. As we discovered in Chapter 10, this situation can be described as a recession—a period of weak economic activity and relatively high unemployment.[2] The amount by which the equilibrium GDP falls short of full-employment, or potential, GDP is known as the **recessionary gap**. In this instance, the recessionary gap is equal to $100 billion, the difference between the full-employment output of $700 billion and the equilibrium output of $600 billion.

What causes a recession? The problem, in Keynesian terms, is *too little spending*. If full employment is to be achieved, the level of planned spending must be increased so that the total expenditure function intersects the 45-degree line at $700 billion. You can see that a function such as $(C + I)_2$ would give such an intersection. With a multiplier of 4, a $25 billion increase in planned expenditure would be sufficient to increase output by $100 billion and bring about full employment.

---

[2] Technically, a recession is a period during which the economy's real output declines. Of course, if less output is produced, fewer employees are needed and unemployment tends to rise.

EXHIBIT 13.9

The Recessionary Gap

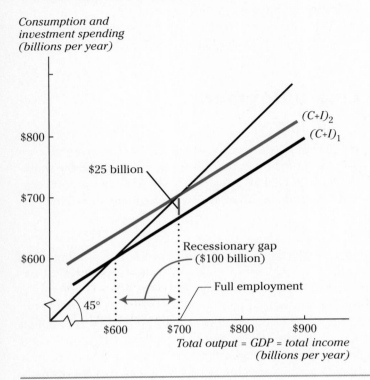

The recessionary gap is the amount by which the equilibrium GDP falls short of full-employment GDP.

THE INFLATIONARY GAP

Although Keynes devoted most of his efforts to studying unemployment, the Keynesian framework can also be used to explain inflation. Referring to Exh. 13.10, let's assume that $(C + I)_1$ is the existing planned expenditure function and that the prevailing level of equilibrium GDP is $800 billion. Recalling that the full-employment output is $700 billion, you will recognize that our hypothetical economy now faces a different problem: inflation.

If $700 billion is the full-employment output, the economy cannot provide more than $700 billion worth of goods and services. In the Keynesian model, full employment implies that the economy is operating at full capacity, that it is not capable of producing any more output. If consumers and investors attempt to purchase more output than the economy is capable of producing, higher prices result as prospective buyers bid against one another. Real GDP, however, will not increase.

EXHIBIT 13.10

The Inflationary Gap

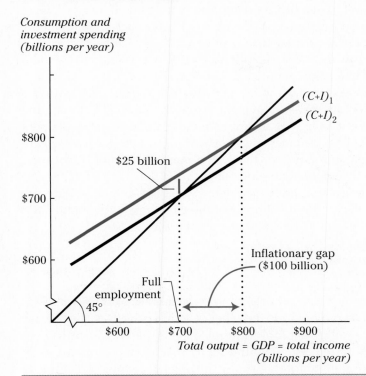

Consumption and investment spending (billions per year)

$(C+I)_1$

$(C+I)_2$

$800

$25 billion

$700

$600

Inflationary gap ($100 billion)

Full employment

45°

$600 $700 $800 $900

Total output = GDP = total income (billions per year)

The inflationary gap is the amount by which the equilibrium GDP exceeds full-employment GDP.

In this simple model, prices are assumed to be constant until full employment is reached. So long as there are unemployed resources, any increase in spending is translated into an increase in output and employment. Once full employment is reached, however, further output increases become impossible. From this point on, increases in spending cannot increase real GDP; they can increase only money GDP. The difference between a GDP of $700 billion and a GDP of $800 billion is not that the larger figure represents more output, but simply that higher prices are being paid for the full-employment output.[3]

The amount by which the equilibrium GDP exceeds full-employment, or potential, GDP is the **inflationary gap**. In this instance, the inflationary gap is

---

[3] In reality, increases in total expenditures or aggregate demand lead to increased output *and* higher prices even before full employment is reached. This possibility is illustrated in the aggregate demand–aggregate supply model, as presented in Chapter 12.

equal to $100 billion, the difference between the full-employment output of $700 billion and the actual output of $800 billion. If inflation is to be eliminated without sacrificing full employment, the level of planned spending must be reduced so that the total expenditure function intersects the 45-degree line at $700 billion. The expenditure function $(C + I)_2$ would give such an intersection. Because the multiplier in our hypothetical ecomony is 4, a $25 billion decrease in planned expenditures would reduce equilibrium GDP by $100 billion, eliminating inflation while still maintaining full employment.

As you can see, the Keynesian model suggests that a market economy does not always come to rest at a full-employment equilibrium. Instead, the equilibrium output may be consistent with unemployment or inflation. The appendix to this chapter will add government spending and taxation to the total expenditure model and will consider how the government's spending and taxing powers can be used to combat unemployment or inflation. Chapter 14 will repeat parts of this discussion in the context of the aggregate demand–aggregate supply model and will consider the impact of the government's spending and taxing decisions on the federal deficit and the public debt.

Summary

According to Keynesian theory, the primary determinant of the level of total output and total employment is the level of total spending. The greater the level of total spending, the more output businesses will want to produce and the more employees they will hire. In a simplified economy with no government sector and no foreign trade, the level of output and employment would be determined by the level of consumption and investment spending.

The most important factor influencing the amount of consumption spending is the level of *disposable income,* or income after taxes. The relationship between disposable income and consumption spending is called the *consumption function.* In Keynesian theory, a positive relationship exists between disposable income and consumption spending; the more people earn, the more they spend.

The way households react to changes in income depends on their *marginal propensity to consume (MPC).* The *MPC* is the fraction of each additional earned dollar that households spend on consumption. The *marginal propensity to save (MPS)* is the fraction of each additional earned dollar that is saved. The *MPC* and *MPS* must add to 1.00, or 100 percent: If *MPC* is 0.80, *MPS* is 0.20.

Profit expectations are the overriding motivation in all investment-spending plans. These expectations are based on a comparison of costs (including the cost of the capital equipment and the cost of borrowing the money to buy that equipment) and revenues (the revenues the investment project is expected to generate). If the investment is expected to generate revenues that exceed all anticipated costs, the investment should be made; if not, the investment should not be made.

In deciding how much output to produce, businesses attempt to estimate the spending plans of consumers and investors. If they estimate demand correctly, they will be able to sell exactly what they produced; hence they will tend to produce the same amount in the next period. If not, they will alter their production plans in order to match demand more closely.

The level of output at which the economy stabilizes is the equilibrium output. The equilibrium output is one that is neither expanding nor contracting and that tends to be maintained. It can be identified by finding the level of output at which total spending (consumption plus investment) is equal to total output. The equilibrium output can be determined graphically by finding the output at which the total expenditures function $(C + I)$ intersects the 45-degree line.

Once the equilibrium output has been established, it will be maintained until there is some change in the spending plans of consumers or investors. To determine the ultimate impact on equilibrium of any change in spending, it is necessary to know the value of the *multiplier (M)*, the number by which any initial change in spending is multiplied to get the ultimate change in equilibrium income and output. The multiplier can be calculated by using either of the following formulas:

$$M = \frac{1}{1 - MPC}$$

or, since $1 - MPC = MPS$,

$$M = \frac{1}{MPS}$$

Perhaps the most important contribution Keynes made was to demonstrate that a market economy can be in equilibrium at less than full employment. He attributed this occurrence to too little spending. The amount by which the equilibrium GDP falls short of full-employment GDP is called the *recessionary gap*. When inflation exists, the problem is too much spending; the economy is attempting to produce too much output. The *inflationary gap* is the amount by which the equilibrium GDP exceeds full-employment GDP.

GLOSSARY

Consumption function. The relationship between disposable income and consumption spending. A consumption function shows the amount that households plan to spend at different levels of income.

Disposable income. Income after taxes. Disposable income is sometimes described as take-home pay.

Dissaving. Taking money out of savings accounts or borrowing in order to finance consumption spending.

Inflationary gap. The amount by which the equilibrium GDP exceeds full-employment, or potential, GDP.

Marginal propensity to consume (MPC). The fraction of any increase in income that is spent on consumption. The formula for the marginal propensity to consume (MPC) is

$$MPC = \frac{\text{Change in consumption spending}}{\text{Change in income}}$$

Marginal propensity to save (MPS). The fraction of any increase in income that households plan to save. The formula for the marginal propensity to save (MPS) is

$$MPS = \frac{\text{Change in saving}}{\text{Change in income}}$$

Multiplier (M). The number by which any initial change in spending is multiplied to get the ultimate change in equilibrium income and output. The formula for the multiplier (M) is

$$M = \frac{1}{1-MPC} \text{ or } M = \frac{1}{MPS}$$

Multiplier effect. The magnified impact on GDP of any initial change in spending.

Recessionary gap. The amount by which the equilibrium GDP falls short of full-employment, or potential, GDP.

Saving. The act of not spending; also, the part of income not spent on goods and services.

STUDY QUESTIONS

Fill in the Blanks

1. According to Keynes, the primary determinant of the level of total output and total employment is the level of

   _____ .

2. The _____ is the fraction of any increase in income that households plan to save.

3. Keynes believed the primary determinant of the level of consumption spending to be

   the level of _____ .

4. In the Keynesian model, if the economy is suffering from unemployment, the problem

   is caused by _____ ;
   if the economy is suffering from inflation,

   the problem is caused by _____ .

5. The _____ shows the precise relationship between income and consumption spending.

6. The level of output that tends to be main-

   tained is called the _____ output.

7. If total spending exceeds the amount necessary to achieve full employment, the economy must be suffering from

   _____ .

8. We can determine the equilibrium output by finding the output at which total

   spending equals _____ .

9. Graphically, equilibrium exists where the total expenditures function (C + I) crosses

   the _____ .

Multiple Choice

1. When Jim's income increased by $1,000, he decided to spend $600 and save the rest. That means his marginal propensity
   a) to save is 0.6.
   b) to consume is $600.
   c) to consume is 0.6.
   d) to consume is 0.4.

2. If the economy's MPS is 0.2, the multiplier would be
   a) 0.8.
   b) 20.
   c) 5.
   d) 4.

   Use the following information to answer questions 3–6.

INCOME	CONSUMPTION
$100 billion	$160 billion
200	240
300	320
400	400
500	480
600	560

3. What is the marginal propensity to consume in this hypothetical economy?
   a) 0.8
   b) 0.5
   c) 0.75
   d) $80

4. At what income level would the consumption function cross the 45-degree line in this hypothetical economy?
   a) $200 billion
   b) $300 billion
   c) $400 billion
   d) $500 billion
   e) None of the above

10. The amount by which the equilibrium GDP falls short of the full-employment

    GDP is called the _____ .

5. If businesses plan to invest $20 billion, what would be the equilibrium level of output in this economy? (*Hint:* Remember what makes up total expenditures.)
   a) $200 billion
   b) $300 billion
   c) $400 billion
   d) $500 billion
   e) None of the above

6. At an income of $700 billion, how much would households desire to consume? (It's not on the schedule, but you can use your previous answers to figure it out.)
   a) $560 billion
   b) $580 billion
   c) $620 billion
   d) $640 billion
   e) $700 billion

7. Assuming that the economy's MPC is 0.8, if autonomous investment spending increases by $15 billion, how much will equilibrium GDP increase?
   a) $15 billion
   b) $30 billion
   c) $45 billion
   d) $60 billion
   e) $75 billion

8. If people expected prices to be higher in the future, this would probably cause
   a) their current consumption function to shift down.
   b) their current saving function to shift up.
   c) their current consumption function to shift up.
   d) the investment function to shift down.

9. Keynes focused particular attention on investment spending because
   a) investment spending is the largest component of total spending.
   b) only investment spending is subject to a multiplier effect.

c) investment spending is very volatile, or changeable.

d) investment spending is the most reliable, or predictable, component of total spending.

10. If the economy produces a level of output that is too small for equilibrium,
   a) there will be an unintended, or unplanned, increase in inventories.
   b) businesses will not be able to sell everything that they've produced.
   c) there will be an unintended, or unplanned, decrease in inventories.
   d) there will be a tendency for output to fall (decline) in the next period.

Questions 11-14 refer to material covered in the appendix to this chapter.

11. Let's assume that the economy is in a significant recession, operating $100 billion below the full-employment output. If the marginal propensity to consume is 0.8, in what direction and by what amount should the level of government spending be changed?
   a) Decrease govenrment spending by $100 billion.
   b) Increase government spending by $100 billion.
   c) Decrease government spending by $20 billion.
   d) Increase government spending by $20 billion.
   e) Increase government spending by $80 billion.

12. Select the best evaluation of the following statement: *Increasing government spending by $10 billion will have a greater impact on the level of equilibrium output than decreasing taxes by the same amount ($10 billion).*
   a) False; both changes will have the same impact on GDP.
   b) False; a $10 billion decrease in taxes will have a greater impact than a $10 billion increase in spending.
   c) True; since only part of the tax reduction will be spent, the remainder will be saved and will not stimulate the economy.
   d) True; a tax reduction will always create twice as much stimulus as a spending increase of equal size.

13. If the marginal propensity to consume is 0.75, a $20 billion increase in personal income taxes will initially reduce consumption spending by
   a) $20 billion.
   b) $80 billion.
   c) $15 billion.
   d) $40 billion.

14. The ultimate impact of the tax increase noted in question 13 would be to
   a) reduce the equilibrium GDP by $20 billion.
   b) reduce the equilibrium GDP by $80 billion.
   c) reduce the equilibrium GDP by $60 billion.
   d) increase the equilibrium GDP by $20 billion.

Problems and Questions for Discussion

1. In the hypothetical economy we explored in this chapter, total income equals disposable income. What assumption makes that true?

2. If the consumption function was a 45-degree line, what would that mean?

3. How do businesses decide which investment projects to pursue and which to reject?

4. Discuss the reasons why the rate of investment spending is less stable than the rate of consumption spending.

5. How can a change in the level of investment spending indirectly cause a change in the level of consumption spending?

6. Referring to Exh. 13.5, assume that the level of autonomous investment is $25 billion instead of $50 billion. What would the equilibrium level of output be?

7. What might cause the level of investment spending to decline, as hypothesized in the preceding question?

8. What is the difference between the equilibrium output and a full-employment equilibrium?

9. What are the recessionary and inflationary gaps? Represent them graphically.

10. What assumption is made about the behavior of prices in the simple model used in this chapter?

ANSWER KEY

Fill in the Blanks

1. total spending
2. marginal propensity to save
3. disposable income
4. too little spending; too much spending
5. consumption function
6. equilibrium
7. inflation
8. total output
9. 45-degree line
10. recessionary gap

Multiple Choice

1. c
2. c
3. a
4. c
5. d
6. d
7. e
8. c
9. c
10. c
11. d
12. c
13. c
14. c

APPENDIX: Incorporating Government Spending and Taxation into the Total Expenditures Model

One conclusion of Keynes's *General Theory* was that government had a responsibility to use its spending and taxation powers to maintain full employment. Today, this is described as *discretionary fiscal policy*—the deliberate changing of the level of government spending or taxation in order to guide the economy's performance. This appendix introduces government spending and taxation into the aggregate expenditures model and then illustrates how fiscal policy can be used to combat unemployment or inflation.

Government Spending and Equilibrium Output

For the sake of our analysis, we assume that the level of government spending is determined by political considerations and is independent of the level of output in our economy.[4] These assumptions allow us to add government spending to the model as an autonomous constant. Recall that investment spending was introduced in the same way in the body of the chapter, as a component of spending that did not vary with GDP.

Exh. A.1 shows how the inclusion of government spending alters the process of determining equilibrium. Let's assume that the government plans to spend $40 billion per year and that it intends to finance its spending by borrowing rather than by imposing taxes. (For clarity, we will introduce government spending first, note the impact on equilibrium output, and then introduce taxation.) To incorporate this decision into our analysis, we need only add the amount of government spending for goods and services *(G)* to the total expenditure function *(C + I)* we constructed in the body of the chapter. In Exh. A.1, total spending is labeled *C + I + G*. Adding government spending raises total spending by $40 billion at every level of output.

The equilibrium output is determined by the intersection of the total expenditure function (now *C + I + G*) and the 45-degree line. You can see that the addition of $40 billion of government spending increases the equilibrium output by $160 billion—that is, from $600 billion to $760 billion. Recall from

---

[4] We use the term *government spending* to mean purchases of goods and services by government. Economists always distinguish between expenditures for goods and services and transfer payments. Government transfer payments are expenditures made by the government for which it receives no goods or services in return (unemployment compensation and Social Security, for example). To avoid unnecessary complexity, our model will ignore transfer payments. The next chapter will discuss the role of transfer payments as "built-in stabilizers" of the economy.

EXHIBIT A.1

Adding Government Expenditures

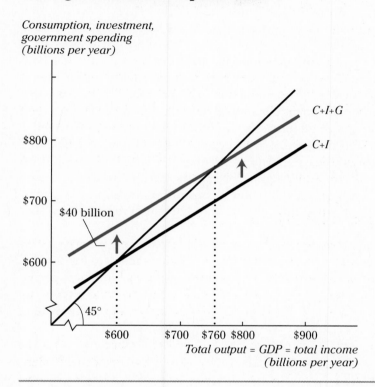

Consumption, investment, government spending (billions per year)

With a multiplier of 4, the addition of $40 billion worth of government spending raises the equilibrium GDP by $160 billion.

Total output = GDP = total income (billions per year)

earlier in the chapter that in our hypothetical economy the marginal propensity to consume is 0.75. The multiplier [$M = 1/(1 - MPC)$], therefore, is 4. This tells us that any change in spending will produce a change in income and output that is four times larger than the initial spending change.

Taxation and Equilibrium Output

Suppose the government decides to collect $40 billion in personal income taxes in order to finance its spending plans. How does this affect the equilibrium level of GDP? The initial impact of this action is to reduce disposable income—income after taxes, or take-home pay—by $40 billion. So long as we ignored taxes, total income (GDP) equaled disposable income (*DI*). But now that we are introducing taxes, this equality no longer holds. The imposition of taxes reduces the amount of disposable income that households have available at any given level of GDP. If disposable income declines, consumption spending will decline. Thus, the ultimate impact of taxation is a reduction in the amount of consumption spending at any given level of GDP. This can be represented by a downward shift of the consumption function, which, in turn, will cause a downward shift of $C + I + G$ (the total expenditure function).

Exh. A.2 shows that the total expenditure function shifts downward by $30 billion when the government imposes taxes of $40 billion. Why doesn't the total expenditure function shift downward by *$40* billion? The answer is that households react to reductions in disposable income by reducing both their consumption and their saving. If the marginal propensity to consume is .75, we know that 75 percent of the reduction in disposable income will come from planned consumption spending, and 25 percent will come from planned saving. Thus, the consumption function—and consequently the total expenditure function—will shift downward by 75 percent of $40 billion, or $30 billion.

Note that in this case the equilibrium level of GDP falls from $760 billion to $640 billion, a reduction of $120 billion. Once again, this represents the impact of the multiplier. The $30 billion reduction in consumption spending is magnified by the multiplier of 4 and thus produces a $120 billion reduction in GDP.

EXHIBIT A.2

The Effect of Taxation

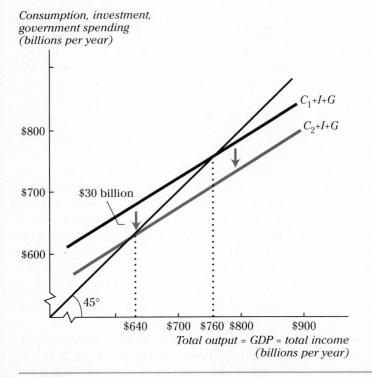

When the government imposes taxes of $40 billion, the total expenditure function shifts down by $30 billion. Because the *MPC* is 0.75, a reduction in disposable income of $40 billion (the amount of the taxes) will reduce consumption spending by 3/4 of that amount, or $30 billion. This $30 billion is then subject to the multiplier of 4; so the ultimate impact of the taxation is to reduce the equilibrium GDP by $120 billion.

Given that government spending and taxation affect total spending and equilibrium output, let's see how changes in government spending and taxation can be used as economic policy tools to combat the problems of unemployment or inflation.

Fiscal Policy to Achieve Full Employment

Suppose our economy's full-employment output is $700 billion. With our present equilibrium of $640 billion, there is a recessionary gap of $60 billion: the economy is experiencing unemployment.

According to the Keynesian model, the source of the problem is too little spending. One corrective approach is the use of discretionary fiscal policy. The appropriate policy response is to increase government spending or reduce taxes (or effect some combination of the two). Let's consider these alternatives.

If government spending is increased while taxes remain unchanged, the amount of total spending in the economy will increase. More spending for goods and services means that businesses will be justified in increasing their production, which will create more jobs.

We must use our knowledge of the multiplier to determine how much more government spending will be necessary. The multiplier in our hypothetical economy is 4; therefore, every additional dollar that the government spends will ultimately produce a $4 increase in total spending and equilibrium output. If we wish to increase GDP by $60 billion, government spending must be increased by $15 billion ($60 billion ÷ 4 = $15 billion). Exh. A.3 shows that a $15 billion increase, when expanded by a multiplier of 4, will produce the needed $60 billion increase in GDP and permit our hypothetical economy to achieve full employment. In an economy with a multiplier of 2, the government would have to increase spending by $30 billion to achieve the same $60 billion increase in GDP. (Recall that studies show the value of the multiplier in the U.S. economy to be approximately 2.)

The goal of full employment can also be pursued by cutting taxes and leaving government spending unchanged. If taxes are reduced, consumers are left with more disposable income, which enables them to increase their consumption spending. This increase in the demand for consumer goods stimulates producers to increase their output and creates additional jobs. Determining the precise amount of a tax reduction to combat unemployment is more complicated than determining the right amount to increase government spending. When taxes are reduced, consumers will not spend all of the additional disposable income the reduction provides; they will save some portion of their increased income.

We saw that $15 billion in increased spending was sufficient to raise equilibrium by $60 billion and eliminate the recessionary gap. By what amount must we reduce income taxes to prompt consumers to spend an additional

EXHIBIT A.3

Expansionary Fiscal Policy

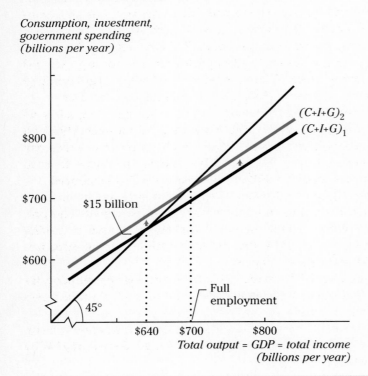

*Consumption, investment,
government spending
(billions per year)*

$800

$700

$15 billion

$600

45°

Full
employment

$640 $700 $800
*Total output = GDP = total income
(billions per year)*

$(C+I+G)_2$
$(C+I+G)_1$

In order to increase the equilibrium output by $60 billion (and achieve full employment), we must either increase government spending by $15 billion or reduce taxes by $20 billion. Either policy will shift the total expenditure function upward by $15 billion. This amount, when expanded by the multiplier of 4, will result in an increase in GDP of $60 billion, the amount needed to reach full employment.

$15 billion? If the *MPC* is 0.75, taxes must be reduced by $20 billion (0.75 × $20 billion = $15 billion).[5] Because consumers will spend 75 percent of any increase in disposable income, a tax reduction of $20 billion will lead to a $15 billion increase in consumption spending and, through the multiplier, a $60 billion increase in equilibrium GDP. Because not all of it will be spent, a tax reduction used to stimulate spending and promote full employment must be somewhat larger than the increase in government spending that would accomplish the same objective.

---

[5] To determine the proper amount to increase or decrease taxes, you must divide the needed change in spending by the *MPC* (needed change in spending ÷ *MPC* = amount of tax change). In this example the needed spending change is $15 billion and the *MPC* is 0.75, and so taxes ought to be altered by $15 billion ÷ 0.75 = $20 billion. Remember that to increase spending, taxes must be *reduced*; so it is a $20 billion tax reduction.

Fiscal Policy to Combat Inflation

When Keynes developed his landmark economic theory in the mid-1930s, his main concern was unemployment. The remedy he prescribed was an expansionary fiscal policy that would increase government spending or reduce taxes to get the economy moving. But Keynes realized that fiscal policy could also serve to combat inflation. If society attempts to purchase more goods and services than the economy is capable of producing, a reduction in government spending or an increase in taxes will help reduce inflationary pressures.

If the government spends less, one component of total spending (G) is reduced directly, and consumption spending (C) is reduced indirectly through the multiplier effect. A tax increase has a different impact. Consumers who pay higher taxes find themselves with less disposable income; this forces them to reduce their consumption spending. Either way, total spending is reduced.

As you might expect, the fiscal policy used to fight inflation is considerably less popular than the policy used to combat unemployment. The prescriptions for dealing with unemployment—reducing taxes and increasing government spending—are generally applauded. Inflation-fighting measures usually meet with less widespread approval.

Test your understanding of the material contained in this appendix by answering the following questions and items 11–14 in the multiple choice section of the study guide.

1. When the government increases spending to combat unemployment, why shouldn't it increase taxes to pay for the increased spending? Why run a deficit instead?

2. Assuming that the economy's MPC is 0.666 and that government spending increases by $20 billion, what would be the impact on the equilibrium level of GDP?

3. If Keynes was correct that consumption spending depends primarily on the level of disposable income, how is it possible for an increase in government spending to lead to an increase in consumption spending?

4. If the prevailing level of output is $800 billion and the full-employment output is $600 billion, and we know that the eonomy's MPC is 0.5, how much should government spending be reduced in order to eliminate the inflation without generating unemployment? If taxes were increased instead, how much would the increase have to be?

5. What advantages can you see to using tax reductions rather than government spending increases to combat unemployment? Can your personal values influence which of these approaches you prefer? Explain.

6. George Humphrey, secretary of the treasury during the Eisenhower administration, once declared. "We cannot spend ourselves rich." What do you suppose he meant? Would Keynes agree? Why or why not?

Fiscal Policy, Debt, and the Deficit

Chapter 12 concluded that a self-correcting mechanism tends to restore the economy to full employment and potential GDP whenever it deviates from those standards. Modern economists are in general agreement about the nature of this adjustment process, though they may disagree about some of the details. One important detail about which there is substantial disagreement is the length of the adjustment process—how long it takes to return the economy to potential GDP when it deviates from that goal. Modern activists, following the lead of John Maynard Keynes, the original activist, accept that the economy will be self-correcting in the long run but recall Keynes's admonition that "In the long-run we're all dead." In other words, we may not want to wait for the adjustment process to run its course. Concern over the speed of the adjustment mechanism led Keynes to call for government intervention to accelerate the process. This chapter examines the possibility that the government's fiscal policy—its spending and taxation policy—can be used to speed the return to potential GDP whenever the economy deviates from that goal. It also considers the limitations of fiscal policy and examines the impact of specific policy measures on the federal budget deficit and the federal debt.

The Existence of Unemployment or Inflation

As we discovered in Chapters 12 and 13, the economy can be in short-run equilibrium at a level of GDP that is larger or smaller than potential. For instance, in Exh. 14.1(a), we find the economy in equilibrium at an output of $800 billion, an output less than the economy's potential GDP of $1,000 billion. Of course, whenever the economy is operating below its potential, the rate of unemployment in the economy exceeds the natural rate. This situation is commonly described as a recession, and the amount by which the equilibrium level of real GDP falls short of potential GDP is known as the **recessionary gap**. In this example, the recessionary gap is equal to $200 billion, the difference between the potential output of $1,000 billion and the actual output of $800 billion.

Exhibit 14.1(b) depicts a different situation. The economy is in equilibrium at an output of $1,250 billion, well beyond the economy's potential GDP.

EXHIBIT 14.1

Recessionary and Inflationary Gaps

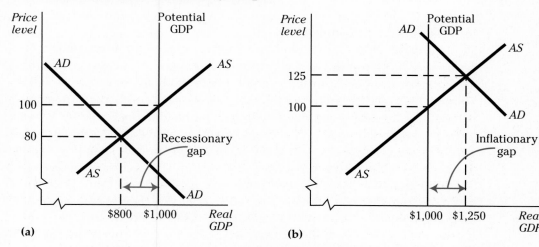

(a)

(b)

A *recessionary gap* exists whenever equilibrium GDP falls short of potential GDP. (a) A recessionary gap of $200 billion, the difference between the potential output of $1,000 billion and the equilibrium output of $800 billion. An *inflationary gap* exists whenever the equilibrium GDP exceeds potential GDP. (b) An inflationary gap of $250 billion, the difference between the potential GDP of $1,000 billion and the equilibrium GDP of $1250 billion.

Because the economy is operating beyond potential, the unemployment rate is less than the natural rate, and the strong demand for labor puts upward pressure on wages and prices. Because operating beyond potential GDP creates inflationary pressures, we describe the excess in equilibrium GDP as the inflationary gap. More precisely, the **inflationary gap** is the amount by which the equilibrium level of real GDP exceeds potential GDP. In this instance the inflationary gap is equal to $250 billion, the difference between the actual output of $1,250 billion and the potential output of $1,000 billion.

Discretionary Fiscal Policy: Combating Unemployment or Inflation

Since the time of Keynes, activist economists have argued that government policies should be used to eliminate recessionary or inflationary gaps rather than waiting for the economy to self-correct. Not all modern economists agree with this activist approach, as you will discover in Chapter 16. In fact, non-activists argue that the economy's performance would be enhanced if government maintained a hands-off approach to the macroeconomy. But policy activism is common throughout the industrialized world and we need to understand the theory behind its use.

One form of policy activism involves discretionary fiscal policy. **Discretionary fiscal policy** is the deliberate changing of the level of government spending or taxation in order to guide the economy's performance. Discretionary fiscal policy attempts to influence an economy's performance by altering the level of spending or aggregate demand in the economy. When a recessionary gap exists and unemployment is above the natural rate, an *expansionary fiscal policy* is called for: Increase government spending, reduce taxes, or do both.[1] Increasing government spending directly increases aggregate demand since it means more government spending at any price level. Tax reductions work indirectly; by reducing taxes, they leave households with more take-home pay which, in turn, tends to stimulate the demand for clothing, furniture, and other consumer items. Either policy would tend to expand the economy to a higher level of equilibrium GDP and lower the

---

[1] We use the term *government spending* to mean purchases of goods and services. Economists always distinguish between expenditures for goods and services and transfer payments. *Government transfer payments* are expenditures made by the government for which it receives no goods or services in return (welfare payments, unemployment compensation, and Social Security benefits, for example).

EXHIBIT 14.2

Using Discretionary Fiscal Policy

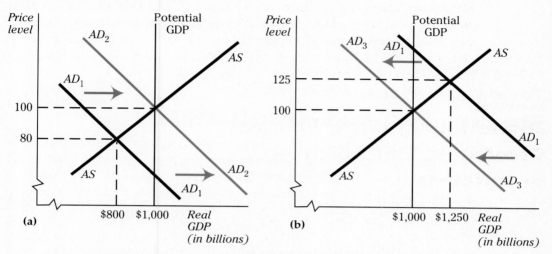

According to activist economists, unemployment can be attacked by using an *expansionary fiscal policy:* increasing government spending or reducing taxes. (a) An expansionary fiscal policy shifts the aggregate demand curve from AD_1 to AD_2, thereby eliminating the recessionary gap and the accompanying unemployment.

Inflationary pressures can be eliminated by employing a *contractionary fiscal policy:* reducing government spending or increasing taxes. (b) A contractionary fiscal policy shifts the aggregate demand curve from AD_1 to AD_3, thereby eliminating the inflationary gap and the accompanying inflationary pressures.

unemployment rate.[2] For instance, in Exh. 14.2(a), we can see that an increase in government spending (or a reduction in taxes) has shifted the AD curve from AD_1 to AD_2, raising the economy's equilibrium GDP from $800 billion to $1,000 billion and the price level from 80 to 100. In short, discretionary fiscal policy has eliminated the recessionary gap and lowered unemployment to the natural rate.

The existence of an inflationary gap would call for a *contractionary fiscal policy:* Government spending should be cut, or taxes should be increased in order to reduce private spending. By reducing aggregate demand, these policies

---

[2] An increase in government spending would actually shift the aggregate demand curve farther than an equal-sized tax reduction would. That's because households will save some portion of the tax reduction.

would tend to contract the level of equilibrium GDP and reduce or eliminate inflationary pressures. For instance, Exh. 14.2(b) shows that by cutting government spending (or increasing taxes), we can reduce aggregate demand from AD_1 to AD_3. This would reduce the equilibrium level of real GDP from $1,250 billion to $1,000 billion (the economy's potential output) and thereby eliminate the inflationary pressures that had existed.

Automatic Fiscal Policy:
The Economy's Automatic Stabilizers

Discretionary fiscal policy, as the term implies, requires Congress to deliberately change the level of government spending and/or taxation. But not all fiscal policy is discretionary; some is automatic. **Automatic stabilizers** are changes in the level of government spending or taxation that occur automatically whenever the level of aggregate income (GDP) changes. This automatic fiscal policy tends to reduce the magnitude of fluctuations in total spending and thereby help prevent wide swings in the level of output and employment.

The federal income tax is one powerful automatic stabilizer. To see how it works, imagine a family earning $50,000 a year and paying $10,000 a year in taxes. (Its average tax rate would be 20 percent since $10,000 is 20 percent of $50,000.) After taxes, our hypothetical family will have $40,000 to spend on food, housing, and whatever else it chooses to purchase.

Now, suppose the economy enters a recession and the family sees its income shrink by $10,000 as a result of reduced hours of work. This will cause the family's tax bill to fall to $8,000, leaving it with $32,000 to spend. The family's ability to purchase goods and services has fallen, but only by $8,000, not by the full $10,000 reduction in income. Other families with falling incomes will have a similar experience; they will receive automatic tax reductions that will cushion the impact of the reductions in income. Because taxes automatically decline with income, the tax system prevents spending from falling as much as it would have if taxes remained constant. This helps to retard the weakening of the economy and prevents unemployment from becoming as severe as it otherwise would.

When the economy strengthens, the tax system operates to dampen inflationary pressures. Increases in income mean higher taxes; consumers are left with less income to spend than they would have if taxes had remained constant. If the higher incomes push families into higher tax brackets (the 30 percent bracket, for example), the increase in after-tax income will be even less.[3]

---

[3] Existing tax law is somewhat progressive; that is, those with higher incomes pay a higher fraction of those incomes in the form of taxes.

Thus, the income tax helps to dampen spending increases and reduce inflationary pressures.

Federal unemployment compensation and state welfare benefits also operate as built-in stabilizers. When the level of economic activity declines and the jobless rate begins to rise, the total amount paid out in the form of unemployment compensation and welfare benefits increases automatically. These expenditures for which government receives no goods or services in exchange are known as **transfer payments**. Government transfer payments compensate somewhat for the declining incomes of the unemployed, and in so doing, they prevent a steeper drop in consumption spending by households. This action retards the downward spiral of spending and slows the deterioration of the economy.

When the economy begins to recover and the unemployment rate drops, these transfer payments automatically decrease, which helps prevent inflation by slowing the growth of spending.

Although automatic stabilizers reduce the magnitude of fluctuations in economic activity, they do not ensure full employment and stable prices. They cannot stop a severe inflation once it is under way, and they cannot pull the economy out of a deep recession. In fact, the same fiscal features that tend to stabilize the economy can also retard the economy's recovery from a recession. As the recovery begins, personal income starts to rise, but higher taxes reduce the growth of spending and therefore slow the recovery. For these reasons, activist economists believe that automatic stabilizers must be supplemented by the kinds of discretionary (deliberate) fiscal policies we examined earlier.

Fiscal Policy and the Federal Budget

When we resort to fiscal policy to combat unemployment or inflation, we are deliberately tampering with the federal budget. That's what discretionary fiscal policy really is—budget policy.

The **federal budget** is a statement of the federal government's planned expenditures and anticipated receipts for the coming year. According to Keynesians, whenever unemployment exists (whenever the unemployment rate is above the natural rate), the federal government should plan a **deficit budget**; that is, it should plan to spend more than it expects to collect in taxes. By taking this action, the government injects the economy with additional spending, or aggregate demand, that should help drive it toward full employment. Inflationary times call for the opposite approach, a **surplus budget**, which expresses the government's intention to spend less than it expects to collect in taxes. A surplus budget helps reduce the amount of aggregate demand in the economy and thereby moderates inflationary pressures. According to the Keynesian model, a **balanced budget**—a plan to match government expenditures and tax revenues—is appropriate only when the economy is operating at full employment, when it has achieved a satisfactory equilibrium and needs neither stimulus nor restraint.

Although the Keynesian, or activist, model indicates that budget deficits make economic sense, that's not the view held by many Americans. In their opinion, deficit spending is always unwise. A government that cannot balance its budget, they contend, is like a spendthrift who lives continually beyond his means; eventually he will suffer financial ruin. But those who voice this blanket condemnation fail to recognize that government deficits arise for a variety of reasons, some of which are legitimate and defensible.

PLANNED AND UNPLANNED DEFICITS AND SURPLUSES

In examining government deficits, we find it useful to distinguish between deficits that are deliberate, or planned, and those that are unintentional, or unplanned. No one preparing the federal budget expects the actual level of government expenditures and tax receipts to agree exactly with the estimates. Changes in the level of national income and employment will mean automatic changes in tax revenues and government expenditures because those changes trigger the automatic stabilizers. The same automatic stabilizers that help reduce the magnitude of economic swings lead to deficits when the economy experiences a downturn and to surpluses during periods of expansion.

Even the most carefully planned budget will be inaccurate if the economy performs in unexpected ways. Consider an experience of the Reagan administration. Early in 1981 President Reagan recommended to Congress a budget with a projected deficit of $45 billion for the 1982 fiscal year. This budget assumed that the economy's real gross domestic product would grow at a rate of 4.2 percent in 1982 and that the unemployment rate would average 7.2 percent for that year. Both assumptions turned out to be incorrect. Real GDP *declined* by 2.1 percent in 1982, and the unemployment rate averaged 9.5 percent. As a result of this unexpectedly weak performance, the federal government's outlay for unemployment compensation and welfare was higher than anticipated, and tax revenues were lower. This produced a budget deficit of approximately $128 billion, a far cry from the administration's $45 billion projection.

Sometimes the economy outperforms the projections of planners. When that happens, the automatic stabilizers have the opposite effect on the government's receipts and expenditures. As the economy expands, tax revenues rise, and expenditures for unemployment compensation decline. This tends to decrease the size of the deficit or increase the size of the surplus. The Clinton administration's experience in 1997 illustrates the point. Prior to the start of the year, the administration estimated a budget deficit of $125 billion. But a booming economy lowered the unemployment rate (and the accompanying payments to the unemployed) and ballooned tax receipts. The result was a deficit of only $22 billion, a much lower figure than anyone had anticipated.

UNEMPLOYMENT AND THE FEDERAL BUDGET

Efforts to balance the budget in the face of a recession can have undesired effects on the economy. Suppose that the economy is initially operating at full employment and that the federal government projects a balanced budget. What will happen to the budget if the economy suddenly weakens and unemployment begins to rise? As you know, the fiscal system's automatic stabilizers will work automatically to retard the downturn. But what will this do to the balanced federal budget? It will push it into deficit.

Suppose that Congress insists on restoring a balanced budget. What should be done to accomplish this objective? The logical response would be to increase taxes and reduce government spending. But wait—this response is clearly inconsistent with the activist remedy for unemployment. The reduced level of government spending and concomitant higher taxes will mean less aggregate demand, which will cause the downturn to deepen and unemployment to worsen. Moreover, because this effort to balance the budget prolongs the recession, it may result in a larger cumulative deficit.

According to the activist model, whenever the economy is in recession, the preferred route to a balanced budget entails a deliberate increase in government spending or a reduction in taxes. Obviously, either measure would increase the short-term deficit, but by stimulating output and employment, either action could help pull the economy out of its depressed state. When the economy improves, tax revenues will rise automatically, and government spending for transfer payments will decline automatically. Thus, expansionary fiscal policy may create a larger deficit in the short run. But by restoring the health of the economy, it can lead to a balanced budget. (How would you expect a Keynesian to react to a law requiring the federal government to balance its budget on an annual basis—the essence of the balanced budget amendment that Congress has been flirting with for several years? The views of Robert Eisner, a long-time activist, are expressed in "Balanced Budget: Bad Economics," on pages 420–421.)

We can see how this process works if we look at the tax cut instituted by President Johnson in the mid-1960s. In 1964 the federal budget was already in deficit when Congress finally approved an $11 billion tax reduction (originally requested by President Kennedy in 1963) designed to push the economy closer to full employment. The stimulus provided by this tax cut helped increase GDP by some $36 billion and lower the unemployment rate from about 6 percent to 4.7 percent. According to Arthur Okun, Chairman of the Council of Economic Advisers under President Johnson, the higher tax revenues that

Use Your Economic Reasoning

Balanced Budget: Bad Economics

By Robert Eisner

Along with two Nobel laureates, Robert Solow of M.I.T. and James Tobin of Yale, I have been soliciting economists' endorsements of a statement opposing a balanced budget amendment to the Constitution. We have initial support from 35 distinguished members of the profession, including seven other Nobel laureates, of various economic philosophy and political persuasion; many hundreds of additional endorsements are now coming in.

I, and many other economists, find the balanced budget amendment personally offensive. We can all understand the views, whether we all share them or not, of those who believe it best to curtail drastically the role of government. But almost all of us recognize that a balanced budget amendment is hardly the best way to accomplish this goal, if it accomplishes it at all. Some conservatives indeed warn that it may prove an invitation either to tax increases to finance still more government expenditures, or to new regulations and mandates on local governments to take the place of federal spending....

Judging from the response we have had thus far, the effort to stop the balanced budget amendment may prove the most concerted attempt by economists to intervene on a matter of public policy since their sadly unsuccessful effort to prevent enactment of the infamous Smoot-Hawley tariff in the 1930s. The failure to stop that protectionist measure is widely viewed as contributing substantially to the Great Depression.

The balanced-budget amendment, if enacted, could similarly turn any future downturn into a major recession. It would perversely destroy the built-in stabilizers of our fiscal system. Currently, tax receipts go down in economic downturns; outlays, such as for unemployment benefits, go up. This tends to cushion the decline by reducing the fall in purchasing power. If a balanced budget were required and a recession started, Congress would be forced, unless a super-majority were to vote an exception, to raise taxes or cut spending; either action would further reduce the public's income.

As proposed in the last Congress, the amendment would allow federal borrowing only if approved by three-fifths majorities of all the members, a very difficult hurdle. Many say, "I balance my checkbook, and state and local governments have balanced budget provisions in their constitutions, why can't the federal government be the same? Why must it borrow?" In fact, almost all of us borrow—to finance our homes, to send our children to college, and to buy cars and other durable goods. Businesses borrow—look at the corporate bond market. State and local governments generally have separate capital budgets; the constraints of balance apply only to current or operating budgets. They borrow for all kinds of capital investment. The balanced budget amendment would put only our federal government under that strict limitation to borrowing.

Finally, the amendment is ludicrous—perhaps fortu-

SOURCE: *Wall Street Journal*, Jan. 22, 1997, p. A14. Reprinted by permission of the *Wall Street Journal*, © 1997 Dow Jones & Company, Inc. All Rights Reserved Worldwide.

nately—in its pretense of enforceability. In one section it declares, "Prior to each fiscal year, the President shall transmit to the Congress a proposed budget for the United States Government for that fiscal year, in which total outlays do not exceed total receipts." What would stop the president from simply estimating prospective receipts high enough to equal outlays? Given the general uncertainty and inaccuracy of such projections, this could be done with reasonable honesty.

Section 1 indeed declares, "Total outlays for any fiscal year shall not exceed total receipts for that year…." But who can say what will actually happen to outlays or receipts? Suppose more people get sick and use more Medicare or Medicaid? Suppose there is a fall in incomes or profits, or employment and tax revenues decline. This section might as well assert that the waves of the Atlantic Ocean shall not cross a certain line. What if they do? Do we put the president or Congress in jail?

On the matter of evasion, I should probably welcome passage of the amendment and set up a consulting firm to make millions by advising how to get around it. One simple technique would be the sale of government assets, which under federal accounting would count as offsets to outlays. We could begin with our national parks, federal

land in general, our oil reserves and all parts of the federally owned transportation infrastructure. I suppose some avid privatizers would welcome all this, but evading the amendment should hardly be the motivation….

Another menace the amendment could spawn would be a great increase in regulations and mandates to states, private business and individuals to pay for out of their own budgets what the federal government could no longer afford to pay for out of its own. In general, federal aid to state and local governments, currently some $200 billion per year, might be the first to take the hit, with disastrous results. One need only recall the near-collapses, in recent years, of the economies in New England, California

and Texas. Who would bail them out if their own tax revenues again declined and there were surges of claims for unemployment benefits, food stamps and general assistance?

The irony of all this is that our budget deficit has come far down without any constitutional amendment. It has fallen from $270 billion in 1992 to $107 billion in 1996. At 1.3% of our gross domestic product, it is the smallest of any major industrial nation. If Congress and the president decide that a balanced budget is to be achieved—regardless of the costs—they can certainly have one. But all economists should band together to stop the passage of a constitutional amendment that would tarnish the economy, the Constitution and our good names.

USE YOUR ECONOMIC REASONING

1. Eisner states that the enactment of a balanced budget amendment could "turn any future downturn into a major recession." How could the amendment produce that result?

2. What does Eisner mean when he says that the amendment would "perversely destroy the built-in stabilizers of our fiscal system"?

3. According to Eisner, declaring that "Total outlays for any fiscal year shall not exceed total receipts for that year…" is similar to asserting that "the waves of the Atlantic Ocean shall not cross a certain line." In what sense are the two statements similar?

4. Eisner believes that it is "perhaps fortunate" that the balanced budget amendment is too vague to be enforceable. Why is this fortunate?

resulted from the improved economy brought the federal budget into surplus in the first half of 1965.[4]

The Public Debt

Whenever the federal government incurs a deficit—be it planned or unplanned—it must finance that deficit by borrowing. This is accomplished by instructing the U.S. Treasury to sell government bonds to individuals, businesses, financial institutions, and government agencies. Each of these transactions increases the **public debt**—the accumulated borrowings of the federal government. The public debt is often referred to as the national debt. At the end of 1997, the U.S. national debt stood at $3.7 trillion, a figure so large that it is virtually beyond the comprehension of most of us. That amount represents all the borrowing it took to finance several wars, numerous economic downturns, and a variety of government projects and programs.

CONCERNS ABOUT THE PUBLIC DEBT

The size and growth of the public debt trouble many Americans. Some of their concerns are justified and some are not. In this section we want to lay to rest some myths and examine the real burden of the debt.

Can We Ever Pay Off the Debt?   A common misconception about the public debt is that it must be paid off at some time in the future. In reality, there is no requirement that the federal government ever pay off the debt. The government simply refinances the debt year after year with new borrowing. As government bonds become due, the Treasury sells new bonds to take their place. So long as there is a market for government bonds, the government will keep issuing them. And because the U.S. government bonds are probably the most secure investment in the world today, that market is not likely to disappear.

If this seems like sleight of hand to you, it really isn't. In fact, it's commonplace outside of government. For example, you might decide to buy a new car before you've finished paying for the one you're driving now. You would pay off the original loan but take out a new, probably larger loan on the new car. Businesses are constantly doing the same thing—paying off some loans as they come due and at the same time borrowing more money to finance additional expansion.

Does the Public Debt Impose a Burden on Future Generations?   Some critics of the debt suggest that it imposes an unfair burden on future generations,

---

[4] Arthur M. Okun, *The Political Economy of Prosperity* (New York: W.W. Norton, 1967), pp. 47–48.

who will be forced to pay higher taxes in order to make the interest payments on the debt.

What this logic overlooks is that one person's debt is another person's asset. Future generations will inherit not only the public debt but also the bonds and other securities that make up the debt. When a future generation pays taxes to service the debt, its members will also be the recipients of the interest payments made by the government. In a sense, this future generation will be paying itself. Of course, some members of the generation will pay more in additional taxes than they receive in interest, while others will receive more in interest income than they pay in additional taxes. This will lead to some income redistribution between the members of the generation; some will be better off, and other will be worse off. If this results in greater inequality, we may not like the result. But it's certainly a far cry from the claim that the debt is burdening an entire generation.

Isn't the Foreign-Owned Debt Particularly Burdensome? It is true that some of our public debt is owed to foreigners, and this portion does threaten to burden future generations. You and your children will pay taxes in order to provide interest payments to foreign investors, whose dollars thus acquired will permit them to claim a share of the goods and services that might otherwise go to Americans. Consequently, our standard of living may be lowered somewhat.

The percentage of the debt owed to foreigners has been increasing since 1984, when foreign interests owned about 13% of the debt. The rate of increase was gradual until 1995, but has been dramatic since then. In 1997, foreigners owned 34% of the debt, and received almost 35% of all interest payments on the debt. These percentages are well above what we have come to expect, and are a source of concern for the reason noted above. The next section will clarify the significance of these changes.

Can Americans Afford the Interest Payments on the Growing Public Debt? Even if the federal government never has to pay off the national debt, it must continue to make interest payments on what it owes. After all, that's why people buy securities—to earn interest.

The ease with which Americans can pay the interest on the debt depends on how rapidly their incomes are growing. As long as incomes are growing at the same rate as the interest payments, those interest payments will continue to absorb the same fraction of the average taxpayer's paycheck. But if interest payments grow more rapidly than income, they will begin to absorb a larger share.

If we all owned equal shares of the public debt, paying higher taxes would be offset by receiving interest payments on our shares. But whereas all people pay taxes, only some hold bonds and receive interest on the national debt. To the extent that bondholders commonly have higher incomes to begin with, this process tends to produce greater inequality. This effect is at least partially modified by our progressive income tax system. Those with higher incomes may receive more in interest payments, but they also pay more in taxes.

The higher tax rates needed to service the debt (that is, to make interest payments on it) may also have a negative effect on the incentive to work and earn taxable income. If individuals are allowed to keep less of what they earn, some may choose to work less. Other may attempt to avoid taxation by performing work that is not reported to taxing authorities—work for friends and barter transactions, for example.

Until about 1975, the burden imposed on taxpayers by the interest charges on the public debt was relatively stable. Exhibit 14.3 shows that although interest payments were growing, so was our GDP—our measure of the economy's income and output. Thus, our ability to make those interest payments was growing also. The last column in Exh. 14.3 shows that from World War II until 1975, interest payments on the debt represented a relatively constant fraction of GDP—between 1.3 and 1.8 percent. Then, in the late 1970s and early 1980s, the interest cost of the debt began to grow much more rapidly than GDP, primarily as a result of the record budget deficits that characterized this period. (Note that interest payments on the debt climbed to 2 percent of GDP in 1980 and to 3.4 percent of GDP in 1990.) This trend has been a major concern for economists and politicians. Fortunately, in 1992 interest payments began to decline as a percent of GDP. By 1995 they had dropped to 3.2% of GDP, and by 1997 to 3.0% of GDP, the lowest fraction since 1984. This new trend reflects the smaller deficits of the last several years, deficits that have fallen partly because of budget restraint but largely because of the strong performance of the economy. For the present at least, interest payments represent a manageable fraction of GDP.

ECONOMIC GROWTH, DEFICITS, AND CROWDING OUT

Ultimately, the public debt is water under the bridge; it represents past decisions that can't be changed. Economists emphasize the importance of focusing on the present—and the future—rather than the past. If we want future generations to live well and to be able to cope with future taxes, we need to make decisions that will ensure the strong growth of the economy, so that future incomes will be high.

Ensuring economic growth requires that we think about how government spends its money. Consider your own spending decisions for a moment. If you spend money to take an accounting class or learn how to use computer software, that's an investment in your future; it will provide you with future satisfaction and future income. But if you spend the same money to pay for a Colorado ski vacation or a trip to Acapulco, that's a form of consumption spending, and all you'll have to show for your expenditures is some pleasant memories. Politicians and government bureaucrats need to recognize the

EXHIBIT 14.3

The Public Debt and Interest Payments in Relation to Gross Domestic Product

YEAR	PUBLIC DEBT (billions)	INTEREST PAYMENT ON DEBT (billions)	GROSS DOMESTIC PRODUCT (billions)	INTEREST AS A PERCENTAGE OF GDP
1930	$ 16.2	$ 0.7	$ 90.7	0.8%
1935	28.7	0.8	68.7	1.2
1940	42.7	0.9	95.4	0.9
1945	235.2	3.1	212.0	1.5
1950	219.0	4.8	265.8	1.8
1955	226.6	4.9	384.7	1.3
1960	236.8	6.9	504.6	1.4
1965	260.8	8.6	671.0	1.3
1970	283.2	14.4	985.4	1.5
1975	394.7	23.2	1,509.8	1.5
1980	709.8	52.5	2,644.1	2.0
1985	1,499.9	129.5	3,967.7	3.3
1990	2,410.7	184.2	5,481.5	3.4
1995	3,603.4	232.2	7,265.4	3.2
1997	3,771.1	244.0	8,083.4	3.0

SOURCE: Economic Report of the President, 1998.

same distinction. If they channel more money into scientific research or education, those decisions are likely to increase future incomes. If they channel more money into Social Security, their decision will make retirees happier, but it won't contribute to the growth of the economy.

One important criticism of deficit spending is that it tends to reduce economic growth by crowding out investment spending. According to this argument, when the federal government borrows money to finance additional spending, it must compete with private borrowers for funds. Under certain circumstances this increased demand for funds will drive up interest rates, which will discourage private businesses from borrowing for investment purposes. This phenomenon is known as **crowding out**: Government borrowing pushes aside, or crowds out, private borrowing.

Crowding out has two important consequences that we need to consider. First, crowding out tends to reduce the expansionary impact of any increase in government spending. To illustrate, suppose that a deficit-financed increase in government spending would (in the absence of crowding out) increase the economy's equilibrium GDP by $100 billion. If the higher interest rates associated with government's borrowing reduce investment spending, that reduction will partially offset the expansionary impact of the government's fiscal policy. As a result the economy's equilibrium will expand by less than $100 billion.

Second, crowding out impacts the economy's rate of economic growth. Unlike consumption spending, investment spending allows businesses to expand their productive capacity and produce more output in the future than they can today. In other words, investment spending permits the economy to grow and, by making more goods and services available, increases the society's standard of living. To the extent that crowding out reduces the level of investment spending, it hinders economic growth and thereby harms future generations.

Keynesians have long argued that crowding out should be a problem only when the economy is operating at, or near, potential GDP. If there are ample unemployed resources (if the economy is operating at less than its potential GDP), the major impact of deficit spending should be to stimulate the economy, raise incomes, and increase the level of saving. With more saving available to be borrowed and with more total spending in the economy, business investment may actually increase rather than decrease as a result of the deficit. But when the economy has reached potential, gains in real income and saving may be slight; then government borrowing may very well crowd out private borrowing.

Modern economists, including activists, add another caution regarding deficit spending. As we've already seen, not all government spending is alike; some forms tend to produce future economic growth while others produce no such benefits. Deficits that go to finance investment in roads or government infrastructure have a twofold impact: They stimulate the economy in the short run, and they allow for income growth in the long run. Consumption spending provides only the short-run stimulus. Therefore, the more we can use our deficits to finance investment-like expenditures rather than consumption, the more likely we are to leave future generations happy for the choices we made.

The Limits to Fiscal Policy

As we've seen, Keynesian theory calls for budget deficits during periods of high unemployment and surpluses during periods of significant inflation. But the recent budget history is one of continuing deficits, even during periods of low unemployment. In short, Congress has been unable or unwilling to reduce spending (or increase taxes), even when Keynesian theory suggests that such changes are appropriate. We conclude our discussion by briefly examining this "expansionary bias" and two other problems that may complicate efforts to use discretionary fiscal policy to guide the economy's performance.

THE EXPANSIONARY BIAS

As you know, activists call for an expansionary fiscal policy to combat unemployment and a contractionary policy to combat inflation. But expansionary policies are more attractive politically than contractionary policies. Incumbent politicians don't want to sacrifice votes, and voters don't want to pay higher taxes—nor do they want to lose the government programs that benefit them. The result is a bias in favor of expansionary fiscal policies. It may be relatively easy for Congress to pass measures to stimulate the economy, but it's quite difficult to muster the votes necessary to trim government spending or increase taxes. This bias has led to ongoing deficits in good times and bad and has significantly tarnished the image of discretionary fiscal policy.

TIME LAGS

Often a substantial interlude passes between the time when a policy change is needed and the economic impact of any change that actually takes place. This lag may reduce the effectiveness of the remedial fiscal policy; in some instances it may even make the change counterproductive.

There are several reasons for this time lag. First, the economy does not always provide clear signals as to what the future will bring. This means that some lag may occur before the need for a policy change is recognized. Second, even after the need is acknowledged, action is historically slow to transpire. It takes a certain amount of time to draft legislation and get it through Congress, even if lawmakers are in general agreement that action is needed. Third, when the bill is finally passed, more time is required for implementation, and still more time is needed for the economy to begin to respond.

These lags mean that by the time the effects of the policy are felt, they may well be the wrong policies for the state of the economy. Remember, the economy has a self-correcting mechanism; it will ultimately eliminate any recessionary or inflationary gap by itself. Of course, it makes no sense to implement a long-awaited tax cut just as the economy has begun to recover from a recession on its own. Extra disposable income at this time could be the stimulus that leads to inflation.

The existence of these policy lags limits the effectiveness of fiscal policy as a vehicle for guiding the economy's performance. Today, even modern Keynesians agree that policymakers should not attempt to use fiscal policy to eliminate every minor increase in unemployment. Instead, discretionary policies should be reserved for major downturns, situations in which the lag will be of less critical importance.

CROWDING OUT—AGAIN

As you already know, when the federal government borrows money to finance its deficit spending, such borrowing may drive up interest rates. This, in turn, may reduce private investment spending. If that happens, the net effect of the increased investment spending will not be as beneficial as it would be if private investment had not been reduced. In addition, the reduced rate of investment spending will mean a slower rate of economic growth.

By now you can see that discretionary fiscal policy is not without its limitations. The significance of these limitations is open to debate. In general, Keynesians believe that fiscal policy can be useful when employed correctly and selectively. But other economists disagree. Monetarists are economists who believe that the problem of crowding out makes fiscal policy essentially useless. New classical economists argue that fiscal policy is ineffective because individuals anticipate its impact and take actions that neutralize the government's efforts. These economists believe that an expansionary fiscal policy does nothing but cause inflation. This isn't the place to take a detailed look at the monetarists and the new classical economists; their views will be examined in Chapter 16. For now, the important point is that economists disagree about the advisability of using discretionary fiscal policy to guide the economy's performance.

Summary

According to the self-correcting model, the economy can be in short-run equilibrium at a level of GDP that is larger or smaller than potential. Whenever the economy is in equilibrium below potential, the rate of unemployment exceeds the natural rate, and a recessionary gap exists. The *recessionary gap* is the amount by which the equilibrium level of real GDP falls short of potential GDP. Whenever the level of equilibrium GDP exceeds potential, the unemployment rate is less than the natural rate, and an inflationary gap exists. The *inflationary gap* is the amount by which the equilibrium level of real GDP exceeds potential GDP.

Activist economists argue that government policies should be used to eliminate recessionary or inflationary gaps whenever they exist. One form of policy activism involves the use of discretionary fiscal policy. *Discretionary fiscal policy* is the deliberate changing of the level of government spending or taxation in order to guide the economy's performance. According to activists, when a recessionary gap exists and unemployment exceeds the natural rate, the appropriate fiscal policy would involve increasing government spending or reducing taxes. Either of these policies would tend to increase aggregate demand and close the recessionary gap. When an inflationary gap exists, government spending should be reduced or taxes should be increased. These policies will reduce aggregate demand and thereby reduce inflationary pressures.

In addition to discretionary fiscal policy, the economy contains automatic stabilizers that help to improve the economy's performance. *Automatic stabilizers* are the changes in the level of government spending or taxation that occur automatically whenever the level of aggregate income (GDP) changes. The federal income tax and unemployment compensation are examples of automatic stabilizers. These features of the fiscal system help to reduce the magnitude of fluctuations in total spending and thereby help prevent wide swings in the level of output and employment.

When we resort to fiscal policy to combat unemployment or inflation, we are deliberately tampering with the *federal budget*. When unemployment exists, the Keynesian model suggests that government should plan a *deficit budget* in order to stimulate the economy. When inflation is a problem, a *surplus budget* is called for. Only when the economy is operating at full employment is a *balanced budget* appropriate.

When the federal government incurs a deficit, it finances that deficit by borrowing. This results in an increase in the *public debt*—the accumulated borrowings of the federal government.

The public debt is a source of concern to many Americans and does impose some burdens on our society. That the government must make interest payments on the debt means that taxes will be higher than would otherwise be necessary. Since not all taxpayers are bondholders, this results in some income redistribution from taxpayers in general to bondholders in particular. In addition, the dollars that foreign investors acquire as interest payments permit them to claim a share of the goods and services produced in our economy.

The burden of the debt is perhaps best represented by interest payments (on the debt) as a fraction of GDP. This ratio increased in the 1980s but has been declining since 1992. In order to keep this ratio low, government must consider the impact of its policies on economic growth. For instance, to the extent that government spending is channeled into investment-like expenditures (such as constructing infrastructure or financing scientific research) rather than expenditures that promote current consumption (Social Security, for instance), its policies can help to expand GDP and provide future generations with the additional income needed to meet future tax obligations.

Critics of discretionary fiscal policy argue that deficit-financed government spending can be harmful to economic growth because it tends to crowd out private investment spending. Crowding out occurs when government borrowing pushes up interest rates and the higher interest rates reduce, or crowd out, investment spending. Because crowding out reduces investment spending, it offsets, at least partially, the expansionary effect of activist fiscal policy. And because investment spending plays a major role in expanding the economy's productive capacity, this reduction in the rate of investment spending will tend to reduce economic growth.

The possibility of crowding out is one criticism of discretionary fiscal policy, but there are others. Another major criticism stems from the often substantial time lags that occur between the appearance of a problem (a recessionary or inflationary gap) and the economic impact of a remedial policy. As a consequence, by the time the policy is felt, it may no longer be appropriate to the state of the economy. Additionally, expansionary fiscal policy is more attractive politically than contractionary fiscal policy. This makes it easy to incur deficits (and expand the public debt) but difficult to generate surpluses (and contract the debt). In spite of these criticisms, modern activists continue to believe that fiscal policy has a role to play in guiding the economy's performance.

GLOSSARY

Automatic stabilizers. Changes in the level of government spending or taxation that occur automatically whenever the level of aggregate income (GDP) changes.

Balanced budget. A plan to match government expenditures and tax revenues.

Crowding out. The phenomenon that occurs when increased government borrowing drives up interest rates and thereby reduces the rate of investment spending.

Deficit budget. A plan to spend more than will be collected in tax receipts.

Discretionary fiscal policy. The deliberate changing of the level of government spending or taxation in order to guide the economy's performance.

Federal budget. A statement of the federal government's planned expenditures and anticipated receipts for the upcoming year.

Inflationary gap. The amount by which the equilibrium level of real GDP exceeds potential GDP.

Public debt. The accumulated borrowings of the federal government; also known as the national debt.

Recessionary gap. The amount by which the equilibrium level of real GDP falls short of potential GDP.

Surplus budget. A plan to collect more in taxes than will be spent.

Transfer payments. Expenditures for which no goods or services are received in exchange.

STUDY QUESTIONS

Fill in the Blanks

1. According to the Keynesian model, if an economy is experiencing unemployment, the federal government should

   _____ or

   _____ or do both.

2. If the federal government spends more than it takes in from tax revenues, we say

   that it is incurring a _____ ;

   if it takes in more in taxes than it spends, it

   has a _____ .

3. The deliberate changing of government spending or taxation in order to guide the economy's performance is

   _____ .

4. _____ tend to

reduce the magnitude of fluctuations in total spending without any action by policymakers.

5. According to the Keynesian model, the appropriate fiscal policy to combat inflation

would be to _____

or _____ or do both.

6. If the economy is experiencing full employment, deficit spending may lead to

_____ .

7. According to activists, a _____

budget would be appropriate if the economy was operating at full employment.

8. The accumulated borrowings of the federal government are called the

_____ .

9. Our economy's automatic stabilizers include unemployment compensation,

welfare benefits, and the _____ .

10. Political considerations may make it particularly difficult to use fiscal policy in

combating _____ .

Multiple Choice

1. According to Keynesian activists, when the economy is experiencing unemployment, the federal government should
   a) increase taxes.
   b) reduce government spending.
   c) deliberately incur a surplus budget.
   d) reduce taxes.

2. When an inflationary gap exists, activists would recommend a
   a) tax reduction.
   b) surplus budget.
   c) increase in government spending.
   d) deficit budget.

Use the following exhibit in answering questions 3–6

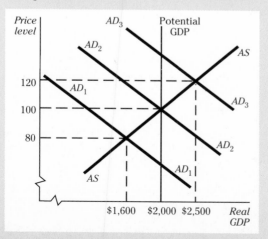

3. If the economy is in equilibrium at the intersection of AD_1 and AS, then
   a) a recessionary gap exists; the gap is equal to $400 billion.
   b) a recessionary gap exists; the gap is equal to $900 billion.
   c) an inflationary gap exists; the gap is equal to $400 billion.
   d) an inflationary gap exists; the gap is equal to $900 billion.

4. If the economy is in equilibrium at the intersection of the AS curve and
   a) AD_1, activists would recommend a surplus budget.
   b) AD_2, activists would recommend a balanced budget.
   c) AD_3, activists would recommend a deficit budget.
   d) AD_2, activists would recommend a deficit budget.

5. **Review Question:** Suppose the economy is in short-run equilibrium at an output of $1,600 billion. If activist policies are not used, the economy will
   a) eventually return to an output of $2,000 billion but at a price level less than 80.
   b) eventually return to an output of $2,000 billion but at a price level of 120.
   c) remain at an output of $1,600 billion indefinitely.
   d) eventually return to an output of $2,000 billion but at a price level of 100.

6. **Review Question.** Suppose the economy is in short-run equilibrium at an output of $2,500 billion. If activist policies are not used, the economy will
   a) return to an output of $2,000 billion when wage contracts expire and the aggregate demand curve shifts to the left.
   b) remain at an output of $2,500 billion indefinitely.
   c) return to an output of $2,000 billion when wage contracts are renegotiated and the aggregate supply curve shifts left.
   d) return to an output of $2,000 billion when the aggregate demand curve automatically shifts back to AD_2.

7. Which of the following is *not* an advantage of automatic stabilizers?
   a) They do not involve the political hassle associated with discretionary fiscal policy.
   b) They help speed recovery from a recession.
   c) They go to work automatically, so that lags are minimal.
   d) They help prevent a minor downturn from becoming a major recession.

8. Because of automatic stabilizers, the budget will
   a) tend toward surplus during a recession.
   b) tend toward deficit during an economic expansion.
   c) tend toward deficit during a recession.
   d) always remain in balance.

9. According to the Keynesian model, when the economy is in a recession, the shortest route to a balanced budget may entail
   a) higher taxes.
   b) less government spending.
   c) lower taxes and more government spending.
   d) both a and b.

10. Which of the following statements is false?
    a) If the economy is operating at full unemployment, a reduction in taxes may increase inflationary pressures.
    b) If the economy is experiencing unemployment, increased government spending may help combat the problem.
    c) Deficit spending is desirable only when the economy is experiencing inflation.
    d) If we attempt to balance the budget during a period of unemployment, we may aggravate the unemployment problem.

11. A legitimate concern regarding the national debt relates to
    a) the higher taxes that are necessary to make the interest payments on the debt.
    b) our inability to pay off such a large sum.
    c) the fraction of the debt owed to foreign factions.
    d) both a and c.

12. "Crowding out" occurs when
    a) U.S. producers lose sales to foreign competition.
    b) an increase in taxes results in a lower level of consumption spending.
    c) foreign interests buy government securities.
    d) government borrowing forces up interest rates and reduces the level of private investment spending.

13. Deficit spending is *least* likely to harm economic growth if it
    a) occurs when the economy is operating at or beyond potential GDP.
    b) is used to finance increases in transfer payments.
    c) crowds out a substantial amount of investment spending.
    d) is used to finance research and development efforts.

14. The lags associated with discretionary fiscal policy
    a) make it more effective.
    b) may make it counterproductive.
    c) apply only to changes in government spending, not to changes in tax rates.
    d) apply only to changes in tax rates, not to changes in government spending.

15. The phrase *expansionary bias* refers to the fact that
    a) discretionary fiscal policy works with a lagged effect.
    b) politicians are more willing to lower taxes and increase spending than they are to do the opposite.
    c) policymakers tend to overestimate the size of the recessionary gap.
    d) deficit-financed government spending can lead to crowding out.

Problems and Questions for Discussion

1. When the government increases spending to combat unemployment, why shouldn't it increase taxes to pay for the increased spending? Why run a deficit instead?

2. Deficit spending for education and scientific research may impose less of a tax burden on future generations than deficit-financed increases in transfer payments. Explain.

3. Some experts argue that the ratio of interest payments (on the debt) to GDP is the most reasonable measure of the burden the public debt imposes on society. Explain.

4. Most deficits are not the result of discretionary fiscal policy; they are the result of downturns in the economy. Explain.

5. Why is the fraction of the debt owed to foreigners more troublesome than the fraction we owe to ourselves?

6. What advantages can you see to using tax reductions rather than government spending increases to combat unemployment?

Can your personal values influence which of these approaches you prefer? Explain.

7. George Humphrey, secretary of the treasury during the Eisenhower administration, once declared: "We cannot spend ourselves rich." What do you suppose he meant? Would Keynes agree? Why or why not?

8. List the various types of lags associated with fiscal policy. Why is the existence of lags a serious limitation of such policies?

9. Suppose the federal government decided to pay off the public debt. How would it go about doing it? What do you suppose would be the impact on the economy?

10. Concern over continuing federal deficits has spawned a movement to amend the Constitution of the United States to require the federal government to balance its budget each year. Can you think of any reasons to argue against a balanced budget amendment? Why would it be difficult to carry out such a rule during a recession?

ANSWER KEY

Fill in the Blanks

1. increase government spending, decrease taxes

2. deficit; surplus

3. discretionary fiscal policy

4. automatic stabilizers

5. reduce government spending, increase taxes

6. inflation

7. balanced

8. public debt, or national debt

9. income tax

10. inflation

Multiple Choice

1. d	4. b	7. b	10. c	13. d
2. b	5. a	8. c	11. d	14. b
3. a	6. c	9. c	12. d	15. b

CHAPTER 15

Money, Banking, and Monetary Policy

1. State the three basic functions of money and explain each.
2. Distinguish between money and near money.
3. Distinguish between the M-1 and M-2 money supply definitions.
4. Explain how depository institutions create money.
5. Calculate the deposit multiplier and explain its purpose.
6. Discuss the functions of the Federal Reserve.
7. Define monetary policy.
8. Describe the three major policy tools the Fed uses to control the money supply.
9. Explain how changes in the money supply lead to changes in output, employment, and prices.
10. Discuss the factors that limit the effectiveness of monetary policy.

Everything you've read thus far in the text has implied a monetary system—the existence of some kind of money. Most of us take the use of money for granted. We pay our bills in money and expect to be paid in money. We compare prices, incomes, and even gross domestic products in terms of money. But exactly what is money, and why is it essential to an economic system? What determines the amount of money in existence, and where does it come from? In this chapter we will provide answers to those questions. We begin by considering the functions performed by money and deciding what constitutes money in the U. S. economy. Next, we examine how banks "create" money, and consider why individuals can't do the same. Then we introduce you to the Federal Reserve—the independent government agency responsible for regulating the money supply and performing other duties related to the banking system. You will discover how the Fed attempts to use monetary policy to guide the economy's performance and what the limitations of its policies are. Let's start by examining what is meant by money.

What Is Money?

Economists define money in terms of the functions it performs; anything that performs the functions of money *is* money. Money performs three basic functions. First, money serves as a **medium of exchange:** the generally accepted means of payment for goods and services. A medium of exchange enables members of a society to transact their business without resorting to barter. In a barter economy, goods are exchanged for goods. A shoemaker who wants to buy a painting must locate an artist in need of shoes. As you can imagine, this requirement makes trading slow and burdensome. Money facilitates trade by permitting the shoemaker to exchange shoes for money and then use the money to purchase a painting or other goods and services.

The second function of money is to provide a **standard of value,** a unit for expressing the prices of goods and services. In a barter economy, we would need an almost endless list of prices, one for each possible exchange. For example, we might find that one painting equals (exchanges for) one pair of shoes and that one pair of shoes equals four bushels of apples and that four bushels of apples equals two shirts. Which is more expensive: a shirt or a pair of shoes? It may take you a moment to figure out the answer because the absence of a standard of value makes the communication and comparison of prices very difficult. The use of money simplifies this process by enabling us to state all prices in terms of a particular standard of value, such as the dollar. Using the dollar as a standard of value, we can easily determine that if a pair of shoes sells for $50 and a shirt sells for $25, the shoes are twice as expensive as the shirt.

Finally, money is a **store of value,** a vehicle for accumulating or storing wealth to be used at some future date. A tomato farmer would find it difficult to accumulate wealth in the form of tomatoes. They don't keep very well! Money is not a perfect store of value, especially in inflationary times, but clearly it is better than a bushel of perishable tomatoes. By exchanging the tomato crop for money, the farmer can begin to build a nest egg for retirement or to save for some major purchase—a tractor or a new barn, for example. In a sense, the availability of a store of value widens the range of spending choices available to individuals and businesses. Their options are no longer limited to what they can afford to buy (trade for) with a single period's income.

MONEY AND NEAR MONEY

What qualifies as money in the U.S. economy? We all know that coins and paper currency are money, and a check is usually as good as cash.

Non-interest-bearing checking deposits at commercial banks[1] are known as **demand deposits** since the bank promises to pay at once, or "on demand," the amount specified by the owner of the account. Checks drawn on demand-deposit accounts are an accepted medium of exchange; they are measured in dollars, the standard of value in the United States, and it is certainly possible to accumulate wealth in your checking account. But although it is relatively easy to agree that currency—coins and paper money—and demand deposits are money, some other assets are more difficult to categorize. An **asset** is anything of value owned by an entity—that is, by an individual or an organization, such as a business. Many assets perform some, but not all, of the functions of money. Others perform all the functions of money but do so incompletely.

One debate among economists concerns the proper classification of **savings deposits**—interest-bearing deposits at banks and savings institutions. The traditional passbook savings account cannot be used directly to purchase goods and services; hence, such deposits do not qualify as a medium of exchange. As a consequence, economists have generally classified savings deposits as **near money**—assets that are not money but that can be converted quickly into money. Not everyone has supported this position, however. Some economists argue that savings deposits should be considered money because they can be converted easily into cash or demand deposits and therefore have essentially the same impact on spending as other financial assets do.

Innovations in banking, moreover, have blurred the distinction between savings deposits and demand deposits. Consider, for example, the negotiable order of withdrawal (NOW) account commonly offered by banks and other financial institutions. The **NOW account** is essentially a savings account on which the depositor is permitted to write checks. Here we seem to have the best of both worlds: the convenience of a checking account plus the earning power of a savings account. Banks have also developed automatic transfer service (ATS) accounts, in which funds from savings can be transferred automatically to a checking account. These types of deposits probably should be considered along with demand deposits as a form of money. But we still face the task of categorizing financial assets that do not function as media of exchange. These include passbook savings accounts, U.S. government savings bonds, and shares in money-market mutual funds.[2] Are such assets money or not? The answer is not clear, even to the Federal Reserve.

---

[1] Commercial banks are so named because in their early days, they specialized in loans to businesses. Today, commercial banks engage in a much wider range of lending, including home-mortgage loans, automobile loans, and other consumer loans.

[2] A mutual fund is an organization that pools people's money and invests it in stocks or bonds or other financial assets. A money-market mutual fund invests in short-term securities, such as U.S. Treasury bills. If you own shares in a money-market mutual fund, you can write checks against your account, but generally they must exceed some minimum amount (commonly $500). This makes money-market funds less useful for everyday transactions involving smaller amounts of money.

CREDIT CARDS AND DEBIT CARDS

If you're accustomed to paying for your books (or your pizza) with a credit card, you probably wonder where that "plastic" fits into this classification system. After all, credit cards seem to work as well as cash, and they are often even more convenient. Actually, credit cards are neither money nor near money; they are simply a means of deferring payment. (Said differently, credit cards are a way of obtaining credit—loans; hence the term *credit card*.) When you pay for something with cash or a check, you have completed the transaction. But when you buy something with a credit card, you are incurring a debt that you ultimately will have to settle by sending the credit card company either cash or a check.

The new cousin of the credit card is the *debit card*, a card that allows you to withdraw money automatically from your checking account. When you use a debit card to make a purchase, you are, in effect, telling your bank to withdraw money from your account and transfer it to the store owner's account. Since a debit card is simply a way of accessing your checking balance, it does not constitute a different type of money.

DEFINITIONS OF THE MONEY SUPPLY

As we noted earlier, the Federal Reserve is responsible for controlling the money supply—the total amount of money in the economy. Before the Fed (as the Federal Reserve is often called) can attempt to control the money supply, it must, of course, decide what money is.

Rather than settling on a single definition of money, the Fed has developed several. The narrowest, **M-1**, is composed of currency in the hands of the public *plus* checkable deposits. **Checkable deposits** are all types of deposits on which customers can write checks: demand deposits at commercial banks; NOW accounts; credit union share draft accounts, which are essentially the same as NOW accounts but are provided by credit unions; and ATS accounts. The primary characteristic of all M-1 money is that it can function easily as a medium of exchange. As you can see from Exh. 15.1, only about 40 percent of this readily spendable money is in the form of currency. Demand deposits account for another 37 percent of the M-1 money supply. The remaining 23 percent is in other checkable deposits.

The Federal Reserve also classifies the money supply according to two broader definitions: M-2 and M-3. The **M-2** portion of the money supply includes everything in M-1 *plus* money-market mutual fund balances, money-market deposits at savings institutions, and certain other financial assets that do not function as a medium of exchange but that can be converted easily into currency or checkable deposits—small savings deposits (less than $100,000) at banks and savings institutions, for example.

EXHIBIT 15.1

M-1, M-2, and M-3 as of January 1998 (billions of dollars)

M-1

Currency (coins and paper money)	$ 427.5
Demand deposits	392.7
Other checkable deposits	253.1
Total M-1	$1,073.3

M-2

M-1 plus small savings accounts and money-market mutual fund balances	$4,064.6

M-3

M-2 plus large savings deposits and other financial assets that provide an outlet for business saving	$5,431.2

Source: *Federal Reserve Bulletin*, April 1998.

An even broader measure of the money supply is **M-3**. It includes everything in M-2 *plus* large savings deposits (over $100,000) and other financial assets that are designed essentially to be used as business savings accounts.

Throughout this chapter and the remainder of the text, we will use the M-1 definition of money: We assume that money consists of currency plus checkable deposits. These assets function easily as a medium of exchange, the function that many economists regard as the most important characteristic of money.

How Depository Institutions Create Money

Where does M-1 money come from? The currency component is easy to explain. It comes from the Federal Reserve, which supplies banks with enough coins and paper money to meet the needs of their customers. (Here and throughout the chapter, we use the term *bank* in a general way, to refer to all types of depository institutions—commercial banks and savings, or thrift, institutions.[3]) But the checkable-deposits element of M-1 is more of a mystery. Checkable deposits are actually created by the numerous banks that offer such accounts.

---

[3] There are three major types of thrift institutions: savings and loan associations, mutual savings banks, and credit unions.

EXHIBIT 15.2

A Hypothetical Balance Sheet: Gainsville National Bank

ASSETS		LIABILITIES AND OWNERS' EQUITY	
Reserves (vault cash plus deposits with the Federal Reserve)	$ 200,000	Checkable deposits	$1,000,000
		Savings deposits	360,000
		Owners' equity	240,000
Securities	450,000		
Loans	800,000		
Property	150,000	Total liabilities	
Total assets	$1,600,000	+ owners' equity	$1,600,000

A BANK'S BALANCE SHEET

To demonstrate how banks create checkable-deposit money, we can use a simple accounting concept known as a balance sheet. A **balance sheet** is a statement of a business's assets and liabilities. The assets of a business are, as we saw earlier, the things of value that it owns. **Liabilities** are the debts of the business, what it owes. The difference between the business's assets and liabilities is the **owners' equity,** which represents the interest of the owner or owners of a business in its assets. These accounting statements "balance"; whatever value of the business is not owed to creditors must belong to the owners: assets = liabilities + owners' equity.

We turn now to Exh. 15.2 to examine the balance sheet of a hypothetical bank, the Gainsville National Bank. The left-hand side of the balance sheet lists the bank's assets. The first entry, *reserves,* includes cash in the bank's vault plus funds on deposit with the Federal Reserve. Banks are required by law to hold a certain amount of their assets as required reserves. The **reserve requirement** is stated as a percentage of the bank's checkable deposits and can be met only by cash in its vault and deposits with the Fed. Because reserves earn no interest income, banks understandably try to maintain only the minimum legal requirement. Reserves greater than the minimum requirement are called **excess reserves,** and they play an important role in a bank's ability to create checkable-deposit money.

The next two entries on the left-hand side, *securities* and *loans,* are the interest-earning assets of the bank. Banks usually have substantial holdings of

U.S. Treasury bills and other securities that are both safe and highly liquid—that is, easily converted into cash. Loans offer less liquidity but generally have the advantage of earning a higher rate of interest.

The final entry on the left-hand side of the balance sheet is *property,* the physical assets of the bank: the bank building, its office equipment, and any other nonfinancial holdings of the organization.

The right-hand side of the balance sheet lists liabilities and owners' equity. In our example the only liabilities entered are *checkable deposits* and *savings deposits.* Although both items are assets for customers, they are debts to the bank. If we write a check on our checking account or ask to withdraw money from our savings account, the bank has to pay. That makes each of those accounts a liability to the bank.

The only remaining entry on the right-hand side of Exh. 15.2 is *owners' equity,* the owners' claims on the assets of the business. As you know, the two sides of the statement have to balance, because whatever value of the business is not owed to creditors (the bank's liabilities) must belong to the owners (owner equity).

THE CREATION OF CHECKABLE DEPOSITS

Earlier we noted that all banks must meet a reserve requirement established by the Federal Reserve. Let's assume that the reserve requirement for our hypothetical bank is 20 percent. Our bank has $1,000,000 in checkable deposits; therefore, it is required by law to maintain $200,000 in reserves ($1,000,000 × 0.20 = $200,000). As you can see from the bank's balance sheet, it has precisely $200,000 in reserves.

Even in the absence of regulation, banks would need to maintain some reserves against their deposits. The bank must have the currency to pay a depositor who walks into the Gainsville Bank and writes a check for "cash." However, the bank does not have to maintain $1 in reserve for every $1 of checkable deposits it accepts, because it is unlikely that all depositors will request their money simultaneously. In fact, while some depositors are writing checks and drawing down their accounts, others are making deposits and thereby increasing their balances.

The key to a bank's ability to create money is this **fractional reserve principle,** the principle that a bank needs to maintain only a fraction of a dollar in reserve for each dollar of its checkable deposits. Once a bank discovers this principle, it can loan out the idle funds and earn interest. That's the name of the game in banking—earning interest by lending money. In the process of making loans, banks create money: specifically, checkable deposits. We can see how this is true by working through the balance sheet entries of the lending bank. In order to simplify things somewhat, we will show only the changes in assets and liabilities for each entry, not the entire balance sheet.

Step One: Accepting Deposits. Let's assume that one of the bank's depositors, Adam Swift, deposits $1,000 in cash in his checking account. We would reflect this change by increasing the bank's checkable deposits by $1,000 and increasing its reserves by the same amount.

The bank now has an additional $1,000 in cash reserves (clearly an asset) and the liability of paying out that same amount if Mr. Swift writes checks totaling $1,000. Because the bank's deposits have increased by $1,000, it must now maintain an additional $200 in required reserves (20 percent of $1,000). The Gainsville Bank now finds itself with excess reserves of $800.

GAINSVILLE NATIONAL BANK

ASSETS			LIABILITIES	
Reserves		+$1,000	Checkable deposits	+$1,000
required	+$200			
excess	+$800			
		+$1,000		+$1,000

What will the Gainsville Bank do with those excess reserves? If it simply let them sit in the vault, it would be sacrificing the interest that could be earned on $800. Because the bank wants to show a profit, it will probably use those excess reserves to make loans.

Step Two: Making a Loan. Let's assume that another resident of Gainsville, June Malthus, walks in and asks to borrow $800. How will we record this transaction? On the asset side, we will record a loan for $800. The bank receives this asset in the form of a note, or IOU, agreeing to repay the $800 plus interest. On the liability side of the balance sheet, we increase checkable deposits by $800 (from $1,000 to $1,800).

GAINSVILLE NATIONAL BANK

ASSETS		LIABILITIES		
Reserves	$1,000	Checkable deposits		$1,800
Loans	+$ 800	Adam Swift	$1,000	
		June Malthus	$ 800	
	$1,800			$1,800

This last entry may seem puzzling to you if you have not yet borrowed money. The way you generally receive money borrowed from a bank is in the form of a checking account with your name on it. This is the money-creating transaction of the bank. Ms. Malthus has exchanged a piece of paper (an IOU) that is *not* money for something that *is* money, checkable deposits. If you think about this process, you'll see the logic of it: The Gainsville Bank is now using $1,000 in reserves to support $1,800 of checkable deposits. And because of the fractional reserve principle, bank officials can be confident that this support is adequate; they know that not all the original depositors will withdraw their money simultaneously.

Not everyone can create money through lending. When you lend money to a friend, your friend ends up with more money, but you have less. The total money supply has not increased. However, when you borrow money from a bank, you end up with more money, but no one has any less. And the money supply actually increases.

How do we explain the difference? Your IOU does not circulate as money, whereas the IOU of a bank does. What happens when you deposit cash in your checking account? You do not reduce your personal money supply as you would if you had made a loan to your friend. Instead, you merely exchange cash (a form of money) for an IOU known as a checkable deposit (a different form of money). Your currency then serves as reserves for supporting loans that result in the creation of additional deposits. Someone else ends up with more money, but you don't have any less. Once you understand this process, you can see that the bank has really "created" money.

Step Three: Using the Loan. Now that we have seen how banks create money, we can ask what happens to that money when it is used to buy something. Let's assume that Ms. Malthus uses her newly acquired checking account to buy furniture in the nearby town of Sellmore—at the Sellmore Furniture Store. Let's also assume that she spends the entire amount of her loan. She will write a check on the Gainsville Bank and give it to the owner of the Sellmore Furniture Store, who will deposit it in the firm's account at the First National Bank of Sellmore. The Sellmore Bank will then send the check to the district Federal Reserve Bank for collection. (One function of the Federal Reserve is to provide a check collection and clearing service. We'll discuss this and other functions of the Fed later in the chapter.) After the Federal Reserve Bank receives the check, it will reduce the reserve account of the Gainsville Bank by $800 and increase the reserve account of the Sellmore Bank by $800. It will then forward the check to the Gainsville Bank, where changes in assets and liabilities will be recorded. Ms. Malthus has spent the $800 in her checking account; so checkable deposits will be reduced by that amount (from $1,800 to $1,000). The bank's reserves have also fallen by $800 (from $1,000 to $200), the amount of reserves lost to the Sellmore Bank.

GAINSVILLE NATIONAL BANK

ASSETS		LIABILITIES	
Reserves		Checkable deposits	
($1,000 − $800)	$ 200	($1,800 − $800)	$1,000
required $200		Adam Swift $1,000	
excess 0		June Malthus 0	
Loans	+$ 800		
	$1,000		$1,000

Note that the Gainsville Bank no longer has any excess reserves. It has reserves of $200, the exact amount required. If the bank had loaned Ms. Malthus more than $800 (the initial amount of its excess reserves), it would now be in violation of the reserve requirement. But each bank realizes that when it makes a loan, it will probably lose reserves to other banks as the borrower spends the loan. For that reason, *individual banks must limit their loans to the amount of their excess reserves.* That's one of the most important principles in this chapter; so be sure you understand it before reading any further.

THE MULTIPLE EXPANSION OF LOANS AND DEPOSITS

Recall that the money lent in the form of checkable deposits circulates. Thus, the money created when the Gainsville Bank made a loan to Ms. Malthus is not destroyed when she uses the loan but rather is simply transferred from one bank to another. The checkable deposits and reserves originally represented on the balance sheet of the Gainsville Bank may now be found on the balance sheet of the Sellmore Bank. This means that the Sellmore Bank will now be able to expand its loans.

We know that each bank can expand its loans to create checkable deposits equal to the amount of its excess reserves. Assuming that the Sellmore Bank also faces a reserve requirement of 20 percent and that it had no excess reserves to begin with, it will now have excess reserves of $640. How did we arrive at that amount? The Sellmore Bank increased its checkable deposits, and thus its reserves, by $800, the amount deposited by the owner of the Sellmore Furniture Store. With a 20 percent reserve requirement, the increase in required reserves is $160 ($800 × 0.20 = $160). That leaves $640 in excess reserves, which can be used to support new loans and create additional checking deposits.

This expansion of loans and deposits continues as the money created by one bank is deposited in another bank, where it is used to support even more loans. In Exh. 15.3, we see that the banking system as a whole can eventually create $4,000 in new loans and new money (checkable deposits) from the initial $800 increase in excess reserves received by the Gainsville Bank. We also see the difference between the ability of a single bank and the banking system as a whole to create money. Whereas an individual bank must restrict its loans—and consequently its ability to create money—to the amount of its excess reserves, the banking system as a whole can create loans and deposits equal to some multiple of the excess reserves received by the system. In our example that multiple is 5; the banking system was able to create loans and deposits five times greater than the initial increase in excess reserves ($800 × 5 = $4,000).

THE DEPOSIT MULTIPLIER

Fortunately we need not work through all the individual transactions to predict the maximum amount of money that the banking system will be able to create. As a general rule, the banking system can alter the money supply by an amount equal to the initial change in excess reserves times the reciprocal of the reserve requirement:

EXHIBIT 15.3

The Creation of Money by the Banking System

BANK	NEWLY ACQUIRED DEPOSITS AND RESERVES	REQUIRED RESERVES (20 percent of checkable deposits)	POTENTIAL FOR NEW LOANS (creating money)
Gainsville	$1,000.00	$200.00	$ 800.00
Sellmore	800.00	160.00	640.00
Third bank	640.00	128.00	512.00
Fourth bank	512.00	102.40	409.60
Fifth bank	409.60	81.92	327.68
Sixth bank	327.68	65.54	262.14
Seventh bank	262.14	52.43	209.71
All others	1,048.58	209.71	838.87
Total amount of money created by the banking system			$4,000.00*

*This figure represents the *maximum* amount of money that the banking system could create from an initial $800 increase in excess reserves. The example assumes that all banks face a 20 percent reserve requirement and that they are all "loaned up" (have no excess reserves) initially.

$$\text{Change in excess reserves} \times \frac{1}{\text{Reserve requirement (written as a decimal)}} = \text{Maximum possible increase in checkable deposits by the banking system as a whole}$$

The reciprocal of the reserve requirement, 1 divided by the reserve requirement, yields a number called the deposit multiplier. The **deposit multiplier** is the multiple by which checkable deposits (in the entire banking system) increase or decrease in response to an initial change in excess reserves.

The reserve ratio in our hypothetical example is .20, and so the deposit multiplier must be 1/.20, or 5. Therefore, an $800 increase in excess reserves will permit the banking system to create up to $4,000 of new demand deposits. This $4,000 figure is really the *maximum* possible expansion in checkable deposits, given the stated change in excess reserves and the existing reserve requirement. The actual amount may, for a variety of reasons, be less than the maximum predicted.

An illustration will help: Suppose that the recipient of Ms. Malthus's check decides not to redeposit the entire amount in a checking account. This event will reduce the amount of money being passed on to the remaining banks in the system and thus reduce the amount the system can create through lending. The expansion in checkable deposits will also be less than the maximum if bankers maintain some excess reserves. For instance, perhaps some bankers anticipate deposit withdrawals and prepare for them by holding, rather than lending, excess reserves. Or banks may be forced to hold excess reserves simply because they cannot find enough loan customers. For all these reasons, the expansion in the checkable-deposit component of the money supply may be substantially less than the maximum predicted by the deposit multiplier.

THE DESTRUCTION OF CHECKABLE DEPOSITS

The deposit multiplier can also work in reverse. Suppose that Adam Swift, our original depositor, withdrew $1,000 in cash from his account at the Gainsville Bank and kept it in his wallet. What would this transaction do to the money supply? The initial transaction merely changes its composition: Mr. Swift is giving up his claim to $1,000 in checkable deposits (a form of money) and is receiving in return $1,000 in cash (another form of money). The size of the money supply remains the same, even though more cash and fewer checkable deposits are in circulation.

What happens next? When Mr. Swift withdraws $1,000 from his checking account, the Gainsville Bank loses $1,000 in deposits and reserves.

GAINSVILLE NATIONAL BANK

ASSETS		LIABILITIES	
Reserves	−$1,000	Checkable deposits	−$1,000

Assuming that the bank had no excess reserves to begin with, it now finds itself with a reserve deficiency; that is, it doesn't have sufficient reserves to meet the 20 percent reserve requirement. What is the amount of the deficiency? It is $800—the difference between the amount that Mr. Swift has withdrawn from his checking account ($1,000) and the reserve that the bank was required to maintain on that deposit ($200). In order to correct this deficiency, the bank has two choices. One is to sell $800 worth of securities (remember, banks hold securities, particularly government securities, which earn interest and can be converted easily into cash); another is to allow $800 worth of loans to be repaid without making new loans. In either case, the next bank in the sequence is going to lose $800 worth of deposits and reserves as its depositors buy those securities or repay those loans. That bank will then be faced with a reserve deficiency; it too may need to sell securities or reduce the amount of its loans to build up reserves.

As you may suspect, this contractionary process can spread to other banks in the system and result in a multiple contraction of loans and deposits that is similar to the multiple expansion we observed earlier. Once again, the limit to this process is set by the reserve requirement and the deposit multiplier derived from that requirement. To predict the maximum contraction in checkable deposits, we multiply the initial reserve deficiency times the deposit multiplier. In our example that would mean a reduction of $4,000 ($800 × 5 = $4,000).

The Federal Reserve System

Now we are ready to examine the role of the Federal Reserve, the central bank of the United States. Virtually every industrialized nation in the world has a **central bank**—a government agency responsible for controlling the national money supply. At one time, the size of a nation's money supply was determined largely by its stock of gold. That's because most of a nation's money supply was currency, and virtually all nations "backed" their currency with gold.[4] But things change. Today, nothing backs the

---

[4] For example, between 1900 and 1933 the United States issued gold certificates that could be redeemed for gold coins. In 1934 the United States stopped *redeeming* currency for gold but continued to maintain 25% gold backing for currency. (The Fed could issue $4 of currency for each $1 of gold it held.) Throughout this period, gold continued to be used to pay international debts, and this gradually caused the U. S. gold supply to shrink to low levels. (The reasons for this gradual outflow of gold are discussed in Chapter 18.) In 1968, the requirement that Fed currency be backed by a gold reserve was eliminated, and in 1971 the United States stopped using gold to settle international debts. That few people noticed either of these events is an indication that the value of our currency stems from what it can buy, not from the backing provided by some scarce commodity.

U. S. dollar (or any other major currency) except the faith that the currency can be used to make purchases. And currency is no longer the most important component of the money supply in most industrialized nations; that role has been assumed by checkable deposits. As a consequence, the size of a nation's money supply is no longer tied to its gold stock. Instead, it is determined by its central bank. In the United Kingdom the central bank is the Bank of England, in Germany the Bundesbank, in the United States the Federal Reserve System.

THE ORIGIN OF THE FEDERAL RESERVE

The Federal Reserve was established in 1913. Its original purpose was to act as a "lender of last resort," to make loans to banks only when all other sources had dried up. It was thought that by performing this function, the Federal Reserve (commonly known as "the Fed") could prevent or stop the financial panics that had characterized this period. A *financial panic* is a situation in which depositors lose confidence in banks and rush to withdraw their money. The panics of this period were usually precipitated by a shortage of cash reserves: Some banks found that they had too little cash to satisfy their customers, and were forced to close their doors. This led to a general distrust of banks and to additional bank closings and business failures. It was felt that by acting as lender of last resort, the Fed could stop

Alan Greenspan, chairman of the Federal Reserve, has been described as the second most powerful person in the world.

any financial panic before it got under way and would thus prevent the bank closings and business failures of previous panics. In addition to this primary function, the Federal Reserve was also authorized to provide an efficient mechanism for collecting and clearing checks throughout the United States and to help supervise banks to ensure the prudence of their investment and lending practices.

Today, the primary responsibility of the Fed is to help stabilize the economy by controlling the money supply. We expect the Federal Reserve to manipulate the money supply in an effort to prevent (or combat) unemployment or inflation, a responsibility much broader than the one envisioned by Congress in 1913. Because the responsibility for controlling the money supply grew as the federal government assumed a greater role in managing the economy, the modern Federal Reserve organization is far more powerful than Congress intended it to be.[5] Some contemporary economists believe that the Fed's powers to influence the economy should be sharply curtailed; others argue that a strong Federal Reserve is necessary to combat unemployment and prevent inflation. (We'll look further at this debate in Chapter 16.)

THE ORGANIZATION OF THE FEDERAL RESERVE SYSTEM

The Federal Reserve System is composed of a board of governors, twelve Federal Reserve banks, and several thousand member banks. The board of governors is the policymaking body of the Federal Reserve. It consists of a chairperson (currently Alan Greenspan) and six members, all appointed by the president of the United States to serve fourteen-year terms. These terms are structured so that only one expires every two years, which helps to provide continuity and to insulate board members somewhat from political pressure. The primary function of the board is to make the major policy decisions that determine how rapidly or slowly the nation's money supply will grow.

To implement these decisions, twelve Federal Reserve banks (plus 24 branches) are located strategically throughout the country. Their primary function is to oversee the actions of the member banks and other depository institutions within their districts. Member banks include all nationally chartered

---

[5] Unlike central banks in other nations, the Federal Reserve is an independent organization that is not required to take orders from any other agency or branch of government. This gives the Federal Reserve at least the appearance of somewhat greater independence than other central banks. Members of Congress periodically threaten to revoke this independence when the Fed pursues policies they disagree with.

commercial banks, which are required to join the Federal Reserve System, as well as any state-chartered banks that have chosen membership.

THE MONETARY CONTROL ACT OF 1980

Prior to 1980, the distinction between member and nonmember banks was significant: Only member banks were subject to the direct regulation of the Fed. Nonmember banks were subject only to regulations imposed by the states that chartered them. Because the Fed's reserve requirements were generally higher than those imposed by the states, member banks were forced to sacrifice more interest income. (Remember, reserve dollars don't earn interest.)

In the days of relatively low interest rates (4–5 percent), many banks were willing to forgo this interest income in order to obtain the check-collection services and borrowing privileges provided by the Fed. But as interest rates rose, the opportunity cost of those idle reserves increased, and Federal Reserve membership grew less and less attractive. As a consequence, more than 300 banks withdrew from the Federal Reserve between 1973 and 1979; 25 of those were relatively large banks with assets of $100 million or more. Faced with declining membership, the Federal Reserve began to search for some way either to stem the loss of member banks or to establish more effective control over the money-creating activities of nonmember banks.

During this time, the Federal Reserve was also concerned about NOW accounts, which enabled savings and loan associations, mutual savings banks, and credit unions (institutions beyond the Fed's control) to create money. The emergence of NOW accounts further threatened the Fed's ability to monitor and control the money supply. To counter this, the Fed pressed for substantial regulatory changes, and Congress responded with the Depository Institutions Deregulation and Monetary Control Act of 1980.

The Monetary Control Act virtually eliminated the distinction between member and nonmember commercial banks and significantly reduced the distinction between commercial banks and other financial institutions. The act required that all depository institutions—member commercial banks, nonmember commercial banks, savings and loan associations, mutual savings banks, and credit unions—meet the same standards with regard to reserve requirements. It lifted many of the regulations that historically had limited competition among various types of financial institutions, and it opened to all such institutions the option to purchase any of the services offered by the Federal Reserve. These changes improved the Fed's ability to monitor and control the money supply and intensified competition among the various types of depository institutions for depositors and loan customers alike.

DEREGULATION, BANK FAILURES, AND CHANGING FINANCIAL MARKETS

Not all the consequences of the Monetary Control Act and subsequent banking reforms were positive. Many analysts argue that the relaxed regulatory environment contributed to an enormous number of bank and savings and loan failures in the 1980s.

The bank failures of the 1980s led to closer regulatory supervision in the 1990s. But increased supervision brings with it higher costs for the supervised institutions, and that can have unintended consequences. Because today's financial markets are increasingly international, countries that impose costly regulations risk driving businesses to other, less regulated countries. (This concern has resulted in growing international coordination of banking regulations.) Another consequence is the diversion of money from depository institutions, such as banks and savings and loans, to nondepository institutions, such as mutual funds and insurance companies. Nondepository institutions have been growing very rapidly, in part because they can afford to pay higher interest rates than the more highly regulated depository institutions with which they compete. But since these nondepository institutions are largely beyond the control of the Fed, its policymakers are concerned that this trend is undermining their ability to control the money supply. It remains to be seen how the Fed will address this challenge.

In addition to undermining the Fed's control, the rapid growth of nondepository financial institutions was initially seen as a signal that traditional depository institutions would play a diminished role in our economy. Recent studies contradict this conclusion. Threatened by increased competition in the borrowing and lending business, depository institutions have increasingly turned to the provision of financial services—services for which they earn fees, as opposed to the interest they earn from loans—to bolster their income. These services include the preparation of payrolls for businesses, the supervision of company pension funds, assistance in arranging mergers, the buying and selling of foreign exchange, and a host of others. This broadening in the role of depository institutions has helped to ensure their financial viability. In fact, some studies indicate that these institutions are becoming more, not less, important to the economy.[6]

THE FUNCTIONS OF THE FEDERAL RESERVE

The foregoing discussion highlights the dynamic nature of our financial institutions and the difficulty of determining the proper level of supervision. Supervising financial institutions is one of the functions of the Fed, a responsibility it shares with the Federal Deposit Insurance Corporation (FDIC), the primary agency insuring deposits at financial institutions.

---

[6] For a discussion, see Mark D. Vaughan, "Bullish on Banking: Surviving in the Information Age," *The Regional Economist*, Federal Reserve Bank of Saint Louis, Jan. 1996.

The Fed also performs a number of other functions. First, the twelve Federal Reserve Banks hold the reserves (other than vault cash) of all the depository institutions in their districts. Second, as lenders of last resort, the Federal Reserve banks stand ready to make loans to depository institutions in temporary need of funds. Third, the Federal Reserve supplies the economy with coins and paper money. Fourth, as we have seen, the Fed provides a system for collecting and clearing checks throughout the United States, making it possible for checks drawn on out-of-town banks to be returned to the home institution for collection. But all these functions are secondary to the Fed's primary responsibility: the control of the nation's money supply. That is the topic we will examine next.

Monetary Policy and the Federal Reserve

Monetary policy is designed to control the supply of money. More precisely, monetary policy is any action intended to alter the supply of money in order to influence the level of total spending and thereby combat unemployment or inflation.

Although the objective of monetary policy is the same as that of fiscal policy (to prevent or combat unemployment and inflation), its methodology is somewhat different. In Chapter 14 you saw how policymakers use the government's spending and taxation powers to alter aggregate demand and thereby eliminate recessionary or inflationary gaps. Likewise, monetary policy works to influence aggregate demand but through a different mechanism: by increasing or decreasing the money supply.

The Fed does not manipulate the amount of money by printing more currency or by removing existing paper money from circulation. Remember, most of our nation's money supply is composed of balances in checking accounts—demand-deposit accounts, NOW accounts, and other forms of checkable deposits. It is this element of the money supply that the Fed's actions are designed to influence. You have seen how depository institutions create checkable deposits when they make loans. Now you will discover how the Federal Reserve can influence the lending ability of depository institutions and thereby alter the supply of money.

The Federal Reserve uses three major policy tools to control the money supply: (1) the buying and selling of government securities, a process known as **open-market operations;** (2) the ability to alter the reserve requirement of depository institutions; and (3) control over the **discount rate**—the interest rate at which banking institutions can borrow from the Federal Reserve. All three policy tools affect the reserve positions of depository institutions. As you have learned, the more excess reserves a bank has, the more loans it can make and the more money (checkable deposits) it can create. By altering the volume of excess reserves, the Fed is able to influence the banking system's ability to make loans. Because making loans means creating more money, the Fed's actions influence the money supply.

OPEN-MARKET OPERATIONS

The Federal Reserve controls the money supply primarily through its open-market operations: buying and selling government securities on the open market. Whenever the U.S. government runs a deficit, the Treasury finances that deficit by selling government securities to individuals, businesses, financial institutions, and government agencies. Most are marketable, or *negotiable*, meaning that they can be held until maturity or resold to someone else.[7] Banks find such securities an attractive investment. They not only earn interest but also convert easily into cash in the event that additional reserves are needed. The Federal Reserve uses the market for negotiable securities as a vehicle for controlling the money supply. Let's see how open-market operations work.

If the Fed wants to increase the money supply by expanding loans, it can offer to buy government securities at attractive prices in the open market. The Fed pays for securities purchased from a commercial bank, for example, by increasing the bank's reserve account at the district Federal Reserve bank. Because this transaction does not increase the bank's deposit liabilities, the additional reserves are all excess and can be used to expand loans and deposits—up to the maximum predicted by the deposit multiplier. As you know, any change in the excess reserves of one bank will lead eventually to a much larger change in the total system's loans and checkable deposits. As commercial banks and other depository institutions make more loans and create more checkable deposits, the money supply will expand.

If the Fed wishes to reduce the money supply, it can shift its open-market operations into reverse and cut the lending ability of banks by selling them government securities. The purchasing banks will experience a reduction in their reserve accounts at district Federal Reserve banks. As their reserves decline, these institutions will have to contract loans or at least limit their expansion. This will cause the money supply to decline or expand at a slower rate.

CHANGING THE RESERVE REQUIREMENT

The Fed can also influence the reserve position of banks by changing the reserve requirement. Under existing law, the Federal Reserve has the power to specify

---

[7] There are different types of marketable government securities. *Treasury bills* are short-term securities with maturities of 91 days to one year. *Government notes* are intermediate-term securities maturing in one to five years. Finally, *government bonds* are long-term securities with maturities of more than five years.

reserve requirements between 8 and 14 percent for depository institutions above a specified size. (At present, most banks must satisfy a ten percent reserve requirement.) This flexibility provides the Federal Reserve with a tool for influencing the money supply by changing the lending ability of depository institutions.

Lowering the reserve requirement would convert some required reserves into excess reserves and thereby expand the lending ability of depository institutions. When these institutions increase their loans, they create checkable deposits, and the money supply expands. Increasing the reserve requirement has the opposite effect. As excess reserves are converted into required reserves, lending contracts and the money supply shrinks.

Modifying the reserve requirement is effective but somewhat dangerous. Even changes as small as one half of one percent can alter by several billion dollars the banking system's ability to make loans. Changes of this magnitude, particularly when they are sudden, can jolt the economy severely. Therefore, the Federal Reserve uses this tool sparingly, adjusting the reserve requirement only infrequently and relying mainly on other tools to control the money supply.

CHANGING THE DISCOUNT RATE

Since the passage of the Monetary Control Act of 1980, any depository institution may ask to borrow reserves from its district Federal Reserve bank to avoid reducing the number of loans it can grant or to increase its volume of loans and thereby earn additional interest income.[8]

Recall that the rate of interest charged by the Federal Reserve on loans to depository institutions is called the *discount rate.* In theory, increasing the discount rate should discourage borrowing from the Federal Reserve and thus force banks to limit or even contract the number of loans they grant. We know that if banks contract their loans, the money supply will fall.

Lowering the discount rate should have the opposite effect. By encouraging depository institutions to borrow from the Fed and create additional loans and deposits, the lowered rate should lead to an increase in the money supply.

Note the use of the words "in theory" and "should." In practice, changes in the discount rate have proved to be a very weak policy tool. Bankers tend to equate loans from the Federal Reserve with money borrowed from in-laws; it's something you avoid unless you have no other options. This attitude is not surprising when one considers the Fed's corresponding view that borrowing is a privilege and not a right: If Federal Reserve authorities

---

[8] When depository institutions repay these loans to the Fed, their reserves decline, and they are forced to contract loans or find other sources of reserves.

believe that a bank has overextended itself through poor planning or has borrowed too often or for the wrong purposes, they can refuse to lend the needed reserves. This disciplinary action forces the wayward bank to contract loans, sell securities, or look elsewhere for reserves. Because bankers don't like such restrictions, they prefer to borrow through the **federal funds market,** a market that brings together banks that need reserves and banks that temporarily have excess reserves. The rate charged on such loans is called the **federal funds rate** and usually applies to reserves borrowed on a very short-term basis—often overnight to meet temporary reserve deficiencies.

Because banks borrow from the Federal Reserve only infrequently, changes in the discount rate have little impact on the banking system's lending ability and thus register little effect on the money supply. In fact, many economists tend to view a change in the discount rate more as an indication of the Fed's intentions than as an effective policy move. Increases in the discount rate are thought to indicate the Fed's intention to contract the money supply or slow its rate of growth; decreases signal a desire to expand the money supply or increase its rate of growth.

Money, Interest Rates, and the Level of Economic Activity

Now that we've seen how the Federal Reserve can expand or contract the money supply, let's explore how changes in the money supply affect the economy. Economic theory suggests that changes in the money supply affect output and employment primarily by altering interest rates. Because a significant amount of consumption and investment spending is financed by borrowing, changes in the interest rate can affect the amount of aggregate demand in the economy and thereby alter the level of equilibrium GDP and the price level. This transmission process can be summarized as follows:

$$\text{Money supply} \rightarrow \text{Interest rate} \rightarrow \text{Aggregate demand} \rightarrow \begin{array}{c} \text{Output,} \\ \text{employment,} \\ \text{and prices} \end{array}$$

INTEREST RATE DETERMINATION

Why would changes in the money supply tend to alter the interest rate? To answer that question, we need to think back to Chapter 3, where we discussed price determination in competitive markets. Like the price of wheat or of

Federal Reserve policies are not always popular. Here, demonstrators protest policies that raised interest rates to slow the economy and prevent inflation.

cattle, the interest rate—the price of money—is determined by the forces of demand and supply. As a consequence, any change in either the demand for money or its supply will affect the rate of interest.[9]

Consider, first, the demand for money. Like conventional demand curves, the demand curve for money slopes downward. That's because the quantity of money demanded by individuals and businesses is inversely related to the interest rate: The higher the rate of interest, the less money is demanded. To understand that relationship, remember that the money you hold (cash in your wallet or money in your checking account) generally pays little or no interest. But other assets you could hold instead of money—bonds, for instance, or bank certificates of deposit—do pay interest. The higher the prevailing interest rate, the more attractive it becomes to hold these assets instead of money. As a consequence, less money will be demanded when interest rates are *high* than when they are *low*. The demand curve in Exh. 15.4 shows that

---

[9] To simplify matters, we will assume a single rate of interest; in fact, there are several. For example, short-term borrowers generally pay a lower interest rate than those who require the money for a longer period. In addition, borrowers with good credit ratings usually pay lower rates than those with poor ratings.

$100 billion would be demanded at an interest rate of 10 percent, whereas $300 billion would be demanded at an interest rate of 6 percent.

The supply of money is depicted as a vertical line in Exh. 15.4 to illustrate that the quantity of money supplied does not respond automatically to changes in the interest rate; instead, it remains constant at the level determined by the Federal Reserve. The intersection of the demand curve and the vertical supply curve determines the equilibrium interest rate: the interest rate at which the amount of money that people want to hold is exactly equal to the amount available. In our hypothetical example the equilibrium interest rate is 8 percent. At that interest rate individuals and businesses are willing to hold $200 billion, exactly the amount being supplied by the Federal Reserve.

MONETARY POLICY AND THE LEVEL OF ECONOMIC ACTIVITY

The Fed attempts to guide the economy's performance by adjusting the money supply and thereby pushing the interest rate up or down. As we've seen,

---

EXHIBIT 15.4

The Equilibrium Interest Rate

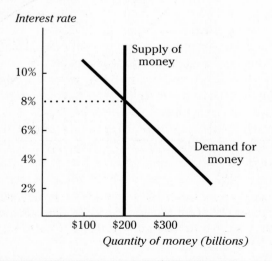

The intersection of the demand curve for money and the supply curve of money determines the equilibrium interest rate—the interest rate at which the amount of money that individuals and businesses want to hold is exactly equal to the amount available. In this example the equilibrium interest rate is 8 percent.

---

changes in the interest rate alter aggregate demand, and changes in the level of aggregate demand lead to changes in equilbrium GDP and the price level.

To illustrate how monetary policy works, let's assume that the economy is suffering from abnormally high unemployment: a recessionary gap exists. The Fed can attack this unemployment problem by increasing the money supply. This could be accomplished by reducing the reserve requirement, buying government securities, or lowering the discount rate. Any of these changes would shift the money supply curve in Exh. 15.5 from S_1 to S_2, denoting an increase in the money supply from $200 billion to $300 billion. Since the demand for money is unchanged, the equilibrium interest rate will fall from 8 percent to 6 percent. At this lower interest rate, businesses will find it profitable to borrow

EXHIBIT 15.5

Using Monetary Policy to Attack Unemployment

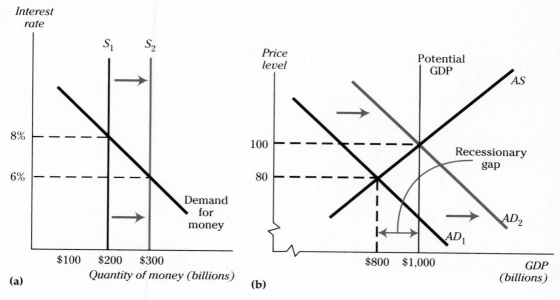

By increasing the money supply from $S_1$to S_2, as in (a),the Fed can lower the interest rate from 8 to 6 percent. The lower interest rate stimulates consumption and investment spending, shifting the aggregate demand curve from AD_1 to AD_2, as in (b), and eliminating the recessionary gap.

Use Your Economic Reasoning

Bogeyman Economics

By Bob Herbert

God help us, there's a chance the unemployment rate will ultimately fall below 5 percent. Can you imagine worse news?

The abject fear that this has engendered was captured in the lead story in the *Washington Post* on Wednesday. You could almost hear the knees of financial analysts knocking as you read that the Federal Reserve will probably have to raise interest rates again next month if this rampaging monster of an economy doesn't hurry up and slow down.

The *Post* story said: "The surge in growth, which began last year…is strong enough that it could soon drive the nation's jobless rate below 5 percent for the first time in nearly a quarter century, the analysts warned."

Warned. This news comes as a warning. It's as if the nation were faced with the threat of a cure for cancer. Be on the alert: Prosperity for the jobless is just around the corner. We have no choice but to confront it, turn it around, and chase it out of the neighborhood altogether. In short, we have to get the unemployment rate up.

Inflation is the bogeyman. No one has seen it in several years, but the mere thought that at any moment it might spring back to life—the financial markets' very own Freddy Krueger—is enough to keep the well-heeled on constant edge.

"Not only do we have to stop inflation when it happens, but the Greenspan position is that we have to anticipate it and stop it before it starts," said Robert Borosage, codirector of the Campaign for America's Future, a pro-

additional money to invest in plants and equipment; households will be inclined to borrow and spend more on new homes, automobiles, and other consumer goods. Thus by lowering the interest rate, an increase in the money supply raises aggregate demand. This is represented in Exh. 15.5(b) by a shift of the aggregate demand curve from AD_1 to AD_2. As you can see, this increase in aggregate demand raises the equilibrium level of GDP from $800 billion to $1,000 billion, eliminating the recessionary gap and restoring full employment.

To attack inflation, the Federal Reserve must raise interest rates by contracting the money supply. This is accomplished by increasing the reserve requirement, selling government securities, or increasing the discount rate. What is the effect of the higher rate of interest? Businesses will tend to gressive advocacy group.

Whatever motives are driving Alan Greenspan, the chairman of the Federal Reserve Board, the result is a brutal catch-22 for the nation's working classes. The route to a brighter future for most men and women—raises for those already working, and increased employment opportunities for those who want to work—is economic growth. There is a consensus on the left and the right that growth is the answer to the persistent and potentially dangerous problem of economic inequality.

For a majority of Americans to do better, an expanding economy is essential. And yet, whenever there is evidence of anything beyond an anemic rate of growth, the policy is to step in and ruthlessly head it off. The effect is to slam the workplace door on millions of men and women in the bottom half, especially the bottom fifth, of the socioeconomic scale....

For a while it was thought that the official unemployment rate had to remain above the 6 percent barrier to keep inflation still. But the jobless rate came down, broke the 6 percent barrier, and nothing happened. The theory had to be adjusted. Perhaps 5.8 percent was the magic figure. Wrong. Unemployment fell through that barrier without a peep from inflation. Well, maybe 5.5, or 5.3, or 5.2.

There is still no evidence of accelerating inflation. But there is plenty of evidence that an awful lot of people are in need of jobs and can't get them....

USE YOUR ECONOMIC REASONING

1. Low unemployment would seem to be a cause for rejoicing. Why is it also a source of concern?
2. Why does Greenspan believe that we have to act to prevent inflation before we see it?
3. Suppose the true "natural" rate of unemployment is 5 percent, but the Fed is convinced that it is 5.5 percent. What would be the consequences of this error?

reduce investment spending, and households will be likely to spend less on new homes, boats, camping trailers, and other itms that they buy on credit or through borrowing. Reducing the money supply thus raises the interest rate and lowers aggregate demand in the economy, which helps to reduce inflationary pressures. (The Fed's efforts to prevent inflation can be quite unpopular, particularly when there is little evidence of an inflation problem. Read "Bogeyman Economics," above, to see why some believe that the Fed's fear of inflation may be costing our society too much.)

As you can see, monetary policy works through its impact on the interest rate. By adjusting the cost of money, the Fed is able to influence the level of aggregate demand in the economy and thereby eliminate recessionary or inflationary gaps.

The Limits to Monetary Policy

The Federal Reserve's independent status gives monetary policy some distinct advantages over fiscal policy. When the Fed's board of governors decides that action should be taken to combat unemployment or inflation, it does not need to wait for Congress to agree. The board can approve the needed policy changes and have them implemented in a very short time. Board members' fourteen-year terms also serve to insulate them from political pressures, although the insulation is not complete in view of the periodic threats to bring the Fed under the direct control of Congress.

But monetary policy has limitations as well. (Recall the limitations of fiscal policy that we examined in Chapter 14.) Here we will look at two problems that may be encountered when monetary policy is used in an attempt to guide the economy's performance.

TIME LAGS

Like fiscal policy, monetary policy is subject to some time lags. Although Federal Reserve authorities don't need the approval of Congress to implement policy changes, they do need time to recognize that a problem exists and to agree on the needed action. As we learned earlier, our economic indicators sometimes send mixed or unclear messages, so that some time may elapse before members of the board of governors identify a problem and prescribe a remedy. Once they take action, additional time passes before their policy change exerts its impact on the economy. If the board members decide to stimulate the economy, for example, it will take time for an increase in lending to trigger the associated increases in spending, output, and employment. If this time lag is too long, the added stimulus may hit the economy when it is already on the road to spontaneous recovery. In that event the Fed's actions may contribute to inflation rather than help reduce unemployment.

UNEVEN EFFECTIVENESS

Monetary policy may be less effective in combating unemployment than in combating inflation. When the Fed reduces banks' reserves to combat inflation, banks are forced to restrict (or even contract) lending. However, when it implements an easy-money policy to combat unemployment and makes more reserves available to depository institutions, bankers may not choose to use those reserves to support loans. If bankers doubt the ability of customers to repay loans, they refuse to lend; if households and businesses are pessimistic about the future, they may decide not to borrow. Without greater lending and borrowing, spending will not increase; thus, the economy will not receive the stimulus needed to pull it from its depressed state.

How significant are the monetary policy limitations noted here? As with fiscal policy, the issue is open to debate. But the performance of the Federal Reserve in the last decade and a half seems to provide evidence that discretionary policy can be successful in guiding the economy's performance. After halting inflation early in the 1980s, the Fed has managed to maintain high employment without allowing significant inflation In fact, in 1997, the unemployment rate dipped as low as 4.8 percent, the lowest in about 25 years, with no noticeable increase in the price level. Many economists argue that this experience demonstrates the wisdom of activist monetary policy.

But all do not agree with this assessment. Monetarists believe that the lags in monetary policy are long and unpredictable. Consequently, they contend, attempts to use monetary policy to guide the economy's performance can result in worse rather than better economic performance. New classical economists also argue against discretionary monetary policy, believing that, as with fiscal policy, the actions of policymakers will be anticipated and neutralized. They argue that an expansionary monetary policy will have no beneficial impact on the economy; it will only lead to inflation. The views of the monetarists and the new classical economists will be considered in detail in Chapter 16.

Summary

Economists define *money* as anything that serves as a *medium of exchange,* a *standard of value,* and a *store of value.* Currency (coins and paper money) and *checkable deposits* (checking accounts at banks and savings institutions) clearly perform all the functions of money. Other *assets*—passbook savings accounts, for example—perform some, but not all, of the functions of money or perform those functions incompletely. Assets that are not money but that can be quickly converted into money are termed *near money.*

In its role as controller of the U.S. money supply, the Federal Reserve defines that supply according to three classifications. The narrowest is M-1, composed of currency in the hands of the public plus all checkable deposits. A somewhat broader definition of the nation's money supply, M-2 includes everything in M-1 plus money-market mutual fund balances, money-market deposits at savings or thrift institutions, and small savings deposits. The broadest definition of the money supply, M-3, includes everything in M-2 plus savings deposits in excess of $100,000.

Approximately 60 percent of the M-1 money supply is in the form of checkable deposits; the remainder is currency. The Federal Reserve provides depository institutions (commercial banks and thrift institutions) with the coins and paper currency they need in order to serve their customers. Checkable deposits, on the other hand, are actually created by the depository institutions themselves when they make loans.

According to the *fractional reserve principle,* a bank must maintain only a given fraction of a dollar in *required reserves* for each dollar in checkable deposits; the balance of those funds can be loaned out to earn interest. In the process of making these loans, banks create checkable deposit money. For example, when a person borrows money from a bank, he or she exchanges something that is not money (an IOU) for something that is money (a checking account balance). This increases the money supply by the amount of the loan.

Each depository institution must limit its loans to the amount of its *excess reserves*—reserves in excess of the sum it is legally required to maintain in the form of vault cash and deposits with the Federal Reserve. This limitation is necessary because as loans are spent, reserves are likely to be lost to other depository institutions. Thus, each institution can expand the money supply by an amount equal to its excess reserves but no more than that.

The banking system (including all depository institutions) does not have to worry about losing reserves. Reserves lost by one depository institution must be deposited in some other bank in the system. The banking system as a whole, then, can create loans and deposits equal to some multiple of its excess reserves. To be precise, it can expand loans and deposits by an amount equal to the initial change in excess reserves times the reciprocal of the reserve requirement (the *deposit multiplier*).

The Federal Reserve, our nation's *central bank,* influences the ability of depository institutions to expand or contract deposits and thereby regulates the size of the nation's money supply. The Fed's board of governors makes all major policy decisions and communicates them to the twelve Federal Reserve banks that oversee the actions of all depository institutions in their districts.

The Federal Reserve has three major tools with which to control the money supply: (1) the buying and selling of government securities, a process known as *open-market operations;* (2) the ability to alter the reserve requirement; and (3) control over the *discount rate*—the interest rate at which commercial banks and other depository institutions can borrow from the Federal Reserve.

All these policy tools affect the reserve position of banks. By influencing the volume of excess reserves, the Fed is able to affect the banking system's ability to make loans and is thereby able to influence the money supply. This control over the money supply enables the Federal Reserve to alter the interest rate, which in turn influences the level of aggregate demand in the economy.

Monetary policy has some distinct advantages over fiscal policy. The lags in monetary policy may be shorter than those in fiscal policy, and because the Fed tends to be somewhat insulated from political pressures, it may have more freedom to pursue long-run goals than Congress does.

Monetary policy is also subject to limitations: (1) The lags in monetary policy have the potential to make Fed action counterproductive. (2) Monetary policy may be more effective in combating inflation than in dealing with unemployment.

GLOSSARY

Asset. Anything of value owned by an entity.

Balance sheet. A statement of a business's assets and liabilities.

Central bank. A government agency responsible for controlling a nation's money supply.

Checkable deposits. All types of deposits on which customers can write checks.

Demand deposits. Non-interest-bearing checking accounts at commercial banks.

Deposit multiplier. The multiple by which checkable deposits (in the entire banking system) increase or decrease in response to an initial change in excess reserves.

Discount rate. The rate of interest charged by the Federal Reserve on loans to depository institutions.

Excess reserves. Bank reserves in excess of the amount required by law.

Federal funds market. A market that brings together banks in need of reserves and banks that temporarily have excess reserves.

Federal funds rate. The rate of interest charged by banks for lending reserves to other banks.

Fractional reserve principle. The principle that a bank needs to maintain only a fraction of a dollar in reserve for each dollar of its demand deposits.

Liabilities. The debts of an entity, or what it owes.

M-1. Federal Reserve definition of the money supply that includes currency in the hands of the public plus all checkable deposits; the narrowest definition of the money supply.

M-2. Federal Reserve definition of the money supply that includes all of M-1 plus money-market mutual fund balances, money-market deposits at savings institutions, and small savings deposits.

M-3. Federal Reserve definition of the money supply that includes all of M-2 plus large savings deposits.

Medium of exchange. A generally accepted means of payment for goods and services; one of the three basic functions of money.

Monetary policy. Any action intended to alter the supply of money in order to influence the level of total spending and thereby combat unemployment or inflation.

Near money. Assets that are not money but that can be converted quickly to money.

NOW account. A savings account on which the depositor can write checks; NOW stands for negotiable order of withdrawal.

Open-market operations. The buying and selling of government securities by the Federal Reserve as a means of influencing the money supply.

Owners' equity. The owners' claims on the assets of the business; it is equal to assets minus liabilities.

Required reserves. The amount of reserves a depository institution is required by law to maintain. These reserves must be in the form of vault cash or deposits with the Federal Reserve.

Reserve requirement. The fraction of a bank's checkable deposits that must be held as required reserves.

Savings deposits. Interest-bearing deposits at commercial banks and savings institutions.

Standard of value. A unit in which the prices of goods and services can be expressed; one of the three basic functions of money.

Store of value. A vehicle for accumulating or storing wealth to be used at a future date; one of the three basic functions of money.

STUDY QUESTIONS

Fill in the Blanks

1. Money functions as a _____ ,

   a _____ , and a

   _____ .

2. Demand deposits, NOW accounts, and ATS accounts are all examples of

   _____ .

3. The primary characteristic of all M-1 money is that it can easily function as a

   _____ .

4. A bank must maintain reserves equal to a specified fraction of its

   _____ .

5. Banks create money when they

   _____ ; the amount of money that a bank can create is

   equal to its _____ .

6. Today, the primary purpose of the Federal Reserve is to regulate or control the

   _____ in order to combat unemployment and inflation.

7. According to economic theory, an increase in the money supply would tend to

   (increase/decrease) _____ the interest rate, which would tend to

   (increase/decrease) _____ aggregate demand, which, in turn, would

   (increase/decrease) _____ GDP.

8. The primary policy tool used by the Federal Reserve to control the money supply

   is _____ .

9. The rate charged by the Federal Reserve on loans to depository institutions is

   called the _____ .

10. Monetary policy may be less effective in

    combating _____

    than _____ .

Multiple Choice

1. Which of the following is the largest component of the M-1 money supply?
   a) Currency
   b) Passbook savings accounts
   c) Checkable deposits
   d) Money-market accounts

2. Which of the following is *not* an example of near money?
   a) A savings account
   b) A government bond
   c) A piece of prime real estate
   d) An account with a money-market fund

3. Which of the following does *not* appear as an asset on the balance sheet of a bank?
   a) Demand deposits
   b) Reserves
   c) Securities
   d) Loans

4. Assuming that the reserve requirement is 30 percent, how much additional money can the bank represented below create? (All figures are in millions of dollars.)

ASSETS		LIABILITIES	
Reserves	$23	Checkable	$50
Securities	25	deposits	
Loans	17	Owner equity	40
Property	25		

   a) $ 8 million
   b) $12 million
   c) $15 million
   d) $25 million

5. Assuming a reserve requirement of 25 percent, how much additional money can the bank represented below create? (All figures are in millions.)

ASSETS		LIABILITIES	
Reserves	$35	Checkable	$80
Securities	30	deposits	
Loans	25	Owner equity	20
Property	10		

   a) $20 million
   b) $15 million
   c) $10 million
   d) $ 5 million

6. If the reserve requirement is 25 percent, the deposit multiplier would be equal to
   a) 4.
   b) 5.
   c) 1/4.
   d) 10.

7. If the balance sheet represented in question 5 were for the banking *system* rather than for a single bank, the system could expand the money supply by an additional
   a) $15 billion.
   b) $30 billion.
   c) $60 billion.
   d) $80 billion.

8. Which of the following was *not* accomplished by the Monetary Control Act of 1980?
   a) It virtually eliminated the distinction between member and nonmember commercial banks.
   b) It enhanced competition between the various types of financial institutions.
   c) It established uniform reserve requirements for all depository institutions.
   d) It eliminated the "lender of last resort" function of the Federal Reserve.

9. If banks hold checkable deposits of $200 million and reserves of $50 million and if the reserve requirement is 20 percent, how much additional money can the banking *system* create?
   a) $20 million
   b) $50 million
   c) $100 million
   d) $200 million

10. Which of the following is *not* a function of the Federal Reserve?
    a) To control the money supply
    b) To make loans to depository institutions

c) To insure the deposits of customers
d) To provide a check-collection service

11. If the Federal Reserve wants to reduce the equilibrium interest rate, it should
   a) increase the reserve requirement in order to expand the money supply.
   b) sell securities on the open market in order to expand the money supply.
   c) buy government securities in order to expand the money supply.
   d) increase the discount rate in order to expand the money supply.

12. When the Federal Reserve sells government securities on the open market, the lending ability of banks
   a) tends to decline; the money supply shrinks, and the interest rate tends to decline.
   b) tends to decline; the money supply expands, and the interest rate tends to rise.
   c) increases; the money supply expands, and the interest rate tends to fall.
   d) tends to decline; the money supply shrinks, and the interest rate tends to rise.

13. Let's assume that all banks in the system are "loaned up" (have no excess reserves) and that they all face a reserve ratio of 20 percent. If the Federal Reserve buys a $100,000 secu-rity from Bank A, how much new money can the banking *system* create? (*Hint:* Remember that the Fed will pay for the security by increasing the reserve account of Bank A.)
   a) $100,000
   b) $1,000,000
   c) $400,000
   d) $500,000

14. If the Federal Reserve wanted to reduce inflationary pressures, what would be the proper combination of policies?
   a) Increase the reserve ratio, decrease the discount rate, and sell securities.
   b) Increase the reserve ratio, increase the discount rate, and sell securities.
   c) Increase the reserve ratio, increase the discount rate, and buy securities.
   d) Decrease the reserve ratio, decrease the discount rate, and buy securities.

15. To combat unemployment, the Federal Reserve should
   a) reduce the money supply by selling government securities.
   b) reduce the money supply by lowering the reserve requirement.
   c) increase the money supply by raising the discount rate.
   d) increase the money supply by buying government securities.

Problems and Questions for Discussion

1. Explain each of the functions of money. Which of these functions does a traditional savings account perform? A NOW account?

2. Explain what is meant by the fractional reserve principle. How is it related to a bank's ability to create money?

3. Why must individual banks limit their loans to the amount of their excess reserves?

4. If a bank can create money, why can't you?

5. What is the deposit multiplier, and how is it calculated?

6. If you asked for your loan in cash rather than accepting a checking account, what impact would this action have on the money-creating ability of your bank? What about the banking system as a whole?

7. Suppose that you have a credit card with a $1,000 limit (you cannot charge more than $1,000). Should that $1,000 be considered part of the money supply? Why or why not?

8. Why might monetary policy be less effective in combating unemployment than in combating inflation?

9. Discuss the reasons for the passage of the Monetary Control Act of 1980.

10. According to Keynesians, monetary policy works through the rate of interest. Explain.

11. Suppose that the Federal Reserve increases the reserve requirement. Explain the step-by-step impact of that change on the economy.

12. Why is the discount rate often described as a weak policy tool?

13. What are the advantages of open-market operations over changes in the reserve requirement?

14. Suppose that the housing industry is depressed. What monetary policy actions would you recommend to help the housing industry? Why do you think they would help?

15. If the Fed buys a government security from a private individual, the money supply will immediately be increased. If the Fed buys a government security from a bank, this action will not affect the money supply until a loan is made. Explain the difference. That is, why does one transaction have an immediate impact while the other does not?

ANSWER KEY

Fill in the Blanks

1. medium of exchange, standard of value, store of value

2. checkable deposits

3. medium of exchange

4. checkable deposits

5. make loans; excess reserves

6. money supply

7. decrease, increase, increase

8. open-market operations

9. discount rate

10. unemployment, inflation

Multiple Choice

1. c	4. a	7. c	10. c	13. d
2. c	5. b	8. d	11. c	14. b
3. a	6. a	9. b	12. d	15. d

The Modern Activist-Nonactivist Debate

In theory, monetary and fiscal policies can be used to maintain full employment and stable prices. But each of these demand-management policies is subject to limitations. Activists argue that in spite of their limitations, these policies can still play an important role in guiding the economy's performance. Nonactivists find the limitations so severe as to make the policies ineffective or counterproductive. This is the controversy that concerns us in this chapter.

As you can see, we have returned to the activist-nonactivist debate that we first encountered in Chapter 11. Just as Keynes and the classical economists disagreed about the advisability of government intervention to guide our economy, today's neo-Keynesians disagree with monetarists and new classical economists (also known as rational-expectations theorists). This chapter introduces you to the views of these competing schools of thought and examines the modern debate about demand-management policies. It also takes a brief look at supply-side economics. We turn first to a short review of the Keynesian, or activist, position.

The Activist Position:
Keynes Revisited

As you learned in Chapter 11, Keynes did not believe that capitalist economies necessarily tend to full employment. Rather, he argued that because of the volatility of spending, particularly investment spending, they could be in equilibrium at a level of output either less or greater than potential GDP. If business executives were pessimistic, they might choose to cut back on investment spending, sending the economy into a tailspin and causing unemployment. If they were optimistic about the future, they might choose to expand investment spending, pushing GDP above potential and causing inflation.

Keynes was an activist economist in the sense that he advocated government action to prevent outbreaks of unemployment or inflation and to combat these problems when they occur. According to Keynes, the central government should use fiscal and monetary policies to ensure sufficient aggregate demand to achieve full employment without inflation.

Fiscal policy, you will recall, is the manipulation of government spending or taxation in order to guide the economy's performance. The appropriate Keynesian fiscal policy for a period of unemployment would be to increase government spending for goods and services or to reduce taxes. These policies would expand aggregate demand, raise the equilibrium GDP, and lower unemployment. Inflation calls for reductions in government spending or higher taxes. By reducing aggregate demand, these policies will reduce inflationary pressures.

Monetary policy—deliberately changing the money supply to influence the level of economic activity—can also be used to combat unemployment or inflation. If unemployment exists, the Federal Reserve (the government agency that regulates the money supply) can increase the money supply in order to drive down the market rate of interest. The lower interest rate will tend to stimulate investment spending and certain forms of consumption spending. By stimulating aggregate demand in this manner, monetary policy can raise equilibrium GDP and lower unemployment. Inflation can be attacked by reducing the money supply and thereby raising the prevailing rate of interest. A higher interest rate will cause businesses and consumers to cut back on their borrowing (and spending) and reduce inflationary pressures.

Even if fiscal and monetary policies work in the manner Keynesians suggest, why would anyone consider using them? If the economy is self-correcting in the long run, why not let it take care of itself? In describing the problems posed by an unemployment equilibrium, the neo-Keynesian response echoes that of Keynes himself more than fifty years ago: "In the long run, we are all dead!" The adjustment process described in Chapter 12 takes time, perhaps a substantial period of time. In the interim, society loses output that will never be regained, individuals suffer the humiliation of being without work, and families deplete their savings or are forced to rely on charity or government assistance. In short, unemployment is costly, and the losses incurred as we wait for self-correction may be unacceptable.

Production above potential also imposes costs on society. As we saw in Chapter 12, when equilibrium GDP exceeds potential, the price level is pushed up, generating inflation. Although society benefits from the additional output and employment, unanticipated inflation tends to redistribute income in an arbitrary way. Moreover, the long-run adjustment process will ultimately eliminate the short-term gain in output and leave the economy with a still higher price level.

In summary, neo-Keynesians believe that capitalist economies are inherently unstable, so that they are always in danger of operating either above or below potential GDP. Although the economy will ultimately return to potential GDP, waiting for this long-run adjustment to occur is needlessly costly to society. Instead, fiscal and monetary policies should be used to prevent deviations from potential GDP or to minimize their duration if they occur.

The Nonactivist Position:
The Monetarists

Not all economists agree with the activist, or neo-Keynesian, position. The two major groups, or schools, of nonactivist economists are the monetarists and the new classical economists (rational-expectations theorists). We will begin by examining the monetarist position.

Monetarism is the belief that changes in the money supply play the primary role in determining the level of aggregate output and prices in the economy. Economists who hold this belief are called *monetarists*.

According to monetarists, an increase in the money supply will tend to stimulate consumption and investment spending, raising equilibrium output and the price level; a reduction in the money supply will have the opposite effect. Neo-Keynesians agree that changes in the money supply can alter output and prices, but they emphasize that other factors—changes in investment or government spending, for instance—can also influence the economy. Monetarists tend to see these other factors as decidedly secondary; changes in the money supply are what really matter.

FISCAL POLICY AND CROWDING OUT

The paramount importance that monetarists attach to the money supply is illustrated by their criticism of Keynesian fiscal policy. According to monetarists, fiscal policy is ineffective unless it is accompanied by monetary policy. To illustrate this view, let's suppose that the economy is suffering from unemployment and that Congress decides to increase government spending to combat the problem. What will happen? The monetarists believe that if the money supply is not increased, government borrowing to finance the larger deficit will drive up the interest rate and discourage, or crowd out, investment spending. In an economy with more government spending but less investment spending, the net effect will be no stimulus to the economy. However, if the Federal Reserve allowed the money supply to expand while the government borrowed, it *would* be possible to provide some net stimulus to the economy. The interest rate would not be bid up, and so investment spending would not be discouraged; thus, total spending would actually expand. Monetarists are quick to point out that the stimulus in this situation results from the increase in the money supply, not from the added government spending.

MONETARY POLICY AND THE MONETARY RULE

Because monetarism focuses attention on the money supply, eager students sometimes conclude that monetarists must favor the use of discretionary monetary policy to guide the economy's performance. But that's not the case. Monetarists believe that changes in the money supply are too important to be left to the discretion of policymakers. Instead, they support a **monetary rule** that would require the Federal Reserve to expand the money supply at a constant rate, something like 3 percent a year.[1]

If the Fed were required to increase the money supply at a constant annual rate, it would no longer be free to use changes in the money supply as a policy tool; it could not increase the money supply more rapidly to combat unemployment or slow the growth of the money supply to combat inflation. In other words, a monetary rule would eliminate the possibility of the Keynesian monetary policies described in Chapter 15. In a sense, the Fed would be

---

[1] Monetarists believe that the money supply should be expanded at 3 percent a year because they think that potential GDP expands at about that rate. If sustainable output is growing at 3 percent a year, a 3 percent larger money supply is needed in order to facilitate this greater volume of transactions. But whether we choose to increase the money supply at 3 percent or 4 percent or 6 percent is not too important, so long as we pick *some* rate and stick with it. If the money supply is growing more rapidly than the economy's ability to produce output, inflation will result. But because it will be a reasonably constant rate of inflation, we will know what to expect and will be able to build it into our wage agreements and other contracts. Thus, it will not tend to redistribute income the way unanticipated inflation does.

Milton Friedman, shown here accepting his Nobel Prize in economics, would like to see the Federal Reserve adhere to a monetary rule.

put on autopilot. Monetarists favor this approach because they are convinced that the Fed's attempts to combat unemployment or inflation have often made things worse rather than better.

POLICY LAGS AND THE SELF-CORRECTING ECONOMY

According to the monetarists, it is time lags that tend to make Keynesian monetary policies counterproductive. Obviously, Fed policymakers cannot take action until they recognize that a problem exists. Unfortunately, the economy commonly sends mixed signals about its performance. For this reason there is a **recognition lag** before agreement is reached that a problem exists. Even after the problem is recognized and policymakers take action, there will be an **impact lag** before the effect on spending is felt in the economy. Moreover, once the policy does begin to influence spending, the effect will continue for some time.

The existence of lags would not be a major argument against discretionary monetary policy if the economy tended to remain in an unemployment or inflationary equilibrium indefinitely. But that's not what happens. As our discussion of the self-correcting mechanism indicates, the economy ultimately begins to solve its own problems. When we recognize this self-correcting tendency, lags can mean trouble for policymakers. To illustrate, suppose that the economy gradually weakens and begins to experience a recession. Fed policymakers eventually recognize the problem and take action to expand the money supply. But if the recognition and impact lags are long enough, the economy may begin to recover on its own before these policies start to take effect. Thus, monetary policy may begin to stimulate spending when such stimulus is no longer welcome. Of course, too much spending can lead to inflation, which is precisely what monetarists believe has happened on several occasions.

In summary, monetarists shun discretionary monetary policy because they believe that it often has a destabilizing effect on the economy—creates additional problems—rather than the stabilizing effect that neo-Keynesians predict. In fact, monetarists believe that government tinkering with the money supply may be the major destabilizing force in the economy. For example, Milton Friedman—who is sometimes referred to as the father of monetarist economics—argues that it was inept monetary policy that caused the Great Depression. According to Friedman, the Fed turned what could have been a serious downturn into a major catastrophe by allowing the money supply to fall substantially in the early 1930s. He contends that a policy of stable money growth would have been vastly superior.[2]

MONETARISM: CONCLUDING POINTS

Perhaps the major source of disagreement between neo-Keynesians and monetarists is about the nature of the economy. Like Keynes, neo-Keynesians tend to see the economy as inherently unstable and relatively slow to recover from demand and supply shocks. Monetarists, on the other hand, believe that the economy is fundamentally stable and returns fairly rapidly to potential GDP whenever deviations occur. If it persists in deviating from potential GDP, it is due to government tinkering, not to the nature of the economy.

Monetarists emphasize that eliminating the Fed's ability to tinker with the money supply would not completely eliminate unemployment or inflation. Fluctuations in spending would still occur, and some unemployment or inflation would result. But the adoption of a monetary rule would eliminate the major source of fluctuations in spending—fluctuations in the growth of the money supply—and would therefore tend to minimize any unemployment or inflation.

CRITICISMS OF MONETARISM

Neo-Keynesian economists disagree with monetarists on several basic points. First, they believe that monetarists attach too much importance to the money supply. Neo-Keynesians agree that changes in the money supply can alter

---

[2] Milton Friedman, "The Case for a Monetary Rule," *Newsweek,* Feb. 7, 1972. Reprinted in M. Friedman, *Bright Promises, Dismal Performance: An Economist's Protest,* published by Thomas Horton and Daughters, Sun Lakes, Arizona, 1983.

GDP, but they argue that other factors are also important—perhaps even more important. These factors include changes in the level of investment or government spending. Neo-Keynesians believe that such autonomous changes can lead to inflation or unemployment even if the money supply expands at a constant rate. For instance, Neo-Keynesians argue that pessimism about the future might cause businesses to cut back on investment and that this might lead to unemployment even if the money supply continues to expand at a steady rate.

Second, although virtually all neo-Keynesians agree with monetarists that crowding out reduces the effectiveness of fiscal policy, neo-Keynesians believe that only a small amount of investment spending will normally be crowded out, so that expansionary fiscal policy can still have a significant impact on equilibrium GDP.

But many modern Keynesians are quite critical of the long lags involved in implementing changes in taxation and government spending. Since the lags in implementing monetary policy are generally shorter than the lags in implementing fiscal policy (though prorule monetarists argue that they are still too long), monetary policy is seen as the primary technique for stabilizing the economy.

Third, neo-Keynesians are critical of the monetary rule because they believe that it could contribute to greater, rather than less, unemployment and inflation. Because neo-Keynesians believe that the economy is *inherently* unstable (due to the volatility of investment spending), they argue that Fed policymakers need discretion to be able to offset fluctuations in spending and thereby maintain full employment without inflation.

The Nonactivist Position:
The New Classical Economists

As you probably noted, monetarists have much in common with the classical economists we discussed in Chapter 11. Both groups see the economy as fundamentally stable and believe in laissez-faire policies. But another school of modern economists has even more in common with the original classical theorists, so much so that this school has been dubbed the "new" classical school of economics.

The new classical economics is based on two fundamental beliefs: (1) wages and prices are highly flexible, and (2) expectations about the future are formed "rationally." The remainder of this section investigates the implications of those beliefs.

WAGE/PRICE FLEXIBILITY AND FULL EMPLOYMENT

Like the classical theorists of old, the economists of the new classical school (of which the most prominent members are Robert Lucas of Chicago, Thomas Sargent of Stanford, and Robert Barro of Harvard) believe that wages and prices are highly flexible. This flexibility permits markets to adjust quickly to changes in supply or demand, so that shortages or surpluses are prevented. In short, highly flexible prices ensure that the quantity of the good or service demanded will equal the quantity supplied; markets will "clear."

New classical economists believe that the market-clearing principle applies not only to individual markets—the markets for shoes or cars or accountants, for instance—but also to the aggregate economy. Its implications for the overall labor market are particularly important. To illustrate, let's suppose that the economy experiences a decline in aggregate demand. Of course, when the overall demand for products declines, the demand for labor must also fall. But the new classical economists do not believe that this reduction in labor demand will result in unemployment. Because wages are highly flexible, the reduced level of labor demand will cause wages to drop. Lower wage rates will both encourage employers to hire more workers and reduce the amount of labor supplied (at the lower wage, some workers will prefer leisure to work). The reduction in wages will thus restore equilibrium in the labor market; everyone who is willing to work at the new, lower wage will find employment, and every employer who is willing to pay that wage will find workers.[3] Any unemployment must be voluntary.

THE IMPORTANCE OF EXPECTATIONS

The belief in highly flexible wages and prices and the voluntary nature of unemployment is not new; this view was held by the original classical economists. But the new classical economists are not clones of the originals; they have made their own distinctive contribution to economic thinking. The distinctive feature of the new classical economics is its focus on expectations and the way that expectations influence people's behavior.

These economists remind us that different expectations about the future can lead to different decisions today. For instance, if consumers expect new-car prices to be lower in a few months, they will probably wait to buy; if they expect prices to be higher, they will buy now. These are commonsense observations that few of us would challenge. But the new classical economists go well beyond these observations. They are interested in how expectations are

---

[3] The new classical economists do not believe that labor contracts make wages so inflexible as to prevent these adjustments.

formed; in other words, they want to know how individuals come to expect whatever they expect—higher car prices, lower interest rates, or more rapid inflation, for instance.

Neo-Keynesians and monetarists disagree about many things, but both groups have assumed that individuals base their expectations only on experience—by looking backward at past events. The new classical economists argue that this assumption implies that individuals are irrational because it presumes that they ignore current events that they know will influence the future. As an alternative, the new classical economists have proposed the theory of rational expectations.

The **theory of rational expectations** suggests that people use all available information to develop realistic (rational) expectations about the future. According to this theory, the public is quite perceptive in forming its expectations. Households and businesses do not merely project past trends into the future; they also take current economic developments quickly into account.

For instance, when forecasting inflation, people will consider the inflation of recent years, but they will also consider the potential impact of upcoming labor negotiations, the rate of productivity growth, the anticipated quality of agricultural harvests (and their impact on food prices), developments in the Middle East (and their impact on oil prices), and—perhaps most important of all—the expected government response to inflation.

RATIONAL EXPECTATIONS AND DISCRETIONARY POLICY

The belief that wages and prices are highly flexible and that expectations are formed "rationally" leads the members of the new classical school to some interesting policy conclusions. According to the new classical economists, *systematic* monetary and fiscal policies cannot alter the level of output or employment in the economy; they can change only the price level. This belief is known as the **policy ineffectiveness theorem.** The implications of the policy ineffectiveness theorem are clear: Government attempts to reduce unemployment are doomed to failure; they will result only in inflation.

The problem, according to the new classical theorists, is that systematic policies whereby the government always responds to a particular set of economic conditions in a given way are *predictable*. But if discretionary policies are predictable, individuals will anticipate those policies and alter their behavior in ways that make the policies ineffective. Thus, individuals, *acting on rational expectations*, make government stabilization policies ineffective.

To illustrate, let's suppose that historically the Fed has expanded the money supply whenever the measured unemployment rate reached 8 percent.[4] Now, let's assume that the unemployment rate reaches that magic number and the Fed feels compelled to take action. Of course, when the money supply is expanded, the aggregate demand curve will shift to the right, as depicted in Exh. 16.1 by the movement from AD_1 to AD_2. This increase in aggregate demand would, ceteris paribus, tend to raise the level of output in the economy. In our example, output would be expanded from the original equilibrium of $900 billion to $1,000 billion (the intersection of AS_1 and AD_2). Because increased output normally means additional jobs, employment would also tend to expand.

But supporters of the theory of rational expectations believe that the assumption of ceteris paribus is unreasonable in this situation. They argue that workers and businesses have learned to anticipate the Fed's policy response to unemployment. Moreover, they have discovered that when the money supply is increased, inflation inevitably follows. (Note that the increase in aggregate demand pushes up the price level along with the level of output.) So when the public perceives that the Fed is likely to increase the money supply, it takes actions to protect itself from the anticipated inflation. Workers ask for higher wages, suppliers raise their input prices, and businesses push up product prices. Because prices and wages are assumed to be highly flexible, these adjustments occur immediately, the moment the public anticipates higher prices. Of course, if wage rates and other costs rise, the aggregate supply curve will tend to shift upward (from AS_1 to AS_2 in Exh. 16.1), and so less real output will be supplied at any given price level. Since the government-mandated increase in aggregate demand has been immediately offset by a *reduction* in aggregate supply, the net effect is to leave output and employment unchanged. The only impact of the expansionary monetary policy has been an increase in the price level from 100 to 110.

---

[4] How can the unemployment rate reach 8 percent if wages and prices are highly flexible? According to the new classical economists, this can occur as a result of *unexpected* shocks in aggregate demand or supply—reductions in planned investment, the outbreak of war, or significant crop failures, for instance. Because these events are unexpected, they may be misperceived by workers. For instance, if the economy experiences a reduction in aggregate demand, some workers may mistakenly assume that the downturn has affected only their industry. Equally important, they may fail to recognize that the overall price level has also fallen, so that the real wage—the purchasing power of their money wage—is unchanged. Suffering from these misperceptions, they are unhappy with their lower money wage. Thus, workers quit their jobs and set out in search of positions that pay as much as they are accustomed to earning. In this way an unexpected shock may lead to unemployment.

EXHIBIT 16.1

Rational Expectations and Economic Policy

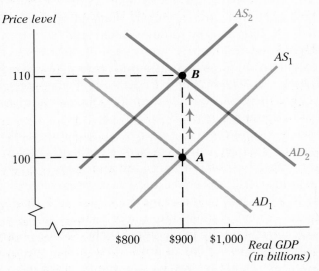

According to the theory of rational expectations, anticipated changes in monetary or fiscal policies cannot alter the level of output or employment; they can change only prices. In this example the expansionary monetary policy that shifts the aggregate demand curve from AD_1 to AD_2 is anticipated, causing workers to ask for higher wages and suppliers to ask for higher input prices. These changes cause the AS curve to shift upward from AS_1 to AS_2, neutralizing the output effect of the monetary expansion and raising the overall price level.

The preceding example focused on efforts to combat unemployment, but the theory of rational expectations has equally interesting implications for the the battle against inflation. To illustrate, let's suppose that the inflation rate rises to some level that Fed policymakers have openly designated as unacceptable. According to the theory of rational expectations, if the public is convinced of the Fed's commitment to reducing inflation, it will expect lower inflation; workers will therefore immediately accept wage cuts, and input suppliers will accept lower prices. As a consequence, the AS curve will quickly shift downward, lowering the price level but preserving the same level of output and employment. Once again, discretionary policy alters only the price level; it has no impact on real output or the level of employment. (Note that this result is quite different from the effect predicted by neo-Keynesians. Neo-Keynesians would argue that because *some* wages and prices are rigid due to contracts, a reduction in aggregate demand would lower *both* the overall price level and the levels of output and employment. In fact, a major concern of neo-Keynesians has been the unemployment "cost" of combating inflation.) Although these examples have dealt with monetary policy, the same conclusions would hold for systematic applications of fiscal policy.

THE NEED FOR POLICY RULES

What conclusions can we reach from the preceding examples? The primary conclusion is that systematic monetary and fiscal policies affect only the price level; they do not alter either the level of output or employment. Of course, for discretionary policies to have the effect intended by neo-Keynesians, they must be systematic; it wouldn't make sense to expand the money supply or to cut taxes at random time intervals. So, in effect, the new classical economists are arguing that discretionary monetary and fiscal policies cannot be used to reduce unemployment.

Because the new classical economists are convinced that government policies cannot be used to alter employment, they believe that policymakers should concentrate on achieving and maintaining a low rate of inflation. This, they suggest, can be best accomplished by permitting a slow, steady growth of the money supply and avoiding large budget deficits. Thus, the new classical economists favor rules much like the monetarists': Increase the money supply at a constant rate, and balance the federal budget over some agreed-on period (not necessarily on an annual basis but over some predictable time frame). These rules will prevent government policymakers from aggravating inflation in their well-intentioned but futile attempts to lower unemployment. (As 1997 drew to a close, the Japanese economy was teetering on the brink of a recession. Did Japanese policymakers respond as Keynesians, monetarists, or new classical economists? Read the article on pages 480–481 to find out.)

CRITICISMS OF THE NEW CLASSICAL ECONOMICS

The new classical economics is quite controversial. Both the assumption of wage/price flexibility and the assumption of rational expectations have been criticized. Few economists seem willing to accept the assertion that wages are sufficiently flexible to ensure that labor markets are continually in equilibrium. These economists point to the prolonged unemployment of the Great Depression and periods in the 1970s and 1980s as evidence that wages adjust slowly, not rapidly as the new classical model implies.

The belief that expectations are formed rationally has also been met with skepticism, both by neo-Keynesians and by many monetarists. Critics argue that the public does not gather and analyze information as intelligently as the theory suggests; nor does it always make fully rational decisions based on

Use Your Economic Reasoning

Is Japan's Rare, Bold Surprise Sufficient to Revive Economy?

By Stephanie Strom

TOKYO, Dec. 17—Prime Minister Ryutaro Hashimoto, facing criticism for sticking to a strategy of fiscal austerity while Japan's economy stands on the brink of recession, stunned his critics today with a surprise package of tax cuts and public spending.

But even as he won praise for changing course, questions quickly arose as to whether his measures were bold enough.

The package includes two trillion yen in income tax cuts—$15.75 billion at current exchange rates, roughly the same amount in spending for public works, and 840 billion yen, or $6.6 billion, in tax cuts for corporations, land owners and investors. In all, the Prime Minister has proposed a stimulus package worth around $38 billion.

It was cobbled together in less than 24 hours, after the Japanese stock market failed to react to leaked reports of a much less ambitious economic plan that would have included just reductions in corporate, land and securities-transaction taxes.

Not all of Mr. Hashimoto's critics, or financial analysts, were mollified by the new package, which includes only about $300 in cuts a year for each Japanese family, and may not be immediately translated into a sufficient stimulus to prime the stalled economy. "It was a necessary step, but it's pretty clear Mr. Hashimoto was dragged to it kicking and screaming," said Alexander Kinmont of Morgan Stanley Japan.

The announcement took bureaucrats here by surprise. Mr. Hashimoto returned to Tokyo late Tuesday evening after a meeting with Asian leaders in Malaysia and began waking colleagues with phone calls to brief them on his plans.

Early today, though, the Finance Ministry seemed to scramble as the announcement was made. "I knew about it at 10:30 this morning—same as you," said Eisuke Sakakibara, the influential vice minister for international affairs. "We are just petty bureaucrats," he said tonight, perhaps only half in jest.

Still, he called the leadership the Prime Minister demonstrated "brilliant," perhaps an indication that his ministry had, after all, been involved in the new plan's preparation.

Bureaucrats from the Finance Ministry polled economists and journalists on Tuesday to get an idea of how certain proposals might be received. That may have led to the additional two trillion yen in public works spending tacked on late this afternoon, apparently in response to analysts' assessments that even a sizable income tax cut, combined with the lowest corporate tax rates since World War II, was not enough to push the economy into a recovery.

Mr. Sakakibara suggested that the package would increase Japan's gross domestic product by at least 1 percent, given that tax cuts usually have an effect beyond their monetary value.

Private economists were less rosy. They estimated that more than half of the income tax cut would find its way into savings accounts, not store cash registers. In 1994, when the Government cut taxes, the savings rate jumped 14 percent after having been flat for the previous three years.

The tax cut announced today is to be for one year only, as Mr. Hashimoto made very clear. And the $300 it would save each taxpayer is to come next June, curtailing any immediate benefit to the economy from increased consumer demand. "It's not enough to create a self-sustaining recovery or send the stock market soaring to new heights," said Mineko Sasaki-Smith, an economist at Credit Suisse First Boston.

The United States was pleased that Mr. Hashimoto had taken at least some action. The prime minister received a call from President Clinton, and Michael D. McCurry, Mr. Clinton's spokesman, praised the measures as a financial package "good for the people of Japan and good for the regional economy of Asia."

Skeptics conceded that any sign of movement on the part of the government would be greeted with relief.

"It's about 1 percent of gross domestic product, but that's really not the point," said Ronald Bevacqua, a Merrill Lynch economist here. "Given how pessimistic everyone has been, this may actually give people some sense of hope. It's about sentiment as much as anything."

The plans for the two trillion yen in public works, which will be contracted and paid for this year, are likely to be controversial. The Government has come under criticism for spending on unnecessary bridges, tunnels and the like that have kept Japan's bloated construction industry afloat for the last few years.

The Prime Minister succeeded in winning applause from critics for his pluck, and got a somewhat more muted reception for the package itself. "I have to think Hashimoto has been wringing his hands over this one a long time," said John F. Neuffer, a political analyst at the Mitsui Marine Research Institue here. "And his timing was so perfect: he rolls in after the party, lackadaisically throws together a package that was sure to be criticized, and steals the show."

In response, the Nikkei index of 225 stocks soared more than 700 points after news of the tax cut got out, and although the index retreated some , it closed the session Wednesday up 3.4 percent....

USE YOUR ECONOMIC REASONING

1. Does the Japanese prime minister sound like a Keynesian, a monetarist, or a new classical economist? Defend your answer.
2. How would a Keynesian expect the Japanese economy to respond to these policy moves? What outcome would a monetarist expect? What about a new classical economist?
3. The Clinton administration praised the prime minister's package of tax cuts and increased public spending as "good for the people of Japan and good for the regional economy of Asia." What model (Keynesian, monetarist, or new classical) is implied by this quote? How could this package be good for the *regional* economy?

that information. Studies of the theory of rational expectations have produced mixed results. Although some early evidence supported the theory, its performance on more recent tests has not upheld its initial promise.

If either of the basic assumptions is incorrect, the policy ineffectiveness theorem of the new classical economists is invalidated. In other words, monetary and fiscal policies would be capable of generating short-run changes in the levels of output and employment. This seems to be the view held by most economists. Of course, whether such policies should be used to change output and employment still depends on the length of the lags involved in policy implementation—the issue raised by the monetarists.

A New Form of Activism: Managing Aggregate Supply

The debate about the desirability of government efforts to manage aggregate demand has been with us for a long time. Given that it is very difficult to prove statistically which of the schools of thought has the most accurate model of the economy, the debate is likely to continue. We'll indicate a few areas of consensus among macroeconomists after we take a brief look at supply-side economics.

Even if monetary and fiscal policies work as Keynesians suggest (which is certainly not the conclusion of the monetarists or the new classical economists), they produce mixed results. As we saw in Chapter 14, efforts to reduce unemployment tend to aggravate inflation, whereas policies to reduce inflation lead to greater unemployment. In addition, demand-management policies are incapable of offsetting supply shocks—unexpected reductions in aggregate supply. Since supply shocks lead to stagflation, they put pressure on policymakers to combat the two problems instead of one. But once again policymakers are confronted by trade-offs. If they choose to combat inflation, they make the unemployment problem even worse; if they decide to attack unemployment, the inflation rate escalates. In the late 1970s these limitations led to an intense interest in supply-side remedies.

SUPPLY-SIDE ECONOMICS

Supply-side remedies are policies designed to shift the aggregate supply curve to the right (downward). Remember, a shift of the aggregate supply curve to the right means an increase in aggregate supply: More is being supplied than before at each price level.

Unlike monetary and fiscal policies, supply-side remedies have the very desirable feature of being able to combat unemployment and inflation at the same time. As you consider Exh. 16.2, suppose that the economy is operating

EXHIBIT 16.2

The Impact of Supply-Side Remedies

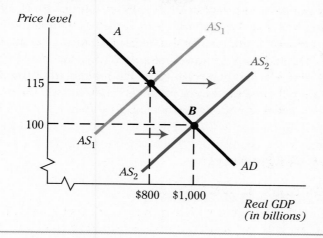

The purpose of supply-side remedies is to shift the aggregate supply curve to the right, thereby reducing the overall price level while increasing output and employment.

at point A, the intersection of AD and AS_1. If policymakers can increase aggregate supply from AS_1 to AS_2, they can move the economy to point B; they will have increased equilibrium output (and employment) in the economy while reducing the overall price level. Policymakers will have succeeded in simultaneously reducing unemployment and inflation.

What policies do supply-side economists advocate? The complete list is too long to present here, but the following are illustrative.

1. *Encourage saving and investment through tax policies.* By encouraging saving through a reduction in taxes on interest income, for example, the government can make more funds available for investment purposes. Various techniques can then be used to encourage businesses to borrow this money and invest it. *Investment tax credits* would allow firms to deduct a certain percentage of their investment outlays from their tax liabilities. To the extent that such policies encourage business to borrow and invest in new factories and equipment, they help to increase the economy's productive capacity so that more output is supplied at any given price level. Of course, if more output is produced at each price level, the aggregate supply curve shifts to the right, as depicted in Exh. 16.2.

2. *Reduce government regulations that drive up the cost of doing business.* We all recognize that government regulations are necessary to protect consumers, the environment, and the health and safety of workers. In some instances, however, regulations may add substantially to the cost of producing goods and services yet may provide little real benefit for the society. For example,

the Food and Drug Administration has been accused of driving up the cost of developing new drugs by needlessly prolonging the testing that is required to gain FDA approval. Reducing such costs should free resources to produce other goods and services; thus, more output can be supplied at each price level.

3. *Encourage individuals to work harder and longer by reducing marginal tax rates.* Marginal tax rates are the tax rates paid on the last increment of income. For example, under a progressive income tax system, an individual earning $15,000 might be required to pay a tax of 15 percent on the first $10,000 and 20 percent on the remaining $5,000. Supply-siders insist that high marginal tax rates discourage work. The way to get people to work more (and thereby increase aggregate supply) is to reduce marginal tax rates and let them keep more of what they earn.

THE REAGAN SUPPLY-SIDE EXPERIMENT

When President Reagan took office, he presented several supply-side features in his Program for Economic Recovery (announced in February 1981). The cornerstone of Reagan's program was the Economic Recovery Tax Act (ERTA) of 1981. Patterned after legislation proposed by two supply-siders, Representative Jack Kemp of New York and Senator William Roth of Delaware, ERTA called for a 5 percent reduction in tax rates in 1981 and a 10 percent reduction in 1982 and 1983. ERTA also contained provisions to encourage saving and to stimulate business investment. According to its supporters, the reduction in tax rates would cause the economy to grow rapidly as the lower tax rates stimulated saving and investment and convinced Americans to work harder. In fact, some supply-siders argued that the economy's growth would be sufficiently rapid that the additional tax revenue generated by the new jobs and expanded hours would more than offset the tax revenue lost through the initial tax cuts. In short, government would take in more revenue at the lower tax rates than it had at the higher rates.[5]

What actually happened? Initially, the effects of the Reagan administration's tax cuts were more than offset by a restrictive monetary policy engineered by the Federal Reserve to combat inflation (which was running at more than 12 percent a year in 1980). While these policies helped to quell inflation, they also pushed the economy into the deepest recession since the Great Depression.

The recession ended in December 1982, and output and employment expanded rapidly through 1984. For the remainder of the 1980s, however, economic growth was unspectacular (President Reagan's term ended in 1988).

---

[5] This possibility was originally suggested by Arthur Laffer, professor of economics at Pepperdine University and one of the early proponents of supply-side measures.

President Reagan's Program for Economic Recovery contained several supply-side features.

Overall, the rate of economic growth experienced in the decade of the 1980s was identical to the experience of the previous decade; in both decades the average annual growth rate of real GDP was 2.7 percent. Clearly, the supply-side measures did not lead to the spectacular economic growth that some supporters expected. In addition, empirical evidence suggests that the supply-side tax cuts did little to encourage work or saving (the personal savings rate actually declined throughout the 1980s). Instead, these tax cuts combined with increases in government spending to result in huge government deficits, which tripled the public debt during Reagan's term in office.

Judged by what some supply-siders initially promised—an explosion in work effort, investment, and saving—the Economic Recovery Tax Act was clearly a failure. Moreover, neo-Keynesian economists attributed most of the economic expansion of the Reagan years not to the supply-side policies but to the demand-side stimulus provided by the substantial budget deficits.

These economists argue that tax cuts shift both the aggregate demand curve (the traditional Keynesian impact) and the aggregate supply curve (the supply-side impact). However, they believe that in the short run, the supply-side impact tends to be minor in comparison with the demand-side effect. Most statistical studies support this view.

THE LONG-RUN IMPORTANCE OF SUPPLY-SIDE MEASURES

Even if neo-Keynesians are correct about the short-run impact of supply-side policies, we should not conclude that measures to enhance aggregate supply are to be ignored. On the contrary, virtually all economists agree that policies designed to expand aggregate supply are crucial to the long-run well-being of Americans. The same policies that cause the aggregate supply curve to shift to the right also cause potential GDP to increase. The ability to increase potential GDP is probably the most important impact of supply-side policies. Although studies suggest that supply-side measures contribute little to the short-run battle against inflation and unemployment, the long-run impact of such policies can be quite important.

To understand why supply-side policies may play an important role in the long run, think about the objective of increasing the living standard of Americans. One measure of a society's standard of living is GDP per person (total GDP divided by population). The first step in ensuring a high standard of living is making the most of our potential, ensuring that the economy operates at full employment. That's the objective of monetary and fiscal policies: to push the economy up to its potential. (As we've already seen, monetarists and new classical economists would argue that these efforts to manage aggregate demand are ill-advised.) But another objective is to keep potential GDP expanding so that it grows more rapidly than the society's population. That objective might be thought of as the domain of supply-side economics.

How do we keep potential GDP increasing more rapidly than population? Consensus holds that the key is in improving labor productivity—output per worker. This means providing workers with more and better capital equipment. (Recall that one of the objectives of supply-siders was to stimulate investment and spending on research and development.) It also means developing a better-educated and more highly motivated workforce. Unfortunately, these changes do not occur automatically. The growth of labor productivity in the United States slowed significantly in the early 1970s and has remained sluggish (though there are some signs of a recent upturn). Economists have been unable to provide a convincing explanation for the slowdown or a palatable plan for remedying the problem. Two things are clear. First, it is more difficult to stimulate labor productivity than the original supply-siders suggested. Second, these efforts generally require society to sacrifice *today* in order to have a higher standard of living in the future. For instance, improving education requires higher taxes, which, in turn, means less disposable income for households. One reason for the productivity slowdown may be a lessening of our willingness to make these sacrifices.

Summing Up: The Current State of Macro Thinking

Economists obviously disagree about the role of government in attempting to maintain full employment and about the possible benefits of supply-side remedies. This section is the author's interpretation of current thinking.

1. Virtually all economists agree that the economy contains, to one degree or another, a self-correcting mechanism. The economy tends to return to potential GDP and full employment in the long run. Economists disagree about how long this adjustment process takes.

2. Economists disagree about the ability of demand-management policies to speed up the adjustment to potential GDP and full employment. Neo-Keynesians support such measures; monetarists and new classical economists do not.

   The differences between activists and nonactivists may not, however, be quite as great as they first appear. Even neo-Keynesians recognize that discretionary policies are subject to lags. Thus, modern Keynesians believe that it is undesirable to attempt to fine-tune the economy—to try to correct every minor increase in unemployment or in the overall price level. Instead, policymakers should confine their efforts to combating major downturns or inflationary threats.

3. The new classical economics has clearly shaken up macroeconomic thinking but hasn't gained very many converts thus far. Most economists do not appear to believe that expectations are formed in a totally "rational" manner. Even fewer economists are willing to accept the classical contention that wages are highly flexible and that markets are continuously in equilibrium. If economists reject these arguments, they must reject the policy ineffectiveness theorem that grows from them.

   Although few economists seem willing to embrace the entire new classical model, most tend to agree that the theory of rational expectations is an improvement on the expectations models previously applied by Keynesians and monetarists. Moreover, there appears to be growing support for a weaker version of the policy ineffectiveness theory: Fully anticipated policy changes have *smaller* effects than unanticipated changes.

4. Virtually all economists support measures to stimulate aggregate supply. But evidence suggests that supply-side measures do little in the short run to stimulate GDP or to lower the price level. The major impact of supply-side policies comes in the long run, when their benefits can be substantial.

Summary

Although economists generally agree about the existence of a self-correcting mechanism, they disagree about the speed with which this adjustment process occurs and about the desirability of government efforts to enhance these naturally occurring forces.

Neo-Keynesians believe that the economy's self-correcting mechanism works quite slowly. Thus, they support an active role for government in speeding the adjustment process through discretionary monetary and fiscal policies.

Monetarists believe that the economy's self-adjustment mechanism works reasonably quickly and that government efforts to aid this process are either ineffective or counterproductive.

According to monetarists, changes in the money supply play the primary role in determining the level of aggregate output and prices in the economy. Government efforts to stimulate the economy through fiscal policy are futile because they lead to the crowding out of investment spending.

The monetarists also argue against the use of discretionary monetary policy. Because of the *recognition lag* and the *impact lag*, the effect of a monetary policy change may be felt when it is no longer appropriate. Thus, discretionary monetary policy has a destabilizing effect on the economy: It contributes to greater unemployment and inflation.

Because monetarists believe that discretionary monetary policy tends to intensify the economy's problems rather than to lessen them, they support a *monetary rule* that would require the Fed to expand the money supply at a constant annual rate.

Monetarists are not alone in opposing the use of discretionary policies to guide the economy's performance; *new classical economists* also argue against such intervention. The new classical economics is founded on two basic tenets: (1) wages and prices are highly flexible, and (2) expectations about the future are formed rationally.

Because new classical economists believe that wages and prices are highly flexible, they believe that the economy quickly tends toward full employment. Reductions in aggregate demand are met by falling wages and prices, which quickly restore equilibrium. Any unemployment is voluntary.

New classical economists emphasize the impact of expectations on behavior; different expectations about the future can lead to different decisions today. The *theory of rational expectations* suggests that people use all available information to develop realistic expectations about the future.

The new classical economists' belief in highly flexible wages and prices and rational expectations led to the *policy ineffectiveness theorem*. According to this theorem, systematic monetary and fiscal policies cannot alter the level of output or employment in the economy; they can change only the price level.

Because the new classical economists are convinced that government policies cannot be used to alter output or employment, they believe that policymakers should concentrate on achieving and maintaining a low rate of inflation. The new classical economists, like the monetarists, favor rules to achieve this objective.

The activist-nonactivist debate has focused on the desirability of demand-management policies. But in the late 1970s, supply-side remedies—policies to increase aggregate supply—attracted a great deal of attention. The desirable feature of such policies is that they can reduce unemployment and inflation at the same time. Available evidence suggests that supply-side measures have a relatively modest impact on aggregate supply in the short run; most of the impact comes in the long run.

GLOSSARY

Impact lag. The time that elapses between the implementation of a policy change and its initial effect on the economy.

Monetarism. The belief that changes in the money supply play the primary role in determining the level of aggregate output and prices in the economy.

Monetary rule. A rule that would require the Federal Reserve to increase the money supply at a constant rate.

Policy ineffectiveness theorem. The theory that systematic monetary and fiscal policies cannot alter the level of output or employment in the economy; they can change only the price level.

Recognition lag. The delay in implementing policy that results from the mixed signals sent by the economy.

Theory of rational expectations. The theory that people use all available information to develop realistic expectations about the future.

STUDY QUESTIONS

Fill in the Blanks

1. Neo-Keynesian economists who advocate government intervention to guide the economy's performance are also known as

   _____ .

2. The two modern schools of thought that oppose the use of demand-management

   techniques are the _____

   and the _____ .

3. The two types of lags associated with discretionary monetary policy are the

   _____ lag and the

   _____ lag.

4. According to the _____

   and the _____ , the Fed should be required to expand the money supply at a constant rate.

5. _____ is often called the father of monetarism.

6. According to the _____, expectations are formed rationally.

7. The belief that systematic monetary and fiscal policies cannot alter the level of output or employment is known as

   the _____ theorem.

8. The requirement that the Fed expand the money supply at a constant rate is known

   as the _____ .

9. The use of monetary or fiscal policy in an attempt to eliminate even minor increases in unemployment or inflation is known as

   _____ the economy and is opposed by virtually all modern economists.

10. Unlike monetary and fiscal policies,

   _____ remedies can be used to reduce unemployment and inflation at the same time.

Multiple Choice

1. Which of the following schools of economists would be described as "activists"?
   a) Classical economists
   b) Neo-Keynesian economists
   c) Monetarist economists
   d) New classical economists

2. Which of the following statements about the activist-nonactivist debate is true?
   a) Monetarists advocate the use of discretionary monetary policy to manage aggregate demand and to ensure full employment.
   b) New classical economists support the use of fiscal policy to guide the economy but believe that monetary policy is ineffective.
   c) Neo-Keynesians advocate government intervention because they believe that the self-correcting mechanism works too slowly.
   d) All of the above

3. According to the monetarists,
   a) fiscal policy is ineffective because of crowding out.
   b) fiscal policy is more effective than monetary policy.
   c) increases in government spending tend to lower interest rates, thus stimulating investment spending.

   d) increases in government spending tend to stimulate investment spending by making business leaders more optimistic.

4. Which of the following is a true statement about the monetarists?
   a) They favor the use of discretionary monetary policy to guide the economy's performance.
   b) They believe that the money supply should be increased at a constant rate.
   c) They favor legislation to provide Fed policymakers with more power to guide the economy's performance.
   d) a and c

5. When monetarists call for a "monetary rule," what they really want is
   a) greater reliance on discretionary monetary policy and less reliance on discretionary fiscal policy.
   b) legislation to provide Fed policymakers with more power to guide the economy's performance.
   c) legislation that would require the Fed to increase the money supply at a constant rate.
   d) bigger paychecks for monetarist economists.

6. The two types of lags in monetary policy are the
   a) policy lag and the implementation lag.
   b) recognition lag and the impact lag.
   c) recognition lag and the policy lag.
   d) identification lag and the implementation lag.

7. The major reason monetarists oppose the use of discretionary monetary policy to guide the economy's performance is that they
   a) do not believe that changes in the money supply have any impact on output or employment.
   b) believe that lags cause monetary policy to have a destabilizing effect on the economy.
   c) believe that monetary policy is not as effective as fiscal policy.
   d) believe that rational expectations make monetary policy changes ineffective.

8. Neo-Keynesians believe that the economy is inherently unstable because of
   a) the instability created by government fiscal policy.
   b) fluctuations in the level of government spending.
   c) the volatility of investment spending.
   d) Federal Reserve monetary policies.

9. Which of the following is *not* a belief of the new classical economists?
   a) Wages and prices are highly flexible.
   b) Expectations are formed rationally.
   c) Unemployment is voluntary.
   d) Labor markets adjust very slowly to changes in demand.

10. According to the theory of rational expectations,
    a) households and businesses base their expectations only on past experience.
    b) people use all available information in developing their expectations about the future.
    c) it is reasonable for households and businesses to ignore the actions of policymakers.
    d) only policymakers have sufficient knowledge to develop accurate estimates of future price levels.

11. According to the policy ineffectiveness theorem,
    a) anticipated changes in monetary or fiscal policy will alter only the price level.
    b) fiscal policy is ineffective unless it is accompanied by monetary policy.
    c) monetary policy is ineffective unless it is accompanied by fiscal policy.
    d) unanticipated changes in monetary or fiscal policy will alter only the price level.

12. The new classical economists believe that any anticipated increase in the money supply will
    a) expand output and employment.
    b) be immediately offset by a reduction in aggregate supply.
    c) immediately cause potential GDP to expand.
    d) lead to an immediate reduction in the price level, with no change in output or employment.

13. According to neo-Keynesians, which of the following is true?
    a) When unemployment is caused by inadequate aggregate demand, expanding the money supply will reduce unemployment but intensify inflation.
    b) When inflation is caused by a supply shock, reducing the money supply will lower the rate of inflation but aggravate unemployment.
    c) When unemployment is caused by a reduction in aggregate supply, increasing the money supply will reduce unemployment but aggravate inflation.
    d) All of the above
    e) None of the above

14. Which of the following is *not* a supply-side remedy?
    a) Use tax credits to encourage investment.
    b) Reduce marginal tax rates to encourage people to work longer and harder.
    c) Increase tax rates on interest income in order to discourage saving and stimulate consumption spending.
    d) Eliminate government regulations that do not serve a valid purpose.

15. In the short run, reductions in marginal tax rates probably increase
a) only aggregate demand.
b) only aggregate supply.
c) both aggregate demand and aggregate

supply but have a greater impact on demand.
d) both aggregate demand and aggregate supply but have a greater impact on supply.

Problems and Questions for Discussion

1. Given that the economy has a self-correcting mechanism, what is the essence of the neo-Keynesian argument for government intervention to combat unemployment?

2. Why do the monetarists believe that fiscal policy cannot be used to stimulate the economy?

3. Discuss the lags involved in the implementation of monetary policy.

4. Neo-Keynesians blame the inherent instability of capitalist economies on the volatility of investment spending. Why do you suppose investment spending by businesses is more volatile than consumption spending by households?

5. What is the nature of the *monetarist* argument for a monetary rule?

6. The new classical economists sometimes argue that only random monetary policy can alter output and employment. Use

their model to explain this conclusion. Does this mean that policymakers should replace Keynesian demand-management policies with random policies?

7. Explain the logic behind the policy ineffectiveness theorem of the new classical economists. Supplement your explanation with a graph.

8. Discuss the similarities and differences between the monetarists and the new classical economists with regard to the issue of demand-management policy.

9. List as many supply-side remedies as you can remember, and discuss the rationale for each.

10. Critics of the Reagan experiment with supply-side economics often argue that it was "oversold." What do they mean? What evidence might they summon to support their position?

ANSWER KEY

Fill in the Blanks

1. activists
2. monetarists, new classical economists
3. recognition, impact
4. monetarists, new classical economists
5. Milton Friedman
6. new classical economists
7. policy ineffectiveness
8. monetary rule
9. fine-tuning
10. supply-side

Multiple Choice

1. b	4. b	7. b	10. b	13. d
2. c	5. c	8. c	11. a	14. c
3. a	6. b	9. d	12. b	15. c

PART FOUR

International Economics: Trade, Exchange Rates, and the Balance of Payments

Chapter 17 introduces the economic rationale for international trade and considers the consequences of barriers to free trade. You will learn the meaning of such concepts as "comparative advantage" and "absolute advantage" and see why these concepts are used to summon support for free trade. Arguments for and against free trade will be presented, and we will look closely at the impact of foreign competition. Chapter 18 considers the financial dimension of international trade and the role of exchange rates. You will see how exchange rates are determined and how changes in exchange rates influence international trade. You will also learn about the balance of payments accounts that nations use to keep track of their international transactions, and why a nation's balance of payments always balances.

International Trade

1. Explain the difference between open and closed economies.
2. Define imports and exports.
3. Explain the principles of absolute and comparative advantage.
4. Describe the benefits of more open trade.
5. Explain why more open trade will benefit some groups and harm others.
6. Describe the different types of trade barriers.
7. Explain why economists prefer tariffs to quotas.
8. Discuss the common arguments for protection from foreign competition and the limitations of each.
9. Describe the roles of GATT, NAFTA, and the World Trade Organization.
10. State the case for trade adjustment assistance.

The first sixteen chapters of the text have included numerous examples involving our economic relationships with other nations. We've previewed the benefits of international trade, and we've considered the impact of trade on our GDP. We've seen how international influences can dominate the process of price determination in competitive markets and how a recession in Europe or some other part of the world can affect the U. S. economy. We've included these examples because, like it or not, the U.S. economy is increasingly an **open economy**—an economy that exchanges goods and services with other nations. (A **closed economy,** by contrast, does not exchange goods and services with other nations.)

The increased openness of the U.S. economy is a matter of some controversy. Many Americans see foreign competition as a destructive force that threatens their jobs and their way of life. Others view foreign competition as a blessing that provides quality products at prices lower than domestic producers charge. Economic policymakers must weigh these costs and benefits as they develop policies to promote or retard international trade. In this chapter we explore the theoretical basis for free, or unrestricted, international trade, and we'll take a closer look at the costs and benefits associated with it.

Interdependent Economies and U.S. Trade

Statistics show that the economies of the world are becoming more interdependent. Consumers in the United States are buying more foreign products, and foreign consumers are buying more U.S. goods. Producers around the world are using more imported parts and raw materials in the products they manufacture. In short, foreign trade is already more important than most Americans realize, and current signs indicate that it will gain even more importance in the future.

IMPORT AND EXPORT PATTERNS

The Sony television sets, Nike tennis shoes, and Raleigh bicycles we see in U.S. stores are all **imports**—goods or services purchased from foreign producers.[1] In the last two decades, trade between the United States and other nations has expanded significantly. More Americans are driving Saabs, Nissans, Peugeots, and Isuzus; are listening to CD players made in Japan; are drinking wine from France and Italy; and are wearing clothes made in Korea, Romania, Taiwan, and other countries. As you can see from Exh. 17.1, imports almost tripled as a fraction of GDP between 1960 and 1997.

U.S. exports are expanding as well. **Exports** are goods and services produced domestically and sold to customers in other countries. For example,

---

[1] The services component of imports includes such items as transportation charges for moving goods and passengers between nations and expenditures made by tourists while traveling in foreign countries.

EXHIBIT 17.1

Trends in U.S. Imports and Exports

	1960	1970	1980	1997
Exports of goods and services	$25.3 billion (4.9% of) GDP	$57.0 billion (5.6% of GDP)	$279.2 billion (10.3% of GDP)	$957.1 billion (11.8% of GDP)
Imports of goods and services	$22.8 billion (4.4% of GDP)	$55.8 billion (5.5% of GDP)	$293.9 billion (10.9% of GDP)	$1,058.1 billion (13.1% of GDP)

SOURCE: Developed from data in *The Economic Report of the President, 1998* and the *Survey of Current Business,* April 1998.

U.S. farmers export wheat and rice and a variety of other agricultural products, while U.S. manufacturing firms export products such as earth-moving equipment, laptop computers, and jet airplanes. Exports of goods and services accounted for less than 5 percent of our gross domestic product in 1960; by 1997 that figure had climbed to almost 12 percent of GDP. That percentage is low compared to Canada (32 percent of GDP), Taiwan (41 percent of GDP), and the Netherlands (61 percent of GDP), but it is a significant fraction of GDP and one that undoubtedly will increase in the future.[2]

INTERDEPENDENCE AND ATTITUDES TOWARD TRADE

We are constantly reminded of the many ways in which national economies are linked to one another. When there is a poor harvest in Brazil, we all pay higher prices for coffee. If the United States undergoes a recession, European businesses suffer a loss of customers. When workers at a German auto-parts manufacturer slow down production to pressure for a wage increase, a Spanish automobile assembly plant is hurt. Like a game of dominoes, events in one part of the world reverberate elsewhere.

Countries often react strongly, almost resentfully, to the actions of foreign nations with whom they trade. When Japanese automobile producers step up production, U.S. producers cry foul. When Federal Reserve policies drive up interest rates in the United States and attract investment funds, complaints ring out from other nations. With increasing frequency, economic events in one part of the world have global repercussions—repercussions that affect each of us.

How should Americans react to this growing interdependence? Does the availability of Japanese automobiles and Taiwanese shoes and other foreign products make Americans better off? Or does the inflow of foreign products simply mean less demand for American products and fewer jobs in domestic manufacturing industries? Should we support U.S. steel and automobile producers and shoe manufacturers when they appeal to our government for protection from "cheap foreign labor"? To respond intelligently to these questions, it is necessary to have some understanding of international economics. We need to understand why countries trade. What are the benefits of trade? Does trade help one country at the expense of another, or is it mutually beneficial? What are the arguments for and against trade barriers? These are the questions we now take up.

---

[2] The percentage figures are for 1996 and are based on information from the *Handbook of International Economic Statistics 1997*, published by the Central Intelligence Agency of the United States.

Domestic workers often protest against imported products.

The Basis for International Trade

Why do countries trade? The various nations of the world are not all equally blessed in terms of either natural resources or capital and labor endowments. Therefore, different nations have different production abilities. Great Britain may be self-sufficient in petroleum products because of oil discoveries in the North Sea. If the British want oranges and grapefruit, however, they will probably have to trade for them because Britain's climate is ill-suited to growing citrus fruits. Americans, by contrast, have no trouble buying domestically grown fruits and vegetables but must rely on other nations for such items as tin, tea, and teakwood furniture. One reason why countries trade, then, is to acquire the products they cannot produce themselves. But that is not the sole—or even the most important—reason for trade.

THE OPPORTUNITY COST
OF DOMESTIC PRODUCTION

Virtually every country is capable of producing almost any product its citizens desire—if it is willing to expend the necessary resources. Lacking alternative sources of supply, the British probably could grow hothouse oranges and grapefruit, and Americans probably would find some way to produce tea domestically. The important point is that neither country chooses to expend its resources this way because other countries can produce these products so much less expensively.

Think of the resources the British would need to use to produce hothouse oranges. More important, think of the other products that Britain could produce with those same resources. Whenever economists talk about the true cost of producing something, they mean the *opportunity cost*. As you will recall, the opportunity cost of anything is what you have to give up to obtain it. The opportunity cost of hothouse oranges would be whatever products the British would sacrifice to produce those oranges. By the same token, the cost of tea or coffee produced in the United States would be whatever other domestic products we could have produced with the same resources.

By making comparisons based on opportunity cost, we can determine which country is the low-cost producer of a particular product without becoming confused or misled as we would if we made comparisons in dollars or some other currency. Economic logic dictates that each country should specialize in the products it can produce at a relatively low opportunity cost and trade for the items that other countries can produce more cheaply. This logic is called the principle of **comparative advantage,** and it is the key to understanding how countries can benefit from trade.

THE PRINCIPLE OF COMPARATIVE ADVANTAGE

The classic example of comparative advantage doesn't involve foreign countries; it has to do with a lawyer and the lawyer's secretary. The lawyer, Ms. Legal Wizard, not only is the best legal mind in the country but also types better than anyone else around. We could say that she has an **absolute advantage** over her secretary (and everyone else in the community) in both jobs. That means that the lawyer is more efficient at those jobs; she can accomplish more work in a given amount of time. If that is the case, why does the lawyer have her secretary, Mr. Average Typist, do the typing? By having the secretary do the typing, the lawyer frees her own time to do legal work.

Consider the high opportunity cost of having the lawyer do her own typing. It would mean the loss of the additional income she could have generated by handling more cases. The secretary, who has almost no talent for legal work, has a comparative advantage in typing because the amount of legal work he gives up to perform the typing duties is insignificant. The secretary does the typing not because he is a better typist than the lawyer (absolute advantage) but because he is better at typing than at legal work (comparative advantage). By allowing individuals to concentrate on the jobs they do best—the jobs in which their absolute advantage is the greatest or their disadvantage the least— the firm is able to handle more clients, earn more money, and thereby raise the standard of living of all its members.

COMPARATIVE ADVANTAGE AS A BASIS FOR TRADE

Countries can benefit from specialization and trade in much the same way that the lawyer and the secretary benefit from their relationship. Consider the possibility of trade between the United States and France. Even if the United States were more efficient than France in the production of everything, specialization and trade along the lines of comparative advantage would allow each country to achieve a higher standard of living than it could possibly attain if it remained self-sufficient.

In order to illustrate that conclusion as simply as possible, let's assume that the United States and France are the only two countries in the world and that they produce only two products: microcomputers and champagne. Exhibit 17.2 summarizes the production abilities of these two nations in terms of a hypothetical unit of resources, with each unit representing some combination of land, labor, capital, and entrepreneurship, some set amount of those resources. For instance, each resource unit might contain 10,000 hours of labor, 1,000 units of raw materials, the use of 10 machines for a year, and 500 hours of entrepreneurial talent. Although each unit contains the same quantities of these resources, the quality of these inputs would vary from nation to nation, giving rise to differences in productive abilities.

With each unit of resources, the United States can produce either 50 microcomputers or 100 cases of champagne. With the same unit, France can produce either 20 microcomputers or 80 cases of champagne. Because the United States can produce more microcomputers and more champagne per unit of resources, we know that it has an absolute advantage over France in the production of both products, just as the lawyer had an absolute advantage over her secretary in both typing and legal work. How is it possible for both countries to benefit from trade when one of them is more efficient, or has an absolute advantage, in producing both products? To answer this question, we must explore the concept of comparative advantage.

EXHIBIT 17.2

Production Possibilities per Unit of Economic Resources

	MICROCOMPUTERS	CASES OF CHAMPAGNE
United States	50	100
France	20	80

In our example the United States has a comparative advantage in the production of microcomputers because the opportunity cost of producing that product is lower in the United States than in France. The United States must sacrifice two cases of champagne in order to free the resources necessary to produce one additional microcomputer. (Each resource unit can produce either 50 microcomputers or 100 cases of champagne, so that each additional computer costs us two cases of champagne.) In France, however, the opportunity cost of each additional microcomputer is four cases of champagne because each unit of French resources can produce either 80 cases of champagne or 20 microcomputers. The United States can produce microcomputers at a lower opportunity cost and therefore has a comparative advantage in that product.

If we switch our attention to champagne production, we note that the French have a comparative advantage in this area. In the United States the production of one additional microcomputer forces the society to sacrifice two cases of champagne. The opportunity cost of producing one more case of champagne is therefore half a computer. In France the cost is lower. Each additional microcomputer requires the sacrifice of four cases of champagne. Therefore the opportunity cost of each case of champagne is one fourth of a computer. The French do indeed have a comparative advantage in the production of champagne.

The Benefits of Trade

Now that you understand how to determine a nation's comparative advantage, let's see how trade based on the principle of comparative advantage can result in a higher standard of living for both trading partners. In the absence of product specialization and trade, both France and the United States would produce some microcomputers and some champagne, with the exact amounts of each depending on the strength of demand for the two products. Prior to trade, we can't say with precision what those amounts would be, but we know that one microcomputer would exchange for two cases of champagne in the United States and for four cases of champagne in France.

Suppose that the United States decides to specialize in the production of microcomputers and offers to trade one microcomputer to France for three cases of champagne. Would the French agree? Of course they would agree! Through trade they can acquire a microcomputer for three cases of champagne, whereas they would have to sacrifice four cases of champagne to produce one domestically. Under such circumstances they are better off to specialize in producing champagne and to trade for the microcomputers they desire.

As U.S. citizens, would we be better off with this arrangement? We certainly would be. We would be getting three cases of champagne for each microcomputer we traded, whereas we would be able to manufacture only two cases of champagne from the resources we used to produce each micro-computer. Clearly, trade based on the principle of comparative advantage will allow both countries to enjoy a higher standard of living.

THE PRODUCTION POSSIBILITIES CURVE AND THE GAINS FROM TRADE

We can see the gains from trade more clearly by using the production possi-bilities curve introduced in Chapter 1. A production possibilities curve (PPC) shows the combinations of goods that an economy is capable of pro-ducing with its present stock of economic resources and existing techniques of production.

Let's assume that the United States and France have 100 units of economic resources each to use in producing either microcomputers or champagne and that these resources are equally suited to the production of either product. When resources are assumed to be equally productive, the production possi-bilities curve appears as a straight rather than a bowed-out line (recall Chap-ter 1). In the United States these 100 resource units can be used to produce either 10,000 cases of champagne or 5,000 microcomputers or any other com-bination of champagne and microcomputers found on its production possibil-ities curve [see Exh. 17.3(a)]. In France the 100 resource units can be used to produce either 8,000 cases of champagne or 2,000 microcomputers or any other combination of champagne and microcomputers found on France's pro-duction possibilities curve [see Exh. 17.3(b)]. Recall that any combination of products we can plot either on or within the production possibilities curve (PPC) is available to the society. Combinations falling outside the PPC are be-yond the economy's production capability and therefore unattainable unless we can trade for them.

Suppose that prior to trade, the United States chooses to produce and con-sume 2,000 cases of champagne and 4,000 microcomputers, whereas France chooses a combination of 5,000 cases of champagne and 750 computers. Total world production would then be 7,000 cases of champagne (2,000 produced by the United States and 5,000 by France) and 4,750 microcomputers (4,000 produced by the United States and 750 by France).

Next, suppose that the two countries decide to specialize along the lines of comparative advantage, agreeing to trade with each other at our hypothet-ical exchange ratio: 1 microcomputer = 3 cases of champagne. The United States has a comparative advantage in microcomputers, so it will use all its

EXHIBIT 17.3

Production Possibilities Curves and the Gains from Trade

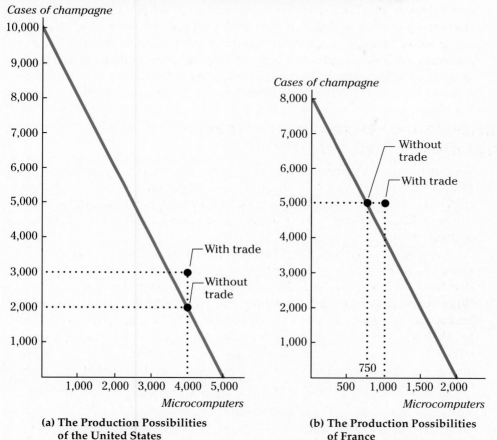

**(a) The Production Possibilities
of the United States**

**(b) The Production Possibilities
of France**

The two production possibilities curves show the combinations of champagne and microcomputers that the United States (a) and France (b) can produce. Without trade, each nation is forced to select a combination of the two products that lies either on the production possibilities curve or inside it. For example, the United States might choose to produce and consume 2,000 cases of champagne and 4,000 microcomputers, whereas France might select a combination of 5,000 cases of champagne and 750 microcomputers. Through specialization and trade, each of these nations can enjoy a higher standard of living. If the United States specializes in producing microcomputers and France specializes in champagne, each of these nations can move to a point beyond its production possibilities curve. For example, if the two countries agree on an exchange ratio of one microcomputer for three cases of champagne, the United States can exchange 1,000 microcomputers for 3,000 cases of champagne. That will leave the United States with 4,000 microcomputers and 3,000 cases of champagne, whereas France will have 1,000 microcomputers and 5,000 cases of champagne; both countries will be better off than they were without trade.

100 resource units to produce microcomputers and will trade for champagne. The French will produce champagne, their product of comparative advantage, and will trade for microcomputers.

We know that the United States is producing 5,000 microcomputers and that France is producing 8,000 cases of champagne. What will be the result if the United States trades 1,000 microcomputers for some champagne? With an exchange ratio of one microcomputer to three cases of champagne, the United States will receive 3,000 cases of champagne in return for its 1,000 microcomputers and will still have 4,000 microcomputers left over. France will have 5,000 cases of champagne left over plus 1,000 microcomputers. The United States will have 1,000 more cases of champagne than it had prior to trade, and France will have 250 more microcomputers.

Trade and specialization have made it possible for each country to move beyond its PPC and to enjoy a combination of products that it could not obtain on its own. Moreover, total world production has increased from 7,000 to 8,000 cases of champagne and from 4,750 to 5,000 microcomputers. The principle of comparative advantage has allowed each of the trading partners to obtain more goods from each resource unit and to enjoy a higher standard of living.

THE TRANSITION TO GREATER SPECIALIZATION: WINNERS AND LOSERS

Trade based on comparative advantage clearly makes sense. And in the absence of **trade barriers**—legal restrictions on trade—we can be confident that the pursuit of self-interest will automatically lead producers to specialize in the products in which their country has a comparative advantage. Consider again our hypothetical world economy. Prior to trade, microcomputers were selling for twice as much as a case of champagne in the United States but four times as much as a case of champagne in France. Enterprising French and U.S. businesses would take advantage of these international price differentials to increase their profits. For instance, suppose that microcomputers were selling for $1,000 in the United States and that a case of champagne was selling for $500. In France, on the other hand, microcomputers were selling for 4,000 francs and a case of champagne for 1,000 francs. U.S. businesses could make a substantial profit by selling microcomputers in France and using the money to buy champagne for resale in the United States. French businesses could do the reverse; they could sell champagne in the United States and use the proceeds to buy computers for resale in France. Because French producers can sell champagne for less, ultimately they would force U.S. champagne producers out of business. The same fate would befall French computer manufacturers: They would be eliminated by competition from the United States.[3]

What would happen to the workers displaced from the French computer industry and the U.S. champagne industry? Our model assumes that all resources are equally suited for champagne production or computer manufacturing and that they move freely between those industries within each country but not between countries. Thus, the economic resources—workers, factories, and equipment—no longer needed by the U.S. champagne industry would flow to the U.S. computer industry, and the resources released by the French computer industry would flow to the French champagne industry. With greater specialization, workers in both countries would become more productive, and they would be paid higher wages by their employers. In this way the benefits of trade would be shared by all members of the society; everyone would benefit from specialization and trade based on comparative advantage.

The transition to greater international specialization, however, is never painless. When a domestic industry is eliminated or reduced in size by foreign competition, difficult adjustments follow. Unemployed workers need time to find other jobs, and factories must be put to other uses. Some of these resources will never be reemployed because firms are reluctant to invest money to retrain a fifty-five-year-old winemaker, for example, or remodel a thirty-year-old computer plant. Even though the total output of both countries will be greater than before trade (see Exh. 17.3), not every individual or group will be better off. Thus, specialization has costs as well as benefits.

LOWER PRICES THROUGH INTERNATIONAL COMPETITION

Even when specialization is incomplete and several countries continue to produce the same products, international trade can benefit consumers by providing them with a wider variety of products from which to choose. Furthermore the availability of foreign products limits the pricing discretion of domestic producers and forces them to be more responsive to consumer demands.

---

[3] Even in the absence of trade barriers, specialization may be less than complete. The United States might continue to produce some champagne, and France might continue to produce some microcomputers.

In order to conclude that foreign trade along the lines of comparative advantage will lead to complete specialization, we have to assume that (1) the products offered by French and U.S. manufacturers are identical—that French champagne is the same as U.S. champagne; (2) all economic resources are equally productive in both uses; (3) economic resources can move freely from one industry to the other but not between countries; (4) transportation costs are not large enough to outweigh the differences in production costs in the two nations; and (5) the computer and champagne industries are purely competitive. To the extent that these assumptions are not met, specialization will be less than complete.

Competition from foreign automobile manufacturers has helped to hold down new-car prices in the United States.

Consider the U.S. automobile market. Foreign competition has not only given U.S. consumers more brands from which to choose but has also spurred domestic manufacturers to develop small, fuel-efficient cars. In addition, competition from foreign producers has helped to keep automobile prices in the United States lower than they would be otherwise. A study by the Council of Economic Advisers concluded that if automobile imports were limited to 10 percent of the U.S. market, new-car prices would increase between 13 and 17 percent. Studies by the Federal Trade Commission and the International Automobile Dealers Association also predicted significant price hikes—up to $3,000 a car.[4] As you can see, international competition can be a powerful force in restraining the market power of domestic oligopolists and promoting a higher standard of living for consumers.

When we consider the benefits of trade in permitting greater specialization along the lines of comparative advantage and fostering greater competition, we can understand why economists generally agree on the

[4] Murray L. Weidenbaum, with Michael C. Munger and Ronald J. Penoyer, *Toward a More Open Trade Policy* (Center for the Study of American Business, Formal Publication 53, Jan. 1983), p. 5.

desirability of **free trade**—trade that is not hindered by artificial restrictions or trade barriers of any type.

Types of Barriers to Trade

We have seen that free trade benefits consumers but often imposes substantial costs on particular groups in a society. Moreover, the benefits of free trade are widely diffused across a large number of people, each of whom is made a little better off, whereas the losses tend to be concentrated in a relatively small segment of the society. Workers who are forced out of jobs by foreign competition provide the best example.

Not surprisingly, the segment that is significantly harmed by foreign competition is likely to be more vocal than the group whose welfare is slightly improved. That's why politicians in the United States and elsewhere hear more often about the costs of free trade than about its benefits. As Michael Oldfather, former chairman of the Kansas Council on Economic Education, has noted,

> [R]emoving import barriers on cars . . . might save every car-buying family a few hundred dollars a year. On the other hand, several thousand families would lose a great deal each (the families of U.S. automobile workers). Even though the total gains of car buyers would far exceed the total losses of car makers, it's not hard to guess whose voice will be the loudest.[5]

Virtually all the nations of the world impose trade barriers of one sort or another, partly in response to political pressure. These trade barriers are designed primarily to limit competition from imports, although export restrictions are sometimes established. The most common devices for limiting import competition are protective tariffs and import quotas.

TARIFFS

A **tariff** is a tax on imported goods. Its purpose is either to generate revenue for the taxing country through a *revenue tariff* or to protect domestic producers from foreign competition by means of a *protective tariff*. Historically, revenue tariffs were the major tool for financing government expenditures. Such tariffs served as the principal source of revenue for the U.S. government through the nineteenth century and remain the principal source in some less developed countries.

Today, most developed countries rely on other forms of taxation for revenue—income and sales taxes, for example. When developed countries, such as the United States, employ tariffs, their main purpose is to protect domestic

---

[5] Michael Oldfather, "Cost of Any Import Ban Outweighs Gain," *Springfield* (Mo.) *News-Leader*, March 9, 1983, p. 7E.

producers. A tariff on a foreign product increases its price and makes it less competitive in the marketplace, thereby encouraging consumers to buy domestic products instead. For instance, the United States imposes tariffs of up to 20 percent on imported luggage, and imports of some synthetic apparel are subject to tariffs of more than 30 percent. Of course, these tariffs make the imported items less attractive relative to domestic products, thereby helping to insulate U.S. producers from foreign competition. We'll have more to say about the impact of tariffs a little later in the chapter.

QUOTAS

Quotas restrict trade in a different way. An **import quota** specifies the maximum amount of a particular product that can be imported. The volume of imported wine, for example, might be limited to 50 million gallons per year, or the quantity of imported steel could be limited to 100,000 tons each year.

Import quotas can be either global or selective. A *global quota* limits the amount of a product that can be imported from the rest of the world. When the limit is reached, all further imports of that item are prohibited. A *selective quota* specifies the maximum amount of a product that can be imported from a particular country. For example, the United States might set a global quota of 500,000 imported automobiles per year and further specify selective quotas: 250,000 cars from Japan and 50,000 from France, perhaps, and the remaining 200,000 from other countries.

Domestic producers generally support import quotas over tariffs. Both trade barriers reduce competition from imported goods, but quotas are considered more effective. If consumers prefer foreign products to those offered by domestic producers, they can continue to buy relatively large amounts of those products in spite of the higher prices caused by the tariff. On the other hand, a quota will completely prohibit imports once the limit has been met.

The impact of quotas can be substantial. For example, the Government Accounting Office (GAO) estimates that sugar quotas cost American consumers $1.4 billion in higher prices each year. (Sugar costs 22 cents a pound in the United States but only 14 cents a pound on the world market. That means higher prices for soft drinks, candy, and numerous other products.) And import quotas on clothing are estimated to cost U. S. consumers something in the neighborhood of $20 billion a year in higher prices for everything from sweatshirts and swimsuits to neckties and dresses.[6] In short, the existence of quotas is not merely of academic interest; it's a pocketbook issue for each of us.

---

[6] "Foot-dragging on Trade Treaty Socks Levi's, GAP," *San Francisco Business Journal,* March 17, 1995.

OTHER RESTRICTIONS

Trade agreements (which are discussed later in the chapter) have helped to discourage the use of quotas and have reduced tariff rates significantly. But other forms of trade protection are more subtle and more difficult to legislate against. For example, health and safety laws are sometimes invoked to prevent or complicate the importation of certain products. (Even labeling can be used as a trade barrier. Read "Seeing Red over Green," on pages 510–511, to learn how.) The acquisition of import licenses can be made difficult or expensive, and government agencies can be required to purchase domestic products. New York requires that state agencies buy American-made steel, for example, and New Jersey requires that all state cars be produced in the United States.[7]

In addition, new forms of trade interference have emerged, largely to bypass, or take advantage of, the rules in existing trade agreements. Among the most troubling is the **voluntary export restraint (VER),** an agreement under which an exporting country "voluntarily" limits its exports to a particular country, often under threat of the imposition of a quota. For example, in 1981 Japan signed a VER that limited its auto exports to the United States to 1.68 million units annually through 1984. And in 1995 Canada agreed to a five-year pact limiting its lumber exports to the United States. Voluntary export restraints have also been used to influence trade in textiles, steel, footwear, motorcycles, machine tools, and consumer electronics.[8] Although VERs have essentially the same effect as quotas, they are not expressly prohibited by existing trade agreements, which discourage the use of *unilaterally imposed* quotas.

Another method of discouraging imports is to accuse a country of dumping. **Dumping** occurs when a product is sold to foreign consumers at a lower price than to domestic buyers. From an economic point of view, selling to different markets at different prices may make perfect sense. In fact, such price discrimination (recall Chapter 7) is a common practice of U.S. businesses. For example, airlines commonly charge a lower fare on routes on which they face substantial competition and charge a much higher fare (for a trip of the same length) on routes from which competition is absent. Economic logic notwithstanding, the United States has long held that dumping is an unfair form of competition (perhaps because, in *rare* circumstances, it can be used to drive a competitor out of business). As a consequence, U.S. laws prohibit dumping and call for additional tariffs to be imposed on products dumped in the U.S. market. (Existing trade laws permit such "antidumping duties.") The U.S. Department of Commerce judges cases involving dumping in the United States

---

[7] Muray Weidenbaum, *Confessions of a One-Armed Economist* (Center for the Study of American Business, Formal Publication 56, Aug. 1983), p. 25.
[8] Jagdish Bhagwati, *Protectionism,* (The MIT Press, Cambridge, Mass., 1988) p.44.

Use Your Economic Reasoning

Seeing Red Over Green

Why big business hates eco-labels

By Marc Levinson

Back in the good old days—say, around 1990— "trade dispute" meant stuff. You know: clothes, cars, computer chips, you buy more of ours or we'll put the screws to yours. Then came the Information Age, with ethereal conflicts over patents and bootleg CDs. If you're perplexed by trade wars over music royalties, get a grip, because the battles only get stranger. Now business lob-

byists are egging U.S. negotiators to arm for a fight over …labels.

Not just any labels. We're talking eco-labels, those symbols certifying that your bedsheets and laundry detergent are ecologically benign. Eco-labels aren't big in America, where only a handful of items bear the imprimatur of Green Seal, Inc., or the cross and globe of its competitor, Scientific Certification Systems. Abroad, through, green consumerism is hot. Almost everyone in Germany recognizes the Fed-

eral Environment Office's blue angel. The white Nordic swan is so popular that Swedish retailers insist on it. Even India has a seal for products whose manufacture, use and disposal are deemed least harmful to the environment. But where environmentalists tout progress, business sees a new form of protectionism. Says Scott Stewart of Procter & Gamble, "Eco-seals potentially create barriers to trade."

Exhibit A: copy paper. Any paper can be sold in the European Union's

and generally finds in favor of U.S. companies. As a consequence, the mere threat of a dumping case is often enough to convince foreign firms to raise their prices. As with VERs, the real loser is the consumer.

Trade Barriers and Consumer Welfare

Economists generally condemn all forms of trade barriers. By reducing competitive pressures on domestic producers, such barriers allow firms with market power to charge higher prices yet be less responsive to the demands of consumers. Moreover, trade barriers interfere with the principle of comparative advantage: They prevent countries from concentrating on the things they do best and enjoying the best products produced by other countries.

15 member nations. But to earn the EU's eco-label, a flower with 12 stars for petals, copy paper must meet criteria covering factory pollution, forest management and recycled content. By no coincidence, U.S. papermakers say, few non-European paper mills qualify for the label. The eco-standard was approved on May 29, and so far it hasn't affected a single sale. But if the EU follows through on its plan to use only eco-labeled paper, importers could be hurt.

In theory, eco-labels should lead to a cleaner environment. "It's a very pure idea," says Phil Evans of Britain's Consumers Association. "The problems come in the actual practice." Paper recycling, for example, might make sense in Holland, but requiring paper made in Canada's sparsely settled west to use recycled pulp may consume more resources than it saves. Or take the EU's eco-label for T shirts. U.S. makers claim the rules permit more pollution from plants that dump wastewater into the sewer than from those that treat it on site, as most U.S. textile plants do.

A problem? Even enviros admit that all-purpose stars and seals can be misleading. But a serious barrier to trade? No, responds Norman Dean of Green Seal, "it's a consumer right-to-know issue." U.S. trade officials are under the gun to launch a push for international eco-labeling rules this month. So far, though, the Clinton administration hasn't figured out whether a green label is worth a bloody fight.

USE YOUR ECONOMIC REASONING

1. How can the use of eco-labels be a form of protectionism?
2. Why might a business resort to eco-labels rather than appealing for tariffs or quotas?
3. GATT negotiations have been more successful in reducing tariffs and quotas than nontariff barriers such as eco-labels. Why do you think that has been true?

Consider the impact of tariffs imposed by the United States on luggage imported from China and the Dominican Republic. These tariffs not only increase the prices consumers have to pay for imported luggage but also permit U.S. producers to charge more for their luggage. If imported luggage were not taxed, it would sell for less, and U.S. producers would be forced to reduce their prices in order to compete. Therefore, U.S. producers desire tariffs even though tariffs are harmful to U.S. consumers.

Tariffs are less damaging to consumer welfare than quotas are, however. When increased demand causes the prices of domestic products to rise, comparable tariff-bearing foreign products become more competitive because the price differential between the foreign and domestic products is reduced. Because foreign products are now a more viable alternative for consumers, domestic producers may be restrained from raising prices further, lest they lose sales to foreign rivals. This is not the case with import quotas. When domestic producers are protected by quotas rather than tariffs, rising domestic prices cannot call forth additional units from foreign suppliers once the quotas have been met. As a consequence, domestic producers have more freedom under a quota system to increase prices without fear of losing their market share to foreign firms. (For example, the voluntary export restraint—in effect, a "voluntary" quota—negotiated with Japan in the 1980s is estimated to have cost U.S. Consumers $2,000 more for their foreign *and domestic* automobiles. By restricting imports, the VER not only drove up the prices of imports, it also increased the pricing discretion of domestic producers.)[9]

Another point in favor of import tariffs is that they provide governments with additional revenue, whereas quotas do not. This additional revenue can be used to reduce personal taxes or provide additional government services. Suppose, for example, that instead of using a voluntary export restraint (in effect, a "voluntary" quota) to restrain Japanese automobile exports, we chose to impose a tariff of $1,000 on each imported Japanese car. If 2 million cars were imported annually, that would amount to an additional $2 *billion* in revenue, not an insignificant sum. None of this is meant to suggest that tariffs are desirable, only that they are preferable to quotas.

The impact of trade barriers on the prices that consumers pay is only part of the story. When the United States erects trade barriers to keep out Japanese motorcycles or South Korean clothing or Canadian lumber, it interferes with the pursuit of comparative advantage. Not only do U.S. consumers get less for their dollars, the United States and the other nations of the world get less from their scarce resources. When we establish import quotas to protect high-cost U.S. motorcycle manufacturers, for example, we allow those firms to stay in business and use resources that could be put to better use in producing airplanes or machinery or other products in which the United States has a comparative advantage. We can acquire more motorcycles by producing aircraft and trading for motorcycles than by producing the motorcycles U.S. consumers demand. If we insist on protecting our motorcycle manufacturers and if Japan insists on protecting its aircraft producers, both societies lose. Their people will have to settle for fewer goods and services than free trade could produce. The price tag for this kind of protection is a lower standard of living for the average citizen.

---

[9] Anne O. Krueger, *American Trade Policy: A Tragedy in the Making* (American Enterprise Institute, Washington, D. C., 1995) p.3.

Common Arguments for Protection

In spite of the costs they impose, trade barriers continue to exist. They exist because they serve the interests of certain powerful groups, even though they penalize society as a whole. Anyone who reads the newspaper or watches television is aware of the ongoing efforts of U.S. shoe manufacturers to maintain import protection against cheaper products from Taiwan and South Korea and Italy. Automobile producers, clothing manufacturers, and steel firms also lobby for protection. They argue that removing import restrictions would mean eliminating some producers and shrinking the output of others. The workers in these industries would have to look for new jobs, learn new skills, and perhaps even relocate to other parts of the country. These adjustments would be easy for some but difficult for others, particularly older workers. For these reasons, employers and employees in industries that suffer from foreign competition have a strong personal interest in appealing to Congress for protection. Invariably the arguments that are used to justify protection mix some truth with at least an equal amount of misunderstanding or distortion. Let's consider three of the most popular arguments.

1. *Infant industries need protection from foreign competition.* The infant-industry argument suggests that new industries need protection until they become firmly established and able to compete with foreign producers. This argument makes little sense in a diversified and sophisticated economy like that of the United States but may have some relevance in less developed countries. Even in that setting, there are dangers. There is no assurance that the new industry will ever be able to compete internationally, and once protection has been granted, it is difficult to take away.

2. *Defense-related industries must be protected to ensure our military self-sufficiency.* This argument suggests that we must protect certain critical industries so that the United States will not be dependent on foreign countries for the things it needs to defend itself in time of war. The national-defense argument is commonly used to summon support for the protection of a long list of industries, including steel, munitions, rubber, and petrochemicals. There is no way to decide which industries are critical to our national defense and which are not. The longer the list, the more expensive protection becomes for U.S. consumers.

3. *U.S. workers need protection from cheap foreign labor.* The cheap-labor argument is heard often today. It claims that U.S. producers and their workers need protection from firms operating in countries with much lower wage rates than the United States, wage rates that constitute an unfair advantage that protection should offset. (A variation of this argument suggests that we

need to prohibit or limit imports from low-wage countries, not only to protect U.S. workers but also to protect foreign workers from sweatshop conditions. The article on pages 516–517, "Estimate of Child-Labor Levels Triples," looks at the implications of this argument as it applies to child labor.)

There are two major flaws in this argument. First, low wages do not necessarily mean cheap labor. Labor is cheap only if the value of the output it produces is high relative to the wage rate. In many industries the United States is very competitive internationally despite its high wage rates. Workers produce more output per hour than their foreign counterparts because U.S. workers tend to work with more and better machinery and tend to be better trained than workers in many other countries.

Second, we must remember that no country can have a comparative advantage in everything. The United States has a comparative disadvantage in the production of products whose manufacture requires large amounts of unskilled labor. On the other hand, we tend to have a comparative advantage in goods that are produced using highly skilled labor or large quantities of land or capital.

If we insist on protecting our labor-intensive industries, other nations have every right to protect their capital-intensive industries. Of course, such protectionism will deprive everyone of the benefits of comparative advantage, and we'll all be poorer for having resorted to protectionist measures.

Reducing Barriers: The Role of Trade Agreements

Arguments in favor of protecting domestic businesses and workers have been with us always. They were heard when our nation was in its infancy, and they are widely heard today. Protectionist sentiments ran particularly high during the Great Depression. The job losses and business failures of that period led to pleas for protection from foreign competition. In 1930 Congress responded by passing the Smoot–Hawley Act, which raised import tariffs to an average of roughly 50 percent. Other countries retaliated, and the result was a lessening of trade, which may have contributed to a deepening of the Depression. Fortunately the remainder of the twentieth century has seen significant, though halting, progress toward eliminating trade barriers.

The Reciprocal Trade Agreements Act of 1934 began the work of undoing Smoot–Hawley. The 1934 act permitted the President to engage in negotiations with individual trading partners of the United States to reduce tariffs. Because negotiations were on an item-by-item basis, progress was slow. But by the end of World War II, substantial progress had been made: U.S. tariff rates had been reduced from the 50 percent range to about half that level.

INTERNATIONAL TRADE AGREEMENTS: GATT

Following World War II, the United States led efforts to reduce trade barriers still further. In 1947 twenty-three countries signed the General Agreement on Tariffs and Trade (GATT), which established some basic rules for trade and created an organization to oversee trade negotiations. Under GATT rules, countries are discouraged from using import quotas. Instead, they are expected to use tariffs as their means of import protection. And although tariffs are viewed as the preferable form of import protection, the primary objective of GATT has been to reduce tariff rates. This has been accomplished through periodic negotiations known as "rounds." Those negotiations have reduced the average tariff applied by industrial nations to less than 5 percent, a far cry from the 50 percent rates of the Depression era.

Although GATT has resulted in steady downward movement of tariff and quota barriers, it has been less successful in dislodging subtle forms of protectionism, such as the use of health and safety regulations, to discourage imports. In addition, the desire to work within the rules of GATT (but still restrain competition) has led to increased use of voluntary export restraints and accusations of dumping. It is these nontariff/nonquota forms of protectionism that constitute the modern threat to free trade.

The most recent round of GATT negotiations, the Uruguay Round (so-named because it was held in Punta del Este, Uruguay), concluded in 1993. The Uruguay Round did little to deter the use of VERs or dumping cases. But it did succeed in lowering tariffs by about one-third and in reducing agricultural subsidies. It also made some headway in reducing nontariff barriers to trade (such as the spurious use of health regulations to keep out imports). The talks also resulted in the formation of the World Trade Organization (WTO) to replace GATT and arbitrate trade disputes between nations.

In its short existence, the WTO has had both successes and failures. The WTO's *dispute settlement body*, which is like a court for resolving trade disputes, seems to work reasonably well. By 1997 it had resolved more than 60 trade disputes. And, unlike those of its predecessor, the WTO's decisions are binding on members; if they fail to comply, they may face trade sanctions. In 1997 the WTO also managed to negotiate an agreement between 69 countries to open their telecommunications markets to competition, most by 2005. But the organization has had little success in liberalizing other areas of service trade or in reducing voluntary trade restrictions. And a host of new issues remain to be tackled—issues that the GATT agreements have never addressed. Among the most important of these issues is how to respond to the spread of regional trading agreements. Some economists view these agreements as a grave long-term threat to trade liberalization. We turn next to a consideration of those agreements.

Use Your Economic Reasoning

Estimate of Child-Labor Level Triples

By G. Pascal Zachary

There are about 250 million child laborers working in developing countries, about three times more than previous estimates, according to a new study.

The International Labor Organization, in a report issued yesterday, estimates that 120 million children between the ages of five and 14 are working full-time and another 130 million work part-time. The organization, a Geneva-based affiliate of the United Nations, attributed the jump in child workers to more accurate survey methods and the inclusion of workers under 10 years old, as well as economic forces that are driving more employers to rely on children. "The problem of child labor has been growing for two decades," said Gabriele Stoikov, the ILO's top expert on child labor. "Employers are willing to hire children not only because they are cheaper but because they are more docile."

Children in developing countries work mainly in agriculture and as domestic servants. But they also toil in mines, construction and on fishing vessels, as well as in rug, glass and match factories. Some of these jobs pose serious health hazards. Children also are being forced to work—sometimes as prostitutes....

Population increases and worsening poverty in some developing countries have resulted in more working children. In countries where many adults are underemployed, children are more apt to work. "Invariably, children work when their parents can't find enough work," said Pharis Harvey, director of the International Labor Rights and Education Fund, a Washington advocacy group.

Most observers believe that only rising incomes in developing countries will lead to the elimination of abusive child labor. But that could take many years. Meanwhile, there is no agreement on the best way to reduce child labor. One proposal is to impose punitive restrictions on trade in products made by children. Others put their hope in voluntary programs—which would be adopted by government, business and social-services agencies—to steer children into schools and out of the workplace...

In the U.S., Sen. Tom Harkins (D-Iowa) has backed a measure to ban imported goods made by children, and some are pressing the World Trade Organization to adopt a social clause that forbids the worst labor abuses. But global trade isn't a big cause of child labor, though certain export-intensive industries rely on child workers, says Jagdish Bhagwati, a leading trade economist at Columbia University.

Trading bans "may make your conscience look good, but [they] won't get the desired results," Mr Bhagwati says, because displaced child workers won't necessarily end up in school, where they belong, and may be forced into even more degrading labor, such as pornography and prostitution. "We need a sophisticated solution that doesn't just rely on sanctions," he says.

SOURCE: *Wall Street Journal*, Nov. 12, 1996, p A2. Reprinted by permission of the *Wall Street Journal*, © 1996 Dow Jones & Company, Inc. All Rights Reserved Worldwide.

The ILO believes "the most humane strategy must ...be to focus scarce resources on the most intolerable forms of child labor such as slavery, debt bondage, child prostitution and work in hazardous occupations...."

The process of weaning industries off child workers may take years, but some multi-national companies can't wait that long. Though child labor is mainly confined within domestic industries, some exported goods are made partly or wholly by children. Talk-show host Kathie Lee Gifford was caught in a barrage of negative publicity this year after it was revealed that foreign children were involved in producing her line of clothes, sold at Wal-Mart stores. That scandal, along with a similar one involving child-stitched soccer balls sold in the U.S., raised doubts about the ability of multi-national companies to monitor contractors in low-wage countries.

To halt a consumer backlash, apparel, sporting-goods and other international companies are seeking ways to make sure their suppliers don't employ children....

USE YOUR ECONOMIC REASONING

1. How do population increases and worsening poverty lead to increases in the number of working children?
2. Senator Harkins has supported a measure to ban imported goods made by children. What flaw does Mr. Bhagwati see in this approach?
3. Suppose U.S. firms are successful in convincing foreign firms to stop hiring children. What would be the likely consequences of that action?

REGIONAL TRADE AGREEMENTS: NAFTA

The GATT agreements and the WTO have as their objective the reduction of trade barriers worldwide. Recently, however, we have seen the emergence of regional trade agreements that attempt to eliminate or reduce trade barriers only among countries in a particular region or trading block. Trading barriers are removed or reduced for members of the trading block but not for nonmembers. For example, the European Union (formerly the European Economic Community) has eliminated most tariff barriers among member countries while continuing to impose tariffs on imports from nonmembers.[10] The North American Free Trade Agreement (NAFTA) created a similar trading block involving the United States, Canada, and Mexico. Under the agreement (signed by the United States and Canada in 1989 and joined by Mexico in 1993), tariffs among the countries are to be eliminated in steps over a ten-year period.

The extension of the NAFTA agreement to Mexico was the subject of much debate. Supporters argued that it would substantially expand employment in the United States. Critics argued that it would lead to major job losses as additional U.S. businesses fled to the lower wages available in Mexico. Recent evidence supports neither view. A study by Raul Ojeda and others at the University of California at Los Angeles concluded that "the impact on trade-related employment during the first three years after NAFTA is estimated to be ...a near zero net impact."[11] This total does not include more than 33,000 jobs lost in the United States because of plant relocations to Mexico. These jobs were not included because the trend toward relocation was well under way before the passage of NAFTA and has continued at roughly the same pace.

Although both the GATT and NAFTA agreements appear to be steps in the direction of more open, or less-restricted, trade, economists are generally more supportive of GATT than of NAFTA. If the world moves toward trading blocks rather than open trade among all nations, the principle of comparative advantage may be compromised. For example, the United States may find itself buying shoes from Mexico (because Mexico can produce shoes at a lower opportunity cost than the United States) but forgoing shoe imports from Taiwan (which may be able to produce shoes at a lower opportunity cost than Mexico) because Taiwan is outside our trading block and thus faces higher U.S. tariffs. If this occurs, the U.S. standard of living will be somewhat lower than it would have been under a system that provided equal access to all foreign producers. As noted earlier, the WTO has yet to address this issue.

---

[10] The EEC was created in 1957 by Belgium, France, West Germany, Italy, Luxembourg, and the Netherlands. They were later joined by Denmark, Greece, Ireland, Portugal, Spain, and the United Kingdom.
[11] Richard W. Stevenson, "Nafta's Impact on Jobs Has Been Slight, Study Says," *New York Times*, Dec. 19, 1996, p. D1. (The full study by Ojeda and his coauthors, entitled "North American Integration 3 Years After NAFTA," is available on the Internet.)

The Case for Trade Adjustment Assistance

Although the UCLA study concluded that NAFTA has caused no net job losses in the United States, that conclusion masks some important details. Ojeda and his coauthors point out that whereas the increased exports resulting from the NAFTA agreement created about 31,000 new jobs in the United States, increased import competition destroyed about 28,000 jobs in other U.S. industries. In short, while the agreement had very little *net* effect on employment, it clearly benefited some workers and harmed others. This is commonly the case when trade barriers are reduced; there are both winners and losers. Unfortunately the losers are often those who can least afford to lose. For this reason many economists believe that efforts to reduce trade barriers should be accompanied by programs to retrain workers and otherwise assist those harmed by foreign competition.

The Trade Adjustment Act of 1962 took an important first step in this direction. Under this act workers losing their jobs because of increased competition from imports become eligible for **trade adjustment assistance** in the form of higher unemployment compensation and funds for retraining. Businesses are granted money to modernize and better prepare to compete with foreign producers. Unfortunately it is difficult to identify those who are harmed by foreign competition rather than by, say, domestic competition or an economic downturn. For example, the U.S. Department of Labor has certified approximately 116,000 workers for NAFTA Transitional Assistance, far more than our earlier estimate of those whose job losses could be attributed to NAFTA. Some economists argue that we would be better served by more general programs that provide financial assistance to those in need of training, for whatever reason.

Even with government programs, the process of retraining and relocating workers is much more complicated than it appears. In some cases displaced workers have very poor educational backgrounds, which make retraining difficult and expensive. Sometimes there are no additional industries in the area for which the workers can be retrained. Additional factors, such as age, family ties, and limited personal savings, often mean that relocation can be accomplished only at the cost of considerable personal hardship.

All these problems complicate the transfer of labor to other industries and increase the human suffering associated with the removal of trade barriers. In fact, some critics argue that the case for free trade is commonly overstated because economists forget that the assumptions of the model—that resources can shift easily from one industry to another, for example—seldom hold true in reality. This important criticism reinforces what we learned earlier in the chapter: Free trade tends to benefit consumers in general, but it usually imposes substantial costs on particular groups in the society. Such criticisms point to the need for adjustment assistance (perhaps available to any worker in need of retraining or relocation) and programs and policies designed to improve the mobility of the workforce—better general education for high school students, for example—so that there will be a greater likelihood that workers released by one industry can find employment elsewhere without an unbearable delay. By approaching the problem this way, we can move closer to the ideal of free trade while minimizing the distress of workers who are displaced by foreign competition.

Summary

The economies of the world are becoming more interdependent. Americans are buying more *imports*—goods or services purchased from foreigners—and foreign consumers are buying more of our *exports*—products produced domestically and sold in other countries. Furthermore, many American-made products have foreign-made components. To know how to react to this growing interdependence, it is necessary to have some understanding of international economics—of why nations trade and how countries can benefit from trade.

One reason why nations trade is to acquire products that they cannot produce domestically. However, this is not the most important reason. Most countries can produce any product their citizens desire, *if* they are willing to expend the necessary resources. But trade may permit countries to import products much more cheaply—at a lower opportunity cost—than they can produce them domestically. This is the major benefit of international trade.

According to the theory of *comparative advantage,* each country should specialize in the products it can produce at a relatively low opportunity cost and trade for the items that other countries can produce more efficiently. This principle will permit each nation to achieve a higher standard of living than it could possibly attain if it remained self-sufficient.

Even when specialization is incomplete, trade can benefit consumers by providing them with a wider variety of products, limiting the pricing discretion of domestic producers, and forcing domestic producers to be more responsive to consumer demands.

Although free, or unrestricted, trade generally benefits consumers, it often imposes substantial costs on particular groups in any society—workers forced out of jobs by foreign competition, for instance. At least partly in response to pressure from these groups, countries erect *trade barriers*—legal restrictions on trade—to protect their domestic industries.

The most common devices for restricting imports are protective tariffs and import quotas. A *tariff* is a tax on imported products. A tariff on a foreign product increases its price and makes it less competitive in the marketplace, thereby encouraging consumers to buy domestic products instead. An *import quota* specifies the maximum amount of a particular product that can be imported.

Nations also employ a variety of other measures to limit import competition. For instance, stringent safety inspections may be imposed on foreign products to deter their importation, and government agencies may be required to purchase domestic products whenever possible. In addition, countries may negotiate *voluntary export restraints*—agreements under which a country voluntarily limits its exports to a particular country—or may accuse foreign firms of illegal *dumping*—selling to foreign consumers at a lower price than they charge domestic buyers.

Economists tend to condemn all forms of trade barriers. Such barriers allow domestic producers to charge higher prices and to be less responsive to consumers. They also prevent countries from concentrating on the things they do best and trading for the best products produced by other countries.

In spite of the costs they impose, trade barriers continue to exist. Three common arguments are used to support trade barriers: (1) Infant industries need protection from foreign competition; (2) defense-related industries must be protected to ensure our military self-sufficiency; and (3) U.S. workers need protection from cheap foreign labor.

In the 1930s the U.S. government was particularly receptive to protectionist arguments. Since that time, tariff and quota barriers to trade have been reduced substantially. The General Agreement on Tariffs and Trade (GATT) has produced seven rounds of negotiations, which have reduced the average tariff applied by industrial countries to less than 5 percent. The most recent round, completed in 1993, led to the formation of the World Trade Organization, a body intended to replace the GATT organization and extend its trade liberalization efforts.

In addition to the GATT agreements, a number of regional trade agreements have been negotiated between particular countries or trading blocks. The North American Free Trade Agreement (NAFTA) and the European Union (EU) are examples of regional trade agreements. Because these agreements reduce trade barriers within the trading block only, economists view them as less desirable than worldwide trade agreements such as GATT.

Although consumers benefit from more open trade, removal of trade barriers often imposes substantial costs on particular groups in society. When businesses are subjected to foreign competition, they may be forced to close their doors and lay off workers, who may have a difficult time finding employment elsewhere. Therefore, efforts to reduce trade barriers should be accompanied by programs to retrain workers and otherwise assist those harmed by foreign competition.

GLOSSARY

Absolute advantage. One nation's ability to produce a product more efficiently—with fewer resources—than another nation.

Closed economy. An economy that does not exchange goods and services with other nations.

Comparative advantage. One nation's ability to produce a product at a lower opportunity cost than other nations.

Dumping. The sale of a product to foreign consumers at a lower price than is charged domestic buyers.

Exports. Goods and services produced domestically and sold to customers in other countries.

Free trade. Trade that is not hindered by artificial restrictions or trade barriers of any type.

Imports. Goods and services that are purchased from foreign producers.

Import quota. A law that specifies the maximum amount of a particular product that can be imported.

Open economy. An economy that exchanges goods and services with other nations.

Tariff. A tax on imported goods.

Trade adjustment assistance. Aid to workers and firms that have been harmed by import competition.

Trade barriers. Legal restrictions on trade.

Voluntary export restraint (VER). An agreement under which an exporting country voluntarily limits its exports to a particular country, often under threat of the imposition of a quota.

STUDY QUESTIONS

Fill in the Blanks

1. Economists advocate that countries specialize in the products they can produce at a lower _____ than other countries.

2. If country A can produce all products more efficiently than country B, country A is said to have a(n) _____ _____ in the production of everything.

3. If country A can produce a given product at a lower opportunity cost than country B, country A is said to have a(n) _____ in the production of that product.

4. A _____ is a tax on imported products.

5. A(n) _____ specifies the maximum amount of a particular product that can be imported.

6. The _____ argument suggests that new industries need protection until they are firmly established.

7. A _____ quota simply limits the amount of a product that can be imported from the rest of the world, whereas a _____ quota specifies the maximum amount of a product that can be imported from each country.

8. Aid to workers who have been harmed by foreign competition is called _____ .

9. In most situations the (benefits/costs) _____ of free trade are widely diffused, whereas the (benefits/costs) _____ tend to be concentrated.

10. Most economists would like to see trade barriers eliminated. However, if they are forced to choose between tariffs and quotas, they would probably

agree that _____ are less damaging to consumer welfare.

11. In 1930 Congress passed the _____

    _____ Act, which raised U.S. import tariffs to roughly 50 percent.

Multiple Choice

Use the following table in answering questions 1–4.

Production Possibilities per Unit of Economic Resources

	FOOD	CLOTHING
Country A	60	240
Country B	100	300

1. Which of the following statements is true?
   a) Country A has an absolute advantage in the production of both food and clothing.
   b) Country B has an absolute advantage in the production of both food and clothing.
   c) Country A has an absolute advantage in food, and country B has an absolute advantage in clothing.
   d) Country B has an absolute advantage in food, and country A has an absolute advantage in clothing.

2. In country A, the opportunity cost of a unit of food is
   a) 4 units of clothing.
   b) 60 units of clothing.
   c) 240 units of clothing.
   d) 1 unit of clothing.

3. According to the table,
   a) country A has a comparative advantage in food.
   b) country B has a comparative advantage in clothing.
   c) country A has a comparative advantage in clothing.

12. Nations may attempt to negotiate voluntary export restraints because the use of import quotas is discouraged by the

    _____ (trade agreement).

13. The _____ replaced GATT as the organization for settling international trade disputes.

   d) country B has a comparative advantage in both food and clothing.

4. According to the principle of comparative advantage,
   a) country A should specialize in food, and country B should specialize in clothing.
   b) countries A and B should each continue to produce both food and clothing.
   c) country A should specialize in clothing, and country B should specialize in food.
   d) country B should specialize in clothing, and country A should specialize in food.

5. Which of the following is *not* a correct statement about trade barriers?
   a) Import tariffs are taxes on imports.
   b) Tariffs encourage consumers to buy domestic products.
   c) Quotas specify the maximum amount of a product that can be imported.
   d) Tariffs are probably more harmful to consumer welfare than quotas.

6. Which of the following is a true statement about trade barriers?
   a) They tend to enhance competition and benefit consumers.
   b) They benefit society as a whole but penalize small groups.
   c) They are needed to protect U.S. workers from cheap foreign labor.
   d) They serve the interests of certain powerful groups, even though they penalize society as a whole.

7. The purpose of trade adjustment assistance is to
   a) assist foreign countries when a tariff or quota is used to reduce imports from that country.
   b) assist domestic workers who are harmed when a quota is levied.
   c) assist domestic workers who are harmed when a tariff is reduced or a quota is eliminated.
   d) a and c

8. Which of the following is an accurate description of the impact of tariffs?
   a) They tend to raise the prices of imported products that are subject to the tariff.
   b) They tend to raise the prices of domestically produced products that are comparable to those being taxed.
   c) They permit inefficient industries to continue to exist.
   d) All of the above

9. Suppose that Italy can produce either 20 bicycles or 100 calculators with a unit of resources and that Taiwan can produce either 10 bicycles or 80 calculators. Which of the following statements is true?
   a) Taiwan has a comparative advantage in calculators.
   b) Taiwan has an absolute advantage in bicycles.

   c) Italy has a comparative advantage in calculators.
   d) Taiwan has an absolute advantage in calculators.

10. Why do economists prefer tariffs to quotas?
    a) Consumers may continue to buy imported products in spite of the tariff.
    b) Tariffs do not really hinder trade; in fact, they may enhance trade.
    c) As domestic products increase in price, foreign products become more competitive.
    d) a and c

11. The General Agreement on Tariffs and Trade has *not* been very successful in
    a) reducing tariff rates.
    b) reducing the use of import quotas.
    c) discouraging the filing of dumping cases.
    d) all of the above

12. Dumping occurs whenever a firm
    a) charges a lower price in foreign markets than it charges in its home market.
    b) sells a lower-quality product in foreign markets than it sells in its home market.
    c) earns economic profits on its sales to foreign markets.
    d) disposes of wastes by shipping them to disposal sites in foreign countries.

Problems and Questions for Discussion

1. Suppose that your roommate can make a bed in three minutes, whereas it takes you six minutes. Suppose also that your roommate can polish a pair of shoes in ten minutes, whereas it takes you fifteen minutes to do the same chore. What can we say about comparative advantage and absolute advantage in this example? How could the principle of comparative advantage be used to make you both better off? Does it make any difference how often each of these tasks must be performed?

2. Explain the difference between comparative advantage and absolute advantage. Why do economists emphasize the concept

of comparative advantage (rather than absolute advantage) as the basis for trade?

3. How is the concept of opportunity cost related to the principle of comparative advantage?

4. The chapter mentions that politicians in the United States and elsewhere often hear more about the costs of free trade than the benefits. Why is that the case?

5. How can specialization and trade allow countries to consume beyond their own respective production possibilities curves?

6. How do trade barriers contribute to the inefficient use of a society's scarce resources?

7. Some economists have suggested that interference with free trade may be legitimate if it is used as a bargaining chip to convince another country to lower its trade barriers. Economist Robert Lawrence has criticized this approach, likening it to a nuclear deterrent—something that is effective only if it isn't used. Explain Mr. Lawrence's position.

8. If resources (including labor) could move freely from one industry to the next, there would be less opposition to the removal of trade barriers. Explain.

9. As Wisconsin University economist John Culbertson once suggested, "There is little comparative advantage in today's manufacturing industries, since they produce the same goods in the same ways in all parts of the world."("'Free Trade' Is Impoverishing the West," *New York Times*, July 28, 1985, p.F3.) How could less developed countries gain access to the same type of capital equipment employed by the United States? Could they operate it if they could obtain it? What are the implications of Mr. Culbertson's statement?

10. State the three most common arguments for trade protection. What are the limitations of each of these arguments?

11. Why are regional trade agreements, such as NAFTA, sometimes viewed as inferior to international agreements, such as GATT?

12. How can domestic firms use antidumping laws to stifle foreign competition?

ANSWER KEY

Fill in the Blanks

1. opportunity cost
2. absolute advantage
3. comparative advantage
4. tariff
5. import quota
6. infant industry
7. global, selective
8. trade adjustment assistance
9. benefits, costs
10. tariffs
11. Smoot–Hawley
12. GATT
13. World Trade Organization (WTO)

Multiple Choice

1. b
2. a
3. c
4. c
5. d
6. d
7. c
8. d
9. a
10. d
11. c
12. a

International Finance

1. Explain what is meant by an exchange rate and how exchange rates influence international transactions.
2. Describe the difference between a system of flexible exchange rates and a system of fixed exchange rates.
3. Illustrate graphically how the equilibrium exchange rate is determined, and identify the factors that can cause it to change.
4. Explain what it means for a currency to appreciate or depreciate in value.
5. Describe the policies that a nation may be required to pursue to maintain a fixed exchange rate, and why those policies may be unpopular.
6. Describe the current exchange rate system and the role of central banks in that system.
7. Describe the content of a country's balance of payments statement, including its four major sections: the current account, capital account, statistical discrepancy, and official reserve transactions.

What are exchange rates, and how do they influence the prices we pay for imported products and even for travel? What do news commentators mean when they say that the dollar has "appreciated in value" or that the "depreciation of the yen" has made Japanese cars less expensive for Americans?

In Chapter 17 our simplified trade model assumed an arrangement whereby two countries exchanged their products directly. In reality, however, international transactions almost always involve money. Indeed, they usually involve two different types of money—the currencies of the two nations participating in the exchange. As we examine the financial dimension of international transactions, we'll learn how the dollars we spend on imported products are converted into the currencies desired by foreign producers, and we'll explore the systems used to determine exchange rates. We'll consider the factors that can cause the exchange value of a nation's currency to change and the impact of those changes on the nation's economy. Finally, we will examine the U.S. balance of payments accounts and learn what it means to have a "current account deficit" and a "capital account surplus." In short, this chapter extends the analysis of Chapter 17, allowing us to gain a more complete understanding of international trade and our economic relationships with other nations.

The Meaning of Exchange Rates

If you want to buy a Japanese radio, you can pay for your purchase with cash or check or credit card. Ultimately, however, Japanese producers want to receive payment in yen, their domestic currency, because their workers and domestic suppliers expect to be paid in yen. That's why French perfume manufacturers seek payment in francs and Scottish producers of cashmere sweaters expect payment in pounds. The need to convert dollars into a foreign currency (or foreign currency into dollars) is the distinguishing feature of our trade with other nations.

The rate at which one currency can be exchanged for another currency is called the **exchange rate;** it is simply the price of one nation's currency stated in terms of another nation's currency. If you have traveled abroad, you know that the exchange rate is of more than passing interest. Suppose that you are having dinner at a quaint London restaurant where steak and kidney pie costs ten pounds (£10). How much is that in U.S. money? If the exchange rate is £1 to $3, you'll be spending $30; if it's £1 to $1.50, the same meal will cost you only $15.

U.S. importers also want to know the dollar cost of British goods. A wool sweater that sells for £25 will cost the importer $75 if the exchange rate is £1 to $3, but it will cost $100 if the exchange rate is £1 to $4. Whenever the pound is cheaper (whenever it takes fewer dollars to purchase each pound), U.S. tourists and importers will find British goods more attractive. If the pound becomes more expensive, fewer tourists will opt for British vacations, and fewer British products will be imported into the United States.

Exchange Rate Systems: Flexible Exchange Rates

Today, exchange rates are determined primarily by market forces, by the interaction of the demand and supply of the various currencies. This is described as a system of **flexible,** or **floating, exchange rates,** since rates are free to move up or down with market forces.

To illustrate how the system works, assume that the United States and France are the only two countries in the world, so that we need to determine only one exchange rate, that between the U.S. dollar and the French franc. As you can see from Exh. 18.1, the demand curve for francs slopes downward, just as the demand curves for jogging shoes and steak did in Chapter 3. The demand curve for francs slopes downward because, ceteris paribus, as the price of the franc falls, Americans will tend to buy more French products. For example, if the dollar price of the franc fell from $0.30 per franc to $0.20 per franc, U.S. consumers would tend to buy more French wine, clothing, and Paris vacations. And, of course, to buy these products, they would demand more French francs. This assumes that the other factors affecting the demand for French francs remain unchanged. The factors that are assumed to be constant include the tastes and incomes of U.S. consumers, interest rates in the United States and France, and the overall price levels in the two countries. If any of these factors changes, the entire demand curve will shift to a new position.

EXHIBIT 18.1

The Equilibrium Exchange Rate

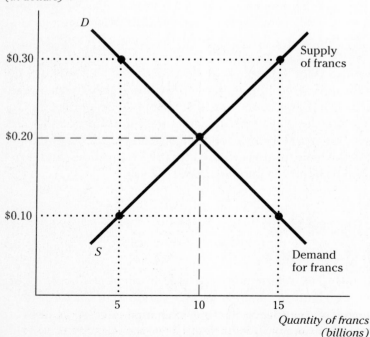

Price of each franc (in dollars)

At the equilibrium exchange rate ($0.20 = 1 Fr), the quantity of francs demanded is exactly equal to the quantity supplied. If the dollar price of the franc is too high for equilibrium, the resulting surplus will tend to reduce the price of the franc. If the price is too low for equilibrium, the shortage of francs will tend to increase its price.

The French supply francs when they want to purchase dollars. If French residents want to buy U.S. products or to visit Disneyland or to invest in California real estate, they exchange their francs to buy dollars. The supply curve of francs slopes upward because, other things being constant, as the value of the franc increases (which means that the dollar becomes less expensive), the French want to buy more U.S. products and will therefore supply more francs. This assumes that the tastes and incomes of French consumers remain unchanged, that French and U.S. interest rates remain constant, and that the price levels in the United States and France are unchanged.

THE EQUILIBRIUM EXCHANGE RATE

The intersection of the supply and demand curves for French francs determines the **equilibrium exchange rate**—the exchange rate at which the quantity of francs demanded is exactly equal to the quantity supplied. In our example these market forces will lead to an equilibrium exchange rate of $0.20 = 1 Fr. At that rate 10 billion francs are demanded and supplied.

If the exchange rate in our example were temporarily above or below the equilibrium level, pressures would exist to push it toward the equilibrium rate. For instance, if the exchange rate were $0.30 to 1 Fr, 15 billion francs would be supplied, but only 5 billion would be demanded. This surplus of francs would drive down the dollar price of the franc, just as a surplus drives

Because manufacturers desire payment in their domestic currency, U.S. importers must convert dollars into Japanese yen, South Korean won, and other currencies in order to purchase foreign televisions.

down the price of wheat or cattle or anything else sold in a competitive market. At an exchange rate of $0.10 per franc, 15 billion francs would be demanded but only 5 billion supplied, and the resulting shortage would tend to push the price of the franc upward. These pressures would exist until the equilibrium exchange rate had been established.

CHANGES IN THE EQUILIBRIUM EXCHANGE RATE

Exchange rates can change frequently and sometimes quite dramatically. Any change that results in a shift of either the demand or the supply curve for a currency will cause the exchange rate to change. The factors that can shift the demand and supply curves include changes in tastes or income levels, changes in relative interest rates, and changes in price levels.

Changes in Tastes or Income Levels. Suppose that the average income in the United States increased. This would cause U.S. consumers to demand more goods and services, including French goods and services. The result would be an increase in the demand for French francs: The demand curve for francs would shift to the right, as depicted in Exh. 18.2. The same thing would happen if Americans suddenly found French fashions more appealing or decided to switch from California wines to those imported from France.

EXHIBIT 18.2

An Increase in the Demand for Francs

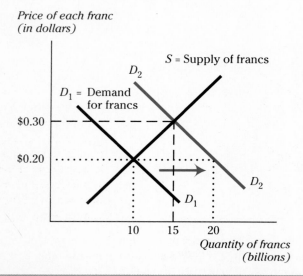

Price of each franc (in dollars)

D_2

S = Supply of francs

D_1 = Demand for francs

$0.30

$0.20

D_2

D_1

10   15   20

Quantity of francs (billions)

An increase in U.S. incomes or an increased preference for French products would tend to increase the demand for francs. This would cause the franc to appreciate in value; each franc would buy more U.S. cents than before. When the franc appreciates, the dollar depreciates; it takes a larger fraction of a dollar to buy each franc.

When the demand curve for francs shifts to the right, the dollar price of the franc is driven up. For example, in Exh. 18.2 you can see that the dollar price of the franc has risen from $0.20 per franc to $0.30 per franc. The dollar has **depreciated** (lost value against the franc) because it now takes a larger fraction of a dollar to buy each franc. Conversely, the franc has **appreciated** (gained value) against the dollar because each franc now buys more dollars (cents) than before.

How would we represent the impact of an increase in French incomes or an increased desire to buy American fashions—Levi's blue jeans, for example? Either of these changes would increase the demand for U.S. products and consequently would increase the demand for U.S. dollars. And the French acquire more dollars by supplying more francs. Remember that! To acquire more dollars, the French must supply more francs! As a consequence, the supply curve of francs will shift to the right, as depicted in Exh. 18.3. Would these changes cause the dollar to appreciate or to depreciate? What about the franc? Take a moment and try to answer these questions before reading further.

The correct answer is that an increase in the supply of francs would cause the dollar to appreciate in value. As you can see from Exh. 18.3, the dollar price of the franc has declined from $0.20 to only $0.10. The dollar must be more valuable—must have appreciated—because it now takes a smaller fraction of each dollar to buy a franc. Conversely, the franc has depreciated in value because each franc now buys fewer cents than before.

EXHIBIT 18.3

An Increase in the Supply of Francs

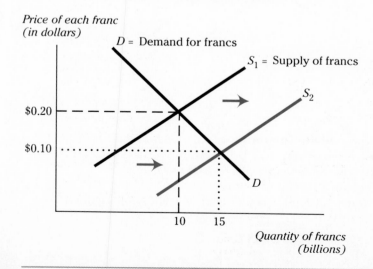

Price of each franc (in dollars)

D = Demand for francs

S_1 = Supply of francs

S_2

$0.20

$0.10

D

10   15

Quantity of francs (billions)

An increase in French incomes or an increased preference for U.S. products would lead to an increase in the supply of francs. This would cause the franc to depreciate and the dollar to appreciate.

Changes in Relative Interest Rates. In the short run, one of the most important sources of changes in exchange rates is changes in relative interest rates. If French interest rates increased relative to those in the United States (as shown in Exh. 18.4), we could expect U.S. households and businesses to buy more French securities in order to earn the higher interest rates. This would shift the demand curve for francs to the right. At the same time, fewer French investors would be willing to buy U.S. securities, and so the supply curve of francs would shift to the left. As the exhibit shows, these changes would cause the dollar price of the franc to rise from $0.20 to $0.30; the franc would appreciate, and the dollar would depreciate.

Changes in Relative Price Levels. Changes in relative price levels also influence exchange rates. To illustrate, imagine a U.S.-made automobile that

EXHIBIT 18.4

The Impact of Higher French Interest Rates

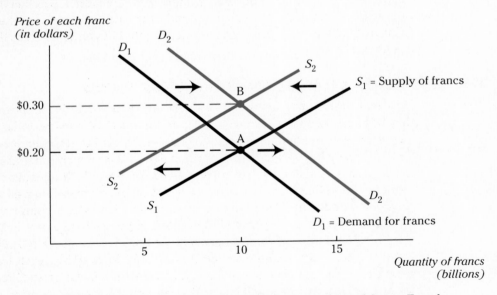

If French interest rates increase in relation to those in the United States, French securities become relatively more attractive. U.S. investors will demand more francs in order to buy French securities, whereas French investors will reduce their purchases of U.S. securities and thus supply fewer francs. These changes will tend to appreciate the franc and depreciate the dollar. (We move from equilibrium point *A* to point *B*.)

sells for $20,000 in the United States and a comparable French auto that sells for 100,000 francs in France. At an exchange rate of $0.20 per franc, these vehicles will have the same sticker prices; the U.S. auto will sell for 100,000 francs in France and the French auto for $20,000 in the United States. Consumers in each country will choose between these vehicles on the basis of design features, available options, and other nonprice characteristics.

Now, suppose that France experiences 20 percent inflation while inflation in the United States is only 10 percent. On average, prices in France will increase by 20 percent, so that the price of the French auto will be pushed up to 120,000 francs. U.S. prices, including automobile prices, will rise by only 10 percent, and so the U.S.-made automobile will now sell for $22,000. At an exchange rate of $0.20 per franc (or $1 = 5 Fr), U.S. automobiles now cost French consumers 110,000 francs, whereas French autos will be available for $24,000 in the United States. The same thing will happen to the prices of the other products traded by the two countries. Since U.S. products have become more attractive in price, the result will be an increase in the supply of francs (as French consumers demand more U.S. products) and a reduction in the demand for francs (as U.S. consumers demand fewer French products). As you can see from Exh. 18.5, these changes will cause the dollar price of the franc to fall from $0.20 to $0.10. The franc has depreciated in value, whereas the dollar has appreciated.

THE IMPACT OF CHANGES IN EXCHANGE RATES

How will Americans react when the dollar appreciates relative to the franc; will they be happy about the stronger dollar or unhappy? (When the dollar appreciates relative to another currency, it is described as getting stronger, whereas the other currency has weakened.) In truth, it depends on which Americans we are talking about. Consider U.S. exporting firms, for example. If the dollar appreciates as it did in Exh. 18.5, U.S. products will become more expensive for French consumers and thus less attractive. To illustrate, consider a computer that is selling for $20,000 in the United States. When the exchange rate is $0.20 per franc (or $1 = 5 Fr), that computer will cost French consumers 100,000 francs. But if the dollar appreciates so that it takes only $0.10 to buy each franc, that same $20,000 computer will cost French consumers 200,000 francs. Predictably, fewer French consumers will buy U.S. computers at the higher price, and U.S. exporters will find their sales suffering as a result of the appreciation of the dollar. And if U.S. exports suffer, some U.S. workers lose their jobs.

The other side of the story has to do with U.S. importers of French products. A stronger dollar means a weaker franc. And a weaker franc means that French products will be cheaper for Americans. Consider a bottle of French wine that costs 200 francs in France. When the exchange rate is $0.20 = 1 Fr,

EXHIBIT 18.5

The Effect of a Rise in the French Price Level

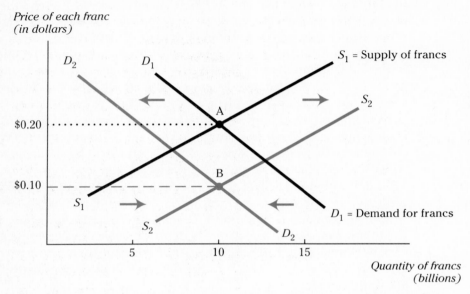

*Price of each franc
(in dollars)*

If prices in France rise in relation to those in the United States, U.S. products will become more attractive. French consumers will supply more francs as they demand more U.S. products, and U.S. consumers will demand fewer francs as they demand fewer French products. The dollar price of the franc will fall from $0.20 to $0.10 (we move from equilibrium point *A* to point *B*).

that bottle of wine will cost a U.S. importer $40. But if the franc depreciates so that the exchange rate is $0.10 = 1 Fr, that same bottle of wine will cost a U.S. consumer only $20. So the strong dollar will be welcomed by U.S. consumers and by U.S. businesses that import foreign products. The point is that whenever the exchange rate changes, there are winners and losers; some individuals and businesses will like the change, and others will not. (The article on pages 536–537 deals with the consequences of a climb in the value of the dollar relative to the Japanese yen and the German mark.)

Although changes in exchange rates are always unpopular with some groups, wide swings in exchange rates—whereby the dollar appreciates or depreciates substantially in a relatively short period of time—are particularly disruptive. For example, from the late 1970s to the mid-1980s, the dollar appreciated an average of approximately 80 percent. Then, over the next half-dozen years, the dollar fell about as much as it had risen. This volatility creates a great deal of risk for firms trading internationally because they cannot know how much imports will cost (in their own country's currency) or how much they will receive for their exports.[1] In addition, wide swings in exchange rates can have a major impact on the competitiveness of exporting firms and firms facing import competition. This, in turn, can translate into undesirable volatility in the levels of domestic employment. These problems have caused some critics to argue for government intervention to "fix" or at least "manage" exchange rates. We will consider those possibilities next.

Exchange Rate Systems: Fixed Exchange Rates

Prior to the emergence of flexible exchange rates, the international monetary system was characterized by one form or another of **fixed exchange rates—** rates established by central governments rather than by market forces.

From the early 1800s to the end of the Great Depression, the international fixed exchange rate system was the **gold standard**; each country's currency was linked to gold. A central government agreed to buy and sell gold to anyone and everyone at a specified price stated in terms of that country's currency. For example, if the United States agreed to buy gold for $20 an ounce and France agreed to pay 100 Fr an ounce, the exchange rate of dollar to franc was $20 to 100 Fr, or $1 to 5 Fr. That rate would prevail until either the United States or France changed the price it was willing to pay for gold.

The gold standard fell apart following World War I for reasons that are beyond the scope of this chapter. From the end of World War I until after World War II, the international community experimented with a variety of temporary exchange rate systems, none of which gained acceptance. Then an international monetary conference held in 1944 at Bretton Woods, New Hampshire, developed a new fixed exchange rate system in which the U.S. dollar played a prominent role. Under what became known as the **Bretton Woods system,** most governments agreed to maintain a fixed value for their currency in terms of the dollar; the United States agreed to redeem dollars (from foreign central banks) for gold at $35 an ounce. This linked all major currencies directly to the dollar and indirectly to one another. For example, if France and the United States agreed that $1 would exchange for 6 Fr and if the

---

[1] Many exporters and importers protect themselves against exchange rate changes by buying and selling foreign currency in the "futures market." For example, if an importer wanted to protect itself against a change in the exchange rate, it would buy forward foreign exchange of the country whose products it was importing. This means that the importer buys foreign currency to be received in the future at an exchange rate agreed on now. This service is not free, and so it increases the cost of foreign trade. And since most futures contracts cover only a few months, long-term importing and exporting agreements remain risky.

Use Your Economic Reasoning

Strong Dollar Creates Winners and Losers

By Michael M. Phillips
Staff Reporter of the Wall Street Journal

Treasury Secretary Robert Rubin has repeated his mantra dozens of times: A strong dollar is in America's interest. The question is, which America is he talking about?

At Computer Network Technology Inc. in Minneapolis, the dollar's climb in the past month has slashed sales of its networking systems to Japan and trimmed earnings as much as $100,000.

In nearby Minnetonka, Minn., however, executives at Insignia Systems Inc. cheer every time the dollar gains further against the yen. In 1997, the company expects to turn its first profit in several years, mainly because the rising greenback has cut the cost of Japanese-made sign-printing machines that Insignia imports and resells to U.S. retailers.

Selecting Winners

The U.S. government has adopted a de facto policy of encouraging the dollar's climb against the Japanese yen and German mark, while trying to keep inflation low and interest rates steady. That combination may encourage stable economic growth for the U.S. as a whole. But in picking that approach, Mr. Rubin and Federal Reserve Chairman Alan Greenspan also are implicitly selecting winners and losers in the U.S. economy.

To be sure, the dollar's surge against the yen and mark hasn't had a big impact on overall U.S. Trade. A big reason is that U.S. exporters are expanding beyond Japan and Europe and selling more goods in Canada, Mexico, Hong Kong, Britain and elsewhere. The dollar also has been relatively stable against the currencies of these other trading partners.

Since April 1995, the dollar has soared 47.5% against the yen, trading at 123.32 yen in late New York trading yesterday, and 18.8% against the mark, trading at 1.64 marks yesterday. But against a basket of currencies representing major U.S. trading partners, the dollar is up only 15.5% during the same period, and just 6.8% in the past year.

"All in all, the latest move up in the value of the dollar is likely to have little restraining effect on U.S. growth," says Robert E. Mellman, vice president and economist at J.P. Morgan....

Beneath the placid surface, however, the pains and profits of the strong dollar policy aren't evenly distributed. The negative impact goes beyond the usual complainers—U.S. auto makers have been most vocal about the rising dollar. On the pain side, there are also small commodities exporters, huge manufacturers, even service providers whose clients or competition are overseas.

As the dollar climbs, these companies face the choice of cutting export prices and accepting lower profits, or passing along the price increase and losing customers. "I'll wind up not passing it along until I see whether [the dollar's] going to stay there for at least a couple of quarters," says Tom Hudson, chief executive and president of Computer Network Technology.

AlliedSignal Inc., a Morristown, N.J., multinational company, ended up losing the customer, in this case a $13 million contract to supply air-bag modules to Japan's Suzuki Motor Corp. "We had a huge cost disadvantage because of the strong dollar against the yen," says Mark Greenberg, vice president for external communications.

Quick Impact

Economists say the impact of the dollar's surge isn't always clear right away. The industries that feel it most quickly are often those competing head-to-head with Europeans or Japanese to sell goods that are roughly indistinguishable. Feedcom Enterprises Inc. of Seattle earns 90% of its revenue exporting livestock feed hay to Japan. The recent weakness in the yen, however, has given North Korean and Australian hay a price edge, and sales are down 15%. "It's a very price-sensitive commodity," says Ed Bitanga, a Feedcom principle and head of international sales.

Another exchange-rate sensitive rate industry is tourism, since one palm-edged beach can quickly substitute for another if prices change. The Hawaii Visitors and Convention Bureau recently revised downward by 120,000 its estimate of how many Japanese tourists would visit in 1997. The reason? The slow economy and the falling yen make it too expensive for many Japanese to travel to the U.S. this year.

On the flip side, U.S. consumers eventually could face lower prices for imported Japanese and European goods, although there may be some delay before discounts appear on the shelves. Many French estate wine growers, for instance, have opted to take greater profits from their U.S. sales, rather than dropping prices.

"They may be farmers, they may be on tractors—but they sure know what currency has to do with the price of their wine," says Robert Kacher, a Washington, D.C., wine importer. Should the franc—which is linked to the mark in the European Monetary System—fall an additional 10% against the dollar, however, consumers could see price cuts, Mr. Kacher predicts.

Some companies that use imported products already are beginning to benefit from the currency realignment.

Rohr Inc., a San Diego aircraft-component manufacturer, has realized some savings on the MD-11 engine pylons it buys in Japan. And since Boeing Co. reports that the rising dollar hasn't hurt jet sales, Rohr has been shielded from the dollar's downside as well. "There's tremendous demand out there for new aircraft," says Laurence Chapman, Rohr's chief financial officer.

Insignia Systems estimates that the dollar's earlier tumble, which bottomed out at 80.63 yen in April 1995, cost the company $2 million a year. The dollar's recent rise should help restore the company to profitability, says G.L. Hoffman, Insignia's president and chief executive….

USE YOUR ECONOMIC REASONING

1. According to the article, the dollar has climbed against the Japanese yen and the German mark. Does that mean that the dollar appreciated or depreciated against these currencies?
2. Which U.S. firms are being hurt by the climb in the value of the dollar, exporters of U.S. products or importers of German and Japanese products?
3. Suppose a product costs an American manufacturer $100 to make and ship to Japan, where (given existing competition) the product can be sold for 11,000 yen. If the exchange rate is $1=100 yen, how much profit will the U.S. firm make? If the dollar exchange rate changes so that $1=110 yen, what will happen to the U.S. firm's profits? Why might the firm be reluctant to increase its price to offset this change?
4. Why is it that firms selling "indistinguishable" products are the first to feel the impact of exchange rate changes? What examples of indistinguishable products are noted in the article?

In 1944, a conference at Bretton Woods, New Hampshire, led to a new fixed exchange rate system. The British economist John Maynard Keynes (seated at the far left) represented Great Britain.

United States and Germany agreed that $1 would exchange for 2 DM (Deutsche marks), 3 Fr would exchange for 1 DM. Each government would then be committed to maintaining that exchange rate, even if market forces wanted to push the exchange rate elsewhere.

FIXED EXCHANGE RATES AND THE BALANCE OF PAYMENTS

To illustrate the consequences of fixed exchange rates, consider the demand and supply curves for francs represented in Exh. 18.6. Suppose that the governments of France and the United States have fixed the exchange rate at $0.20 per franc ($1 = 5 Fr) and that this initially represents the equilibrium exchange rate. Now, suppose that an increase in U.S. incomes causes the demand for francs to increase from D_1 to D_2. Under a system of flexible exchange rates, the dollar price of the franc would increase to $0.30 = 1 Fr. But that can't happen under a system of fixed rates because the governments are committed to maintaining an exchange rate of $0.20 = 1 Fr. At the fixed exchange rate of $0.20 = 1 Fr, 15 billion francs will be demanded but only 10 billion supplied; there will be a shortage of 5 billion francs.

This shortage of francs represents a balance of payments deficit for the United States. A **balance of payments deficit** exists when a nation's foreign expenditures exceed its foreign receipts in a given year. In our hypothetical example the U.S. deficit is 5 billion francs (or $1 billion at an exchange rate of

EXHIBIT 18.6

Fixed Exchange Rates and the Balance of Payments

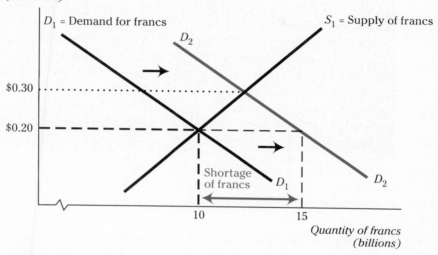

If the exchange rate is fixed at $0.20 = 1 franc, an increase in the demand for francs would lead to a shortage of the French currency. This shortage of francs represents a balance of payments deficit for the United States and a balance of payments surplus for France.

5 francs per dollar). Of course, if the United States has a balance of payments deficit, France enjoys a **balance of payments surplus**; its foreign receipts exceed its foreign expenditures.

As we've already noted, with flexible exchange rates the shortage of francs would push the price of the franc up to $0.30. This would eliminate France's balance of payments surplus (and the U.S. balance of payments deficit). That's one of the desirable features of flexible exchange rates; they automatically eliminate balance of payments deficits and surpluses. But because the United States and France are committed to maintaining an exchange rate of $0.20 = 1 Fr, that can't be allowed to happen. Instead, something must be done to maintain the agreed-on rate.

Intervention in Foreign Exchange Markets. One approach to maintaining the fixed exchange rate would be for the Federal Reserve, the U.S. central bank, to use its accumulated reserves of francs to supply francs to the foreign exchange market. This would tend to shift the supply curve of francs to the right, as represented in Exh. 18.7, and allow the exchange rate to be maintained at $0.20 = 1 Fr. Alternatively, the French central bank could directly demand dollars. (Remember, in order to buy dollars, the central bank would need to supply francs.)

As long as the equilibrium exchange rate is sometimes above and sometimes below the fixed exchange rate (and relatively close to it), this type of intervention can go on indefinitely. Central banks will sometimes be required to use their reserves of foreign currencies, but during other periods they will be accumulating reserves. But when a more or less permanent change in demand or supply causes the equilibrium exchange rate to remain consistently above or below the fixed rate, something has to give. In our example the Federal Reserve cannot intervene forever; eventually its reserves of francs will run out. And the French central bank won't be willing to buy dollars forever. After all, the French are accumulating dollars without any guarantee that they will ever want to use them.

EXHIBIT 18.7

Intervention in Exchange Markets

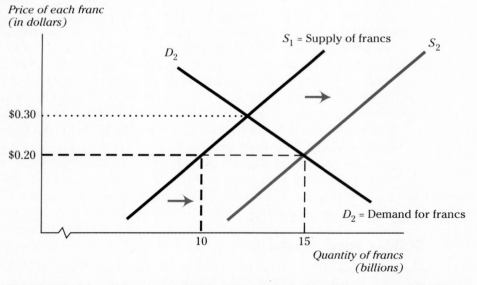

To maintain the exchange rate at $0.20 = 1 Franc, the Federal Reserve must be willing to use its reserves of francs to buy dollars. By supplying francs to buy dollars, the Fed can shift the supply curve of francs to the right and maintain the fixed exchange rate.

Intervention in the Domestic Economy. When persistent balance of payments problems exist, they can be eliminated by using fiscal and monetary policy to alter the demand and supply of foreign exchange. For example, the United States could eliminate its balance of payments deficit with France by increasing income taxes. This would reduce the disposable incomes of U.S. consumers and cause them to buy fewer French imports, shifting the demand curve for francs back to D_1 in Exh. 18.6. Reducing government spending in the United States could accomplish the same objective, since it would also tend to reduce income levels in the United States. Alternatively, the country with a surplus (France) could employ an expansionary fiscal policy, cutting taxes and increasing government spending. This would tend to increase income levels and cause France to import more U.S. products, reducing the U.S. balance of payments deficit.

Monetary policy could be used in a similar manner. By reducing the money supply, the Fed could push up interest rates in the United States and slow spending for goods and services, including imported products. This would tend to reduce the demand for francs. In addition, the higher interest rates available in the United States would tend to attract money from French investors, who would need to buy dollars (supply francs) for that purpose. This would also help to reduce the U.S. balance of payments deficit. The alternative would be for France to expand its money supply. By driving down French interest rates, the French central bank would cause spending to increase, including spending for U.S. products. And the lower French interest rates would cause French investors to buy more U.S. securities.

Curing balance of payments problems by using monetary and fiscal policies can be tough medicine. In effect, the country with the deficit is forced to reduce employment and income as the price it must pay to eliminate the deficit. Alternatively, the country with the surplus is asked to accept the inflation that results as it expands its economy to eliminate the surplus. It was the unwillingness of either party to accept this harsh medicine that led to the breakdown of the Bretton Woods system, the fixed exchange rate system that prevailed from World War II until 1971.

The Current System:
The Managed Float

As we've seen, neither fixed exchange rates nor flexible exchange rates provide nations with everything they want. Flexible exchange rates can lead to undesirable fluctuations in exchange rates, but fixed rates force countries to sacrifice domestic employment (or price stability) in order to stabilize exchange rates. Perhaps because neither of these systems is fully satisfactory, the system that has emerged can best be described as a system of managed exchange rates for major industrialized countries.

Managed exchange rates combine the flexible exchange rate system we described earlier in the chapter with intervention by central banks. Rather than completely fixing exchange rates (as in the fixed rate system), the purpose of central bank intervention is to limit or narrow exchange rate movements. In some instances they may even attempt to reverse exchange rate changes they consider inappropriate or to hasten exchange rate changes they see as desirable. This system of quasiflexible exchange rates is sometimes described as **managed float.**

Like flexible exchange rates and fixed exchange rates, the managed float has also been subject to criticism. Even with intervention, exchange rates have proved to be quite volatile. This is not surprising when you recognize that the amounts central banks can spend to intervene in foreign exchange markets are small in comparison with the total amounts traded. For example, when central banks intervene, they spend something on the order of $1 or $2 billion a day. That compares with approximately $200 billion in foreign currency trading taking place on the average day. So while central banks may be effective in offsetting minor changes in supply and demand conditions or in slowing the pace of more fundamental changes, it is unlikely that central banks can preserve exchange rates that are significantly out of line with prevailing demand and supply conditions for the currencies in question. As a consequence, exchange rates have remained quite volatile, and the search continues for an exchange rate system that can provide greater stability in exchange rates without the problems posed by the fixed rate systems of the past. (The countries in the European Union have agreed on a novel solution to the problem of exchange rate volatility.[2] They are adopting a common currency, the euro, to replace their individual national currencies. Read "Clinging to Its Past, Europe Is Warily Awaiting the Euro," on pages 544–545, to learn about the impact of this upcoming change.)

The U.S. Balance of Payments Accounts

Regardless of the exchange rate system adopted, countries will always want to keep track of their transactions with other nations. They want to know how dependent they are on imported products and how well their own exports are selling. And they're interested in where their residents are investing and in how much foreign money is being invested in their land. The answers to these questions and others are contained in a nation's balance of payments statement.

---

[2] The European Union includes Belgium, France, Germany, Italy, Luxembourg, the Netherlands, Denmark, Greece, Ireland, Portugal, Spain, United Kingdom, Austria, Finland, and Sweden.

The U.S. **balance of payments (BOP) statement** is a record of all economic transactions between the United States and the rest of the world during a given year. Like other accounting statements, the BOP statement records credits and debits. Transactions that provide us with foreign exchange (the sale of exports, for example) are recorded as credits and are entered with a plus sign. Transactions that require us to use foreign exchange (such as the purchase of imports) are recorded as debits and are entered with a minus sign.

To simplify the recording of these debits and credits, the BOP statement is divided into four main sections: the current account, the capital account, the statistical discrepancy, and official reserve transactions. These categories are clearly indicated in Exh. 18.8 on page 546, which depicts the U.S. balance of payments statement for 1997.

THE CURRENT ACCOUNT

The first entries listed under the **current account** are merchandise exports and imports. The exports figure (a credit) reflects the value of the computers, airplanes, agricultural products, and other merchandise sold by U.S. firms to buyers in other countries. The figure for imports (a debit) reflects our purchases of Japanese automobiles, Brazilian coffee, Canadian lumber, and any other merchandise purchased from foreign sellers. As you can see from Exh. 18.8, in 1997 U.S. merchandise imports exceeded exports by $199 billion. This means that the United States experienced a **trade deficit** in 1997. If merchandise exports had exceeded merchandise imports, the United States would have enjoyed a **trade surplus.**

The next entries in the current account are the exports and imports of services. This category includes such items as shipping and banking services, insurance, and tourist expenditures. For example, if Colombian rose growers decide to use U.S. air carriers to ship their flowers to market, the transportation charge will be recorded as a credit in the services category of our balance of payments statement. On the other hand, when U.S. citizens vacation in Paris, their expenditures are recorded as a debit under services. Exhibit 18.8 reveals that in 1997 the value of service exports exceeded the value of service imports by $85.3 billion.

The final entries in the current account record investment income paid to and received from foreigners. This includes interest and dividend income earned by U.S. residents on investments in other countries (a credit) and interest and dividend income earned by foreign residents on investments in the United States (a debt). If you're earning interest on money in a Swiss bank account, that interest payment will be recorded as a credit in the U.S. balance of payments. On the other hand, when General Motors makes dividend payments to British stockholders, that payment will be recorded as a debit. According to the exhibit, in 1997 U.S. interest and dividend payments exceeded receipts by roughly $53 billion.

Clinging to Its Past, Europe Is Warily Awaiting the Euro

By Roger Cohen

MOSBURG, Germany—Franz Schmid is old enough to have suffered his share of European upheaval, and now, as the century wanes, he is convinced that the Continent is on the brink of another disaster, one that will wipe out all he has slowly built from the ruins of Hitler's war.... [L]ike about 60 percent of his fellow Germans, he is alarmed by a plan to ditch the world's second-largest reserve currency, the mark, and use a new money to change Europe. "The mark is part of us," Mr Schmid said. "What do we need a worthless new money for?" But several European governments—including Germany's—appear ready to scrap their national currencies and replace them with a single money, the euro, by 1999. They are set to impose the currency on restive, sometimes openly hostile, citizens, for whom union has become synonymous with stagnation and sacrifice. The political risk is enormous....

The Case for the Euro Unshackling Europe to Take On the U.S.

The economic logic behind the plan is simple. "What," asked Jean-Claude Trichet, governor of the French Central Bank, "would the single American market be without a single money in Texas and California?" In other words, the European Union's single market in goods and services is incomplete without a single currency and will be invigorated by having one. Over 60 percent of the trade of European Union states is with other countries in the union: the euro will simplify and stimulate this trade.

Like many European executives, Horst Teltschik, a member of the executive board of BMW, the German auto maker, sees the case for the new money as self-evident. "We export one-third of our production to other European Union countries, and we've suffered a lot from exchange rate fluctuation. The euro will eliminate that risk." For example, since BMW bought the British Rover auto company three years ago, sterling has appreciated more than 10 percent against the mark. As a result, the new Rover dealerships opened by BMW in Germany are having difficulties. "We should raise Rover Prices to match the mark's level," Mr. Teltschik said, "but we can't, so for now we take losses." Of course, companies trading between New York and Phoenix do not face such fluctuations. In this sense, the euro is intended to make Europe more like America.

Corporations including Siemens and Unilever have made clear that they believe they will benefit greatly from the change. Executives say that business will be spurred by easier corporate planning, pricing, and billing. European financial markets will be opened up to new competition; inefficient policies will be less sustainable; pressure will rise on countries to make their economies attractive to business. The dollar will at last have a real rival.

The union's economy is roughly the same size as America's; it accounts for 20.9 percent of world trade, more than the United States' 19.6 percent;

its population is bigger by about 100 million people, providing the largest single market in the world. Why, therefore, should the euro not eventually make strong inroads into the dollar's international dominance, expressed in the fact that the dollar is the currency for close to 60 percent of international trade and 80 percent of financial operations?...

Such visions are by no means shared by everyone... Up to now, Britain, Denmark and Sweden have indicated that they will probably not join the planned "first wave" because of their reservations about the project. To these countries, the economics look too risky and the politics of a formal abandonment of national sovereignty too sensitive. But they may join later.

The Case Against the Euro in Monetary Policy, Can One Size Fit All?...

By minting a money without making a government, and by surrendering control of monetary policy to a central bank while shunning the creation of other federal institutions, European states are heading into largely uncharted territory... The planned European Central Bank will—if the euro is broadly adopted—set a single monetary policy from Rotterdam to Rome, from Berlin to Barcelona. National room for economic maneuvering after January 1, 1999, will be limited.

Thus, if Italy hits a recession as the Netherlands booms, Italian authorities will no longer be able to lower interest rates to stimulate activity. They will not be able to devalue the lira. Italians are unlikely to migrate en masse to Amsterdam for jobs, as Americans might move to a booming Arizona from a depressed Vermont. Europeans, in general, do not like to move. Nor will a European federal budget transfer resources to Italy, as the United States Federal budget transfers money to depressed areas through Medicare and Social Security payments. Nor, finally, will there be room for generosity in national budgets, because of the new fiscal discipline: no deficits larger than 3 percent of output...

Europe, in other words, had better be a truly convergent economy, more or less responsive to the same economic medicine from Helsinki to Lisbon, or there will be tensions that will find a readily available target in the European Central Bank.

"How will a Europe with the euro deal with regional recessions?" asked Paul Krugman, a professor of economics at M.I.T. "I would put the odds of a collapse at one in four...."

"One can certainly imagine potential disasters in the one-size-fits-all approach to monetary policy," Eddie George, governor of the Bank of England, said in an interview. "I am feeling nervous for the whole of Europe...."

USE YOUR ECONOMIC REASONING

1. How will a single currency encourage intra-European trade? What will it mean for businesses located outside the European Union?
2. By facilitating intra-European trade, the adoption of a single currency is supposed to force European firms to become more efficient, thus making them more effective rivals for U.S. firms. Explain how the move to a common currency might have this impact.
2. How will the adoption of a single currency (and a single central bank) reduce a particular nation's ability to combat unemployment or inflation?
3. To participate in the new monetary union (the common currency), countries must agree to limit their budget deficits to less than 3 percent of GDP. Activist economists might see this as an undesirable limitation on a nation's ability to combat unemployment, particularly when coupled with the move to a single central bank for the entire European Union. Explain this concern.

EXHIBIT 18.8

The U.S. Balance of Payments Accounts: 1997 (Billions of Dollars)

Current Account

Merchandise exports*	+ 678.3	
Merchandise imports	− 877.3	
Merchandise balance	− 199.0	
Service exports	+ 253.2	
Service imports	− 167.9	
Service balance	+ 85.3	
Receipts of investment income	+ 236.0	
Payments of investment income**	− 288.8	
Balance on investment income	− 52.8	
Balance on current account		− 166.5

Capital Account

Capital inflows	+ 672.3	
Capital outflows	− 426.1	
Balance on capital account		+ 246.2

Statistical Discrepancy   − 96.9

Official Reserve Transactions

Increase (−) in U.S. reserve assets abroad	− 1.0	
Increase (+) in foreign reserve assets in the U.S.	+ 18.2	
Official reserve balance		+ 17.2

*The figures for exports and imports are preliminary and will differ slightly from those presented in earlier chapters.

**This entry includes unilateral transfers such as gifts and charitable contributions made to people and organizations in other countries and aid provided to foreign governments.

SOURCE: U.S. Department of Commerce, *Survey of Current Business,* March 1998.

The current account balance gives us the net result of all transactions involving merchandise, services, and payments of investment income. In 1997, the United States spent $166.5 billion more for these purposes than it received, and so it had a current account deficit of that amount. (If it had earned more than it spent, it would have enjoyed a current account surplus.)

THE CAPITAL ACCOUNT

Like individuals, nations can spend more than they earn either by selling assets to raise money or by borrowing. For example, one of the ways that the United States can pay for a current account deficit is by selling some of its capital assets—real estate or factories or entire businesses—to foreigners. So if a group of Japanese businesspeople buys a quaint San Francisco hotel or a small midwestern brewery, that transaction will be recorded as a credit under our **capital account.** The United States can also finance its current account deficit by borrowing money. This is accomplished when foreigners purchase U.S. stocks and bonds and bank accounts. Since these transactions also provide us with foreign funds, they too are recorded as credits under the capital account. Of course, while some U.S. residents are selling assets and borrowing money, others may be buying foreign assets and lending abroad. If a U.S. resident purchases an Italian winery or buys stock in a new Canadian company or opens a bank account in Japan, these transactions are recorded as debits under the capital account.

As you can see, the United States enjoyed a large capital account surplus in 1997. The $246.2 billion surplus was more than enough to finance the substantial current account deficit it experienced that year.

STATISTICAL DISCREPANCY

If we compare the balance on current account and the balance on capital account, it appears that the United States experienced a balance of payments surplus of $79.7 billion in 1997. That is, the country's foreign earnings exceeded its foreign spending by $79.7 billion. But that figure misrepresents the true situation. When information is collected for the balance of payments accounts, some transactions are missed or improperly recorded. The entry entitled **statistical discrepancy** reflects an adjustment to compensate for these transactions. After adjustment for the statistical discrepancy ($96.9 billion), we find that the U.S. actually had a balance of payments deficit of $17.2 billion in 1997.[3]

OFFICIAL RESERVE TRANSACTIONS

Whenever a balance of payments deficit exists, it must be financed in some way. The primary method is through **official reserve transactions** by central banks.

The Federal Reserve and foreign central banks maintain reserves of foreign currencies that they can use to intervene in exchange markets. The Fed maintains reserves of Japanese yen and German marks, for example, whereas Germany's central bank, the Bundesbank, maintains reserves of yen and dollars. Exhibit 18.8 indicates that in 1997 the Fed increased its holdings of reserve assets

---

[3] Recall that before adjusting for the statistical discrepancy the U.S. had a BOP surplus of $79.7 billion. If we subtract the statistical discrepancy of $96.9 billion, the result is a deficit of $17.2 billion.

by $1 billion. (It was using dollars to buy foreign currencies.) This entry is recorded as a debit because, like U.S. imports, it increases the demand for foreign currency. Over the same period, foreign central banks increased their holdings of reserve assets (dollars) held in the United States by $18.2 billion. By buying dollars (and supplying foreign currencies), these central banks, in effect, loaned U.S. residents another $18.2 billion to finance their expenditures abroad. The net effect of these two official reserve transactions is to provide a credit of $17.2 billion, exactly enough to finance the U.S. balance of payments deficit.

As you can see from this example, a nation's balance of payments statement always balances. The only question is *how* it will balance. If a country experiences a current account deficit, it must be offset by a capital account surplus or by official reserve transactions or by some combination of the two. If a country experiences a current account surplus, the surplus must be offset either by a capital account deficit or by official reserve transactions or some combination of the two.

The common wisdom is that a nation cannot run current account deficits indefinitely; ultimately it must learn to "live within its means." But the United States has recorded such deficits for roughly a decade. Clearly our capacity to spend more than we earn depends on our ability to attract foreign investment funds (to generate a surplus in the capital account). When foreigners no longer see the United States as an attractive place to invest, the dollar will tend to depreciate, and the current account deficit will shrink. But as long as foreign residents and central banks are willing to loan us the foreign exchange we need to finance our present spending habits, our current account deficits can continue.

SUMMARY

The feature that distinguishes international trade from trade within a nation is the need to convert the currency of one nation to the currency of some other nation. The rate at which one currency is exchanged for some other currency is called the *exchange rate*. The exchange rate plays a critical role in determining each country's level of imports and exports. Whenever the dollar is cheaper—that is, whenever it takes fewer pounds or yen or francs to purchase each dollar—importers find U.S. goods more attractive, and Americans will find British and Japanese and French goods more expensive. On the other hand, if the dollar becomes more expensive, U.S. goods will become less attractive and foreign goods a better buy.

Under a system of *flexible*, or *floating, exchange rates*, exchange rates are determined by market forces, by the interaction of demand and supply. At the *equilibrium exchange rate,* the quantity demanded of a currency is equal to the quantity supplied, and there is neither a shortage nor a surplus of the currency.

The equilibrium exchange rate will change in response to changes in the demand or supply of the currency being exchanged. When the exchange value of a nation's currency increases relative to other currencies, the currency has *appreciated* in value; when its exchange value declines, it has *depreciated* in value. Factors that will shift the demand and supply curves of currencies include changes in the tastes and income levels in the trading countries, changes in relative income levels in the trading countries, and changes in relative prices in the trading countries.

The alternative to flexible exchange rates is a system of fixed exchange rates. *Fixed exchange rates* are established by central governments rather than by market forces. Under a system of fixed exchange rates, nations are expected to use central bank intervention or monetary and fiscal policies to maintain the established rate. The *gold standard* and the *Bretton Woods system* are examples of fixed exchange rate systems.

Neither fixed nor flexible exchange rates provide nations with everything they desire. Flexible exchange rates can lead to undesirable fluctuations in exchange rates, whereas fixed rates may force countries to sacrifice domestic employment or price stability in order to stabilize exchange rates. Because neither system is fully satisfactory, most nations have turned to a system of managed exchange rates. *Managed exchange rates* combine the flexible exchange rate system with occasional intervention by central banks.

Regardless of the exchange rate system, countries want to keep track of their transactions with other nations. This is facilitated through a balance of payments statement. A *balance of payments statement* is a record of all economic transactions between a given country and the rest of the world.

Each country's balance of payments statement is divided into four parts: the current account, the capital account, the statistical discrepancy, and official reserve transactions. The *current account* is the portion of the balance of payments statement that records the exports and imports of goods and services. The *capital account* records the purchase and sale of capital assets, including factories and businesses, as well as stocks, bonds, and bank accounts. The *statistical discrepancy* adjusts for missing or improperly recorded transactions. The *official reserve transactions entry* is a record of the purchase or sale of reserve assets—including reserve currencies—by central banks. These reserve transactions commonly reflect central bank intervention in exchange markets.

When all transactions have been completed, each country's balance of payments statement must balance. If a country has a deficit on current account, that deficit (after adjustment for any statistical discrepancy) must be offset by a surplus on capital account or official reserve transactions.

GLOSSARY

Appreciation of currency. An increase in the exchange value of a currency relative to other currencies.

Balance of payments deficit. Total payments to other countries exceed total receipts from other countries for an unfavorable balance of payments.

Balance of payments (BOP) statement. A record of all economic transactions between a particular country and the rest of the world during some specified period of time.

Balance of payments surplus. Total receipts from other countries exceed total payments to other countries for a favorable balance of payments.

Bretton Woods system. A fixed exchange rate system whereby nations agreed to fix a value on their currency in terms of the dollar, and the United States agreed to redeem dollars from other central banks for gold.

Capital account. The portion of a nation's balance of payments statement that records the purchase and sale of capital assets.

Current account. The portion of a nation's balance of payments statement that records the exports and imports of goods and services.

Depreciation of currency. A decrease in the exchange value of a currency relative to other currencies.

Equilibrium exchange rate. The exchange rate at which the quantity of a currency demanded is equal to the quantity supplied.

Exchange rate. The price of one nation's currency stated in terms of another nation's currency.

Fixed exchange rate. An exchange rate established by central governments rather than by market forces.

Flexible exchange rate. An exchange rate that is determined by market forces, by the supply and demand for the currency. Also described as a floating exchange rate.

Floating exchange rate. See *flexible exchange rate.*

Gold standard. A fixed exchange rate system whereby the value of each country's currency is directly tied to gold.

Managed exchange rates. Exchange rates that are determined by market forces with some intervention by central banks. Also described as a managed float.

Managed float. See *managed exchange rates.*

Official reserve transactions. The purchase and sale of reserve assets by central banks.

Statistical discrepancy. The entry in a nation's balance of payments statement that adjusts for missing or improperly recorded transactions.

Trade deficit. Merchandise imports exceed merchandise exports for an unfavorable balance of trade.

Trade surplus. Merchandise exports exceed merchandise imports for a favorable balance of trade.

STUDY QUESTIONS

Fill in the Blanks

1. The price of one currency in terms of another currency is called the

   _____ .

2. Another term for foreign currency is

   _____ .

3. When imports exceed exports, a country is

   experiencing a _____ ;

   when exports exceed imports, a country is experiencing

   a _____ .

4. The _____
   refers to merchandise imports and exports,

   whereas the _____ refers
   to all economic transactions between nations.

5. There are essentially two types of exchange rate systems: those involving

_____ exchange rates and those

involving _____ exchange rates.

6. Under a system of flexible exchange rates, if it takes more French francs than before to buy a U.S. dollar, we can say that the

dollar has _____ and that

the franc has _____ .

7. If per capita incomes increased in the United States as a result of an economic expansion, U.S. imports of foreign products would probably (increase/decrease)

_____ .

8. If a country's exports of goods and services exceeded its imports of goods and services, it would experience a

_____ account

_____
(deficit/surplus).

9. If interest rates are higher in the United States than they are abroad, foreign investors will tend to invest more money in the United States, and the dollar will tend to (appreciate/depreciate)

_____ in value.

10. If the dollar appreciates in value, it will

be (harder/easier) _____
for U.S. producers to sell their products abroad.

Multiple Choice

1. If total merchandise exports by the United States exceed total merchandise imports, the United States is experiencing a
   a) balance of payments deficit.
   b) balance of payments surplus.
   c) trade deficit.
   d) trade surplus.

2. Which of the following is not a source of foreign exchange for the United States?
   a) Foreign tourists visiting the United States
   b) U.S. exports to France
   c) U.S. imports from Japan
   d) German investments in the United States

3. For which of the following transactions must the United States acquire foreign exchange?
   a) Buying Japanese automobiles
   b) Investing in French companies
   c) Paying dividends to Arabs on their U.S. investments
   d) All of the above

4. If Americans decide to buy more Japanese automobiles,
   a) the demand curve for Japanese yen will shift to the left.
   b) the demand curve for American dollars will shift to the right.
   c) the demand curve for Japanese yen will shift to the right.
   d) the supply curve of Japanese yen will shift to the right.

5. The Bretton Woods system
   a) preceded the gold standard.
   b) was identical to the gold standard.
   c) was established after World War II.
   d) lasted until 1982.

6. If German interest rates increased relative to those in the United States,
   a) Americans would tend to demand fewer German marks.
   b) Germans would tend to supply more marks.
   c) the mark would tend to appreciate relative to the dollar.
   d) the dollar would tend to appreciate relative to the mark.

7. If the price level in Japan increases more rapidly than the price level in the United States,
   a) the Japanese will tend to supply more yen, appreciating the dollar relative to the yen.

b) the Japanese will tend to supply fewer yen, appreciating the dollar relative to the yen.

c) U.S. consumers will tend to demand more yen, depreciating the dollar relative to the yen.

d) U.S. consumers will tend to demand more yen, appreciating the dollar relative to the yen.

8. If the German central bank intervenes in the foreign exchange market by buying dollars for marks, the intervention would tend to
a) depreciate the dollar relative to the mark.
b) appreciate the mark relative to the dollar.
c) depreciate both the mark and the dollar.
d) appreciate the dollar.

9. The purchase of a French company by a U.S. business would be recorded in the U.S. balance of payments accounts as a
a) credit in the current account.
b) debit in the current account.
c) credit in the capital account.
d) debit in the capital account.

10. Interest payments to foreign residents would be recorded in the U.S. balance of payments accounts as a
a) credit in the current account.
b) debit in the current account.
c) credit in the capital account.
d) debit in the capital account.

11. If the British decide to purchase more U.S. products,
a) the demand curve for the British pound will shift to the right.
b) the supply curve of the British pound will shift to the right.

c) the supply curve of the American dollar will shift to the right.
d) the supply curve of the American dollar will shift to the left.

12. If a $40,000 U.S. computer costs a German importer 120,000 DM, the exchange rate must be
a) 1 Deutsche mark to 3 dollars.
b) 1 Deutsche mark to 1/4 dollar.
c) 1 dollar to 1/3 Deutsche mark.
d) 1 dollar to 3 Deutsche marks.

13. Under a system of flexible exchange rates, if U.S. citizens started buying more British goods,
a) the dollar would tend to appreciate relative to the pound.
b) the price of the pound (in dollars) would begin to fall.
c) the dollar would tend to depreciate relative to the pound.
d) the price of the dollar (in pounds) would begin to rise.

14. If the yen price of the dollar (the price of a dollar stated in terms of Japanese yen) declined,
a) Japanese cars would cost Americans fewer dollars.
b) Japanese tourists would find American meals less expensive.
c) American cars would cost Japanese consumers more yen.
d) American tourists would be encouraged to tour Japan.

15. The existing exchange rate system is best described as a
a) gold standard.
b) system of fixed exchange rates.
c) system of flexible exchange rates.
d) managed float.

Problems and Questions for Discussion

1. If you were visiting London, which exchange rate would you prefer: $4 to £1 or $3 to £1? Why?

2. Suppose that we are operating under a system of flexible exchange rates. If Americans demand more British automobiles, will the dollar tend to appreciate or depreciate? Show this result graphically. What about the pound?

3. How was the Bretton Woods system different from the gold standard? What did the two systems have in common?

4. We sometimes read about balance of payments deficits or surpluses, but a nation's balance of payments statement must always balance. Clarify this apparent contradiction.

5. Japan's central bank has often intervened to buy dollars and prevent the dollar from depreciating relative to the yen. What is the rationale for such intervention?

6. Japan's central bank is in a better position to keep the dollar from depreciating than is the U.S. central bank (the Fed). Why? (*Hint:* How would the Fed go about trying to appreciate the dollar?)

7. If a nation is experiencing persistent balance of payments deficits, how could monetary and fiscal policies be used to remedy this problem? Why might a nation be reluctant to use such remedies?

8. Suppose that the Fed pursues a restrictive monetary policy to combat inflation in the United States. What impact would these policies be likely to have on the current account balance, the capital account balance, and the exchange value of the dollar relative to other currencies?

9. Federal government deficits are thought to drive up domestic interest rates. How could this indirectly hurt our merchandise exports?

10. If the German economy entered a recession, what impact would this have on the exchange rate between the German mark and the U.S. dollar? Why would it have this impact?

ANSWER KEY

Fill in the Blanks

1. exchange rate
2. foreign exchange
3. trade deficit; trade surplus
4. balance of trade, balance of payments
5. fixed, flexible
6. appreciated, depreciated
7. increase
8. current, surplus
9. appreciate
10. harder

Multiple Choice

1. d
2. c
3. d
4. c
5. c
6. c
7. a
8. d
9. d
10. b
11. b
12. d
13. c
14. b
15. d

Photo Credits

Index